D0023133

★★★★★★★★★★★

American Politics in a Changing World

★ About the Authors

Janet A. Flammang, Dennis R. Gordon, Timothy J. Lukes, and Kenneth R. Smorsten are young professors in touch with today's issues and today's students. Together, they provide a blending of diverse areas of expertise: Dr. Flammang specializes in public policy, federalism, and women and politics; Dr. Gordon, in international relations, comparative politics, and American foreign policy; Dr. Lukes, in American political behavior; and Dr. Smorsten, in interest groups, public opinion, and institutions, especially the presidency.

Janet A. Flammang (Ph.D., University of California, Los Angeles) has taught at Santa Clara University since 1978, serving as department chair since 1986. She has also taught at San Diego State University and Whittier College. She is active in academic circles as a lecturer, panelist, and writer and served as president of the Women's Caucus and Committee on the Status of Women of the Western Political Science Association from 1986 to 1987. In 1987, she received the Phi Beta Kappa Northern California Association Award for Excellence in Teaching. She has edited the book *Political Women: Current Roles in State and Local Government* (Sage, 1984) and written numerous articles and papers, especially on comparable worth and feminism.

Dennis R. Gordon (Ph.D., University of California, Santa Barbara) has taught at Santa Clara University since 1979. He has also taught as an instructor at Solano Community College and as a teaching assistant at the University of California at Santa Barbara. Dr. Gordon has published numerous articles on Central America, South America, and the Caribbean and is currently director of Santa Clara's International Studies Program. His article on the Falkland/Malvinas war was awarded the 1987–1988 DeBenedetti Prize in Peace History. He was president of the Northern California Political Science Association from 1987 to 1988.

Timothy J. Lukes received his Ph.D. in political economy from the University of Toronto and has taught at Santa Clara University since 1983, serving as department chair from 1985 to 1986. In 1984–1985 and in 1988–1989, he was a visiting professor at The Loyola University Rome Center of Liberal Arts. He directs Santa Clara University's Public Service Internship Program and, since 1983, has served as commissioner of the San Jose Commission on the Internment of Local Japanese Americans. He has written two other books, *The Flight into Inwardness* (Associated University Presses, 1985) and *Japanese Legacy* (California History Center, 1985).

Kenneth R. Smorsten received his Ph.D. in politics and public administration from the London School of Economics at the University of London and subsequently taught at several colleges on the central coast of California, including San Jose State University, the College of San Mateo, and City College of San Francisco. He has served as a field representative for the office of California State Senator Nicholas Petris in Oakland and as assistant program administrator for the Adult Center of the Mission Neighborhood Centers in San Francisco in the late 1960s. In 1983 he received the Outstanding Contribution Award, Pi Sigma Alpha Honor Society, San Jose State University. He has written a previous textbook, *A Preface to Action: An Introduction to American Politics* (Goodyear, 1976; Scott Foresman, 1980).

By combining their individual strengths and lending their individual dimensions to the content, coverage, and emphasis of *American Politics in a Changing World,* the authors have produced a text that is unusually well balanced and well researched throughout. ★

American Politics in a Changing World

Janet A. Flammang
Santa Clara University

Dennis R. Gordon
Santa Clara University

Timothy J. Lukes
Santa Clara University

Kenneth R. Smorsten

Brooks/Cole Publishing Company
Pacific Grove, California

Brooks/Cole Publishing Company
A Division of Wadsworth, Inc.

Printed in the United States of America
10 9 8 7 6 5 4 3 2 1

Library of Congress Cataloging-in-Publication Data
American politics in a changing world / Janet A. Flammang . . .
[et al.].
p. cm.
Includes bibliographical references.
ISBN 0-534-12342-2
1. United States—Politics and governmment. I. Flammang, Janet A.
JK274.A5625 1990
320.973—dc20 89-27694
CIP

Sponsoring Editor: *Cynthia C. Stormer*
Project Development Editors: *John Bergez, Pat Gadban, and Janet M. Hunter*
Editorial Assistants: *Mary Ann Zuzow and Cathleen Sue Collins*
Production Coordinator: *Fiorella Ljunggren*
Production: *Cece Munson and Sue Ewing*
Permissions Editor: *Carline Haga*
Interior and Cover Design: *Katherine Minerva*
Cover Photos: Sky: *Comstock, Inc., Mike and Carol Werner;* Column: *Comstock, Inc., R. Michael Stuckey*
Art Coordinator: *Cece Munson*
Interior Illustrations: *Pat Rogondino*
Illustrations for the Essays: *Pat Rogondino and Mary Burkhardt*
Photo Researchers: *Marquita Flemming, Mary Kay Hancharick, and Research Plus*
Photo Researchers for the Essays: *Yvonne Gerin, Marion Paone, and Stephen Forsling*
Typesetting and Color Separation: *Graphic Typesetting Service*
Cover Printing: *Lehigh Press Lithographers*
Printing and Binding: *Arcata Graphics/Hawkins*
"Let America Be America Again" reprinted by permission of Harold Ober Associates Incorporated. Copyright 1938 by Langston Hughes. Copyright renewed 1965 by Langston Hughes.
(Credits continue on p. 815.)

★★★★★★★★★★★

To our families:

Joseph, Gloria, Richard,

Barbara, Lee, Alexander,

Jacob

Penelope,

Clare Elizabeth, Gerry,

Robert, Linda

Betty Ann, John, Paul,

Elaine

Jenny, Sonja, Ken, Dana,

Raymond

Preface

In this American politics text, we emphasize certain themes to help students come to terms with the complex nature of our political system in the 1990s. One major theme is the growing importance of global affairs in American political life. In the past, it was only during times of war that the line between domestic and foreign affairs was significantly blurred. Today, the line has been virtually erased. Consider, for example, the impact of foreign trade on our domestic economy. Although protectionism has been a long-standing issue, with roots deep in our past, today most Americans recognize that their prosperity is directly linked not just to foreign competition but to such issues as global interest rates, "off-shore" investment, access to raw materials in the Third World, and even defense spending. It is, therefore, important to understand how these links have been forged.

Moreover, the issues and problems raised by an increasingly fragile world ecology, expanding global communications, the arms race, and other international political, economic, and social forces greatly affect the development of our governmental institutions. A major reason for the growth in the power of the modern presidency, for example, has been the need to respond effectively and decisively to changing international crises and events. Congress, too, has had to face new issues dictated by both positive and negative aspects of global interdependence. The attachment of human rights criteria to foreign aid, the overseeing of intelligence-gathering activities, and the appropriation of funds to combat the international drug trade, have all reflected the changing focus and agenda of the legislative branch.

Thus, although our primary goal is to offer the essential information traditionally covered in introductory government courses, we present that information in a global perspective when it seems appropriate. International examples are used alongside more traditional domestic examples and case studies. We hope that the results of our efforts will be a student well versed in the basics of American politics who is also sensitive to the undeniable impact of global forces.

In addition to considering the interdependence of foreign and domestic affairs, we try to take advantage of the tools developed by policy analysts. The growing complexity of American politics requires more precise and sophisticated tools of investigation. The field of public policy assumes we cannot understand change and its consequences by focusing only on the traditional institutions and processes of American government. Thus, we have included chapters on public policies to introduce students to the methods used by decision makers and analysts to sort through the costs and benefits of different policies. By looking at public policies from a problem-solution perspective, students can better appreciate how difficult it is to evaluate a simple program or determine why one program should be favored over another.

In the chapter on national character, we also acknowledge the rebirth of a more traditional mode of analysis, such as that used in Robert Bellah et al.'s *Habits of the Heart* (New York: Harper & Row, 1985). That title is derived from an expression used by the nineteenth-century French observer Alexis de Tocqueville to describe the mix of traits he thought essential to our national character. In the tradition of Tocqueville, we recognize the benefits of investigating how key values play a role in defining what a country is all about. National-character analysis lends itself to cross-country comparisons, which is in keeping with our efforts to help students see how they fit into the global political puzzle.

In addition to these basic themes, the book contains several other useful features. To help the reader understand that politics is the activity of human beings, a more personal look has been given to the presidency, Congress, the Supreme Court, and other major governmental institutions. These institutions are all examined in terms of the individuals who occupy them. Presidents, members of Congress, and Supreme Court justices are portrayed as citizens who have reached positions of significant political power and who can be expected to wield that power in terms of their own values and ambitions, as well as with regard to the rules and regulations of their respective offices.

The importance of the human element also underscores our belief that a clear and accurate picture of American politics demands constant, not intermittent, attention to the contributions of women and ethnic minorities. Thus, our analysis, examples, and language have been chosen so as not to diminish the importance of the rich diversity of influences and values in the American political system.

In addition, the book offers several tools to help students think creatively. For example, we present varying interpretations of the American power structure in a separate chapter describing the ruling elite, pluralist, and bureaucratic interpretations of American politics. The implications of these theories reappear at various times throughout the text, drawing the student into the controversies and debates surrounding the relationship between people and government.

Because many students are not going to study political science beyond the introductory course, the book also examines politics in ways useful to them as citizens. At appropriate times, it presents and evaluates specific action strategies open to the citizen, ranging from voting to joining interest groups. Even if students do not intend to engage in political activities, these evaluations will help them understand the obstacles and rewards of trying to effect change in our political system.

At all times, we have tried to limit political science jargon to tolerable levels. Although the introductory course is crucial for political science majors, it is also taken by nonmajors whose future is better served by an enhancement of citizenship skills than by specialized vocabulary skills. Thus, we have aimed for a lively style of writing that, we hope, will stimulate, rather than inhibit, interest in the subject.

Finally, we have assembled a package of learning aids to help the reader understand the material. For example, key terms are highlighted when they first appear in the text, then listed at the end of each chapter, defined in the glossary, and discussed in the *Study Guide* and *Instructor's Manual.* In addition, we have provided a summary of the main points covered in each chapter and punctuated the text with self-contained vignettes. We also offer suggested reading lists at the conclusion of each chapter to assist in term papers and other forms of student research.

Acknowledgments

An undertaking of this magnitude involves the assistance and talents of many creative people. We extend our gratitude to our friends and colleagues at Santa Clara University: Eric Hanson and Leslie Bethard of the Political Science Department, Joseph L. Subbiondo and Timothy O'Keefe of the College of Arts and Sciences, and student assistants Regina Weaver and Angela Clifford.

Critical external peer review of a manuscript is essential. We were fortunate to receive three separate sets of reviews as the project developed, and we wish to thank our colleagues for their thoughtful comments. They are James E. Anderson of Texas A. & M. University, Janet K. Boles of Marquette University, Earl W. Cobill of Freed-Hardeman College, Byron W. Daynes of DePauw University, James Dull of the University of New Haven, Larry Elowitz of Georgia College, Elizabeth N. Flores of Del Mar College, Michael Gunter of Tennessee Technological University, John Havick of Georgia State University, Harry Holloway of Oklahoma University, John Iatrides of Southern Connecticut State University, David H. Johns of San Diego State University, Michael W. McCann of the University of Washington, Keith Nicholls of Arizona State University, Henry Steck of the State University of New York at Cortland, and Eric Uslaner of the University of Maryland.

A special note of thanks is also extended to Lucy Valentine Wurtz, who prepared the *Instructor's Manual* and the *Study Guide.* Ms. Wurtz is a graduate of Santa Clara University and a fellow at the Coro Foundation. Her dedication to scholarship and its translation into political action reaffirms our commitment to the teaching profession.

Authors are not the only ones who burn the midnight oil. The editing, production, and marketing professionals involved in our project performed amazing feats with style and grace. Cindy Stormer, Political Science Editor at Brooks/Cole, has been with us from the start. Her encouragement, steadfastness, and good humor were crucial. And we are grateful for the first-rate contributions of manuscript editor Barbara Salazar, production coordinator Fiorella Ljunggren, production editors Cece Munson and Sue Ewing, and designer Katherine Minerva. We also wish to acknowledge the developmental help by Janet Hunter on the main text and Pat Gadban on the photo essays.

Janet A. Flammang
Dennis R. Gordon
Timothy J. Lukes
Kenneth R. Smorsten

★★★★★★★★★★★

Brief Contents

Contents

PART ONE

Log Cabins and Apple Pie: The Foundations of the American Political System

CHAPTER ONE

Those who labor in the earth are the chosen people of God . . . whose breasts he has made his peculiar deposit for substantial and genuine virtue. . . . While we have land to labor then, let us never wish to see our citizens occupied at a work-bench. . . . For the general operations of manufacture, let our work-shops remain in Europe. . . . It is the manners and spirit of a people which preserve a republic in vigor. A degeneracy in these is a canker which soon eats to the heart of its laws and constitution.

—*Thomas Jefferson*

At no time in our peacetime history has the state of the Nation depended more heavily on the state of the world; and seldom, if ever, has the state of the world depended more heavily on the state of our Nation.

—*Gerald R. Ford*

INTRODUCTION

★★★★★★★★★★★★★

From Small Town to Global Village: The Political Experience in the United States

In the 1980s, thousands of young people flocked to benefit concerts staged by superstar music idols in the hope of raising money for famine victims, political prisoners, and many other international causes. Charity benefits, even for politically controversial causes, were of course nothing new. In the 1960s, film and music stars raised money for the civil rights movement and the campaign to end the Vietnam war. In the 1970s, other stars were active in support of the women's rights, gay rights, and the antinuclear movements. But in the 1980s, when the stars and their fans joined together to sing "We Are the World," they reflected not only the age-old desire to help one's neighbors but also the changing nature of the world around them. Today Americans are part of a world community unimagined just decades ago. As former president Gerald Ford has reminded us, our well-being is inextricably linked to the well-being of the more than five billion other humans who inhabit this planet.

Thomas Jefferson may have longed for a republic of virtuous yeoman farmers, unsullied by degenerate industrialization. As we enter the last decade of the twentieth century, however, the United States is intertwined with other nations and peoples through a vast web of political, economic, military, and cultural relationships. These relationships, expressed sometimes as subtly as by the singing of "We Are the World" and sometimes as dramatically as by a terrorist's bomb blasting an airliner from the heavens, have a great impact on our way of life. This is not to say that foreign nations and diplomacy have not always been factors in American politics. After all, President Jefferson doubled the size of our agrarian republic in 1803, when he and Congress purchased the Louisiana Territory from a beleaguered France. What has changed is the intensity and scope of foreign influences. Historically, only a handful of citizens have been involved in international economics and politics. Now millions of Americans feel a direct connection with events occurring around the globe, and they are kept informed about the changing world by a vast array of electronic news sources beamed into their homes each day. Certainly, it is no longer possible, if indeed it ever was, to think of the United States as an autonomous nation isolated by vast oceans.

This is a book about American politics. As such it is concerned primarily with the basics of the U.S. political system: the Constitution, elections, parties, interest groups, federalism, and the three branches of government. But this book also takes notice of America's increasing involvement in a global political, economic, and cultural system. Today the student of American government, while never losing sight of traditional topics, must also consider international influences on our polit-

★ International stars performed around the world to aid the hungry in Africa.

ical life. Let us begin by exploring some of the changes that have "globalized" American politics during the past fifty years. These changes will be developed and highlighted throughout the book. We will then offer brief definitions of "power," "politics," and other important concepts. The chapter concludes with an overview of some of the problems inherent in the study of politics and government.

★ American Politics and the Changing Global Environment

How has the world changed during the past fifty years? Clearly, everyone's list carries a distinctive emphasis, depending on one's perceptions and interests. Our list, emphasizing the most obvious global influences on American politics, makes no pretense at being comprehensive. Nor do we feel compelled to support each item on the list with mounds of statistical proof at this point. The "proof" is what the rest of the book is about. The list of global changes is intended to serve as a conceptual road map, alerting readers to themes that we will expand upon in the chapters that follow.

Since 1945, American society and politics have been globalized by at least six interrelated developments: high-tech global communications, new superpower responsibilities, a continuing conventional and nuclear arms race, increased involvement in a world economy, the increasing integration of the global ecosystem, and an emerging global culture. Let us consider each development in turn.

★ Satellite broadcasting facilities can provide nearly instantaneous coverage of major news events. They are also helping to create a global television audience.

★ Modern communications bring information, entertainment, news, and political propaganda to the remote corners of the globe.

High-Tech Global Communications

Technological developments have indeed made the world smaller, creating a virtual **global village.** From supersonic jets linking London and New York to the South American peasants watching an old episode of *Dallas* dubbed in Spanish, interaction among the world's peoples has increased at a dizzying pace. Transactions between the world's financial centers, which once required weeks, are now completed in seconds with the aid of computers and satellites. Containerized freighters, loaded with goods, ply the seas with the aid of computerized navigation systems, which chart the fastest route to any destination in an instant. As figure 1-1 shows, a transatlantic crossing that once required seventy-two days can now be made in three and a half hours. Changes in communications, dramatic in their own right, are also important in the subtle ways they affect our thinking. Not only are we more involved with the rest of the world, but we are more aware of our involvement. The global flow of information tends to raise the level of citizens' concern about issues that used to be the exclusive province of specialists. During America's involvement in the Vietnam war, for example, the live images captured by hand-held video cameras brought news of the war into our homes in ways never before experienced by the general public and heightened political tensions. Improved information about the world has thus created new issues and demands on the American political system.

New Superpower Responsibilities

At the end of World War II, the European powers lay in ruins. Winner and loser alike found their economies and political systems in turmoil. In Asia, Japan's bid

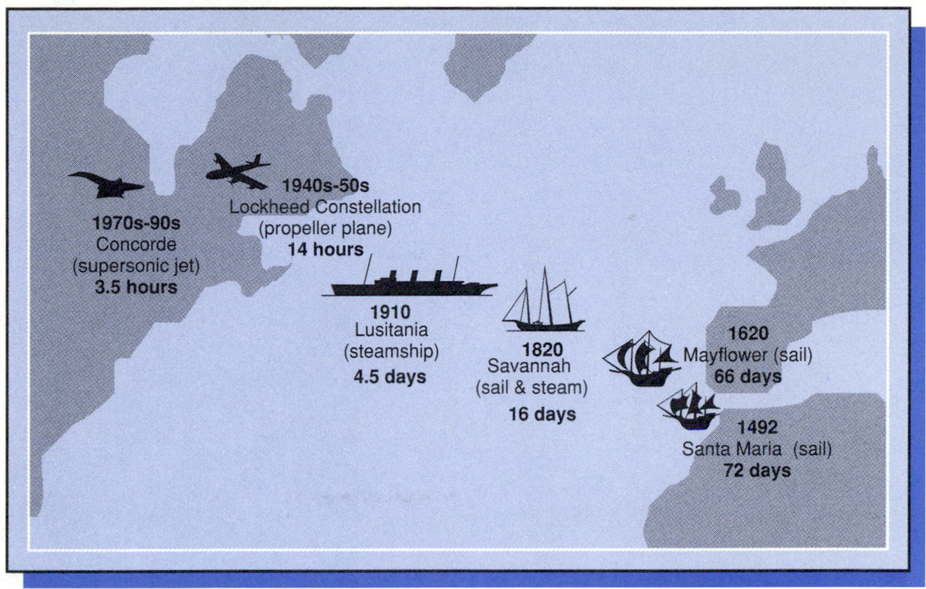

★ **Figure 1-1**
Transatlantic travel times, 1492–present
SOURCE: Rolf H. W. Theen and Frank L. Wilson, *Comparative Politics: An Introduction to Six Countries* (Englewood Cliffs, N.J.: Prentice-Hall, 1986).

for regional dominance ended with two devastating atomic blasts. The war also encouraged the European colonies in Africa, Asia, and the Middle East to seek independence, and eventually nearly one hundred new nations were created in the "Third World."

Unlike Europe and Japan, the United States emerged from the war as an economic, military, and political superpower. Whereas before the war the United States had been selective about its international commitments, it soon became the leader of the Western world. When challenged by the Soviet Union, America became the "world's policeman," creating military and economic alliances around the globe to contain this new threat.

The ensuing cold war with the Soviets had far-reaching political consequences at home. America's role as a world leader whipped up public support for military spending and a global activism unheard of in peacetime. A politician's credentials as an anticommunist frequently became a key concern of the voters. As the Vietnam war and the trillion-dollar arms race raised the cost of global activism in the 1960s and 1970s, Americans found a new set of issues complicating their political system. In the 1980s, the economic and political costs of America's superpower responsibilities continued to be a major source of controversy among citizens and political leaders alike.

A Continuing Arms Race

The development of atomic weapons has changed America and the world profoundly. Missiles and other long-range weapons have made America vulnerable in ways unimagined fifty years ago. In the quest to maintain the delicate nuclear

★ The threat of nuclear war has redefined America's role in the world. Once protected by vast oceans, today America's cities can be devastated by nuclear attack with as little as ten minutes' warning.

balance of power, the United States embarked on an intense arms race with the Soviet Union, created a vast system of alliances with friendly nations, and established more than three hundred military facilities abroad, with major bases in Europe, Africa, Asia, the Middle East, and Latin America. The atomic era also produced an entirely new vocabulary for Americans to digest—mutually assured destruction, Star Wars, nuclear winter, ICBM, nonproliferation, Strategic Arms Limitation Talks—and a new set of political controversies for voters to tackle.

Atomic weapons made it crucial for the superpowers to avoid direct military confrontation. When a face-to-face showdown loomed—the Cuban missile crisis of 1962 is a good example—one side or the other backed down. But the cold war and the arms race did not lead the superpowers to abandon military activity altogether. Both the United States and the Soviet Union supported their allies in distant armed struggles: Korea, Vietnam, Angola, Nicaragua, Afghanistan. Thus Americans (and Soviets) have watched their children march off to war (and seen billions of tax dollars spent) in countries that may not have even existed fifty years ago.

As the 1980s came to a close, the United States and the Soviet Union were enjoying a period of improved relations and reduced tension. The Intermediate-Range Nuclear Force Treaty, ratified in 1988, was an important first step in limiting the expensive and potentially destabilizing competition in high-tech nuclear weapons. In 1989, bold superpower initiatives to reduce conventional forces in Europe, labeled a "historic transition" by President George Bush, heightened the public's expectations that the cold war was finally coming to an end. But as the superpowers seek to reduce their nuclear stockpiles, other nations, some in the Third World, are working hard to develop their own atomic devices and delivery systems (see figure 1-2). Nuclear weapons, moreover, are only one dimension of global military competition. Today the nations of the world spend billions of dollars on conventional forces, including deadly chemical and biological weapons (see figure 1-3 on p. 10).

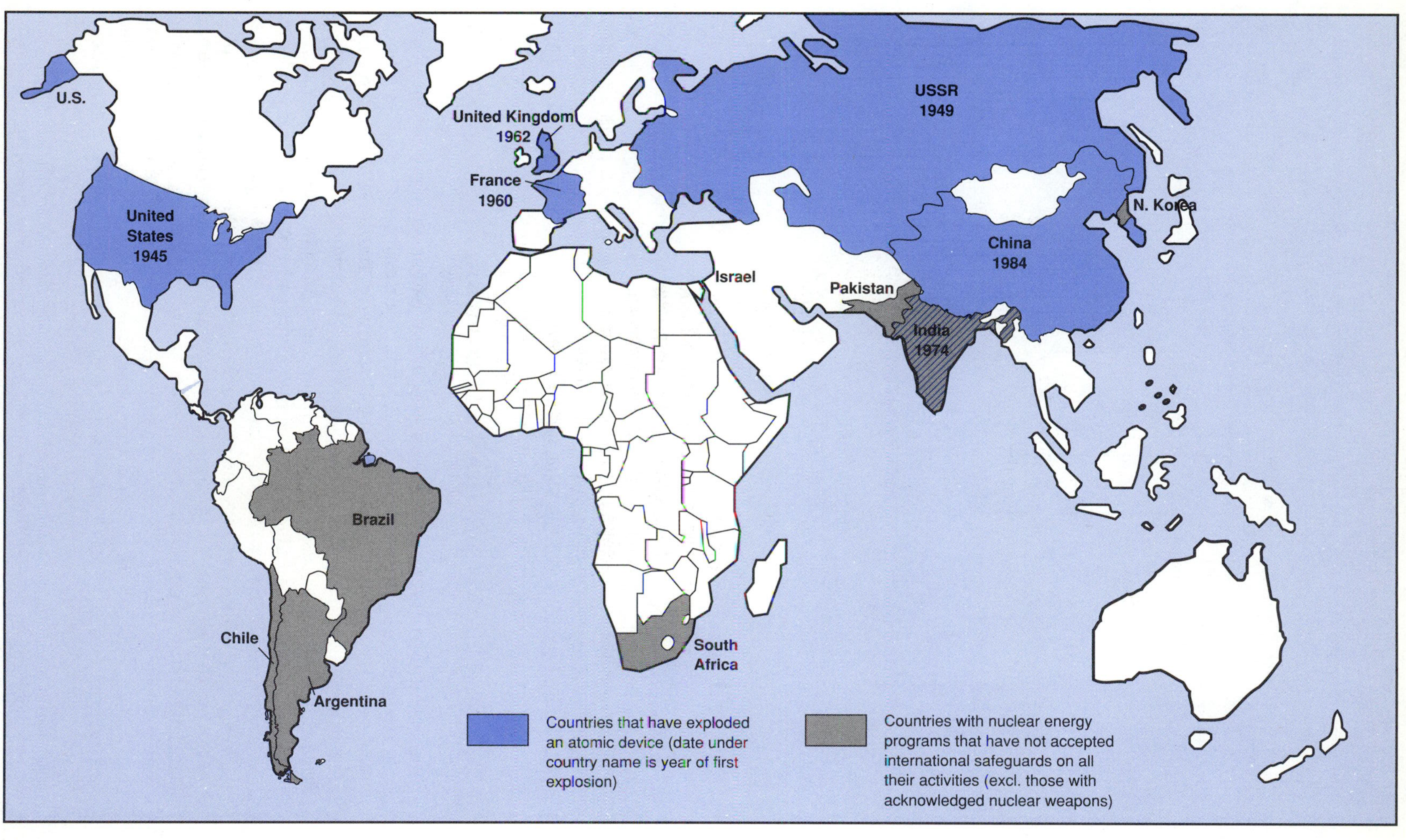

★ **Figure 1-2**
Nuclear weapons—haves and have-nots
SOURCE: United States Department of State, *Atlas of United States Foreign Relations,* 2d ed. (Washington, D.C.: Bureau of Public Affairs, 1985).

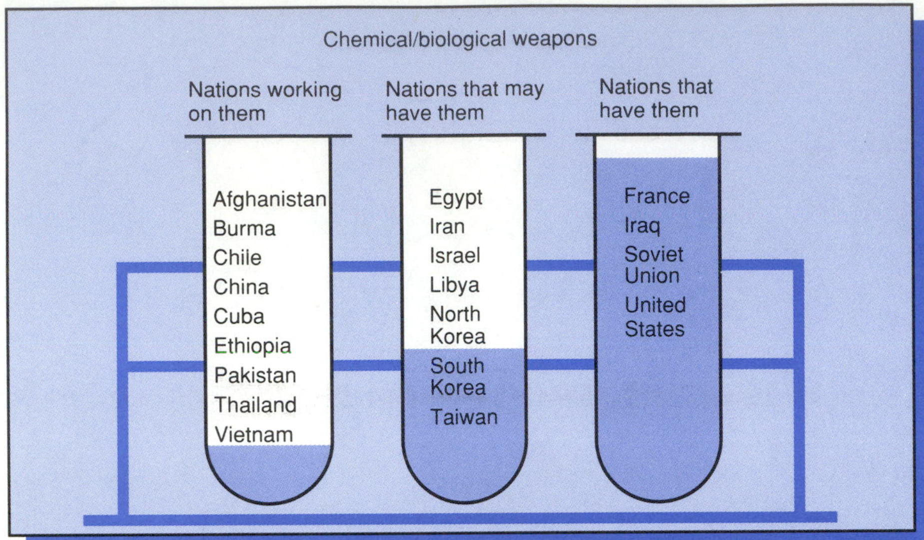

★ **Figure 1-3**
The threat of chemical/biological weapons
SOURCE: John J. Fialka, "Fighting Dirty: Chemical Weapons Spread in Third World," *Wall Street Journal* (September 15, 1988), pp. 1, 26.

According to the U.S. government, worldwide military spending increased from $650 billion in constant dollars (adjusted for inflation) to $900 billion over the ten years between 1976 and 1986.[1] As these weapons spread around the globe, U.S. national interest requires close attention to and involvement in international political and economic conflicts (see figure 1-4).

Increased Involvement in a World Economy

The postwar expansion of America's role in the global economy has also been extraordinary. At the end of World War II, about 5 percent of the U.S. gross national product (GNP) was in foreign trade and investment. Today nearly 30 percent of America's GNP is generated by foreign activity. The United States has benefited tremendously from access to foreign markets and new sources of raw materials. Today more than five million Americans work directly in export-related jobs. At the same time, the future of many American jobs and the availability of such consumer goods as imported cars and electronic items have come to be heavily influenced by other nations. The emergence of the Third World as a source of materials and labor, moreover, has shifted the basis of America's economy from manufacturing to service industries. The shift to a service economy has created many new jobs for women, who have flooded the labor market since World War II. But it has also forced many citizens to develop new skills or go without jobs. In the face of increased competition from the European Community, Japan, and other nations, the United States, once a creditor nation, has become the world's largest debtor.

Involvement in the global economy has also made the United States vulnerable in other ways. During the 1970s, for example, the nation was rocked by the

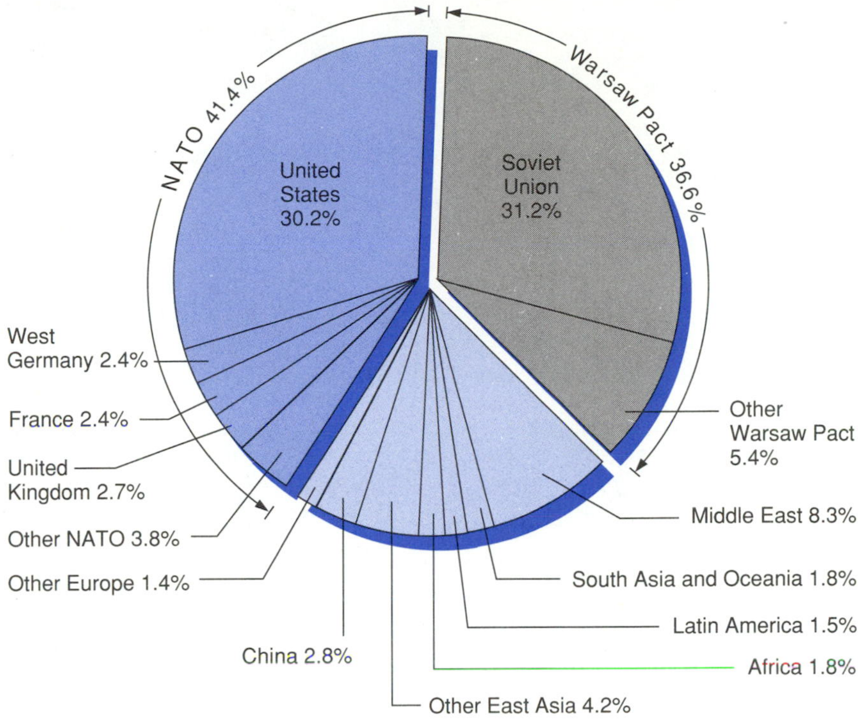

★ **Figure 1-4**
Shares of world military expenditures, 1985
SOURCE: United States Arms Control and Disarmament Agency, *World Military Expenditures and Arms Transfers, 1987* (Washington, D.C., 1988).

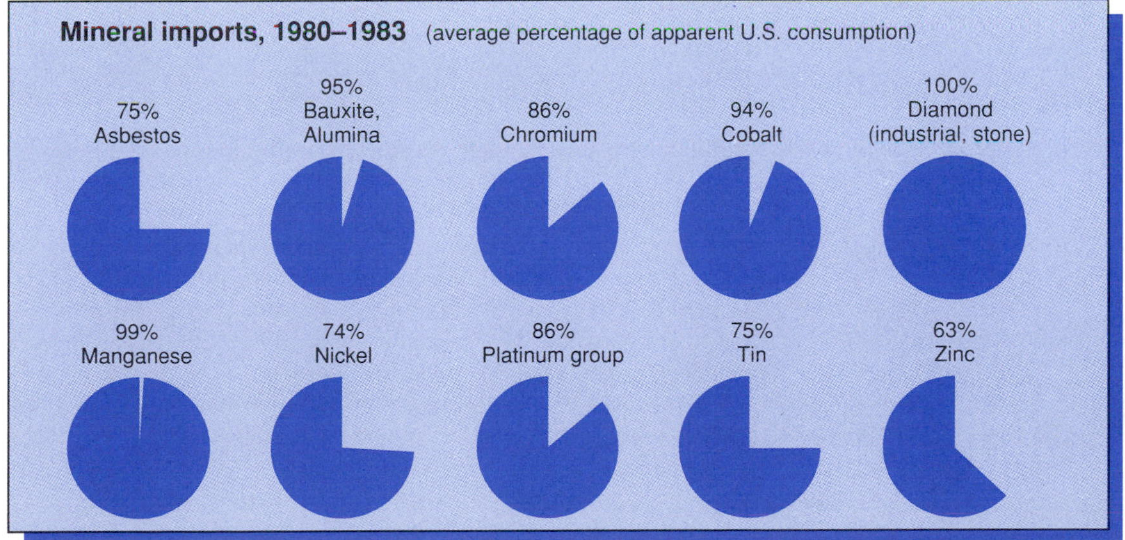

★ **Figure 1-5**
U.S. reliance on imported minerals
SOURCE: United States Department of State, *Atlas of United States Foreign Relations,* 2d ed. (Washington, D.C.: Bureau of Public Affairs, 1985).

★ The use of foreign workers in "offshore" plants by U.S. manufacturers has become quite controversial. Labor leaders often accuse business of exporting jobs and encourage their fellow citizens to "buy American."

soaring prices of imported oil, and oil was also used as a political weapon by some Middle Eastern nations in the aftermath of the 1973 Arab-Israeli war. Figure 1-5 illustrates the United States' reliance on imported minerals; global food production is shown in figure 1-6. Both figures demonstrate reliance on other countries for supplies and staples. The lag in economic development in many of the poorer nations of the Third World has led to political unrest in areas of vital strategic importance to the United States. Since many Third World nations owe billions of dollars to U.S. banks, a global recession or other economic problems not directly the result of U.S. actions can still be highly disruptive to the American economy. While the United States still holds a commanding lead among the world's economies in most respects, its leadership is increasingly tested by other nations and its prosperity is tied to economic decisions made in foreign lands.

The Global Ecosystem

In 1988, two "natural" events dramatically revealed that the nations of the world are subject to the forces of a global ecosystem. The first event was a drought that hit many parts of the world, including the North American continent, drying up crops and raising food prices. Droughts, of course, have been a constant feature of humankind's experience on this planet. But this drought, according to many scientists, was not the result of naturally occurring wet and dry cycles. The drought of 1988 appeared to be a product of the so-called greenhouse effect. The greenhouse effect, a gradual warming of the earth's atmosphere, is thought to result from the growing use of fossil fuels for transportation, industry, and many of the technological necessities of modern life.

The North American drought had several immediate economic effects in the United States and around the globe. Beyond the short-run changes in food supplies and prices lay the lesson that national boundaries are meaningless to Mother Nature. While the developed nations of the world are primarily responsible for the global warming (because of their high energy use), all countries will eventually suffer from the changes in the earth's climate (see figure 1-7 on p. 15).

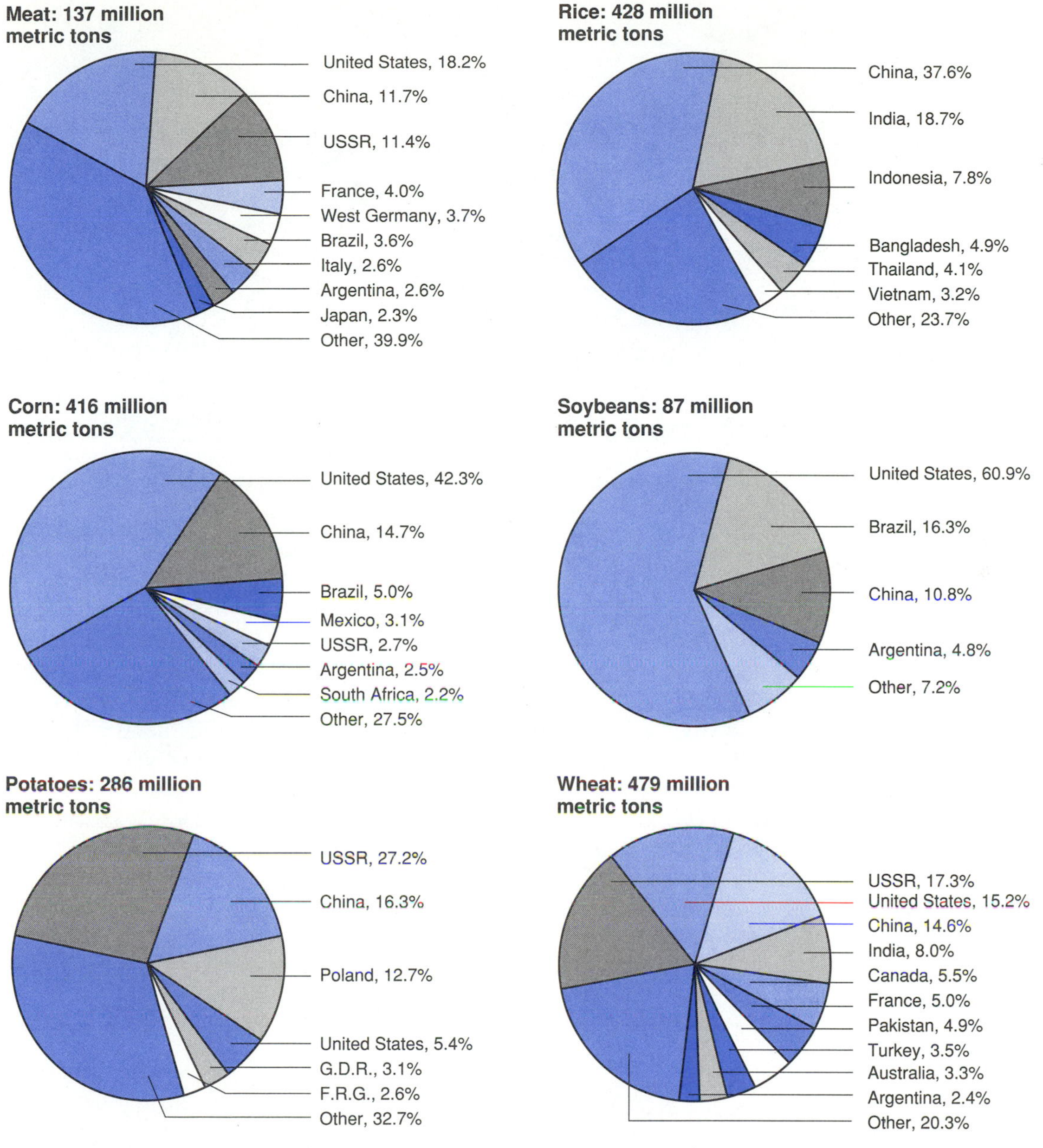

★ **Figure 1-6**
Global food production: The United States is a main source of agricultural goods for many nations.
SOURCE: United States Department of State, *Atlas of United States Foreign Relations,* 2d ed. (Washington, D.C.: Bureau of Public Affairs, 1985).

The second event of 1988 involved several California gray whales that had become trapped by ice as winter advanced in the frozen reaches of Alaska. Whales, which at one time had been hunted nearly to extinction, had come to enjoy support from many citizen groups around the globe. Thus a massive rescue effort was launched, which ultimately involved experts from the United States, the Soviet

★ Drought in North Dakota threatens American agriculture. Many feel that changes in the weather are one result of the "greenhouse effect" and other human changes to the environment. Such problems, often the product of pollution occurring thousands of miles away, require global political and technological solutions.

Union, and many other lands. Working against the clock, local citizens, U.S. naturalists, and a Soviet icebreaker worked to free the seemingly doomed mammals. Using everything from hand labor to satellite photos, the rescuers worked on as an anxious world was kept informed through the latest electronic news-gathering devices. In the end, most of the whales were saved and humans could savor the tiny victory that international cooperation made possible.

Today the world faces a lengthy list of global environmental threats: pollution, spread of new diseases, major oil spills, nuclear contamination from atomic power plants, acid rain. "These trends," according to Jessica Tuchman Mathews, a former

"This past summer, I got deeply depressed about our planet—as if I didn't have enough problems of my own."

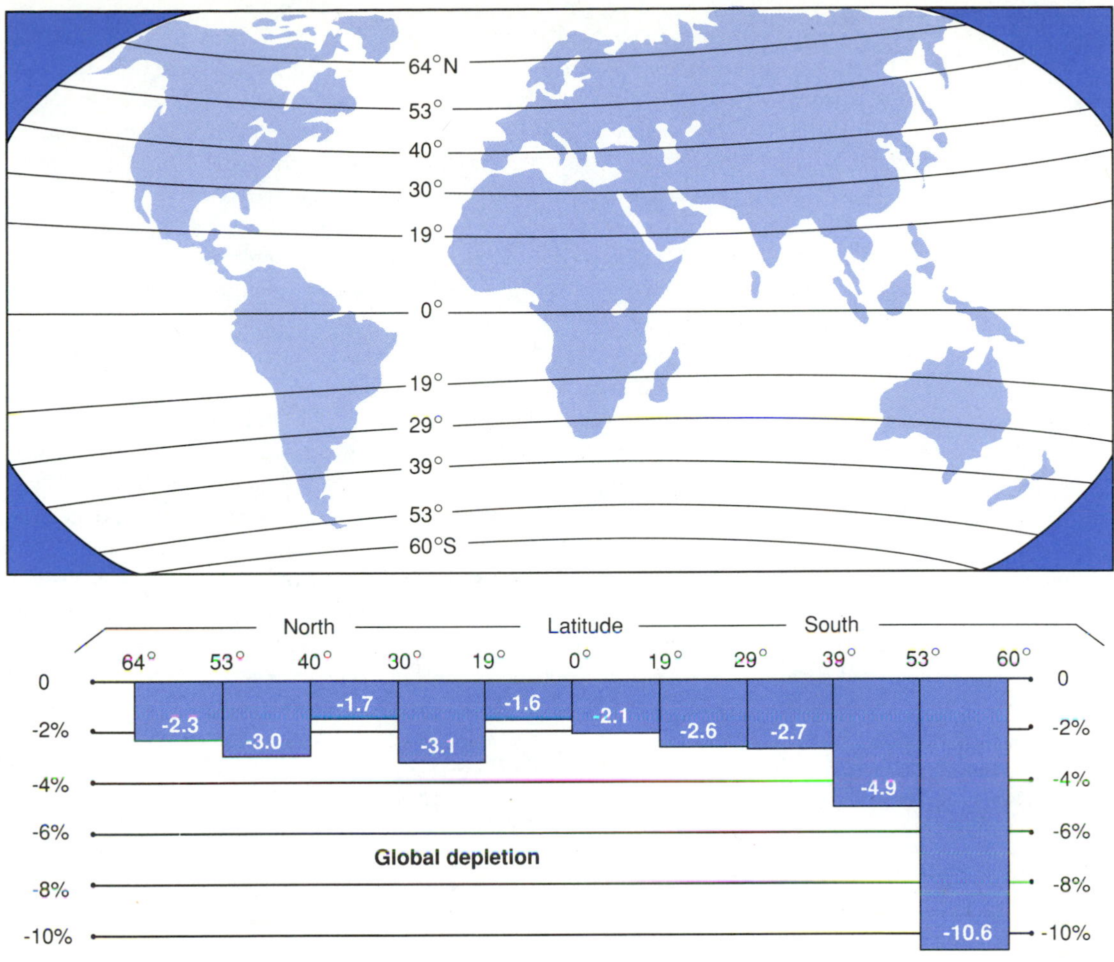

★ **Figure 1-7**

Global areas of highest ozone depletion, by latitude

SOURCE: NASA Ozone Trends Panel. Reprinted in *South, 103,* May 1989, p. 75.

adviser to the National Security Council, "are already affecting international relations, and will more and more. Soil erosion, drought, flooding, local weather cross borders with impunity."[2] As more nations become economically developed, previously unforeseen problems arise. The fruits that the United States and other lands have reaped from postwar economic changes have dramatically increased the wear and tear on Mother Earth. Neither the most intimidating army nor the most clever diplomacy can defeat the forces of nature. As awareness of global ecological problems has grown, American political institutions have had to respond.

An Emerging Global Culture

All of the changes we have mentioned contribute to what may be the most pervasive postwar development: the emergence of a global culture. Today people in many lands wear the same fashions, listen to the same music, eat the same fast food, and watch the same films and videos. Whether or not these consumption patterns

Ozone Depletion: A Crisis without Borders

Only a few years ago ozone was hardly a household word, let alone the subject of examination in a textbook on American politics. Today government leaders in the United States and around the globe are working together to prevent the depletion of ozone in the earth's atmosphere.

The layer of ozone gas in the stratosphere prevents dangerous levels of solar ultraviolet radiation from reaching the earth's surface. In the 1970s, scientists began to detect small amounts of manufactured chlorofluorocarbons (CFCs) in the upper atmosphere. CFCs, chemicals first produced in the 1920s, are used in a variety of products ranging from air conditioners to plastic containers. Though beneficial to society, CFCs are believed to be harmful to the ozone layer. In 1978 the U.S. government banned aerosol sprays that used CFCs as a propellant. By the mid-1980s, however, research indicated that a growing hole in the ozone layer had developed over Antarctica. The development of such a hole over a populated area, scientists warned, could pose serious health risks. A 1 percent drop in ozone over the United States, for example, could cause 10,000 additional cases of skin cancer per year.

Government leaders and environmentalists in the United States and in many other countries responded to the ozone problem. Since the scientific community was fairly certain the CFCs were the main cause of ozone depletion, steps were taken both nationally and locally to curtail use of the chemical compounds. Many communities banned foam containers at fast-food restaurants, since they have a high CFC content. A variety of international forums, including the United Nations, met to discuss this global threat. In 1987 the Montreal Accord was signed by twenty-four nations, which pledged to reduce production of CFCs by 50 percent by the year 1999. While welcoming the Montreal Accord, many scientists indicated that much greater reductions are needed if the dangers of ozone depletion are to be escaped.

The threat to the ozone layer is a classic global technology-inspired political issue. Since Mother Nature knows no borders, CFC pollution in one country can cause cancer thousands of miles away. It would be hard to find a better example of the globalization of our life: local city councils responding to an international problem by acting to change the packaging of that sacred American institution, the cheeseburger to go.

SOURCE: Michael D. Lemonick, "The Heat Is On," *Time,* October 19, 1987, p. 61.

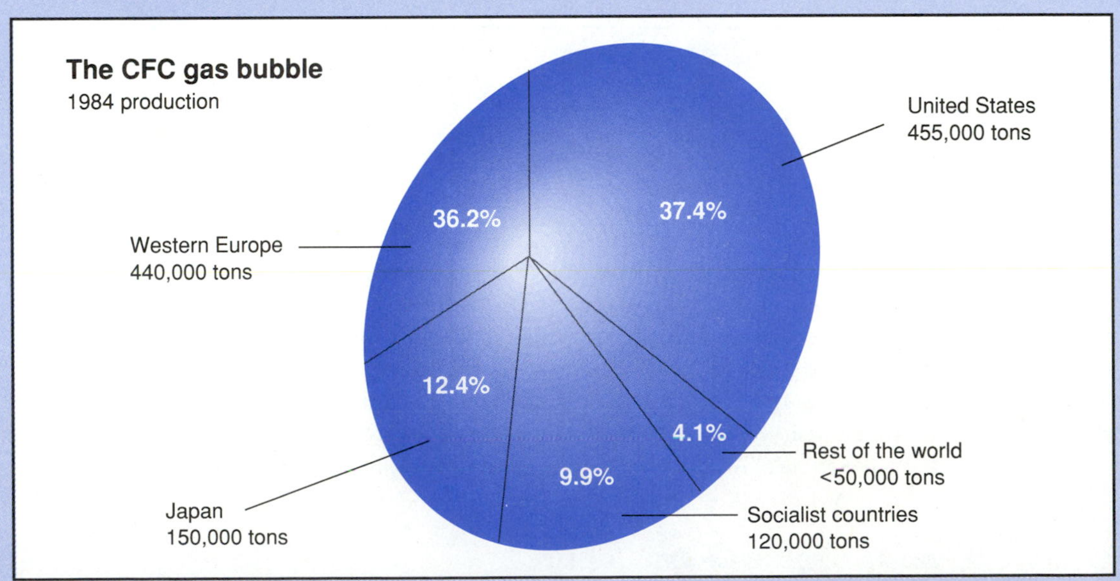

 **Figure 1-8**

CFC production in 1984: Who is destroying the ozone layer?

SOURCE: Courtesy of Greenpeace, 1989.

★ The lovable characters produced by America's entertainment industry help to create a global culture. Could their world-wide popularity begin to destroy local traditions and values?

indicate more than a superficial global culture is a matter of debate. The fact that people in many countries wear the same designer clothes and enjoy the same soft drinks or that most university students in the Western world study English does not mean that they share the same basic values or world view. Many Americans are too quick to assume that people in other nations think just as we do simply because they like the same things. Indeed, some Third World peoples condemn America and Western society as culturally and politically decadent. This potential clash of cultures became apparent in 1989, when Iran's Ayatollah Khomeini called for the murder of an author, Salman Rushdie, whose novel *The Satanic Verses,* published in the West, was reported to be offensive to the Islamic faith. Thus, while the world's peoples remain divided on many levels, the emerging global market, combined with improved travel and communication, increasingly exposes Americans to other nations and heightens their awareness of the ways in which international events influence their lives.

The challenge we face as students of politics is to understand both the obvious and the subtle ways in which economic, political, and social interdependence with other nations affect American politics. This book aims to encourage students to recognize that the Organization of Petroleum Exporting Countries (OPEC) is as much a part of American society as baseball (a major sport in Japan and Cuba) and

★ Two demonstrations symbolize the clash of cultures heightened by globalization. Protesters in New York denounce stores that hesitated to carry *The Satanic Verses.* Iranian women, protesting the publication in the West of the controversial book, call for the death of author Salman Rushdie.

apple pie (sometimes made with fruit imported from South America). Of course this lesson can be learned in more direct ways, as when you drive your Honda (made in Ohio, in a plant owned by Japanese) down to the local fast-food outlet (perhaps owned by investors from Asia and serving beef raised in Central America), or when you travel abroad and are attacked by terrorists firing an antitank missile (made in the United States but sold to the terrorists by a South American drug baron, who obtained it with the help of an Eastern European diplomat). Contrary to popular myth, what you don't know can hurt you when it comes to politics.

★ Politicization and Interdependence

Since World War II, the rapidly unfolding political, technological, economic, and cultural changes have linked Americans and once-distant peoples into a web of complex **interdependence.** Interdependence is a relationship in which two or more nations come to rely on each other to satisfy their economic, political, or other needs. Interdependence can provide great benefits. America's economic prosperity, for example, has been due in part to the expansion of global trade since World War II.

Thus our lives have become increasingly bound up with decisions and events that take place thousands of miles from our shores. Reliance on other nations, of course, can also have its costs, as the United States learned during the energy crisis of the 1970s and the terrorist attacks of the 1980s. It is precisely the uncertain nature of interdependence, offering both dangers and opportunities, that has made foreign affairs such a complex and controversial part of our everyday political life.

One result of growing interdependence is that American life seems to have become increasingly politicized. By **politicization** we mean that the average citizen has come to see more of society's problems as falling within the realm of politics and government. Sixty years ago unemployment was seen by many people as the result of laziness. The cure for unemployment was to be found in education or a good swift motivational kick in the pants. While many Americans still hold this view, many others now blame the "economy" or "foreign competition." Politiciza-

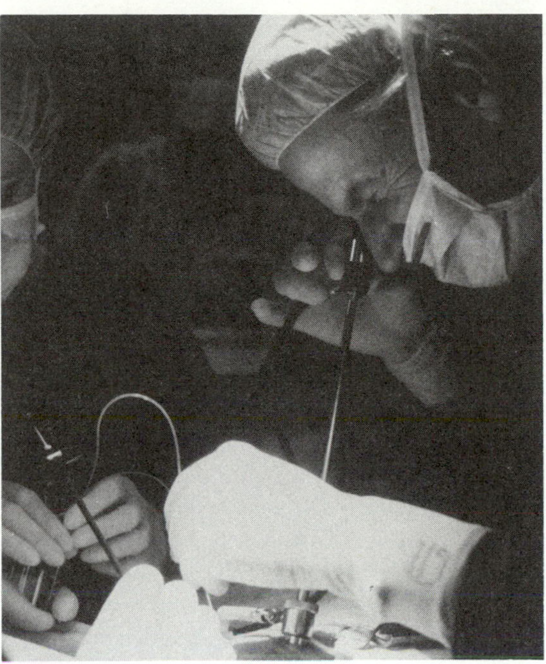

★ The development of new medical procedures, like in vitro fertilization for couples unable to bear children, presents government with many new difficult and controversial issues.

tion is also reflected in the fact that such problems as import quotas, acid rain, and human rights in South Africa are not just issues to be handled by State Department specialists or elected officials. Today these matters are the subjects of everyday debate in American communities large and small. And government, by either design or default, is assigned the task of finding solutions that will satisfy 250 million Americans while not making the other 5 billion people of the earth fighting mad.

Politicization has also increased as technological innovations have created new issues that were not even imagined fifty years ago. Thanks to science and technology, the courts are asked to decide when human life begins, and when it should end. Legislators and bureaucrats must grapple with issues ranging from fetal tissue transplants to the acceptability of abortion pills. Issues that once confounded philosophers and theologians are now the subjects of routine political debate. Interest groups and political movements have sprung up to promote every conceivable cause. From city hall to the United Nations Security Council, citizens and government officials confront an astounding array of issues and challenges.

★ Some Views of "Politics" and "Power"

To say that issues have become increasingly politicized raises the next question: What is "politics"? While some people argue that "politics" refers simply to the activities of government, others view it more broadly as the totality of everyday experience. Many feminists say that "the personal is political." In the opinion of the late antiwar activist Abbie Hoffman, politics is "the way you live your life." In fact, a major problem faced by political scientists is how to determine what politics is and what, therefore, they should study. The concept has become so ambiguous and controversial that no universally accepted definition of it exists. Because of its ambiguity, political scientists have been charged with "riding off in many directions, evidently on the assumption that if you don't know where you are going, any road will take you there."[3]

How may a political act or event be distinguished from other kinds of acts or events? How may one determine when labor leaders and corporate presidents are engaged in political as opposed to economic activity? When do inexpensive imported products from abroad cease to be a boon for consumers and instead become a political headache for politicians worried about unemployment? And when should a terrorist act against Americans be seen as a coolly calculated maneuver by some organization to obtain political advantage, rather than the work of crazed fanatics?

These diverse issues have one common element: they all involve some form of conflict. Indeed, many political scientists view **politics** as the process of settling conflicts and distributing benefits. They point out that in most societies, controversy rages over who should receive whatever happens to be of value, whether it be material possessions, such as money and land, or intangibles, such as prestige and power.

Politics, in other words, involves the allocation of values. In regard to some issues, such as determining who benefits from a tax cut, the values may be relatively easy to define. In regard to other issues, such as deciding the right to teach religion in public schools or the right of terminally ill patients to die, the values may be complex and highly philosophical. One thing is clear: people tend to want their own needs and desires satisfied, craving benefits that are likely to be demanded by others. Unless they receive these benefits (or become convinced by reason or force that they cannot have them), disorder and violence may ensue. Consequently, many political scientists see politics as the means of deciding how wealth, power, and other values are to be distributed and how conflicts and disagreements are to be managed. As Harold Lasswell succinctly put it, politics is the process of deciding "who gets what, when, and how."[4]

A broad definition of politics is necessary because a narrow definition can limit our understanding of the way nations are governed. The U.S. government, for example, has for years supported an organization called the American Institute for Free Labor Development (AIFLD), a group dedicated to helping "nonpolitical" labor unions in Latin America. According to AIFLD, a nonpolitical union would ban communist members and shun political controversy to focus on such technical issues as job safety. Negotiations over wages and working conditions in this nonpolitical atmosphere would be conducted in a spirit of goodwill and mutual cooperation. Latin America, however, suffers from rampant unemployment, hunger, and poverty. AIFLD's desire for nonpolitical unions thus seems unrealistic to many people. In nations where conflicts over "who gets what, when, and how" have historically led to rebellion and violence, labor unions frequently play a part in the battle over the allocation of values. For critics of AIFLD, its goal of nonpolitical unions is at best naive and at worst a thinly disguised effort to protect governments friendly to the United States from hostile workers.[5] Needless to say, in this book our definition of politics is broad enough to include labor unions and a host of other nongovernmental organizations and institutions.

★ Deterioration of the environment has created an entirely new set of political controversies for Americans to tackle.

Indeed, it is important to note that politics is not necessarily the same as **government.** "Government" usually refers to the rules and institutions that form the basis for the organization and operation of the political system. A quick look at the table of contents of this book indicates that the study of American political life includes forces ranging from interest groups to protest movements and public opinion. Still, while many groups and institutions may help decide how benefits will be distributed, governmental institutions are the principal agencies of social control. They make most of the rules for society and have a virtual monopoly on the use of force (such as the police and the military) to carry them out. In short, if politics is the process of resolving disputes and allocating benefits, then government is the principal machinery by which the tasks are accomplished.

Government seems to have many tools at its disposal to resolve disputes and allocate benefits. The key element, of course, is **power.** A glance at the dictionary tells us that power has many characteristics: capacity to act, strength, control, authority, influence, and domain, to name a few. On the surface the link between government and power may seem obvious—the government passes a law and uses its power to punish violators. It certainly does, as anyone who has run afoul of a parking meter can attest, but power for modern governments includes much more than brute force. Government officials use power both positively and negatively: to get us to do certain things and to prevent us from doing other things. It teaches us a pledge of allegiance to foster patriotism and it jails us for tax evasion. Government gives foreign aid to build friendly relations abroad and it goes to war when necessary. The legitimate exercise of power is the essence of government.

★ For many people, the town meeting symbolizes citizen participation in the political process and the best of American democracy.

Thus we can see why power is such an integral part of the study of politics and government. So long as conflicts continue over who gets what, when, and how, people will struggle for the power to make these decisions. Furthermore, political power shapes our thinking about the way benefits should be distributed and disputes settled. Power is wielded to determine, for example, whether major oil companies should receive special tax breaks, whether defense spending or social security payments should be cut in an effort to balance the federal budget, or whether women should receive pay equal to that of men in similar jobs. In short, the study of politics leads to an analysis of the way power is pursued, achieved, used, and lost. It leads to an examination of political campaigns, back-room deals, voting, the media, the links between corporate wealth and governmental policy, the influence of other nations, and even personal motivations and drives—the process, in other words, that determines who will make the major political decisions affecting society's welfare. When we examine power more fully in a later chapter, we will see that the analysis of power has resulted in sharply conflicting views of how important political decisions are made in the United States and of who makes them.

★ The Study of Politics

The study of politics covers many subjects and draws upon many fields, including history, sociology, geography, economics, and psychology. Still, many aspects of the study of politics—**political science**—are unique. While each discipline no doubt has its own justifications for existence, none makes so bold a claim of providing citizenship training as does political science. It is said that political science helps prepare students for their roles as productive members of a democratic society and global community. By acquiring the skills of political analysis and improving

★ Helping to shape the views of future generations is a key ingredient of political power. By using national symbols and rituals—the Pledge of Allegiance and the flag—government instills loyalty and love of country at a young age.

their understanding of government, they learn to influence the political decisions that affect their lives. As one scholar has put it, "The best reason for improving one's skill in political analysis is this: political analysis helps one to understand the world he [or she] lives in, to make more intelligent choices among the alternatives he [or she] faces, and to influence the changes, great and small, that are an inherent aspect of all political systems."[6]

Political scientists have also developed new techniques to explore the expanding world of politics and government. Inventive scholars have been working to expand the discipline, seeking contact with researchers in fields ranging from biology to mathematics. The research methods used to study political behavior, including sophisticated polling techniques and computer modeling, reflect the most up-to-date thinking in the scientific community. In fact, some political scientists see no outer limits to their research; they are constantly involved with the progress and findings of other areas of study, regardless of labels. As one scholar has concluded, "A political scientist cannot close any doors. He [or she] must use the historian's evidence of past human experience; the economist's analysis of wealth, value, and distribution; the sociologist's explanation of status and group interrelations; the geographer's comparative data on natural resources; the psychologist's insights and findings about human behavior; and the philosopher's analysis of political ends."[7]

There is also some controversy within the discipline over its true "scientific" capabilities. While some political scientists claim that the study of politics is empirical and objective, others insist that politics—whether studied or practiced—cannot and should not be divorced from personal values.

The controversy will probably never be resolved, because the nature of "science" is primarily a matter of definition. If science is regarded simply as a way of gathering information through careful and deliberate observation—an effort to treat the subject matter with as much precision as possible—then perhaps political science can rightly be thought of as a science. But if science implies, instead, an ability to submit the subject matter to controlled experiments that other scholars can duplicate and test under the same laboratory conditions, as well as an ability to produce general laws capable of yielding accurate predictions about future behavior, then the label may be less accurate.

In any event, it would be a mistake to think of political scientists as solely engaged in lofty scholarship, pondering the great issues of the day and debating whether their findings are "scientific." Many students of political science have chosen to practice rather than study politics. From the White House (Woodrow Wilson was a political scientist) to the storefront community center in America's poorest ghetto, many political scientists take a hands-on approach to the nation's thorniest issues. Our courts, moreover, are packed with lawyers and judges who began their careers with the study of political science. Other political scientists staff the so-called think tanks—private research and lobbying institutes, which analyze and propose solutions for problems ranging from waste treatment to verification of superpower arms-control treaties. Still others, working in the United Nations or in interest groups, pursue a personal dream of world peace. Political science, in other words, involves much more than classroom contemplation of the electoral college and voting districts.

Given the broad focus of political science, we are therefore likely to find a relative paucity of simple and established conclusions. Although political scientists may feel comfortable describing certain features of the political scene, such as the number of citizens who voted in an election or support arms control, they will have to be a great deal more tentative in offering explanations, such as why people voted a certain way or how diplomats forge their treaties with formidable adversaries. As we will discover throughout this volume, political scientists are rarely in agreement on the major questions of politics, especially on how a citizen may fit into the political scheme of things. We will find that, to arrive at some definite conclusions about our own role in the politics of this country and the world, ultimately we will have to furnish our own explanations. But do not despair, our lack of pat answers is a challenge, not a limitation.

★ Summary

Since the end of World War II, American society and politics have become increasingly globalized by six interrelated developments: improved high-tech global communications, new superpower responsibilities, a continuing arms race, increased involvement in a world economy, the increasing interaction of the global ecosystem, and the emergence of a global culture. These developments constitute the strands of a web of complex interdependence, linking American politics to global concerns. As a result of these developments, numerous aspects of our everyday lives have become politicized.

Politics is the means of settling conflicts and distributing benefits. Government, consisting of the rules and institutions that form the basis for the organization and operation of the political system, is the primary machinery by which these tasks are accomplished. Government officials and citizens alike pursue power, the ability to do desired things and prevent undesired things. Politics involves a struggle for power to decide who gets what, when, and how.

Political science is the study of politics, government, and power. It draws on the insights of many disciplines and is "scientific" to some degree. The ultimate purpose of political science, and of this book, is to prepare citizens for informed participation in a democratic society and a global community.

★ Key Terms

global village
government
interdependence
political science
politicization
politics
power

★ Notes

1. U.S. Arms Control and Disarmament Agency, *World Military Expenditures and Arms Transfers, 1987* (Washington, D.C., 1988), p. 1.
2. Jessica Tuchman Mathews, interviewed on *Bill Moyers' World of Ideas,* PBS, September 13, 1988.
3. Heinz Eulau, "Political Science," in *A Reader's Guide to the Social Sciences,* ed. Berthold F. Hoselitz (New York: Free Press, 1959), p. 91.
4. Harold D. Lasswell, *Politics: Who Gets What, When, and How?* (New York: McGraw-Hill, 1936).
5. See Penny Lernoux, *Cry of the People* (New York: Doubleday, 1980).
6. Robert A. Dahl, *Modern Political Analysis,* 3d ed. (Englewood Cliffs, N.J.: Prentice-Hall, 1976), p. 1.
7. Robert E. Murphy, *The Style and Study of Political Science* (Glenview, Ill.: Scott, Foresman, 1970), p. 7.

★ For Further Reading

Barnes, James F., Marshall Carter, and Max J. Skidmore. *The World of Politics: A Concise Introduction.* 2d ed. New York: St. Martin's Press, 1984.

Best, Paul J., Kul B. Rai, and David F. Walsh. *Politics in Three Worlds: An Introduction to Political Science.* New York: Wiley, 1986.

Keohane, Robert. *After Hegemony: Cooperation and Discord in the World Political Economy.* Princeton, N.J.: Princeton University Press, 1984.

Lasswell, Harold D. *Politics: Who Gets What, When, and How?* New York: McGraw-Hill, 1936.

Olson, Gary L., ed. *How the World Works: A Critical Introduction to International Relations.* Glenview, Ill.: Scott, Foresman, 1984.

Pirages, Dennis. *Global Technopolitics: The International Politics of Technology and Resources.* Pacific Grove, Calif.: Brooks/Cole, 1989.

Rosenau, James M. *The Dramas of Politics: An Introduction to the Joys of Inquiry.* Boston: Little, Brown, 1973.

What the delegates had accomplished was truly remarkable. It was the first constitution of its kind in all human history. They drew on the wisdom of the past going back as far as Pericles, but particularly the great French thinkers, the English thinkers and the thinkers of the Scottish enlightenment. Dreamed about by philosophers and thinkers, it had never been tried out on that level.

—*Chief Justice Warren E. Burger*

CHAPTER TWO

THE CONSTITUTION

★★★★★★★★★★★★

A Written Foundation: The United States Constitution

To understand American politics, we must know something about the historical roots of our society and the constitutional arrangements fashioned by a talented band of individuals gathered in Philadelphia two centuries ago. Their perceptions of the political world—and of human nature—led to a body of laws and principles that continue to define the boundaries of our political behavior.

Like most of the other subjects discussed in this book, the United States Constitution cannot be fully understood without giving some attention to the political and international setting in which it emerged. Although the framers of the Constitution could not have foreseen the growing importance of international affairs in American politics, the document they wrote reflected many of the philosophical views and political concerns prominent on the world stage at that time.

Moreover, the provisions contained in the document they forged greatly affect the ways in which we confront the problems and dangers imposed by international influences and events today. Whether dealing with a crisis in the Persian Gulf, a revolution in Central or South America, or an imbalance in international trade, this country must respond with an often unwieldy system of checks and balances and separation of powers devised by people who lived and died more than two centuries ago. Yet, because of their wisdom and foresight, they also gave us a document flexible enough—and with enough built-in safeguards—to accommodate many of the changes imposed by a world they could not have anticipated.

In this chapter we will examine the events that led to the adoption of the Constitution, and consider just how well the Constitution has adapted to the changing conditions of modern times.

★ The Nature of a Constitution

Just what is a constitution? By its nature, a **constitution** is something special and unique. It is the principal legal statement of a political system, prescribing the powers and procedures of its governmental institutions. A constitution may be a single document, a group of documents, or even a series of laws and unwritten rules developed over many centuries, as in Great Britain. Although most countries can lay claim to a constitution, not all may be considered true constitutional states. **Constitutionalism** implies a limited government in which rulers may not arbitrarily do anything they please. Thus, although the Soviet Union, for instance, may

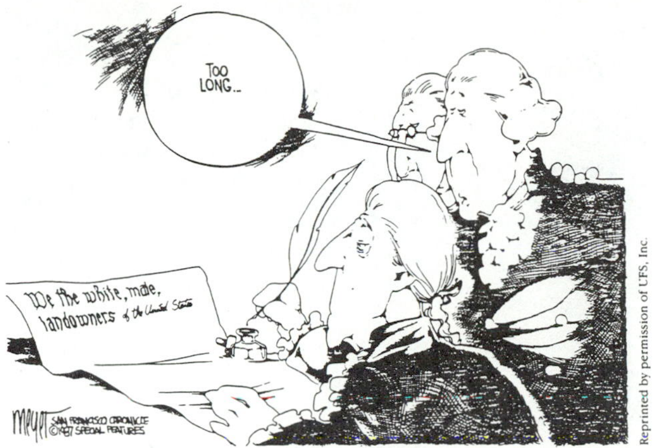

have a written constitution, it may bear little relation to the powers commanded by Soviet leaders.

In the broadest sense, our own Constitution includes more than just the historical document preserved under glass in the National Archives. The Constitution of 1787 is only the original foundation for an entire structure of amendments, Supreme Court rulings, and statutes that form the legal framework of our society. In fact, many vital elements of our political system—such as the political parties and the federal bureaucracy—are not mentioned in the original document, but can be included as part of our "unwritten constitution."

As our political system continues to evolve, so will our Constitution. We will face a constant need to reexamine what the framers had in mind when they drafted the original document and to consider whether we still agree with their intentions. Since it was first drafted in 1787, the Constitution has undergone many important changes in form and interpretation. Scholars and judges over the years have produced a rich literature of judicial analysis based on interpretations of the framers' motives and the changing needs of our society. Let us begin, therefore, with a brief analysis of what the framers had in mind when they assembled to devise a constitution.

★ The Framers' Agenda

The Constitution was drafted in Philadelphia during the hot summer of 1787 by a gathering of fifty-five delegates representing twelve of the original thirteen states (Rhode Island did not send delegates). Although seventy-four delegates were named to the Philadelphia convention, only fifty-five showed up, and only thirty-nine eventually signed the document.

As a group, the delegates embodied the political, intellectual, and commercial elite of American society—"an assembly of demigods," according to Thomas Jefferson. They were not representative of the general population. Most of the delegates were college-educated and had considerable political experience as members of the Continental Congress or as state governors; most were successful lawyers,

Our Founding Mothers

Though no women attended the Constitutional Convention, women were actively involved in the revolutionary ferment that produced our founding document. Women applied the explosive ideas of the time to their own condition. If man was endowed with certain natural and inalienable rights, why not woman too? If civil authority was derived from reason and the consent of the governed rather than from divine right, how could men keep women in a state of subjection on the authority of the Bible?

On March 31, 1777, Abigail Adams expressed the rebellious sentiments of many women in a letter to her husband, the future president John Adams:

> In the new code of laws which I suppose it will be necessary for you to make, I desire you would remember the ladies and be more generous and favorable to them than your ancestors. Do not put such unlimited power into the hands of husbands. Remember, all men would be tyrants if they could. If particular care and attention is not paid to the ladies, we are determined to foment a rebellion, and will not hold ourselves bound by any laws in which we have no voice or representation.

Colonial women organized anti-tea leagues to protest the tax imposed by the British on tea imported by colonies. The British had no right, they protested, to levy taxes on people who had no voice in their own government. To defuse the situation without abandoning the right it claimed, the British government reduced the tax to a trifling amount, but still the protests continued. For both sides it wasn't the money that mattered, it was the principle it stood for. Women popularized substitutes for tea made from such things as raspberry, sage, and birch. The most popular concoction was called "Liberty Tea." Such groups as the Daughters of Liberty aided the boycott of British

★ Abigail Adams, a Founding Mother.

merchants, landowners, and financiers. No women, blacks, or Native Americans attended, and only a few small farmers and tradespeople were present.

Nor were many of the old revolutionary firebrands on hand. Although some of the famous leaders of the Revolution attended—George Washington, Benjamin Franklin, James Madison, Alexander Hamilton—other notables were absent. Thomas Jefferson was serving as a diplomat in Paris, John Adams was in London, and Thomas Paine was busy spreading the gospel of revolution in Europe. Patrick Henry declined to come because he "smelt a rat." In all, only eight of the fifty-six signers of the Declaration of Independence attended the convention.

The motives of the delegates have inspired considerable scholarly debate. Generations of historians have argued whether the framers were motivated by personal or national interests. Until 1910, historians commonly viewed the framers as farsighted statesmen inspired only by the noblest sentiments to produce the best possible system of government. Under the impetus of the Progressive movement, however, scholars began to reevaluate this view. The most shocking reinterpretation was provided by the historian Charles Beard in his 1913 classic, *An Economic Interpretation of the Constitution.*

Beard unearthed archival information on the delegates' financial holdings, revealing that many owned government bonds that had depreciated in value. Beard insisted that the delegates wanted to establish a strong central government that goods by spinning and making their own clothes and publicly pledging to buy only domestic products.

During the Revolutionary War, women helped the Continental Army as cooks, nurses, and tailors. Some even disguised themselves as men and fought in battle. Organizations of female patriots in Philadelphia and New Jersey collected funds for Washington's troops. Broadsides that accompanied these fund-raising drives proclaimed that American women were "born for liberty, disdaining to bear the irons of a tyrannic Government," and that women had "borne the weight of war and met danger in every quarter."

Mercy Otis Warren rallied public sentiment for independence with her political writings. Warren shared her political ideas in correspondence with John and Abigail Adams and Thomas Jefferson. After independence had been won, she was disturbed by the failure of the proposed constitution to protect the rights of individuals through a bill of rights. She became a prominent Anti-Federalist pamphleteer. Under a pen name (A Columbian Patriot), she wrote a scathing argument against the proposed constitution; the number of copies distributed in New York during the ratification debates—more than 1,600—exceeded the circulation of the *Federalist* essays of Hamilton, Madison, and Jay.

★ Mercy Otis Warren, prominent Anti-Federalist pamphleteer.

Despite their contributions to America's founding, women are usually treated as a historical footnote to this era during which their rights were not recognized. In fact, after the Constitution was adopted, women lost some of the rights they had had, such as the right of some women to vote. For all the talk of liberty and equality, these "natural rights" belonged only to men; women were not seen as "people." The only reference to women in *The Federalist Papers* occurs in no. 6, which warns against the dangers posed to the safety of the state by the intrigues of courtesans and mistresses. And there is no mention of women in the Constitution. ★

SOURCES: Eleanor Flexner, *Century of Struggle: The Woman's Rights Movement in the United States,* rev. ed. (Cambridge, Mass.: Belknap Press of Harvard University Press, 1975); Linda K. Kerber, *Women of the Republic: Intellect and Ideology in Revolutionary America* (Chapel Hill: University of North Carolina Press, 1980), pp. 104–105; Linda Grant De Pauw, *The Eleventh Pillar: New York State and the Federal Constitution* (Ithaca, N.Y.: Cornell University Press, 1966), p. 113.

would restore the value of their holdings, protect their property, and preserve their elite status. As he put it, "the members of the Philadelphia Convention which drafted the Constitution were, with few exceptions, immediately, directly, and personally interested in, and derived economic advantage from, the establishment of the new system," so that "the Constitution was essentially an economic document."[1]

Beard's analysis aroused a storm of criticism. Later historians challenged Beard's interpretations, claiming that he overstated the founders' economic motives. Robert E. Brown, for instance, said he found little relation between the delegates' financial holdings and their actions at the convention. "We would be doing a grave injustice to the political sagacity of the Founding Fathers," Brown wrote, "if we assumed that property or personal gain was their only motive."[2]

The debate is by no means ended. Ruling-elite theorists (see chap. 5) often cite Beard's study when they argue that our elitist political system has deep historical roots, while others contend that the framers' economic motives played only an incidental part in the Constitution's creation.

In all likelihood, the framers saw little conflict between their own interests and the well-being of the country. Their desires for personal gain were mixed with practical concerns about the state of society and with broad philosophical views on human nature and the proper role of government. They had to resolve the problems of a new society torn by what they believed were serious sectional and

Table 2-1
Chronology of events, 1776–1791

Year	Event
1776	Declaration of Independence signed
1777	Articles of Confederation drafted
1781	Articles of Confederation adopted
1783	Peace with England
1786	Shays's Rebellion in Massachusetts
1787	Constitutional Convention in Philadelphia
1788	Required nine states have ratified Constitution
1789	George Washington elected president
1790	Last state (Rhode Island) ratifies Constitution
1791	Bill of Rights (first ten amendments) ratified

economic cleavages, and by an inability of the weak confederation to deal with foreign trade and diplomacy and even with threats from England and France. Yet they were also concerned with constructing a governmental system capable of safeguarding personal liberties. Indeed, we can gain a better understanding of the Constitution if we consider (1) the political challenges that faced the delegates and (2) their perspectives on human nature and human rights, as expressed in the writings of James Madison and several European philosophers.

Hammering Out Some Compromises

A major reason the delegates gathered in Philadelphia was the failure, in their view, of the existing government to deal with serious national problems. The **Articles of Confederation,** drafted ten years earlier during the Revolutionary War (see table 2-1), left virtually all governmental power in the hands of the states. Having rebelled against the tyranny of centralized British rule, many of the delegates felt the Confederation went too far in the opposite direction. The weak central government, embodied in the Continental Congress, lacked the power to tax and regulate interstate commerce, to deal effectively with foreign governments, and to protect against foreign invasion. It could not prevent the states from coining their own money, setting up tariffs and trade barriers, or violating treaties. And it had no direct authority over the people, who were subject only to the governments of their states. The Confederation, as one scholar has stated, was hardly more than "a league of friendship entered into by sovereign states."[3]

In addition, the Articles of Confederation provided for only one national branch of government: a **unicameral** (one-house) **congress.** There was no judicial system to settle disputes between states, no executive branch to enforce the laws. Executive and judicial functions were exercised primarily by committees selected by and responsive to the Continental Congress. The raising of armies for national defense was also left mostly to the states.

Clearly the delegates to the Philadelphia convention had expected more from

★ Shays's Rebellion (1786–1787). An engraving of a brawl between a Massachusetts government supporter and a rebel.

the Revolution than a faltering economy and an impotent government. They feared that unless the central government was strengthened, financial chaos and anarchy would result. This fear was reaffirmed by Shays's Rebellion in 1786, a revolt staged by several thousand poor farmers and laborers in Massachusetts who were unable to pay their taxes and mortgages.

At first many delegates believed that their task was simply to revise the Articles of Confederation, as they had been instructed to do by the Continental Congress. But it soon became apparent that a revision would not be enough: an entirely new constitution was needed. The question then became: What groups and regions would control the new government?

One bitter dispute erupted over the question of state representation in the new government's legislative body. While the delegates from some of the larger states, such as Virginia, were eager to form a strong central government with a legislature they could dominate, the delegates from some of the smaller states, such as New Jersey, wanted to avoid losing the powers they enjoyed under the Articles of Confederation.

In fact, the first proposal before the convention was the **Virginia Plan,** introduced by Governor Edmund Randolph. It called for a new structure of national government having three separate branches: legislative, executive, and judicial. The legislature would consist of two houses, in which the states would be represented on the basis of population or the amount of taxes paid. Thus a state with 600,000 people would have twice as many representatives as a state with 300,000 people. Congress would appoint both the executive and the judiciary, and could veto any state law it felt violated the Constitution, thus ensuring national supremacy.

Not surprisingly, this proposal alarmed delegates from some of the smaller states. They feared that the larger states would band together in Congress and lord it over the smaller ones. They backed instead the **New Jersey Plan,** introduced by William Paterson, which called for keeping the one-house legislature provided by the Articles of Confederation. Under this plan, all states would continue to be represented equally in Congress, so that New Jersey's vote would count the same as Virginia's. And although Congress would have the expanded power to levy taxes and regulate interstate commerce, it would not appoint the judiciary; judges would be appointed by the president, who would be chosen by Congress.

In a sense, both sides had valid points. Why should Virginia, say, allow its vote to be counted the same as New Jersey's, when Virginia contained more people and thus paid more taxes? At the same time, why should New Jersey voluntarily hand over the equal status it enjoyed under the Articles and become dominated by the larger states?

When the convention threatened to break up in hopeless deadlock, the delegates from Connecticut (a medium-sized state) offered a compromise. They suggested a **bicameral** (two-house) **congress,** allowing for equal representation in the Senate (two senators from each state) and representation by population in the House of Representatives. This arrangement would grant a veto power to both large and small states, since any legislation passed by Congress would need the approval of both chambers. In addition, since the larger states would bear the major burden of taxation, all revenue bills would originate in the House, where population determined voting strength. Reluctantly the delegates agreed to the **Connecticut Compromise,** and it was written into the Constitution. They then proceeded to hammer out compromises concerning the executive and judicial branches, providing for a president to be selected every four years by a "college" of citizens chosen by the states, and a Supreme Court to be appointed by the president with the Senate's approval.

The Slavery Question

The sharp dispute over state representation was coupled with the question of slavery. Northern delegates did not want slaves to be counted when the southern states' representation in the House was determined. At the same time, southern delegates did not want slaves to be counted when their tax burdens were determined. A compromise was eventually reached—incredible from our perspective today—defining each slave as three-fifths of a human being for both purposes. As Article I noted, a state's population would be determined "by adding to the whole number of free persons . . . excluding Indians not taxed, three-fifths of all other Persons." (The term "slave" does not appear in the Constitution.) Eighty years later, in 1868, this formula was eliminated by the Fourteenth Amendment.

Another "compromise" in regard to slavery betrayed the framers' concern with international trade. The southern delegates, many of whom owned large plantations, wanted to ensure free trafficking in slaves from Africa, while some northern delegates were uncomfortable with a limitless guarantee. Thus the **1808 Compro-**

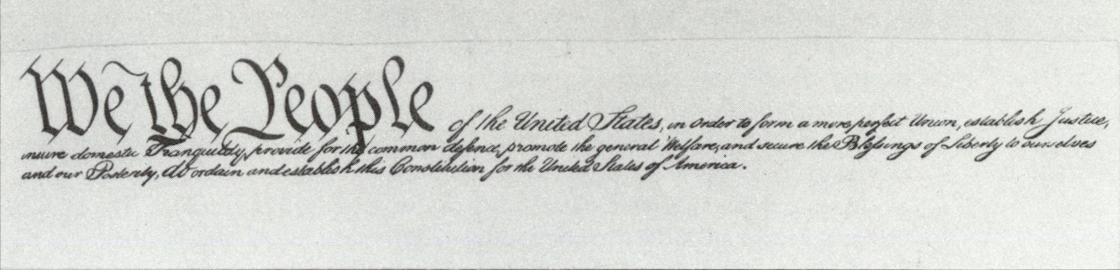
We the People of the United States, in Order to form a more perfect Union, establish Justice, insure domestic Tranquility, provide for the common defence, promote the general Welfare, and secure the Blessings of Liberty to ourselves and our Posterity, do ordain and establish this Constitution for the United States of America.

★ The preamble of the Constitution of the United States of America.

mise was reached, whereby the slave trade would be allowed until 1808. This was hardly a compromise, however, since the plantation interests were sure that they could import enough slaves before the deadline to maintain the slave population domestically. In fact, slave owners were hopeful that prices might go up after the deadline, and anticipated sharp increases in their profits.

Indeed, foreign trade and foreign competition were issues nearly as big during the Constitutional Convention as they are today. The southern states, concerned mainly with agriculture, were indifferent to the idea of supporting American industry with tariffs on European finished products, and fledgling manufacturing interests in the North were growing increasingly impatient with this lack of concern. The northern delegates lobbied for the right of Congress to impose uniform tariffs on goods entering the country. Because northern industry was suffering from start-up costs that had long since been overcome in Europe, the northerners needed the tariffs to make their goods competitive. Southerners were willing to go along with the idea as long as they were assured that their cotton and other raw goods would never be taxed upon leaving the country. Eventually the delegates arrived at the **Exportation Compromise:** the Constitution contains the simple statement "No tax or duty shall be laid on articles exported from any state."[4] Virtually all other trade and international economic issues were left to the legislative process and continue to this day to fuel regional political controversy.

★ The Constitution's Philosophical Base

The disputes between the large and small states and between the northern and southern delegates should not obscure the important philosophical aspects of the Constitution. Although the document was hammered out by individuals facing serious economic and political problems, it was not solely the product of pragmatic compromise. The Constitution also reflected the framers' perspectives on the nature of human conflict and the values of limited government.

In a sense, the Constitution was partly the product of the eighteenth-century Age of Enlightenment. Many of the delegates were familiar with the writings of English and Continental philosophers, such as John Locke, who contended that government should be based on the consent of the governed and that each person has certain natural rights. The framers accepted the idea, for example, of a government that, as James Madison stated, is "derived from the great body of the society and not from an inconsiderable proportion or a favored class of it."[5]

Yet most of the framers were equally certain that the people could not be trusted. Shays's Rebellion had merely reinforced their belief that an unrestrained citizenry could pose as great a threat to individual liberty as any despot and that government should be carefully designed to impede majority rule. "The evils we experience," Elbridge Gerry of Massachusetts thundered, "flow directly from the excesses of democracy."

Thus apprehension permeated the drafting of the Constitution. The framers were afraid that an individual or group might take hold of the government and rule the people in a manner reminiscent of the British aristocracy. At the same time, they also feared too much popular rule; the average American was not to be trusted to deal with political issues that required intelligence and dispassion. As we shall see, they dealt with the fear of despotism by designing a system of checks and balances, in which each branch of government would be more occupied with maintaining its powers than with expanding them. To alleviate their fear of the chaos that would accompany pure popular rule, the framers invented ways of preventing direct popular access to many areas of government.

A good deal of the framers' fear was based on their views of human nature—views that can be traced to the thought of the English philosophers John Locke and Thomas Hobbes. Hobbes described the lives of human beings in their natural state as "nasty, brutish, and short." In this same vein, Alexander Hamilton exclaimed, "Sir, your people is a great beast." It would be imprudent, the framers felt, to build a system that depended heavily on the limited virtue and wisdom of the people. "If men were angels," Madison declared, "no government would be necessary. If angels were to govern men, neither external war nor internal controls over government would be necessary. In framing a government which is to be administered by men over men, the great difficulty lies in this: You must first enable the government to control the governed; and in the next place, oblige it to control itself."[6]

The writings of James Madison in *The Federalist* (a series of essays urging the ratification of the Constitution in New York State)[7] provide perhaps the best clue to some of the principles accepted by the delegates. His analysis in *Federalist* no. 10 of "factions" and the need for a mixed government reveals some interesting perspectives on the nature and problems of a political society.

In Madison's view, politics in America was primarily a struggle among competing groups or factions, each pursuing its own selfish goals. He defined a faction as any group of citizens whose passions or interests were "adverse to the rights of other citizens, or to the permanent and aggregate interests of the community." Like Karl Marx in the following century, Madison believed that the main divisions in society were between those with property and those without, between those who were creditors and those who were debtors. As he put it, "the most common and durable source of factions is the unequal distribution of property. Those who hold and those who are without property have ever formed distinct interests in society." Unlike Marx, however, he saw more than just two contending classes. He recognized divisions not only between the haves and have-nots but also between different sectors of the economy: "a landed interest, a manufacturing interest, a mercantile interest, a moneyed interest," and so forth.

Because factions were based on the pursuit of selfish goals, Madison continued, they were hardly desirable. They divided the society and undermined the public good. More important, there was a danger that one faction might become a permanent majority, threatening the liberties of others. "To secure the public good and private rights against the danger of such a faction," Madison stated, "and at the

★ James Madison (1751–1836) played an important role at the Constitutional Convention, acting as reporter for the proceedings. He penned 29 of *The Federalist Papers* and proposed the first ten amendments to the Constitution known as the Bill of Rights. While in Congress, he parted company with *Federalist* co-author Alexander Hamilton and became a leader of the Jeffersonian Republicans. Madison served as Jefferson's Secretary of State, and as President for two terms, during which his popularity waned as a result of inept leadership in the War of 1812.

same time to preserve the spirit and form of popular government, is then the great object to which our inquiries are directed."

In short, the problem facing the framers was how to curb the influence of factions without imposing a tyrannical government. What sort of system would be capable of insulating individual liberties against both the power of the state and the excesses of the mob?

Madison's answer was a masterpiece of political theory. Because factions can be seen as a disease, he contended, either a "cure" or a means of "controlling its effects" was needed. A cure was impossible, since there were only "two methods of removing the causes of faction: the one, by destroying the liberty which is essential to its existence; the other, by giving to every citizen the same opinions, the same passions, the same interests." That is, destroying the liberties that permit factions to flourish would be "a cure worse than the disease." And to eliminate factions by sweeping away people's selfish interests, one would have to change human nature—an impossible task. As Madison put it, "The latent causes of faction are thus sown in the nature of man."

Thus the answer must lie in controlling the *effects* of factions. Because people have to be taken as they are and because the main task of government is to secure order without threatening liberty, good institutional arrangements that will render factions harmless must be found.

One solution would be to combine the thirteen states into a nation large enough to contain many kinds of interests. In a large territory, he wrote, "it is less probable that a majority of the whole will have a common motive to invade the rights of other citizens." In fact, it would be difficult for groups even to stay in touch; not only would they be unaware of their common interests, but it would be difficult for them to impose their will on others.

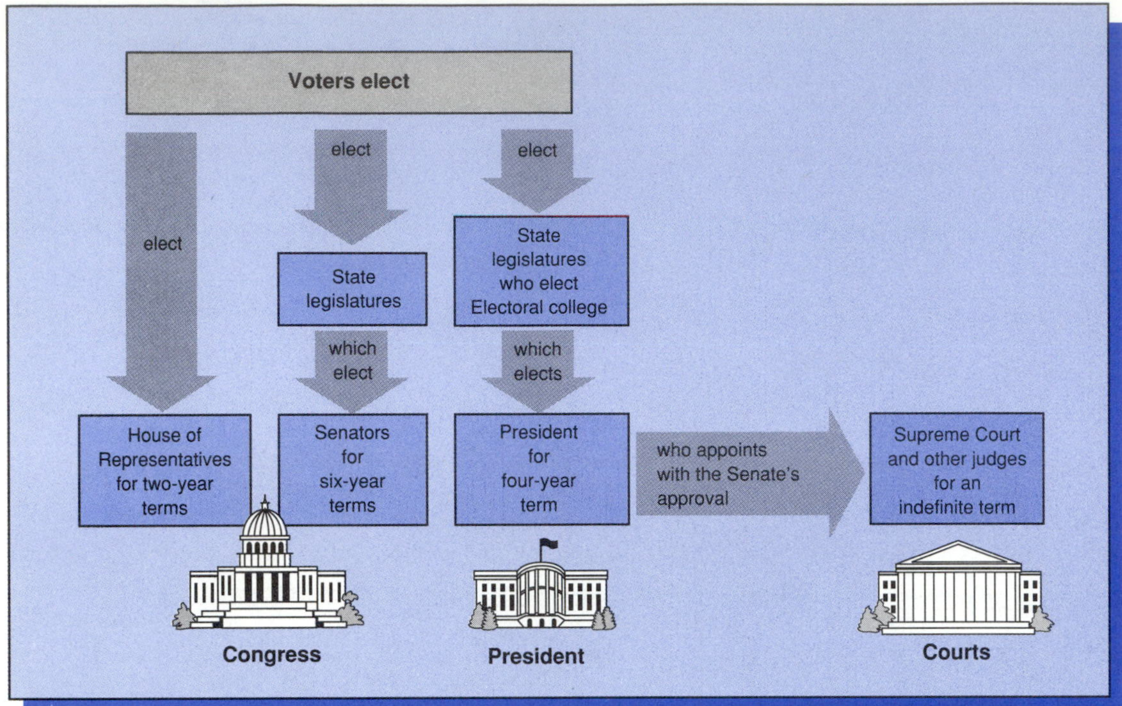

★ **Figure 2-1**
How the Madisonian model used separation of powers to thwart a majority faction: The original plan

NOTE: Originally, only members of the House of Representatives were elected directly by the voters. Senators were chosen by state legislatures, presidents were picked by electors chosen by the states, and judges were appointed. However, under present rules, senators are also directly elected by the voters and the electoral college mainly reaffirms voters' preferences.

A second solution would be to design a system of staggered elections that would prevent any faction from gaining control of government. If the president and members of the House and Senate were elected for terms of different lengths and by different procedures, no group could dominate all three offices at the same time. (See figure 2-1.) Thus representatives would serve for two years, presidents for four, and senators for six, with a third of the senators elected every two years rather than all at once. In addition, only members of the House would be elected directly by the people. Senators would be elected by state legislatures, while presidents would be chosen by "electors" selected by the states. Justices of the Supreme Court would be appointed for life terms by the president with the consent of the Senate. (Since Madison's time, of course, several of these arrangements have changed. As we will see, the electoral college has evolved largely into a rubber stamp, and the Seventeenth Amendment in 1913 provided for the popular election of senators.)

It should be noted that the framers' concern over factions was closely tied to their fear of too much popular rule. They deliberately avoided the direct election of senators, for example, in order to mix aristocratic with popular government. As Madison put it, the Senate, comprised of older citizens with great personal property, would be likely to proceed with "more coolness, with more system, and with more wisdom, than the popular branch." And although members of the House would be chosen at the polls, the states would decide who was qualified to vote. In most states, only white male property owners were given the franchise; nonwhites, women, and propertyless men were generally excluded. Not until 1870 was the constitutional right to vote extended to nonwhites (by the Fifteenth Amendment), and not until 1920 was the vote granted nationally to women (by the Nineteenth Amendment).

Even the size of the territory would help limit citizens' participation. Millions of people could not possibly squeeze into a town hall to make national policy decisions, as in a direct democracy, but would have to choose the most qualified among them to serve as their representatives. In this way, a representative democracy (a **republic**) would help filter the opinions of the masses. It would "refine and enlarge the public views by passing them through the medium of a chosen body of citizens, whose wisdom may best discern the true interests of their country." One might wonder how Madison would respond to the capacity of modern communications technology to expand the "town hall."

Yet even these arrangements were not considered sufficient. In addition to a large union, a system of staggered elections, and a representative legislative body, Madison and the other framers insisted on "auxiliary precautions." Indeed, they felt that the most effective way to prevent tyranny—by a majority or a minority—was to scatter power among various levels and institutions of government, with each imposing restraints on the others. As Madison declared, "ambition must be made to counteract ambition."[8]

★ Our Separated Institutions: Ambition to Check Ambition

One such "auxiliary precaution" (actually more essential than auxiliary, in the minds of the framers) was a **separation of powers.** The framers adopted the idea from several sources, especially from the eighteenth-century French philosopher Montesquieu.[9] Admiring the British political system, the Baron de Montesquieu asserted that the secret of its success lay in the separation of power among the executive (the king), the legislature (the Parliament), and the judiciary (the House of Lords). Unfortunately, Montesquieu was somewhat mistaken on a number of points about the British political system, not least of which is the fact that it is based more on a fusion—rather than a separation—of power between the Parliament and the cabinet executive.

Despite Montesquieu's errors, however, the framers accepted his notion that the way to avoid tyranny was to divide constitutional authority among three branches of the national government. "No political truth is certainly of greater intrinsic value, or is stamped with the authority of more enlightened patrons of liberty," Madison wrote, "than that . . . the accumulation of all powers, legislative, executive, and judiciary, in the same hands . . . may justly be pronounced the very definition of tyranny."[10] Thus the Constitution declares that the legislative power will be vested in Congress (Article I), the executive power will be in the hands of the president (Article II), and the judicial power will rest with the courts (Article III).

In actuality, of course, the separation of powers is not absolute. The Constitution also provides for a sharing of powers. The president, for example, wields the legislative power to propose and veto bills, and the Senate exercises the executive power to confirm or reject presidential appointments and treaties.

In fact, the three branches were not designed to be entirely separate. Because there was always the danger that ambitious politicians in one branch might try to assume command of the government, the framers also provided for a system of **checks and balances,** which would enable each branch to have some say in the operation of the other two, as illustrated in figure 2-2. Just as one faction in society would balance another, so one branch of government would prevent another from abusing its powers. Thus Congress can pass a bill, but the president can veto it. Congress can then override a veto by a two-thirds vote in both houses. The president can negotiate a treaty, but it cannot become effective unless the Senate approves it. And although the president carries out the laws, Congress appropriates the money to keep his administrative apparatus running. The Supreme Court, in turn, as a result of interpretation and precedent, can invalidate a law passed by Congress and signed by the president, but the president appoints the justices with the consent of the Senate. In short, each branch balances the others by commanding independent and overlapping powers, and also checks them by limiting their actions.

One point should be noted, however. The system of checks and balances devised by the framers was not based solely on abstract principles; it was also the product of political compromise. For example, the appointment of Supreme Court justices by the president with the potential for veto by the Senate was a compromise between those delegates who favored judicial selection by the legislature and those who preferred selection by the executive. While this provision might help prevent tyranny, it also provided a convenient compromise between two opposing views.

Over the years, the fragmentation of political authority has sparked considerable criticism. Many critics have seen the separation of powers as an unwieldy system of governing that encourages needless delay, impedes social reform, and favors the status quo. "In their effort to protect basic rights," one scholar has observed, "what the framers did in effect was to hand out extra chips in the game of politics to people who are already advantaged, while they handicapped the disadvantaged who would like to change the status quo."[11]

Indeed, from the standpoint of citizen action, the fragmentation of power seems to impose severe limitations on what people seeking social reform are likely to achieve. Even if a group wins the support of the House of Representatives in its efforts to bring about a change in policy—whether it be handgun control, support for arms control, tax reform, or improved medical care for the elderly—there is no assurance that support will also come from the Senate or the White House. By scattering power among many centers of decision making, the framers created many potential veto points to frustrate reform.

From another perspective, however, the scattering of power among several institutions has also provided alternative avenues of access to government. Groups unable to penetrate one branch of government have been able to gain access to another branch, where they have won support in bringing about a change of policy. In the 1950s and 1960s, for example, the National Association for the Advancement of Colored People (NAACP) found a powerful ally in the Supreme Court in its drive for civil rights, when both Congress and the White House were slow to move. In the 1980s, business and labor turned to Congress for protection from foreign competition when the executive branch continued to push a free-trade policy. Thus the separation of powers can both frustrate and encourage citizen action, depending on the goals and the circumstances.

Nor has the system of checks and balances escaped the notice of critics. Many observers have pointed to periods in history when the president has been dominated by a more powerful Congress (as during the post–Civil War years), and to other periods when Congress has been virtually eclipsed by the president (as during

★★★★★★★★★★★★

Global Culture

La Realidad ni Pintada (Vermeer y Mondrian) by Herman Braun/Vega © Pestana

The more we travel and know about others' cultures, the more cultures intertwine to create a complex social reality. Peruvian artist Herman Braun-Vega encapsulates all that in his painting *Reality Not Even Painted... Vermeer and Mondrian.* It depicts the Dutch painter Jan Vermeer (1632-1675) apparently painting a contemporary Peruvian beach scene framed in the geometric style of Dutch painter Piet Mondrian (1872-1944), while two Peruvian boys watch us as we watch. And what do we see?

Tom McHugh, 1972

Terence White/Picture Group

Economics are responsible for much of world culture. Western consumer goods and products and their attendant values have spread throughout the non-Western and the Third Worlds.

Colonel Sanders shows up in Kuala Lumpur, Malaysia; Coca-Cola is part of the collage behind the mujahideen in Afghanistan; Marlboro provides the backdrop in Cairo, Egypt; and, of course, there's American pizza in Moscow. American pizza? Since when is pizza American?

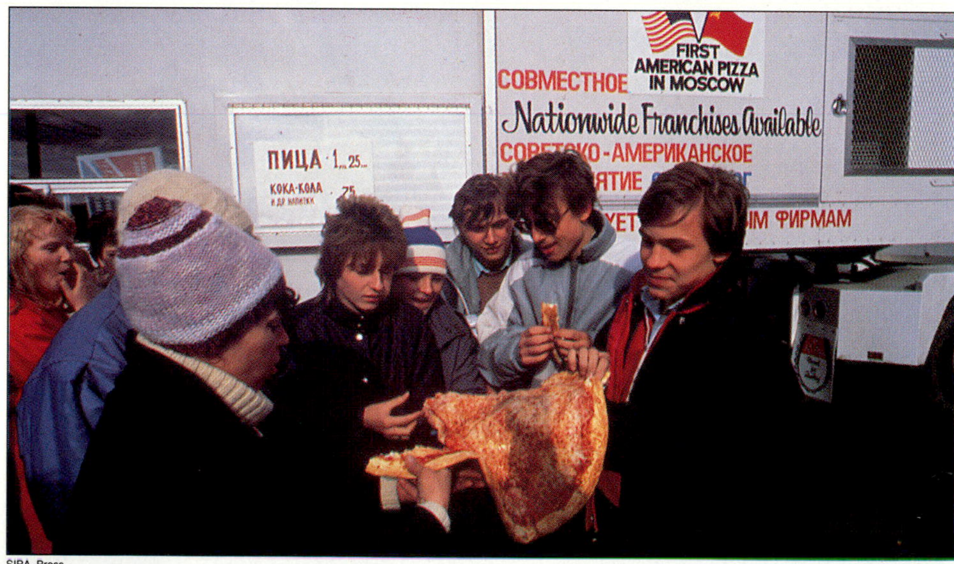

SIPA–Press

Alex Webb/Magnum Photos, Inc.

K. Cohens

Peter Turnley/Black Star

One of the ways global culture is brought into people's homes is through video cassettes. You can find videos of all nationalities in the United States, videos in the USSR, and videos even in this out-of-the-way mining town in South Africa.

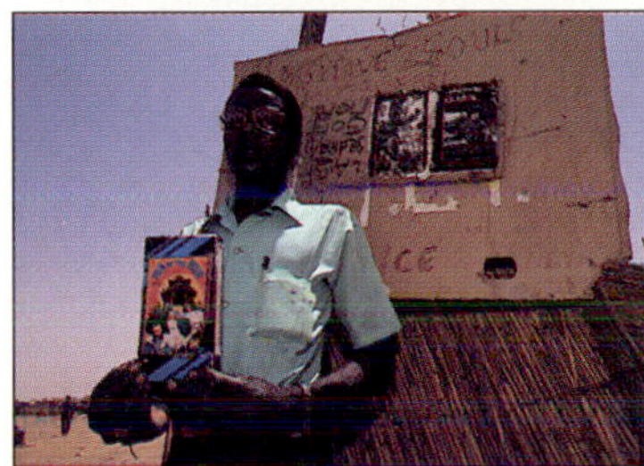
Jeremy Nicholl/JB Pictures

In some countries, political dissidents exchange videos or smuggle them abroad to gain sympathy for their plight.

St. Franklin/Magnum Photos, Inc.

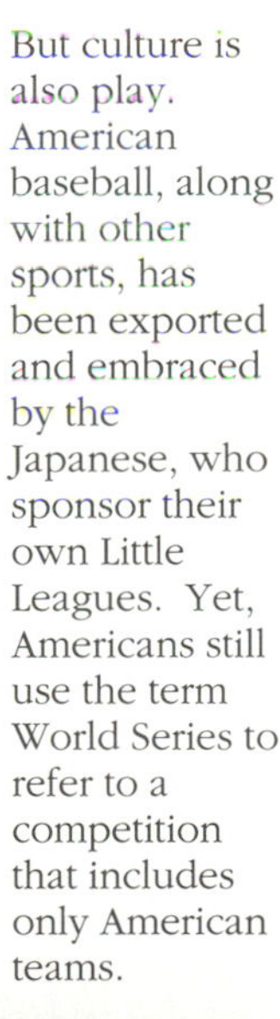
But culture is also play. American baseball, along with other sports, has been exported and embraced by the Japanese, who sponsor their own Little Leagues. Yet, Americans still use the term World Series to refer to a competition that includes only American teams.

Even within the Brazilian forests, where migrants come looking for land, we see the pervasiveness of the global culture. While the stereo plays American music, the posters tell a deeper story. Exported for the global market are Western models of sexuality—the macho militant Rambo and the blond, blue-eyed poster girl. Would you have expected to see something else on his wall?

Gustano Gilaberi/JB Pictures

Ricki Rosen/Picture Group

From art to architecture, there is not only co-mingling but, many say, an increasing homogeneity. Can you tell the players without a program? These heavy metallists are not in the graffitied halls of New York City; they are Soviet citizens in Moscow.

Patrick Frilet/SIPA–Press

And the punk rockers? Japanese.

As more of us participate in this global culture, will we create mutual understanding that can reach to the levels of political agreement?

Does it mean we have more in common? If we share these forms of dress, music, and movement, will we become closer? Does such sharing decrease diversity? Does it matter that Chicago and Rio de Janeiro look surprisingly alike in these aerial views?

Steve Kagan/Gamma–Liaison

Ricardo Azourylfy/Picture Group

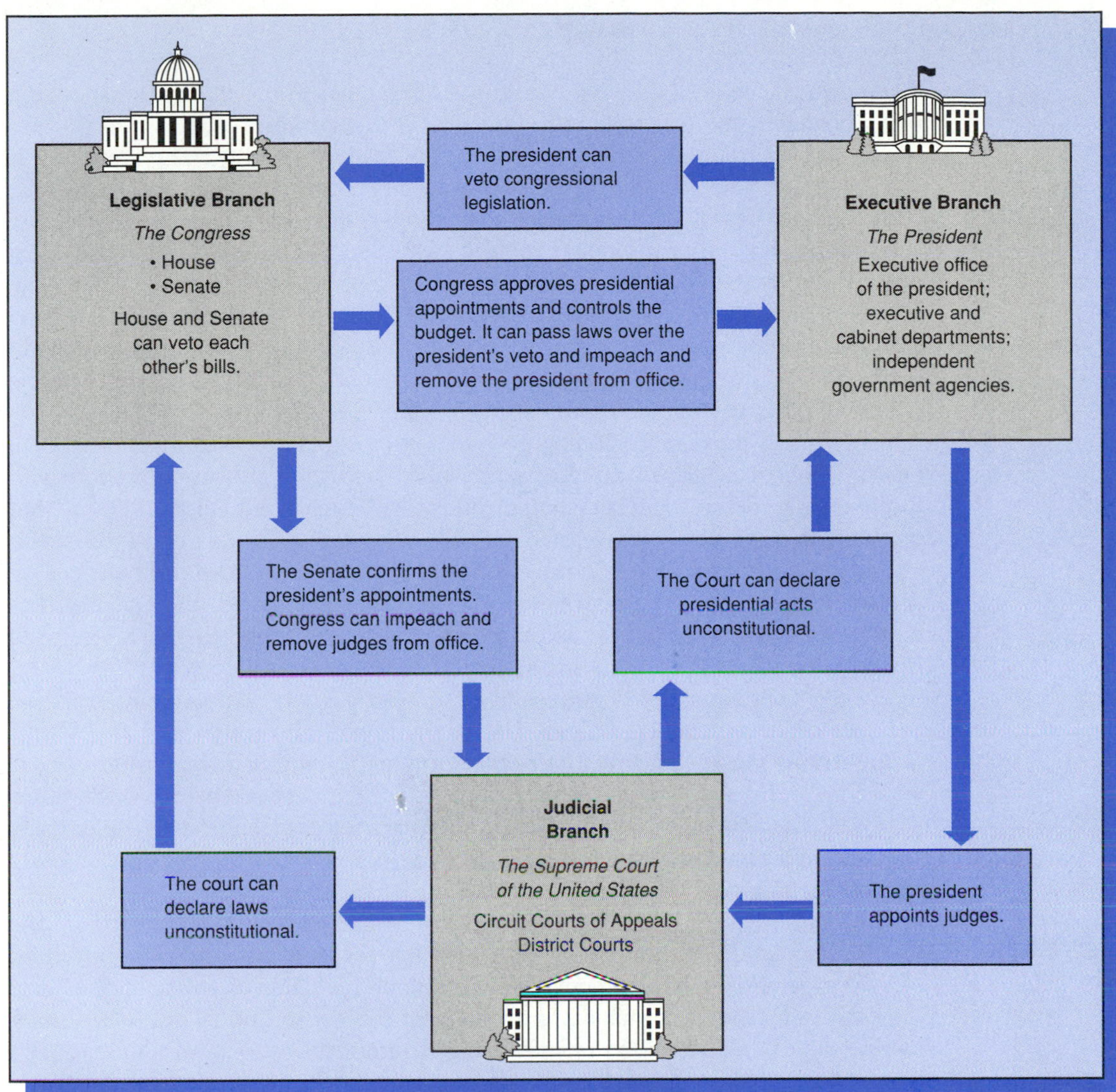

★ **Figure 2-2**
Separation of powers and checks and balances in the Madisonian system
NOTE: As shown in this diagram, the system of separation of powers and checks and balances devised by the framers enables each branch of government to have some say in the operation of the other two.

the Vietnam war). Other critics have asked how a proper check on presidential warmaking powers can be applied in the nuclear age. The Watergate scandal and the Iran-Contra affair revealed how one branch of government can overstep its constitutional boundaries and threaten to undermine the principle of checks and balances.

But the battles between Congress and the executive branch also reveal how the system of checks and balances can be triggered into action. Congress's drive to impeach Richard Nixon in 1974, eventually forcing him from office, dramatically brought the system into focus for many Americans.

★ The Constitution in a Changing World

Many experts feel that the post–World War II changes in the international system that globalized American politics have tested the Constitution, especially its systems of checks and balances between the branches of government.[12] The argument is that too much power has migrated to the executive branch. Ironically, the specific constitutional powers of the president in foreign affairs are surprisingly few. In recognition that military conflicts require swift, decisive leadership, the president was named by the Constitution as commander in chief of the armed forces. The president also appoints ambassadors and makes treaties. But the founders, fearing that Tom Paine was correct when he said that "a king has little more to do than to make war and give away places," provided a variety of checks and balances on the president's warmaking and diplomatic powers.[13]

Congress, in contrast, seems to have more explicit power in international affairs. Congress declares war, sets the military's budget, regulates commerce with foreign states, defines and sets the penalties for "Piracies and Felonies committed on the high seas," and approves treaties and the appointment of ambassadors with a two-thirds majority of the Senate. In fact, congressional checks and balances on presidential actions in the international sphere are quite broad, and Congress has intervened in the president's diplomacy many times, as when the Senate refused to ratify President Woodrow Wilson's prized Treaty of Versailles in 1919.

Still, over time the president has acquired a great deal of latitude in the conduct of foreign policy. Indeed, vast technological and political changes have propelled the president to the forefront of diplomacy. Without formal congressional approval, presidents have dispatched troops to fight undeclared wars in such places as Korea, Vietnam, and Central America. Many presidents (as we shall see in chap. 13) have avoided consulting Congress on deals with other nations by substituting executive agreements for formal treaties.

Congress, for its part, has attempted to restore legislative input through the War Powers Act, its authority to oversee intelligence agencies, and refusal to fund military operations. Enforcement of congressional restraints on the president's use of troops and other diplomatic acts involves serious constitutional questions, some of which have been avoided by informal accommodations by both branches, and some of which have led to direct confrontation.

International Adventures: A Challenge to the Constitution?

The Iran-Contra congressional hearing of 1987 (discussed in chap. 19) revealed how far the executive branch may go in pursuit of a foreign policy against the will of Congress. Since 1981, Congress and the executive branch had disagreed on how to respond to the radical government in the Central American nation of Nicaragua. Seeking to get around a legislative cutoff of funds to the Nicaraguan Contra rebels, the presidential aide Oliver North and his associates in the executive branch worried about constitutional checks and balances: "I didn't want to show Congress a single word on this whole thing," North testified. After offering congressional investigators a glimpse into the shady world of secret Swiss bank accounts and the clandestine operations of deep-cover foreign agents, North outlined a classic executive–legislative confrontation: "Congress is to blame because of the fickle, vacillating, unpredictable, on-again-off-again policy."[14]

★ Oliver North testifying at the Iran-Contra hearings.

In order to circumvent congressional limits on covert military operations, North, along with National Security Adviser John Poindexter and CIA chief William Casey, created a complex network of arms merchants, former military and CIA personnel, and mercenaries to ensure the training and arming of antigovernment rebels in Nicaragua. But President Reagan's staff sought more than just a way to get around Congress on the question of Nicaragua. According to North, the ultimate goal was to establish a permanent structure to engage in foreign political and military operations without the knowledge of the American people or the approval of Congress. Such a secret organization, hidden away in the White House, the Pentagon, and the CIA, would, in the view of many constitutional scholars, directly challenge the basic principles of checks and balances.

The Iran-Contra affair can also be offered as yet another instance of the Constitution's success in weathering an attempt by one branch of government to exclude another from the process of government. Although members of Congress knew nothing about the matter until the story appeared in a newsmagazine in Lebanon, they eventually did investigate the Iran-Contra affair and put pressure on the executive branch to mend its ways.

The Constitution and the Pace of Global Change

Is the pace of global technical, military, and political change outstripping the Constitution's ability to adapt? The Constitution's framers certainly attempted to build in the means to conduct foreign affairs without permitting unrestrained power by government or by a narrow faction or interest. Yet America's emergence as a superpower has led to many unanticipated developments. Picture, for instance, the president flying at 40,000 feet in his 747 command post, conflicting reports of a nuclear attack pouring in from around the globe, trying in less than ten minutes to decide the fate of humanity. The notion that Congress could "advise and consent" in such circumstances seems a cruel joke. One need not conjure up a situation as extreme as nuclear war to see that the growth of technological and international developments demand quick decisions that are not amenable to deliberation by a body as large and cumbersome as the U.S. Congress, not to speak of the U.S. electorate.

★ The framers of the Constitution signing their handiwork.

★ Federalism: Dispersing Political Power

In addition to splitting the national government into three branches, the framers provided a second "auxiliary precaution" in the form of federalism. As we will see in chapter 3, **federalism** can be defined as a division of governmental power between a central (national) government and local or regional (state) governments coexisting within the same territory. Local units of government in this country (the states) are more than just administrative branches or departments of a central government, as in the **unitary system** of Great Britain or France. Each of the fifty states boasts its own constitution and judicial system, and can make and enforce its own laws. In effect, all of us possess dual citizenship: we are citizens of both the entire nation and our state, paying taxes to keep the governments of both in operation.

To Madison and the other delegates, the division of powers between the national government and the states offered an additional means to control factions. As Madison put it, "The influence of factious leaders may kindle a flame within their particular states but will be unable to spread a general conflagration through the other states."[15]

In addition, federalism was a way to unify the nation and strengthen its central government while preserving the integrity of the states. Most people at the time regarded themselves as New Yorkers, Georgians, or Virginians rather than as Americans, and would not have allowed their states to become totally submissive to a powerful central authority. By dividing powers between the national government and the states, the framers achieved the compromise necessary to win approval for their newly forged document.

The Constitution therefore lays out a framework for dividing power between the two levels of government. It assigns the federal government certain **delegated** or **enumerated powers** to be distributed among the three branches. Article I,

Section 8, for instance, declares that Congress alone has the power to coin money, establish federal courts, raise armies, make treaties, and declare war. Congress is also granted **concurrent powers**—powers that it shares with the states, such as the right to levy taxes and borrow money.

The powers of the states are not spelled out in the Constitution, but are classified as **reserved powers.** The Tenth Amendment (1791) states that "the powers not delegated to the United States by the Constitution, nor prohibited by it to the states, are reserved to the states respectively, or to the people." Traditionally, those who oppose a strong central government have interpreted this "reserve clause" to mean that the national government can wield only those powers granted by the Constitution and that all other powers belong to the states. In their view, the reserve clause prohibits the national government from stepping into any area not specified in the Constitution.

To a large extent, however, the delegated powers of the national government have been broadened by the famous **necessary and proper clause** at the end of Section 8. This clause (also known as the "elastic clause") allows Congress to "make all laws which shall be necessary and proper for carrying into Execution the foregoing powers, and all other Powers vested . . . in the Government of the United States." In carrying out a delegated power such as raising an army, for instance, Congress may find it "necessary and proper" to draft young men and women into the armed forces, even though the draft is not mentioned in the Constitution. The draft is an **implied power** that may reasonably be inferred from Congress's delegated powers. Section 8 also authorizes Congress to tax and spend for the "general welfare" and to "regulate commerce . . . among the several states." Congress has frequently used these broad phrases, together with the necessary and proper clause, to extend its powers beyond those spelled out in the Constitution. It has initiated programs in a wide range of areas on the grounds that they involve interstate commerce or are aimed at the "general welfare."

Generally, whenever the national government and the states have become embroiled in a dispute over the proper boundaries of their authority, the Supreme Court has acted as the umpire of the federal system. It has wielded its powers of judicial review both to strike down acts of Congress that invade the reserved powers of the states and to overturn state laws that are contrary to the Constitution.

Indeed, Supreme Court justices have played a major part in shaping the evolution of federalism through their interpretations of nation-state issues. Although the justices have supported the claims of states over the national government at various times over the years, support for a strong central authority was demonstrated as early as 1819 in the celebrated case of *McCulloch* v. *Maryland.* The case developed when the state of Maryland tried to tax the politically unpopular Bank of the United States, which had been chartered by Congress. The tax was levied in a thinly disguised attempt to drive the bank out of the state. The cashier of the bank's Baltimore branch, James McCulloch, refused to pay the tax, arguing that a state could not tax an instrument of the national government. Maryland countered that the Constitution gave Congress no authority to charter a national bank, and even if it did, a sovereign state could do as it wished within its own boundaries.

In a classic statement on the doctrine of implied powers, Chief Justice John Marshall supported Congress. In his majority opinion, he stated that the creation of a national bank by Congress was a "necessary and proper" means of carrying out its constitutional powers to borrow money, collect taxes, raise and support armies, and regulate commerce. Chartering a national bank was a power "implied" by other powers listed in the Constitution. In addition, Marshall ruled, the national government is constitutionally superior to the states and in cases of conflict the former must prevail. The states cannot use their reserved powers to hinder the national government's performance of its duties. This ruling echoed Article VI, which states that federal law "shall be the supreme law of the land." Thus Marshall's opinion affirmed both the supremacy of the national government and the breadth of its implied powers, paving the way for countless federal programs—ranging from atomic energy to urban renewal—not anticipated by the framers.

It should be understood, of course, that conflict between the national government and the states has been only one feature of federalism in this country. Despite Madison's call for divided powers, cooperation among the various levels of government has also been common. As we will see in chapter 3, the federal government and the states have joined forces to provide essential services in such areas as health, education, law enforcement, and transportation.

★ The Struggle for Ratification

After the delegates had signed the Constitution in September 1787, they had to persuade the states to adopt it—a task so difficult that eventually it took two and a half years to complete. One formidable obstacle was the need to obtain the unanimous consent of all thirteen state legislatures, as the Articles of Confederation required. Because some of the states might veto the newly forged document, the delegates searched for a different scheme.

They decided to appeal to the people over the heads of both the Continental Congress and the twelve state legislatures that had sent delegates. They provided in Article VII that the consent of only nine states—not the entire thirteen—was needed to ratify the Constitution. And because state legislatures might spurn a document that weakened their powers, the delegates proposed that the ratifying bodies be popularly elected state conventions. This scheme would make the Constitution appear as a compact among all the people rather than simply as an agreement among state politicians.

The delegates knew that the Constitution would not be enthusiastically applauded by all segments of society. Many people were satisfied with the Articles of Confederation and were wary of change. Indeed, a debate soon erupted between those who championed the new Constitution (the **Federalists**) and those who opposed it (the **Anti-Federalists**). Many of the Anti-Federalists were small farmers who feared that a strong central authority would devour the states and suppress individual rights and local interests. They objected that the president had too much independence, that the Senate was too aristocratic, and that the Constitution lacked a bill of rights to safeguard citizens against governmental tyranny. They even charged a frame-up. They cried that the delegates had met in secrecy to forge a document that was essentially extralegal, exceeding their instructions from Congress merely to patch up the Articles of Confederation. In fact, the picture they drew of the Philadelphia convention was similar to that drawn by Charles Beard more than a century later: as a gathering of aristocrats who secretly fashioned a strong central government designed to protect their own economic and political interests.

The supporters of the Constitution responded with a well-organized newspaper campaign to whip up support. In New York State, for example, a series of essays known collectively as *The Federalist* (or ***The Federalist Papers***) was published in local newspapers. Written under the pen name "Publius" by Alexander

★ **Table 2-2**
Ratification of the Constitution

State	*Date*	*Vote in convention*	*Rank in population*
Delaware	December 7, 1787	Unanimous	13
Pennsylvania	December 12, 1787	46 to 23	3
New Jersey	December 18, 1787	Unanimous	9
Georgia	January 2, 1788	Unanimous	11
Connecticut	January 9, 1788	128 to 40	8
Massachusetts	February 6, 1788	187 to 168	2
Maryland	April 28, 1788	63 to 11	6
South Carolina	May 23, 1788	149 to 73	7
New Hampshire	June 21, 1788	57 to 46	10
Virginia	June 25, 1788	89 to 79	1
New York	July 26, 1788	30 to 27	5
North Carolina	November 21, 1789	195 to 77	4
Rhode Island	May 29, 1790	34 to 32	12

Hamilton, James Madison, and John Jay, the essays compared the defects of the Articles of Confederation with the virtues of the proposed constitution. They emphasized that the new government would be strong enough to meet its obligations and safe enough to respect the liberties of the people. Though strongly partisan, these essays eventually gained recognition as perhaps the most significant contribution to American political thought. They offered a penetrating analysis of the American political system and revealed a great deal about the framers' intentions.

For the most part, the debate did not involve the general population. Although delegates to the ratifying conventions were popularly elected, only a small percentage of eligible voters turned out to vote. As one historian concluded, "The Constitution was adopted with a great show of indifference."[16]

But it was adopted. Less than three months after the framers departed from Philadelphia, Delaware became the first state to ratify the Constitution, in December 1787. Six months later, New Hampshire became the ninth state to do so, and it was soon followed by the two critical states of Virginia and New York. By the summer of 1790, all thirteen states had approved the document (see table 2-2).

★ The Demand for a Bill of Rights

Certainly the Constitution could not have been ratified without a promise to add a bill of rights once the document had been approved by the states. Although the original text guaranteed trial by jury and protected citizens against being held for crimes without cause (writ of habeas corpus), singled out for punishment (through a legislative bill of attainder), or punished for acts that were not illegal when they were committed (ex post facto laws), it did not provide for other basic rights. It did not guarantee freedom of religion, speech, or assembly, or prohibit cruel and unusual punishment or unwarranted searches and seizures.

Most of the delegates felt it was unnecessary to draft a bill of rights, since the federal government could exercise only those powers granted by the Constitution. In their view, the system of government they fashioned, with its separation of powers and checks and balances, provided adequate safeguards against despotism. The addition of a list of rights would only be dangerous, since it would suggest that any rights *not* listed could be denied by the government.

The Anti-Federalists were not persuaded, however. They insisted that without a bill of rights, citizens would have no protection against abuses of governmental power. They demanded, as their price for supporting the Constitution, that a bill of rights be attached as soon as a new government was formed. Thus, when the first Congress convened in 1789, more than one hundred amendments were considered. Of this number, ten amendments (mostly the work of James Madison) were finally adopted by the states in 1791, three years after the required nine states had ratified the Constitution (1788) and four years after the delegates had assembled in Philadelphia (1787) (see table 2-3).

These ten amendments, it should be noted, guarded citizens only against the powers of the national government. They did not specifically guard against the powers of state governments. Only through the Supreme Court's interpretations of the "equal protection" and "due process" clauses of the Fourteenth Amendment (1866) was the protection of the Bill of Rights gradually extended to the states (see chap. 4).

★ What the Constitution Leaves Out

In addition to the protections afforded by a bill of rights, other key elements of American government were not touched on by the delegates. Many of our most prominent political institutions and processes came into being through custom or legislation or in response to complex technological changes and the demands of national security in the modern era.

For example, the Constitution makes no mention of political parties. Although parties affect many aspects of our government, they have no written constitutional base. The framers had little experience with parties and probably could not have foreseen the important roles they would play in the future. In fact, as we will see in chapter 8, they abhorred the whole idea of parties, believing they would only encourage factionalism. Not until after the Constitution was drafted did organized parties begin to take shape as various groups clashed over economic issues, foreign policy, and the proper role of the federal government.

Similarly, the Constitution makes no provisions for the major departments and agencies of the federal bureaucracy. Although the Constitution authorizes the president to "require the Opinion, in writing, of the principal Officer in each of the executive Departments," it is silent about the way these departments should be organized and the duties they should perform. All of the agencies of the federal bureaucracy—the Labor Department, the Food and Drug Administration, the Central Intelligence Agency, and so on—owe their existence to congressional statutes, not to the intentions of the framers.

Nor does the Constitution provide for the president's cabinet, the congressional committee system, the civil service system, nominating conventions, or presidential primaries. Not even the Supreme Court's sweeping power of judicial review or the structure of the lower federal courts is specifically provided for in the Constitution. They all evolved in response to changing political needs and circumstances, gradually filling in the gaps left in the original document.

★ Table 2-3
Provisions of the Constitution

Original Articles

Preamble	Statement of purpose of the Constitution
Article I	Establishment of legislative branch
Article II	Establishment of executive branch
Article III	Establishment of judicial branch
Article IV	Regulation of intergovernmental relations
Article V	Provisions for amending the Constitution
Article VI	Supremacy of the national government
Article VII	Provisions for ratifying the Constitution

Bill of Rights (1791)

1. Freedom of religion, speech, press, assembly, and petition
2. Right to bear arms
3. Right of homeowners to refuse to quarter soldiers
4. Protection against unreasonable searches and seizures
5. Rights of accused persons and due process of law
6. Right to a speedy, public, and fair trial
7. Right to a trial by jury in civil cases
8. Prohibition of excessive bail and of cruel and unusual punishment
9. Rights retained by the people
10. Protection of powers reserved to the states

Later Amendments

11. Reduction of judicial power of national courts (1795)
12. Separate election of president and vice-president (1804)
13. Abolition of slavery (1865)
14. Privileges of U.S. citizens, due process, and equal protection of the laws (1868)
15. No prohibition of right to vote because of race (1870)
16. Establishment of federal income tax (1913)
17. Direct popular election of senators (1913)
18. Prohibition of intoxicating liquors (1919)
19. No prohibition of right to vote because of sex (1920)
20. New dates for terms of president, vice-president, and Congress (1933)
21. Repeal of the Eighteenth Amendment (1933)
22. Limitation of president to two terms (1951)
23. The right to vote in presidential elections granted to residents of Washington, D.C. (1961)
24. Elimination of poll tax as prerequisite for voting in federal elections (1964)
25. Regulation of presidential succession and continuity of power in case of disability (1967)
26. Voting age set at eighteen years for federal, state, and local elections (1971)

★ Changing the Constitution

The growth of new institutions and procedures should remind us that the process of constitution making did not end when the delegates packed their bags and departed from Philadelphia in 1787. The document they fashioned was extremely brief (about 7,000 words) and contained statements of broad principles that would require specific application and interpretation.

In fact, the framers did not expect their handiwork to endure without change. They knew, as one scholar put it, that "no amount of drafting skill could be expected to eliminate the necessity of revision and development to adapt the Constitution to the unforeseen and unforeseeable."[17] Through a variety of processes, federal court judges, members of Congress, and even ordinary citizens could make their mark on the Constitution.

Interpretation by the Courts

One important way the Constitution is changed is through federal court interpretation. Each time a question of the Constitution's meaning is raised—as in a dispute over the proper authority of Congress—judges must decide what the document means in that particular case. In fact, former Chief Justice Charles Evans Hughes was exaggerating only slightly when he said that "we live under a Constitution, but the Constitution is what the judges say it is."

Through their power of judicial review (which is discussed more fully in chap. 15), Supreme Court justices can rule on the constitutionality of legislative and executive acts. The nine Court justices can overturn a decision of Congress, the president, or a state legislature if in their opinion it conflicts with the Constitution, thereby interpreting the document's meaning. Although this sweeping power is not mentioned in the Constitution, its use in overturning more than one hundred national and one thousand state acts makes the Supreme Court one of the most powerful tribunals in the world. Few judges elsewhere wield such power. In Great Britain, for example, a statute passed by Parliament cannot be overturned by the courts, even if it violates such long-standing "constitutional" principles as freedom of speech. Members of Parliament, not judges, have the final say on fundamental law.

Because Supreme Court justices can wield the power of judicial review, they are among the principal agents of constitutional change. As Woodrow Wilson concluded, the Supreme Court represents "a kind of Constitutional Convention in continuous session."

Congressional Statutes

Supreme Court justices are not alone in affecting the Constitution. Members of Congress also command the power to amend the document through legislative interpretation. The Constitution grants Congress the authority "to make all laws which shall be necessary and proper" to carry out its enumerated powers, thus giving senators and representatives an opportunity to make changes not anticipated by the framers. As we saw, Congress in 1816 created a national bank, even though the Constitution makes no provision for such an institution. Congress insisted that it was "necessary and proper" for it to charter the bank in order to carry out financial responsibilities—such as coining money and collecting taxes—dictated by the Constitution. Chief Justice Marshall supported Congress's claim, stating that the Constitution was "intended to endure for ages to come and, consequently, to be adapted to the various crises of human affairs."[18]

Since then, members of Congress have affected the structure and powers of the federal government in many ways, from creating the executive departments and federal courts to determining the order of succession to the presidency. Presidents also have contributed to constitutional change over the years, as when they developed executive agreements as instruments of foreign policy making (see chap. 13).

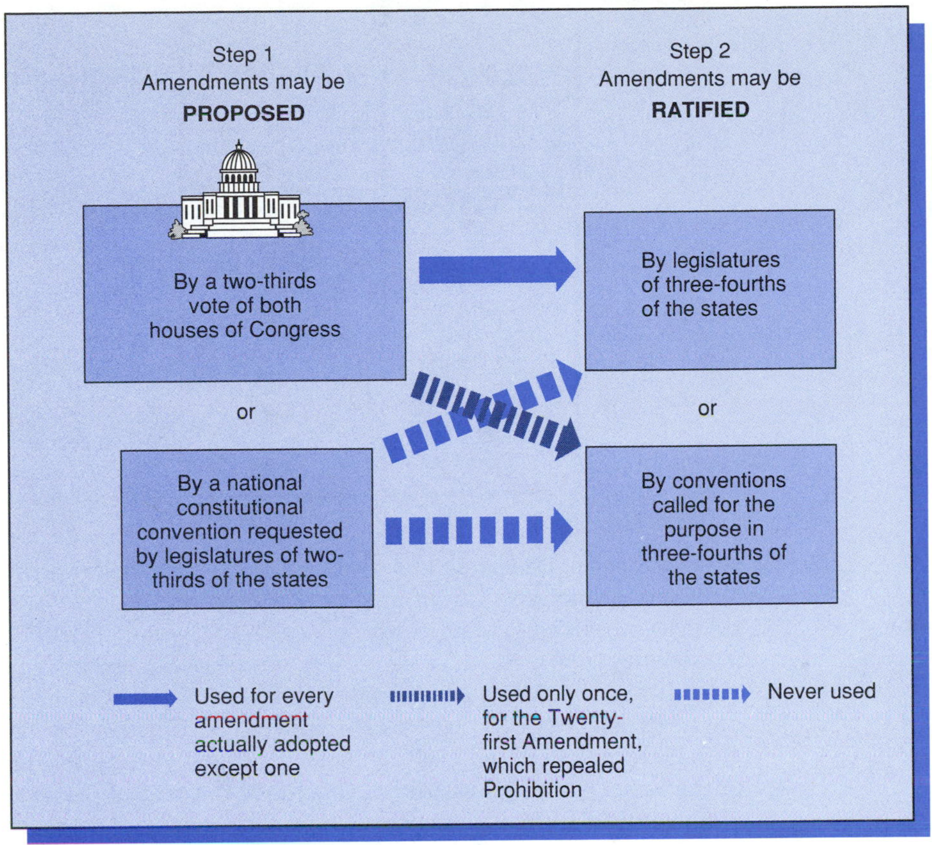

Figure 2-3
How the Constitution can be amended.

Constitutional Amendments

The most dramatic means of changing the Constitution has been through amendment. Because the framers believed that no constitution could remain unchanged for all time, they provided four procedures for amending the original document: two ways to propose an amendment and two ways to ratify one (see figure 2-3).

A constitutional amendment can be proposed either by a two-thirds vote of both houses of Congress or by a national convention called by Congress at the request of two-thirds of the states. All existing amendments were proposed by Congress, although there have been movements to propose amendments by the convention method. By 1986, for instance, several states had passed resolutions calling for a constitutional amendment to balance the federal budget.

Once approved by Congress, an amendment must be ratified either by three-fourths of the state legislatures or by special ratifying conventions in three-fourths of the states. Only the Twenty-first Amendment, repealing prohibition, was ratified (in 1933) by the convention method.

A striking aspect of this procedure is that the president has no legal power to veto an amendment. In fact, not even the Supreme Court can overturn an amendment. An amendment ratified by the states becomes part of the Constitution, and

in no way can the Court declare part of the document itself "unconstitutional." Thus members of Congress can use the amending power to reverse a Supreme Court ruling. For example, Congress proposed the Sixteenth Amendment, establishing the federal income tax, after the Court had declared such a tax unconstitutional.

Congress has formally proposed two additional amendments in recent years, but neither has won enough state support to become part of the Constitution. In 1978 Congress proposed to give full voting rights and congressional representation to the residents of the District of Columbia, the seat of the federal government. Although the district is represented in Congress, its single delegate cannot vote on any measure before the House, and its residents have no representation in the Senate and cannot vote in congressional elections. The proposed amendment would have delivered full voting rights to district residents and entitled them to two U.S. senators and one or two representatives.[19] However, it failed to be ratified by the states.

An amendment that would have banned discrimination on the basis of sex had been proposed (once again) in 1972. The struggle to ratify it reveals the kinds of obstacles new amendments may face. After whizzing through thirty-five state legislatures (twenty-two in 1972 alone), the Equal Rights Amendment (ERA) stalled three states short of ratification. Because of a surge of strength by stop-ERA forces, it appeared as though the amendment would fail to be ratified before the March 1979 deadline. A resolution accompanying the amendment had set the usual seven-year deadline for ratification by three-fourths of the states. (Although the Constitution says nothing about the length of time the process should take, Congress in 1917 set a seven-year time limit for ratification of all new amendments. In 1921 the Supreme Court ruled that approval should come "within some reasonable time after the proposal."[20])

All the same, ERA supporters persuaded Congress in 1978 to take an unprecedented step: to add thirty-nine months to the original seven-year period. The extension resolution set a new deadline of June 1982, thus keeping the amendment alive for several years. Although disagreements flared among constitutional experts over the legality of the extension, it was not rescinded.[21] As former senator Birch Bayh declared, "It has been clear in every court decision and in every action by the U.S. Congress that Congress has the authority to determine what is a reasonable time for ratification of a constitutional amendment. . . . Ten years is a reasonable

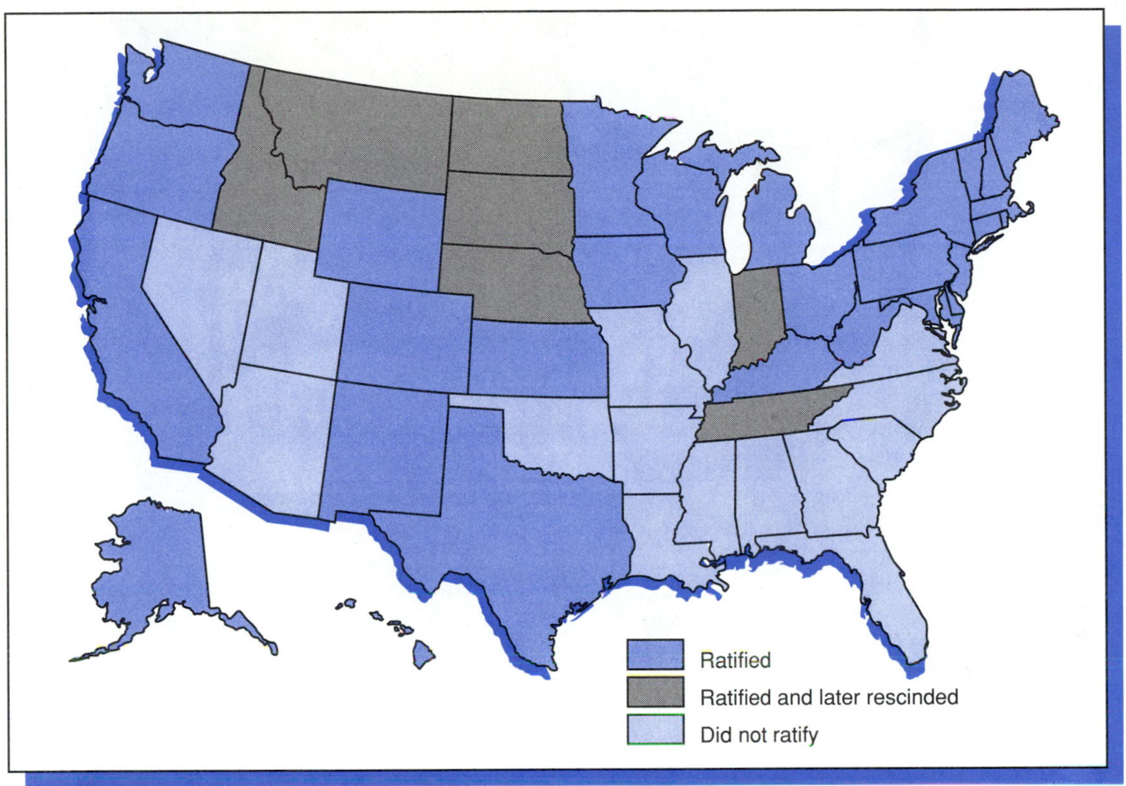

Figure 2-4
State ratification of the ERA

time for the ERA. This is no ordinary constitutional amendment. We are dealing with the rights of over half the people in this country."[22] Nevertheless, despite the extension, the amendment failed to win enough remaining states to become part of the Constitution, as shown in figure 2-4.

The push by women's rights organizations to win ratification of the ERA also reveals the kind of role that can be played by ordinary citizens in stimulating constitutional change. In fact, many Americans have tended to see the amendment process as a means of last resort in their efforts to achieve policy goals. When pleas to legislators and judges have been exhausted, citizen groups have tried to persuade Congress (and state legislatures) to support a constitutional amendment. Amendments suggested in the 1980s would have abolished the federal income tax, outlawed abortion, permitted prayer in public schools, required a balanced federal budget, prohibited the burning of the flag, and elected Supreme Court justices by popular vote.

The prognosis for most such proposals is not good. Amending the Constitution remains difficult, not only because of the reluctance of members of Congress to take such a bold step but also because of the need to secure the approval of three-fourths of the states. Apart from the first ten amendments (the Bill of Rights), which were tacked on as part of the politics of ratification, only sixteen amendments have been proposed by Congress and ratified by the states during the past two hundred years. While the Constitution is constantly undergoing change, it will not easily be rewritten to accommodate the passing concerns and passions of the times.

★ Betty Ford and other prominent ERA supporters gather at a rally.

★ Summary

The provisions of the U.S. Constitution, drafted more than two centuries ago, greatly affect the way our nation deals with modern problems and events, both domestically and in foreign affairs. The Constitution is the principal legal statement of our society, prescribing the powers and the limits of our major governmental institutions.

Though there has been considerable debate over the motives of the framers, it is apparent that they were influenced by both practical and philosophical considerations. They debated many aspects of the new constitution, and their differences required them to compromise on a variety of issues, including the nature of state representation in Congress and the question of slavery.

When we read *The Federalist Papers,* we get some idea of the philosophical and practical issues facing the framers. In the end, they created a system of separation of powers, checks and balances, and federalism. Each of these aspects of our system has brought both problems and benefits to our nation.

Once the Constitution was drafted, the framers faced the difficult task of persuading the states to ratify it. A debate soon erupted between the Federalists, who championed the Constitution, and the Anti-Federalists, who initially opposed it. Eventually it was ratified by the states, and ratification was followed three years later by the adoption of the Bill of Rights.

In the two hundred years since its ratification, the Constitution has undergone numerous changes brought about by the interpretations of the courts, by congressional statutes, and by constitutional amendments.

★ Key Terms

Anti-Federalists
Articles of Confederation
bicameral congress
checks and balances
concurrent powers
Connecticut Compromise
constitution
constitutionalism
delegated (enumerated) powers
1808 Compromise
Exportation Compromise
federalism
The Federalist Papers
Federalists
implied powers
necessary and proper clause
New Jersey Plan
republic
reserved powers
separation of powers
unicameral congress
unitary system
Virginia Plan

★ Notes

1. Charles Beard, *An Economic Interpretation of the Constitution* (New York: Macmillan, 1954; first published 1913), p. 324.
2. Robert E. Brown, *Charles Beard and the Constitution of the United States* (Princeton, N.J.: Princeton University Press, 1956), p. 198.
3. C. Herman Pritchett, *The American Constitution,* 2d ed. (New York: McGraw-Hill, 1968), p. 11.
4. Art. I, sec. 9, para. 5.
5. *Federalist* no. 39.
6. *Federalist* no. 51.
7. James Madison, Alexander Hamilton, and John Jay, *The Federalist Papers* (1788).
8. *Federalist* no. 51.
9. Baron de Montesquieu, *The Spirit of the Laws* (1748).
10. *Federalist* no. 47.
11. Samuel Hendel, "Separation of Powers Revisited in Light of Watergate," *Western Political Quarterly,* December 1974, pp. 575–588.
12. See, for instance, Arthur M. Schlesinger, Jr., *The Imperial Presidency* (Boston: Houghton Mifflin, 1973).
13. Thomas Paine, *Common Sense,* reprinted in *Directions in American Political Thought,* ed. Kenneth M. Dolbeare (New York: Wiley, 1969), p. 31.
14. *New York Times,* July 8, 1987, p. 7; July 10, 1987, p. 4.
15. *Federalist* no. 10.
16. Brown, *Charles Beard and the Constitution,* p. 170.
17. Pritchett, American Constitution, p. 33.
18. McCulloch v. Maryland (1819).
19. See *Congressional Quarterly Weekly Report,* August 26, 1978, pp 2277–2278.
20. Dillon v. Gloss (1921). See also Coleman v. Miller (1939).
21. See *Congressional Quarterly Weekly Report,* November 26, 1977, pp. 2493–2495.
22. Associated Press, October 12, 1978.

★ For Further Reading

Beard, Charles A. *An Economic Interpretation of the Constitution.* New York: Macmillan, 1913.

Brown, Robert E. *Charles Beard and the Constitution of the United States.* Princeton, N.J.: Princeton University Press, 1956.

Corwin, Edward S. *The Constitution and What It Means Today.* Rev. Harold W. Case and Craig Ducat. Princeton, N.J.: Princeton University Press, 1981.

Hamilton, Alexander, James Madison, and John Jay. *The Federalist Papers,* 1788. Various editions.

Kelly, Alfred, Herman Belz, and Winfred Harbison. *The American Constitution.* New York: Norton, 1983.

McCann, Michael W., and Gerald L. Houseman. *Judging the Constitution.* Glenview, Ill.: Scott, Foresman, 1989.

Peltason, J. W., and Edward S. Corwin. *Understanding the Constitution.* 10th ed. New York: Holt, Rinehart & Winston, 1985.

Wills, Garry. *Explaining America: The Federalist.* Garden City, N.Y.: Doubleday, 1981.

The different governments will control each other, at the same time that each will be controlled by itself.

—*James Madison*
Federalist *no. 51*

CHAPTER THREE

FEDERALISM

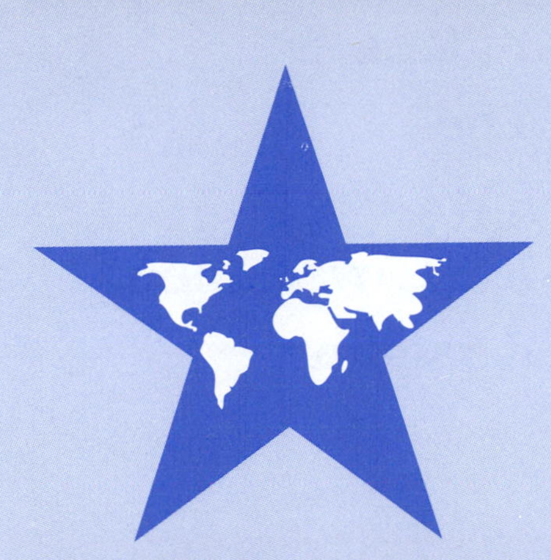

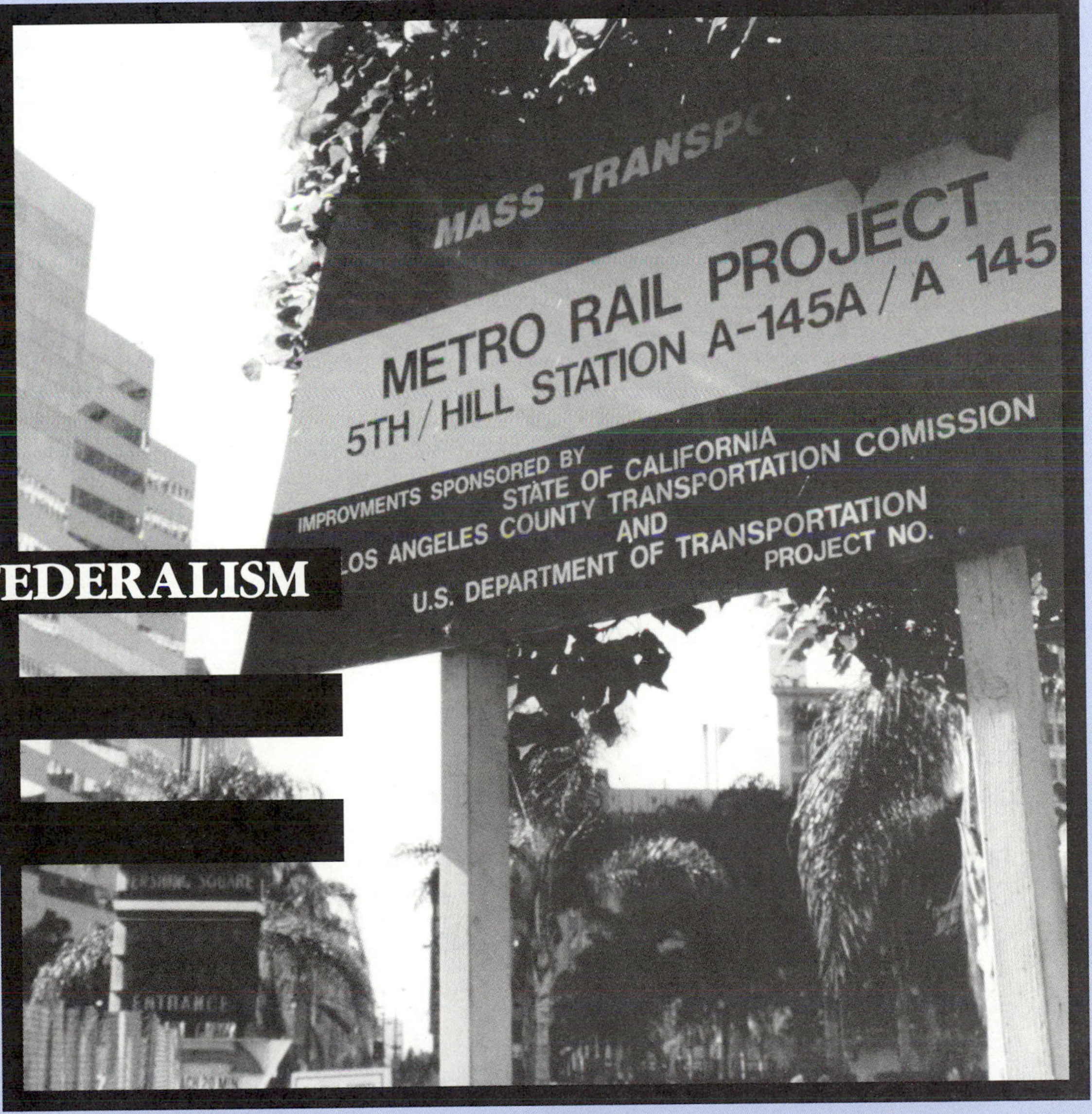
METRO RAIL PROJECT
5TH / HILL STATION A-145A / A 145
IMPROVMENTS SPONSORED BY
STATE OF CALIFORNIA
LOS ANGELES COUNTY TRANSPORTATION COMISSION
AND
U.S. DEPARTMENT OF TRANSPORTATION
PROJECT NO.
ENTRANCE

★★★★★★★★★★★★★

Federalism: The Maze of Intergovernmental Relations

When we think of American government, what typically comes to mind is the president and Congress, and perhaps the Supreme Court. But our lives are influenced not only by our national government but also by fifty state governments and more than 80,000 counties, cities, and special districts (see table 3-1).

Indeed, each of us is affected every day by these layers of government. Driving to school or work, we slalom around potholes the city should repair, turn onto a federally funded highway, and probably pay a toll to a state agency for crossing a bridge or entering a turnpike. Our local police and state highway patrol direct us around traffic and may even cite us for speeding if we are late to class. We also pay a federal excise tax for the gasoline in our cars, which have to meet state emission-control standards. And if we do not have a car, the bus or the subway we take is probably subsidized by local sales taxes and federal grants.

How did we end up with so many governments? Are there any advantages to this system, with its governmental powers divided among national, state, and local jurisdictions? What kinds of conflicts have developed over the years between national and state governments? In this chapter we will look at the legal and historical origins of American federalism. We will consider how the national government's powers have grown in relation to those of states and localities. We will also discuss how levels of government have become increasingly interdependent as America has become more involved in the global community since the end of World War II. And we will conclude with an evaluation of the pros and cons of our federal system.

★ Inventing America: The Legal and Historical Origins of Federalism

In most nations, ultimate legal authority and political power rest in a central government, or what scholars call a unitary government. In a federal system, by contrast, power and authority are shared between a central government and one or more levels of subgovernments. In the United States, the national government (also called the federal government) shares powers and functions with states and localities. Although unitary governments may also have subnational units, those units carry out policies formulated at the national level; they lack the independent constitutional authority to act on their own. Only a handful of the world's 170 nations—Australia, Canada, India, Nigeria, Switzerland, the United States, and West Ger-

★ **Table 3-1**
Governmental units in the United States: 1952–1982

Type of government	*1952**	*1957**	*1962*	*1967*	*1972*	*1977*	*1982*	*1987*
U.S. Government	1	1	1	1	1	1	1	1
State government	50	50	50	50	50	50	50	50
Local governments	166,756	102,341	91,186	81,248	78,218	79,862	81,780	83,166
County	3,052	3,050	3,043	3,049	3,044	3,042	3,041	3,042
Municipal	16,807	17,215	18,000	18,048	18,517	18,862	19,076	19,205
Township and town	17,202	17,198	17,142	17,105	16,991	16,822	16,734	16,691
School district	67,355	50,454	34,678	21,782	15,781	15,174	14,851	14,741
Special district	12,340	14,424	18,323	21,264	23,885	25,962	28,078	29,487
Total	116,807	102,392	91,237	81,299	78,269	79,913	81,831	83,217

*Adjusted to include units in Alaska and Hawaii, which adopted statehood in 1959.

SOURCES: U.S. Bureau of the Census, *Census of Governments: 1967,* vol. 1, No. 1; *Governmental Organization, 1982,* vol. 6, No. 4; *Historical Abstracts on Governmental Finances and Employment* (GC82(6)–4); and *Government Units in 1987,* Preliminary Report, No. 1, *Census of Governments: 1987.*

many—have a true federal political system. Some other countries, such as Brazil, Mexico, and the Soviet Union, have a federal system in theory, but the central governments actually determine local activities.

Why bother setting up a political system with specially protected subnational governments? When the framers drafted the Constitution, federalism, along with the separation of powers and judicial review, was largely a new social invention. The legal and historical origins of federalism are found in the philosophical and practical concerns of the framers. Federalism is embodied in certain key provisions of the Constitution and in subsequent Supreme Court interpretations of these provisions.

As we saw in chapter 2, both philosophical and practical interests drove the framers to establish a federal system. Philosophically, they wanted to prevent tyranny and promote individual liberty. In order to prevent concentration of power, they dispersed it among multiple units: horizontally among the branches of the central government, and vertically between the central and state governments. In their view, citizens could protect their liberty by playing the two levels of government against each other. As Alexander Hamilton explained, "If their rights are invaded by either, they can make use of the other as the instrument of redress."[1]

There were also practical reasons for federalism. As we know, the United States was a confederation in the decade following the Revolutionary War. Under the Articles of Confederation, the central government could not tax, regulate interstate commerce, deal effectively with other nations, or protect against foreign invasions. Federalists at the Constitutional Convention advocated a system that would give these powers to a central government. Alexander Hamilton was such a staunch proponent of central power that today the supporters of this position are known as Hamiltonians.

The Federalist experiment faced certain doom, however, unless concessions were made to protect the powers of the states. The states had existed as colonies

Native Americans: Inventors of American Federalism

When European settlers arrived in America, the League of the Iroquois was the most extensive political unit north of the Aztec civilization. Benjamin Franklin, in his capacity as official printer for the colony of Pennsylvania, became acquainted with the operation of this league, which united five principal Indian nations—the Mohawk, Onondaga, Seneca, Oneida, and Cayuga. Franklin became a lifelong champion of the Indian political structure and advocated its use in the new nation.

The League of the Iroquois, founded sometime between A.D. 1000 and 1450, controlled territory from New England to the Mississippi River. Each of the five nations had a council composed of delegates called sachems, who were elected by the tribes of that nation. Each nation's council governed its own territory. The fifty sachems also formed a grand council, which met to discuss issues of common concern—declaring war and making peace, sending and receiving ambassadors, entering into treaties, regulating the affairs of subjugated nations, and receiving new members into the league.

Unlike European governments, the league united several sovereign units in one government—precisely the solution to the problem of juggling state and federal power faced by the framers of the U.S. Constitution. The historian Henry Steele Commager said that even "if Americans did not actually invent federalism, they were able to take out an historical patent on it." The framers may have taken the credit, but Native Americans provided the model for our federal system, in which states retain power over some matters while a national government regulates affairs common to all. ★

SOURCES: Jack Weatherford, *Indian Givers: How the Indians of the Americas Transformed the World* (New York: Crown, 1988), pp. 135–137; Henry Steele Commager, *The Empire of Reason: How Europe Imagined and America Realized the Enlightenment* (Garden City, N.Y.: Anchor/Doubleday, 1978), p. 207.

for several generations before they won their independence, and they had developed their own economic, religious, and political traditions. Small states feared being bullied by large states. Southern states worried that tariffs would be placed on cotton exports and that slavery would be severely restricted. Northern states wanted uniform tariffs to protect their fledgling industries. Thus the Federalists made concessions to regional and state concerns. As chapter 2 explains, Article V provides that the Constitution cannot be amended to deny states equal votes in the Senate, and Section 9 of Article I prohibited a ban on the slave trade before 1808; slaves counted as three-fifths of a person for the purpose of calculating the number of representatives each state could send to the House (art. I, sec. 2), and Congress cannot tax exports from any state (art. I, sec. 9).

Federalism as Law: The Constitution and Supreme Court Decisions

Federalism is partly a matter of law, based on the Constitution and interpretations by the Court. The Constitution is ambiguous, however, about the division of responsibilities between national and state governments, and it is silent about the powers of local governments.

Article IV of the Constitution contains the most explicit references to state powers. According to the "full faith and credit" clause in Section 1, states are bound to respect each other's laws and judicial proceedings. Section 2 says that a person

★ Benjamin Franklin (1706–1790) was an influential statesman in colonial times. He was impressed with a Native American version of what today we call a federal political system. Franklin signed the Declaration of Independence and was a member of the Constitutional Convention, where he played a key role in framing the compromise between large and small states on the question of representation in the House. He is also known as the author of *Poor Richard's Almanack* and as a scientist and inventor.

who is charged with a crime in one state and flees to another state must be returned to the state where charges have been brought. This section initially applied to runaway indentured servants and slaves as well as to criminals, but this application was superseded by the Thirteenth Amendment, abolishing slavery and involuntary servitude, in 1865. Section 3 gives Congress the power to admit new states to the Union, but bars it from forming a state within an existing state or joining together two states without the consent of the states concerned. This section also gives Congress power over U.S. territories and "other properties." (Currently, Congress governs American Samoa, the District of Columbia [under art. I, sec. 8], Guam, Puerto Rico, and the Virgin Islands, which send nonvoting delegates to Congress.) Finally, Section 4 guarantees every state a republican form of government and protection from foreign invasion and domestic insurrection.

These provisions did not inhibit disputes, however. Once the Constitution was adopted, a battle erupted over the respective powers of federal and state governments, with the Supreme Court serving as referee.

The Constitution's ambiguity in regard to the respective powers of levels of government can be traced in part to the framers' disagreement over the question of central versus state power. The Federalists, led by Hamilton, wanted a strong central government, while the proponents of state power, led by Thomas Jefferson, were suspicious of such centralization. This controversy has continued to rage throughout American history and sparks debate today. While liberal Democrats tend to look to the federal government to protect individual liberties and solve social problems, conservative Republicans tend to believe that state and local governments are more effective problem solvers and protectors of individual rights.

Both sides of this debate can point to "elastic clauses" in the Constitution to support their claims. Elastic clauses are general statements whose meaning can be

How American Federalism Was Shaped by the Global System

It was not until 1959, when Alaska and Hawaii joined the Union, that the United States' map included the fifty states we see today. The territorial growth of the United States was shaped in part by global forces. Competition among rival empires and global migration account for some of the political differences we observe among the states today.

At various times in U.S. history, Great Britain colonized much of the land east of the Mississippi River, along with territory in the Pacific Northwest; France controlled the Louisiana Territory (a swath of land from today's Montana in the north to Louisiana in the south); and Spain ruled over what is today Florida and the Southwest (from California to Texas). One legacy of this colonial past can be seen in state family law. States that had been British territories based their family law on common law, which is a body of law developed in England primarily from judicial decisions founded on custom and precedent. Under common law, for example, a woman lost her legal standing when she married. In many common law states, wives could not own property, sue in the courts, sign contracts, or keep their wages. Many states originally controlled by France and Spain, by contrast, had community property systems, under which each spouse owned half of the earnings of the other and all property acquired during the marriage was jointly owned.

Global migration has also put its stamp on American federalism. The United States' involvement in the international slave trade brought Africans to work on southern plantations. The legal, political, and cultural legacies of a slave labor economy had dramatic effects on southern states, from the Civil War to the legal disfranchisement of blacks to what the political scientist Daniel Elazar calls a "traditionalistic" political culture, in which politics was left to a small elite.

Between the Civil War and the 1920s, more than 33 million people immigrated to the United States, most of them from Europe, in search of economic opportunity and political liberty. Many of them settled in the large cities in the industrialized states, such as New York, Pennsylvania, and Ohio.

According to Elazar, an individualistic political culture has been typical of the large band of industrial states of the East and Midwest, with their large populations of immigrants from Eastern and Southern Europe and Ireland. Politics in these states has been viewed practically as a kind of business in which the ambitious could engage to get things for themselves and for their ethnic group. The traditional machine politics of New York, Jersey City, Cleveland, and Chicago are typical of an individualistic political culture. By contrast, states of the upper Midwest and New England, populated largely by Scandinavians and descendants of English Puritans, have a more moralistic political culture, characterized by a lack of corruption and an emphasis on citizen participation and community improvement. ★

SOURCES: Jo Freeman, "The Legal Revolution," in *Women: A Feminist Perspective,* ed. J. Freeman (Mountain View, Calif.: Mayfield, 1989), pp. 371–394; Daniel Elazar, *American Federalism: A View from the States* (New York: Harper & Row, 1984).

stretched to cover an ever-expanding range of issues. Those who favor a strong central government, for example, cite the necessary and proper clause in Article I, Section 8, which enumerates seventeen specific powers of Congress (among them the powers to levy taxes, regulate interstate commerce, coin money, maintain an army and navy, and declare war) before concluding with a catchall provision: Congress may "make all laws which shall be necessary and proper for carrying into Execution the foregoing Powers." Proponents of centralization also focus on the **supremacy clause** of Article VI, which states that the Constitution and the laws made under it "shall be the supreme Law of the Land; and the Judges in every State shall be bound thereby, any Thing in the Constitution or Laws of any State to the Contrary notwithstanding."

Advocates of state power, in contrast, favor the Tenth Amendment's **reserved powers clause,** which states that powers not delegated to the national government

★ Thomas Jefferson (1743–1826) favored decentralizing governmental powers. His many accomplishments include drafting the Declaration of Independence and serving as Washington's first secretary of state. He resigned in protest over Secretary of the Treasury Alexander Hamilton's fiscal and centralizing policies. His presidency (1801–1809) was marked by simplicity and economy. President John Kennedy summarized Jefferson's contributions when he remarked to a group of Nobel Prize winners at a White House dinner that they were "the most extraordinary collection of talent . . . that has ever been gathered at the White House—with the possible exception of when Thomas Jefferson dined alone."

★ Alexander Hamilton (1755–1804) advocated centralizing governmental powers. He wrote more than half of *The Federalist Papers*. As the first secretary of the treasury, he recommended several measures that enhanced the role of the federal government in the nation's economy. Hamilton foresaw America as a commercial power, in contrast to Jefferson's vision of a society of self-sufficient free farmers. While Hamilton would be pleased to see the United States as the industrial giant it is today, Jefferson would take pleasure in noting how a suspicion of centralized power has remained as an enduring part of America's political tradition.

or forbidden to the states "are reserved to the States, respectively, or to the people." Proponents of state power see this clause as implying a fundamental limit to national government: central authority extends only to those functions explicitly outlined in the Constitution; all other powers go to the states or to no government at all (see table 3-2). The necessary and proper clause, they say, must be narrowly interpreted: unless a power can be traced directly to the Constitution, it is not proper for the national government to exercise it. Proponents of centralized power respond that the meaning and scope of the Tenth Amendment are highly ambiguous. They point out that it was a last-minute addition to the Bill of Rights, a sop to the states to secure their support for the Constitution.

Many of the disagreements between these two sides have been taken to the Supreme Court. Under Chief Justice John Marshall, the Federalist view prevailed, and the necessary and proper clause was broadly interpreted. In *McCulloch* v. *Maryland* (1819), as we saw in chapter 2, the Court ruled that a state could not tax a federal bank. "The power to tax," it declared, "involves the power to destroy," and the power to destroy a federal agency would give states unconstitutional supremacy over the federal government.

★ Table 3-2
National and state powers delineated in the Constitution

Clause or provision	*Coverage*
Necessary and proper clause	Congress can make laws to carry out the powers enumerated in the Constitution (enhances federal power)
Supremacy clause	The Constitution, treaties, and laws of the United States are the supreme law of the land (enhances federal power)
Reserved powers clause	Powers not granted to the national government by the Constitution are reserved to the states or the people (enhances state power)
Exclusively national powers	Foreign affairs, military affairs, interstate commerce, commerce with foreign nations, currency
Powers denied to the states	States may not impair the obligations of contracts, deprive any person of life, liberty, or property without due process of law, or deny equal protection under the law.
Powers shared by federal and state governments	Regulation of elections, taxation, regulation of commerce, spending for general welfare, judicial functions, law enforcement

The Nineteenth Century: Layer-Cake Federalism

Marshall's successor as chief justice, Roger B. Taney, attempted to settle the constitutional ambiguity. He ushered in a judicial philosophy that dominated most Court decisions throughout the nineteenth century: **dual federalism.** According to this idea, there was a fixed distribution of power between the two levels of government, with the states operating on an equal basis with the federal government. The reserved powers clause was interpreted as carving out areas of exclusive state jurisdiction that the national government's supremacy and necessary and proper clauses could not touch. For example, dual federalism was used to prevent the federal government from establishing a minimum wage and adopting child labor laws.

This approach has often been referred to as **layer-cake federalism:** the federal governmental structure consists of two layers of equal importance, with the Supreme Court preserving a neat boundary between them. This neatness is illusory, however. The battle of states' rights versus national supremacy migrated to Congress, where, in the 1840s, Senator John C. Calhoun of South Carolina espoused the **nullification doctrine.** This doctrine held that the Constitution was a compact among states, not citizens, and that any state was free to nullify this compact by refusing to enforce within its boundaries any law it believed exceeded federal authority. Echoing a debate over trade and foreign competition that continues today, Calhoun advanced this view to oppose the federal tariff, or tax on imports. Southern states regarded the tariff as a Yankee tactic to force southern consumers to subsidize fledgling industries in the North. Southern opposition to the tariff, and to federal limits on the admission of slave states to the union, contributed to a series of crises that culminated in the bloodiest war in this nation's history: the Civil War (1861–1865).

★ John C. Calhoun (1782–1850) of South Carolina was the leading proponent of states' rights in the pre–Civil War period. He served as vice-president under John Quincy Adams and Andrew Jackson. He resigned after breaking with Jackson on the question of nullification. As a U.S. senator and John Tyler's secretary of state, he championed the admission of slave states and opposed the admission of free states. Calhoun (*right*), along with Daniel Webster of Massachusetts (1782–1852) and Henry Clay of Kentucky (1777–1852), formed the great senatorial triumvirate of the decades preceding the Civil War. While all three were known for their oratorical skills, Webster (*left*) and Clay (*center*) were willing to compromise when it came to the battle between state and national interests. They backed the Missouri Compromise of 1820 and the Compromise of 1850, both of which tried to strike a balance between the interests of slave and free states.

The Civil War established the supremacy of the national government over the states. Once this constitutional issue was resolved, the two layers of government settled into a half century of dual federalism, in which each layer had its respective responsibilities carved out by the courts. The most important issue concerning federalism in the last half of the nineteenth century was government regulation of an emerging industrial economy. A pro-business judiciary struck down national laws passed in an attempt to regulate commerce. The courts argued that while Congress could regulate commerce *between* states (in keeping with the interstate commerce clause of art. I, sec. 8), all other commercial matters should be left to the states. Industrialization got another boost from a federal court's ruling that corporations were legal "persons," covered by the Fourteenth Amendment's guarantee of due process of law. (The Fourteenth Amendment had been enacted at the end of the Civil War to protect the freed slaves of the South.) The courts struck down many state laws regulating minimum wages, maximum working hours, and workplace safety. So, in effect, the federal courts said that neither the states (because of the Fourteenth Amendment) nor Congress (because of the interstate commerce provision) could regulate the economy.

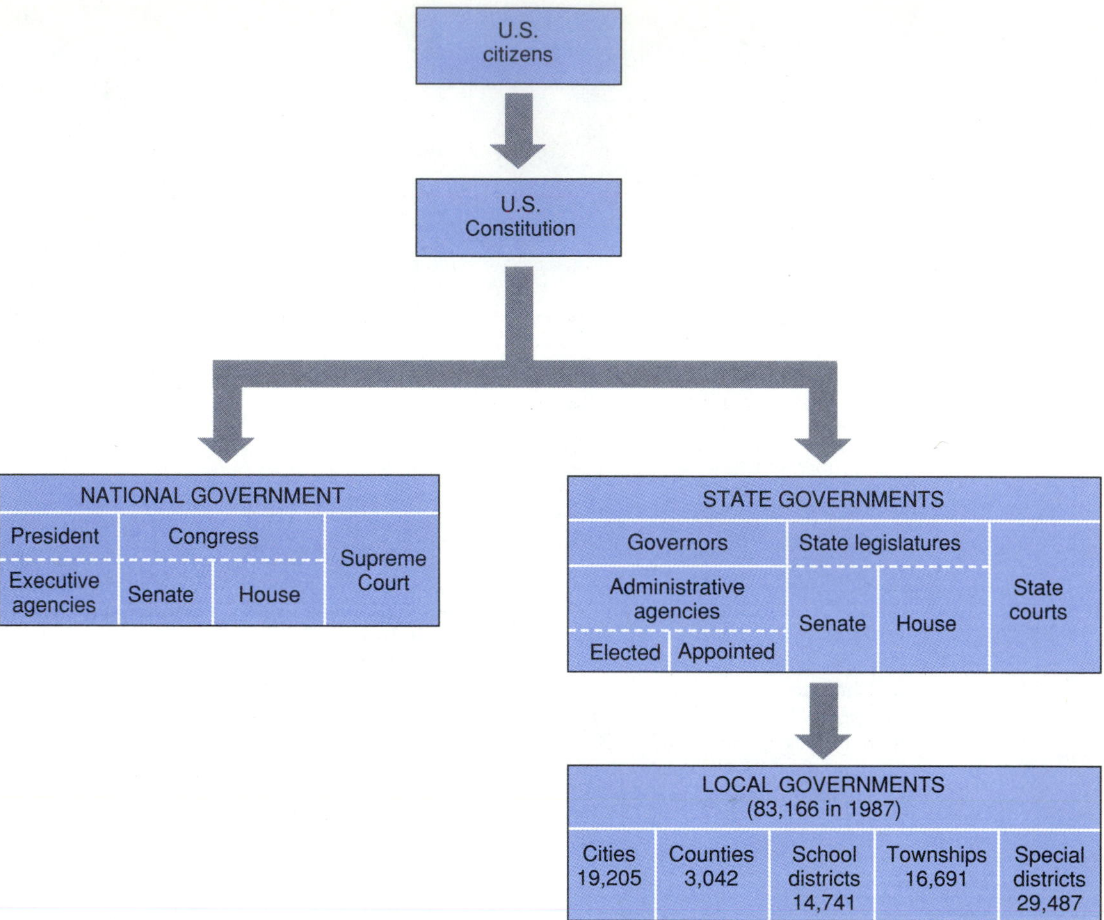

★ **Figure 3-1**
Governments in the United States: Systems and structures
SOURCE: Deil S. Wright, *Understanding Intergovernmental Relations,* 3d ed. (Pacific Grove, Calif.: Brooks/Cole, 1988). [Based on U.S. Bureau of the Census, *Census of Governments, 1987.*]

The Twentieth Century: Marble-Cake Federalism

During the twentieth century, local and national governments began to increase their powers in relation to those of the states (see figure 3-1). Urbanization expanded the importance of local governments, and national crises broadened the scope of the central government. Many state legislatures, under the control of rural and agricultural interests, failed to redraw district boundaries to reflect the movement of population to the cities. This intransigence forced many cities to turn to the federal government for a sympathetic ear.

In the 1930s and 1940s, the powers of the central government expanded with President Franklin Roosevelt's emergency measures in response to two crises: the Great Depression, which was tackled with a variety of programs known collectively as the New Deal, and World War II, which saw the federal government take unprecedented control of the nation's economy. These measures prompted a new meta-

How Do State and Local Governments Fit into the Marble Cake?

State Governments

Each state has its own constitution, which can contain provisions not found in the federal Constitution. California's constitution, for example, mentions an explicit right to privacy. However, state provisions cannot violate the U.S. Constitution. Like the federal document, each state constitution embodies the principles of separation of powers and checks and balances. The actions of state executives, legislatures, and courts must conform to the U.S. Constitution.

The governor is the chief executive of each state. Like presidents, most governors serve four-year terms (three states have two-year terms). Governors in half of the states, again like presidents, are limited to two consecutive terms in office. Governors oversee the administration of state laws and develop a state budget. In many states, the governor shares administrative powers with other independently elected officials (such as a lieutenant governor, an attorney general, and a secretary of state). When these officials do not belong to the same party as the governor, partisan differences may arise in a way not found among the president's top administrators. All governors (except North Carolina's) can veto laws passed by the legislature, and in forty-three states governors have the item veto, the power to reduce or eliminate individual items in state budget bills.

All state legislatures except one (Nebraska's) are bicameral (made up of two houses). Like the U.S. Congress, they are composed of a house of representatives (in some states called an assembly or house of delegates) and a senate. Nebraska's unicameral legislature is called the legislature and its members are called senators.

The U.S. Supreme Court has ruled (*Baker* v. *Carr,* 1962, and *Reynolds* v. *Simms,* 1964) that representation in state legislative chambers, both senate and house, must be based on districts of equal populations. Every ten years, when a census is taken in accordance with the constitutional mandate, the boundaries of state legislative districts must be redrawn to reflect changes in their populations. The sizes and sessions of state legislatures vary enormously. Lower chambers range in size from 40 members in Alaska to 400 in New Hampshire; senates from 20 in Alaska to 67 in Minnesota. In thirty-seven states, legislatures have annual regular sessions, while many other states place severe restrictions on the length of time their legislatures may meet (Wyoming's limit, for instance, is twenty days in even-numbered years and forty days in odd-numbered years).

Among the state courts are municipal or local courts, general district trial courts, courts of appeal, and a state supreme court. Judges of state appellate and supreme courts are popularly elected in about half of the states (unlike federal judges, all of whom are appointed). In the other half of the states, judges are appointed or selected through a combination of appointment and election. State courts play an important role in family law, the regulation of professions, and the definitions of crimes, all of which vary considerably from state to state.

Local Government

Local governments—counties, townships, towns, cities, and school and other special districts—are creatures of the states. They are established under the authority of state constitutions and laws, which can alter or abolish them. Some local governments serve large populations (8 million in Los Angeles county, 7 million in New York City) and others perform such specialized functions as mosquito abatement.

States determine the amount of autonomy enjoyed by local governments. A county serves as a kind of political outpost of the state government. Counties are set up by the state on its own initiative to administer state business at the local level. Some counties, however, have become vehicles for local self-government. These counties, along with many cities, have home-rule charters, state documents allowing a jurisdiction freedom to do largely what it wants within the realm of local concerns where the state has no paramount interest. About half of the states allow for home rule. Most cities are chartered by states under a general law applying to all its cities.

Unlike the federal government, states are unitary systems. Thus counties and cities do not have independent constitutional status equivalent to that of the states in our federal system. ★

★ President Franklin D. Roosevelt (1882–1945) answered calls for help from states and localities during the Great Depression. Unlike his predecessor, Herbert Hoover, Roosevelt supported direct relief to the poor. His New Deal measures called for the cooperation of state and local agencies in administering federal programs.

★ The Great Depression was a watershed in the history of American federalism. As industrial production slowed and workers lost their jobs, cities were forced to find ways to feed the unemployed, who stood for hours in breadlines such as this. Strapped for funds, city officials turned to Washington for help.

phor, **marble-cake federalism:**[2] federal, state, and local activities are seen as so interdependent that distinctions among them are blurred. Throughout the twentieth century, marble cakes have come in three varieties: the "cooperative federalism" of the Roosevelt years (1930s–1940s), the "creative federalism" of Lyndon Johnson's administration (1960s), and the "new federalism" of Presidents Richard Nixon, Gerald Ford, and Ronald Reagan.

During the early years of Franklin Roosevelt's administration, in the 1930s, hundreds of localities and many states faced bankruptcy under the growing weight of the Depression. When they could no longer meet their financial commitments to the poor and the jobless, they turned in desperation to Washington for solutions to record levels of unemployment and farm foreclosures. The chief mechanism used to coordinate national, state, and local efforts was the **grant-in-aid,** a direct transfer of money from the national government to a state or local government. While such grants existed before the New Deal, they were far more limited in size and scope than those of this watershed period in the history of federal government aid. New Deal programs provided direct relief to the poor and families with dependent children, as well as unemployment insurance and jobs. This system has been termed **cooperative federalism** in part because many of these programs were administered by state and local agencies, which used their discretion in setting eligibility and benefit levels.

Interdependence reached a peak in the **creative federalism** of President Lyndon Johnson's Great Society (1962–1968). In an effort to wage a "war on poverty" and promote civil rights, this administration used federal grants as carrots and sticks to induce states and localities to undertake controversial programs. Left to their own devices, many localities would have avoided such measures as job training, urban renewal, remedial educational programs, a minimum wage, and food stamps. Creative federalism envisioned a partnership in which all three levels of government would devise solutions to social problems. If existing government agencies were inadequate, new governmental bodies, such as community action agencies staffed by local activists, would be created. Frequently these new bodies met with resistance from established government agencies and local politicians. Confusion often resulted over who was eligible for what money and how one should apply for it.

Largely in response to what they saw as the excesses of the intrusive, centralized federalism of liberal Democratic administrations, conservative Republicans coined the term **new federalism** to describe their state-centered philosophy. The administrations of Richard Nixon and Gerald Ford (1969–1976) stressed the importance of sharing between levels of government; but they also maintained that the federal government had become too deeply involved in state and local politics with the proliferation of narrowly defined grants and webs of costly restrictions. New federalism programs thus gave greater discretion to states and localities to spend money as they saw fit. The new federalism of President Ronald Reagan (1981–1988) placed even greater emphasis on reducing the federal government's role in domestic policy making.

However, Republican administrations have not been able to curb the central government's role in intergovernmental relations as much as they would like. Let us take a closer look at the origins and significance of the national dominance of our federal system.

★ National Dominance in Our Federal System

One way to measure the power of each level of government is to look at **fiscal federalism.** This term refers to the nature and size of revenues and spending at each level of government. In this century there have been three important trends in fiscal federalism. National dominance is the most important of these trends in terms of the changes in American federalism over time. But fiscal federalism reveals two other significant trends as well.

First, there has been an overall increase in revenues generated and spent at all levels. At the turn of the century, all governments combined spent less than $2 billion, or less than half the price tag of the Department of Energy's new atom-smasher. By the mid-1980s, total government spending topped $1.2 trillion. Combined government spending has grown at a faster rate than the economy as a whole: from less than 8 percent of the GNP (gross national product, or the value of all goods and services produced per year) at the turn of the century to roughly one-third of the GNP in the mid-1980s.[3] (See figure 3-2 on the next page.)

A second twentieth-century trend has been a dramatic shift in the proportion of revenues generated at each level of government. National and state revenues have grown, while the local share has declined. Between the turn of the century and the mid-1980s, the national government's share of revenues grew from 38 percent to 62 percent; the state share doubled, from 11 to 23 percent; but the local share plummeted from 51 to 15 percent.[4]

Finally, there has been the trend toward national dominance. Lower levels have increasingly relied on federal funds. At the turn of the century, national grants accounted for less than 1 percent of state and local revenues. By the mid-1980s,

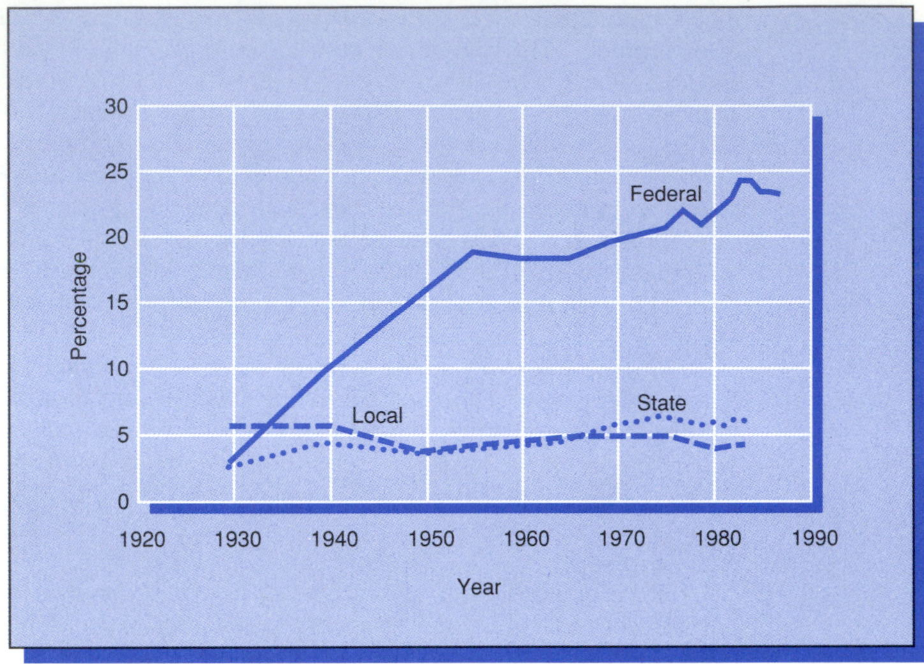

★ **Figure 3-2**
Government spending as a percentage of GNP, 1929–1986
NOTE: State and local figures unavailable for 1984–1986.
SOURCE: Harold W. Stanley and Richard G. Niemi, *Vital Statistics on American Politics,* (Washington, D.C.: Congressional Quarterly Press, 1988). [Data for 1929–1984 based on U.S. Advisory Commission on Intergovernmental Relations, *Significant Features of Fiscal Federalism, 1985–1986,* 6; 1985–1986: Office of Management and Budget, *Budget of the U.S. Government, Fiscal Year 1988, Historical Tables,* Table 15.2.]

this figure had risen to 20 percent. The most dramatic change was at the local level, where grants as a revenue source rose from 6 to 40 percent.[5] Obviously, local governments cannot afford to ignore the politics and policies of higher levels, since nearly half of the funds they handle come from above (see figure 3-3). The power of the purse clearly resides at the national level.

Reasons for National Dominance

There are six reasons why the central government has eclipsed states and localities in the fiscal federalism game. The most important reason is the adoption in 1913 of the Sixteenth Amendment to the Constitution, which gave the national government the authority to impose an income tax. The federal government has maintained its revenue edge ever since. Eventually, most states also adopted an individual income tax. Some states tax at a flat rate between 2 and 5 percent, but most state taxes are graduated, like the federal tax. A few states impose no taxes on wages, only on income from interest, dividends, and capital gains. In 1982, all but four states taxed corporate income.[6] But overall, the federal government outpaces subnational governments in income tax revenues. In 1985 the federal government generated $330 billion from individual incomes and $61 billion from corporate

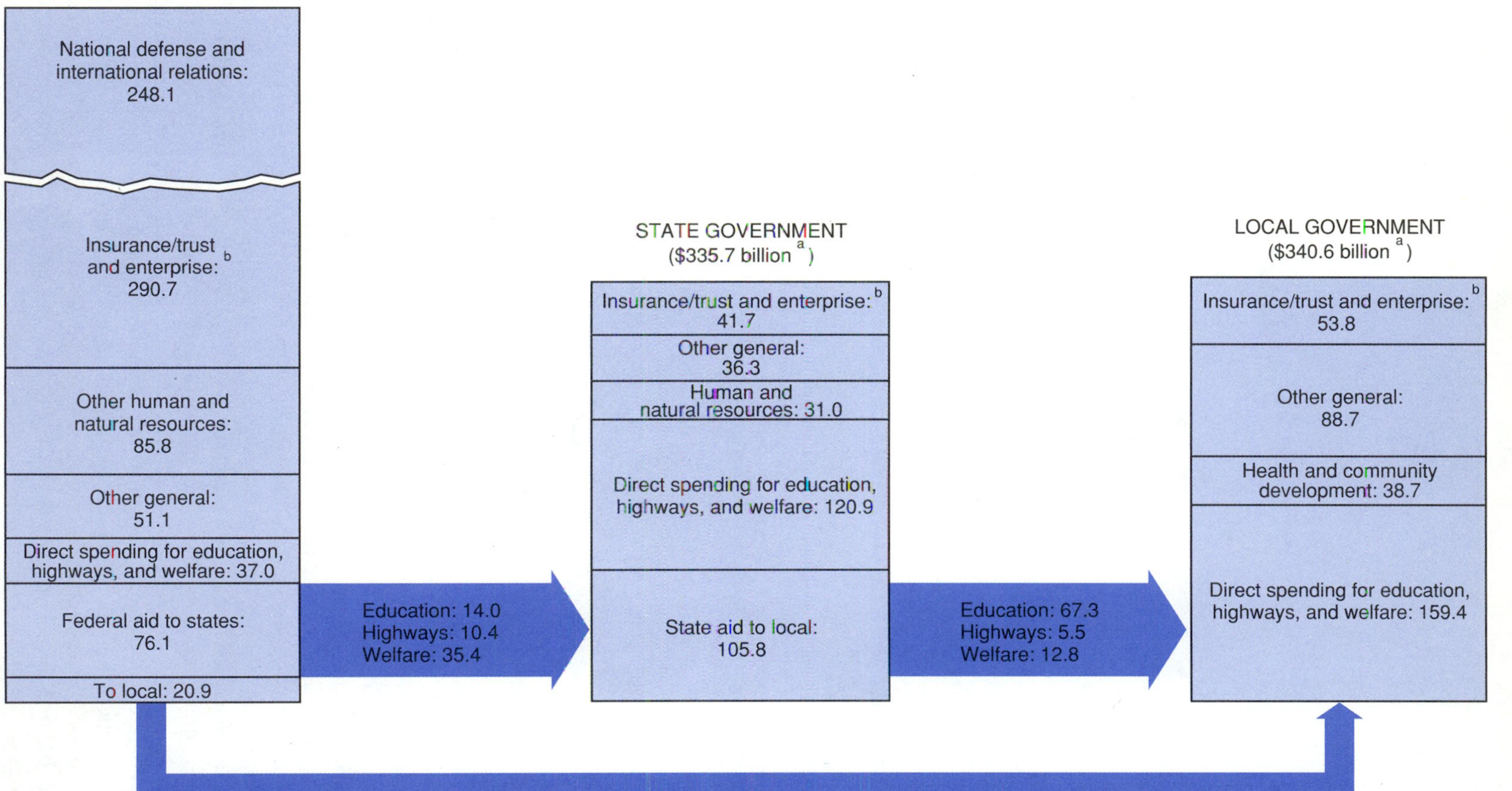

★ **Figure 3-3**

State and local governments' dependence on federal funds: Fiscal year 1984

[a]Excludes interest on the national debt of $109.2 billion, the state debt of $13.7 billion, and the local debt of $20.7 billion.

[b]Insurance/trust includes government benefits for unemployment compensation, workers' compensation, old age, survivors' disability, and health insurance. Enterprise includes spending on government-run facilities such as utilities and liquor stores.

SOURCE: Deil S. Wright, *Understanding Intergovernmental Relations,* 3d ed. (Pacific Grove, Calif.: Brooks/Cole, 1988).

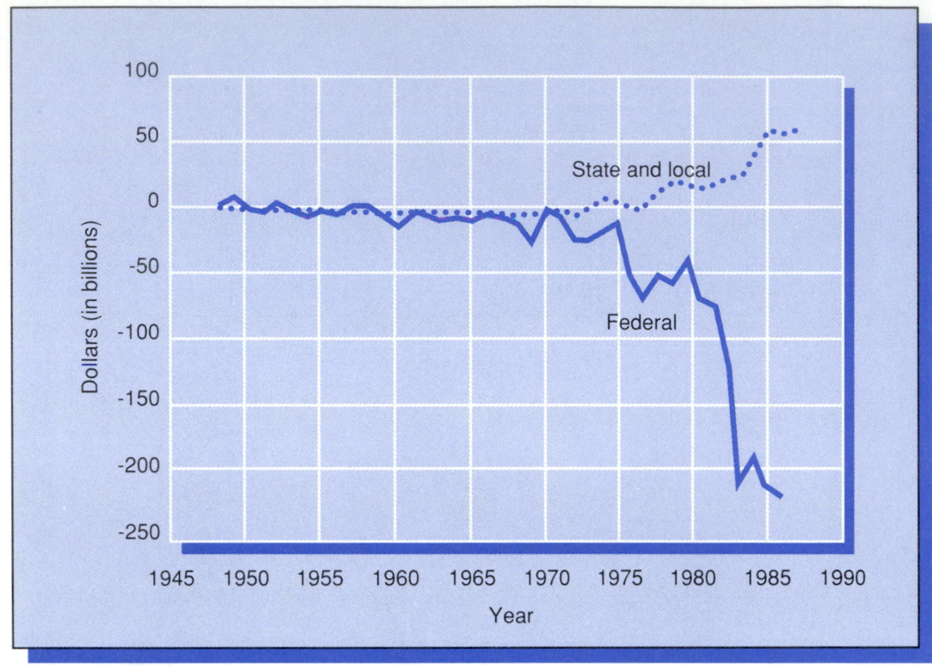

★ **Figure 3-4**
Surpluses and deficits in government finances, 1947–1986
SOURCE: Harold W. Stanley and Richard G. Niemi, *Vital Statistics on American Politics* (Washington, D.C.: Congressional Quarterly Press, 1988). [Based on Office of Management and Budget, *Budget of the U.S. Government, Fiscal Year 1988, Historical Tables.*]

incomes, while state and local governments reaped only $70 billion from individuals and $19 billion from corporations.[7]

A second reason for national growth is the expansion of federal programs in response to national crises. We have already looked at the escalation of social welfare programs during the Great Depression and the War on Poverty. The cold war and the arms race locked in vast amounts of federal spending after World War II, an increase that the states could not match. Twentieth-century military involvements, as in the two world wars and the Korean and Indochina conflicts, have increased the scale of both defense-related and other sectors of the federal bureaucracy, which retains most of its wartime growth despite initial postwar layoffs.[8] Once programs begin, it is difficult to terminate them.

A third reason for national expansion is the fact that many states require a balanced budget and have otherwise restricted their growth in ways the federal government has not done (see figure 3-4). The Constitution does not mandate a balanced federal budget, but many state constitutions do, and many also limit local government debt to a fixed percentage of property value in the community and require a local referendum to approve any increase in local debt.[9] In the face of competitive pressures that the federal government is spared, some states and localities restrict their tax levels. They provide special tax breaks in order to attract businesses, investments, or affluent residents from other areas. Florida, for example, banned the inheritance tax in 1924 to lure wealthy retirees away from other states.[10]

Fourth, the central government has also grown as a result of increased interdependence and social mobility. Such problems as acid rain, toxic wastes, economic recession, traffic congestion, and drug dealing do not respect state or local boundaries. They force local officials to seek regional or national cooperation. When local politicians have been unresponsive to such problems, citizens have appealed to the national government for redress.

Fifth, federal dominance is also attributed to what economists call the superior elasticity of the personal income tax, in comparison with the property and sales taxes on which states and localities rely. The income tax is more responsive to changing economic conditions than either property or sales taxes. A tax with high elasticity produces a disproportionate increase in revenue as taxable incomes rise. A 10 percent increase in economic activity, for example, will automatically yield a rise in revenue greater than 10 percent. As the "automatically" suggests, elastic taxes have the political advantage of increasing revenues without the need to legislate any increase in taxes. With an average growth in the nation's GNP, the federal treasury automatically expands by $6 billion or $7 billion annually.[11]

And sixth, federal dominance is indirectly related to the fact that an income tax is a progressive tax; that is, the higher one's income, the larger the percentage of that income one pays in taxes. Property and sales taxes, by contrast, are regressive; that is, they take a larger share of the income of low-income people than of the affluent. So an important political debate over "federalism" is really a question of fairness: should a service be provided by the relatively progressively funded central government or by the relatively regressively funded state and local governments?

Let's consider briefly why property and sales taxes are regressive. It would seem at first glance that since low-income people are renters, only the affluent who own property are liable for property taxes. But in fact renters pay property taxes when landlords include their tax costs in the rents they charge their tenants. Besides, people with high incomes have most of their wealth in untaxed forms of property. As for sales taxes, low-income people devote a larger share of their income to purchases than do people with high incomes, who have more money to save. While some states exempt necessities such as food, the sales tax is still more regressive than the income tax.[12]

In light of the national government's superior revenue-generating capacity, states and localities feel compelled to drink from the tap of federal funds. The term "grantsmanship" has been coined to designate the ability to compete successfully for federal grants-in-aid. Both the public and state and local officials tend to see grants as "free money" that one would be foolish not to grab.

Grants-in-Aid: Federalism with Strings Attached

There is a distinctive politics to the kind of grant the national government provides. Grants vary in the amount of discretion allowed the recipient: the greater the discretion, the less federal control over the way the money is spent. Recipients usually want as few strings as possible. The predominant form of national aid is the **categorical grant,** money that is to be spent for a specific purpose defined by federal law, such as interstate highways, public housing, or welfare payments. Such grants are usually "matching" ones: states and localities must pay for part of the program. When the federal government grants funds for highway construction,

★ Interstate highways such as this one are built largely with your federal income tax dollars, which are returned to your state government in the form of categorical grants.

for example, Washington pays about 90 percent of the costs and the state pays 10 percent. In 1972, 90 percent of all national grant funds were distributed in categorical grants; by the end of the decade, however, the share of such grants had fallen to 75 percent, reflecting the increased popularity of block grants and revenue sharing.[13]

The **block grant** covers a broad functional area, such as law enforcement or community development. Such grants were initiated under the Nixon administration, as a way to combine several categorical grant-in-aid programs into a single "block" devoted to a policy area. Local officials have discretion in regard to the way the money is spent within that given area. Community development block grants, for example, have been used for community facilities, public works projects, social services, and economic development.[14] Recipients of block grants have much more flexibility than those who receive categorical grants.

Flexibility is even greater under **revenue sharing.** Developed in 1972 under President Nixon, revenue sharing allows recipients to use the money for almost any purpose, with few strings attached. Federal funds are distributed to localities (and, until recently, to states too) according to a statistical formula that takes into account population, local tax effort, and the wealth of the local area. As a result, poorer, heavily taxed communities get more money than better-off, lightly taxed ones. No matching funds are required.[15]

As we mentioned earlier, the new federalism of such conservative Republican presidents as Nixon and Reagan was based on the desire to return responsibilities back to states and localities. While this orientation has resulted in increased reliance on block grants and revenue sharing, the shift away from categorical grants has not been so extensive as the proponents of the new federalism would like. States and localities have been hesitant to rely on revenue-sharing funds for three reasons.

Principal Areas of Responsibility of the Various Levels of Government

Primarily Federal Government

Air terminals
Farm subsidies
Foreign policy
Immigration
Interstate commerce
Medicare
National defense
Naturalization
Natural resources
Passports
Postal service
Public housing
Social security
Space research and exploration
Urban renewal
Veterans' benefits
Water transport

Joint Federal/State/Local Governments

Affirmative action
Food stamps
Medicaid
National Guard
Unemployment compensation
Welfare

Primarily State and Local Governments

Adoption
Animal control
Building permits and inspection
Drivers' licenses
Education, elementary
Education, secondary
Fire protection
Gambling
Garbage collection
Gun control
Jails
Libraries
Marriage and divorce
Parks and recreation
Police and highway patrol
Property and contracts
Sewage treatment
Smoking restrictions
Street maintenance
Voter registration
Water and power services
Zoning and land use ★

First, since 1972 revenue-sharing money has accounted for less than 10 percent of national grants. Second, the funds have not kept pace with inflation. And third, revenue-sharing programs have never been in force for more than six years at a time, so local officials are reluctant to rely on them for ongoing programs. These funds have been used primarily for hardware-oriented programs, such as fire protection, law enforcement, and streets, and only minimally for social services and health programs.[16] By the late 1980s, the virtual elimination of general revenue-sharing programs had left states and localities to rely on categorical and block grants.

Whatever the pitfalls of various forms of federal aid, states and localities have come to rely on these funds. State and local officials have recognized the necessity of lobbying the federal government for their fair share of the grant pie, and have formed various organizations to advance their causes. The twentieth century has seen a proliferation of so-called **intergovernmental lobbies,** associations of officials at one level of government organized to influence officials at other levels. At the turn of the century there were only five such groups; by 1968 that number had grown to eighty-six.[17]

The two most important urban lobbies are the National League of Cities, formed in the 1920s, and the U.S. Conference of Mayors, established by big-city mayors during the Great Depression to solicit federal help. Other governmental lobbies are the National Governors' Association, the National Conference of State Legislatures, and the National Association of Counties.[18]

★ Table 3-3
Responses to the question: "Which level of government is most effective?" 1972 and 1984 (percent)

Year	Federal	State	Local	No opinion
1972	40%	20%	22%	18%
1984	24	26	38	12

SOURCE: Advisory Commission on Intergovernmental Relations, *Significant Features of Fiscal Federalism* (Washington, D.C.: U.S. Government Printing Office, 1984).

Federal Expansion into State and Local Policy Domains

The dependence of lower levels of government on federal money has led the national government to extend its reach into several policy areas that once were the province of states and localities. While the Constitution clearly allots certain functions (such as defense, foreign policy, postal service, and naturalization) to the federal government, it says little about the respective policy responsibilities of the three levels of government. These responsibilities have evolved historically by custom. One way to tell which government is responsible for what is to turn to the community service list at the beginning of your local telephone book. You will find federal, state, county, and municipal telephone listings for dozens of services, ranging from adoption and animal control to garbage collection and street maintenance.

A possible response to this array of services is to say that it does not matter which level of government is responsible, as long as the job gets done. In fact, most Americans would probably fail a quiz asking which level of government was responsible for which functions. At the same time, many Americans have opinions about the relative virtues of the various levels of government. Conservative proponents of the new federalism say that Washington is inefficient, removed from local needs and preferences, and intrusive; liberals note that Washington has often responded to the needs of the disadvantaged in the face of inaction by local governments, particularly in the area of civil rights.

Public satisfaction with levels of government seems to have shifted away from the federal and toward the state and local levels in recent years. The Advisory Commission on Intergovernmental Relations (ACIR), a federal research agency, conducts frequent opinion polls, asking Americans, "Which level of government—federal, state, or local—is most effective?" Table 3-3 shows the 1972 and 1984 responses. Satisfaction appears to depend in part on one's economic status. A 1982 ACIR study found that, in response to the question "From which level of government do you feel you get the most for your money?" lower-income people tended to choose the federal government; better-off respondents preferred their local government.[19]

While the federal government has entered into several policy areas formerly controlled by states and localities, including law enforcement, criminal justice, and

Education: A Close-Up Look at the Marble Cake

When we think of education, we probably picture the schools of our childhood and the university we attend. Most of the people responsible for our elementary and secondary education—teachers and administrators—are employed by the states and operate out of the nation's fourteen thousand school districts. States and school districts control most of the decisions affecting the quality of education, such as the licensing of teachers and hiring of administrators, the building and maintenance of school buildings, control of class size and curriculum, adoption of textbooks, and provisions for extracurricular programs. In addition, most states run one or more institutions of higher education.

In recent years, however, the federal government has become an active partner in the education of Americans. Federal affirmative action guidelines are aimed at increasing the number of female and minority faculty members in institutions of higher learning. Funds provided by the National Science Foundation and appropriated under the National Defense Education Act are targeted to improve education in science and mathematics. The Department of Education grants funds for research in elementary and secondary education. The federal government provides guidelines for the education of disabled students. The National Endowment for the Arts promotes arts education. And federal reports such as *A Nation at Risk* have placed the federal government squarely in the movement for school reform.

The recent decline in the United States' economic position in the world has prompted the federal government to take a closer look at the way we are preparing students for the demands of the twenty-first century. Students in Japan and West Germany, our strongest economic competitors, are required to attend class for more hours and to take more math and science classes than American students are. Concern is growing that young Americans are not being adequately educated to fill the kinds of jobs that will allow the United States to keep its competitive edge in the global marketplace. ★

health care, we will look at just three of the more controversial areas: education, employment practices, and election procedures.

Education. Traditionally, education has been the province of state and local governments. Most parents want schools to be responsive to local needs and preferences in regard to such matters as textbooks, teachers, curriculum, and discipline. Yet it is often forgotten that the first federal grant programs gave land to the states in order to finance education. Throughout the country, state universities were built with the proceeds from the sale of these lands (hence "land-grant colleges").

Federal involvement has more recently been felt in desegregation measures. In 1954, local schools were ordered to desegregate in the wake of the U.S. Supreme Court decision in the case of *Brown* v. *Board of Education of Topeka, Kansas.* In 1957, when the school board of Little Rock, Arkansas, attempted to implement its court-ordered desegregation plan, Governor Orval Faubus ordered out the Arkansas National Guard to prevent black children from entering a public school previously reserved for whites. In the face of growing mob violence, President Dwight D. Eisenhower federalized the Arkansas National Guard and sent in paratroopers to restore order and implement desegregation.

Education was also an important target for President Johnson's War on Poverty. The Head Start Program provided preschool instruction for low-income chil-

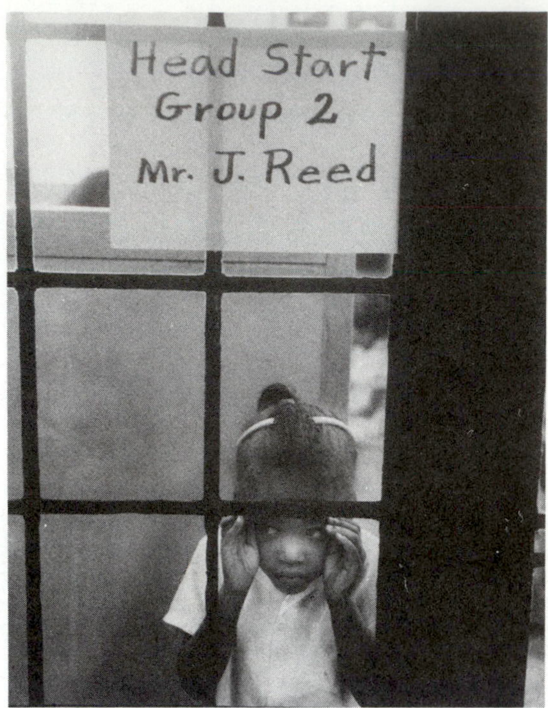

★ The federal government has lent a hand to states and localities in their efforts to educate young Americans. Head Start is one of the most popular federal programs. In the 1980s, Congress allocated about $1 billion a year for the program, which prepares low-income children for elementary school.

dren. Free and reduced-price lunches were provided for low-income children in participating schools, along with a general subsidy for all meals served in those schools.

Employment Practices. Federal laws have also had a major impact on the employment practices of state and local governments. Since the 1950s, the number of federal civilian employees has remained about the same (between 2.5 and 3 million), while the number of state and local government employees has tripled, from roughly 4 million to 13 million.[20] (See figure 3-5.) The federal government has imposed certain restrictions on state and local governments' employment practices. The 1931 Davis-Bacon Act mandates that locally prevailing wages be paid to construction workers employed under national government contracts and financial assistance programs. The Hatch Act (1940) prohibits public employees from engaging in certain political activities.

State and local governments are also subject to three important antidiscrimination laws. The 1964 Civil Rights Act bars discrimination on the basis of race, color, sex, or national origin in federally assisted programs. The 1972 Equal Employment Opportunity Act prohibits discrimination in employment on the basis of race,

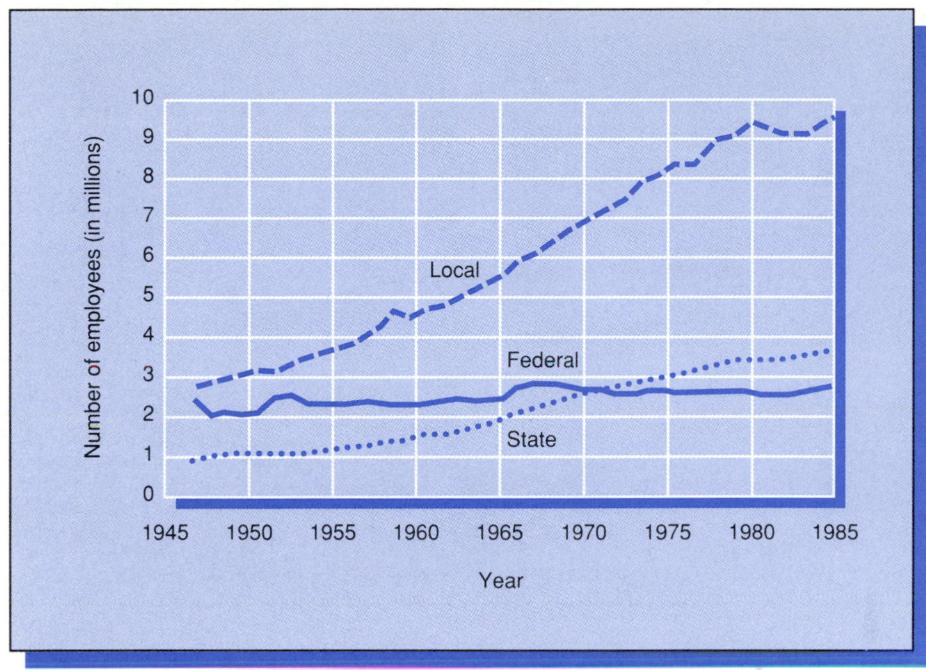

★ **Figure 3-5**

Number of government employees: Federal, state, and local, 1946–1985

SOURCE: Harold W. Stanley and Richard G. Niemi, *Vital Statistics on American Politics* (Washington, D.C.: Congressional Quarterly Press, 1988). [Data for 1946–1970: *Historical Statistics of the U.S.*, 1971–1984: U.S. Advisory Commission on Intergovernmental Relations, *Significant Features of Fiscal Federalism, 1985–1986* (Washington, D.C.: U.S. Advisory Commission of Intergovernmental Relations, 1986); *Statistical Abstract of the U.S., 1987*.]

color, religion, sex, or national origin. And the 1974 Age Discrimination in Employment Act outlaws discrimination on the basis of age.

Election Procedures. Finally, states have experienced federal intervention in the area of election procedures. In the case of *Baker* v. *Carr* (1962) the U.S. Supreme Court ruled that state legislatures had to reapportion their legislative districts to reflect the principle of "one person, one vote." State legislatures, reflecting a rural bias, had failed to give equal voice to more populous urban areas. Along similar lines, according to the provisions of the 1965 Voting Rights Act, the U.S. attorney general, acting on evidence of voter discrimination, can replace local registrars with federal registrars, abolish literacy tests, and register voters under simplified federal procedures.

The political debate surrounding increased federal involvement in state and local government activities is cast in terms of "encroachment" and "equity." Opponents cite federal interference as a violation of states' rights. Proponents point to increased equity for the poor, women, and minorities. Yet the federal government is not always found on the progressive side of the federalism debate. Some state constitutions, for example, grant more rights than the federal Constitution. Localities have been much more active than the federal government in the areas of gay rights, smoking restrictions, and comparable worth. Some local health officials have

★ Federal registrars such as these can be brought into any area suspected of discriminatory election procedures. An example would be a predominantly black county where only a fraction of blacks are registered to vote and an overwhelming majority of whites are registered. Federal attempts to rectify such imbalances are often resented by local government officials.

refused to take part in federal civil defense preparedness measures, arguing that such measures give the public a false sense of security about surviving a nuclear war.

Federal Creation of the Social Welfare State

Not only has the federal government expanded into areas previously controlled by states and localities, it has also carved out new policy areas over time. In recent years these new areas have been largely the legacy of Democratic administrations, which have gone far toward the creation of a social welfare state. This term refers to a government with extensive social insurance programs. Many of today's most costly and controversial programs—social security, food stamps, Medicaid, Medicare, affirmative action—are relatively recent developments.

Social security became law under President Franklin Roosevelt in 1935. For the first time, the federal government required workers to save for their retirement. Social security taxes are withheld from paychecks, matched by employers, and placed in a fund that accounts for nearly one-third of Treasury revenues.

President Lyndon Johnson's Great Society initiated new antipoverty and civil rights programs. Food stamps are federally financed and state-administered coupons redeemable for food. Medicaid, which provides medical benefits to low-income people, is jointly financed by federal and state governments and administered by the states. Medicare, a health insurance program for the elderly, is financed by social security taxes and administered by the federal government. In the area of civil rights, President Johnson issued executive orders requiring employers who hold federal contracts (one-third of the labor force works for such employers) to refrain from race and sex discrimination in employment practices and to establish affirmative action programs to rectify the effects of past discrimination.

The political debate about the social welfare state often divides along partisan lines. Republicans typically object to the further expansion of the federal government into functions they consider to be the proper domain of the private sector—insurance, health care, employment practices. Most Democrats defend such programs, citing the inability of other governments and the private sector to handle pressing social problems adequately.

Whether one thinks of the federal government as a helper or as a usurper of the functions of the states and the private sector, one must recognize that the interdependence of all levels of government shows no signs of subsiding. The marble cake seems to be here to stay, though the relative proportions of the ingredients may change.

★ Federalism in a Changing World

Federalism changed dramatically following World War II. Not only did the federal government extend its reach into such previously state and local domains as education, health, welfare, and civil rights, but state and local governments began to have a greater say in the presumably impervious national domains of defense and foreign policy. Let us see how governmental interdependence increased in four areas—national security, immigration, anti-apartheid activity, and the National Guard.

National Security

Since the inception of the cold war between the United States and the Soviet Union following World War II, national security has been a major preoccupation of the federal government. While the concern for national security was overtly reflected in foreign policy—the arms race, the wars in Korea and Vietnam, the invasion of Grenada—it also had a tremendous impact on domestic policies. Concern for national security led to a fervent search for local "subversives" during the 1950s, and it led to mock air-raid drills that had schoolchildren diving for cover under their desks. It had a direct influence on state and local governments as well.

During the Eisenhower administration of the 1950s, for example, a concern for national security was partially responsible for the expansion of interstate highways. True, a network of interstate highways would create jobs and help the trucking industry. But it would also facilitate the movement of troops and supplies during a national emergency, as the title of its enabling legislation suggests: the National Defense Highway Act. This act, passed in 1956, changed the grant-in-aid formula so that the federal government's contribution toward the costs of the projects rose from 50 percent to 90 percent.[21] State governments were happy to have the construction jobs that the money paid for and they were delighted to have the roads.

State education programs also received a boost from the federal preoccupation with national security. In 1957, when the Soviet Union launched *Sputnik,* the

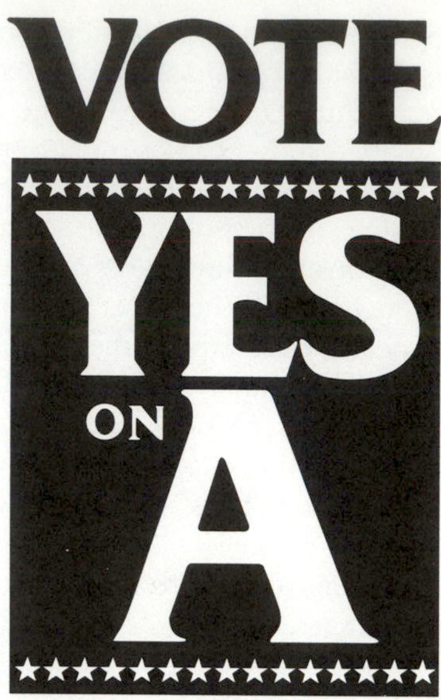

★ As a result of the nuclear freeze movement, many states, counties, and towns have passed freeze resolutions.

first satellite to orbit the earth, the federal government became concerned that American education in the sciences, math, and technology was lagging. In an effort to catch up with the Soviets, the 1958 National Defense Education Act gave financial assistance to states and public school districts to improve their offerings in science, mathematics, and foreign languages. It also bolstered guidance counseling and testing, improved statistical services, and offered loans and fellowships.[22]

Many states and localities have certainly not been passive onlookers at the race for national security. State and local governments have fought long and hard to secure and maintain military bases and defense contracts for local industries. Indeed, many American communities would suffer tremendous economic hardship should a base or defense-related industry leave the area. Along with these economic concerns, state and local governments have become active in the more overtly political and controversial aspects of the national security debate. Consider, for instance, the nuclear freeze movement, which began to gather momentum in the early 1980s. Arguing that the vast nuclear stockpiles of the superpowers could lead only to global destruction, freeze proponents wanted both sides to stop the testing,

★ **Table 3-4**
Immigration to the United States from around the world, 1961–1986

Country	*1961–1970*	*1971–1980*	*1981–1986*
Europe[a]	1,238,600	801,300	348,300
Asia[b]	445,300	1,633,800	1,644,500
North America[c]	1,351,100	1,645,000	1,093,400
South America	228,300	284,400	225,900
Africa	39,300	91,500	94,500
Other[d]	19,100	37,300	23,500
Total	3,321,700	4,493,300	3,466,100

[a]Western and Eastern Europe and the Soviet Union
[b]Far East and Middle East
[c]Canada, Mexico, Caribbean, Central America
[d]Australia, New Zealand, and other countries

SOURCE: U.S. Bureau of the Census, *Statistical Abstract of the U.S., 1988* (Washington, D.C.: Government Printing Office, 1988), p. 10.

production, and deployment of warheads and delivery systems. By 1983 the legislatures of eleven states (Connecticut, Delaware, Hawaii, Iowa, Maine, Massachusetts, Minnesota, New York, Oregon, Vermont, and Wisconsin) had passed freeze resolutions. In the elections of November 1982, the voters passed freeze referendums in nine states (California, Massachusetts, Michigan, Montana, New Jersey, North Dakota, Oregon, Rhode Island, and Wisconsin). And by 1983, 348 city councils, 444 New England town meetings, and 64 county councils had done the same.[23]

In addition, several localities—among them Amherst, Massachusetts; Berkeley, California; and counties in Washington and Oregon—declared themselves "nuclear-free zones."[24] Their resolutions contained such features as prohibition of city contracts with or investments in firms producing nuclear weapons or components; a ban on the transport of any nuclear weapons or components through the town; the barring of local scientists from research on nuclear weapons; refusal to participate in war-related civil defense programs; and the posting of "nuclear-free zone" signs on major roads. While parts of these ordinances resulted in protracted court challenges and others led to threatened cuts in federal funds, their successful adoption in enough communities could possibly hamper research and production of nuclear weapons.[25]

Immigration Policy

Another foreign policy area of conflict between local and federal officials is immigration policy, especially in regard to refugees from economic hardship or political strife in Central America, Southeast Asia, and the Middle East (see table 3-4). One dimension of this local–federal controversy involves money: some local communities refuse to burden taxpayers with the cost of searching out undocumented

★ Throughout the 1980s, many communities made their own foreign policy by harboring Central American refugees against the wishes of federal officials in the INS. In these "sanctuary" communities, local law enforcement officials were told not to cooperate with the INS in locating undocumented aliens, such as those from El Salvador pictured here with a pastor who supported their claims as political refugees.

immigrants. Many cities, including San Diego, San Jose, Phoenix, New York, and San Antonio, instructed city employees to leave the pursuit of undocumented immigrants to the federal Immigration and Naturalization Service (INS). Edward Koch, mayor of New York, captured the feelings of many local officials worried about the cost of pursuing immigrants when he said, "It's a federal responsibility and they're not carrying it out."[26]

The question of immigration also had a more controversial dimension: what to do with the hundreds of thousands of people fleeing political persecution and seeking asylum in the United States? The number of political refugees grew from a few hundred each year in the 1970s to an average of 40,000 a year by the mid-1980s.[27] Some communities, in recognition of the politically inspired terror launched by death squads in El Salvador and Guatemala, declared themselves "sanctuaries" for Central American refugees. Federal officials, contending that many of these people were simply leaving Central America for economic reasons and alleging political persecution in order to enjoy the greener pastures of the United States, sought to deport these undocumented immigrants. Local leaders accused federal officials of playing politics with people's lives and admitting refugees from regimes the Reagan administration disapproved of while excluding those fleeing regimes it liked. In 1984, for example, 1,018 refugees from Nicaragua were granted asylum, while only 328 of the thousands fleeing El Salvador were permitted to remain in the United States.[28] To prevent unauthorized refugees from being deported, sanctuary communities (which included such major cities as San Francisco and Seattle) instructed their law enforcement and other employees not to cooperate with the INS in locating undocumented aliens.

★ Critics of U.S. policy toward South Africa, such as these students at Columbia University, urged universities and state and local governments to exert economic pressure on firms doing business in South Africa. To the extent that U.S. firms withdrew from South Africa in response to such pressure, state and local governments had an indirect role in making U.S. foreign policy, traditionally the exclusive province of the federal government.

The federal government responded to this challenge to its authority in several ways. In Los Angeles, for instance, the head of the regional INS office waged a successful public campaign to force the city council to rescind a sanctuary resolution. In 1986 the Justice Department threatened the city of Sacramento, California, with a cutoff of law enforcement funds if local officials failed to cooperate with the INS. The effects of these local–federal confrontations, dramatic as they were, were ultimately more symbolic than real. After a few highly publicized cases, immigration officers found themselves so overwhelmed by the tasks of enforcing the amnesty and employment provisions of the 1987 immigration reform law that most political refugees are likely to escape the scrutiny of the INS.

Anti-Apartheid Activities

State and local governments waged a guerrilla war against President Ronald Reagan's policy of "constructive engagement" with the white regime in South Africa. Disgusted by that regime's apartheid system, which denies important rights to the black majority, some Americans wanted the Reagan administration to break all political and economic ties with South Africa. Unable to change Reagan policy, critics resorted to action in their local communities.

Like many other protest movements, the effort to change U.S. policy toward South Africa gained momentum on college campuses. In the mid-1980s, students joined with civil rights groups to demand "U.S. out of South Africa." Students wanted universities to sell or "divest" their stocks in firms doing business in South Africa. By 1986, more than a hundred colleges and universities had sold over $410 million of their holdings in companies doing business in South Africa.[29]

Moving from the campuses, students joined community leaders to influence local and state government policies. By 1987, nineteen states, seventy cities, and thirteen counties had passed laws requiring the withdrawal of investments (especially pension funds) from companies doing business in South Africa. At the time it was estimated that over $18 billion had been divested by local and state governments.[30] Some cities, such as New York, Chicago, and San Francisco, passed so-called selective purchasing laws, which gave preference in local contracts to firms that pledged not to do business with South Africa. Though these laws were frequently hard to enforce and provided for many exceptions, local and state governments undeniably made an impression on foreign policy makers in Washington.

Washington's response was twofold. On the one hand, Reagan administration officials hoped to dissuade local officials from passing selective purchasing laws. Federal transportation officials, for instance, threatened to cut road projects in New York City, a move that would have cost the local community $500 million in grants.[31] On the other hand, senators and representatives in Washington began to feel the heat from constituents and pressured President Reagan to apply federal sanctions against South Africa. In October 1986, Congress overrode a presidential veto, thus putting into law measures denying South African airlines landing rights in the United States, prohibiting new loans to the South African government, and banning the importation of Krugerrands (investment-quality gold coins).

Whose National Guard?

Another instance of state influence on foreign policy occurred when governors tried to prevent the federal government from sending their state's National Guard on training missions in Central America. National Guard units are composed of civilians who serve a few hours a week in military training. They are normally under the control of state governors, who call upon their assistance in emergencies, such as natural disasters or riots. Congress has the power to make these state militias part of the national armed forces. When the military draft ended in the 1970s, the army planned to rely on National Guard units for about half of its combat positions in case of war. Accordingly, the army required Guard troops to train around the world.

The federal government had sent some Guard contingents to Honduras to build roads and other facilities that several governors believed would be used by the Contra rebels fighting the leftist Sandinista government in neighboring Nicaragua. Ten thousand Guard troops served in Honduras in 1985, and a more or less permanent contingent of six thousand troops remained through 1986 and 1987. In 1986 some governors had withheld consent for Guard missions to Central America. That fall Congress passed a law permitting governors to withhold consent for a foreign mission only when their units were needed for local emergencies. Minnesota sued to have this provision voided on the grounds that though the Constitution gave the federal government the right to call out a state's militia, it reserved to the state the authority over its training. About a dozen states joined Minnesota's suit. It was dismissed in 1987 by a federal district judge, who said that Congress had authority over the training of the National Guard while it was on active duty.[32]

We must remember that foreign policy is ultimately the responsibility of the federal government. State and local intervention in foreign policy is primarily symbolic, a public statement that draws attention to an issue. But we should not underestimate the importance of symbolic influence. The same voters who select state and local officials also elect the president and members of Congress. As we shall see in chapter 19, the remoteness of foreign policy issues sometimes creates a lag in voter response. Once voters are aroused, however, they can have the final word. As in the case of Central American refugees and the nuclear freeze movement, the actions of local governments can forge links in the chain of public arousal.

★ Advantages and Disadvantages of Federalism

Is a federal system worth the trouble? Scholars have heaped both praise and blame on our cumbersome experiment in divided political authority. The political scientist Daniel J. Elazar maintains that federalism has promoted governmental strength, political flexibility, and individual liberty.[33] Another political scientist, William H. Riker, argues that the main effect of federalism since the Civil War has been to perpetuate racism.[34] For every virtue cited, a corresponding drawback has been noted. Let us compare the most important advantages and disadvantages of American federalism.

Advantages of Federalism

Federalism has certain advantages: it checks power, promotes competition, encourages flexibility, spurs innovation, enhances participation, creates a vital Congress, and allows for local autonomy.

A Check on Power. A system that provides for several levels of government makes a concentration of political power less likely than does a unitary system. When decision making is dispersed, political elites have many points of potential resistance to contend with. As we have seen, even though the central government has grown in power over time, its authority is by no means absolute. Levels of government share authority over many social welfare policies, and the federal government has to contend with state and local attempts to influence foreign policy as well.

The federal government does monopolize the nation's most critical life-and-death decision—whether to engage in a war. But we tend to forget that life-and-death decisions are made daily by subnational governments as well. During World War I, for example, more American women died in childbirth than American soldiers died in the war.[35] At that time, health care was primarily a function of local governments. During the Vietnam war, as many Americans died in motor vehicle accidents each year as died fighting during the entire war (about fifty thousand).[36] Subnational governments are responsible for such traffic functions as maintaining safe roads and bridges, setting speed limits (subject to a federal upper limit), issuing and suspending drivers' licenses, and providing traffic patrols. And state courts mete out the death penalty. Thus life-and-death decisions are dispersed in a federal system.

Competition. Federalism can promote healthy competition among jurisdictions. In 1987, for example, states competed for the right to build the Department of Energy's $4.4 billion atom-smashing supercollider, the largest scientific instrument ever built. California, Colorado, Illinois, New York, and Texas tried to outdo each other in offering financial incentives—funds, lands, roads, facilities. Illinois reportedly intended to give project scientists season tickets to the Chicago Symphony![37] Texas won the competition.

Jurisdictions constantly compare themselves with each other in order to promote a desired policy. Advocates of increases in expenditures for education, for example, will note with alarm their state's ranking in annual public school expenditures per pupil. In 1987 these figures ranged from Alaska's $8,842 to Utah's $2,455.[38] Another example is comparable worth, or equal pay for jobs of comparable value to the employer, a wage-setting policy that would benefit women and minorities. In the 1980s, proponents of the policy pointed to its successful implementation in Minnesota. Opponents of policies use the same tactics. Antidevelopment forces in Oregon in the 1970s sported a bumper sticker reading "Don't Californicate Oregon." Critics of unplanned urban growth often cite Houston and Los Angeles as horrible examples they want to avoid emulating.

Another healthy form of competition, in keeping with Alexander Hamilton's intentions, is seen in the ability to appeal to a higher form of government if one level fails to meet a citizen's needs. Such appeals are usually made through the court system, when citizens sue governmental bodies for denying their rights. In 1986 a rural Florida school district barred three brothers carrying the AIDS virus from attending school. The boys were hemophiliacs believed to have been exposed to the virus through plasma-based medications they took. Their parents sued the school board, and a federal judge ordered them reinstated as pupils. (As it turned out, the family had to move from the area after they received death threats and their house burned down under suspicious circumstances.)[39] Federal court decisions prevail over school district decisions in our federal system.

Flexibility. A federal system has the virtue of being sufficiently flexible to accommodate the diverse regional, economic, and cultural needs of more than 250 million Americans scattered over thousands of miles. Only once in U.S. history has a region—the South during the Civil War—sought to secede from the federal experiment.

In setting national policies, unitary governments are often insensitive to important regional differences. The English unitary government is often faulted for its treatment of Scotland and Wales. In Peru, the major part of the government's expenditures goes to Lima and the coastal area, while the bulk of the population in the Andes Mountains often go without. A federal system is designed to give regions a voice.

Consider the "Sagebrush Rebellion" of 1979–1981. During the 1970s, the Interior Department's Bureau of Land Management tightened restrictions on the use of federally owned land for grazing cattle and other activities harmful to the environment. The federal government owns over three-quarters of the land in Alaska and Nevada, and over half of that in Idaho and Utah. Real estate developers, loggers, miners, and other commercial interests pressured state legislatures in several western states not only to protest the Carter administration's attempts to revise long-standing arrangements in regard to land and water use, but also to lay claim to federally owned land in their states. Similar proposals were drawn up by western senators in Congress. But when President Reagan's first interior secretary,

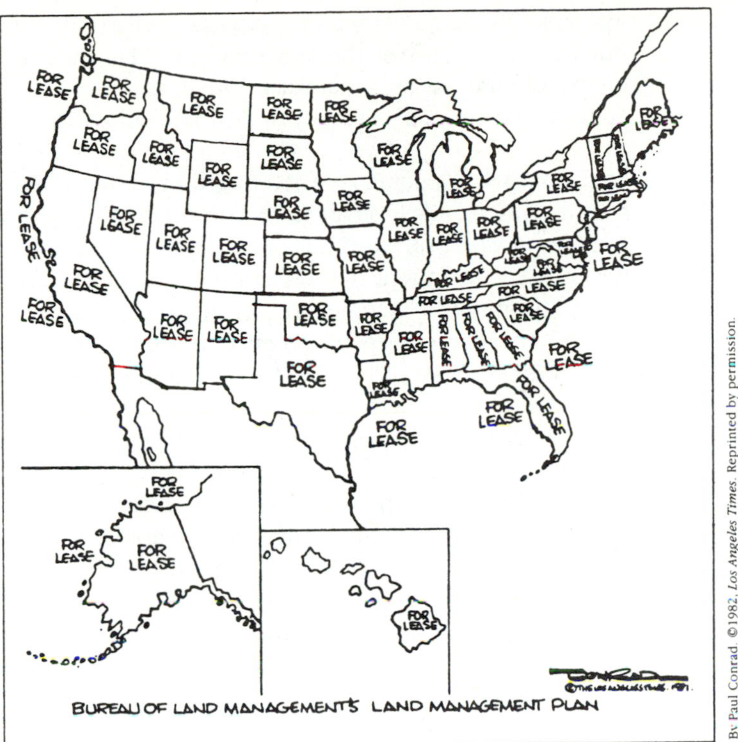

James Watt, took a pro-development stance, frustrations eased and the regional rebellion died out.[40]

Federalism allows for economic as well as regional differences. The wide variations in the benefits paid to recipients of Aid to Families with Dependent Children (AFDC), for example, can be explained in part by differences in the cost of living from state to state. Rent, food, and transportation cost a lot more in California and New York than in South Carolina and Mississippi. So it is only reasonable for states to set their own AFDC benefit levels. Interstate differences in tax burdens have also been reflected in national policies. States vary enormously in the combined state-local tax burden they place on their citizens. In 1985 this burden averaged more than $2,000 in Alaska, Wyoming, and New York. And it averaged less than $1,000 in Tennessee, Alabama, Arkansas, and Mississippi.[41] The Tax Reform Act of 1986 retained deductions for state taxes on federal income tax returns largely because the states with high taxes lobbied for these reductions.

Federalism's flexibility extends to cultural diversity as well. Anthropologists define a culture as a customary way of life, with shared values and guides to appropriate behavior.[42] The American political culture has been divided into state or regional subcultures by some scholars. For example, observers have contrasted two subcultures: the Frostbelt (North and Midwest) and the Sunbelt (South and West).[43] Frostbelt "Yankees," they say, hail from old wealth, Ivy League universities, Wall Street, and eastern law and investment firms; Sunbelt "cowboys" are newly rich, flamboyant, restless, open-collar, and can-do. Cowboys are said to be self-made, competitive, strongly anticommunist, and parochial, while Yankees have an international perspective and are social welfare liberals, imbued with a responsibility to "do good" for the less privileged. During the 1973 oil crisis Texans displayed bumper stickers that read "Drive fast, freeze a Yankee." Federalism permits cultural and regional diversity to flourish within the limits of national laws.

Innovation. Federalism encourages innovation. The American public benefits from having relatively small-scale experimental programs. If they fail, the costs are small in comparison with those of a nationwide failure. If they succeed, the federal government can adopt the tested program, and perhaps even take credit for the idea. The modern income tax, for instance, was first introduced in Wisconsin, spread to other state governments, and eventually was adopted by the central government in 1913. When the Nineteenth Amendment, which granted women the right to vote, was passed in 1920, several states had already approved female suffrage: California, Colorado, Kansas, Michigan, Montana, New York, Utah, Washington, and Wyoming.[44]

In the current period, states are ahead of the federal government in two important policy areas: acid rain and comparable worth. In 1982 Minnesota adopted an innovative program to control sulfur dioxide emissions and foster research and public education on acid rain. Illinois has enacted some of the country's strongest laws to reduce sulfur dioxide emissions from coal-burning plants. Canada followed Maine's lead in issuing weekly reports on acid rain levels. Several northeastern states have filed suits against several midwestern states, citing them for failure to enforce the federal Clean Air Act.[45]

Minnesota is also a trendsetter in the area of equal pay for jobs of equal value to the employer. In 1982 it became the first state to pass comparable worth legislation. It covered all state employees and had a specific implementation timetable of four years. In 1984 it became the first state to require all local jurisdictions—cities, counties, school boards, and special purpose governments—to prepare plans to implement comparable worth for their employees.[46]

Participation. A federal system enhances citizen participation by providing multiple decision-making centers. Citizens are more likely to get involved in politics if they think that someone will listen. The typical metropolitan area has ninety separate local governments. Numerous elections and hearings invite citizen participation. The more local the government body, the lower the costs of citizen action in time, transportation, and media expenses. The same factors apply to citizens who seek elective office. Federalism provides numerous training grounds for higher political office. The United States has more than 83,000 governments and roughly half a million elected officials.[47]

Federalism in America has spawned electoral mechanisms for direct citizen involvement that are not available at the national level: the direct primary, initiative, referendum, and recall. These mechanisms are called "clean government" or Progressive reforms. They were introduced into state and local governments in the early twentieth century by the Progressives, who were urban, middle-class reformers trying to do away with the "dirty politics" of party bosses—patronage, graft, bribery, corruption. Clean government mechanisms weakened political parties by circumventing legislative bodies and putting issues directly to popular vote.

As we shall see in chapter 9, the direct primary substitutes party members in the general electorate for party bosses in the selection of candidates to run in general elections. The initiative and recall are measures placed on the ballot after

★ The nose and chin of this statue outside a Chicago museum show the effects of acid rain. The control of acid rain through laws aimed at reducing sulfur dioxide emissions from coal-burning plants is one of the policy areas in which states are ahead of the federal government.

a requisite number of citizens have signed a petition calling for a vote on an issue (initiative) or for the removal of an official from office (recall). In a referendum, a legislature submits a measure directly to the people for their yes or no vote. In California, for example, since 1912 more than 170 proposals have been submitted to voters by means of initiatives and referenda.[48] Local recalls are permitted in thirty-seven states. Few statewide recalls have ever qualified for the ballot, and most of them occurred more than fifty years ago.[49] In recent years, initiatives around the country have asked voters if they want to cut property taxes, permit gambling, support a nuclear freeze and nuclear-free zones, authorize prayer in schools, forbid state funding of abortions, and approve the death penalty.[50]

A Vital Congress. Some people argue that federalism makes the American Congress more vital than the legislatures of unitary nations. One scholar attributes this vitality in part to the opportunities federalism provides for responding to pressures for action while limiting the risks of response. The grants-in-aid system in particular, she writes, allows Congress

> to commit itself to serving very broad national purposes (such as "more adequate" welfare) without assuming the burden of making all the political choices it would have to make in a unitary system (how much welfare, for whom?). The difficult choices may be left to other governments.[51]

Local Autonomy. Finally, federalism allows for a local autonomy unheard of in most other nations. Recall the odyssey of the infamous garbage barge in 1987. Where else could a city (Long Island City, New York) send a barge loaded with 3,000 tons of garbage on a 6,000-mile search over 155 days for a jurisdiction willing to accept its noxious cargo and see it be rejected by six states (North Carolina, Alabama, Mississippi, Louisiana, Texas, Florida), not to mention three nations (Mexico, Belize, the Bahamas), before it was deposited a few miles from where it started (Brooklyn, New York) to be incinerated?

Localities are increasingly acting as autonomous agents in the world of international trade. Cities organize overseas investment and trade missions, establish

★ Beginning in the 1970s, women seeking political office have found a welcome reception in local governments, where their numbers have tripled in two decades. Pictured here is El Paso Mayor Suzie Azar, one of the six female mayors of major Texas cities. Local political office is often a stepping stone to state and federal positions.

foreign trade zones and one-stop export assistance shops, set up export trading companies (authorized by Congress in 1982), and run international development offices. By 1981, foreign investment in the United States had reached $400 billion, including $180 billion in property, plants, and equipment, resulting in more than 2 million jobs. Five percent of U.S. workers owe their jobs to foreigners, up from 2 percent in 1975. Foreign investment is concentrated in Texas and California, with sizable amounts in Alaska, Louisiana, New York, and New Jersey as well. Andrew Young, former ambassador to the United Nations in the Carter administration and former mayor of Atlanta, put his city at the forefront of municipal competition for foreign investment. Other cities in the running are the Sunbelt's San Antonio, San Diego, Miami, New Orleans, and Los Angeles, and the Frostbelt's Philadelphia, New York, and Battle Creek.[52]

Disadvantages of Federalism

For each advantage of our federal system one can point to a corresponding disadvantage. Our system promotes inefficiency, inequity, lack of accountability, and obstructionism; it has harmful spillover effects; it leads to weakness in our political parties, creates a parochial Congress, and hinders our efforts to present a united front to the world.

Inefficiency. Redundant levels of government may prevent the concentration of political power, but they also promote inefficiency. The framers of the Constitution purposely set up an inefficient system with federalism, separation of powers, and a bicameral congress. They reasoned that duplication of effort and contentious deliberation were necessary prices to pay to prevent an efficient tyranny. This insight is lost on most Americans, who want their government to be as efficient as some private firms, and who think of government as a bastion of red tape and bureaucracy.

Republicans have been the most vocal in their desire for governments to imitate the cost-cutting measures of private industry. The Reagan administration's

Grace Commission Report, for example, listed several ways for the federal government to cut costs and reduce duplication of efforts. In one efficiency move, President Reagan proposed that the federal government take over the health-care programs of Medicare and Medicaid and let the states and localities take over AFDC and food stamps. Congress rejected the proposal, largely because of opposition by state and local officials.

The form of inefficiency experienced most directly by state and local officials is the red tape involved in securing federal grants-in-aid. They tell horror stories—applications being rejected on narrow technical grounds, grants going disproportionately to affluent communities skilled in grantsmanship, restrictive categorical grants distorting local priorities, grants being disapproved after state or local funds have been spent. Many officials are hesitant to entrust vital services for their constituents to the whims of the unreliable federal grants game.

Another frustrating form of inefficiency is seen when government programs work at cross-purposes. In the 1950s and 1960s, for example, Washington helped destroy the tax base of inner cities by encouraging a flight to the suburbs with highway construction funds and home loan and mortgage assistance programs. At the same time, many local governments were trying to revitalize downtown areas through urban renewal programs.

Inequity. While competition certainly has its advantages, as we have seen, it also has the disadvantage of rewarding people who already have resources, thus perpetuating certain inequities. For example, many state and local officials worry about the erosion of their tax base. They fear losing jobs, investments, and affluent taxpayers to other communities. Therefore, they compete to see who can spend the least, sometimes at the expense of needed programs. They compete for defense contracts and military bases. They favor incentives to attract new wealth. Poor people contribute little to the tax base and require costly government services. In a federal system, states are free to impose the kinds of taxes they wish in order to pay for the levels of services they are willing to provide. We saw how income taxes tend to be more equitable than either property or sales taxes. And service levels vary dramatically by state. In 1985, for example, the average monthly AFDC payment per family in California was $514; in Mississippi it was $104.[53]

Lack of Accountability. In addition to fostering inequities, federalism promotes a lack of accountability. One level of government can always pass blame along to another level. In the mid-1980s, for example, governors blamed the federal government for the lack of a comprehensive acid rain policy. There was little one state could do when a neighboring state's industries produced pollutants that blew across its borders. Canada was just as frustrated when winds blew the problem north. Whom should Canada approach? Minnesota? Wisconsin? Maine? Or Washington, D.C?

Similarly, local school districts often blame state governments for problems stemming from lack of funds. Consider the arguments raised before the U.S. Supreme Court in the case of *San Antonio Independent School Board* v. *Rodriguez* in 1973. It was pointed out that the poorest districts in Texas taxed their residents at twice the rate of rich districts. Yet poorer districts could raise only $60 per pupil, while those with strong tax bases raised nearly ten times as much. Demetrio P. Rodriguez claimed that Texas school financing laws prevented his son from receiving an equal opportunity to acquire an education. The court disagreed, saying that education was not a "fundamental right" protected by the U.S. Constitution, and that there was no evidence that the education provided in the poorest districts was inadequate in an absolute, rather than in a relative, sense.[54]

Obstructionism. While federalism has the virtue of flexibility, the other side of this coin is obstructionism. The will of the majority of Americans has sometimes been thwarted by states in strategic decision-making positions. In the 1950s and early 1960s, for example, southern Democrats in Congress were able to prevent the passage of civil rights legislation because they chaired important committees in the House and Senate. Southern legislators held "safe seats." They were virtually assured of reelection because of the Democratic party's domination of southern politics. Facing little opposition in election after election, southern Democrats acquired the seniority needed to rise to the rank of committee chair, where they stalled or killed measures that would have expanded the voting and economic rights of blacks, as many of their white constituents relied on them to do.

States can also obstruct majority will through the constitutional amendment process, as we saw in the case of the Equal Rights Amendment (ERA). In the 1970s, every public opinion poll on the subject showed that a majority of Americans supported this amendment.[55] Yet when the ratification deadline came in 1982, only thirty-five of the required thirty-eight states had ratified it, and the amendment went down to defeat.

Harmful Spillover Effects. We have seen that state and local actions can be beneficial for other jurisdictions, but they can be harmful, too. Economists talk about harmful "spillover effects" or "negative externalities." These are unintended consequences of a decision made in one jurisdiction that cause harm to another. The important political question here is whether government should force the party responsible for the problem to meet the costs of solving it. As we saw in the case of acid rain, northeastern states want to force midwestern states to take responsibility for a problem they export on the wind. In local politics, neighboring cities often face a "jobs–housing imbalance": a job-rich city gets the higher tax base provided by lucrative businesses, while its housing-rich neighbor has to provide public transportation, low-income housing, and costly social services for residents who commute to the job-rich area. The job-rich city reaps the benefits of a labor force while passing along the costs of providing for them to its neighbor.

Unless a higher level of government is willing and able to look at the larger question of who ought to bear the costs and benefits of a government's political decisions, federalism's free-for-all does not provide redress. And what happens if the central government itself inequitably divides up certain benefits? Since the end of World War II, federal defense contracts have gone disproportionately to the Sunbelt at the expense of the Frostbelt. Sunbelt growth has also been encouraged by federally sponsored water projects in the West. As we shall see, regional caucuses in Congress are trying to prevent such regional disparities in the future.

Weak Parties. While we have praised such state mechanisms as the direct primary and initiative for promoting direct citizen participation, we should also point out that such measures have severely weakened the national party system in the United States. They allow candidates to bypass the party apparatus in running for office and citizens to bypass party-dominated state legislatures in making laws. Federalism has dealt an equally crippling blow to parties. Of the half a million

★ Acid rain is a problem that crosses state and international borders.

elected officials in the country, only two are chosen on a national basis (the president and vice-president). All the rest are selected on a state or substate basis: senators, representatives, governors, state legislators, county supervisors, mayors, city council members, and so on. Most elected officials are not going to risk offending local voters in order to remain loyal to a national party platform. As a result, federalism makes party unity difficult to achieve. Party officials have a fair amount of autonomy at each level of the party structure. There is no centralized chain of command to enforce discipline.

Political scientists are divided on the question of the chicken–egg relationship between decentralized party structure and federalism. Some, such as David Truman, argue that federalism produces fragmented political parties because of the important role played by the states in the national electoral system. Others, such as Morton Grodzins, maintain that the American party system contributes to as well as reflects the decentralized pattern of policy making in our federal system.[56]

A Parochial Congress. Just as federalism adds to Congress's vitality, it also creates a parochial Congress. The public wants Congress to be sensitive to state and district needs. When asked what their legislators in Washington should do when forced to choose between the interests of their constituency and those of the nation as a whole, most Americans say that constituents' interests should prevail. Indeed, votes in Congress are often split more along regional lines than along party lines. While the Democratic party tends to support liberal measures and the Republican party usually favors conservative ones, the votes of some northern Republicans (nicknamed "gypsy moths") are frequently more liberal than those of some southern Democrats (dubbed "boll weevils"), particularly on such issues as civil rights, welfare, prayer in schools, defense, and foreign aid.

Regional interests are also reflected in congressional caucuses, or informal associations of like-minded members. In 1973, for example, House members formed the New England Congressional Caucus with the help of regional business leaders, who saw the caucus as a means for Congress and the private sector to discuss regional economic concerns and monitor public opinion and legislative action on such issues as energy, the environment, job training, and exports. There is also a Frostbelt association, the Northeast-Midwest Congressional Coalition, and a Sunbelt Council.[57]

Weakened Nationalism. Finally, though we have praised the virtues of local autonomy, we should also note that this federal system, created to present a united front to the outside world, occasionally speaks to that world with many governmental voices. We have already discussed several state and local attempts to influence foreign policy: efforts to prevent the National Guard from training in Honduras, declarations of support for a nuclear freeze and nuclear-free zones, provision of sanctuary for Central American refugees, resistance to South African apartheid, and promotion of foreign trade. These and other measures baffle foreign observers.

Take the matter of whether the supersonic Concorde would be permitted to land at U.S. airports. Efforts to prevent the landings were helped by the fact that airports are locally rather than nationally operated. While opponents were blocked in England and France, where the national governments control such matters, they managed to persuade the Port of New York Authority to deny landing rights to this noisy aircraft. (Eventually the courts ordered the lifting of these restrictions.)

Most of the recent attempts to obstruct national defense or trade policies have been minor irritations rather than significant roadblocks to federal policy initiatives. And they are typically resolved by the courts in favor of the central government. Nonetheless, they do serve notice to Washington and the global community that our federal experiment is alive and well. Anyone who attempts to understand American politics had better take into account the complex interactions among the three levels of government.

★ Summary

The American system of federalism has its origins in the framers' attempt to prevent a concentration of power, to improve upon the weaknesses of the confederation, and to persuade the states to ratify the Constitution. The Constitution is ambiguous in regard to the respective powers of the federal and state governments, and it says nothing about the powers of local governments. The Supreme Court mediates disputes among governments. Conflicts in the nineteenth century pitted the federal government against state authority (dual federalism), culminating in the Civil War.

In the twentieth century, the term "intergovernmental relations" has come increasingly to replace "federalism," an indication of the importance of the city as a third layer of government and the growing reliance of subnational governments on Washington. Today the United States has more than 83,000 governments and half a million elected officials.

States get about one-fifth and localities get about two-fifths of their revenues from the federal government, which has demonstrated a revenue-generating edge over other levels ever since the national income tax went into effect. The dominance of the federal government is also due to its growth during crises, the absence of budget limits found at other levels, social interdependence, and the elasticity and progressivity of the income tax. Jurisdictions compete for federal grants-in-aid, preferring the discretion associated with revenue sharing and block grants to the restrictions imposed by categorical grants. Intergovernmental lobbies pressure Congress for their share of the federal grant pie.

Governments divide up policy responsibilities, with the federal government increasingly expanding into state and local policy domains and creating new areas of public policy. But it is also the case that the various levels have become increasingly interdependent in recent years. Just as the federal government is having a growing say in this nation's educational policies, subnational governments are attempting to influence our foreign policies. And more than one level controls many social welfare programs.

For every advantage of our federal system there is a corresponding disadvantage. Federalism checks power but promotes inefficiency. It encourages healthy competition, but it also fosters inequities and lack of accountability. Flexibility has its flip side: obstructionism. Federalism has the virtue of innovation and the vice of harmful spillover effects. It both encourages political participation and weakens political parties. And it creates a Congress that is vital yet parochial.

★ Key Terms

block grant
categorical grant
cooperative federalism
creative federalism
dual (layer-cake) federalism
fiscal federalism
grant-in-aid
intergovernmental lobbies
marble-cake federalism
new federalism
nullification doctrine
reserved powers clause
revenue sharing
supremacy clause

★ Notes

1. *Federalist* no. 28.
2. Martin Grodzins, *The American System* (Chicago: Rand McNally, 1966).
3. David C. Nice, *Federalism: The Politics of Intergovernmental Relations* (New York: St. Martin's Press, 1987), p. 45.
4. Ibid., p. 46.
5. Ibid., p. 47.
6. Thomas R. Dye, *Politics in States and Communities,* 5th ed. (Englewood Cliffs, N.J.: Prentice-Hall, 1985), pp. 478–479.
7. U.S. Bureau of the Census, *Statistical Abstract of the United States, 1988* (Washington, D.C.: U.S. Government Printing Office, 1987), p. 258.
8. Bruce D. Porter, "Parkinson's Law Revisited: War and the Growth of American Government," *Public Interest* 60 (Summer 1980): 50–68.
9. Dye, *Politics,* p. 36.
10. Nice, *Federalism,* p. 214.
11. Michael Reagan and John Sanzone, *The New Federalism* (New York: Oxford University Press, 1981), p. 39.
12. Dye, *Politics,* pp. 482–483.
13. George Break, *Financing Government in a Federal System* (Washington, D.C.: Brookings Institution, 1980), pp. 123–124.
14. J. Richard Aronson and John L. Hilley, *Financing State and Local Governments,* 4th ed. (Washington, D.C.: Brookings Institution, 1986), p. 66.

15. Jeffrey R. Henig, *Public Policy and Federalism: Issues in State and Local Politics* (New York: St. Martin's Press, 1985), p. 17.
16. Nice, *Federalism,* p. 56.
17. Jack Walker, "The Diffusion of Innovation among the American States," *American Political Science Review* 63 (1969): 880–899.
18. Donald H. Haider, *When Governments Come to Washington* (New York: Free Press, 1974).
19. Advisory Commission on Intergovernmental Relations, *Changing Public Attitudes on Government and Taxes* (Washington, D.C.: U.S. Government Printing Office, 1982).
20. George Gordon, *Public Administration in America,* 3d ed. (New York: St. Martin's Press, 1986), pp. 306–307.
21. Dennis R. Judd, *The Politics of American Cities: Private Power and Public Policy* (Boston: Little, Brown, 1979), p. 285.
22. Dye, *Politics,* pp. 412–413.
23. Victoria Baldwin, Ann Cahn, and Lou Karestesy, "Nuclear Weapons Freeze," in *American States: A Citizen's Agenda, 1983–84* (Washington, D.C.: Conference on Alternative State and Local Policies, 1983), pp. 231–235.
24. Susan Tifft, "Taking Matters into Their Own Hands," *Time,* November 19, 1984, p. 15.
25. André Ryerson, "Small Town Freeze," *New Republic,* October 15, 1984, pp. 14, 16.
26. *New York Times,* October 19, 1985, p. 31.
27. *New York Times,* February 8, 1986, p. 8.
28. *New York Times,* May 25, 1985, p. 5.
29. *New York Times,* May 5, 1986, p. 8.
30. *New York Times,* February 9, 1987, p. D1.
31. *New York Times,* May 1, 1986, p. B3.
32. *New York Times,* August 5, 1987, p. 4.
33. Daniel J. Elazar, *American Federalism: A View from the States,* 2d ed. (New York: Crowell, 1972).
34. William H. Riker, *Federalism: Origin, Operation, Significance* (Boston: Little, Brown, 1964).
35. Patricia Schroeder, "Forward," in *Women, Power and Policy,* ed. Ellen Boneparth (New York: Pergamon, 1982).
36. *Statistical Abstract, 1982–83,* p. 80.
37. *San Francisco Chronicle,* August 17, 1987, p. 4.
38. *Statistical Abstract, 1988,* p. 133.
39. *New York Times,* August 25, 1987, p. 8.
40. Gordon, *Public Administration,* p. 168.
41. *Statistical Abstract, 1988,* p. 264.
42. Clyde Kluckholn, "The Concept of Culture," in *The Science of Man in the World,* ed. Ralph Linton (New York: Columbia University Press, 1945).
43. Kirkpatrick Sale, *Power Shift* (New York: Random House, 1975).
44. Eleanor Flexner, *Century of Struggle: The Woman's Rights Movement in the United States,* rev. ed. (Cambridge, Mass.: Belknap Press of Harvard University Press, 1975), p. 329.
45. David Jones, "States Put Up Umbrellas," *Environmental Action,* April 1984, pp. 1–2.
46. Barbara J. Nelson, "Comparable Worth: A Brief Review of History, Practice and Theory," *Minnesota Law Review* 69 (May 1985): 1199–1216.
47. Nice, *Federalism,* pp. 18, 220.
48. *Los Angeles Times,* March 26, 1982.
49. Charles M. Price, "Recalls at the Local Level: Dimensions and Implications," *National Civic Review* 72 (April 1983): 199–206.
50. Tifft, "Taking Matters into Their Own Hands," p. 15.
51. Martha Derthick, *The Influence of Federal Grants: Public Assistance in Massachusetts* (Cambridge, Mass.: Harvard University Press, 1970), p. 196.
52. Carol Steinbach and Neal R. Peirce, "Cities Are Setting Their Sights on International Trade and Investment," *National Journal,* April 28, 1984, pp. 818–822.
53. *Statistical Abstract, 1988,* p. 354.
54. Henig, *Public Policy and Federalism,* p. 355.
55. Jane J. Mansbridge, *Why We Lost the ERA* (Chicago: University of Chicago Press, 1986), p. 14.
56. Both arguments are found in Aaron Wildavsky, ed., *American Federalism in Perspective* (Boston: Little, Brown, 1967).
57. John di Ferrari, "Congress' Own Special Interest Groups," *Nation's Business,* August 1983, pp. 39–40.

★ For Further Reading

Elazar, Daniel J. *American Federalism: A View from the States.* 3d ed. New York: Harper & Row, 1984.

Hale, George, and Marian Palley. *The Politics of Federal Grants.* Washington, D.C.: Congressional Quarterly Press, 1981.

Howitt, Arnold. *Managing Federalism.* Washington, D.C.: Congressional Quarterly Press, 1984.

Peterson, Paul E., Barry G. Rabe, and Kenneth K. Wong. *When Federalism Works.* Washington, D.C.: Brookings Institution, 1986.

Reagan, Michael D., and John G. Sanzone. *The New Federalism.* 2d ed. New York: Oxford University Press, 1981.

Walker, David B. *Toward a Functioning Federalism.* Cambridge, Mass.: Winthrop, 1981.

Wright, Deil S. *Understanding Intergovernmental Relations.* 3d ed. Pacific Grove, Calif.: Brooks/Cole, 1988.

The Advisory Commission on Intergovernmental Relations publishes reports on the state of the federal system. The commission is located at Suite 2000, Vanguard Building, 111 Twentieth Street, N.W., Washington, D. C. 20006; phone, 202-653-5540.

> We hold these truths to be self-evident, that all men are created equal, that they are endowed by their Creator with certain unalienable Rights, that among these are Life, Liberty and the pursuit of Happiness.
>
> —*Declaration of Independence*

CHAPTER FOUR

CIVIL RIGHTS

★★★★★★★★★★★

Don't Tread on Me: Individual Freedom, Civil Liberties, and Human Rights

Our ability to influence governmental decision making obviously depends on whether we can freely communicate our political views and question governmental decisions. Without freedom of expression and the right to organize into groups, we would enjoy few opportunities to voice our objections to governmental policies and to work actively against them. The battle to win and maintain individual rights has been a constant theme in American politics. The fight began with the pursuit of a bill of rights. The fight continued as blacks, women, and other disadvantaged persons struggled to ensure that the Bill of Rights protected all Americans. As the United States matured into a major world power and global interdependence brought a greater realization of political repression abroad, the nation sought to promote its vision of freedom around the world. Today human rights has become a major issue in American politics, both at home and abroad.

★ The Evolution of Political Rights in America

The document framed in Philadelphia in 1787 contained no specific provisions guaranteeing freedom of expression or most other basic rights. In fact, the lack of such provisions was one of the major criticisms lodged against it by the Anti-Federalists, who demanded that a **bill of rights** be added as their price for supporting the Constitution. The original document did impose certain restraints on government. It prohibited Congress from suspending, except during rebellion or invasion, the writ of **habeas corpus.** This provision requires officials to bring anyone whom they apprehend before a court to state their reasons for the detention or arrest. In many nations around the world, citizens can languish in jail for years without ever being formally charged with a crime, and the state has no need to defend the legality of their confinement. President Lincoln suspended writs of habeas corpus during the Civil War.

The Constitution also forbade Congress to enact **bills of attainder** or **ex post facto laws.** Bills of attainder are legislative acts applying to named individuals or members of a group in such a way as to inflict punishment on them without a judicial trial. Legislation requiring that all members of the Ku Klux Klan be thrown in jail, whether or not they had been accused or convicted of a crime, would constitute a bill of attainder. Ex post facto laws apply retroactively to actions taken before the law was passed; although such actions were not forbidden at the time they were taken, the persons who took them can be punished as criminals. The original document also guaranteed the right of trial by jury in criminal cases and imposed limits on punishments for treason.

But the principal foundation of American **civil liberties** came with the addition of the Bill of Rights (especially the first eight amendments) in 1791 and the passage of the Thirteenth, Fourteenth, and Fifteenth Amendments shortly after the Civil War. For the most part, these amendments are couched in negative terms. They are aimed at restricting government from interfering with the rights of the individual. Congress is prohibited, for example, from abridging a citizen's freedom of speech or religion, and from depriving a citizen of life, liberty, or property without **due process of law.** These amendments protect not only the individual's right to participate *in* government—as by exercising freedom of speech and assembly—but also, to some extent, the individual's freedom *from* intrusion by government into his or her affairs.

Despite the adoption of the Bill of Rights, the Constitution gave the nation no overall principle to follow in regard to the protection of civil liberties. The Bill of Rights was drafted principally to restrain the actions of the federal government, not those of the states. The First Amendment declares that "*Congress* shall make no law . . . respecting an establishment of religion . . . or abridging the freedom of speech, or of the press." It says nothing about the states. At the time the amendments were drafted, most people tended to fear the power of the new federal government more than that of the states, believing that state governments were closer to the people and thus easier to control. In addition, many state constitutions already included a bill of rights limiting the actions of state officials. In fact, in *Barron* v. *Baltimore* (1833), the Supreme Court rejected the idea that the Bill of Rights applied to the states. If the framers had intended the states to be covered by the Bill of Rights, Chief Justice Marshall stated, "they would have declared this purpose in plain and intelligible language."

The result was that for years the nation had no consistent policy in regard to civil liberties. Some states imposed severe limits on individual rights, denying their citizens the right to legal counsel and jury trial and even tolerating such brutal practices as mob lynchings.

The states' autonomy in regard to civil rights was substantially reduced by the adoption in 1868 of the Fourteenth Amendment, which proclaims that no state shall deprive any person of "life, liberty, or property, without due process of law," or deny any person "the equal protection of the laws." Following World War I, the Court gradually began to use the language of the Fourteenth Amendment to make the Bill of Rights binding on the states. The major turning point came in *Gitlow* v. *New York* (1925), in which the Court ruled that a state that denied a person's First Amendment right of freedom of speech or freedom of the press would be depriving that person of "liberty" without due process of law, an action barred by the Fourteenth Amendment. Freedom of speech and of the press are such fundamental rights, the Court stated, that they should be "incorporated" in the Fourteenth Amendment and protected from impairment by the states. During the next four decades, the Court rigorously pursued the process of **selective incorporation,** applying most of the protections of the Bill of Rights to the states, including the First Amendment freedoms of assembly, petition, and religion, the right to legal counsel in criminal cases, protection against unlawful search and seizure, and the prohibition of "cruel and unusual punishments." The liberties ensured by the sixteen amendments to the Constitution are detailed in table 4-1.

The impact of the Supreme Court on our civil liberties should not be underestimated. Basically, the amount of freedom we enjoy is determined not only by

★ Table 4-1
Civil liberties ensured by constitutional amendments

Amendment	*Year passed*	*Provisions*
1*	1791	Freedom of religion, speech, press, assembly; petition for redress of grievances
2*	1791	The right to bear arms
3*	1791	Restrictions on quartering of soldiers in private homes
4*	1791	Prohibition of unreasonable search and seizure of persons and their property
5*	1791	Guarantee of grand jury indictment for serious crimes; protection against double jeopardy, self-incrimination, and deprivation of life, liberty, or property without due process of law; guarantee of compensation for private land taken for public use
6*	1791	The right to a speedy and public trial by an impartial jury, to be informed of charges brought against one, to be confronted with witnesses against one, to obtain witnesses in one's favor, and to have counsel for one's defense
7*	1791	The right of trial by jury
8*	1791	Prohibition of excessive bail or fines and of cruel and unusual punishments
9*	1791	Citizens' rights are not limited to those specifically listed in the Constitution
10*	1791	Powers not delegated to the federal government or expressly denied the states are reserved to the states or the citizens
13	1865	Abolition of slavery and involuntary servitude
14	1868	States may not deny the privileges and immunities of citizenship; deprive any person of life, liberty, or property without due process of law; or deny any person the equal protection of the laws
15	1870	The right to vote shall not be denied on account of race, color, or previous condition of servitude
19	1920	The right to vote shall not be denied on account of sex
24	1964	Elimination of the poll tax as a prerequisite for voting in federal elections
26	1971	Voting age set at 18 years in federal, state, and local elections

*Original Bill of Rights.

the Bill of Rights and other amendments but by the way the nine justices of the Supreme Court interpret them. With their power of judicial review—the power to overturn laws that, in their opinion, conflict with the Constitution—Supreme Court justices tend to serve as the final arbiters on questions of civil liberties. Indeed, to understand American civil liberties one must trace their evolution through the history of Court rulings and interpretations, a history marked by both enlightened and repressive judicial decisions.

★ Political Participation and the First Amendment

The First Amendment states that "Congress shall make no law respecting an establishment of religion, or prohibiting the free exercise thereof; or abridging the freedom of speech, or of the press; or the right of the people peaceably to assemble, and to petition the Government for a redress of grievances." No other amendment is so central to the operation of our democratic society. Freedom of speech, the press, assembly, religion, and petition are all vital elements of effective citizen action

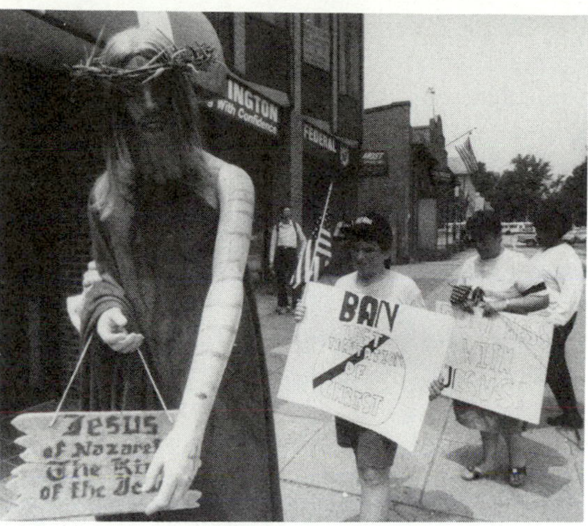

★ Different religious views can ignite strong emotions, as in 1988 when some people protested the showing of Martin Scorsese's film *The Last Temptation of Christ.*

and are closely intertwined. Without freedom of assembly, for example, freedom of speech would be nothing but the right to talk to oneself. Likewise, the right to petition government would be meaningless without a free press to provide information on what government is doing. And without freedom of religion as a form of personal expression and conscience, freedom of speech and assembly would be hollow concepts for many people.

At the same time, none of these First Amendment freedoms and rights is absolute. The rights of the individual need to be properly balanced against the rights of others. As Justice Oliver Wendell Holmes observed, "The right to swing my fist ends where the other man's nose begins." Finding that balance, of course, has been one of the Court's major problems. Let us consider, then, the nature and evolution of these freedoms and rights, beginning with freedom of religion.

Freedom of Religion

Religious belief, as a form of personal expression, was so important to the authors of the Bill of Rights that they put it at the top of the list. They knew that deep religious feelings can sometimes spark intolerance, and that people have been persecuted for their religious beliefs. In fact, the desire to escape religious persecution was a major reason that many of the early settlers fled Europe and came to America. Like many other aspects of America's culture, the desire for religious freedom was influenced and nourished by events and experiences beyond its own shores. Even today we can see in other countries how religion and politics have become intertwined. The civil strife in Northern Ireland stems in part from the long-standing hostility between Catholics and Protestants, while in the Middle East, Africa, and elsewhere, religious differences fuel political conflict.

The First Amendment deals with two aspects of religion. It states that "Congress shall make no law respecting an establishment of religion, or prohibiting the free exercise thereof." The courts have interpreted the first provision—prohibiting the establishment of religion—to mean not only that government may not set up a state religion but also that it may not favor any religious sect. Thus the Supreme Court has struck down some government attempts to give financial aid to religious schools and has banned Bible study and prayer in public school classrooms.[1] In an effort to overcome the Supreme Court's objections, President Reagan pushed for a constitutional amendment that would allow "voluntary" prayer in public schools, but in 1984 the proposal failed to win the necessary two-thirds vote in the Senate to be submitted to the states for ratification.

This is not to say that church and state have been kept entirely separate, however. The Supreme Court has allowed states to provide free bus transportation, textbooks, and equipment for students in parochial schools, arguing that such aid benefits the children, not the schools. In fact, government has even tended to sustain religious practices in a variety of ways: religious organizations are exempted from taxation; our coins and paper money carry the motto "In God We Trust"; sessions of Congress open with prayers; the Pledge of Allegiance contains the phrase "one nation, under God"; court witnesses usually are asked to swear on the Bible; and in 1984 the Supreme Court ruled that a city could include a Nativity scene in its Christmas display.

In addition to prohibiting the establishment of religion, the First Amendment prohibits the government from interfering with religious observances. This means that an individual is free to believe or disbelieve as he or she chooses. But like all other rights, religious freedom is not absolute. A person may not engage freely in human sacrifice, for instance, just because his or her religion condones it. The Supreme Court has consistently ruled that government may prohibit religious groups from practicing their beliefs if those practices are harmful or offensive to others. Thus in 1879 the Court upheld laws banning polygamy (the practice of having more than one mate at a time), even though it was part of the Mormon faith. Mormons had the right to believe that God allows plural marriages, the Court ruled, but they could not practice that belief because it was "in violation of social duties or subversive of good order."[2]

Still, the Court has tended to give religious groups broad support in their exercise of their religious convictions. It has backed the right of Jehovah's Witnesses, for instance, to distribute and sell their religious literature without a city permit or payment of a license fee. It has also upheld the right of Witnesses' children to refuse to salute the flag because of their belief that the pledge violates the biblical injunction against worshiping graven images.[3] It has upheld the right of Amish parents to establish their own school system and has supported the right of conscientious objectors to avoid military service for religious reasons.[4]

One controversy in recent times has centered on the proliferation of religious cults. The Jonestown tragedy in 1978, in which more than nine hundred members of the People's Temple died in a mass ritual of suicide and murder in the South American nation of Guyana, triggered national debate over whether cults can—and should—be curbed. Many people argued that for a society to grant special status and privileges to any group that calls itself a religion is to invite such tragedies as Jonestown. Legislators introduced various proposals designed to forbid cults to use "mind control" techniques and to force cult recruiters to reveal their affiliations and goals to potential converts at an early stage.

Civil libertarians, however, responded that such proposals would be hard to reconcile with the First Amendment. How could government, they argued, define what is and what is not a true "religion" or determine which recruiting practices were good and which were bad? In their view, it would be better to remove the

★ An Amish first-grader exercises the religious freedom to attend an Amish school in Maryland.

status and privileges given to all religious groups than to single out certain ones for punishment. The controversy over cults exemplifies the traditional problem facing government: how to balance society's right to be protected from harmful practices and individuals' rights to exercise their religious beliefs.

Freedom of Speech

Throughout history, it has been observed that no democratic society can exist without freedom of expression. If people are to press their demands on government, they must be able to voice their political views. They must be able to engage in free and open discussion with others and to criticize the actions and policies of their leaders.

In fact, justification for freedom of speech goes even beyond the requirements of a democracy. The English philosopher John Stuart Mill argued in his essay *On Liberty* (1859) that without a free exchange of ideas, individuals cannot reach their full potential and society as a whole cannot advance. "The worth of a state in the long run," he declared, "is the worth of the individuals composing it; and a state which . . . dwarfs its men, in order that they may be more docile instruments in its hands even for beneficial purposes, will find that with small men no great thing can be accomplished." In fact, Mill argued, because it is often difficult to distinguish "good" ideas from "bad" ones, all views need to be expressed. Even if an idea turns out to be false, it can at least help make the truth easier to see by comparison. The

★ John Stuart Mill offered a classic defense of free expression in *On Liberty* (1859).

only way we can achieve progress is by considering all ideas, no matter how unpopular or "wrong" they may appear.

It is largely for these reasons that the American Civil Liberties Union (ACLU) and other strong advocates of free speech have backed the rights of all members of our society to express their views. Freedom of speech, they point out, benefits not merely the speakers but also those who wish to hear what they have to say. Even would-be tyrants should be allowed to speak, not because they necessarily deserve to exercise that right but because others need to be aware of their positions. By denying someone's freedom of speech, one also denies the rights of others to understand the meanings and implications of certain views.

Do these justifications mean there should be no limits on expression? According to former justices Hugo Black and William O. Douglas, when the Constitution says that "Congress shall make no law ... abridging the freedom of speech," it literally means *no law.* In their view, freedom of speech is such an important and basic right that it should not be curbed in any way.

The majority of Supreme Court justices, however, have tended to take a less absolutist position. They have held that though free speech is important, it may have to yield to other interests. If certain kinds of speech lead directly to actions that threaten society, for example, then society has both a right and a duty to restrict them. The problem has been to decide where the line should be drawn between the rights of the individual and those of society. At what point should a person be compelled to step down off the soapbox and be silent?

The Court offered one answer in the famous case of *Schenck* v. *United States* (1919). During World War I a pacifist named Charles Schenck was convicted and sent to prison under the Espionage Act of 1917 for distributing leaflets urging potential draftees not to serve in the armed forces. Schenck appealed his conviction to the Supreme Court, arguing that the Espionage Act was unconstitutional because it stripped him of his First Amendment rights of freedom of speech and of the press. The Court disagreed, ruling that his actions represented a "clear and present danger" to national security and thus his conviction was valid. "The question in every case," Justice Oliver Wendell Holmes wrote, "is whether the words are used

★ In 1916, antiwar demonstrators exercised their First Amendment rights in a May Day parade.

in such circumstances and are of such nature as to create a clear and present danger that they will bring about substantive evils that Congress has a right to prevent." As an analogy, Holmes noted that even "the most stringent protection of free speech would not protect a man in falsely shouting fire in a theater and causing panic."

Obviously, this "clear and present danger" test tends to be highly subjective. The applicability of the example of a person falsely shouting fire in a crowded theater is limited. Whether in fact the theater was on fire could surely be proved in short order; but how does one determine when a political speech or pamphlet presents a "danger" to society? Is it not possible that governmental officials could use the clear and present danger test to suppress opinions with which they disagree? During the Vietnam war, students and others who protested administration policies were sometimes accused of giving "aid and comfort" to the "enemy" and even of committing "treason." Should protesters against the war have been thrown in jail because some high-ranking officials regarded their criticisms as a danger to America's war effort? Still, many scholars insist that the clear and present danger test actually helps bolster freedom of expression because it places the burden on government to prove that curbs are needed to prevent some identifiable evil from occurring.

In 1925, in *Gitlow* v. *New York,* the Court once again tried to draw a line between the rights of the individual and those of society. In this case, the Court seemed to come down harder against the individual's right of free speech with the "bad tendency" rule. Benjamin Gitlow had been convicted in New York State for publishing a pamphlet calling for the violent overthrow of the U.S. government. In upholding Gitlow's conviction, the Court ruled that the government could ban speeches or publications that merely had a *tendency* to pose a danger to society.

★ Antiwar protestors face the military police outside the Pentagon during the Vietnam war, threatening to cross the line separating peaceful protest and violent confrontation.

In other words, despite lack of evidence that Gitlow's tract had had any adverse effects, government could take steps to protect society against some act that conceivably might occur.

Nor did the Court stop there. As the fear of communism gripped the nation during the cold war era of the 1940s and 1950s, the criteria for curtailing speech became even broader. In 1948 Eugene Dennis and ten other leaders of the homegrown American Communist party were convicted and sent to prison for violating the Smith Act. Passed by Congress in 1940, the Smith Act made it a crime to advocate overthrow of the government or to belong to any group that advocated such action. The Court upheld the group's convictions, arguing that the criteria for restricting speech included not only its possible effects but the "gravity of the evil" to be avoided.[5] The fact that Dennis and the other plaintiffs advocated the use of force to overthrow the government was justification enough, the Court stated, to curtail their activities. (Six years later, the Court modified this formula by noting that people could be convicted under the Smith Act only for promoting illegal *action* against the government, not for their political beliefs alone.)[6]

Since the 1950s, the Court has continued to apply these and other formulas in interpreting the constitutionality of restrictions on speech. As the fear of internal communism has ebbed, however, the Court has shown less willingness to accept restraints on the rights of Communists and other groups. It has, for example, overturned laws denying passports to American Communist party members and requiring them to register with the government.[7] It has also struck down laws requiring private citizens to take a loyalty oath in certain cases.[8] Nevertheless, the Court has not denied in any sweeping fashion the right of government to curtail speech on national security grounds.

Various kinds of free-speech issues have occupied the Court's attention over the years. Protests against the Vietnam war, for example, raised the question whether the Constitution protects "symbolic speech" (the expression of political views through actions rather than words). The Court upheld the right of students to protest the

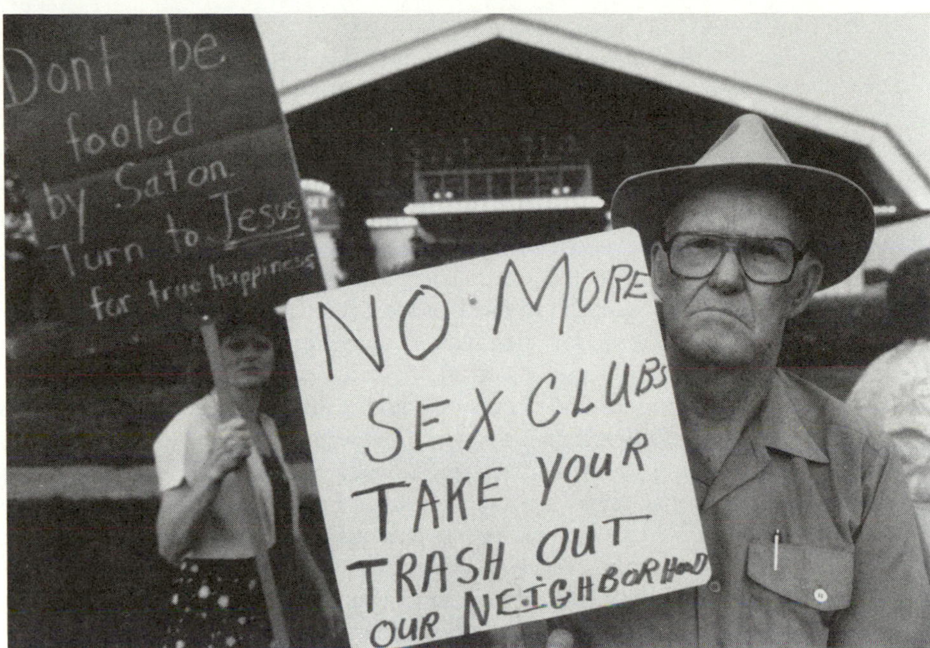

★ Protestors denounce the presence of an "adult" movie theater in their neighborhood.

war by wearing black armbands in school, but in another case it contended that the burning of draft cards was not a legitimate exercise of symbolic speech.[9] In 1989, the Court ruled that burning the American flag as a political protest was protected by the First Amendment.[10] The Court even has become involved in controversies involving "commercial speech." During the 1970s, for example, it overturned state laws that barred pharmacies from advertising their prices for prescription drugs and lawyers from advertising their services and rates.[11]

One free-speech issue that has generated considerable emotion over the years has been that of "obscenity." The balance between the freedom of individual expression and the rights of society has taken on new meaning as the Court has tried—somewhat unsuccessfully—to define the constitutional status of obscene material. For years people have contended that material depicting sex or violence offends public morality or leads to criminal behavior and thus should be banned. But because material that appears obscene to one person may not appear so to another, judges have had a difficult time defining obscenity in precise terms. As one judge cracked, "To come to grips with the question of obscenity is like coming to grips with a greased pig."[12]

In 1957, in *Roth* v. *United States,* the Supreme Court tried to tackle the obscenity issue head on, stating that "obscene" material did not enjoy the protection of the First Amendment. The definition it offered, however, proved to be slippery. The Court defined obscenity as material that appeals to "prurient interests," that is considered objectionable by the "average person," and that lacks any "redeeming social importance"—concepts almost as vague, and therefore difficult to apply, as the word "obscenity" itself. The Court clouded the issue even more by ruling in

1966 that "the constitutional status of an alleged obscene work must be determined on the basis of a national standard." Moreover, it said, no work could be judged obscene unless it was "utterly without redeeming social value."[13] Because opinions varied on what this "national standard" might be and because nothing could be banned unless it appeared to be *utterly* without social value, obscenity laws became almost impossible to enforce. "Adult" bookstores flourished, and producers of X-rated movies and sex magazines raced to see who could offer the public the most explicit details of human anatomy and violence.

In 1973 the Court tried a different approach. It abandoned the idea of a national standard in favor of local standards, giving each community more discretion to define for itself what is obscene. "It is neither realistic nor constitutionally sound," the Court ruled in *Miller* v. *California,* "to read the First Amendment as requiring that the people of Maine or Mississippi accept public depiction of conduct found tolerable in Las Vegas or New York City." The Court also changed its earlier position by saying that a questionable work might be adjudged obscene if it lacked "serious literary, artistic, political, or scientific value." Because it is easier to demonstrate that a work has no "serious" value than it is to establish that it is entirely without value, convictions became somewhat easier to obtain. Thus Larry Flynt, publisher of *Hustler* magazine, was convicted in 1977 by an Indianapolis jury for offending local community standards.

Civil libertarians' fears that some citizens would ban everything in sight were somewhat relieved in 1974, when the Court overturned the conviction of a Georgia theater owner for showing the film *Carnal Knowledge.* The justices did not find the film "patently offensive" and said that local juries could not use "unbridled discretion" in defining obscenity.[14] In 1982 the Court ruled that a local school board could not ban books (such as Kurt Vonnegut's *Slaughterhouse-Five* and Eldridge Cleaver's *Soul on Ice*) from school libraries on the grounds that they were "anti-American" and "just plain filthy."[15] Thus local communities and judges alike would have to continue to wrestle with the definition of obscenity case by case.

In the 1980s, some communities tried to pass ordinances defining and penalizing pornography as discrimination against women. Such laws, however, were struck down by the courts. In a case dealing with an Indianapolis law, an appellate court, while accepting the legislation's basic premise that pornography exploited and degraded women, nonetheless held that such material was protected by the First Amendment. The Supreme Court, in a 1986 decision upholding the lower court, concluded that "depictions of subordination tend to perpetuate subordination. The subordinate status of women in turn leads to affront and lower pay at work, insult and injury at home, battery and rape on the streets." But it went on to say that "this simply demonstrates the power of pornography as speech," which, like other dangerous speech, must be protected by the First Amendment, because "any other answer leaves the government in control of all the institutions of culture, the great censor and director of which thoughts are good for us."[16]

Some communities, in efforts to deal with the spread of "adult theaters," have tried to bypass definitional problems by using zoning laws to regulate their location—an approach upheld by the Court, with some reservations. And some states have moved to counter child pornography by passing laws prohibiting material that depicts sexual conduct by children. These laws, rather than trying to define and thereby prohibit "pornography," merely outlaw the production and distribution of material showing children engaged in sexual acts, as a form of child abuse. So far, the courts have sided with the states.

Whatever one's position may be on the issue of obscenity, one must still face the difficulty of deciding who should set the standards. Should anyone be handed the authority to determine what other adults may read or see? Civil libertarians argue that a distinction should be made between "private" and "public" activities. People should not be forced to confront obscenity in public places (as on highway billboards), but they should be free to read or watch anything they wish in the relative privacy of a home or theater. (Whether the charging of admission makes entering a theater a "private" or "public" activity remains a matter of definition.) In view of the ongoing controversy surrounding obscenity, the issue will hardly be resolved by any Supreme Court decision.

Freedom of the Press

"One of the most powerful hopes advanced by theories of representative government," two scholars have noted, "is that news media remain free so they may educate the public in making political choices. Ignorance condemns people to sway with the most available rhetoric."[17] A free press has always been considered indispensable to the public's "right to know." Without a press free to criticize government officials and to provide information on their activities, citizens could not determine whether to keep the officials in office or to throw them out. In fact, government control and censorship of the press is clear proof for many Americans of a lack of political freedom in South Africa, the Soviet Union, and many other nations. Freedom of the press means that government may not censor what is published. It means that government may not exercise **prior restraint** on what a journalist reports, even though the reporter may have to answer later for what he or she has written.

The issue of prior restraint gained national attention in the early 1970s, when the government tried to block publication of the "Pentagon Papers" by the *New York Times* and *Washington Post.* The papers were copies of classified documents smuggled out of the Pentagon by the defense analyst Daniel Ellsberg, which constituted evidence that successive administrations had withheld information from the public on the conduct of the Vietnam war. The Nixon administration tried to prevent their publication, claiming they would cause "injury to the defense interests of the United States." The Supreme Court, however, ruled 6 to 3 against the government, arguing that publication would not threaten national security and that the press could not be muzzled except to prevent "direct, immediate, and irreparable" damage to the nation.

The issue of prior restraint arose again later in the decade when the government obtained a court order preventing *The Progressive,* a monthly journal, from publishing an article describing how an H-bomb is built ("The H-Bomb Secret: How We Got It, Why We're Telling It"). Government lawyers argued that the article violated sections of the 1954 Atomic Energy Act prohibiting disclosure of secret detailed information about atomic weapons. The article, they said, could be used to help other countries or even terrorists to develop the bomb, thus causing "irreparable damage" to the nation. Press champions feared that a permanent ban on the article would set a dangerous precedent. As a *Washington Post* editorial noted, "Once the door is open to advance judicial scrutiny of what the press may publish, it will never close." (Following publication of similar information by other papers, the federal government abandoned efforts to stop *The Progressive* from publishing the article.)

Press freedom, of course, has never been absolute. It has not protected journalists, for example, who damage a private citizen's reputation with irresponsible accusations. Only when the press has commented on public figures or government officials has it enjoyed substantial protection against **libel** suits. In an effort to prevent libel laws from being used to shield politicians and other public figures from criticism, the Supreme Court ruled in 1964 that public figures must prove "actual malice" as well as falsehood to establish libel.[18]

In 1979, however, the Supreme Court eroded some of the protection it had given the press. It ruled that a public official, in trying to prove actual malice by a reporter, can ask the court to evaluate the reporter's "state of mind"; that is, the plaintiff can demand to know what the reporter was thinking while the story was being prepared.[19] By declaring that a reporter can be hauled into court and questioned about his or her thought processes, the Supreme Court appeared to open the door wider to libel suits. As James Goodale of the *New York Times* put it, the decision hampers investigative reporting because reporters now know they "are going to have to stand naked in front of the courts with respect to all their thought processes."[20]

Journalists have been dismayed, in fact, by a series of Court rulings against the press. During the 1970s, for example, the Court ruled that a judge may close a pretrial hearing to the press and the public if the defendant and the prosecutor believe the publicity will harm the defendant's chances of a fair trial. Neither the press nor the public, the Court stated, has a constitutional right under the "public trial" guarantee of the Sixth Amendment to attend a hearing that takes place before a criminal trial.[21] To many journalists and legal scholars, this ruling was a serious contradiction of the First Amendment, which guarantees freedom of the press so that the public may be informed on what is going on.

Moreover, the Court held that police, after obtaining an ordinary search warrant, could conduct unannounced searches of newsrooms to gather evidence, including reporters' notebooks and phone records.[22] This ruling followed another in which the Court held that reporters could not withhold information from grand juries investigating potential crimes.[23] Several reporters have been sentenced to jail and their employers fined for refusing to surrender their notes for possible use in criminal investigations. A defense attorney, for example, may argue that a reporter's sources could help clear his or her client. Reporters usually insist that the confidentiality of their sources must be protected. If reporters complied with orders to identify their sources, they would become an investigative arm of the government and jeopardize their ability to gather news. The courts, however, have tended to deny reporters' claims, stating that the First Amendment guarantee of a free press is superseded by a defendant's Sixth Amendment right to a fair trial.

The government has tended to regulate radio and television more closely than the print media. A radio or television station, for example, must obtain a federal license to use one of the limited number of frequencies or channels on the "public airwaves." These licenses are granted by the Federal Communications Commission (FCC) and must be renewed at regular intervals.

Until 1987, the FCC required stations to honor the "fairness doctrine" by providing opportunities for conflicting views to be aired on important issues. Now television and radio stations are as free as newspapers to present only one side of an issue without having to grant air time to opposing views. This situation is likely to change in the future.

★ AIDS activists and sufferers used the right to assemble and petition the government for a redress of grievances, demanding more government support in the fight against AIDS and discrimination.

Freedom of Assembly and Petition

As we will see in later chapters, an important way to change government policies is through concerted group action. Interest groups, not single individuals, have become the basic units of influence in our society. Thus our ability to influence government requires not only freedom of expression but also the right to organize into groups and exchange political views—that is, the right "peaceably to assemble, and to petition the Government for a redress of grievances."

Over the years, the Supreme Court has tended to give substantial protection to freedom of assembly and petition. It has upheld the right of groups and individuals not only to petition government directly but also to engage in peaceful protests and demonstrations. During the early civil rights demonstrations in the 1960s, for example, a group of about two hundred black students assembled on the grounds of the South Carolina state capitol to protest discrimination. A crowd of several hundred onlookers gathered, some threatening violence, and the police ordered the students to disperse. When the students failed to comply, they were arrested and convicted of breach of the peace. The Supreme Court reversed their convictions, stating that "the Fourteenth Amendment does not permit a state to make criminal the peaceful expression of unpopular views."[24] When an audience's hostility may erupt in violence, the Court declared, the police must try to control the crowd rather than disperse the demonstrators. In the decades since, the courts have tended to uphold the right of peaceful demonstrations, even those in support of unpopular causes. Members of the American Nazi party, for example, were granted a permit to parade through Skokie, Illinois, where many Jewish survivors of the Nazi concentration camps had settled.

At the same time, the Supreme Court has recognized that the right to assemble may conflict with the needs of local governments to prevent violence or maintain the free flow of traffic. It has upheld the right of local officials to regulate public meetings and demonstrations in the streets, parks, and other public places through the use of parade permits and other regulatory devices. Such devices are constitutional, the Court has held, so long as they are "reasonable" and are applied equally to all groups.

The problem, of course, is to define "reasonable." It is sometimes difficult to determine the motives of local officials who refuse to permit certain groups to express their views. Groups on both the political left and the political right have been denied permission to stage marches or demonstrations on the grounds that violence might ensue. Although concern over violence has often been genuine, some groups have been denied the right to assemble simply because local officials disapproved of their views.

The Supreme Court also has recognized a related freedom—that of association—even though it is not specifically mentioned in the First Amendment. In 1958 the Court overturned an Alabama state law requiring the local chapter of the National Association for the Advancement of Colored People (NAACP) to reveal the names of its members. The Court said it could find no legitimate reason that Alabama would need the names of the members, except perhaps as a way to harass the association and impede its activities. "Freedom to engage in association for the advancement of beliefs and ideas," the Court stated, "is an inseparable aspect of the 'liberty' assured by . . . the Fourteenth Amendment, which embraces freedom of speech."[25]

★ Due Process: The Rights of the Accused

The Bill of Rights affords other protections besides those covered in the First Amendment, including the **procedural rights** found in the Fourth through the Eighth amendments. These are the rights that governments must honor in its dealings with individuals, the rights of people who run afoul of the law.

Procedural rights are not just the rights of criminal suspects; they are also society's assurance that prosecutors and judges will act in a fair and proper manner. Although society has a right to protect itself against those who disobey its laws, the citizen also has the right to be protected against government harassment in the name of "law and order." Without such protection, no person could feel secure against threats of imprisonment or even death at the hands of the state. A person who criticizes governmental policies could be carted off to jail for committing unspecified "crimes against the state" and for an unspecified prison term—a fate encountered by political dissidents in many parts of the world.

Although the application of procedural rights in this country has been spotty at best—local officials and judges sometimes ignore them with impunity—the Constitution gives considerable attention to procedural safeguards. The Fourth through the Eighth amendments guarantee, for example, the right to have legal counsel, to have a "speedy and public trial" by an impartial jury, to cross-examine hostile witnesses, to call friendly witnesses on one's own behalf, and to be protected against self-incrimination and **double jeopardy** (being tried twice for the same crime). They also guarantee protection against "cruel and unusual punishments" and "excessive bail." These rights have gradually been incorporated in the due process

★ In *Powell* v. *Alabama* (1932), the conviction of four young men in Alabama was overturned by the Supreme Court. The Court decided that those accused of crimes under state judicial systems deserved appointed counsel if they could not afford it.

clause of the Fourteenth Amendment and applied to the states as well as to the federal government.

Protection against Unreasonable Searches and Seizures

Throughout history, one of the most feared uses of governmental power has been the sudden midnight rapping at the door and the forced entry into one's home by agents of the state. Such forced entry has been a common tool of authoritarian regimes, used to terrorize their subjects and force their compliance. Indeed, such a fear was well understood by the framers of the Bill of Rights. The Fourth Amendment guarantees "the right of the people to be secure in their persons, houses, papers, and effects, against unreasonable searches and seizures." Before agents of the state can search a suspect's home, they must show "probable cause" and secure a warrant describing "the place to be searched, and the persons or things to be seized."

The framers of the Fourth Amendment did not ban all warrantless searches and seizures; they banned only "unreasonable" ones. They knew that in some situations there would be probable cause for a search to be carried out without a search warrant. The courts have ruled, for instance, that a police officer making a lawful arrest does not need a warrant to search a suspect for weapons or evidence. Moreover, an officer who hears someone scream for help inside a house has probable cause to suspect that a crime is in progress and thus can enter the building without waiting for a warrant. In a borderline case, an officer may believe there is probable cause, but the judge may disagree and let the suspect go.

In *Mapp* v. *Ohio* (1961), the Supreme Court applied the so-called **exclusionary rule** to both the states and the federal government. This rule bars improperly seized evidence from being used against a suspect (although the Court noted some exceptions in the 1970s and 1980s).[26] The purpose of the rule is to protect suspects against the sometimes excessive zeal of the police. For example, the Court overturned the conviction of a man who was charged with drug possession after the police had his stomach pumped to recover some morphine capsules he had swallowed.[27] The Court realized that the only way to discourage the police from engaging in such practices—from making illegal searches and seizures—was to bar evidence obtained in this manner from being admitted at a trial. In 1984, however, the Court did undermine the exclusionary rule by noting the "inevitable discovery" exception: if evidence obtained by an illegal search would have been discovered in the normal course of events, it may be admissible in court.

But what about electronic means of surveillance, such as wiretapping? Does electronic eavesdropping on people's private conversations represent "unreasonable search and seizure"? In 1928 the Court said no. It stated that wiretapping someone's telephone does not violate the Fourth Amendment because it does not involve actual physical entry into a person's home.[28] Nearly forty years later, however, in 1967, the Court reversed itself. It held that the Fourth Amendment "protects people, not places," and thus electronic snooping without a proper warrant does represent an unlawful form of search and seizure.[29]

Note that the Court did not actually prohibit electronic spying: it said only that a valid warrant authorizing such spying had to be obtained. Thus, following the Court's ruling, Congress enacted the Omnibus Crime Control and Safe Streets Act of 1968, which authorizes court-approved wiretaps and other forms of electronic snooping. It also allows governmental officials to proceed without a warrant in cases involving possible threats to "national security," provided that a warrant is obtained within forty-eight hours after surveillance has begun. In the years since the act's passage, the government has tapped the phones, opened the mail, and bugged the homes and offices of thousands of American citizens, ranging from suspected gangsters to political "radicals." And as the Watergate and other investigations revealed, not all of these activities were lawful.

There is clearly a relationship between protection against unreasonable searches and seizures and a right to privacy. As technology has become increasingly sophisticated, with listening devices that can be concealed in a martini olive or implanted under a person's skin, the potential for unlawful invasion of privacy has become increasingly frightening. The framers of the Constitution had little reason to be concerned about invasion of privacy. As there were no phones to tap or computer files to enter, about the only real threat to privacy was the town gossip. In fact, the Constitution does not specifically mention a right to privacy. The Court has come gradually to recognize such a right as one of the "penumbras" of the Constitution. The general right to privacy, in the Court's view, is implied not only by the Fourth Amendment's protection against unreasonable searches and seizures but also by the First Amendment's protection of freedom of religion and association, the Third's restrictions on the quartering of soldiers in private homes, the Fifth's protection against self-incrimination, and the Ninth's assertion that the rights listed in the preceding eight do not exhaust all existing rights.

In recent years the Court has extended the right to privacy to cover a variety of personal activities, ranging from the use of birth control devices to having an abortion.[30] The Court's decision in *Roe* v. *Wade* (1973) to overturn states' restrictions on a woman's right to abortion have sparked numerous efforts to add an antiabortion amendment to the U.S. Constitution. Though these efforts have been unsuccessful, Congress and several states have prohibited the use of public funds for most abortions for women who receive government support, such as Medicaid.

★ A group of movie celebrities arrives at the Capitol on October 27, 1947, to protest the tactics of the House Committee on Un-American Activities' investigation into alleged Hollywood communism.

In 1989, in fact, in the case of *Webster* v. *Reproductive Health Services,* the Supreme Court approved significant new restrictions in U.S. abortion law. Although it did not specifically overturn *Roe* v. *Wade,* it upheld, among other provisions, the constitutionality of a Missouri law that barred the use of public funds to "counsel or encourage" abortion, inasmuch as, according to its preamble, "the life of every human being begins at conception." Hundreds of thousands of people marched in Washington, D.C., in support of the right to abortion as a privacy issue and against the imposition of any restrictions by the institution that had recognized that right in the first place.

Self-incrimination and the Right to Counsel

Closely related to the protection against unreasonable searches and seizures is the Fifth Amendment's guarantee that no one "shall be compelled in any criminal case to be a witness against himself." A person may "take the Fifth" when being interrogated by the police, a prosecutor, or even a legislative committee. This right has been vigorously defended to discourage the use of coercion (the "third degree") to wring confessions or other incriminating statements from suspects; they may be innocent of the charges.

One of the most famous uses of the Fifth Amendment was made by the "Hollywood Ten" in the 1947 hearings of the House Committee on Un-American Activities. The committee heard testimony from film actors, writers, directors, and producers about alleged communist influence in their profession. "The climax of the hearings," one writer noted, "was reached when ten witnesses refused to answer questions about their past and present political affiliations, were quickly dismissed, hollering from the witness chair, then were publicly charged by the committee staff with being Communist party members on the basis of FBI information, and eventually were sent to jail for contempt of Congress."[31] Once the charges were made public, the Hollywood movie industry "blacklisted" (conspired to deny employment to) any person accused of communist affiliations who did not deny such charges. The Hollywood Ten, many of whom were forced out of the industry (or began to write under assumed names), showed that the Fifth Amendment may not always afford the protection the authors of the Bill of Rights envisioned.

Since most people are untutored in the technicalities of the law, the Sixth Amendment guarantees them the right to legal counsel. Until the 1960s, however, this right applied almost exclusively to cases tried in the federal courts. Even though the bulk of criminal laws (from auto theft to murder) are enacted by the states and applied in state courts, suspects in many states have not always been provided with an attorney. In *Gideon* v. *Wainright* (1963), the Court finally held that states must furnish counsel to all persons facing serious criminal charges who cannot afford one. It also ruled, in *Escobedo* v. *Illinois* (1964), that legal counsel must be provided by the states at the time a suspect is arrested, not just at the time of trial.

One of the most important—and controversial—due process decisions handed down by the Supreme Court came in 1966, in the case of *Miranda* v. *Arizona*. Ernesto Miranda was arrested in 1963 for kidnapping and raping an eighteen-year-old woman near Phoenix. After being interrogated by the police for two hours, he confessed to the crimes and was convicted. The Supreme Court overturned his conviction on the grounds that Miranda confessed without being told of his right to remain silent and to be represented by a lawyer. The Court declared that a person arrested must be informed that anything he says may be used against him, that he has a right to remain silent, that he has a right to have a lawyer present, and that a lawyer will be provided if he cannot afford one.

Some people denounced the *Miranda* ruling, accusing the Court of "handcuffing" the police. They claimed that the Court misread the Constitution by putting the rights of criminals above those of their victims. Because the majority of criminal convictions stem from confessions, they charged, curbs on police interrogation procedures limit the police's ability to bring dangerous criminals to justice.

Under the direction of Chief Justice Warren Burger, the Court began to whittle away at the *Miranda* decision. In 1971, for example, the Court held that statements made by a suspect before police warned him of his rights could be used later to discredit his testimony on the witness stand.[32] In 1975 the Court also ruled that incriminating statements made after a suspect had asked for an attorney (but before the attorney arrived) could be used to cast doubt on his or her credibility.[33] And in 1984 the Court ruled that in situations in which public safety is involved, an officer may try to obtain information from a suspect before administering the *Miranda* warning.[34] Generally, however, the *Miranda* decision has been upheld and continues to guide police when they make arrests.

Protection against Cruel and Unusual Punishments

A person convicted of a crime must have some protection against "cruel and unusual punishments." The framers provided such protection in the Eighth Amendment in order to bar such practices as torture, maiming, and lingering death. Although the amendment has rarely been invoked, a few cases have attracted the Court's attention. In one case the Court held that a state law under which drug addicts were sent to prison, rather than to a hospital for treatment, was unconstitutional because the treatment it mandated was cruel and unusual.[35]

The controversy over cruel and unusual punishments has focused principally on the death penalty. Movements to abolish the death penalty have been with us for centuries, all of them based on the argument that it is immoral and cruel and does not serve as a deterrent. In *Furman* v. *Georgia* (1972), the Court struck down the states' death-penalty laws, declaring that they were often applied "wantonly and freakishly" and were exercised mainly against poor and uneducated defendants.

A number of states responded by passing new death-penalty laws designed to avoid the features to which the Court objected. In 1976 the Court heard five related cases involving the constitutionality of the death penalty and upheld the laws of three states.[36] The Court ruled that the death penalty was not inherently cruel and unusual punishment so long as it was not mandatory and provided that judges and juries considered the character and record of the defendant and any mitigating circumstances. In 1977 Gary Gilmore, convicted of murdering two people, died before a Utah firing squad, the first person to be executed in the United States in almost ten years. Since then, dozens of other people have been executed in the United States.

★ The Struggle for Equal Rights

A crucial element of constitutional rights is that they must be applied equally to all. A guarantee of free speech or due process would mean little if government could arbitrarily exclude certain groups from the protection of the law. If one group can be denied the rights enjoyed by others—because of skin color, sex, religion, age, or physical disabilities—then no group can consider itself safe from discrimination. Denial of basic rights to one group increases the potential for their denial to all.

Over time, the struggle for equal rights has expanded to include demands for legal, political, economic, and social equality. When Thomas Jefferson noted in the Declaration of Independence that "all men are created equal," he was referring mainly to equality before the law. This concept of legal equality was later coupled with the idea of political equality, an idea best expressed by the concept of "one person, one vote." In recent decades the concept of equal rights has also included the notion of equal opportunity in education, employment, and housing.

Political action has perhaps no more meaningful purpose than to remove the sting of prejudice and discrimination. The achievement of equality has long been a struggle for black Americans, who were deprived of their constitutional rights and liberties first as slaves and then as second-class citizens. On paper, black Americans appeared to have achieved legal and political equality immediately after the Civil War. The Thirteenth Amendment abolished slavery in 1865. The Fourteenth Amendment guaranteed to all citizens "due process of the law" and "equal protection of the laws" in 1868. And in 1870 the Fifteenth Amendment ensured that the right to vote "shall not be denied or abridged by the United States or by any State on account of race, color, or previous condition of servitude." In addition, Congress passed a series of acts designed to protect Americans' civil rights in the 1860s and 1870s. The Civil Rights Act of 1875, for example, prohibited any operator of a hotel, theater, or other public facility from discriminating against anyone on the basis of race or color.

★ In 1955, Mrs. Rosa Parks challenged segregation by sitting in the front of a Montgomery, Alabama, city bus. Her arrest led to a year-long boycott of the bus system that ended with a court order forbidding segregation on buses.

★ Segregated restrooms in a South Carolina gas station in the late 1950s.

But hopes for equality soon evaporated. In 1883 the Supreme Court struck down the Civil Rights Acts of 1875 on the grounds that Congress had no authority to prohibit one citizen from discriminating against another. The Fourteenth Amendment, the Court stated, applied only to the actions of states and not to those of private individuals. This ruling was followed in 1896 by the case of *Plessy* v. *Ferguson,* in which the Court upheld a state law requiring separate accommodations in railroad coaches for black and white passengers. Separate accommodations, the Court ruled, were not inherently a denial of equality. For more than half a century, this "separate but equal" rule was used to justify segregation in virtually all areas of southern life, from restaurants and theaters to restrooms and water fountains. Many states also employed such discriminatory devices as literacy tests and poll taxes to deny black citizens their voting rights. (These practices will be explored more fully in chap. 9.)

It was not until 1954 that the Supreme Court finally overturned the separate but equal doctrine. In the landmark case of *Brown* v. *Board of Education,* the Court held that separate facilities for black and white schoolchildren were inherently unequal. A year later, the Court demanded that desegregation in public schools be achieved "with all deliberate speed." Congress joined the crusade by passing the Civil Rights Act of 1957. The act created a permanent Commission on Civil Rights to investigate charges of discrimination, as well as a new Civil Rights Division in the Justice Department to enforce federal civil rights laws.

These actions, however, were hardly sufficient to abolish segregation. Resistance to change was substantial. In fact, many of the local officials who had been enforcing segregation were now expected to enforce the Court's rulings. Thus it became increasingly apparent that citizens themselves had to work to erase the discriminatory practices that flourished throughout the South and in other parts of the country.

A major step came in December 1955, when a black woman named Rosa Parks was arrested in Montgomery, Alabama, for refusing to give up her seat on a bus to

★ **Table 4-2**
Percentage of white and black voting-age populations registered to vote in eleven southern states, 1960 and 1986

	1960		*1986*	
	White	*Black*	*White*	*Black*
Alabama	64%	14%	77%	69%
Arkansas	61	38	67	58
Florida	69	39	67	58
Georgia	57	29	62	53
Louisiana	77	31	68	61
Mississippi	64	5	92	71
North Carolina	92	39	67	58
South Carolina	57	14	53	52
Tennessee	73	59	70	65
Texas	42	35	79	68
Virginia	46	23	60	56

SOURCE: U.S. Bureau of the Census, *Statistical Abstract of the United States, 1978* and *1988* (Washington, D.C.: U.S. Government Printing Office, 1978, 1988), pp. 519 and 250, respectively.

a white man. Under the leadership of Martin Luther King, Jr., a year-long boycott of the bus company led to a court order ending segregation on Montgomery city buses. Soon strategies of nonviolent direct action—marches, sit-ins, "freedom rides"—were launched throughout the South. With national television focused on the spreading protests by black and white Americans alike, the struggle for equality was brought to the attention of people everywhere. An emotional climax was reached in the summer of 1963 when a quarter of a million people gathered in Washington, D.C., to demand an end to policies of discrimination.

The impact of the civil rights movement was registered in a series of congressional laws passed between 1960 and 1975. The most significant of these laws, the 1964 Civil Rights Act and the 1965 Voting Rights Act, were major steps toward equality for all Americans. The 1964 Civil Rights Act barred discrimination in public accommodations, authorized the attorney general to file suits in civil rights cases, and outlawed discrimination in any program receiving federal money, among other things. By banning the use of voter-qualification tests in southern states where black voter turnout was markedly low, the 1965 Voting Rights Act made it easier for black adults to register and vote (see table 4-2). Black voter participation was also bolstered in 1964 by a constitutional amendment that outlawed the poll tax. As a result, the number of black officeholders grew from fewer than 500 in 1965 to more than 7,000 in 1988. More than two hundred cities, including Atlanta, Detroit, Chicago, Oakland, Washington, D.C., and Los Angeles, have been governed in recent years by black mayors.

Yet the civil rights acts and the growing number of black officeholders have not retarded the spread of **de facto segregation**—segregation established not by law but by housing patterns and custom. Predominantly black ghettos continue to be plagued by unemployment, crime, drug addiction, and other evils that feed frustration and anger. Nor have black Americans achieved economic equality with

Major Provisions of the 1960–1975 Civil Rights Laws

Civil Rights Act of 1960

Provided for federal referees to help register black voters in southern states; strengthened provisions against obstruction of voting.

Equal Pay Act of 1963

Provided for equal pay for equal work, requiring employers to pay men and women the same wages if they perform the same work in the same establishment, under the same working conditions.

Civil Rights Act of 1964

Barred discrimination in restaurants, hotels, theaters, and other public accommodations; outlawed discrimination in employment on account of race, sex, religion, or national origin; created the Equal Employment Opportunity Commission to administer these provisions; authorized the attorney general to file civil rights lawsuits; authorized the cutoff of federal funds for programs that practiced discrimination.

Voting Rights Act of 1965

Authorized federal examiners to register voters in counties where patterns of discrimination were found; suspended the use of literacy tests for voting in a number of southern states.

Civil Rights Act of 1968

Prohibited discrimination in the sale or rental of housing; made it a crime to interfere with the legal activities of civil rights workers.

Voting Rights Act of 1970

Extended the life of the 1965 Voting Rights Act for another five years and broadened its provisions to include states in the North as well as in the South.

Equal Employment Opportunity Act of 1972

Applied the employment provisions of the 1964 Civil Rights Act to the states; gave the Equal Employment Opportunity Commission power to file suits to end discriminatory practices in the private sector.

Title IX of Educational Amendments of 1972

Outlawed sex discrimination in educational programs receiving federal funds; gave the Office of Civil Rights the power to resolve complaints and investigate school programs.

Voting Rights Act of 1975

Extended the provisions of the 1965 Voting Rights Act until 1982 and broadened its provisions to cover "language minorities," such as the Spanish-speaking. ★

whites. The vicious circle of poverty, lack of educational opportunity, and unemployment in which black people have been trapped for generations remains to be broken. As one civil rights worker commented, "What good is a seat in the front of the bus if you don't have the money for the fare?" The unemployment rate for black adults—double that for whites—has remained virtually unchanged since the early 1960s. Moreover, according to 1986 Census Bureau statistics, the median income for black families in the United States is still only 57 percent of that earned by white families—only 7 percent higher than that estimated for 1947. And one in three black Americans still lives below the poverty line ($11,203 for a family of four)—compared to one in ten for whites. This gap in income and employment between whites and blacks leaves the civil rights movement with major unfinished work in the 1990s.

Black Americans, of course, are not the only citizens who have been struggling to achieve their constitutional rights. Native Americans, people of Asian ancestry, Spanish-speaking Americans, women, and other groups have also been victims of discrimination in varying degrees. They have been denied equal opportunity in education, employment, and other aspects of their economic and social lives. Native Americans, for example, did not win the right to vote until 1924. They have the highest unemployment rate, the lowest income level, and the lowest life expectancy

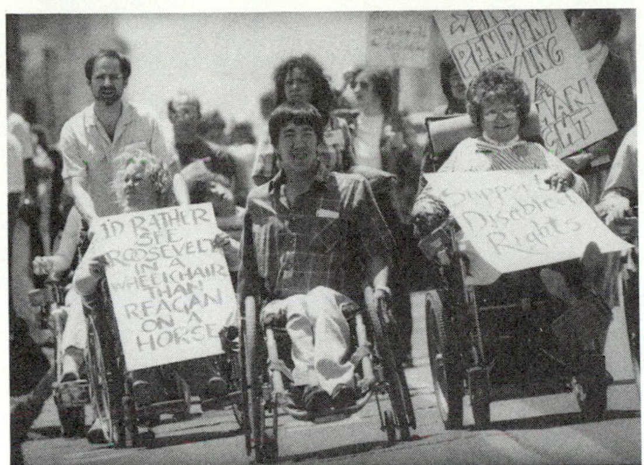

★ Like other groups, disabled Americans have at times resorted to direct action and symbolic protest to demand their full civil rights.

of any major ethnic group. Like black Americans, they and other groups have had to rely on a variety of tactics, ranging from litigation to demonstrations, in their efforts to remove legal and social obstacles to equality. Moreover, as social and political strife continues around the globe—in Asia, Central America, the Middle East, and elsewhere—many other disadvantaged people will immigrate to America in the hope of a better life. The civil rights of all these people will continue to be a major political issue.

The largest "minority" group in America is the majority of the population: women. Although women represent more than 51 percent of the population, they have held less than 1 percent of all major governmental positions since 1789. Even today they account for only 15 percent of state legislators, 5 percent of the members of Congress, and less than 20 percent of the nation's doctors, lawyers, and college teachers. They are usually paid less than men who do similar work and are less likely to wind up in high corporate and management positions. One estimate is that 75 percent of all working women are still in low-level clerical and service occupations. In response to these conditions, such groups as the National Organization for Women (NOW) and the National Women's Political Caucus (NWPC) have been formed to press for women's rights. Building on the achievements of black civil rights activists, these and other groups have won a variety of legislative battles, ranging from the passage of the Equal Credit Opportunity Act of 1974 to revisions in state laws concerning rape. The Equal Rights Amendment (ERA), however, stalled three states short of the three-fourths needed for ratification.

Inspired in part by the black civil rights and women's movements, still other groups, such as homosexuals, the physically disabled, and the elderly, have organized to combat discriminatory laws and practices. A group that has recently attracted national attention to its cause has been the physically disabled. In 1977, disabled Americans staged protest demonstrations in cities throughout the country to force the federal government to implement the Rehabilitation Act of 1973. Among other things, the act prohibits employers from refusing to hire the disabled and mandates that all schools, hospitals, and other institutions receiving federal funds make their buildings accessible to such people by providing ramps, elevators, and other conveniences. As the American Coalition of Citizens with Disabilities noted, the implementation of the act represented an important first step toward bringing the physically disabled into the mainstream of American life.

The Equal Rights Amendment

Both proponents and opponents of the Equal Rights Amendment (ERA) to the Constitution have tended to talk about it in terms of outrage. Proponents are outraged that this effort to have women mentioned in the Constitution has not been successful even though such an amendment has been introduced in every session of Congress since 1923, soon after women were granted suffrage. Opponents claim the ERA would have outrageous effects on the traditional role of women—it would disrupt family life, force women to work, legalize homosexual marriage, and require single-sex bathrooms. What is the legal significance of this amendment that has stirred so much controversy?

The proposed amendment that was passed by Congress in 1972 provided (in its entirety) that "equality of rights under the law shall not be denied or abridged by the United States or by any state on account of sex." Thirty-eight states were required to ratify the amendment by 1982, and only thirty-five did so. Six of the states that ratified the amendment later rescinded their action, raising the unanswered constitutional question whether a state could rescind its decision.

The legal purpose of the ERA is to make gender a "suspect classification," just as the Fourteenth Amendment does for race. If a law contains a suspect classification, it will be struck down by the courts unless there is compelling evidence that it achieves governmental purposes that can be reached in no other way. As matters stand now, without the ERA, laws that appear to discriminate against women must be challenged in court one by one. If the ERA were to become part of the Constitution, the courts would substitute a rule by which laws that made illegal gender distinctions could be held unconstitutional. Such a rule would have a far greater reach than the present case-by-case approach. About five hundred federal and countless state laws would thus have to be rewritten if the ERA should be ratified.

Opponents of the ERA favor "protective" laws for women, such as those that exempt women from

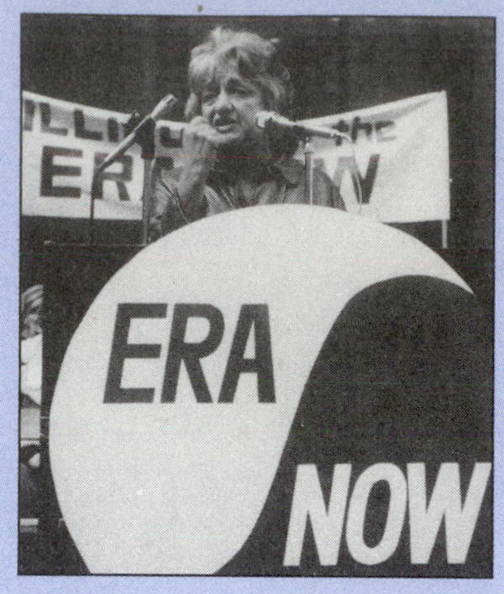

★ Author and activist Betty Friedan speaks out at a pro-ERA rally.

the military draft and from combat, and those that require husbands to support their wives and children. Supporters of the amendment point to the records of the sixteen states that already have equal rights measures in their constitutions. These provisions have no effect on privacy issues in regard to bathrooms, dormitories, and the like. They do, however, affect laws that provide opportunities or benefits for one sex and place restrictions on the other. The constitutions of such states have eliminated laws that provided scholarships for men only at colleges of those states and assigned ownership of all household goods to the husband in divorce proceedings. ★

A major question facing our society is how far government should go to ensure equality of opportunity. How far should it go to help minorities and women succeed in a society dominated by white males? Just as the courts have faced the difficult problem of balancing the rights of the individual against those of society in free speech and criminal justice cases, so they have faced the problem of balancing the demands of one group against those of another in civil rights cases.

For a number of years, schools and businesses have employed **affirmative action** programs and quota systems in an effort to improve educational and job opportunities for disadvantaged persons. While these policies have been touted as an important means of remedying past discrimination, they have also raised charges of "reverse discrimination" against whites. In the mid-1970s a white engineer named

Alan Bakke sued the regents of the University of California after he was refused admission to medical school at that school's Davis campus. Bakke charged the school with reverse discrimination because his test scores were higher than those of sixteen minority students admitted under a special program. In 1978 the Supreme Court ruled in favor of Bakke, stating that Davis's admissions program was unfairly biased against white applicants. The use of rigid quotas, the Court ruled, violated the Civil Rights Act of 1964, which outlaws racial discrimination by institutions receiving federal funds (as the Davis medical school did). At the same time, however, the Court held that affirmative action programs for minority applicants are legal, so long as race is not the only criterion used and quotas are not rigidly applied.

Obviously, this decision left the issue of reverse discrimination—and the future of affirmative action—far from settled. In 1979 the Court spoke again on the issue. In *United Steelworkers of America* v. *Weber,* the Court held that private companies can legally give preference to minority workers in hiring, training, and promotion. Specifically, the Court ruled that a white worker, Brian Weber, was not the victim of illegal racial bias when two black co-workers with less seniority were picked ahead of him for an on-the-job training program, in which half the positions were reserved for minorities and women. Voluntary affirmative action plans, the Court held, even those containing quotas, do not automatically violate Title VII of the 1964 Civil Rights Act, which bars racial discrimination in employment. "It would be ironic," Justice William Brennan wrote in his majority opinion, "if a law triggered by a nation's concern over centuries of racial injustice . . . constituted the first legislative prohibition of all voluntary, private, race-conscious efforts to abolish traditional patterns of racial segregation and hierarchy." Thus the Supreme Court not only upheld the principle of affirmative action but also supported the use of quotas in certain instances to eliminate "manifest racial imbalances" in jobs traditionally reserved for whites.

In the 1980s, however, with the three new Reagan appointees on the bench, the Court began to waver on affirmative action. While it supported some affirmative action plans, it struck down others. In 1989, in *Richmond* v. *Croson,* the Court struck down a Richmond, Virginia, ordinance that assigned 30 percent of all city construction subcontracts to minority firms. Any government program that favored one race over another, the Court stated, was "highly suspect" and should be subject to "strict scrutiny." The Reagan administration, in fact, had largely opposed the vigorous enforcement of affirmative action. It became one of the key points of contention during the Senate's hearings on the nomination of the conservative Robert Bork to the Supreme Court in 1987. (Bork's nomination was not confirmed.)

In 1987 the Supreme Court also ruled for the first time in an affirmative action case regarding gender-based preference (*Johnson* v. *Transportation Agency, Santa Clara County*). It found the use of affirmative action plans for women constitutional. In order to achieve a balanced work force, employers may promote women and minorities ahead of better-qualified white males even if the employer in question has never intentionally discriminated.

Affirmative action is not the only controversial civil rights issue that has been brought to the courts. Another is the question of education programs that discriminate against women. Title IX of the Education Amendments of 1972 prohibits sex discrimination "under any educational program or activity receiving federal financial assistance." Throughout the 1970s the proportion of college degrees granted to women increased dramatically, and more intercollegiate sports were being opened up to women's teams. Many women on the 1984 Olympic volleyball team, for example, said that they would not have been able to develop their athletic skills were it not for the experience they had gained through Title IX–inspired programs in college.

Title IX programs have not escaped controversy, however. Originally, school officials applied the law to all activities of schools receiving federal funds. Opponents wanted local school officials to apply Title IX nondiscrimination provisions only to programs specifically funded by the federal government. Thus a school sports program that was totally funded by local sources, in this view, would not have to allocate equal resources to men's and women's sports. This program-specific approach was upheld by the Supreme Court in its 1984 decision in *Grove City* v. *Bell.* Liberal Democrats in Congress immediately tried to counteract the *Grove City* ruling by introducing the Civil Rights Restoration Bill, which stated that the purpose of Title IX was to prohibit gender discrimination in all aspects of the American educational system. The bill became bogged down in Congress as opponents sought to remove many educational activities from Title IX coverage, such as student clubs, athletic programs, housing, financial aid, and health services. Congress finally passed the Civil Rights Restoration Act in 1988, overriding a veto by President Reagan, who claimed the measure would "vastly and unjustifiably expand the power of the federal government over the affairs of private organizations."

Perhaps someday our society will overcome prejudice and discrimination and thus have no need for federal intervention or affirmative action measures. As Justice Harry Blackmun remarked, "At some time . . . the United States must and will reach a stage of maturity where [such] action is no longer necessary. Then persons will be regarded as persons, and discrimination of the type we address today will be an ugly feature of history that is instructive but that is behind us."

★ Civil Liberties in a Changing World

> Human rights is at the core of American foreign policy because it is central to America's conception of itself. . . . Human rights is not something added to our foreign policy, but its ultimate purpose: the preservation and promotion of liberty in the world. . . . This Administration believes that human rights is an issue of central importance . . . to link foreign policy with the traditions of the American people.
>
> —*U.S. Department of State, 1982*

Americans have always felt that the Constitution and Bill of Rights set them apart from other nations. Indeed, the Monroe Doctrine proclaimed in 1824 that American democracy was superior to other forms of government and warned the monarchs of Europe to keep to their own part of the world. The United States' participation in the Spanish-American War in 1898 and the two world wars was justified in part as an effort to promote democracy around the globe. Although the United States has sometimes found that political or economic necessity required it to work with foreign tyrants and dictators, the desire to support democracy and human rights abroad has remained a constant theme in American politics.

Historically, the average U.S. citizen probably has had only a vague appreciation of the political situation in other countries. In the late nineteenth century the

U.S. press often depicted foreigners, especially Latin Americans and Asians, as ignorant children oppressed by overstuffed dictators. A reluctant Uncle Sam was seen as a paternalistic father figure lecturing recalcitrant tyrants, with a "big stick" firmly in hand.

As international communications, travel, and trade have expanded, especially since World War II, Americans have grown more aware that many foreign governments abuse and oppress their citizens. At first American attention focused on the victims of communism behind the "Iron Curtain" in Eastern Europe and the Soviet Union. By the early 1960s, Americans were also becoming better informed about the plight of political prisoners in Latin America, Africa, the Middle East, and the Far East. Many Americans experienced a growing sense of hypocrisy when they realized that while their own rights were ensured, their government was supporting dictatorships abroad. By the 1980s thousands of citizens, politicians, and interest groups considered human rights abroad a major priority of American foreign policy. Americans by the thousands supported such groups as Amnesty International and the International Committee of the Red Cross.

Human Rights Defined

America's traditional concern for freedom and civil rights at home has gone global. Human rights are a little like motherhood, apple pie, and baseball: most Americans are for them. But what exactly are human rights? As more than one president has found, the answer to this deceptively simple question can be very difficult.

As we have seen, the rights to speak freely, to vote and be represented, to practice or not practice religion, and to be safe from discrimination form the core of American "human rights." But the Bill of Rights may be too specific to American society to be applied universally to other societies. Does England, for instance, deny human rights and democracy to its citizens by the Official Secrets Act, which limits some types of expression? Obviously, America's leaders know that our own conceptions of human rights cannot be applied literally abroad.

Americans' definition of human rights draws not only on the Bill of Rights but on international law and custom as well. The most important international documents outlining human rights are the United Nations Charter and the Universal Declaration of Human Rights. The UN Charter sets standards for the conduct of nations and, in theory, provides mechanisms to punish those that wage war or violate human rights.

The **Universal Declaration of Human Rights,** adopted by the UN General Assembly in 1948, enumerates in great detail the basic rights that all humans should enjoy. The declaration's thirty articles enumerate a wealth of political, economic, and personal rights, including freedom from slavery, freedom of thought, the right to a fair public trial, the right to employment, to an adequate standard of living, and to education. The declaration is supplemented by several later agreements, including the International Covenant on Economic, Cultural, and Social Rights, the Covenant on Civil and Political Rights, the Convention on Racial Discrimination, and the Genocide Convention. The United States recognizes and has formally supported the Declaration of Human Rights, but for many years the Senate failed to ratify all of the supporting conventions and covenants. The Genocide Convention, which had been submitted to the Senate by President Truman in 1949, was ratified nearly forty years later in 1986. After initial reservations, President Reagan signed enabling legislation in 1988 and the United States became a full adherent to the Genocide Convention at last.

Human Rights in Action

As with most foreign policy issues, the application of the United States' policy on human rights abroad depends on the will of the president and Congress. President Jimmy Carter entered office in 1977 with a firm commitment to promoting respect for human rights abroad. Governments that jailed, tortured, or murdered political opponents, Carter warned, would get little support from the United States. Making good on this threat, he severely curtailed military and economic foreign aid to some dictators in Latin America. With the help of Congress, Carter insisted that U.S. representatives on the boards of international lending organizations vote against loans to governments that violated human rights. On at least 112 separate occasions during the Carter years, U.S. representatives helped to deny such loans to nations with poor human rights records.[37] The Carter administration also urged the Senate to approve the Genocide Convention and other unratified conventions and covenants, but without success.

Despite this record, Carter's human rights policies had many critics. Some senators complained that the president was not forceful enough in arguing for ratification of the outstanding conventions and covenants. Others complained that while the Carter administration recognized the Universal Declaration's economic and social components, it tended to employ a narrow *political* definition of human rights. Is it enough to be able to vote and speak out, many people asked, if one does not have food, shelter, and sanitation? In the Third World, America was seen as a well-fed and self-righteous giant, pushing voting rights while children starved.

When Reagan assumed office in 1981, he brought a different definition and focus for promoting human rights abroad. Reagan rejected virtually any notion that economic and social needs are part of basic human rights. Human rights policy during the Reagan years thus focused on traditional political rights—self-government, civil liberties, and freedom from government denial of life, liberty, and the pursuit of happiness. Economic and social rights, on the other hand, were "really more in the nature of aspirations and goals than rights."[38] Economic and social benefits were not, in Reagan's view, inherently the responsibility of government. Economic and social progress, however, would be the natural product of a free society and an open market.

Reagan also changed the target of American human rights policy. Carter, in Reagan's view, had applied too much pressure on America's friends in the Third World, while letting communist nations off the hook. Although the Reagan administration recognized human rights abuses in Latin America, Asia, and Africa, it reserved its harshest criticism for the Soviet Union and its allies. With nations more friendly to the United States, the administration promoted human rights through so-called **quiet diplomacy**—subtle economic and political pressure on the government to change its ways. U.S. representatives constantly reminded the dictators of Chile and Paraguay, for instance, of America's preference for an open political system and worked behind the scenes to protect and encourage noncommunist opposition groups. On some gross violators of human rights, such as South Africa, the U.S.

Human Rights in Nicaragua: The Somoza Family

Were it not for the tremendous human suffering they caused, the Somoza family's fifty-year domination of Nicaragua would make a great adventure film. Through intrigue, conspiracy with a foreign power, and the murder of a national hero, Anastasio Somoza took power in 1936. At his death in 1947, his son—another Anastasio, called Tachito—inherited Nicaragua. The country's political and economic life was under the total control of the Somoza family and their friends. Rigged elections were held to present a facade of democracy. Political opponents were hunted down by the police, and the feared National Guard stifled public protest. Before his assassination in 1978, Pedro Joaquín Chamorro, editor of the opposition newspaper *La Prensa,* described his treatment at the hands of the Somozas:

> I received thousands of blows all over my body—I especially remember those below the belt. I heard unspeakable insults, was forced to physical exercise to the limits of total exhaustion, had applied to my eyes powerful spotlights that burned my pupils and the skin of my face until my brain seemed to explode.

Given the Somozas' systematic denial of human rights, one might have expected strong opposition from the United States, especially to such a government right in its own "backyard." During most of the family's fifty-year rule, however, the United States supported the Somozas. They provided political stability and welcomed foreign investment. They were fiercely anticommunist and loyal allies of the United States. On several occasions the Somozas allowed Nicaragua to be used as a staging area for clandestine U.S. operations in Central America and the Caribbean. Between 1946 and 1979 the Somoza regime received $225 million in economic and military assistance from the United States.

By the mid-1970s, popular opposition had begun to threaten the dictatorship. Tucked away in his heavily fortified residence, known as the Bunker, Tachito Somoza assumed that his friends in Washington would come to his rescue. But for Jimmy Carter, with his concern for human rights, Nicaragua presented a real dilemma. On the one hand, Somoza represented all that was wrong with past American policy in Latin America. If real democracy was to grow, in Carter's view, dictators like Somoza had to go. On the other hand, he did not altogether trust the Nicaraguan opposition, especially the Sandinistas (some of whom were Marxists).

In the past the United States would have stayed with the dictator, a distasteful but known quantity. But Somoza's brutal repression of his own people, including the bombing of civilians and the murder of an American reporter from the ABC television network, could not be ignored. Alternately applying carrots and sticks, Carter attempted to nudge Somoza from power. If the symbol of repression could be removed, the United States reasoned, a new government not led by the Sandinistas could be established.

The Sandinistas and the Nicaraguan people, however, would not wait for Carter's subtle maneuvers. Slowly they gained the upper hand on the battlefield and in the crucial arena of world public opinion. In July 1979 Somoza fled to Miami and the vestiges of his National Guard scattered to neighboring Honduras. Remnants of the National Guard were later recruited by the CIA to form the anti-Sandinista Contras. Tachito Somoza was killed by assassins in Paraguay in 1980. ★

SOURCE: John A. Booth, *The End and the Beginning: The Nicaraguan Revolution* (Boulder, Colo.: Westview, 1982).

applied more overt pressure, including economic sanctions, while still hoping to maintain generally friendly relations with a strategically and economically important nation.

With communist nations, Reagan's efforts to promote human rights were anything but quiet. In diplomacy with the Soviets, the Reagan administration made it clear that no progress would be made on arms control and other issues unless the human rights situation improved. Tremendous public pressure was applied on

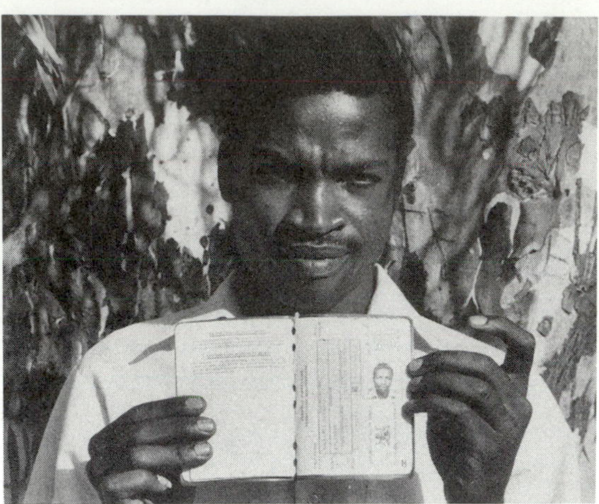

★ Americans have become increasingly aware of the continuing struggle for individual rights in other countries. In South Africa, a black worker shows the "passbook" he needs to travel and work within his own country.

Poland and other Eastern European nations, and a near-total economic boycott of Cuba was maintained. The Reagan administration trained, funded, and armed groups opposed to the governments of Nicaragua and Angola.

At the end of his eight years in office, President Reagan pointed with pride to the Philippines, Haiti, and even the Soviet Union as nations where U.S. pressure helped improve the human rights situation. Critics of the Reagan administration, of course, produced a lengthy list of other nations where little progress had been made for the thousands of victims of government-sponsored repression and terror.

Theory and Practice in Human Rights

Historically, the United States has done business with an international rogues' gallery of petty dictators, such as the former president-for-life of Haiti, Jean-Claude "Baby Doc" Duvalier, who considered the national treasury his personal bank account. On more than one occasion the U.S. military and the CIA have put and kept such dictators in power. The United States has always justified its tolerance of foreign dictators by reference to the "national interest" or the need to maintain military bases in strategically important nations, such as the Philippines and Iran. Cyrus Vance, secretary of state during the Carter administration, making the classic "realist" appeal, argued that "in each case, we must balance a political concern for human rights against economic and security goals." The Reagan administration, echoing this sentiment, stated that "human rights is an important but not the only consideration in determining the course of U.S. relations with foreign countries. Other factors have to be taken into account."[39]

As we have seen, globalization of American politics has made more citizens aware of human rights abuses, and many are uncomfortable with the moral compromises a pragmatic foreign policy seems to require. But even when the United States does go after a foreign dictatorship, controversy can develop over tactics.

What are the proper tactics to promote global human rights? Should the United States, for example, deny military assistance to a nation as strategically important as Panama because its government violates its citizens' rights? Should we halt shipments of surplus food and other types of aid for the poor people of Haiti because the military has taken over the government? By voting against development loans for poor nations, doesn't the United States prevent the very economic growth that might provide a climate of social calm on which democracy could be built?

An aggressive human rights policy can also hurt segments of American society. At the height of the so-called détente between the United States and the Soviet Union in 1972 (discussed in chap. 19), the two nations signed a trade agreement designed to open up economic exchanges. Implementation of this agreement was stalled in 1974, however, when Congress passed the Jackson-Vanik amendment to a trade bill, making trade concessions contingent on a liberalization of Soviet policy in regard to Jewish emigration. The Soviets, angered over what they viewed as interference in their internal affairs, claimed the 1972 trade agreement had been violated. American business thus lost vital opportunities to penetrate the potentially lucrative Soviet market. Moreover, when President Carter embargoed grain shipments to the Soviets following their invasion of Afghanistan in 1979, U.S. exports were cut in half.[40] When the United States takes the moral high ground in support of human rights, some American businesses can founder in a sea of red ink.

At a more philosophical level, we can wonder what gives America the right to tell other nations how to run their lives. When a hulking superpower demands to examine their polling booths and prisons, is it not violating their national sovereignty? Is funding opposition parties and even launching massive military operations, such as the Contra war in Nicaragua, really the best way to ensure a people's right to self-government and local autonomy? As long as racism, sexism, and other forms of discrimination exist in American society, other critics ask, should we not set our own house in order before telling the rest of the world how to live? These are extremely tough, controversial questions. The political debates they spawn among the American people are not likely to disappear in the 1990s.

★ Public Opinion and Individual Rights: Where We Stand Today

A fundamental aspect of a democratic society is that the people themselves, and not just the government, support its underlying principles. After all, curbs on individual freedoms can be just as readily imposed by one's neighbors as by governmental officials. This country, then, seems to have a problem, for many people appear to have little tolerance for individual rights, although evidence does suggest that such tolerance is increasing. While many people say they believe in the right of free speech, for example, they do not always endorse the right of specific groups to exercise it in all situations.

In the early 1950s political scientists began to examine the public's attitudes toward individual rights to find out how many Americans supported or rejected the constitutional "rules of the game." One of the first to undertake such a study was Samuel Stouffer, who found in 1954 that most Americans would not permit certain groups to exercise their right of free speech. He discovered that 60 percent would not permit an individual to speak in their community against churches and religion. He also found that 31 percent would not permit a socialist to speak; 68 percent would not permit a communist to speak; and 21 percent would not allow a speech by an individual whose loyalty had only been *questioned* by a congressional committee.[41] The people in this sample were not asked to support any criminal activity; they were asked only whether an individual with generally unpopular beliefs should be allowed to express his or her views.

Stouffer's findings were validated by later studies that revealed a similar lack of support for individual rights. In 1964 Herbert McClosky reported that, although a favorable consensus emerged on most general statements concerning civil liberties and procedural justice in his surveys, the consensus evaporated when specific examples were presented. He found that freedom of speech was generally supported as a concept, but not necessarily when it was applied to schoolteachers. Similarly, legal rights were strongly defended in principle, but not always for those who "hide behind the laws" when they are questioned about their activities.[42]

One interpretation of these findings is that people tend to react positively to such popular phrases as "free speech" and "legal rights and protections" and negatively to such loaded concepts as "foreign ideas" and "unorthodox political views." If the persons questioned had a real commitment to the principles of civil liberties and procedural justice, their responses would have been more consistent, no matter what emotionally charged terms were used. In McClosky's view, the evidence clearly indicated that "a large proportion of the electorate has failed to grasp certain of the underlying ideas and principles on which the American political system is based."[43]

More recent studies indicate, interestingly, a gradual shift toward greater tolerance of individual rights. In 1987 the National Opinion Research Center at the University of Chicago asked a national sample of Americans some of the same questions Stouffer had asked in 1954 and obtained somewhat different results. For instance, whereas in 1954 only 27 percent of respondents would allow a communist to speak in their community, 59 percent would do so in 1987 (see figure 4-1). Similarly, when asked whether a person who wants "to make a speech in your community against churches and religion should be allowed to speak," 68 percent said yes in 1987, as compared with only 37 percent in 1954.[44] Apparently either pressures to appear tolerant toward such persons have increased during the past three decades or more Americans generally feel unthreatened by these persons' views and opinions. Despite the rise in tolerance, however, a significant proportion of Americans in 1987 did not support specific applications of individual rights—39 percent in the case of communists and 30 percent in the cases of atheists and homosexuals.

An incident in Fairfield, California, some years ago suggests that unwillingness to support individual rights is related to lack of knowledge about our system of government. High school students in an American Studies class made a door-to-door survey in a residential neighborhood to ask support for what they described as "a possible amendment to the Constitution." After reading the proposed amendment, one resident exclaimed it was "unconstitutional"; another said it was "gibberish"; and a third was afraid it "would increase the sale of marijuana." Out of a total of 850 Fairfield residents surveyed, only 290 agreed that the proposed amendment should be added to the Constitution and only 64 (8 percent) recognized it as being, in fact, a verbatim copy of the First Amendment: "Congress shall make no law respecting an establishment of religion, or prohibiting the free exercise thereof; or abridging the freedom of speech, or of the press; or the right of the people peaceably to assemble, and to petition the Government for a redress of grievances."

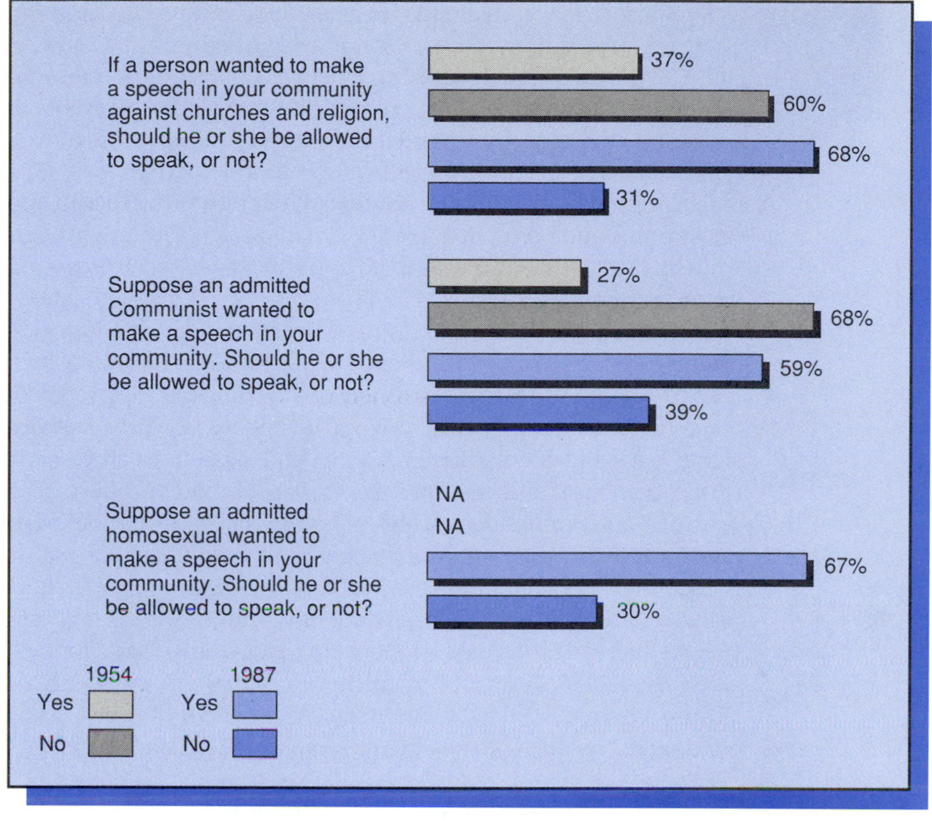

★ **Figure 4-1**
Free speech for whom?
NOTE: NA = not asked. "Don't know" responses are omitted.
SOURCE: Samuel A. Stouffer, *Communism, Conformity, and Civil Liberties* (New York: Doubleday, 1955), pp. 28–41. [Based on data from National Opinion Research Center, University of Chicago, 1987.]

★ Summary

We often take our basic freedoms and rights for granted, forgetting that liberty and protection from government intrusion are the products of many hard-fought struggles at the ballot box, in the courtroom, on the streets, and even on battlefields. Most of our basic freedoms and rights are expressed in the Bill of Rights and other amendments to the Constitution. The basic freedoms—religion, speech, press, assembly, and petition—and the basic procedural rights—due process of law, protection against unreasonable searches and seizures, protection from self-incrimination and cruel and unusual punishments, access to legal counsel—have been interpreted and elaborated by Supreme Court decisions. Following the Civil War, important amendments struck down slavery and racial discrimination in voting, and applied the Constitution's protection of due process to the states. In 1920, the Nineteenth Amendment granted voting rights to women.

None of our freedoms and rights are absolute. They often have to be balanced against other values, against the rights of other people, even against each other. Finding that balance has been one of the major challenges facing the courts.

Another major challenge has been the constitutional and moral imperative to apply the protections and benefits of these freedoms and rights equally to all. The Bill of Rights, subsequent amendments, and Court interpretations did not in practice guarantee that all Americans enjoyed the same political rights and civil liberties. Local laws and racism prevented millions of Americans from fully participating in American society. The civil rights movement helped provide equal political rights and economic opportunities. But the job of eradicating racism and providing equal opportunity and protection for all is not complete. Other segments of our society—women, homosexuals, the disabled, the elderly—continue to work for their political rights and civil liberties.

In the post–World War II era of interdependence and a globalized American political system, many citizens and political leaders have become concerned about human rights abuses abroad. America's dealings with foreign dictatorships have come under increasing scrutiny. While definitions of what exactly constitutes "human rights" vary, Presidents Carter, Reagan, and Bush have all voiced their strong concern for political and economic conditions abroad and have taken visible steps to pressure and sometimes punish governments that repress, torture, and murder their political opponents. Moreover, a fundamental aspect of a democratic society is that the people themselves, not just the government, support its underlying principles. Studies suggest that while most Americans strongly support freedom of speech and the other basic rights in general terms, that support tends to dwindle when these rights are applied to specific situations, especially to individuals who express controversial views. Individual rights, civil liberties, and human rights will continue to be major issues in American domestic and international politics.

★ Key Terms

affirmative action
bill of rights
bills of attainder
civil liberties
de facto segregation
double jeopardy
due process of law
exclusionary rule
ex post facto laws
habeas corpus
libel
prior restraint
procedural rights
quiet diplomacy
selective incorporation
Universal Declaration of Human Rights

★ Notes

1. Lemon v. Kurtzman (1971); Abbingdon School District v. Schempp (1963); Engel v. Vitale (1962).
2. Reynolds v. United States (1879).
3. West Virginia State Board of Education v. Barnette (1943).
4. United States v. Seeger (1965).
5. Dennis v. United States (1951).
6. Yates v. United States (1957).
7. Aptheker v. Secretary of State (1964); Albertson v. Subversive Activities Control Broad (1965).
8. Elfbrandt v. Russell (1966); Whitehall v. Elkins (1967).
9. Tinker v. Des Moines Independent Community School District (1968); United States v. O'Brien (1968).
10. Texas v. Johnson (1989).
11. See, for example, Virginia State Board of Pharmacy v. Virginia Citizens Consumer Council (1976).

★★★★★★★★★★★★

Human Rights

Patrick Harbron/SYGMA

Peter Magubane/Gamma–Liaison

Diego Goldberg/SYGMA

Pater Magubane/Gamma–Liaison

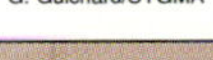

G. Guichard/SYGMA

Singly and together, the people of the world are speaking out against the suppression of human rights and the torture of both the body and the spirit. Musicians joined with Amnesty International in 1989 to heighten awareness of this group's work in gaining the release of political prisoners across the globe. South African supporters of opposition leader Nelson Mandela march for his release while U.S. activists protest apartheid. And Argentinean mothers and grandmothers protest in the 1980s about the disappearance of their husbands and children in the 1970s. "Los Desaparecidos" (those who disappeared) were abducted, imprisoned, tortured, and killed by the military, who allegedly gave the children of the disappeared to families more supportive of the regime.

Associated Press

Sometimes a lone voice speaks out, as when this Chinese student stood in front of the tanks on their way to disperse the protesting Chinese students in Tiananmen Square in June 1989. The student was pulled aside by friends before the tanks rolled on. But Rodrigo Rojas, a U.S. resident originally from Chile, was not so lucky. While participating in an antigovernment demonstration in Santiago, Chile, on July 2, 1986, soldiers doused his body with gasoline and set him on fire. His mother accepts consolation and recognition for her son from Senator Ted Kennedy of Massachusetts.

Miguel Sayago

Stuart Franklin/Magnum Photos, Inc.

In December 1988, this Pan American airliner exploded over Scotland, killing everyone aboard, including many American exchange students from Syracuse University on their way home for the Christmas holidays. A terrorist bomb was suspected.

Vera A. Lentz/Black Star

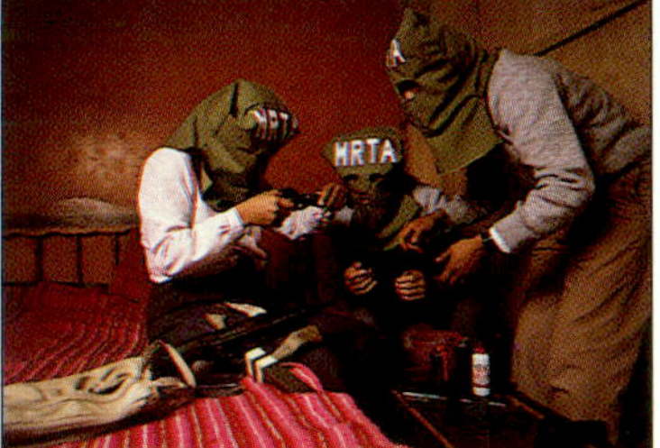

Vera A. Lentz/Black Star

In Peru, MRTA rebels took credit for bombings in Lima in the 1980s. Many continue to die as torture and terrorism combine to undermine trust in government and underscore the need for global solutions to what once were considered "internal" problems. Terrorist tactics are meant to create uncertainty and insecurity. Hitting civilian targets in public places creates a situation in which everyone "pays" for the crime of being on the other side.

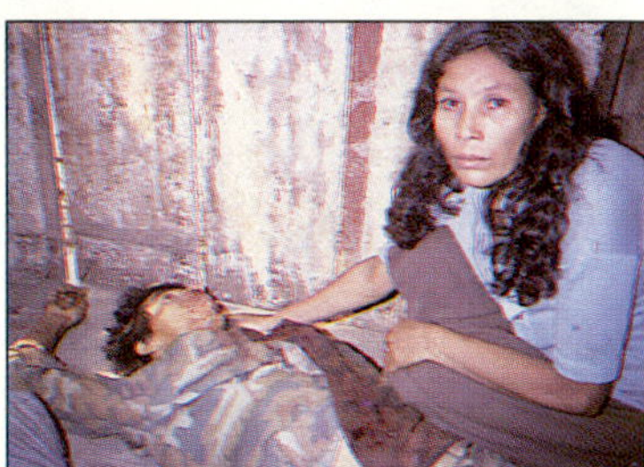

© Witness for Peace Organization/Gamma–Liaison

While the death toll increases, news reports cite statistics. But each statistic is an individual; each death is someone's suffering or loss—be it a peasant in the civil war in Nicaragua or the urban victim of the French terrorist group Directe Action.

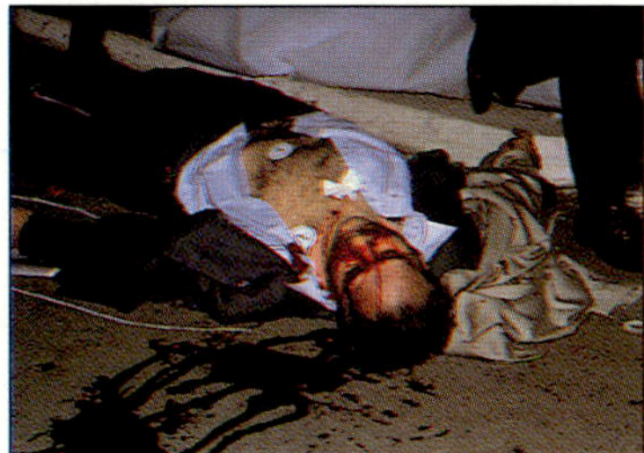

George Besse/Gamma–Liaison

Mass killings of civilians, such as these Kurdish villagers in Afghanistan, through chemical warfare produce shock and despair in the face of a weapon against which there is little protection.

Irna Halabia/SYGMA

Mass atrocities are not the only form of human rights violation. Individuals are often taken one by one and kept hostage, pawns in an international bargaining game where the stakes are usually a matter of life and death.

Maurice Spira, courtesy of Jacqueline M. Gallery, Vancouver, B.C.

Colonel William Higgins, kidnapped on February 2, 1988, was hanged; an Israeli newspaper shows a picture of his body, released by his captors . . . a public execution for the world to see.

SYGMA

השיעים: היום נתלה
עוד שני בני־ערובה

Ricki Rosen/Picture Group

Hostages Currently Held

Name	Nationality	When Kidnapped	Comments (All kidnapped in Beirut area unless otherwise stated)
Terry Anderson	U.S.	3/16/85	AP Journalist, claimed by Islamic Jihad.
Alec Collett	British	3/25/85	UNWRA journalist. Believed dead. Claimed by the Revolutionary Organization for Socialist Muslims (Abu Nidal pseudonym).
Thomas Sutherland	U.S.	6/8/85	Dean of American University of Beirut. Claimed by Islamic Jihad.
Alberto Molinari	Italian	9/11/85	No claim. Long-time Lebanon resident.
Brian Keenan	Irish/British	4/11/86	No claim. Teacher at American University of Beirut.
John McCarthy	British	4/17/86	No claim. World TV News journalist, picked up on way to airport.
Fa'ek Wareh	U.S./Syrian	6/29/86	No claim.
Joseph Cicippio	U.S.	9/12/86	Accountant at AUB. Claimed by Revolutionary Justice Organization.
Edwin Tracy	U.S.	10/21/86	Claimed by Revolutionary Justice Organization. Writer.
Terry Waite	British	1/20/87	No claim. Archbishop of Canterbury's special political advisor.
Alan Steen, Jesse Turner, Robert Polhill	U.S.	1/24/87	Beirut University College. Academics kidnapped with Indian professor Midhileshwar Singh, who was released on 10/4/88. Claimed by the Islamic Jihad for the Liberation of Palestine.
Houtekins family (5 members)	Belgian	11/8/87	Abu Nidhal kidnapped the Houtekins and Valente families from their yacht in the Mediterranean, claiming them to be Israeli agents. The two daughters were released on 12/29/88.
Jaqueline Valente (plus baby born in captivity and another baby expected)	French	11/8/87	
Jack Mann	British	5/12/89	74 years old. Former pilot, long-time resident of West Beirut.
Heinrich Strubig	German	5/16/89	48 years old. Member of West German ASME Humanitas Relief Agency.
Thomas Kempner	German	5/16/89	ASME Humanitas Relief Agency.
Emmanuel Christen, Elio Erriquez	Swiss	10/6/89	No claim. Medical technicians.

SOURCE: *Geographical Magazine*, August 1989.

At stake in the quest for human rights are the lives of future generations. Human rights involve more than being free from torture, persecution, and warfare.

Kai Muller, 1980/Woodfin Camp & Assoc.

Most people today feel that those born into this world have the right to enough food, to an education, and to proper health care. Yet these rights are denied to a great portion of the world's population. Very often, civil wars and the superpowers' struggle over the balance of power have disastrous effects on food supplies, economic development, and human rights. Can Americans, who take pride in the protection of their own civil rights, stand idly by as the rights of other countries' citizens are trampled?

12. Paul Blanchard, *The Right to Read: The Battle against Censorship* (Boston: Beacon, 1955), p. 148.
13. Memoirs v. Attorney General of Massachusetts (1966).
14. Jenkins v. Georgia (1974).
15. Board of Education, Island Trees Union Free School District v. Pico (1982).
16. *New York Times,* February 25, 1986, pp. 1, 12.
17. Peter Clarke and Eric Fredin, "Newspapers, Television, and Political Reasoning," *Public Opinion Quarterly,* Summer 1978, p. 143.
18. New York Times v. Sullivan (1964).
19. Herbert v. Lando (1979).
20. Associated Press, April 20, 1979.
21. Gannett Co. v. De Pasquale (1979).
22. Zurcher v. Stanford Daily (1978).
23. Branzburg v. Hayes (1972).
24. Edwards v. South Carolina (1963).
25. NAACP v. Alabama (1958).
26. See, for example, United States v. Calandra (1974) and Stone v. Powell (1976).
27. Rochin v. California (1952).
28. Olmstead v. United States (1928).
29. Katz v. United States (1967).
30. Griswold v. Connecticut (1965); Eisenstadt v. Baird (1972); Roe v. Wade (1973).
31. Robert Justin Goldstein, *Political Repression in Modern America* (Cambridge, Mass.: Schenkman, 1978), p. 307.
32. Harris v. New York (1971).
33. Oregon v. Hass (1975).
34. New York v. Quarles (1984).
35. Robinson v. California (1962).
36. See, for example, Gregg v. Georgia (1976).
37. Lars Schultz, "Politics, Economics, and U.S. Participation in Multilateral Development Banks," *International Organization* 36 (Summer 1982): 546–547.
38. Paula Dobriansky, *U.S. Human Rights Policy: An Overview,* U.S. Department of State, Current Policy no. 1091 (June 3, 1988), p. 2. Dobriansky was deputy assistant secretary of state for human rights and humanitarian affairs in the Reagan administration.
39. Ibid., p. 3.
40. Charles W. Kegley, Jr., and Eugene R. Wittkopf, *American Foreign Policy: Pattern and Process,* 3d ed. (New York: St. Martin's Press, 1987), p. 238.
41. Samuel A. Stouffer, *Communism, Conformity, and Civil Liberties* (New York: Doubleday, 1955), pp. 28–41.
42. Herbert McClosky, "Consensus and Ideology in American Politics," *American Political Science Review,* June 1964, pp. 365.
43. Ibid., p. 365.
44. National Opinion Research Center, University of Chicago, 1987.

★ For Further Reading

Abernathy, Glen M. *Civil Liberties under the Constitution.* Rev. ed. New York: Harper & Row, 1985.

Abraham, Henry J. *Freedom and the Court.* New York: Oxford University Press, 1982.

Freeman, Jo. *The Politics of Women's Liberation.* New York: David McKay, 1975.

King, Martin Luther, Jr. *Why We Can't Wait.* New York: Harper & Row, 1964.

Lewis, Anthony. *Gideon's Trumpet.* New York: Random House, 1964.

McCann, Michael W., and Gerald L. Houseman. *Judging the Constitution.* Glenview, Ill.: Scott, Foresman, 1989.

Mill, John Stuart. *On Liberty.* New York: Norton, 1975. First published 1859.

The government of the Union is emphatically and truly a government of the people. In form and substance it emanates from them. Its powers are granted by them, and are to be exercised directly on them and for their benefit.

—*Chief Justice John Marshall*

CHAPTER FIVE

WHO GOVERNS?

★★★★★★★★★★★★★

Fat Cats or Grass Roots: Who Governs in the United States?

The question "Who governs?" has probably puzzled most Americans at one time or another; and when the issue is raised, it often stirs strong opinions. Political scientists have been especially caught up in the controversy and have spent years trying to resolve several pertinent questions: Who makes most of the important political decisions? How widely is political power shared? What impact do economic and other elites have on governmental policies? How accountable are these elites to the general public?

The dispute over the way power is distributed has been most vigorously waged between the advocates of two currently popular alternatives: the ruling elite theory and the pluralist theory. Both theories have been prominent in studies of community power structures. They have also been applied to the national scene, where the implications of global interdependence and America's role in the world are most profound.

Briefly stated, the **ruling elite theory** holds that power is concentrated in the hands of a relatively small group of people subject to little or no control by the rest of society; the **pluralist theory** states that power is widely dispersed among many separate groups, all held in check by the public and by each other. Each of these two theories has certain implications. For one thing, exploring "who governs" in America provides a way of determining who has the power to steer America through the challenges posed by an increasingly interdependent world. If the pluralist view is correct, a variety of views shape America's response to the rest of the world. But if the ruling elite theory comes closer to the truth, only certain views prevail in the debate over where America should be headed. Moreover, the issue of who governs is crucial to those of us who wonder how we fit into the political system. Clearly our ability to accomplish anything meaningful in the political system depends on how power is distributed and how difficult or easy it is to gain access to that power. If the pluralist view is correct, it would seem that most of us can gain meaningful access to and influence over decision making. But if the ruling elite theory prevails, then the opportunity for effective action is more limited. As we examine these two conflicting theories, each of us ultimately must decide which one better describes the conditions of American politics, what are its full implications for individual action, and who has—and should have—the power to speak for America on the global stage.

Keep in mind that few political scientists accept all the tenets of either the ruling elite or pluralist theory. Nor does either theory necessarily refute point for point all the assumptions of the other. As we will see in the following chapters,

"Fetch me the law for the rich, will you?"

each is unique in several of its interpretations of the American political scene and should be evaluated on its own merits. And one should not be surprised to discover that disagreements about "who governs" will continue to arise, no matter how persuasive one theory may seem. Despite the elaborate evidence offered in support of each theory, the problems inherent in defining key terms, such as "elite" and "power," and in circumventing the long-standing prejudices on each side probably will continue to prevent either theory from becoming universally accepted.

The concept of **elite** is especially troublesome, despite the many good definitions that have been proposed. Perhaps the most widely accepted view is that an elite consists of the few who have the most of anything valued in society, whether it happens to be money, fame, status, or power. In political terms, an elite includes the people who exercise the most control over the major decisions affecting other people's lives, those who determine how desirable goods and values (such as money, security, and even influence) will be distributed. Thus a political elite may comprise not only high governmental officials, such as the president and members of Congress, but also corporation executives, labor union leaders, and people with influence in the media. After all, the decisions of oil companies to raise their prices, of unions to call a strike, and of media figures to expose a government scandal can affect the distribution of benefits as greatly as can any single governmental policy.

A similar problem of definition arises with the concept of power. At best, we can say that power is relational: power is not something that can be possessed in a vacuum or stored, but arises only in relations among people. Thus social scientists often assert that **power** is the ability to affect the behavior of others, to compel them to do something they might otherwise not do. As president of the United States or as corporation executive, a person can compel others to support a policy he or she advocates. Of course it may be extremely difficult to determine how that individual is able to get his or her own way. A person may succeed in securing compliance from someone by relying on **authority** (power that is regarded as legitimate and right by virtue of one's position, as that of a mother in relation to her son), on force (as by putting a gun to another person's head), on **influence** (persuasion that is based on reason or tangible rewards), or even on manipulation

★ "Charlie Chan" actor speaks out at a protest rally against the ethnic stereotypes that have been perpetrated by the film industry.

(the use of subtle, underhanded methods that leave the subject unaware of what is taking place). And a person's success in the matter may depend as much on his or her position as on any personal talents or attributes.

Power can also be described as institutional. Society's key institutions, such as schools, churches, and the media, socialize Americans to characteristic ways of thinking. Control over the thoughts of citizens is a subtle form of power. For years many textbooks and magazines perpetuated harmful stereotypes of women, blacks, and ethnic groups. In their attempts to remedy this discrimination, these groups pointed out the harmful effects of **institutional power.** Institutions, not individuals per se, were said to be responsible for reinforcing the power of white males. One need only watch movies made in the 1930s and 1940s (and later) to see the degrading and stereotypical way in which blacks, Asians, and other minorities were often portrayed to the American public. Representatives of the film industry responded to such criticism by saying that they were only depicting "real life" and that no racism was intended. Whatever the intentions, the film industry, in the view of its critics, needed to show minorities in more positive roles. Thus institutional solutions, such as affirmative action, were advocated even though no individual intent to discriminate could be identified.

In view of the many forms of power available, it is often difficult to pin down precisely not only *who* wields the power to make major political decisions in this country but also *how* that power is exercised.[1] Ruling elite theorists are convinced that a privileged few get their way by virtue of their access to key resources, while pluralists are predisposed to find many powerful groups checking one another's power. Both sides tend to conduct the type of research that will yield results supporting their preconceived ideas about power.

Interestingly, ruling elite theorists tend to be found on the left and right of the political spectrum, while pluralists are usually in the center. On the left, such democratic socialists as Michael Harrington talk about a dominant ruling class of

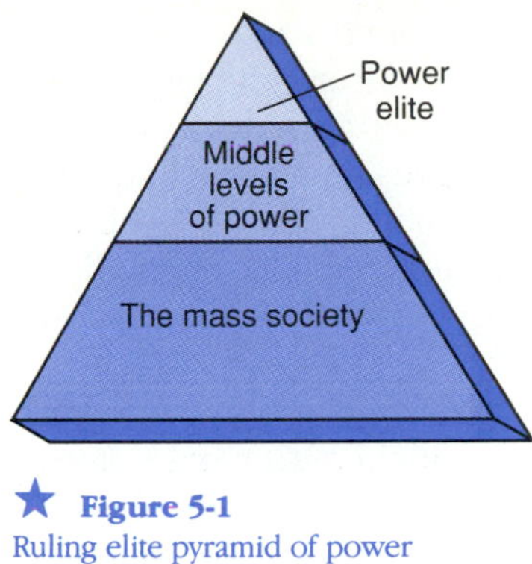

Figure 5-1
Ruling elite pyramid of power

corporate capitalists, while power elite theorists such as C. Wright Mills and G. William Domhoff describe a cohesive elite with a common background. On the right, George Wallace, former governor of Alabama and presidential candidate, spoke of an East Coast liberal "establishment" that was "soft on communism" and permissive on social issues. Some Christian fundamentalist groups link this establishment with a "secular humanism" that is destroying the moral fabric of American life. In the center, pluralists say that for every corporate capitalist there is a labor leader thwarting his power; for every East Coast newspaper espousing secular humanism there are scores of influential churches; and for every conciliatory business person trading with the Soviets there is a hawk in the Pentagon suspicious of the Soviets' every move.

Ruling Elite Theory

The ruling elite theory holds that power in the United States is concentrated in the hands of a relatively small, cohesive group.[2] This theory appeals to people who believe the country is run by a "military-industrial complex," a "ruling class," an "establishment," or a behind-the-scenes political machine. It is a view often expressed by those who are unhappy with the current political scene, who believe that a system of elite or upper-class rule is contrary to American democratic ideals. As one scholar has remarked, "This kind of view . . . is simple, compelling, dramatic, 'realistic.' It gives one standing as an inside-dopester. For individuals with a strong strain of frustrated idealism, it has just the right touch of hardboiled cynicism."[3] Although the ruling elite theory includes a variety of views, certain assumptions are made.

A Pyramid of Power

First, the ruling elite theory holds that only a relatively small number of people dominate policy making in American society. According to the late C. Wright Mills, a sociologist and leading proponent of the ruling elite view, the basic pattern of power in the United States takes the shape of a pyramid (see figure 5-1). At the apex of this pyramid stands the *power elite,* a triumvirate of top corporation executives, military officers, and high-ranking politicians, such as the president and his advisers. Together these three groups control most of the wealth, weapons, and other political resources that underlie the major or "important" decisions in government and the economy—whether to plunge the nation into war, recognize or trade with other countries, or overhaul current economic policies. Members of the power elite wield this enormous power not because they have seized command by design but primarily because they occupy top positions in great and powerful institutions. They get their own way mainly because they serve as chief of staff of the army, president of General Motors, secretary of state, or chairman of the board of Citicorp.

Beneath this powerful triumvirate is a second layer consisting of judges, interest groups, members of Congress, and media executives, who constitute what Mills termed the "middle levels of power." Although they exert a great deal of influence on policies, they usually cannot match the influence of the power elite. At best they can muster a limited veto power (for example, through congressional committees) that may thwart the designs of the power elite temporarily. But they lack the capacity to initiate or implement major new policies or permanently to block programs enthusiastically favored by the president, large corporations, and the military, especially in economic and foreign affairs.

At the bottom of the pyramid sit the rest of the population—the **mass society**—who not only have little say on policy but are controlled or dominated from above. They have no access to the top decision-making levels of government except through elections, which are manipulated by the elite. They are not united in any politically meaningful way by interest groups or political parties. Without such groups to guide their thinking, citizens in a mass society fall prey to the manipulative techniques of a corporate-dominated mass media that entertains more than informs. "The bottom of this society," Mills concluded, "is politically fragmented, and even as a passive fact, increasingly powerless: at the bottom there is emerging a mass society."[4]

A Cohesive Power Elite

A second contention is that an interlocking relationship exists among the top leadership in the United States. Although a balance of power may prevail among interest groups, members of Congress, and judges at the middle levels of power, the members of the power elite—the president, corporation executives, and the military brass—have been drawn together into a fairly cohesive group who know one another and who usually get what they want by pooling their resources. In other words, the top elites are not only more powerful than other groups but also interlock in several important respects.

In the first place, the career patterns of the elite frequently overlap. Many former military and governmental officials, for example, eventually join major industries as executives and lobbyists, helping their firms win lucrative government contracts, price supports, and other political favors through their ties with former colleagues in the military and government. Former senator William Proxmire noted at one point that more than two thousand retired military officers of the rank of colonel or higher were on the payrolls of the top one hundred military defense contractors.[5]

"Mr. Browley was in Vietnam, too, albeit on business."

In similar fashion, many top corporation executives and military officials move into important appointive positions in government. Among those who held cabinet-level posts during the Reagan administration were George Shultz, former president of Bechtel Corporation and a director on the boards of General Motors and Sears, Roebuck; Malcolm Baldridge, chairman of Schoville Corporation; Caspar Weinberger, vice-president of Bechtel Corporation; and Donald Regan, chairman of Merrill Lynch. For his cabinet George Bush tapped Richard Darman of Shearson Lehman Brothers; James D. Watkins, a former high-ranking navy official; and Robert Mosbacher, an oil baron. He also relied heavily on what some critics call the "old-boy network," selecting people from his own exclusive social and political orbit or with close ties to the Reagan administration.

Even Jimmy Carter, the modest Georgia peanut farmer who campaigned for the presidency as an outsider, filled the executive branch with traditional establishment figures. For secretary of the treasury he picked Michael Blumenthal, president of Bendix Corporation. For director of the Office of Management and Budget he chose Bert Lance, president of the National Bank of Georgia. He even picked James Schlesinger, a familiar face during the Nixon and Ford administrations (as defense secretary and CIA director), to head the new Department of Energy. And when Schlesinger was sacked in 1979, Carter picked Charles Duncan, former head of Coca-Cola, to replace him. Although Carter's election to the presidency in 1976 seemed at first to contradict the ruling elite scenario, he kept many of the traditional establishment figures out of the unemployment lines.

The cohesion of the power elite is also maintained through a basic overlap of interests among the military, the government, and many large corporations, especially those seeking defense contracts. A sizable number of major companies—including Lockheed, McDonnell Douglas, General Dynamics, and Grumman—depend on military contracts for a significant portion of their business. In 1986, for instance, the Pentagon awarded military contracts totaling more than $158 billion to major U.S. industries.[6] According to the ruling elite interpretation, because a corporation such as Lockheed wants lucrative military contracts and the Pentagon needs the hardware the corporation produces, each strives to cooperate with the other.

But the close partnership between the government and corporation officials, according to the ruling elite view, is not based solely on defense contracting. They

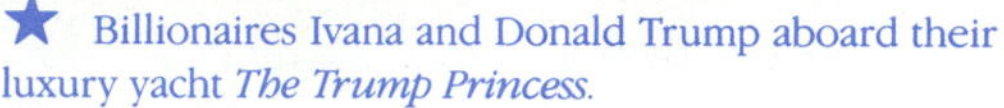

★ Billionaires Ivana and Donald Trump aboard their luxury yacht *The Trump Princess*.

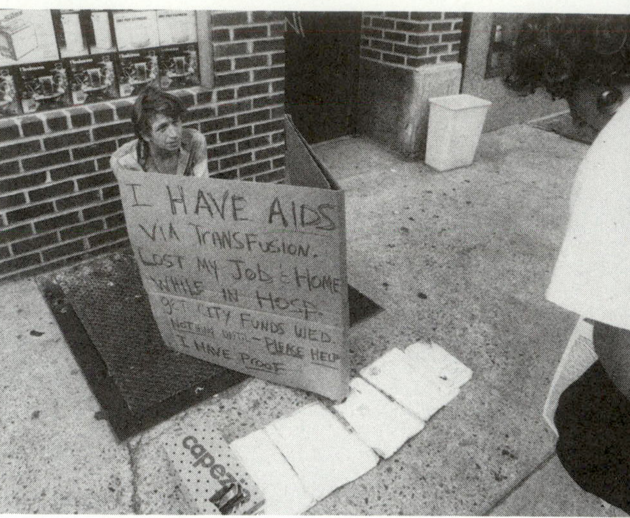

★ In dramatic contrast, a homeless person with AIDS asks passers-by for assistance.

share the conviction that policies that benefit such major corporations as General Motors and Exxon will also benefit the government and the economy as a whole.

One explanation commonly given for this overlap of interests between big business and government is that corporations contribute heavily to political campaign funds. Although corporations are prohibited from giving corporate funds directly to candidates, they have continued to do so either clandestinely or through political action committees (PACs). As the Watergate investigations of the 1970s revealed, some of the biggest corporations in America—including Gulf Oil, American Airlines, and Greyhound—admitted to illegally scratching up large sums of money for Richard Nixon's 1972 reelection campaign. Another explanation is that no administration can afford to ignore the views and interests of industry leaders, whose decisions may create jobs and augment private income, making an administration look good in the eyes of the public. As a result, from one administration to another, industries involved in such activities as shipping, oil exploration, sugar production, mining, and farming reap subsidies and special tax breaks in the billions of dollars to enhance their profits and reduce their losses. Our tax system, critics say, constitutes a form of "welfare for the rich."

For these reasons, according to the ruling elite view, the ties between government and business are hardly confined to Republican administrations. Corporations exert a great deal of influence on government regardless of which party controls the White House. As John L. Lewis, founding president of the United Mine Workers, once complained, "The only difference between Republicans and Democrats is that the Republicans stay bought. Democrats keep coming back for more."

Concentration of Economic Resources

Complementing the view of a closely knit power elite, then, is the argument that economics and politics are inevitably intertwined. Wealth provides the means to

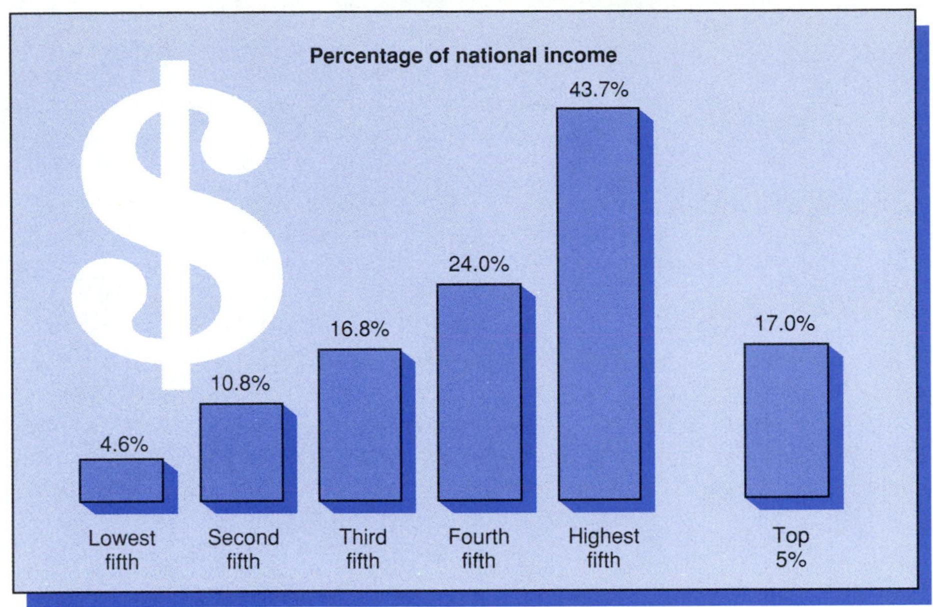

★ **Figure 5-2**
Income distribution in the United States, 1986
SOURCE: U.S. Bureau of the Census, *Statistical Abstract of the United States, 1988* (Washington, D.C.: U.S. Government Printing Office, 1987), p. 428.

gain access to elected officials, as well as to sustain the lobbyists, lawyers, and experts needed to promote one's special interests. In the opinion of one scholar, "Wealth . . . is doubly powerful, not only for what it can purchase now but for what it can buy in the future. In this double sense, wealth negates, or at least frustrates, other more fleeting power factors that unquestionably are dispersed—ethnic popularity, ingenuity, luck, and others. Men of wealth can afford to wait, to bide their time while maintaining continual pressure on behalf of their interests."[7]

For this reason, advocates of the ruling elite theory consider it significant that the structure of economic power and resources in America also assumes the shape of a pyramid. As figure 5-2 reveals, the richest 20 percent of the families in the United States received 43.7 percent of the total private income in the country in 1986, while the poorest 20 percent received only 4.6 percent—a distribution that has not changed substantially since the 1940s.

A similar concentration of resources prevails among major corporations. By 1986 the one hundred largest industrial corporations had laid claim to more than 71 percent of all industrial assets. Some of the same people sat on the boards of directors of many of these corporations. A study of the Rockefeller family by G. William Domhoff and Charles L. Schwartz, presented to Congress in the mid-1970s, revealed that fifteen members of the Rockefeller family were directors of forty corporations with total assets of $70 billion. The boards on which the Rockefellers sat had interlocking combined assets of $640 billion.[8]

Moreover, according to a report issued by two Senate Government Operations subcommittees, "a few institutional investors, principally six superbanks headquartered in New York," held enough stock in competing corporations to influence entire industries. Of these six, the Chase Manhattan Bank, headed by David Rockefeller, was the biggest bank stockholder in twenty major corporations. Chase Man-

Key System Streetcars in the Bay Area

Forty years ago, the Key System provided 260 miles of track and more than 500 electric streetcars to carry one-quarter million commuters a day between San Francisco and Oakland, California, and around the East Bay. A person could board a train in San Francisco and disembark in Oakland or Berkeley twenty-eight minutes later. In the East Bay area the trains ran on the city streets, stopping in front of grocery stores and banks. Like Los Angeles and most other American cities, the Bay Area had a clean, efficient electric transit system, and by 1960 that system had disappeared. What happened to the streetcars?

Although many factors contributed to the demise of the streetcars—including the growing popularity of the automobile—they were doomed after the Key System was acquired by National City Lines in 1946. Financed by, among other firms, General Motors, Firestone Tire Company, and Standard Oil, National City Lines already controlled dozens of other city transit systems in the country. In the mid-1950s the Key System asked the California Public Utilities Commission for permission to scrap the rail network. By 1960 the tracks had been paved over, and buses had replaced the streetcars. The buses were purchased from General Motors, ran on Firestone tires, and operated on Standard Oil fuel. ★

hattan held more than 5 percent of the stocks of four airlines and was a substantial stockholder in the firms that own the three major television networks. Altogether the banks held 38.1 percent of the stock of Columbia Broadcasting System and 34.8 percent of the American Broadcasting System. The report concluded that control of even small blocks of stock "by a single or few like-minded financial institutions provide them with disproportionately large powers."[9]

A Sharing of Values

According to the ruling elite interpretation, the top corporate, governmental, and military elites are united, not only because they share common economic interests but also because they subscribe to similar values, in particular a commitment to private property and capitalism and a conservative attitude toward change. Though members of the top elite do disagree over policies from time to time and even compete for power and profits, they agree on the basic rules of the game, on preserving the system and their privileged positions within it.

This sharing of values filters down even to the middle levels of power in the Democratic and Republican party leadership. Although the two major parties may reflect somewhat different perspectives on the issues (as we shall see in chap. 8), their overall programs tend to be similar and moderate. Though Democrats and Republicans may disagree over the extent to which government should regulate the economy, for example, neither group advocates the nationalization of major industries. If either party offered radical policy alternatives, ruling elite theorists proclaim, it would only alienate voters and undermine the consensus of values shared by prominent officials of both parties and by other elites. As a result, the Democratic and Republican parties offer voters only a narrow range of policy alternatives, a range confined to the interests and values of the ruling elite.

This analysis naturally raises an important question. If a small, cohesive elite with shared values actually governs, how do significant changes in policy ever see the light of day? Why do policies that appear to conflict with elite interests ever emerge? Why do we have minimum wage laws, collective bargaining, and environmental restrictions on industry? Part of the answer, according to the ruling elite view, is that the elites themselves sponsor and support such changes. Dramatic new policies are occasionally enacted when a major crisis threatens the economic system; witness Franklin Roosevelt's New Deal in response to the Great Depression. By remaining flexible—by tolerating some regulation of commerce and industry, social security programs, and fair labor practices—members of the elite can incorporate policy changes to satisfy the public while still preserving the system's basic features and their control of it.

Elites Unrepresentative

Supporters of the ruling elite theory are quick to point out that top corporate and governmental elites—including the second layer of elites, such as members of Congress—are not representative of the general population. In addition to possessing considerably greater wealth, members of the elite are drawn disproportionately from a certain social background: white, male, Anglo-Saxon, Protestant. Neither the House nor the Senate, for example, truly reflects a cross-section of American society. Most seats in Congress are filled by lawyers, bankers, or business executives who belong to the white upper middle class and are overwhelmingly male. Other groups—including the poor, most minority groups, and women—have a great deal less representation in Congress than their proportions in the society might lead us to expect. Similarly, almost all presidents, vice-presidents, Supreme Court justices, and cabinet officials have been white, male, and Protestant. Many, such as Ronald Reagan, George Bush, and Dan Quayle, have also laid claim to considerable wealth.

These unrepresentative qualities of the top elite convince some scholars, such as G. William Domhoff, that there is a "governing class" in America, composed of people from prominent families with great wealth. A disproportionate number of these people serve as corporate directors, network executives, cabinet officials, and foundation presidents. They are closely knit, says Domhoff, "by such institutions as stock ownership, trust funds, intermarriages, private schools, exclusive city clubs, exclusive summer resorts, debutante parties, fox hunts, charity drives, and, last but not least, corporation boards."[10]

Each year more than two thousand of the richest and most powerful men in the country gather at Bohemian Grove, up the coast from San Francisco. They are all members of the Bohemian Club, an exclusive fraternity of top corporate, social, and governmental elites (all men). The privileged few who receive invitations to attend one of the annual "summer encampments" (also known as "the greatest men's party on earth") play golf and drink expensive bourbon with such luminaries as former president Gerald Ford, Bank of America president A. W. Clausen, former secretary of state Henry Kissinger, and assorted corporation executives, millionaires, entertainers, and other celebrities. Such gatherings, according to Domhoff, provide an opportunity for members of the elite to exchange views and establish new social ties that in the long run help maintain the cohesiveness of the ruling class.

Access Not Open

Supporters of the ruling elite theory further contend that the ranks of the elite are virtually closed to most members of our society. Although persons of humble origin occasionally do reach elite positions (as Ronald Reagan's meteoric rise from a small town in Illinois to president certainly testifies), the instances are rare, especially in the high corporate and social spheres. The opportunities for social and occupational mobility remain slight for most people, particularly for minority groups and the poor. As one study revealed, most upward mobility occurs within the middle range of society: at both the rich and poor extremes, sons and daughters tend to remain at the same levels as their parents.[11] In other words, those who possess few financial and political resources are not likely to be admitted into the ranks of the elite.

And even if they should acquire those resources, only people who subscribe to the values of the present elite and are willing to play by their rules—to accept compromise, go slowly, and submerge their individuality—will be accepted. "Personal relations," C. Wright Mills wrote, "have become part of 'public relations,' a sacrifice of selfhood on a personality market, to the sole end of individual success in the corporate way of life . . . the elite careerist must continually persuade others and himself as well that he is the opposite of what he actually is."[12]

Elites Unaccountable

Many supporters of the ruling elite view also strongly criticize the present distribution of political and economic power. They charge that elites are subject to little control by the rest of society and, as the numerous Washington and corporate scandals that flash on the news reveal, can be extremely corrupt and irresponsible. "The men of the higher circles," Mills concluded years ago, "are not representative men; their high position is not a result of moral virtue; their fabulous success is not firmly connected with meritorious ability. Those who sit in the seats of the high and mighty are selected and formed by the means of power, the sources of wealth, the mechanics of celebrity which prevail in their society."[13] Although power is supposed to reside ultimately in the people and their elected representatives, in reality it rests with those who control the corporations, bureaucracies, and military. It rests with those who are neither elected by the people nor morally responsible to them.

Indeed, ruling elite theorists charge, not even such elected officials as the president and members of Congress are truly accountable. Although voters are able to choose among alternative party candidates at election time, their choices are narrow and their power is limited almost exclusively to the act of voting. Because only a relative few participate in other kinds of political activity or even know what their elected representatives are doing (as we shall see in chap. 7), politicians tend to cater to the interests of those few influentials who keep informed and voice their demands. "Policy questions of government," Thomas R. Dye and L. Harmon Zeigler have written, "are seldom decided by the masses through elections or through the presentation of policy alternatives by political parties. For the most part, these 'democratic' institutions—elections and parties—are important only for their symbolic value. They help tie the masses to the political system by giving them a role to play on election day and a political party with which they can identify."[14]

In fact, according to the ruling elite view, elites influence the public more than the public influences them. Corporate executives and politicians, for instance, employ the mass media to manipulate public opinion through sophisticated advertising and slick public relations techniques. Because elites dominate the mass media, the public has few opportunities to get radically different points of view or to voice

★ Many dramatic symbols exist of the disparities in wealth and position discussed by the ruling-elite theorists.

their own views and opinions. In fact, the views and opinions of most Americans probably have been conditioned to a significant degree by the media, anyway. As a result, governmental policies and social values do not ultimately reflect the needs and interests of the public as much as they mirror those of the power elite.

Elites in a Changing World

In light of the growing importance of international relations, one might expect average citizens to have a greater voice in the making and executing of U.S. foreign policy. To be sure, our withdrawal from Vietnam and the limiting of our commitment of troops in Central America seem to suggest that the public can influence the foreign policy agenda. According to the ruling elite view, however, American foreign policy making, with only a few dramatic exceptions, is determined and carried out by a small but highly influential business, military, and governmental elite.

Given the technical nature of many foreign policy decisions and the need for secrecy in a potentially hostile world, foreign policy has always been the responsibility of a relatively small inner circle. The constitutional powers of the president further concentrate foreign policy decisions and relegate Congress to the second tier of power. The foreign policy elite fill important diplomatic posts and ensure continuity in America's dealings abroad. This elite group is seen to be a "self-selecting, self-recruiting, and self-perpetuating governing body, a group of individuals who 'guard' American foreign policy by advising incumbent administrations and ensure that those who enter into policy-making roles share the views and attitudes of their predecessors."[15]

To support their contention that a small elite dominates American foreign policy, ruling elite theorists point to the existence of such organizations as the **Council on Foreign Relations.** The council is a highly influential private research and planning organization that draws its limited membership from the most powerful business, military, financial, and governmental circles. Its membership list has included many major foreign policy decision makers of the last fifty years:

President George Bush
President Jimmy Carter
Cyrus Vance (former secretary of state)
Harold Brown (former secretary of defense)
George Shultz (former secretary of state)
Alexander Haig (former NATO commander and secretary of state)
Donald Regan (former secretary of the treasury)
William Casey (former director of the CIA)

In all, more than thirty advisers to Presidents Bush and Reagan have been members of the Council on Foreign Relations.[16]

The council, according to ruling elite theorists, performs two basic tasks in influencing American foreign policy. First, it provides opportunities outside of government for the elite to come together informally to discuss America's international policies. Second, the council develops specific policy proposals, which are then passed on to government officials, leaders in the private sector, and the media. Among the council's proposals that have become official American policy are the Marshall Plan to aid postwar Europe, the "containment" of the Soviet Union, U.S. involvement in Vietnam, and the pressuring of dictatorships to improve their records on human rights. "The history of Council recommendations and U.S. foreign policy proposals and actions," observers note, "have shown remarkable consistency."[17]

The council thus helps establish the basic goals of American foreign policy, and many of its programs are carried out by the executive branch with little public input. The public, according to the ruling elite view, can react to decisions only by waiting for the next election to change a policy that may have been in place for several years. The next election, of course, may be contested by candidates who, while representing different political parties, all belong to the Council on Foreign Relations.

Ruling elite theorists have noted that the elites of several nations have formed similar organizations to discuss global problems. The most noted in recent years has been the **Trilateral Commission,** founded by David Rockefeller in the early 1970s. The Trilateral Commission, so named because its members came from the three pillars of advanced capitalism—the United States, Western Europe, and Japan—worked to coordinate their economic and political policies. By the late 1970s, nineteen members of the commission were members of the Carter administration, including the president himself, Vice-President Walter Mondale, Secretary of State Cyrus Vance, and National Security Adviser Zbigniew Brzezinski. Indeed, Carter's rise from relative political obscurity as a former governor to presidential contender in 1976 is often attributed to his contacts on the Trilateral Commission. When Ronald Reagan entered office in 1981, his administration included thirteen members of the commission, including Secretary of Defense Caspar Weinberger.

One version of the ruling elite theory is the view that American foreign policy is dictated by a **military-industrial complex.** This idea was first given wide publicity by President Eisenhower in his farewell address in 1961:

> This conjunction of an immense Military Establishment and a large arms industry is new in the American experience. The total influence—economic, political, even spiritual—is felt in every city, every statehouse, every office of the Federal Government. . . . We must never let the weight of this combination endanger our liberties or democratic processes.[18]

The military-industrial complex is said to consist of career military personnel, executives in the arms industry, government bureaucrats whose agencies are involved in national defense, and members of Congress whose districts benefit from military bases and defense industries.[19] Members of this group influence policy in order to ensure a high level of military spending, not necessarily because it is essential to the national security but because it is in their own interest. Critics have accused the military-industrial complex of distorting the threat posed by the Soviet Union in 1945 to raise tension, start the cold war, and guarantee continued high levels of defense spending.[20] Others cite more recent examples, such as U.S. involvement in Central America during the 1980s. By exaggerating the threat to the United States from Nicaragua, in this view, the military-industrial interests could maintain high levels of defense spending, introduce troops into Honduras and other nations, and build public support for their political agenda. The close relationship between arms merchants and the group in the White House responsible for the Iran-Contra scandal of 1986–1987 (see chap. 19) is seen as symptomatic of the power of the military-industrial complex.

Those who fear the military-industrial complex sometimes portray American foreign policy as held captive by a conspiracy of special interests. This is an image that many citizens cannot accept. As we will see when we discuss the alternative theory, many people see American foreign policy as being set by competing interests and persuasions. Still, with the words of President Eisenhower echoing in our ears, we must remember that the argument that U.S. foreign policy is heavily influenced by a small economic and political elite is quite strong.

★ Political Implications of Ruling Elite Theory

In summary, the ruling elite theory sees little opportunity for most of us to work effectively within the existing political system, at least not for any significant reform. Although we may believe we can play a major role in the political system (through such processes as elections), our participation remains more symbolic than real. The true power rests with a small, fairly cohesive elite drawn from top corporate, military, and governmental circles. Members of this elite share interlocking relationships based on mutual self-interest, overlapping careers, and a commitment to the same basic values. They not only are unrepresentative of the general population but also resist efforts to gain access by people who lack wealth, proper social connections, and a world view similar to their own. And instead of being controlled by public opinion, they usually are in a position to dominate and manipulate that opinion. They, not the public, mark the boundaries of political activity for the majority of society.

One other implication is clear. The ruling elite theory implies that if significant political change is to be achieved, it may become necessary to engage in actions more extreme or radical than would be necessary in a truly competitive political system. A system that remains closed to large segments of society offers justification for direct action and even violence. Although not everyone who opposes a ruling elite system will resort to violence, it is not just coincidental that groups favoring radical means of political action have viewed the system as hopelessly controlled by an establishment bent on thwarting any kind of major reform. Ironically, however, the ruling elite theory also offers justification for the decision not to engage in any political action at all. It gives those who might ordinarily be motivated to work for political change the excuse that such actions would be futile in the face of an indomitable elite.

A final implication stems from our increasingly interdependent world. This interdependence cuts two ways. On the one hand, as foreign policy plays an ever-expanding role in American politics, the influence of the power elite expands correspondingly, given its dominance of foreign policy making. On the other hand, the global communications network can shine light on a foreign policy elite used to working in secret. The news that the Reagan administration was secretly selling arms to Iran, for example, first broke in a Lebanese magazine and soon thereafter hit the international wire services.

★ The Pluralist Theory

Despite widespread support for the ruling elite theory, many political scientists do not accept its basic tenets. While they agree that elites exist, they believe ruling elite theorists greatly exaggerate the concentration of political power in the United States.[21] One of the leading critics of the ruling elite view, the political scientist Robert Dahl, described political power in this country as "pluralistic"—that is, widely dispersed among many separate elites kept in check by numerous social and political forces. The underlying assumption of Dahl and other pluralists is that any theory of who governs must be supported by evidence of participation in decision making. It must not be assumed that, simply because persons occupy important positions of power, they constitute a single, cohesive ruling elite whose decisions usually prevail. According to one scholar, "Only if it can be shown that such a group is a cohesive one with a sense of group identity, and that it has a grip on the governmental power in that community approaching a monopoly, can it be argued that it constitutes a 'ruling elite.'"[22] Nor must it be assumed that people with considerable economic or military resources actually employ those resources to exert great power. Even though the military controls armaments, for example, it does not employ them to determine defense policy.[23] In other words, one must study the actual decisions made and not simply assume that persons in high positions or in possession of great wealth actually constitute a single powerful ruling group.

In effect, pluralists contend that their examinations of political power are more objective and precise than those of ruling elite theorists (a view not shared, of course, by the latter), and that their studies paint a considerably more diversified picture of who governs in America. Although the pluralist theory, like the ruling elite theory, embraces a variety of interpretations, certain basic assumptions stand out.

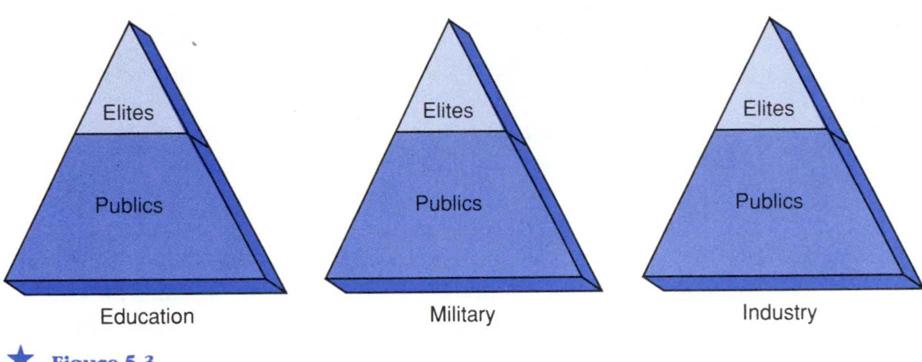

★ **Figure 5-3**
Pluralist pyramids of power

Many Pyramids of Power

First, pluralists reject the idea that a single elite makes most of the important decisions in America. (Indeed, they question how we can even determine which decisions are "important" and which are not.) Although they agree with ruling elite theorists that powerful groups exist, they contend that the power structure is too decentralized and complex to permit such groups to act together in a common design. Whereas ruling elite proponents see the power structure as a single pyramid dominated by a unified power elite at the top, pluralists see it as a range of pyramids, with shifting **coalitions** of groups dominating separate areas of policy making (see figure 5-3). They do not find that the same military, corporate, and governmental leaders determine most major policies; they find rather that different groups exercise power in different spheres and at different times, depending on the issue.

In studying community power in New Haven, Connecticut, for instance, Dahl found that the people who made the major decisions in the area of urban renewal were not the same as those who made the major decisions in education. "Leaders in redevelopment," he noted, "are with a few exceptions officially, professionally, or financially involved in its fate. Most of the leaders in the public schools have a professional connection of some kind with education . . . a leader in one issue-area is not likely to be influential in another."[24]

Part of the reason for this dispersal of power, Dahl and other pluralists contend, is that many different resources of power exist in our society. Whereas ruling elite theorists assume that economic resources and position are the major keys to power, pluralists find that power is based on a variety of factors—wealth, expertise, access to the media, prestige, position in a major institution—each of which may be decisive in one area but not in others. That is, although pluralists do not dispute the fact that most economic resources are controlled by a small proportion of society, they do insist that other resources may be equally if not more consequential in determining who wields influence. Further, although these other resources may not be equally distributed among the population, no single individual or group can claim a monopoly on any of them.

Competition among Elites

Adding still more fire to the controversy, most pluralists insist that a great deal of competition prevails among elites. Whereas ruling elite proponents believe the top elites are unified and mutually supportive—squabbles, they say, occur mainly at the middle levels of power, as among interest groups and members of Congress—pluralists find significant competition at all levels. They see power spread widely among many different **veto groups,** which balance one another. Echoing Madison in *Federalist* no. 10, pluralists say that the ambitions of one group are tamed by the conflicting ambitions of another. Industry, the government, and the military are all fragmented by numerous subgroups that have conflicting interests and policy goals.

Thus among major corporations one finds vigorous competition not only among businesses operating within a general field (such as transportation) but also among those whose interests differ in regard to governmental policies. Whereas one industry may applaud price supports or import quotas, another may condemn them as disastrous. Import quotas on textiles are a boon to fabric manufacturers, for example, but raise prices for clothing retailers. Even the Vietnam war (which many observers considered to be economically inspired) revealed a considerable division within industry. While some companies clearly benefited from defense contracts, other companies suffered, especially those geared to a peacetime, consumer-oriented economy. (Indeed, it may be significant that the *Wall Street Journal* and *Business Week,* which generally reflect business values, were among the first publications to take an editorial stance against the war.)

Similarly, as the evening news keeps demonstrating, conflict frequently erupts among the various branches of government. The president, members of Congress, and the officials of each of the fifty states represent diverse constituencies and do not necessarily have the same policy goals. Indeed, pluralists argue, the competition that occurs in government often thwarts powerful elite interests, as when Congress or the Supreme Court succeeds in blocking presidential initiatives. History is full of conflict between governmental elites:

1920 The U.S. Senate refused to ratify the Treaty of Versailles, dashing President Wilson's personal plan to end World War I and establish the League of Nations. For Wilson this was a crushing defeat, both personally and politically.

1937 President Franklin Roosevelt's plan to reorganize the Supreme Court, labeled by opponents as the "court-packing scheme," failed to win the support of Congress.

1952 The Supreme Court declared President Truman's plan to send the army to operate steel mills in Youngstown, Ohio, an unconstitutional exercise of legislative power by the executive branch. Truman sought control of the mills to end a labor dispute that he claimed threatened U.S. military operations in Korea.

1970 Congress halted development of the supersonic transport (SST), which both President Nixon and major aerospace corporations wanted. Although Congress was under great pressure to support the program, it eventually succumbed to the outcries of scientists and environmental groups who argued that the plane posed an environmental hazard.

1971 The Supreme Court refused to halt publication of the so-called Pentagon Papers. The papers, a secret history of U.S. engagement in Vietnam, were leaked to the *New York Times* by Daniel Ellsberg, a former Defense Department employee. The Pentagon Papers revealed a detailed effort on the part of several administrations to mislead the public and Congress on America's role in Vietnam.

1980 President Jimmy Carter withdrew the SALT II treaty from consideration by the Senate. Carter was unable to convince opponents in both parties that this major arms limitation treaty with the Soviet Union would maintain American military superiority.

1987 Congress investigated the Reagan administration's secret plan to sell arms to Iran in the hope of securing the release of American hostages held in the Middle East. In this major scandal, dubbed the Iran-Contra affair, administration officials used the money from the sale of arms to Iran to circumvent Congress's ban on arming the Contra rebels in Nicaragua. The scandal led to the prosecution of several Reagan appointees.

The pluralist argument is thus boosted by inter-elite conflict in the government. As figure 5-4 shows, presidents' success in bargaining with Congress has fluctuated wildly during the past twenty years, and reached the lowest point with Richard Nixon during the Watergate scandal.

One of the most dramatic conflicts among the governmental elite occurred in 1974, when probes by Congress and the federal courts into the Watergate scandal pressured Richard Nixon into resigning from the presidency. Although supporters

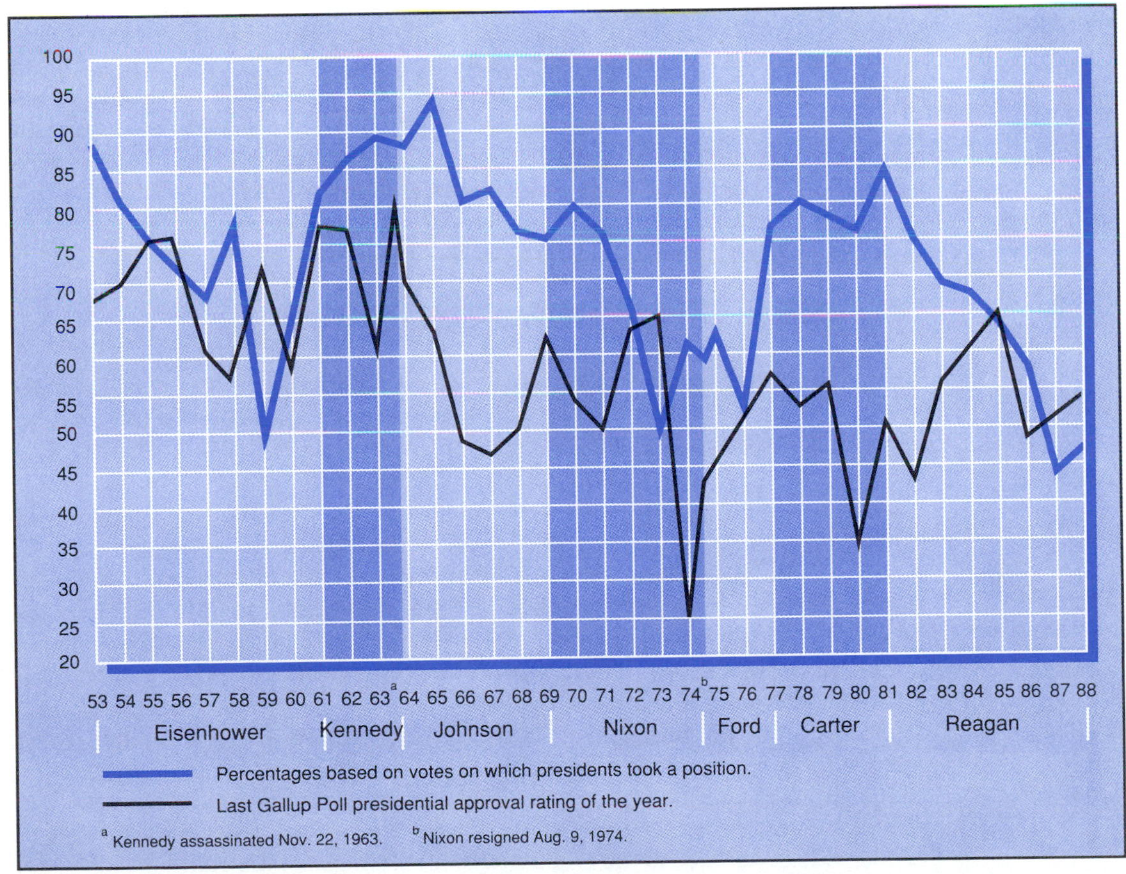

Figure 5-4
Presidential popularity and measures voted upon in Congress, 1953–1988
SOURCE: *Congressional Quarterly Weekly Report,* January 7, 1989, p. 5.

of the ruling elite theory point to the scandal as evidence of elite conspiracy and corruption—and, in fact, insist that Nixon's downfall was hastened by other elites who never fully accepted him—the head-on collision between Nixon and Congress revealed to pluralists the presence of true institutional pluralism. Only in a decentralized power structure, they argue, could a president be compelled to resign his office and the attorney general and White House aides be carted off to prison. In other words, from a historical perspective, presidents have not been able perpetually to strong-arm either Congress or the courts, or to force unpopular issues and behavior on the American people.

Further, according to the pluralist view, it would be a mistake to interpret presidential actions in terms principally of the benefits accorded the ruling elite. Presidents sometimes find themselves locked in battle with top corporate and military elites, as Jimmy Carter discovered with his energy proposals in 1977. His emphasis on conservation, as opposed to incentives for exploration and production of new oil, resulted in outcries from oil companies and increased lobbying pressure on Congress to reject Carter's energy package. Similarly, Carter was hardly the instrument of military or corporate interests in the B-1 bomber controversy. Despite appeals from the Air Force, prime contractors such as Rockwell International, and even organized labor, Carter decided to honor his campaign pledge on defense policy by rejecting the $20 billion bomber project. (It was later restored under President Reagan.)

What makes this competitive situation significant, according to pluralists, is that as long as governmental and corporate elites hold each other in check, average citizens have some protection from abuse. As long as corporations must compete for consumers' dollars and as long as presidents and members of Congress must vie for voters' support, the interests of most citizens can be neither ignored nor ultimately repressed.

Distinction between Elites and Masses Blurred

Pluralists find the distinction between "elites" and "masses" less clear than the ruling elite theory suggests. How is it possible, they ask, to draw precise lines between an elite and a nonelite when groups with wide public membership, such as labor unions, wield such enormous influence on policy? Not only do unions threaten major industries with strikes, but they flex their muscles in Congress and contribute money and organizational skills to political campaigns.

In addition, pluralists hold, there is really little difference between the social and economic values of elites and those of most other Americans. Although business and governmental leaders may not be truly representative of the general population in education, wealth, and social composition, elites and nonelites alike tend to subscribe to similar values: the sanctity of private property, capitalism, a belief in compromise, and a conservative attitude toward change. These and other shared values, in effect, restrain business and governmental leaders, forcing them to act within the boundaries of society's overall expectations. "How leaders act," Dahl concludes, "what they advocate, what they are likely to believe, are all constrained by the wide adherence to the creed that exists throughout the community."[25] (Ruling elite theorists, of course, counter that these values ultimately are propagated by elites, through their control over the mass media and other institutions, and hence elites are not constrained at all.)

★ Pluralists point to Andrew Young—the first black mayor of Atlanta, meeting here with other city leaders—as an example of how access to elite positions remains open in America.

★ In January 1989, Elizabeth Dole was sworn in as secretary of labor. Her appointment by President Bush made her the first woman to hold that position.

Access Is Open

Pluralists, furthermore, toss out the ruling elite thesis that access to decision making is blocked for most members of society. They point out that many persons from relatively poor families and with diverse social and ethnic backgrounds have managed to reach positions of political and economic power. Contrary to the ruling elite interpretation of sociological studies, pluralists argue that upward mobility has been increasing during the past several decades. According to one study, the proportion of high-level executives who actually "started at the top"—the percentage of board chairmen, presidents, and vice-presidents of the six hundred largest industrial corporations in the United States who inherited their positions—has steadily declined, until it is now down to only about 3 percent. Most of the other 97 percent rose through the ranks after twenty or twenty-five years of service in the company; very few of them had any family connections in the firms they now head.[26]

In fact, pluralists feel that access to elite positions probably will continue to improve, especially as more women and members of minority groups are elected to public office and work their way into higher positions in industry and finance. Although women and minority groups are still underrepresented in Congress and the executive branch, they have been making significant inroads in other areas. Chicago, Detroit, Los Angeles, Washington, D.C., and Atlanta have been headed in recent years by black mayors. Moreover, such major cities as San Francisco, Chicago, San Jose, and Phoenix have been headed by female mayors, while in Connecticut, Vermont, Nebraska, Washington, and Kentucky, women have been elected governors. And although President Bush was criticized by many observers for resorting to the old-boy network in selecting his cabinet in 1989, he also picked a black educator, two Hispanics, and two women.

In any event, continues the argument, if access to elite positions is restricted, society as a whole is to blame, not just the elites. The history of prejudice and low levels of popular support for equal opportunity have set up the roadblocks that

★ Many Native Americans, like other groups, have fought for their full voting rights in the belief that participating in elections is more than just a symbolic activity.

prevent certain groups from reaching positions of power. The fact that individuals must support certain values and codes to join the ranks of the elite reflects the prevailing ideas of society at large, not just those of elites.

Elites Are Accountable

The proposition that economic and other elites are unaccountable to the rest of society is similarly rejected by pluralists. While they agree that important decisions affecting society are passed down by nonelected, frequently invisible corporate heads, military brass, and bureaucrats, they believe these elites can be kept in check by elected governmental representatives who are subject to public scrutiny. After all, they contend, elected governmental officials ultimately hold the most powerful positions in America. Only they have the authority and access to the legitimate use of physical force (as through the armed forces and the Justice Department) to make and enforce decisions affecting the whole society. Only the president and members of Congress have the authority to establish the limits of the military budget, set up new regulatory agencies, and (together with the courts) break up monopolistic enterprises.

All of these considerations, according to the pluralist view, mean that ordinary citizens ultimately can exert a great deal of influence. Citizen influence can be felt through elected officials who must remain alert to public reaction at the polls.

Although corporate and military elites are not directly accountable to the public, their independence is curtailed by governmental elites who are accountable through elections. Presidents and members of Congress often must initiate policies that do not favor prominent corporate executives or military brass—or risk the loss of public office. Even though presidents and most members of Congress share backgrounds similar to those of other powerful elites, the institutional imperatives of their offices—their public reputations and need of voter support—compel them to respond to influences other than corporate wealth or military lobbying. The necessity of responding to a wider public interest, pluralists argue, accounts for the succession of laws that protect the individual citizen and consumer: truth-in-labeling laws, statutes that curb deceptive advertising, antitrust laws, pollution controls, and regulation of labor practices. Admittedly, such protections often are poorly enforced or only minimally applied, but their existence testifies nonetheless to the frequently opposing interests of corporate and governmental elites. (It should be noted, however, that ruling elite theorists do not necessarily view elites as unsympathetic to public needs. They argue that elites are capable of being "public-minded" and will support policy changes that benefit society, but only when those changes do not cause their own interests to suffer.)

The fact that elites occasionally must "walk the line" to preserve their privileged positions therefore signifies a degree of latent power among the citizenry. Although only a relatively small number of citizens actually throw themselves into the political fray, the voice of the majority is still heard because politicians must remain attentive to opinion polls, votes, and the views of influential community spokespersons. As Dahl puts it, "The leaders who directly control the decisions of political associations are themselves influenced in their own choices of policies by their assumption as to what the voting populace wants."[27]

Elites and Democratic Values

Pluralists and ruling elites conflict also in their views of public apathy. As we shall discuss in chapter 9, many Americans turn their backs on politics and are poorly informed about the most rudimentary facts of government. While these findings generally disturb ruling elite theorists, who fear that nonparticipation and apathy give elites even greater freedom to ignore public needs, some pluralists (though certainly not all) conclude that nonparticipation may, to some degree, be beneficial to the political system. First, those who are politically uninvolved and uninformed often have a low commitment to such principles as freedom of speech. It might be a mistake, some pluralists warn, to call for greater participation from people who are relatively uninformed and who reject many of the nation's basic political values. Further, a more politically active populace might only interfere with the work of elected representatives chosen to create policy. A highly active electorate marked by extreme ideological differences might only lead to increased fragmentation of the political system.

In any event, the argument goes, it is the elites, not the general public, who protect and safeguard the American political system. Research on political opinion reveals that leaders in government, education, and industry—those with higher education, social prestige, and positions of power—generally show greater support for freedom of speech, freedom of the press, and equality of opportunity than do most other Americans. (Of course, there may be a distinction between what people say and what they actually feel. Persons in high positions may be under greater pressure to appear more tolerant than those not in the limelight.)[28] Thus both apathy and rule by elites are regarded not as malfunctions of the political system but as conditions for preserving American political values. So long as governmental leaders remain accountable to the public through periodic elections and the people enjoy freedom of speech and choice, pluralists contend, a political system responsive to the interests of most Americans will prevail.

Pluralism in a Changing World

As we saw in our discussion of the ruling elite theory, a strong case can be made for the power of an international elite composed of political and military leaders, transnational corporations, financiers, and the media. Those who adhere to the pluralist perspective do not deny the existence of a loosely interconnected international elite. Pluralists acknowledge that international relations, diplomacy, and foreign policy, more than any other dimension of government, fall within the purview of an elite.

Indeed, since national security concerns dictate that diplomacy and military planning must often be conducted in secret, pluralists recognize that the average citizen is going to be somewhat distant from the inside world of foreign policy making. This distance is increased by the technical nature of military strategy in the nuclear age and by the complex economic relationships that lie behind international trade and finance. Pluralists even accept the fact that an old-boy network of men from elite schools and wealthy families has dominated recruitment for the State Department, Central Intelligence Agency, and other key government and diplomatic posts. But pluralists deny that the insular and technical nature of international relations has allowed American foreign policy to be dictated solely by a tiny elite.

Foreign policy, according to the pluralist perspective, has been one of the most contentious arenas of American political life. The Constitution itself, which divides the responsibility for war and diplomacy between the president and Congress, provides a system of checks and balances that, in the pluralist view, has prevented the president from totally dominating foreign policy. Major issues—war and peace, trade, U.S. involvement in Latin America—have sparked heated debate among America's political leaders as well as among the general public. Consider the lessons of history. War hawks in Congress, for example, dragged a reluctant President Madison into war against Britain in 1812. More than a century later, isolationist sentiments in Congress prevented the United States from entering World War II, contrary to the wishes of President Roosevelt, until the Japanese bombed Pearl Harbor in 1941. While in the past most citizens were not often directly affected by the outside world (or particularly well informed about it), an aroused public could balance the influence of a small elite over the formulation of U.S. foreign policy. Public fear of "another Vietnam," for instance, thwarted the Reagan administration's designs for a major military buildup in Central America.

The growing political and economic interdependence of the world's nations, in the pluralist view, has made it even more difficult for a small elite to dominate U.S. foreign policy. In recent years numerous interest groups have sprung up to influence government policy on trade, military security, human rights, and a wealth of other issues (as we shall see in chap. 10). A military-industrial elite may attempt

★ The harsh experience of the Vietnam war still elicits strong public reactions whenever the administration considers a major military buildup.

to push development of a Star Wars antimissile system, for example, but a scientific or economic counter-elite will soon move to block what it sees as an excessively costly and dangerous program. With more information about international affairs available, citizen groups will soon join the battle. In recent years many international issues, including the Vietnam war, arms control, Central America, and trade policy, have involved both the foreign policy establishment and the general public in protracted political debate and conflict.

Pluralists see interdependence and globalization as limiting elite domination in another important way. The sheer volume and scope of the United States' involvement with the rest of the world makes implementation of policy quite difficult. A policy favored by one sector of the American elite, therefore, can be circumvented, sometimes with surprising ease, by a countervailing elite. A good example of inter-elite conflict is seen in the international economic policies of President Carter during the late 1970s.

The Carter administration considered a stable dollar the key to low inflation and a healthy economy at home. The U.S. dollar and many other national currencies were fluctuating wildly on international markets during the 1970s as a result of rising oil prices and a host of other economic and political factors (international economics is discussed in chap. 18). Accordingly, President Carter ordered the Treasury Department to take steps to stabilize the value of the dollar. Although Carter's policy made good sense to many economists and business leaders, other members of the foreign policy establishment disagreed. The disagreement, especially among the nation's banking and financial elite, was partly philosophical and partly practical. The bottom line, for many banks, was that they could make millions of dollars overnight by buying and selling different currencies in the world's financial centers—New York, Tokyo, London, Zurich, Hong Kong. Citibank of New York, for example, recorded a 700 percent increase in profits from foreign currency deals between 1977 and 1978. So the U.S. government pursued one economic policy while America's banks pursued another. "If a foreign exchange trader gets patriotic," declared one banker, "he's an idiot."[29] From the pluralist perspective, then, the banks' currency deals revealed a U.S. economy that was hardly dominated by a single-minded elite. The banks' actions, of course, also show one of the ways in which international interdependence can influence American life.

Pluralists admit nonetheless that government secrecy and other factors make foreign policy an area somewhat more vulnerable to elite domination. In the area of military technology, for example, public debate may often be limited by a lack of information, or even by deliberate government misinformation. In foreign affairs the public's role, according to the pluralists, thus may be more reactive than proactive. In the long run, nonetheless, countervailing elites and an aroused public can have an impact on policy.

★ Political Implications of Pluralist Theory

We may conclude that those who accept the pluralist interpretation of the American political system tend to be considerably more optimistic about the opportunities for effective citizen action than those who adopt the ruling elite view. According to the pluralist interpretation, the political system in the United States offers many ways for persons with motivation and skill to gain access to positions of power and help mold public policy. Women and minorities can organize to pressure the political system. Their numbers can often substitute for their lack of financial resources. Because power does not depend exclusively on wealth and social position, a variety of groups and individuals can play major roles in the policy-making process. Under existing conditions, no single power elite can continually restrict access to positions of power. The system is too decentralized and complex to permit any cohesive group to act out a comprehensive design. Rather, many different groups exercise power in separate policy spheres. These groups not only tend to balance one another but are kept in check by a variety of social and political forces.

This is not necessarily to say that political access is wide open under the pluralist interpretation. Obviously, social prejudices—not to mention the ever-present obstacles facing the poor—continue to prevent many groups from achieving their political goals. The main difference between the pluralist and ruling elite views is that pluralists regard the system as considerably more flexible and capable of responding to internal pressures for needed social and political reforms.

★ Evaluation: The Two Theories

Reviewing the differences between the ruling elite and pluralist theories, one gets the distinct impression that advocates of the two theories do not really speak the same language. Although both groups refer to hierarchy in American society, they disagree about the nature of that hierarchy and about the way it affects the chances of ordinary citizens to influence the political process. Although they occasionally depend on the same data and statistics (as when they evaluate various groups' degree of access to elite positions), they arrive at entirely different conclusions. Part of the reason for this difference is that the two groups employ different research methodologies. That is, ruling elite theorists say that power flows from position and background, while pluralists emphasize that power has to be demonstrated in actual decisions. These differences in methodology result in endless debates on many complex issues, ranging from definitions of power to the value and meaning of such vague concepts as **nondecisions.**[30] Nondecisions are matters that never make it onto the formal political agenda. Elite theorists point out that such matters often say more about who has power than do formal government decisions.

It is clear, too, that each theory represents an overview of the entire political system in the United States. Each is essentially an abstract model that attempts to diagram and explain the distribution of political power. Indeed, most texts on American government tend to view political institutions and behavior from the vantage point of one of these two overarching theories. Specific conclusions reached by pluralist and elitist analysts will be provided throughout this text.

Actually, both theories are persuasive in some respects, particularly at the community level, where the amounts of pluralism and ruling elitism seem to vary considerably from one city to another.[31] Also, one can accept one proposition of a theory without necessarily accepting all its other propositions. Even if one adopts the pluralist view that separate elites dominate in different policy areas, for instance, one need not agree that these elites are restrained by competition among themselves or that they are responsive to the wishes of the community.[32]

Advocates of the two theories even agree on some points, such as the inequality of influence. Though they disagree about the true potentials for citizen action, both groups acknowledge that the ideal of American democracy, in which most citizens wield equal influence over policy making, hardly prevails. Not only are there elites who exert considerably greater influence on government than most people do, but it is also true that many citizens become only minimally involved in political life. Many people remain pessimistic about their chances to affect the political process and do not especially care whether the society is governed by a single cohesive elite or a plurality of elites.

★ A Third Theory: The Politics of Bureaucracy

> The functionaries of every government have propensities to command at will the liberty and property of their constituents.
>
> —*Thomas Jefferson*

A third, and increasingly popular, theory of power in America holds that ultimately *no one* is in charge. It states that the political system in the United States has become so enveloped in the tentacles of bureaucracy, so divided by a system of internal checks and balances, and so beset by a growing complexity of national and international problems and proposed solutions that effective control over policy making by any group has become virtually impossible. The powerlessness many people feel results neither from the concentration of power in the hands of a few remote elites nor from the dispersal of power among a large number of competing groups and institutions. It results rather from the fact that no one ultimately has responsibility for policy. The system is running by itself, out of control; no group is capable of controlling it.

Some of us probably have suspected as much for quite some time. There is something compelling about this theory, especially in light of the growing use of computers that tolerate no backtalk, the pervasive reliance of government and industry on those long, forgettable numbers marking our credit cards, bank accounts,

★ The spread of computer networks and data banks is closely associated with the increasing bureaucratization of our society.

and driver's licenses, and the proliferation of faceless bureaucrats who refuse to budge from "the policy of this office."

Although this theory embraces a variety of concepts and concerns, it is ultimately a response to the seemingly pervasive bureaucratization of American society. In government, especially, bureaucracy seems to be everywhere, creating and enforcing rules affecting virtually all aspects of our lives. To those who accept this theory, the most alarming aspect of this sprawling bureaucracy is the power it exerts over the individual. And at no time, they say, is this power more evident than when federal agencies are engaged in the secret surveillance of people's private lives. The spread of government investigators, computer networks, and data banks has made each citizen subject to the prying eyes of countless civil servants. It has been estimated that at least ten separate dossiers exist in government files on the average American, detailing his or her medical history, financial status, educational achievements, and political activities. Occasionally the existence of such surveillance is revealed in newspaper headlines, as when it was disclosed during the 1970s that the Postal Service had been turning over citizens' letters to the Central Intelligence Agency and that the Federal Bureau of Investigation had been collecting information on the drinking and sexual habits of U.S. presidents, members of Congress, and other high-ranking officials. Former attorney general Edward Levi testified before a House subcommittee that 883 entries on senators and 722 on House members existed among the FBI's general files on 6.5 million Americans.[33]

The question is: Who is to be held responsible for such acts? Officials who carry out the surveillance claim merely to be obeying orders of superiors, who in turn claim to be following instructions from above. In many instances—especially when publicity does not accompany a bureaucratic policy—the maze of specialized departments and the devotion to secrecy make it virtually impossible for an outsider to trace the source of a decision. Although responsibility can always be placed on the president's desk, it is unlikely that any chief executive could maintain control over all bureaucratic decisions. Presidents often experience the same frustrations as the rest of us in dealing with bureaucratic obstinacy and red tape. Meanwhile, those responsible remain hidden in the impenetrable jungle of federal office buildings and executive suites.

Thus, in view of the seemingly ubiquitous presence of bureaucracy in the lives of Americans at all levels of the political system, the alternative theory that ultimately no one can maintain effective control over policy making offers few promises for effective citizen participation. Indeed, the implications of this theory may be even more pessimistic than those of the other two theories we have considered. If no one is in charge—if no one is in control—then no group can be singled out as the target for reform. Those of us who are intent upon influencing the political process will have to wander through a maze of agencies and bureaus simply to try to locate the pressure points. And for each policy decision we wish to affect, we will have to seek an entirely different and obscure locus of power. (More will be said about the bureaucracy in chap. 14.)

★ Summary

The question "Who governs?" sparks one of the liveliest debates in American politics. Although America takes pride in its democratic heritage and institutions, there is strong evidence that a small number of wealthy men in government and business enjoy tremendous influence. The ruling elite theory holds that the distribution of political power in America is shaped like a pyramid, with a small but cohesive power elite at the top. The elite's influence stems from its economic resources, shared values, and access to the key institutions of government and society. The existence of a power elite is undemocratic because the general public does not enjoy the same access and the elite is not accountable. Growing global interdependence, moreover, has expanded the influence of elites around the world.

Despite widespread support for the ruling elite theory, many political scientists do not accept its basic tenets. While acknowledging the existence of a power elite, they see American politics as a vast arena of competing groups. The pluralist theory recognizes that power has many sources in addition to the wealth and contacts of the elite. Workers, minority groups, and special interests can mobilize their resources to have a say in the formation of public policy. Furthermore, the power elite, according to the pluralist theory, is hardly cohesive. The globalization of American politics, rather than expanding elite influence, has produced a wide-ranging debate on foreign policy and led to the creation of many new interest groups.

An answer to the question "Who governs?" does not come easily. Both the ruling elite and the pluralist theories are persuasive in some respects. Foreign policy making is strongly influenced by a small elite who enjoy direct access to the president and the executive branch of government. At the community level, on the other hand, policy is often made by a vast array of competing groups and interests. Other observers argue that to cast the debate only in terms of elitism and pluralism is to exclude the most pervasive political influence in the United States. According to this view, America has become enveloped in a web of bureaucracy, with competition between branches of government making effective control over policy making by an elite or by special-interest groups impossible. As local and international issues continue to politicize American life, it seems certain that the debate over "who governs" is likely to continue among both scholars and the American public.

★ Key Terms

authority
coalitions
Council on Foreign Relations
elite
influence
institutional power
mass society
military-industrial complex
nondecisions
pluralist theory
power
power elite
ruling elite theory
Trilateral Commission
veto groups

★ Notes

1. For an excellent discussion of power and its alternatives, see Peter Bachrach and Morton S. Baratz, "Decisions and Nondecisions: An Analytical Framework," *American Political Science Review,* September 1963, pp. 632–642.
2. See, for example, C. Wright Mills, *The Power Elite* (New York: Oxford University Press/Galaxy, 1959); Floyd Hunter, *Community Power Structure* (Chapel Hill: University of North Carolina Press, 1953); G. William Domhoff, *Who Rules America?* (Englewood Cliffs, N.J.: Prentice-Hall, 1967); Thomas R. Dye and L. Harmon Zeigler, *The Irony of Democracy,* 7th ed. (Pacific Grove, Calif.: Brooks/Cole, 1987).
3. Robert Dahl, "A Critique of the Ruling Elite Model," *American Political Science Review,* June 1958, pp. 463–469.
4. Mills, *Power Elite,* p. 324.
5. U.S. Congress, Senate, *Congressional Record,* 91st Cong., 2d sess., March 24, 1969.
6. U.S. Bureau of the Census, *Statistical Abstract of the United States, 1986* (Washington, D.C.: U.S. Government Printing Office, 1985), p. 316.
7. David M. Ricci, *Community Power and Democratic Theory* (New York: Random House, 1971), pp. 168–169.
8. *Statistical Abstract, 1988,* p. 513.
9. *Time,* January 21, 1974, p. 71.
10. Domhoff, *Who Rules America?,* p. 4.
11. Joseph A. Kahl, *The American Class Structure* (New York: Holt, Rinehart & Winston, 1965), p. 272.
12. Mills, *Power Elite,* p. 348.
13. Ibid., p. 361.
14. Dye and Zeigler, *Irony of Democracy.*
15. Charles W. Kegley, Jr., and Eugene R. Wittkopf, *American Foreign Policy: Pattern and Process,* 3d ed. (New York: St. Martin's Press, 1987), p. 264. For a further discussion, see G. William Domhoff, *Who Rules America Now?: A View for the '80s* (Englewood Cliffs, N.J.: Prentice-Hall, 1983).
16. See, for example, ibid., p. 140.
17. Kegley and Wittkopf, *American Foreign Policy,* p. 265.
18. Ibid., pp. 268–269.
19. See Steven Rosen, ed., *Testing the Theory of the Military-Industrial Complex* (Lexington, Mass.: Lexington Books, 1973).
20. See Gabriel Kolko, *The Roots of American Foreign Policy.* (Boston: Beacon Press, 1969); Alan Wolfe, The Rise and Fall of the "Soviet Threat": Domestic Sources of the Cold War Consensus. (Washington, D.C.: Institute for Policy Studies, 1979).
21. See, for example, Robert A. Dahl, *Who Governs? Democracy and Power in an American City* (New Haven, Conn.: Yale University Press, 1961); Nelson Polsby, *Community Power and Political Theory* (New Haven, Conn.: Yale University Press, 1963); Arnold Rose, *The Power Structure* (New York: Oxford University Press, 1967).
22. Carl Friedrich, *Man and His Government* (New York: McGraw-Hill, 1963), p. 326.
23. See Dahl, "Critique of the Ruling Elite Model."
24. Dahl, *Who Governs?* p. 183.
25. Ibid., p. 325.
26. "The Big Business Executive, 1964," *Scientific American,* lithographed report, 1965.
27. Dahl, *Who Governs?* p. 101.
28. See Robert W. Jackman, "Political Elites, Mass Publics, and Support for Democratic Principles," *Journal of Politics,* August 1972, pp. 753–773.

29. Michael Moffitt, *The World's Money: International Banking from Bretton Woods to the Brink of Insolvency* (New York: Simon & Schuster, 1983), pp. 146, 148.
30. See Bachrach and Baratz, "Decisions and Nondecisions"; Raymond E. Wolfinger, "Nondecisions and the Study of Local Politics," followed by comments, *American Political Science Review,* December 1971, pp. 1063–1104; Geoffrey Debnam, "Nondecisions and Power: The Two Faces of Bachrach and Baratz," followed by comments, *American Political Science Review,* September 1975, pp. 889–907.
31. See, for example, Robert Presthus, *Men at the Top: A Study in Community Power* (New York: Oxford University Press, 1964).
32. See, for example, Wallace S. Sayre and Herbert Kaufman, *Governing New York City* (New York: Norton, 1965).
33. *Newsweek,* March 10, 1975, p. 16.

★ For Further Reading

Dahl, Robert A. *Who Governs? Democracy and Power in an American City.* New Haven, Conn.: Yale University Press, 1961.

Domhoff, G. William. *Who Rules America Now?: A View for the '80s.* Englewood Cliffs, N.J.: Prentice-Hall, 1983.

Dye, Thomas R. *Who's Running America?: The Conservative Years.* 4th ed. Englewood Cliffs, N.J.: Prentice-Hall, 1986.

Mills, C. Wright. *The Power Elite.* New York: Oxford University Press, 1956.

Polsby, Nelson. *Community Power and Political Theory.* 2d ed. New Haven, Conn.: Yale University Press, 1980.

Prewitt, Kenneth, and Alan Stone. *The Ruling Elites.* New York: Harper & Row, 1973.

Ricci, David. *Community Power and Democratic Theory.* New York: Random House, 1971.

O, yes,
I say it plain,
America never was America to me,
And I swear this oath—
America will be!
An ever-living seed,
Its dream
Lies deep in the heart of me.

—Langston Hughes,
"Let America Be America Again"

CHAPTER SIX

NATIONAL CHARACTER

★★★★★★★★★★★★

The American Personality: Freedom, Equality, and Achievement

Can a nation, especially one as diverse as the United States, be said to have a personality? The purpose of this chapter is to entertain such a possibility. Although Americans have come from Africa, Europe, Asia, and South America, they seem different from Africans, Europeans, Asians, and South Americans; despite the proliferation of ethnic, religious, and cultural groups in the United States, there appears to be a national personality—a personality strong enough to influence the behavior and policies of our political system.

Like an individual's personality, a national personality can affect behavior in subtle and important ways. In terms of politics, the national personality may predispose a country to favor one political choice over another. Ancient Sparta, for instance, was known for its militant and confrontational disposition, and given a choice between battle and negotiation, the Spartans tended to favor war.

The term often used to describe a nation's "personality" is **national character**—a term somewhat inclined, unfortunately, to vagueness and generalization. It is hard enough to describe one person's character, let alone the character of 250 million individuals. And the task is made even more challenging by the fact that national character, like an individual's character, is a complicated combination of the ideal and the real. If people and nations value honesty but sometimes stoop to lies, it would be a mistake to omit either inclination from a discussion of their character.

So let us start with a working definition of the term "national character." Generally speaking, it refers to the ideals shared among citizens of a nation, along with the often imperfect application of those ideals in the real world. The achievement of these ideals tends to be exaggerated, especially by leaders, while the imperfections are often ignored.

Obviously, the extent to which individual citizens reflect their national character varies enormously. Many Americans are recent immigrants and thus carry the culture of their national origin. Other Americans are highly influenced by their subculture, be it ethnic, economic, or social. This chapter examines the possibility that despite the differences, most Americans do partake in a general national character, which is facilitated by a dominant history and a dominant language, and which has an effect on the political system.

This chapter begins with a discussion of American ideals and their origins. Then it considers why American ideals have not always been realized, and why some Americans have been prevented from pursuing them. The chapter concludes with a discussion of potential changes in the American national character in the

National Character: A Controversial Subject

Perhaps the most formidable opposition to the idea of a national character comes from those who believe that the entire concept is faulty. The famous communist philosopher Karl Marx argued that there are just too many economic distinctions between groups of people in a country to allow the formation of any true or important national traits.

But consider this: for many years investigators have been asking people in a variety of countries to comment on their political attitudes. In many of these countries the investigators run into problems; often the respondents are reluctant to voice their opinions. Some are fearful that they might say something at odds with the beliefs of the ruling regime, while others feel genuinely unworthy of political opinions. The citizens of many countries feel that only those who rule can handle political decisions; those who don't rule feel incapable of understanding important and complex political issues.

Americans, on the other hand, whether they know much about a political issue or not, are usually quite willing to express an opinion. It doesn't matter whether they are rich or poor, highly educated or high school dropouts, they will probably have something to say. Such controversial issues as welfare, abortion, and mass transit are bound to get Americans talking. In contrast to citizens of many other countries, Americans have little trouble projecting themselves into positions of political power, and they do not hesitate to express their political opinions to others. ★

SOURCE: Gabriel A. Almond and Sidney Verba, *The Civic Culture: Political Attitudes and Democracy in Five Nations* (Boston: Little, Brown, 1965).

1990s and beyond, focusing on international influences. The discussions are designed to provide some broad cultural and historical reasons why American politics has evolved into its present state. Our hope is to capture the national political mood to which we refer in later chapters.

★ Langston Hughes (1902–1967), one of America's premier poets, provided the inspiration for this chapter. In his poem "Let America Be America Again," Hughes celebrated American ideals but was painfully aware that American reality often fell far short.

★ Three Ideals: Freedom, Equality, and Achievement

Three ideals stand out as particularly important aspects of the American national character: **freedom, equality,** and **achievement.** The members of Hell's Angels, for example, fight motorcycle helmet laws with the rhetoric of freedom; they argue that they should be free to crush their own skulls if they wish. Likewise, a concern for equality is spread across the "employment opportunity" section of our daily newspaper. Firms declare that they are "equal opportunity employers," ratifying the American ideal that everyone deserves an equal shot at a job regardless of age, sex, or race. And we are encouraged to "be all that you can be" by an Armed Forces ad that promises an opportunity for unlimited achievement.

Of course, these values are not uniquely American. Obviously, a country as new as the United States, and home to so many immigrants, cannot avoid sharing traits with other nations. On the other hand, the United States has never had a king or queen, never suffered a devastating famine or plague, and never fought a world war on its own soil; consequently, we may be justified in believing that these and other distinctively American phenomena have created a climate in which the three values have come to mean something different to Americans than to citizens of other nations.

The Foundation of National Character: Nature or Nurture?

In the field of human psychology, a debate has long raged over the way human personality is formed. The debate centers on the relative importance of inherited, genetic traits and learned traits—"nature versus nurture." This debate may be extended, after some alteration of the terms, to the formation of national character.

Some explanations focus on nonhuman factors, such as geography, climate, and natural resources, in the development of national character. The Russian winter, for example, often enters into discussions of the Soviet outlook on world affairs, and as we shall see, the American frontier has been discussed as equally important in the development of American attitudes. This type of explanation, akin to the "nature" position on the formation of human personality, may be called the **environmental explanation.**

Social explanations of national character emphasize distinctly human contributions, such as political philosophies and events, religious beliefs, and other factors of human causation. This perspective, of course, parallels the "nurture" position on human personality. If some people argue that the Soviets' preoccupation with security is an outgrowth of their bitter climate (a harsh world from which protection is always a paramount concern), just as many say that the Russians' history of strong, paternalistic leaders and many invasions of their homeland is a better explanation of a concern for national security.

★ Frederick Jackson Turner and the Environmental Explanation of National Character

The environmental argument in regard to the American national character was best put forward by the historian Frederick Jackson Turner. Turner argued that the success of the American experiment was due not to the intellectual greatness of its

★ Frederick Jackson Turner (1861–1932) was concerned that the settlement of the Western frontier would deprive the American character of its most valuable attributes.

founders but to the vastness and richness of the continent. The values of freedom, equality, and achievement could not have survived and prospered unless the physical environment had supported those values. In other words, it was the physical environment of the North American continent that allowed those values to prevail.

Freedom and the Frontier

As president of the American Historical Association in 1900, Turner was asked to address his fellow members on what the new century might hold in store for the United States. Turner's response was not hopeful, for he believed that the settlement of the frontier posed a serious threat to the personality of the American citizenry. Most threatened was the American infatuation with freedom.

Turner believed that freedom and open space were closely intertwined, and that the settlement of the frontier would induce a national sense of claustrophobia. For Turner, the American sense of freedom depended on the wilderness, which was accessible to anyone who found civilization too constricting. It did not matter that most people remained in developed communities; what was important was that they felt they *could* move on if they chose. As Turner put it: "Who would rest content under oppressive legislative conditions when with a slight effort he might reach a land wherein to become a co-worker in the building of free cities and free states on the lines of his own ideal?"[1]

During colonial times America presented a sharp contrast to Europe. Whereas the American continent provided vast, untapped wilderness at every turn, the European nations had long since developed their outlands. Britain, for instance, had fully implemented a system of "enclosure" (even the term inspires a feeling of being trapped), which pushed the peasantry off lands previously in the public domain. Rural settlements were replaced by herds of sheep, which grazed on large tracts of land and needed little in the way of human labor. The result was a great human displacement and migration to the ever-growing cities. In 1700, London had barely 500,000 residents, Edinburgh 35,000; of the other cities only Bristol and

Norwich had more than 20,000 inhabitants. Only 13 percent of the population lived in cities. Between 1700 and 1800, however, the percentage of city dwellers in England doubled. Such towns as Manchester and Glasgow, stimulated by the woolen industry, grew threefold.

The American colonies provided a much freer environment. The space and mobility available to European settlers inspired a sense of liberation from the more constricting confines of their origins. They came from crowded cities to a country whose rural population greatly outnumbered its urban population. For Turner, this distinction was crucial to the development of the American sense of freedom, and reinforced his concern about the occupation of the continent's open spaces.

There is little doubt that Americans have continued to connect freedom with open space. Getting away from familiar and cramped surroundings is a common American fantasy. The Gateway National Recreation Area in New York, the Golden Gate National Recreation Area of San Francisco, and the Indiana Dunes and Cuyahoga parks of urban Ohio occupy prime real estate and provide costly evidence that Americans put a high premium on easy access to open space. And, of course, these urban parks are complemented by millions of acres of more distant wilderness areas. The naturalist John Muir, not wanting to underestimate the importance of wilderness parks, likened them to a national spiritual home:

> Thousands of nerve-shaken, overcivilized people are beginning to find out that going to the mountains is going home; that wilderness is a necessity; and that mountain parks and reservations are useful not only as fountains of timber and irrigating rivers, but as fountains of life.[2]

But national parks have not been the only response to Turner's concern about the loss of the frontier. In fact, the taming of the wilderness may have been only a temporary setback to Americans' love affair with open spaces. Indeed, it was no accident that in 1960 John F. Kennedy campaigned on the promise to open a "new frontier." Kennedy was convinced that the possibilities of exploration had not ended with the winning of the West; although one frontier may have been tamed, many more frontiers remained to be explored and conquered. Outer space was merely the most obvious of these possibilities. In any case, Turner's pessimism may not have been warranted; freedom may still be environmentally encouraged even for a nation whose wilderness has been settled.

Environment and Equality

Turner's environmental explanation for our national character can also help account for the American interest in equality. During the phase of European settlement, the United States was what modern economists call an undeveloped area. When newly arrived Europeans set out to build communities and businesses to their imported specifications, they had to start from scratch. Their difficulties were compounded by the fact that they brought little more than their experience to the new continent. Most new immigrants were not wealthy, and few had even a slight financial head start in their efforts to develop the unsettled areas.

Thus, according to the environmental argument, Americans started to value equality because the environment forced them to do so. In the face of a vast wilderness, all immigrants started on a very primitive and equal footing. Turner explained:

> The frontier is the line of most rapid and effective Americanization. The wilderness masters the colonist. It finds him a European in dress, industries, tools, modes of travel, and thought. It takes him from the railroad car and puts him in the birch canoe. It strips off the garments of civilization and arrays him in the hunting shirt and the moccasin.[3]

Thus an English aristocrat's gentility would be of little use in clearing a virgin acre of land for a grain crop. Nor would a London street urchin's coarseness prevent him from clearing the plot just as well as the aristocrat. The primitive conditions of the new colony acted as a leveler, and the legitimacy of factors that gave one European precedence over another was seriously questioned in an environment where those factors made little sense.

Indeed, the rough, undeveloped American environment has often been associated with an indifference to stuffy aristocracy. Such heroes as Andrew Jackson and Daniel Boone sought to rid American politics of creeping gentility. As politicians, both exploited their backgrounds as "country folk," successfully tapping the American tendency to trust simplicity and common sense. City slickers might think that their exaggerated manners gave them some right to rule, but people like Boone and Jackson helped to deflate their pretensions and demonstrate the simple competence of ordinary Americans.

★ Colonel Daniel Boone (1734–1820) impressed many Americans with his simple, rugged lifestyle. Upon first meeting Boone, naturalist J. J. Audubon was taken by Boone's disdain for modern amenities: "On retiring to the room appropriated to that remarkable individual and myself for the night . . . he merely took off his hunting-shirt, and arranged a few folds of blankets on the floor, choosing rather to lie there, as he observed, than on the softest bed." So impressed was Audubon with Boone's primitive behavior that he developed the "impression that whatever he uttered could not be otherwise than strictly true."
[FROM: Cecil B. Hartley, *The Life and Times of Colonel Daniel Boone* (New York: Derby and Jackson, 1860), pp. 310–311.]

★ Women's rights were achieved sooner in the West than in the East. Scholars have argued that because of their participation in traditionally "male" roles, frontier women were in a better position to demand equal treatment.

That the frontier contributed to the American appreciation of equality is no better demonstrated than in the experiences of pioneer women. Upon examining diaries of pioneers on the Kansas prairie, Joanna L. Stratton concluded that, "faced with a chronic shortage of labor on the frontier, the working family needed all the help it could muster. When the strength of the frontiersman and his sons proved inadequate, the mother and the daughters assisted with the traditionally male tasks of planting and harvesting, tending livestock, hauling water, gathering fuel, and even hunting."[4] Many western territories and states gave women political and economic rights before they were granted in the more "civilized" East and South. In the 1870s, for example, women in Wyoming could vote, control their own property, and serve as jurors.[5] In Wyoming and other western states, the frontier proved to be a force for greater equality between the sexes.

Environment and Achievement

> The Western wilds, from the Alleghenies to the Pacific, constituted the richest free gift that was ever spread out before civilized man.
>
> —*Frederick Jackson Turner*

More than any other environmental factor, the sheer abundance of riches on the North American continent has aroused people's interest. Virtually every European visitor who made a written record of his or her American experience has commented on the embarrassment of resources available to the American settlers, and each new generation has looked back fondly to a past of fruited plains and amber waves of grain. Hunger and disease may have occurred intermittently in American history, but the mainstream belief is that the environment was uncommonly receptive to settlement and exploitation.

It is no surprise, then, that many scholars have argued that this original experience with abundance helped mold the American national character. One student

★ Horatio Alger, famous for his rags-to-riches tales, wrote that hard work and perseverance are always rewarded handsomely.

of Turner's, the historian David M. Potter, focused on the connection between the continent's untapped abundance and the American intoxication with achievement, thus offering a third environmental explanation for the American national character.

Potter pointed to two factors that he believed fostered this country's achievement orientation. First, the new continent was primitive by European standards; if the settlers wanted to copy the amenities of their former homes, they had much work to do. Communities had to be *achieved*, not inherited. But even more important was the extent to which efforts to achieve were rewarded. Hard work was often rewarded richly; harsher environments would not have been so generous.[6]

This combination of bounty and effort is seen clearly in the case of John Pratt of seventeenth-century New England. Upon arriving in the colonies, Pratt wrote back to England that "here was nothing but rocks and sands, and salt marshes, etc." Later he was compelled to draft a retraction, which included references to the more hidden wealth of the environment: "And as for the barrenness of the sandy grounds, I spoke of them as then I conceived, but now I find that such ground as before I accounted barren, yet being manured and husbanded, doth bring forth more fruit than I did expect."[7] Thus, while the environment may not have caused the achievement orientation, the abundance in America did provide a prime breeding ground for it. Achievement came to be valued, according to the environmental perspective, because the environment was receptive to achievement.

American folklore has consistently reinforced the idea that the environment favors hard workers and "pays off" those who are energetic, even during times when reality has not quite matched the ideal. During the hard economic times of the late nineteenth century, the inspiration to achieve was provided by an author whose name has become synonymous with rags-to-riches stories. Horatio Alger (1832–1899) wrote more than one hundred novels about young waifs who climbed from the depths of poverty to positions of industrial greatness. In one such book,

The Errand Boy, ambitious young Phil accidentally meets the president of a large railroad. Informed of the errand boy's aspirations, the industrialist booms: ". . . but I had a hard struggle before I reached that position." Phil responds confidently, "I am not afraid to work, sir."[8] And, of course, Phil worked and prospered. By promoting the environment's susceptibility to hard work, Alger reinforced the belief that "only in America" could a person with so little achieve so much.

When Franklin Roosevelt was asked what book he would have placed in the hands of each Russian citizen, Roosevelt suggested the Sears, Roebuck catalogue. For Roosevelt, the material bounty available to American consumers was the most compelling aspect of the American system.[9] Even today, Americans continue to believe that their environment yields rewards for those who seek them, buoyed by the continuing ability of the American system to fill catalogues with attractive and accessible goods. In a national survey conducted in 1987, participants were asked whether hard work, luck, or help from other people leads to success. Of the 1,500 people polled, 64 percent said that hard work was the most important factor in success, while 24 percent said that success was a combination of work and luck. Only 12 percent excluded hard work from the factors necessary to get ahead.[10] It seems as if, from the nation's founding to the present time, the resources of the American continent have blessed its inhabitants with success. And for Potter and Turner, it is no wonder that Americans have come to place so much value on achievement.

★ The Social Explanation of National Character

It has become clear to most psychologists that both nature and nurture are involved in the formation of human personality. Similarly, there are compelling arguments to support the proposition that national character owes as much to human factors as to environmental ones. Is it really fair, for instance, to imply that the Sears catalogue owes its bounty to the physical characteristics of the North American continent? Must we not also discuss the human energy that took advantage of the natural wealth? Let us consider, then, some of the human, social forces that have helped shape the American character.

Don't Tread on Me: Freedom from British Domination

As we have seen, the environmental explanation for Americans' reverence for freedom focuses on the vastness of the unsettled continent. The social explanation focuses on the experiences of early Americans under the thumb of British rule, and the resultant pledge that Americans would never again experience the political and economic exploitation they suffered before the Revolution.

The North American colonies were settled during a time of great political strain in England. Many British subjects were becoming increasingly dissatisfied with the monarchy and were setting out on the bumpy road toward a government more representative of their interests. By 1640, Charles I had recognized the need for consultation with Parliament on important and expensive public policies; and from 1649 to 1658, England had no monarch. British subjects everywhere, even in America, began to think about an expanded role for ordinary citizens in the governing of their affairs. Even though the monarchy returned after the rule of Cromwell, no later king or queen could easily disregard the will of Parliament.

These new ideas on responsible government and freedom from arbitrary decree took hold in America. In fact, the colonies were a haven for radicals who were impatient with the sluggish pace of change in the mother country. Unfortunately, this parliamentary fervor ran headlong into a second British political development: the colonial mentality. Rather than consider America as a parallel community made up of citizens of the realm, the British elite believed that America and its colonists should serve the political and economic needs of the mother country, regardless of hardships.

The so-called Navigation Acts of 1660 and 1663 were among the most blatant examples of this British colonial mentality. These acts established a virtual English monopoly on shipping between the American colonies and Europe. Foreign ships were denied access to New England harbors, and American goods, with few exceptions, could only go to England. In addition, Americans were forced to import all their foreign goods through English ports and were subject to taxation. The message to the colonists was clear: the political and economic interests of England were supreme.

It is no wonder, then, that the American battle cry was "No taxation without representation!" This simple phrase expressed the growing collision between the American desire for more responsive government and the British desire to exploit the colonies. The conflict could not be resolved short of a violent revolution; and the sacrifice of lives and property made it even more essential to the builders of the new republic that their government would allow more personal freedom than any that had come before it. Americans wanted to be free from taxes imposed to pay for a war with France in which they had no part. They were not eager to house British troops in their inns, taverns, and barns, as required by the Quartering Act of 1765. And they wanted to be free of British attempts (the "Intolerable Acts" of 1774) to punish and intimidate the colonists who objected to the British presence.

When the First Continental Congress convened in Philadelphia in September 1774, the delegates expressed their desire for a representative and limited government, under which the colonists would enjoy greater latitude to pursue their own interests. In their "Declaration and Resolves," the Congress asserted that as

> the English colonists are not represented, and from their local and other circumstances, cannot properly be represented in the British parliament, they are entitled to a free and exclusive power of legislation in their several provincial legislatures, where their right of representation can alone be preserved in all cases of taxation and internal polity.[11]

Thus, while the vast spaces of the frontier may have inspired American freedom, it would be difficult to ignore the role of these more human, social factors.

Equality and Liberalism

The American concern for equality also has roots in a political philosophy known as **liberalism**. Planted by the famous political philosopher Thomas Hobbes (1588–1679), the seeds of liberal thought blossomed in the works of John Locke (1632–1704) in Britain and in those of Baron de Montesquieu (1689–1755) in France. The writings of both these men were very influential among the founders

★ In 1668, John Locke endeared himself to his patron for life. The Earl of Shaftesbury was afflicted with a suppurating cyst on the liver. Locke, who was a physician, performed an operation in which it is believed he inserted a metal tube from which the "corrupt humours" could drain. The tube probably was of little use, and it was a miracle that the earl did not die from infection. He fully recovered, however, and continued to support Locke in his philosophical projects.

of the United States. James Madison admitted that when he considered the structure of the new American system of government, he "always consulted and cited [Montesquieu] on the subject."[12] And it is not difficult to pluck passages from the Declaration of Independence that are almost identical to passages in Locke's *Second Treatise*.[13]

Advocates of liberalism rejected the idea known as the "divine right of kings," which held that the king and his heirs were destined by God to rule, and that they had special talents to do so. Rejecting the divinity of the monarchy, the liberals believed that everyone had the capacity to contribute to the political destiny of the nation, and should do so if for no other reason than to keep monarchs who claimed divinity from gaining power. To combat the monarch who claimed superiority to the common people, liberals argued that people are basically equal; and they backed their case by discussing traits they believed to be common to everyone. Each person, according to the liberals, sought his or her own **self-interest** above the interests of others and had the intellectual, rational power to know how to pursue it. Self-interest and the ability of humans to *reason* formed the basis of the liberal defense of equality.

Self-Interest. Indeed, at the base of seventeenth- and eighteenth-century liberal thought was the idea of self-interest. According to liberal philosophers, the most important thing to each individual is his or her own preservation and the preservation of the immediate family. While liberal thinkers were aware of human charity, they did not see charity as so basic that the individual could always be trusted to exhibit it. To Locke, individuals could *always* be trusted to pursue their own interests,

> God having made Man, and planted in him, as in all other Animals, a strong desire of Self-preservation, and furnished the World with things fit for Food and Rayment and other Necessaries of Life, Subservient to his design, that Man should live and abide for some time upon the Face of the Earth.[14]

Locke and other liberal thinkers were careful, then, to justify their political philosophies with arguments of self-interest. The political institutions they advo-

★ It really stretches the term to call Thomas Hobbes a liberal, because he suggested that the general brutality and meanness of humankind could be squelched only by an all-powerful "sovereign." What allows us to place Hobbes near the liberal camp, however, is his belief that *everyone* has the *rational* ability to see his or her predicament and to do something about it.

cated were to be supported only because each individual realized that he or she would be better off under the new system. No other form of allegiance could be trusted.

The Common Capacity of Reason. Having established the primary importance of self-interest, the liberals went on to demonstrate that each individual was intellectually qualified to pursue it, without outside guidance or interference. Though Thomas Hobbes expressed many ideas that were far from liberal, he nevertheless argued effectively that cleverness could make the weak fully equal to the strong:

> Nature hath made men so equall, in the faculties of body, and mind; as that though there bee found one man sometimes manifestly stronger in body, or of quicker mind than another; yet when all is reckoned together, the difference between man, and man, is not so considerable, as that one man can thereupon claim to himselfe any benefit, to which another may not pretend, as well as he. For as for strength of body, the weakest has strength enough to kill the strongest, either by secret machination, or by confederacy with others, that are in the same danger with himselfe.[15]

In other words, even the most pitiful weakling has the intellectual ability to lure a bully to a spot where a rock may be strategically dislodged to fall on the bully's head. Hobbes goes on to say that individuals may differ in education or in manners, but when all such things are peeled away, not too much brilliance or strength separates one person from another.

American history abounds in instances of homespun simplicity and practicality overcoming intellectual posturing. Benjamin Franklin charmed the European aristocrats with his uncluttered insights, becoming famous not for any philosophical tracts but for collecting and inventing popular and simple guides to everyday behavior. President Harry S Truman spoke in simple and coarse language, and had little patience with advisers of professorial demeanor. And James Earl Carter, who spoke of the wisdom of his Sunday school teachers, insisted that he be inaugurated as "Jimmy." Popularity in American politics is gained not by stunning displays of mental superiority but by evidence of the uncluttered wisdom of the "common people."

Liberalism and Equality. In many respects, the concepts of liberalism and equality are intertwined. When one believes that each individual is self-interested and has the capacity to pursue that self-interest, one can no longer justify a **paternal** relationship between politicians and citizens. Such a relationship—like that of parent to children, warden to prisoners, or dictator to subjects—presumes that the paternal figure knows better than the subordinates what is best for them. Liberalism shattered the legitimacy of the paternal relationship (as far as politics is concerned) and replaced it with an egalitarian one that puts politicians on short leashes—to be drawn in even closer if the public wills it. Perhaps the most powerful statement of liberalism and rejection of paternalism is contained in the Declaration of Independence:

> We hold these truths to be self-evident, that all men are created equal, that they are endowed by their Creator with certain unalienable Rights, that among these, are Life, Liberty, and the pursuit of Happiness. That, to secure these rights, Governments are instituted among Men, deriving their just Powers from the consent of the governed. That, whenever any form of Government becomes destructive of these ends, it is the Right of the People to alter or to abolish it.

Here, government is not the ultimate recourse of humble people seeking answers to questions of goodness and justice. Rather, government is limited to serving the rights of individual citizens, and if in their wisdom they decide they are not being well served, they can abolish the government. Only the citizens themselves, not paternalistic proxies, can represent their concerns.

Paternalism in America was not scrapped entirely by the Declaration of Independence, however. It was not until 1848, for example, that American women openly demanded the rights promised in the Declaration. The "Declaration of Sentiments" issued at the first American women's rights convention in Seneca Falls, New York, paraphrased the Declaration of Independence in applying it to women:

> When in the course of human events, it becomes necessary for *one portion of the family of man* to assume among the people of the earth a position different from that they have hitherto occupied . . .
>
> We hold these truths to be self-evident: that all men *and women* are created equal . . .
>
> The history of mankind is a history of repeated injuries and usurpations on the part of *man toward woman*, having in direct object the establishment of an absolute tyrrany *over her*. To prove this, let the facts be submitted to a candid world.[16]

The list of grievances that accompanied the "Declaration of Sentiments" was clear in its rejection of paternalistic practices directed at women: no franchise, no property rights, taxation without representation, limited education, and a moral double standard. Like the liberal sentiments expressed in the Declaration of Independence, the sentiments expressed at Seneca Falls portrayed women as best capable of deciding their own fate, rather than having their fate imposed upon them by men.

Religion and the Achievement Orientation

Perhaps the most important social contribution to the American value of achievement has been religion. (This and other contributions to the development of national

Values	Environmental explanation	Social explanation
Freedom	The "wide open spaces" of the frontier (Turner)	Opposition to British colonialism and support for representative government–culminating in the American Revolution
Equality	The undeveloped state of the new continent	Liberalism: Self-interest Common reasoning
Achievement	The richness of the new continent. Hard work required, but also richly rewarded	Religious factors: Puritanism (Winthrop) and the drive to display chosenness

★ **Figure 6-1**
Environmental and social factors that contributed to the development of American values

character are contrasted in figure 6-1.) With few exceptions, the early European settlers of the American continent were Christians of some denomination. In light of the Christian emphasis on heavenly rather than earthly matters, the linkage of American religious creeds with the American concern with achievement may at first seem unusual. Nevertheless, the term "Protestant work ethic" has crept into common usage and hints at the connection.

The Christian sects that contributed most to the achievement orientation were those that have come to be lumped together under the label "Puritan." **Puritanism** began as a reform movement within the Church of England during the late sixteenth and early seventeenth centuries. The movement sought a further distancing from what was seen as a moral decline in the Catholic church, caused by a concentration of power in the hands of the church hierarchy. In order to rid Christianity of this problem, John Calvin and other reformers preached a relationship with God that bypassed the pope and his hierarchy.

One of the strongest elements of puritanism, which did much to reduce the power of the church hierarchy, was Calvin's doctrine of predestination. Predestination is the idea that before birth a few human beings are chosen by God for eternal happiness. These individuals are invested with God's grace. No amount of prayer, dispensation, good works, or priestly intervention can help the person who has not been chosen for salvation by God, nor can any human act or earthly power deprive the chosen of heavenly bliss. The covenant is between God and the elect, and nothing can break the seal.

A belief in predestination seems unlikely to contribute to earthly achievement. If you are destined for the devil, why bother to exert yourself? For that matter, if you are predestined for heaven, why not sin while you can? The answer is that no one ever receives earthly confirmation of his or her "election" for heaven. All

★ John Winthrop (1588–1649) was elected governor of the Massachusetts Bay Colony even before the *Arbella* had set sail from England. He offered these inspired words during the treacherous journey: "Now the onely way to avoyed this shipwracke and to provide for our posterity is to followe the Counsell of Micah, to doe Justly, to love mercy, to walke humbly with our God, for this end, wee must be knitt together in this worke as one man."
[FROM: Edmund S. Morgan, ed., *Puritan Political Ideas* (New York: Bobbs-Merrill, 1965), p. 92.]

believers want to think that they are among the elect. Though salvation cannot be won by good works, all people are under a moral obligation to do good; and the experience of grace is so powerful that the elect are impelled to perform good works. Therefore, the free expression of diligence and piety is a strong sign that one has been chosen, and surely prosperity is a sign of God's grace. Conversely, if you detect doubt or sloth in yourself, or if you fail to achieve earthly success, you may reasonably suspect that you are not among the elect.

This commitment to "works" as a sign of grace was present in the first Puritan community in Massachusetts. Even before John Winthrop and his fellows landed at Salem in 1630, they agreed to demonstrate their chosenness by forging a new community unparalleled in the world. They felt that the eyes of the world would be on them, and were determined to demonstrate to all other religions that theirs was the most pure. Winthrop admonished his Puritan associates, "Wee must Consider that wee shall be as a Citty upon a Hill, the eies of all people are uppon us; soe that if wee shall deale falsely with our god in this worke wee have undertaken and soe cause him to withdrawe his present help from us." Winthrop was convinced that his religion was the most godly, but he needed to demonstrate his conviction to the world. By achieving greatness as a community—by becoming a **city upon a hill**—the Puritans intended to send an unmistakable advertisement of their worthiness.

★ Harry R. Truman (1896–1980) is pictured toasting Washington State's Mount St. Helens in the background. A few days after this photo was taken, the volcano buried him under thirty feet of ash and debris.

★ The Values Today: Three Case Studies

To what extent have the three values worked their way into contemporary political attitudes? Do twentieth-century Americans retain the historical commitment to freedom, equality, and achievement? Three case studies demonstrate that we do, and that the values continue to reflect their historical origins.

Freedom and the Harry Truman Who Wasn't President

On May 18, 1980, Harry R. Truman (no relation to President Harry S Truman) was buried under about thirty feet of volcanic ash. He had been warned by officials that his life was in danger, and that his Spirit Lake Resort in the shadow of Washington's Mount St. Helens was not long for the world. He even received letters from schoolchildren in England asking him to evacuate. He did not heed the warnings, preferring instead to stay in the surroundings that had become familiar to him over his fifty-one-year residence. After all, he had survived a German U-boat attack during World War I. His younger sister, Geraldine, probably put it best: "Nobody in this world could make him leave that mountain when he was told. We all knew that it was for his own good, but he was so hardheaded."

There is, of course, a moral to this story. It would have been quite easy for the police to step in and forcibly remove Harry from the premises, and in many

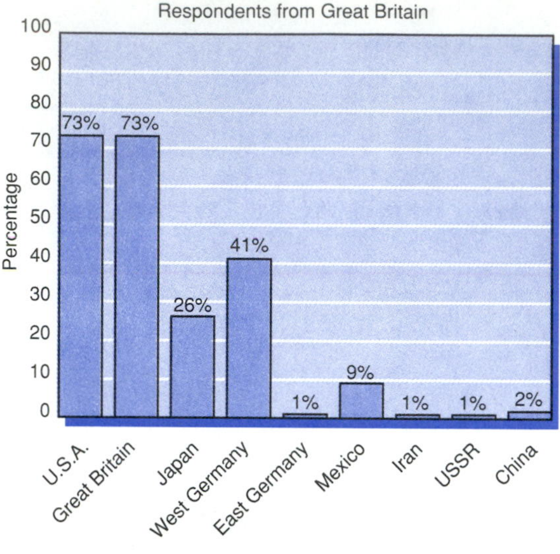

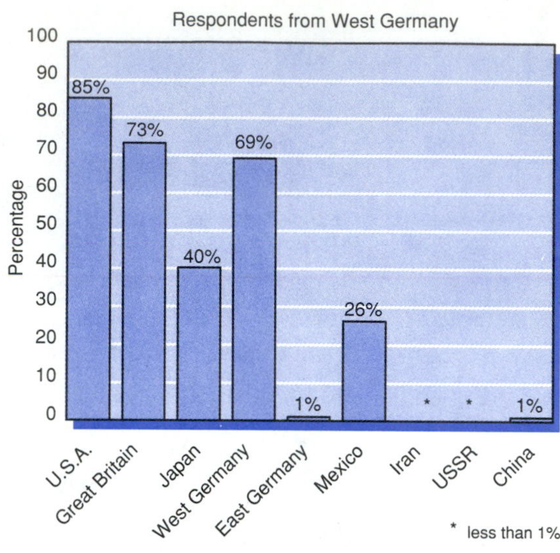

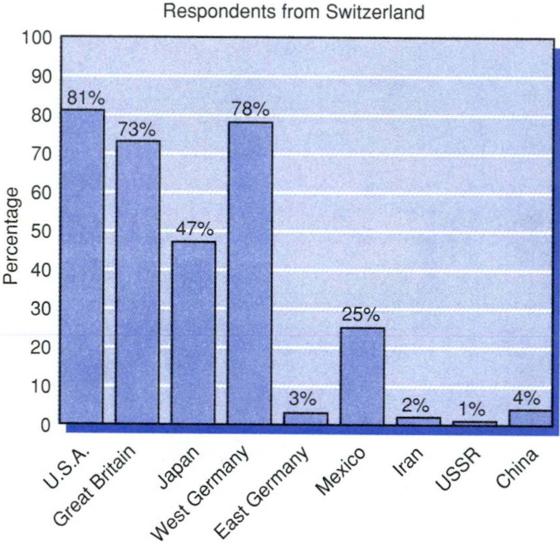

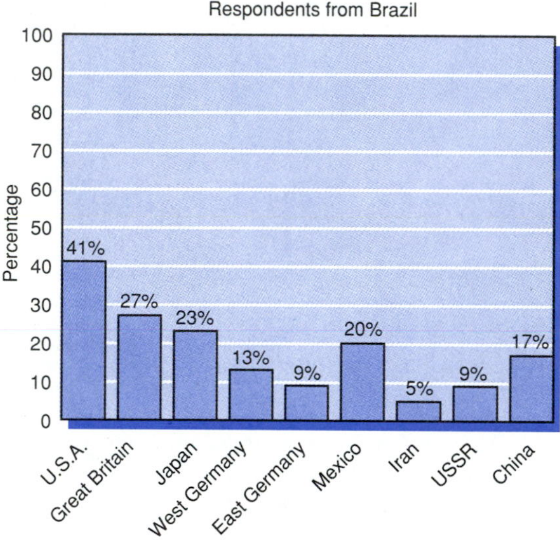

★ Figure 6-2

International perspectives on freedom. These graphs represent the responses of residents in five countries who answered the question, "For each of the following countries please tell me if you think the people of that country now have a great deal of freedom, only some freedom, very little freedom, or no freedom at all." The percentages given for each graph correspond to those who answered that a great deal of freedom exists in the countries listed.

SOURCE: Data taken from *Gallup Report,* Jan./Feb. 1984, p. 54.

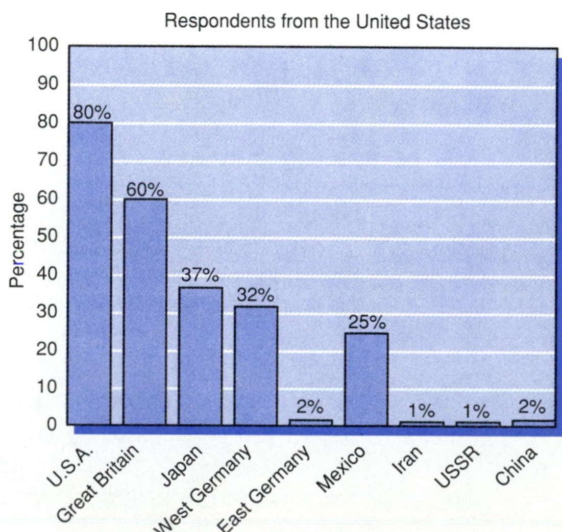

Allan Bakke

countries they undoubtedly would have done precisely that. In America, however, a sanctity surrounds individual decisions, so that they are often protected even when they are obviously flawed. The logic of this protection is that individuals must be allowed to make their own mistakes. If Harry Truman had been evacuated against his own will, the basic freedom of making his own decision would have been violated. He made his choice and was allowed to continue living in danger. A free society cannot impose decisions on people if it expects to maintain freedom. Individuals must have the feeling that they are responsible for a good portion of their lives. (Seat belt and helmet laws pass not only because of concerns for the irresponsible individual, but also out of concern about skyrocketing insurance rates.) The Reverend James Conrad was certainly correct when, at Harry's funeral, he said: "He chose to live there, and he chose to die there."

Affirmative Action: Equality at the Starting Line?

On June 4, 1982, the oldest student ever to attend the medical school of the University of California at Davis took his seat at the graduation ceremony. He had not planned to be so old when he graduated, but he had taken a five-year detour. Allan Bakke, who was forty-two years old when he finally graduated, gained entrance to medical school as a result of a Supreme Court case that was decided in his favor (as we saw in chap. 4). Bakke, who was white, argued that a less qualified black student was given preference over him for admission because of a quota system that had been implemented to ensure ethnic balance in the medical school. (Sixteen out of one hundred slots had been reserved for black students.)

Bakke's supporters argued that he suffered "reverse discrimination," and that he was not given an equal shot at admission. Supporters of the quota system and of other affirmative action programs argued that government intervention in some instances enhances the likelihood that all Americans will have an equal shot—that such programs balance out the discrimination faced by members of minority groups in America. Notice that both sides of this heated debate claimed to promote the cherished concept of equality. The ideal of equal opportunity for every citizen to choose his or her destiny remains strong.

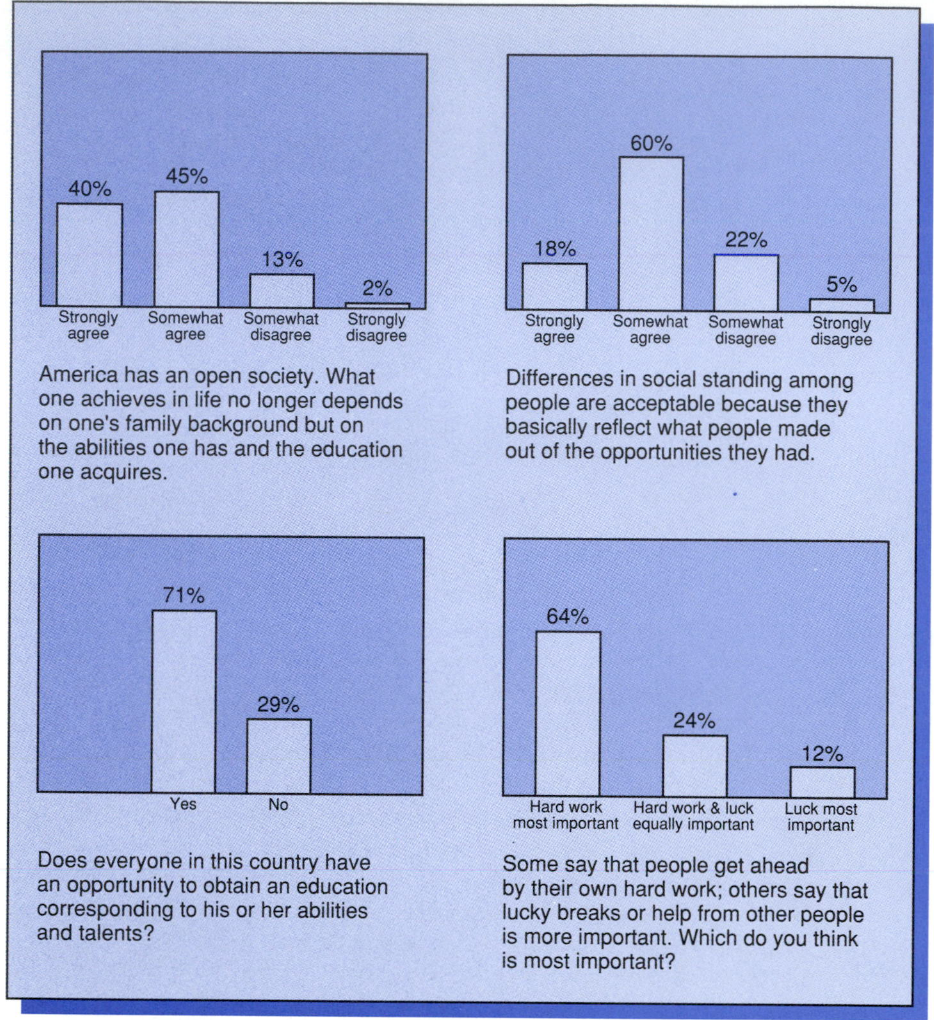

★ **Figure 6-3**
American support for equality of opportunity
SOURCE: James Allan Davis and Tom W. Smith, *General Social Survey, 1972–1988* (Chicago: National Opinion Research Center, 1988), subfile 1988 (machine-readable data file).

Sputnik: A Test of Determination

O little *Sputnik*, flying high
With made-in-Moscow beep,
You tell the world it's a Commie sky,
And Uncle Sam's asleep.

—*G. Mennen Williams, former governor of Michigan*

On October 4, 1957, the Soviet Union successfully launched the first earth-orbiting satellite. The United States had some cause for concern, for clearly the launch demonstrated that the Soviets had the capability to deliver an atomic bomb by means of an intercontinental ballistic missile. There was also a legitimate concern about the increased surveillance capabilities of orbiting satellites. Thus President Dwight Eisenhower was quick to inform American leaders and citizens of the facts, and to reveal the scientific progress that was being made in American laboratories.

Eisenhower did not anticipate the emotional response to the launching of ***Sputnik,*** however. Rather than focusing on specific problems attached to the Soviet launch, comments were framed in the language of doom. The *New York Times* said that the Soviets had initiated a "race that is not so much a race for arms or even prestige, but a race for survival." The nuclear physicist Edward Teller lamented that we had lost a battle "more important than Pearl Harbor." And Speaker of the House of Representatives John McCormack feared that the United States faced "national extinction" if it did not respond immediately to the Soviet space efforts.[17]

These dire predictions were not called forth by a mere scientific setback. They can be understood only as responses to a cherished principle—the American attachment to achievement. *Sputnik* achieved heights that the United States had not achieved, and in so doing it touched a raw nerve in the American citizenry. It was unacceptable that such an important achievement had not been American, and politicians and scientists scurried quickly to place blame and promote solutions. In later chapters—especially in chapter 19, on foreign policy—we will show how the American concern with achievement has affected political decisions. Americans continue to occupy a "city upon a hill."

★ The Other Side of the Coin: The Liabilities of Freedom, Equality, and Achievement

While it may be argued that freedom, equality, and achievement are important aspects of the American national character, the United States has not fully lived up to its dreams about them. The imperfect application of these values is as much a part of the American character as the values themselves. Until 1865, African American slaves were legally the property of their masters and had no rights as persons, much less as free persons. Until 1920, women were considered so unequal to men that they were not allowed to vote in national elections or to control their own earnings. And many generations of Americans were deprived of their chance for achievement by devastating depressions and wars, and by laws that favored factory owners over workers.

Freedom, equality, and achievement are not easy values to maintain; they tend to break down in application. Unfortunately, it is all too easy for freedom to lead to irresponsibility, for equality to lead to mediocrity, and for achievement to lead to materialism. No one has recognized the risks to American ideals better than Alexis de Tocqueville, a nineteenth-century French aristocrat who visited the United States in 1831 and recorded his impressions of the country. The following discussions are based on reservations first raised by Tocqueville.

Freedom and Irresponsibility

In the summer of 1978 the American Nazi party petitioned the officials of Skokie, Illinois, for a permit to hold a rally. It was no accident that the Nazis chose Skokie,

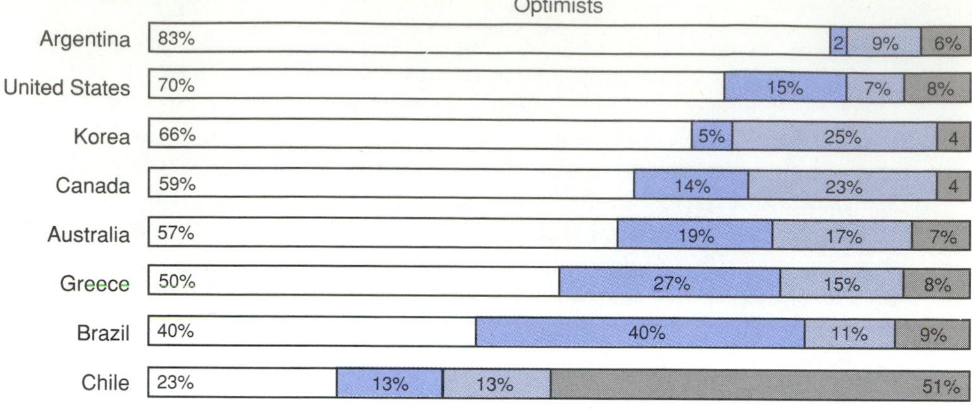

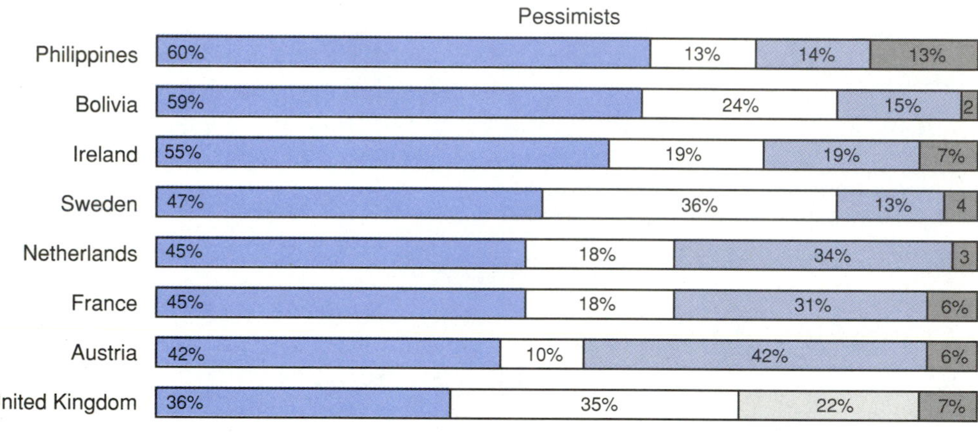

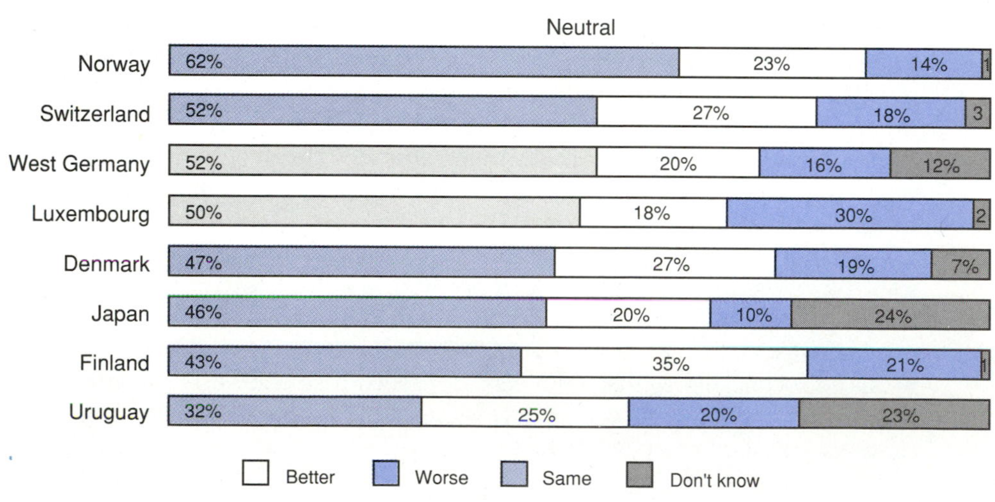

★ **Figure 6-4**

International optimism. Despite the gloomy predictions of George Orwell, Americans ranked second only to Argentinians in believing 1984 would be a year of continuing achievement and prosperity.

SOURCE: Based on *The Gallup Report*, Jan./Feb. 1984, p. 33.

Alexis de Tocqueville

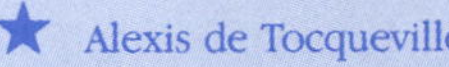
Alexis de Tocqueville

On May 9, 1831, a twenty-six-year-old French nobleman, Alexis de Tocqueville, and a close friend and associate, Gustave de Beaumont, landed at Newport Beach, Rhode Island, to begin a nine-month, seven-thousand-mile trek through the United States. Tocqueville's aristocratic heritage did not prevent him from developing a fascination with the burgeoning liberal movement. He was disenchanted with the remnants of aristocracy that hung on in France (and England), and with the compromises that were being made with the surviving culture of the *ancien régime*. Thus he was anxious to examine the American political system, which was known to have gone farthest in implementing liberal reforms.

Their scheme was a clever one. Both men had been appointed as magistrates of the French court, and in order to obtain leaves of absence, they pretended that the purpose of the journey was to study American prison reform. Indeed, they did submit a report on prisons, and it was well received, but it was not their true purpose.

Tocqueville was much more interested in recording general impressions of the American political and social atmosphere. In fact, the written outcome of his curiosity, titled *Democracy in America*, is still known as the best account of the American national character. It is ironic (and worthy of some contemplation) that such a work was drafted by a foreigner.

Tocqueville's optimism regarding liberal democracy was dulled after his firsthand observation of it. And it is his reservations about the American system that have made his work important. Among his many keen predictions were that the executive branch would become too powerful, that the emphasis on equality would lead to mediocrity, and that the best Americans would not be drawn to political careers but would choose instead to make money. Perhaps most famous are his comments on slavery and the disastrous consequences he was sure lay ahead:

> Whatever may be the efforts of the Americans of the South to maintain slavery, they will not always succeed. Slavery, now confined to a single tract of the civilized earth, attacked by Christianity as unjust and by political economy as prejudicial, and now contrasted with democratic liberty and the intelligence of our age, cannot survive. By the act of the master, or by the will of the slave, it will cease; and in either case great calamities may be expected to ensue.

SOURCE: Alexis de Tocqueville, *Democracy in America*, 2 vols. (New York: Knopf, 1945); quotation on p. 263 of vol. 1.

as this Chicago suburb is home to a substantial Jewish population. The Nazis were interested in the publicity that would surely follow the inevitable collision.

The community was faced with a tough decision: should the Nazis be allowed the freedom to plot and advertise the denial of freedom to others? Or to put the question more generally, can a free society tolerate those who strive to reduce the general level of freedom in the society? In the end, officials decided to let the Nazis speak. They claimed that free speech included the expression of ideas generally held to be repulsive.

The officials, of course, were far from condoning the Nazi position. They valued an atmosphere in which the citizens, not governmental censors, could decide on what is and is not valid information. The American Civil Liberties Union, known as a strong defender of free speech, simultaneously defends Nazis and Communists. The ACLU does not defend a single ideology or political position; rather, it holds

★ Skinheads, with sympathies for "white power" and Nazi tactics, demonstrate the irony that an atmosphere of freedom can generate ideas that promote the disruption of freedom for others.

that a society can prosper only when all opinions can be heard, no matter how absurd and even dangerous they may seem.

A question remains, though: How can a society that claims such an attachment to freedom and individual rights give birth to individuals and groups so intent on destroying freedom? Indeed, the United States has suffered an embarrassing array of incidents in which the freedom to speak and assemble has been misused to encourage the elimination of freedoms. The Ku Klux Klan takes advantage of its right to free speech by preaching the most severe infringements on the freedoms of American minorities. President Franklin Roosevelt gave in to irresponsible expressions of fear in World War II and signed an order that caused more than 100,000 American citizens of Japanese ancestry to be placed in concentration camps without any proof that they threatened American security. And in 1952 Senator Joseph McCarthy of Wisconsin tried to deprive many citizens of their political freedom by launching unsubstantiated attacks on their loyalty. Sadly, many Americans during the McCarthy era were quite willing to ostracize individuals tainted with the label "communist," paying scant attention to evidence or to the specific criticisms that the individuals may at one time have expressed.

Tocqueville was well aware that a society that leans toward freedom risks irresponsibility. Freedom is not in itself, he argued, enough to maintain a free environment; a free environment can easily collapse into a repressive one. Just as a small child who is permitted to use sharp scissors can do serious harm, Tocqueville believed, free citizens who are immature and ignorant are dangerous.

Thus Tocqueville introduced the concept of "self-interest rightly understood." What he meant was that individuals ought to be free to pursue their self-interest, but not at the expense of others. Freedom does not mean blaming one's problems on an easily identifiable ethnic minority. Nor does it mean a macho, unreflective interference in the affairs of other nations. For Tocqueville, freedom was to be exercised only after a thoughtful, careful examination of the situation. Only then would one see that freedom is fragile, and that freedom without thought often leads to the erosion of freedom.

★ The 1950s have become notorious for the promotion of mindless conformity and indifference to serious problems. David Riesman's book *The Lonely Crowd* chastised American society for accepting the equality of "the most common denominator." The immediate popularity of hula hoops was a symbol to some people that Riesman's assessment was correct.

Equality and Mediocrity

Tocqueville was also concerned about the unfortunate possibilities of an egalitarian society; in a society of equals, politics must be conducted with the consent of the majority rather than just by an elite. As politicians appealed to the majority, Tocqueville found, ideas were being watered down, and novel approaches were not given a proper forum.

For Tocqueville, a possible consequence of majority rule was mediocrity. When one attempts to mobilize majority opinion, he argued, the easiest tactic is to promote simple and uncontroversial ideas. Thus an idea is expressed with the hope not that it is sophisticated and well reasoned but that it will catch on quickly. The result is a watered-down commonplace, and the public happily accepts it because it is the will of the people.[18]

In 1950 an unusual book climbed to the top of the nonfiction best-seller list. Written by the sociologist David Riesman, *The Lonely Crowd: A Study of the Changing American Character* was a modern expression of Tocqueville's original concerns, and its popularity indicated that Riesman had hit a nerve among the reading public. Riesman argued that the American character was losing its depth and sophistication, that Americans' addiction to equality had put at risk the excellence they pursued. Americans were settling for the easy equality of assembly-line jobs and hula hoops for all, instead of pursuing an equality of intellectual, thoughtful citizens. According to Riesman, American equality had become conformity to superficial values and mindless pursuits.

The most visible target of Riesman's criticism was the student population of the 1950s.[19] These collegians were depicted as concerned with little more than determining the number of live goldfish a fraternity brother could swallow in one sitting, or the number of sorority sisters who could be jammed into a telephone booth. For Riesman, as for Tocqueville, equality was a hollow concept if it meant that everyone was equally foolish and immature. Just as freedom can turn to irresponsibility, equality can engender mediocrity and conformity.

Achievement and Materialism

Almost as soon as achievement took its place among the most esteemed American values, people became concerned that the motivation to achieve might be transformed into a simple, selfish desire to amass material wealth at the expense of other worthy concerns. Even John Winthrop, who inspired his Puritan followers to build a "city upon a hill," expressed concern that in constructing such an impressive monument, its builders would forget the purpose of the achievement, and would begin to live only for the benefits the city could provide. He saw that the Puritans were beginning "to embrace the present world and prosecute [their] carnal intentions."[20] For Winthrop, achievements had to be related properly to their heavenly purpose.

Tocqueville, too, was concerned about the connection between achievement and selfish materialism. He saw that, unlike aristocratic regimes, where common people were restricted from amassing material wealth, American democracy offered the chance of material gain to all citizens. Thus the achievement drive was most quickly and reliably directed toward the getting of wealth. Tocqueville identified a kind of addiction to this newfound ability to accumulate things, arguing that the first taste of affluence "haunts the mind" with ever more grandiose dreams of material riches. The most serious side effect of the addiction was the growing shortsightedness of the addicts; Americans, Tocqueville thought, tended to live for the day, sacrificing their future for present consumption. For Tocqueville, this constant search for material gain "hides the future, which becomes indistinct, and men seek only to think about tomorrow."[21]

There is little doubt that materialism and shortsightedness continue to overshadow the more admirable aspects of the American achievement orientation. Americans have long since discovered that they do not need money to buy things. Since World War II, consumer credit has increased more than tenfold; and whereas the families of other industrialized nations typically save between 10 and 20 percent of their income, Americans refuse to save even 5 percent. Americans prefer spending to saving; they tend to measure achievement by the cars, houses, electronic gadgets, and wardrobes they can collect.

Consumerism has the unfortunate effect of sacrificing future concerns for immediate gratification. The infatuation with large luxury automobiles, for instance, blinded consumers to their growing dependence on foreign oil. Only the sharp rises in gasoline prices that accompanied the Arab oil embargo convinced Americans that long-range plans for energy distribution were sorely needed. Similarly, America is the ultimate in throwaway societies, where manufacturers keep consumers consuming at a frantic pace by designing goods to last only a short time. "New and improved" continues to be one of the most effective guns in the advertisers' arsenal, while planned obsolescence continually pushes consumers back to the marketplace. Given this conviction that conspicuous consumption is a sign of achievement, one cannot fault Tocqueville for worrying about Americans' neglect of anything but the very short-term future.

A focus on the accumulation of material wealth may also have harmful effects on the fabric of the community. Tocqueville was one of the many people who have lamented the fact that many talented Americans have no interest in politics, preferring instead to pursue careers in business. Tocqueville was critical of the self-centeredness of citizens who refused to serve or even recognize the public good as they pursued their private interests. In the early 1980s, the Reagan administration had difficulty recruiting talented individuals from the business community to serve in government, and many of the reluctant recruits returned to their six- and seven-figure incomes before Reagan left the White House.

The United States has indeed prospered, and its citizens can be proud of their material achievements. But it is no less true that despite the bounty available to many citizens, a substantial minority of Americans continue to live in poverty and do not benefit from the material wealth that surrounds them. Many Americans seem to have narrowed their vision to shut out this kind of social failure. Achievement, like freedom and equality, can have unfortunate consequences if it is not carefully monitored and evaluated.

★ America in a Changing World: Toward a Global Culture

Nowhere is the United States' involvement with the rest of the world more evident than in the growing effect of American culture on other nations. At the same time, changes in the American national character are being stimulated by international developments.

The American Cultural Empire

In many ways, the United States today dominates an empire far bigger than any known by ancient Rome or China. We have achieved our domination not by force of arms but by cultural influence. American culture is known worldwide (not always accurately), and there is no doubt that countless lives in many countries have been changed by contact with American tourists, American music, American advertising, and American products.

Our history is replete with efforts to export American values. American revolutionaries were pleased to offer advice to their French counterparts; indeed, George Washington proudly received the key to the Bastille, symbol of despotism and oppression, after French revolutionaries stormed the building in 1789. In 1823 President James Monroe warned European powers that the United States would not tolerate European interference with the new "democracies" of Latin America. Later still, the Spanish-American War was fought under the banner of democracy for Cuba, and a world war was fought to keep the world "safe for democracy." And every day U.S.-supported Radio Free Europe beams its messages to Eastern European nations and the Soviet Union. During his two terms in office, Ronald Reagan spoke often of the need to support the "freedom fighters" in Nicaragua, and of the importance of keeping the United States' concept of democracy alive in Central America.

★ The United States often supports its foreign policies with arguments related to American values. In an effort to win public support and associate the cause with American tradition, former president Reagan referred to the anticommunist Nicaraguan Contras as "freedom fighters."

Ironically, it is not the values of freedom and equality that have taken hold in foreign countries. Despite attempts to export American democratic institutions and values, it is the American commitment to achievement, particularly material achievement, that has most impressed foreigners. In 1932 the sociologist André Siegfried said: "What has been borrowed from us, as I have so often observed, is our mechanisms. Today, in the most remote, most ancient villages, one finds the automobile, the cinema, the radio, the telephone, the phonograph, not to mention the airplane."[22]

Nor should we underestimate the influence of American materialism in the fundamentalist Islamic movements in the Middle East. Some Muslim leaders see America as consumed by the desire to amass material wealth at any cost and to spread this "disease" to the Middle East. Thus some Muslim leaders seek to isolate their countries from American cultural influences. In the hope that spiritualism will prevail over materialism, they discourage the accumulation of material goods. Tocqueville's concern that American materialism would undermine the community has taken on international dimensions.

The Newest Frontier: Modern Technology

Not only does the American national character affect the international environment; international developments also influence the domestic American character. The days when politicians could win votes by promoting isolationism are over. The American economic, manufacturing, educational, and communication systems (to name a few) are fundamentally and unavoidably affected by developments in other nations.

Spurred on by the virtual explosion in global communications, the world has become more or less a single economy, with ideas, jobs, products, and finance

★ Steve Jobs, one of the founders of Apple Computer, Inc., has come to symbolize the "technology revolution." Here, he shows off his NeXT computer.

flowing from one country to another. In the past, industrialized nations such as the United States and Britain designed and manufactured products and then sold them to less industrialized nations, which supplied raw materials and agricultural products in exchange for them. Today, thanks to technology and the economics of world trade, the relationship has been altered dramatically, with ramifications spreading to the American national character.

The developing nations of Latin America and Asia are now competing directly with (and within) the United States for markets. A major factor in this change has been the willingness of such nations as Japan, Korea, and Brazil to employ high technology, and the willingness to keep wages below those of American workers. The well-known result: U.S. nonagricultural exports grew by only 6 percent between 1980 and 1986 while imports of goods (exclusive of oil) grew by 99 percent.[23]

In 1985 the President's Commission on Industrial Competitiveness clearly pointed to high technology as the key to maintaining American success in the new world economy:

> Technology propels our economy forward. Without doubt, it has been our strongest competitive advantage. Innovation has created whole new industries and the renewal of existing ones. State-of-the-art products have commanded premium prices in world markets, and technological advances have spurred productivity gains. Thus, America owes much of its standard of living to U.S. preeminence in technology.[24]

American high-technology service industries link us to an integrated global economy. They supply loans to foreign manufacturing clients, provide insurance to underwrite international construction firms, and use computer-controlled inventory systems to ensure customer satisfaction. All of these endeavors have required the American worker to be on the cutting edge of technological innovation—in computers, biotechnology, investment, currency manipulation, even the exploration of outer space for private industry. The emphasis is on specialized training and exotic research facilities; and while American students may understandably become excited about the possibilities they see ahead, these developments have less attractive implications for the American national character.

High Technology and the American National Character

Alvin Toffler predicts that radical social change will result from these new technologies. He paints a picture of an America caught in the riptide between a receding "second wave" and a cresting "third wave" form of civilization. The first wave, representing agricultural civilization, has long since subsided; in America, the primacy of agriculture was finally overcome after the Civil War, with the fall of the agricultural South. The old agricultural civilization was displaced by the industrial civilization of the North. This second-wave society was typified by the factory: it was highly centralized, produced identical goods in massive quantities, was highly organized to coordinate the activities of large groups of cooperating individuals, and demanded long hours of work at routine tasks. According to Toffler, the result was a "mass society" that seemed to peak in the "boring 50s." Like the parts that made up the industrial mechanisms, Americans themselves seemed to be susceptible to standardization. One member of the society could be replaced by an identical one just as easily as one General Motors exhaust manifold could be replaced by another.

According to Toffler, this situation is changing. Because American manufacturers are unable to compete with other nations in second-wave industries, Toffler anticipates a breathtaking transition to a third-wave economy (see figure 6-5). He sees the third wave as a liberating force. Americans are carving out a new niche in specialization, designing complex custom goods to suit the unique needs of the individual customer. Thus the assembly line and its routine are endangered species in the American economy. As the old factories are scrapped, Toffler points out, they are replaced by quiet and inconspicuous buildings that have no need to be shoved into the gritty corners of the community. Nor are the jobs of third-wave people so repetitive and noxious; the third wave needs highly trained specialists, whose tasks are challenging and rewarding. And America's superior educational facilities ensure competitiveness in third-wave ventures that cannot be achieved in second-wave pursuits.

Silicon Valley: On the Crest of the Third Wave. Toffler and others mention Northern California's Silicon Valley as the model of things to come—the highest development to date of third-wave technologies. Here engineers and scientists brainstorm products and services that eventually will be taken offshore for manufacture and refinement. Thus it might be interesting to look at Silicon Valley in the light of Toffler's predictions, and consider what these changes may portend for the American national character. There are "Silicon Valleys" all over the country now, in Massachusetts, North Carolina, and Texas, for example, and this discussion is relevant to those places also.

Toffler's term for the new technological society of Silicon Valley is **blip culture**. In such a society the mere quantity of information and stimulation keeps people from spending much time wrapped up in any single idea or theme. Repet-

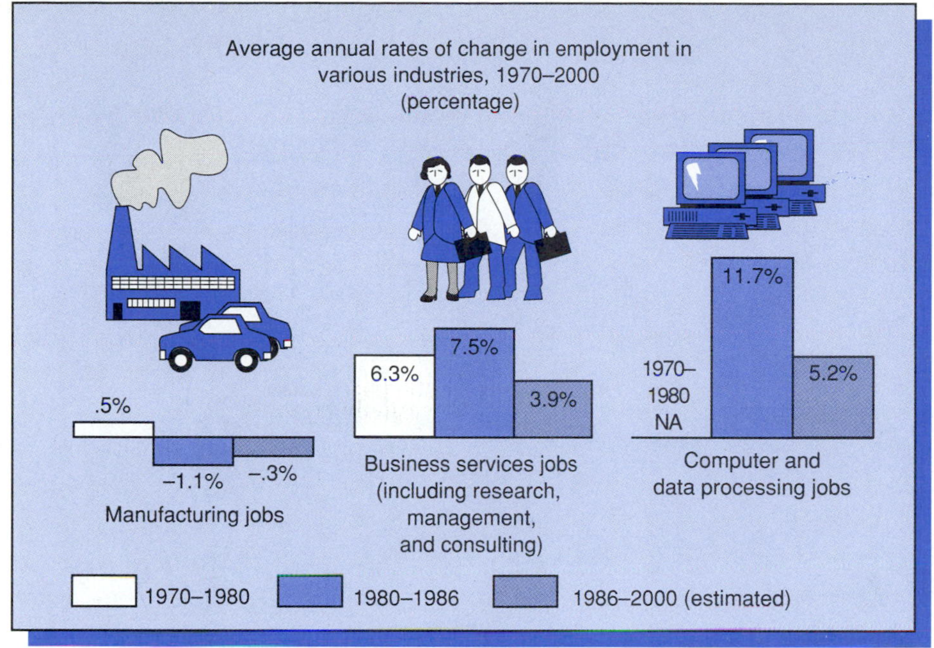

★ **Figure 6-5**
Rising tide of third-wave industries
NOTE: NA means not available
SOURCE: U.S. Bureau of the Census, *Statistical Abstract of the United States, 1988* (Washington, D.C.: U.S. Government Printing Office, 1988), p. 380.

itive tasks can be left to second-wave societies. Here is how Toffler compares the third-wave, blip-culture person to the "dinosaurs" of the second wave:

> Instead of receiving long, related "strings" of ideas, organized or synthesized for us, we are increasingly exposed to short, modular blips of information—ads, commands, theories, shreds of news, truncated bits and blobs that refuse to fit neatly into our preexisting mental files. The new imagery resists classification, partly because it often falls outside our old conceptual categories, but also because it comes in packages that are too oddly shaped, transient, and disconnected. Assailed by what they perceive as the bedlam of blip culture, Second Wave people feel a suppressed rage at the media.[25]

Thus members of a blip culture make no effort to connect the dots of their existence; rather, every experience is taken individually, and appreciated without the bias of prior experiences. High technology fosters this kind of existence because it is too complicated and too specialized to allow the interconnection of pursuits. Individuals need to concentrate on the tasks before them, and cannot clutter their minds with connections to other projects or concerns. Greek and Latin have been sacrificed to Fortran and Cobol.

Indeed, blip culture seems to have taken hold in Silicon Valley. People there have little sense of connection with the past. The only historical site that receives much attention is the Winchester Mystery House—and that only because of the weird old lady who lived there. Everything that succeeds in the Valley is new and flashy; if one should slip into a nostalgic mood, one may retreat to the manufactured

★ Blip individuals enjoy the explosive, fast-paced, flashy diversion of video games.

quaintness of Old Town in nearby Los Gatos, which opened in the late 1960s. Cultural forms that demand some facility in linear, thematic thinking, such as classical theater, have given way to thrill-packed amusement parks (Marriott's Great America has a collection of roller coasters unparalleled in the civilized world) and giant-screened movie theaters that specialize in overwhelming sound systems and breathtaking visual stimulation. According to 1980 Census Bureau figures, Santa Clara County supports 749 employees in the movie theater business while only 146 people work in theatrical production and service. Second-wave San Francisco County to the north, which is much smaller, supports 583 theatrical workers.

Toffler is hopeful that this migration to blip culture will lead to unheard-of freedom. He believes that the multitude of blips will cause a great diversity in society, with each individual choosing a unique combination of pursuits. Each specialty will have a group of expert leaders, and the complexity of the blips will prevent any one person or group of people from gaining too much power. Blip culture demands autonomy and authority for individuals within their specialized niches. The result, according to Toffler, is unprecedented freedom.

We may discern some problems in Toffler's analysis; for just as easily as the blip culture could lead to freedom, it could detract from it. Toffler does not admit that many blips are relatively mindless diversions. Is the next generation of video games really an expression of expanded human freedom? Are 500 watts per channel combined with a graphic equalizer really a way to promote human autonomy? There is a strong possibility that the freedoms created by blip culture may be superficial, and that in order to protect and enhance the freedom to criticize the system or to challenge the leadership of a large public bureaucracy, we need the kind of knowledge and interest that Toffler would call "second wave." We need to maintain a sense of our connection with our past and with other people's present. We need to maintain an overarching value system under which some experiences may be dismissed as superficial, while others are recognized as important.

Blip culture is the result of a massive technological revolution, which is spurred on in part by a belief that if the United States is to maintain its preeminence in the world, it needs to carve out a niche as pioneer in research and development. Problems may occur, however, if in the quest for new frontiers the pioneers lose touch with their cultural, ethical, and political roots.

★ Summary

National character is a complex mix of the ideals and the reality of a country's political and social life. In the United States, three of the most important ideals are freedom, equality, and achievement. Two theories compete to explain the formation of national character. One, advanced by Frederick Jackson Turner, has it that national character is a result of environmental forces that are largely beyond human control. Jackson pointed to the abundance of land, resources, and opportunities on the undeveloped frontier as determinants of the American national character. The competing theory—the social explanation—holds that human beings play a crucial role in the formation of their national character. This theory finds the roots of the American character in the colonists' opposition to domination by Great Britain; in the founders' adherence to the ideas of eighteenth-century liberalism, with its emphasis on self-interest and reason; and in the Puritans' drive to demonstrate by diligence and achievement that they were the elect of God.

The values that have shaped the American character have their dark side. Freedom can lead to irresponsibility, equality to mediocrity, and achievement to crass materialism. America has a difficult time living up to its lofty ideals.

The United States' commitment to material achievement has spread American influence around the world. Other countries complain about American materialism as their citizens eagerly embrace American fashions, music, and technology. As industrial strength has increasingly shifted to countries with large and undemanding labor pools, the United States has moved to carve out a niche as the world's developer of advanced technologies. In this effort the American character may also be undergoing a shift. The specialists who develop the new technologies are so deluged by fragments of seemingly unrelated information that they tend to lose sight of their connection with the past and with other people's present. In such a culture our overarching value system may fade from view and the superficial may no longer be easily distinguished from the important.

★ Key Terms

achievement
blip culture
city upon a hill
environmental explanation
equality
freedom
liberalism
national character
paternalism
puritanism
self-interest
social explanation
Sputnik

★ Notes

1. Frederick Jackson Turner, "Contributions of the West to American Democracy," in *The Turner Thesis Concerning the Role of the Frontier in American History*, ed. George Rogers Taylor (Lexington, Mass.: D. C. Heath, 1956), p. 28.
2. Quoted in Freeman Tilden, *National Parks* (New York: Knopf, 1986), p. 24.
3. Frederick Jackson Turner, "The Significance of the Frontier in American History," in Taylor, *Turner Thesis*, p. 2.
4. Joanna L. Stratton, *Pioneer Women: Voices from the Kansas Frontier* (New York: Simon & Schuster, 1981), p. 61.
5. Eleanor Flexner, *Century of Struggle: The Women's Rights Movement in the United States*, rev. ed. (Cambridge, Mass.: Belknap Press of Harvard University Press, 1975), pp. 163–164.
6. See David M. Potter, *People of Plenty: Economic Abundance and the American Character* (Chicago: University of Chicago Press, 1954).
7. Quoted in Lucy Lockwood Hazard, *The Frontier in American Literature* (New York: Barnes & Noble, 1941), pp. 23–24.
8. Horatio Alger, Jr., *The Errand Boy* (New York: A. L. Burt, 1888), p. 39.
9. Potter, *People of Plenty*, p. 80.
10. James Allan Davis and Tom W. Smith, *General Social Survey, 1972–1988* (Chicago: National Opinion Research Center, 1988), subfile 1988 (machine-readable data file).
11. "Declaration and Resolves of the First Continental Congress, October 14, 1774," in *Documents of American History*, ed. Henry Steele Commager, 9th ed. (New York: Appleton-Century-Crofts, 1973), p. 83.
12. Alexander Hamilton, James Madison, and John Jay, *The Federalist Papers* (New York: Mentor, 1961), p. 301 (no. 47).
13. John Locke, *Two Treatises of Government* (New York: Mentor, 1965). See especially chaps. 2, 6, and 7 of the *Second Treatise*.
14. Ibid., p. 242.
15. Thomas Hobbes, *Leviathan* (New York: Dutton, 1973), pt. I, chap. 13, p. 63.
16. "Declaration of Sentiments," in *The Feminist Papers*, ed. Alice S. Rossi, pp. 415–418 (New York: Bantam, 1974) (emphasis added).
17. Quoted in Tom Wolfe, *The Right Stuff* (New York: Farrar, Strauss & Giroux, 1979), chap 3.
18. "The authority of a king is physical and controls the actions of men without subduing their will. But the majority possesses a power that is physical and moral at the same time, which acts upon the will as much as upon the actions and represses not only all contest, but all controversy. I know of no country in which there is so little independence of mind and real freedom of discussion as in America" (Alexis de Tocqueville, *Democracy in America*, 2 vols. [New York: Knopf, 1945], 1:263).
19. The concern seems to have resurfaced with the publication of Allan Bloom's best-seller, *The Closing of the American Mind* (New York: Touchstone, 1988).
20. Quoted in David E. Shi, *The Simple Life: Plain Living and High Thinking in American Culture* (New York: Oxford University Press, 1985), p. 13.
21. Tocqueville, *Democracy in America*, 2:150.
22. Quoted in Isabel Cary Lundberg, "World Revolution, American Plan," *Harper's Magazine*, December 1948, pp. 38–46.
23. The causes of the decline in U.S. exports and the rise in imports are quite complex; they include consumer purchasing power in other countries and the strength of the U.S. dollar abroad, as well as direct competition from foreign products.
24. President's Commission on Industrial Competitiveness, *Global Competition: The New Reality*, vol.1 (Washington, D.C.: U.S. Government Printing Office, 1985), p. 18.
25. Alvin Toffler, *The Third Wave* (New York: Bantam, 1981), p. 166.

★ For Further Reading

Alger, Horatio, Jr. *The Errand Boy*. New York: A. C. Burt, 1888.

Almond, Gabriel A., and Sidney Verba. *The Civic Culture: Political Attitudes and Democracy in Five Nations*. Boston: Little, Brown, 1965.

Bellah, Robert, et al. *Habits of the Heart*. Berkeley: University of California Press, 1985.
Hartz, Louis. *The Liberal Tradition in America*. New York: Harcourt Brace, 1955.
Lipset, Seymour Martin. *The First New Nation*. Garden City, N.Y.: Anchor/Doubleday, 1967.
McLuhan, Marshall. *Understanding Media*. New York: McGraw-Hill, 1964.
Potter, David M. *People of Plenty: Economic Abundance and the American Character*. Chicago: University of Chicago Press, 1954.
Shi, David E. *The Simple Life: Plain Living and High Thinking in American Culture*. New York: Oxford University Press, 1985.
Stratton, Joanna L. *Pioneer Women: Voices from the Kansas Frontier*. New York: Simon & Schuster, 1981.
Taylor, George Rogers, ed. *The Turner Thesis Concerning the Role of the Frontier in American History*. Lexington, Mass.: D. C. Heath, 1956.
Tocqueville, Alexis de. *Democracy in America*. Various editions.
Toffler, Alvin. *The Third Wave*. New York: Bantam, 1981.
Wolfe, Tom. *The Right Stuff*. New York: Farrar, Strauss & Giroux, 1979.

PART TWO

Practicing Citizenship: From Couch Potato to Activist

[To understand the adult] we must begin higher up; we must watch the infant in his mother's arms; we must see the first images which the external world casts upon the dark mirror of his mind, the first occurrences which he witnesses; we must hear the first words which awaken the sleeping powers of thought, and stand by his earliest efforts, if we would understand the prejudices, the habits, and the passions which will rule his life.

—Alexis de Tocqueville

CHAPTER SEVEN

PUBLIC OPINION

★★★★★★★★★★★★

Political Attitudes and Opinions: What Americans Think about Politics

Saturday morning is sacred to most American families. While parents catch up on a week of lost sleep, children are exiled to the television room, where they can fixate quietly on their favorite cartoon show. One of the most popular shows features the Smurfs, a band of cute, mushroom-dwelling creatures who each week must frustrate the forces of evil that threaten them.

The simple life of the Smurfs may hold a complex political lesson, for these shows condition their young audience to long-established stereotypes of masculinity and femininity. The Smurf leaders, Papa and Grandpa Smurf, are quintessential male figures. They are wise, and they are held in great respect by the community. Papa Smurf, according to a seven-year-old friend of ours, "makes potions." Though "Brainy reads books" and "Sleepy writes poems," Papa is "the smart one." Brainy and Sleepy are "both boys." The one girl in the family is known as Smurfette, a name that indicates that she is somehow tied to but not quite the same as the more numerous Smurfs. When asked about the activities of Smurfette, our friend tells us that "she picks flowers all the time" and that the others "are pretty good to her." Sometimes "the bad guy gets her but the other Smurfs save her."

A 1988 survey revealed that 34 percent of Americans felt that women are "unsuited for politics."[1] (Figure 7-1 reveals some other attitudes toward women in politics.) In this age of equal rights and a strong American feminist movement, this figure seems very high. It is less surprising, however, if one examines how we acquire our political attitudes, and how we tend to hold on to attitudes learned early in life. As an isolated phenomenon, the Smurfs would not be a significant influence on the development of gender roles. But the Smurfs are only a small part of an environment in which parents admonish boys to assert themselves and girls to smile, and in which 85 percent of elementary school teachers are women while 78 percent of the principals are men. It would be unwise to examine political attitudes without paying some attention to early and pervasive conditioning of this sort.

In this chapter we will examine the political attitudes and opinions of adult American citizens; but we will first look at how American children acquire the general outlooks that shape their adult political opinions. When we examine the political beliefs of adults, we will pay special attention to the sophistication—or lack of it—of Americans' opinions on political issues and candidates. Finally, we will discuss some recent and important changes in public opinion regarding America's role in world affairs, as well as attitudes that seem to be leading to a "new conservatism." In short, we will consider how people behave in the political realm, and why they behave as they do.

Do you agree or disagree with this statement? Women should take care of running their homes and leave running the country up to men.

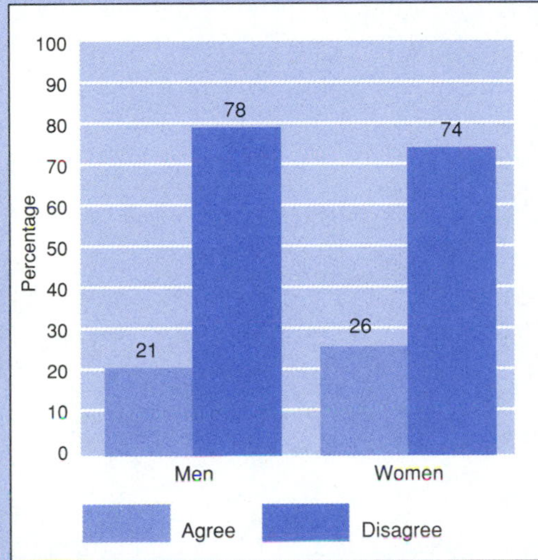

If your party nominated a woman for president, would you vote for her if she were qualified for the job?

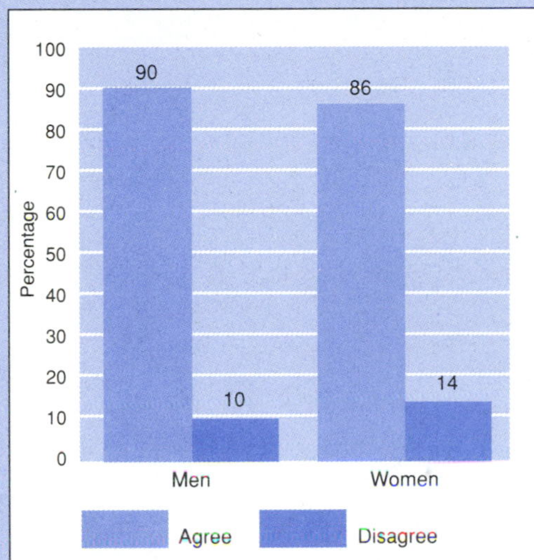

Tell me if you agree or disagree with this statement: Most men are better suited emotionally for politics than are most women.

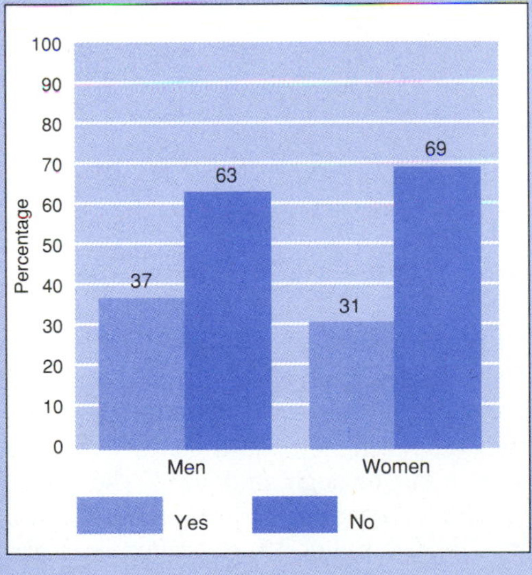

★ **Figure 7-1**

Attitudes toward women in politics

SOURCE: James Allan Davis and Tom W. Smith, *General Social Survey, 1972–1988* (Chicago: National Opinion Research Center, 1988), subfile 1988 (machine-readable data file).

★ Flags are simple and effective representations of a shared community. Old Glory is a well-known and cherished symbol of the American tribe, as evidenced by the recent controversy over flag-burning.

★ Political Socialization: Learning the Facts and Values of Political Life

Like gender roles, many political attitudes can be traced to childhood experiences. It is not accidental that we are taught the Pledge of Allegiance in kindergarten and are encouraged to sing "The Star-Spangled Banner" at baseball games. Politicians know that if they can reach their audience early, they can inspire feelings of loyalty and patriotism that last through adulthood. The process through which we gain our knowledge about the facts and values of the political system is called **political socialization.** Through political socialization we learn such details as the names of famous presidents, but we also learn a value system through which we can interpret the details; we learn that Theodore Roosevelt and his Rough Riders helped to free Cuba from "the Spanish yoke" and that Woodrow Wilson sent American troops to Europe to "make the world safe for democracy." Thus political socialization is also the process through which we internalize the national character described in chapter 6.

★ Police officers make substantial efforts to establish friendly and helpful relationships with young people.

The Importance of Socialization

Political socialization is important for both the individual and the political system as a whole. It is important for the individual to acquire a favorable first impression of political authority. In societies where agents of political authority are feared and mistrusted, a child's adjustment to the world of laws and external authorities can be traumatic and troublesome.

Infants come to believe that their parents are all-powerful. They expect their parents to change the temperature if it is uncomfortable and instantly remove pain or alleviate hunger. Soon enough, however, children realize that their parents have limited powers and that mom and dad must submit to a variety of external authorities who have power over the entire family.

Among the first external authority figures that children remember are agents of the police department. Uniforms, badges, and guns are impressive to a youngster, as are the occasional blaring sirens that make usually confident parents nervous. Police officers are aware of their impact on children, and they visit day-care centers and kindergartens to demonstrate their humanness and dedication to helping. The idea is to promote a healthy recognition of external authority, and to set the foundation for a lifelong relationship of cooperation and trust.

It is not only police officers that attempt to ensure a healthy socialization to their authority. As children mature, they are told stories about the virtues of other political authorities. George Washington, Abe Lincoln, and Thomas Jefferson are portrayed as virtuous and gifted leaders. The flag becomes a source of pride, and

American democracy is depicted as the most generous and advanced system of government. Children engage in imaginary battles with Russians or other "aliens." All of these influences tend to promote an acceptance of and submission to political authority. Children are taught to feel good about obeying laws *and* about participating in the political process.

Thus successful socialization can make the job of the police officer, and of the political system as a whole, much easier. Socialized citizens are more likely to abide by the laws and customs of the society, without the need for coercion. Indeed, no society can afford to plant an agent of authority on every street corner. Authorities must maintain order by socializing citizens to believe that their system is worthy of voluntary support. Thus leaders reinforce American values, and they portray themselves as vitally connected to those values, with the hope that their authority will be seen as normal and desirable.

From Cherry Trees to Crooks in Congress: Three Levels of Socialization

The political scientists David Easton and Jack Dennis have identified three levels through which individuals travel as they become socialized to politics.[2] The first level is socialization to the community. This is the stage at which children begin to conceptualize an American "tribe," which is distinct from other tribes. They learn to appreciate the distinctions between "us" and "them," and to recognize and revere the symbols of the community. Even before entering school, most children can identify the American flag, and believe it to be the most attractive. They sense that police officers perform important tribal functions, and some can even identify the president as "tribal chief." Beyond a general feeling of community, however, youngsters at this level of socialization know very little of political things.

The next level discussed by Easton and Dennis is socialization to the regime. At this level, during the first few years of elementary school, children begin to internalize the values of freedom, equality, and achievement, and they begin to associate those values with their country. At this stage, such images as the Statue of Liberty and the Washington Monument act as important cues to children who are beginning to understand that the community shares certain values and aspirations. At this level, almost all American children retain positive feelings about their country. Most know who the president is, and most speak of him in glowing terms.

At the next level, socialization to particular political authorities, more critical perceptions creep in. Whereas children cannot separate the president from the myths they are learning in the regime phase, they now begin to understand that they can love their country without necessarily loving the people who run it. At this stage, which occurs at about the fourth grade, children begin to learn about political parties, voting, and the foibles of political leaders.

Figure 7-2 illustrates the transition from a regime to an authorities orientation. Children were asked questions about the presidency, first at the height of President Kennedy's popularity (1962), then twelve years later, during the worst shocks of Nixon's Watergate scandal. Second- and third-graders seemed a little less positive in the Watergate era, but the discrepancies were nowhere near so great as those found among fourth-, fifth-, and especially sixth-graders. It seems that political facts register later than political values as the process of socialization proceeds.

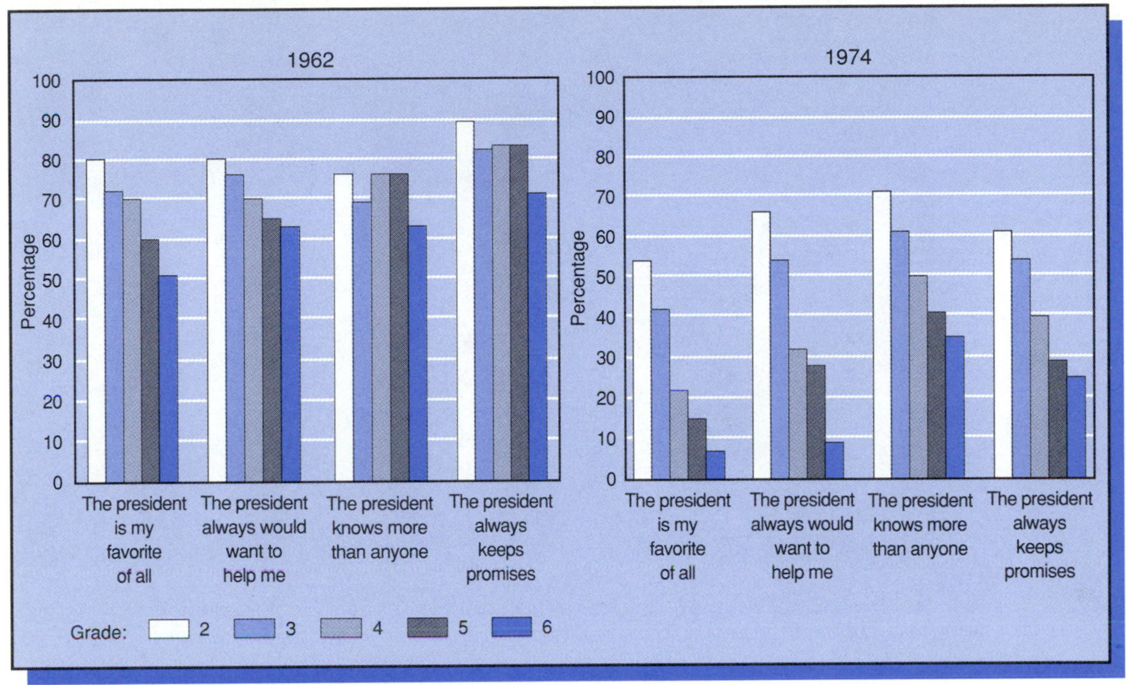

★ **Figure 7-2**

Children's responses to questions about the president, 1962 and 1974 (by grade level and by agreement)

SOURCE: Adapted with permission from F. Christopher Arterton, "The Impact of Watergate on Children's Attitudes toward Political Authority," *Political Science Quarterly* 84 (June 1974): 269–288.

★ The Agents of Political Learning

Although the factors that influence people's lives are virtually limitless, a few of them seem to bear the major responsibility for inculcating political views and opinions: the family, the schools, the peer group, and the mass media. The most fundamental of these agents is the family.

The Family

In both political science and folklore ("As the twig is bent, so grows the tree"; "The hand that rocks the cradle . . ."; "Like father, like son"), the family is regarded as an important influence on the development of attitudes and values. In the nineteenth century, Alexis de Tocqueville stressed the importance of the family in the early stages of political learning. To understand the adult, he said, "we must watch the infant in his mother's arms."[3]

When most of us first come into contact with the political world, we have already acquired a set of social values from our family. Depending on the family we are born into, we are given at birth a race, a sex, a religion, and an economic

★ The family plays an important role in the socialization of children, especially preschoolers. This child is receiving an early introduction to a politically based rally through his concerned parents.

background, all of which may strongly influence our political actions in later life. According to one scholar, by the time a child enters "kindergarten—where many adults naively think his learning is about to start—this new semisocial being has already acquired the equivalent of 350 college courses, enough for an A.B. degree more than eight times over, in learning the values, customs, and attitudes that are sanctioned by his own unique family."[4]

Although many changes have been taking place in the American family, it continues to play a vital role in the development of political attitudes. One reason is that the family tends to have the primary influence over the child during the preschool years, a period many psychologists believe is the most emotionally critical part of an individual's life. During this early period, even when parents or other caregivers are not consciously trying to teach their children values and attitudes, children are picking them up anyway, just as they are picking up their parents' habits and expressions.

When both parents support the same political party, for example, their children often inherit a similar way of ordering the political world that they will carry with them through their lives. They learn to separate the good guys from the bad by party labels long before they understand the real differences between the parties. One political scientist found that many fourth-graders in Connecticut considered allegiance to a political party—or revulsion for one—to be a family trait. As one ten-year-old girl put it, "All I know is we're not Republicans."[5] Only a few of the children said their party preference differed from that of their parents.

If family influences tend to be so exclusive at an early age, why is it that apparently one of every three people eventually adopts a preference that differs from that of her or his parents? Why do parents of the radical 1960s produce children who join the Young Republicans and wear Italian designer sport coats?

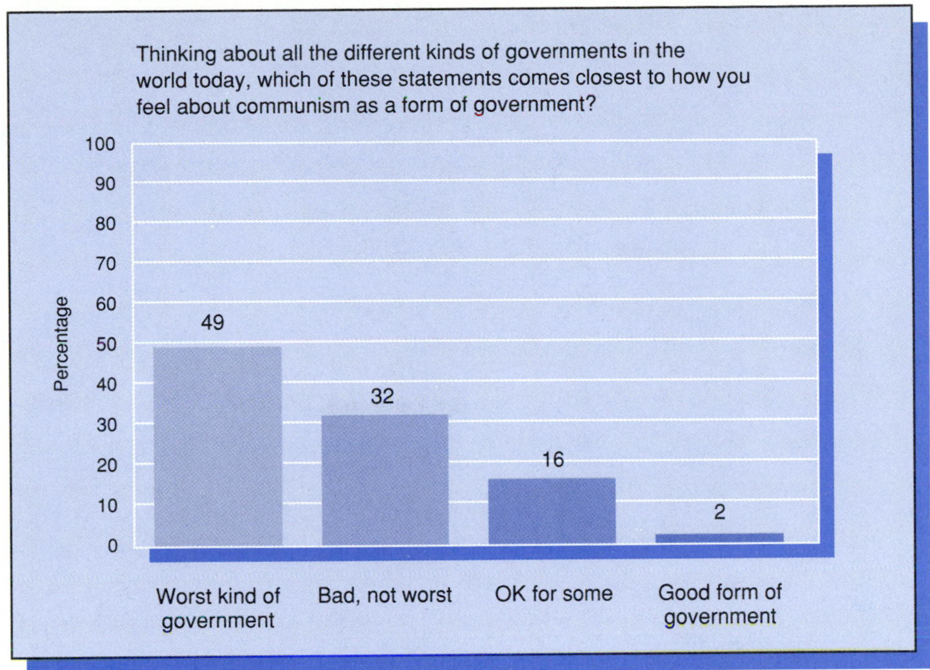

★ **Figure 7-3**
Americans are socialized to be wary of alternative political systems.
SOURCE: James Allan Davis and Tom W. Smith, *General Social Survey, 1972–1988* (Chicago: National Opinion Research Center, 1988), subfile 1988 (machine-readable data file).

The answer, of course, is that many other socializing agents come into play as children mature. Although they may continue to hold many of the attitudes and values shaped early on by the family, such as their general attitudes toward authority, their specific views and opinions on political issues may change in response to new influences.

The Schools

A seven-year-old child, when asked what she learned in school about American presidents, replied, "They do much more work and they're much importanter." A ten-year-old, when asked what he had learned about communism, answered, "Well, communism is sort of—it's a different way of people; well, sort of like . . . to me it's bad."[6] (See figure 7-3.)

While other social forces may greatly affect a person's way of thinking about politics, no institutions are handed so much responsibility for spreading the basic symbols of the political system as are the schools. Most of us probably can recall learning about the country's early political heroes and celebrating our national holidays. We can recall solemnly saluting the flag, raising our voices in "The Star-Spangled Banner," and perhaps identifying with the rowdy young George Washington and his infamous cherry tree. And we can remember being herded into American history and civics classes in junior high and high school.

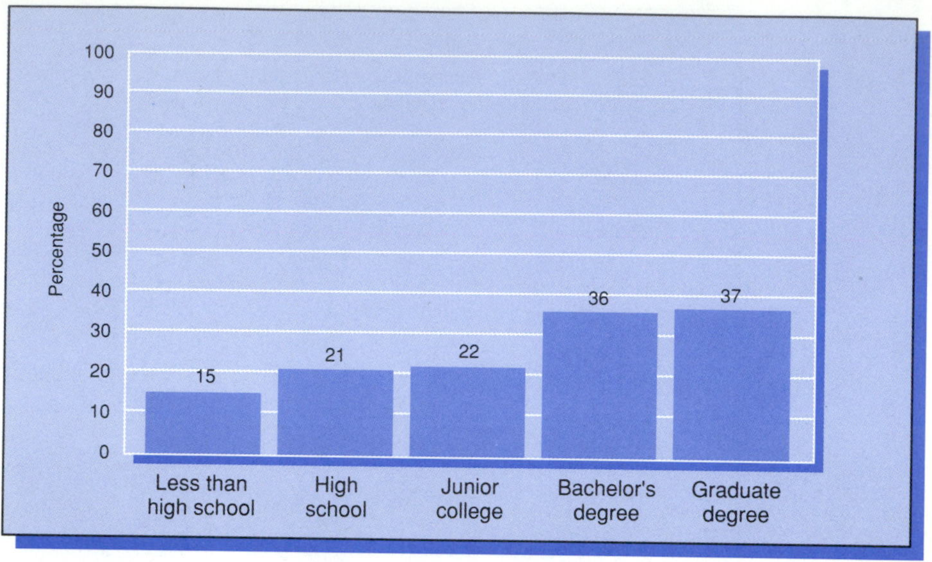

★ **Figure 7-4**

Percentage of respondents who said they were "very interested" in politics (1988, by level of education)

SOURCE: James Allan Davis and Tom W. Smith, *General Social Survey, 1972–1988* (Chicago: National Opinion Research Center, 1988), subfile 1988 (machine-readable data file).

Yet, despite these political symbols and civics classes, the role of the schools in political socialization is not really clear. What are the schools actually teaching children about politics and how are they teaching it? Do the schools reinforce loyalty to the system, or do they stimulate pessimism by introducing students to the "real world"? Most of the fourth-graders interviewed in Connecticut, for example, felt a personal attachment to the president, regarding him as wise and worthy of great trust. As one child volunteered, "The President is doing a very good job of making people be safe."[7]

For many youngsters, however, the lessons in school are undermined by personal experience and conflicting family attitudes. The positive feelings about "America" which seem to infect most kindergarteners often turn sour for underprivileged children, who must face the undeniable contrast between their existence and the idealistic views of society and government touted in the school curriculum. Children whose parents are distrustful and disapproving of the political system often develop similar doubts and negative feelings.[8]

A persistent finding, however, is that people's perceptions of their place in the political system correspond to the amount of formal education they acquire (see figure 7-4). As their educational level advances, so does their level of participation and interest in politics. The more education people acquire, the more confidence they gain in their ability to understand the political world and to play an effective role in it. Thus, there is some hope that childhood alienation can be overcome with educational opportunities.

But school experiences influence children's political learning in ways that go beyond what the curriculum formally teaches. Many informal lessons of the classroom and playground also influence children's political views. One social scientist, for example, made the following observations about his visit to a third-grade class:

> As I was sitting in the back of the classroom shortly after school started, three boys larger than those in the class came in and asked for Mike Smith. The teacher asked the boys what he had done, and she was told that he had pushed in line. She called Mike to the front, made disapproving sounds, and commanded Mike to leave the room with the boys. The leader of the three placed one monitor in front of Mike and one behind, and, with the leader directing, Mike was marched from the room. As an observer I felt very uneasy and a bit like it must have felt to watch the Gestapo come for an enemy of the state . . .
>
> A little later this same morning, after the lesson on current events, which was notable for the vapidity of the items discussed, mass movement began in the class. Soon I discovered that all the boys had—at some unseen signal—lined themselves up on the opposing side of the room from the girls and both groups stood patiently waiting for the teacher to do something. I became alarmed at this bizarre behavior until I realized that they were preparing to march to the bathrooms simultaneously. No one was allowed to remain behind. . . . I found this regimentation as disconcerting as the fact that earlier mere accusation had been enough to establish Mike's guilt in the teacher's mind. Relating the two events, I thought the children were being well trained for a life of regimentation.
>
> [In such a classroom] the accused child learns that punishment is capricious, not judicious. He learns that it depends on factors over which he has no control and little understanding, that accusation is more important than investigation, and that, in the distribution of punishments, some are privileged, and some are not.[9]

What the school teaches in theory about democracy and justice, then, may or may not conform with the informal lessons children learn in their dealings with teachers, classmates, and school administrators.

The Peer Group

The views we acquire in our family environment often are affected later by our peers—our friends, classmates, co-workers, and neighbors. Although peers may become influential at almost any time in our lives, their influence is especially strong in early adolescence, when most of us begin the process of acquiring an identity apart from the family.

As time goes on, the opinions and views of the people we see face to face each day are usually more powerful than those voiced by more distant acquaintances or expressed through the mass media. One's spouse, close friends, roommates, other associates—especially those who seem better informed and more articulate than we are—enjoy a unique influence not shared by other social forces.

In fact, if people close to us strongly voice a preference for a political party other than the one favored by our parents, they may succeed in drawing us away from the family's chosen party. According to one study, when the majority of a voter's peers do not support the party favored by his or her family, the chances are more than eight in ten that the voter will shift his or her support to the opposition.[10]

Peer group pressure can be substantial. Psychologists have found that people often support a group's views even when those views conflict with their own judgments. This tendency has been most strikingly demonstrated in experiments in which people yield to group pressure in their perceptions of inanimate objects and shapes. When a group of college students was told to state incorrectly that one of several unequal lines was shortest (even though it clearly was not), many other

★ Children spend more time watching television than they spend in school. Although we are aware that television and other media influence us politically, we do not know exactly how.

unsuspecting students repudiated the evidence before their eyes and echoed the group's false response.[11] It has been hypothesized that the students' desire to be accepted by their peers was stronger than the clues supplied by their senses. They echoed the group's false reply because they feared ridicule and rejection if they did not. If people willingly respond to group pressure by ignoring their own perceptions of inanimate objects and shapes, they may also conform by altering their views of less concrete political and social issues, especially if they are not strongly committed to any particular viewpoint. Clearly, one's peers can have a strong effect on political opinion, competing with and sometimes even surpassing that of family and school.

The Mass Media

Most of us pass a great part of our lives tranquilized by television, absorbed in magazines, newspapers, and books, listening to the radio and going to the movies. American families spend an average of six hours a day watching television, and the average child spends more hours before the TV set than he or she spends in school. Thus it is not surprising that the mass media—television, radio, films, books, newspapers, and magazines—now compete with the family, schools, and other institutions to shape our political views and attitudes.

Yet the nature and degree of the media's influence on political views is far from clear. On the one hand, the media's ability to change specific opinions on current issues appears to be limited. The media tend more to reinforce political opinions acquired from the family and other social agents than to create new ones. Most people tend to pay attention to news reports, editorial opinions, and political ads that conform to their present views and tune out those that contradict them. Of course we cannot completely avoid information that conflicts with our views, any more than we can avoid repetitious television commercials that peddle toothpaste and deodorants. But "the audiences of the mass media," as one scholar reflects, "tend toward a selectivity that supports rather than weakens their pre-existing outlooks."[12]

Moreover, some of the information provided by the media goes through a two-step flow. Rather than persuading people directly, the information often is interpreted by a small number of opinion leaders who pass on their views. Whether these opinion leaders happen to be schoolteachers, union officials, or just friends and neighbors, their views on the information conveyed by the media may have greater impact than the original information. Thus the television program watched on Monday may have less effect on a person's opinions than what someone he or she respects says about the program on Tuesday.

The media may be more effective, however, in shaping political perceptions over the long term. Children may be especially susceptible to the messages of television and other media because their world views and values are rarely so well developed as those of adults. Children are constantly exposed to lessons of social importance in comic books, television dramas and commercials, magazines, and films. All of these popular means of communication promote, whether intentionally or not, certain social concepts and stereotypes, such as the idea that violence is an appropriate way for a man to settle a dispute, or that a woman who "sacrifices" home and children for a career will come to realize her folly.[13]

Additional Influences

Because each person is a unique product of many social forces, no one influence will apply equally to all. In fact, many social influences can play important parts in political learning.

In view of the potential impact of a job on a person's income, choice of residence, and exposure to other people, one's occupation can significantly influence one's political orientation. As we will see later, a person's desire to participate in politics and to pay attention to current issues can often be related to such occupational factors as income and personal contacts. The same is true for party preferences. Well-paid professional people, such as doctors and corporate executives, tend to vote Republican, whereas factory workers and teachers tend to vote Democratic. Obviously, such related factors as education and family upbringing also influence party choice.

A person's political orientation may be affected also by whether he or she is brought up in a large city, a suburb, or a rural area: each may have its own traditions and social customs that can affect long-term political views.

Sometimes political events and social crises can create pressures for adjustments in political thinking. History is made up of major events that have produced dramatic breaks with the past. The Great Depression of the 1930s, the Vietnam war and civil rights protests of the 1960s, the Watergate scandal of the 1970s, and the international terrorist attacks of the 1980s have all changed many people's political orientations.

The same can be said for a personal crisis, such as the loss of a job or the death of a spouse. One's normal interest in and perspective on the political world can change abruptly in the face of a personal problem or tragedy.

Finally, people's broad political orientations are affected by the social and cultural traditions of their society. They learn not only the specific values of their families and friends but also the general values that make their culture (or subculture) unique. Families, schools, peers, and the media do not invent their positions from whole cloth; rather, long-standing national characteristics—such as the inclinations to value freedom, equality, and achievement discussed in chapter 6—represent a major source of political socialization.

★ Survey Research: "According to a Recent Poll . . ."

Before we turn our attention to the way political attitudes are carried into adulthood, let us consider briefly how we acquire information about public opinion. Many of the generalizations made in this and other books on American politics are based on information collected in political surveys. Theories about the recent decline in the importance of political parties or about voters' growing distrust of politicians are supported by survey data. There are experts in the techniques of drawing a random and unbiased sample of the population. There are experts in writing clear and simple questions. There are experts in administering surveys, and there are experts in interpreting the results. Computers and statistical techniques are used at virtually every stage of the survey process.

Basically, a **political survey** is a set of political questions asked of a group of people. Usually the opinions of the group are expected to reflect those of the general population. In addition, researchers like to ask similar questions over a long period of time in order to uncover areas of stability and change. Sometimes, though, even with the most careful preparation, the questions miss the target. Survey research has suffered some spectacular miscues.

Perhaps the most embarrassing error occurred in 1936, when *The Literary Digest* predicted a landslide victory for the Republican presidential candidate, Alfred Landon. Landon's opponent, Franklin Roosevelt, ended up with over 60 percent of the popular vote. The magazine poll was dead wrong, despite the fact that the pollsters had asked the same questions of more than two million Americans. *The Literary Digest* folded soon thereafter.

Unfortunately for *The Literary Digest,* the size of a survey is irrelevant if the survey is biased in terms of the kind of individuals who are contacted. *The Literary Digest* used automobile registrations and phone directories as its population list; in 1936, however, many Americans had neither a car nor a phone. And of course it was these lower-income Americans suffering through the Depression who had grown to appreciate Roosevelt's reform policies.

Since 1936, pollsters have applied a variety of techniques to ensure that their surveys represent the population accurately. Surprisingly, none of the techniques calls for an increase in the sample size. It is generally accepted that 1,500 to 2,000 people in a national survey will yield accurate responses (responses that can be duplicated) within 3 percentage points 95 percent of the time (see table 7-1).

Much more effective in improving accuracy are various techniques to ensure a **random sample.** In a random sample each citizen has the same chance to be

★ **Table 7-1**
Gallup Poll accuracy record, 1936–1988 (percent)

Year	*Gallup final survey*		*Election results*		*Deviation*
1936	55.7%	Roosevelt	62.5%	Roosevelt	−6.8
1938	54.0	Democratic	50.8	Democratic	+3.2
1940	52.0	Roosevelt	55.0	Roosevelt	−3.0
1942	52.0	Democratic	48.0	Democratic	+4.0
1944	51.5	Roosevelt	53.3	Roosevelt	−1.8
1946	58.0	Republican	54.3	Republican	+3.7
1948	44.5	Truman	49.9	Truman	−5.4
1950	51.0	Democratic	50.3	Democratic	+0.7
1952	51.0	Eisenhower	55.4	Eisenhower	−4.4
1954	51.5	Democratic	52.7	Democratic	−1.2
1956	59.5	Eisenhower	57.8	Eisenhower	+1.7
1958	57.0	Democratic	56.5	Democratic	+0.5
1960	51.0	Kennedy	50.1	Kennedy	+0.9
1962	55.5	Democratic	52.7	Democratic	+2.8
1964	64.0	Johnson	61.3	Johnson	+2.7
1966	52.5	Democratic	51.9	Democratic	+0.6
1968	43.0	Nixon	43.5	Nixon	−0.5
1970	53.0	Democratic	54.3	Democratic	−1.3
1972	62.0	Nixon	61.8	Nixon	+0.2
1974	60.0	Democratic	58.9	Democratic	+1.1
1976	48.0	Carter	50.0	Carter	−2.0
1978	55.0	Democratic	54.6	Democratic	+0.4
1980	47.0	Reagan	50.8	Reagan	−3.8
1982	55.0	Democratic	56.1	Democratic	−1.1
1984	59.0	Reagan	59.1	Reagan	−0.1
1988	56.0	Bush	53.9	Bush	−2.1

Average deviation for 26 national elections:
2.2 percentage points

Average deviation for 19 national elections since 1950, inclusive:
1.5 percentage points

Trends in deviation

Elections	*Average error*
1936–1950	3.6%
1952–1960	1.7
1962–1970	1.6
1972–1988	1.4

SOURCE: *Gallup Report,* December 1988, p. 44. Reprinted with permission from *Political Science Quarterly*.

interviewed as any other citizen. The use of random sampling is generally preferred to the quota method, which calls for interviews with a certain number of people in major ethnic, age, religious, and other social groups. This method allows the researcher too much discretion in deciding beforehand which social characteristics are important to consider. Instead, survey researchers often compare the characteristics of their respondents after the survey is taken with characteristics of the whole population as reported in the national census. Researchers begin to worry only if groups are over- or underrepresented in their samples.

Other problems remain, however. For instance, there can be problems with the types of questions that are asked in the survey. Most surveys use multiple-

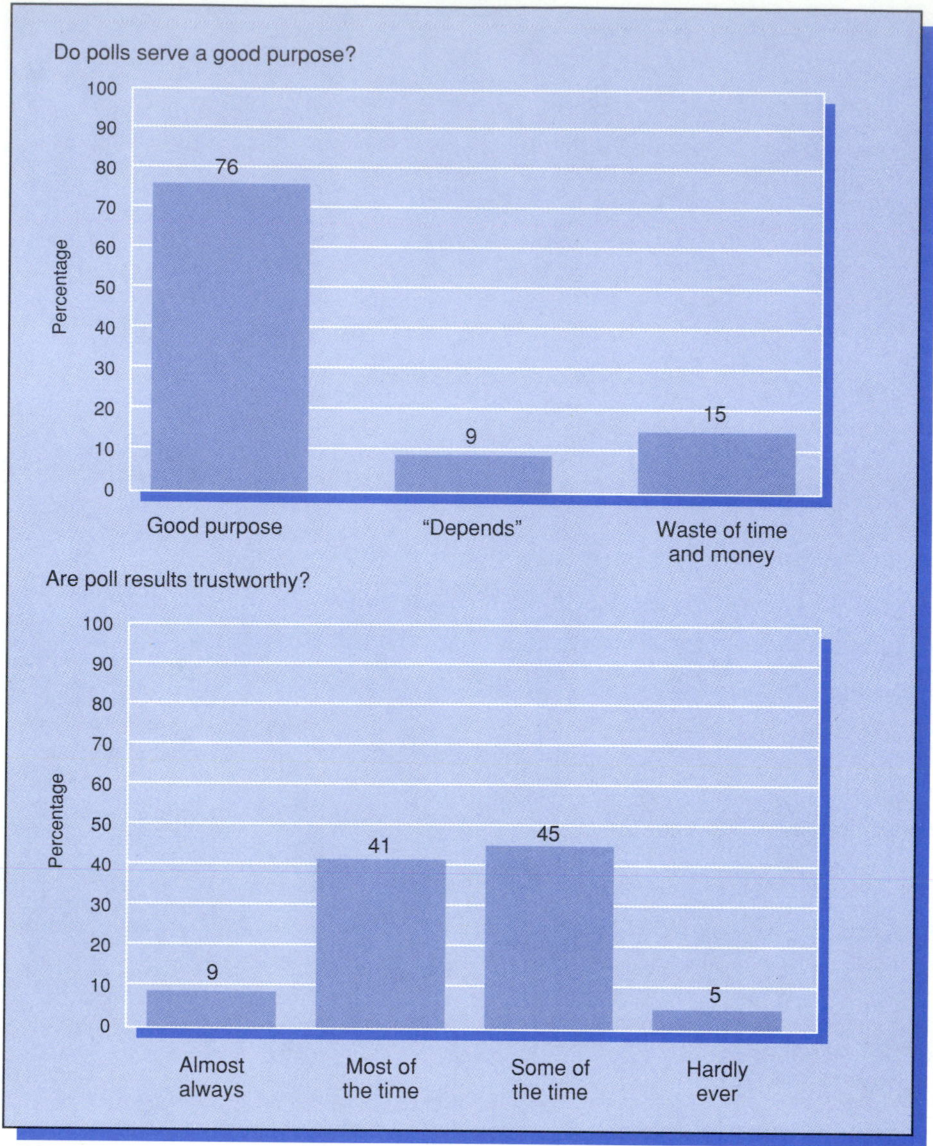

★ **Figure 7-5**
What does the public think about polls?
SOURCE: James Allan Davis and Tom W. Smith, *General Social Survey, 1972–1988* (Chicago: National Opinion Research Center, 1988), subfile 1988 (machine-readable data file).

choice questions: respondents choose an answer among a series of possibilities. The possibilities are chosen by the researcher and not the respondent, and the questions lack detail and nuance. In addition, in order to appear knowledgeable or merely to be courteous, individuals may express an opinion just for the sake of the survey, and thus attach themselves temporarily to one of the choices offered. (The public's opinion about polls is shown in figure 7-5.)

The questions may also be biased. In 1988 the Senate held hearings to determine if Judge Robert Bork was qualified to serve on the Supreme Court. Many of

★ Polls are common occurrences in American life. You may encounter either a person conducting a door-to-door poll as shown here or someone conducting a telephone survey.

Bork's opponents claimed that public opinion was strongly against him. Supporters of the judge (who eventually lost his quest) argued that the survey questions asked by the Harris polling organization stacked the deck against Bork. Certainly the questions could have been better phrased. One of the supposedly pro-Bork questions read: "If President Reagan says that Judge Bork is totally qualified to be on the Supreme Court, then that's enough for me to favor the Senate confirming his nomination. Agree or disagree?" Only 27 percent agreed, but it is not clear whether those who disagreed did so because they opposed Bork or because they wanted to avoid the implication that the president did their thinking for them.[14]

The moral of this story is that we should look at survey data with a skeptical eye. Although the best surveys have shown remarkable consistency over the years, the reputation of the surveyor and the fairness of the questions should be scrutinized. Survey research can be valuable, however, especially now that almost all universities and colleges have facilities that allow students hands-on experience with computerized analyses of high-quality survey data.

★ Name Your Congressmember: How Much Do People Know about Politics?

For many years political observers assumed that because the United States claimed to be a democracy, it fully satisfied the ideals of a democratic society. They believed, for example, that the citizenry made thoughtful decisions regarding the political fate of their country. One of the early political observers who embraced the notion of an informed, ideological electorate also served as president. In one of his academic works written as a political science professor at Princeton, Woodrow Wilson suggested that political problems could be substantially reduced only if "the people could have . . . daily knowledge of all the more important transactions of the governmental offices."[15] Wilson's assumption, of course, was that the people were willing and able to appreciate all this political information.

After Wilson's presidency, however, something occurred that raised doubts about the coincidence of ideal democratic citizens and the American reality. Scholars actually began to ask the electorate specific questions about the way they made their political decisions. Of course, there had been presidential "straw polls" back in the nineteenth century, but only in the 1940s (with substantial boosts from computer technology and social scientists who had gained research skills on war-related projects) did experts begin systematically to study the opinions and political preferences of the electorate. The experts used new techniques in survey research, and found that the reality of the American electorate fell short of the democratic ideal.

Political Views without Politics: A Shock from the Sociologists

To the dismay of the political science community, the first shock was delivered by a team of sociologists. Starting with a survey of Erie County, Ohio, in 1940, and expanding and refining their project in the 1944 and 1948 elections, Paul Lazarsfeld and his associates collected hard data that challenged the notion of the informed democratic citizen. Citizens did not carefully weigh political factors before they cast their votes, Lazarsfeld found; politics often had little to do with the way people acted politically. These conclusions set in motion a debate that continues today. Just how rational are Americans when they choose among alternative positions on local, national, and international issues? Do they in fact have a goal in mind and select the best candidate or policy approach to achieve it?

The sociologists boldly asserted that they could predict with surprising accuracy the way individuals would vote, not by asking them about politics but by asking them only about their socioeconomic status (income, education, and occupation), where they lived, and what church they attended. In the 1960s, when the elimination of discriminatory poll taxes and tests made it possible for black Americans to vote in large numbers, race was also used as a predictor of the way an individual would vote. On the whole, the sociologists found that Protestant, upper-income, well-educated, professional white northerners tended to be the strongest supporters of the Republican party. Working-class, Catholic or Jewish, less-educated voters tended to favor the Democratic party. And if they happened to be black or lived in the South, the chances were even greater that their loyalty lay with the Democrats. If individuals were cross-pressured—that is, if they had sociological traits that pulled in opposite directions—they tended to withdraw from interest in politics, and often made quick, uncommitted, last-minute decisions as to how they would vote.

There is of course some logic to this finding. The Republican party is known to be the more conservative of the two major parties. Republicans tend to be more

Can Twelve Million People Be Wrong?

Nancy Reagan caused quite a stir in 1988 when she announced that she consulted the stars on important matters; her husband even admitted that the presidential schedule had sometimes been changed to accommodate her astrological advice.

Seven percent of the American population—about twelve million people—admit to having changed their behavior in response to astrological advice. Could it be that astrology and American politics are related? The matter is open to debate. According to a report in *Public Opinion* magazine, party preferences are scattered evenly among the signs of the zodiac.

A closer analysis, however, reveals a stunning contradiction. Data on the 1984 election indicate that the Aquarian Ronald Reagan (February 6) and the Capricorn Walter Mondale (January 5) held dramatically different appeal for astrological segments of the electorate. Reagan did very well with voters born under Taurus, Leo, Libra, and Pisces; Mondale fared better with citizens born under Aquarius and Sagittarius. ★

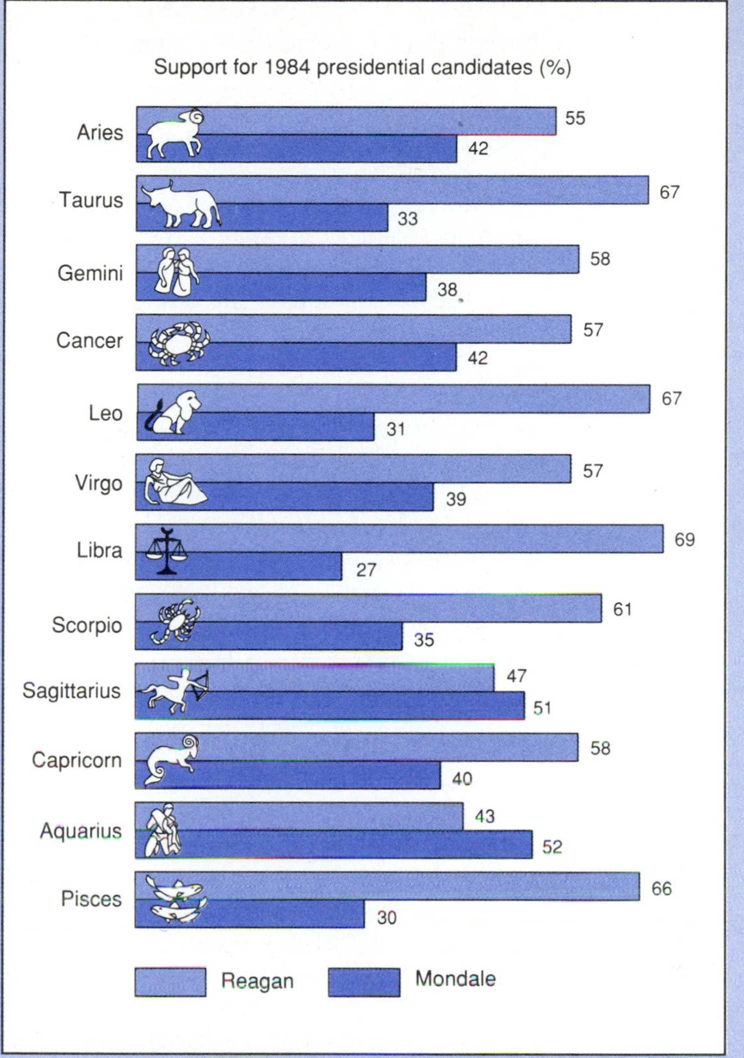

SOURCE: James Allan Davis and Tom W. Smith, *General Social Survey, 1972–1988* (Chicago: National Opinion Research Center, 1988), subfile 1985 (machine-readable data file).

interested in retaining, or conserving, what they see as good aspects of American society than in changing its less desirable aspects. People who feel they have much to lose if the system's rewards are altered or redistributed therefore tend to be sympathetic to the Republican party. And those who feel they have much to lose tend to be those with substantial wealth, education, and attachment to the older, more traditional American religious movements. People who belong to religions more recently founded, or who are less educated or wealthy, have reason to want to change the system to increase opportunities for people like themselves. Thus they are more likely to align themselves with the Democratic party.

Four Levels of Political Knowledge

If people tended to vote on the basis of broad sociological attachments, then one thing was clear: specific political issues and sharp ideologies were not so important to people as the democratic idealists had hoped. Following the Lazarsfeld studies, therefore, political scientists set out to determine just how much people knew and cared about American politics. Their findings were not too encouraging to those in search of an informed citizenry.

The most famous of these studies were conducted by Philip Converse at the University of Michigan's Survey Research Center. Using survey data collected during the 1956 presidential campaign, one study divided the electorate into four groups, each representing a different level of political knowledge and sophistication. At the top was the group Converse called "ideologues." These people most closely represented the ideal democratic citizen, although even at this level the researchers found "their commentary . . . neither profound, stimulating nor creative."[16] These people had knowledge of specific political issues, and they were able to connect their issue preferences with the general philosophies of parties and candidates. One person classified as an ideologue gave this answer to the question "What don't you like about the Republican party?"

> Well, I think they're more middle-of-the-road—more conservative. They are not so subject to radical change. Oh, I like their foreign policy—and the segregation business, that's a middle-of-the-road policy. You can't push it too fast. You can instigate things, but you have to let them take their course slowly.[17]

At the next lowest level were the "group benefits" people. They knew nothing more about their party or candidate than whether or not a particular group benefited from the policies of that party or candidate. When asked what was good about the Democrats, a voter from Ohio replied: "I think they have always helped the farmers. To tell you the truth, I don't see how any farmer could vote for Mr. Eisenhower."[18] It comes as no surprise to learn that this person happened to live in a farming community. The group-benefits people tended to evaluate politics in terms of what it meant to their particular niche in society, and then only in very general terms. Specific agricultural policies were beyond the political knowledge of the Ohio voter, for example, and beyond the knowledge of the group-benefits level as a whole.

An even more primitive level of political knowledge was found among the "nature of the times" group. These were people who knew virtually nothing of the specifics of politics. They could only associate "good times" or "bad times" with particular parties or candidates. A voter from New York City was asked why she liked the Republicans: "My husband's job is better. Well, his investments in stocks are up. They go up when the Republicans are in. My husband is a furrier and when people get money they buy furs."[19]

At the bottom of the scale were the "no issue content" group. These people functioned with only the most minute political knowledge. If they had anything at all to say about political candidates, it was a superficial comment about their looks or their family. If they belonged to a political party, they could not say why except that they "liked" it or it was their family's party from "way back." Figure 7-6 shows the percentage distribution of the four types.

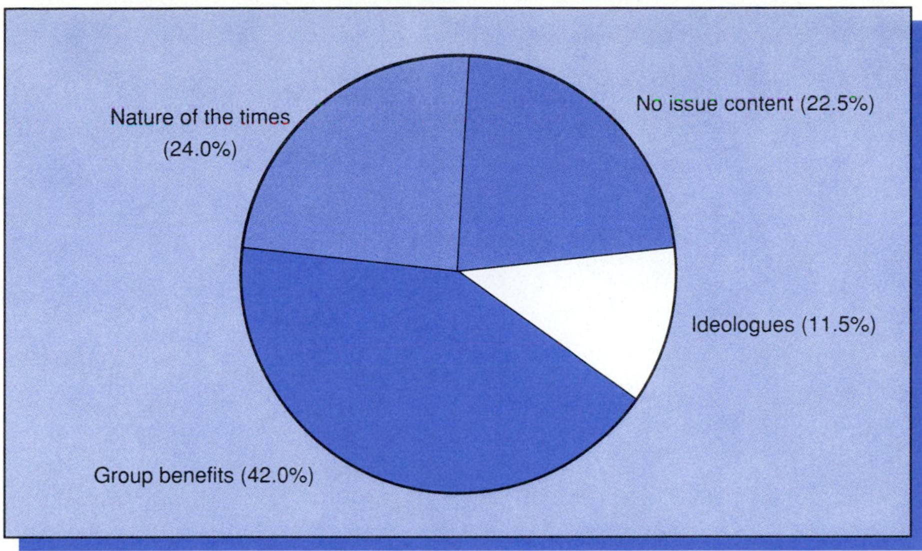

★ **Figure 7-6**
Converse's levels of rationality, 1956
SOURCE: Adapted from Angus Campbell, Philip E. Converse, Warren E. Miller, and Donald E. Stokes, *The American Voter: An Abridgment* (New York: Wiley, 1964), p. 144.

Citizen Ignorance: Abraham Who?

On the face of it, things do not seem to have changed much since the mid-1950s. The journalists Diane Ravitch and Chester E. Finn, Jr., revealed in 1987 that citizens about to enter the voting ranks knew little about their political system.[20] Only one of every three seventeen-year-olds knew in what half-century the Civil War took place, and only 43 percent had heard about the controversy that surrounded Senator Joseph McCarthy in the 1950s. Only 15 percent could identify Tocqueville as the foreign observer who visited the United States more than a century ago and recorded his insights in *Democracy in America.*

Adults do no better. A *Washington Post*-ABC News poll taken in August 1987, as the Robert Bork controversy was steaming in Washington, revealed that 55 percent of American adults had not read or heard about his nomination to the Supreme Court. Other polls have revealed that 63 percent of the adult public did not know which countries engaged in the SALT talks.[21] And polls have shown consistently that less than half of American adults can name their representative in Congress. (See figure 7-7.) Perhaps Americans are just a bunch of inveterate know-nothings who lack the curiosity or even the intelligence to appreciate politics. Indeed, many scholars support this position.[22] Another interpretation, however, is that the public's ignorance reflects not just lack of interest but a dearth of significant information. If meaningless campaign slogans and superficial news accounts dominate the airwaves, the blame belongs at least as much to the transmitters of information as to the public.

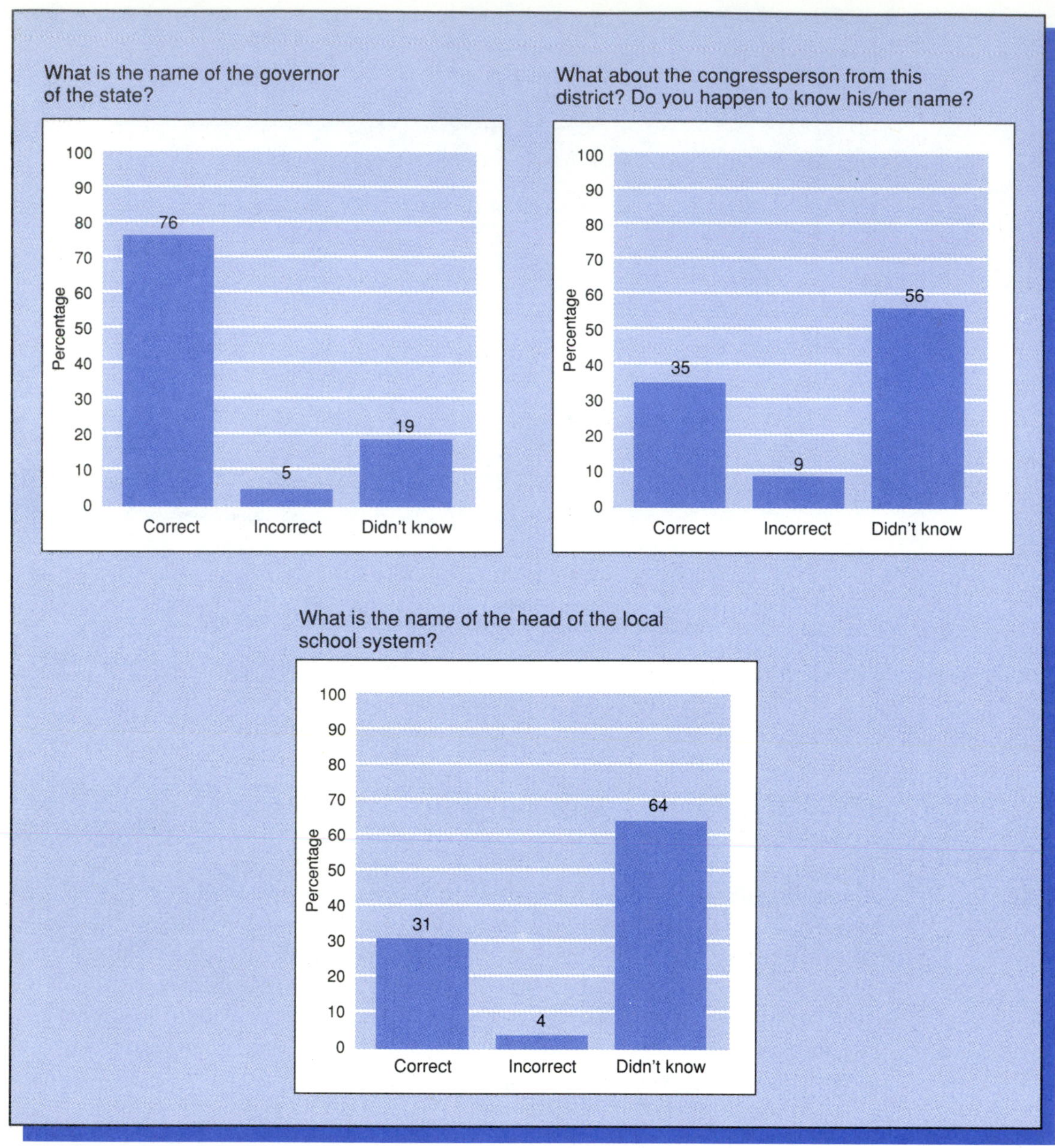

★ **Figure 7-7**

Can you name your governor, congressmember, and school district superintendent? Here is how your fellow citizens fared in 1987.

SOURCE: James Allan Davis and Tom W. Smith, *General Social Survey, 1972–1988* (Chicago: National Opinion Research Center, 1988), subfile 1987 (machine-readable data file).

Television especially can be criticized for rarely fulfilling its potential to stimulate and educate. Although most people report television to be their main source of news, public affairs programming gets far less air time than soap operas, game shows, and commercials. Except for coverage of unusual or dramatic events, such

as the Iran-Contra hearings of 1987, current political and social issues are rarely explored in a meaningful way. The nature and quality of programming reflect instead a commercial desire to reach the largest number of viewers and to present programs that "arouse no controversy, irritate no sensitivity, irritate no brain cells."[23]

People *can* be aroused to higher levels of political awareness when they see an issue as particularly significant to them. The debate over the Vietnam war and the social upheaval that surrounded the debate played substantial roles in the 1972 presidential race between Richard Nixon and George McGovern. In fact, for the first time since the Converse studies, political scientists were able to predict the way people would vote on the basis of where they stood on the issues rather than on the basis of their party or social class. Perhaps Converse found the electorate to be uninvolved because the elections he examined (1952 and 1956) seemed to many voters to lack important issues. Whether the fault lies in poorly transmitted information or in a lack of interesting issues, the people themselves are not entirely to blame for being uninformed and unexcited about politics.

When Issues Do Count: The Shift in Black Voters' Party Allegiance

The ability of issues to influence political behavior was evident among black voters in the aftermath of the 1964 election. In 1965 the Survey Research Center at the University of Michigan surveyed 1,500 high school seniors. The researchers discovered that when the black students were looked at individually, parental influences appeared to have little effect on partisan choice. In fact, by 1965 almost all of the black students were leaning toward the Democratic party, even if their parents were Republicans. Something other than long-term social attachments seemed to be at work.

During the 1964 elections a large number of black voters suddenly shifted their party preference. Before 1964 the Republican party had maintained a moderate level of support among black voters. But loyalty to the party of Abraham Lincoln all but vanished in the presidential election of 1964. Not only did black voters switch to the Democratic party in substantial numbers, but the strength of this allegiance to the party quickly surpassed that of white Democrats (see figure

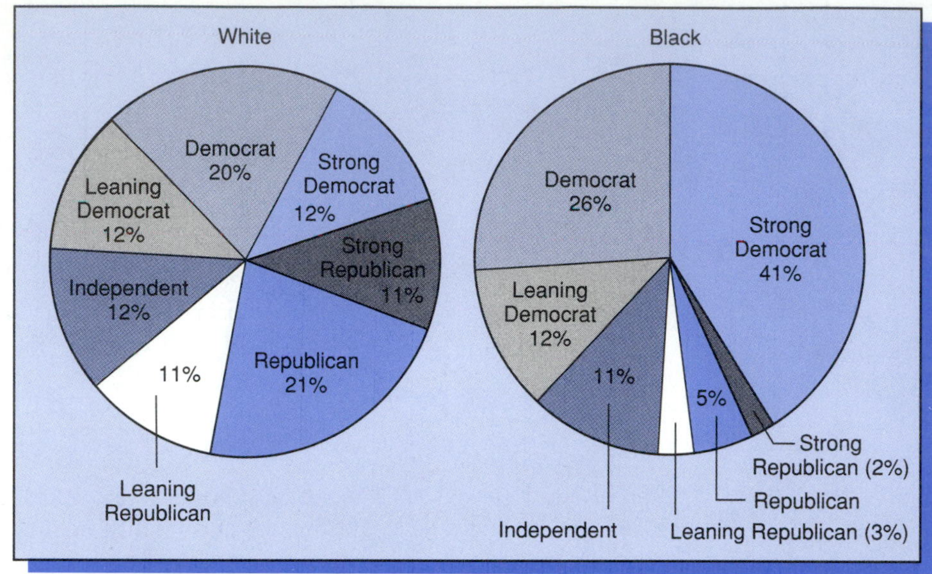

★ **Figure 7-8**
Party choice of black and white Americans, 1988
SOURCE: James Allan Davis and Tom W. Smith, *General Social Survey, 1972–1988* (Chicago: National Opinion Research Center, 1988), subfile 1988 (machine-readable data file).

7-8). Obviously, something had mobilized black voters that could not be accounted for by sociological explanations.

What probably accounted for the shift were the particular issues and candidates of 1964. The Democratic party, and especially its presidential candidate, Lyndon Johnson, became increasingly committed to the civil rights movement, and supported legislation to expand the political and economic freedoms of black Americans. Barry Goldwater, in contrast, was seen as the most conservative Republican presidential candidate in many elections, and black voters especially were concerned about his apparent lack of interest in civil rights. Everett Carll Ladd called the Goldwater candidacy of 1964 "an act of supreme stupidity":

> Richard Nixon, for instance, received the support of only one black voter in eight in his 1972 landslide victory, but he was backed by almost *one-third* of black Americans in his narrow 1960 defeat. . . . The key event in this shift of black allegiances was the 1964 election. Until that year, it was a question as to which of the two parties would be the party of civil rights.[24]

Thus, while it may be idealistic to see American voters as consistently keen on political issues, it may be equally misleading to see them as lazy drones who mindlessly conform to political patterns dictated by parental and sociological influences. There do seem to be times when issues capture the interest of voters, who then abandon their long-standing, often weak sympathies for informed concern. Seekers after ideal democracy mourn the fact that such interest seems to occur most often in the wake of wars and scandals. More pragmatic commentators respond that at least the public rises to the occasion when it really counts.

★ A role reversal: In the 1960s, radical youths warned against trusting anyone over forty. The 1980s brought "Family Ties," where it was the Keaton parents who tried to hold the fort against the onslaught of conservatism—represented by their yuppie son, Alex.

★ The New Conservative: A Volvo in Every Garage?

A good deal of attention has been paid to changes in the attitudes and opinions of young Americans. Universities are now brimming with morose middle-aged professors who roam the hallowed halls complaining to each other about the values and aspirations of the contemporary student. They grow teary-eyed as they reminisce about their part in a meaningful demonstration or daring sit-in during the 1960s; tears turn to sobs when they overhear their students, dressed in yachting sportswear, discussing their stock portfolios.

This new generation gap is the subject of television shows and comic strips. Younger Americans are being type-cast as yuppies who drive a Volvo but crave a Mercedes, who read the *Wall Street Journal,* play golf, and think Woodstock is a lumber investment. We are told that there is a resurgence of **conservatism**, and many professors are certain it is true.

Until now, a kind of iron law has said that conservatism comes with age. Financial security, for instance, tends to arrive in middle age, if it arrives at all, and a conservative stance is attractive to people who want to retain their material comforts. It has also been argued that as children leave the nest, parents have a

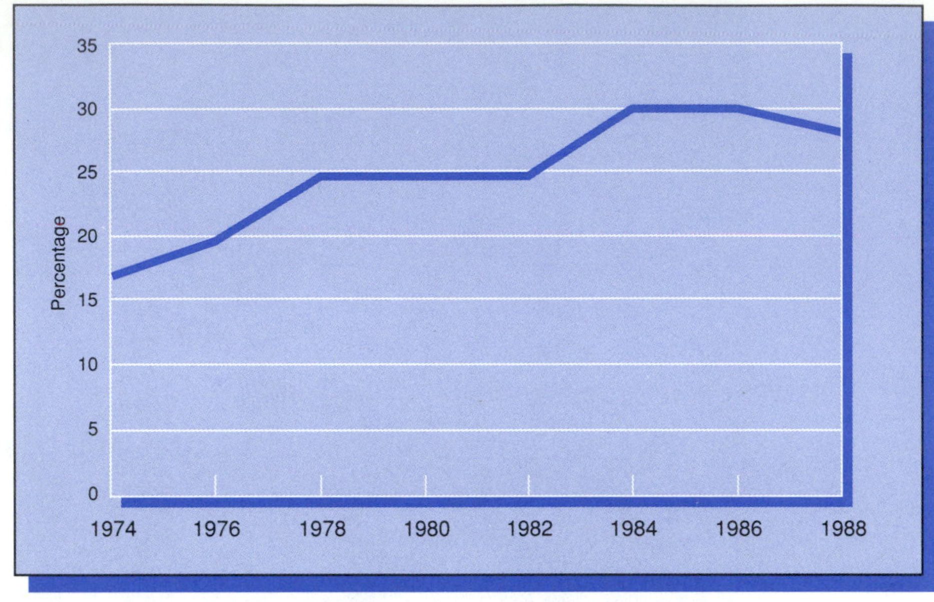

★ **Figure 7-9**

Percentage of 18–25-year-olds who considered themselves "conservative," 1974–1988

SOURCE: James Allan Davis and Tom W. Smith, *General Social Survey, 1972–1988* (Chicago: National Opinion Research Center, 1988) (machine-readable data file).

tendency to downplay the importance of public expenditures for schools, parks, and recreation facilities. Reluctance to see one's taxes spent on public works is often perceived to be typical of American conservatives.

Other observers say that as Americans approach their twilight years, they worry more about the legacy they will leave behind to their family and posterity. Older people, it is argued, want to achieve the trappings of success in order to convince themselves and others that they have led a valuable life. Thus large houses, impressive wardrobes, foreign travel, and prestigious automobiles become increasingly important. Older Americans want to be seen as part of the successful "establishment," even to the extent of adopting establishment politics. And, of course, establishment politics tend to be conservative. As we noted earlier, it makes sense that the pillars of the community want to maintain rather than change a structure that serves them well.

A New Breed?

Despite these traditional arguments, today's young Americans seem to be increasingly attracted to conservative politics. Although the proportion of all adults who consider themselves conservative has increased only slightly in the years from 1974 to 1986, the story changes when young citizens are looked at separately. Figure 7-9 shows that in 1974 only 17.2 percent of citizens aged eighteen to twenty-five considered themselves conservative; by 1986, the ranks of young conservatives had swelled to 30.4 percent of that age group. Note, too, that the stability of the trend seems to refute the idea that the new conservatism is only a Reagan glitch.

What It Means to Be a New Conservative

It may be true that younger Americans are now almost as willing as their elders to describe themselves as conservative. It is far from certain, however, that both age groups define "conservative" in the same way. The terms "conservative" and "liberal" have come to mean many things, and definitions change with each new political era. Since the Civil War, to be conservative has meant to some people to be opposed to civil rights legislation. Since the age of industrialization, others have equated conservatism with a laissez-faire attitude toward the activities of corporations. Since Roosevelt's New Deal, conservatism has meant to still other people resistance to tax increases to support government programs. After the presidential campaign of the liberal Democrat George McGovern in 1972, many people equated conservatism with opposition to the three *A*'s—amnesty, acid, and abortion. What, then, does it mean to be a "new conservative"?

On one set of issues, at least, young conservatives seem to reflect the long-time concerns of their conservative predecessors. Whereas a few years ago young Americans were not nearly so concerned about crime as older Americans were, all age groups now seem to be attentive to such issues. On the whole, young Americans are increasingly conforming to the long-time conservative position that criminals are not being sufficiently punished for their crimes, that murderers deserve to die for their crimes, and that more energy should be devoted to law enforcement.

Some traditional conservative issues, however, do not seem so attractive to younger conservatives. For instance, young voters continue to be strong environmentalists, wary of an unbridled assault by the private sector on the globe's scarce resources. Nor have young people shifted to the right on issues of civil rights or welfare policy. Young Americans continue to think that the poor deserve public assistance, and that the rights of minorities need and deserve government protection.

Some observers believe that the new conservative represents a turn to a hawkish international policy. After all, a majority of people aged eighteen to twenty-five supported Reagan's emphasis on increased military expenditures, even after older voters had begun to sour on the massive increases in military spending. The issue is complicated, however, because at the same time that young citizens were favoring a military buildup, they were also supporting increased expenditures for foreign aid—usually seen as a liberal stance. The explanation for the seeming paradox may be that young Americans are simply placing more importance on foreign affairs. They see simultaneously the need for peaceful diplomacy and aid on the one hand and a strong defense posture to meet international challenges on the other.

One aspect of American conservatism is given new emphasis by younger citizens: a "moral conservatism" in regard to a few key issues, such as religion and school prayer. In 1972, for instance, 30.2 percent of adult citizens under twenty-six believed that an antireligionist should not be allowed to teach in a public school. By 1984, the proportion had risen to 40.6 percent. And an even stronger jump was registered on the issue of the legalization of marijuana, as figure 7-10 indicates.

Perhaps coming years and elections will show that although young American voters are tolerant of various moral positions, they are intolerant of those who flout or criticize conventional morality in general. A Muslim might be welcomed as a teacher while a militant atheist would not. Both drugs and atheists may be seen as threats to a fragile moral fabric. Thus young Americans may be rejecting the "anything goes" attitude that they associate with the generation of the 1960s.

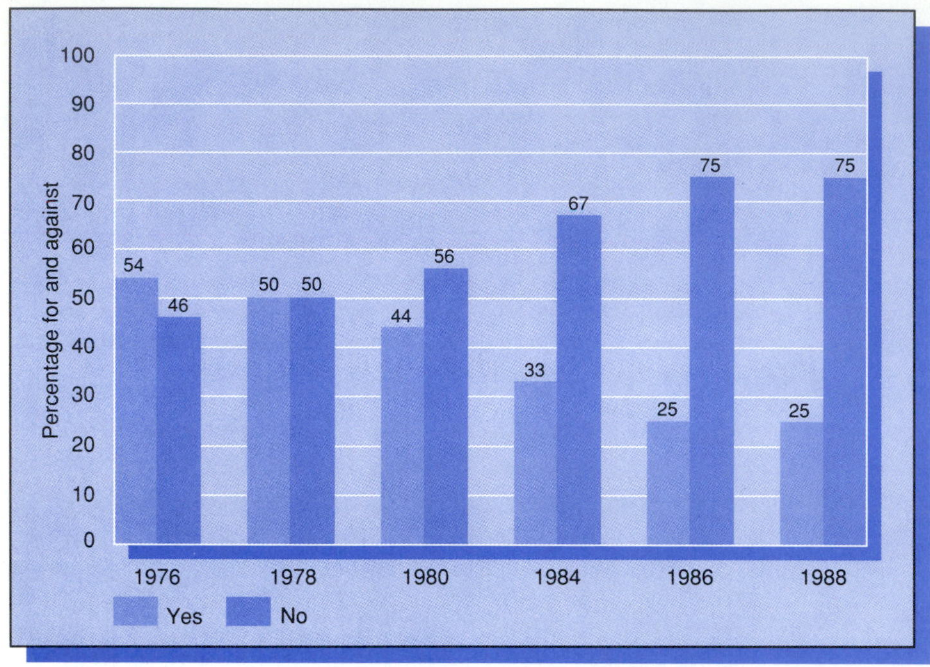

★ **Figure 7-10**
One measure of moral conservatism is seen in 18–25-year-olds' reported attitudes about the legalization of marijuana
SOURCE: James Allan Davis and Tom W. Smith, *General Social Survey, 1972–1988* (Chicago: National Opinion Research Center, 1988) (machine-readable data file).

★ Public Opinion in a Changing World

We have argued that the United States' relations with other nations have greater importance today than ever before. To what extent do American citizens recognize and understand the relevance of international developments to their own lives? Let us examine the status of American attitudes toward international developments.

When we turn our attention to the international sphere, we discover some curious facts about citizens' opinions and core values. Americans seem to subscribe to certain values or philosophies in regard to this nation's role in the world, yet they are often uninformed about foreign affairs. Moreover, public opinion on specific countries and issues—Central America, arms control, South Africa—is subject to a dramatic shift at any given time. How, then, can the student of American politics understand public opinion on international issues?

To begin, let's review what we know about public opinion and American foreign policy. Since 1949, Americans have in general admitted the importance of foreign affairs; international issues have been at the top of the list of political problems two-thirds of the time.[25] Paradoxically, however, although Americans consider international events important, they can be woefully ignorant about them. Examples of our lack of knowledge about the world and international politics abound. In 1950, as the nation became embroiled in the bloody Korean conflict, only 66 percent of Americans could name the U.S. secretary of state. In 1964, 38 percent believed that the Soviet Union was a member of NATO, the military alliance created specifically to defend Western Europe from Soviet attack, and 28 percent did not know that China was a communist nation.[26] During the 1980s, the controversial and much-publicized policy of aiding the antigovernment Contra rebels in Nicaragua was equally a mystery to many Americans. At the height of the debate over funding of the Contras in 1986, of those who said they favored financial aid, only 40 percent knew which side the U.S. government was supporting in the conflict.[27]

How can we explain the gap between the general recognition that world events are important and the lack of knowledge and understanding of them? One obvious answer involves access to information. It may be difficult to imagine a time when news of the world did not flash across our television screens as events unfolded. Yet we must remember that global communication by satellite and electronically printed national newspapers are recent developments. Before the advent of modern jet transports, relatively few Americans traveled abroad. Except in times of war or other crises, most people's lives were not routinely influenced by political, economic, or cultural events in other countries. Thus most Americans enjoyed the luxury of selective attention to world events, perhaps offering an opinion when prodded by an inquisitive pollster but otherwise remaining content with their superficial knowledge of complex foreign policy issues. Wars and other dramatic foreign events were seen as important, but it was easy for the average American to avoid the details.

A second reason why the public has only a poor understanding of the details of foreign policy is people's willingness to leave the problems of war, peace, diplomacy, and trade to the experts in Washington. The nation's foreign policy decisions are often left to specialists from academia, the military, and the business community—those whom David Halberstam, in his Pulitzer Prize–winning book on our government's involvement in Vietnam, called "the best and the brightest."

One can point to many examples of the power of presidential influence in shaping people's attitudes toward foreign affairs. During the Vietnam conflict, for example, public opinion often flipflopped as the president searched for a workable policy. Before the decision to begin bombing North Vietnam, a majority of Americans opposed such an escalation of the conflict. After President Lyndon Johnson ordered the bombing of targets around Hanoi and Haiphong in 1965, however, polls showed that 85 percent of the people supported this switch in policy. When Johnson decided in 1968 to halt the bombings in the interest of promoting peace talks, 64 percent went along with this change of direction.[28]

Politicians, presidents, and researchers alike have discovered that immediately following a quick and daring military operation, the president's popularity soars. Even the disastrous Bay of Pigs invasion in 1961 and President Carter's failed effort to rescue hostages in Iran in 1980 provoked strong favorable public opinion. And after a bomb killed 241 United States Marines in Lebanon in 1983, the public's support for President Reagan's policy climbed from 36 percent to 48 percent.[29]

Can we conclude that Americans have been duped by propaganda and manipulation, and that they have made the task easy because they lack underlying values and firm opinions about how their nation should operate in the world? Such an explanation ignores the persistent appearance of broad public attitudes and core values in regard to America's behavior in the world. Despite a lack of knowledge of world events, certain values or philosophies do play a role in the way citizens interpret the sparse details they manage to collect.

The Growth of Internationalism

Before the international environment became as complex as it is today, two general philosophies dominated American public opinion about the outside world: isolationism and internationalism. Advocates of **isolationism,** which has strong roots in American history (as we shall see in chap. 19), believed that the nation should avoid entanglement in international affairs. They saw the global environment as hostile and the people of other nations as ungrateful for American assistance. For the isolationists, the solution to an unfriendly world was straightforward: America, protected by vast oceans, would be better off enjoying the bounty of its own continent with people of "their own kind." As late as the mid-1960s, 20 percent of the American public were categorized as isolationists.[30]

At the opposite pole were the **internationalists,** who contended that America's proper role in the world was to be a political, economic, military, and moral leader. Internationalists believed that the world's richest and most powerful country could not realistically stick its head in the sand. Since World War II, all American presidents and the vast majority of the foreign policy elite have been firm internationalists.

The general public, however, has been slower to adopt the internationalist perspective. A substantial barrier to such acceptance was the Vietnam war, which provoked a public withdrawal from international concerns. In response to the question "Should the United States mind its own business internationally and let other countries get along as best they can on their own?" 41 percent answered yes in 1974, whereas only 19 percent agreed in 1964.[31]

This last gasp of isolationism did not last long, however. Such events as the oil crisis of 1973 drove home the importance of global influences on the American economy. Ronald Reagan and other politicians raised serious questions about the nation's influence abroad, and public opinion responded. As the 1970s came to a close, Democrats and Republicans alike were expounding on the Soviet military threat and the need to "put Vietnam behind us." The public's response was evident in the debate over the military budget. In 1973, 15 percent of Americans felt that too little was being spent on defense. But by 1980, 55 percent of those asked the same question responded that defense expenditures were too small. After Reagan launched his military buildup plan in October of 1981, public opinion has receded to a basic satisfaction with America's military preparedness.[32]

Hard-liners and Accommodationists

Despite the short bout of isolationism following the Vietnam war, then, evidence indicates a growing acceptance and recognition of the importance of international developments. Thus the basic split between internationalists and isolationists is disappearing. In its place we find a more subtle, perhaps more complex philosophical distinction. Researchers have discovered that citizens no longer question whether the United States should be entangled in world events; their concern is rather *how* the nation should be involved. For the most part, Americans now see the impossibility of isolationism; but they disagree as to the kind of internationalism we should pursue.

The disagreement has divided public opinion into two camps—hard-liners and accommodationists.[33] **Hard-liners** feel that the best defense is a good offense. Rather than seek agreement with potential adversaries such as the Soviet Union, hard-liners counsel action. Adversaries need to be confronted and contained, with military force if necessary. Hard-liners tend to be distrustful of arms control and believe that in international affairs, actions speak louder than words.

Accommodationists, by contrast, believe that confrontation in the age of nuclear bombs and intercontinental missiles is a recipe for global annihilation. They believe that negotiation, arms control, and international cooperation offer the best path to peace and security.

Whether the public tends toward the position of either hard-line or accommodationist often depends on recent developments. During periods of stress between the superpowers—as in the early 1980s, when President Reagan described the Soviet Union as an "evil empire"—opinion tended to run strongly toward the hard-liner perspective. A series of successful summits between Reagan and the Soviet president, Mikhail Gorbachev, which culminated in the signing of the Intermediate-Range Nuclear Forces Treaty in 1987, encouraged many Americans to move toward the accommodationist point of view. In response to a 1988 Gallup poll that asked "Do you think that in the future the Soviet Union will be more likely or less likely to live in peace with its neighbors?" 76 percent said that it was "more likely" and only 16 percent said "less likely."[34]

★ Summary

Many of our political attitudes and values can be traced to our childhood experiences. The process through which we gain our knowledge and views of the political world is called political socialization. Among the many agents of political learning, the family, the schools, the peer group, and the mass media bear the major responsibility for inculcating political views and opinions.

To obtain reliable information about people's political opinions and preferences, researchers have turned to surveys or opinion polls. By asking detailed questions of a select sample of people, they hope to gain an understanding of the opinions and views of the general population. While surveys have at times been inaccurate or biased, the use of random sampling has provided insights into what American voters believe about government and politics at a given time.

One finding is that many Americans are poorly informed about politics, although the reasons are not clear. Whereas some observers blame the American people themselves for lack of interest in the affairs of their country, others point to the failure of the media and other institutions to stimulate and inform.

When surveys focus on the opinions of young Americans, the findings suggest that today's young people are more conservative than their predecessors on many issues, although the findings are not always consistent.

When we seemed to have a choice in regard to involvement in world affairs, Americans tended to be either isolationists or internationalists. Now that the influence of international developments on our lives can no longer be ignored, we tend to be either hard-liners or accommodationists. That Americans subscribe to these broad philosophies, though, does not mean that they are strongly held or always based on factual knowledge.

★ Key Terms

accommodationists
conservatism
hard-liners
internationalists
isolationism
political socialization
political survey
random sample

Notes

1. James Allan Davis and Tom W. Smith, *General Social Survey, 1972–1988* (Chicago: National Opinion Research Center, 1988), subfile 1988 (machine-readable data file).
2. David Easton and Jack Dennis, *Children in the Political System* (New York: McGraw-Hill, 1969), pp. 58–60.
3. Alexis de Tocqueville, *Democracy in America,* 2 vols. (New York: Schocken, 1961), 1:12.
4. David Wallace, *First Tuesday: A Study of Rationality in Voting* (New York: Doubleday, 1964), p. 231.
5. Fred I. Greenstein, *Children and Politics* (New Haven, Conn.: Yale University Press, 1965), p. 23.
6. Ibid., pp. 34, 62.
7. Ibid., p. 39.
8. See, for example, Edward S. Greenberg, "Black Children and the Political System," *Public Opinion Quarterly* 34 (Fall 1970): 333–345; Harrell R. Rodgers, Jr., "Toward an Explanation of the Political Efficacy and Political Cynicism of Black Adolescents: An Exploratory Study," *American Journal of Political Science,* May 1974, pp. 257–282; John S. Jackson, "Alienation and Black Political Participation," *Journal of Politics,* November 1973, pp. 849–885.
9. Norman Adler and Charles Harrington, "Concluding Essay," in *The Learning of Political Behavior,* ed. Adler and Harrington (Glenview, Ill.: Scott, Foresman, 1970), p. 190.
10. Herbert McClosky and Harold E. Dahlgren, "Primary Group Influences on Party Loyalty," *American Political Science Review* 53 (September 1959): 772.
11. S. E. Asch, "Effects of Group Pressure upon the Modification and Distortion of Judgments," in *Group Dynamics: Research and Theory,* ed. Dorwin Cartwright and Alvin Zander, pp. 151–162 (New York: Harper & Row, 1960).
12. V. O. Key, Jr., *Public Opinion and American Democracy* (New York: Knopf, 1961), p. 355.
13. For a brief review and bibliography of studies on television, see Douglass Cater and Richard Adler, eds., *Television as a Social Force* (New York: Praeger, 1975).
14. We thank Senator Orrin Hatch of Utah for supplying us with the particulars of this illustration.
15. Woodrow Wilson, *Congressional Government: A Study in American Politics* (Boston: Houghton Mifflin, 1885), p. 299.
16. Angus Campbell, Philip E. Converse, Warren E. Miller, and Donald E. Stokes, *The American Voter: An Abridgment* (New York: Wiley, 1964), p. 129.
17. Ibid., p. 130.
18. Ibid., p. 136.
19. Ibid., p. 140.
20. Diane Ravitch and Chester E. Finn, Jr., *What Do Our Seventeen-Year-Olds Know?* (New York: Harper & Row, 1987).
21. "What Americans Should Know," *U.S. News & World Report,* September 28, 1987, pp. 86–94.
22. One scholar has even gone so far as to argue that the stability and health of the system is maintained by the electorate's lack of interest in politics. See Bernard Berelson et al., *Voting: A Study of Opinion Formation in a Presidential Campaign* (Chicago: University of Chicago Press, 1954), chap. 14.
23. Key, *Public Opinion,* p. 386.
24. Everett Carll Ladd, *Where Have All the Voters Gone?* (New York: Norton, 1977), p. 8.
25. Eugene R. Wittkopf, "Elites and Masses: Another Look at Attitudes toward America's World Role," *International Studies Quarterly* 31 (March 1987): 132.
26. Charles W. Kegley, Jr., and Eugene R. Wittkopf, *American Foreign Policy: Pattern and Process,* 3d ed. (New York: St. Martin's Press, 1987), p. 288.
27. *New York Times,* April 15, 1986, p. 4.
28. James M. McCormick, *American Foreign Policy and American Values* (Itasca, Ill.: F. E. Peacock, 1985), p. 278.
29. Ibid., p. 279.

30. Lloyd Free and William Watts, "Internationalism Comes of Age . . . Again," in *Perspectives on American Foreign Policy,* ed. Charles W. Kegley, Jr., and Eugene R. Wittkopf (New York: St. Martin's Press, 1983), p. 215.
31. Ibid.
32. Kegley and Wittkopf, *American Foreign Policy,* p. 296.
33. Wittkopf, "Elites and Masses," p. 146.
34. *Gallup Report,* November 1987, p. 35.

★ For Further Reading

Adler, Norman, and Charles Harrington. *The Learning of Political Behavior.* Glenview, Ill.: Scott, Foresman, 1970.

Asher, Herbert. *Polling and the Public: What Every Citizen Should Know.* Washington, D.C.: Congressional Quarterly, Inc., 1988.

Dawson, Richard E., and Kenneth Prewitt. *Political Socialization.* 2d ed. Boston: Little, Brown, 1977.

Easton, David, and Jack Dennis. *Children in the Political System.* New York: McGraw-Hill, 1969.

Erickson, Robert, Norman Luttbeg, and Kent Tedin. *American Public Opinion.* New York: Wiley, 1980.

Greenstein, Fred I. *Children and Politics.* New Haven, Conn.: Yale University Press, 1965.

Hennessy, Bernard. *Public Opinion.* 5th ed. Pacific Grove, Calif.: Brooks/Cole, 1985.

Holloway, Harry, and John George. *Public Opinion.* New York: St. Martin's Press, 1985.

Jennings, M. Kent, and Richard Niemi. *Generations and Politics.* Princeton, N.J.: Princeton University Press, 1981.

McCormick, James M. *American Foreign Policy and American Values.* Itasca, Ill.: F. E. Peacock, 1985.

Neuman, W. Russell. *The Paradox of Mass Politics: Knowledge and Opinion in the American Electorate.* Cambridge, Mass.: Harvard University Press, 1986.

Critical observers are fond of referring to the Democrats as the War Party and the Republicans as the Depression Party. No one has ever explained who started all the wars and depressions before there were Republicans and Democrats.

—*Will Stanton*

CHAPTER EIGHT

POLITICAL PARTIES

★★★★★★★★★★★★

Adaptive Organism or Endangered Species? Political Parties in the United States

★ Deadly Factions: Early Opposition to Parties

Two gunshots sounded almost simultaneously in the muggy summer air, and Dr. David Hancock prepared to treat yet another victim of a gunshot wound. He had followed the customary procedure, staying out of sight but within earshot of the disputants, so that he could claim ignorance of the details if the police arrived. He wasn't much worried about that, though, since the showdown had occurred across the Hudson River from New York in the more permissive surroundings of Weehawken, New Jersey, where hundreds had fallen dead or been injured in earlier duels.

As anticipated, Dr. Hancock was summoned to come quickly, but not so quickly that he might see the departure of the victor. The wound was to the abdomen, and very serious. Dr. Hancock could do little more than escort the victim by barge to the Greenwich Village home of a close friend and attend him until his death, which came the next day, July 12, 1804.

The dead man was none other than Alexander Hamilton, general of the Revolutionary War and a major architect of the Constitution. Three years earlier, his son Philip had died the same way, at the same place, with the same pistol in his hand. This time the nation went into shock. Thousands attended memorial ceremonies, and newspapers devoted entire issues to the fallen hero. Philadelphia, the center of Hamilton's national vision, was paralyzed with mourning.

The duel spelled disaster of a more subtle variety for the victor, Aaron Burr. Although he was vice-president of the United States at the time, Burr was soon to succumb to a political system that could not tolerate powerful individuals who refused to align themselves with one side or another. Burr had been an irritant to Hamilton, not because he always opposed him but because he was unpredictable. Thus, when the choice for president in 1800 came down to Burr or Jefferson, Hamilton had supported Jefferson. Although Jefferson's politics were more distant from Hamilton's, at least Jefferson was predictable. In a letter to his friend James A. Bayard, Hamilton explained:

> The truth is, that Burr is a man of very subtle imagination, and a mind of this make is rarely free from ingenious whimsies. Yet I admit that he has no fixed theory, and that his peculiar notions will easily give way to his interest. But is it a recommendation to have *no theory?* Can that man be a systematic or able statesman who has none? I believe not.[1]

From *Totally U.S.* by Simon Bond. Copyright ©1988 by Polycart, Ltd. Reprinted by permission of Harper & Row, Publishers, Inc.

In their many political encounters in the state of New York, Burr had supported Hamilton's positions on some issues but opposed him on others. Hamilton considered Burr an opportunist at best, a scoundrel at worst. (Burr challenged him to a duel when Hamilton said so in public.) Burr's resistance to political factions eventually caused him to be distrusted by almost everyone, and the duel with Hamilton hastened his decline.

It is ironic that Aaron Burr, who tried to remain independent of party ties, in the end suffered for his independence. Just a few years before the duel, many of the founders had criticized the whole idea of parties, on the grounds that they would undermine a legislator's independence and encourage undesirable divisions and factions. Indeed, parties have no written constitutional base. Although the Constitution spells out many of the duties of Congress, the president, and the Supreme Court, it does not even mention political parties.

President George Washington, in his farewell address to Congress in 1796, cautioned against "the baneful effects of the spirit of party." He feared that parties, in encouraging the pursuit of selfish partisan goals, might destroy national unity at a time when the new country was struggling to survive. John Adams, his vice-president, agreed with him, saying, "There is nothing I dread so much as the division of the Republic into two great parties. . . . This, in my humble opinion, is to be feared as the greatest political evil under our Constitution." Even Thomas Jefferson, who later became a key figure in the creation of strong rival parties, declared in 1789, "If I could not go to heaven but with a party, I would not go there at all."

Needless to say, parties developed anyway. Even though the founders considered a party system to be, as Frank Sorauf puts it, "an extraconstitutional excrescence not to be dignified by mention in the constitutional document," parties began to take shape as different groups clashed over economic issues, foreign policy, and the proper role of the federal government. As the eighteenth century came to a close, there were two national parties: the Jeffersonian Republicans (officially called Democratic-Republicans) and the Federalists. And by the middle of the nineteenth century, the American party system was so established that it has been called the "first truly national party system, one in which both parties were established and competitive in all the states."[2]

In this chapter we will trace the development of this partisan division. We will also examine the major shake-ups that have rocked the American political structure from time to time, jolting the ideological orientation of the major parties. Of course, special attention will be given to the two main parties today—Republican and Democratic—and to their relevance to contemporary American politics. We will also look at the interesting phenomenon of third parties in American politics, and at the role of parties on the world stage and in the years to come.

★ The Trademark of a Party

What exactly is a **political party**? How do we distinguish between a party and, say, an interest group or a political movement? Like many other concepts in political science, a party is difficult to define. "As there are many roads to Rome and many ways to skin a cat," one scholar has quipped, "there are also many ways to look at a political party."[3]

One traditional way to distinguish a party from other kinds of political groups is to examine its purpose. According to most political scientists, the unique goal of a party is to capture public office, to wield the powers of government. An interest group, in contrast, strives merely to influence governmental policy on specific issues. It does not attempt to assume responsibility for running the government itself. The American Medical Association, for instance, may try to affect policies relating to medical practices, but it is not interested in determining foreign policy as well, or in having the association's president in the White House.

While this distinction is a valid one, it fails to take into account those parties that are more concerned with advancing causes than with winning elections. Members of the Socialist and Prohibition parties, for instance, often concede that they have little realistic chance of gaining political control and say their chief interest is in using elections to publicize their cause and sway public opinion. They reason that, even though they have little hope of winning an election, they can attract more attention by fielding a candidate for office than by working behind the scenes as an interest group. As John Hospers, the 1972 presidential candidate of the Libertarian party, once confessed, "We're not even going to watch the votes very closely. But as a mouthpiece for ideas, I happily consented to run."[4]

Perhaps, then, we also need to differentiate between parties and other groups by their method of satisfying their objectives: only parties run candidates for public office under their own banners. Although other kinds of political organizations, such as interest groups, may try to mobilize public support for their views, they do not do so by nominating candidates for public office. No one runs for Congress, for example, under the banner of the National Rifle Association or the United Brotherhood of Carpenters.

But aside from running candidates for office and trying to gain control of government, parties serve a variety of functions for both the political system and the individual citizen.

Political parties

- provide a channel for political action.
- offer information on current issues and candidates.
- provide financial and other help to those seeking public office.
- promote the smoother running of governmental machinery.

Most of these functions, in fact, bear directly on the opportunities for participation at various levels of the political system, not only for political elites but for ordinary citizens as well.

One of the most important functions of parties is to provide a channel for people who want to affect policy making in some direct way. Several important party activities, including the political campaign and the nomination of candidates for office, draw upon the resources of ordinary citizens. Those who seek expanded opportunities for political action may serve as delegates to county and state party conventions, sit on local party platform and policy committees, or help recruit candidates for local offices. In fact, those willing to spend the time learning how the party in their state chooses delegates to its quadrennial national convention may even help decide who will be their party's nominee for president. As we will see later, major parties have encouraged grass-roots participation in the presidential nomination process.

If political action is to have any significance, it must be based on some understanding of current issues and problems. Even voting would be largely meaningless if one knew nothing about what was at stake, about what the policy proposals touted by the various candidates would mean for the country. In this respect, parties are also looked to for information. People looked to party platforms, press releases, and the speeches and media ads of George Bush and Michael Dukakis for information on current issues and solutions to national problems in 1988. They depended on the candidates to point out the errors of the opposition and to acquaint them with alternative policy ideas. Of course, the parties and their candidates do not always provide the kind of information voters need. Some critics charge that, although the parties do occasionally focus public attention on issues, party candidates rely too heavily on emotional speechmaking and on negative and simplistic media campaigns that exploit voters' needs and insecurities. To many people who watched the candidates hurling barbs and innuendos at each other, the 1988 presidential election appeared to be a particularly negative one. Yet this criticism is nothing new. More than twenty-five years ago, one scholar scoffed: "The claim that parties educate the public is open to serious reservation if education means mobilizing facts . . . and impartially appraising problems and solutions. Hyperbole, exaggeration, the oversimple solution, and demagoguery too often characterize the educational efforts of party activists."[5] (More will be said about the style of political campaigns in chapter 9.)

Party support is also regarded as an important asset for people who seek public office. Candidates still rely on the party label to gain the support of voters who habitually champion that party, whether or not the voters agree with or even understand the specific views and positions that the candidates take. As a consequence, candidates and their supporters are helped by knowing the affiliations and backgrounds of party members, as well as others they may hope to sway to their side. (See figure 8-1.) Candidates knock on the door of the local party headquarters seeking campaign workers and party volunteers eager to encourage potential supporters to register and vote. As we shall see, the future of parties in America may depend on their ability to develop and deploy sophisticated campaign organizations.

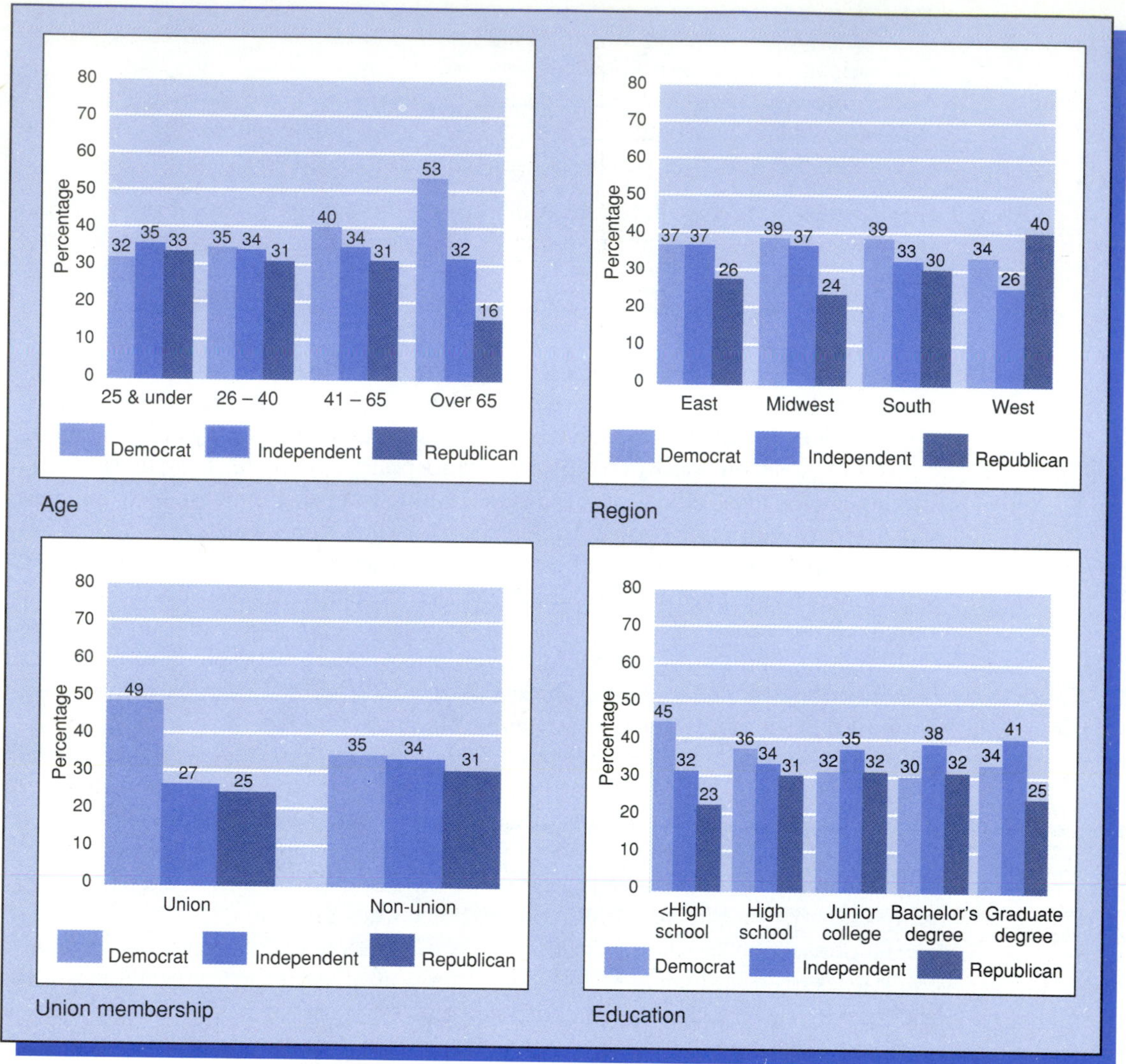

★ **Figure 8-1**

Political party affiliation, 1988, by characteristics of respondents (percent)

SOURCE: James Allan Davis and Tom W. Smith, *General Social Survey, 1972–1988* (Chicago: National Opinion Research Center, 1988), subfile 1988 (machine-readable data file).

Finally, parties assist the people who presumably have made it to the summits of power. National, state, and local officials look to their party organizations for help in creating public policy. Members of Congress, for example, often rely on the party leadership to steer a program over the various legislative hurdles and to help them staff committees, define responsibilities, and select presiding officers (such as the Speaker of the House). The parties additionally are viewed as a bridge between Congress and the White House. A president frequently appeals to fellow party members in the House and Senate to support his prized legislative proposals. He knows their common party ties and mutual desire to fashion an effective party

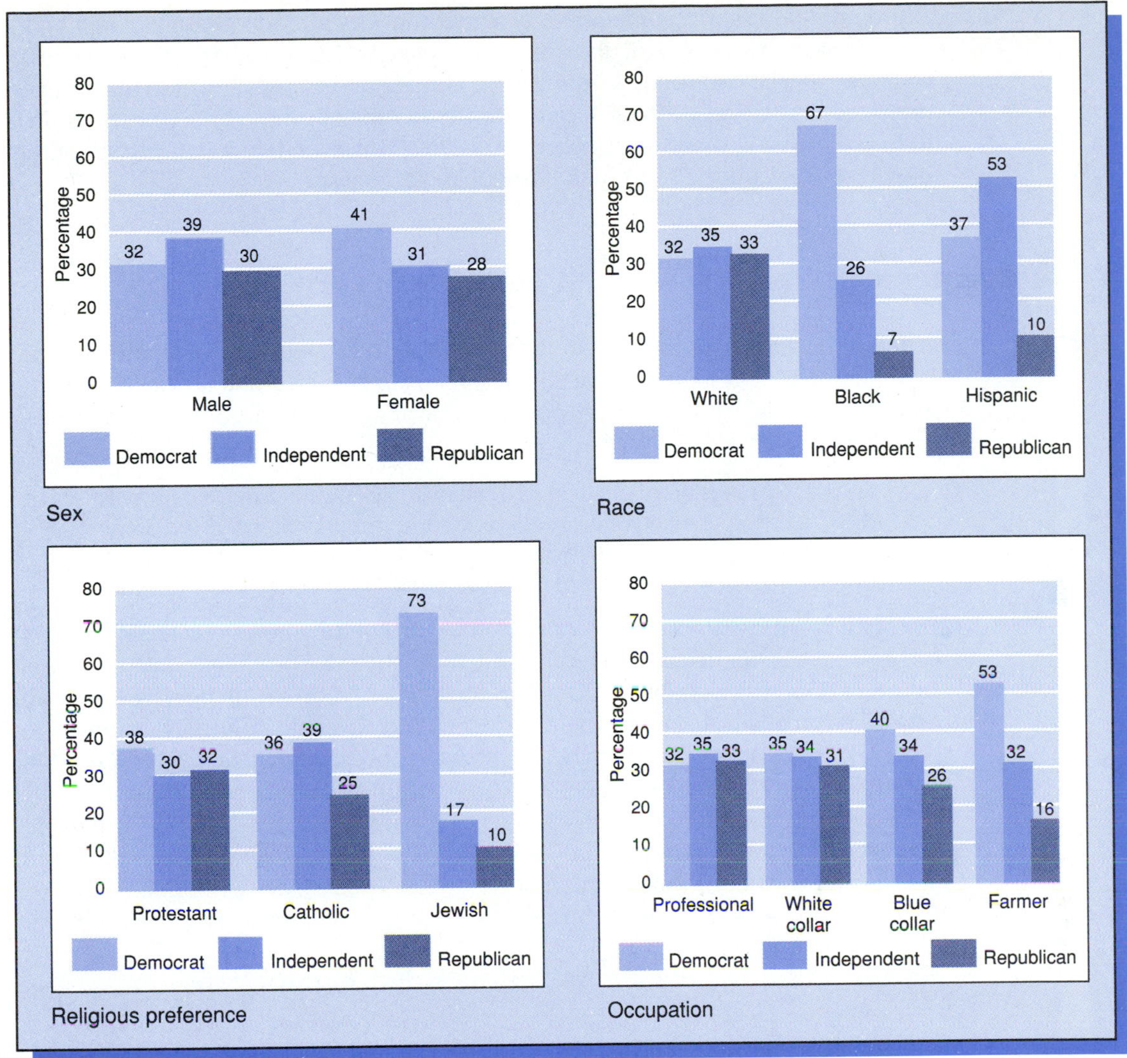

★ **Figure 8-1 *(continued)***

program can provide an incentive for cooperation between the two branches of government.

It should be kept in mind that neither the Democratic nor the Republican party has performed these tasks in a particularly effective manner, at least not in recent years. As we will see, each party has fallen short as a coordinator of the government's policy-making activities. And both have fallen short of their stated aim of representing voters' interests. As we noted in chapter 5, ruling elite theorists contend that the Democratic and Republican parties have been too similar and moderate to represent all segments of our society. Many Americans—especially among the poor and the members of some minority and ideological groups—do not believe either party articulates their interests. And since third parties have been too weak to take control of government, a climate of dissatisfaction and tension has persisted in some areas of our society that neither major party seems able to resolve. Before discussing these more recent problems, however, let us return to the time of Aaron Burr and the birth of the American party system.

★ The American Party System: A Historical View

At least one framer of the Constitution was not so fearful of partisan divisions as President Washington was. In fact, James Madison believed that American society would inevitably break up into opposing political groups or "factions." In *Federalist* no. 10 he wrote:

> From the protection of different and unequal faculties of acquiring property, the possession of different degrees and kinds of property immediately results; and from the influence of these on the sentiments and views of the respective proprietors, ensues a division of the society into different interests and parties.

For Madison, the purpose of the Constitution, and of the new government, was not to prevent factions from developing but to ensure that no single faction could suppress opposing factions. Madison saw the size and diversity of the new American nation as a real advantage; it would be difficult for a single political movement to control so much territory. Nevertheless, he was concerned that Alexander Hamilton and other colleagues were so determined to suppress competing factions that they were creating a unified central organization with too much power. He had no qualms, then, about joining forces with the growing opposition to Hamilton and his allies, thus contributing to the first partisan split in American politics.

Hamiltonian Federalists vs. Jeffersonian Republicans

The ratification of the Constitution put Hamilton and his allies in the driver's seat. George Washington was swept into office as the first president on a tide of nationalism and an eagerness to expand the powers of the central government. John Jay, co-author of the *Federalist Papers,* was nominated and confirmed as the first chief justice of the United States, and Hamilton was named secretary of the treasury.

It was not long before these Federalists, as they were called, began to stimulate a strong, organized opposition. Hamilton's fiscal program, for instance, called for excise taxes designed to permit quick repayment of the Revolution's wealthy supporters—at the perceived expense of less favored citizens, who had also made financial and personal sacrifices. The Federalists also supported the fledgling industrial and commercial interests of the North, to the dismay of many southern farmers and plantation owners. (This North–South split led to a bitter fight over the location of the new capital.) In addition, there was a growing belief that the Federalists were becoming clones of the British aristocracy, by shutting out popular input and participation.

If a single issue polarized the two camps and pushed them into full-fledged partisan organizations, it was the Jay Treaty of 1795. Washington and Hamilton were interested in the economic benefits that would accompany expanded trade relations with Britain. Thus Chief Justice John Jay was dispatched to England to negotiate a treaty that would create a most favorable trade status between the two countries. At the time, however, Britain and France were at war, and it seemed to some American revolutionaries (Jefferson and Madison among them) that their allegiance ought to be to France. After all, France had assisted in the American Revolution, and in 1789 it had fought its own antimonarchical revolution. It seemed to the treaty's opponents that the economic gain of an alliance with Britain would be outweighed by unacceptable ethical compromises. Not that the opponents of Jay's treaty were beyond ethical reproach. They also opposed the treaty because it had no stipulations for compensation for the slaves taken by the British during the Revolutionary War. It is no coincidence, then, that many of Hamilton's strongest opponents were southern plantation owners.

Therefore, by 1797 Congress had two distinct voting blocs that lacked only official names to become fully operative political parties. A representative's vote could be predicted on the basis of the company he kept. The Federalists were mostly from New England and the coastal regions of the middle states, and from South Carolina. They represented commercial interests, were sympathetic to England, and favored political institutions that retained elements of aristocracy. The Jeffersonian Republicans, who came to power in the presidential election of 1800, were from the American interior or from the South, represented agrarian interests, were sympathetic to the French Revolution, and favored political institutions that approached direct democracy.[6] It is interesting to note that trade and foreign affairs were controversial in America's early years, and helped to galvanize our first political parties. The difference between then and now lies in the magnitude, intensity, and number of lives directly affected by American ties to other nations.

To see the workings of our fledgling party system, let us return to the saga of Aaron Burr. Before his stint as vice-president, Burr had become a respected leader of the New York wing of the Democratic-Republican Party (the official name adopted by the Jeffersonian Republicans). He had joined the party not out of any strong ideological commitment but because of various ties of friendship and family. His specialty was campaigning, and he was credited with masterminding a dramatic turnaround in New York from Federalist to Republican control. And since New York was seen as crucial to Jefferson's presidential hopes, Burr was rewarded with an invitation to join the Virginian on his ticket in 1800.

The ensuing election created a headache for Jefferson and a crisis for the Constitution. Article II specified that the electoral college winner would be president and the runner up would be vice-president. Burr and Jefferson tied with 76 electoral votes each, and in accordance with the Constitution, the contest was transferred to the House of Representatives, where each state delegation would cast one vote. Through lengthy discussions and thirty-five ballots, neither candidate could muster the required majority.

Although Burr had always been considered his party's vice-presidential candidate, he was tempted by the Federalists (who preferred Burr's independence to Jefferson's partisanship) to use a loophole in the Constitution to advance to the presidency. Burr resisted the temptation, however, thus turning the Federalists' hopes to anger. Jefferson was angered even more when Burr proved unwilling to state that, since his shot at the presidency was based on a technicality, he had no right to the office. (By the 1804 election, the states had ratified the Twelfth Amendment to the Constitution, which called for the electors to cast ballots for both president and vice-president.) Thus, when Jefferson was finally elected on the thirty-sixth ballot, he vigorously pursued a now well-established practice of locking the vice-president out of important matters of state.

THE POLITICAL SITUATION.

For what he saw as gross disloyalty, Jefferson held a grudge. But it was only years later that Burr obliged Jefferson with an appropriate opportunity to take revenge. Burr's fame had dissipated; he was ostracized from Jefferson's second administration, he had shot and killed an American hero, and he had suffered a crushing defeat in the New York gubernatorial race. So he decided to enhance his political, financial, and military reputation by a dramatic and daring "western campaign." After conducting various missions of exploration and settlement, Burr found himself suspected of planning an attack on Spanish territory and of plotting the separation of the western territories from the eastern United States. Jefferson, smelling revenge, had Burr tracked down and hauled under guard to Virginia to face charges of high treason.

It looked as if Burr was done for. Only the greatest of ironies saved him. His talent for getting caught in the middle of partisan disputes had always brought him trouble, but now it was to be his salvation. For the judge assigned to try Burr for treason was John Marshall, the Federalist chief justice of the United States and long-time adversary of Jefferson and his Democratic-Republican party.

Although it was a jury trial, Marshall proceeded to make technical legal rulings that made conviction impossible. Legal scholars have argued that Marshall's actions were motivated as much by his desire to frustrate Jefferson as by a desire to see justice done to Burr.[7] In any case, we can see that intolerant squabbling between parties had already put its stamp on American politics.

★ Realigning Elections

Political parties may have been important to Hamilton and Jefferson, but even in its heyday the American party system had only a weak hold over the population. In many other countries, to be a party member is to carry a membership card, pay

★ **Table 8-1**
Issues and realigning candidates and parties in realigning elections, 1800–1932

Year	*Issue*	*Realigning candidate and party*
1800	Opposition to growing power of central government; fear that the United States was becoming a copy of Great Britain	Thomas Jefferson, Democratic-Republican party
1828	Expansion of political power to "common Americans" and opposition to the "establishment"; mythification of frontier existence	Andrew Jackson, Democratic party
1860	Political opposition to expansion of slavery in U.S. territories and moral opposition to slavery in the South	Abraham Lincoln, Republican party
1896	Rejection of the benevolence of big government and big business; demand for governmental opposition to big-business practices for protection of common citizens	William Jennings Bryan,* Democratic party
1932	Recognition of the need for government intervention in economic recovery, including substantial expansion of government welfare programs	Franklin Roosevelt, Democratic party

*Bryan lost the election, but Theodore Roosevelt and succeeding presidents adopted his perspective on big business.

dues, and go to periodic meetings. Party members support a cohesive and secure party philosophy. In the United States, party membership is almost as simple as declaring one's political preference. As the humorist Will Rogers used to say, "I don't belong to any organized party. I'm a Democrat." (In most states, to vote in a presidential primary, one must register with a party. To vote in a general election, one does not have to declare support for any party.) In many other countries, party members, including high government officials, can be booted out of a party for disloyalty, or failure to follow the "party line."

Because American parties have such a weak hold on their members, they must quickly reflect major shifts of public opinion. In other words, if a new issue comes on the scene, the parties had better address that issue immediately or be left in the dust. American parties don't have the power to maintain discipline among their members, whether citizens or elected officials.

Every once in a while, the American party system has had to respond to major public issues. The result has been a periodic reshaping of what the parties stand for. The first major partisan division, as we have seen, occurred between the Jeffersonian Anti-Federalists and the Hamiltonian Federalists. Since that time, the American party system has undergone four more upheavals strong enough to alter dramatically the political personalities of American parties. Such upheavals are called **realigning elections.** (See table 8-1, and for more specific data on presidential elections, see Appendix C.)

Realigning elections share certain characteristics.

- They signify a time of substantial political upheaval.
- The normal debates seem stale in the light of newer, more exciting issues.
- Participation and voting rates increase sharply.
- Many people (up to one-third of the electorate) change parties.
- Realignments have seemed to occur at roughly equal intervals—about every thirty years.

Let us briefly investigate the realigning elections that followed the original shake-up of 1800.

The Second American Party System

By 1824, the old divisions between Federalists and Anti-Federalists had grown stale. Even though the Jeffersonian Democratic-Republican party had come to dominate national elections, forceful resistance to a powerful central government had faded. In fact, many new states were entering the union with hardly a memory of the Hamilton-Jefferson dispute. The system was ready for a new issue over which the parties could squabble. The issue was the extension of political participation to the "common American," and its chief proponent, Andrew Jackson, exploited his own humble origins.

It is not surprising that the realignment of the 1820s focused on the common citizen, since that era was the first to offer true popular input in national elections. In 1800, for instance, only two states selected their members of the electoral college by popular vote; the rest were selected by state legislatures. By 1832, however, only South Carolina had resisted the pressure for popular input in presidential elections. Given this trend toward popular democracy, it makes sense that politicians would lay claim to the interests of the average hard-working American.

In 1828 Andrew Jackson succeeded in bringing his Democratic party to power on his reputation as a Tennessee country lawyer and brash military strategist. Born in a Carolina log cabin and lacking the landed-gentry background of the early presidents, he was able to sell the Democratic party as the best representative of popular interests. He attracted the planters and farmers of the South and West, the small entrepreneurs in all parts of the country, and artisans and factory workers in the towns and cities. Jackson's opponent in 1828, John Quincy Adams (of the rival National Republican party, later known as the Whig party) was able to win states in the Northeast and New England, thus establishing his party's reputation as representing the "establishment" interests.

Jackson justified his politics with populist arguments. He opposed Supreme Court decisions based on what he saw as the Court's aristocratic characteristics. He also justified his dramatic expansion of the "spoils system" (giving government jobs to friends and supporters) in the federal bureaucracy, arguing that rapid turnover would rid the system of bureaucrats whose lengthy tenure made them feel impervious to the popular will. He was a strong supporter of westward expansion, often praising the hard work and simplicity of the yeoman farmer. Although the Whig candidate, William Henry Harrison, was elected president in 1840, his untimely

★ Andrew Jackson, born in a Carolina log cabin in 1776, commander in the battle of New Orleans in the War of 1812, and champion of the common American. He was elected president of the United States in 1828.

death and the incompetence of his successor, John Tyler, ensured the success of the Jacksonian revolution until the tumult of the Civil War era.

The Civil War Realignment: Democrats vs. Republicans

In the 1850s, the axis dividing partisan attachments was rotated from an east–west to a north–south position (see figure 8-2). Many northern politicians were dissatisfied with the unwillingness of both the Jacksonian Democrats and the Whigs to respond to the crisis of slavery in the territories. They formed an entirely new party, called the Republican party, which gained immediate success, supplanting the Whigs and dividing the Democrats. Within two years the new Republican party had promoted a presidential candidate, John C. Fremont, who came within one state of winning the 1856 election.

By 1860 the pressure for a realigning election could not be resisted. Abraham Lincoln attracted factions from both parties of the earlier realignment. The antislavery Whigs, called "Conscience Whigs," most of them in the North, were allied in the new Republican party with antislavery Democrats, called "Barnburners." In the meantime, the Democratic party, with its stronghold in the South, had come to represent pro-slavery sentiment. The minority of pro-slavery Whigs bolted their party to become Democrats, having first been appropriately labeled "Cotton Whigs."

The new lines of partisanship were drawn so sharply—ideologically and geographically—that it was impossible for the political tension to be resolved. The result was civil war, and a partisan split that lasted long after the last shot was fired.

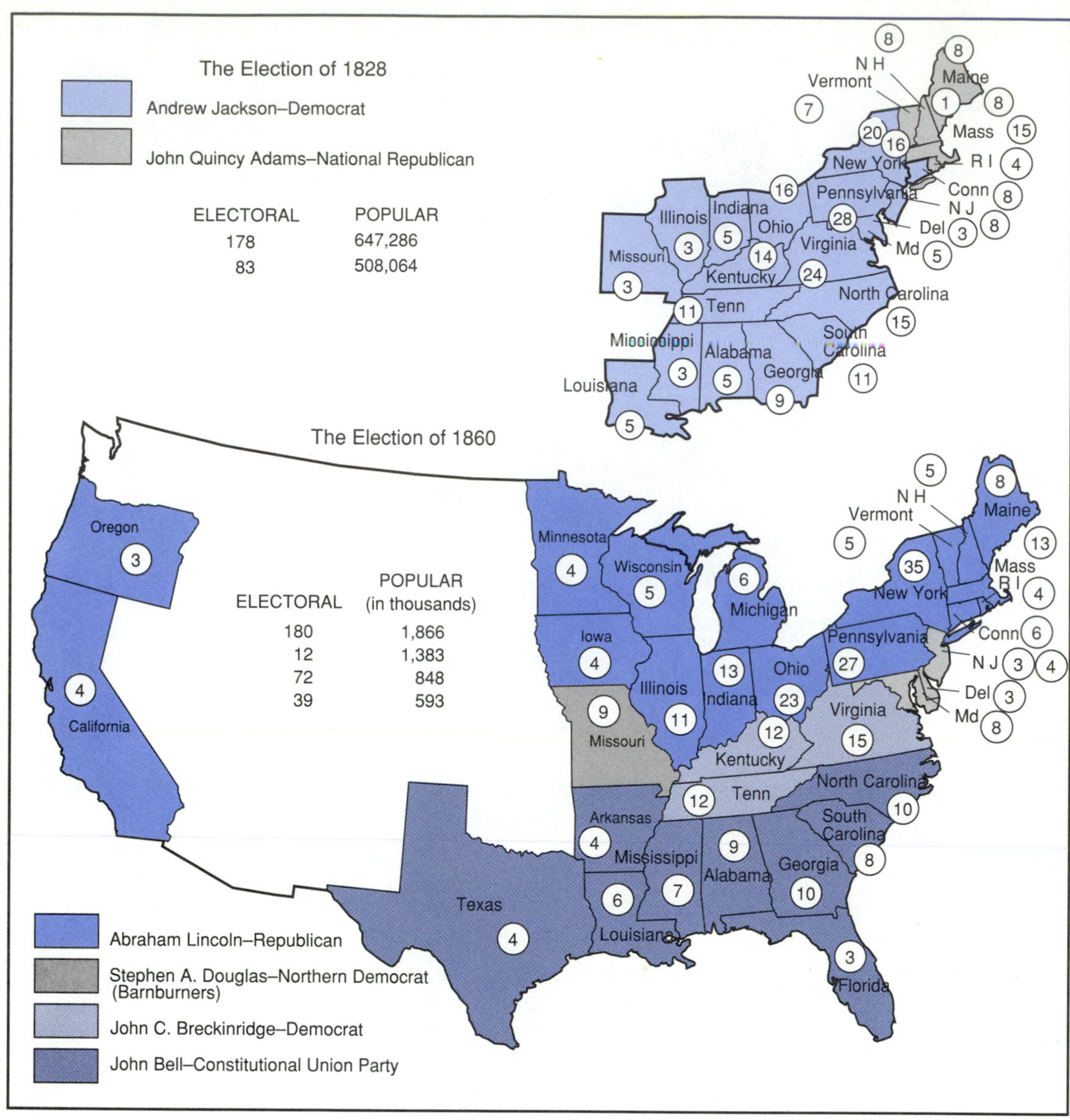

★ **Figure 8-2**
The geography of realignment: These maps show how the East–West division cracked by Andrew Jackson's appeal to the "common American" was replaced by the North–South division created by the slavery issue.

Silver and Gold

The next realigning election, in 1896, was not nearly so dramatic as its predecessor, and its effects were not so deep. Just like other realigning elections, however, this one occurred at a time when the issues of the past realignment had largely lost their relevance.

Until 1896 the role of government in America's industrialization had sparked little debate. The interest of the government was seen to coincide with the interests of the large banking, manufacturing, and railroad establishments. But 1893 had brought a severe depression, and complaints that earlier had been restricted to the Socialist and Populist parties began to be heard in the speeches of a major party.

William Jennings Bryan was the Democratic presidential candidate in 1896, and his fiery speeches stirred up a controversy that was to become a bone of partisan contention for years to come. As a so-called Silver Democrat, Bryan split away from the traditional Democratic party to prevent what he saw as the strangulation of America's economy by such high rollers as J. P. Morgan and Jay Gould. Bryan wanted to devalue the wealth and power of the magnates by devaluing their currency; thus he favored a silver over a gold standard. He hoped to fracture the grip of monopolies with strong antitrust legislation. And he constantly claimed to be the champion of skilled and unskilled factory labor.

Although Bryan did not win the 1896 election, he did succeed in establishing the idea that government should serve as a "watchdog" over business as a legitimate partisan issue. A drive to cut the strings connecting "manipulative industrialists" and their "seedy political puppets" motivated both parties. Accountability and professionalism became partisan battle cries in the new war against political and industrial fat cats. In Democratic strongholds, mostly in the mountain and southwestern states, reforms included provisions for the initiative, referendum, and recall, the direct election of U.S. senators, and the nomination of candidates for public office by direct primaries. Republicans began to press for competitive exams for public jobs, more trained professionals in state and local administration, and more accountable budget-making procedures. These "clean government" measures were advocated at the turn of the century by the Progressive party, whose ideas, like those of the Populist party, seeped into the two major parties.

The New Deal Realignment

The next realignment was triggered by an even more devastating economic catastrophe, the Great Depression. President Hoover tried "politics as usual" to deal with the 1929 crash; he decided that governmental restraint and the good intentions of private business interests would be enough to turn the economy around. But when it became clear that his philosophy of "limited intervention" was not working, the Democrats fielded a candidate who stood for more vigorous government intervention in economic affairs. With unemployment standing at 24 percent on the eve of the 1932 presidential election, it was clear that a novel approach was needed. In fact, the ideas being considered were so alien to traditional ideologies and programs that a realigning election was almost certain.

Franklin Roosevelt's convincing triumph in 1932 cemented a new realignment. Roosevelt, like Jackson, Lincoln, and Bryan before him, ushered in a new cluster of issues for the parties to debate. His New Deal set the stage for a new generation of political discussion. Government was to take a more active role in economic affairs, on the understanding that poverty and unemployment were not always the fault of the individuals involved, but could be due to more distant and powerful factors. For Roosevelt, those factors had to be dealt with through strong government programs for economic recovery. Thus the New Deal promoted federal development of energy sources, federal establishment of agricultural price supports, and federal welfare programs that provided jobs and training for the unemployed.

In one of the ironies of American political history, urban blacks began to transfer their loyalty to the party that only a couple of generations earlier had been the stronghold of pro-slavery sentiment. Other groups joined them in what has been called the **New Deal coalition:** city dwellers, organized labor, Catholics and Jews. Town dwellers, big business, and white Anglo-Saxon Protestants coalesced on the Republican side. In various degrees, these coalitions have continued to the present.

Where Is the Modern Realignment?

The intervals separating 1800, 1828, 1860, 1896, and 1932 are all about thirty years, give or take a few years. Since the late 1960s, therefore, scholars have been predicting that a realignment of the party system is just around the corner. Many experts believed that opposition to the Vietnam war would cause a long-term alteration of the party system. Others believed that the civil rights movement of the 1960s and 1970s would usher in its own partisan realignment. But many observers see no modern realignment and an entire generation of political scientists feel cheated that they have not experienced the excitement and tension of a realigning election. They ask, as do we: Why not a modern realigning election?

First of all, there may be just too many issues. In the past it was easier to paint the political world in only two colors. In the years leading up to the Civil War, for instance, the more simple political environment allowed full focus to be paid to the North–South dispute. Today, as important domestic issues become crowded by international concerns, it may be impossible to assemble attitudes on a myriad of specific concerns into one of two comprehensive ideologies. This diversity of concerns helps to explain the proliferation of interest groups (discussed in chap. 10), which make no attempt to integrate disparate concerns under one political umbrella. In fact, some scholars are convinced that political issues have multiplied so enormously that interest-group politics has superseded party politics in America for good.[8]

There is also the matter of the complexity of modern American politics. It may have been possible in 1860 to be either for or against slavery in the territories, but is it possible in the 1990s to be for or against control of nuclear arms? More likely, American attitudes on arms control are spread across a complex field of considerations, including levels of verification, types of weapons, and cost. It does not seem possible that we could ever refer, for instance, to the Democrats as the party for arms control and the Republicans as the party opposed. The issues seem too complex to inspire the kinds of party realignments that occurred in the past.

And finally, it may be that American voters, who seem disinclined to adopt strong party loyalties, do not need simple two-way divisions of political reality. After all, a major reason for dividing politics into two broad ideologies is to make choices easier for citizens. Perhaps modern American voters have outgrown the need to have their political information processed into two simple positions. Many of those who claim to be "independent" of partisan labels feel capable of evaluating candidates and issues without the cues provided by party labels.

In any case, the lack of a modern realignment has taken much of the excitement out of party politics. The percentage of Americans who identify strongly with

★ Table 8-2
Party affiliation, 1950–1988 (percent)

Year	*Democratic*	*Independent*	*Republican*
1988	37%	34%	29%
1986	40	34	26
1984	37	36	27
1982	47	33	20
1980	38	38	23
1978	40	36	23
1976	42	37	21
1974	42	31	22
1972	47	26	22
1960	47	23	30
1950	45	22	33

NOTE: Independents include pure independents and independents who consider themselves "near" to one party or the other. Rows do not always add up to 100 percent because of third-party affiliation.

SOURCES: James Allan Davis and Tom W. Smith, *General Social Survey, 1972–1988* (Chicago: National Opinion Research Center, 1988) (machine-readable data file); Gallup Opinion Index, December 1977.

a political party has declined since the 1950s. In 1980, the number of **independents**—people who do not identify with a political party—reached a record 38 percent (see table 8-2). In 1988, 34 percent claimed to be independents.

One significant result of the apparently decreasing relevance of party labels has been an increase in **split-ticket voting:** voters cast their ballots for congressional and presidential candidates of different parties. In the period of 1920–1944, split-ticket voters made up only about 15 percent of the electorate. From 1944 to 1964, ticket splitting rose to about 30 percent. And in 1972, the phenomenon reached an all-time high of 44 percent. Since then it seems to have settled at about 30 to 35 percent.[9] Thus it is not surprising that despite the near landslide victory of George Bush in 1988, the Democrats strengthened their hold on both the Senate and the House of Representatives.

★ Democrats and Republicans: Group Support and Ideology

Although the absence of a recent realignment may have lowered the profile of American political parties, we cannot conclude that the parties are irrelevant or completely indistinguishable. Many of the people who continue to identify with one of the two parties believe their party embodies the country's major virtues. Although they may be confused at times about the essential differences between the two parties, they are likely to subscribe to some popular notion about what distinguishes Democrats from Republicans. One observer irreverently summed up the differences this way: "A gathering of Democrats is more sweaty, disorderly, offhand, and rowdy than a gathering of Republicans; it is also more likely to be

★ During his first presidential campaign, former President Jimmy Carter partook in the difficult and messy job of shucking oysters. Is he more likely to be a Democrat or a Republican?

more cheerful, imaginative, tolerant of dissent, and skillful at the game of give-and-take. A gathering of Republicans is more respectable, sober, purposeful, and businesslike than a gathering of Democrats; it is also more likely to be more self-righteous, pompous, cut-and-dried, and just plain boring."[10] Behind the humor of this statement is the common perception that a major remaining difference between the parties involves the kinds of people that each party attracts. And, in fact, although no stark lines can be drawn, it does seem that Republicans and Democrats differ in their social makeup.

Group Support

Surveys reveal, first of all, that the two parties tend to attract differing occupational, ethnic, and other social groups. The Republican party tends to do relatively better among whites, Protestants, people unaffiliated with a labor union, and white-collar workers, whereas the Democratic party tends to attract Hispanic and black voters, blue-collar union members, and Jewish voters. (For more information, refer back to figure 8-1.) The most recent political division between groups (beginning about 1980) is that between the sexes—the "gender gap." In 1987, 48 percent of women considered themselves Democrats, compared to only 42 percent of men; and in the 1988 election, Republican George Bush won 57 percent of the men's vote but only 50 percent of the women's vote.

Obviously, these are only tendencies. Neither party commands the exclusive support of any group. Many Democrats are college-educated, attend a Protestant church, or own a business. Likewise, many Republicans are Jewish or Hispanic or belong to a union. Nor does either party historically draw support always from the same groups. Before the 1930s, for instance, Jewish and black voters tended to be predominantly Republican. In addition, new groups can alter the party balance.

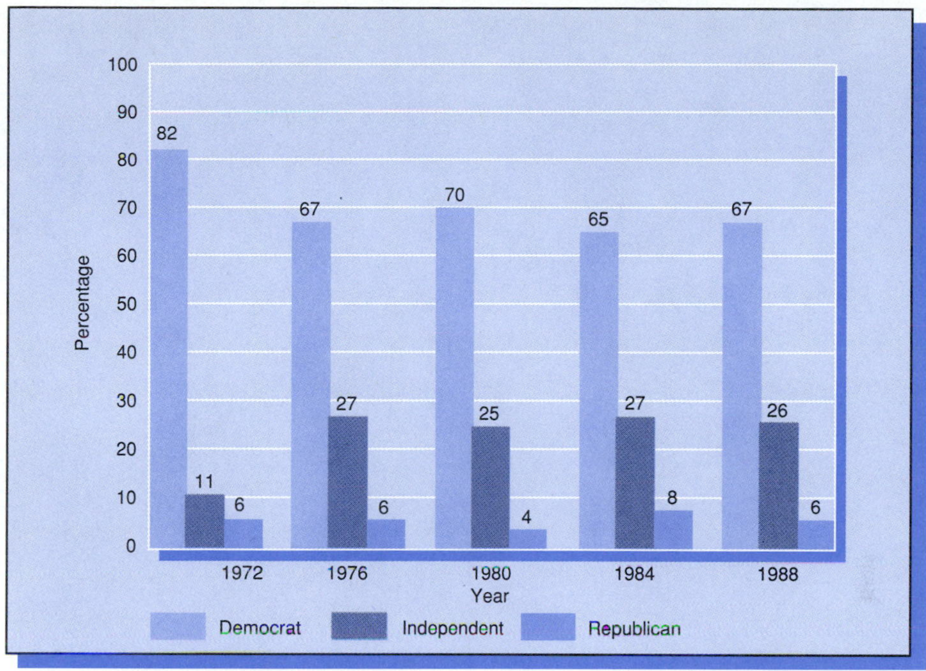

★ **Figure 8-3**
Party choice of black voters, 1972–1988 (percent)
SOURCE: James Allan Davis and Tom W. Smith, *General Social Survey, 1972–1988* (Chicago: National Opinion Research Center, 1988) (machine-readable data file).

The more than one million Cuban refugees who have come to South Florida since the Cuban Revolution of 1959 have helped turn the state into a conservative Republican stronghold. Whether a similar mini-realignment will occur on the West Coast among the thousands of refugees and immigrants from Central America and Southeast Asia (many of whom are not yet eligible for citizenship) remains to be seen.

Although defections are common among most of these groups, some groups within each party provide a significant basis of continuing support. Such loyalty is most clearly seen in the overwhelming support black voters have given to the Democratic party (see figure 8-3). As the authors of one study point out, "The Democratic party now draws almost a fifth of its support from blacks. They are crucial to Democratic dominance in general; and in some states they are the segment of the electorate that keeps the party competitive."[11]

This crucial support has not escaped the notice of either black leaders or Democratic politicians. Jimmy Carter, for example, quickly discovered that his support for black needs and aspirations was expected in return for the overwhelming support he won from black voters in 1976. As Vernon Jordan of the National Urban League commented, "Much has been made of regional loyalties that gave Carter a solid south, but without black voters the Republican ticket would have cracked Carter's southern bloc, with devastating results for his candidacy. . . . It was a heavier than expected black vote that put Carter over the top in some key states he needed to win. That's something Jimmy Carter should not forget, nor should black people allow him to forget it."[12]

★ Jesse Jackson's "Rainbow Coalition" in 1984 not only helped him personally in his bid to run for president but also tied the black vote very closely to the Democratic party.

The candidacy of Jesse Jackson in 1988 is a vivid demonstration of the impact of the black contingent on the Democratic party. Jackson's remarkably successful campaign and his popularity at the 1988 Democratic National Convention were a tribute to the size and strength of his "Rainbow Coalition." With nearly 90 percent of the black vote going to Dukakis in 1988, the overwhelming loyalty of black voters to the Democratic party continued to be one of the party's most valuable assets.

Ideology

In addition to group support, the two parties differ in their ideological tendencies. Political observers have found that Democrats (especially those in leadership positions, such as governors, members of Congress, and campaign workers) tend to take a more liberal stand on many political issues than Republicans do. Democrats are more inclined than Republicans to experiment with new governmental programs, to favor expanded regulation of the economy (including, recently, the erection of trade barriers to protect domestic industry from cheaper foreign goods), and to support more extensive health and welfare programs. Of course, this tendency is due at least in part to the kind of group support the Democrats have maintained. The backbone groups of the Democratic party—women, lower-income voters, ethnic minorities, and city dwellers—are often among the strongest supporters of social welfare programs.

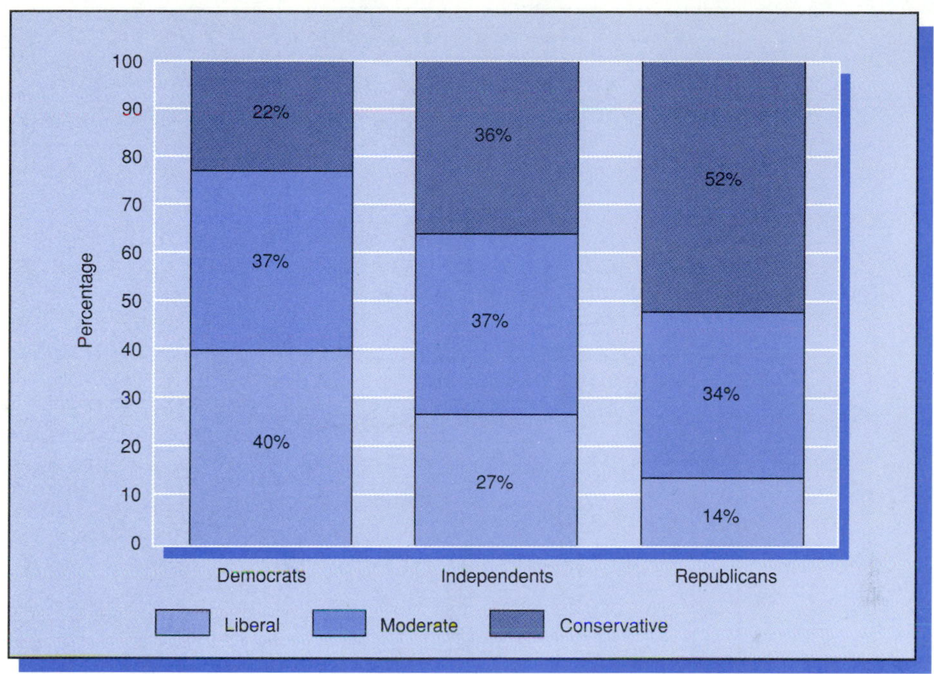

★ **Figure 8-4**

Percentage of Democrats, Independents, and Republicans who considered themselves liberal, moderate, and conservative, 1988

SOURCE: James Allan Davis and Tom W. Smith, *General Social Survey, 1972–1988* (Chicago: National Opinion Research Center, 1988), subfile 1988 (machine-readable data file).

One way to determine the ideological differences between Democrats and Republicans, at least among the leaders, is to examine the voting records of members of Congress. For some years now, the American Conservative Union (ACU) and the liberal Americans for Democratic Action (ADA) have been doing just that—rating the votes of Democratic and Republican members of Congress on key legislation. Generally speaking, the conservative ACU awards its highest rating to members who seem committed to a strong defense posture, a competitive market system, and states' rights. The ADA, on the other hand, awards its top marks to members who favor a reduction in defense spending, welfare reform, civil rights, and environmental protection. In the 1986 congressional session, twenty-nine Democrats and only three Republicans in the Senate received positive scores of 70 percent or better from the liberal ADA. As for ACU scores, thirty-one Republican senators scored 70 or higher, while only one Democrat did so. While these scores indicate ideological consistency in the expected direction, it is also clear, from the number of senators who did not rank high on either scale, that congressional leaders do not vote as ideological blocs.

What, then, about the voters? Are there ideological differences also among the rank and file? There do appear to be such differences, although they are not so marked as among policy makers. Surveys indicate that Democrats are far less likely than Republicans to identify themselves as conservative (see figure 8-4).

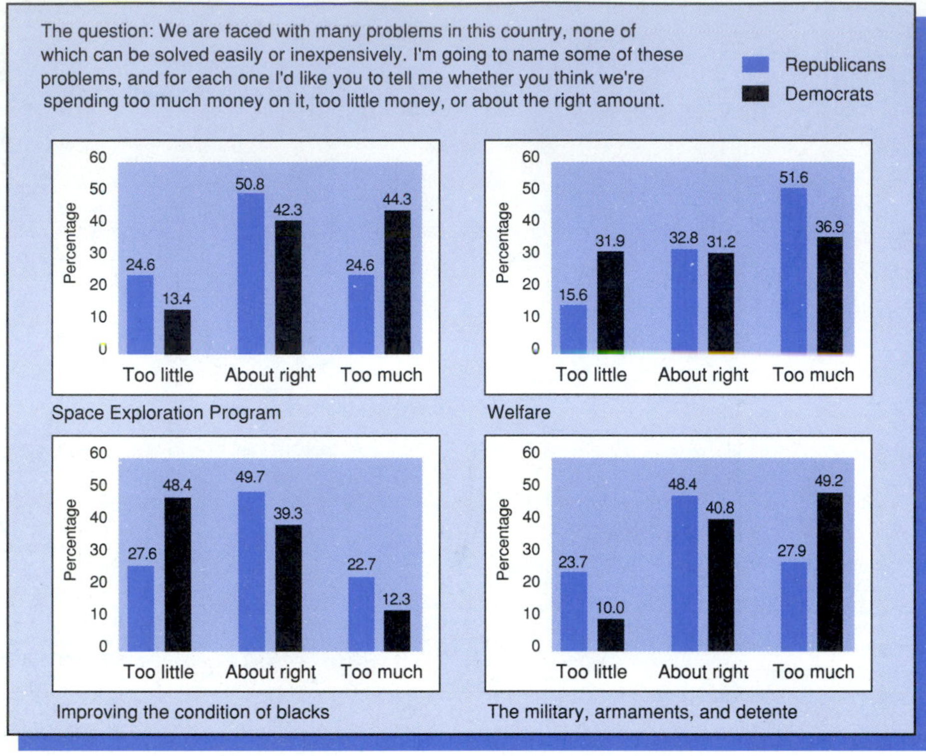

★ **Figure 8-5**

Republicans' and Democrats' opinions on four issues, 1988 (percent)

SOURCE: James Allan Davis and Tom W. Smith, *General Social Survey, 1972–1988* (Chicago: National Opinion Research Center, 1988), subfile 1988 (machine-readable data file).

Moreover, as we can see in figure 8-5, Democratic and Republican voters express different degrees of support for certain political and social issues. Democratic voters give substantially more support than Republicans to such issues as increased spending for social programs and reductions in defense spending, and are more likely to oppose prayer in public schools and a ban on abortion.

★ Party Characteristics and Citizen Confusion

Despite these apparent differences in ideology and group support, many Americans are still confused about what the two parties represent. They cannot easily distinguish between the Democratic and Republican parties on many controversial issues, especially in state and local elections. This confusion was hardly clarified in 1988, when it was only during the last gasps of a losing campaign that Michael Dukakis declared himself to be a liberal.

Confusion about what the parties stand for is not a recent phenomenon. The British writer James Bryce, after visiting this country in the late nineteenth century, observed that a European is always asking Americans to explain the differences between the two parties. "He is always asking," Bryce quipped, "because he never gets an answer."[13] Although many factors may account for this confusion, some observers believe several features of the parties themselves are to blame. Let us take a look at these features.

Our Fragmented Parties

Certainly one factor that contributes to the confusion has been the fragmentation of party leadership. Although most of us may regard the Democratic and Republican parties as national bodies, they are in fact loose alliances of national, state, and local organizations. For most of American history, each of the states—and not any national body—has directed party operations. This arrangement reflects the federal system in this country, in which power is constitutionally divided between the national government and the states, as we saw in chapter 3. Each state boasts its own constitution and its own rules concerning elections and the operations of parties. As a result, the Democratic and Republican parties differ in form and membership from one state to another, with each local party responding to its own rules, policy needs, and constituencies.

This decentralization has been criticized not only for confusing voters but also for making it difficult for either party to maintain unity on the issues. The Democrats and Republicans have been unable to forge their diverse state and local organizations into unified party machines capable of implementing policies desired by voters. Voters have had no assurances that the party they support will carry out even the vague policies stated in their platforms. Hence voters have little incentive to remain loyal to either party.

Consider the situation in Congress. Because members of Congress have tended to draw most of their campaign support from local organizations and special-interest groups, many of them have succeeded in building their own bases of power independent of the congressional party leadership. Thus members of Congress often ignore pleas for party unity when they vote on issues. **Party whips** are members of Congress whose job it is to get members to vote the party line. They have few sanctions to impose on wayward members. Even given the parties' increased organizational vitality (discussed later in this chapter), in 1986 the average Democrat or Republican in Congress voted contrary to the majority of his or her partisan colleagues one out of every four times.

Not all party reformers wish to see the parties become more centralized and uniform. Some contend that party decentralization actually encourages citizen participation in party affairs. Because many important party decisions, including the choosing of candidates for local offices, are made at the local and state levels, in decentralized parties citizens remain relatively close to the real power centers of their party. If all major decisions were centralized at the national level, most citizens would find it more difficult to have an impact on party policy.

A Potpourri of Ideology

In addition to sharing a tradition of decentralization, the Democratic and Republican parties have tended to be ideologically mixed. Both parties have continued to elect members who span the spectrum of liberal and conservative philosophies.

In fact, there are almost as many ideological differences within each party as there are between them. The Democratic party, for instance, attracts not only liberals such as Jesse Jackson but also conservatives such as Sam Nunn. Similarly, the Republican party embraces not only conservatives such as Pat Robertson but also moderate liberals such as New York Senator Alfonse D'Amato. Obviously, the decentralized tradition of the two parties has a great deal to do with this ideological potpourri. As long as state and local party organizations maintain some autonomy, politicians will tend to reflect the unique values and interests of their own local power bases.

What, then, holds the members of the Democratic and Republican parties together? Aside from sharing a party tradition, most members of a party have some common views. Although Democratic Senators Robert Byrd and Edward Kennedy, for example, have hardly seen eye to eye on such policies as national health insurance and tax reform, both have subscribed in principle to some basic concepts, such as an active governmental role in the economy, which distinguish them from most Republicans. Shared views and a mutual desire to see the party come out on top in elections have helped to hold members of a party together despite policy differences. And, as we shall see, the national party organizations are amassing some impressive campaign machines that candidates may find increasingly difficult to forsake.

Just the same, the tensions have sometimes reached the breaking point, as in 1968, when George Wallace, former governor of Alabama, bolted from the Democratic party to form his own American Independent party, or when John Anderson left the Republican party to run an independent campaign in 1980. Similar defections occurred in 1948, when Henry A. Wallace left the Democratic party to run for president on the Progressive party ticket and southern Democrats stormed out of the Democratic national convention over the civil rights issue to support Strom Thurmond as their "States' Rights" candidate for president. (Thurmond later switched to the Republican party.) Even the generally less turbulent Republican party has suffered major defections. In 1912 the followers of Theodore Roosevelt bolted to support his Progressive party candidacy for another term in the White House.

A Blurring of Differences

A third characteristic of the two major parties—and one subject to many criticisms—is that they do not seem to be very different from each other. While there were clear party differences in the realigning elections discussed earlier, George Wallace summed up the feelings of many contemporary Americans when he complained in his 1968 presidential campaign that "there's not a dime's worth of difference" between Democrats and Republicans. Similarly, James Bryce once charged that "the two major parties are like two bottles, identical in size, shape, color, bearing different labels, but both empty."[14]

These are of course exaggerations. As we have seen, the two parties do express somewhat different views and draw support from different social groups. Even in the lackluster campaign of 1988, the two parties' presidential nominees, George Bush and Michael Dukakis, expressed opposing views on such social issues as abortion and prayer in public schools. In fact, one's perceptions of party differences are likely to depend on one's political views. One who abides by the ruling elite model of American politics (see chapter 5), for example, will perhaps perceive a less significant difference between the two parties than an advocate of the pluralist model.

Still, in comparison with the range of political parties in other countries, where the spectrum may run from the extreme left to the extreme right, the Democratic and Republican parties do seem similar and moderate. Although they may differ over how much government should regulate business, neither party promotes the nationalization of industry. And though they may differ over the merits of governmental economic assistance, few Democrats or Republicans advocate the abolition of social security or the graduated income tax. In fact, Democratic and Republican politicians tend to espouse many of the same values: free public education, a strong military defense, law and order, governmental subsidies for key industries, and so forth.

The parties' similarity and moderation stem not only from their mutual support for certain traditions (such as capitalism) but also from the pressures of two-party competition. When only the Democratic and Republican parties have a reasonable chance to gain control of government (for reasons we will discuss shortly), each party must attract a wide spectrum of the population to win an electoral majority. Each must offer programs and candidates having as broad an appeal as possible.

Moreover, because both parties must appeal to voters of many persuasions, they cannot afford to be ideologically extreme. A party that proposes dramatic changes in current policies or that caters only to a small segment of society risks alienating more voters than it attracts. The dramatic failures of both George McGovern in 1972 and Barry Goldwater in 1964 suggest that strong policy statements can be a handicap in a presidential election. During the 1988 Democratic National Convention, the Dukakis delegates blocked efforts to include more liberal policy statements in the party platform. Facing a potentially close election in November, they did not wish to alienate moderate Democratic voters. In fact, however, the plan may have backfired, as Dukakis seemed to suffer from an image as a bland "manager" rather than an inspirational leader. Only near election day did he inject his political ideology into the campaign.

The blurring of differences between the parties carries interesting implications for citizen action. If the two major parties often fail to offer clear policy alternatives, then access to party decision making (when one can get it) may not seem very meaningful. After all, if the pressures of two-party competition demand a bland policy approach, efforts to use the parties as channels for political action may accomplish little in the way of significant policy reform. As long as both parties try to attract as many people as possible without simultaneously alienating their own partisan loyalists, they will remain low-keyed and equivocal. Both parties (and their candidates) will continue to indulge in what have been described as "verbal exercises in calculated ambiguity."

★ The Fall and Rise of the National Conventions

Although many citizens may find it hard to distinguish Republicans and Democrats in tangible ways, it is easy to distinguish them symbolically; and those symbolic differences are celebrated and strengthened every four years at the national **party**

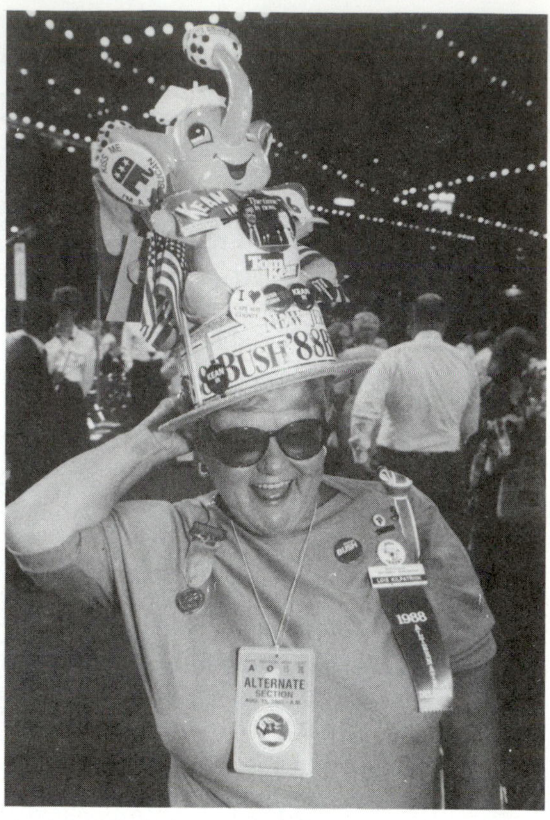

★ National party conventions are a strange combination of business, entertainment, hype, and celebration.

conventions. These conventions, held in midsummer of the presidential election year, provide a dramatic media backdrop to the official selection of the parties' nominees. Here the supporters of each candidate make their final attempts to persuade wavering delegates that their candidate is the one most likely to capture the White House, and elephants and donkeys transcend their positions in the animal kingdom to become visual symbols of proud and energized political communities.

The political wrangling at the conventions has been played down recently, however, in favor of the carnival atmosphere. The convention is not so important as it was in times past, when veteran party hacks turned into kingmakers in the notorious smoke-filled rooms that were hidden from public view. Now the parties have deprived delegates of much of their former latitude in an attempt to encourage greater grass-roots participation in the nomination process.

More than any other change in the nomination process, it has been the proliferation of direct primaries (see chap. 9) that has deprived the conventions of their former importance. With so many states now using the primary method, the result is more delegates who are committed to one candidate rather than to "broad party goals," heretofore emphasized by delegates selected by and from the states' party elites. In 1968, thirty-four states selected their delegates by the caucus method, which ensured the input of state party bosses. By 1980, only eighteen states had

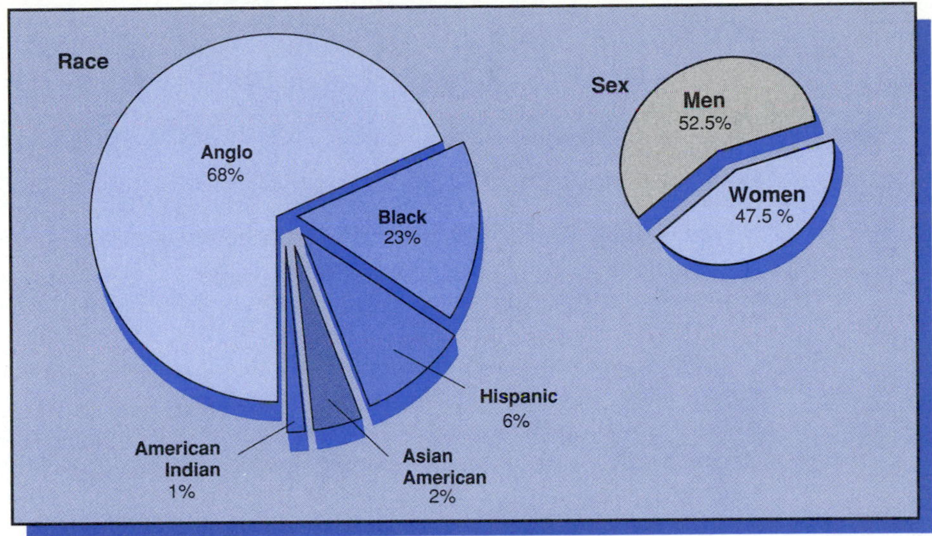

★ **Figure 8-6**
Characteristics of delegates to 1988 Democratic National Convention
SOURCE: *San Jose Mercury-News,* July 17, 1988, p. 2. Reprinted by permission.

retained the caucus. With the change to the primary system, candidates for the Republican or Democratic nomination for the presidency can bypass the party bosses and appeal directly to the people. And the parties have been even further hampered by state laws that in many cases prohibit the party organizations from even indicating which candidate they prefer in the primary.

In addition, the parties have devised their own regulations to restrict candidate horse trading at the convention. These rule changes, most pronounced in the Democratic party, have disadvantaged the old party hacks in favor of a new cadre of delegates who represent more disparate elements of their party. Following the turmoil of the 1968 Democratic Convention in Chicago, a reform-minded commission, headed by Representative Donald M. Fraser (Minnesota) and Senator George McGovern (South Dakota), set new guidelines for delegate selection. The party was directed to increase the number of women, minorities, and young people in state delegations "in reasonable relationship to their presence in the population of the state."

Thus the delegates of today are more diverse and more committed to their chosen candidate (see figure 8-6)—traits that make convention compromises more difficult. In fact, the political scientist Nelson Polsby has complained that the convention has become a rubber stamp that only ratifies a choice long since made in the primaries. Polsby mourns the loss of rational deliberation at the convention, which he believes might at times produce a better candidate.[15]

Those who supported the transition to primaries and delegate diversity claimed an increase in democracy. Candidates were compelled to enter all the state primaries, and they had to cater to all the major subgroups of their party. But the increase in democracy brought some unanticipated problems. It became clear that the rank-and-file party faithful—citizens motivated enough to register and vote in their party's primary—did not necessarily represent the broader electorate. In order to win the presidency, both parties must attract independent voters and voters of the other party. Thus George McGovern won many primary elections in 1972 but could carry only Massachusetts and the District of Columbia in the general election. He was popular with the hard-core Democrats, but he lost miserably among the fence-sitters.

The 1984 and 1988 conventions represented efforts to reintegrate the input of party leaders in a primary-dominated process. The logic of the changes is based on the belief that party leaders are better equipped to determine *who can win* in the general election. The Democratic party has implemented rule changes that ensure more independence and compromise among the convention delegates, thus partly relieving the convention of its growing reputation as a rubber stamp.

Prior to the 1984 Democratic Convention, the party organization made two important rule changes. The first reform, which produced the most controversy, was a provision that would bring party and elected officials back into the nominating process. About 550 slots were reserved for senators, representatives, governors, other state officials, big-city mayors, and state party chairs and vice-chairs. These **superdelegates** were to be unpledged and chosen by party leaders in Congress.

The second change in the direction of flexibility was provoked by Senator Edward Kennedy (D-Massachusetts), who was disgusted in 1980 that delegates were compelled to vote for the candidate to whom they were originally pledged. This so-called robot rule was eliminated in 1984 with the stipulation that although delegates are no longer bound to their original candidates, they must "in all good conscience reflect the sentiments of those who elected them." Obviously, these changes represented an attempt to deal with the criticism that the convention was only a rubber stamp. So far, even under these new regulations, nominees have gone over the top in the primaries; but clearly there is now a real potential for a close primary race to be ultimately decided at the convention.

★ Third-Party Alternatives

Some Americans who have become fed up with the similar and moderate traits of the Democratic and Republican parties have put their faith in **third parties,** which often favor policies neither major party has been willing to support. In doing so, however, they have had to accept the enormous difficulties third parties have faced in trying to carry out their programs. During most of American history, only two parties at any given time have had sufficient strength to compete for control of the national government with any chance of success.

The Variety of Third Parties

Third parties have played an active role throughout the nation's history. Since the Constitution permits any native-born American over thirty-five years of age to become president, elections in this country have brought out an abundance of eager competitors for the job. In 1988, voters had an opportunity to vote for a score of presidential aspirants other than George Bush and Michael Dukakis. None of these candidates, however, came close to receiving the 13.5 percent captured by George

Table 8-3
Third-party showings in the 1988 presidential election

Candidate	*Party*	*Votes*
Ron Paul	Libertarian	409,412
Lenora B. Fulani	New Alliance	201,430
David Duke	Populist	44,135
Eugene McCarthy	Consumer	30,074
James Griffen	American Independent	26,053
Lyndon Larouche	National Economic Recovery	23,713
William Mara	Right to Life	22,560
Ed Winn	Workers League	18,645
James Warren	Socialist Workers	11,435
Earl F. Dodge	Prohibition	7,868
None of the above		6,923
Larry Holmes	Workers World	6,628
Herbert Lewin	Peace and Freedom	3,968
Delmar Dennis	American	3,443
Willa Kenoyer	Socialist	3,412
Jack Herer	Grass Roots	1,949
Louie Youngkite	Independent	363
John Martin	Third World Assembly	229

SOURCE: *New York Times,* November 22, 1988, p. B6.

Wallace in 1968, or the 7 percent won by the independent John Anderson in 1980. Together they garnered fewer than 1 million votes of the more than 91 million cast in 1988, a total of less than 1 percent (see table 8-3).

There have been many kinds of third parties. Some, such as the American Communist party, have been highly doctrinaire, advocating the overhaul of the entire economic and political system. Others, such as the Progressives in 1912 and the States' Rights party in 1948, have been basically splinter parties that broke off in protest from the Democratic or Republican party. Still others, such as the Prohibitionists and the Vegetarians, have used the electoral process to gain publicity for their ideas. Other third parties have included the Anti-Masons, who in the 1830s contested only one presidential election and then disappeared; the Know-Nothings, an anti-Catholic, anti-Irish nativist party in the 1850s, so secretive that its members pretended to know nothing about it (hence the name); and the Mugwumps, Republicans who bolted from their party in 1884 in protest against the presidential nomination of James C. Blaine. Their name was a slang term derived from an Indian word, but predictably it soon became a joke: "I am a mugwump . . . my mug is on one side of the fence and my wump is on the other."

Some third parties have attained sufficient strength to affect the outcome of a presidential election or to elect members to Congress. One of the most successful, although short-lived parties was the Populist, a coalition of agricultural and labor interests that gained prominence in the 1890s. Although it failed to attract a national following, it was able to win the election of six senators and seven representatives

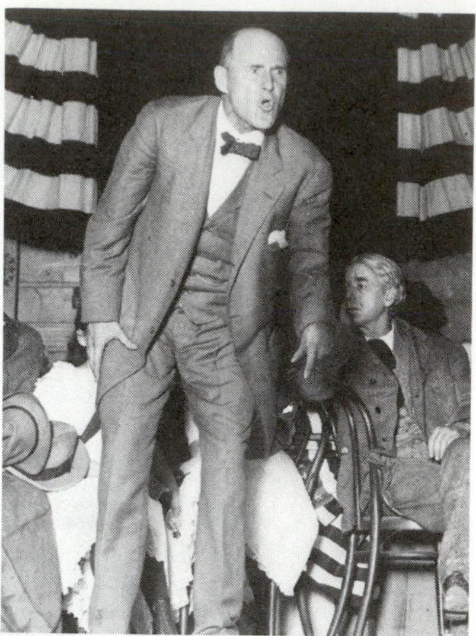

★ Eugene V. Debs (1855–1926) garnered 6 percent of the presidential vote in 1912 as a candidate for the Socialist party. He was the founder of that party and ran for president on that ticket five times between 1904 and 1920.

to Congress in 1894. In this century, the most impressive national third-party showing was made by Teddy Roosevelt's "Bull Moose" Progressive party, a group of liberal Republicans who left the party in 1912. The Progressives captured 27 percent of the popular vote that year—more than the Republican incumbent, William H. Taft—and thus brought victory to the Democratic candidate, Woodrow Wilson.

Third parties have also enjoyed some success in state and local politics. The Socialist party, for example, has elected mayors in Bridgeport and Hartford, Connecticut, and in Milwaukee, Wisconsin. In Minnesota during the 1920s and 1930s, the Farmer-Labor party—not the Democratic party—provided the main opposition to the Republican party in most state and congressional elections; in the 1940s, the Farmer-Labor party even won the governorship. Similarly, in New York State, the Conservative party in 1970 sent James Buckley to the U.S. Senate, where he served for one six-year term.

The Reasons for Third Parties' Failure

Ordinarily, however, third parties have won few victories at the polls in either state or national elections. No third party has ever captured the presidency, and only a few have occupied more than a handful of seats in Congress. As table 8-4 shows, only five third parties since 1832 have collected more than 10 percent of the popular vote in a presidential election.

In a sense, the absence of powerful third parties seems rather surprising in view of the many regional, economic, and social differences in this country. We might expect many parties to flourish in Congress and in state legislatures, each representing a different segment of our society. Yet the United States is one of the few democracies in the world where strong third parties have not been able to thrive. Norway, Italy, West Germany, and Switzerland, for example, have all had several competitive parties.

Political scientists have been unable to agree on any overall explanation for the persistence of only two major parties in this country. Of the several hypotheses

★ **Table 8-4**
Percentage of popular vote won by third parties, 1832–1988

Year	*Party*	*Percent of popular vote*
1832	Anti-Masonic	8.0%
1844	Liberty	2.3
1848	Free Soil	10.1
1852	Free Soil	4.9
1860	Constitutional-Union	12.6
1880	Greenback	3.4
1884	Greenback	1.7
1888	Prohibition	2.2
1892	Populist	8.5
1904	Socialist	3.0
	Prohibition	1.9
1908	Socialist	2.8
	Prohibition	1.7
1912	Progressive	27.4
	Socialist	6.0
1916	Socialist	3.2
1920	Socialist	3.4
1924	Progressive	16.6
1932	Socialist	2.2
1936	Union	2.0
1948	States' Rights	2.4
	Progressive	2.4
1968	American Independent	13.5
1972	American	1.4
1976	American Independent	0.2
1980	Libertarian	1.1
1984	Libertarian	0.3
1988	Libertarian	1.2

that have been offered, one of the most plausible is that the system of electing candidates reinforces two-party competition.[16] In this country, the **single-member district system** is used in all federal elections, meaning that only one representative may be elected from a congressional district regardless of the number of candidates running: it is simply a case of winner-take-all. (The same applies to the presidential election: the candidate who receives the most popular votes in a state receives all of its electoral votes.) Thus even if a third party wins 20 or 30 percent of the votes all over the country, it may still not be rewarded with a single seat in Congress. Democracies with proportional representation, by contrast, send third-party legislators to parliament, where they form coalitions with other parties. (Comparative election systems are fully described in chap. 9.)

Nevertheless, the election of only one member per district does not fully explain why no third party has been able to gain enough support to displace either the Democratic or the Republican party. Another popular hypothesis is that the United States has simply had a historical tradition of two-party competition, inher-

The Prohibition Party

In 1892, Brigadier General John Bidwell of California received 271,058 votes for president of the United States, which came to 2.3 percent of the national total. He ran as the candidate for the Prohibition party, which had been gaining strength since its first national campaign in 1872. The Prohibitionists were mostly renegades from the Republican party who felt betrayed by the Republicans' support of big business and the eastern establishment. Bidwell was a rugged individualist who detected an erosion of the American spirit. He believed that common people were being stupefied and alienated under the thumbs of the tycoons, and he believed that the major instrument of the alienation was liquor. Instead of banning liquor, the Republican elite was placing excise taxes on it, lining their pockets while they immobilized the general public. Bidwell was made of sterner stuff: he yanked all the grapevines from his 25,000-acre Rancho Chico in northern California.

By 1916, buoyed by their recent alliance with the powerful Anti-Saloon League, the Prohibitionists launched a 20,000-mile whistle-stop campaign for their political candidates. In New York, the Prohibitionist Dr. C. E. Welch ran for governor, having already become famous as the president of Welch's grape juice, which he promoted with pictures of young women saying: "My lips only touch lips that touch Welch's." And on January 16, 1919, the Eighteenth Amendment to the Constitution was ratified, initiating a fifteen-year dry spell, during which "the manufacture, sale, or transportation of intoxicating liquors . . . within the United States . . . [was] prohibited."

★ From 1919 to 1933, thanks in part to the work of the Prohibition party, "the manufacture, sale, or transportation of intoxicating liquors" was forbidden in the United States. Those willing to break the law frequented "speakeasies," like the one pictured here.

Although the Prohibition party has seen better days, in 1988 its candidate, Earl F. Dodge, appeared on the ballots in four states (Arkansas, Colorado, New Mexico, and Tennessee) and was able to garner 7,868 votes. And while the Prohibition party takes stands on such issues as social security, right to life, agricultural subsidies, and ballot reform, the alcohol problem remains the linchpin of its party platform. From the 1988 version of its platform:

> The liquor traffic is linked with and supports a nationwide network of gambling, vice and crime. It also exercised a great measure of control over both the Democratic and Republican parties and much of the governmental life of our nation.
>
> Our party alone offers a program of publicity, education, legislation, and administration leading to the prohibition of the manufacture, distribution, and sale of all alcoholic beverages.

SOURCE: Roger C. Storms, ***Partisan Prophets: A History of the Prohibition Party, 1854–1972*** (Denver: National Prohibition Foundation, 1972), p. 36.

ited from the split between the Whigs and Tories in England and reinforced by the division between the Federalists and Anti-Federalists over ratification of the Constitution. The pattern of two dominant, competitive parties became entrenched at this early stage and has been perpetuated ever since.

Moreover, the traditional allegiances of voters to the two dominant parties have been difficult for third parties to break. After more than 130 years of Democratic and Republican supremacy, most voters have become used to supporting one of these two parties. Because partisan loyalties tend to pass from generation to generation, the Democratic and Republican parties have enjoyed a tremendous historical and psychological advantage over smaller and more sporadic third parties.

It is also possible that many third parties are too ideologically extreme or specialized to gain widespread support. Not enough people feel strongly about single issues, such as prohibition or vegetarianism, to cast their votes for special-interest third parties, especially when the tradition of electing only one member per district may discourage them from "wasting" their votes. When people do feel strongly about single issues, they are more likely to pursue these issues through interest groups, which, unlike parties, do not have to compromise across a broad political spectrum to achieve their goals.

Third parties also face tremendous financial obstacles, especially in presidential elections. As we will see in chapter 9, the Federal Election Campaign Act provides public funds for Democratic and Republican presidential candidates in the general election. Third-party candidates are eligible for such support only if their party obtained 5 percent of the total vote cast in the preceding election—a high percentage for most third parties. Without funds, third-party hopefuls find it difficult to gain publicity; and without publicity, they cannot hope to win enough support to carry out a credible campaign. This problem is compounded by the fact that state legislatures control access to the ballot in state elections. Third parties often have to use most of their limited funds to gather signatures for petitions to gain the right to appear on the ballot.

Finally, the failure of third parties often results from the ability of the Democrats and Republicans to steal their thunder. A third party sometimes proposes a promising idea—such as the direct election of senators, the progressive income tax, or the regulation of banks—only to have the two major parties appropriate the idea when it becomes popular. The unique appeal of the third party is thus undercut, and it loses whatever support it had started to gain.

The Value of Third Parties

Do third parties make any contributions to our political system? Despite their inability to gain mass public support or play a major role in policy making, these parties do provide some important services.

In the first place, third parties often express the desires of people who are dissatisfied with the Democratic and Republican parties. Although third parties normally are unable to translate these demands into concrete policies, they do provide a forum for alternative views. Without third parties, in other words, many more citizens might abstain from voicing their political concerns.

In addition, third parties sometimes draw public attention to controversial issues ignored by the two major parties. Whether it is because third-party candidates tend to be more ideological or because they see little hope of gaining control of government anyway, they have tended to be more outspoken on the issues. Third-party candidates in the past, for example, called for the primary election, old-age pensions, universal and compulsory education, women's suffrage, and the initiative and referendum well in advance of their acceptance by Democratic and Republican candidates.

In addition, third parties sometimes directly affect the programs of the two major parties. By threatening to steal votes away from the Democrats and Republicans with a popular campaign issue—as George Wallace attempted to do with the "law and order" issue in 1968—third parties sometimes compel the other two parties to alter their long-term policy orientations and to adopt ideas endorsed by third-party candidates. In the 1890s, for example, the Democratic party absorbed the Populists and in 1924 it adopted many of the Progressive programs of Robert La Follette. "The evidence seems to suggest," one scholar has concluded, "that the rather large-scale, episodic, nonrecurring minor-party movements must be regarded . . . as integral elements of the so-called two-party system. They spring from the center of the political melee, and in turn affect the nature of the major parties and the relationship between them as they cumbersomely make their way from election to election."[17]

★ The Metamorphosis of American Political Parties

American Parties in a Changing World

We have already mentioned that the complexity and diversity of international issues makes it increasingly difficult for the parties to exhibit clear and distinct alternative positions, thus reducing the chance of an electoral realignment.

Another important factor that emerges when a nation's attention is drawn increasingly outward is the phenomenon of nationalism. **Nationalism** may be defined as the propensity of citizens to drop their differences and promote what they feel are shared national values. It can take the form of simple patriotic demonstrations or it can fuel a military invasion. When international events impinge on Americans' sense of security, political leaders speak in nationalistic terms, often asking the nation to "put partisan differences aside" and face the problems with a "united front." During the Iranian hostage situation, for instance, when Ronald Reagan was a candidate for the presidency, he was very careful not to criticize President Carter's handling of the situation, fearing to appear to be capitalizing on the nation's distress if he did so.

The perceived need to face international problems with a united front, then, is yet another force in the erosion and blurring of party differences. As international affairs take a stronger role in American politics, leaders have more opportunities to deemphasize partisan differences. Since World War II there have been few substantive partisan debates on foreign affairs. As we will see in chapter 19, the cold war of the 1950s and 1960s was carried out with the same intensity by Republicans and Democrats alike. Communism was seen as a threat to "all Americans," and CIA plots to overthrow unfriendly governments and assassinate obstinate foreign leaders flowed smoothly from Eisenhower's Republican administration to Kennedy's Democratic administration. Likewise, the United States' involvement in the Vietnam war evolved through four administrations, two Republican and two Democratic. In fact, the student revolts of the 1960s were in large part a response to a party system that did not seem to offer any valid alternatives to status quo international policies.

Evidence indicates, however, that international issues of a less threatening nature might stimulate partisan disputes. In the coming years, American politicians will have to deal with such international issues as the so-called second debt—the United States' substantial **trade deficit.** Simply put, the foreign goods we bring into the country exceed in value the American goods we sell overseas.

The political parties disagree as to the best solution. Democrats tend to favor **protectionism**—the practice of taxing foreign imports to make them more expensive and so less attractive to American buyers. The 1988 presidential primary campaigns of Richard Gephardt centered on protectionist legislation. Republicans, on the other hand, lean toward attempts to persuade other nations (particularly Japan) to reduce tariffs on American goods so that they may be more attractive to foreign buyers. Advocates of **free trade** believe that in a worldwide free market system, American goods would hold their own in cost and quality, and would not need to be protected.

It is also clear that experience in foreign affairs is an important asset to a candidate of either party. Polls continue to demonstrate that international issues are increasingly important to American citizens. In fact, one of the major negatives of the candidacy of Michael Dukakis in 1988 was his lack of foreign policy experience. In the future, the parties may be more hesitant to select the likes of a peanut farmer from Georgia or an actor from California as their presidential candidate.

Thus there can be no easy formula regarding the effect of growing international concerns on American parties. We can say that some international events—those of the crisis variety—may tend to contribute to the blurring of party lines. Yet we can also see the possibility that less explosive, long-term international issues (such as trade issues) may lead to substantial partisan differences.

The Future of American Political Parties

Given the various factors that are eroding the traditional relevance of American political parties, it seems unlikely that the party system will ever return to what it was in the past. It is doubtful that an issue will come along that has the simplicity and substance to divide the electorate into two distinct and compelling factions. It is more likely that the parties will continue to be loose alliances of shifting elements, and interest groups will continue to represent conviction and unity of purpose.

But this does not mean that parties will continue to decline in overall importance to the political system. It only means that parties, in order to maintain their relevance, will have to adapt to present conditions; indeed, there are signs that the parties are carving out new niches.

For one thing, although parties may not be so important to rank-and-file voters as they once were, they are developing stronger local, state, and national organizations. Despite the public's lack of interest in partisan affairs, candidates for public office are taking advantage of services and financial support from party organizations that did not even exist in earlier years. In fact, party workers are contacting three times the number of voters they contacted in the 1950s.[18] Thus the strength of American parties may be growing, not in the most obvious ways but behind the scenes.

Just why the parties are enhancing their organizational strength is an interesting question. The parties have been aided by post-Watergate legislation that was really intended to diminish their financial role in elections. The Federal Campaign Finance Act (discussed in chapter 9) limits the amount of money that an individual can contribute to the national party organization. Thus, in order to maintain their financial support, the parties have been forced to reach out to a multitude of small contributors; and in the process of contacting people to make contributions, the parties have been able to establish a wider popular base.

Moreover, in the late 1970s Congress enhanced the ability of the parties to contact voters by granting them postal rates comparable to those of nonprofit organizations. The Republican party especially has been successful with the direct mail approach. By 1984, the Republican party had a mailing list of more than two million proven contributors. Defying those who believe the party is dependent on the financial elite, the party brags that through its mail campaign it raises more than three-fourths of its revenue with an average contribution of less than $35.[19]

Mass mailings are not the only valuable services now provided by the party organizations. By 1986, the Republican party had established seventeen regional phone centers from which millions of voters have been contacted. And both parties have established sophisticated polling departments. In 1985, for instance, the Democratic party spent $200,000 on a poll in an effort to understand what kinds of issues were important to various population groups, so that the party could target its advertisements. The parties also support media divisions that help their candidates develop high-tech campaigns. The Republican party even supports a "Congressional Campaign Academy," which offers a ten-week, expenses-paid training course to campaign managers interested in the newest techniques in campaign management. And finally, the parties offer their candidates computer time and technical expertise in fulfilling the complicated reporting requirements established by the Federal Election Campaign Act.

Thus, because these organizations now have much to offer candidates, the candidates are paying more attention to the political parties. Especially when they are involved in close elections, candidates are admitting the indispensability of their national and congressional party organizations.[20] This new obligation to the party may be part of the reason why the Ninety-ninth Congress, which sat in 1985–1986, produced the most clear-cut partisan voting record in thirty years.[21]

So for the near future it looks as if the parties will not represent two clear perspectives on one monumental issue. It seems more likely that the party organizations will increase their mastery over a variety of sophisticated, high-tech goods and services that will allow candidates to tailor their campaigns to the particular issues that are most important to their constituents. Thus, while we may not expect any grand ideological battles on a national scale, we ought not to underestimate the parties' importance in American politics.

★ Summary

The party system traveled a rocky road to legitimacy, and in the process Aaron Burr became a victim. The party system has also been subject to major disruptions, called realignments.

Realignments occurred at fairly regular intervals until recent years. Instead of periodically revitalized parties, we now see instead a party system that is fragmented, that blurs their differences on issues, and that can tolerate great internal ideological diversity. Yet the parties do seem to retain some general and consistent differences, and voters display at least weak ties to the parties that best represent their social and ideological positions.

The future does not seem to hold a return to the distinct and vital parties of the era of Aaron Burr. Modern, often international issues do not conform well to the more simplistic partisan divisions of times past. If the parties are to remain relevant, they will need to expand the organizational services that they can provide candidates behind the scenes.

★ Key Terms

free trade
independents
nationalism
New Deal coalition
party convention
party whip
political party
protectionism
realigning elections
single-member district system
split-ticket voting
superdelegates
third parties
trade deficit

★ Notes

1. Quoted in Paul Goodman, ed., *The Federalists vs. the Jeffersonian Republicans* (New York: Holt, Rinehart & Winston, 1967), p. 54.
2. Frank J. Sorauf and Paul Allen Beck, *Party Politics in America,* 6th ed. (Glenview, Ill.: Scott, Foresman, 1988), pp. 23–24.
3. Frank J. Sorauf, *Political Parties in the American System* (Boston: Little, Brown, 1964), p. 1.
4. Quoted in *Newsweek,* October 23, 1972, p. 47.
5. Hugh A. Bone and Austin Ranney, *American Politics and the Party System,* 3d ed. (New York: McGraw-Hill, 1965), p. 662.
6. John F. Hoadley, *Origins of American Political Parties: 1789–1803* (Lexington: University of Kentucky Press, 1986), p. 171.
7. Edward S. Corwin, *John Marshall and the Constitution* (New Haven, Conn.: Yale University Press, 1919), pp. 108–109.
8. Advisory Commission on Intergovernmental Relations, *The Transformation in American Politics: Implications for Federalism* (Washington, D.C., 1986), pp. 40–41.
9. Martin P. Wattenberg, *The Decline of American Political Parties, 1952–1980* (Cambridge, Mass.: Harvard University Press, 1984), pp. 18–19.
10. Clinton Rossiter, *Parties and Politics in America* (Ithaca, N.Y.: Cornell University Press, 1960), p. 117.
11. Norman H. Nie, Sidney Verba, and John R. Petrocik, *The Changing American Voter* (Cambridge, Mass.: Harvard University Press, 1976).
12. *Newsweek,* November 22, 1976, p. 15.
13. James Bryce, *The American Commonwealth,* 3 vols. (London: Macmillan, 1888), 1:353.
14. Ibid., p. 354.
15. Nelson Polsby, *Consequences of Party Reform* (New York: Oxford University Press, 1983).
16. See, for example, Maurice Duverger, *Political Parties* (New York: Wiley, 1955).
17. V. O. Key, Jr., *Parties, Politics, and Pressure Groups,* 5th ed. (New York: Crowell, 1964), p. 279.
18. University of Michigan Survey Research Center data.
19. Larry J. Sabato, *The Party's Just Begun: Shaping Political Parties for America's Future* (Glenview, Ill.: Scott, Foresman, 1988), p. 77.
20. Paul S. Herrnson, "Do Parties Make A Difference? The Role of Party Organizations in Congressional Elections," *Journal of Politics* 48 (August 1986): 612.
21. *Congressional Quarterly Weekly Report* 44 (November 15, 1986): 2901.

★ For Further Reading

Burnham, Walter Dean. *Critical Elections and the Mainsprings of American Politics.* New York: Norton, 1980.
Crotty, William. *American Parties in Decline.* Boston: Little, Brown, 1984.
Eldersveld, Samuel J. *Political Parties in American Society.* New York: Basic Books, 1982.
Mazmanian, Daniel. *Third Parties in Presidential Elections.* Washington, D.C.: Brookings Institution, 1974.
Polsby, Nelson. *Consequences of Party Reform.* New York: Oxford University Press, 1983.
Sabato, Larry J. *The Party's Just Begun: Shaping Political Parties for America's Future.* Glenview, Ill.: Scott, Foresman, 1988.
Sorauf, Frank J. *Party Politics in America.* 5th ed. Boston: Little, Brown, 1984.
Sundquist, James L. *Dynamics of the Party System: Alignment and Realignment of Political Parties in the United States.* Washington, D.C.: Brookings Institution, 1973.

"Do you know how to bake blueberry muffins?"

—Reporter's question to Geraldine Ferraro, 1984 Democratic Vice-presidential candidate

CHAPTER NINE

ELECTIONS

★★★★★★★★★★★★

Would You Buy a Used Car from This Person? Elections and Campaigns in the United States

One often hears that this country boasts a viable democratic system that offers its citizens numerous ways to articulate their demands and influence governmental policy. But many countries and ideologies describe themselves as democratic. The concept of **democracy** is among the most vague and value-laden in all political thought. It has been estimated that there are as many as two hundred separate definitions of the concept. In this country, for example, many people equate democracy with rule by the majority—that is, an electoral process in which a candidate who garners more than 50 percent of the votes represents all of the people (including those who did not lend their support). A problem with this definition is its failure to fit a system with multiparty elections, in which the winning candidate may not have a clear majority.

To many other people, "democracy" ultimately implies support for liberty and equality, protection of minority rights, respect for the individual, a fundamental written law, and the availability of choice. To still others, it simply suggests rule in the interests of "the people," regardless of the legal and institutional forms. The word itself stems from two Greek roots: *demos,* the common people, and *kratos,* strength or power. Thus the term implies that power ultimately is vested in the people.

The literature on democracy is so exceedingly rich and controversial that we could hardly do full justice to the concept. For our purposes, we may adopt a procedural interpretation of democracy. That is, we may describe a system as democratic if its citizens enjoy a relatively high degree of access to and influence over their government. But "relatively" is the key word. In no system is public influence over government totally absent, and in no system is that influence absolute. Hence the political system in this country may be more or less democratic than others, depending on one's perception of citizens' ability to affect policy.

When Americans are asked to identify the basic ingredients of democracy, fair elections are usually included in the list. Along with the First Amendment rights—freedom of speech, press, assembly, and religion—the opportunity to select the people who govern, from those in the White House to those in the county courthouse, forms the basis of the American political system. From the Boston Tea Party of 1773 to the Voting Rights Act of 1965 to today's presidential extravaganzas, elections have played an important part in our national history.

Elections and the right to vote affect the way we view the rest of the world. Nations that hold American-style elections are considered to be good democratic governments, while those with other methods of choosing their leaders are often

★ Elections are not always synonymous with democracy. Dictatorial governments, trying to promote their legitimacy, often stage elections that are anything but democratic. Here, a wounded woman is carried from the scene of an election-day massacre in Haiti in 1987. Fifteen people were killed by gunmen at the polling station.

considered irresponsible and undemocratic. As we shall see, passing judgment on the electoral procedures of other nations has not been just an idle pastime. On several occasions the United States has invaded and occupied nations in Central America and the Caribbean because, among other reasons, we did not approve of the way their leaders were chosen.

In this chapter we will look at the way the United States selects its leaders. We will begin with a brief historical account of the gradual extension of the right to vote to more and more segments of the population. We will then discuss the nuts and bolts of American elections and compare them with elections in other countries. We will also discuss an issue that has received much attention in recent years: low voter turnout. Finally, we will examine political campaigns and some criticisms that have been leveled at contemporary campaign practices and strategies.

★ The Road to Universal Suffrage

In view of our tendency to pass judgment on the electoral procedures of other nations, it may seem ironic that our own historical record reveals a bumpy road to citizen participation and universal suffrage. Although the founders sought to involve ordinary citizens in government, they were hesitant to remove all elements of aristocracy. Supreme Court justices were given lifetime appointments so that they would be insulated from popular hysteria. The president was to be elected by an "electoral college," which could serve as a buffer between the executive and the general population. Senators (until 1913) were elected by state legislatures rather than by popular vote. And even in local contests and in elections for the House of Representatives, various barriers kept many citizens from voting.

Under our federal constitutional system, the states were allowed to determine their own voting qualifications, although Congress could intervene in cases of gross malfeasance. Some of the original states chose to prohibit Jews from voting, while others blocked those citizens who remained loyal to Great Britain, and still others demanded a long period of residence before a citizen became eligible to vote. The most consistent and substantial restrictions, however, were based on gender, race, and property. The first American electorate was decidedly male, white, and propertied.

The Erosion of Property Requirements

The first obstacle to universal suffrage to be scrubbed was the need to own property in order to vote. Early Americans found it increasingly difficult to support such grand phrases as "all men are created equal" when men were categorized according to their property holdings. Likewise, it was difficult for those who had fought under the banner of "no taxation without representation" to be told that they owed taxes to the new government but could not vote for it.

Perhaps most unhappy, however, were soldiers of the Revolution, who were prevented from contributing peacefully to the establishment of their new government. In Maryland, where property qualifications were particularly harsh, groups of Revolutionary soldiers disrupted local elections, and in a few instances forcibly replaced stubborn election judges with their own people.[1] By the time the thirteen states ratified their own constitutions, seven had substantially reduced property qualifications; and those that remained were eliminated during the time of Andrew Jackson and his commitment to the "common man." Extending the vote to black Americans proved much more difficult and complex.

The Struggle to Enfranchise Black Americans

"The right of citizens of the United States to vote shall not be denied or abridged by the United States or by any State on account of race, color, or previous condition of servitude." So reads Section 1 of the Fifteenth Amendment, which was ratified in 1870. Although it seemed to sound the death knell of racial discrimination in voting, it was really only the beginning of a long struggle.

Southern state legislatures discovered a variety of ways to prevent the Fifteenth Amendment from being implemented. Among the earliest tactics was the use of **literacy tests,** which supposedly ensured that voters could read and write. In reality, these tests were designed to maintain a white electorate. The tests were often designed so that virtually no one could pass them. A fill-in question from the 1964 version of the test administered in Hattiesburg, Mississippi, reads "Appropriation of money for the armed services can be only for a period limited to ____ years." Few voters know their political system in such detail. Most whites did not

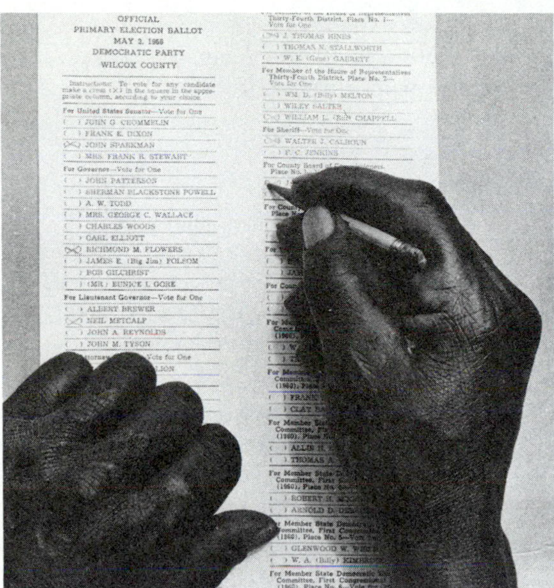

★ The ratification of the Fifteenth Amendment in 1870 was only the beginning of a long struggle for equal voting rights for black Americans.

need to take these tests, since the legislation establishing them normally included a **grandfather clause,** which exempted any voter whose grandfather had voted. Of course, a citizen whose grandfather was a slave and ineligible to vote was required to take the test.

A similarly restrictive tactic was the use of poll taxes. A **poll tax** is simply a fee charged to vote, and in many states the fees were cumulative: in order to vote in an election, one had to have paid the fees for all other elections in which one had been eligible to vote. Of course, these fees imposed a much greater burden on poor citizens, many of whom were black.

In tandem, literacy tests and poll taxes were quite effective. In 1958, Mississippi was one of three states to retain both practices, and in that year the black voting rate was 3.4 percent. Poll taxes were eliminated with the ratification of the Twenty-fourth Amendment in 1964, and literacy tests were virtually outlawed in 1975 with the passage of an extension of the 1965 Voting Rights Act. As a result, black Americans have nearly reached parity with whites in terms of voter turnout; in the 1986 congressional election, only four percentage points (47 to 43) separated the turnout rates of white and black Americans.[2]

Another tactic used to impede black voters was the **white primary.** Because the South was firmly in the grip of the Democratic party, the primary election really decided the eventual winner. Black voters were kept from participating in these crucial primary elections because the state Democratic party organizations claimed that their party was a private club, and that they could restrict membership to the people of their choice—all of whom, as it happened, were white. It was not until 1944 that the Supreme Court declared that primaries were a normal aspect of the electoral process, and thus subject to the stipulations of the Fifteenth Amendment.[3]

These legislative and judicial victories were bolstered in the 1960s by grassroots efforts to encourage black citizens to exercise their voting rights. The agendas of such people as Martin Luther King, Jr., Medgar Evers, and Malcolm X (all assassinated) included strategies to enhance the political action of previously disenfranchised and disillusioned black Americans. The various voting rights acts and civil rights acts passed in the 1960s and 1970s contained provisions intended to put in practice the laws and decisions of earlier years.

The Battle for Women's Suffrage

The enfranchisement of black Americans was not the only outcome of the abolitionist movement; the cause of women was soon associated with that of racial minorities. In 1840 the abolitionists Elizabeth Cady Stanton and Lucretia Mott attended the World Anti-Slavery Convention in London. Along with other women in the American delegation, they were denied seats as delegates and told to sit quietly in a curtained gallery during the ten-day convention. Struck by the contradiction of facing discrimination in a movement pledged to end discrimination, Stanton and Mott returned to the United States determined to end such abuses. After years of careful preparation, they convened the first American women's rights convention, in Seneca Falls, New York, in 1848. Three hundred women and several men attended. The most controversial section of the convention's Declaration of Sentiments called for women's "sacred right to the elected franchise." Subsequent conventions brought the names of such abolitionists/woman suffragists as Lucy Stone, Sojourner Truth, and Susan B. Anthony to public attention.

During the 1860s woman suffragists channeled their energies into the Civil War and passage of the Fifteenth Amendment, which guaranteed the right to vote to black freedmen. Anthony and Stanton wanted to include the word "sex" in this amendment, but such a drastic national change was not politically feasible at that time. However, women's suffrage was slowly creeping into laws across the nation, beginning with the right to vote in school board elections. In 1869 the territory of Wyoming became the first member of the Union to grant women's suffrage.

That same year, the suffrage movement divided along strategic lines. The National Woman Suffrage Association (NWSA), headed by Stanton and Anthony, pursued a national strategy to provide women's suffrage through a constitutional amendment. The American Woman Suffrage Association (AWSA), led by Julia Ward Howe (author of "Battle Hymn of the Republic") and Lucy Stone, adopted a more cautious state-by-state approach and eschewed the more radical causes with which the NWSA had become associated: rights for working women, criticisms of the church (Stanton published the *Women's Bible*), divorce, and free love.

When the NWSA and the AWSA finally merged in 1890 to form the National American Woman Suffrage Association (NAWSA), it was not because the AWSA had increased its support for wider causes, but rather because the NWSA had abandoned its association with more radical pursuits, especially the labor movement. This move revealed the fundamentally middle-class orientation of the suffrage movement at the turn of the century. With the decline of the old guard and the rise of a new breed of suffragist came a shift in the arguments advanced by the movement, from voting as a matter of justice to voting as a matter of practicality and expediency.[4]

Stanton and Anthony had advocated women's suffrage as a "natural right." They believed all persons were created equal, with an inalienable right to consent to the laws by which they were governed. A woman was a human being first, then a citizen, then a woman, and then a mother, wife, sister, or daughter. The expediency argument, by contrast, was voiced by Carrie Chapman Catt, who succeeded Susan B. Anthony as NAWSA president and led the movement until women's suffrage was

★ Elizabeth Cady Stanton, Susan B. Anthony, and Sojourner Truth (*left to right*) were each active in the suffrage movement. None of them, however, lived to see the passage of the Nineteenth Amendment, which gave women the vote in 1920.

achieved in 1920. Catt, who was called the "general of the suffrage movement," said that expediency required that women be given the vote to counteract the "ignorant foreign male vote." Some southern suffragists even advanced white supremacist arguments, objecting to a system that defined "refined white women" as political inferiors to former slaves. Obviously the movement had drifted far from its abolitionist roots.

More radical and militant women left NAWSA and used semimilitant tactics to secure passage of a federal suffrage amendment. In 1914 Alice Paul organized the Congressional Union for Woman Suffrage, which focused attention on Washington, D.C. Paul had staged a march of five thousand women the day before Woodrow Wilson's inauguration in 1913. It degenerated into a near riot but gained sympathy for the suffragists' cause. Grass-roots petition drives culminated in the presentation of 200,000 signatures to a group of senators. Delegations met with President Wilson, who remarked that the matter of women's suffrage had never been brought to his attention.

In 1916 the Congressional Union organized the National Woman's Party, which picketed the White House during World War I, with banners reading, "Democracy Should Begin at Home," "Kaiser Wilson," and "Free Russia" (Russian women received the vote in 1917, after the overthrow of the tsar). When envoys from the new Soviet government called at the White House, the banners read that America was a democracy in name only, precipitating mob violence and the arrest of some of the women demonstrators. They were sentenced to up to six months in jail. Eventually more than two hundred women from twenty-six states were arrested; ninety-seven of them went to prison, where many engaged in hunger strikes and were subjected to force-feeding. In 1918, on the day before the **Nineteenth Amendment** was scheduled for a House vote, Wilson declared himself to be in favor of it and set to work to secure congressional support. He urged the Senate to pass the suffrage bill as a war measure: "We have made partners of the women in this war; shall we admit them only to a partnership of suffering and toil and not to a partnership of privilege and right?"[5]

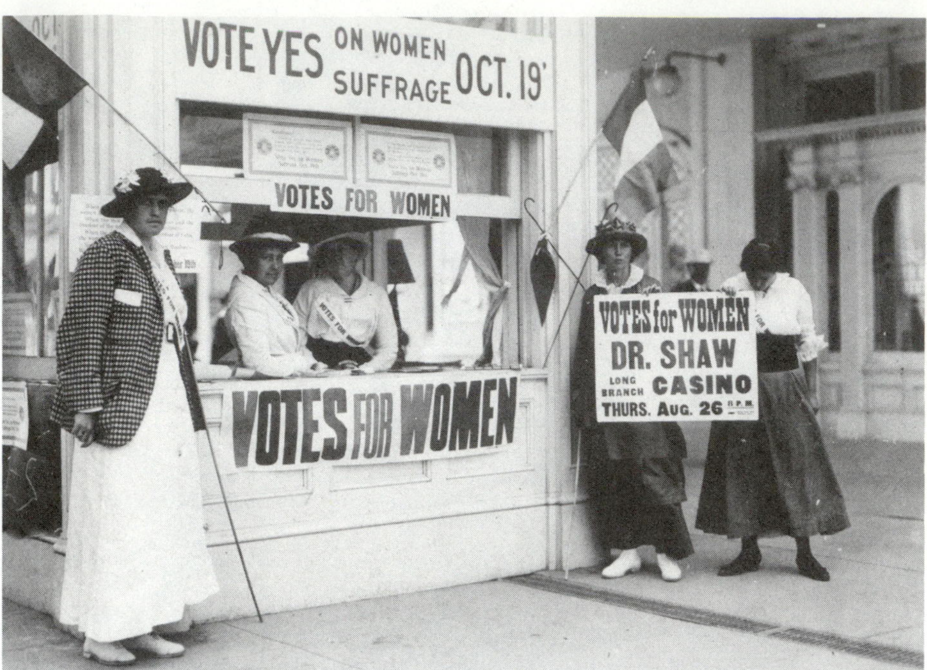

★ Women's suffrage was finally won after a long battle in which many types of tactics were used. In this photo, women are openly asking men to support women's right to vote.

Carrie Chapman Catt summarized the less militant tactics women used for fifty-two years to achieve at last the right to vote in 1920:

> They were forced to conduct 56 campaigns of referenda to male voters; 480 campaigns to get Legislators to submit suffrage amendments to voters; 47 campaigns to get State constitutional conventions to write woman suffrage into state constitutions; 277 campaigns to get state party conventions to include woman suffrage planks; 30 campaigns to get presidential party conventions to adopt woman suffrage planks in party platforms; and 19 campaigns with 19 successive Congresses.[6]

These efforts reveal the complexity of the American election system. Whether one is seeking radical political change, as the suffragists and civil rights activists were, or just trying to be an informed voter, knowledge of the nuts and bolts of the American electoral system is a crucial prerequisite.

★ The Nuts and Bolts of the American Election System

From the playground to the boardroom, those with the most votes win in America. In politics, too, with the exception of some presidential primaries and state and local contests, virtually all major elections require a candidate to win a plurality to claim victory. A **plurality** is the largest number of votes cast for any candidate in the race; it is not necessarily an absolute majority, which is at least one vote more than 50 percent of the total votes cast.

★ **Table 9-1**
Armageddon as a single-member/plurality system

Party	*Percent of popular vote*	*Number of seats*	*Percentage of seats held*
Nuke'em	40%	50	100%
Peace with Care	30	0	0
Peace Now	30	0	0

The second basic characteristic of the American electoral system is the **single-member district.** The U.S. House of Representatives and state legislatures are divided into districts, each district serving approximately the same number of citizens. Each district elects one representative, hence "single-member district." (In respect to the U.S. Senate, the entire state becomes, in effect, a single-member district at election time.) As we shall see, many nations in other parts of the world have **plural-member districts:** a single district may elect several representatives to the legislature. Members of some local city councils and county governing boards are elected "at large," but they are exceptions to the general rule; single-member districts are a basic part of the American way of life. Though we seem to be discussing mere technicalities of interest only to calculator-toting political scientists, election rules can influence everything from the formation of parties to the power of the average citizen.

The Effects of Single-Member/Plurality Elections

In football the shape of the ball determines the nature of the game and sets the sport apart from basketball or golf. Plurality elections and single-member districts have likewise determined major aspects of American politics. A hypothetical example will help make this point clear.

Imagine that three political parties dominate the mythical nation of Armageddon: Peace Now, Peace with Care, and Nuke'em. Imagine further that 40 percent of the voters, spread evenly throughout fifty single-member electoral districts, support the Nuke'em party, while each of the remaining parties enjoys a 30 percent following. If party loyalty remained strong in a single-member/plurality district election, the distribution of seats in the legislature would look like the results in table 9-1. For the Nuke'em party faithful (and perhaps the manufacturers of bomb shelters) the election results would seem fair and just. But what about the 60 percent of the voters who did not support the Nuke'em candidates? Would they feel that democracy had triumphed in such a situation? What solutions could the losers seek to gain representation in the legislature?

In many countries such a situation could lead to violence and revolution. A less drastic solution, however, would be for the two peace parties to reconcile their differences and join forces to defeat their Nuke'em opponents. Should voter loyalty remain the same in the next election, we would expect the results to be reversed,

Table 9-2
Armageddon as a plural-member/proportional representation system

Party	*Percent of popular vote*	*Number of seats*	*Percentage of seats held*
Nuke'em	40%	200	40%
Peace with Care	30	150	30
Peace Now	30	150	30

with the Peace with Care/Peace Now coalition vanquishing the Nuke'em party 50 to 0.

Such a scenario, though technically possible, is not likely even in the fantasy world of Armageddon. It is unlikely that all supporters of the two peace parties would be happy with the compromises necessary to bring their groups together. A more probable scenario would find some cautious Peace with Care supporters, worried about the compromises necessary to build the alliance, defecting to the Nuke'em party. Ultimately, the original three-party system would probably evolve into a competitive two-party system.

Indeed, a two-party system is the logical outcome of the single-member electoral system. Third parties must unite or die in a system that shows no generosity to third parties. All of the nations that use this method of voting—Great Britain, Australia, Canada, most British Commonwealth democracies—are virtual two-party systems. Not surprisingly, the American political system soon became a two-party system after the Constitution was ratified (as we saw in chap. 8).

Alternatives to the Single-Member/Plurality System

Another possibility would be for the mythical Armageddon to adopt the plural-member/**proportional representation** system. This system is used in many nations in Europe, Latin America, Africa, and other regions of the globe. Rather than elect a single representative for each district, a plural-member system selects a number of individuals from one district to serve in the legislature. The mechanics of the system can be quite simple or numbingly complex, with literally hundreds of candidates vying for office in each district. The basics, however, are as follows: Each party presents a list of candidates for seats available in a given district. After the election, seats are apportioned among the parties on the basis of the percentage of votes each party has received. If a party wins 20 percent of the votes in a district, then it will be allocated roughly 20 percent of the seats.

Let's again consider our hypothetical nation of Armageddon, with its three political parties. Recall that support for the parties broke down like this: Nuke'em, 40 percent; Peace with Care, 30 percent; and Peace Now, 30 percent. A plural-member/proportional representation election with fifty districts, in which each district has ten seats and similar partisan divisions, is represented in table 9-2. The plural-member system obviously distributes more power to nonwinners than the single-member system does.

Proportional representation in plural-member legislative districts influences a nation's political parties. Since parties can enjoy electoral success even with a relatively small following, they tend to proliferate. Parties tend to represent more specific ideological positions, ethnic groups, and special interests. Ultraright and ultraleft parties, which would not stand much of a chance in the United States, may enjoy a small but visible presence in the national legislature of France, Argentina, or Sweden.

Small parties, in fact, can enjoy influence greater than their numbers would indicate. If no single party holds a majority of seats in the legislature, some parties must form coalitions in order to pass bills into law. When a small party holds key swing votes, it can drive a hard bargain with much larger and more powerful parties. Thus temporary and fragile alliances are part of a proportional representation multiparty system. In the United States' two-party system, the compromise and negotiation among groups and interests usually takes place within the Republican and Democratic parties, especially during nominating conventions and strategy sessions.

Thus the way officials are elected can have a decisive effect on the entire political system. The single-member system tends to produce large coalition parties that avoid controversial issues in their efforts to maintain broad-based support. Because splinter groups are discouraged, this type of system tends to promote long-term stability (although exceptions do exist), and often at the expense of solutions to issues that arouse controversy. The plural-member arrangement tends to encourage a multiplicity of parties, which can result in a volatile political structure because coalitions tend to shift. Politics may seem more exciting in such a system, but stability may be sacrificed.

★ A Remnant of the Past: The Electoral College

There is a wrench in our discussion of the nuts and bolts of the American election system. Most people assume that a president is elected directly by the voters in November, but such is not the case. Rather than choose between the candidates, voters in each state actually cast their ballots for rival slates of presidential electors (usually loyal party workers) selected by state party organizations. Not until the electors vote in December is a president officially chosen.

Direct election of the president was opposed by most of the founders, who believed the people were not competent to make informed decisions. "It would be as rational to refer the choice of a proper character for Chief Magistrate to the people," George Mason declared, "as it would be to refer a trial of colors to a blind man." As a result, during the early years of American history, state legislatures picked the electors, who in turn voted for the president; ordinary citizens had no direct say over who would be the chief executive. Only with the passage of time have the state legislatures allowed citizens to vote directly for members of the **electoral college,** who now reflect the voters' preferences. (In most states voters are unaware that they are voting for electors because their names do not even appear on the ballot.) Although such an eventuality is highly unlikely, state legislatures could legally change the rules again and discontinue the popular election of electors.

Over the years, the electoral college has played a significant role in presidential selection, focusing the attention of candidates on the most populous states. The Constitution grants each state as many electoral votes as it has senators and

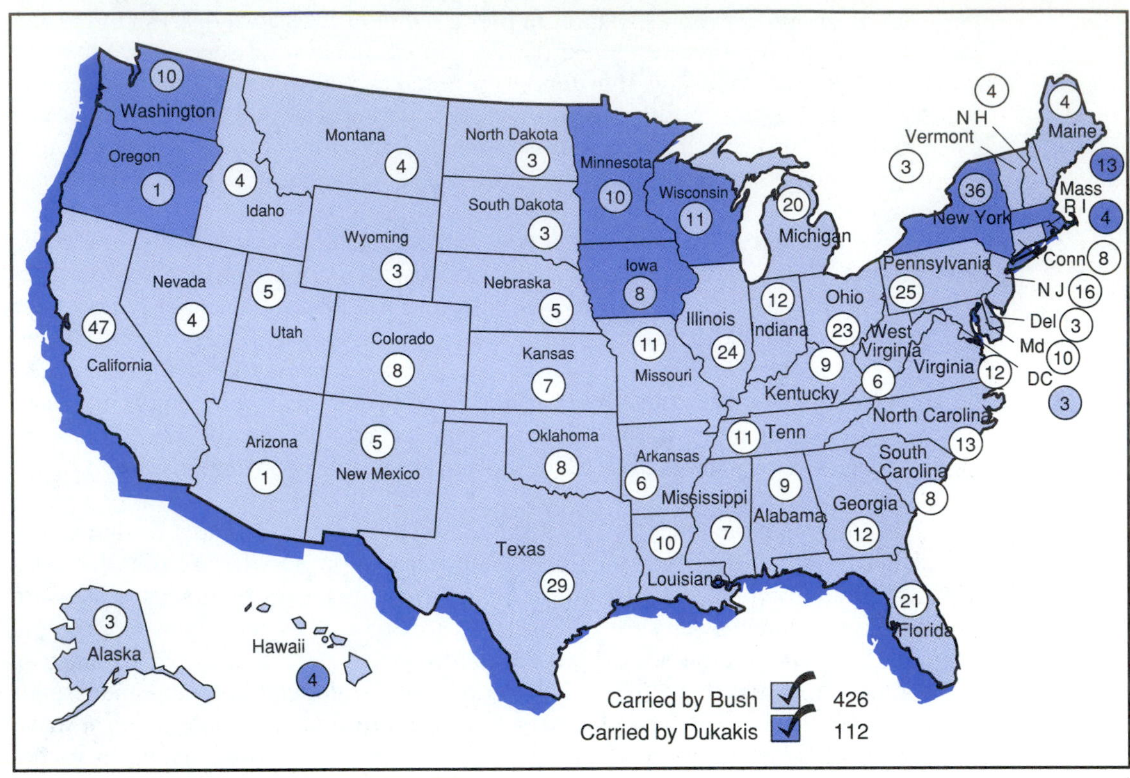

★ **Figure 9-1**
Electoral votes by state, 1988
SOURCE: *Congressional Quarterly Weekly Report,* November 12, 1988, p. 3242.

representatives, so the most populous states have the most electors. Since all electoral votes in most states (Maine is an exception) go to the candidate who captures the most popular votes (a custom, not a constitutional requirement), it is to the candidate's benefit to win the largest states. Figure 9-1 shows how the electoral votes were cast in 1988.

The fear, of course, is that the electoral outcome could frustrate the popular will. A candidate who wins enough large states by narrow margins could beat an opponent with more popular votes nationwide. Indeed, in three elections (1824, 1876, and 1888), the winner of the popular vote failed to obtain an electoral majority and lost the presidency. Although no such upset has occurred in this century, a small shift in the popular vote in 1976 could have given the election to Ford instead of Carter. A change of only 9,000 votes in Ohio and Hawaii would have given Ford more electoral votes than Carter, even though Carter beat Ford by 1.7 million votes nationwide. Moreover, in the event that no candidate wins a majority in the electoral college (perhaps as the result of a strong showing by a third-party candidate), the election would be thrown into the House of Representatives. The House members would choose from among the top three candidates, with each state delegation having a single vote. The possibility would exist that a candidate with less popular support could be named president.

Despite these drawbacks, the abolition of the electoral college has been vigorously opposed by many party officials. In their view, such an action would deprive them of their ability to swing a state and all its electoral votes to one candidate or another. They also insist that the change could further weaken the two major parties by encouraging the growth of third parties. Most proposals for the direct popular election of the president provide that if the winning candidate receives no more than 40 percent of the popular vote, a runoff election has to be held. Thus a third-party candidate could amass enough popular votes to bargain for favors and affect the electoral outcome—a prospect, of course, that many third parties would welcome.

★ Before the General Election: Selecting the Finalists

Clearly, it is the general election that receives the most attention. In general elections, candidates of all political parties vie for coveted political offices. Yet equally important is the process by which the parties choose candidates to represent them in the general election. And just as general elections have become increasingly accessible to the American citizenry, the candidate selection process has developed in the direction of popular input.

In the early nineteenth century, a party's candidate was usually chosen in a legislative **caucus,** or a closed meeting among the party's leaders. Presidential candidates, for example, were selected in caucuses attended by influential party members of the Senate and the House of Representatives. The problem with the caucus system was that it failed to represent all party elements and excluded the participation of those at the grass-roots level. It even appeared to violate the separation-of-powers principle by having legislators pick candidates for executive offices.

By the 1830s, a more representative method of selecting candidates—the **convention system**—began to be adopted by the political parties. Delegates chosen by local party members gathered at state or national conventions (as they still do today) to nominate slates of candidates. But though it was an improvement over the caucus method, the convention system still tended to exclude most rank-and-file members from the nomination process. Generally, only the most active of the party faithful turned out to select convention delegates, and the conventions themselves were frequently dominated by party bosses. Efforts to open the candidate selection process to more diverse elements in each party led to the adoption of the direct primary form of candidate selection.

Primary Elections

The **direct primary** came into being in the early twentieth century as part of the Progressive movement, which also brought about the popular election of senators and the initiative process—all attempts to carry decision-making power to the populace. In contrast to the convention system, in which delegates freely pick the party's candidates, the primary system allows voters themselves to choose delegates who are pledged to support candidates competing for the party's endorsement. Most states today use the **closed primary,** in which voters may cast ballots only for the candidates of their own party. Only a few states maintain an **open primary,** in which citizens are free to vote for the candidates of either party. Table 9-3 shows the systems used in the various states as of 1987.

★ **Table 9-3**
Summary of state rules and statistics (1987)

	Delegates		Form of delegate selection	Method of allocation		Registered voters		
							Percent	
	Dem.	Rep.		Dem.	Rep.	Total	Dem.	Rep.
Alabama	61	38	Open primary	PR	PR/WTA	2,341,264	—	—
Alaska	17	19	Closed caucus	BPR	NFS	257,429	22	21
Arizona	40	33	Closed caucus	PR	NFS	1,464,071	43	46
Arkansas	43	27	Open primary	PR	PR	1,188,831	—	—
California	336	175	Closed primary	PR	WTA	12,121,051	51	38
Colorado	51	36	Closed caucus	BPR	NFS	1,807,156	31	33
Connecticut	59	35	Closed primary	PR	PR	1,672,949	40	27
Delaware	19	17	Closed caucus	PR	NFS	293,119	44	35
Florida	146	82	Closed primary	BPR	WTA	5,631,188	57	36
Georgia	86	48	Open primary	BPR	WTA	2,575,819	—	—
Hawaii	25	20	Closed caucus	PR	NFS	419,794	—	—
Idaho	23	22	Open C(D)/P(R)	PR	PR	514,801	—	—
Illinois	187	92	Open primary	DE	DE	6,003,811	—	—
Indiana	85	51	Open primary	PR	WTA	2,878,498	—	—
Iowa	58	37	Open caucus*	PR	NFS	1,544,902	35	31
Kansas	43	34	Closed caucus	PR	NFS	1,102,641	29	42
Kentucky	60	38	Closed primary	PR	PR	1,936,025	68	28
Louisiana	71	41	Closed primary	PR	WTA	2,139,861	78	14
Maine	27	22	Open caucus*	PR	NFS	773,966	34	30
Maryland	78	41	Closed primary	DE/PR	WTA	2,139,690	67	25
Massachusetts	109	52	Open primary*	BPR	PR	2,933,364	47	13
Michigan	151	77	Open caucus	PR	NFS	5,597,748	—	—
Minnesota	86	31	Open caucus	PR	NFS	2,447,273	—	—
Mississippi	45	31	Open primary	PR	WTA	1,643,191	—	—
Missouri	83	47	Open primary	BPR	PR	2,775,654	—	—
Montana	25	20	Open primary	BPR	NFS	443,935	—	—
Nebraska	29	25	Closed primary	PR	DE	849,762	42	51
Nevada	21	20	Closed caucus	PR	NFS	367,596	50	43
New Hampshire	22	23	Open primary*	PR	PR	551,257	30	37
New Jersey	118	64	Open primary*	DE	DE	3,647,886	34	20

	Delegates		Form of delegate selection	Method of allocation		Registered voters		
							Percent	
	Dem.	Rep.		Dem.	Rep.	Total	Dem.	Rep.
New Mexico	28	26	Closed primary	PR	NFS	499,180	60	34
New York	275	136	Closed primary	BPR	DE	7,650,666	47	33
North Carolina	89	54	Closed primary	BPR	PR	3,080,990	69	27
North Dakota	20	16	Open C(D)/P(R)	PR	PR	—	—	—
Ohio	174	88	Open primary*	BPR	WTA	5,856 552	31	20
Oklahoma	51	36	Closed primary	PR	WTA	2,014,578	67	30
Oregon	51	32	Closed primary	PR	PR	1,422,226	48	40
Pennsylvania	193	96	Closed primary	DE	DE	5,384,375	54	42
Rhode Island	26	21	Open primary*	PR	PR	524,662	—	—
South Carolina	48	37	Open C(D)/P(R)	PR	WTA	1,184,133	—	—
South Dakota	19	18	Closed primary	PR	PR	428,097	43	49
Tennessee	77	45	Open primary	PR	PR	2,543,597	—	—
Texas	198	111	Open P & C(D)/P(R)	PR	PR/WTA	7,340,638	—	—
Utah	27	26	Open caucus	PR	NFS	763,057	—	—
Vermont	19	17	Open caucus	PR	NFS	328,466	—	—
Virginia	85	50	Open P(D)/C(R)	PR	NFS	2,546,345	—	—
Washington	72	41	Open caucus	PR	NFS	2,230,254	—	—
West Virginia	44	28	Open primary*	DE	DE	946,039	67	31
Wisconsin	88	47	Open primary	PR	WTA	—	—	—
Wyoming	18	18	Closed caucus	PR	NFS	187,302	33	59

Open—Voters may participate in either party's event.
Closed—Event restricted to registered party voters.
*—Open to independents, but not to members of the other party.
C(D)/P(R)—Democratic caucus and Republican primary.
P(D)/C(R)—Democratic primary and Republican caucus.
DE—Direct election of delegates independent of vote for candidates (winner-take-all possible).
PR—Proportional representation system.
BPR—"Bonus" proportional representation; candidate receives a bonus delegate for each district won.
WTA—Winner-take-all system.
NFS—No formal system for allocating delegates to candidates; method determined by participants.

SOURCE: Rhodes Cook, *Race for the Presidency: Winning the 1988 Nomination* (Washington, D.C.: Congressional Quarterly, 1987), p. 3.

In reality, primaries have tended to express the popular will less than they were intended to; although primaries allow substantially wider participation in the candidate selection process, few voters take advantage of the opportunity. Fewer than 30 percent of the eligible voters turn out for most primary elections, and those who do are generally not representative of the party membership as a whole. Voters in primary elections tend to be more well-to-do, better educated, and more ideological than those who participate only in general elections. This circumstance sometimes favors candidates with sharp ideological views who are difficult to elect in November. Some observers noted, for instance, that George McGovern's primary victories in 1972 helped him capture the Democratic presidential nomination even though he did not enjoy widespread support among the electorate.

Primaries can also lead to divisiveness. Following a bitter primary fight, supporters of the losing candidate may refuse to support the victor in the general election. In 1976, for example, some of Ronald Reagan's supporters refused to back Gerald Ford's presidential bid in the wake of the Republican primaries, and in 1980, Senator Edward Kennedy's hesitant and lukewarm endorsement of Jimmy Carter hardly inspired Kennedy supporters to jump on the Carter bandwagon. The primary system can also divide the party faithful because candidates can bypass the party organization and appeal directly to the voters. Both McGovern and Carter gained a good deal of their popularity by openly confronting the Democratic party line. Among recent Democratic presidential hopefuls, only Walter Mondale and Michael Dukakis did not openly campaign as outsiders.

Despite these problems, more and more states have adopted the primary as a means of choosing delegates to the national presidential conventions. In 1968, fewer than half of the delegates to the Democratic and Republican national conventions were chosen in primaries. Most of the states continued to select delegates in state caucuses or conventions. As a result, Hubert Humphrey was able to garner enough delegates to win the Democratic presidential nomination even though he did not enter a single primary.

By 1976, however, more than three-fourths of the delegates were picked in primary elections scattered from February until June in thirty states. With little doubt, this spurt in the number of primaries greatly affected the nomination contests in both the Democratic and Republican parties. Because most of the delegates were chosen in primary elections, none of the major candidates could hope to win the nomination through state party conventions alone. Ronald Reagan, for instance, took advantage of the primaries in 1976 to mount a strong challenge to the incumbent president, Gerald Ford. Faced with possible defeat by the former movie star and Republican governor of California, Ford was forced to enter the primaries in order to win the Republican party nomination.

Even more significant, Jimmy Carter's victories in the early primaries transformed him from a relative unknown into a successful contender for the Democratic party nomination. By entering most of the primaries, he was able to attract national media attention and demonstrate his popularity with the voters. In 1976 the Democratic party scrapped winner-take-all primaries, in which candidates with the most votes won all of a state's convention delegates, and encouraged instead a system of proportional representation. With this change, although Carter did not win all of the primaries he entered, he collected enough delegates to convince party leaders that he could not be stopped and that he offered the party's best chance of defeating the Republican candidate (Ford) in November. Ironically,

★★★★★★★★★★★★

Ecology

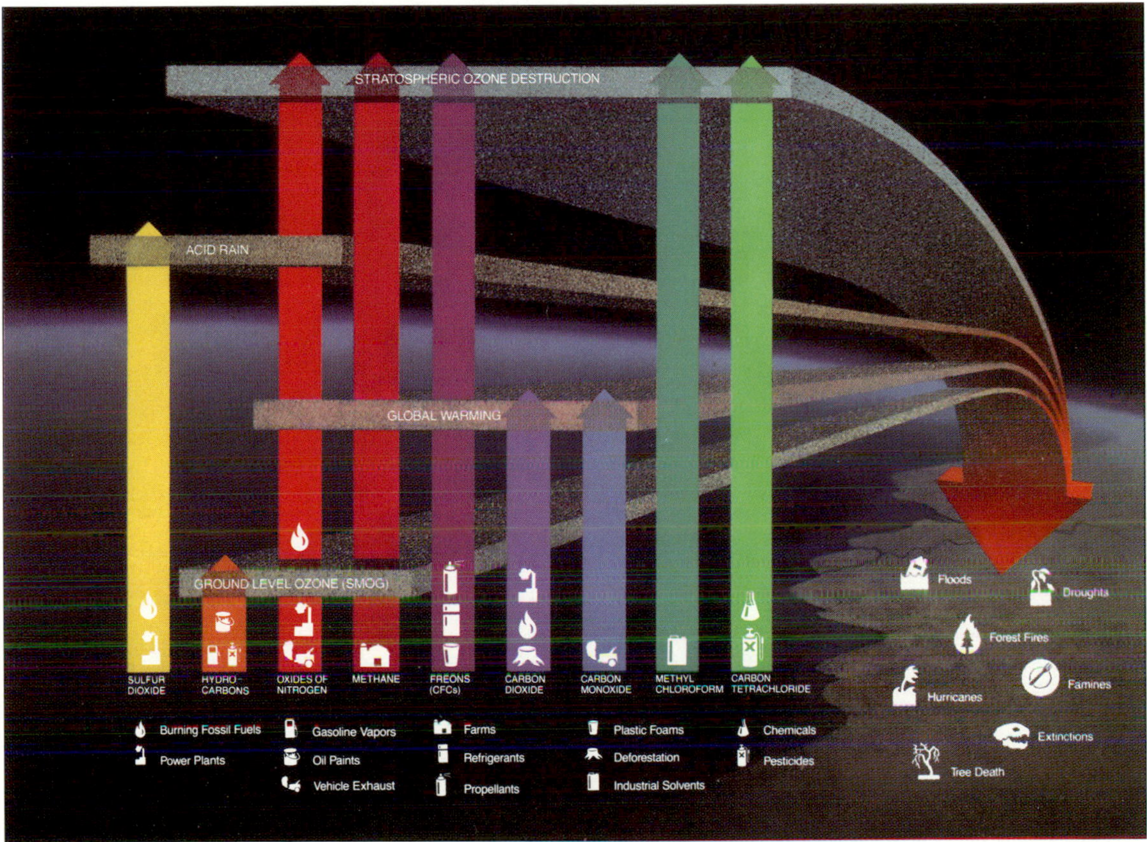

Rob Wood

Larry Lefever/Grant Heilman Photography, Inc.

Gay Charneau/Gamma–Liaison

UNICEF/Stephenie Hollyman/Picture Group

Global warming is one of the most significant threats to our environment, along with acid rain, the destruction of the ozone layer, and ground-level pollutants. Global warming is caused by the greenhouse effect, the process of warming that occurs in the atmosphere because of the heat-trapping abilities of certain gases, notably carbon dioxide, methane, and nitrous oxide. These gases allow energy from the sun to reach the earth's surface but keep the radiant energy from leaving the earth. Chlorofluorocarbons (CFCs) exacerbate the global warming by destroying the fragile

Louis Psihoyos/Contact Press Images

Sebastio Salgado/Magnum

ozone layers. The result is a rise in the average temperature, the melting of polar ice, and a change in climate that, in turn, affects the type of vegetation that will grow in a particular region. You can see the effect in the pictures on the preceding page of the summer drought of 1988 in the United States, France, and Ethiopia.

Bossu–SYGMA/Regis

Gustavo Gilabert/JB Pictures

Industrial pollutants also threaten the earth's fragile ecosystem, from the industrialized cities of North America and Western Europe to the vacation paradises of Jamaica in the West Indies as well as in Brazil.

Burning garbage in the open air adds to the deterioration of the atmosphere. In addition, acid rain, the fallout from industrial pollutants discharging in the air, creates great destruction of vegetation, as seen above in the Black Forest in Germany.

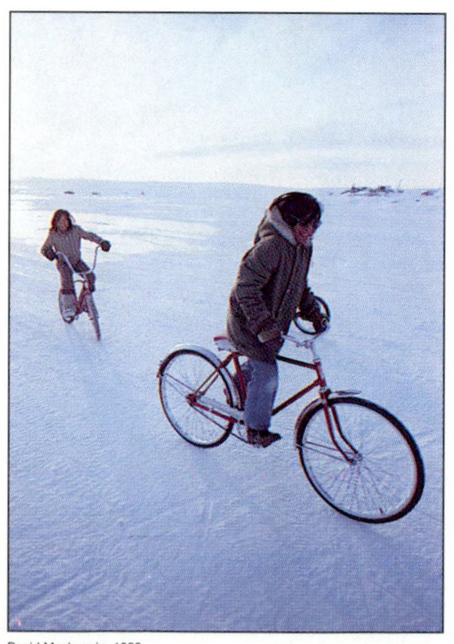

David Mackenzie, 1989

Even in the arctic regions of Canada, tests have shown radioactive elements in the breast milk of Inuit mothers and in the caribou that the Inuit eat. This contamination has been traced to the testing of nuclear weapons in the USSR and to the accident at the Soviet Chernobyl nuclear power plant. The Inuit are trying to protect their future and that of their children by protesting a projected uranium mine in their territory, which would leave uranium tailings in the area after the mining was done.

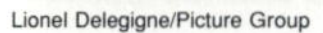

Lionel Delegigne/Picture Group

Hans Silvester/Photo Researchers, Inc.

The Inuit are not the only indigenous people trying to protect their environment. The Indians of the Amazon, notably the Xingu, called a summit at Altamira, Brazil, to protest the destruction of the Amazonian rain forest, their home. The forest is being burned to clear land for cattle ranchers and the millions of landless poor in Brazil. However, this forest is a major source of the world's oxygen, as well as the land from which the Xingu and others make their living. The musician Sting, among others, attended the Altamira summit, calling attention both to the global effects of this destruction and to the global aspects of the support. This support increases as people become more aware of how their fate hinges on the fate of a faraway Amazonian rain forest. In fact, environmental groups in the United States have pressured the government to link U.S. economic policy toward Brazil with rain-forest protection. People from many countries also came together in an effort to clean up the damage when the tanker *Exxon Valdez* ran aground, spilling oil in Alaska's Prince William Sound and killing countless wildlife. And when three California gray whales were trapped in Alaska, rescuers, including representatives of both the U.S. and the Soviet governments, worked round the clock to release them.

Burlington Free Press

JL Atlan/SYGMA

Brandon/SIPA–Press

These are not isolated efforts; they represent a growing pattern of ecological awareness and concern. More and more, international politics and ecology are linked hand in hand. For example, the Green Party, recognized as a political force in Western Europe, is now a growing party in the United States, standing for sound ecological principles, social responsibility, grass-roots democracy, and nonviolence. Seen above are the Burlington, Vermont, Greens taking a stand on a housing issue.

Industrial pollution, acid rain, and global warming touch us all, as does the problem of everyday garbage disposal. In 1988, each American generated about 1,300 pounds of solid waste. Where does it go? In this text you saw the "homeless" garbage barge

EDP/Ad Council

Patrick Frilet/SIPA–Press

Michael Macintyrer/Hutchins Library

David Mackenzie

of New York trying to find a berth, a place to throw it all away. Where is away? Is it on Japan's island of garbage *(far left),* with its mountains of filled plastic bags? Is it in the Philippines' "Garbage Mountain" *(middle)*, which actually houses many of its citizens who forage and work there? Or is it in the Keewatin District of the Northwest Territories of Canada *(right),* where nondegradable garbage and the disposal of human waste are a growing problem? Where is away?

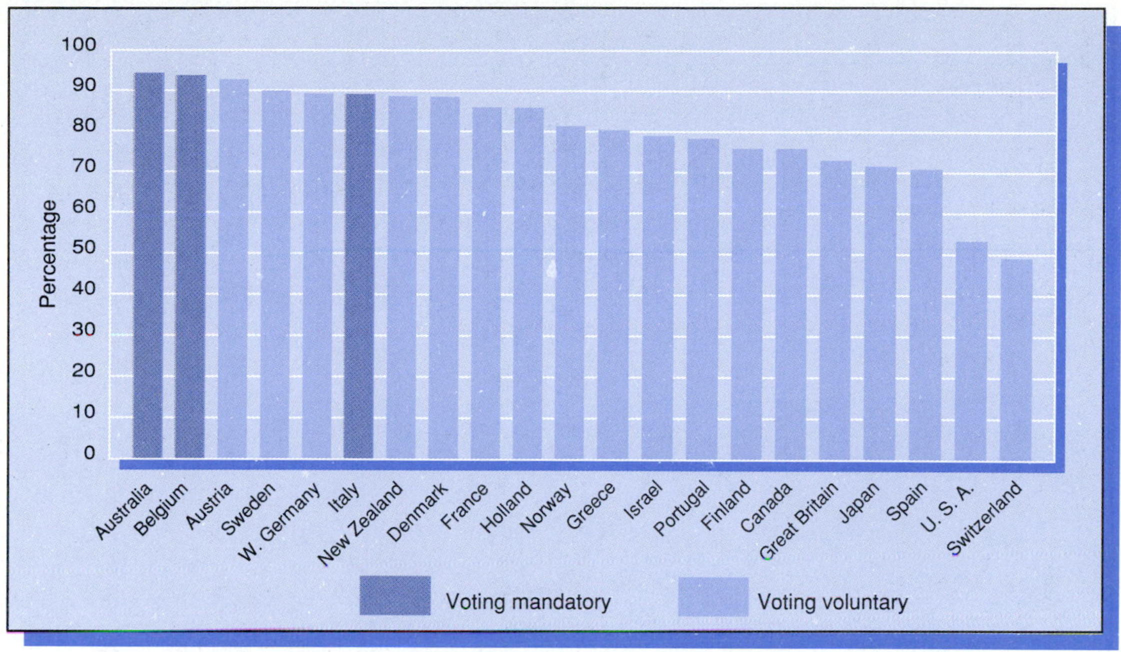

★ **Figure 9-2**
International voter turnout rates (percent), based on elections in 1981–1986
SOURCE: Adapted from *Congressional Quarterly Weekly Report*, April 2, 1988, p. 863.

with yet another increase in the number of primaries in 1980, Carter faced a tough challenge from Edward Kennedy, who sought to wrest the party's nomination from him.

★ Citizens and the Election Process

A Modern Scandal?

After the 1988 presidential election, some observers declared the winner to be neither George Bush nor Michael Dukakis but "none of the above."[7] As only 50.1 percent of the voting-age population had bothered to vote, Bush may have become president more by default than by popular mandate.

A consistent finding is that most people do not participate actively in politics. This lack of participation is most conspicuous during elections. An international survey of electoral systems shows that only Switzerland has a lower turnout rate (see figure 9-2). As figure 9-3 shows, turnout in presidential elections since 1972 has not exceeded 55 percent. In fact, it has declined each year since 1960, rising again only slightly in 1984. The 1988 turnout of only 50.1 percent was the lowest in sixty-four years. Out of a potential electorate of about 180 million, then, fewer than 92 million registered voters marched to the polls to vote for their presidential choice. More than 88 million other Americans—a number greater than the population of either England or France—failed to show up on election day.

Turnout is even lower in midterm congressional elections, when the entire

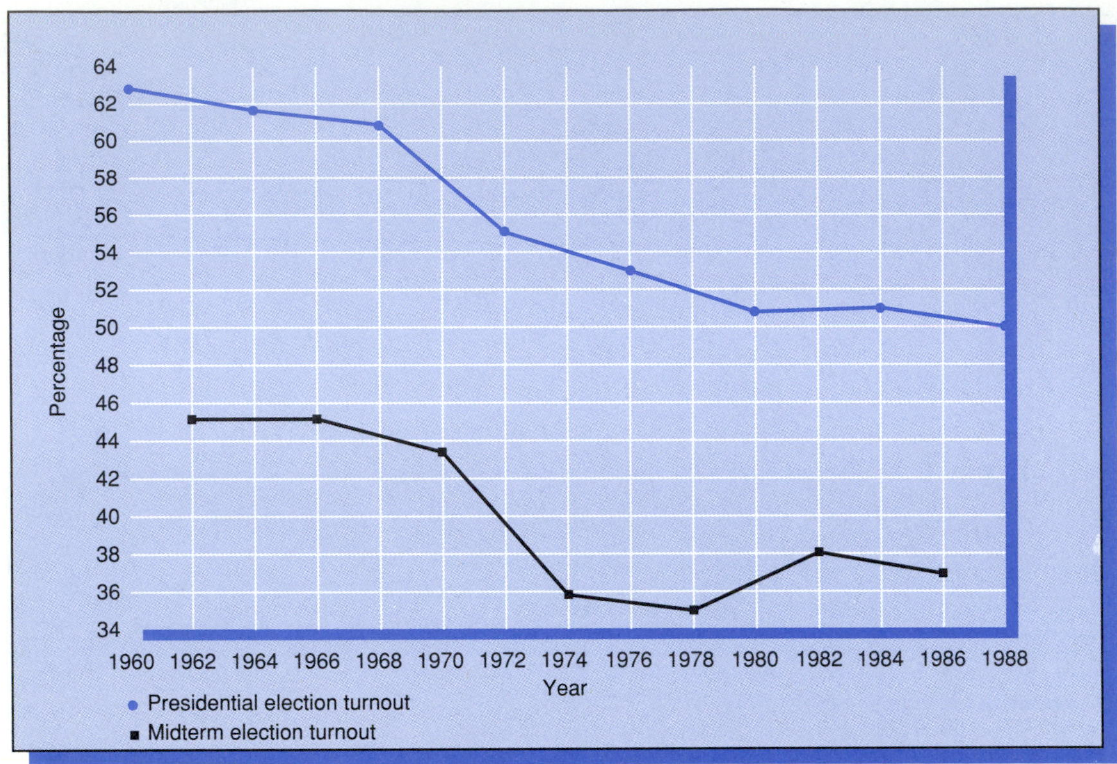

Figure 9-3

Percentage of eligible citizens who voted in presidential and midterm elections, 1960–1988

SOURCE: U.S. Bureau of the Census, *Statistical Abstract of the United States, 1987* (Washington, D.C.: U.S. Government Printing Office, 1986), p. 243; figure for 1988 from *Congressional Quarterly Weekly Report,* January 21, 1989, p. 2.

House of Representatives and one-third of the Senate are chosen. In the seven midterm congressional elections between 1962 and 1986, an average of only about 40 percent voted. And in statewide and local elections involving the choosing of governors and mayors, turnout frequently dips below 30 percent.

These figures seem to compare unfavorably with those of other countries, such as Italy, France, Denmark, and Japan, where turnout is commonly about 80 to 90 percent. In some respects, however, comparisons with other countries are unfair.

- The United States is the only country that computes its turnout statistics on the basis of eligible citizens; all other democracies provide turnout statistics as a proportion of those registered.
- Americans are asked to vote more often than citizens in other nations, and in many states and localities the ballots can be extremely long and complex.
- Some state constitutions contain provisions for initiatives and referendums, in which citizens vote directly on constitutional amendments and other legislation.

Thus it is harder to be a consistently attentive voter in the United States than in many of the countries with which American turnout is unfavorably compared.

Those Americans who go beyond voting to engage in other kinds of political activity represent an even smaller fraction of the voting-age population (see figure 9-4). One political scientist, Lester Milbrath, stratified the population into several

During elections, do you ever try to show people why they should vote for one of the parties or candidates?

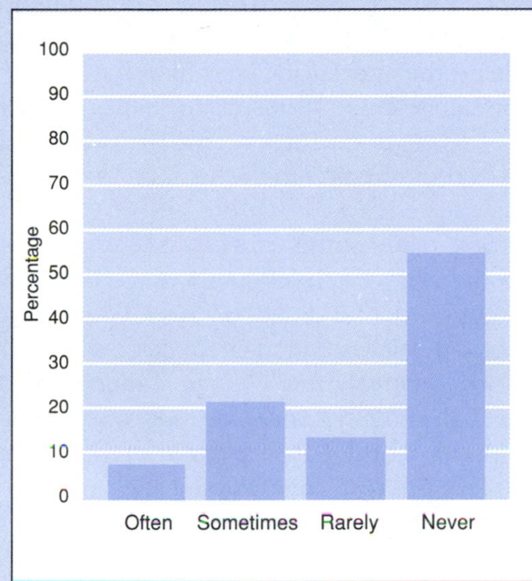

Have you done work for one of the parties or candidates in most elections, some elections, only a few, or never?

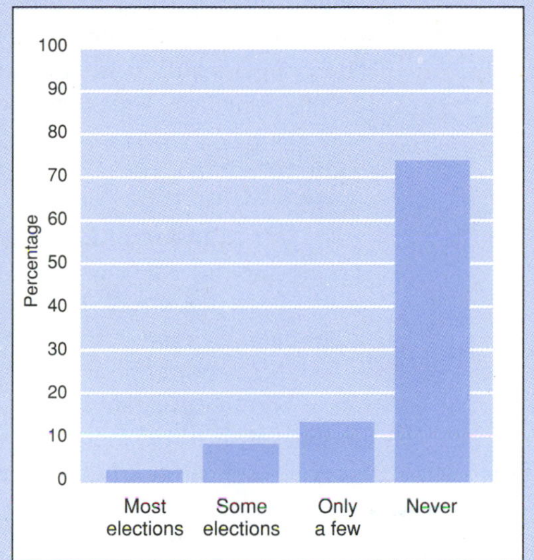

In the past three or four years, have you attended any political meetings or rallies?

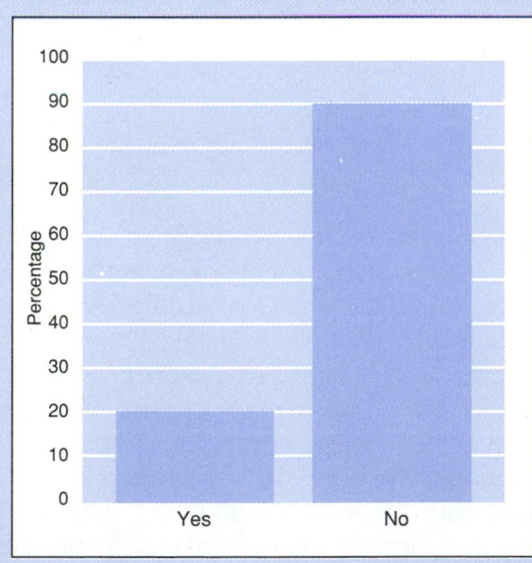

Have you ever personally gone to see, or spoken to, or written to some member of local government or some other person of influence in the community about some needs or problems?

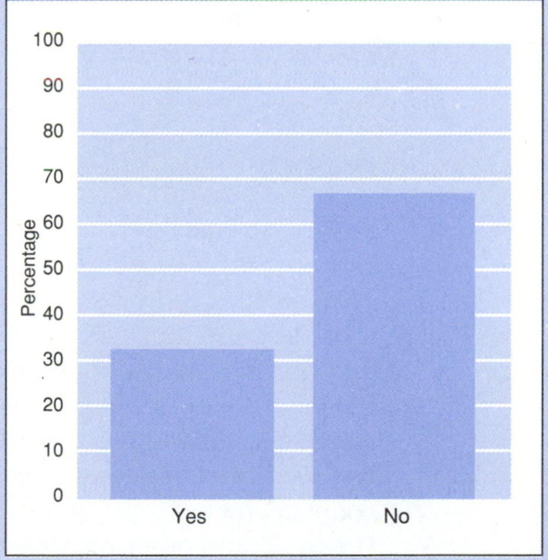

★ **Figure 9-4**
The more active aspects of citizenship, 1988
SOURCE: James Allan Davis and Tom W. Smith, *General Social Survey, 1972–1988* (Chicago: National Opinion Research Center, 1988), subfile 1988 (machine-readable data file).

basic types, including "gladiators" (who become active in party politics or run for office), "spectators" (who seek information and vote), and "apathetics" (who either participate minimally or abstain altogether). According to Milbrath, those "gladiators" who engage in one active form of political participation, such as raising campaign funds, tend to be active in other ways as well. "This division," Milbrath reflected, "is reminiscent of the roles played at a Roman gladiatorial contest. A small band of gladiators battle fiercely to please the spectators, who have the power to decide their fate. The spectators in the stands cheer, transmit messages of advice and encouragement, and, at given periods, vote to decide who has won a particular battle (election). The apathetics do not bother to come to the stadium to watch the show."[8]

Thus, although most Americans have made some effort to vote and express a political opinion, only about 15 percent have written letters to an elected official and only 12 percent have contributed money to a candidate or party.[9] Voting aside, it has been estimated that more Americans participate in amateur stage shows than in politics. And, contrary to expectations, relatively few college students take an active part in campaigns. Following the 1970 congressional elections, when student antiwar protest was at its peak, a Gallup poll found that 91 percent of the students interviewed had not been involved at all in political campaigning.[10]

★ Obstacles to Voter Participation

Political scientists have been greatly interested in discovering the factors that inhibit participation in politics. Because voting is a particularly important ritual in American life, scholars have tried to explain why millions of people stay home on election day. Though we do not yet have a definitive answer to this question, a few explanations have been offered.

Registration Requirements

First of all, the low turnout of voters may be partly explained by institutional barriers, such as state registration requirements. In the 1984 presidential election, 31 percent of those interviewed by the Gallup organization claimed not to have voted because they had failed to register.[11] In 1988, an estimated 37 percent said they had not registered. State laws usually require voters to register in person and to renew their eligibility whenever they move or miss a major election. Sometimes these registration procedures are seen as awkward or burdensome, or are too far removed from the election itself; someone who normally is interested in the outcome of an election may not feel sufficiently excited a month before it to register. For these and other reasons, there is a significant discrepancy in turnout among the various states (see figure 9-5).

In 1977 President Carter handed Congress an "instant registration" proposal that would have allowed any citizen to vote in a federal election by merely walking up to the polling place on election day and flashing a driver's license or other acceptable identification. In the few states that already have such a system—Maine, Minnesota, and Wisconsin—voter turnout has tended to be higher than the national average, even when other factors are taken into account. Many members of

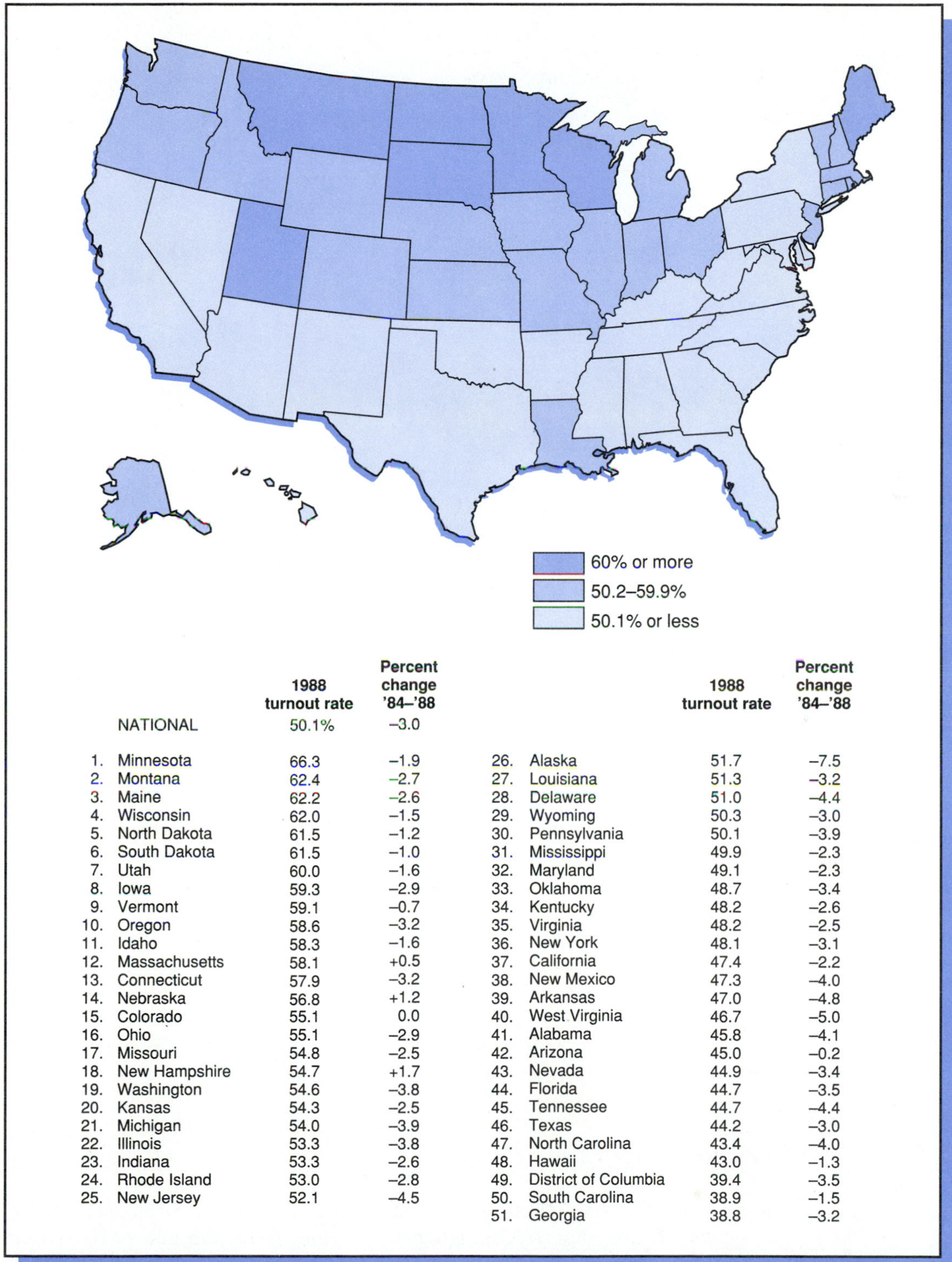

		1988 turnout rate	Percent change '84–'88
	NATIONAL	50.1%	–3.0
1.	Minnesota	66.3	–1.9
2.	Montana	62.4	–2.7
3.	Maine	62.2	–2.6
4.	Wisconsin	62.0	–1.5
5.	North Dakota	61.5	–1.2
6.	South Dakota	61.5	–1.0
7.	Utah	60.0	–1.6
8.	Iowa	59.3	–2.9
9.	Vermont	59.1	–0.7
10.	Oregon	58.6	–3.2
11.	Idaho	58.3	–1.6
12.	Massachusetts	58.1	+0.5
13.	Connecticut	57.9	–3.2
14.	Nebraska	56.8	+1.2
15.	Colorado	55.1	0.0
16.	Ohio	55.1	–2.9
17.	Missouri	54.8	–2.5
18.	New Hampshire	54.7	+1.7
19.	Washington	54.6	–3.8
20.	Kansas	54.3	–2.5
21.	Michigan	54.0	–3.9
22.	Illinois	53.3	–3.8
23.	Indiana	53.3	–2.6
24.	Rhode Island	53.0	–2.8
25.	New Jersey	52.1	–4.5

		1988 turnout rate	Percent change '84–'88
26.	Alaska	51.7	–7.5
27.	Louisiana	51.3	–3.2
28.	Delaware	51.0	–4.4
29.	Wyoming	50.3	–3.0
30.	Pennsylvania	50.1	–3.9
31.	Mississippi	49.9	–2.3
32.	Maryland	49.1	–2.3
33.	Oklahoma	48.7	–3.4
34.	Kentucky	48.2	–2.6
35.	Virginia	48.2	–2.5
36.	New York	48.1	–3.1
37.	California	47.4	–2.2
38.	New Mexico	47.3	–4.0
39.	Arkansas	47.0	–4.8
40.	West Virginia	46.7	–5.0
41.	Alabama	45.8	–4.1
42.	Arizona	45.0	–0.2
43.	Nevada	44.9	–3.4
44.	Florida	44.7	–3.5
45.	Tennessee	44.7	–4.4
46.	Texas	44.2	–3.0
47.	North Carolina	43.4	–4.0
48.	Hawaii	43.0	–1.3
49.	District of Columbia	39.4	–3.5
50.	South Carolina	38.9	–1.5
51.	Georgia	38.8	–3.2

★ **Figure 9-5**
1988 presidential election turnout as percentage of voting-age population, by state
SOURCE: *Congressional Quarterly Weekly Report,* January 21, 1989, p. 136.

★ Table 9-4
Percentage of adults who reported they voted, 1972–1988, by category

	1972	*1976*	*1980*	*1984*	*1988*
Sex					
Male	64.1%	59.6%	59.1%	59.0%	56.4%
Female	62.0	58.8	59.4	60.8	58.3
Race					
White	64.5	60.9	60.9	61.4	59.1
Black	52.1	48.7	50.5	55.8	51.5
Hispanic	37.4	31.8	29.9	32.6	28.8
Age					
65+	63.5	62.2	65.1	67.7	68.8
45–64	70.8	68.7	69.3	69.8	67.9
25–44	62.7	58.7	58.7	58.4	54.0
18–24	49.6	42.2	39.9	40.8	54.0
Education					
College	83.6	79.8	79.9	79.1	77.6
High school	65.4	59.4	58.9	58.7	54.7
Grade school	47.4	44.1	42.6	42.9	36.7
Employment					
Employed	66.0	62.0	61.8	61.6	58.4
Unemployed	49.9	43.7	41.2	44.0	38.6

SOURCE: U.S. Bureau of the Census, *Statistical Abstract of the United States, 1988* (Washington, D.C.: U.S. Government Printing Office, 1987), p. 249. Figures for 1988: U.S. Bureau of the Census, *Voting and Registration in the Election of November 1988 (Advance Report)* (Washington, D.C.: U.S. Government Printing Office, 1989), pp. 1–10.

Congress opposed the plan, however, fearing it would lead to widespread voter fraud. Republican members were especially unhappy with the idea, insisting that instant registration would only swell the ranks of Democratic voters, who are less likely to register than Republicans. As a result, despite the continuing decline in voter turnout, the proposal was rejected.

Still, the reasons many people fail to register in the first place is puzzling. Also, even after accounting for those who were sick or away from home on election day, we find that about 38 million registered voters did not turn out in 1988; and a much larger number ignored other kinds of political activity. To account for these no-shows, we must consider some additional factors.

Group Differences

Political scientists have found that certain groups or categories of people tend to participate less than others. Although many potential group differences have been noted, those related to age, income, and education have been found to be the most important (see table 9-4). The younger people are, the less formal schooling they have, and the less income they draw, the more likely they are to abstain from voting. Thus those under twenty years of age tend to show their faces at the polls less often than the middle-aged; fewer people with only grade school education tend to show up than those with college degrees; and the unemployed tend to show up less reliably than those who are employed.

These group differences appear to result from a variety of personal and social factors. Studies suggest, for instance, that people under twenty years of age are less likely to vote than those of middle age, in part because they are more unsettled and are less exposed to political information. Similarly, those without high school diplomas or who are out of work are less likely to vote than those with college degrees or good salaries, because they have fewer resources (including knowledge and confidence) to deal with the political world. Indeed, it is not hard to understand why someone under twenty years of age struggling to find even a low-paying job is likely to suffer special hardships and disillusionments that dampen his or her political interest.

The differences in group turnout also reflect a disturbing fact: people who are most likely to benefit from governmental assistance, such as the poor and less educated, participate less than those who already enjoy considerable advantages. The same lack of resources that deprives many people of a decent standard of living also contributes to their failure to vote or their inability to participate in campaigns or contribute money to candidates. And their failure to participate renders the poor and less educated ineffective in communicating their needs and exerting pressures on politicians to implement policies that would directly benefit them.

Attitudes and Perceptions

Participation in the political process is also related to people's political attitudes and perceptions. In the 1984 presidential election, for example, 8 percent of those interviewed cited lack of interest as their reason for not voting. Another 10 percent said they did not like the candidates, and 8 percent gave no special reason at all.[12]

Such responses frequently hide more specific attitudes toward politics, ranging from general boredom or complacency to a lack of faith in the political process. These attitudes often are shaped early by family or friends, and may be affected by such social factors as education and income.

Some people, for example, simply see no meaningful connection between politics and their personal lives. Though they may occasionally view the political world with some interest, it still remains distant from the more immediate concerns of day-to-day living. A hard-working couple with four children may spend more time worrying about automobile repairs and the high cost of food for their family than about the country's balance-of-payment problems or who will win the next election for county supervisor. Or a single parent may not be able to squeeze voting in between work, shopping, and collecting the kids at daycare. Their neighbors, meanwhile, may simply be too busy following the progress of the Detroit Redwings or driving their new Buick to pay much attention to politics. One study even suggested that such lack of interest can be reinforced by the behavior of others. People who initially feel some guilt about their inactivity lose it when they see how common apathy is among their friends and neighbors.[13]

Other people (although perhaps not so many as we might expect) abstain from voting as a form of political expression. Some scorn politics because it appears to be dishonest or self-serving, or are disgusted by a lack of meaningful choice between the parties.[14] We may sympathize with the elderly voter who, when asked

How Important Is Voting?

Given the fact that each person is only one of approximately 90 million voters in this country, does it make sense to believe that one person's participation, one vote, will have any impact on a major election? Simply to raise the question "What if everyone felt the same way?" does not remove the lingering impression that a single person is dwarfed by the enormous number of people who do trek to the polls, especially in a national election.

Supporters of the ruling elite theory insist that even though voters are given a choice among candidates, their choice is restricted to a narrow range of similar-minded individuals sanctioned by the ruling elite. Elections do not express what most people want or need, nor do they provide guidance for politicians (even if they want it) on what policies to enact. In this view, elections are primarily just rituals that perform a symbolic function for society.

Still, since most people continue to show their faces at the polls at one time or another, what arguments can be made in favor of voting? One argument is that voting does have significance, if not in individual impact, then in group pressure. Because citizens collectively have the power to give or withhold votes, they directly control the tenure of elected officials. Even if the choice is between Tweedledee and Tweedledum, Tweedledee knows that a day of reckoning is fixed by law and that minimally he or she must strive to avoid displeasing the constituents or lose the job.

★ (*left to right*) Row 1: George Washington, Adolf Hitler, Richard Nixon, Franklin Roosevelt, Lyndon Johnson. Row 2: Charles DeGaulle, Idi Amin, Mao Zedong, Ulysses S. Grant, Jawaharlal Nehru. Row 3: Theodore Roosevelt, Muammar Qaddafi, Golda Meir, Hideki Tojo, Herbert Hoover. Row 4: Joseph Stalin, Benito Mussolini, Leonid Brezhnev, Anwar Sadat, Indira Gandhi. Row 5: Margaret Thatcher, Helmut Schmidt, John Kennedy, Winston Churchill, Abraham Lincoln.

But perhaps political efficacy and impact in voting is not the only consideration anyway. People do not vote only to influence policy. Millions go to the effort to register and vote for a variety of other reasons as well. Some people may participate just to avoid feeling guilty about not voting. They may have been taught that it is their patriotic duty to vote and that they have no right to complain about the outcome if they stay at home. Still others may vote to derive satisfaction from feeling that they are somehow participants, not just spectators, in an exciting electoral contest. Even if their one vote may not be crucial to the outcome, it nevertheless affirms their role in and support for the political process. Indeed, perhaps it is this final need that fuels the desire for full democratic participation among people in many nations around the world. ★

which candidate she was going to vote for, replied, "I never vote. It only encourages 'em."[15]

Voter interest can even be affected by the type and nature of the election. As we have seen, more people show up for presidential elections, which are given wide coverage in the media, than for congressional or state elections. Also, in contests in which one party has no more than a slim chance of defeating the other, feelings of futility may halt further political involvement. Some people may decide that, even with their participation, their party's candidate will fail at the polls anyway (or, conversely, that their candidate will coast to an easy victory and does not need their support). This situation is most likely to occur in such regions as the South, where one party traditionally dominates most congressional and state elections. People who favor the minority party may prefer to stay home rather than experience again the frustration of defeat.

Indeed, another commonly cited reason for reduced electoral participation is the changing role of political parties. In the past, the party label served as an easy way to solidify an allegiance, especially for people who had neither the time nor the inclination to study the positions of all the candidates. Candidates and voters alike thought it was important whether they were Republicans or Democrats, and voting served to rekindle a partisan bond. Nowadays, candidates and voters have had to take positions without the benefit of a strong partisan community, as we saw in chapter 8. As a result, according to some observers, many voters have become confused or disenchanted with the detachment from partisan cues, and have abandoned the voting booths.

But perhaps the most disturbing reason given for nonparticipation is a feeling of futility that reaches beyond the outcome of any single election. Many people are deterred from participating in politics by the belief that their involvement would not make not make a significant difference.[16] They feel lost among the millions of other voters and sense that those who make the major political decisions—politicians, corporate executives, and bureaucrats—will not pay any attention to what they need or want. Many even accept the ruling elite view (see chapter 5) that elections are just rituals anyway, and the outcome will make no difference in their lives. Consequently, they see little point in doing anything, least of all voting.

A feeling of powerlessness may derive to some degree from the enormous size and complexity of modern society. In a large country where government can seem remote and out of reach, people may see little chance of personally influencing the decision-making process. In fact, one of the most dramatic problems facing the country is the lack of public confidence in government's responsiveness to the individual. Many Americans have come to believe not that they can control and regulate government but that government controls and regulates them. They sense that much of government has fallen into the hands of corrupt and self-serving scoundrels who pursue their own selfish interests with little regard for the welfare of the nation as a whole. A substantial number of Americans are disheartened about both the American political process and their own roles in it, as figure 9-6 shows. They feel ineffective against the wishes of powerful interests and believe governmental officials are largely unresponsive to their needs.

It is hardly surprising that such feelings of inefficacy tend to be most pronounced among minority groups and the poor. People in these groups are particularly likely to feel estranged from government and to believe they have little control over their political environment.[17] Nor is this pessimism necessarily unrealistic. The poor, especially, have been served badly by the political system. They have experienced a long history of futility in trying to draw some kind of govern-

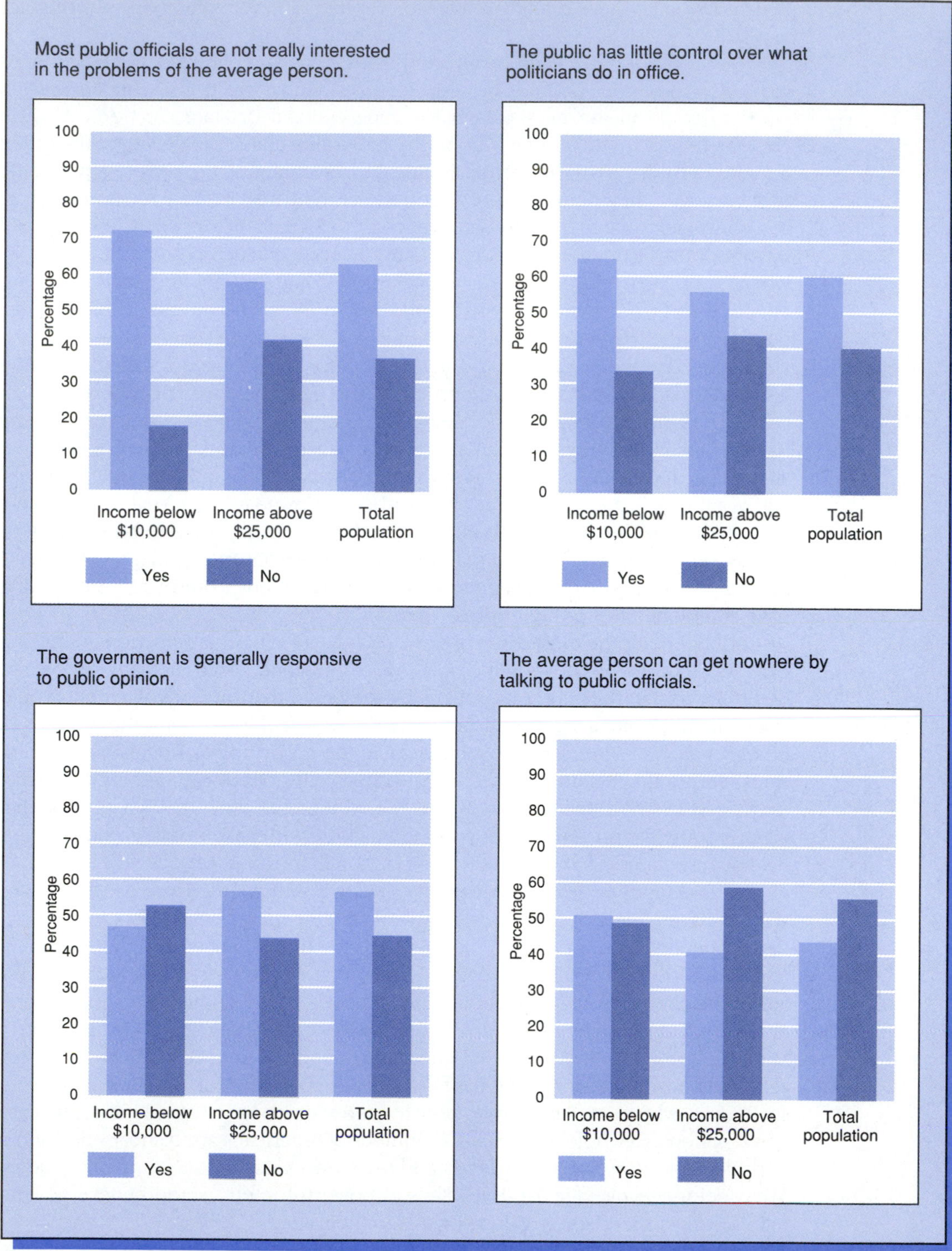

★ **Figure 9-6**

Do you make a difference? The relationship between feelings of efficacy and income, 1988

SOURCE: James Allan Davis and Tom W. Smith, *General Social Survey, 1972–1988* (Chicago: National Opinion Research Center, 1988), subfile 1988 (machine-readable data file).

mental response to their needs. American political institutions have been notable for being slow to help those who lack organized or meaningful representation of their interests. If one accepts the ruling elite view that money talks in politics, then one can understand why a poor person might feel that his or her political actions would be futile.

If dissatisfaction with the system can result in withdrawal, satisfaction with the system can promote voter laziness. A substantial number of Americans choose not to participate because they are generally pleased with the way things are going, and they see no need to "interfere."[18] Political scientists have labeled these people **positive apathetics,** because their apathy stems from a sense of positive satisfaction with the status quo.

In any event, we may ask whether nonparticipation is, in some ways, an understandable response to the political system. In view of the fact that government can often seem remote and unresponsive, the desire to avoid the disappointments of politics becomes an understandable psychological defense. Similarly, the tendency to remain unaware of public issues may stem from a desire to draw a veil over distressing situations one would rather not confront. The news media can impose a frightening picture of a world of violence—political kidnappings, payoff scandals, murders—over which people have no control. Although awareness of current issues may be a positive goal, it may be unreasonable to expect people to feel guilty about screening out events that increase their sense of helplessness.

Still, we may hope that the political world will never become so oppressive that we are forced into a permanent cocoon of apathy. As the anthropologist Margaret Mead warned many years ago, "We must never see the government as something other than ourselves, for then automatically we become children; and not real honest children, but adults dwarfed to childhood again in weakness and ineffectiveness."[19]

★ At the Corner of Pennsylvania and Madison Avenues: The Campaign

During his bid for the 1984 presidential nomination of the Democratic party, Walter Mondale escaped his reputation for dullness by asking his closest opponent, Gary Hart, "Where's the Beef?" Hart had not been forceful in articulating his positions on tough issues, and Mondale's taunt seemed to crystallize a growing public feeling that Hart was more style than substance. Mondale knew a good slogan when he saw one, so he asked his rhetorical question almost as many times as the fast-food restaurant chain that had originated it.

It is ironic that a slogan designed to sell hamburgers could become a tool of a political campaign; for many of us, national campaigns resemble an advertising war over voters' allegiance to one hamburger over another. Indeed, there are similarities between the launching of a candidate and the launching of a new product. Before selling a new fast-food item, McDonald's conducts extensive market research, asking thousands of people what they think of the packaging, look, smell, and taste of the product. Politicians hire their own version of market analysts, called pollsters, who try to tap current tastes and cravings. Often with the aid of moonlighting advertising professionals, the candidate is given an "image" that is intended to exploit the market cravings.

In 1980, for example, pollsters discovered a craving for someone optimistic and decisive, in opposition to the Carter image of preoccupation with details and negativity. The result was the full-speed-ahead image of Ronald Reagan. But after eight years of Reagan and the questions raised about his style in the wake of the Iran-Contra affair and the savings and loan crisis, some pollsters detected a desire for change. As the 1988 presidential election approached, some Democratic image experts believed the public was looking for "youth and truth."[20] They detected impatience with Reagan's detached optimism, and a longing for an injection of straightforward facts by a person with a sharp, youthful mind capable of vigorously digesting and communicating those facts, however complex. Whether, in the end, George Bush fulfilled this desire is open to discussion.

How Important Is the Campaign?

When products fail in the marketplace, the producers invariably blame the advertising campaign rather that the product itself. Likewise, when politicians lose, they complain that their opponent spent more money, and they vow to "campaign harder" next time. Thus, just as a great deal of attention is given to product advertising, so is the campaign seen as of utmost importance to the politician. Speeches, press releases, and even items in the candidate's wardrobe are analyzed in terms of their contribution to the proper product image. Precious little is extemporaneous; candidates and their staffs strive to anticipate controversial questions and situations and conduct lengthy rehearsals to prepare for them.

Yet are we to believe that the product itself has nothing to do with its success in the marketplace? If we like the taste of a Big Mac better than that of a Whopper with cheese, is our preference based only on the winner of the ad war? Similarly, if we have a long-standing appreciation for the Republican party, will we be seduced by the Democratic candidate solely because of a glitzy campaign?

Despite the losing politician's lament that the campaign is all-important, political science research has reached some more sober conclusions regarding the efficacy of campaign strategies. For the most part, it has been discovered that campaign slogans and rhetoric do not change most people's minds about candidates so much as they reinforce and enhance opinions developed far in advance of the campaign onslaught. As we mentioned in chapter 8, most voters maintain vague and unsophisticated attachments to party labels, even if they call themselves independents. The campaign, then, allows these individuals to place more specific information about candidates within the framework of their general preexisting preferences.

Psychological research tends to support this **reinforcement theory.** Psychologists tell us that it is common for individuals to ignore a good deal of the information that bombards them daily. People tend to focus on stimuli that relate to preexisting interests. Psychologists call this phenomenon **selective attention,** and early voting studies discovered that individuals tended to ignore the campaign pleas of candidates to whom they were not already sympathetic:

> With the appealing devices of mass communications and their widespread use as habit, duty, or pastime, people are exposed to miscellaneous information about a far greater range of things than those in which they are genuinely interested. But, at the same time, they really follow only the few topics that genuinely concern them.[21]

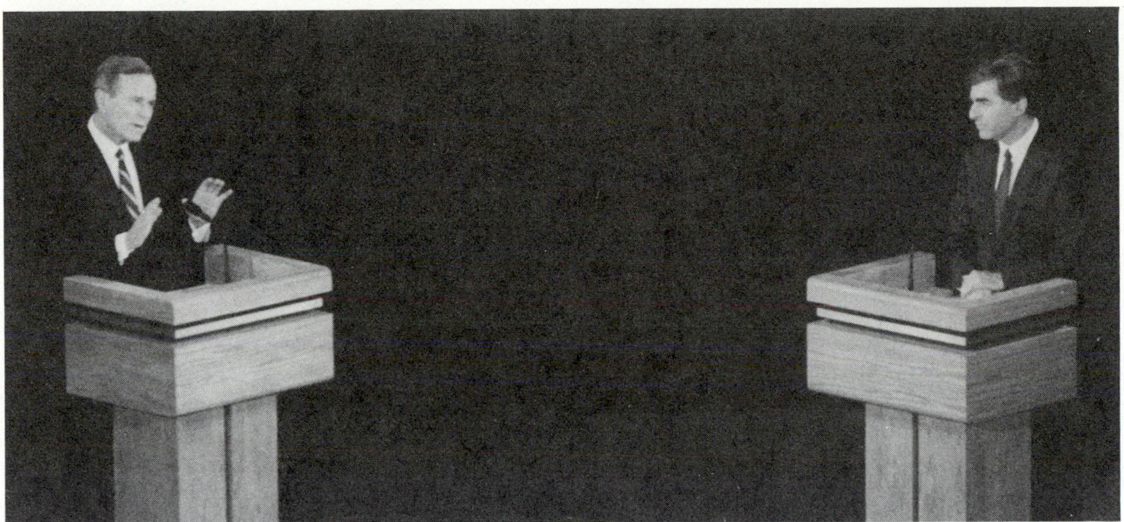

★ The phenomena of reinforcement and selective perception are fully operative in the case of presidential debates. That does not mean, however, that debates are completely ineffective at changing voters' minds. Dukakis did very well in the first 1988 presidential debate, closing his deficit from five to two percentage points almost overnight. In the second debate, Bush fared much better and solidified a strong lead that he never relinquished.

Even neutral information is often processed in a way that supports rather than challenges preexisting attitudes. News coverage of a political rally, for instance, may contain information both favorable and damaging to the rally's cause, but many supporters of the cause tend to see only the positive information, while the opponents register the negative. This psychological phenomenon is called **selective perception.** People tend to perceive what they want to perceive; thus, while the Iran-Contra hearings may have strengthened the commitment of Reagan's opponents to replace him with a more active, capable leader, Reagan fans saw the incident as a trumped-up ploy to damage the Republican cause just before the 1988 presidential campaign.

Though these psychological findings may detract from the myth of the all-important campaign, they do not preclude the possibility of campaign effectiveness. First of all, the concepts of selective attention and selective perception assume that the individual already has some opinions. What about the person who has no preference among candidates? How can the reinforcement theory work when there is nothing to reinforce? Why can't the campaign work effectively on people who are undecided?

The political scientists who first applied the reinforcement theory to politics had a simple answer. They argued that the undecided, those who might be most susceptible to an effective political campaign, paid little or no attention to politics. Thus the campaign faced a Catch-22 situation. The people who were most interested in politics didn't believe the campaign messages, and the people most likely to be swayed by a campaign message were least likely to be listening.

As we will see in chapter 11, television has interrupted this argument. It seems that people who are quick to turn the page of a newspaper or push the button on a car radio to escape a political announcement are willing to suffer through a candidate's commercial as long as they know that *Wheel of Fortune* will reappear

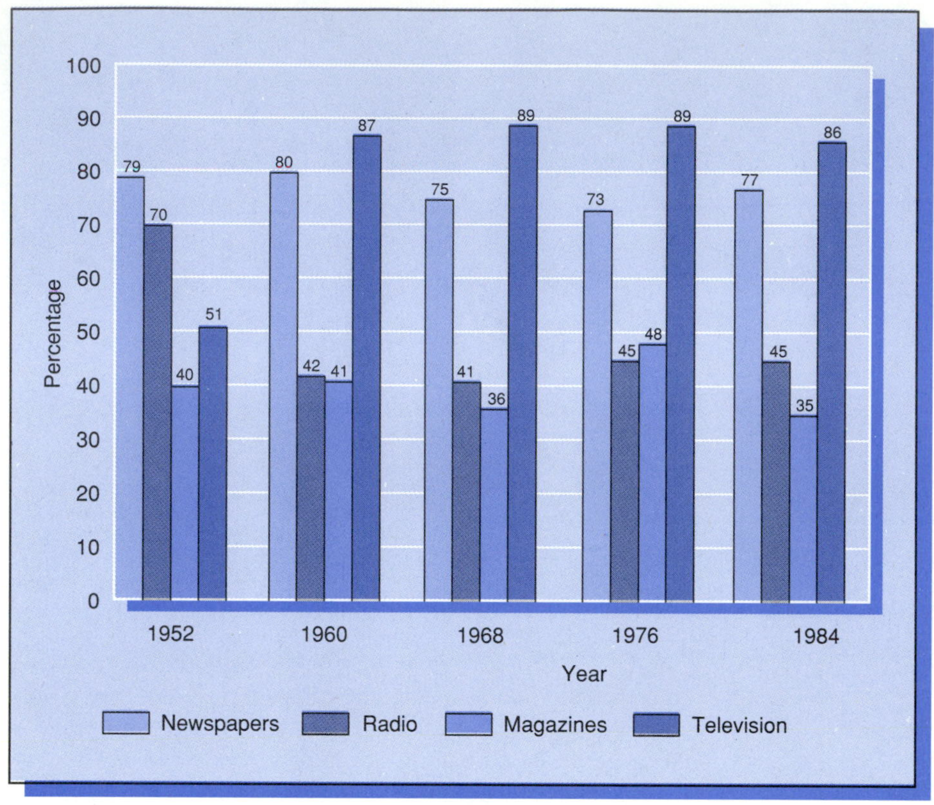

★ **Figure 9-7**
Percentage of Americans who used various media as a primary source of information on political campaigns, 1952–1984

SOURCE: Adapted from Herbert S. Asher, *Presidential Elections and American Politics,* 4th ed. (Pacific Grove, Calif.: Brooks/Cole, 1988), p. 249.

in sixty seconds (see figure 9-7). Admittedly, these people do not vote religiously, but some do go to the polls out of a sense of civic duty. Certainly these "uninterested" voters are numerous enough to change the course of a close election.

Television does reach uninterested voters, and thus seems to have the best chance of actually changing people's political inclinations. Politicians have recognized the special possibilities of televised campaigning. With each election, the percentage of campaign funds used for televised messages has increased. And the sheer expense of television advertising has reinvigorated the importance of financial contributions.

★ Campaign Finance

Perhaps no aspect of American politics has been subjected to harsher criticism than the relationship between campaigns and money. To some extent, the problem began with the broadening of the electorate. American politicians early in this country's history realized that in their zeal to extend the vote to greater portions of the citizenry, they were creating a situation that demanded an extension of the campaign. In 1757 George Washington won a seat in the Virginia House of Burgesses with campaign expenditures amounting to only 152 gallons of various alcoholic beverages. But Fairfax County at that time listed only 391 qualified voters. As the rapid expansion of the electorate required each member of Congress to represent thousands of voters, politicians could look forward to a sodden constituency if they had to buy nearly two quarts of booze for each vote.

It had become clear that the achievement of political office in America demanded a wide solicitation of votes. As early as 1783, Edmund Randolph contemplated a late entry in the race for a seat in the Virginia Assembly, but backed out when he reflected that "the candidates having been active, and indefatigable, I might possibly expose myself to a mortification, were I to step forward at this late hour."[22] To win an American election, it became increasingly necessary to mount a campaign that extended well beyond the personal resources of the candidate. Money, and the misuse of money, thus became crucial aspects of the American electoral system.

By the end of the nineteenth century, many people had come to see the American system of campaign finance as a disgrace. Large corporations used their money imaginatively to gain control over the votes of legislators. An executive of Standard Oil was heard to say: "We've done everything to the Pennsylvania legislature except refine it."

Cleanup Attempts

By the turn of the century, such progressive politicians as Elihu Root and Theodore Roosevelt successfully promoted legislation intended to stifle corporate purchase of the political system. The Tillman Act of 1907 barred corporations from making contributions to candidates for federal office. Despite good intentions, however, this law merely ushered in a tradition, which continues today, of bypassing campaign finance legislation through loopholes and other evasive tactics.

The next law to test the cleverness of the evaders was the Federal Corrupt Practices Act of 1925. This law was intended to limit spending by congressional candidates to 3 cents per eligible voter, with a maximum expenditure of $5,000 by candidates for the House and $25,000 by candidates for the Senate. But this legal limit was never enforced. Because the limit applied only to expenditures made with the "knowledge and consent" of the candidate, funds could simply be channeled through campaign committees that were not required to file reports.

Similarly, the Hatch Act of 1940 was supposed to prohibit any person from contributing more than $5,000 to a candidate for federal office, but loopholes rendered it largely ineffective. A person who wished to part with more than $5,000 could contribute to a variety of separate party committees or make the contributions in the names of relatives. And in the absence of any serious intention to enforce the law, even blatant violations went unpunished. When corporations were donating as much as $250,000 each, $5 or $10 contributions from ordinary citizens tended to be virtually meaningless. These citizens were simply priced out of the political system.

It was not until 1971 that Congress rekindled the legislative fires by passing the **Federal Election Campaign Act.** Among its provisions was the requirement

"He's targeting his campaign at the cynical voter."

that candidates for federal office file detailed reports on all donations and expenditures in excess of $100. The new law also set limits on the amounts candidates could spend on media advertising (although these limits were later removed by new legislation and Supreme Court rulings).

By ironic coincidence, in the same year that the new Federal Election Campaign Act became law, the Watergate scandal became public. In fact, the revelations of the scandal may have been aided by the law's disclosure provisions. The General Accounting Office, for example, issued a series of reports citing apparent violations of the 1971 act by the Committee for the Reelection of the President (Nixon's campaign organization, also known as CREEP). These reports led to the indictment of the committee by the Justice Department on eight separate counts of campaign spending violations. Federal investigators charged that CREEP had raised $10 million more than it reported, that top Nixon hands had skimmed money for their personal use, and that campaign funds had been converted into Watergate hush money.

The Watergate scandal inspired Congress to pass even more stringent legislation in 1974. The new legislation, which made its initial impact on the 1976 presidential election, set new limits on the amount of money that could be contributed by individuals or groups to congressional and presidential candidates. The 1974 Federal Election Campaign Act (as amended in 1976) provides that

- No individual can give more than $1,000 to any presidential or congressional candidate in any primary or general election, and not more than $25,000 to all candidates for federal office during one campaign season.
- No group or organization can give more than $5,000 to any congressional or presidential candidate in any one election.
- Candidates in presidential primaries who raise a minimum of $100,000 in amounts of $5,000 in each of at least twenty states, through gifts not exceeding $250, will receive matching federal funds up to $5.5 million.
- In the general election, each major-party candidate for president is entitled to federal funds (in 1984 it was $41 million) on the condition that no private contributions will be accepted.

- Each major party is entitled to $2 million in federal funds to finance its national convention.
- Third-party candidates will be eligible for federal funding if their party obtained at least 5 percent of the total votes cast in the preceding election.
- A six-member bipartisan Federal Election Commission will administer the law. Criminal violations of the law will be handled by the Justice Department.

Thus presidential candidates of the two major parties now have the choice of either accepting public financing of their general campaigns or raising their own funds, without limits. If they decide to accept public funds—as all presidential candidates have done since 1976—they can accept no private contributions. According to the Center for Public Financing of Elections, which lobbied actively for the measure, the 1974 Federal Election Campaign Act (also known as the Campaign Reform Act) represented the "only decent legacy of Watergate."

Originally the law also set limits on the amounts congressional candidates could spend on their campaigns. But this provision provoked considerable opposition and resulted in a court challenge by a coalition of conservative and liberal members of Congress, who felt that spending limits violated the constitutional right of free expression. They insisted that ceilings on campaign spending would give an unfair advantage to incumbents, who usually enjoy greater public recognition than challengers. Only by spending large sums of money, they argued, could unknown challengers, particularly third-party candidates, compete effectively with incumbents. Thus, except at the presidential level (where optional spending limits remain), the main thrust of the legislation continues to be the disclosure of sources of federal campaign support and contribution limits for individuals and organizations.

Problems with the Present Legislation

As might be expected, strategies for evading the law quickly developed. The law declares that an individual cannot contribute more than $25,000 a year to all federal campaigns; but individuals who want to give more have discovered that they can funnel the money through associates or other family members, or they can establish a political action committee (PACs will be discussed in detail later), which is allowed much higher levels of contribution. Additionally, there are ways to support a candidate at "arm's length" and bypass the legislation altogether. This practice was so blatantly used by organized labor in support of Walter Mondale in 1984 that Mondale was forced to denounce some of his support by PACs. Michael Dukakis refused all PAC contributions in 1988.

And the provisions for public disclosure have been no panacea. Knowledge of the sources and recipients of campaign money does not in itself eliminate unwarranted influence. We know, for instance, that in 1980 the various automobile dealer associations spent $675,000 (up from $14,000 in the previous election) on congressional campaigns. We also know, however, that of the 286 House members who voted to overturn legislation requiring used-car dealers to tell buyers about existing defects in a car, 242 had received money from the dealers. Problems obviously remain even under the present campaign laws, including the sheer amount of money being spent, the sources of the money, and where the money goes.

★ Campaign Spending

The amount of money being spent in campaigns arouses some concern. No longer can it be claimed that campaign costs are merely keeping up with inflation. Despite federal legislation, total federal campaign expenditures since 1980 have increased three to four times as much as the consumer price index. In 1988, congressional races alone cost an estimated $458 million. In California in 1986, Alan Cranston and Ed Zschau spent $25 million on just one Senate contest, by far the largest portion on television commercials. Cranston refused to debate Zschau, and Zschau seemed content to run ads that emphasized the proper pronunciation of his name.

Financial concerns consume the energies of candidates and their helpers. Candidates, who feel that success depends on matching their opponents commercial for commercial in the expensive television market, dine on countless rubbery chickens in efforts to pluck wealthy supporters. And the present legislation has proved to be not much of a barrier to candidates intent on amassing ever greater stockpiles of donations.

Money now also pervades campaign organizations, especially at the higher levels of federal office. Except for the valuable commodity of college students earning internship credits, few politicians are able to attract workers solely on a voluntary basis. Even most of the door-to-door hawkers are salaried, sometimes campaigning for candidates and issues they know little about or, worse yet, oppose ideologically. And at the top of the campaign pyramid, traditional campaign managers have been replaced by expensive media, demographic, and advertising consultants who flock to the highest bidder. Because of the big money involved (see figure 9-8), campaigning has changed from a part-time diversion to a full-time industry.

The Sources of the Money

Many observers are as troubled by the sources of campaign funds as by the amount of money being spent. In years past, candidates could rely on campaign money from their political party. These days, candidates rely more and more on special-interest money, much of it contributed by **political action committees (PACs).** These entities, officially sanctioned by the Campaign Reform Act, were intended to permit close tabs to be kept on large contributions by organizations. Instead, the law seems to have stimulated the political participation of a multitude of groups, which some observers believe are suffocating Congress under the weight of narrow yet well-funded and highly organized interests. Some members of Congress have amassed impressive war chests.

The problem is that in order to maintain the PACs' financial support, politicians sometimes deny the broad public interest in favor of pleasing the sources of money. Thus many members of Congress who personally do not wish to encourage smoking continue to support legislation that gives financial breaks to tobacco growers. And of course the growers are eager to contribute, as they see the possibility of saving millions of dollars by smartly investing only thousands.

During the negotiations over the 1987 tax bill, Dan Rostenkowski, chairman of the House Ways and Means Committee, became enraged by the blatant way some members of his committee were pursuing campaign funds by supporting special-interest amendments to the bill: "There was on the part of three to five members,

	1984	1988	Increase
Overall limit on individual contributions to campaign	$1,000	$1,000	0%
One ream of Xerox paper	$3.39	$3.67	8.2%
One bumper sticker (bought in lots of 1,000)	$.10	$.11	10%
First-class postage stamp	$.20	$.22	10%
One night, double room, Marriott Hotel, Des Moines	$85	$95	11.7%
Charter 12-seat Gulfstream jet from Teterboro, N.J., to Manchester, N.H., to Des Moines and back to Teterboro	$19,200	$21,600	12.5%
Overall limit on prenomination spending by campaign, if federal funds are accepted	$20.2 million	$23.0 million	14.1%
One-hour postproduction editing of campaign commercial	$490	$560	14.2%
One campaign flyer, one-page three-fold (bought in lots of 1,000)	$.10	$.11 1/2	15%
Purchase of American Telephone & Telegraph phone system with two incoming lines and six phones	$3,000	$3,500	16.6%
One telephone interview by poll taker, including phone, salary, and processing costs	$25	$35	40%
30-second commercial in top-rated prime-time show, Des Moines	$1,100	$1,800	63.6%
One campaign button (bought in lots of 1,000)	$.15	$.25	66.6%
Computer list of Iowa's Democratic voters and caucus attenders from state Democratic party	$5,000	$10,000	100%

★ **Figure 9-8**
The rising cost of campaigns
SOURCE: *New York Times,* February 6, 1988, p. A9. Copyright © 1988 by The New York Times Company. Reprinted by permission.

on both sides of the aisle, a definite string attached to some corporate lobbyist outside in the hall—in one instance a direct link with respect to how much money he could raise in a campaign. That got me nauseated. . . . There were two members in my opinion that flagrantly violated ethical codes."[23]

Representatives of PACs claim that they have no intention of buying any candidate's vote on the particular issue they represent; they only want "access" to the candidate. Yet as we will see (in chap. 13) in regard to the gatekeeping function so cherished by close presidential advisers, access is an important requisite of power.

Unfortunately, not all positions on all issues have equal backing; obviously, people who have money, time, and an organization are highly advantaged. Thus the interests of "the people" or of "future generations" may become lost in a competition with myopic and narrow interests. Politicians often forsake political philosophies to adopt views that seem better calculated to win campaign support.

Where the Money Goes

A look at the recipients of campaign support reveals that over 80 percent of all campaign contributions goes to incumbents—the candidates who are most likely to win an election. (House incumbents have a 90 percent success rate in their bids for reelection.) In 1986, for instance, the 333 incumbents in the House of Representatives who won by a landslide (receiving more than 60 percent of their constituents' votes) spent an average of $274,766 on their campaigns.[24] In fact, substantial contributions often go to candidates who run unopposed. Representative Sam Gibbons of Florida, for instance, spent $550,000 for his 1986 campaign, though he had no opponent. Contributors are not always motivated by a desire to help an ideological counterpart in a close race; rather, money is spent where dividends on the investment are most secure. Conservative corporation PACs give money to liberal Democrats as long as they are the front-runners, and as long as the PACs detect potential support on one or two pet bills. And when there is no apparent front-runner, PACs have been known to give money to both candidates. In the 1986 senatorial races, for instance, there were 494 instances of "double giving'" by PACs in the nine states selected for study by the public interest group Common Cause. According to Fred Wertheimer, Common Cause's president, "Double-giving PACs want to be assured of access in January no matter which candidate wins in November."[25]

When so much money goes to so many sure winners, it comes as no surprise that campaign funds are not always spent judiciously. Representative Charles Wilson, Democrat of Texas, sponsors an annual domino tournament, and then sends the two winners on an all-expenses-paid trip to Washington, D.C., courtesy of his campaign. Kika de la Garza, chairman of the House Agricultural Committee, charged his campaign for trips to San Francisco, Washington state, Brazil, and Japan.[26] When John Rhodes, Republican of Arizona, retired as House minority leader, he spent $11,272 of his campaign chest to commission two oil paintings of himself. In fact, it was not until 1979 that retiring members of Congress were prohibited from keeping leftover campaign funds for their personal use. (In order to pass the prohibiting law, Congress included a clause stipulating that anyone elected before the law's passage would be exempt from this provision.)

Sometimes campaign funds are put to uses that border on the illegal and unethical. Representative James Weaver, Democrat of Oregon, withdrew from the Senate race in August 1986 after it was revealed that he had borrowed $80,000 from his campaign funds to invest in the commodities market. Senator Paul Trible, Republican of Virginia, reluctantly returned 60 cents on the dollar to his campaign contributors after he decided not to run in 1986; and although he withdrew on September 19, he still charged $3,400 to his campaign for a December 11 restaurant bill. Republican party officials in North Carolina determined that Democratic Representative Charlie Rose borrowed $63,995 from his campaign chest over a seven-year period, and that he used some of the money to buy a Jeep and put a down payment on a beach property.[27]

★ John Glenn, first known to the public as an astronaut, used that experience to boost his senatorial and presidential aspirations.

★ The Modern Campaign: Too Much Isolation and Superficiality?

When Mitch McConnell won the Kentucky Senate race in 1984, one of the first orders of business was to establish the "McConnell Senate Committee '90," which promptly raised over $200,000. Campaigning is no longer a distasteful detour that is postponed to the last phase of a politician's term. Candidates now feel that they must carry on a continual campaign in order to raise the vast amounts of money needed to win office.

The need for large contributions not only leads to the compromises mentioned earlier but also puts pressure on the candidates to retreat from activities that might detract from their popularity. The continued service of high-powered media consultants requires the candidate to maintain the impressive image the consultants have created. Thus the candidate is advised from the start to say or do nothing that might divert him or her from the script. Whereas old-fashioned campaign managers might have had some interest in what the candidates said, even to the extent of supporting the candidate in an unpopular cause, the new style of perpetual campaigning and Madison Avenue direction has focused attention on the way issues are presented. Candidates have been known to hide from the public behind television makeup and a prepared script, sure that any departure from it will blast their hopes for reelection. In the 1988 presidential election, for example, Republican vice-presidential candidate Dan Quayle was kept as far as feasible from potentially unfriendly reporters and their cameras, for fear that one more controversy might derail the Bush candidacy. Under these conditions, candidates can become isolated and inaccessible even to people who would like to offer their support.

Another effect of this preoccupation with style over substance is the temptation for candidates to make only bland and noncontroversial statements. Barry Nova, a New York advertising executive, represented John Glenn in his 1970 bid for the Senate. Nova took the job despite his feeling that his candidate was "shallow of thought" and "an egocentric." Nova, concerned that Glenn was unclear on major issues, encouraged his candidate to speak out on the burning questions of the day. Unfortunately, the resulting commercials were far from enlightening, and they provide humorous evidence of some candidates' hesitation to say anything of substance. Here is the script for a thirty-second "clarification" of Glenn's position on pollution:

VIDEO	AUDIO
Camera up on woman voter, asking candidate Glenn what he intends to do about pollution.	Glenn: "That is a very important question. I'm glad you asked it. Pollution blows and flows across state lines. We have to stop it now. Strong laws against polluters would help. It's really an important issue. I'm glad you asked that question. I hope I've answered it well."
Closing graphic (words superimposed over Glenn picture): "Once in a great while a man like John Glenn comes along."	

To this day, Nova, who helped Glenn with his later attempts to win nomination for the presidency, claims that he still does not know what Glenn stands for.

★ Elections and Campaigns in a Changing World

In 1938, Congress passed the Foreign Agents Registration Act, which was designed to ensure that foreign governments would not interfere with the American electoral system. Under the act, Congress required all foreign agents to register with the Justice Department. They also banned any foreign contribution to domestic political campaigns.

On October 14, 1976, the *Washington Post* broke a story that clearly demonstrated that the act was not being enforced. The *Post* held that a South Korean businessman, Tongsun Park, had distributed up to $1 million in gifts and campaign contributions to various members of Congress. At the time of Park's activities, a plan was circulating to withdraw one-third of the U.S. troops in Korea, and Park's contributions went to politicians who were likely to oppose such reductions. Although Park never admitted to being an agent of the Korean government, Special U.S. Prosecutor Leon Jaworski said, "This whole thing was run right out of the Korean embassy . . . and the Korean government might as well be kidding itself. We're not going to rest until we've got everything."[28]

In the end, Congress was able to escape serious embarrassment, in part because ethical violations are investigated by committees within Congress itself. Jaworski complained bitterly about a system in which it was possible to have potential co-conspirators as judges. In any case, a few members of Congress were reprimanded, and one California Democratic representative, Richard Hanna, pleaded guilty to

★ Presidential candidate Michael Dukakis wears a sombero while campaigning in 1988 to remind voters of his interest in Mexico and Latin America.

conspiracy to defraud the government. Park testifed to giving Hanna $262,000 in unreported campaign contributions.

Although the so-called Koreagate incident did not blossom into a full-fledged political disaster, it demonstrated the extent to which foreign nations can become involved in American campaigns and elections; and although foreign leaders may have become more cautious since the Park scandal, they still use some not-so-subtle tactics to boost the reputations of their favorite candidates.

Although foreign leaders seem to be observing the ban on financial contributions, they continue to make contributions of another kind. For instance, China's former leader, Deng Xiaoping, told American officials on September 7, 1988, that he hoped Vice-President Bush would become the next president. Deng had come to know Bush when he was American ambassador to China, and Deng believed Bush to be a good and pragmatic politician.[29] Likewise, in June 1988, Great Britain's foreign secretary at the time, Sir Geoffrey Howe, boosted the Bush candidacy by saying that "obviously, it would be less than human if we didn't recognize the value of working with George Bush, with whom we've worked for a long time."[30] And Italy's prime minister, Ciriaco de Mita, stated that Republican presidents tend to do better with negotiations with the Soviet Union.

Most analysts believe that it is not really philosophical similarities that draw foreign leaders to particular candidates, but merely familiarity and predictability. Mikhail Gorbachev made it clear in 1984 that he supported Reagan's reelection not for ideological reasons but because Reagan was a known quantity. Conversely, Mexican officials grew wary of Jimmy Carter during his presidency because he often departed from normal American positions. A Mexican expert on Mexican-American relations put it like this: "Mexicans always feel more comfortable with a president who behaves predictably like an American, who fulfills our expectations of having to stand up to the gringo."[31]

The Democrats had their share of support in 1988. Michael Dukakis and Lloyd Bentsen were able to take advantage of their ties to Mexico. Both candidates spoke Spanish, and tried hard to promote their connections to Latin America. Their efforts paid off when a senior adviser to Mexico's president, Miguel de la Madrid, said that "the selection of Lloyd Bentsen was good for Mexico. We regard him as a friend of

Mexico."[32] And Michael Dukakis was pleased when Israel's defense minister, Yitzhak Shamir, flew to Boston to hold lengthy talks with the Democratic candidate. Obviously, these types of meetings and endorsements add to the prestige and legitimacy of the candidates. Dukakis, who was inexperienced in foreign affairs, had much to gain by such contacts.

Nor is it just foreign leaders who have developed a keen interest in American elections. For a few years now, many European television stations have broadcast delayed versions of the CBS, NBC, and ABC nightly news. Armed with surprising proficiency in English, foreign audiences are becoming increasingly interested in American politics. During the 1988 campaign, for instance, the Cable-Satellite Public Affairs Network (C-Span) broadcast in twenty European nations the Democratic and Republican national conventions. (For more on C-Span, see chap. 11.) And despite the early-morning broadcast times, the audience was even larger than anticipated. Stated one Dutch viewer, "For us Europeans, it is very unusual to see what looks like entertainment but seems to be politics."[33]

Perhaps the most ironic demonstration of international involvement in the 1988 election came when Dukakis made what he thought was a blistering speech against foreign ownership of industries in the United States. Believing that Moog Automotive Corporation in Wellston, Missouri, was a bastion of purely American productivity, Dukakis told the assembled employees: "Maybe the Republican ticket wants our children to work for foreign owners and pay rent to foreign owners and owe their future to foreign owners, but that's not the kind of future Lloyd Bentsen and I and Dick Gephardt and all of you want for America." As Dukakis was delivering the speech, workers informed reporters that in fact Moog Automotive was owned by I.F.I. International of Luxembourg. Later that evening Dukakis responded meekly to reporters' questions: "I have no problem with foreign investment at a plant like the one I was at."[34]

Obviously, it is this seemingly unavoidable blending of American and foreign interests that stimulates international involvement in the American electoral process. Citizens and leaders of foreign nations recognize the ripple effects that can accompany what may seem to be purely domestic policy changes. Thus they become especially concerned when changes are sudden or unanticipated.

★ Summary

Over time, the right to vote has gradually been extended to more and more segments of the population. Many of the barriers based on property, race, ethnicity, and gender have been removed through a combination of legislative and judicial decisions. Often these decisions came about as a result of grass-roots efforts by ordinary Americans seeking to claim their rights as citizens.

Perhaps the two most decisive features of American elections are (1) the requirement that candidates for most offices obtain a plurality in order to win, and (2) the single-member district system. Many other countries have a system of proportional representation, which tends to give several political parties a chance to gain representation in the legislature.

One unique feature of the American election system is the role of the electoral college in selecting the president. Rather than choosing directly between the candidates, voters in each state are actually casting their ballots for rival slates of electors selected by the parties. Not until the electors vote in December is a president officially chosen. Both advantages and disadvantages of the electoral college can be noted.

Another important feature of American elections has been the growing role of primaries, which permit voters to decide directly who the nominees of their parties will be in the general election. Primaries have been criticized for, among other things, being unrepresentative and encouraging party divisiveness. Yet most states have adopted the primary as a means of choosing delegates to the national presidential conventions.

One consistent finding is a relatively low turnout of voters in elections. During the past several decades, only about half of the eligible voters turn out in presidential elections and usually even fewer vote in other elections. Among the explanations for the low turnout are registration requirements, people's perceptions of and attitudes toward politics, and the influences of age, income, and education.

Perhaps no aspect of American politics has been subjected to harsher criticism than the relationship between election campaigns and money. Congress has passed legislation designed to limit campaign spending by candidates, to prohibit contributions over certain amounts by individuals and groups, and to require candidates for federal office to disclose donations and expenditures. Yet the vast amounts of money required to run an effective campaign and the influence that inevitably accompanies substantial donations continue to cloud the electoral scene.

Finally, it has become increasingly clear that American elections have effects that transcend American boundaries, and that foreign leaders and their constituencies are showing increased involvement in the American electoral process.

★ Key Terms

caucus
closed primary
convention system
democracy
direct primary
electoral college
Federal Election Campaign Act
grandfather clause
literacy tests
Nineteenth Amendment
open primary
plurality
plural-member district
political action committees (PACs)
poll tax
positive apathetics
proportional representation
reinforcement theory
selective attention
selective perception
single-member district
white primary

★ Notes

1. Robert J. Dinkin, *Voting in Revolutionary America: A Study of Elections in the Original Thirteen States, 1776–1789* (Westport, Conn.: Greenwood Press, 1982), p. 31.
2. *Wall Street Journal,* December 4, 1987, p. 10D.
3. Smith v. Allwright (1944).
4. Aileen S. Kraditor, *The Ideas of the Woman Suffrage Movement, 1890–1920* (New York: Doubleday/Anchor, 1971).
5. Ray Stannard Baker and William E. Dodd, eds., *The Public Papers of Woodrow Wilson,* vol. 1, *War and Peace* (New York: Harper, 1925), pp. 236--237.
6. Carrie Chapman Catt and Nettie Rogers Shuler, *Woman Suffrage and Politics: The Inner Story of the Suffrage Movement* (Seattle: University of Washington Press, 1970), p. 107 (first published 1923).

7. See *Congressional Quarterly,* January 21, 1989.
8. Lester W. Milbrath, *Political Participation* (Chicago: Rand McNally, 1965), p. 20.
9. Survey Research Center, University of Michigan.
10. Gallup Opinion Index, February 1972.
11. George Gallup, Jr., *The Gallup Poll: Public Opinion, 1984* (Wilmington, Del.: Scholarly Resources, 1985), p. 259.
12. Ibid.
13. Morris Rosenberg, "Some Determinants of Political Apathy," *Public Opinion Quarterly,* Winter 1954, pp. 349–366.
14. For a discussion of the relationship between cynicism and participation, see Arthur H. Miller, "Political Issues and Trust in Government, 1964–1970," followed by comments, *American Political Science Review* 26 (September 1974): 951–1001.
15. Quoted in Robert Sherrill, *Why They Call It Politics,* 2d ed. (New York: Harcourt Brace Jovanovich, 1974), p. 316.
16. Angus Campbell, Philip E. Converse, Warren E. Miller, and Donald E. Stokes, *The American Voter* (New York: Wiley, 1960).
17. Milbrath, *Political Participation;* Jack Citrin et al., "Personal and Political Sources of Political Alienation," *British Journal of Political Science* 5 (January 1975): 1–32.
18. For instance, 31 percent of the people who did not bother to vote in the 1984 presidential election said they trusted that the government does the right thing "most of the time" or "almost always." See James Allan Davis and Tom W. Smith, *General Social Survey, 1972–1988* (Chicago: National Opinion Research Center, 1988), subfile 1987 (machine-readable data file).
19. Margaret Mead, *And Keep Your Powder Dry: An Anthropologist Looks at America* (New York: Morrow, 1942), pp. 165–166.
20. *Christian Science Monitor,* April 29, 1987, p. 1
21. Bernard R. Berelson, Paul F. Lazarsfeld, and William N. McPhee, *Voting* (Chicago: University of Chicago Press, 1954), p. 244.
22. Quoted in Dinkin, *Voting in Revolutionary America,* p. 74.
23. *Wall Street Journal,* July 18, 1986, p. 1.
24. *Congressional Quarterly Weekly Report,* September 12, 1987, p. 2185.
25. *Washington Post,* October 17, 1986, p. A10.
26. *Congressional Quarterly Weekly Report,* September 12, 1987, p. 2187.
27. Ibid., June 20, 1987, p. 1331.
28. Congressional Quarterly, *Congressional Ethics* (Washington, D.C., 1980), p. 39.
29. *New York Times,* September 8, 1988, p. B10.
30. Ibid., July 2, 1988, p. A29.
31. Ibid., September 13, 1988, p. D24.
32. Ibid.
33. Ibid., August 2, 1988, p. B4.
34. Ibid., October 8, 1988, p. A34.

★ For Further Reading

Alexander, Herbert E. *Financing Politics: Money, Elections, and Political Reform.* Washington, D.C.: Congressional Quarterly Press, 1983.

Asher, Herbert B. *Presidential Elections and American Politics.* 4th ed. Pacific Grove, Calif.: Brooks/Cole, 1988.

Campbell, Angus, Philip E. Converse, Warren E. Miller, and Donald E. Stokes, *The American Voter.* New York: Wiley, 1960.

DeVries, Walter, and Lance Torrance, Jr. *The Ticket-Splitter.* Grand Rapids, Mich.: William B. Eerdmans, 1972.

Flanigan, William H., and Nancy H. Zingale. *Political Behavior of the American Electorate.* Boston: Allyn & Bacon, 1983.

Kraditor, Aileen S. *The Ideas of the Woman Suffrage Movement, 1890–1920.* New York: Doubleday Anchor, 1971.

Nie, Norman, Sidney Verba, and John Petrocik. *The Changing American Voter.* Cambridge, Mass.: Harvard University Press, 1976.

Polsby, Nelson, and Aaron Wildavsky. *Presidential Elections.* New York: Scribner's, 1984.

Sorauf, Frank. *Money in American Elections.* Boston: Little, Brown, 1988.

Wolfinger, Raymond, and Steven J. Rosenstone. *Who Votes?* New Haven, Conn.: Yale University Press, 1980.

In no country in the world has the principle of association been more successfully used, or applied to a greater multitude of objects, than in America . . . .

—*Alexis de Tocqueville*

CHAPTER TEN

INTEREST GROUPS

★★★★★★★★★★★

A Blessing or a Curse? Interest Groups in the United States

American Postal Workers Union
National Rifle Association
American Association of Witloof Endive Growers
Underwear-Negligee Associates
American Israel Public Affairs Committee
National Association of Manufacturers
Sierra Club
National Coalition for the Homeless
Morality in Media

At first glance these diverse organizations may seem to have little in common. On closer inspection, however, we see that among the many services such groups provide, they have the common goal of influencing public opinion and government policy to the benefit of their members. These organizations, to use political terminology, are interest groups.

Although the number and scope of these groups have mushroomed in recent years, they are hardly a new or unexpected phenomenon in American politics. Politicians and scholars alike have noted that collective rather than individual action offers the greatest promise for affecting government policy. By joining an organized group and working with people who share similar goals, an individual can overcome his or her feelings of political isolation and impotency.

Yet in spite of their effectiveness, interest groups are frequently criticized by politicians, the media, and the general public. Just mention pressure groups, or the lobbyists who represent them, and many people conjure up images of shady characters with suitcases stuffed with cash, skulking in and out of doorways to buy up politicians' votes. Lobbyists have won a reputation for corruption and shady dealing that while occasionally is deserved, tends to obscure the important ways interest groups help link citizens with the governmental process.

In this chapter we will take a close look at interest groups in an effort to understand more about their activities and the controversy that surrounds them. Among the questions we will explore are:

- What are interest groups?
- How do they affect governmental policy?
- Who joins interest groups?
- How has the globalization of American politics influenced interest group activity?
- What are the benefits and limitations of membership in an interest group?
- Whose interests do they tend to represent?

★ Interest Group Defined

What is an **interest group?** In the broadest sense, an interest group can be defined as a collection (large or small) of people with shared attitudes and goals who band together to influence public opinion and government policy. Although interest groups are often referred to as "pressure groups," the term is somewhat more limited because "pressure" carries a strong negative connotation and because direct contact with government officials is only one of many techniques employed to influence policy. The same is true of the term "lobby." While interest groups are often described as lobbies, "lobbying" usually denotes direct dealings with policy makers and is only one of many activities engaged in by organized groups. The word **"lobbyist"** can be traced back more than a century. It was first used to identify people who tried to corner legislators in a corridor or lobby outside the legislative chamber. Today most interest groups still employ lobbyists to approach legislators directly. During the Senate hearings on tax reform in the 1980s, for example, the halls outside the chambers were dubbed Gucci Gulch in honor of the well-heeled lobbyists representing clients seeking loopholes in the new tax law. But some interest groups also promote their causes behind the scenes, preferring to conduct letter-writing and other publicity campaigns from a high-tech computer work station or "boiler room" telephone operation.

Types of Groups

So many types of groups operate on the political scene that they defy any simple classification. Some groups, such as the National Association of Manufacturers, may be concerned primarily with improving the economic situation of their members. Other groups may be more ideological or idealistic, focusing on religious and moral controversies, from defense spending to prayer in public schools and abortion. Still others represent the interests of identifiable ethnic or social segments of American society. The National Association for the Advancement of Colored People (NAACP), for instance, seeks to represent the interests of black Americans, while the National Organization for Women (NOW) hopes to advance the cause of women in America.

Indeed, the concerns and activities of interest groups may be quite diverse, and not strictly economic, ideological, or limited to a specific segment of society. The National Education Association, for instance, is concerned with teachers' economic interests as well as a variety of ideological issues involving national education policy. The National Rifle Association serves its members not only by opposing gun-control legislation but also by offering group insurance, publishing hunting and shooting magazines, and acting as the national governing body for a number of shooting competitions (including the U.S. Olympic shooting teams).[1] Defense contractors may pursue their economic interest by supporting the Committee on the Present Danger, an overtly ideological group that pushes military spending. And finally, there are umbrella groups that claim to speak not for individual segments or economic interests but for the American public at large. In this category we find consumer groups and the so-called citizens' lobbies, such as Common Cause. We will have more to say about these types of groups later in the chapter. Figure 10-1 shows public perceptions of some prominent interest groups.

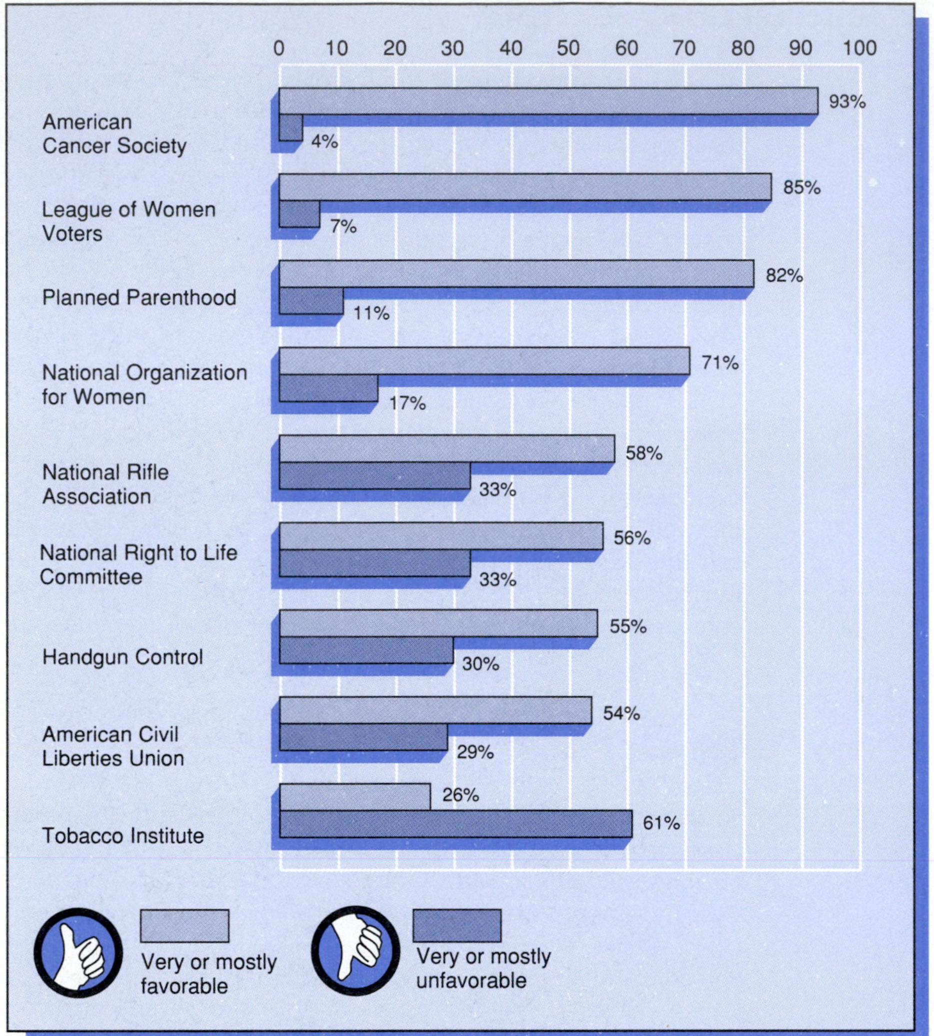

★ **Figure 10-1**
How various interest groups were ranked by the public in 1989 (percent)
NOTE: The favorable and unfavorable opinions do not add to 100 percent; the remaining percentages represent those whose response was "No opinion."
SOURCE: George Gallup, Jr., "Cancer Society Is Top-Rated Special Interest, *San Jose Mercury-News*, April 16, 1989, p. 9A.

In categorizing interest groups, it is necessary to make a distinction between actual and potential groups. As David Truman has pointed out, many, if not all, Americans are members of potential groups: farmworkers, music video fans, Southeast Asian refugees, ice cream eaters.[2] But most of these potential group members do not formally link up with each other. An actual group, on the other hand, consists of those from the pool of potential members who choose to join together to form a group. The success of an actual group depends in large part on its ability to attract members from the pool of potential participants. Some groups, such as the NAACP and the National Urban League, may claim to speak for all black citizens, but they

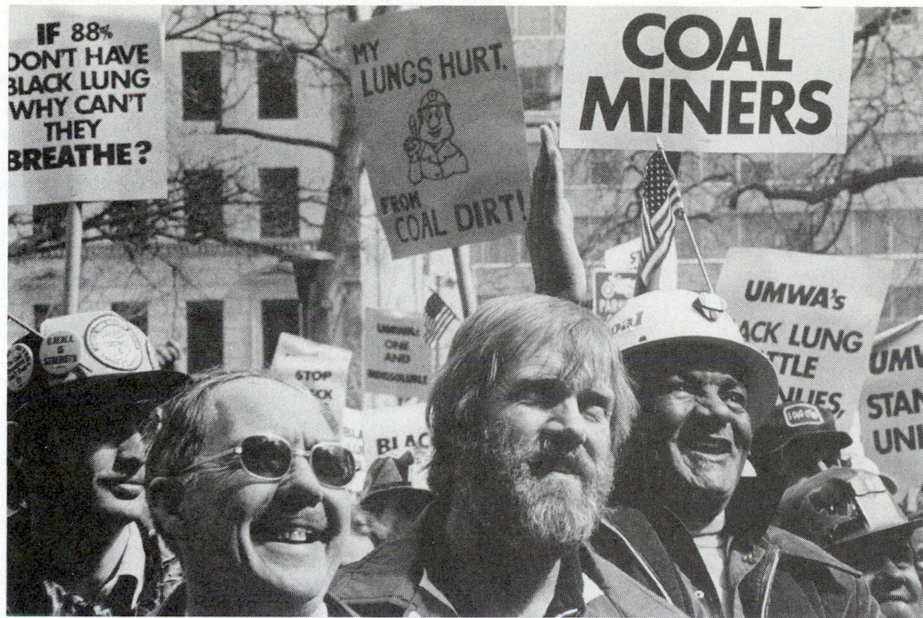

★ An interest group in action: United Mine Workers members protest against black-lung disease, one of the many health hazards they face on the job.

must amass the money, voter loyalty, and other resources needed to capitalize on this claim.

It is also important to remember the differences between interest groups and our two major political parties. The Democratic and Republican parties bring together citizens of diverse backgrounds and points of view with the goal of nominating candidates, winning elections, and controlling the federal and state governments. In order to be successful, they must reconcile conflicting interests—labor and management, developers and environmentalists, hawks and doves. They often avoid taking a strong stand on controversial issues as they try to please the widest audience. Once in office, they also organize legislative bodies and help determine the way government conducts its business.

Interest groups, on the other hand, may represent a very narrow segment of society and have little concern with overall government policy. **Single-issue groups** support or oppose a candidate solely on the basis of his or her stand on a single issue, such as abortion, trade policy, arms control, or programs for the elderly. Whereas political parties may seek to reconcile differences on specific issues in order to win votes, interest groups consider elections only one of many weapons in the service of their cause.

★ The Growth of Interest Groups

In several respects, the activities of interest groups lie at the heart of the American political system. They reflect the enormous diversity of opinion in our society, representing a wide range of causes at virtually every stage of the policy-making

The Saga of an Interest Group: The National Organization for Women

The story of the National Organization for Women (NOW) illustrates many of the dynamics of interest groups in the United States and shows why they have grown so rapidly in recent times. It all began when the outrage of a few individuals coincided with an increasingly sympathetic political climate. In 1961, President John Kennedy established the Presidential Commission on the Status of Women, and by 1966 almost every state had named a comparable state-level commission to investigate the extent of sex discrimination.

In 1966 the Presidential Commission issued a report documenting twenty-four areas in need of immediate attention. But it failed to recommend a course of action. Some members of the commission soon felt that the time of conferences and talk was over; the time had come to act. They wanted not only to act on the federal commission's findings but also to pressure the Equal Employment Opportunity Commission (EEOC) to enforce the provisions of Title VII of the 1964 Civil Rights Act, outlawing sex discrimination in employment. Many EEOC officials had treated these provisions as a joke; certainly they did not consider sex discrimination as serious as race discrimination. Other EEOC members argued that sex discrimination would be taken more seriously if, as Jo Freeman wrote in *The Politics of Women's Liberation* in 1975, there was "some sort of NAACP for women to put pressure on the government. As government employees they could not organize such a group, but they spoke privately with those whom they thought could do so."

EEOC members met to discuss the possibility of forming a civil rights organization for women. At this meeting was Betty Friedan, author of *The Feminine Mystique*, a 1963 best-seller that launched a wave of American feminism. The book led many women to question their lives and some to urge Friedan to form a new organization to address women's problems. Twenty-eight women paid $5 each to join the new National Organization for Women, a name chosen by Friedan, who was its first president. Once established, NOW built on the communications networks and research collected by the various state commissions.

The federal and state governments that had created the commissions that helped get NOW off the ground soon became the targets of NOW lobbying efforts. By the 1980s, NOW had become the largest feminist interest group, with over 220,000 members, 700 chapters in all fifty states, and an annual budget of $13 million. It has weathered internal debates on matters ranging from political strategy to abortion.

In order to maximize fund-raising and lobbying flexibility, NOW has developed several offshoots. The NOW Legal Defense and Education Fund raises money to pursue court

(continued)

process. Although interest groups are not mentioned in the Constitution, the right to influence government through collective action is based firmly on the First Amendment freedoms of speech and assembly and on the people's right to "petition the Government for a redress of grievances." As we noted in chapter 2, James Madison and some of the other framers viewed the division of society into many competing groups (or "factions") as a natural outcome of economic and social differences. Even though they were worried about the potential dangers posed by a few powerful groups, they also recognized the value of providing these groups with access to government officials.

What the framers could not foresee was the phenomenal growth in the number and variety of groups pressing their claims on government. During the past two centuries, as the federal government has ballooned into a bureaucratic colossus that touches the lives of all Americans, interest groups have proliferated and their representatives have flocked to Washington (and to state capitals) by the thousands to influence legislation and public opinion. From the 1970s to the 1980s the number of formally registered lobbyists grew by over 20 percent, to roughly 5,000. Fur-

★ Politics in the media age. Many interest groups use figures from the world of entertainment to publicize their cause. Hollywood personalities Marlo Thomas, Whoopi Goldberg, and Cybill Shepherd *(left to right)* take part in a NOW rally.

cases involving women's rights. The Project for Equal Educational Rights monitors enforcement of equal educational opportunities for women. And NOW political action committees mount battles at the ballot box. NOW also lobbies on such issues as sex-based employment discrimination in regard to wages, working conditions, sexual harassment, maternity leave, and child care.

NOW is probably best known for its efforts to secure passage of the Equal Rights Amendment (ERA) to the Constitution. The passage of the ERA out of Congress and on to the state legislatures in 1972 was achieved by a broad coalition of groups, including NOW. Other women's groups, however, were formed to work against ratification of the ERA. These other groups sought to promote women's traditional roles as mothers, wives, and homemakers. Such groups as STOP-ERA, Females Opposed to Equality (FOE), and Happiness of Motherhood Eternal (HOME) opposed not only the ERA but also affirmative action, reproductive freedom, sexual freedom, and gay rights.

In one of the ironies of American interest group history, NOW's success spawned groups that ultimately led to the defeat of one of feminism's most important goals, the passage of the ERA. When the ERA fell three states short of ratification, NOW shifted its efforts to increasing the number of women in the state legislatures. The story of NOW reveals how changing times have produced new interest groups on the American political scene. ★

thermore, it is estimated that 30,000 to 40,000 people in Washington now spend some time lobbying.[3] This growth has many causes, but the most obvious factors include the changing nature of political parties, changes in campaign spending laws, changes in public relations campaigns, and the general politicization and globalization of American society.[4]

The Nature of Political Parties

As we mentioned earlier, the two major political parties seem to deemphasize ideology and avoid a strong stand on any issue in their efforts to win elections. With the parties attempting to make their message appealing to a broad range of voters, people vitally concerned with specific questions—such as abortion, the environment, policy toward certain foreign nations, and gun control—have turned to interest groups to press their agenda. These groups are not interested in compromise; they have been known to support or reject legislators on the basis of a single roll-call vote, paying little attention to their overall voting record, service to their local constituency, or party affiliation.

Changes in Campaign Finance

Also encouraging the formation of interest groups has been Congress's efforts to curb influence-buying through campaign spending. As we saw in chapter 9, the Campaign Reform Act of 1974 limited individual contributions to $1,000 per candidate. Group contributions were not to exceed $5,000. Wealthy interests, nonetheless, found a way around the 1974 spending limits by creating thousands of political action committees (PACs). Corporations, labor unions, and citizens' groups seeking to gain favor with a candidate can establish and fund a PAC, which can pass out checks of up to $5,000 as it sees fit. As we will see, PACs have become a major avenue of influence for interest groups.

Changes in Public Relations Campaigns

The development of high-tech methods of organizing supporters, raising money, and spreading the message through direct mail and media campaigns has also encouraged the formation of interest groups. In the past, publicizing one's cause usually required a great deal of money or a large number of enthusiastic volunteers. While money and bodies are still very helpful in efforts to promote a cause, almost anyone with a personal computer and roll of postage stamps can mount a respectable publicity campaign. As we will see, direct mail campaigns can be very successful in raising money and mobilizing supporters.

The proliferation of television news, including specialized cable programs that deal exclusively with political topics, have also opened new avenues by which interest groups can take their case to the public. Television news programs need interest groups and the occasionally controversial causes they espouse nearly as much as the groups need public exposure. In the highly competitive TV news business, interest groups can provide the information, color, and drama essential to successful programming.

The Politicization and Globalization of Society

As we saw in chapter 1, the overall growth of government and the variety of political, economic, and technological changes that have occurred throughout the world have further politicized life in America. Before scientists began to develop successful commercial applications for DNA, for example, there was little need for a group to represent genetic engineering interests. While hunger and disease are hardly new to parts of Africa, it took the development of a global media and entertainment industry to spread the news of mass starvation and mobilize public relief efforts in America and Europe. Today, with more and more people seeing government as responsible for solving new problems and the major political parties shunning strong stands on specific issues, citizens, corporations, universities, local governments, and even foreign governments have formed interest groups and employed lobbyists.

★ Interest Groups in a Changing World

> Everybody needs a Washington representative to protect their hindsides, even foreign governments.
>
> —*Senator Paul Laxalt*

Given the United States' many economic, political, and cultural links with other countries, it is not surprising that lobbying has become a global activity. From its base in Switzerland the International Committee for the Red Cross seeks to influence American policy makers (as well as leaders of many other nations) to protect the rights of refugees and prisoners of war. Such groups as Amnesty International and Greenpeace, although founded abroad, have recruited thousands of members in the United States who support their political and environmental agendas. Some American groups push more narrow causes, such as the United Nations Association's efforts to build support for the world body. Others tackle such complex problems as the plight of Palestinian refugees in the Middle East, arms control, global hunger, and the suffering of political prisoners in Latin America and the Soviet Union.

American ethnic groups also have organized to influence foreign policy. For nearly twenty years after the Chinese revolution in 1949, the so-called China lobby worked effectively to prevent American recognition of the Chinese communist government. Many Cuban American groups have lobbied for strong sanctions against Fidel Castro's communist government in Cuba. Jewish Americans have formed the American Israel Public Affairs Committee, an extremely successful and well-funded group that seeks favorable U.S. policy toward Israel. Irish Americans, Polish Americans, and many other ethnic-based interest groups also have sought to influence U.S. policy toward their ancestral homelands.[5] New immigrants and refugees from Central America and the Far East, following the example of other ethnic and national groups in America, have also banded together to influence government policy on a wide range of national and international questions. Organizations with an interest in American policy toward other nations include:

Action Committee on Arab-American Relations
American Chilean Council
American Committee on U.S.–Soviet Relations
American Israel Public Affairs Committee
Committee in Solidarity with the People of El Salvador
Japanese American Citizens League
National Association of Arab Americans
National Committee on U.S.–China Relations
National Conference on Soviet Jewry
Polish American Congress
Washington Office on Africa
Washington Office on Latin America[6]

American labor and industry have also formed associations and lobbied on tariffs and many other trade issues. Steel manufacturers, with the support of organized labor, have joined together for years to pressure the government to cut imports from Japan, Korea, and other competing nations. Supporting trade with Japan, on the other hand, is the United States–Japan Trade Council, comprising more than 900 American and Japanese companies, including General Electric, Stan-

Getting It Right: The American Israel Public Affairs Committee

> Without question, the most effective lobby in Congress.
> —*Representative Mervyn M. Dymally*

The American Israel Public Affairs Committee (AIPAC) is the envy of just about every interest group in Washington. Though some people disagree with its tactics and goals, most acknowledge that AIPAC has elevated the art of lobbying to a new height. AIPAC is an American interest group dedicated to ensuring that U.S. foreign policy remains unfailingly committed to Israel. In pursuing its goals AIPAC employs all of the tools of effective lobbying:

Information. AIPAC employs a variety of experts, including academics and former government officials. Strong ties with the government of Israel lend credibility to AIPAC information. Congress and the executive branch sometimes consult with AIPAC experts before planning moves in the Middle East.

Contacts. AIPAC has excellent relations with all branches of the government. Personal and professional ties ensure access to the centers of power. An image of power in Washington, in turn, brings more power. According to one observer, "Each election year, AIPAC is proud to point out, hundreds of candidates for the House and Senate solicit the lobby's support."

Resources. AIPAC boasted a membership of 55,000 in 1987, and an annual budget of $6 million. Though it does not formally endorse candidates, AIPAC draws attention to politicians who support Israel. Pro-Israel PACs contributed $3.8 million to candidates in the 1986 elections.

Singleness of purpose. AIPAC, like other groups, is concerned with one narrow goal: in this case, influencing U.S. policy toward Israel. Although the Middle East represents only one of many trouble spots for U.S. foreign policy makers, AIPAC judges candidates and issues solely in relation to their effect on Israel.

Public confusion over America's proper role in the Middle East presents an excellent opportunity for a special interest group to influence policy making. By employing the most sophisticated lobbying techniques, AIPAC has shown the significant influence that a relatively small group can have on U.S. foreign policy. ★

SOURCE: Edward Tivnan, *The Lobby: Jewish Political Power and American Foreign Policy* (New York: Simon & Schuster, 1987); Robert Pear and Richard L. Berke, "Pro-Israel Group Exerts Quiet Might as It Rallies Supporters in Congress," *New York Times*, July 7, 1988, p. 7.

dard Oil of California, Japan Airlines, and the Bank of Tokyo. Overall the Japanese are said to spend in excess of $40 million on lobbying and often join forces with U.S. interests favoring free trade policies. Japanese auto companies, for example, have worked with American farm groups to increase trade between the two countries.[7] Even Harley Davidson, sainted manufacturer of redblooded American macho motorcycles, had to lobby the government for protection from imported Japanese superbikes.

Lobbying in high-tech areas is also strong. The computer industry persuaded the Reagan administration to impose wide-ranging tariffs on many products from Brazil. The Brazilians, computer interest groups argued, were borrowing hardware designs, copying software, and using other "intellectual products" without honoring patents or otherwise compensating American firms.

Foreign governments too have increasingly turned to lobbyists and public relations firms to create a favorable impression among the American people and government officials. The creation of nearly a hundred new nations since World War II has increased the volume of voices clamoring to be heard in Washington. New and old nations alike have felt the need to employ American lobbyists and encourage the formation of interest groups to supplement the activities of their formal diplomatic representatives. Foreign governments routinely spend large sums of money on interest group activities, which can range from promoting tourism and trade to obtaining military aid and the right to purchase the latest in American weapons technology. Nondiplomatic representatives of foreign governments are required by law to register as lobbyists. In 1985, 850 individuals and firms registered as agents of foreign countries and spent $150 million on their lobbying activities.[8]

How important can the right representative or media consultant in Washington be? Lobbying by foreign governments is especially important for a nation with a poor public image in the United States. In the early 1980s Saudi Arabia was reported to be paying one of its several lobbyists $400,000 a year.[9] Before his downfall in 1986, President Ferdinand Marcos of the Philippines was reported to be paying $950,000 for advice on his media image in the United States.[10] In October 1988, El Salvador's right-wing political party ARENA (National Republican Alliance) registered as a lobby with the federal government in Washington. The ARENA leadership, fearful that its alleged ties to death squads in El Salvador would hurt its image in the United States, hired a Washington law firm and sent its presidential candidate, Alfredo Cristiani, to Capitol Hill. With hundreds of millions of dollars in U.S. economic and military aid at stake, Cristiani wanted to convince the Congress that ARENA would respect human rights. Cristiani was elected president of El Salvador in the spring of 1989.

★ How Interest Groups Influence Policy: The "Washington Insider" Approach

In order to influence policy, interest groups use the primary resource of politics—power. Power, as we saw in chapter 5, has many dimensions, and the resources that provide power for interest groups are as varied as the organizations and the causes they espouse. Power for one interest group may involve contributions of money to help elect sympathetic candidates, or it may involve the establishment of personal connections with important officials and agencies of government. Some groups may use their expertise on specific issues to sway public opinion or politicians; others may employ lawsuits to win a favorable court decision, and still others may mobilize large numbers of people in support of their cause. The most successful groups often use a wide variety of tactics in pursuit of their goals.

Not only do tactics and resources vary, but interest groups also pursue their agenda at many levels of the American political system. Sometimes the best tactic is the "Washington insider" strategy—an attempt to gain support in Congress, the executive branch, and the courts. At other times, groups may go beyond Washington to appeal directly to the public.

Washington Insider Tactic 1: Lobbying Congress

A lobbyist is someone who seeks to influence the passage, defeat, or content of policy, usually through direct contact with decision makers. Today many interest group representatives are highly skilled (and highly paid) professionals with backgrounds ranging from advertising and business to law and government. Some interest group representatives dislike the term *lobbyist* because of its traditional negative connotation. For clarity, nonetheless, we will stick to that term here, noting

that interest group representatives nowadays come from diverse professional backgrounds and use a variety of tools and resources in their efforts to influence public policy.

Essentially two kinds of lobbyists operate on Capitol Hill: full-time employees of single organizations, who roam the halls of Congress drumming up support for their organizations' interests; and the lobbyists for hire, who may represent several organizations at once. Among the most prominent of the latter is the Washington law firm of Patton, Boggs, and Blow and its superstar lobbyist partner, Thomas Boggs, Jr., whose parents Hale Boggs and Lindy Boggs both have served in Congress. The firm's lobbying and fund-raising skills, along with its contacts in Washington, have won it such clients as the government of Oman, MCI Corporation, *Reader's Digest*, and a Guatemalan business group called Los Amigos del País (Friends of the Country).[11]

The approaches used in congressional lobbying vary with the issue, the interest group the lobbyist represents, and the resources available. Some lobbyists have succeeded in winning the support of senators and representatives through bribes, lavish entertainment, and promises of future employment. People who thought open bribery was a thing of the past were shocked when the so-called Abscam scandal broke in 1980. Abscam was an undercover investigation of corruption by the Federal Bureau of Investigation. FBI agents, posing as Arab businessmen, offered bribes to members of Congress and other elected officials in exchange for help with commercial ventures, immigration problems, and federal grants. Six representatives and a senator were eventually convicted of charges ranging from bribery to conspiracy.[12] Though increased public scrutiny has reduced the more blatantly illegal tactics, money still plays a large part in lobbying through campaign contributions, handsome speaking fees, and other means of capitalizing on a seat in Congress.

Still, money is but one weapon in the arsenal of interest groups and their lobbyists on Capitol Hill. "Lobbying," according to an important study of interest groups, "has gone professional. Gone are the days of the old-style, cigar-smoking lobbyist who is free with his money and short on solid information. Lobbyists today are professional people, tacticians, strategists. . . . They are public relations experts with astute political savvy."[13] The lobbyists' savvy often involves more than just knowledge of politics. With Congress dealing with issues ranging from depletion

★ Going one-on-one with the government: Yet another legislator is buttonholed by a lobbyist advocating a cause.

of the ozone layer to organ transplants, technical knowledge has become an important tool for the lobbyist. Indeed, information and expertise are crucial for interest groups and the lobbyists they employ. Many interest groups develop a substantial body of technical information to influence Congress and build support among the public. Through the use of consultants, pollsters, and other experts, interest groups can supply legislators and bureaucrats with a wealth of information that their busy staffs may not have the time or resources to produce. By supplying officials with detailed information through committee testimony, personal discussions, and even suggested drafts of bills, lobbying groups can often incorporate their own ideas into the final version of proposed legislation.

The objectivity of information supplied by lobbyists may of course be open to question. A report on smoking and health supplied by the Tobacco Institute, for instance, will have to be balanced by information available from other sources. The cautious legislator may consult his or her staff as well as the Library of Congress's Congressional Research Service or the Office of Technology Assessment before taking a lobbyist's information as the final word.

A lobbyist's political savvy and technical knowledge must be combined with an understanding of the way Congress operates. As we will see in chapter 12, much of the legislative process takes place in committees. Each bill introduced on Capitol Hill is referred to a committee for consideration; and it is in a committee, not on the floor, that its fate usually is determined. Interest groups know that busy committee members are often hungry for information, especially on how pending legislation may affect their districts. They also know that in fights over specific bills, it is easier to influence a handful of committee members than the entire Senate or House, and that a committee's recommendations tend to be accepted by other senators and representatives. Rather than waste their time on legislators strongly opposed to their views, interest groups focus instead on wavering members who may tip the balance in their favor; and they carefully nurture the friendship of members who have supported their concerns in the past.

Not only do interest groups work to build mutually beneficial relationships with legislators, they also seek strategic coalitions with other groups. By pooling their resources, groups may compete with larger, better-financed opponents. Labor unions and business leaders, for example, may join forces to stem the tide of foreign competition. This type of coalition, though often a marriage of convenience, has been instrumental in obtaining or preventing passage of major legislation.

Washington Insider Tactic 2: Lobbying the Executive Branch

Interest groups do not, of course, limit their lobbying energies to Congress. Once bills are passed by the House and Senate, interest groups must also make sure that the president signs them into law and that the bureaucracy carries them out (or, conversely, that the bills are vetoed, or made ineffective by administrators' failure to enforce them).

Laws passed by Congress often leave considerable room for interpretation. Bureaucrats are given great discretion in deciding how laws are to be put into practice. Congress may pass legislation establishing strict federal standards for clean water supplies, for example, but the actual requirements of the law will probably be defined by administrators. As a result, interest groups try to develop friendly ties with bureaucrats whose decisions may advance or retard their efforts. Farmers seek ties with the Department of Agriculture, teachers with the Department of Education, and airlines with the Federal Aviation Administration. And bureaucrats honor those ties because they value the information interest groups can supply and because they may need the groups' support in lobbying Congress for adequate budgets for their programs.

Interest groups and executive agencies form two sides (along with congressional committees) of an **iron triangle** (see figure 10-2). These iron triangles, sometimes called subgovernments, are especially evident in the area of military spending, where officials at the Pentagon (eager for new weapons) work with private-sector defense contractors (eager for sales) and members of Congress (eager for new jobs for their constituents in their districts) to ensure approval of their pet projects.

How do interest groups seek to influence executive-branch officials? They employ some of the same tactics used to influence members of Congress, adapting these measures to the decision-making processes of administrative agencies. They testify or "intervene" at agency hearings in an effort to shape the rules and regulations that the executive branch issues every day. Thus such interests as General Motors and the Sierra Club often find themselves on opposite sides when the Environmental Protection Agency holds hearings on a regulation to set clean air

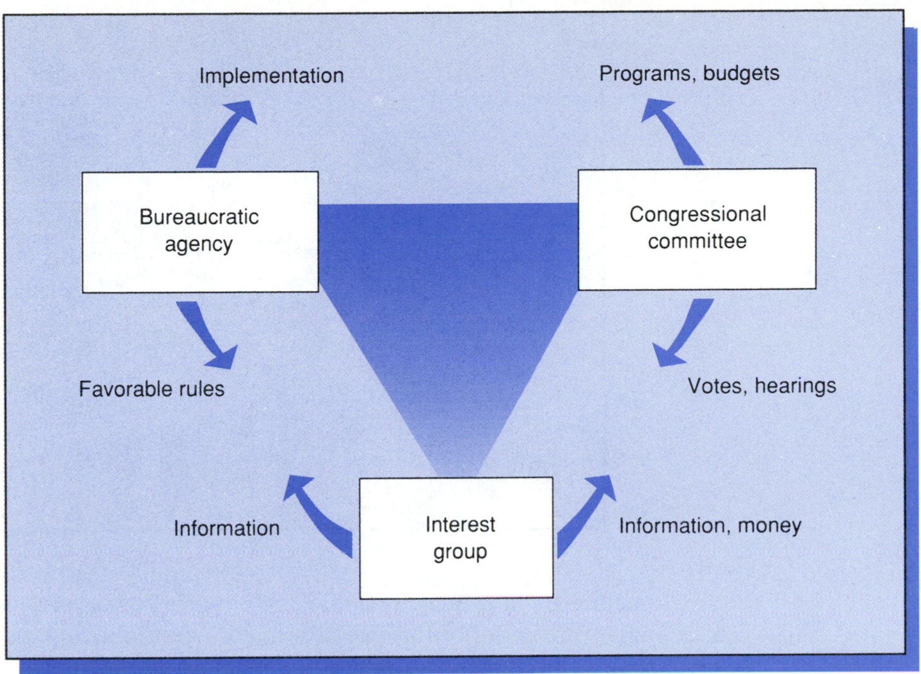

★ **Figure 10-2**
One example of the reciprocal exchanges that form an iron triangle, or subgovernment

standards. Food manufacturers and consumer or public interest groups tangle over food labeling or ingredient regulations before the Food and Drug Administration. They also seek direct meetings with senior agency officials to express their views. They do not neglect to send telegrams and letters, issue special appeals, or insert advertisements in the press to publicize their concerns. Interest groups even seek to influence appointments made to administrative agencies; environmental groups and mining interests clash over appointments to the Bureau of Mines, and one can expect Ralph Nader and toymakers to disagree over appointments to the Consumer Product Safety Commission.

There are other important differences between Congress and the executive branch that interest groups try to exploit. Many top officials of the executive branch are political appointees, whose tenure lasts no longer than the president they serve. The fact that many former government officials find lucrative employment in businesses that they used to regulate is not lost on interest groups. Interest groups often serve as gatekeepers for the infamous "revolving door" that connects government to industry. Although they must take care not to violate the laws that govern the employment of former government officials, interest groups often are able to establish close working relationships with agency personnel based in part on potential future employment or business contacts.

Sometimes former officials have little besides their insider contacts to offer special interests. Take the case of former secretary of the interior James Watt. Watt, a key ideological force in the Reagan administration's war on big government, was hired as a consultant by developers seeking lucrative housing contracts from the Department of Housing and Urban Development. Although he openly admitted to Congress that he knew very little about the housing business, Watt received $300,000 in consulting fees from the developers.

Sometimes, unfortunately, former members of the executive branch do not take enough care in following the laws that govern lobbying. Such was the case with a former official of the Reagan administration, Michael K. Deaver. Deaver, who had been associated with Ronald Reagan since his days as governor of California, founded a consulting firm in Washington when he left the government in 1985. Using contacts established while he was on the president's staff, M. K. Deaver and Associates was soon doing $3 million in business. Deaver's instant success led many observers to conclude that he was exploiting his close contacts with his friends in the Reagan White House, and he was investigated by a federal grand jury and a congressional committee. In 1987 Deaver was convicted of lying about his lobbying activities.[14]

Interest groups can also be helpful to career bureaucrats in government service. Department heads must convince the boss (the president or cabinet-level official) of the worthiness of their programs, and interest groups can provide vital information, a vocal public constituency, and other kinds of support. The inter-governmental battle of the budget can be bloody, and a wise bureaucrat deploys all of the weapons available, including the support of interest groups. As with the revolving-door problem, critics often complain of too cozy a relationship between government bureaucrats and interest groups.

Because of its domination of foreign policy, the executive branch tends to be more directly involved than Congress with interest groups that espouse international causes. Groups that want to influence foreign policy have proliferated as America's involvement in the world has grown. While Congress certainly receives its share of lobbying on behalf of foreign trade, human rights, national security, and other causes, it is the president and executive-branch departments—State, Commerce, Defense—that are the favorite targets of international interest groups.

Washington Insider Tactic 3: "Lobbying" the Courts

If pressure on members of Congress and the executive branch prove to be ineffective, interest groups and their lobbyists can try to challenge a law or executive action in the courts. Interest groups have learned that they can often achieve results by using the court system, usually through the filing of a lawsuit.

Some groups have discovered that the courts are more sympathetic to their cause than Congress or the president, especially if the issue threatens to spark a controversy that election-conscious politicians wish to avoid. Historically, the NAACP has been especially successful in gaining the support of the Supreme Court in overturning discriminatory laws at both federal and state levels. One of its most notable achievements was the landmark 1954 decision in *Brown* v. *Board of Education,* which declared segregated schools unconstitutional. More recently, environmental groups, anti-abortion organizations, women's groups seeking equal treatment at the workplace, and foes of capital punishment have been but a few of the many interests seeking to influence public policy through the courts. During the 1970s, for example, environmental groups were the plaintiffs in 636 cases before federal district courts. The Center for Public Interest Law has estimated that more than 150 interest groups have pursued their agendas in the courts.[15] The Supreme Court has made it clear that litigation is a legitimate and useful tactic for influencing public policy:

> In the context of NAACP objectives, litigation . . . is a means for achieving the lawful objectives of equality of treatment. . . . It is thus a form of political expression. Groups which find themselves unable to achieve their objectives through the ballot turn to the courts. . . . And under conditions of modern government, litigation may well be the sole practical avenue open to a minority to petition for redress of grievances.[16]

This is not to say that litigation is a tactic available equally to all groups. Litigation can prove to be a costly and time-consuming undertaking, especially if a case goes all the way to the Supreme Court. Groups that have the money to pay for high-powered attorneys and that are willing to endure the long delays of the judicial process usually enjoy a great advantage over groups struggling to make ends meet.

Partly for this reason, an interest group may prefer to become involved in a court action as an amicus curiae (friend of the court). Instead of bringing suit directly, it submits a written argument, known as an amicus brief, outlining its legal views on the issue in question. Between 1970 and 1980, more than half of the amicus briefs filed with the Supreme Court in noncommercial cases came from interest groups.[17]

★ The Outside-Washington Approach: Mobilizing the Public

Interest groups have placed increased emphasis on generating grass-roots support in recent years. While the Washington insider approach can be effective in influencing Congress and executive agencies, many groups also take their case directly "to the people." They have learned a great deal from advertising and public relations specialists about how to target sympathetic segments of the public, build a reliable following, and mobilize their members to apply pressure on legislators and government officials. Such tactics may be especially important for groups that lack significant financial resources. Grass-roots tactics may include letter-writing campaigns, a media blitz, even public demonstrations.

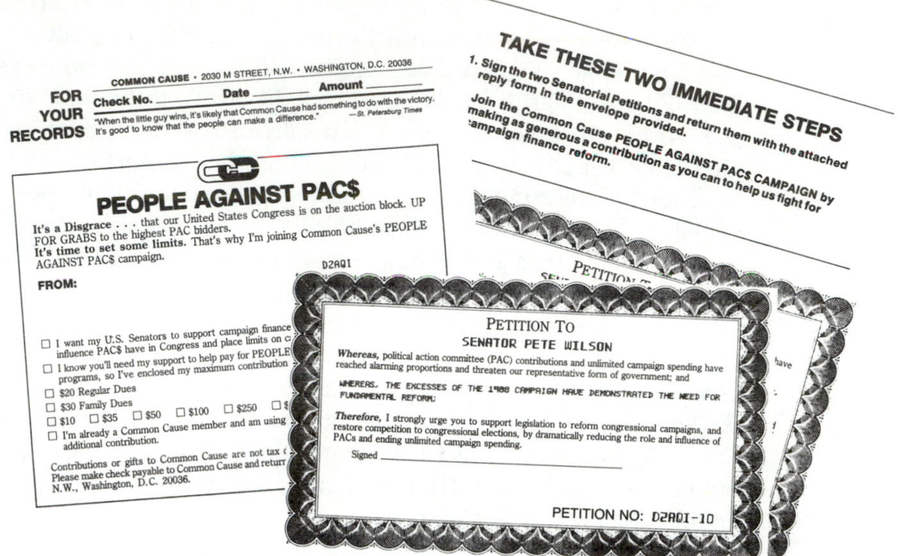

★ Direct mail *is* direct. This Common Cause mailer does it all: states its case, offers a petition suitable for sending to the appropriate politician, asks for a monetary contribution, and provides a receipt all in one page!

Letter-Writing Campaigns

An intensive letter-writing campaign may be waged to whip up citizen support for or opposition to a particular policy or cause. Some groups employ the latest in computer and communications technologies to maintain up-to-date mailing lists, "phone trees," and other means to alert members and supporters that an issue of concern is under consideration by federal, state, or local officials. Such tactics can be quite successful. The National Conservative Political Action Committee, for instance, raised $9.6 million for the 1982 congressional elections; and the government reform group, Common Cause, reported that it received $1 in donations for every 16 cents spent on mailings.[18]

While the financial and other resources of groups vary, the goals remain the same: bombard government officials with letters, phone calls, telegrams, or any other means of communication in sufficient quantity to get their attention. The National Rifle Association, for example, operating on the premise that nothing shakes a politician like a pile of angry letters from home, has been using its large mailing lists to turn aside gun laws since the 1930s. Proponents of gun control, of course, have turned to the same tactics.

Government officials and politicians are certainly moved by an outpouring of public sentiment on a given issue, but they have become quite sophisticated in assessing the nature of letter-writing campaigns. A computer-generated letter carries much less weight than a handwritten note from a long-time supporter back home. Armed with opinion polls, reports from the local district office, and their own political instincts, legislators weigh the mounds of mail that come in on a given issue and act accordingly. In other words, well-financed direct mail campaigns are no guarantee that an interest group's goals will be realized.

★ Pro- and anti-gun-control groups take their cases to the public in dramatic fashion. Publicity campaigns are one of the many weapons in the interest-group arsenal.

Media Blitz

A second method of mobilizing the public—a massive media advertising campaign—is aimed at all citizens and thus broader in scope than a letter-writing campaign, which targets specific segments of society. The goal of the media blitz remains the same: to create a favorable public (and government) attitude toward a group's basic aims. Many large corporations, for instance, launch elaborate public relations campaigns to sell their political views as well as their commercial products to the public. During the oil shortage of the 1970s the major oil companies ran numerous television commercials intended to assure the public that they were not reaping enormous profits from the soaring price of gasoline and that the search for oil, including drilling off some of the nation's most scenic coastal areas, must continue to "keep America strong." More recently, the aerospace giant Northrop ran a series of newspaper advertisements extolling the virtues of the proposed F-20 Tigershark jet fighter and other weapons. Clearly Northrop was not hoping to put a jet in every American's garage. Rather, the firm sought to build a favorable public image that would spread to the people in the Pentagon who buy its weapons and to the legislators who raise the revenue to pay for them.

★ Thousands of civil rights marchers convened in Washington, D.C., in 1963. Public protest and mass demonstrations provide another route for interest groups to influence public opinion and government policy.

Public Protest

Perhaps the most dramatic kind of mobilization takes the form of rallies, demonstrations, boycotts, and even violence to publicize a group's cause and apply direct pressure on the government. From the veterans marching for benefits after the Civil War to the farmers converging on Washington during the 1980s, Americans have frequently taken to the streets to state their case and influence policy. By resorting to direct action, such groups hope to call attention to injustices and stimulate others to take action. For a group long on members but short on funds, a series of public demonstrations can, in some instances, be as effective as a well-heeled professional lobbyist plying the Washington cocktail-party circuit.

Like all other strategies, however, direct action has limitations. For one thing, it may be disadvantageous for a group that seeks wide-based public support. Strikes, sit-ins, and demonstrations run the risk of alienating potentially sympathetic people who may agree with the goal but reject the methods used to achieve it. While many Americans welcome the correction of injustices, they tolerate only a narrow range of corrective approaches. They reject the use of any tactic that violates their norm of political conduct. During the height of civil rights and anti-Vietnam war demonstrations, Sam Hayakawa, an obscure college president in California, was able to mount a successful campaign for the Senate by appealing to what he called the "silent majority" of citizens who disapproved of violent political protest.

Influencing Elections

In addition to grass-roots efforts, interest groups often throw themselves directly into the political fray by aiding candidates for public office. Although interest groups (unlike parties) do not run candidates for office under their own banners, they do contribute money and other forms of political support. Indeed, how better to

★ **Table 10-1**
Contributions of leading PACs to political candidates, 1987–88 eighteen-month election cycle

PAC	Contributions
Democratic Republican Independent Voter Education Committee	$4,000,000
Campaign America	3,300,000
National Congressional Club	3,200,000
American Citizens for Political Action	2,900,000
American Medical Association	2,800,000
Realtors Political Action Committee	2,700,000
National Security Political Action Committee	2,600,000
League of Conservation Voters	2,600,000
National Conservation Political Action Committee	2,100,000

SOURCE: Federal Election Commission data

influence government policy than by ensuring that favorable legislators are elected or reelected in the first place?

Groups employ a variety of tactics in support of candidates, including public education and direct mail campaigns. Many groups keep score cards on legislators and rate their performance on a numerical scale or award a letter grade, which is then made public through press releases and mailings. Some legislators decry this rating system as too narrow an assessment of their overall service to their constituency and the nation, but most recognize the value of a good rating by the Sierra Club or the National Rifle Association, especially when the time comes to seek campaign contributions.

Interest groups also form political action committees to raise funds and provide campaign volunteers. Corporate PACs, for example, may seek contributions from stockholders and executives and their families or anyone else who supports policies that are good for business.

By the end of 1984, seventeen U.S. senators reported that they had received more than $1 million in contributions from PACs during their careers. Only two years later the number of senators who had received in excess of $1 million had risen to forty-six. By 1987, a full year before the 1988 election, incumbent candidates for the Senate had already raised a total of over $20 million from PACs.[19] The impact of PACs on races for the House of Representatives has been equally strong. According to the Federal Elections Commission, 3,152 PACs contributed to House campaigns in 1985–1986; some individual candidates received as much as $1.4 million.[20] Overall, PACs provided 34 percent of all funding for House campaigns and 21 percent for Senate races. Most of the PAC money for House campaigns, moreover, went to incumbents. By the end of 1987, House incumbents had gathered $24.3 million from PACs while their challengers had received less than $250,000.[21] Overall, House and Senate incumbents received $115.3 million in PAC contributions by election day in November 1988. Table 10-1 shows the contributions made by leading PACs in the eighteen months preceding the 1988 presidential election.

While PACs provide an avenue for those who can afford to play the traditional game of big-money politics, they also open a channel for poorer people who get out their jars of pennies and send them off in support of refugees from civil war in Central America or to protect the long-toed salamander. Many interest group PACs are nonpartisan, basing support not on party but on a candidate's stand on their pet issue. Some are even cagey enough (or unprincipled enough, depending on one's point of view) to hedge their bets by contributing to candidates of both parties; no matter which candidate loses, the interest group wins.

What most interest groups are trying to achieve through PACs and campaign contributions, of course, is access. When legislation affecting their interests comes up in Congress, they want to be sure they will receive a warm reception when they come to lobby. They see a campaign contribution not as a bribe for support on a particular policy but as a down payment on a long-term friendly relationship—a relationship the member of Congress will not easily let dissolve if he or she desires future campaign support.

★ Winners and Losers: In Whose Interest?

From the oak-paneled boardrooms of corporate America to the basement office pumping out mailings in support of migrating salmon, interest groups play an integral part in the formation of government policy. Despite the enormous number and variety of groups in this country, many people wonder if most Americans are well represented in the game of interest group politics. Indeed, one of the major controversies in regard to interest groups is whether they express the needs and concerns of a broad spectrum of our society, or whether they serve instead only to advance the goals of powerful foreign and domestic elites.

As we saw in chapter 5, supporters of the pluralist theory insist that power in America is widely dispersed among many groups, whose competing ambitions help keep them in check. In their view, American politics is principally interest group politics. They argue that rival groups are likely to represent a variety of alternative views on any given issue. For each oil company seeking the right to drill offshore, for example, there will be a coalition of citizen groups trying to frustrate it. For each group trying to protect the American worker from "unfair" foreign competition there will be an organization of importers pushing for free trade. Over the long run, pluralists believe, the policies that emerge from this group competition will reflect the broad diversity of opinion in our society; each group will take its turn winning and losing in the struggle for political influence.

Pluralists also contend that membership in interest groups is spread so widely among the population that practically all Americans have an opportunity to air their views and push their agendas. In 1988, nearly 70 percent of Americans belonged to some kind of organization. Of this number 4.5 percent said they belonged to a political club, 13 percent to a labor union, and 13.7 percent to a professional organization.[22] Figure 10-3 shows memberships in various types of organizations. Although 30 percent of citizens reported no memberships, pluralists still insist that groups provide an important channel of influence for citizens who wish to express their political views. Groups, the pluralists contend, offer a way for citizens to feel more effective in influencing policy by bringing them into contact with like-minded individuals who share the same goals.

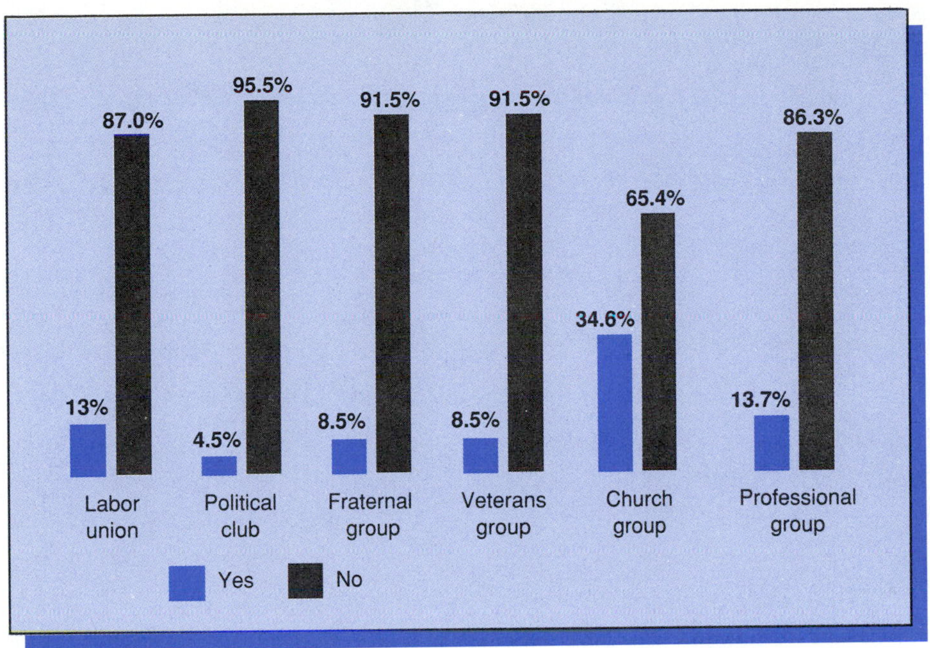

★ **Figure 10-3**
Memberships in six types of organizations, 1988 (percent)
NOTE: Individuals with multiple memberships are included in the data.
SOURCE: James Allan Davis and Tom W. Smith, *General Social Survey, 1972–1988* (Chicago: National Opinion Research Center, 1988), subfile 1988 (machine-readable data file).

Pluralists like to cite the case of Candy Lightner of California. In 1980 her thirteen-year-old daughter was walking to a church carnival when she was struck and killed by a drunk driver. Less than a week earlier, the driver had been released on bail on a hit-and-run drunk-driving charge. Lightner, turning her grief into political action, pressured the governor to appoint a task force on drunk driving and took her crusade to the media. She founded a group, Mothers Against Drunk Drivers (MADD), which persuaded all fifty states to tighten their drunk-driving laws. MADD also helped persuade the federal government to reduce federal highway grants to any state that failed to raise the drinking age to twenty-one. In just five years, the organization mushroomed to 375 chapters and 600,000 members nationwide.

As the MADD crusade shows, the pluralists are correct in pointing out that an interest group often can represent an individual in ways that a political party or an elected representative cannot. As we noted in chapter 8, the Democratic and Republican parties are not strictly issue-oriented. Both parties tend to offer only the broadest and vaguest programs in an effort not to alienate voters. Lacking party discipline, moreover, candidates sometimes abandon the principles and positions stated in the party platform hammered out during the presidential nominating convention. Furthermore, members of Congress and state legislators are elected on a geographical basis and represent districts comprising hundreds of conflicting groups. Under these circumstances, it is difficult to imagine how any individual can feel adequately represented as part of a large, mixed constituency. Interest groups,

★ Table 10-2
Number of group memberships, by income and education, 1988 (percent)

	Income			Education		
Number of memberships	*Less than $15,000*	*$15,000–25,000*	*$25,000+*	*Below high school*	*High school*	*Some college*
0	42.9%	27.9%	19.1%	45.7%	29.3%	12.6%
1	26.9	26.2	24.9	34.1	24.5	19.5
2	16.6	21.3	20.2	12.1	21.8	18.1
3+	13.6	24.6	35.8	8.2	24.4	49.8

SOURCE: James Allan Davis and Tom W. Smith, *General Social Survey, 1972–1988* (Chicago: National Opinion Research Center, 1988), subfile 1988 (machine-readable data file).

on the other hand, provide supplementary representation for specific groups by serving their unique ideological, occupational, or other goals. The American Medical Association, for instance, can speak for the interest of doctors in ways that a party or a legislator alone cannot.

Ruling elite theorists challenge many of these claims made for interest groups. They contend that interest groups do not serve a broad spectrum of our society. With the exception of such associations as the National Coalition for the Homeless and welfare rights organizations, interest groups and lobbyists work primarily for middle- or upper-class causes. "The flaw in the pluralist heaven," one scholar has quipped, "is that the heavenly chorus sings with a strong upper-class accent."[23] Indeed, polls confirm the ruling elite theorists' view that income, education, ethnicity, and other socioeconomic factors influence participation in interest groups. As table 10-2 shows, over 40 percent of people with an annual income of less than $15,000 and 45 percent of those who have not completed high school do not belong to any organized group.

Many people who depend on public and private assistance—single mothers, the elderly poor, the mentally ill, the homeless—do not belong to any effective organization that speaks on their behalf. Although examples abound of heroic efforts by disadvantaged citizens to present their case, by and large such people possess neither the financial resources nor the leadership necessary to influence the government successfully.

Advocates of the ruling elite view also reject the notion that group competition leads to a general equality and balance among interests. They see no guarantee that "ambition will counteract ambition" or that "cross-cutting allegiances" will dilute a member's devotion to a single cause. Although consumer groups and other so-called public interest lobbies may win an occasional battle, they cannot, over the long run, effectively compete against powerful corporate interests. Industry groups, such as the oil and utility lobbies, tend to be the best organized and well financed of all interests operating on the national scene. They employ legions of experts whose full-time responsibility it is to promote the group's interest, while citizen groups may be staffed by volunteers who can spare only a few hours a week away from family and work.

Powerful industry groups also have large budgets with which to court legislators and bureaucrats and to build up public support for their policy goals. They often enjoy the support of many top governmental officials who share their economic concerns and who have held, or hope to hold, managerial positions in industrial and financial institutions. And there is little indication that the influence of corporate lobbies will wane. According to recent estimates, over 80 percent of the nation's largest companies support an organized lobbying effort in Washington.

But perhaps the most significant aspect of interest group representation, ruling elite theorists insist, is that it tends to favor the status quo. Although interest groups' goals may vary, few organizations that acquire a stake in the existing order are likely to push for major social and political change. "Interest group conflict," one pair of scholars concludes, "reflects merely the most visible disputes between factions within the established elite. Business and labor may contest over the raising of the minimum wage, but both unite to keep demands for radical reform out of the pressure system."[24]

Which of these two conflicting views of interest groups is right? Is it possible that interest groups can provide ordinary citizens with added opportunities to participate effectively in politics and also can serve as the tools of powerful elites? People's perceptions of the role played by interest groups in our society, like those of other political issues, vary with their views of the political order. Our increasingly interdependent world will certainly continue to serve up new and complex disputes, and most political activists will see the collective action engaged in by interest groups as the most promising way to affect public policy. Even if ruling elite theorists are right in perceiving an imbalance in group representation—and their arguments are persuasive—groups, not single individuals, will remain the basic units of influence in our society. One relatively new type of group, the so-called citizens' lobby, may provide an avenue for even greater public involvement in government.

★ Battling Special Interests: The Rise of Citizens' Lobbies

One of the most interesting developments over the years has been the spread of **public interest groups** or citizens' lobbies, organized to promote the "public interest." Seeking to extend interest group representation to a broader segment of society, many individuals have put their faith in such groups as Common Cause, the Environmental Defense Fund, and the Moral Majority. These and other citizens' lobbies purport to represent the interests of society as a whole rather than just those of their own members. They claim to provide a necessary counterbalance to vested interests, such as the corporate and labor lobbies, which have tended to dominate the Washington political scene and the national dialogue on issues.

Common Cause is one of the best known of these organizations and among the best financed. Founded in 1970 by John Gardner, a former secretary of the Department of Health, Education, and Welfare, Common Cause has pressed for what it regards as common public goals, with an emphasis on structural and procedural reform, a more equitable tax system, and reform of campaign financing.

★ Ralph Nader and staff from various public interest groups prepare a frontal assault on the Capitol. These and other citizens' lobbies hailing from across the ideological spectrum claim to battle special interests in the name of all Americans.

Its members are regularly polled to learn which national and local issues require the most immediate attention.

Over the years, Common Cause has achieved some notable legislative and legal victories. By filing suits in federal courts and by employing the same professional lobbying techniques used by other interest groups, it spearheaded the effort to ratify the Twenty-sixth Amendment, which lowered the legal voting age to eighteen, and helped force the enactment of the 1974 Federal Election Campaign Act. More recently Common Cause has turned its attention to the role of political action committees, launching a major publicity and lobbying campaign to reduce their financial impact on political campaigns.

Also prominent is Ralph Nader's group, Public Citizen, an umbrella organization that has raised and distributed funds for a variety of affiliated groups. Although not strictly a membership-based organization like Common Cause, Public Citizen has been supported by thousands of contributors, as well as by foundation grants, book sales, and Nader's own lecturing and writing fees. With dozens of paid professionals on its staff and hundreds of volunteers, Public Citizen has pursued a broad range of consumer, environmental, legal, and economic issues.

The techniques employed by Nader's Raiders, as they have been called, have been similar to those used by other interest groups. While they may not have plied members of Congress with campaign contributions, they have prepared testimony for committee hearings, helped draft legislation, stimulated grass-roots lobbying campaigns, and filed lawsuits in federal courts. And they have been able to claim some striking successes. They helped force the repeal of the oil depletion allowance, effectively petitioned the Food and Drug Administration to ban a number of hazardous products, prevented states from prohibiting advertising of prescription drugs, and helped form dozens of independent, student-run public interest research groups around the country. In 1988 Nader even helped win passage of a proposition intended to slash automobile insurance rates in California.

As the founder and principal spokesperson for the group, Ralph Nader has commanded the kind of media attention no ordinary lobbyist can match. With his rumpled suits and drooping socks, Nader has become a familiar figure on the political scene, a crusading folk hero to millions of disgruntled citizens. He first gained national attention in 1965 with the publication of his book *Unsafe at Any Speed,* in which he charged that the Chevrolet Corvair had such fundamental safety defects that it was dangerous to drive. (General Motors stopped producing the Corvair shortly thereafter.) After winning an out-of-court settlement against General Motors for invasion of privacy (the company presumably had tried to discredit him by prying into his sex life and attempting to lure him with a prostitute), Nader used the funds to institutionalize his activities by forming the Center for the Study of Responsive Law in 1969 and Public Citizen in 1973. Not all of his actions have been popular. He has been criticized both for his intentions and for his methods. Some people have accused him of attacking the free enterprise system, and others have scolded him for battling too long on too wide a range of issues.

The most persistent criticism of public interest groups in general has been hurled against the use of the term "public interest." Citizen groups claim that their interests deserve special attention because they are looking out for the general good of society. Some critics argue, however, that most public interest groups are liberal and aligned with the Democratic party, and thus cannot claim to represent all major elements of American public opinion. In fact, they argue, many policies favored by public interest groups are detrimental to large segments of society. As one scholar puts it:

> There are those who argue that consumer, environmental, and other so-called "public interest" issues are in reality middle and upper-middle class concerns which are addressed for the most part at the expense of the poor, the aged, and urban and ethnic minorities. Environmentalists often advocate strict zoning laws and growth curbs on city developments, while others argue that these policies discriminate against the less affluent and translate directly into loss of jobs and local economic growth.[25]

Indeed, many of the so-called special-interest groups representing industry, business, and the medical profession also contend that their goal is to serve all of the public, not just their membership.

Public interest groups, in response, contend that the term "public interest" does not apply strictly to middle-class or liberal concerns, because consumer, health, and environmental issues affect everyone. The prospect that some jobs may be lost over the short term does not contradict the fact that all segments of our society—not just one social or economic group—will benefit from safer prescription drugs, cleaner air, campaign spending reform, and more responsive government. As David Cohen, former president of Common Cause, remarked, "We are *a* citizens' lobby, *a* public interest group. The difference between 'a' and 'the' is very important. We don't define 'the public interest' in the sense that one group represents it while others don't."[26]

Many conservatives remain convinced nonetheless that public interest lobbies are interested primarily in liberal causes. Their response in the late 1970s was to

★ Jerry Falwell and the Moral Majority added a new dimension to lobbying efforts. His organization provided a forum for the religious right who felt their views were being ignored by liberal interest groups.

establish their own groups to counter what they saw as the liberal agenda. Perhaps the best-known conservative public interest lobby to emerge on the political scene was the Moral Majority. Founded by the Reverend Jerry Falwell, a Baptist minister from Virginia, the Moral Majority helped focus public attention on many of the New Right's causes, including abortion, prayer in schools, and a hawkish policy toward the Soviet Union. The Moral Majority also provided strong support for conservative candidates, including Ronald Reagan, who found common ideological ground with the religious right. At the height of its popularity the Moral Majority boasted a mailing list of six million citizens. In 1984 the group raised $11 million for political lobbying.

The religious right suffered a series of setbacks, however, beginning in 1987, when scandal tainted the reputation of some television evangelists. Moreover, the Reverend Falwell, not personally accused of any wrongdoing, withdrew from the Moral Majority's leadership to tend his flock in Virginia. Another television evangelist, Pat Robertson, promoted New Right causes not by lobbying but by seeking the Republican nomination for president in 1988. Although Robertson's bid for the nomination failed, his campaign attracted a significant amount of support in some states, and he vowed to return in 1992. With 35 percent of the American public identifying themselves as conservative, the potential political influence of New Right public interest groups remained strong.[27]

Despite the battle over which groups can legitimately claim to represent the public interest, the citizens' lobbies have had an impact on policy making. Few sectors of our society and government have escaped the probes and challenges of consumer advocates, environmentalists, antipornography activists, civil rights leaders, pro- and anti-abortion groups, and others who claim to champion the public good. One student of public interest groups concludes that "these organizations are slowly changing the overall environment within which governmental officials formulate public policy. . . . The opinion they can arouse, the bad publicity they can generate, the lawsuits they can file, are all factors that are relevant to the deliberations of those who must make policy decisions."[28]

★ Joining a Group: The Benefits and Limitations

We may wonder why some people, and not others, join an interest group. Why do some people spend the time and money to belong to a civic organization, labor union, or citizens' lobby, while others whose interests and goals are similar remain part of the potential and not the actual group? Are those who join an interest group more politically motivated and aware than the rest of society, or do they expect to derive benefits that have little to do with politics?

The question is an intriguing one, in part because observers sometimes wonder whether the disadvantages of joining an interest group outweigh its advantages. Despite the appeal of engaging in collective action, membership in an interest group has some limitations and drawbacks. Because many interest groups have evolved into large organizations with thousands of members, the individual member may become only a small cog in a large machine. Few exciting opportunities for political action may be offered, even in a public interest group such as Common Cause, which claims to be a "citizens' lobby." The member who pays dues and receives information on its activities may regard his or her contribution as insignificant in comparison with the efforts of those who work directly to influence policy makers. Volunteers often find themselves doing menial chores, such as stuffing envelopes, that are not likely to satisfy the desire to be directly involved in policy making.

In addition, many interest groups tend to be led by a small cadre of active elites. The members of a large interest group often elect their leaders from among candidates sanctioned by a dominant or ruling clique that represents the group year after year in its relations with governmental officials. Though some organizations may place great emphasis on democratic controls over internal policy making, the members of others wonder whether the ruling clique accurately reflects their own policy views. An individual may contribute money and other means of support to an organization with only limited knowledge of the group's day-to-day operations and policies.

In fact, some groups that raise big money face potential disputes as to how the funds are spent. The conservative National Congressional Club raised $9.3 million in 1982, but gave only $150,000 in support of candidates; the remaining 98 percent of the money reportedly went to the club's operating expenses.[29] Thus while a member may obtain satisfaction from belonging to a large organization, he or she will be unlikely to have a strong personal influence on its policies and tactics.

What, then, are the advantages of belonging to an interest group? Why do many Americans join and continue to maintain their membership in a large organized group? Part of the answer can be found in our earlier discussion of types of interest groups. Obviously, people create and/or join such groups to meet a need or solve a problem, either ideological, ethnic, economic, or associated with (for want of a better term) the public interest. Helpful as these categories may be, we still need to dig deeper into the human motivations that lead people to spend the time, money, and energy on group activity.

One of the most intriguing explanations is offered by the economist Mancur Olson.[30] Olson argues that it is not rational for people to join a large organization where their influence will probably not be felt, especially if they can benefit from its activities without having to pay dues or other costs. Why should a college professor, for example, join a union pressing for higher teacher salaries and smaller classes if she will gain these benefits whether or not she is a dues-paying member? Unless she is forced to join through peer pressure or other means, why not simply sit back and reap the rewards of other people's labors?

Olson maintains that people will join an interest group such as a labor union or professional association only if their individual participation is considered significant (thus the size of the group becomes a relevant factor), if they are coerced into joining (for instance, through a "union shop"), or if they expect to receive **selective benefits** available only to members. If the professor joins the union, she will do so not necessarily because the union will press for higher wages but because it may provide her with new professional contacts, low-cost health insurance, or the opportunity to attend a convention in Hawaii.

In effect, Olson challenges the pluralist view that interest groups arise out of common political interests and serve primarily to translate people's political dreams into reality. He insists that, on the contrary, most large economic groups arise—and succeed—by also supplying members with selective benefits that are essentially nonpolitical. "The common characteristic which distinguishes all of the large economic groups with significant lobbying organizations," he writes, "is that these groups are also organized for some *other* purpose. The large and powerful economic lobbies are in fact the by-products of organizations that obtain their strength and support because they perform some function in addition to lobbying for collective goods."[31]

Olson's view also suggests why many people remain part of an interest group despite the absence of internal democratic controls. As long as the organization does a good job of providing benefits and achieving its goals, the individual member may not care about the nature of its internal operations or its responsiveness to the membership.

Is Olson correct in his assumptions? Do people tend to join interest groups for nonpolitical reasons? Labor unions and business lobbies certainly offer their members potential financial benefits. Good scholarship and not just cynicism leads us to recognize that when unions unfurl the banner of worker solidarity or a business leader speaks with reverence about the sanctity of government noninterference in the private sector, personal finances as well as political ideology may be at stake.

But what of interest groups that provide no apparent economic benefit to their members? What leads citizens to toil endlessly (and donate millions) for a nuclear freeze, animal rights, or protection of political prisoners in Latin America? True, a citizen who works for arms control may hope that reduced military spending will lead to lower taxes. The reasons for joining interest groups, however, can also satisfy social, moral, and even psychological needs.

A desire for social contacts is one explanation for individuals' desire to take part in noneconomic interest groups. The wish to be with like-minded citizens, to make new friends, and in general to enjoy the personal bonds of community activity probably helps fill the ranks of some groups.

★ These concerned citizens made their point directly to their state representative (*back to camera*) at the Georgia capitol. Their efforts in working for the passage of the Equal Rights Amendment were not rewarded, but they might have derived some satisfaction from being an integral part of the ratification process.

Few people would deny, moreover, that while economic reward is a value held dear in our capitalistic and highly materialistic society, many Americans are also willing to make large sacrifices in the pursuit of moral and ideological goals. In a recent survey, both liberal and conservative contributors to PACs were asked why they were willing to spend money on political issues. Over 60 percent of conservatives and 45 percent of liberals listed "influencing policy" as their major goal. A little more than 25 percent of liberals and conservatives said that furthering their career was the most important reason for political contributions.[32] Indeed, citizens may spend large amounts of money pressing a legal challenge to laws banning prayer in public schools, while others risk life and limb to block trains carrying nuclear weapons to America's military bases. Historically, Americans have pursued cherished political ideals with missionary zeal at home and abroad. Increasingly these ideals have been pursued through collective action, by citizens joined together to muster their resources in an interest group.

Take the case of Dr. Helen Caldicott, president emeritus of Physicians for Social Responsibility (PSR) and founder of Women's Action for Nuclear Disarmament (WAND). During the course of her work as a pediatrician, Caldicott realized that doctors were in a unique position to communicate to the public the medical and psychiatric consequences of the arms race and nuclear war. She and other physicians in PSR crisscrossed the nation to describe the medical consequences of a nuclear war, labeling it a "final epidemic" that would defy treatment by the world's medical community. PSR chapters around the country provided 1,500 speakers committed to public education about nuclear war. Partly as a result of PSR actions,

professional medical associations passed resolutions urging physicians to try to prevent nuclear war, two-thirds of American medical schools began to teach about the medical effects of nuclear war, and Congress resisted President Reagan's requests for increases in what PSR described as futile civil defense programs. Showing that interest groups and lobbying can be a global operation, PSR even took its case to the Soviet Union.

In 1980 Caldicott founded WAND to mobilize women, who polls showed were overwhelmingly in favor of ending the nuclear arms race. WAND made an explicit pitch to mothers to protect their children's futures. WAND's members have included such celebrities as Joanne Woodward, who described how she first became politically aware when, after the birth of her first child, she agonized over the dilemma of raising her child in a world threatened by weapons of mass destruction.

★ Regulating Interest Groups

As we have seen, the value of interest groups is a subject of continuing controversy. Some critics take the extreme view that the activities of interest groups are inconsistent with democratic government. They believe that interest groups represent narrow concerns that are antithetical to the general welfare of society and therefore should be suppressed. Others insist, however, that the problems and dangers surrounding interest groups stem mainly from secrecy and the excessive amounts of money their lobbyists throw around. They contend that most abuses could be prevented if interest groups' activities were given greater visibility and if lobbyists' spending were restricted and fully reported.

In any case, the growing strength and influence of interest groups have not been ignored by government. Congressional efforts to control lobbying have focused on three major areas: public disclosure of interest groups' lobbying activities, limits on campaign spending by PACs, and monitoring of lobbying by former government officials. Although the public has been concerned about lobbying since the founding of the nation, it was not until the 1930s that Congress began to pass legislation designed to regulate interest group activities. In 1935 and 1936, it passed laws requiring the registration of lobbyists for public utilities and shipping firms who appeared before congressional committees or certain regulatory agencies. In 1938 the Foreign Agents Registration Act required lobbyists for foreign governments to register with the Justice Department.

In 1946 Congress passed the omnibus Federal Regulation of Lobbying Act, designed not to restrict the activities of interest groups but merely to disclose them. Enacted as part of a general scheme to reorganize Congress, this law requires the registration of any group that "solicits, collects, or receives money or any other thing of value to be used principally to aid . . . the passage or defeat of any legislation by the Congress of the United States." Lobbyists are required to register with the House and the Senate, and to file quarterly financial reports with the House.

The 1946 Lobbying Act, however, contained significant loopholes and was virtually unenforceable. Under the language of the law and subsequent Supreme Court interpretations,[33] only those groups whose "principal purpose" is to influence Congress need to register and report their lobbying expenses. Many large lobbying groups, such as the National Association of Manufacturers, have been able to avoid the law's reporting requirements for years by claiming that lobbying is only an incidental part of their overall program, not their principal purpose.[34] The 1946 act, moreover, pertains only to the lobbying of Congress. Groups that lobby the executive branch or use some other method to influence public policy are not required to disclose their activities.

Numerous efforts have been made since 1946 to tighten the loopholes in the Lobbying Act and expand its regulations. Congress has been deluged with proposals to replace it with more comprehensive controls. It has resisted almost all of them. Despite disagreements over details, most reformers contend that a good lobby disclosure law should contain at least four provisions: (1) coverage of the executive branch as well as Congress; (2) a broader definition of lobbying groups to include all organizations that attempt to influence legislation; (3) comprehensive reporting of all major lobbying expenditures and activities, including those aimed at the grassroots level; and (4) strict enforcement provisions.

Although Congress has not confronted the problem of lobbying directly, it has found other means to place some limits on interest group activities. One method has been the regulation of campaign contributions by PACs. As chapter 9 explains, interest groups are prohibited from directly contributing money to a candidate's campaign, and must channel funds to candidates through political action committees. While campaign spending legislation has not eliminated the importance of PACs or their money, their disclosure provisions and oversight by the Federal Elections Commission have forced candidates to let the public know which interest groups are paying their bills.

A final approach to control of lobbying involves the activities of former government officials. A successful lobbyist, as we have seen, often relies on inside information and contacts within the government. Not surprisingly, former high government officials often become lobbyists, sometimes representing interest groups before the very agencies where they used to work (see table 10–3). Congress,

★ Table 10-3
Percentage of lobbyists with previous government experience, 1983

	Percent	
Federal government		45.0%
Congressional	16.9%	
Executive commissions	22.0	
Other	6.1	
State and local governments		9.4
All levels of government		54.4%

SOURCE: Robert A. Salisbury, "Washington Lobbyists: A Collective Portrait," in *Interest Group Politics,* eds. Allan J. Cigler and Burdett A. Loomis, 2d ed. (Washington, D.C.: Congressional Quarterly Press, 1986), p. 153.

recognizing the unfair advantage former officials may have in dealing with friends and associates in government, passed the **Ethics in Government Act** in 1978. This act prohibits former high officials from engaging in lobbying activities for one year after leaving government service. During the Reagan administration, dozens of officials and former officials were accused of profiting from their positions in government, and several were brought to trial for violating the Ethics in Government Act.

In late 1988, Congress passed a bill to place further restrictions on lobbying by former federal officials. For the first time, lobbying by members of Congress and their top aides would be restricted for one year after they left office. The bill also would have provided additional restrictions on lobbying by former executive officials. President Reagan, however, arguing that such restrictions were unnecessary and counterproductive, pocket-vetoed the measure; that is, he neglected to sign it before Congress adjourned, thus letting it die.

Congress's limited efforts to control lobbying activities highlights the dilemma that interest groups represent. On the one hand, interest groups provide the government and the public with information on a wealth of public issues. In many respects, lobbyists have become integral to the legislative process in America. On the other hand, interest groups also represent the worst of big money, influence peddling, and privileged special access to government. Because money is crucial in elections, it is easy to understand why incumbent politicians, engaged in never-ending fund raising and campaigning, are reluctant to kill the golden goose. In seeking to limit interest group influence, moreover, they also risk depriving citizens of the opportunity to pool their meager resources and help shape public policy. One thing is certain: given the increasing politicization of many aspects of life, citizens with special interests will continue to band together to publicize their causes and fill politicians' campaign war chests in the hope of staking a claim on America's national agenda.

★ Summary

Interest groups and lobbying have long been part of the American political scene. Historically, special interests have been looked upon with distrust by many citizens, who have feared that these well-financed organizations could buy influence in Washington. While many people remain suspicious of interest groups, others see them as offering an opportunity for average people to work together to influence public policy.

Recent years have seen an explosion of interest groups in response to the emergence of such issues as abortion, women's rights, consumer protection, and the environment. Globalization and interdependence have also spawned new foreign policy interest groups. The importance of the United States in the world has led many foreign governments and interests to launch lobbying and public relations campaigns in Washington. The personal economic benefits that interest group membership can bring have also encouraged many citizens to join such organizations.

Along with the proliferation of groups have come many new tactics to influence public policy. The lobbyists' traditional tools—campaign contributions and other monetary inducements—are now supplemented by technical expertise and data, media campaigns, and mobilization of the public. Clever use of these resources by interest groups has in turn created a degree of dependency on the part of politicians. Congressmembers' dependency on interest groups makes them reluctant to limit the groups' activities and to deemphasize the role of money in politics. Although interest groups have succeeded in providing access to the public policy process for many citizens whose influence would be marginal if they acted alone, it is still big business, big labor, and well-educated and well-paid individuals who join and benefit most from membership in interest groups.

★ Key Terms

Ethics in Government Act
interest group
iron triangle
lobbyist
public interest groups
selective benefits
single-issue groups

★ Notes

1. Robert J. Hrebenar and Ruth K. Scott, *Interest Group Politics in America* (Englewood Cliffs, N.J.: Prentice-Hall, 1982), p. 21. Additional information provided by the National Rifle Association.
2. See David B. Truman, *The Governmental Process: Political Interests and Public Opinion,* 2d ed. (New York: Knopf, 1971).
3. Burt Solomon, "How Washington Works," in *American Government 87/88,* ed. Bruce Stinebrickner (Guilford, Conn.: Dushkin, 1987), p. 185.
4. This list is adapted from Burdett A. Loomis and Allan J. Cigler, "Introduction: The Changing Nature of Interest Group Politics," in *Interest Group Politics,* 2d ed., ed. Cigler and Loomis (Washington, D.C.: Congressional Quarterly Press, 1986), p. 1.
5. See Eric M. Uslaner, "One Nation, Many Voices: Interest Groups in Foreign Policy Making," in Cigler and Loomis, *Interest Group Politics,* pp. 236–257.

6. The list is partially based on Thomas L. Brewer, *American Foreign Policy: A Contemporary Introduction,* 2d ed. (Englewood Cliffs, N.J.: Prentice-Hall, 1986), p. 86.
7. Ibid., pp. 83–84.
8. Charles W. Kegley, Jr., and Eugene R. Wittkopf, *American Foreign Policy: Pattern and Process,* 3d ed. (New York: St. Martin's Press, 1987), p. 278.
9. Steven Emerson, "Dutton of Arabia," in *Behind the Scenes in American Government: Personalities and Politics,* 5th ed., ed. Peter Woll (Boston: Little, Brown, 1985), p. 93.
10. Allan J. Cigler and Burdett A. Loomis, "Moving On: Interests, Power, and Politics in the 1980s," in their *Interest Group Politics,* p. 312.
11. Albert R. Hunt, "The Washington Power Brokers," in Woll, *Behind the Scenes,* pp. 84–90.
12. "The Washington Lobby: A Continuing Effort to Influence Government Policy," *Congressional Quarterly Guide to Current American Government,* Fall 1987, p. 79.
13. Hrebenar and Scott, *Interest Group Politics,* p. 137.
14. Evan Thomas and Thomas M. De Frank, "Mike Deaver's Rise and Fall," *Newsweek,* March 23, 1987, pp. 22–23.
15. Lee Epstein and C. K. Rowland, "Interest Groups in the Courts: Do Groups Fare Better?" in Cigler and Loomis, *Interest Group Politics,* p. 280.
16. NAACP v. Button (1963).
17. Epstein and Rowland, "Interest Groups in the Courts," p. 279.
18. Tina Rosenberg, "Diminishing Returns: The False Promise of Direct Mail," in Stinebrickner, *American Government 87/88,* pp. 173–174.
19. *New York Times,* August 10, 1987, p. 13.
20. *New York Times,* July 7, 1988, p. 7.
21. *Wall Street Journal,* March 22, 1988, p. 1.
22. James Allan Davis and Tom W. Smith, *General Social Surveys, 1972–1988* (Chicago: National Opinion Research Center, 1988), subfile 1988 (machine-readable data file).
23. E. E. Schattschneider, *The Semisovereign People: A Realist's View of Democracy in America* (New York: Holt, Rinehart & Winston, 1960), p. 35.
24. Thomas R. Dye and L. Harmon Zeigler, *The Irony of Democracy,* 4th ed. (Pacific Grove, Calif.: Brooks/Cole, 1978), p. 214.
25. D. Stephen Cupps, "Emerging Problems of Citizen Participation," *Public Opinion Review* 37 (September–October 1977): 481.
26. Quoted in *Congressional Quarterly Weekly Report,* May 15, 1976, p. 1197.
27. Davis and Smith, *General Social Surveys,* subfile 1986.
28. Jeffrey M. Berry, *Lobbying for the People: The Political Behavior of Public Interest Groups* (Princeton, N.J.: Princeton University Press, 1977), p. 289.
29. Rosenberg, "Diminishing Returns," p. 173.
30. Mancur Olson, Jr., *The Logic of Collective Action,* rev. ed. (Cambridge, Mass.: Harvard University Press, 1971).
31. Ibid., p. 132.
32. John C. Green and James L. Guth, "Big Bucks and Petty Cash: Party and Interest Group Activists in American Politics," in Cigler and Loomis, *Interest Group Politics,* p. 106.
33. United States v. Harris (1954).
34. Norman J. Ornstein and Shirley Elder, *Interest Groups, Lobbying, and Policymaking* (Washington, D.C.: Congressional Quarterly Press, 1978), p. 104.

★ For Further Reading

Berry, Jeffrey. *Lobbying for the People: The Political Behavior of Public Interest Groups.* Princeton, N.J.: Princeton University Press, 1977.

Cigler, Allan J., and Burdette A. Loomis, eds. *Interest Group Politics.* 2d ed. Washington, D.C.: Congressional Quarterly Press, 1986.

Greenwald, Carol S. *Group Power.* New York: Praeger, 1977.

Hrebenar, Ronald J., and Ruth K. Scott. *Interest Group Politics in America.* Englewood Cliffs, N.J.: Prentice-Hall, 1982.

Lowi, Theodore. *The End of Liberalism.* New York: Norton, 1969.

MacFarland, Andrew S. *Common Cause: Lobbying in the Public Interest.* Chatham, N.J.: Chatham House, 1984.

Olson, Mancur, Jr. *The Logic of Collective Action.* Rev. ed. Cambridge, Mass.: Harvard University Press, 1971.

Ornstein, Norman J., and Shirley Elder. *Interest Groups, Lobbying, and Policy Making.* Washington, D.C.: Congressional Quarterly Press, 1978.

Sabato, Larry. *PAC Power: Inside the World of Political Action Committees.* New York: Norton, 1984.

Sorauf, Frank. *Money in American Elections.* Boston: Little, Brown, 1988.

Ted Koppel, host of ABC's Nightline: Talk about television for a moment. It has a tendency because so many people get everything of what they savor, flavor from a campaign through television, it has a tendency to dominate and—

Presidential candidate Michael Dukakis (breaking in): That may be the understatement of the night.

CHAPTER ELEVEN

MEDIA

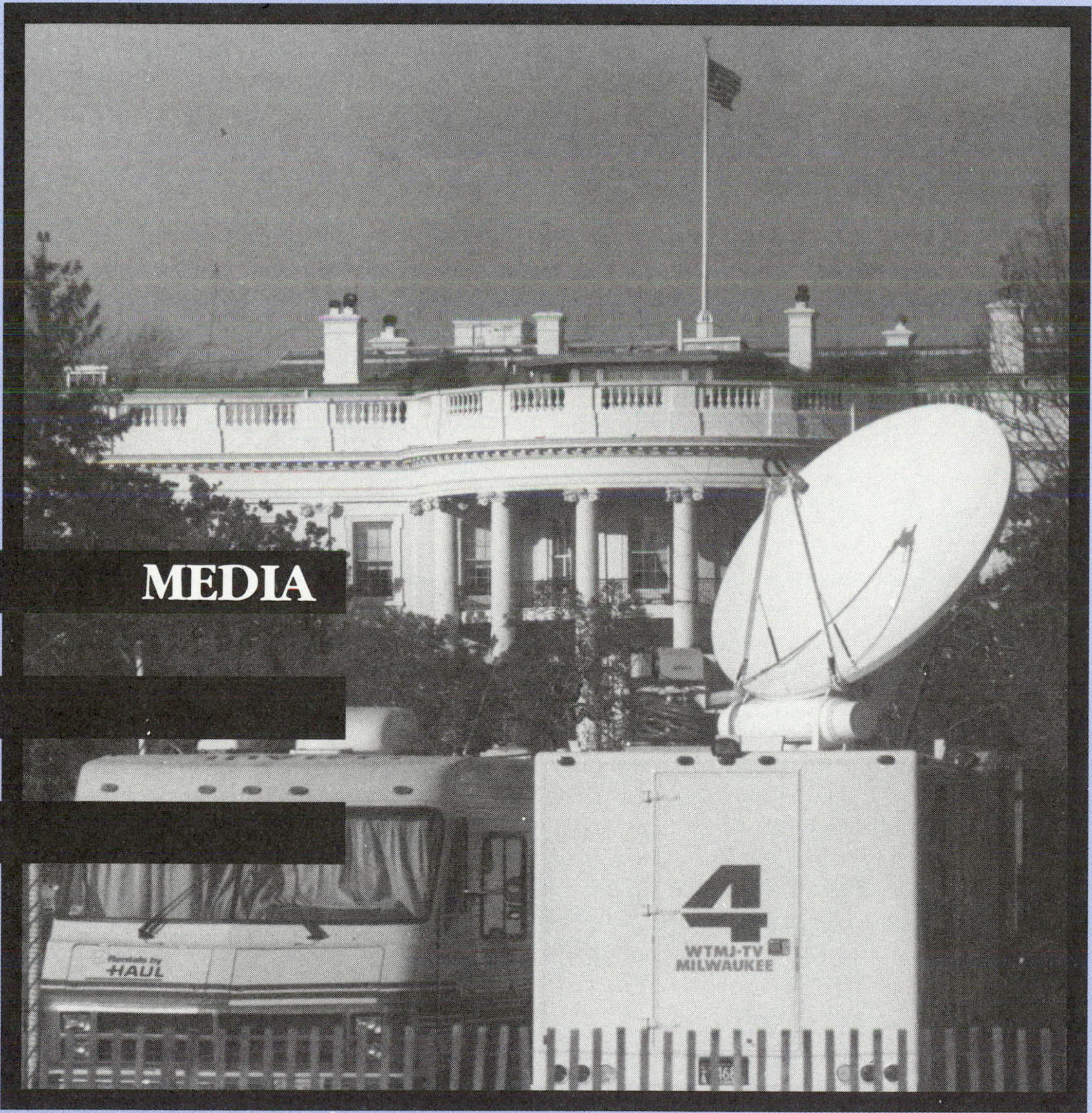

Spreading the Word: The Media, Global Telecommunications, and American Politics

At first the image on the TV screen seems blurred, but the reporter's commentary helps orient the viewer. Sharing a sight heretofore seen only by combat pilots, millions of viewers watch as American F-111 supersonic bombers attack a Libyan airfield. Air Force video cameras, mounted in the bellies of the bombers, record the attack and only hours later an anxious world views—in the comfort of their own homes—these startling images of America's latest international confrontation.

Battle scenes, of course, are nothing new. Since its invention, photography has been used to record battles for subsequent viewing by military analysts and the general public. What was significant about the video of the Libyan bombing raids in 1986 was the speed with which the pictures were broadcast, affording millions of people almost instant access to this important story. Only hours after the bombers returned to their bases in Great Britain, the attack had created controversy and conflict at home and abroad.

Most of us in America take for granted the electronic telecommunications marvels that bring news from the farthest reaches of the globe. But the ways in which news is reported have vast political and social implications. Because of their commanding presence, television and other media have great relevance to students of politics and government. The media, after all, supply much of the information on which we base our political judgments and actions. Because most citizens have few alternative sources of information, we are enormously dependent on the media for our awareness of current issues, political candidates, and changes in the ongoing struggle for power. We depend on the media particularly to keep us informed of national and international events at great distances from us.

Television and radio have become so pervasive that they not only provide the bulk of family entertainment but have become the main sources of information about world events. Table 11-1 shows the growth of broadcasting since 1950. Some observers fear that the people who control television may be able to manipulate our views and opinions. If we do indeed receive most of our information about world events from television—and are not very critical about what we receive—those who dominate the medium may have inordinate power to mold our perspectives on politics. In this chapter we will examine the media and American politics in order to find answers to these questions:

- What are the various media and how do they report on politics and society?
- How have changes in global communications technology influenced foreign policy?

- What is the media's role in political campaigns?
- What is the relationship between the media and the government?
- Who owns the media?
- Are the media biased in reporting the news?

★ Defining and Categorizing the Media

When the sociologist Marshall McLuhan remarked nearly thirty years ago that "the medium is the message," many observers of society nodded sagely, though many may have wondered in private what he was talking about. Today McLuhan's point should be easily understood by a generation raised on television: though the news may be important, it is also important *how* we obtain our news. News is flashed instantly around the globe by satellite and fiber optic cable. News is often interpreted, condensed, manufactured, or even ignored by the enormous media corporations and government information agencies. Thus the "story" for students of politics and society is not just the event being reported but also the way the story is presented by the **mass media.**

Any form of communication generally accessible to large numbers of people can be labeled a mass medium. The most important mass media in terms of news in the United States are television, newspapers, radio, and magazines.

Television

It is difficult for anyone born after 1940 to remember a time without television. Today television is the common denominator of American society, providing us with our news, our entertainment, and, according to some analysts, our view of the world. Regular television broadcasts began in the United States in 1941. After wartime restrictions on the manufacturing of receivers were removed, the television industry blossomed. By 1949 a million receivers were in use in the United States.

★ Table 11-1
Number of radio and television stations in the United States, 1950–1989

	1950	*1960*	*1970*	*1980*	*1989*
Radio					
AM	2,086	3,398	4,269	4,558	4,932
FM	733	688	2,476	4,190	5,529
Television	97	573	872	1,013	1,395

SOURCE: *Broadcasting/Cable Yearbook, 1989* (Washington, D.C.: Broadcasting Publications, 1989), p. H59.

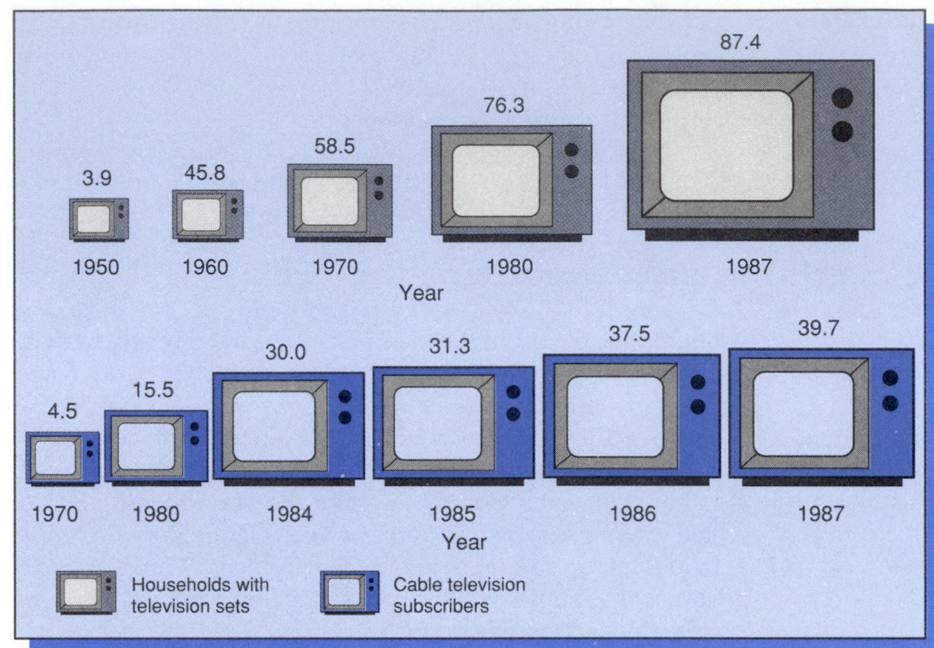

Figure 11-1
Number of households in the United States with television sets, 1950–1987, and with cable, 1970–1987 (millions)
SOURCE: U.S. Bureau of the Census, *Statistical Abstract of the United States, 1988* (Washington, D.C.: U.S. Government Printing Office, 1989) p. 523.

Two years later the number of TV sets totaled ten million. Figure 11-1 chronicles the growth of the television industry in America. As access grew, so did America's reliance on television as its primary source of information about the world.

Despite the rapidly increasing popularity of TV, the television industry was slow to develop its news and information programming. Until 1956, the major networks devoted little more than fifteen minutes a day to newsreels and headlines. Technology severely restricted television's mobility, and political coverage was usually limited to staged speeches and news conferences.[1] In 1956 the NBC network began broadcasting *The Huntley-Brinkley Report,* with Chet Huntley and David Brinkley, a nightly review that established the basic format of the news and information programs seen on television to this day.

By the end of the 1960s, television news had become big business. It earned the networks millions of dollars and proved more profitable than all but a handful of entertainment programs. As equipment became more portable, it became possible to provide more coverage of live events. Television's often dramatic coverage of the Vietnam war focused the nation's attention on what had been an obscure and distant conflict. Television also became a vehicle through which opposition to the war was expressed:

> As protest against the war rose, the nation and the world witnessed demonstrations, marches, riots, and acts of government repression. . . . Television's expanded news delivery function gave rise to new strategies to capture the attention of television news. Politicians saw the importance and power of television in campaigning and in governing, and protest groups developed techniques to make themselves "newsworthy."[2]

★ Images of war: children fleeing a napalm bomb attack in Vietnam. This powerful photo, along with a nightly barrage of others on television, fueled the anti-Vietnam war movement in the United States.

Other technological changes, especially the proliferation of cable television delivery systems, have also had dramatic influence on news reporting. Cable systems, once found only in remote areas where broadcast reception was poor or nonexistent, now serve most urban and rural areas of the nation. The 9,300 cable systems in the United States, reaching 25,000 communities, have expanded the national audience that was originally served by the three major commercial broadcasting networks (along with the smaller educational stations).[3] As any viewer soon learns, cable networks provide a vast array of programming, from sports to twenty-four-hour-a-day shopping from the comfort of one's own home. Today nearly 50 percent of American households subscribe to cable service. The major networks have seen their share of the TV market fall by 25 percent as increasing numbers of viewers tune in movies and news offered by cable systems.[4]

Cable's most noted commercial news service is the Cable News Network, or CNN. Though other networks would disagree with its boast of being "the world's most important network," CNN does provide round-the-clock news service nationwide. Along with the standard "nightly news" format employed by the major networks, CNN provides nearly continuous and unedited coverage of events as they unfold. Many government agencies, foreign embassies, and lobbyists in Washington stay tuned to CNN to keep up with the latest news.[5] During a Middle East hostage crisis in the summer of 1989, President Bush reportedly kept abreast of the latest developments by watching CNN. The public's ability to view events in "real time" can be unnerving for political media specialists, who seek to manage the news and protect the image of a candidate or government official who may mis-speak in front of the cameras.

Another politically significant service offered by the cable networks is C-SPAN, a cable-delivered service that offers continuous live coverage of Congress and other political events in Washington. Although the coverage is strictly managed by the

★ Community cable systems and inexpensive satellite receivers have brought television to virtually every corner of America. Satellite dishes have also made it possible for college students and other interested viewers to receive programming from the Soviet Union and many other nations as they are broadcast.

leaders of Congress (to avoid, among other things, having a member caught napping or chatting during a colleague's speech), C-SPAN does provide a glimpse inside the workings of government previously available to only a few Americans. Surveys indicated that in 1988, 21.6 million households watched C-SPAN.[6]

Cable service has also brought the American viewer local news not always found on the commercial stations. Many companies set aside a channel for local stories ranging from high school sports to city council meetings. Cable companies are also required to set aside time and production facilities for community access programming, open to the general public. These "electronic soapboxes" offer a chance for various political groups that are too obscure to attract the attention of commercial stations to make their case to the public.

Despite the many new sources of information provided by cable systems and such specialized services as C-SPAN, some observers suspect that these systems may actually diminish the general public's exposure to news about politics and government. As specialized news services proliferate, the major networks may actually reduce the amount of programming devoted to "hard news" about politics. Although citizens and experts with a special interest in politics enjoy a wealth of news on their pet subjects, viewers whose only exposure to political news comes from ABC, CBS, or NBC at the dinner table may actually learn less about the outside world than they did before the advent of the cable services.

Newspapers and Other Print Media

Americans consider a free press essential for democracy, and newspapers have long been a major source of information about government and the world. With the

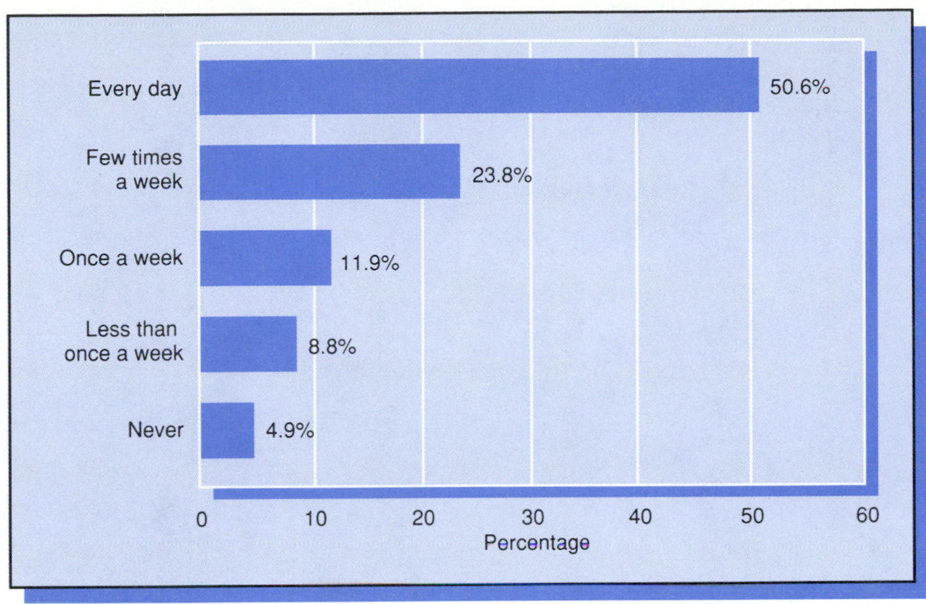

★ **Figure 11-2**

Frequency with which respondents read a daily newspaper, 1988 (percent)

SOURCE: James Allan Davis and Tom W. Smith, *General Social Survey, 1972–1988* (Chicago: National Opinion Research Center, 1988), subfile 1988 (machine-readable data file).

establishment of the *New York Sun* in 1833, the nation's first true mass medium was born. Before 1833, newspapers had been simple pamphlets or small journals available to a limited readership. From then on newspapers became available on the street at a price that the average citizen could afford: one penny. The *Sun*'s circulation grew from 2,000 to 8,000 in six months. Technological advances spread the press's news-gathering abilities. In the 1840s, the telegraph made it possible to offer direct reports from remote locations. America's first **wire service,** the Associated Press, was established in 1848 to provide news stories for papers unable to maintain their own reporters in distant cities and nations.[7] The wire services established bureaus or, in small towns, used local reporters to cover stories of regional and national interest. By 1850 nearly four hundred daily newspapers were published in the United States. Increasing literacy has continued to expand their potential readership, until today about half of all Americans read a newspaper every day (see figure 11-2).

America's early newspapers were usually highly partisan, each representing the views of one of the major political parties and expounding its own political perspective. President Andrew Jackson is said to have had sixty full-time journalists on the government payroll. As the newspapers pushed their own political agenda, they employed sensationalism to boost their circulation. By reporting (and often exaggerating) dramatic stories involving violence and sex, the papers hoped to secure the paid advertising essential to financial success. Newspapers often adopted a moralistic and crusading attitude toward real and imagined political corruption and deplored the "decadence" infesting society. Employing what came to be known as **yellow journalism,**[8] papers used dramatic headlines and graphic drawings to report (and distort) a national or international political story.

★ Newspapers remain a major source of information about politics and the world. Although most cities are served by only one major daily paper, modern printing and transportation have made the latest edition from Washington, New York, Miami, or Los Angeles available on street corners across the nation.

Yellow journalism often permeated reporting on America's foreign relations. Using racist and degrading images of other nations and peoples, yellow journalism was an essential part of "manifest destiny" (see chap. 19), the doctrine that America was ordained to lead the world.

The use of sensationalism and yellow journalism, of course, varied enormously; many publishers took their responsibility to inform the public very seriously. Aldolph Ochs, for example, who took over publication of the *New York Times* in 1896, promised to present "news impartially, without fear or favor, regardless of any party, sect or interest involved."[9] Many of the more tasteless aspects of yellow journalism were eventually abandoned by most major papers. Advertising sales, nonetheless, remained linked to a paper's popularity, and many publishers today still rely on flamboyance and sensationalism to attract readers. The debate over objectivity and the media's role in interpreting the news is hardly a new controversy in American political life.

Another important aspect of America's journalistic heritage—**muckraking**—joins sensationalism with a publisher's desire to expose corruption in government. The term, inspired by the practice of spreading manure with a rake to fertilize a garden, was applied by President Theodore Roosevelt to journalists' investigations of corruption and other scandal-laden problems in government.[10] Muckraking, which today goes by the more respectable-sounding name of **investigative reporting,** has become a major occupation for journalists and all mass media reporters. Investigative reporters helped expose the Watergate scandal, the Iran-Contra affair, and the alleged extramarital romantic activities of 1988 presidential candidate Gary Hart.

Today newspapers rank second only to television as the public's primary source of news about government and politics. Newspapers usually cover stories in greater depth than television and many endeavor to present alternative points of view in their opinion sections. Technological innovations have also changed the newspaper industry. Global telecommunications and computerized operations have reduced the time needed for a story and photos to travel from the reporter in the field to the front page of the latest edition. These same technical innovations have also spawned *USA Today,* the first "national" newspaper, and the regional editions of the *New York Times,* which can hit the streets in San Francisco the same day they appear in Boston or Miami.

Weekly newsmagazines also offer coverage of politics and current events on a national basis. Such publications as *Time* and *Newsweek* can offer in-depth and ongoing coverage of events in a much more comprehensive manner than all but the very best newspapers. Whether or not newsmagazines and other print media actually provide broad coverage and alternative points of view, of course, is a matter of serious debate, one we will consider shortly.

Radio

Like television today, radio once provided the nation with dramatic coverage of important events. When the major networks were established in the late 1920s, people across the country were exposed to politics in ways never before possible. David Halberstam describes the power of a radio address by Franklin Roosevelt:

> He was the first great American radio voice. For most Americans of this generation, their first memory of politics would be of sitting by a radio and hearing *that* voice, strong, confident, totally at ease. . . . Most Americans in the previous 160 years had never even seen a President; now almost all of them were hearing him, *in their own homes.* It was literally and figuratively electrifying.[11]

Through the Great Depression and World War II, the nation lived and died by their radios, often listening to dramatic accounts of war and suffering by such news legends as Edward R. Murrow. Radio still plays an important role in informing the public about natural and other disasters. Most large cities have at least one station that broadcasts news and information continuously, thus providing news when a television set is not handy.

★ The Media in a Changing World

Like the Industrial Revolution and the development of atomic energy, the **communications revolution** has changed the way people talk, learn, and act all over the world. A little more than thirty-five years ago, the invention of the battery-powered transistor radio opened up the outside world to millions of people in the poorest and most remote nations on earth. More recently, miniaturization, satellites, fiber optics, and computerization have linked the world's nations in an almost

★ "News, weather, sports, and a whole lot more." Television has had a tremendous impact in most nations of the Third World. Control of the airwaves is a major aspect of political power around the globe.

continuous flow of information, data, and visual images. These changes have had profound political, social, and economic influence on the United States and the world.

At the simplest level, the communications revolution has made it possible for people to know more about the world and how people in other nations live. Whether this knowledge comes from news programs or from American movies and soap operas dubbed in the local language, people have the opportunity to compare their lives with those of people in other regions. Knowledge, of course, is never neutral. Political scientists recognize that when people realize that social conditions can be improved, they may experience the phenomenon of "rising expectations." Rising expectations can lead to political unrest. The international media are among the most potent means of raising people's expectations, especially in poor nations. Figures 11-3 and 11-4 show the proliferation of television and radio receivers and VCRs around the world.

International News: America's Window on the World

According to the U.S. government, roughly one-half of 1 percent of the American people travel outside of North America each year. Thus most people come by their information about other nations secondhand, primarily from the media. Reporting the world's news is big business.

Approximately 80 percent of the news copy produced around the world each day is generated by four news-gathering agencies, the descendants of the early wire services: Associated Press and United Press International (U.S.), Reuters (Great

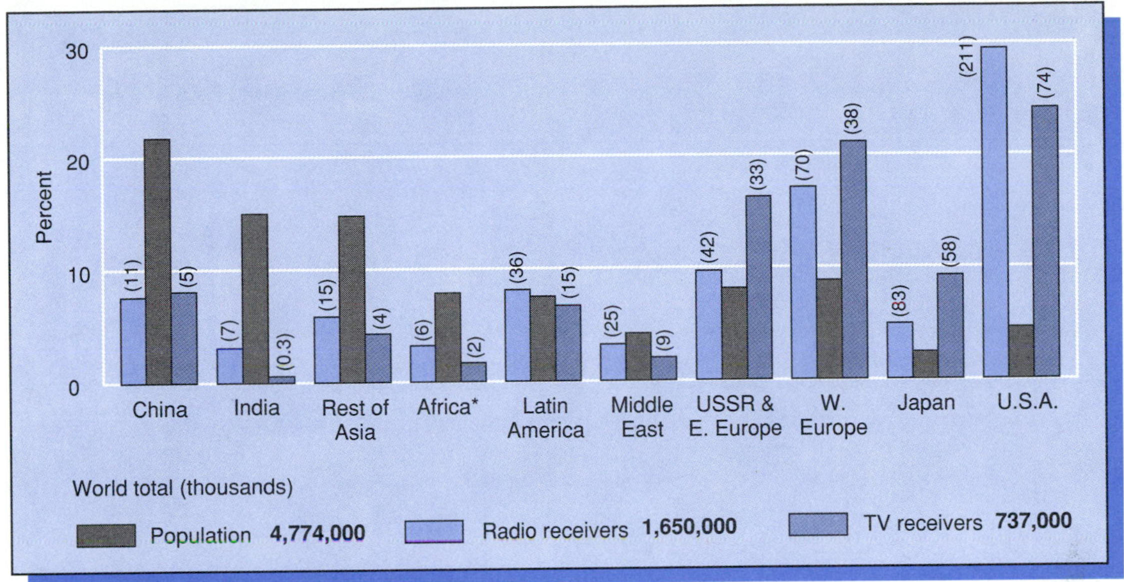

★ **Figure 11-3**

Percentage of world's total radio and television receivers in ten regions, 1985 (estimated)

*Excluding South Africa.

NOTE: Figures in parentheses are numbers of radio and TV receivers per 100 population.

SOURCE: Bernard Anderson, "Broadcasting: Tuning In to Development," *South,* August 1986, p. 97.

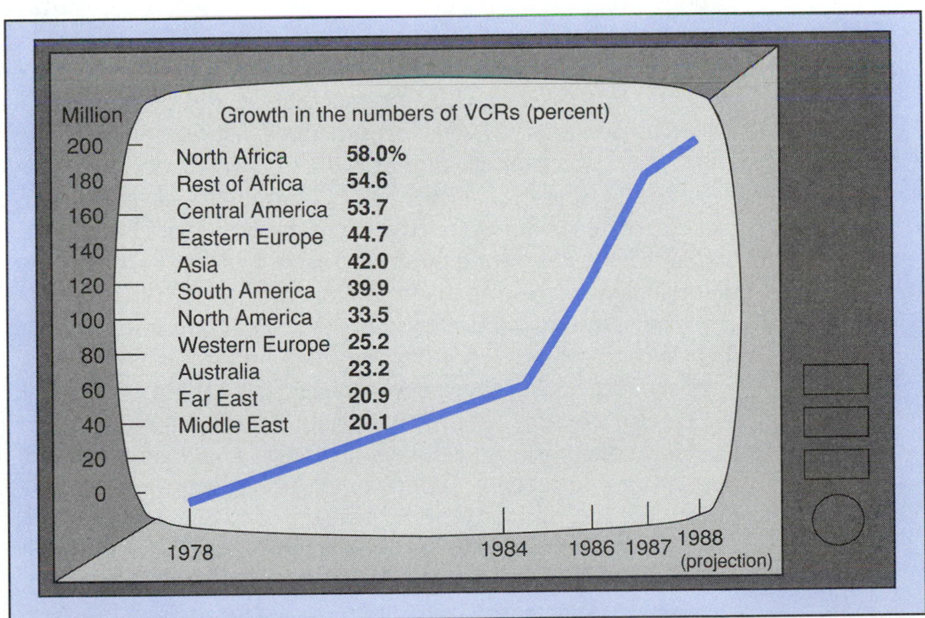

★ **Figure 11-4**

Estimated number of video cassette recorders in operation worldwide, 1978–1988 (millions) and growth in numbers of VCRs to 1987, by region (percent)

SOURCE: *South,* November 1988, p. 12, from figures supplied by *Screen Digest.*

★ Table 11-2
Percentage of coverage given to world regions by major news agencies

Region	*Agence France-Presse*	*Reuters*	*United Press International*
North America	11.1%	14.0%	71.2%
Latin America	5.1	5.0	3.2
Western Europe	38.7	40.9	9.6
Africa	13.2	9.3	1.8
Middle East	7.7	8.2	3.0
USSR/Eastern Europe	3.5	4.1	1.5
Asia/Far East	13.3	6.3	3.3
Other	7.4	12.2	6.4

SOURCE: Anthony Smith, *The Geopolitics of Information: How Western Culture Dominates the World* (London: Oxford University Press, 1980), p. 93.

Britain), and Agence France-Presse (France). (See table 11-2.) The British Broadcasting Corporation (BBC) and the Soviet news agency Tass provide much of the rest.[12] Specialized television services such as Visnews, based in London, supply video feed or complete stories to broadcasters in more than one hundred nations. Although major newspapers and television networks in the United States station correspondents abroad, they also depend heavily on the major news agencies for much of their copy. Roughly 75 percent of American foreign correspondents are stationed in Western Europe or Asia. The rest of the world, always interested in America, had a total of 1,278 correspondents stationed in the United States in 1987.[13]

American coverage of international events is frequently criticized as superficial and lacking in analytical depth. Although this situation is changing rapidly, many reporters still do not have sufficient language skills and familiarity with the nations they are covering. American reporters often apply their own cultural prejudices when they use such terms as "democracy," "freedom," and "dictatorship" to describe complex political systems in foreign countries. But some reporters risk their lives to get to the bottom of a story. And sometimes they become part of the story themselves. The journalist Michael Herr's dramatic book about Vietnam, *Dispatches,* for example, offers a poignant account of how a war correspondent faced the moral dilemma of picking up a weapon to defend himself in a conflict that he opposed. More recently, American and other reporters have been kidnapped in the Middle East and have risked being shot in China.

Coverage tends to be crisis-oriented. News teams are sent to "hot spots," and once the action dies down, the underlying causes and ongoing political events tend to be ignored. Many reporters, moreover, have seemed to accept without question official U.S. explanations and policy. Since the Vietnam experience, however, reporters have become more skeptical. Reports on events in Central America, for instance, while still crisis-oriented, have occasionally been critical of U.S. policy in the region.

Bill Stewart: Foreign Correspondent on the Front Line

On June 20, 1979, a television reporter for the ABC network, Bill Stewart, was detained at one of the many roadblocks erected by the Nicaraguan dictator Anastasio Somoza's National Guard. The Somoza dynasty was coming apart at the seams as it faced an armed insurrection by a citizenry tired of its human rights abuses and domination of the economy. Stewart was obviously unarmed as he approached the soldiers manning the roadblock, and his press credentials were in plain view. This sort of encounter had become routine for the corps of reporters risking life and limb to cover an important international story. Rather than engage in the usual perfunctory check and minor chitchat, one of the soldiers, in clear view of a camera operator filming just a few feet away, murdered the reporter in cold blood. The taped account of Stewart's murder, beamed back to the United States in time for the nightly news, produced an outpouring of condemnation for Somoza and helped remove the last vestiges of U.S. support for the Central American dictator. ★

SOURCE: John A. Booth, *The End and the Beginning: The Nicaraguan Revolution* (Boulder, Colo.: Westview, 1982), p. 175.

Governments and the Global Communications Revolution

The technical innovations that spawned the communications revolution are of great importance to governments. Satellites and other electronic wizardry have vital military applications. The economic dimension is equally important. The manufacture of industrial and consumer electronics products is one of the world's most competitive industries, with America, Europe, and Asia fighting for shares of the market. Competition to establish a new high-definition broadcast standard for television may determine who dominates program production and sales well into the twenty-first century. Though in annual production of television sets, the Japanese have come to dominate the global market, America remains highly competitive in many other areas. For instance, in 1989 the United States commanded 85 percent of the world's export market for movies, cable and satellite broadcasting, and video cassettes.

But government concern about the communications revolution goes beyond military and economic applications. Most governments, of course, have tried to manage the way their citizens learn about other nations and political systems. They have also sought to manage their nation's image abroad. In today's interdependent global village, governments are more concerned about such matters than ever. The United States, the Soviet Union, and many other nations routinely use the international media to promote a favorable image abroad (see table 11-3). Broadcasting on the shortwave band, the Voice of America and its sister stations, Radio Free Europe, Radio Liberty, and Radio Martí, present America's views to the world. The Soviet Union, Cuba, and other nations have frequently tried to prevent American and European shortwave broadcasts from reaching their people by jamming the signals. As relations between the Soviets and the Americans improved in the late 1980s, efforts to jam radio signals slackened.

★ Table 11-3
Major government broadcasts on international shortwave

Country	Hours per week	Languages
Soviet Union	2,177	83
United States	2,004	49
China	1,424	45
West Germany	789	39
Great Britain	720	37

NOTE: The numbers given are total hours of simultaneous broadcasting.
SOURCE: *South,* August 1986, p. 97.

Nations attempt to influence international public opinion also through direct manipulation of the media. America's Central Intelligence Agency (CIA) is reported to have had secret dealings with more than four hundred journalists and paid agents in the foreign bureaus of the Associated Press and United Press International.[14] The Soviet intelligence service, the KGB, is equally well known for its efforts to penetrate media at home and abroad. Planting stories favorable to a friend or damaging to an enemy is a classic technique to promote foreign policy goals.

Governments also place strict limits on what national and international journalists may report. Many countries, including El Salvador, Nicaragua, South Africa, the Soviet Union, and even the United States, have denied entry to or expelled foreign journalists. Governments also deny reporters access to satellite ground facilities and other technical equipment needed to send stories overseas. Repressive governments and leaders routinely imprison, torture, and kill local journalists who dare to criticize or oppose them.[15]

Try as they may, governments are never completely successful in controlling the media. In May 1989, hundreds of international journalists descended on the People's Republic of China to cover the first meeting in thirty years between Soviet and Chinese leaders. Chinese students and workers, who had been pressing the government for political reforms, welcomed this historic visit by Mikhail Gorbachev (the architect of increased political freedom in the Soviet Union) as an opportunity to show the strength of their movement to the world.

With the international media present in large numbers to cover the Gorbachev visit, Chinese officials were forced to tolerate the presence of an estimated one million peaceful demonstrators in Beijing's Tiananmen Square. Much to the leaders' consternation, the demonstrators (and the international television crews) stayed on long after the Soviets had gone home. With the government unable to decide how to respond to the demonstrators, China soon faced one of the worst crises of its modern era.

As the demonstrations swelled and spread to other cities in the ensuing weeks, hard-line factions within the government gained the upper hand. Fearing the pres-

★ Reporting and making news, China, May 1989: An American television crew covers political protests in Tiananmen Square.

ence of the international media, the government closed satellite ground stations, thus making it more difficult to transmit coverage abroad. Government pressure against the foreign media was sometimes dramatic. "On Friday night—May 19—CBS interrupted its presentation of the season finale of 'Dallas' for an extraordinary real-life drama," the journal *Broadcasting* reported: "Chinese officials, speaking Chinese through CBS News consultant and translator Bette Bao Lord . . . were telling Dan Rather and the CBS crew to stop their satellite transmissions. CBS was not alone. CNN was also covering itself, live, being ordered off the air by another set of Chinese."[16] The television medium, as it so often does, had become part of the story.

Government pressure presented hardships for the international media in China, but did not silence them. When the military brutally mowed down the demonstrators, many reporters were still able to get the story out. Video tapes, shot at great personal risk, were smuggled out of the country and transmitted by the nearest friendly satellite ground station. Even tourists with miniature video cameras got into the act.

The video images of the massacre in Tiananmen Square shocked the world. The impact on Chinese foreign policy was immediate. The United States and many other nations, encouraged by their outraged publics, curtailed their economic and political exchanges with China. Western coverage of the violence in China, broadcast over the Voice of America, BBC, and other shortwave networks, also helped the demonstrators circumvent the news blackout imposed by their own leaders. After the massacre, the Chinese government used its monopoly of the domestic news media to assure its citizens and the world that the only people killed had been soldiers, who had been attacked by "counterrevolutionaries."

Terrorism: The Whole World Is Watching

In 1972 people around the world sat stunned before their TV screens as they watched the Black September faction of the Palestine Liberation Organization attack Israeli athletes at the Munich Olympic games. Today terrorism in all its forms is an all but constant feature of the global political scene. Between 1980 and 1986 there were more than three hundred terrorist attacks against airlines and tourist offices. Diplomats and diplomatic offices were attacked more than eleven hundred times. Many of these attacks were intended, at least in part, to attract the world's attention to the terrorists' political cause.

The international media often play a crucial part in terrorist incidents. In the view of the U.S. Department of State, journalists have a special responsibility because terrorists equipped with simple radios have "the ability to track outside responses to their actions in real or near-real time . . . journalists are not just narrating the passing scene. They are players; like it or not, they are involved." Reporting the nationalities of passengers on a hijacked airliner, for example, can greatly increase their risk.

Suggestions have been put forward to limit the international media's utility to terrorists. Some people say the media should refuse to give live coverage to terrorist incidents. Others, pointing out that government and airline officials had received threats before the bombing of a Pan American jumbo jet over Scotland in 1988, argue that the public has a right to know about any and all terrorist activities. As the controversy over the media and terrorism rages, one thing seems certain: as long as desperate and violent people seek international redress for their real or imagined grievances, the media will be part of the story. ★

SOURCE: L. Paul Bremer III, *Terrorism and the Media* (Washington, D.C.: U.S. Department of State, June 25, 1987).

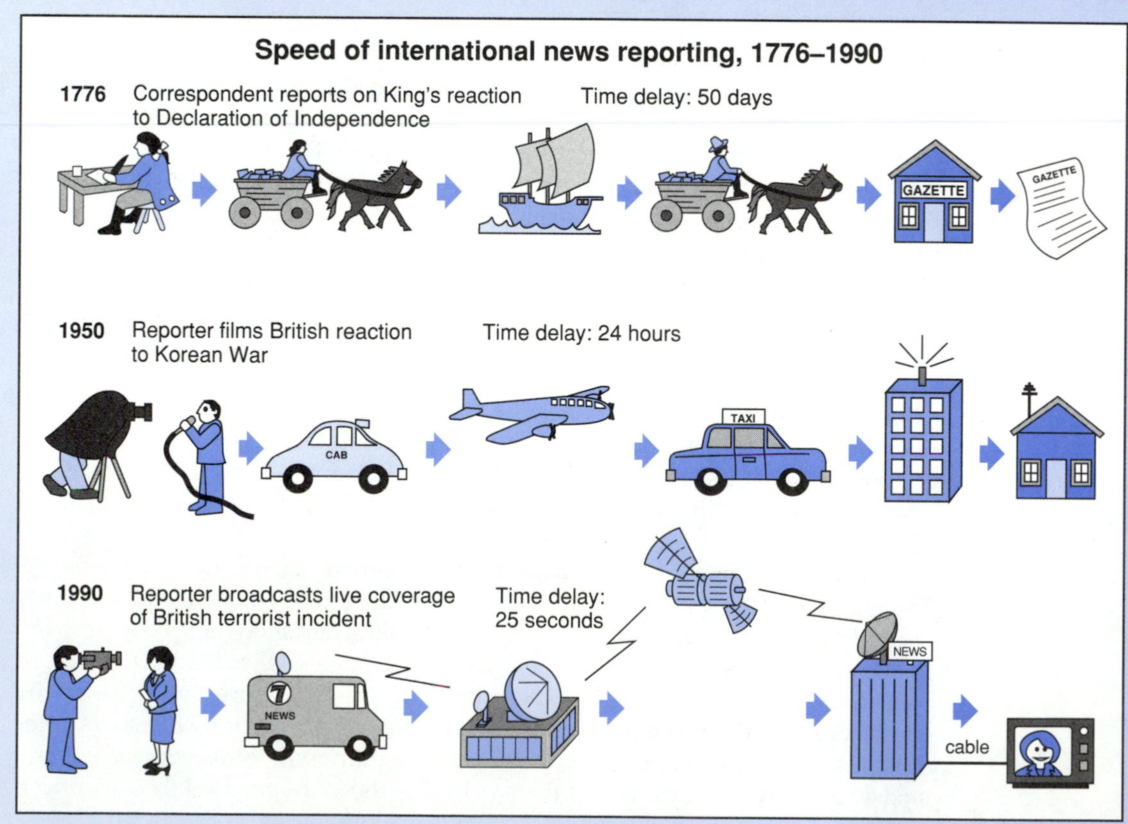

★ As camcorders, personal computers, and telefax machines become more common throughout the world, governments will have difficulty trying to control the flow of information about politics and social or cultural events.

Governments are not alone in their desire to influence international public opinion. Numerous nongovernmental organizations—human rights, environmental, religious—expend a great deal of time and money in efforts to get their messages across. International terrorists, of course, commit some of their most violent acts in the hope that their cause will be publicized around the world.

Many nations of the Third World are concerned about the effects that the international media have on their people. Since much of the news and entertainment programming comes from Europe and America, they feel that their people receive a distorted view of the world and that traditional cultural values may be undermined. And, as we said earlier, they fear that knowledge of the lifestyles and material benefits enjoyed by citizens in economically more developed nations may lead to unrealistic expectations and political unrest at home.

Acting through the United Nations and other organizations, Third World leaders have called for the creation of a "new international communications order." Such a new order would place limits on the flow of international news stories, encourage international reporting to be sensitive to the needs of local communities, promote global interest in problems of poverty, and require codes of conduct for reporters. Negative reporting, such as predicting a famine in an already underfed nation, could, according to some Third World leaders, produce panic and political unrest.[17] The United States, by and large, has not been sympathetic to the call for a new communications order. The Reagan administration denounced the notion of a code of conduct as a violation of freedom of speech and of the press, and argued that governments should stay out of the business of regulating the flow of news and information.

The communications revolution has made it difficult for authoritarian governments to silence opponents. Desktop publishing, easily duplicated audio and

1960. John Kennedy *(left)* and Richard Nixon *(right)* took part in the first televised presidential debates.

video cassettes, and even telefax machines have become powerful tools in the fight for political rights. In 1988 opponents of Panama's military-dominated government discovered an electronic weapon:

> A group of Panamanian expatriates living in Washington, D.C., avoided the Noriega government's press restrictions by sending censored news reports to their homeland via telefax. The articles arrived at business offices in Panama City and then were transmitted to churches, schools, and labor union headquarters. From there, opponents of the regime distributed the information to large numbers of people throughout the country.[18]

The communications revolution, like interdependence itself, is a double-edged sword. It provides economic and political benefits, and it gives governments great power. But it also can provide knowledge, knowledge which can be used to counterbalance the power of government.

The Media in America: Elections

As television evolved into America's window on the world, politicians began to use the medium to their advantage. Truman was the first president to use television to address the nation, yet he made little use of the medium. Neither did Eisenhower. Television first became a potent political tool in 1960, when Nixon and Kennedy publicly debated their respective qualifications for the presidency. Most people who listened to the debate on the radio told pollsters that Nixon had won it, but most of those who saw it on television said that Kennedy had prevailed. The difference lay in the visual images projected by the two men: Nixon with his five-o'clock shadow and shifty eyes, Kennedy with his handsome looks and dashing style. The era of **image politics** had begun; style had become more important than substance.

David Halberstam describes the effects of image politics on Representative Sam Rayburn, legendary Democratic Speaker of the House. Rayburn, watching a speech by presidential candidate Richard Nixon, was troubled by the power of television:

> It was clear . . . that Rayburn was appalled by the entire new process of politics, the new and different tempo, television, modern advertising, polls, all that. The new modern manipulation was so different from the manipulation that Rayburn knew and trusted and practiced.[19]

Voters pay a great deal of attention to the media at election time. The mass media play a crucial role in political campaigns through presentation of paid advertising and news coverage of campaigns.

Campaign Advertising

> News coverage and politics are increasingly influenced by the marketing trade. As a matter of fact, I think politics is now in the era of the marketer. And just as bad money drives the good from circulation, marketing strategies have now driven substance from politics. The new kings are pollsters, film makers, political consultants, focus-group organizers, computer mail experts and, of course, the fund raisers who make it all happen.
>
> —*Walter Mondale*

As we are all aware, it is virtually impossible to enjoy our favorite television shows without facing endless commercials imploring us to buy this or that car, chewing gum, or floor wax. Commercials are as much a part of our viewing entertainment as the programs they interrupt. Indeed, some specialty cable channels that broadcast travel advice, investment and financial planning, or music videos offer little more than full-time commercials. Commercials often deliver inflated promises of beauty and youth, social acceptance, and heightened sexual prowess, frequently exploiting people's personal and social insecurities. Other commercials play on people's fears, offering life insurance, home security systems, and health-care products.

In this way television commercials can serve as powerful formulators of public opinion, socializing people to define their needs and desires in accordance with the financial interests of the advertisers. They create new images—often false and absurd—to which viewers are expected to compare themselves and their lives. In a nation characterized by ethnic diversity, an aging population, and significant poverty, commercials paint a one-dimensional portrait of an eternally youthful and affluent America. Commercials, moreover, can subtly influence the political culture by

> redefining individualism in ways that would dismay the Founding Fathers. It becomes the consumption of material goods in conformity with the styles and standards set by advertising. No longer does individualism mean control over political decisions—or even personal ones; no longer does it involve altering or abolishing outmoded or oppressive structures. Advertising defangs American individualism, working against its socially and politically revolutionary meaning, channeling individual strivings toward easily controlled non-political outlets.[20]

What about advertising in political campaigns? Can commercials similarly sell candidates for public office by compelling voters to buy exaggerated claims and promises? Can media experts package presidential and congressional hopefuls as they do shiny automobiles and "all-natural" breakfast cereal, making them consumable by exploiting people's fears and insecurities? Recent local and national campaigns indicate that media experts certainly have this goal in mind.

During every major election, television screens throughout the country become showcases for the modern wizards of American politics, the creators of political commercials. In many expensive campaigns, the same technical experts who peddle cat food, cosmetics, and beer are employed to sell politicians to the voters. Jack Tinker and Partners, for instance—the firm responsible for many of the popular Alka-Seltzer commercials—was hired in the late 1960s to create ads for Nelson Rockefeller's reelection campaign for governor of New York, in large part because the Alka-Seltzer ads were so clever. And the firm accepted the challenge because, as managing partner Myron McDonald unabashedly put it, "we looked at the Governor almost as though he were a product like Alka-Seltzer."[21]

The most common form of television and radio campaign advertisement is the **spot commercial,** a thirty-second or one-minute political advertisement that typically has a single dramatic theme. It is commonly employed to build a favorable image of a candidate or to present an unfavorable view of an opponent, sometimes by exploiting public fears and anxieties. One of the most controversial one-minute spots was used briefly by the Democrats in 1964 against Senator Barry Goldwater. To convince the voters that Goldwater would lead the nation toward a dangerous confrontation with the Soviet Union, the Democrats ran an ad showing a little girl standing innocently in a meadow, picking petals from a daisy. As she finished counting the petals, the scene dissolved into a countdown to an atomic explosion, concluding with a billowing mushroom cloud. "The stakes," a voice warned, "are too high for you to stay home."

In the post-Watergate election of 1976, both Jimmy Carter and Gerald Ford attempted to soothe a public wary (if not openly distrustful) of all politicians. Consultants for both candidates believed voters would be swayed more by low-keyed, upbeat commercials than by negative, opponent-baiting advertising. Ford's ads, for example, showed him delivering his State of the Union message to Congress or working at the White House, emphasizing the traditional virtues of the incumbent: "President Ford is your President. Keep him." Similarly, the Carter spots featured him on his Georgia farm sifting peanuts through his fingers, proclaiming that government should be "as good and honest and decent and truthful . . . and as filled with love as the American people."

Positive spots, however, proved to be the exception after 1976. As we discussed in chapter 9, negative campaigning is often perceived as more effective. In 1988, strategists for George Bush continuously used a spot showing convicts entering and leaving prison through a revolving door—the point being that the Democratic candidate, Michael Dukakis, as governor of Massachusetts had let dangerous criminals back into society prematurely. Though such early-release programs are found in many states, the Republicans hoped that the voters would see Dukakis as "soft on crime." The Democrats also employed a variety of negative spots, including several that attacked the Republican vice-presidential candidate, Dan Quayle.

Without a doubt, advertising is a crucial weapon in the candidates' battle plan. It is especially important for new or aspiring politicians who seek public recognition. In 1984 media expenses represented 30 to 50 percent of campaign spending at all levels of government. The Democrats spent $18.2 million and the Republicans

1988: A Tale of Two Ad Campaigns

In July 1988 Michael Dukakis had reason for optimism. At the end of the Democratic convention he was doing well, despite the fact that he was facing a sitting vice-president who could take some credit for the peace and relative prosperity the nation enjoyed. The Dukakis campaign strategy aimed at stressing the candidate's character, leadership, and integrity. He would attack Bush's part in the Iran-Contra scandal and the budget deficit. When it came time to be nasty and negative, the Dukakis campaign would attack Bush's leadership during the Reagan era by asking, "Where was George?" and speaking of the "sleaze factor" that tainted former administration officials with a hint of corruption.

The Bush strategists, though certainly not running scared, planned an aggressive ad campaign. Bush's advertising would depict Dukakis as a liberal who was both unwilling to require students in Massachusetts schools to recite the Pledge of Allegiance and a "card-carrying" member of the American Civil Liberties Union. Dukakis, the voters were told, would raise taxes while cutting the defense budget. When it came to mudslinging, the Republicans attacked with the dramatic Willie Horton ad campaign, which implied that Dukakis was personally responsible for the weekend pass issued to a convicted murderer who seized the opportunity to kill again.

When the dust had settled (and Bush had won by a comfortable margin), the Republicans figured that about 50 percent of their campaign advertising had been negative. The Democrats reported running 60 percent negative and 40 percent positive ads. It is, of course, not just the tone of the ads that counts. Most observers agree that the Bush campaign was able to get through to the voters while the Dukakis campaign lacked focus and definition. "Dukakis ads," according to the campaign analyst Larry Sabato, "have either been absent or out of sync or poorly done." Though election victories are the result of a complex mix of factors, pollster Louis Harris felt that advertising was crucial: "The simple story of this election is that the Bush commercials have worked and the Dukakis commercials have not." ★

SOURCE: Marjorie Randon Hershey, "The Campaign and the Media," in *The Election of 1988: Reports and Interpretations,* ed. Gerald M. Pomper (Chatham, N.J.: Chatham House, 1989), pp. 73–102; and Michael Oreskes, "TV's Role in '88: The Medium Is the Election," *New York Times,* October 30, 1988, pp. 1, 19.

spent $22.9 million of their federal allotments on presidential campaigns *after* the candidates were nominated. In all, 1984 campaign spending on the media for all races came to an estimated $500 million.[22]

Given the expense of buying media time, it is not surprising that the candidates and political parties go to great lengths to ensure that the money is well spent. Media experts and consultants have become crucial to most campaigns. Candidates not only must be competent to hold office but must *appear* competent to the public, especially when they are seen on television. Makeup, lighting, and perhaps an attractive spouse or grandchild situated just within the camera's range, have become part of the winning television image. Candidates are trained in television techniques by media consultants and are repeatedly coached throughout the campaign. The campaign's in-house pollsters continually sample public opinion to learn if the message is succeeding. It is not surprising that a former actor (Ronald Reagan) and a former astronaut (John Glenn) have become successful politicians. According to an astute observer, "candidates no longer 'run' for office; they 'pose' for office."[23] In short, "candidates . . . sell themselves. That's what people do in television commercials—they sell things—and they sell them by using provocative images, not by using appeals to principles and beliefs."[24]

Photo Ops and Sound Bites: How Candidates Make the Evening News

Campaigns are more than just opportunities for the media to sell advertising slots to the candidates; they are also big news. From a candidate's perspective, news coverage is an opportunity for free exposure, an almost invaluable commodity when millions of dollars may be needed to run for high office. Gaining the media's attention is a major aspect of any campaign strategy, especially during the preelection primaries, when the media can play an important role in determining which candidates seem capable of winning and which are destined to lose. And since election news can boost ratings and sell newspapers, the media and candidates develop a relationship of interdependence: each side needs the other.

The media cover elections in a variety of ways. Though media styles vary, reporters are usually assigned to a major candidate and accompany him or her throughout the campaign. They monitor the candidate's daily comings and goings, hear the same speeches day in and day out, check out leads, and work to meet deadlines.

Candidates, for their part, seek to manage the flow of information and the visual images crucial to creating the proper impact on television. A practice used to perfection by the Reagan and Bush presidential campaigns was to set a theme for the day and then make sure that the press was fed the information early enough to meet deadlines. Once the theme was set, the preselected photo opportunities were arranged and a catchy phrase or "sound bite," providing the desired verbal accompaniment to the pictures, was included in the day's speech. With national defense as the theme, for instance, the candidate would be shown meeting with workers at a factory, preferably with a shiny new fighter plane or navy ship in the background, and the speech would include a brief phrase—often emotional and patriotic—to bring the candidate's point home.

The major television networks and newspapers tend to accept the "theme for today" approach to campaigning. This is certainly the easy and safe approach for reporters facing strict deadlines. At the same time, reporters often feel that candidates are evasive and unwilling to give specific answers on controversial issues. One of the ways in which the media attempt to get beyond the photo-opportunity and sound-bite style of the campaign managers is to try to arrange one-on-one interviews with the candidates. Commercial television and radio news programmers, for example, invite candidates to take part in "newsmaker" broadcasts, such as CBS's long-running *Face the Nation* and NBC's *Meet the Press.* In this interview format, the candidate faces several print and electronic journalists who endeavor to ask probing questions. Candidates, of course, attempt to turn the conversation toward themes that they are comfortable with and to avoid subjects that may make them look bad. Tom Brokaw, host of NBC's *Nightly News,* explains the need to control or "mediate" a candidate's appearances on TV: "I think it is part of the risks of having an open-ended live interview on the evening news. . . . Politicians all over the world understand that there is no retrieving that time once you're on live television. That is, if they continue to consume it, at some point they'll begin to control the medium on which they appear."[25]

In general, newspapers fare a little better at probing a candidate's position on issues. Newspapers and magazines can often devote more space to campaign issues than the two or three minutes available on the major TV network news programs. Print journalists can do background stories, outline the candidate's posi-

★ Ronald Reagan *(left)* and Walter Cronkite *(right)* are two old pros who understand the power of the media. Presidents and superstar reporters, although often locked in verbal combat, need each other to succeed.

tion on the issues over time, and identify inconsistencies. Television, Brokaw points out, "leaves no footprints. It's hard to retrieve that complicated information unless you've got it on tape."[26]

Hoping to get beyond staged events and packaged press releases, the media also put the candidate's personal life under the microscope. A great deal of information on candidates—their incomes, their business interests—is a matter of public record and relatively easy for a reporter to dig up. But media investigators, using undercover surveillance, sometimes delve deep into a candidate's personal life. During the 1988 race for the Democratic party's nomination for president, front-runner Gary Hart temporarily withdrew his candidacy after media disclosures about alleged extramarital affairs. Vice-presidential candidate Dan Quayle's college grades and military service during the Vietnam war were also subjected to close scrutiny by the media. Such investigations were widely criticized as unfair and irrelevant intrusions. Some critics wondered if qualified individuals would avoid seeking public office for fear that a seemingly insignificant episode of twenty years ago would be blown out of proportion and create lasting embarrassment.

Others congratulated the media on exposing potential character flaws in candidates for the nation's highest offices. Muckraking, they argue, is hardly a new development on the American political scene. Given the vast powers of the president in the era of nuclear warfare, citizens have a right to know what kind of individual they are electing. According to the Pulitzer Prize–winning journalist Jack Nelson, candidates' "lives, their personalities, their finances, families, friends and values are all fair game for fair reporting." Former presidential candidate Walter Mondale concurs: "People will always want to know about character, and they should . . . whether [candidates are] able or honest or strong physically and mentally healthy is the most important of all questions."[27]

A final means by which the media can bring the candidates into the American home is a **televised debate.** A debate offers the public the opportunity to see the candidates together on the same stage and compare their styles and positions on some issues. A debate can reveal a candidate's strengths and weaknesses. During

★ Edmund Muskie, a strong contender for the 1968 Democratic nomination for president, saw his support dwindle after an emotional speech before the TV cameras. Muskie's tearful response to a newspaper article critical of his wife led some voters to conclude he lacked the strength necessary to lead the nation.

★ Gary Hart, another casualty of the media? Hart, who once led the field for the 1988 Democratic presidential nomination, was reduced to an also-ran after reporters turned up stories of extramarital affairs.

the first nationally televised debate in 1960, for example, John Kennedy's performance helped overcome the charge that he was too young and inexperienced for the presidency. Ronald Reagan's image in his first debate with Walter Mondale in 1984, on the other hand, suffered when he seemed confused and faltering in response to some questions.

Candidates and campaign managers clearly view a debate as a mixed blessing. Incumbents, especially if they are confident of reelection, are reluctant to risk a public confrontation with the opposition. A debate tends to give the lesser-known challenger needed exposure, provides him or her with a stature equal to the incumbent's in the eyes of the voters, and puts the incumbent in a position of having to defend the government's policies. It was largely for these reasons that Lyndon Johnson backed away from a confrontation with Barry Goldwater in 1964 and that Richard Nixon refused to debate George McGovern in 1972. In 1976, however, Gerald Ford was far behind in the polls and felt he had more to gain than to lose from a televised showdown with his challenger, Jimmy Carter.

Since 1976, debates have become a fixture of the American electoral system. In 1980, more than one hundred million Americans watched the Reagan/Carter debate.[28] Debates were held in 1988 for the presidential primary elections and for state and local races across the nation. For many viewers, vice-presidential candidate Lloyd Bentsen's sharp retort to Dan Quayle when the young Republican compared himself to the nation's youngest president—"Senator, you're no Jack Kennedy"—was excellent television, if not the high point of the entire campaign.

Drama aside, many observers wonder if the debates really help voters assess the qualifications of the candidates. By and large, the presidential debates are not really debates in the strict sense of the word. The candidates are fed questions—usually by journalists—and then take turns responding. There is usually no real opportunity for direct give-and-take between the opponents. Unhappiness with the media-dominated format for the Bush/Dukakis debate in 1988 led the well-respected League of Women Voters to refuse to sponsor the event. Other critics decry the overpreparation of candidates by campaign staff. Before a debate the candidates are thoroughly briefed by their staffs and then put through practice sessions that simulate the real thing right down to the glaring lights. Such rehearsals, according to critics, give the public little opportunity to glimpse the real person behind the robot perfection of the TV image created by the media consultants. Still, the voter who is willing to watch several different TV news programs and plow through newspapers and magazines can gain much more information on candidates than ever before. Public television and radio, CNN, and C-SPAN provide extensive and accessible coverage on nearly all candidates and issues during major election campaigns. Unlike the citizens of many countries of the world, Americans do have the chance to become well acquainted with the individuals they select to govern, if they are willing to endure campaign hype and learn to separate image from reality.

★ The Media and Government

Aside from the occasional traffic violation or panic-provoking letter from the Internal Revenue Service, most people acquire their experience with the government and its policies at secondhand. The distance between people and political issues, moreover, has been amplified by global interdependence and international events that influence our lives. Thus the media, always important in spreading news about politics and government, take on added significance.

Muckraking and aggressive media coverage of the government have deep historical roots. Many analysts believe that an adversarial relationship exists between the media and government, and they cite such examples as the press's relentless pursuit of Richard Nixon during the Watergate scandal of the 1970s. The interactions of the media and government, often rife with conflict, are also quite complex.

Like political candidates, government officials have a love/hate relationship with reporters. Each needs the other if they are to perform their functions for society. But each has a *different* function to perform. The media representatives' primary tasks and goals are

- to inform the public about government and current events.
- to provide critical and subjective analysis of events.
- to enhance their professional standing as journalists.
- to make money through advertising and subscriptions (if they are private broadcasters and publishers).

Government officials, on the other hand, must

- set national priorities and provide leadership.
- make and implement policy.
- convince the public and other officials that its policies are worthwhile.
- get reelected.

Government, even in a democracy, will at times mislead the people and other governments. The media, in theory, seek the truth. Thus cooperation between the media and government often gives way to conflict.

In many ways, the media's coverage of government parallels their coverage of campaigns. Reporters are assigned to cover the White House, Congress, the courts, and the bureaucracy. Coverage is not equal, however, and tends to focus on the latest crisis or major news event.

The Media and the President

> When information which properly belongs to the public is withheld by those in power, the people soon become ignorant of their own affairs, distrustful of those who manage them, and—eventually—incapable of determining their own destinies.
>
> —*Richard Nixon*

The presidency and modern television were made for each other. The American president, perhaps the most powerful person on earth, is an excellent source of the glamour and high drama on which television news thrives. Television, from the president's perspective, is the perfect outlet to inform the public while building support for his political party. As we shall see in chapter 13, the media have played a major role in the emergence of today's powerful "imperial presidency."

Presidential media coverage is a mixture of formalized, routine relations and informal news-gathering by reporters. At the formal level, most major media assign reporters to the White House press corps. These reporters work closely with the president's press secretary and public relations staff. As with most press–politician interaction, reporters and those who manage the presidential public image have an interdependent relationship that is characterized by both cooperation and conflict. The White House press staff provides reporters with volumes of background and other information. Reporters gratefully accept these tidbits (often slanted) while searching for the real story that will scoop their media competition.

Most presidents complain that they are not treated fairly by the press. Reporters, for their part, often believe they are manipulated and/or ignored by the White House. On occasion—during the Watergate scandal of the 1970s, for example—the press has seemed to have the upper hand in its dealings with the executive branch of government. Although Watergate demonstrated the power of the press, subsequent events have shown that the press's dominance was a very exceptional occurrence. The Iran-Contra story, for instance, was first reported by an obscure journal in Lebanon, and the major American papers with reporters covering the White House and Pentagon day and night were taken by surprise. By and large, the president and the White House press managers usually are quite adept at controlling the flow of news.

The president's staff works hard to control the daily flow of information. The staff plans the day's events, gives the press a timetable, and hopes that coverage will be limited to the president's media agenda. One method of controlling the news is to stage **pseudo-events.** Pseudo-events—including photo opportunities and sound-bites—are similar to tactics used to dominate the media during campaigns. These events are not spontaneous but are planned or even incited events.[29] With the proper planning and use of pseudo-events, the White House can avoid discussing controversial issues.

Another way in which news can be managed is through the use of **strategic leaks** of information: a member of the government passes information surreptitiously to the press. Leaks can be used to test public reaction to a proposed policy or to embarrass an opposing politician. By rewarding reporters with inside information, the White House can build a loyal following among them. Indeed, providing access and information is one of the president's most powerful tools for managing the media. Access is crucial to a reporter's career. A reporter who has fallen out of favor with the White House may be of little use to his or her editor or network news director.

Leaks can be turned against the government as well. Disgruntled officials can leak information that is politically damaging to the White House. The most famous leak of all, the crucial guidance reportedly provided by the mysterious "Deep Throat" to the *Washington Post,* played a major role in the downfall of Richard Nixon. Members of Congress are also routinely criticized by the president for leaking information to the press. Fear of leaks, especially those involving foreign policy, have led some presidents to try to limit congressional access to some types of information.

Between the White House's tightly structured pseudo-events and the anarchy of uncontrolled leaks lies the politically important middle ground of partially controlled news. A presidential press conference, for example, is an opportunity for the press to try to pose questions that will put the president on the spot. The White House staff, of course, attempts to prepare the president for every conceivable question and to script prepackaged answers. President Reagan is reported to have rehearsed answers as if studying lines for a movie role.

Reporters can be persistent, and "the struggle over partially controlled political turf is an ongoing one, with the victories generally going to high-status officials who can use prestige, power, and other resources . . . to define their relations with the press. When those rare moments of spontaneous political exchange do occur, the news most often records only the patented political avoidance terms like 'no comment' or those windy bursts of political rhetoric that seem to have nothing to do with the issue at hand."[30] President Reagan's favorite trick was to fire off a brief statement as he left the White House and then let reporters' questions be drowned out by the noise of his waiting helicopter.

The Media and Foreign Policy

Given the physical distance that separates most Americans from international events, media reporting can be crucial to an informed and open discussion of foreign policy. As we have seen, the communications revolution has spawned expanded real-time coverage of international events. Though American leaders generally welcome expanded coverage of foreign affairs, they do not give their support without reservation. Unlike other political issues, foreign policy often requires secrecy. During wartime and when weapons and other military secrets are involved, the public and reporters alike recognize the need for discretion in foreign affairs. But when foreign policy is surrounded by controversy, as it was during the Vietnam war, government secrecy and censorship can be harshly criticized.

During the Vietnam conflict both the Johnson and Nixon administrations misled the American public in order to maintain political support for the increasingly unpopular war. Professional journalists, who considered themselves capable

★ October 1983. U.S. forces invade the tiny Caribbean island of Grenada. Government restrictions on reporting of the military operation troubled the media and the American public.

of judging when secrecy was appropriate to maintain security, were outraged by the government's brazen attempts to mislead the public. The adversarial relationship between the government and the media, fostered by the Vietnam war and enhanced by the Watergate scandal, led many reporters to develop a healthy skepticism in regard to government explanations, at least in regard to highly controversial issues.

The U.S. invasion and occupation of the tiny Caribbean microstate of Grenada in 1983 led to further controversy between the media and the government. No reporters were allowed onto the island until three days after U.S. troops had landed. The military contended that reporters were excluded to maintain secrecy and for their own protection. NBC television commentator John Chancellor saw media restrictions differently. Chancellor labeled the invasion "a bureaucrat's dream: Do anything. No one is watching." The American people seemed to agree. A Harris poll in December 1983 discovered that 65 percent of Americans felt that reporters should have accompanied the troops into Grenada.[31]

In the aftermath of the invasion, the Pentagon and the press met to establish guidelines for the media's role in future military actions. The Pentagon promised to allow "pool" coverage by a select group of journalists in any future Grenada-style operation. America, of course, is not the only democracy to have limited press access to a combat zone. During the 1982 war over the Falkland/Malvinas Islands, the British severely limited the activity of reporters, and their stories were subject to censorship by military officials.

Although technology has greatly expanded the media's ability to cover foreign affairs, they still tend to concentrate primarily on hot spots and major events. Doris Graber has found that only 11 percent of newspaper coverage is devoted to foreign affairs when there are no major crises. Coverage is often taken from wire services and from State Department briefings and press releases.[32] As coverage is not consistent, it is difficult for the people to see events around the world in their historical

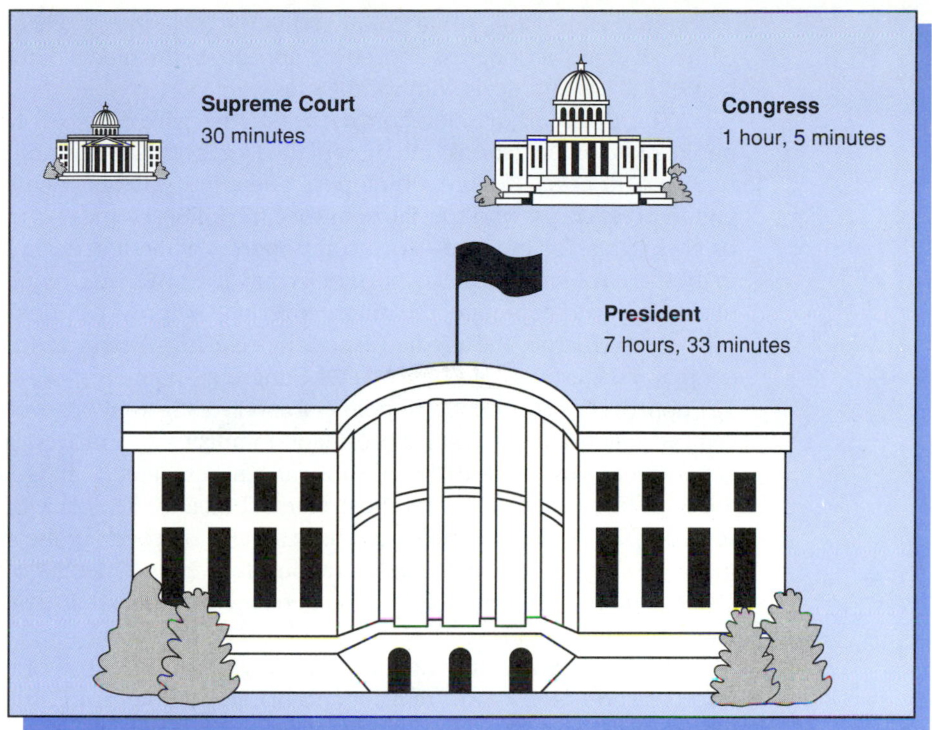

★ **Figure 11-5**
Average time per month allotted by the major television networks to coverage of the three branches of government on prime-time evening news (July 1986–June 1987)
SOURCE: Doris A. Graber, *Mass Media and American Politics,* 3d ed. (Washington, D.C.: Congressional Quarterly Press, 1989), p. 237.

perspective. Still, for the citizen willing to consult a variety of sources, the media can provide enough information to keep the politicians in Washington on their toes.

The Media and Congress

Congress, with its 535 senators and representatives, does not lend itself to the dramatic and highly personalized media attention that the president receives. The presidency, especially in the hands of a professional actor such as Ronald Reagan, is made for modern television. Congress's routine activities—lengthy and detailed budget debates, long-winded speeches aimed at a specialized constituency in the home district—are not so captivating as the president's bold moves in foreign policy.

Given these differences, one might assume that the president receives the lion's share of media coverage. As figure 11-5 shows, this is indeed the case as far as national television is concerned. Researchers have found, however, that when newspapers and magazines are included, the president and Congress enjoy roughly the same amount of attention from the media.[33] The type and focus of the coverage of the branches of government, however, vary greatly. The president receives more attention on television, while Congress has the edge in newspaper coverage. Much of the coverage of Congress, moreover, appears in the media of the representatives' home districts and deals with local issues.

The three major television networks, the wire services, major private and public radio organizations, and most of the larger newspapers and magazines assign reporters to cover Congress on a permanent basis. Other members of the Washington press corps, who specialize in specific political topics—the budget, defense, or civil rights, for instance—focus on Congress when it is dealing with legislation in their area of interest. Since much of its time is consumed by lengthy and technical discussions and committee hearings, covering Congress can be tedious.

By and large, the media (especially television) tend to focus on the more controversial aspects of Congress. Of Congress's many responsibilities (see chap. 12), approval of presidential appointees and investigation of government programs can be quite dramatic. When a president nominates a controversial figure to a high government post, such as Ronald Reagan's nomination of Judge Robert Bork for the Supreme Court or George Bush's first choice for secretary of defense, former senator John Tower, the media can have a field day covering the story. Not content merely to report the Senate deliberations, the media's sleuths conduct their own investigations of a nominee, and sometimes dig up embarrassing or downright damaging information.

Media coverage of Congress's oversight of the executive branch also has produced some of the most dramatic and historic moments in American politics. At the height of the Watergate scandal during the spring and summer of 1973, the nation sat glued to its TVs and radios as witness after witness paraded in front of the Senate Select Committee. "By the time the hearing began on May 17," according to David Halberstam, "it was the biggest story in the country. . . . Those regular watchers of soap operas who had at first complained because their favorite programs were being crowded off soon became hooked. The ratings were very good."[34] The power of televised congressional hearings has not diminished. Fourteen years later, the Iran-Contra hearings again captivated the nation and revealed the power of the media to make information about politics available to the general public.

The media also seek the big story by looking for scandal in the personal and business dealings of members of Congress. The media's snooping, which begins with the campaign for office, does not end when the politicians enter the hallowed halls of Congress. Over the years members of the House and Senate have been involved in all kinds of scandals—corruption, conflict of interest, sexual misconduct—and the media have reported every sordid detail. The media themselves, through their own investigative efforts, sometimes contribute to the chain of events that lead to the bringing of charges against a politician and help turn the tide of public opinion.

Even the most powerful members of Congress are not immune. In 1989 the Speaker of the House, Jim Wright, was forced to resign from Congress when his personal finances came under investigation. According to Wright, the media's reporting of charges against him before House rules permitted him to respond formally played a substantial part in his demise: "For the past year, while the Committee on Standards has had these matters under advisement, I have ached for the opportunity to speak. . . . But before those charges were issued, as press leaks filtered out almost daily, tarnishing my reputation and by inference spilling over onto the reputation of this institution [Congress], I pleaded for the privilege to come and answer those questions."[35]

Ironically, most members of Congress feel that they do not receive enough attention from the media. Unlike the president, who often avoids or evades the media's questions, America's 535 senators and representatives openly pursue the press. A significant portion of their staffs' time is devoted to preparing press releases, and they work hard to promote the boss's image in the home district and the nation. Congress, as we have seen, established the C-SPAN cable network to provide the public an opportunity to view its proceedings live on television. Members of Congress complain that the media spend too much time on the negative side—scandal, inefficiency—and too little time on the many hard-working legislators who become expert on highly technical issues.

The Media and the Courts

Of the three branches of government, the Supreme Court receives the least amount of the media's attention. One study found that during a single Supreme Court term the *New York Times* did not report on nearly a quarter of the Court's decisions, and regional papers covered fewer than half of the cases.[36] The major television and radio networks, wire services, and newspapers do assign reporters to cover the Court's term. An often-heard complaint is that the reporters lack the legal knowledge to analyze the Court's decisions accurately. The legal issues the justices discuss are technical and not always considered newsworthy, and television in particular places a premium on entertainment.

Another impediment to detailed media coverage of the Supreme Court is the privacy in which much of its work is conducted. The justices themselves (after their confirmation hearings) are not always well known by the public:

> Whereas coverage of the president and Congress is often personalized, Supreme Court reporting is quite the reverse. We rarely learn much about sitting justices as people or even as lawyers and legal philosophers. Unlike other politicians, their peccadillos and predilections are not dissected; personal or ideological conflicts are not seized upon and played up. Indeed, except in their written opinions, justices are quoted rarely. They are shadowy (though not shady), mysterious figures.[37]

The courts are not totally ignored by the media. Famous and controversial cases—*Brown* v. *Board of Education, Roe* v. *Wade*—receive detailed coverage. Political activities aimed at influencing the Court, such as the mass pro- and anti-abortion demonstrations that took place in the 1980s, receive wide media attention. On occasion the media have become part of the story by going to court in defense of First Amendment rights of speech and press. In the celebrated *New York Times Company* v. *United States* in 1971, the paper won the right to publish the controversial Pentagon Papers, a revealing account of the United States' involvement in Vietnam that the government argued should remain secret.

The Quality of Media Coverage of Government

Americans enjoy as much information about their government as any people on earth, perhaps more. Still, critics raise many probing questions about the way the media report on government in the United States and events abroad. One question

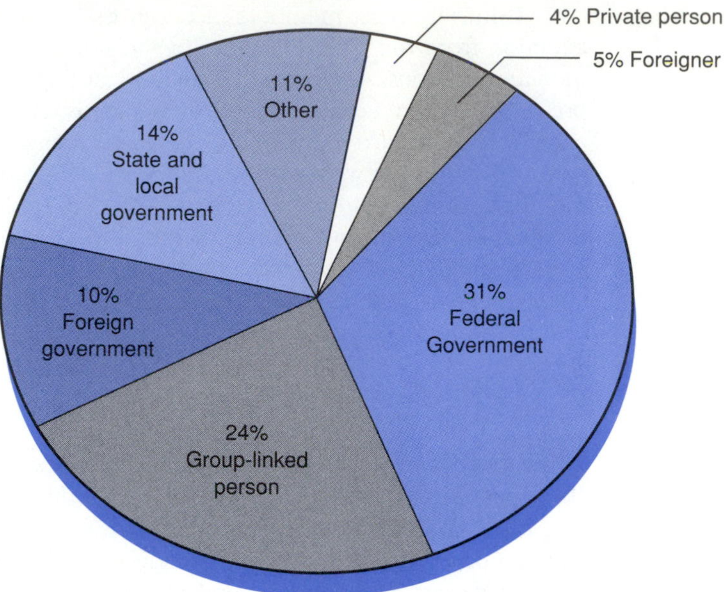

★ **Figure 11-6**

Sources for the front page stories for major newspapers

NOTE: The survey findings are from *New York Times, Washington Post,* and some smaller newspapers.

SOURCE: Doris A. Graber, *Mass Media and American Politics,* 3d ed. (Washington, D.C.: Congressional Quarterly Press, 1989), p. 79. Adapted from material originally presented by Jane Delano Brown, Carl R. Bybee, Stanley T. Wearden, and Dulcie Murdock Straughan, "Invisible Power: Newspaper News Sources and the Limits of Diversity," *Journalism Quarterly,* 64 (Spring, 1987), p. 49.

involves sources, or where reporters obtain their information on government. Popular mythology holds that reporters are supersleuths, murky figures draped in trench coats, haunting the back alleys of government. While there is some truth to this image, most information is gained directly from government press releases and other mundane sources. As figure 11-6 shows, government was the reporters' primary source nearly 50 percent of the time. Analysis of the *New York Times* and *Washington Post* shows that through press conferences, press releases, and official announcements, the government newsmakers control the flow of information nearly half of the time. The reporters' own analyses of events accounted for 1 percent of a story's content.[38]

As we saw in our discussion of the president and the media, the government goes to great lengths to manage and control the news. Agencies routinely leak information or give statements not to be attributed to them in order to influence public opinion. Government information about itself, in other words, is not always reliable or objective. Yet despite the government's efforts to manage the news, many reporters still depend heavily on government sources for their information.

Reporters are sometimes criticized for having a "herd mentality." The major networks and wire services, Robert Sherrill points out, tend to congregate in the same places (especially Washington, D.C., London, Paris, and Moscow) and to cover the same stories:

> Laziness, an unwillingness to offend friendly political sources, peevish envy of successful colleagues, devotion to journalistic "stylishness"... philosophical uncertainty and anxiety that induce the press to move with extreme caution—what does all of that add up to? It often adds up to herd journalism.... There's a clubby, lazy, selfish reason why reporters covering the same beat are content to follow the pack: if one of them should break away and dig up a hard-hitting story on his or her own, others would be obliged to get out and do some extra work, too.[39]

Related to the herd mentality is what is called **pack journalism.** Pack journalism comes to the fore when several reporters are assigned to the same subject or story. Reporters assigned to accompany the president on foreign trips, for example, often work, eat, and live in the close company of one another. Faced with daily deadlines and fearful of running a story that is factually incorrect, many reporters and news directors take the safe, noninnovative course. They use "pool" reports written by colleagues appointed by the pack, and rely on the press-kit handouts prepared by the president's public relations experts. One study of television news found that at least two of the major networks ran the same lead story 91 percent of the time.[40] The herd mentality and pack journalism do not preclude thoughtful, critical reporting by the media. These tendencies do not make it impossible to find varying points of view. They do mean that inquisitive citizens may have to search the back pages of several newspapers or tune in a public broadcasting station. But most Americans do not have the time or interest to seek out such commentary, and thus are fed a daily diet of news that differs only in the personalities of the various network anchors.

★ Government Regulation of the Media

By now it should be clear that the media play a crucial role in any society's political life. One might therefore assume that politicians and government officials would seek to control such a potentially powerful force. Indeed, in many countries the media are just another branch of government, held in the firm grip of political leaders. But such rigid control would obviously violate many of America's most cherished political rights.

In the United States, the print media (newspapers, magazines, books) fully enjoy the First Amendment's protections of free speech and press. Aside from the few legal limits resulting from Supreme Court decisions, the press is virtually free from censorship. Once a story appears, of course, private citizens (but usually not politicians) can bring suit if they feel they have been libeled. Television and radio, on the other hand, historically have been subject to tighter government control of their operations.

Government Control of the Airwaves

In 1934 Congress passed the Communications Act and created the **Federal Communications Commission (FCC).** The commission, appointed by the president and approved by the Senate, is empowered to regulate all radio and television broadcasting. The FCC's most important regulatory function is to grant licenses to all of the nation's radio and television stations.

In exercising its control over the airwaves, the FCC deals with many technical aspects of the industry: broadcast frequencies, competence of station personnel, and strength of signal, to name a few. The FCC also controls ownership patterns among the electronic media. As a general rule, the FCC's one-to-a-customer rule does not permit a single owner to acquire more than one AM, one FM, and one TV station in a single market. This rule does not prohibit owners from acquiring several stations in many different markets. Television broadcasting companies may own as many as twelve TV stations, provided that they don't reach more than 25 percent of the nation's homes.[41] In the climate of deregulation and corporate mergers that prevailed in the 1980s, the electronic media, like other aspects of American business, came increasingly under the control of a few large corporations.

The FCC's most important political function involves its requirements that broadcasters provide useful information to the public, treat different points of view fairly, and offer listeners and viewers an opportunity to express their opinions on the air. The FCC promotes the dissemination of information by its requirement that broadcasters include public affairs programming in their schedules. In 1973 the FCC passed a series of regulations called the "5-5-10 rule." Under this rule, stations were required to devote 5 percent of their air time to local affairs, 5 percent to news and public affairs, and 10 percent to nonentertainment programming.[42] These regulations were relaxed during the 1980s, when President Reagan's deregulation policies reduced direct government control of the media. Yet many broadcasters continue to provide significant public affairs programming.

Another regulatory requirement of the FCC is the **equal time requirement.** This rule requires broadcasters to give equal air time to candidates for public office. If a radio or TV station sells or gives air time to one candidate, all other candidates for the same office must receive equal treatment. This rule does not apply to straight news stories, interviews, or other news-related coverage. Many broadcasters oppose this rule, as it requires them to grant as much time to third-party and independent candidates as to those representing the Democrats and Republicans. In 1960 Congress removed the equal time rule for presidential elections, thus eliminating one of the broadcasters' biggest complaints.

In 1987 a long-standing FCC requirement, the so-called fairness doctrine, was eliminated. Under the fairness doctrine, broadcasters were required to present many points of view on controversial subjects and allow reasonable time for rebuttal to opinions expressed on the air. Broadcasters claimed that adherence to the fairness doctrine was difficult, expensive, and an intrusion on their right of free speech. When, they argued, is a presidential speech news, and when is it a partisan political statement deserving rebuttal by representatives of the opposing party? Supporters of the fairness doctrine, on the other hand, believed that some broadcasters would fail to provide the public with fair representation of all points of view on controversial issues.

The FCC's licensing authority gives it great influence over broadcasters. Since the number of frequencies available in any geographical area is limited, licenses are quite valuable. Revocation of a license can mean the end of a business empire for a broadcaster who has run afoul of the FCC's dictate to "serve the public interest, convenience, and necessity." At renewal time, the FCC invites the public to give testimony as to broadcasters' compliance with regulations and their service to the local community. This opportunity for public input permits citizens to have some say in the quality and political objectivity of their local broadcast media. In the past, some citizen groups have managed to persuade the FCC to lift the licenses of unpopular stations. With deregulation, however, the FCC has adopted a more hands-off attitude toward broadcasters.

★ Are the Media Biased?

> In this mass communications society, if you don't exist in the media, for all practical purposes, you don't exist.
>
> —*Daniel Schorr*

Political scientists have identified four basic functions of modern media: (1) surveillance of the world to report ongoing events, (2) interpretation of the meaning of events, (3) socialization of individuals into their cultural settings, and (4) deliberate manipulation of the political process.[43] The first function, surveillance (or reporting), we have already examined in depth. The remaining functions—interpretation, socialization, and manipulation—are highly controversial.

Many reporters, in keeping with long-standing traditions of journalism, claim that they are objective. Events, they insist, are to be reported without coloration or injection of personal preferences. When a journalist editorializes, it is to be made clear that this is opinion, not fact. But is the media's reporting really objective? In order to assess the media's impact we need to consider three questions: (1) Who controls the media? (2) Do the media attempt to manipulate the public? (3) What impact do the media really have on citizens' opinions?

Media Ownership

The media in the United States are owned by a relatively few large corporations and conglomerates. Of America's approximately 25,000 mass media (television channels, publishers, newspapers, radio stations, magazines), the majority are owned by twenty-nine corporations. Whereas 80 percent of newspapers were locally owned before World War II, now 72 percent are owned by fifteen large corporations.[44] In 1987, moreover, four companies controlled nearly 20 percent of the national television market.[45]

Recent years have also seen the emergence of large corporations with multiple ownership of different types of media. The Gannett Company, publisher of *USA Today,* owns more than a hundred daily and weekly newspapers and twenty-four radio and television stations. Another firm, Park Communications, owns 103 newspapers and nineteen broadcast outlets.[46] Some members of Congress have also noted with concern that mergers and acquisitions in the communications-entertainment-publishing industry have concentrated ownership in relatively few large corporations. The acquisition of newspapers, television stations, and film distributorships by foreign investors, such as the Australian Rupert Murdoch, is also of concern to some media analysts.

The media *are* big business. In 1988 the three major television networks earned total revenues in excess of $10.1 billion from broadcasting and related operations. ABC's total earnings rose 38 percent in 1988, and CBS's 1988 profits climbed 154 percent over those of 1987.[47] In defending their interests, the media employ many of the same lobbying tactics as other large corporations. Between 1985 and August 1988, according to one report, the National Cable Television Association donated $446,240 to federal candidates. The National Association of Broadcasters (NAB) gave $307,986 during the same period. The speaking fees paid by the NAB to politicians were second only to the American Trucking Association's among trade associations in 1987. Politics can be big business for broadcasters in its own right: candidates, political parties, and political action committees buy hundreds of millions of dollars' worth of advertising. Television stations alone received more than $300 million for political advertising during the 1986 congressional election.[48]

Whether or not one finds media ownership patterns significant depends on one's theory of politics. In chapter 5 we asked the crucial political question "Who governs?" According to the ruling elite theory of American politics, government and other important institutions are controlled by a small economic, intellectual, and political elite. The pluralist theory, by contrast, takes the view that American political life is shared by many groups—labor, business, ethnic groups, political parties—and that public policy is the product of competition and cooperation among these groups. For various groups to compete successfully, they must have access to powerful institutions, including the media. While corporate domination of the media does not preclude citizen access (especially through public television and radio), it does imply that some economic and/or political interests may enjoy much greater access than others.

The Media's Monopoly of Information

The media are often charged with being too conservative or too liberal. What constitutes liberal or conservative, of course, depends on the political views of the accuser. Rather than fight over labels, let us agree that the media accept the basic values of American life—capitalism, Western-style democracy, consumerism, individualism, global activism, and entrepreneurship. Within these basic premises the media recognize a relatively narrow band of alternative views, ranging from the moderate liberal left to the conservative right.

The media's ultimate power lies not in their ideological preferences for the left or the right but in the way they define reality for the American people. The media, in deciding to cover some stories and not to cover others, determine the crucial issues of the day. The few people who select stories for coverage by the newspapers and the networks are sometimes called **gatekeepers.** Gatekeepers include editors, assignment planners, TV network anchors, and radio disk jockeys. Some major stories demand coverage. But many others are selected by media decision makers.

Gatekeepers are especially important in selecting the international events to be reported. Most major media stories on the international scene focus on dramatic events and crisis situations. To the casual reader or viewer, international events seem to fade in and out of view. This week's crisis may be forgotten in a few days. During the 1980s, a bloody civil war raged almost continuously in the Central American nation of El Salvador. Coverage by the American media, however, was highly sporadic. Though American taxpayers sent over $150 million a year in foreign aid to El Salvador, they received (and demanded) relatively little mass-media coverage of the situation in that embattled nation.

Gatekeepers can become kingmakers at election time. By focusing on frontrunners during the presidential primaries, the media can help elevate a candidate into a position of national prominence. Media attention, based on public opinion

"And as the campaign heats up, the latest poll shows the Dan Rather news team running slightly ahead of the Peter Jennings news team, with the Tom Brokaw team just two points back and gaining."

polls and performance in the early primary elections and caucuses, is crucial to a candidate's success. The success of a virtual unknown, Jimmy Carter, in the 1976 primaries is widely attributed to his good showing early in the contest. A poor showing in New Hampshire or Iowa, on the other hand, can lead the media to demote a front-runner to a has-been in a week's time.

The media are widely criticized for their horse-race approach to primary elections. The focus on early results from Iowa and New Hampshire, according to some critics, sets the tone for the election, and reduces the importance of primaries held later in the more populous states. In 1984, for instance, while the snow still lay on the ground, New Hampshire, with 0.4 percent of the nation's population, received 19.2 percent of all media coverage during the presidential nomination campaign. Sunny California, with its 10.8 percent of the population basking in the June sun, received 6.9 percent of total media coverage.[49] Many Californians felt disenfranchised by their diminished role in the primary process.

The media's horse-race approach, according to Doris Graber, with its clear designation of winners and losers, "may become a self-fulfilling prophecy because supporters and money, as well as media coverage, flow to the front-runner, especially when lesser contenders have dropped out of the race after poor showings in early contests."[50] Campaign strategists, in recognition of the media's kingmaker role, have abandoned traditional party structures and "smoke-filled rooms" for well-crafted campaigns aimed at securing the prized front-runner slot on TV and in the press. Thus the media's real power lies in its story selection process and role of gatekeeper and kingmaker.

The Media's Impact: Is Anyone Listening?

> The spectrum of information in America has become so crowded and so cacophonous that the people who are out there attempting to get real information from it have a hard time picking out what's real and what's just noise.
>
> —*Tom Brokaw*

It is clear that Americans spend a great deal of time watching television and that

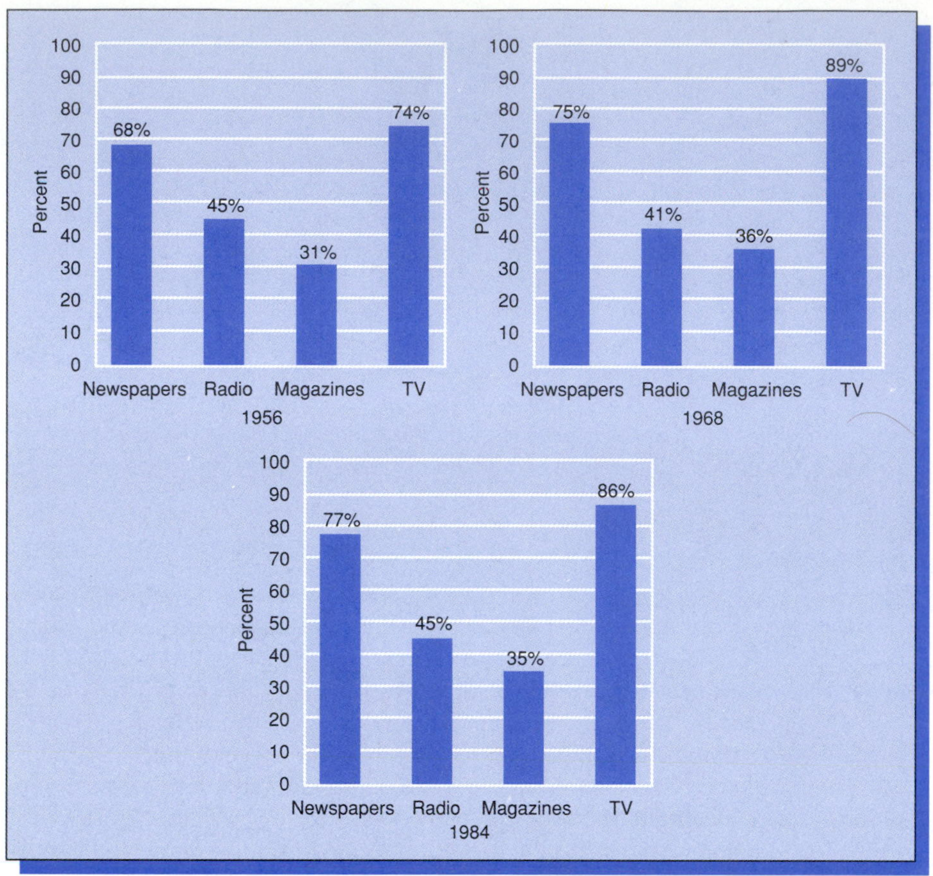

★ **Figure 11-7**
Public reliance on media for campaign information
SOURCE: Herbert B. Asher, *Presidential Elections and American Politics,* 4th. ed. (Pacific Grove, Calif.: Brooks/Cole, 1988), p. 249.

they receive most of their news about politics from the media (see figure 11-7). And there is significant evidence that the media do help shape their political opinions. In a 1988 poll, one in four voters reported that campaign advertising helped them make a choice between presidential candidates.[51]

Still, it is difficult to measure how much real impact the media have on political opinions. The public is certainly skeptical of the media's reliability. In 1987 Norman Ornstein found that 44 percent of the public felt that media news reporting was accurate while 48 percent felt it was not. As figures 11-8 and 11-9 show, overall public confidence in television and the press is not high. Aside from accuracy, one of the biggest problems the public faces is to sort through the flood of information available through the modern mass media. One obvious coping strategy is to ignore a good part of the information available. A major network prime-time interview with Soviet leader Mikhail Gorbachev in 1987, for example, was watched by only 15 percent of the national audience. Newspaper readers usually exclude two out of three stories in their daily paper, and only 18 percent of the stories are read in full. Of the fifteen to twenty events covered on TV's evening news, viewers may recall the substance of only one or two.[52]

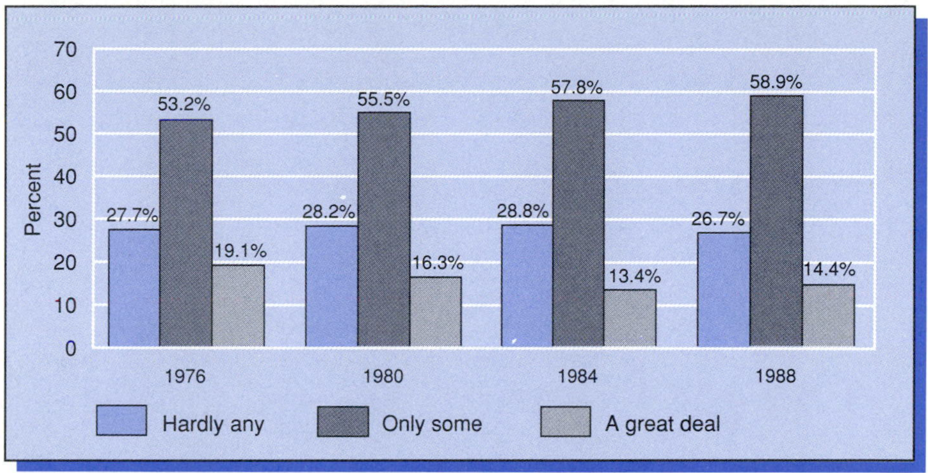

Figure 11-8
Degree of confidence expressed in television, 1976–1988 (percent)
SOURCE: James Allan Davis and Tom W. Smith, *General Social Survey, 1972–1988* (Chicago: National Opinion Research Center, 1988), subfiles 1976, 1980, 1984, 1988 (machine-readable data file).

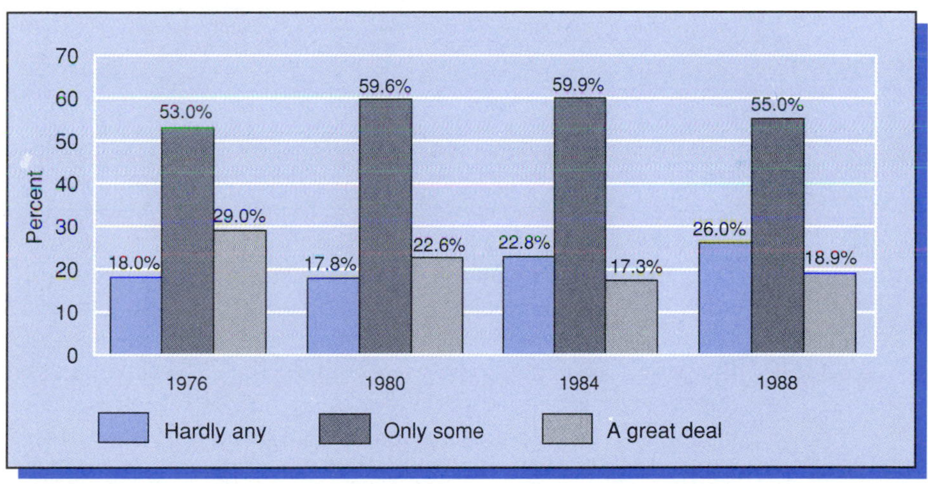

Figure 11-9
Degree of confidence expressed in press, 1976–1988 (percent)
SOURCE: James Allan Davis and Tom W. Smith, *General Social Survey, 1972–1988* (Chicago: National Opinion Research Center, 1988), subfiles 1976, 1980, 1984, 1988 (machine-readable data file).

The public filters information in other ways as well. Through conscious or unconscious selective perception, the public screens out or modifies messages. Selective perception involves what Doris Graber calls the schema process. The schema, based on the person's background and belief system, represents a definition of reality that leads the individual to extract from a story only information that conforms with his or her own opinions and expectations. If you believe, for example, that the Soviet Union is an aggressive nation that seeks to dominate the world, you will dismiss information to the contrary. As we saw in our discussion of public

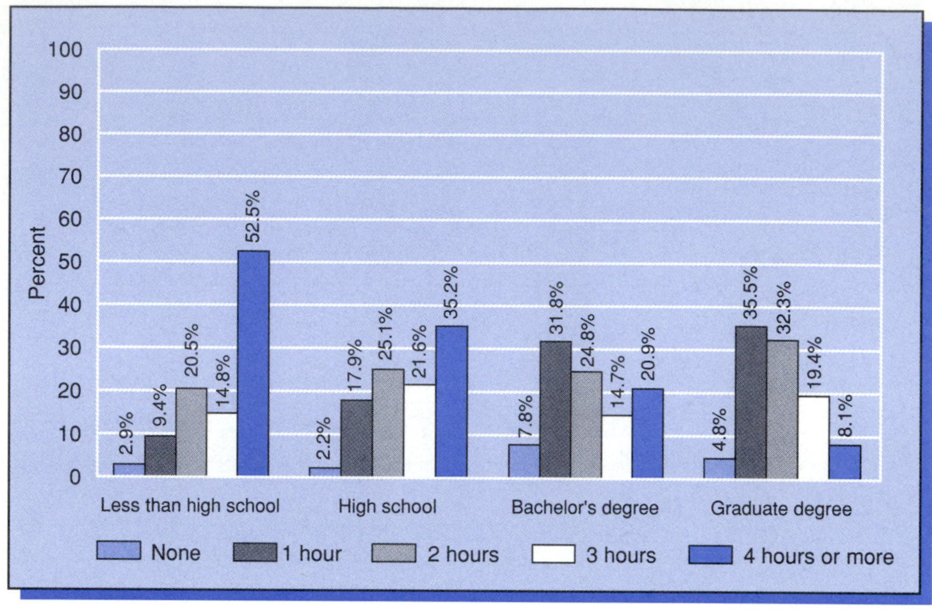

★ **Figure 11-10**
Hours of television viewed per day, 1988 (by level of education)
SOURCE: James Allan Davis and Tom W. Smith, *General Social Survey, 1972–1988* (Chicago: National Opinion Research Center, 1988), subfile 1988 (machine-readable data file).

opinion and international relations (chapter 7), internationalists and isolationists tend to cling to their view of the world. Learning can and does take place, but reporters and politicians who attempt to influence public opinion cannot be certain that their message will be received as they intended.

Overall, the public's interest in the news remains relatively low. At the same time, many people feel that, as good citizens, they should try to keep informed. But the public's exposure is somewhat haphazard—people tend to wade through the hard news to get to the sports and weather. The situation is complicated by the fact that media news, especially television news, is itself fragmented and inconsistent. Since television viewing is related to level of education (see figure 11-10), the least educated in our society may also be the least informed about the news.

In order to attract a somewhat disinterested audience, the media, as a big business in search of big profits, must entertain while informing. Viewers may watch dramatic accounts of troops killing unarmed demonstrators in China, but they are offered little comprehensive analysis of the origins of the conflict. Instead of analysis, the media concentrate on crisis and drama. Their international reporters become globetrotters, chasing the latest big story. This partial flow of information leads to superficial conclusions: "America is powerless," or "All Muslims are political fanatics."

Still, the communications revolution continues to change the way we view the world. Although there is ample room to criticize the media, the situation is not hopeless:

> On balance, the verdict is clear. Average Americans are capable of extracting enough meaningful political information from the flood of news to which they are exposed to perform the moderate number of citizenship functions that American society expects of them.[53]

★ Summary

Global interdependence, along with rapid technological developments in electronics, has led to a communications revolution. The mass media, always an important force in American politics, have used the tools of the communications revolution to expand their coverage of local, national, and international events. At the global level, the communications revolution has made it possible to learn about international events as they occur. With the expansion of television to nearly every American home, most citizens can gain access to the news at the push of a button.

Television and newspapers are America's primary sources of political news. The media cover elections, the three branches of government, and foreign affairs. The modern presidency benefits significantly from television coverage. Governments attempt to influence the media and public opinion in many ways. But relations between the media and politicians are not always smooth. They need each other to perform their societal functions, but they have different goals. Although the media and government cooperate on many levels, an adversarial relationship often exists between politicians and the media.

The media are sometimes criticized for relying too heavily on the government as the source of their news. Ownership of the media by a relatively few large corporations is also cited as a threat to open access and wide-ranging discussion of all points of view. The charge that the media are politically biased, however, is more difficult to substantiate. Above all, the media seem to represent mainstream American life, and accept with few questions its economic, social, and political institutions.

The media's overall impact on public opinion is unclear. By serving as gatekeepers of the news, the media are able to determine which issues will be brought to the public's attention. Media news, by and large, is fragmented and lacking in sophisticated analysis. Business and financial considerations often compete with good journalistic practices. Still, if a citizen is willing to consult a variety of sources and media, it is possible to become a well-informed participant in the American political system.

★ Key Terms

communications revolution
equal time requirement
Federal Communications Commission (FCC)
gatekeepers
image politics
investigative reporting
mass media
muckraking
pack journalism
pseudo-events
spot commercial
strategic leaks
televised debate
wire services
yellow journalism

★ Notes

1. Ronald Berkman and Laura W. Kitch, *Politics in the Media Age* (New York: McGraw-Hill, 1986), p. 39.
2. Ibid., p. 41.
3. *Broadcasting/Cable Yearbook, 1989* (Washington, D.C.: Broadcasting Publications, 1989), p. D3.
4. "Pipeline to the U.S. Viewer," *South,* November 1988, pp. 12–13.
5. *New York Times,* December 16, 1987, p. A32.

6. John Schachter, "Congress Begins Second Decade under TV's Watchful Glare," *Congressional Quarterly,* March 11, 1989, p. 507.
7. Berkman and Kitch, *Politics in the Media Age,* p. 21.
8. Yellow journalism gets its name from a comic strip, *The Yellow Kid,* published in color.
9. Berkman and Kitch, *Politics in the Media Age,* p. 25.
10. Doris A. Graber, *Mass Media and American Politics,* 3d ed. (Washington, D.C.: Congressional Quarterly Press, 1989), p. 12.
11. David Halberstam, *The Powers That Be* (New York: Knopf, 1979), p. 15.
12. Bernard Anderson, "Broadcasting: Tuning In to Development," *South,* August 1986, p. 95.
13. Graber, *Mass Media,* p. 334.
14. David L. Paletz and Robert M. Entman, *Media-Power-Politics* (New York: Free Press, 1981), p. 217.
15. See Jacobo Timmerman, *Prisoner without a Name, Cell without a Number* (New York: Vintage, 1981).
16. "China with a C: CBS and CNN," *Broadcasting* 116 (May 29, 1989): 59.
17. See Anthony Smith, *The Geopolitics of Information: How Western Culture Dominates the World* (New York: Oxford University Press, 1980).
18. Samuel C. Florman, "Liberating Technologies," *Technology Review,* October 1988, p. 18.
19. Halberstam, *Powers That Be,* p. 6.
20. Paletz and Entman, *Media-Power-Politics,* pp. 179–180.
21. Quoted in Robert MacNeil, *The People Machine: The Influence of Television on American Politics* (New York: Harper & Row, 1968), p. 210.
22. Graber, *Mass Media,* p. 203.
23. Marquis Child, quoted in ibid., p. 202.
24. Berkman and Kitch, *Politics in the Media Age,* p. 319.
25. Tom Brokaw, comments at "The People, Press, and Politics," a panel discussion presented by the *Los Angeles Times and Times Mirror,* January 29, 1988.
26. Ibid.
27. Jack Nelson and Walter Mondale, comments at ibid.
28. Berkman and Kitch, *Politics in the Media Age,* p. 131.
29. W. Lance Bennett, *News: The Politics of Illusion* (New York: Longman, 1983), p. 47.
30. Ibid., pp. 48–49.
31. Carl Sessions Stepp, "In Time of War: Grenada Skirmish over Access Goes On," in *Main Currents in Mass Communications,* ed. Warren K. Agee et al. (New York: Harper & Row, 1986), p. 80.
32. Graber, *Mass Media,* p. 328.
33. See ibid., p. 255; and Stephen Hess, *The Washington Reporters* (Washington, D.C.: Brookings Institution, 1981).
34. Halberstam, *Powers That Be,* p. 696.
35. Quoted in *New York Times,* June 1, 1989, p. A17.
36. David Ericson, "Newspaper Coverage of the Supreme Court: A Case Study," *Journalism Quarterly* 54 (Autumn 1977): 605–607.
37. Paletz and Entman, *Media-Power-Politics,* p. 105.
38. Bennett, *News,* pp. 53–54.
39. Robert Sherrill, *Why They Call It Politics: A Guide to America's Government,* 4th ed. (New York: Harcourt Brace Jovanovich, 1984), p. 331.
40. Graber, *Mass Media,* p. 87.
41. Companies that are more than half owned by ethnic minorities may own up to fourteen stations and reach 30 percent of the national market.
42. Berkman and Kitch, *Politics in the Media Age,* p. 52.
43. The first three functions are identified by Harold Lasswell in "The Structure and Function of Communication in Society," in *Mass Communication and Society,* ed. James Curran et al. (Urbana: University of Illinois Press, 1969); the fourth function is identified by Graber, *Mass Media,* p. 5.
44. Ben H. Bagdikian, *The Media Monopoly,* 2d ed. (Boston: Beacon, 1987), p. 4.
45. "Concentrating on Concentration," *Broadcasting* 116 (June 5, 1989): 48.
46. *Broadcasting/Cable Yearbook, 1989,* pp. A56–A62.
47. "The Top 100," *Broadcasting* 116 (June 5, 1989): 54.
48. Sheila Kaplan, "The Powers That Be: Lobbying," *Washington Monthly,* December 1988, pp. 38, 46.
49. William C. Adams, "As New Hampshire Goes . . . ," in *Media and Momentum: The New Hampshire Primary and Nomination Politics,* ed. Gary R. Orren and Nelson W. Polsby (Chatham, N.J.: Chatham House, 1987), p. 45.

50. Graber, *Mass Media,* p. 199.
51. Michael Oreskes, "TV's Role in '88: The Medium Is the Election," *New York Times,* October 30, 1988, p. 19.
52. Doris A. Graber, *Processing the News: How People Tame the Information Tide* (New York: Longman, 1984), pp. 201–202.
53. Ibid., p. 204.

★ For Further Reading

Agee, Warren K., Phillip H. Ault, and Edwin Emery, eds. *Main Currents in Mass Communications.* New York: Harper & Row, 1986.

Bagdikian, Ben H. *The Media Monopoly.* 2d ed. Boston: Beacon, 1987.

Bennett, W. Lance. *News: The Politics of Illusion.* New York: Longman, 1983.

Berkman, Ronald, and Laura W. Kitch. *Politics in the Media Age.* New York: McGraw-Hill, 1986.

Crouse, Timothy. *The Boys on the Bus.* New York: Random House, 1973.

Graber, Doris A. *Mass Media and American Politics.* 3d ed. Washington, D.C.: Congressional Quarterly Press, 1989.

——. *Processing the News: How People Tame the Information Tide.* New York: Longman, 1984.

Halberstam, David. *The Powers That Be.* New York: Knopf, 1979.

Herr, Michael. *Dispatches.* New York: Knopf, 1977.

Lamb, Brian. *C-SPAN: America's Town Hall.* Washington, D.C.: Acropolis, 1988.

McLuhan, Marshall. *Understanding Media: The Extensions of Man.* New York: McGraw-Hill, 1965.

McQuail, Denis, and Karen Siune. *New Media Politics: Comparative Politics in Western Europe.* London: Sage, 1986.

Mowlana, Hamid. *Global Information and World Communication.* New York: Longman, 1986.

Nimmo, Dan, and James E. Combs. *Nightly Horrors: Crisis Coverage by Television Network News.* Knoxville: University of Tennessee Press, 1985.

Stover, William James. *Information Technology in the Third World.* Boulder, Colo.: Westview, 1984.

PART THREE

Behind the Granite Walls: The Nuts and Bolts of the American Political System

Representative Michael Synar . . . was addressing a Cub Scout pack in Grove, Oklahoma, not far from his home town of Muskogee. Synar asked the young boys if they could tell him the difference between the Cub Scouts and the United States Congress. One boy raised his hand and said: "We have adult supervision."

—Gregg Easterbrook

CHAPTER TWELVE

CONGRESS

★★★★★★★★★★★

The Legislative Labyrinth: The United States Congress

When it comes to influencing policy, senators and representatives seem to be in enviable positions. Members of Congress share a unique responsibility for enacting or blocking legislation that affects the health and well-being of millions of Americans. As America's role in the world grows, moreover, Congress's influence on U.S. defense policy, foreign aid, and trade regulations also affects people in many other nations. Indeed, to many people who seek political power, Congress has the allure of an exciting arena in which new legislation is constantly being created. The men and women in Congress are seen as participants in a dynamic process in which they share a great opportunity to translate their dreams into political reality. Undoubtedly it is this vision that compels many citizens to try to influence their senator or representative, to sway his or her vote on pending legislation. In this chapter we will examine Congress's role as the primary representative of the American people. And we will see that Congress is both plagued by parochialism and determined to help to guide America's role on the global stage.

★ A Sense of Impotence?

In some ways, a vision of the creative potential of serving in Congress is deceptive. One's view of power in Congress depends greatly on which senators and representatives one chooses to examine. If one looks at those committee chairs who work on behalf of wealthy and powerful interests—the oil companies, the banking lobby, the military—then the opportunities for influence may seem boundless. But if one examines instead those members who come to Washington to work on behalf of people without strong representation, such as the homeless or the elderly poor, then the chances of achieving meaningful goals in Congress appear more remote. As newly elected members soon discover, Congress does not easily gratify the thirst for power or the desire for reform that may have been the driving force behind their campaigns. "A new Congressman," former representative Shirley Chisholm has written,

> faces a lot of disappointments. One most freshman House members share is the discovery that, while getting elected made him a big man back home, Washington has seen green representatives arrive by the thousands and is not very impressed. Then, unless he has had legislative experience, he will be frustrated to learn that his plans for laws that will solve the problems of the country, whatever he deems them to be, are doomed because he is a very junior member of a rather large group.[1]

Nor are such frustrations confined to freshman members. Even seasoned congressional veterans can find their efforts blocked. With its many committees and subcommittees that decentralize decision making, its complex procedures, the power of the executive branch, and the strong influence of special interests, Congress can be a source of irritation even to those familiar with its ways. Members seeking solutions to social problems complain time and again that Congress is a difficult place in which to assume a constructive role. Explaining why he chose to retire from the House after serving fourteen years, one representative snapped, "It's the system. I can't do anything unless I'm chairman of an important committee—and I could wait forever for that."[2]

Even senators occasionally feel discouraged. Though they have advantages that House members do not enjoy—greater prestige, a six-year rather than two-year term, and a smaller chamber with less rigid rules and procedures—each remains only one voice among many. Even if a senator's bill wins the support of a majority of senators, it still must secure the support of a far more numerous majority of House members. The major differences between the two legislative bodies are shown in table 12-1 on page 413.

Also, members of Congress cannot count on basking in the warmth of public adulation once they have reached this lofty position. On the basis of past failures, citizens often take a skeptical and cynical attitude toward their representatives' claims of noble intentions. Indeed, senators and representatives would have to go to considerable lengths to restore public confidence in their lawmaking abilities. According to a 1988 Gallup poll, only about one-third of Americans had a great deal of confidence in Congress (see chap. 7).

In fact, Congress has long been chided for lacking the will to confront global problems and for serving as an obstacle to reform. Generations of commentators, satirists, and cartoonists have decried what the nineteenth-century writer Alexis de Tocqueville once described as Congress's "vulgarity and its poverty of talent." Even the venerable satirist Mark Twain had scathing things to say about Congress:

> It could probably be shown by facts and figures that there is no distinctly native American criminal class except Congress.
>
> I . . . was a reporter in a legislature two sessions and the same in Congress one session—and thus learned to know personally three sample-bodies of the smallest minds and the selfishest souls and the cowardliest hearts that God makes.
>
> . . . those burglars that broke into my house recently . . . are in jail, and if they keep on they will go to Congress. When a person starts downhill you can never tell when he's going to stop.

Though most Americans today may be amused by Twain's iconoclastic views of Congress, many harbor similar negative feelings. They hear tales of senators and representatives traveling abroad on pleasure junkets at taxpayers' expense, attending cocktail parties when they should be legislating, and accepting bribes for political favors. Indeed, how can a favorable view of Congress be expected when scandals involving legislators, even the Speaker of the House, continue to leap out of the front pages of newspapers? During the past two decades, more than a dozen members of Congress have been indicted for crimes ranging from tax evasion to bribery. But perhaps the most widespread feeling is that Congress remains unresponsive to people's needs. Crime still rages in the streets, pollution and toxic wastes continue to contaminate our environment, and millions of homeless citizens roam the streets while members of Congress seem to coast along making promises that are rarely fulfilled.

© Signe Wilkinson

Yet there is some irony here. Despite generally low opinions of Congress as a whole, people seem to be generally content with the performance of their own representative. During the past twenty years, more than 90 percent of House incumbents seeking reelection have won, and about 80 percent of senators have returned to office.

Some reform-minded members have been heartened by efforts to reform the legislative machinery. As we will see, Congress has approved a variety of changes in the way it does business, including the curbing of the seniority system and of the powers of committee chairs. It also has made significant strides to regain some of the powers lost to the White House, as when it placed limits on the president's war powers and assumed greater control over the federal budget. With these changes has come the hope that Congress can respond more decisively to national and global social and economic ills, and that each member can play a more assertive role in policy making.

To understand the action potential of serving on Capitol Hill, we will examine some of the powers and duties of senators and representatives. We will also look at the evolving power structure in Congress, especially at the suitability of that structure to the goals of individual members. Obviously, those of us who desire to feed our own ideas into the legislative labyrinth also need to know what our senators and representative can and cannot do for us—what sorts of obstacles we as citizens can expect to face.

★ The Powers of Congress

An incredible diversity of powers and duties is the most striking feature of a congressional career. In addition to such rarely exercised powers as those of declar-

Table 12-1
Major differences between the House and the Senate

House	*Senate*
Larger (435)	Smaller (100)
Shorter term of office (2 years)	Longer term of office (6 years)
More procedural restraints on members	Fewer procedural restraints on members
Narrower constituency	Broader, more varied, constituency
Policy specialists	Policy generalists
Less press and media coverage	More press and media coverage
Power less evenly distributed	Power more evenly distributed
Less prestigious	More prestigious
More expeditious in floor debate	Less expeditious in floor debate
Less reliance on staff	More reliance on staff
Less staff	More staff
Equal populations represented	States represented
Important Rules Committee	Less important Rules Committee
Nongermaine amendments (riders) not allowed	Nongermaine amendments (riders) allowed
22 major committees	16 major committees
	Special treaty ratification power
	Special confirmation power

SOURCE: Walter J. Oleszek, *Congressional Procedures and the Policy Process*, 2d ed. (Washington, D.C.: Congressional Quarterly Press, 1984), p. 22.

ing war, proposing amendments to the Constitution, and removing federal officials through impeachment, members of Congress have several major responsibilities: to forge new laws, to oversee the executive branch through investigations, to advise the president and give or withhold consent to his actions, to raise and spend money, and to help **constituents** back home. (A senator's constituents are all of the residents of an entire state—whether tiny Rhode Island or populous California. A representative's constituents are residents of the state congressional district in which he or she was elected.) On any given day, a senator or representative may cast the crucial vote on a foreign aid bill, chair an important committee hearing on bureaucratic waste, or help trim or fatten the federal budget; and he or she may also help one constituent retrieve a lost social security check. Let us take a look at how each of these powers and duties may be exercised.

Forging New Laws

As we would expect, the greatest potential for political power enjoyed by members of Congress is the opportunity to forge new laws. Because the Constitution declares that "all legislative powers herein granted shall be vested in a Congress of the United States," each senator and representative may introduce and help pass legislation designed to promote the general welfare of the country (or at least of some special group).

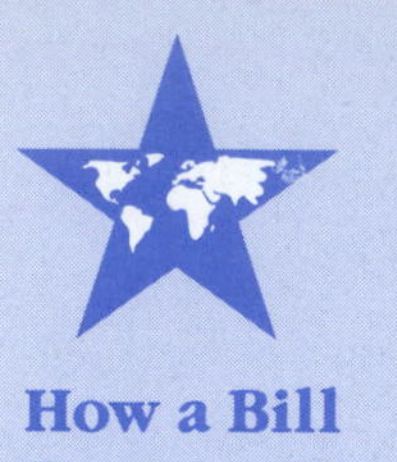

How a Bill Becomes Law

With the exception of revenue bills, which must originate in the House of Representatives, a bill may be introduced first in either the House or the Senate or simultaneously in both.

House of Representatives

A bill is introduced. A bill is received from the Senate or introduced by a representative, usually with cosponsors and perhaps as suggested or even drafted by the president. It is given an identification number and then referred to the appropriate standing committee.

The committee considers it. If the committee does not kill the bill outright, it may refer it to a subcommittee and also may add amendments. After the bill wins a majority vote in the committee, it is usually sent to the Rules Committee (most appropriations and revenue bills bypass the Rules Committee).

The Rules Committee considers it. If the Rules Committee decides not to kill the bill outright, it determines *when* the bill will be heard on the floor, *how long* debate on it may last, and *whether* it can be amended on the floor.

Floor action. The bill goes before the entire House, where it is debated and voted on.

Final action. Once the bill wins House approval, it may be sent either (1) directly to the president for signature or veto, (2) back to the Senate for approval of amendments added in the House, or (3) to a conference committee of Senate and House members, where the differences may be hammered out (in which case another vote on the bill must take place in both chambers).

Senate

A bill is introduced. A bill is received from the House or introduced by a senator, usually with cosponsors and perhaps as suggested or even drafted by the president. It is given an identification number and then referred to the appropriate standing committee.

The committee considers it. If the committee does not kill the bill outright, it may refer it to a subcommittee and hold hearings. After the bill wins a majority vote in the committee (possibly with amendments), it is scheduled for debate on the floor.

Floor action. The bill goes before the entire Senate, where it is debated and voted on.

Final action. Once the bill is passed (possibly with amendments), it is sent to the House of Representatives, where it must clear similar hurdles. ★

It is important to remember, however, that the actual amount of influence on policy making varies from member to member. Some senators and representatives are clearly more or less ambitious than others and expect or refuse to wield the maximum power they can draw from their positions. Moreover, the hurdles of Congress can at times seem insurmountable. Because most policy making takes place in committees, for example, a member may find it difficult to push through legislation unless the proper committee shares his or her concerns (see figure 12-1). Not only may the committee members not share those concerns, but many other bills may be competing for their attention. After all, Congress receives legislative proposals from a grab bag of sources: lobbyists pushing interest group causes, leftover bills not passed earlier, or policy brainstorms of powerful committee chairs and budding presidential hopefuls. And because the president has been handed the responsibility to set much of Congress's legislative agenda, a senator or representative may find his or her own pet project placed on the back burner while the president's policy recommendations receive priority. Since the president largely controls the foreign policy agenda and can make executive agree-

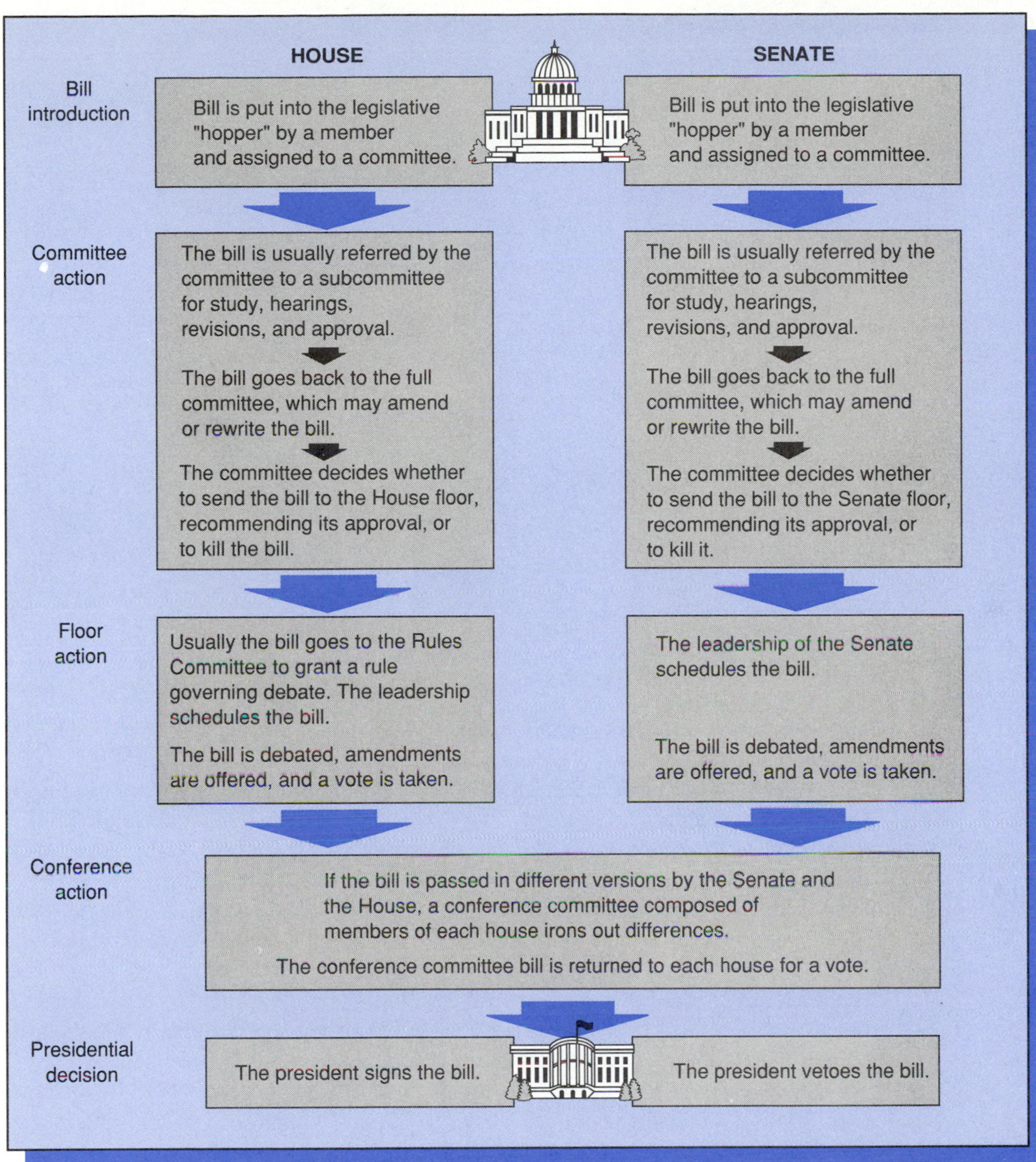

Figure 12-1
How a bill becomes law

ments with other nations without Congress's advice or consent, the legislator can also feel quite restrained or ineffective in dealing with international issues.

Thus, while constituents back home dash off letters urgently pleading for legislation to help working families with day care, to apply sanctions to South Africa, or otherwise to cure society's ills, the policy maker in Congress struggles with cumbersome legislative machinery. Despite pressures from home, few members of Congress actually succeed each year in getting important new legislation passed.

★ Rep. William Gray of Pennsylvania, the first black majority whip in the House, confers with fellow Democrat Rep. George Miller of California.

Although some members remain indebted to special interests and have little interest in serving constituents, others find their dreams of legislative knighthood vaporized. One representative once lamented, "I came here thinking I would immediately share in the drafting of legislation. As all of us soon discover, the likelihood of first or second termers, and particularly minority members, doing any major drafting of legislation that passes is slim if not completely unknown."[3]

Nor does the average member of Congress wield tremendous influence with his or her vote on the floor. Although voting is one of a member's most important legislative responsibilities—after all, it is through their votes that senators and representatives theoretically express the will of their constituents—few members perceive their votes as decisive on most pieces of legislation. This is particularly true in the House of Representatives with its 435 members. "Since I've been here," one representative has noted, "only one major bill has been decided by a single vote. If you try to evaluate your incremental impact, you have to decide that, unless you're Speaker, chairman of an important committee, or part of the House leadership, you just can't have much impact on normal Congressional operations."[4]

As we will see, however, a member can wield significant influence in his or her own committee or subcommittee, where a single vote can determine the life or death of a bill. The question then becomes how to decide whether to support or reject a bill. One standard view is that members of Congress ultimately are "delegates" of their constituents and should honor constituents' wishes. As one representative has stated, "You cannot buck district sentiment on certain issues. In my area, oil, coal, and mining are extremely important, and if you're 'right' on these things you have a much easier time of it. But you are opening yourself up to criticism if you vote against them often."[5]

As we saw in chapter 5, supporters of the ruling elite theory insist that most members of Congress are the delegates of powerful local elites. They point out that senators and representatives tend to communicate more with active special interests in their home states and districts than with the majority of their constituents, who are ignorant of congressional activities. In a district where the main industry is computers, for instance, the key and relevant constituency is the people who dominate that industry. Whether the interests of the local elite necessarily conflict with the interests of a majority of the legislator's constituents is another question. Conceivably, a majority of the people back home may feel that congressional policy that benefits local industry also benefits them, as it secures them jobs and other economic advantages.

In any event, how can legislators know what the majority of their constituents want on every issue? Although sophisticated tools are available to sample opinions—including polls and mailed questionnaires—they are impractical on an issue-by-issue basis. As John Kennedy discovered when he served in Congress, "In Washington I frequently find myself believing that forty or fifty letters, six visits from professional politicians and lobbyists, and three editorials in Massachusetts newspapers constitute public opinion on a given issue. Yet in truth I rarely know how the great majority of voters feel, or even how much they know of the issues that seem so burning in Washington." Such doubts have convinced many legislators that they are ultimately "trustees" of the people, and must make their own decisions as to what is to their district's best advantage. "The voters selected us," Kennedy concluded, "because they had confidence in our judgment and our ability to exercise that judgment from a position where we could determine what were their own best interests, as part of the nation's interests."[6]

In practice, the views of most members of Congress toward lawmaking vary from policy to policy. On issues that do not specifically pertain to their districts, such as foreign aid, lawmakers often act in response to their own sentiments, or to the wishes of colleagues or the party leadership; but on matters closer to home, such as economic and social issues, they tend to vote more in accordance with local interests.

Serving Constituents

Although senators and representatives face interesting challenges in legislating for the nation, they are not solely lawmakers. As the federal bureaucracy expands its influence over people's lives, members of Congress must spend an increasing amount of time helping constituents cut red tape or correct bureaucratic injustices by **casework.** Perhaps a constituent quickly needs a visa to travel, or perhaps a family wants to help relatives emigrate from the Soviet Union. One representative discovered that "much of the work that comes across a Congressman's desk has absolutely no relationship to legislation. All of these casework problems probably could not easily be sent elsewhere. Certainly the people don't know where else to take them."[7]

The only complaint is that the need to deal with constituents' requests takes time away from purely legislative matters. Even though most of the mail that pours into the office is handled by a hired staff, the average representative, according to one estimate, spends almost 30 percent of his or her time receiving visitors, answering letters, and handling constituents' problems.[8] Although members of Congress prefer to remain cordial and diplomatic when they deal with constituents, diplomacy sometimes evaporates. In one famous incident, John Steven McGroarty of California wrote back to a constituent: "One of the countless drawbacks of being in Congress is that I am compelled to receive impertinent letters from a jackass

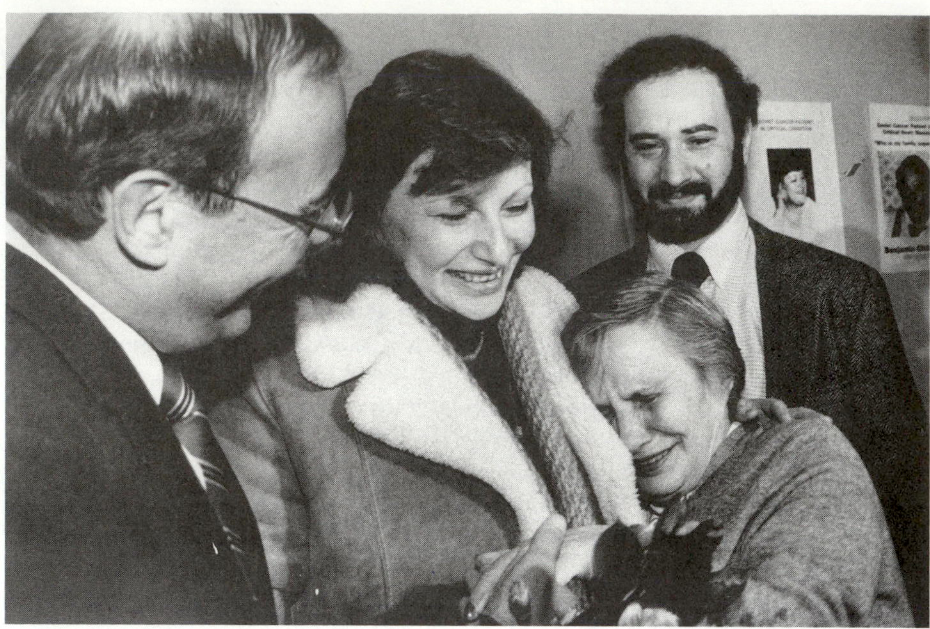

★ Sen. Alfonse D'Amato (R-N.Y.) *(left)* watches as his constituent Dr. Khana Anbinder greets her daughter Rimma Bravve on her arrival from the Soviet Union. The senator helped smooth the way for Rimma to come to the United States to undergo cancer treatment. Another constituent, Leon Charney *(right)*, whose brother has cancer and would like to come to the United States for treatment, is also seeking Sen. D'Amato's help.

like you in which you say I promised to have the Sierra Madre mountains reforested and I have been in Congress two months and haven't done it. Will you please take two running jumps and go to hell."[9]

Still, most senators and representatives place great importance on their constituent-service function. They believe their continuation in office depends in large part on satisfying those who request personal assistance. Even though most voters may not be familiar with the work of their legislators, few Congress members are willing to alienate those who do contact them with a problem. Later in the chapter, we will consider this point further, taking a look at the constituent-service function of Congress members from the point of view of the citizens who write the letters.

Investigating

Over the years, members of Congress have been able to broaden their influence by using an implied power not spelled out in the Constitution. The right to hold committee hearings and conduct investigations has come to be part of their responsibilities to make laws and conduct **legislative oversight**—that is, to review actions by the executive branch. In fact, senators and representatives have come to rely on hearings and investigations to serve several crucial functions: (1) to gather information on proposed bills; (2) to haul up existing policies for review; (3) to oversee the executive branch; and (4) to inform the public on current issues and problems. When bills of an important or controversial nature are being considered, hearings

★ Sen. Sam Ervin of North Carolina *(seated)* chaired the Senate Select Committee on Presidential Campaign Activities. Investigations by and hearings of this committee in 1973 revealed the full scope of the Watergate scandal and provided evidence used by the House in its impeachment proceeding against President Richard Nixon.

and investigations can last for weeks, during which testimony may be obtained from dozens of experts, lobbyists, and other citizens.

One of the most sensational investigations in recent years was the so-called Iran-Contra probe in the spring of 1987. A **joint committee**—that is, a committee composed of members of both chambers of Congress—focused public attention on a scandal that threatened to undermine the Reagan presidency. During weeks of televised testimony from key White House officials, most notably National Security Adviser John Poindexter and his aide Colonel Oliver North, the committee sought to unravel a confusing complex of events that tied the sale of arms to Iran to millions of dollars in aid sent illegally to the Contra rebels fighting the Sandinista government in Nicaragua. As we will note more fully in chapter 19, the Iran-Contra hearings sought to answer important questions about the lengths to which officials in the Reagan administration had gone to bypass formal congressional opposition to funding the Contra forces. It brought the confusing tale of U.S. foreign policy initiatives to life for many Americans who probably had had little interest in or understanding of this country's involvement in Iran and Nicaragua before the hearings.

Fourteen years earlier, in 1973, in an even more absorbing televised investigation, the Senate Watergate Committee riveted the nation's attention on the scandals that eventually led to President Nixon's resignation from office. Chaired by Senator Sam Ervin, a constitutional law expert from North Carolina, the committee (known officially as the Senate Select Committee on Presidential Campaign Activities) set out to investigate the break-in at the Democratic party headquarters in Washington's Watergate complex during the 1972 presidential campaign. Its ostensible purpose was to uncover the part played in the burglary by the Committee for the Reelection of the President (CREEP) and to recommend legislation to prevent future campaign abuses. In the process, the committee heard weeks of televised testimony by key Nixon aides, most notably John Dean, who implicated Nixon in the subsequent cover-up of the affair. The next year, as its final official action, the

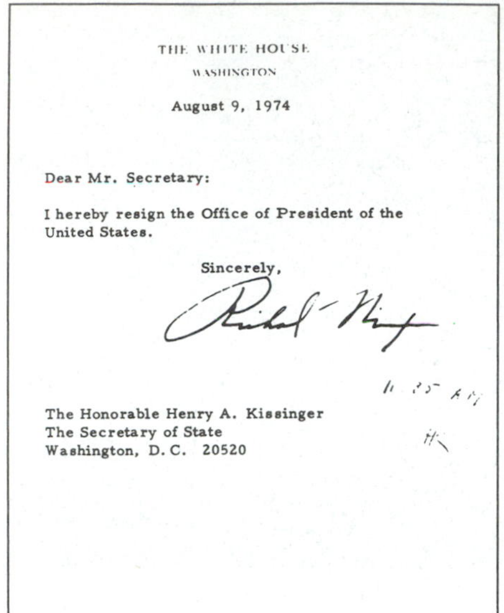

THE WHITE HOUSE
WASHINGTON

August 9, 1974

Dear Mr. Secretary:

I hereby resign the Office of President of the United States.

Sincerely,

Richard Nixon

11:35 AM

The Honorable Henry A. Kissinger
The Secretary of State
Washington, D.C. 20520

HK

★ In 1973, Richard Nixon resigned the presidency shortly after the House Judiciary Committee concluded its investigations into his conduct in office and recommended his impeachment.

committee released a ponderous three-volume report spelling out some recommendations for reform. Among them was the suggestion (later carried out) that an independent commission be created to supervise and enforce campaign finance laws.

Equally sensational were the deliberations of the House Judiciary Committee in 1974. The thirty-eight-member committee, headed by New Jersey's Peter Rodino, was delegated the historic responsibility, in Rodino's words, "to investigate fully and completely whether sufficient grounds exist for the House of Representatives to exercise its constitutional power to impeach Richard Milhous Nixon, President of the United States of America." After months of research, hearings, and heated debate, the committee played out its final days of deliberations over network television. As cameras panned along the long mahogany bench to capture the aye or no of each member, the committee handed down the first recommendation for the impeachment of a president since 1868. It charged Nixon with obstruction of justice in the Watergate cover-up, abuse of power in his dealings with governmental agencies, and contempt of Congress by his defiance of congressional subpoenas.

One significant aspect of these committee investigations is that they were watched on television and discussed by more people than perhaps any other investigations before or since. Indeed, the televised coverage of the committees may have done more to elevate public interest in Congress's activities—normally overshadowed by those of the president—than anything else undertaken by Congress during the past several decades. In 1979 the House began to televise its proceedings, and, after considerable controversy, the Senate agreed to permit TV cameras in 1986. It is estimated that about a quarter of a million people watch the coverage of Congress on cable television through C-SPAN, and that about one-quarter of cable subscribers watch C-SPAN occasionally.[10]

Congressional investigations can also take legislators to the far corners of the globe. As the U.S. economy becomes increasingly linked to the economies of other nations, legislators may travel to Japan to discuss trade policy or to Latin America

"This problem is too serious for us to procrastinate any longer. We've got to form a blue ribbon commission to study it right away!"

to search for new sources of raw materials. Legislators may make strong ideological statements by visiting antigovernment activists or political prisoners in other lands. Some foreign fact-finding missions can be little more than an excuse for a trip to the Caribbean while Washington is blanketed with snow. But some missions can also be deadly. In 1978, California Representative Leo Ryan was murdered while looking into the People's Temple religious cult in Guyana. In 1989, Texas Representative Mickey Leland died in a plane crash while overseeing U.S. famine-relief work in Ethiopia.

Congressional investigations are not always praised, of course. A common complaint is that committee hearings and investigations are sometimes used as a political copout, as a smokescreen for inaction. Some representatives and senators, eager to appear concerned about toxic waste or housing conditions in urban slums, hold public hearings, though information is already abundant and the problem cries for immediate solution. In the opinion of one former representative,

> most congressional hearings are ridiculous. They are held to impress the public, to get someone's name in the papers and on television. . . . Witnesses come in and earnestly testify about something they know and care about, hoping that the committee will be moved. They think if they give Congress the truth, they will get justice in return. Then their testimony is printed in book after book of hearing records, which are piled on shelves to gather dust.[11]

Another complaint is that investigations are often carried out in an incompetent and unproductive manner. One of the most common uses of investigations is to see whether the federal bureaucracy is properly administering the laws passed by Congress, but such investigations often prove to be inadequate. Administrative errors and fraud, cost overruns, and general bureaucratic incompetence frequently slip by unnoticed or are tacitly accepted with a mutual shrugging of shoulders by administrators and members of Congress. In 1988, for example, the House and Senate Armed Services committees were criticized for failing to check abuses by the Department of Energy in the operation of plants that produce nuclear weapons.

Committee members admitted that oversight in this area had low priority, given the national security and secrecy issues involved in producing weapons-grade plutonium and tritium. In deferring to the executive branch, Congress allowed dangerous levels of radioactive air and water contamination to go unchecked.

Some members complain that they are at a disadvantage when they try to check the activities of the executive branch. They are unable to compete with the thousands of experts and enormous technical resources of the federal bureaucracy, and thus are unable to catch or prevent every irresponsible policy decision. While this complaint has some justification, the disadvantage in resources could be lessened by additional staff or new legislation that stiffened penalties for bureaucratic mismanagement if the will existed to do a vigorous job of legislative oversight. Unfortunately, as some critics note, the will to do so often seems to be lacking.

Raising and Spending Money

Many members of Congress find that a great deal of their power rests with their constitutional authority to regulate the flow of money. Although the president draws up elaborate budget recommendations each fiscal year, members of Congress help decide where the money will come from (such as taxes and government bonds) and how much will be spent. In other words, without their agreement, no money can be doled out for foreign aid, salaries for army generals, or paper clips for bureaucrats.

Members of the House of Representatives have traditionally exercised most financial control. If the president requests more money for defense or some other purpose, bills must be introduced in the House to authorize (approve) and appropriate (instruct the Treasury to spend) such funds. By custom, the House Appropriations Committee, which has the primary authority for spending, is the first to review the president's budget requests. It then sends its recommendations to the Senate Appropriations Committee, which may add amendments. Members of the House also have the constitutional authority to initiate revenue bills (art. I, sec. 7). Therefore new tax bills usually go first to the House Ways and Means Committee, whose members consider the ways and means of raising money. After a tax bill wends its way through this committee and the House, it will reach its Senate counterpart, the Finance Committee, for review. (There are exceptions to this order of business, as when Reagan's tax-cut proposal was first passed by the Senate before being voted on in the House.)

Controversy has raged for years over the effect of Congress's power of the purse on its relations with the White House. Ever since the Bureau of the Budget (now the Office of Management and Budget) was created in 1921, members of Congress have often had to play by the president's rules, making only slight alterations in a budget sent over from the White House. Yet control over the purse strings also provides representatives and senators with their greatest influence over the executive branch. Because few of the president's programs can succeed without funds, a decision to boost or slash his budget requests can drastically affect his administration's performance. Throughout the eight years of the Reagan administration, for example, the president's desire to aid the antigovernment Contra rebels in Nicaragua was stymied by Congress's indecisiveness and then resistance to such action.

In fact, over the years Congress has taken steps to expand its influence over the budget. In 1974 it passed the Budget and Impoundment Control Act, establishing new House and Senate Budget committees and a joint Congressional Budget Office of fiscal experts. The act was designed to improve Congress's ability to determine what the total of government spending should be each year. That is, instead of just looking piecemeal at the budget proposals offered by the president, Congress can now set its own overall spending target for each broad area of governmental activity. The revenue and appropriations committees (and the president) must keep these targets in mind when they consider new tax laws and spending bills.

The importance of cooperation and compromise on budgetary matters between Congress and the president was evident in the successful passage of the Tax Reform Act of 1986 (see chap. 18). The act eliminated the old system of fourteen separate tax brackets for individual taxpayers in favor of only two rates of 15 and 28 percent. In addition, citizens at the bottom rung of the economy were removed from the tax rolls, and many deductions and exemptions were scrapped. Some members of Congress took an active leadership role in pushing the reform package past the objections of powerful interest groups and helped gain broad congressional and public support for the act, which was signed into law by President Reagan in October 1986.

The Budget and Impoundment Control Act also contained a provision to limit presidential **impoundments,** or refusals to spend money appropriated by Congress. This provision coincided with a series of lower federal court rulings curtailing the president's power to hold back funds. Ever since Thomas Jefferson's term, presidents have occasionally balked at spending money appropriated by Congress. When the House and Senate authorized $25 billion to clean up the nation's polluted rivers in 1972, for example, President Nixon vetoed the bill in an effort, he said, to hold down federal spending. Then, after Congress overrode his veto, Nixon simply impounded $6 billion by ordering that it not be spent. He argued that, as chief executive, he had the authority to impound any funds allotted by Congress. Many members of Congress objected, however, that under the Constitution the president may veto a bill only in its entirety; he may not veto any specific item. As a result, the 1974 Budget Act was passed, limiting the president's power to hold back funds appropriated by Congress.

Providing Advice and Consent

Although members of the House may have an edge over senators in revenue matters, senators have the sole constitutional authority to oversee the White House by reviewing the president's appointments and treaties. Just as the president can veto bills passed by Congress, so senators can "veto" his appointments and treaties.

The Constitution stipulates that the president's appointments of federal officers—such as department heads, ambassadors, and federal court judges—are subject to the **advice and consent** of a simple majority of senators present and voting. Members of the House do not share this duty with the Senate, except when a president must pick a new vice-president (under the Twenty-fifth Amendment). When President Nixon selected Gerald Ford to replace Spiro Agnew in 1973 and when President Ford, a year later, selected Nelson Rockefeller, both houses of Congress were called upon to give formal approval by a majority vote.

★ Between 1974 and 1976, the country was headed by two men who were appointed, not elected, to office. President Gerald Ford *(right)* had been appointed by Richard Nixon to serve as his vice-president after Spiro Agnew resigned. Nelson Rockefeller *(left)* was chosen by Ford to be his vice-president when Nixon resigned.

Although most appointees are confirmed without difficulty, senators on occasion do turn thumbs down on a nominee. The Senate rejected two of Nixon's nominees to the Supreme Court, for example, and in 1987 Reagan's nominee to the Supreme Court, Robert Bork, was turned down by the Senate following a vast public outcry against the nomination. Bush's nominee for secretary of defense, former senator John Tower, was rejected by the Senate in early 1989. Presidents must bear in mind that even though senators give them considerable freedom to appoint federal officers (fewer than a dozen cabinet nominees have been rejected since 1789), it is still wise to clear prospective nominees with key senators—especially those from a state in which an appointee such as a federal judge is to serve—before making an appointment. This informal practice, known as **senatorial courtesy,** helps to build a good working relationship between the legislative and executive branches.

The same need for Senate consultation exists in regard to treaties, which, unlike appointments, require the approval of two-thirds of the senators present and voting. The possibility that the Senate may reject a treaty compels the president to seek the support of key senators in advance, especially those on the powerful Foreign Relations Committee, who are the first to review new treaties. Although

★★★★★★★★★★★★

Communications

Woodfin Camp & Assoc.

Jeremy Nicholl/JB Pictures

Information is a source of power for people and their governments around the world. In recent years, information has been transmitted and received more quickly, over greater distances, and in more innovative ways than ever before.

S. Petean/SIPA–Press

Sepp Saitz/Woodfin Camp & Assoc.

Much information is still communicated "by word of mouth," but no longer necessarily face to face. The telephone is available nearly everywhere, from the vast deserts of Saudi Arabia to the bustling streets of London. In remote areas where there are no telephones, such as the Amazon jungle, citizens can communicate by radio. And in some cities, the intimacy of face-to-face conversation is made possible by the modern wizardry of the teleconference, which enables people to carry on a dialogue using telephone and television.

John Nordell/JB Pictures

The telephone allows us to send facsimiles of documents across its lines, and "faxing" has become an important political resource. For example, during the student demonstrations in China in June 1989, these Massachusetts students "faxed" information to the students in Beijing, who would have otherwise had no idea what the outside world knew about their cause. We knew about what was happening because of television, which showed us the demonstrations as well as Chinese officials taking news reporters off the air. Satellite transmission makes much of this international communication possible. Satellite imaging combined with computer processing allows experts to track the temperature changes in ocean currents such as El Nino along the coast of South America. This imaging makes it easier to predict the cyclical warm flows that wreak havoc with coastal industries like fishing. Computer imaging is also used in medical databases, where patient records can be combined with sophisticated tests to get a more accurate overview of a patient's condition. Telecommunications

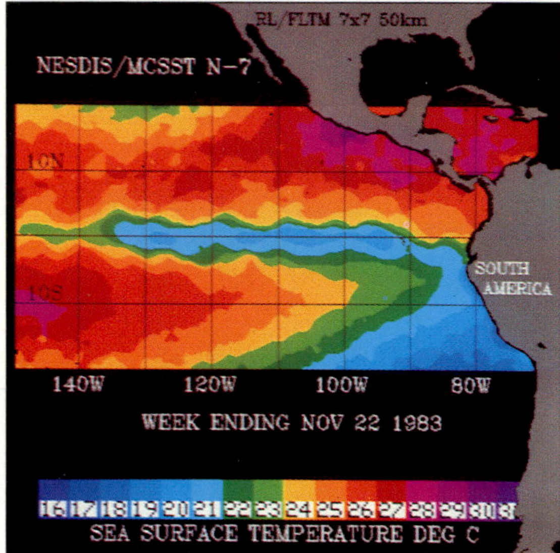

Legeckis, 1983

© 1989 CNN

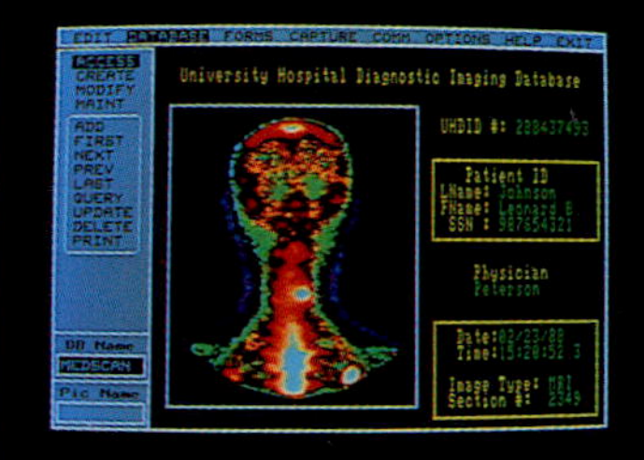

SIPA–Press

John Chiasson/Gamma–Liaison

are increasingly available throughout the world. Even in the remote grasslands of Kenya, a television provides information for all to see. The source of information is no longer the village elder or the local community; it is the larger, global community.

John Nordell/JB Pictures

Robert Morris/JL Atlan/SYGMA

Of course, the defense of a country requires the most up-to-the-minute information, and in the White House situation room *(top)* computers, TV monitors, and other information sources provide the president's staff with the data with which he can make informed decisions.

But every innovation and technological development brings with it problems and dangers. In 1988, Robert T. Morris, Jr. *(top left),* a student at Cornell University, created a "virus" that intruded into the Defense Department's computer research network. Viruses are programs designed to proliferate in a system, destroying data or otherwise jamming the system. There is, for example, a virus called "the brain" that originated with two software developers in Lahore, Pakistan. It infected thousands of computers in the United States, Malaysia, Indonesia, and the Philippines. Ronald Austin *(middle right)*, a student at UCLA, also penetrated the Defense Department's computer system in 1983 and was uncovered by David Dalva *(bottom right)*, another student at UCLA. Exploits such as these are not always perpetrated out of malice but out of the very sense of adventure and challenge that these technologies stimulate. But what would happen if one day someone maliciously tampered with computers tracing incoming missiles or tallying votes at the local precinct?

Ron Mark Autino/Bill Nation/SYGMA

Bill Nation/SYGMA

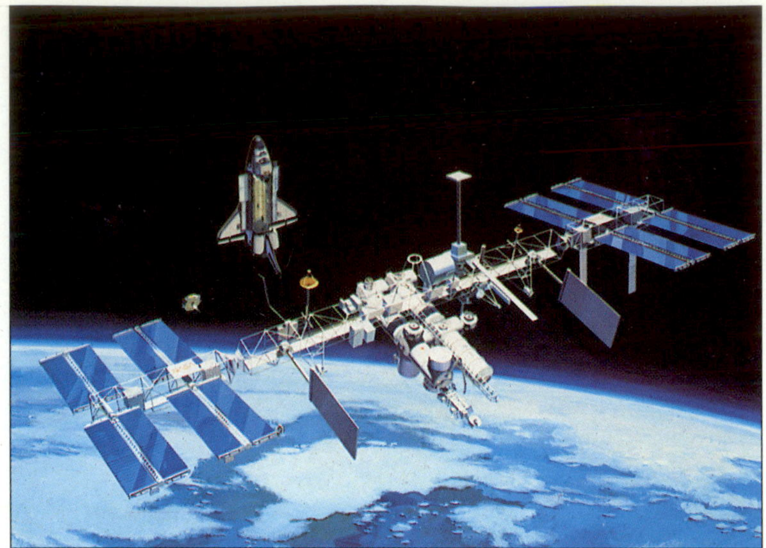

NASA

If the United States ever maintains a permanent station in space, such as the Space Station Freedom shown here in an artist's rendering, we will need to use all the technologies at our disposal and ones yet undeveloped. A space station not only will gather information but will be able to send it back to earth or to whatever other planet that humans might occupy. And we will also have to keep those in space in continual communication with people on earth.

We already have the benefits of almost instantaneous feedback from our space shuttles as they cruise into space beaming back data that only science fiction writers once envisioned. Neptune *(below)* became part of our consciousness thanks to satellite transmissions. The earth, seen here as you might see it while coming in for a landing on the moon, was once seen as the center of the universe; now it is only one player in an increasing cast of characters in our solar system. America's frontier has shifted to the heavens, altering not only our sense of time and place but also our sense of being and consciousness. What political concepts will we carry with us into space? Shall we explore the heavens in unity with other countries, or shall we try to divide the universe as we have tried to divide the globe? What thoughts go through the minds of astronauts as they peer down on a planet Earth without political boundaries?

NASA

NASA

the Senate historically has approved more than 90 percent of the treaties submitted, senators occasionally have demanded last-minute changes as their price for support (as they did before approving the two Panama Canal treaties in 1978). In 1919, Woodrow Wilson made the disastrous mistake of not compromising with the Senate Republican leadership on the Treaty of Versailles, and thereby helped doom the League of Nations. Of course, as we will see in chapter 13, one response of presidents to the risk that a treaty may be rejected has been to rely on executive agreements, which do not require formal Senate approval.

★ Congress in a Changing World

Congress has usually been eclipsed by the president in the formation of U.S. foreign policy. But as American involvement in the world has grown since World War II, Congress has confronted a wealth of new questions and problems created by expanding global communications, the arms race, and the political, economic, ecological, and cultural interdependence of the world's nations. While Congress's formal role has not changed in recent years, the consequences of international interaction at the national, state, and local levels have forced legislators to play an increased role in crafting foreign policy.

On paper, Congress's foreign policy responsibilities seem formidable. The Constitution gives Congress the authority to declare war, regulate commerce with foreign nations, provide for the common defense, and raise and support armies. Congress's general powers in setting the national budget and in keeping an eye on other branches of government through its oversight function also provide many opportunities to influence foreign policy. The Senate's role in approving treaties and diplomatic appointments is yet another dimension of the legislative branch's formal role in international affairs. In 1988, for instance, the Senate voted 95 to 5 to ratify the Intermediate-range Nuclear Force (INF) Treaty, a major arms-control agreement with the Soviet Union to ban intermediate-range nuclear missiles.

Yet it is the president who makes American foreign policy. Indeed, Congress's power is very much subordinate to the president's in the formulation and execution of American foreign policy. As we shall see in chapter 13, the president's power as commander in chief, the unity and speed with which the executive branch can act, and its access to and control of vital information have tended to leave Congress in the awkward position of reacting to the president's initiatives.

Nonetheless, Congress does not sit idly by while the president monopolizes foreign policy. The globalization of American politics and some controversial presidential initiatives—such as the Vietnam war and the Contra war in Nicaragua—have focused congressional interest on the international realm. Representative Lee Hamilton described Congress's expanding role in foreign affairs this way:

> The important role of the Congress in the foreign policy process is recognized here and abroad. Lobbyists for foreign policy issues stream to Capitol Hill. In public meetings across America constituents . . . plead with their Congressman or Congresswoman about foreign policy issues. Visiting heads of government a few years ago used to come to Washington and visit the President, the Chairman of the World Bank, . . . the Secretary of State, and go home. Now they insist on coming to Capitol Hill to meet with members of the Congress. Ambassadors who are assigned to Washington parade the halls of Congress on a daily basis.[12]

Historically, Congress and the president have not always been in general agreement on major foreign policy matters. In the post–World War II era, as the president has solidified control over the making of foreign policy, Congress has felt at times like a junior partner in the process. Unpopular wars, such as Vietnam, certainly created friction between Congress and the president. The recent trend toward Republican control of the White House and Democratic domination of the Congress, reaffirmed in the 1988 elections, has also amplified the potential for disagreement on foreign policy. With these factors in mind, let's examine how Congress applies its constitutional authority in the areas of war and defense, treaties, international economics, and oversight of other branches of government.

War and the Common Defense

Congress's warmaking powers are clearly spelled out in Article I, Section 8, of the Constitution. A congressional declaration of war is not subject to a presidential veto. Most wars and military actions in American history, however, have been conducted without a formal declaration of war. Congress has declared war only five times: in the War of 1812 against Britain, the Mexican-American War of 1846, the Spanish-American War of 1898, and World Wars I (1917) and II (1941). But according to a State Department study, U.S. troops have been sent overseas more than 125 times in the nation's history. In justifying his unilateral decision to send American troops to Korea in 1950, President Harry Truman cited eighty-seven instances of similar presidential action.

Many of these military engagements have produced marked conflict between the president as commander in chief and Congress. When we consider the Constitution's imprecise sharing of warmaking authority between the legislative and executive branches, we would do well to remember Edward S. Corwin's observation that the Constitution is basically an "invitation to struggle." For many observers, the struggle has been won by the executive branch:

> Congress has been thoroughly vanquished. The President stands virtually unchallenged in his unilateral ability to commit the United States to war. . . the White House has been able to seize and monopolize the war-making power. No recent president has seriously shared it with Congress.[13]

Although most wars have been undeclared, historically presidents have usually consulted Congress on major uses of American troops abroad. Harry Truman's use of troops in Korea, without prior consultation with Congress, was quite controversial but did not produce a significant movement for reform of the president's warmaking prerogatives. The manner in which Presidents Johnson and Nixon conducted the Vietnam war, however, pushed Congress beyond griping about being left out. Some people argued that Congress had given its approval for U.S. involvement when it passed the Tonkin Gulf Resolution in 1964, but others felt that it clearly had not sanctioned the deployment of more than 500,000 troops or the massive bombing of North Vietnam. Feeling misled by Johnson and generally fearing the growing power of the "imperial presidency," Congress acted against President Nixon.

The **War Powers Resolution,** passed in 1973 over Nixon's veto, limits the president's unilateral use of troops abroad to major national emergencies resulting

★ U.S. marines board the SS *Mayaguez* to regain control of the ship after it had been hijacked by Cambodia. President Gerald Ford ignored the War Powers Resolution when he ordered soldiers to rescue the civilian crew of the ship. Was his action unconstitutional?

from a direct attack on U.S. forces, territory, or possessions. The specific provisions of the resolution include the following:

1. Troops must be withdrawn after sixty days unless Congress approves further action.
2. Congress can order withdrawal of troops at any time.
3. The president must consult with Congress before sending troops.

Nixon and every president after him have labeled the War Powers Resolution an unconstitutional limitation of the commander in chief's authority. Nixon contended that the decision to use military force has always been the prerogative of the president and that the act would "seriously undermine the nation's ability to act decisively and convincingly in times of international crisis."[14] Rather than assault the resolution by direct defiance or court action, subsequent presidents have paid lip service to it while doing as they pleased.

The first major test of the War Powers Resolution came during the administration of Gerald Ford. In 1975 an American merchant ship, the *Mayaguez*, and its civilian crew were seized in international waters by the Cambodian navy. President Ford ordered a rescue effort and military retaliation against Cambodian facilities. Arguing that his actions were based on the president's traditional power as commander in chief, Ford informed but did not consult Congress, as the War Powers Resolution required.

Congress's response to Ford's unilateral use of troops in the *Mayaguez* incident set the tone for future applications of the War Powers Resolution. While some legislators complained openly of Ford's disregard for the resolution, most decided not to force a confrontation and risk a constitutional crisis. Congress, reflecting the public's approval of Ford's action, openly embraced the rescue mission. Although the *Mayaguez* incident is now a minor footnote in U.S. diplomatic history, it signaled the practical demise of the War Powers Resolution only two years after its passage.

Since 1975, U.S. presidents have ordered military actions numerous times without fulfilling the letter of the War Powers Resolution: in 1980 President Carter attempted to rescue U.S. hostages in Iran; President Reagan sent troops to Lebanon in 1982 (and 241 of them died there), ordered the invasion of Grenada in 1983, sent military advisers to El Salvador, sent planes to bomb Libya in 1986, and dispatched warships to the Persian Gulf in 1987. In some cases, Reagan informed Congress only after the action was under way. Although American troops had been in Lebanon for more than a year, it was only after they suffered severe casualties that the president formally discussed the matter with Congress. In agreeing to an eighteen-month limit on the use of troops, Reagan made it clear that he did not feel bound by the War Powers Resolution: "I do not and cannot cede any of the authority vested in me under the Constitution. . . . Nor should my signing be viewed as any acknowledgment that the President's constitutional authority can be impermissibly infringed by statute."[15]

It is not surprising that the War Powers Resolution failed to expand significantly Congress's control over the use of U.S. troops abroad. The resolution was passed at the height of the Watergate crisis, a brief period when presidential prestige was very low. If Congress would not press its case against Presidents Ford and Carter, how could it stand up to Ronald Reagan, one of the nation's most popular presidents? Yet the War Powers Resolution is not totally irrelevant. Ronald Reagan and other presidents have not gone out of their way to violate its provisions. The resolution, by its very existence, publicly raises the issue of consultation any time troops are sent abroad. Though the president may be relatively unrestrained in the use of force, the resolution offers Congress a way to influence foreign policy *should* it choose to do so.

Another tool Congress possesses in the area of foreign affairs is its constitutional charge to "provide for the common defense." Through its power of the purse, Congress can influence foreign policy (and rein in a president) in a variety of ways. In 1976, for example, Congress passed the Clark Amendment, which prohibited direct economic assistance to rebels fighting the government of Angola, in Africa. This prohibition was not successfully removed until 1985. During the early years of the Reagan administration, Congress reduced the deployment of a new generation of missiles, the ten-warhead MX. And in perhaps the most celebrated case in recent years, Congress passed the Boland Amendment, prohibiting direct financial aid to the Contra rebels fighting the Nicaraguan government in Central America. While a dynamic president can overcome congressional opposition, as President Reagan did in forcing through a bill that allowed the sale of advanced AWACS radar planes to Saudi Arabia in 1981, his victory may require major compromises and expenditures of large sums of presidential capital on Capitol Hill.

Treaties

The Constitution requires that all treaties with foreign nations be approved by a two-thirds vote of the Senate. The Foreign Relations Committee has primary responsibility for considering treaties, and its members are the Senate's foreign policy specialists. Although some treaties can be extremely controversial, such as the Panama Canal Treaty, approved in 1977, the Senate historically has ratified most agreements set before it. Between 1900 and the mid-1980s, for instance, the Senate failed to ratify only six treaties.

One reason that most treaties enjoy such acceptance is that important senators are usually consulted by the State Department and other administration officials while the treaties are still being negotiated. Treaties generally represent the highest statement of U.S. foreign policy, and as such reflect general agreement between the political parties. Another reason for the low rejection rate of treaties is that a president may choose not to submit a treaty that faces a serious fight in the Senate. In 1979, for example, President Carter decided not to push ratification of the controversial SALT II arms-limitation treaty with the Soviet Union. (Instead he promised informally to follow the limits set by the treaty and challenged the Soviets to do likewise.)

Senators may pursue a more active role in setting the terms of some treaties. They can attach a reservation to a treaty stipulating terms they consider essential. Some reservations may actually require the president to renegotiate the treaty with the foreign nation before final approval is granted. Other reservations may simply state the Senate's interpretation of a treaty without actually changing the nature of the agreement. At times, disagreement between the Senate and the president over treaty interpretation can lead to major controversy. President Reagan's reinterpretation of the 1972 Anti-Ballistic Missile Treaty to allow deployment of the Star Wars antimissile system enraged some senators, who vowed to take the president to court if necessary to prevent what they saw as an unconstitutional abrogation of the Senate's right to advise and consent on treaties.

The increasing use of executive agreements by the president has lessened the importance of formal treaties in the setting of U.S. foreign policy. Since World War II, as we will see in chapter 13, when presidents have stationed troops abroad, promoted commerce and trade, and pursued other international goals, they have used executive agreements to do so nearly 95 percent of the time. By and large, Congress is consulted on most executive agreements, as they require legislation to put their provisions into force. Still, many observers see executive agreements as a way for the president to avoid the close scrutiny of the Senate on such controversial issues as the sending of troops abroad and clandestine activities against other governments. The Case Act, passed in 1972, requires the executive branch to inform Congress of all secret executive agreements within sixty days of their signing.

International Economics

Congress also influences America's economic role in the world. Its control over the national budget determines how much money goes to foreign aid, how the Treasury Department and Federal Reserve Board adjust the value of the dollar abroad, and how the United States participates in such international economic organizations as the World Bank and the International Monetary Fund. Congress also regulates trade and sets the terms by which tariffs and other import restrictions are applied. Over the years Congress, working closely with the president, has outlined the basics of American trade through the Reciprocal Trade Agreement Act of 1934, the Trade Expansion Act of 1962, the Trade Act of 1974, and the Trade Act of 1988. The Senate also was called upon to ratify such major trade treaties as the General Agreement on Trade and Tariffs of 1947 (GATT) and the Canadian-American Free Trade Agreement of 1988.

As global interdependence has politicized American economic life, members of Congress are often pressured to curtail foreign competition. With a $171 billion

★ Col. Oliver North is sworn in before the Iran-Contra committee. Like the Watergate hearings before it, Congress's televised investigation of the Iran-Contra affair captivated the nation during the spring and summer of 1987.

trade deficit in 1987, legislators were forced to become better informed about the effects of international trade on their districts and the nation. While presidents typically pursue a national economic policy of free trade, local legislators tend to protect the interests of their constituents. Congress included agricultural export subsidies as part of the Farm Act of 1985, for instance, and in 1988 American businesses were required to give prior notice of plant closings to their workers despite the opposition of President Reagan. In chapter 18 we will consider the question of international trade and economics in depth.

Oversight and Investigation

Aside from its infrequent declarations of war, Congress's oversight of government operations and its investigations connected with legislation provide the most dramatic involvement in foreign affairs. As we will see, Congress functions largely by committees, and the committees gather data and conduct hearings to write legislation and measure the effectiveness of existing laws. From the prestigious Senate Foreign Relations Committee to a lowly House subcommittee, American foreign policy is discussed, examined, dissected, exhumed, and debated from every conceivable angle. Sometimes the hearings are dramatic, as when Colonel Oliver North, his Marine uniform bedecked with medals, defended his Iran-Contra operation. Sometimes the hearings are secret, as when the Senate Intelligence Committee hears the CIA's latest plan to topple the government in Nicaragua. Mostly the hearings are boring, as when the House Armed Services Committee adds up the price of every nut and bolt that hold together a C5 military aircraft.

Congressional oversight and investigation of foreign affairs can be highly partisan and political. Staff researchers, such as those in the House's Office of Technology Assessment, provide information (and political ammunition) to counter presidential policies. During Reagan's first term, for example, the Office of Technology Assessment released studies that disputed the administration's views on nuclear war and the balance of strategic forces. Oversight and investigation also provide opportunities for legislators to try to balance the president's domination of the public discussion of foreign affairs. More than one aspiring politician has seized the limelight (or TV camera) during a committee meeting to boost his or her image as a foreign policy expert in the eyes of the public.

On the whole, Congress has been reluctant to attack the fundamentals of administration foreign policy through its oversight and investigative functions. With some major exceptions (Iran-Contra, arms control), Congress has focused instead on minute details of policy implementation rather than on the larger political questions. Robert J. Art has found that between 1976 and 1983, the Senate Armed Services Committee spent approximately 20 percent of its time studying defense policy matters and 80 percent of its time looking into the management of programs and spending.[16] Thus, unless the president clearly ignores Congress, senators and representatives are generally content to investigate the carrying out of foreign policy rather than play a dynamic role in its creation.

Congress and Foreign Policy in the 1990s

Two things seem certain about Congress and foreign policy in the 1990s: globalization will continue to increase the number of international issues that affect the nation and the local congressional district, and the president will continue to dominate the making of American foreign policy. Although both Reagan and Bush have criticized Congress for attempting to fine-tune foreign policy, for the most part legislators have acknowledged the preeminence of the president in the international sphere. Democratic Representative Lee Hamilton offered this assessment of why the executive branch should lead in the making of foreign policy:

1. Diplomacy requires speed, but Congress moves very slowly.
2. Diplomacy requires secrecy; Congress often leaks sensitive matters.
3. Diplomacy requires a long view of the national interest; Congress is influenced by short-term interests and often has its eye too much on the coming election.
4. Diplomacy requires expertise, but Congress is often ignorant of foreign affairs.
5. Diplomacy requires sustained interest; Congress's approach is sporadic and eclectic.
6. Diplomacy requires strong leadership, but power in Congress is diffused.[17]

Hamilton does see an important role for Congress, especially in its ability to study and deliberate fundamental foreign policy issues. Many legislators do, in fact, develop expertise on technical international issues. Senator Bill Bradley (D-New Jersey), for example, became an expert on international banking even though the subject did not directly concern his constituency. And Congress, especially the House of Representatives, provides the closest link with the public. When a citizen wishes to make his or her voice heard on a foreign policy issue, it is most likely the local representative who will receive (and probably answer) the letter or telephone call.

Although most legislators accept Congress's reactive role in foreign affairs, they often feel snubbed by the executive branch. During the Reagan administration, for instance, certain congressional leaders were informed of the decisions to invade Grenada, bomb Libya, and take other major foreign policy initiatives when it was too late for a significant dialogue between branches of the government. To many members of Congress, prior consultation involves much more than the briefing of a handful of senators while the troops are landing.

★ Recruitment to Congress

Now that we have considered the growing range of powers and responsibilities of members of Congress, the next question becomes: What kinds of people serve in Congress? The Constitution stipulates only a few legal qualifications for election to Congress: that representatives (who serve two-year terms) must be at least twenty-five years old, and senators (who serve six-year terms) must be at least thirty; that the former must have been American citizens for at least seven years and the latter for at least nine; and that they must reside in the states in which they are elected.

Although most American adults are legally qualified to serve in Congress, neither the House nor the Senate truly reflects a cross section of our society. The vast majority of the people who serve on Capitol Hill are white males, and the professional backgrounds of most of them have been in either law, business, banking, or education. As table 12-2 shows, women are remarkably underrepresented in Congress; although they make up more than half of the nation's population, they account for only 5 percent of the 101st Congress (1989–1991), with a total of twenty-seven members. Minority groups are similarly underrepresented: although 12 percent of the population is black, for example, the 101st Congress has twenty-four black members, or 4 percent of the total membership of both houses. Other minority groups, such as Hispanics, Asians, and Native Americans, have few or no members in the House or Senate.

Congress probably will never reflect a true cross section of the population in every respect (it is not surprising that lawyers predominate in a lawmaking body). Yet it is difficult to justify such underrepresentation of women and other large groups in our society. Such underrepresentation may lead not only to disillusionment with the governing process but also to a neglect of social problems that many senators and representatives simply do not identify with or understand. Though it may be true that members of Congress do not need to resemble their constituents to represent their interests, we may wonder how a group of predominantly white, college-educated male senators can possibly understand the problems of a poor, aging black woman trying to raise her grandchildren in an urban slum. How broader representation can be achieved, however, is a perplexing question. Certainly the prejudices of many voters, the inequalities of campaign financing, and other roadblocks need to be overcome to erase the inequalities of representation.

★ The Structure of Power: Implications for Action

Although the ability of senators and representatives to gain significant political influence has much to do with their talents and ambitions, ultimately it depends on the positions they attain in the congressional power structure. Like most organizations, Congress is not a body of equals. Some senators and representatives, by virtue of their committee assignments and leadership roles, can attain positions of power that elude other members.

Indeed, as we noted earlier, many newly elected members are shocked to find how little influence they can exert outside the limited policy areas of their committees and how often Congress can tear apart meaningful legislation. They discover not only that the procedures and power structure in Congress can be quite forbidding but that a handful of legislators can impede or permanently block

★ Table 12-2
Characteristics of the 101st Congress, 1989–1991

	House	Senate
Sex		
Men	410	98
Women	25	2
Race		
White	399	100
Black	24	0
Hispanic	12	0
*Prior occupation**		
Agriculture	19	4
Business or banking	138	28
Education	42	11
Engineering	4	0
Journalism	17	8
Labor leader	2	0
Law	184	63
Law enforcement	8	0
Medicine	4	0
Other	17	8
Religion		
Baptist	43	12
Episcopalian	43	20
Jewish	31	8
Methodist	63	13
Presbyterian	42	9
Roman Catholic	120	19
Other or none named	93	19

*Some senators had more than one prior occupation.

SOURCE: Adapted from *Congressional Quarterly Weekly Report,* November 12, 1988.

bills favored by a majority of members and the public. The seniority tradition, the Senate filibuster, and other hallowed procedures have been the targets of reform efforts, but disturbing questions about the responsiveness of Congress remain.

Many historians point out that the framers of the Constitution never intended Congress to be a particularly responsive institution. The fact that they created a bicameral (two-house) legislature composed of an often competitive and mutually hostile House and Senate (the latter originally not even directly elected by the voters) suggests a willingness to allow delay and deadlock in its lawmaking. As we saw in chapter 2, many of the framers were wary of creating a national legislature that might respond too speedily to the changing moods of future majorities.

Let us, then, consider some of the main features of the congressional power structure—features that can often frustrate our hopes of seeing constructive policies emerge from the legislative labyrinth.

Table 12-3
The standing committees of Congress

House committees	Senate committees
Agriculture	Agriculture, Nutrition, and Forestry
Appropriations	Appropriations
Armed Services	Armed Services
Banking, Housing, and Urban Affairs	Banking, Finance, and Urban Affairs
Budget	Budget
District of Columbia	Commerce, Science, and Transportation
Education and Labor	Energy and Natural Resources
Energy and Commerce	Environment and Public Works
Foreign Affairs	Finance
Goverment Operations	Foreign Relations
House Administration	Governmental Affairs
Interior and Insular Affairs	Judiciary
Judiciary	Labor and Human Resources
Merchant Marine and Fisheries	Rules and Administration
Post Office and Civil Service	Small Business
Public Works and Transportation	Veterans Affairs
Rules	
Science and Technology	
Small Business	
Standards of Official Conduct	
Veterans Affairs	
Ways and Means	

The Committees

With rare exceptions, all legislative craftsmanship in the House and Senate takes place in committees and subcommittees. Each bill introduced on Capitol Hill is referred to a committee for consideration; and it is in the committee or subcommittee, not on the floor, that its fate usually is determined. After being ushered into the House and Senate galleries, tourists are often amazed to see perhaps only a dozen or so members on the floor, speaking to rows of empty seats. Unless an important vote is about to be taken, most members are in their offices or attending to the business of their committees.

Congress relies on committees to divide the work load and to enable each member to specialize in a few fields. (It is common today for most representatives to serve on about six committees and subcommittees, and for senators to serve on about ten.) With thousands of bills introduced each session on Capitol Hill, few members can become familiar with the details of each bill. As a result, each committee in the House and Senate has jurisdiction over a certain broad area, such as foreign relations, education, or agriculture (see table 12-3). In addition to proposing legislation, the committees engage in legislative oversight, monitoring the administration of laws by bureaucratic agencies.

At present there are sixteen permanent or **standing committees** in the Senate and twenty-two in the House. Because each standing committee is supposed

★ Typically both the House *(left)* and the Senate *(right)* are empty because much of the Congressmembers' work is done in committee sessions. The seats in the House are filled by representatives and senators listening to President Reagan deliver a State of the Union message to the nation in January 1983.

to mirror the party composition of the entire body, each is bipartisan, with its seats distributed according to the relative strength of the two major parties. Thus in the 101st Congress (1989–1991) a majority on each committee—as well as *all* committee chairs—are Democrats, because Democrats are in the majority in both houses.

To most of the men and women in Congress, their committee assignments are of crucial importance: it is in their committees, not on the floor, that they will have the best chance to guide legislation and establish their reputations. Obviously, some committees, such as the Foreign Relations Committee in the Senate and the Appropriations Committee in the House, have greater prestige and more important responsibilities than others, and thus positions on them are highly prized.

Basically, the decision as to who gets assigned to which committee is made by special committees dominated by the party leadership in each house. An effort usually is made to help members politically by assigning them to committees that reflect their interests or the concerns of voters back home. However, it is not unknown for new members (particularly in the House) to be placed on committees that have little to do with their concerns. Shirley Chisholm, for example, was shocked to find herself at one time assigned to the House Agriculture Committee. She objected vehemently to the appointment, insisting that service on that committee was an absurd way for her to represent her urban and mostly black district in Brooklyn. "Apparently, all they know here in Washington about Brooklyn," she commented sarcastically, "is that a tree grew there."[18] Her committee assignment was eventually changed to Education and Labor.

The standing committees are themselves broken down into several hundred smaller subcommittees to handle specialized subjects. The House Judiciary Committee, for instance, has subcommittees on civil and constitutional rights, crime and monopolies, and commercial laws. Over the years, subcommittees have become increasingly powerful forces in Congress. Because the members of subcommittees tend to become specialists in their own narrow policy areas, other Senate and House members, including the members of their parent standing committees, usually defer to their decisions. Thus, on issues ranging from atomic energy to tax legislation, a few subcommittee members often rule the day. In fact, the House Democrats in 1973 passed a "subcommittee bill of rights" granting the Democrats on each standing committee (rather than the chair) the authority to select subcommittee chairs and stipulating that no member could head more than one subcommittee. This ruling in effect reduced the powers of committee chairs and caused power in the House to be even more fragmented than it had been before. Subcommittee chairs were dispersed widely among the Democrats, so that more members had a chance to play a major role in at least one narrow policy area. By 1989, almost half of the members of Congress were in charge of one committee or another.

Congress also relies on **conference committees** to iron out differences in bills passed by both houses, and on **select committees** to conduct special investigations. Two of the latter were the 1974 Senate Watergate Committee and the 1987 select committee that investigated the Iran-Contra affair.

A great deal of criticism has been leveled against the committee system. One major complaint is that much of what Congress *does not do* is determined by the committees. Because committees have the power to change bills drastically or to refuse to consider them at all, only a small fraction of the bills introduced (about 5 to 10 percent) ever show up on the floor for a vote. When a bill is referred to a committee, Woodrow Wilson once remarked, it "crosses a parliamentary bridge . . . to dim dungeons of silence whence it will never return."[19]

Although many bills undoubtedly deserve this fate, important bills that have wide public and congressional support sometimes are killed in committee by a small number of lawmakers. Indeed, few representatives and senators (not to mention concerned citizens) have escaped the disappointment of seeing a desired bill destroyed by a handful of hostile committee members.

In fact, even if a senator or representative succeeds in propelling a bill through both houses, it may still become useless because of an appropriations committee's actions. Any bill approved by Congress, especially one that sets up a new federal program, is only an "authorization" for the program: money still has to be raised to put it into effect. To get that money, the appropriations committees in the House and Senate must support a new bill to allot the funds. Historically, many programs have never been given full funding simply because an appropriations committee or one of its subcommittees did not support them.

It is not only members of Congress who may find their will obstructed by a committee's actions; ordinary citizens may be similarly affected. Because the destiny of most bills is decided in committee, special-interest groups—oil companies, labor unions, banking interests, foreign governments—can concentrate pressure on a handful of committee members known to be sympathetic to their concerns. If they wish to bury a bill favored by a majority of the public, the support of a simple majority of members on the right committee can do the trick. The diffusion of power among committees, each of which virtually monopolizes policy decisions in a given area, makes Congress particularly susceptible to the pressures of well-organized interests. Such interests can have considerably greater impact on legislation than they could if they had to deal with the entire membership of Congress, often to the detriment of an unalerted public.

Moreover, the committee system encourages unequal representation. Those of us fortunate enough to live in a district served by a member who sits on or possibly even heads a powerful House committee—Appropriations, say, or Ways and Means—can sometimes count on more immediate returns for our votes than people who live in a district served by a junior representative with little experience and no position of consequence. Although a working relationship between citizens and their representative depends on many factors, a representative who has been assigned to a minor committee and who commands little influence imposes a handicap on constituents who hope for an effective political voice in the House.

In fact, it has been said that the benefits constituents derive from legislation depend greatly on the length of time their representative has served in Congress and on the position he or she holds. Chairs of committees can be especially effective in catering to the economic interests of constituents and local industry alike, helping to channel funds into their districts for such projects as military installations and veterans' hospitals. Meanwhile, other districts may go hungry.

The Rules Committee

One striking example of committee influence on legislation is found in the House Rules Committee. Because the House of Representatives has 435 members to the Senate's 100, more bills are introduced in the House than in the Senate. To save the members from drowning in endless pieces of legislation, most bills approved by the standing committees must pass through the Rules Committee on their way to the House floor. The committee determines (1) the sequence in which bills will be taken up by the entire House (they do not have to be reported out in the order in which they come in from other committees), (2) the time that will be allotted for debate, and (3) whether amendments can be offered on the floor.

Although these functions seem to be necessary, the Rules Committee occasionally has been lambasted for lacking objectivity and for wielding too much influence over legislation. Members of the committee have been known to insist that a bill be amended as the price for permitting it on the floor and even to substitute an entirely new bill for the one originally proposed. In fact, whenever a majority of the committee has decided to delay or table a bill, it has usually died, even when it has been favored by most House members and by the public at large. This was the case with civil rights legislation in the 1950s. Although a majority of members can petition to "discharge" a bill from the committee, such action has been rare. One reason is that few members have been willing to antagonize the committee that can decide the fate of their own bills.

Even so, the power of the Rules Committee is less dramatic than it was in the past. As a result of reforms passed in the mid-1970s, the committee has tended to behave less dictatorially. The Speaker now has the power to name its majority-party members and thus to keep them more in line with the party leadership.

The Filibuster

Although the Senate operates without a rules committee, it has its own procedures that can obstruct the flow of legislation—most notably, the **filibuster.** Because the Senate, unlike the larger and more unwieldy House, permits almost unlimited discussion on a bill, any senator can try to stop a bill by talking continuously or otherwise procrastinating (as by asking for endless roll-call votes and points of order). To filibuster, all he or she must do is remain standing and keep talking; the subject does not even have to be relevant to the bill at hand. A senator may entertain colleagues with nursery rhymes or recipes from a cookbook. Passage of the 1957 Civil Rights Act, for example, was delayed by Strom Thurmond of South Carolina, who bored the Senate for more than twenty-four hours by reading editorials in southern newspapers and the opinions of former chief justice William Howard Taft on jury trials in contempt cases.

Because individual senators cannot rely on iron vocal cords to carry them through, the most effective filibuster strategy is for a group of senators to speak in succession. When one senator tires, he or she can simply yield the floor to a colleague, who continues the "debate." Such a group filibuster may drag on for days or even weeks. The longest group filibuster in the Senate's history was staged by a coalition of southern senators who tried unsuccessfully to block passage of the 1964 Civil Rights Act. Their filibuster lasted more than eighty-three weary days.

Senators can cut off debate by invoking the **cloture rule**. If three-fifths of all senators (60 of 100) support a petition to restrict debate, all further discussion on a bill is limited to one hour per member. Since 1975, a majority of cloture votes has been successful.

But why should a filibuster pose a threat at all? Why should senators be afraid of seeing a few of their colleagues taking control of the floor for an extended period of time? The major reason is that as long as a filibuster continues, the Senate is unable to enact other important legislation. Even when most senators support a bill, they may have a difficult time trying to muster the necessary sixty votes to stop a minority talkathon. A filibuster can be especially effective toward the end of the year, when time is running short and members have pet legislation they wish to pass. A handful of senators can threaten to bury dozens of bills simply by gaining the floor and refusing to yield until their demands are met.

Yet, despite the filibuster's apparent threat to majority rule, many senators continue to champion its use. One reason is that it allows added influence over legislation by a senator who, although greatly affected by a bill, has not been part of the crucial legislative machinery. By filibustering, he or she can try to stop a bill viewed as disastrous for the home state. The filibuster may also be used by a majority against a minority. One or two senators may stage a filibuster as a holding action to prevent a minority of their colleagues from passing legislation while the rest of the members are not present. Whether these justifications surmount the criticisms of the filibuster remains a matter of dispute.

The Committee Chairs and the Seniority Tradition

Although their style and influence vary, most committee chairs exercise considerable influence over policy making. In addition to hiring staff and appointing subcommittees, they usually determine the order in which bills will be considered. When hearings on a bill are held, the chairs often decide who will testify and how much time each member has to cross-examine a witness. And, in rare instances, they have even been known to kill a bill outright simply by refusing to schedule any hearings at all. When Emanuel Celler of New York, the former chair of the House Judiciary Committee, was asked how he stood on a bill, he replied defiantly: "I don't stand on it. I am sitting on it. It rests four-square under my fanny and will never see the light of day."

For years, committee members had done little to change matters. But during the 1970s and 1980s, the autocracy of committee chairs was challenged through an assault on the **seniority system** and through the growing powers of subcommittees (and their chairs). During most of this century, power and position have been determined not by expertise, intelligence, or party loyalty but primarily on the basis of time spent on a committee. Whenever a member of a committee dies, resigns, or is defeated at the polls, everyone remaining moves up a step on the seniority ladder. And the member of the majority party who has served longest on the committee usually becomes its chair.

One might ask why this custom has been followed. What could justify the selection of chairs on the basis of longevity? One popular argument in favor of seniority has been that it promotes internal harmony in Congress by providing a peaceful route to power. If the heads of committees were selected solely by the will of the majority, conflict and bitterness might result. Another is that it encourages the selection of experienced and able legislators. It rewards those who know the technicalities of the legislative process and who have had long exposure to the subject areas dealt with by their committees.

The drawback, however, has been that seniority does not reward experience gained outside of Congress by newer members. Nor does it seem to be consistent with the fact that other important positions in Congress, such as the Speaker of the House and the floor leaders, have been filled through open elections.

Of equal concern has been the tendency of the seniority tradition to favor members from certain states and districts. To gain enough seniority to head a committee, members usually have had to be continually reelected from "safe" districts where they face little stiff opposition from the other major party. Until the mid-1970s, southern Democrats used to get the lion's share of the chairs because two-party competition tended to be weakest in the Democratic-dominated South.

In 1975, for instance, half of the standing committees in the House were headed by southerners. As Republicans have made more inroads in the South, however, and as older southern Democrats have left Congress, the picture has been changing. In fact, some of the safest seats are now held by black members of Congress, who represent mostly black urban districts in the North.

But perhaps the strongest criticism against the seniority system has been that it splinters party responsibility and makes Congress less internally democratic. If chairs are not selected on the basis of party loyalty and service, they cannot be held accountable to other committee members or to the elected party leadership. As long as their power derives from just staying alive and getting reelected, they can continue to wield significant power.

Thus it is not surprising that critics of the seniority tradition applauded the actions of the House Democrats in 1975. In a major break with the seniority tradition, the House Democratic caucus (comprising all the Democratic members) voted to depose three crusty old Democratic chairs, all from the South. The three were removed in a wave of resentment among young liberal members, many of whom had been swept into the House in the 1974 post-Watergate Democratic landslide. In 1985, House Democrats even went so far as to replace the chair of the Armed Services Committee, Melvin Price, with Les Aspin, the seventh-ranking Democrat on the committee.

This assault was made possible by a number of changes in House rules. In the early 1970s, the House Democrats (following a similar move by the Republicans) voted to allow any ten members of a committee to demand a vote before the party caucus on the status of their chair. Realizing later that an open challenge to a chair might intimidate some members, the Democrats decided to make any chair subject to a secret vote if 20 percent of the party members asked for it. This ruling was then strengthened when secret ballots were required to choose *all* House committee chairs every two years. Senate Democrats also caught the fever of reform and voted to select their committee chairs by secret ballot whenever 20 percent of their colleagues demand it.

Yet seniority has not been entirely abandoned as a result of these reforms. Most of the current chairs have accumulated many years of congressional service, and seniority, especially in the Senate, is still the principal guide in the selection of committee chairs.

★ The Parties and the Party Leadership

When tourists visit the Senate and House chambers, they notice that the Democrats sit on one side of the aisle and the Republicans on the other, and that the members of the two parties enter and leave through separate swinging doors. Although the two major parties, as we saw in chapter 8, are fragmented and undisciplined bodies, they provide some important cues to senators and representatives on how to vote and help bring some order to the chaos on Capitol Hill.

One of the major contributions of the parties is in providing some organization to manage the flow of legislation. In fact, some of the most powerful and prestigious positions in Congress are held by a handful of senators and representatives chosen by their party to keep other members in line and provide policy leadership (see figure 12-2). In many respects, the job of these party leaders is one

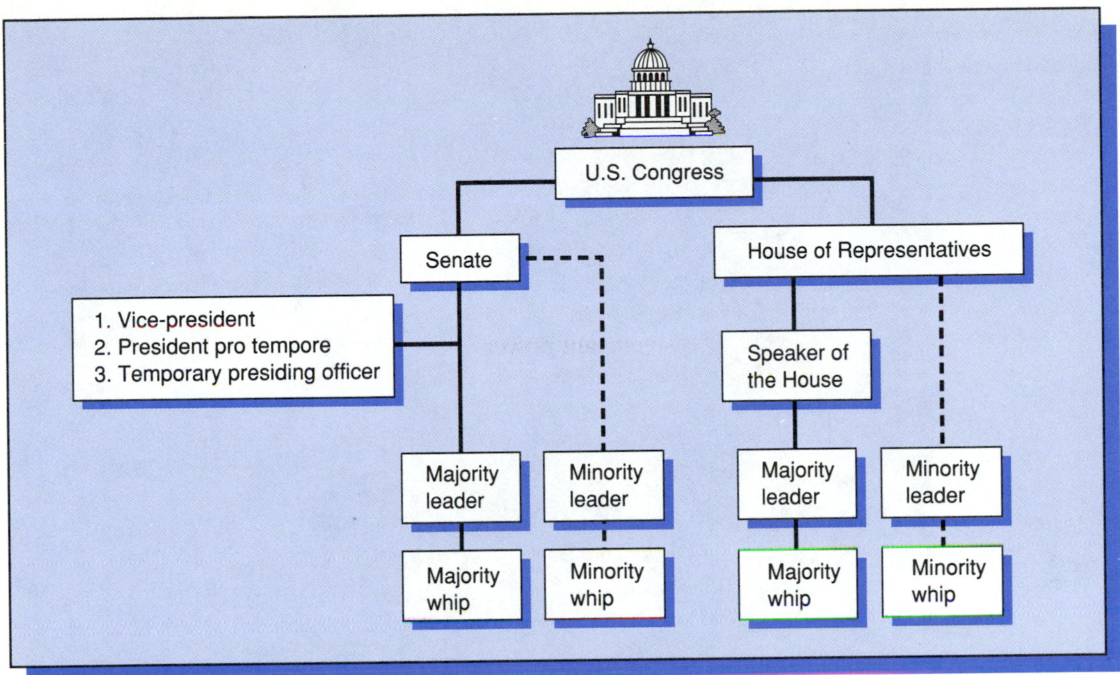

★ **Figure 12-2**
A small number of senators and representatives hold a large amount of power in Congress through their elected party positions.

of the most challenging in Congress. Who are these elected party leaders? And what do they do? Let us begin with those in the House.

The House

The most powerful elected representative is the **Speaker of the House,** who serves not only as presiding officer but also as the majority party leader. He is elected by the entire House every two years and, because of a straight party-line vote, is always a member of the majority party.

In presiding over the House, the Speaker has the power to recognize members on the floor and to interpret parliamentary rules. He refers bills to committees and appoints members to select and conference committees. When he is a Democrat, he also chairs the Democratic Steering and Policy Committee, and he selects members of the Rules Committee. And although such a crisis has never occurred, the Speaker may even assume the presidency if both the president and vice-president die or become incapacitated.

In the past, such Speakers as Thomas Reed and Joseph Cannon wielded enormous power by virtue of formal rules—the ability to control committee appointments, for instance. One of the longest reigning Speakers was the Texan Sam Rayburn, who held the post for most of the years from 1940 to 1961. His power was based more on his ability to persuade than on formal rules, which had come

★ In 1989, Jim Wright became the first Speaker of the House of Representatives to resign his office for alleged misconduct. One charge, among many, was that he used sales of his book as a means to evade financial limits on outside speaking fees.

under attack in the 1910 revolt against Cannon's arbitrary use of the Speaker's power. This revolt democratized the House, but it also weakened party influence, because the Speaker could no longer punish members with loss of committee assignments.

In the final analysis, the extent of the Speaker's power depends on his style and character. Some Speakers have used their position to great advantage—serving effectively as their party's contact with the president, deciding who gets the best committee seats, and so on—but others have made much less effective use of the position.

The Speaker is assisted by a majority **floor leader,** who is chosen by the party caucus. The floor leader helps the Speaker plan party strategy, bargain with committee chairs, and resolve disputes among party members. The job usually serves as a stepping-stone to the Speaker's post, as when Jim Wright of Texas rose from House majority leader to Speaker in 1986. When Wright resigned as Speaker in 1989 under charges of unethical conduct, the post of Speaker thus fell to newly-elected majority leader Thomas S. Foley of Washington state. Helping the floor leader is a majority **whip,** who communicates the wishes of the leadership to the party rank and file, and rounds up members for important votes on the floor. (The title "whip," incidentally, comes from the term "whipper-in," used in Britain to describe the person assigned to keep the dogs from straying during a fox hunt.)

The minority party also elects a floor leader and whip to help manage the legislative programs of their party, direct party strategy, and work occasionally with

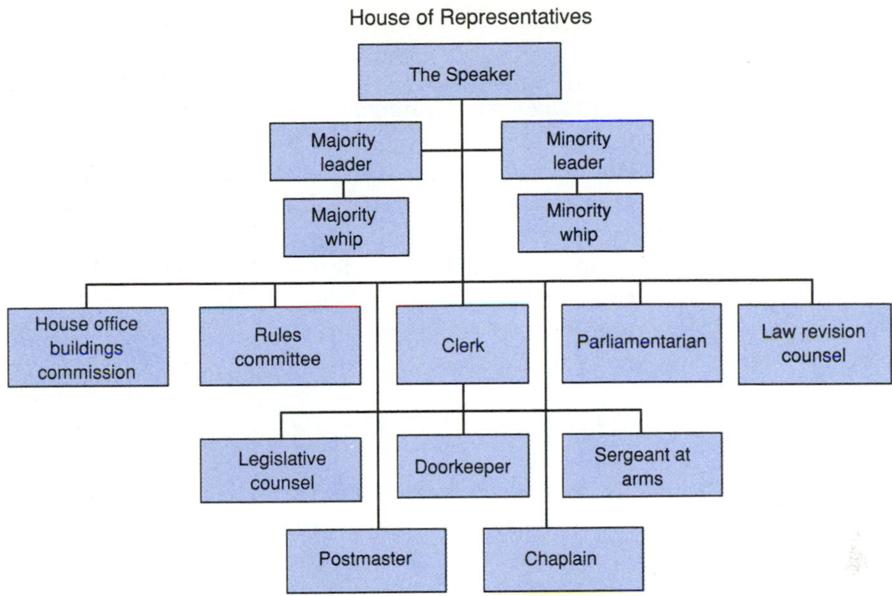

★ **Figure 12-3**
A flowchart of the hierarchies in the House of Representatives

the majority leader and the president to iron out differences on bills (see figure 12-3). The members of each party in the House also occasionally come together as a group, called a **party caucus** by the Democrats and a **party conference** by the Republicans. The caucus and conference vote on committee assignments, elect party leaders, and discuss party policy.

The Senate

The Senate has no powerful counterpart to the Speaker of the House. The vice-president holds the constitutional office of president of the Senate and has the power to cast a vote only in the case of a tie. The **president pro tempore,** a post typically given the member of the majority party with greatest seniority, presides in the vice-president's absence. But neither official wields much clout. In fact, the job of presiding usually falls to junior senators, who take turns wielding the Senate gavel.

The **majority leader** of the Senate is actually the most influential party leader of that body. Like the Speaker of the House, the majority leader is the chief strategist of the majority party in his chamber, mobilizing the members behind bills the leadership decides are in the party's best interests. Naturally, in view of the decentralized, undisciplined character of American parties, this is quite an ambitious task. Generally, the majority leader strives to achieve as much party unity as possible. To this end, this party official helps parcel out committee assignments to other party members, works with the minority leader to determine the sequence of bills on the floor, and serves with the Speaker of the House as a party liaison with the president. The majority leader's success, however, like that of other party leaders, depends ultimately on persuasiveness—the ability to coax, bargain with, even flatter other senators in the party. Lyndon Johnson was a master at this sort of thing during his tenure as majority leader, before he became vice-president under Kennedy. A leader who is unpersuasive will have little success in keeping other party members in line.

As in the House, the Senate majority leader is assisted by a whip, who performs many of the same duties as the House counterpart (see figure 12-4). The minority party also has a floor leader and a whip, and both parties hold caucuses. Ironically, George Bush's election forced him to work with a Senate minority leader, Robert Dole, who had waged a bitter campaign against him for the Republican party nomination for president in 1988.

The Effectiveness of Congressional Leadership

Despite the assaults on the seniority tradition and the powers of committee chairs, the party leaders have experienced considerable difficulty in achieving party unity. Members of Congress continue to be responsive to local pressures and interest groups independent of the congressional party leadership. Legislators thus frequently vote in special-interest blocs that cross party lines. The conservative coalition of Republicans and southern Democrats, for example, and the rise of informal groups (such as the Congressional Black Caucus and the Northeast-Midwest Economic Advancement Coalition) provide potent challenges to the authority of the elected party leaders.

The term "caucus" is also applied to the dozens of legislative special-interest groups that have sprung up in recent years on Capitol Hill. **Congressional caucuses** are informal associations of like-minded members who meet to discuss policy concerns. Some caucuses are regional (border states, rural, territories, New England, Sunbelt), some are economic (auto, steel, and textile industries), some are policy-specific (arms control and foreign policy, science and technology, human rights, space, the environment, exports, and military reform), and others are aimed at a group interest (blacks, Hispanics, and women).

There are more than sixty of these caucuses, which have both positive and negative features. On the one hand, they serve as clearinghouses for information, dialogue, and new legislation. On the other hand, they may challenge the traditional legislative process and often weaken party discipline in the two chambers. Caucuses are more numerous and formal in the House than in the smaller Senate.

★ Legislative Staffs: Our Nonelected Lawmakers

Senators and representatives are not the only policy makers in Congress. Scurrying in and out of their offices and through the halls are groups of shadow lawmakers who write the speeches, handle the constituent mail, do the research, and occasionally even help draft new pieces of legislation. These are the roughly fifteen thousand men and women who staff the committees and offices of members of Congress (about twenty eight for each legislator). Most of them are under forty years of age, have college degrees, and earn anywhere from $30,000 to $60,000 a year.

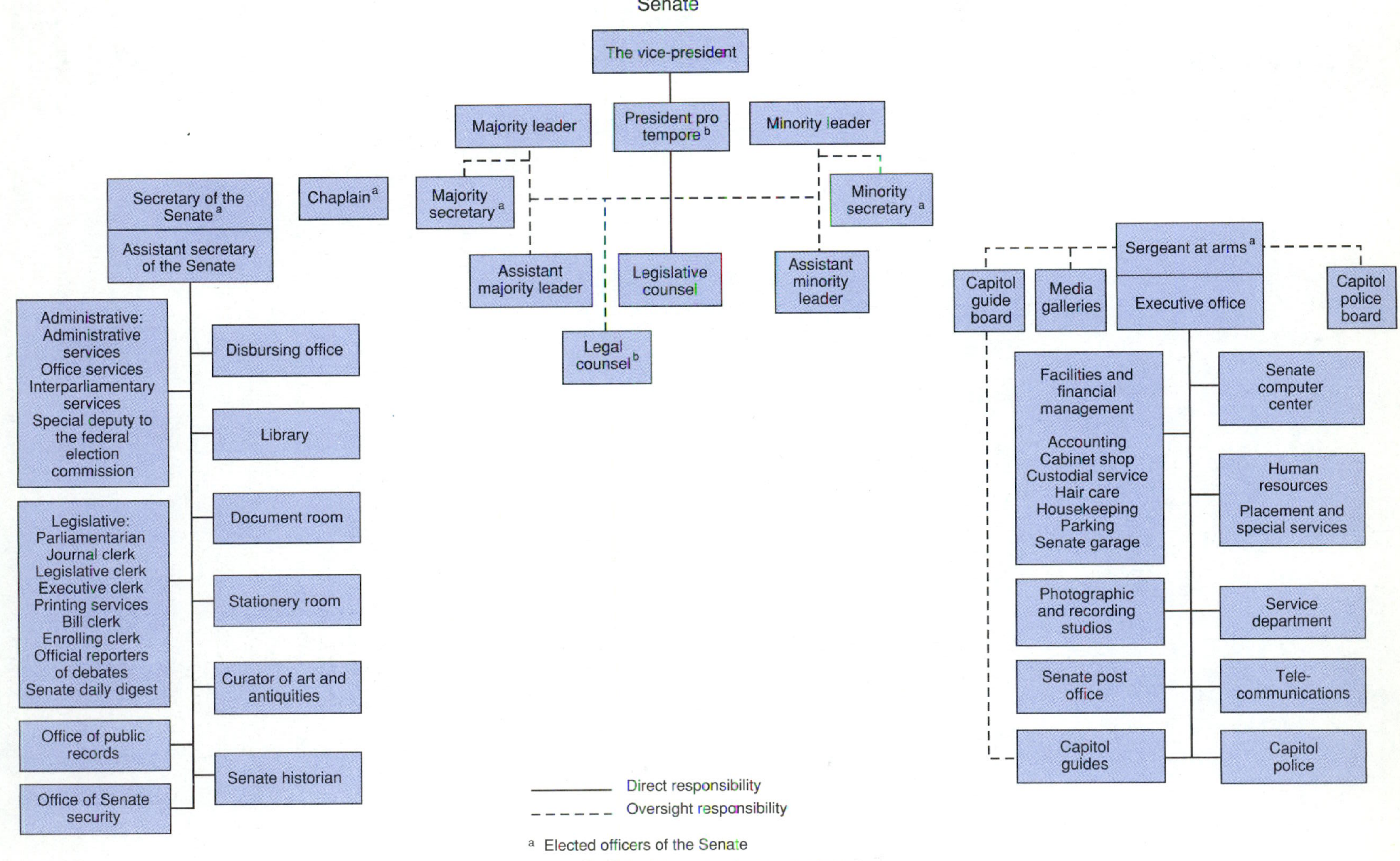

Figure 12-4
A flowchart of the hierarchies in the Senate

Challenges to the White Male Club

Congress may be a white male club, but those women and minorities who have managed to get elected to Congress have formed caucuses to further their policy goals. The Congressional Black Caucus has been a powerful force in securing U.S. sanctions against the white-supremacist regime in South Africa. The Congressional Hispanic Caucus is vitally concerned with U.S. immigration policy, particularly as it affects discrimination against Hispanic Americans. And the Congressional Caucus for Women's Issues is a powerful clearinghouse for legislation affecting women.

The Congressional Caucus for Women's Issues is a bipartisan organization, which in recent years has been co-chaired by Representatives Patricia Schroeder (D-Colorado) and Olympia Snowe (R-Maine). In 1988 there were eighty-five men in the caucus, whose executive committee was staffed by two female senators (Barbara Mikulski, D-Maryland, and Nancy Kassenbaum, R-Kansas) and sixteen of the female representatives. The caucus has been instrumental in many key policy areas, such as welfare reform, enforcement of child support, child care, family violence services, maternal and child health, pay equity, equal credit, parental leave, and family planning. The caucus not only introduces new legislation but also keeps an eye on funding levels for favored programs, implementation of legislation by the executive branch, and court decisions affecting women. In 1988, for example, the caucus co-chairs circulated an amicus brief and collected the signatures of ninety-two members of Congress. The brief was filed in an appellate court to oppose family planning regulations issued by the Department of Health and Human Services. ★

★ Rep. Patricia Schroeder (D-Col.), the senior woman member of Congress, has gained national attention in her support for such causes as women's rights, curbing military spending, and protecting the environment.

As the role of government has increased, this growing army of anonymous congressional aides has played an ever-expanding role in policy making. In order to oversee the vast federal bureaucracy and to keep up with the growing complexity of legislation, members of Congress have become increasingly dependent on their staffs to gather, process, and evaluate information, much as the president has come to rely on his personal White House assistants. Although many aides have little say on policy—they sit in cramped offices all day answering constituent letters—other aides are actively involved in legislative decision making. This is particularly the case for committee staff aides, who arrange the hearings, select the witnesses, prepare the questions, brief the members, and draft the bills. (We will look at a case study of one of these staffers in chap. 16.)

Many aides develop more technical expertise than the senator or representative they serve and provide the advice that may determine how a busy legislator will vote on a bill. During a vote on the Federal Election Commission (FEC) in 1976, for example, a top staff aide was on the Senate floor telling his boss to vote against an amendment that would cripple the commission. "I did what I thought was the responsible thing," the aide recalled. "As it turned out, the amendment was defeated by a single vote. . . . If I had told him to vote the other way, the FEC would be out of existence now. . . . I had the power—me, an appointed staff member, elected by nobody and responsible to nobody—to overturn a major law in this country. It's scary."

The power may indeed be scary, but it is also a source of excitement to many aides, who as ordinary citizens would have little political clout. By attaching themselves to a senator or representative, they can help think up new laws, tell pushy bureaucrats where to place their pencil sharpeners, and write impassioned speeches on current issues without once having to endure the hardships of a political campaign. In fact, aides with long tenure who serve in key positions are often as likely to initiate bills as the senator or representative they serve.

The danger comes when aides begin to think of themselves as senators or representatives, manipulating the process to satisfy their own policy goals. Aides have been known to influence legislative decisions by giving only selected information to their bosses, neglecting to mention items that conflict with their own political views. A few aides have even used their positions for private gain, with resultant scandals that have undermined the reputations of their elected bosses.

But perhaps the most important consequence of an ever-expanding professional staff is that Congress has been creating its own bureaucracy, with all the features (good and bad) of the executive bureaucracy it is supposed to oversee. Instead of just 435 representatives and 100 senators, Congress now comprises thousands of hopeful policy makers stumbling over one another in their efforts to see their ideas embodied in legislation.

★ Citizen Access to Congress

When voting is an inadequate means to express one's opinions, one can get in touch with one's legislators directly. Public opinion surveys reveal that most Americans have given thought to picking up a pen to express their concerns, although only about 15 percent have ever done so. While letters may be addressed to practically any official—including the president, the mayor, the governor, or a bureaucrat—the congressional representative has become the principal target of citizen mail.

People try to get in touch with their representative for at least two major reasons: either they wish to influence legislation or they need assistance with a personal problem. If they want to influence the vote of a member of Congress on a bill, they need to time their letters for the best effect. Probably the best time to write is when a bill is about to reach the House or Senate floor for debate, or when it is pending before a committee. The latter is a particularly crucial time because the fate of most bills is sealed in committee. For maximum effectiveness, letter writers must understand the committee process and keep track of the bill at its various stages. One useful source of information on such matters has been offered by the League Action Service (a service of the League of Women Voters), which keeps a watchful eye on the status of legislation and suggests when action should be taken.

Naturally, citizens who desire to influence policy must also take into account the committee position held and power commanded by their representative. If they want to influence tax policy, for example, and their representative happens to sit on the Agriculture Committee and is still wet behind the ears, then pressure may have to be directed elsewhere. Indeed, a few letters to the chair of the Ways and Means Committee may have considerably greater impact than four hundred letters to the young upstart from home. Unfortunately, many people fail to take notice of the position held, talent exhibited, and clout exercised by their representative before taking action. They also fail to consider the difficulties many members face in seeing their bills enacted into law. When they expect immediate returns on their minimal letter-writing efforts, they ignore the special requirements of an effective citizen campaign.

Many people also are unaware of the impersonal way their letters often are handled. Their carefully composed letters are not likely to reach their representative directly, but will be read by an administrative or legislative assistant. Typically, only the most important letters are brought directly to a legislator's attention. In fact, most members of Congress do not compose their own replies to constituents' letters; rather, an office assistant types out letters to be signed by the Congress member, giving constituents only the appearance of a personal reply.

Moreover, any letter is bound to be only one among many pouring into a legislator's office. In most instances, a letter from a constituent will not determine how a member of Congress votes on a bill. Members of Congress often place greater importance on their own opinions of a bill, especially if they feel they have researched the issue more thoroughly than their constituents have done. In such an instance, a hapless citizen may simply receive a smug, precomposed reply stating the reasons for the representative's support or rejection of the bill in question.

Occasionally notice is taken of constituents' views, especially if many people correspond on an issue. Such was the case in 1987, when many senators were stunned by the enormous volume of letters against Reagan's nomination of Robert Bork to the Supreme Court. And in early 1989, after being battered by constituents' complaints and adverse press reports, members of Congress decided to shelve their proposed 51 percent salary increase. In fact, many people believe that the only effective way to sway legislators is to trigger a mass letter-writing campaign in order to flood their offices with petitions from home. This strategy is designed to convince legislators that constituents are deeply concerned about an issue and want immediate action. Indeed, many letter-writing campaigns today are not the work of individuals but are massive direct mail assaults by interest groups.

However, even mass letter-writing campaigns have limitations. An avalanche of correspondence may not be very effective if the letters are not spontaneous and personal. Members of Congress know that only a few citizens are behind some letter-writing campaigns and that most of the other correspondents have a low commitment to the issue. Such campaigns lose their forcefulness when members learn that letters containing essentially the same information and language are handed to people on the street to sign and mail. "Most experienced Senators and Representatives," former Speaker Jim Wright reflected, "suspect one of these organized campaigns when the first batch of mail begins to hit their desks. The repetition of certain phrases and slogans and the coincidence of several hundred communications in a given day on a certain subject in which little interest previously has been evinced by the constituency almost invariably tip the hand of those who would deluge the lawmakers with numbers. The design sticks out all over, like a well-developed case of hives."[20] Thus interest groups often advise their members to state in their own words why they support or reject a bill under debate. Be courteous, they are advised, for more flies can be caught with honey than with vinegar.

Most people probably will have more success in asking for help with a per-

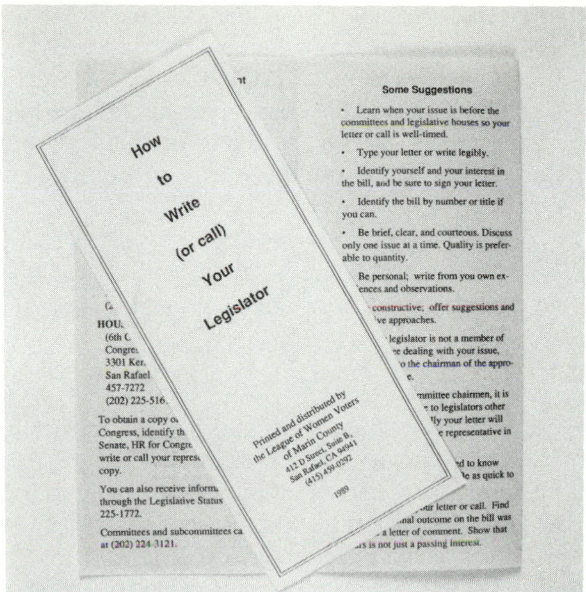

★ Writing letters to elected officials can help influence the way they vote on issues. Groups such as the League of Women Voters publish pamphlets with hints about how to write effective letters.

sonal problem. Although they may not obtain such help directly from their representative (few members of Congress, in fact, personally respond to constituents' requests for aid in most circumstances), they will be assisted by one of the caseworkers in the legislator's office. Each month those caseworkers may accept hundreds of requests for help in untangling a snarl with Medicare, speeding a relative through immigration, or acquiring information on a bill. Naturally, a person's ability to obtain results depends on the scope of the problem. It is easier to get help from a legislator's office in tracking down a lost social security check, for example, than in trying to stop a new federal highway from cutting through the neighborhood. To find the lost check an aide may need to do little more than persuade an otherwise recalcitrant clerk to thumb through the constituent's records. But to halt the invasion of a highway the legislator may personally have to battle contractors, unions, and other special interests that make up the highway lobby and cajole high officials into taking appropriate action. In such instances, unless public sentiment runs strongly against the proposed highway, a simple request for help from a legislator's office probably is doomed to failure.

Furthermore, success often depends on the motivations and talents of the caseworkers. While some respond speedily to a problem and know exactly what strings to pull, others are less committed to constituents and have no talent for cutting through bureaucratic red tape on their behalf.

Still, letters to a legislator's office can have spectacular results. Legislators have, on occasion, responded to a constituent's misfortune by introducing new legislation to rectify it. This is as true at the state level as in Congress. In the early 1970s, for example, an elderly woman wrote to her California state senator, Nicholas

Petris, complaining that, under existing law, she would not be eligible for senior citizen's property tax assistance. She had been denied eligibility because she had been unable to meet her tax obligations the previous fiscal year. Her letter inspired Senator Petris and his caseworker to put together a new bill easing the eligibility requirements. The bill, passed by the full legislature, ultimately benefited not only the woman who wrote the letter but countless other citizens who faced a similar problem.

★ Reform of Congress

The feelings of impotence and frustration that overcome some of the men and women in Congress largely reflect the difficulty in getting Congress as a whole to move. As the country's primary lawmaking body, Congress has not been adept at setting policy priorities and responding to many of the major social and economic problems facing the country, let alone the globe. Crime and drug abuse continue to make neighborhoods unsafe, poverty and environmental pollution still ravage the nation, and people in large numbers cast a weary and cynical eye on government.

Advocates of congressional reform have tended to argue that the rules and customs that frustrate many members of Congress, such as the emphasis on seniority and the wide dispersion of power among committees, also interfere with Congress's ability to fulfill many of its lawmaking responsibilities. Even when a major social problem has reared its ugly head, Congress has been too splintered by internal bickering, too indebted to special interests, too encumbered by an antiquated, slipshod organization to do much about it.

In many respects Congress has become a different institution in recent years. Although the dispersion of power among committees and a lack of party discipline continue to block passage of important legislation, many of the old procedures and rules have been reformed. The seniority system has been weakened, the filibuster has been modified, autocratic committee chairs have been deposed, and Congress as a whole has become a more open institution by exposing most committee sessions to the public and the press. Many members of Congress and others have been heartened by these reforms. Congress is now in a better position than ever before, they say, to respond to the nation's social and economic ills, and to play an increasingly important role on the world stage.

Yet there is another perspective on Congress worth considering. Many observers insist that the ability of Congress to respond to social problems depends on more than the reform of its procedures. They argue that the very goals of Congress are shaped and limited by the power structure of the society in which it thrives. Congress simply mirrors the prevailing inequities of the political and economic system, serving mainly as an instrument of elite interests. "As long as Congress reflects the distribution of economic power in the wider society," one writer has argued,

> it is not likely to change much even if liberals in both houses manage to gain control of the major committees, and even if the cloture rule is changed to enable the Senate to rid itself of the filibuster . . . and even if seniority is done away with. For what remains is the entire system of organized corporate power

> with its elitist institutions, business-controlled media and mass propaganda, organized pressure groups, high-paid lobbyists and influence-peddling lawyers, campaign contributions and bribes—all of which operate with such telling effect on legislators, including most of the professedly liberal ones.[21]

These are harsh criticisms. Undoubtedly Congress does serve elite interests and has often been slow to respond to the needs of a large part of our society. But if we have to wait until the present system is overhauled before meaningful improvements in the responsiveness of Congress are realized, we are probably in for a long wait. In the meantime, we can continue to debate the role of Congress and find new ways to make it responsive to those who, up to now, have been slighted in the struggle for political favors.

★ Summary

Despite Congress's major role in policy making, many members feel frustrated in their efforts to achieve even modest political goals. Because of the influence of committees, the impact of interest groups, and its complex procedures, Congress can be a source of irritation even to those familiar with its ways. For years Congress has been chided for lacking the will and the ability to confront many of the important problems facing the nation.

Still, an incredible diversity of powers and duties are wielded by members of Congress. In addition to such rarely exercised powers as declaring war, proposing amendments to the Constitution, and impeaching federal officials, members of Congress have four major responsibilities: forging new laws, overseeing the executive branch, raising and spending money, and helping their constituents.

Although Congress is usually eclipsed by the president in the formation of foreign policy, its members have had to confront a wealth of new questions and problems created by expanding global communications, the arms race, and other international political, economic, and social forces. Congress's role in foreign and military policy making can be seen clearly in its authority to declare war, to ratify treaties, and to regulate commerce with foreign nations. Theoretically, the president's power to send troops abroad is balanced by Congress's authority under the War Powers Resolution, though presidents have uniformly ignored it.

Although the success of members of Congress in their efforts to have significant influence is contingent on their abilities, ultimately it depends even more on the positions they attain in the congressional power structure. Congress is not a body of equals. Committee assignments and other leadership roles affect the impact members can have on policy. Congress relies especially on committees to divide the work load and to enable each member to specialize in a few fields. It is in the committees that members have the best opportunity to influence legislation. Moreover, to help manage the flow of legislation, Congress relies on the elected party leaders in each house and on specialized rules and procedures, such as the filibuster and the seniority system. It also depends on a growing staff of assistants who play a major role in policy making. Citizens who desire to have an impact on legislation must, like their representatives, understand the complex ways in which Congress tries to grapple with the problems of the modern era.

★ Key Terms

advice and consent
casework
cloture rule
conference committees
Congressional caucuses
constituents
filibuster
floor leader
impoundment
joint committee
legislative oversight
majority leader
party caucus
party conference
president pro tempore
select committees
senatorial courtesy
seniority system
Speaker of the House
standing committees
War Powers Resolution
whip

★ Notes

1. Shirley Chisholm, *Unbought and Unbossed* (Boston: Houghton Mifflin, 1970), p. 100.
2. *U.S. News & World Report,* March 25, 1974, p. 96.
3. Quoted in Charles L. Clapp, *The Congressman: His Work as He Sees It* (Washington, D.C.: Brookings Institution, 1963), p. 426.
4. Donald Riegle, *O Congress* (New York: Doubleday, 1972), p. 65.
5. Quoted in Clapp, *Congressman*, p. 377.
6. John F. Kennedy, *Profiles in Courage* (New York: Harper, 1955), pp. 18, 16.
7. Quoted in Clapp, *Congressman*, p. 54.
8. Donald G. Tacheron and Morris K. Udall, *The Job of the Congressman,* 2d ed. (Indianapolis: Bobbs-Merrill, 1970), pp. 303–304.
9. Quoted in Kennedy, *Profiles in Courage,* p. 10.
10. Ronald Garay, *Congressional Television: A Legislative History* (Westport, Conn.: Greenwood Press, 1984).
11. Chisholm, *Unbought and Unbossed*, p. 104.
12. Lee H. Hamilton, "Congress and the Presidency in American Foreign Policy," *Presidential Studies Quarterly* 17 (Summer 1988): 508.
13. John T. Rourke and Russell Farnen, "War, Presidents, and the Constitution," *Presidential Studies Quarterly* 17 (Summer 1988): 513.
14. Charles W. Kegley, Jr., and Eugene R. Wittkopf, *American Foreign Policy: Pattern and Process*, 3d ed. (New York: St. Martin's Press, 1987), p. 444.
15. Ibid., p. 447.
16. See Robert J. Art, "Congress and the Defense Budget," *Political Science Quarterly* 100 (Summer 1985): 227–248.
17. Hamilton, "Congress and the Presidency," p. 509.
18. Quoted in Mark J. Green et al., *Who Runs Congress?* 4th ed. (New York: Bantam, 1972), p. 56.
19. Woodrow Wilson, *Congressional Government* (New York: Meridian, 1956), p. 63; first published 1885.
20. Jim Wright, *You and Your Congressman* (New York: Coward-McCann, 1965), pp. 189–190.
21. Michael Parenti, *Democracy for the Few* (New York: St. Martin's Press, 1974), pp. 205–206.

★ For Further Reading

Davidson, Roger, and Walter J. Oleszek. *Congress and Its Members*. 2d ed. Washington, D.C.: Congressional Quarterly Press, 1985.

Dodd, Lawrence C., and Bruce I. Oppenheimer, eds. *Congress Reconsidered*. 3d ed. Washington, D.C.: Congressional Quarterly Press, 1985.

Fenno, Richard F., Jr. *Congressmen in Committees*. Boston: Little, Brown, 1973.

Fox, Harrison, and Susan Webb Hammond. *Congressional Staffs*. New York: Free Press, 1977.

Green, Mark J., et al. *Who Runs Congress?* 4th ed. New York: Dell, 1984.

Mayhew, David R. *Congress: The Electoral Connection*. New Haven, Conn.: Yale University Press, 1974.

Redman, Eric. *The Dance of Legislation*. New York: Simon & Schuster, 1973.

Sinclair, Barbara. *Majority Leadership in the U.S. House*. Baltimore: Johns Hopkins University Press, 1983.

Smith, Steven, and Christopher Deering. *Committees in Congress*. Washington, D.C.: Congressional Quarterly Press, 1984.

Energy in the Executive is a leading character in the definition of good government. It is essential to the protection of the community against foreign attacks; it is not less essential to the steady administration of the laws.

—Alexander Hamilton,
Federalist *no. 70*

CHAPTER THIRTEEN

THE PRESIDENCY

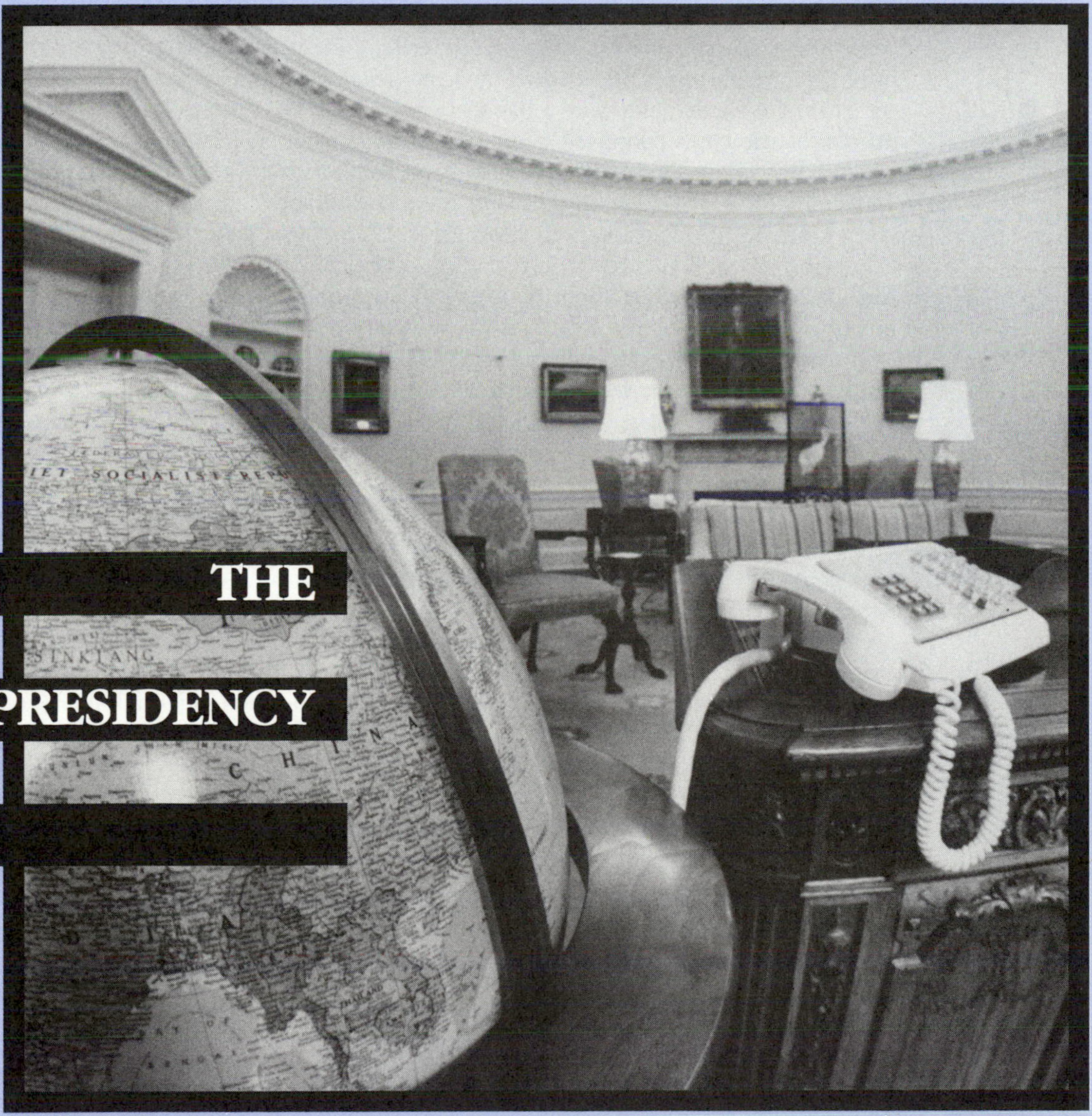

★★★★★★★★★★★

The President of the United States: Imperial or Imperiled?

In 1989 George Bush joined his immediate predecessors as the preeminent decision maker in today's interdependent world. The international press often refers to the president of the United States as the most powerful person on earth. He shares with only a handful of world leaders the power to order a nuclear attack. He is constantly reminded of this power, as he is accompanied at all times by a military aide whose wrist is manacled to a black briefcase, or "football," containing the secret code used to launch nuclear weapons.

A president's decisions can alter our relations with other nations in many ways. He can sanction covert operations to destabilize unfriendly governments. He can reward an ally with millions of dollars in aid. His visit to one nation can tip the uneasy balance among the world's superpowers.

His decisions can also affect the global economy and ecology. His efforts to remedy the U.S. trade and budget deficits can send shock waves through the financial centers of New York, Tokyo, London, and Bonn. A presidentially convened conference on acid rain or the greenhouse effect can draw international attention to global ecological problems.

When a newly elected president assumes the responsibilities of the highest office in the land, he quickly learns the importance of his global role. President-elect Kennedy, for example, was startled to learn from outgoing President Eisenhower about secret plans to invade Cuba. And when President Carter met with President-elect Reagan, he said that he briefed Reagan on "such matters as the management of our nuclear forces in time of attack on our nation. I urged him to take plenty of time to learn about these arrangements before Inauguration Day, so that he could be thoroughly instructed on the procedures to be followed in an emergency. I described some top-secret agreements we had with a few other nations."[1]

America's global responsibilities have so coalesced in the executive branch that some observers have written with alarm about an "imperial presidency" that runs a "secret government." These analysts say that Tocqueville was right when he predicted that the president's strength lay in foreign affairs, and that, as U.S. military power grew, so would that of the presidency.

In this chapter we will consider whether we have an imperial presidency, or whether we have instead, as some observers have countered, an "imperiled presidency," hamstrung by an unwieldy bureaucracy and overzealous Congress. After considering the framers' ambivalence about presidential power, we will investigate the foreign policy powers and skillful use of the media that have encouraged an

★ In one of his first trips as president, George Bush *(right)* visited Chinese leader Deng Xiaoping *(left)* in 1989 to signal good Sino–U.S. relations. Bush had served as ambassador to China and was interested in furthering economic ties between the two world powers. (These relations soon soured, however, when Chinese troops massacred hundreds of unarmed protesters in June 1989.)

imperial presidency to flourish. We will then see that a president's hands are often tied by his own bureaucracy and by Congress, with which he shares domestic policy powers. Finally, we will consider a job description of the presidency and the public's ambivalence (mirroring that of the framers) about presidential power.

★ The Framers' Ambivalence about Presidential Power

The framers of the Constitution found themselves between a rock and a hard place when it came to the chief executive. On the one hand, the last thing they wanted was a king like George III of England, with arbitrary and unchecked powers. As Thomas Jefferson wrote in the Declaration of Independence, "a Tyrant is unfit to be the ruler of a free people." On the other hand, the framers feared an omnipotent legislature with direct ties to the people. As we saw in chapter 12, this fear drove them to create a bicameral body, whose members served terms of different lengths and represented different constituencies.

To resolve this dilemma, the framers arrived at what was at the time a novel American solution—the president. His powers differed not only from those of previous heads of state (such as kings, tsars, and emperors) but from those of subsequent rulers as well (such as premiers, shahs, junta strongmen, and party secretaries general). Today many other democracies are headed by prime ministers, whose power rests in control of the legislature. While these nations may also have a president, his or her role is often limited to symbolic functions—dedicating public works, greeting visiting dignitaries, and the like. The French presidency, created to enshrine Charles de Gaulle as head of state in 1958, came close to the

American model. Interestingly, in recent years, previously authoritarian regimes on both the right and the left have moved in the direction of an American-style presidency: in the Philippines, the dictatorship of Ferdinand Marcos gave way to the presidency of Corazon Aquino; and Mikhail Gorbachev became the first Soviet leader since Lenin to permit an open election.

While the U.S. presidency may seem like a model of checked power to a growing number of nations around the world, when our Constitution was being considered by the states for ratification, it was the "awful squint towards monarchy," as Patrick Henry put it, that was foremost on many people's minds. The framers enlisted Alexander Hamilton to make the case (in *Federalist* nos. 67 through 77) that the president was no king and, indeed, wielded power similar to that of the governor of New York.

Hamilton pointed out that, unlike a king, the president was elected by an electoral college for a four-year term, had no absolute veto, could not declare war, needed the Senate's approval for treaties and for ambassadorial and court appointments, and could be impeached. Like the governor of New York, the president had the power to serve as commander in chief of the military, to recommend measures to the legislature, to execute the laws, to grant reprieves and pardons, and to convene extraordinary sessions of the legislature.

The powers of the presidency, as outlined in Article II of the Constitution, are less detailed than those provided Congress by Article I. The framers figured that many powers of the office would be established by precedent, and the precedent setter they had in mind was General George Washington. He was held in high esteem by the men who drafted the Constitution. They felt confident that he would be the first president and would resist any monarchical tendencies implicit in the office. They knew that a single chief executive was needed for "decision, activity, secrecy and dispatch,"[2] features lacking in a divided Congress. What they could not have foreseen was that the commander-in-chief provision and the possibility of acting in secret would become a Pandora's box for the accumulation of presidential power as America assumed global responsibilities in the post–World War II era.

★ The Ascendancy of the Presidency

History has shown that the framers' system of checks and balances tilts in favor of the White House whenever Congress abdicates its war powers to the president as **commander in chief** of the military. Furthermore, presidents have accumulated power as their foreign policy powers have become translated into domestic policy powers, creating what some analysts have termed the "imperial presidency."[3] Throughout American history, the executive and legislative branches have alternated as the dominant force in the making of foreign policy.

The Nineteenth-Century Tug-of-War

During the first half of the nineteenth century, presidential warmaking gradually increased: first against Native Americans on this continent and "pirates" in the Mediterranean, then against Mexico and the Confederacy. The 1846 war against

Mexico, for example, was popularly known as "Polk's war," since President James Polk sent U.S. troops into disputed territory and then secured a declaration of war by a Congress outraged that our troops had been "attacked." At the time, Representative Abraham Lincoln objected to one man's ability to compel Congress to declare war. Polk took his commander-in-chief role seriously, supervising the entire operation—from devising military strategy to purchasing army mules, settling disputes among military surgeons, and assigning cargo ships.

Similarly, Congress never declared war against the Confederacy; to do so would have been implicitly to recognize its sovereignty. President Lincoln's extraordinary war powers, seen as expedient measures at the time, marked the beginning of a fateful development that has seen several of his successors invoking the powers of commander in chief in times of emergency. President Lincoln delayed the convocation of Congress for twelve weeks while Fort Sumter was fired upon; he called up the militia and enlarged the army and navy beyond congressional authorizations; he instituted a naval blockade of the Confederacy; he called out volunteers for service; and he spent funds without congressional approval.

Extraordinary war powers spilled over to domestic powers as Lincoln set bold restrictions on civil liberties. He approved measures that suspended the writ of habeas corpus, proclaimed martial law behind the lines, ordered people arrested without warrants and siezed property, suppressed newspapers, and barred treasonable correspondences from the mail. He also proclaimed that all persons who resisted the draft or aided rebels would be subject to martial law and tried by the military. In all, about thirteen thousand Americans were arrested by the military for offenses ranging from theft of government property to treason. Most received mild sentences at their courts-martial and were pardoned when the war ended.

After the Civil War, Congress recoiled against presidential domination. It impeached Lincoln's successor, President Andrew Johnson, for trivial offenses, hardly the "high crimes and misdemeanors" for which the Constitution authorized **impeachment.** The main charge was that Johnson violated the Tenure of Office Act (which was later found to be unconstitutional) by firing a Radical Republican member of his cabinet. Among the other high crimes and misdemeanors of which Johnson was accused was delivering speeches "in a loud voice."

Congress's intent was obviously political—to end Johnson's systematic sabotage of the Republicans' reconstruction efforts in the South. As there was no vice-president (Johnson had assumed the presidency upon Lincoln's assassination), Radical Republicans would see their president pro tempore of the Senate become the next president if Johnson were removed from office (the law designating the Speaker of the House as next in line after the vice-president to succeed the president was not passed until 1947). Johnson narrowly escaped conviction by the Senate, and Congress's impeachment power was never used again in such a partisan fashion.

The cycle of congressional domination was rounded out with restraints on Presidents Ulysses S. Grant (who wanted to annex Santo Domingo) and Rutherford B. Hayes (who tried to use troops for whom Congress had not appropriated money). And between 1871 and 1898, the Senate ratified no important treaty.

Twentieth-Century Presidential Dominance

The turn of the century brought about a return of presidential dominance of foreign affairs that lasted until the end of World War I. The Spanish-American War of 1898

★ **Table 13-1**
Treaties and executive agreements approved by the United States, 1789–1986

Year	*Number of treaties*	*Number of executive agreements*
1789–1839	60	27
1839–1889	215	238
1889–1929	382	763
1930–1932	49	41
1933–1944 (F. Roosevelt)	131	369
1945–1952 (Truman)	132	1,324
1953–1960 (Eisenhower)	89	1,834
1961–1963 (Kennedy)	36	813
1964–1968 (L. Johnson	67	1,083
1969–1974 (Nixon)	93	1,317
1975–1976 (Ford)	26	666
1977–1980 (Carter)	79	1,476
1981–1986 (Reagan)	92	2,019

NOTE: Varying definitions of what constitutes an executive agreement and its entry-into-force date make the above numbers approximate.

SOURCE: Harold W. Stanley and Richard G. Niemi, *Vital Statistics on American Politics* (Washington, D.C.: Congressional Quarterly Press, 1988), p. 226.

strengthened the executive branch. President William McKinley began the twentieth-century trend of relying on **executive agreements** instead of treaties (see table 13-1). As we saw in chapter 12, executive agreements are agreements between nations drafted by the executive branch without Senate approval. McKinley used executive agreements to help settle the Spanish-American War and to promote his Open Door policy in the Far East, whereby European nations agreed to equal trade opportunities in China. He also sent five thousand U.S. troops to China to suppress the Boxer Rebellion and prop up the Chinese Empire. Congress neither declared war nor objected to sending troops to China.

After McKinley was assassinated by an anarchist in 1901, his successor, Theodore Roosevelt, continued to conduct foreign policy by executive agreement. In 1905 he acted without Senate consent to place Santo Domingo's customhouses under U.S. control, and signed a secret agreement with Japan approving of its military protectorate in Korea.

Theodore Roosevelt, famed for his provocative foreign policy ventures, ironically became the first American to win a Nobel peace prize, awarded for his mediation of the 1905 Treaty of Portsmouth, ending the Russo-Japanese War. Roosevelt had instigated a "revolution" to separate Panama from Colombia in 1901 and secured the Canal Zone on his own terms. This feat was a source of great pride to him and he boasted that he "stole Panama fair and square."

In another provocative move, Roosevelt sent the "Great White Fleet" of sixteen U.S. battleships on a year-long, round-the-world mission to flex American muscle abroad. (Actually, he sent the ships halfway and then asked Congress for the funds

★ President Woodrow Wilson *(right)* met in Versailles in 1919 with the leaders of our allies during World War I: *(from left)* Lloyd George (England), Vittorio Emanuele Orlando (Italy), and Georges Clemenceau (France). The Senate, however, was miffed at being excluded from Wilson's peace agreements, and it dealt him a humiliating defeat by not ratifying the Treaty of Versailles.

to bring them home.) Upon leaving the White House, Roosevelt stated imperially, "The biggest matters, such as the Portsmouth peace, the acquisition of Panama, and sending the Fleet around the world, I managed without consultation with anyone; for when a matter is of capital importance, it is well to have it handled by one man only."[4]

In a final gesture of turn-of-the-century presidential dominance of foreign affairs, President Woodrow Wilson sent troops against the regime of Victoriano Huerta in Mexico in 1914 and reinforced an allied expeditionary force in Siberia in an attempt to overthrow the Bolsheviks in 1918.

Our involvement in World War I demonstrates that a president's foreign policy power can reverberate on the home front. Wilson was elected in 1916 because "he kept us out of war;" seven months later the United States had declared war on the Central Powers. It was an unpopular war, and more than 335,000 eligible men dodged the draft. Wilson called war resisters unpatriotic and sponsored an auxiliary police force called the American Protection League to enforce the draft. Resisters were beaten, tarred and feathered, and even lynched by the league.

Wilson secured a series of laws that effectively ended freedom of speech for war resisters. It became a crime to oppose the war. Judges convicted people for such offenses as stating that conscription was unconstitutional, supporting a mandatory popular referendum before war could be declared, saying that the war was contrary to the teachings of Christ, and giving antiwar speeches. The socialist Kate Richards O'Hare was sent to the Missouri state penitentiary for saying that "the women of the United States were nothing more nor less than brood sows, to raise children to get into the army and be made into fertilizer."[5]

After the war, thousands of resisters and other dissidents were rounded up in the so-called Palmer raids, conducted by Wilson's attorney general, A. Mitchell Palmer, between 1919 and 1920. The "Red scare" of the 1920s was the executive branch's attempt to repress any American sympathy for the Bolshevik revolution against the tsarist regime in Russia.

The end of the war in 1918 was celebrated by a swift but brief reaction to Wilson's power. The Senate refused to ratify the Treaty of Versailles, which Wilson had drafted without consulting Senate leaders. In 1921 Wilson's successor, President Warren Harding, promised a "return to normalcy" in an emotional speech from a New Jersey dock, where ships were unloading five thousand American war dead.

Congress became so isolationist that it almost handed its warmaking power over to the people. In 1935 Representative Louis Ludlow of Indiana proposed a constitutional amendment requiring that, except in the event of invasion, "the authority of Congress to declare war shall not become effective until confirmed by a majority of votes cast in a Nation-wide referendum." According to a 1937 Gallup poll, three-quarters of the American people supported the Ludlow (or Peace) Amendment. But the proposal was narrowly defeated in the House after successful lobbying against it by President Franklin Roosevelt.

The shock of the Japanese attack on Pearl Harbor in December 1941 jolted Congress from its isolationist mood. Arthur Schlesinger, Jr., sums up the legacy of the interwar period: "No one for a long time would trust Congress with a basic foreign policy. The grand revival of the presidential prerogative after Pearl Harbor must be understood as a direct reaction to what happened when Congress tried to seize the guiding reins of foreign policy in the years 1919 to 1939."[6]

The Flowering of the Imperial Presidency

In the post–World War II period, the imperial presidency emerged in full bloom. During the 1930s, the Supreme Court had quietly laid the groundwork for presidential ascendancy by proclaiming the president's authority in foreign affairs (*U.S.* v. *Curtiss-Wright Corporation*, 1936) and by upholding the constitutionality of executive agreements in a case regarding recognition of the Soviet Union (*United States* v. *Belmont*, 1933).

President Roosevelt's 1940 lend-lease agreement with war-torn Britain was also reached by executive agreement. The United States lent Britain destroyers in exchange for leased bases while the United States was still technically neutral in the European war. Congress gave the deal implicit sanction by voting money to build the bases. In 1941 Roosevelt entered into an executive agreement with Denmark to send American troops to Greenland and then ordered the navy, without express congressional consent, to protect American convoys on the high seas.

After the Japanese attacked Pearl Harbor and Congress declared war, Roosevelt unilaterally created several executive agencies to command the wartime economy. By **executive order** (a presidential directive to an executive agency) he instructed the military to intern thousands of Japanese-Americans. Both Congress and the Supreme Court upheld this tragic violation of the civil rights of a target group of American citizens. (In 1988 Congress finally approved reparations to these victims of wartime hysteria.)

Roosevelt died while the war was still raging. His successor, Harry Truman, became the first American president to confront the decision that has become the hallmark of contemporary presidential power: whether to use nuclear weapons. His decision to drop atomic bombs on Hiroshima and Nagasaki, killing more than 100,000 civilians and bringing the war to a halt at last, remains controversial to this day. At the time, it was justified as resulting in less loss of life than an invasion of Japan would have entailed. Japan's army of 5 million had already killed 300,000 Allied personnel and countless civilians.[7] Critics charge, however, that we had an ulterior motive in dropping the bombs when we did: government leaders hoped to forestall the entrance of the Soviet Union into the war on the Pacific front, so that it would not be in a position to extend its power over Eastern territories after

★ At the height of the cold war in June 1961, President John F. Kennedy *(second from right)* greeted Soviet Premier Nikita Khrushchev *(left)* at the U.S. Embassy in Vienna.

an Allied victory. Moreover, critics contend that a demonstration bomb dropped in the ocean could have had the effect of ending the war without such a devastating loss of life.

Though Truman is the only president who has actually used nuclear weapons, subsequent presidents have offered or threatened their use as foreign policy tools. According to Daniel Ellsberg, a former Defense Department analyst, "Every President from Truman on (with the exception of Ford) has had occasion in an ongoing, urgent crisis to direct serious preparations for possible imminent U.S. initiation of tactical nuclear warfare, preparations in every case 'leaked' to the enemy, and in several cases accompanied by secret, explicit, official threats."[8] Presidents issued public warnings on several occasions: Kennedy during the Berlin crisis of 1961 and during the Cuban missile crisis of 1962, and Carter and Reagan in proclamations on the defense of Middle East oil lanes.

Secret presidential threats have also come to light. Eisenhower threatened to bomb the Chinese if they did not meet his terms to end the Korean war in 1953. The following year, his administration offered the French three U.S. tactical nuclear weapons for their defense of Dienbienphu in Indochina. In 1958, Eisenhower instructed the Joint Chiefs of Staff (the heads of the army, navy, air force, and marines) to develop plans to use tactical nuclear weapons should the Chinese attempt to invade the island of Quemoy, in the China Sea. During the Vietnam war, the Joint Chiefs advised President Johnson that nuclear weapons would have to be considered to rescue marines surrounded at Khe Sanh unless the weather cleared. (Fortunately, it did.) And President Nixon made direct secret threats to the Hanoi regime. Thus Ellsberg concludes that nuclear weapons have in an important sense been "used" by virtually every postwar president. Indeed, nuclear weapons are the trump card in a president's foreign policy "invitation to struggle" with Congress, let alone our adversaries.

Control over the bomb is not the only reason postwar presidents have gained an edge over Congress. Another important reason is their substitution of the executive's commander-in-chief power for a congressional declaration of war. President

Truman relied on his powers as commander in chief to commit American air and sea forces to support South Korea after it was invaded by North Korea in 1950. Two days after he sent the troops, Truman met with congressional leaders, who gave him their support. But Congress never declared war. The Korean war lasted over two years, cost more than 50,000 U.S. lives, and brought the United States perilously close to war with China. It also marked the first time in American history that the two branches of government came to a showdown over who should control the commitment of U.S. troops abroad.

The Supreme Court entered the fray, too. In one of the most famous instances in which the executive has brought its foreign policy prerogatives to bear on domestic matters, President Truman ordered his secretary of commerce to seize and operate steel mills threatened by a nationwide strike. Truman proclaimed a national emergency, fearing that the strike would stop the flow of military supplies to U.S. troops in Korea. Eight weeks later, the U.S. Supreme Court pronounced the seizure unconstitutional. As one justice quipped, the Constitution, in making the president commander in chief of the army and navy, did not also constitute him "Commander in Chief of the country, its industries and its inhabitants."[9]

Another weapon in the president's postwar arsenal is **executive privilege**—presidential discretion to withhold information from Congress. While this sounds like an old term, it does not appear in the Constitution and was first used during the Eisenhower administration to deny Senator Joseph McCarthy access to the executive department's personnel files. McCarthy wanted access to these files to find evidence of communist sympathizers in the Eisenhower administration. Later, President Richard Nixon invoked executive privilege in an attempt to prevent congressional committees from obtaining access to tapes that implicated him in a cover-up of the Watergate scandal.

The Secret Government

A final postwar weapon that has contributed to the president's ascendancy in foreign affairs is the intelligence community, particularly the **Central Intelligence Agency (CIA).** Created by the National Security Act of 1947, the CIA marked the first U.S. peacetime effort to set up a worldwide network of agents to collect and analyze intelligence. Over the years, agents have also engaged in overt and covert operations. The covert operations in particular have become subjects of great controversy. While some observers have defended covert operations as necessary measures in a world threatened by international communism, others have questioned whether such undemocratic means can be justified in the pursuit of democratic ends. President Eisenhower, for example, used the CIA as the primary instrument of American intervention to overthrow governments in Iran (1953) and Guatemala (1954) and to install governments in Egypt (1954) and Laos (1959). The CIA was unsuccessful in its attempts to topple regimes in Indonesia (1958) and Cuba (1960–1961).

In the post–World War II period, executive intelligence agencies have resorted to controversial means in pursuit of their overarching goal of preventing the spread of communism. In the view of some observers, this "secret government" of the intelligence community has become a threat to our Constitution.[10] Some of its operatives, such as Lieutenant Colonel Oliver North and former National Security Adviser John Poindexter, felt they were justified in circumventing the law of the land (in this case, the Boland Amendment, which prohibited military aid to the Nicaraguan Contras) in the name of a higher purpose: preventing the establishment of communism abroad. Ironically, in the last decade of the twentieth century, the United States is being led by George Bush, the first president in its history to have once served as director of the CIA.

The "secret government" was in part responsible for planning two of the most controversial postwar presidential actions: the 1961 Bay of Pigs invasion and the war in Vietnam. At their last meeting before Kennedy's inauguration, Eisenhower told the new president that it was "the policy of this government" to aid the anti-Castro guerrilla forces training under the CIA in Guatemala "to the utmost."[11] The Bay of Pigs invasion failed miserably.

The U.S. involvement in Vietnam, which began with covert CIA operations when the French pulled out of Indochina in 1954, was an even more costly failure. When American destroyers were allegedly attacked off the coast of North Vietnam in 1964, President Lyndon Johnson stampeded the Tonkin Gulf Resolution through Congress. This blank check from Congress said that it "approves and supports the determination of the President, as Commander in Chief, to take all necessary measures to repel any armed attack against the forces of the United States and to prevent further aggression." This resolution substituted for a formal declaration of war.

Seven years later, as the war wore on, a skeptical Congress revoked the Tonkin Gulf Resolution. But President Nixon continued the war without the resolution, citing his authority as commander in chief. When he had ordered the invasion of Cambodia the year before, Nixon had proclaimed, "The legal justification is the right of the President of the United States under the Constitution to protect the lives of American men."[12]

Watergate and a Resurgent Congress

A major setback to presidential ascendancy was Congress's response to the **Watergate scandal.** Never had foreign policy concerns reverberated on the domestic front more strongly than when the Nixon administration attempted to plug alleged national security leaks with a band of men who called themselves "plumbers." The name of the scandal stems from their attempts to bug the phones of the Democratic Party National Headquarters at the Watergate complex in Washington, D.C. These former CIA operatives also burglarized the office of the psychiatrist of Daniel Ellsberg, the Defense Department analyst who had leaked to the press the documents known as the Pentagon Papers, detailing secret U.S. operations in the Vietnam war.

As the Watergate scandal unfolded, the nation learned of the Nixon administration's illegal wiretapping of members of the National Security Council (the president's top foreign policy advisers) and newspaper reporters; its "enemies list" of Nixon critics, such as Joe Namath, Carol Channing, Barbra Streisand, and Gregory Peck; its hiring of *agents provocateurs* to infiltrate student and veterans' groups, among other "dirty tricks"; and the ambitious Huston plan. This CIA-backed scheme to plant undercover agents in universities, spy on Americans, listen to international phone calls, and open and copy private letters was stopped by the FBI.

The scandal first broke in the *Washington Post*, when two reporters probed to find higher-ups involved in the Watergate burglary. Subsequent investigations were conducted by congressional committees. The House was about to vote on articles of impeachment when Nixon resigned.

Public Opinion, the Presidency, and the War in Vietnam

As the Vietnam war wore on, Americans increasingly came to think that the U.S. entrance into the war had been a mistake. Some Americans, including some veterans who had risked their lives fighting in the Vietnamese jungle, actively protested U.S. involvement in this war.

Throughout the course of his administration, President Lyndon Johnson was keenly aware of changes in public opinion about the war. He carried around in his pockets newspaper clippings describing the latest polls about the war. Mounting public opposition to the war was a key factor in Johnson's decision to abandon plans to run for reelection in 1968. ★

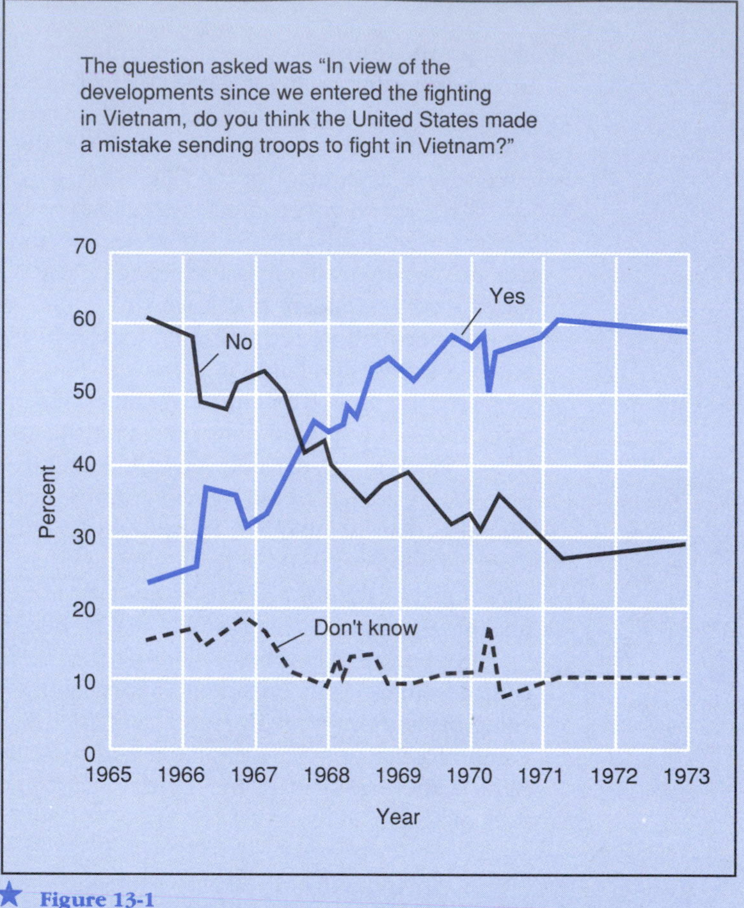

★ **Figure 13-1**
Public opinion on the Vietnam war, 1965–1973
SOURCE: Harold W. Stanley and Richard G. Niemi, *Vital Statistics on American Politics* (Washington, D.C.: Congressional Quarterly Press, 1988), p. 299.

The courts added their weight to the effort to curb presidential power. Nixon was so outraged by the release of the Pentagon Papers that he sought an injunction to prevent the *New York Times* from publishing them, and sought sanctions against Senator Mike Gravel of Alaska for reading them into the *Congressional Record.* In 1971 the Supreme Court ruled against Nixon and refused to impose prior restraint on the *Times,* which proceeded to publish the documents. The following year, the Court struck down Nixon's illegal wiretaps, stating that the government did not have the power to eavesdrop without prior judicial approval unless it could show evidence of foreign intelligence links.[13] In a final blow to Nixon, the Court ordered him to release tapes that implicated him in the cover-up of the Watergate scandal.

Thus the press, Congress, and the courts reined in the presidency once again. Nixon's resignation in 1974 and the presidency of Gerald Ford ushered in yet another return to "normalcy." The congressional elections of 1974 brought the Watergate generation of reformers to Congress. As we saw in chapter 12, they reformed congressional procedures and deposed some committee chairs. And they instituted several measures to forestall another runaway president.

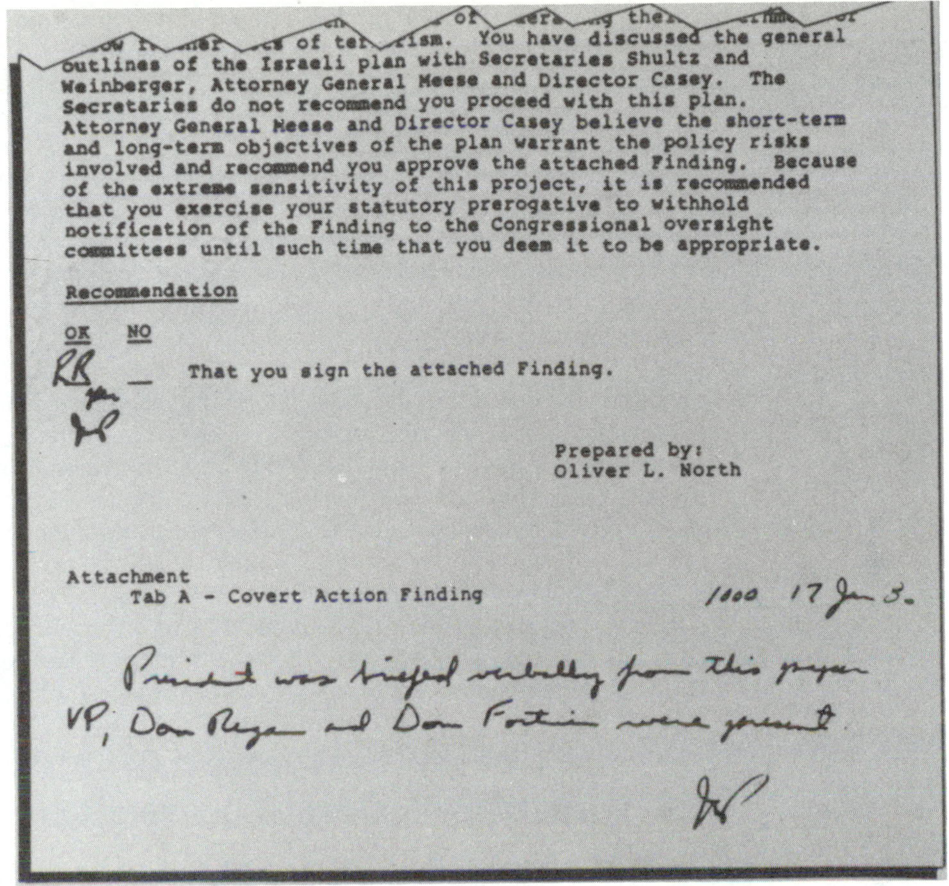

... of ter...ism. You have discussed the general outlines of the Israeli plan with Secretaries Shultz and Weinberger, Attorney General Meese and Director Casey. The Secretaries do not recommend you proceed with this plan. Attorney General Meese and Director Casey believe the short-term and long-term objectives of the plan warrant the policy risks involved and recommend you approve the attached Finding. Because of the extreme sensitivity of this project, it is recommended that you exercise your statutory prerogative to withhold notification of the Finding to the Congressional oversight committees until such time that you deem it to be appropriate.

Recommendation

OK	NO	
RR	_	That you sign the attached Finding.

Prepared by:
Oliver L. North

Attachment
Tab A - Covert Action Finding

★ In this memorandum released by the Reagan White House in January 1987, President Reagan agreed to sign a finding authorizing covert action by the CIA. The handwritten line by National Security Adviser John Poindexter reads, "President was briefed verbally from this paper[.] VP [George Bush], Don Regan [Chief of Staff] and Don Fortiere [deputy NSC adviser] were present." Note that North recommends withholding notification of the finding from the congressional committees that oversee U.S. intelligence activities.

Paramount among these curbs was the War Powers Resolution, passed over Nixon's veto the year before he resigned. This measure (discussed in chap. 12), which emerged from Congress's frustration over Nixon's war powers, represents an attempt to force the president to submit to the will of Congress each time he decides to send U.S. troops abroad. Equally important are laws mandating congressional oversight of CIA covert operations by the House and Senate Select Committees on Intelligence. Each covert operation must now be accompanied by a written document, called a finding, signed by the president. The CIA is required to notify Congress whenever a finding is issued.

Congress also sought to crack down on executive agreements, emergency authority, and unauthorized arms sales. Secret executive agreements were banned in 1972 by a law requiring the secretary of state to send the text of any international agreement other than a treaty to Congress within sixty days after it takes effect.

The 1976 National Emergencies Act retains most of the 470 wartime and emergency powers that presidents have accumulated from past crises, but it creates a system for declaring and terminating national emergencies. And a 1974 law requires the president to give Congress advance notice of any offer to sell abroad arms or services valued at $25 million or more.

This muscle flexing by Congress in foreign affairs was respected for the most part by the Ford and Carter administrations. But it was challenged by those in the Reagan administration who wanted to support the Contras in Nicaragua. As the Iran-Contra congressional hearings revealed, top officials, with the CIA's blessings, sold U.S. arms to the Khomeini regime in Iran and diverted some of the money they gained from these sales to the Contras. The operation was carried out covertly, to bypass the Boland Amendment, whereby Congress expressly forbade military assistance to the Contras. (This scandal will be discussed further in chap. 19.)

To many members of Congress, the press, the courts, and the public, the Iran-Contra scandal was the latest manifestation of an executive branch run amok. The only new twist was that this time members of the National Security Council (NSC) and the Central Intelligence Agency tried to create an autonomous, profit-making venture to conduct U.S. foreign policy not only outside the purview of the public and Congress, but even independent of the NSC and CIA.

We can probably expect further cycles of presidential action and congressional reaction in the tug-of-war of foreign policy making. And we can anticipate significant domestic consequences of such policy struggles.

★ Masters of the Media: Presidents Steal the Spotlight

Despite congressional efforts to restrain presidents, chief executives have used the media to enhance their visibility and power. Television is much better at covering the president than it is at capturing the performance of the 535 members of Congress. Television conveys the image of a president who takes charge and a raucous Congress where no one seems to be in charge.

Television also brings dramatic images from around the globe into our living rooms. From anti-U.S. riots in the Middle East to flag-draped coffins of fallen marines, television rivets our attention on the world stage. It also shows the president responding to world events. While Congress debates and holds hearings, the president takes dramatic action, ordering troops into battle and laying wreaths on their graves. Modern telecommunications have revolutionized our access to the world, and the presidency is uniquely suited to take center stage.

As we saw in chapter 11, the mass media are of two types: broadcast (radio and television) and print (newspapers and magazines). Presidents have enjoyed a symbiotic relationship with the broadcast media especially, each side using the other for its own advantage. A president gets his message across to the public, and the media cash in on coverage of the president's activities on the six-o'clock news. Presidents' relations with the print media have not been so rosy. Newspapers and magazines are more likely than radio and television to adopt an adversarial stance toward a president; the two sides tend to be much more critical of each other, as we saw in the case of President Nixon.

The first presidential master of the medium of his day was Franklin Roosevelt. During his four terms in office he was opposed by most newspaper owners, so he

★ President Franklin D. Roosevelt mastered the medium of his day, radio, in "fireside chats" with the American public. He also held press conferences more frequently than any subsequent president.

took his case directly to the people in a series of "fireside chats" on the radio. He had an impressive speaking voice and an ability to reach the average citizen. He was so popular that he was given as much air time as he wanted. Though newspaper owners opposed him, he was extremely popular with reporters. They agreed never to photograph him in his wheelchair and were delighted by his availability. Roosevelt held press conferences, meetings at which reporters were free to ask questions, twice a week—a rate no other president has matched.

Roosevelt's immediate successors, Truman and Eisenhower, were the first presidents to use television to address the nation, but neither one of them made much use of the medium. It was not until the presidency of John Kennedy that the era of image politics began.

Press Conferences

Kennedy was the first president to allow live television broadcasts of his press conferences, complete with a seating chart for reporters. Subsequent presidents and their aides have transformed press conferences into carefully orchestrated media events. Some administrations have even limited questions to certain topics. Presidents have routinely rehearsed answers to likely questions, and have preferred to call on reporters who they know will ask soft questions. Even though press conferences have become staged events, reporters still value them and chide presidents who fail to hold them. While the president faces the media, reporters jockey for a chance to bask in the limelight and to please their editors.

★ **Table 13-2**
Average number of presidential press conferences per month and total press conferences, 1929–1987

President	*Term*	*Average per month*	*Total*
Herbert Hoover	1929–1933	5.6	268
Franklin D. Roosevelt	1933–1945	6.9	998
Harry S Truman	1945–1953	3.4	334
Dwight D. Eisenhower	1953–1961	2.0	193
John F. Kennedy	1961–1963	1.9	64
Lyndon B. Johnson	1963–1969	2.2	135
Richard M. Nixon	1969–1974	0.5	37
Gerald Ford	1974–1977	1.3	39
Jimmy Carter	1977–1981	1.2	59
Ronald Reagan*	1981–1987	0.5	42

*The figures cover only the first seven of Reagan's eight years as president.

SOURCE: Harold W. Stanley and Richard G. Niemi, *Vital Statistics on American Politics* (Washington, D.C.: Congressional Quarterly Press, 1988), p. 50.

Photo Opportunities

Though presidents can stage-manage press conferences to a great degree, they still run the risk of being embarrassed by the occasional tough question. As table 13-2 shows, presidents of the television era have held fewer conferences than their pretelevision counterparts did. Increasingly, presidents are taking the safe way out by staging photo opportunities. These media events are designed to convey an image of the president's position on some issue. Often the image prevails over the substance of a president's policy. For example, when polls showed that the public disapproved of President Reagan's action in cutting federal money for student loans and aid to schools, he traveled across the country to meet with teachers and students in a series of televised photo opportunities. Then, in the words of an aide, "the polls absolutely flip-flopped. He went from a negative rating to a positive rating [on education] overnight."[14] Yet there had been no change in Reagan's educational policies.

Photo opportunities are not opportunities to discuss policy. They offer only short, pithy slogans or buzzwords, short "sound bites" that television crews will pick up for the evening news. Critics charge that television has taken substantive discussion out of presidential politics and replaced it with media manipulation by public relations experts.

Presidential public relations were honed to a fine art during Reagan's terms in office. Reagan aides had seen how the relentless televised coverage of the hostages in Iran had doomed President Carter's chances for reelection in 1980. They combined Reagan's natural talents as "the great communicator" with a public relations strategy to produce an extremely effective image. As his former aide Michael Deaver put it, "Television elects presidents."

★ Television news thrives on photo opportunities of the president as commander in chief. Here President Ronald Reagan speaks from Liberty Bell Camp, part of the demilitarized zone that separates communist North Korea from capitalist South Korea.

Every morning Reagan's top aides met to go over the president's calendar and plan what they called "the line of the day"—the questions he would probably be asked and the answers he should give. Then they briefed Reagan. After his public appearances, his aides called the networks to learn what stories about the president they planned to run on the evening news. Sometimes the aides tried to persuade the networks to change the lineup. Each evening they met to evaluate the success of their strategy.[15]

Reagan aides capitalized on the fact that television loves good pictures of the president as commander in chief. When Reagan visited the demilitarized zone separating North and South Korea in 1983, the evening news programs (along with newspapers and newsweeklies) were filled with photos of Reagan dressed in a flack jacket, staring down the communists through field glasses. His aides, following their usual practice, had visited the site in advance, accompanied by representatives of the major networks, to plan the photo opportunity down to the smallest detail. According to one reporter, they even provided toe marks. "When he didn't stand on his toe mark he was signaled by one of the advance men to move over into the sunshine."[16]

In the opinion of one Reagan aide, the Korean photo opportunity "was great television. I think every White House would rather see its President in what amounts to a heroic situation . . . and it sure is a hell of a lot better picture than a guy like Carter stumbling up in Camp David when he's jogging. . . . One picture builds support for the President. The other, I think, destroys him."[17]

Television is a medium much better suited to the presidency than it is to Congress. As the former press secretary to long-time Democratic Speaker of the

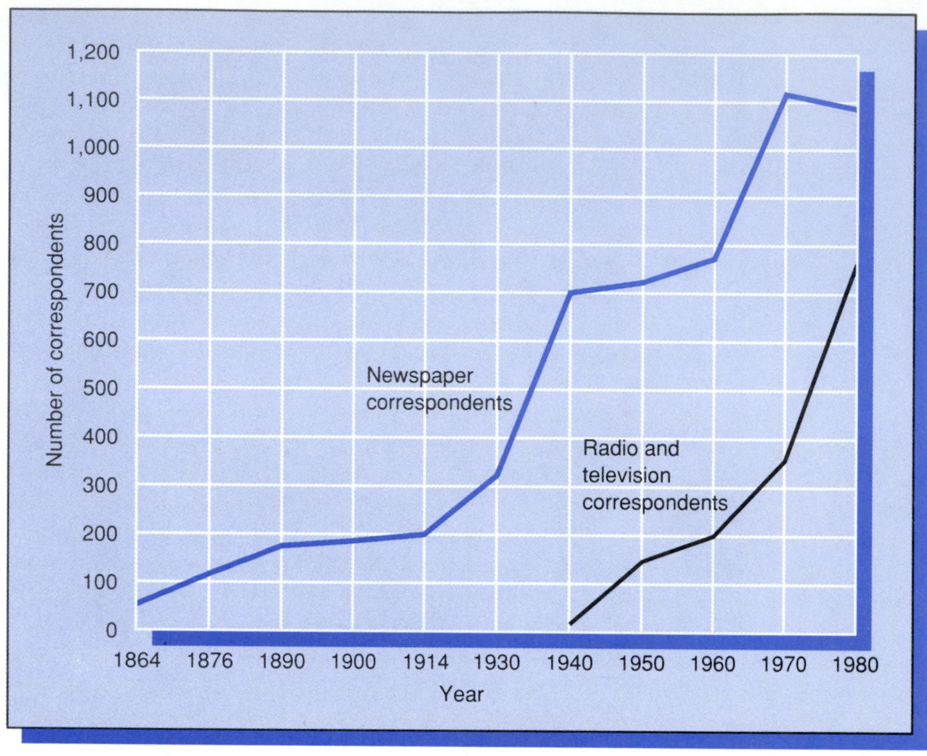

★ **Figure 13-2**
Growth of the Washington press corps, 1864–1980
SOURCE: Samuel Kernell, *Going Public: New Strategies in Presidential Leadership* (Washington, D.C.: Congressional Quarterly Press, 1986), p. 67.

House Thomas P. "Tip" O'Neill remarked, Reagan's aides "know that the presidency is ideally suited for the television age, because it is one person, there is all the *People* magazine aspect—what is he like, what is Nancy like? It is amazing how the monarchy translates so well into the television age and legislatures do not."[18]

Controlling the White House Press Corps

Today about 80 percent of all television coverage of government affairs is devoted to the president, due in part to the number of correspondents assigned to cover the White House (see figure 13–2).[19] Thus the American public gets a distorted view of the three branches of government: legislative and judicial branches seem to do nothing simply because they are less amenable to prime-time TV coverage.

Additional distortion results from White House correspondents' reliance on the president's press office as the sole source of their news stories. All too often they are charged with failing to conduct independent investigations of White House stories. The glitter of covering the White House clouds their objectivity. It was a Beirut reporter, not the White House press corps, that broke the Iran-Contra story.

A former press officer in the Nixon and Reagan administrations compared the tactics the two presidents used to control the White House press corps. While the Nixon staff provided only bits and pieces of information, Reagan's staff engaged in "manipulation by inundation."

> They've got to write their story every day. You give them their story, they'll go away. As long as you come in there every day, hand them a well-packaged, premasticated story in the format they want, they'll go away. The phrase is "manipulation by inundation."... As long as you do that long enough, they're going to stop bringing their own stories and stop being investigative reporters of any kind, even modestly so.[20]

Occasional Adversarial Relations

There have been times when the media have been critical of presidents. Adversarial relations date back to John Adams's administration, when Federalists passed the Alien and Sedition Act of 1798, which prohibited criticism of the government and was used to imprison Jeffersonian newspaper editors.

In the modern era, adversarial relations developed during the early cold war years. In 1960, for instance, the *New York Times* dutifully reported that a U.S. weather plane had been shot down over the Soviet Union. The paper later learned that it was a U.S. spy plane. After the U-2 affair, the *Times* became more skeptical of government sources.

President Kennedy became so upset by the *New York Times*' coverage of the Vietnam war that he asked the paper to transfer one of its correspondents. President Nixon felt positively persecuted by the press. When he lost the 1962 gubernatorial race in California, he told the press, "You won't have Dick Nixon to kick around any more." As president, he had his vice-president, Spiro Agnew, lash out at the press (he called them "nattering nabobs of negativism," among other things). Nixon ordered the Justice Department to investigate some media corporations for possible antitrust violations and the Internal Revenue Service to audit a newspaper and a reporter for possible income tax violations.

The Vietnam war and Watergate scandal sparked a flurry of investigative journalism, and reporters went to great lengths to confirm or refute official government versions of a story. But suspicion and adversarial relations have been the exception rather than the norm in postwar presidential relations with the media. Like Congress and the courts, the press is anxious to defer to the president as commander in chief in matters of national security. In 1961, for example, the *New York Times* found out about the imminent invasion of Cuba at the Bay of Pigs and agreed to withhold the story on national security grounds. The following year, when the *Times* learned about the Cuban missile crisis, its editor reminded President Kennedy that he had regretted suppressing the story that could have stopped the ill-fated venture at the Bay of Pigs. But again Kennedy persuaded the *Times* to withhold its story, promising that no blood would be shed or war started during the period of silence.

As commander in chief, the president is in a unique position to block access to information, whether or not the claim of national security is warranted. As a practical matter, the press should not be allowed to jeopardize military operations. As a matter of fact, when reporters have been told not to publish secret information

★ In 1962, U.S. spy planes photographed the installation of Soviet missiles in Cuba, triggering the Cuban missile crisis, which brought the United States and the Soviet Union closer to direct confrontation than at any time during the Cold War. The *New York Times* got wind of the story but agreed not to publish news about the missile installation until President Kennedy had addressed the nation on television about the crisis.

that could endanger American lives, they have usually cooperated. The press participated in the momentous D-Day invasion of German-occupied France during World War II, parachuting in with the airborne troops and landing on the beaches with amphibious forces. When President Reagan ordered the invasion of Grenada in 1983, by contrast, he excluded reporters from the invasion force and ordered the military to turn back reporters who later arrived on the island on their own. For two days the administration controlled all news coverage of the assault, calling it both necessary and successful. Some reporters subsequently challenged this characterization of the invasion, but the image of its success had already been firmly implanted in the public's mind.

Television has enhanced the power of the president as commander in chief and has been the medium of the postwar imperial presidency. The president has stolen the spotlight from the less telegenic Congress and courts. Even the print media, with their more adversarial bent, tend to defer to the president's definition of national security.

★ Who's Who in the President's Bureaucracy

Presidents do not spend all their waking hours, of course, agonizing over foreign policy concerns and posing for photos. The arena of domestic policy calls for them to haggle with Congress over legislation and preside over their nearly three million

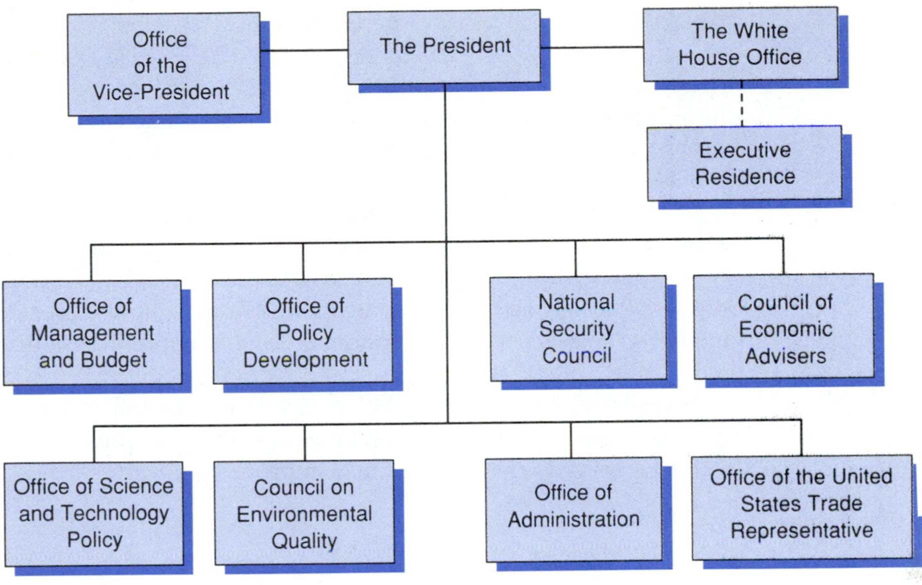

★ **Figure 13-3**
Executive Office of the President
SOURCE: *U.S. Government Manual 1987–1988* (Washington, D.C.: Government Printing Office, 1988), p. 86.

assistants in the executive branch. If the presidency appears to be imperial in the area of foreign policy, it has also been called "imperiled" and "impossible," constrained by an unwieldy bureaucracy.[21]

As chief executive, the president administers the laws of the land. In the early days of the republic, this was a relatively easy task, requiring few personal aides. George Washington had a full-time staff of one—his nephew, whom he paid out of his own pocket. Not until 1857 did Congress provide money for an executive clerk. Even though Abraham Lincoln had a staff of four, he opened and answered all of his daily mail himself. Grover Cleveland personally answered the White House telephone, and Woodrow Wilson typed many of his own speeches.[22]

The Institutionalized Presidency: The White House Office and the Executive Office of the President

In 1939 President Franklin Roosevelt issued a call for help to save him from the mass of detail that was threatening to paralyze the modern presidency. By executive order, he created the **Executive Office of the President (EOP),** sheltering a host of agencies that help the president make administrative decisions (see figure 13-3). He also secured congressional funding for a **White House Office (WHO)** with a staff of about forty-five. WHO staff has direct contact with the president, providing personal services (barbers, chefs, press secretaries) and serving as policy advisers. Today the White House staff numbers around 350 and the Executive Office of the President employs about 1,500 people.

According to the presidential scholar Thomas Cronin, the presidential establishment has grown as presidents have taken on new roles during national emergencies. In times of crisis, Congress and the public have looked to the president for decisive responses. Staff increases followed the Great Depression, World War II, the Soviet success with *Sputnik,* and the Bay of Pigs fiasco.[23] Congress deferred to the executive in key policy areas when it authorized funds for the three most important agencies in the EOP: the National Security Council, the Council of Economic Advisers, and the Office of Management and Budget.

The National Security Council (NSC), which received so much publicity when some of its members masterminded the Iran-Contra connection, was created in 1947 to advise the president on national security matters. The Council of Economic Advisers (CEA) consists of three economists who help the president interpret and attempt to manage national economic developments. The Office of Management and Budget (OMB) helps prepare the federal budget that the president submits each year to Congress. The OMB reviews the financial requests of other federal agencies, makes sure the requests conform with the president's overall program, and suggests ways the agencies may improve their performance.

The Struggle between Staff and Cabinet

Cronin cites a second reason for the growth of the presidential establishment—White House distrust of the "permanent government" of civil service bureaucrats. Over 90 percent of federal employees are career civil servants who are not appointed by the president. They are typically more loyal to their profession or agency than they are to the president. Indeed, recent administrations have felt a tension between a White House staff loyal to the president and a cabinet more often loyal to the agencies they oversee.

The **cabinet** consists of the heads of the fourteen executive departments (Agriculture, Commerce, Defense, Education, Energy, Health and Human Services, Housing and Urban Development, Interior, Justice, Labor, State, Transportation, Treasury, Veterans Affairs). They are referred to as the secretaries of the departments they head (except for the attorney general, who presides over the Justice Department). Cabinet officials are appointed by the president with the consent of the Senate. Many people do not realize that the cabinet stems not from the Constitution but from a politically expedient tradition honored by successive presidents. Although the Constitution calls for the appointment of a "principal officer in each of the Executive Departments," it says nothing about an institution that groups these department heads in an advisory council. Yet each president has formed a cabinet to help him administer the executive branch.

Unlike the British cabinet, in which elected members of Parliament share responsibility with the prime minister for policy direction, members of the American cabinet often remain on the fringes of presidential decision making. The cabinet in this country rarely has the influence commanded by its counterparts in most parliamentary systems.

Cabinets typically enjoy a one-year honeymoon with their presidents, who begin their administrations with an open mind. Before long, however, presidents become preoccupied by crises, rebuff their cabinet advisers, and hold purely symbolic meetings with them. One cabinet member tried forty-three times to get an appointment with President Kennedy, whose aides shielded the president without Kennedy's knowledge. In the face of such neglect, cabinet members tend either to become allies of Congress or to "go native" and ally themselves with their depart-

★ President George Bush *(third from left)* is pictured here meeting with his cabinet. In recent years, cabinet secretaries have had to compete with members of the White House staff for the president's attention.

ment's goals. After all, Congress appropriates departmental funds and bureaucrats can make a persuasive case for their pet projects, even when they may conflict with a president's priorities.

This cycle of estrangement seems to be inevitable, even when presidents come to office eager to make use of their cabinets to counter the palace-guard image of the White House staff of the previous administration. Jimmy Carter, for example, wanted to counter the legacy of Nixon's palace guardians, John Ehrlichman (presidential counsel) and H. R. Haldeman (chief of staff), who blocked access to the president. Carter held a record sixty cabinet meetings in the first two years of his tenure (every Monday morning from 9:00 to 11:00). These meetings, however, had little policy content. Policy contributions came rather through task forces associated with the National Security Council or the domestic policy council staff. These task forces were coordinated by a White House staffer, who developed policy options to pass along to the president. Within two years, the honeymoon was over.

President Reagan tried a novel approach to the problem in instituting cabinet councils. Recognizing that the president does not need to have every cabinet member at every cabinet meeting, he divided his top advisers into seven policy areas (in addition to the NSC), each constituting a cabinet council. Some members of the cabinet were on each council, along with members of the White House Office and the Executive Office of the President. The Cabinet Council on Economic Affairs, for example, consisted of the secretaries of treasury, state, commerce, labor, and transportation, along with the OMB director, the U.S. trade representative, and the chair of the Council of Economic Advisers. This mechanism reduced friction between cabinet members and other presidential advisers. It also gave the cabinet a voice in policy making. During the first year and a half of its operation, recounted Ed Meese, then counselor to the president, "nearly 200 major policy issues were considered by these cabinet councils and then as pros and cons were developed, the cabinet council met with the President as its chairman for a fuller debate prior to a final presidential decision."[24]

In spite of some presidents' attempts to make the best use of their cabinet advisers, the White House staff usually prevails in the contest for the president's attention. The staff members are the generals in the president's battle to control his own bureaucracy. As one Kennedy aide put it, "Everybody believes in democracy until he gets to the White House and then you begin to believe in dictatorship, because it's so hard to get things done. Every time you turn around, people resist you and even resist their own job."[25]

According to former presidential aide Bill Moyers, the two main sources of power in Washington are information and access to the president, both of which tilt the balance of power in favor of the White House staff. "The White House staff now has information more quickly or just as quickly as the Secretary of State or Secretary of Defense, and they certainly have physical access to the President more readily than the Cabinet Secretaries do. This tends to give the initiative to the White House staff operation."[26]

Members of this inner circle are not subject to Senate confirmation and are selected primarily for their technical expertise, political savvy, and/or personal loyalties. Each president molds the White House staff according to his own style, assigning titles and duties to suit his needs. Some staff members serve as links with Congress and executive agencies. Others smooth the president's relations with the press and handle his appointments. Still others advise him on foreign policy, provide legal counsel, or write his speeches.

Occasionally a struggle may develop between a president's policy advisers and his political advisers, the first prodding him to fight for what the adviser thinks is right, the second urging him to be careful and work for a second term. It is up to each president to decide how much to compromise between the two, how much to ignore the "political realities" and fight legislative battles of the moment.

At least two clear dangers may arise from a president's use of the White House staff. One is that he may become too insulated in the White House, shielded by overzealous aides from outside influences and information sources. Only too late a president may discover that he received one-sided information or was shielded from advice he should have heard. Of course, most presidents, by selecting assistants who share their policy views, encourage this one-sidedness. They set the tone of the White House by choosing aides who are most like themselves. It is difficult for advisers to escape the trap of only answering "yes."

The other danger is that a president may delegate too much responsibility to his aides. Assistants eager to please their boss may on his behalf take independent actions that go well beyond the confines of the law. The Senate Watergate hearings of 1973 revealed that top Nixon aides had employed the White House Office—apparently with Nixon's encouragement—as a private instrument to intimidate political opponents and carry out assorted forms of espionage. The congressional Iran-Contra hearings of 1986 uncovered a similar pattern of an overzealous national security staff working out of the White House basement to bypass the law by selling arms to Iran and funneling some of the proceeds of the sales to Contra forces in Nicaragua.

To curb the excesses of White House aides, some observers have suggested expanding congressional oversight and making aides subject to Senate confirmation. We might wonder, however, whether these or other reforms would do much good. After all, the White House aides ultimately reflect the character and style of the president they serve and usually behave the way he wants them to behave.

The Vice-President

In addition to his White House staff, cabinet secretaries, and other advisers in the Executive Office of the President, the president can rely for counsel on his vice-president. While the presidency has evolved into one of the most powerful offices in the world, the vice-presidency has remained, in the words of Clinton Rossiter, merely a "hollow shell of an office."[27] Some of the framers even doubted the need for a vice-president. In fact, several vice-presidents have felt that the office has been only a source of humiliation. John Adams, the first person to hold the job, lamented that "my country in its wisdom contrived for me the most insignificant office that the invention of man contrived or his imagination conceived." John Nance Garner, vice-president under Franklin Roosevelt, went even further, contending that "the vice-presidency isn't worth a pitcher of warm spit." Roosevelt's last vice-president, Harry Truman, quipped, "It's the easiest job in the world. All you do is get up in the morning and ask, 'How is the president?' "

The vice-president actually draws only three clear duties from the Constitution: (1) to serve as the constitutional heir to the president; (2) to preside over the Senate; and (3) to exercise a vote in case of a Senate tie. As a measure of the insignificance of the last two tasks, former vice-president Spiro Agnew presided for only two and a half of the 667 hours the Senate sat during the first half of its 1973 session.[28] During the rest of the time, either the Senate president pro tempore or a junior senator wielded the gavel. And during his entire term as vice-president Agnew cast a deciding vote in the Senate only once: to break a tie in favor of the Alaskan oil pipeline in July 1973.

Most contemporary vice-presidents, of course, are assigned other duties by the president. They serve on the National Security Council, attend cabinet meetings, travel abroad as the president's personal ambassador, and make public speeches the president may not wish to make. Jimmy Carter even used Vice-President Walter Mondale as a close personal adviser, breaking precedent by installing Mondale in an office in the White House. Ronald Reagan gave his vice-president, George Bush, more authority than almost any other vice-president had enjoyed. Bush participated in some major policy decisions and was in charge of regulatory reform and the war on drugs. This experience was of immense help in maintaining executive branch activities after Reagan was shot and hospitalized in 1981. But because these duties are carried out at the president's request, they do not provide an independent power base. In other words, a vice-president's powers are generally what the president chooses to make them.

If the vice-presidency seems to be such an insignificant office, why would any prominent politician want the job? One reason, perhaps, apart from the high salary and fringe benefits, is that it may offer a convenient springboard to the presidency. Although only George Bush and four other vice-presidents have advanced to the White House by their own efforts (John Adams, Thomas Jefferson, Martin Van Buren, and Richard Nixon), eight other vice-presidents have been thrust into the presidency as a result of the death of the incumbent, and one (Gerald Ford) suc-

★ **Table 13-3**
Vice-presidents who became presidents, 1797–1989

Year	*Vice-president*	*President with whom he served*	*Reason for obtaining office*
1797	John Adams	George Washington	Elected to office
1801	Thomas Jefferson	John Adams	Elected to office
1837	Martin Van Buren	Andrew Jackson	Elected to office
1841	John Tyler	William Henry Harrison	Harrison died
1850	Millard Fillmore	Zachary Taylor	Taylor died
1865	Andrew Jackson	Abraham Lincoln	Lincoln killed
1881	Chester A. Arthur	James A. Garfield	Garfield killed
1901	Theodore Roosevelt	William McKinley	McKinley killed
1923	Calvin Coolidge	William G. Harding	Harding died
1945	Harry S Truman	Franklin D. Roosevelt	Roosevelt died
1963	Lyndon B. Johnson	John F. Kennedy	Kennedy killed
1968	Richard M. Nixon	Dwight D. Eisenhower	Elected to office
1974	Gerald R. Ford	Richard M. Nixon	Nixon resigned
1989	George Bush	Ronald Reagan	Elected to office

ceeded as the result of his predecessor's resignation. As of 1989, fourteen of the forty-four vice-presidents in history—one-third—eventually became president (see table 13-3).

In view of these statistics, we might expect the selection of a vice-president to be a careful process, aimed at choosing a person with great leadership capabilities. Yet the choice of vice-president, Theodore White observed, "is the most perfunctory and generally the most thoughtless in the entire American political system."[29] Traditionally, the vice-president is chosen by the presidential nominee in the closing hours of the national convention, with an eye to "balancing the ticket," adding regional or ideological strength to the campaign.

To many critics, this method of hurriedly picking a vice-president for purposes of political expediency is a mistake. The selection of Thomas Eagleton had a disastrous impact on George McGovern's candidacy in 1972. (Senator Eagleton's history of treatment for mental health problems was attacked in some quarters.) Nixon's vice-president, Spiro Agnew, became the second vice-president to resign, and the only one to do so after pleading "no contest" to a charge of federal income tax evasion. (John C. Calhoun resigned the office in 1832 to become a U.S. senator.) In 1984 the Democratic nominee, Walter Mondale, chose Geraldine Ferraro as his running mate too hurriedly to uncover her husband's questionable financial practices. And in 1988, George Bush lost some support at the polls because of his choice of the relatively inexperienced and lackluster Dan Quayle for the vice-presidential post. The conservative pundit William F. Buckley, Jr., fired a typical barb when he wondered whether Quayle was capable of uttering a grammatically correct and complete sentence.

Although no way can be devised to guarantee that a vice-presidential choice will not turn into a disaster, pressure has been mounting for a change in the process of selecting the person "a heartbeat away from the presidency." In addition to the suggestion that the vice-presidency simply be abolished,[30] at least two major reform proposals have been discussed. One is to force presidential and vice-presidential candidates to pair up for the primary races. The other is to have a separate primary for all people campaigning solely for the vice-presidency. In each case, vice-presidential candidates would be exposed to the voters during the long ordeal of the primaries, offering the voters a chance to decide for themselves who was best suited for the job.

Given the high odds that a vice-president will have to step in to fill the president's shoes, either permanently or temporarily, the institution seems to be here to stay, for all its faults. The United States has managed to limp along without a vice-president sixteen times, for a total of more than forty years. Before the ratification of the Twenty-fifth Amendment in 1967, there was no provision for filling the vice-presidency between elections if the office became vacant. The provisions of that amendment were first put into effect when Agnew resigned in 1973. Richard Nixon became the first president to select a new vice-president (Gerald Ford) during his administration, confirmed by a majority vote of both houses of Congress. (Interestingly, when Nixon resigned in 1974 and Ford chose Nelson Rockefeller as his vice-president, both the president and the vice-president were appointed, not elected, for the only time in U.S. history.)

★ Domestic Powers of the President

Under the assumption that the president can muster enough control over his own institutionalized presidency to get down to the business of governing, what are the domestic policy powers at his disposal in his struggle with Congress?

The Constitution and tradition have assigned the presidency a number of domestic duties to perform. In addition to directing the executive branch, he is supposed to propose new federal programs, serve as ceremonial head of state, lead his party, and make judicial appointments. These domestic duties often entail a power struggle with Congress, which, along with the bureaucracy, can frustrate a president's efforts.

An Architect of Policy

A president is judged by the kinds of programs he proposes to Congress. Although the Constitution does not specifically refer to him as an architect of policy, it does outline a number of major legislative responsibilities.

One of these duties is to deliver an annual **State of the Union message** to Congress, in which the president spells out what needs to be done to relieve the nation's woes. The constitutional basis for this message is found in the statement that he "shall from time to time give to the Congress information of the State of the Union, and recommend to their consideration such measures as he shall judge necessary and expedient."

Usually the president addresses both houses of Congress after the opening of each session in January, taking full advantage of television coverage. Because he cannot personally introduce a bill into the House or Senate, he can use this annual address—as well as more detailed messages later on—to persuade members of

his party to enact certain policies. Most members of Congress, in fact, look to the president for policy leadership. Because the president heads the federal bureaucracy and enjoys a national constituency, they regard him as a focal point of legislation. For example, when George Bush was elected in 1988 on a platform that ruled out any increase in taxes to erase the budget deficit, leaders of the Democratic-controlled Congress said they would not consider any revenue-enhancing measures until Bush proposed one.

Obviously a president cannot always count on success (see figure 13-4). It is easier for members of Congress to thwart his plans than to initiate constructive policies of their own. Jimmy Carter, for example, after running for the presidency as an outsider against the Washington establishment, discovered how difficult it was to win support for his proposals in an independent-minded Congress. His lack of long-term congressional relationships and experience with Washington's political ways got him into immediate trouble on several of his major energy and economic programs. He had to learn the same tricks as his predecessors: how to soothe congressional egos, do a little mutual back-scratching, and otherwise acquire allies for his legislative battles. Such intimates of Capitol Hill as Lyndon Johnson, Gerald Ford, and George Bush came to the White House with these skills already honed.

Indeed, ruling elite theorists and pluralists alike contend that the powers of the presidency over legislation vary with the personalities of those who occupy the

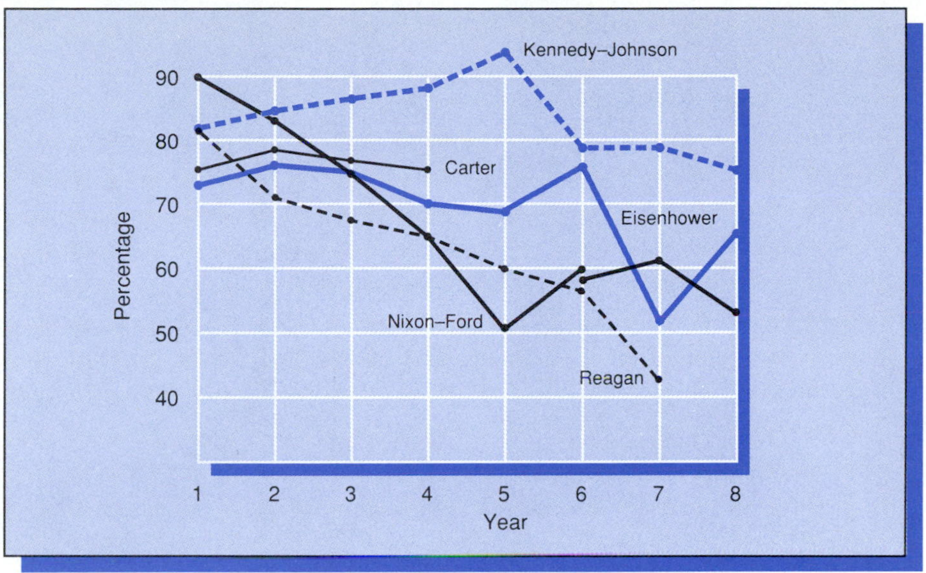

★ **Figure 13-4**

Presidential scorecards in Congress, Eisenhower to Reagan

NOTE: This figure shows the percentage of votes won by the president in Congress. Presidential averages are as follows: Eisenhower 72%; Kennedy-Johnson 84%; Nixon-Ford 65%; Carter 76%; Reagan 64%.

SOURCE: Charles O. Jones, "Ronald Reagan and the U.S. Congress: Visible Hand Politics," in Charles O. Jones (ed.), *The Reagan Legacy: Promise and Performance* (Chatham, N.J.: Chatham House, 1988), p. 53.

office, and that a president's real power depends on his ability to persuade. To win support for his programs, he must be able to bargain aggressively, employ publicity, and do anything else necessary to convince skeptical legislators that, as Richard Neustadt noted, "what the White House wants of them is what they ought to do for their own sake and on their authority."[31] Harry Truman once said, "There are a lot of other powers written in the Constitution and given to the President, but it's that power to persuade people to do what they ought to do anyway that's the biggest. And if the man who is President doesn't understand that, if he thinks he is too big to do the necessary persuading, then he's in for big trouble, and so is this country."[32]

Proposing legislation is, of course, only the beginning. Another important legislative responsibility is to provide an occasional check on Congress by wielding the potent constitutional weapon of the **veto**—a weapon, incidentally, that plays no minor role in his ability to persuade. Because all new bills must be signed by the president, he has virtual life-or-death power over policy. The mere threat of a veto may force a bill's sponsors in Congress to scurry to shape it to the president's desires.

The reason the veto is such a potent weapon is that two-thirds majorities in both the House and the Senate are required to override it. In fact, any bill the president receives within ten days before Congress adjourns and does not sign (a practice called a **pocket veto**) automatically dies and cannot be overridden. Between 1933 and 1988, as we can see in table 13-4, Congress was able to override only about 3 percent of all presidential vetoes.

★ **Table 13-4**
Number of presidential vetoes and of vetoes overridden, 1933–1988

President	Term	Vetoes	Vetoes overridden
Franklin D. Roosevelt	1933–1945	635	9
Harry S Truman	1945–1953	250	12
Dwight D. Eisenhower	1953–1961	181	2
John F. Kennedy	1961–1963	21	0
Lyndon B. Johnson	1963–1969	30	0
Richard M. Nixon	1969–1974	43	7
Gerald Ford	1974–1977	66	12
Jimmy Carter	1977–1981	31	2
Ronald Reagan	1981–1988	78	9

SOURCE: *Congressional Quarterly*, January 7, 1989, p. 7.

One major limitation of the veto is that if the president wishes to eliminate one part of a bill of which he otherwise approves, he has to reject the whole bill. Most state governors command even greater power than the president's over some kinds of legislation, for they can employ an **item veto;** that is, they can strike out any part of an appropriations bill they disapprove of, while leaving the remainder intact. Because the president cannot use an item veto, members of Congress sometimes can push through policies by attaching riders (amendments) to bills the president is known to want. They know that the president must either accept or reject the entire package; he cannot veto just the amendment. This was the very strategy that enabled Congress to end the bombing of Cambodia and Laos in 1973. By attaching the measure to an emergency supplementary $3.4 billion appropriations bill, members of Congress averted a veto of the antiwar amendment by President Nixon.

Both Reagan and Bush have tried to persuade Congress and the public to support a constitutional amendment granting the item veto to the president. However, it is not likely that Congress will readily hand the president even greater power over legislation than he now has.

The Ceremonial Side

In addition to his political chores as head of government, the president can find his calendar clogged by endless ceremonial functions as the nation's symbolic head of state. In such countries as England, Spain, and Norway, the two jobs are performed by different persons: as titular head of state the queen or king discharges most of the ceremonial duties—such as knighting prominent public figures and welcoming visiting heads of state—while the prime minister wields the real political power as head of government. But because the president by tradition holds both jobs at once, he may spend his time not only proposing and vetoing legislation but decorating (or mourning) astronauts, rolling out the first Easter egg on the White House lawn, and hosting delegations of Campfire Girls and Vietnam veterans. When he enters a hall on state occasions, he is usually welcomed by the presidential anthem, "Hail to the Chief" (so far only President Carter has discouraged the practice), and is inaugurated with all the ceremony and pomp reserved in other countries for royalty.

Although these ceremonial duties and trappings may seem unimportant, they are not. Often a president's personal magnetism and appeal can be augmented by his activities as the symbolic representative of the American people. Indeed, a good performance as chief of state can greatly enhance a president's prestige, and thus becomes a useful political tool.

Naturally, the president's featured role in the spotlight can also attract attention to his character and style in ways not entirely flattering. Certainly most presidents have been subjected to typecasting: Nixon as the used-car salesman, Johnson as the Texas wheeler-dealer, Kennedy as the youthful sophisticate, Carter as the down-home peanut farmer, Ford as the amiable bumbler, Reagan as the great communicator, Bush as the blueblooded oilman.

But whatever relationship exists between a president's popular image and his role as a ceremonial leader, his image can have a decided effect both on his popularity and on public confidence in the presidency. Though the nation laughed when Johnson described Ford as a man who couldn't walk and chew gum at the same time, Ford seemed to offer to many Americans a welcome contrast to his predecessor. Whereas Nixon's presidency had been widely viewed as insular and devious, Ford's was immediately regarded as open and relaxed. Apparently the public mood had been so depressed by the Watergate revelations as to be at least temporarily bolstered by seeing the presidency pass from the "used-car salesman" to the "supermarket clerk."

The President and His Party

An interesting paradox each president must face is that he not only must serve as the ceremonial representative of the entire nation but must provide partisan leadership for his party as well. Because of his powerful position he is expected to lead his party from the moment he is nominated at the national convention—to select the party's national chair, campaign for local and state candidates, use his prestige to attract needed campaign contributions, and help set policy goals. "He is at once," Clinton Rossiter observed, "the least political and the most political of all heads of government."[33]

Yet the president's leadership of the party can never extend too far. Because of the decentralized nature of the Democratic and Republican parties, the president has little direct control over state and local party organizations; for instance, he can impose only marginal discipline over most congressional members of his party. Some presidents have exercised more leadership than others, but on the whole a president's relations with other members of his party tend to rest on mutual benefits: he requires their support for his legislative proposals, and they depend on his prestige, policy direction, and special favors, such as appointments.

If a president loses credibility and public support, he cannot provide his party with effective leadership. Such misfortune has befallen several presidents, including Andrew Jackson, Warren Harding, Harry Truman, and, most recently, Richard Nixon and Jimmy Carter. Nixon's rapid decline in popularity during the Watergate investigations prompted a majority of Republicans to disavow ties to his policies. During the special off-year elections in the spring of 1974, many Republican candidates, instead of seeking his appearance in their districts, pleaded for his absence. Similarly, many Democratic candidates in 1980 did not want to be tarnished by Carter's legacy of high inflation and the hostage crisis in Iran.

The Judicial Side

Although the Constitution assigns "the judicial power of the United States" to the courts, the president (as a check on the judicial branch) also undertakes certain judicial tasks. For one thing, he may overturn a court ruling by pardoning a person convicted of a federal (but not a state) crime. He may also reduce a sentence by granting a commutation, or temporarily delay a punishment by granting a reprieve. In rare instances, he may even pardon an entire group, as both Ford and Carter did in limited form for Vietnam war resisters.

A pardon may stir considerable public controversy, as when President Ford stunned the nation in August 1974 by granting "full, free and absolute" pardon to Richard Nixon. In an unprecedented display of presidential judicial prerogative, Ford pardoned his White House predecessor before any official charges could be brought. The pardon covered not only Watergate-related activities but all other federal crimes Nixon might have committed as president. Although Ford claimed his pardon was an act of mercy in view of Nixon's deteriorated health at the time, and that a trial would only "cause prolonged and divisive debate" in the country, most critics felt it was premature and violated the principle of equal justice.

In addition to the pardoning power, a president has the authority to fill all vacancies on the federal courts, including the Supreme Court. This power can leave the stamp of the president's judicial philosophy on federal courts across the nation long after his term has ended. Before Ronald Reagan left the Oval Office, for example, he appointed close to half of all lower federal court judges, more than any other president had had an opportunity to do.

The power to appoint Supreme Court justices—which, as we will see in chapter 15, has tended to be guided by partisan considerations—is one of the president's most sweeping powers. Because justices are appointed for life, their selection can influence national policy long after a president's term has ended. Thurgood Marshall, for example, one of the most outspoken liberal forces on the Court during the 1970s and 1980s, was appointed by Lyndon Johnson in 1967.

This important power is restricted in three ways. For one thing, presidents do not always get the judicial philosophy they thought they could count on. Dwight Eisenhower appointed Earl Warren, who presided over one of the most liberal Courts in U.S. history. Byron White, appointed by John Kennedy, issued moderate to conservative rulings on the whole. A second limitation is the fact that only a few vacancies on the Court may occur during a president's term. On the average, each president has been able to select only two Supreme Court justices, although Nixon appointed four and Reagan three. Moreover, the president's power to appoint Supreme Court justices is limited constitutionally by the fact that a majority of the Senate must confirm his choices. Although the Senate has approved most appointments to the Court, it nevertheless has turned down 30 of the 145 Supreme Court nominations made through 1988. Most recently, the Senate has rejected two nominations put forth by each of three presidents—Johnson, Nixon, and Reagan.

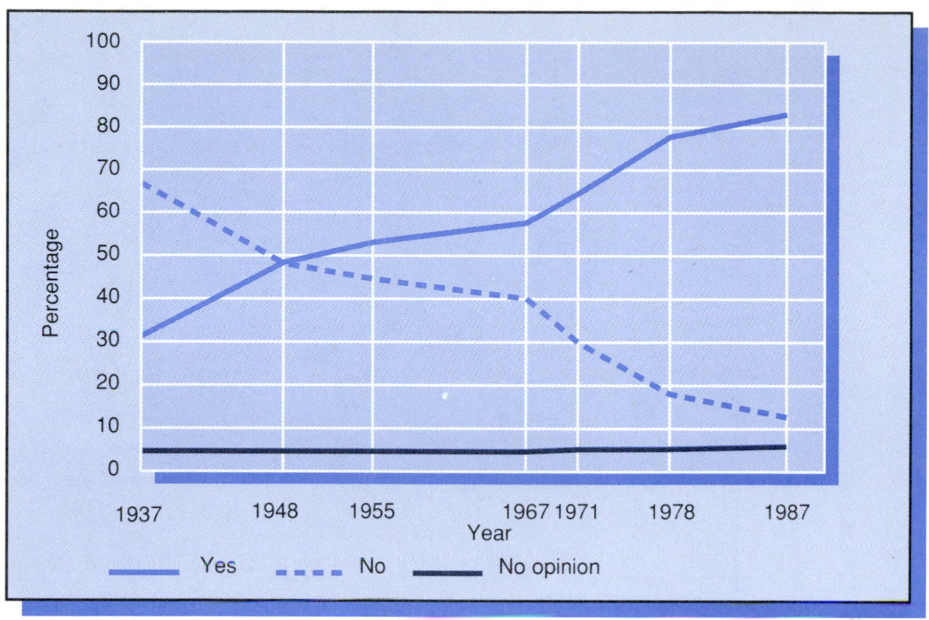

★ **Figure 13-5**
Would you vote for a woman candidate for president? 1937–1987 (percent responses)
SOURCE: *Gallup Report,* No. 262, July 1987, p. 17.

★ Job Description of the Presidency

The Constitution spells out only a few qualifications for the job of president: the person who holds the office must be a natural-born citizen, at least thirty-five years old, and a U.S. resident for at least fourteen years before taking office. The informal job specifications that have evolved by custom are more telling. It helps if one is a white male Protestant. There has never been a Jewish president or nominee. In 1960, John Kennedy became the first Catholic to win the presidency.

Moreover, no major party has slated a woman for the presidency. It was not until 1984 that a major party nominated a woman for the number-two post, when the Democrats selected Representative Geraldine Ferraro to join Walter Mondale's presidential bid. The Democrats hoped to cash in on the "gender gap" revealed by polls showing that women were more critical than men of Ronald Reagan's policies. Though women's support for Reagan in the 1984 election was lower than men's, the gender gap was not great enough to unseat the incumbent, who was overwhelmingly favored by men.

Public support for a woman for president has risen dramatically since the 1930s, when two-thirds of the public said they would not vote for a woman for president. Today only about 12 percent of the public holds this view (see figure 13-5). Still, we have yet to join the growing list of nations headed by women in the twentieth century: Great Britain, Iceland, the Philippines, Argentina, Israel, India, Sri Lanka, Dominica, and Pakistan.

Along with sex, race has been a formidable barrier to potential presidential candidates. The Reverend Jesse Jackson's national candidacies in 1984 and 1988

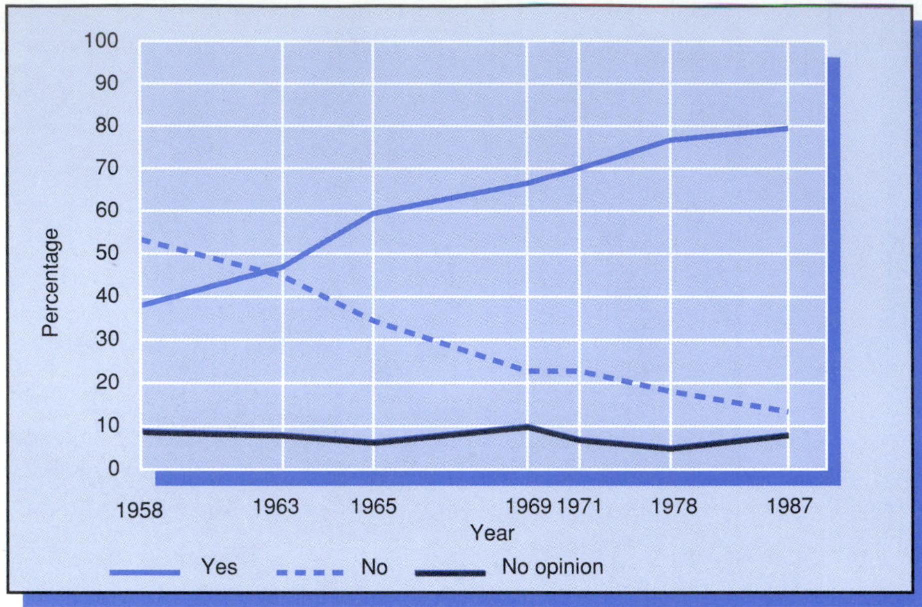

★ **Figure 13-6**
Would you vote for a black candidate for president? 1958–1987 (percent responses)
SOURCE: *Gallup Report,* No. 262, July 1987, p. 19.

reflect growing acceptance of a black chief executive. Today about 80 percent of the American electorate say that they would vote for a black candidate for president (see figure 13-6).

Political experience also limits the number of potential candidates. In the past, it was helpful to be a popular war hero. Former generals who became presidents include George Washington, Andrew Jackson, William H. Harrison, Zachary Taylor, Ulysses S. Grant, and Dwight Eisenhower. Most modern presidents have been either members of Congress (Truman, Kennedy, Nixon, Johnson, Ford, Bush) or governors (Franklin Roosevelt, Carter, Reagan).

As we noted earlier, vice-presidents have a good chance of becoming president. But despite Bush's success in 1988, their ascension to office results more often from the death of the incumbent than from election in their own right. Fourteen former vice-presidents have become president, but only five by their own efforts.

Tenure of Office

Although the original Constitution permitted presidents to serve an unlimited number of four-year terms, until 1940 presidents by tradition served no more than two terms. Then Franklin Roosevelt, having been elected in 1932 and reelected in 1936, ran for an unprecedented third term. Elected again, he ran for and won a fourth term in 1944. (The winners of all presidential elections and their opponents are listed in Appendix C.) In 1951 congressional Republicans secured the passage of a constitutional amendment limiting a president to two terms—a move some would later regret when their party basked in the reflected popularity of Presidents Eisenhower and Reagan. The Twenty-second Amendment further specifies that presidents may serve ten years if they complete the term of an incumbent who dies or resigns. Eight presidents have died in office as a result of illness or assassination and one president has resigned.

The Constitution is vague when it comes to presidential succession, saying only that presidential powers and duties "shall devolve on the Vice President" if a president dies, resigns, or cannot fulfill his responsibilities. The Constitution instructs Congress to choose a successor if there is no vice-president. In 1947, two years after Roosevelt's death in office, Congress passed the Presidential Succession Act, which spells out the order in which officers should succeed the president if there is no vice-president: the Speaker of the House of Representatives, the president pro tempore of the Senate, the secretaries of State, Treasury, and Defense, and other department heads in the order of their department's creation.

This act has never been implemented, as in recent years there has always been a vice-president when a president's term has been cut short. According to the Twenty-fifth Amendment, ratified in 1967, if the vice-presidency falls vacant (as it did under Nixon and Ford), the president names a new vice-president acceptable to both houses of Congress. This amendment also provides for a substitute in the event of presidential disability. In the past, it was unclear who should act as president when the president was disabled. When James Garfield was shot in 1881, he lingered incapacitated for two months before his death. Woodrow Wilson suffered a nervous collapse and stroke while in office. More recent presidents (Eisenhower, Lyndon Johnson, Reagan) have undergone extensive surgery while in office. Under the terms of the Twenty-fifth Amendment, the vice-president and a majority of the cabinet (or some other body named by Congress) determine if a president is able to do his job. If they find the president incapacitated, the vice-president becomes "acting president." The president resumes his responsibilities after notifying Congress of his recovery.

Of course the most dramatic way a president may be forced to end his tenure in office is impeachment. When the House brings charges of high crimes and misdemeanors against a president, he is said to be impeached. The term "high crimes and misdemeanors" is meant to refer to serious abuses, not the sort of partisan charges brought against Andrew Johnson, the only U.S. president to be impeached. Following impeachment, the president stands trial in the Senate, where a two-thirds majority is needed for conviction. If he is convicted, the president is removed from office. The only president since Andrew Johnson who came close to being impeached was Richard Nixon, who resigned when it became clear that the House would impeach him.

In Payment for Services

As confirmation of the special place of the presidency in American politics, special compensations and benefits have been bestowed on the incumbent. In addition to being served by a large personal staff, the president enjoys a salary of $200,000 a year (taxable), plus an annual expense allowance of $50,000. For his personal comfort and convenience, he has at his disposal a fleet of jets and helicopters, a staff of gourmet cooks and chefs, a tennis court, and even a White House projection room for private showings of first-run films. He and his family can also retreat to

Does the President's Personality Make a Difference?

Naturally, the degree to which a president allows the trappings of the office to go to his head depends a great deal on the individual. Jimmy Carter seemed to be more aware than his recent predecessors of the dangers of presidential isolation, and he took pains to keep in touch with ordinary Americans. He sold the presidential yacht, *Sequoia*, and lounged around the office in levis and a cardigan sweater. Early in his term, he took phone calls from citizens on a nationwide radio show and stayed overnight with several American families.

A president's personality may have a profound impact on national and international affairs. The political scientist James David Barber suggests that we analyze each future chief executive to predict his likely performance under stress, insisting that we can make such a prediction if we study his psychological makeup. By examining his earliest childhood and adult experiences, we can anticipate what he will do in the White House.

Barber contends that early experiences usually result in one of four presidential types: active-positive, active-negative, passive-positive, and passive-negative. Barber uses "active" and "passive" to describe the amount of energy a president invests in the office, and "positive" and "negative" to indicate how a president feels about what he does. Thus active-positive presidents want most to achieve results and enjoy exercising power. They tend to have relatively high self-esteem and an ability to adapt to changing circumstances (Franklin Roosevelt, Truman, Kennedy, Ford, Carter). Active-negatives also seek results, but they seldom get much pleasure from the task. Their actions seem more compulsive, and they tend to view life as a hard struggle to gain and maintain political power (Wilson, Hoover, Johnson, Nixon). Passive-positive presidents search for affection as a reward for being agreeable. They do not accomplish much, but they enjoy the adulation that comes with the office (Taft, Harding, Reagan). The passive-negatives not only accomplish little but retreat from the demands and conflicts of the job by stressing vague civic virtues (Coolidge, Eisenhower).

Barber issues a special warning about the second type of presidential character: the active negative. This type of individual, Barber believes, tends to be motivated by anxieties and guilt, and has difficulty controlling his aggressions. Because such a person sometimes confuses national and international policy with his own ambitions and becomes fixated on a policy regardless of the consequences—as Johnson did with Vietnam and Nixon did with the Watergate cover-up—the active-negative president can be an especially dangerous individual who may bring on disaster.

Some critics have question-

(continued)

Camp David in rural Maryland. It has been estimated that an ordinary citizen would require an annual salary of more than $50 million to live in the style of an American president.

About 1,600 Secret Service agents provide continuous protection for the president and his family at an annual cost of $100 million. This protection continues at a reduced scale for the rest of a former president's life. When a president leaves office, he receives a lifetime annual pension of $60,000, free office space, and up to $96,000 a year for staff assistance.

We might wonder whether all the perquisites of the office—especially the doting assistants who inevitably come with the job—do not eventually take their toll, sheltering a president from the life the rest of us know. George Reedy, former special assistant to Lyndon Johnson, observed after serving in the White House, "A President moves through his day surrounded by literally hundreds of people whose relationship to him is that of a doting mother to a spoiled child. Whatever he wants

★ President Jimmy Carter *(center)* has been described as an active-positive president, one who seeks results and adapts to changing circumstances. One of Carter's most notable achievements was the 1979 Camp David Accords, a peace plan signed by President Carter, President Anwar Sadat of Egypt *(left)*, and Prime Minister Menachem Begin of Israel *(right)*.

ed Barber's categories, pointing out that even active-positive presidents can act aggressively and irresponsibly. President Kennedy, for example, may have had a more healthy view of life, but he was still capable of approving a debacle such as the invasion of Cuba at the Bay of Pigs in 1961. Still others question the advisability of painting presidents in the flat strokes of two dimensions. Besides, when it comes to predicting presidential behavior, it may be difficult to know which early experiences were truly relevant; some childhood events may be simply picked out to account for later actions.

Whatever flaws may be discerned in Barber's theory, his approach underscores the importance of examining the character of the world's preeminent decision maker. ★

SOURCE: James David Barber, *The Presidential Character*, 3d ed. (Englewood Cliffs, N.J.: Prentice-Hall, 1977).

is brought to him immediately—food, drink, helicopters, airplanes, people, everything but relief from the political problems."[34]

★ Public Ambivalence about Presidents

The singularity and visibility of the American president make him a popular political figure. He and the vice-president are the country's only nationally elected officers. He is the first major political figure American children recognize. As we saw in chapter 7, studies reveal a rally-around-the-flag effect—public opinion often rallies to support a president when he embarks on foreign policy ventures, even such disastrous ones as the Bay of Pigs invasion and the escalations of the Vietnam war.

However, the rally-around-the-flag effect is usually temporary. When the international crisis subsides, so does the need to stand behind the symbol of the nation.

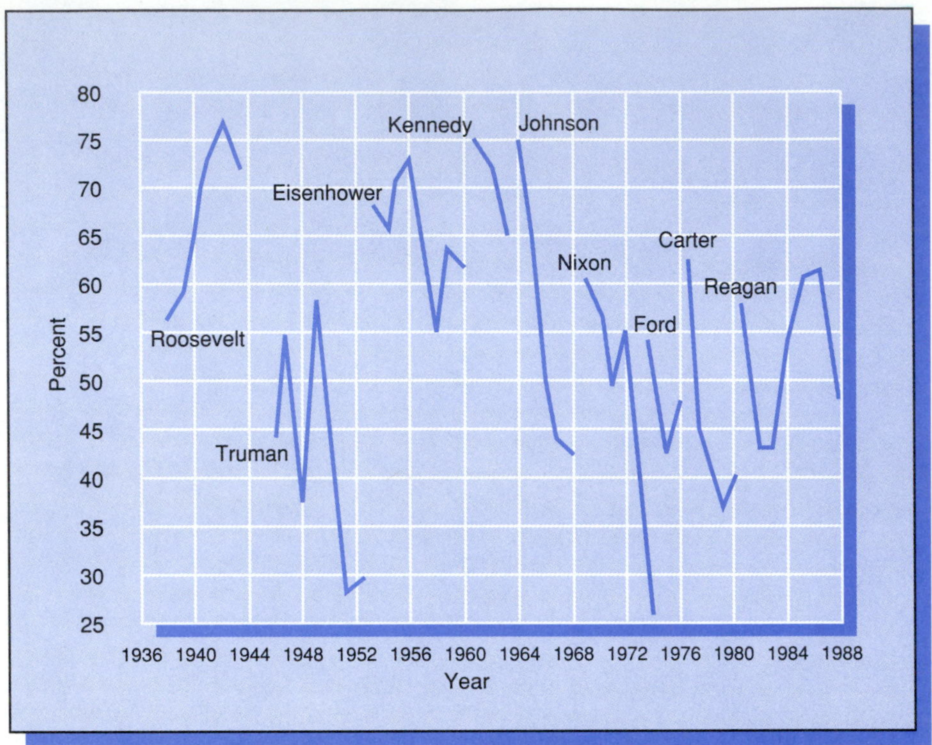

Figure 13-7
Percentage of respondents expressing approval of presidents, 1938–1988
NOTE: The question asked was: "Do you approve or disapprove of the way — (last name of president) is handling his job as president?" Actual poll results fluctuated more widely; these are averaged by year.
SOURCE: Harold W. Stanley and Richard G. Niemi, *Vital Statistics on American Politics* (Washington D.C.: Congressional Quarterly Press, 1988), p. 227.

In fact, presidents are often the scapegoats of the public's high expectations. In the post–World War II years, Gallup public opinion surveys have shown a high rate of public approval at the outset of a presidency—usually higher than the president's percentage of the popular vote just a few months earlier. This euphoria is typically followed by a decline in support (see figure 13–7). Ronald Reagan was one of the few presidents who left office as popular as when he arrived.

Some observers draw the analogy between the president and a parent: the object of childhood idealization and adult disillusionment. The president is *the* authority figure in American politics, and it is not surprising that Americans are ambivalent about him. Americans become particularly upset when presidents engage in deception and cover-ups. It was Nixon's cover-up of the Watergate scandal and related illegalities and the secret bombing of Cambodia that led to his greatest public disapproval. When it is revealed that a president is saying one thing and doing another, congressional committees swing into action, not to assess the policies in question but to determine whether the president has taken part in the deception.[35] The people can also be remarkably forgiving, however, if they feel the president is doing his best. At first critical of the Reagan administration's efforts to circumvent a congressional ban on aid to the Nicaraguan Contras, a majority of the

★ **Table 13-5**
Impact of events on presidential popularity

President/Event	*Type*	*Immediate impact on popularity in percent*
Johnson		
Great Society speech	Domestic	5.8
Intervenes, Dominican Republic	Foreign	7.0
Gallbladder operation	Personal	5.8
Escalates Vietnam war	Foreign	6.4
Urban riots	Domestic	−6.6
Glassboro summit	Foreign	8.3
Nonproliferation weapons treaty	Foreign	7.4
Christmas message from Vietnam	Foreign	5.1
Pueblo ship seized	Foreign	−6.8
Nixon		
Midway meeting about Vietnam	Foreign	−7.9
Silent-majority speech	Foreign	11.8
Invasion of Laos	Foreign	−6.7
Mining of Haiphong	Foreign	5.1
Return to bombing Hanoi	Foreign	−10.4
Vietnam peace announcement	Foreign	15.3
Price freezes	Domestic	−5.3
Vice-President Agnew resigns	Scandal	−6.2
John Dean Watergate testimony	Scandal	−6.4
Watergate*	Scandal	−24.5
Ford		
Nixon pardon	Domestic	−8.0
Tax-cut proposal	Domestic	7.0
Mayaguez ship rescue	Foreign	12.9
Captures Republican nomination	Domestic	6.6
Carter		
Bert Lance hearings	Scandal	−9.4
Panama Canal Treaty signed	Foreign	−8.7
Camp David peace treaty	Foreign	11.7
National malaise speech	Domestic	8.9
Iran embassy takeover	Foreign	6.6
Permits Shah to enter United States	Foreign	11.4
Failed hostage rescue mission	Foreign	10.1

*Cumulative impact of Watergate over 17 months

SOURCE: M. B. MacKuen, "Political Drama, Economic Conditions, and the Dynamics of Presidential Popularity," *American Journal of Political Science*, 27, May 1983, pp. 165–192. Reprinted by permission of the University of Texas Press.

public quickly accepted the president's explanation that he was misled by his staff, and his rating in the polls soared.

But there is more to the story than psychological idealization and disillusionment (see table 13-5). A president's fall from grace can be traced to other factors

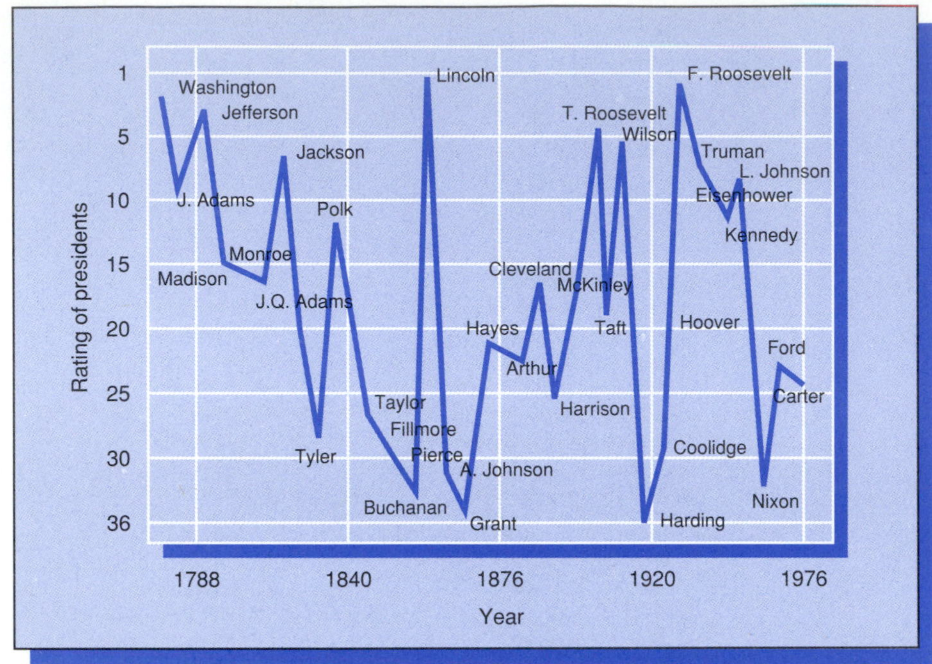

★ **Figure 13-8**

Presidents as ranked by historians

SOURCE: Robert K. Murray and T. H. Blessing, "The Presidential Performance Study: A Progress Report," *Journal of American History*, 1983, 70:335–355. Reprinted by permission.

as well. First, the White House magnifies the incumbent's shortcomings, whether they be Carter's preoccupation with detail or Reagan's neglect of it. Second, a zealous White House staff of loyalists can try to pursue a president's agenda with Hamiltonian "secrecy and dispatch" despite the wishes of Congress, as was the case with the Watergate and Iran-Contra affairs. Third, a president's popularity surges with a robust economy and plunges with economic downturns. For example, President Reagan's approval ratings dipped to less than 40 percent following the recession of 1982 and climbed during the subsequent economic recovery. Fourth, a protracted unpopular war can take its toll on a president's popularity, as Truman learned in the case of the Korean war. And finally, given the weakness of political parties in the United States, the public tends to fix blame for policies on individual presidents, not their political parties.

Presidents are acutely aware that history will judge them. Sometimes they rely on family members to give them perspective on the big picture. President Kennedy, for example, turned to his brother Robert, the attorney general, for advice during the Cuban missile crisis. And President Reagan sought the counsel of his wife Nancy, particularly in regard to the thaw in the cold war sought by the Soviet leader, Mikhail Gorbachev.

Scholars and the public alike enjoy playing the game of ranking great presidents (see figure 13–8). It is interesting to note that even such greats as George

Washington and Thomas Jefferson were not always popular in their own day. Washington barely secured ratification of the Jay Treaty, and Jefferson lost popular support with his trade embargo of France and Britain. But with hindsight we can see a difference between a president's short-term popularity and his long-term leadership record. Great presidents are typically those who have seen the country through wars or crises (Washington, Lincoln, Franklin Roosevelt) or inspired its philosopical direction (Jefferson, Kennedy).

In the great-presidents game, it is interesting to speculate whether many former "greats" could survive the scrutiny of the television age. Washington was reserved in public and could smile only slightly for fear of losing his primitive dentures. While Jefferson was a brilliant writer and charming in small groups, he was a poor public speaker and left the job of defending his Declaration of Independence before the Continental Congress to John Adams. James Madison tended to wear outdated clothing and had a face that Washington Irving described as "a withered little Apple-John." Lincoln's looks were routinely panned in the popular press. Indeed, the three presidents from the past who probably had the best telegenic images were the unforgettable Franklin Pierce, Chester A. Arthur, and Warren G. Harding.[36]

★ Summary

The framers were ambivalent about giving the president a great deal of power, but they did give him the edge over the other two branches in foreign policy. In the view of some observers, twentieth-century presidents have parlayed this edge into an institution that has accumulated too much power: an imperial presidency heading a secret government. This commanding position in American politics has been bolstered by sympathetic media, especially television, which presidents have used to their advantage.

Other analysts counter that the president is more imperiled than imperial. He can barely ride herd on his bureaucracy of three million employees. Even his closest advisers in the White House and Executive Office of the President have their turf battles. Nor can he control an assertive Congress, which is eager to put its own stamp on domestic policies.

The presidency is a difficult job to which individuals have brought their own energy and leadership styles. While the American public idealizes its presidents, it shares with the framers an uncertainty about presidential power. In the end, it is leadership rather than popularity that determines who will go down in history as one of the great American presidents.

★ Key Terms

cabinet
Central Intelligence Agency (CIA)
commander in chief
executive agreement
Executive Office of the President (EOP)
executive order
executive privilege
impeachment
item veto
pocket veto
State of the Union message
veto
Watergate scandal
White House Office (WHO)

★ Notes

1. Jimmy Carter, *Keeping Faith: Memoirs of a President* (New York: Bantam, 1982), p. 577.
2. *Federalist* no. 70.
3. Arthur Schlesinger, Jr., *The Imperial Presidency* (Boston: Houghton Mifflin, 1973).
4. Quoted in ibid., p. 89.
5. Nicholas Von Hoffman, *Make Believe Presidents* (New York: Pantheon, 1978), pp. 168, 172.
6. Schlesinger, *Imperial Presidency,* p. 99.
7. Henry L. Stimson and McGeorge Bundy, "The Atomic Bomb and the Surrender of Japan," in *On Active Service in War and Peace* (New York: Harper, 1948).
8. Daniel Ellsberg, "First Strike: An Interview with Daniel Ellsberg," *Inquiry*, April 13, 1981, p. 3.
9. Justice Robert Jackson, quoted in Schlesinger, *Imperial Presidency,* p. 144.
10. Bill Moyers, *The Secret Government* (Washington, D.C.: Seven Locks Press, 1988).
11. Quoted in Schlesinger, *Imperial Presidency,* p. 172.
12. Quoted in ibid., p. 187.
13. United States v. U.S. District Court, *Supreme Court Reporter,* July 15, 1972.
14. Steven R. Weisman, "The President and the Press," *New York Times Magazine,* October 14, 1984, p. 71.
15. Mark Hertsgaard, *On Bended Knee: The Press and the Reagan Presidency* (New York: Farrar, Strauss & Giroux, 1988).
16. NBC reporter Andrea Mitchell, quoted in ibid., p. 25.
17. David Gergen, quoted in ibid, p. 25.
18. Christopher Matthews, quoted in ibid., p. 51.
19. Shanto Iyengar and Donald Kinder, *News That Matters* (Chicago: University of Chicago Press, 1987).
20. Leslie Janka, quoted in Hertsgaard, *On Bended Knee*, p. 52.
21. See, for example, Harold M. Barger, *The Impossible Presidency* (Glenview, Ill.: Scott, Foresman, 1984).
22. Thomas E. Cronin, *The State of the Presidency* (Boston: Little, Brown, 1975), p. 118.
23. Ibid., p. 121.
24. Edwin Meese III, "The Institutional Presidency: A View from the White House," *Presidential Studies Quarterly,* Spring 1983, Vol. 13, pp. 191–197.
25. A Kennedy aide, quoted anonymously in Cronin, *State of the Presidency,* p. 153.
26. Quoted in ibid, p. 153.
27. Clinton Rossiter, *The American Presidency,* rev. ed. (New York: Harcourt Brace Jovanovich, 1960), p. 129.
28. *Newsweek,* August 27, 1973, p. 11.
29. Theodore H. White, *The Making of the President, 1972* (New York: Atheneum, 1973), p. 193.
30. See, for example, Arthur M. Schlesinger, Jr., "Is the Vice-Presidency Necessary?" *Atlantic,* May 1974, pp. 37–44.
31. Richard E. Neustadt, *Presidential Power* (New York: Wiley, 1960), p. 34.
32. Quoted in Merle Miller, *Plain Speaking: An Oral Biography of Harry S Truman* (New York: Berkley, 1974), p. 10.
33. Rossiter, *American Presidency,* p. 128.
34. George E. Reedy, *The Twilight of the Presidency* (New York: New American Library, 1970), pp. 33–34.
35. Donald L. Horowitz, "Is the Presidency Failing?" *Public Interest,* no. 88 (Summer 1987), p. 17.
36. Robert Bendiner, "Charisma? Washington? Jefferson? Madison?" *New York Times,* August 28, 1984.

★ For Further Reading

Barber, James David. *The Presidential Character: Predicting Performance in the White House.* 3d ed. Englewood Cliffs, N.J.: Prentice-Hall, 1985.

Barger, Harold M. *The Impossible Presidency*. Glenview, Ill.: Scott, Foresman, 1984.

Cronin, Thomas E. *The State of the Presidency.* Rev. ed. Boston: Little, Brown, 1980.

Fisher, Louis. *Constitutional Conflicts between Congress and the President.* Princeton, N.J.: Princeton University Press, 1985.

Kernell, Samuel. *Going Public: New Strategies of Presidential Leadership.* Washington, D.C.: Congressional Quarterly Press, 1986.

Koenig, Louis. *The Chief Executive.* 4th ed. New York: Harcourt Brace Jovanovich, 1981.

Lowi, Theodore J. *The Personal President: Power Invested, Promise Unfulfilled.* Ithaca, N.Y.: Cornell University Press, 1985.

Neustadt, Richard E. *Presidential Power: The Politics of Leadership from FDR to Carter.* New York: Wiley, 1980.

Schlesinger, Arthur, Jr. *The Imperial Presidency.* Boston: Houghton Mifflin, 1973.

It is hard to feel individually responsible with respect to the invisible processes of a huge and distant government.

—*John Gardner*

CHAPTER FOURTEEN

BUREAUCRACY

★★★★★★★★★★★★★

"Alphabet Agencies" Spell Power: The American Bureaucracy

As we saw in chapter 5, the debate between the ruling elite theorists and the pluralists over who governs in America has been joined by a third group of theorists who contend that ultimately no one is in charge. They argue that our political system has become so enveloped in the tentacles of bureaucracy, so beset by a growing complexity of problems and solutions, that control over policy making by any group has become virtually impossible. This theory, which embraces a variety of concepts and concerns, is ultimately a response to the seemingly pervasive bureaucratization of American society. In the federal government especially, the bureaucracy seems to be everywhere, a potent and independent "fourth branch" elected by and seemingly accountable to no one. With its labyrinth of departments, agencies, and bureaus, the federal bureaucracy has become so vast that neither the president nor Congress nor even the people who work within it can fully comprehend its scope. Some critics suggest that the bureaucracy merely feeds upon itself, swelling under its own internal pressure, as a perfect illustration of Parkinson's Law: "Work expands so as to fill the time available for its completion."[1]

In this chapter we will examine some features of the federal bureaucracy and the impact it has on our lives. We will address a number of questions, including:

- How did we end up with it?
- Are there dangers when such vital concerns as national security are entrusted to giant departments that seem to be more interested in competing with each other than in defending the country?
- What opportunities (if any) exist for citizens to make the bureaucracy work for them?

★ The Nature and Growth of Bureaucracy

It is said that the word **bureaucracy** was first coined in eighteenth-century France, a combination of *bureau* (which originally referred to a cloth covering the desk of a government official and later to the place where an official worked) and *cracy* (signifying rule of government).[2] As used today, the word "bureaucracy" suggests certain arrangements and conditions. In the broadest sense, it implies an organization having a hierarchy of command, with a specialization of roles and a division of labor, and governed by formal rules and regulations. To some observers, it also

★ **Table 14-1**
Number of federal civilian employees, 1986, by cabinet department

Cabinet department	Employees
Agriculture	113,147
Commerce	34,397
Defense	1,067,974
Education	4,554
Energy	16,647
Health and Human Services	133,842
Housing and Urban Development	11,843
Interior	73,980
Justice	65,529
Labor	17,487
State	25,325
Transportation	61,281
Treasury	135,628
Veterans Affairs	240,423

SOURCE: U.S. Bureau of the Census, *Statistical Abstract of the United States, 1988* (Washington, D.C.: U.S. Government Printing Office, 1987), p. 310.

signifies certain ideals: an emphasis on rationality and expertise, and political neutrality. If a group of people suddenly found themselves stranded on a deserted island (pardon the familiar analogy), they would not constitute a bureaucracy—not, that is, unless they formed a pyramidal chain of command, with each person assigned responsibilities on the basis of his or her expertise. (If they began to sit behind desks piled with paper, gave themselves pompous titles, and erected massive wooden huts to house alphabet-soup agencies, they would certainly be on the bureaucratic track.)

Bureaucracies can be found almost everywhere, from large corporations and universities to church organizations and hospitals. In the federal government, the bureaucracy consists principally of the executive agencies and departments under the president's command that carry out the laws passed by Congress.

During the early part of American history, few people thought much about the bureaucracy. As late as the 1880s, fewer than 150,000 people were employed by the federal government. Only a handful of executive departments and agencies existed, performing such tasks as collecting taxes, printing money, and delivering the mail.

Today approximately three million civilians work for Uncle Sam (see table 14-1) and another two million are employed in the armed forces. The Department of Veterans Affairs alone has more employees than the total number of federal bureaucrats on hand at the turn of the century. Only during the past few decades, in fact, has the number of federal employees leveled off. Since the 1950s, the number of people employed in federal bureaus has remained generally around three million. (Federal agencies now "contract out" many of their activities to private firms, thus indirectly employing many additional people. And where the federal

Bureaucratic Inertia

Bureaucracies are like avalanches: they are a bit hard to start, but once they get going, there is little if any way to stop them. Thus the most important and vulnerable period for a bureaucracy is its infancy. Analysts use such terms as "the wedge" and "the camel's nose" to signify strategies that bureaucracies use to get a foot in the door. Once a bureaucracy is established, it seems to have a life of its own. A case in point the Commission for the Standardization of Screw Threads.

On May 31, 1918, Representative John Tilson of Connecticut expressed concern about the apparent chaos in the world of nuts and bolts, which he felt was hindering the war effort. His idea was to establish a commission to look into the problem. Eventually Congress okayed the commission, but imposed a six-month time limit on it.

World War I ended without a report, but the commission prospered. Commission members went to Europe to discuss the screw-thread problem with foreign sympathizers. Money and personnel were acquired from various resources as the commission members became skilled at bureaucratic politics.

On January 16, 1922, John Tilson proudly announced in Congress that the commission had issued a "tentative report" after five years on the job. Eventually the commission managed to legitimize its existence by a congressional resolution establishing the commission's permanence. In 1966, the commission's executive secretary, Irwin Fullmer, retired. He had held the post for forty-seven years. ★

SOURCE: Jim Clark, "The International Screw Thread Commission," in *The Culture of Bureaucracy*, ed. Charles Peters and Michael Nelson, pp. 8–11 (New York: Holt, Rinehart & Winston, 1979).

bureaucracy has remained constant, state and local bureaucracies have been taking up the slack. Almost five times as many people today are employed by state and local governments as by the federal government.) In terms of money spent, the federal budget exceeded $1 trillion a year by the end of the 1980s. And during the past thirty years, close to 250 new agencies and bureaus have been added, while only a few dozen have been scrapped.

It seems likely that the framers did not anticipate the enormous growth of the federal bureaucracy. As we noted in chapter 2, the Constitution is silent about the bureaucracy's structure and the duties it should perform. The document makes only a few casual references to the bureaucracy, such as the provision that the president "may require the Opinion, in writing, of the principal Officer in each of the executive Departments." Although the framers realized that some apparatus would be needed to carry out the laws passed by Congress, they did not foresee how the government would expand. They did not foresee that as Congress faced growing demands for legislation to cure society's ills, more agencies and administrators would also be needed to carry out that legislation.

Indeed, the federal bureaucracy did not spring into being overnight. It evolved gradually in response to new economic forces, technological developments, and a changing population. It grew in response to demands that government solve such problems as unemployment, inadequate housing, and the need for education and transportation. The emergence of giant industrial corporations in the late 1880s, for example, spurred demands for regulatory legislation to protect workers and to preserve a competitive market system. Similarly, the Great Depression of the 1930s stimulated the need for new federal programs and agencies (such as the Social Security Administration) to provide greater financial security for citizens and to help maintain the economic order. These pressures continued to mount over the years and reached a peak in the 1960s, during the Johnson administration, when

★ A retired worker applies for his social security benefits, one of the continuing legacies of the federal government's response to the Great Depression of the 1930s.

in the name of the "Great Society" a massive new program was offered as a solution to virtually every major social problem.

Increased interdependence with other nations has also expanded the bureaucracy. At the end of World War II roughly 65 nations formed the global community; today there are more than 170, each requiring the attention of the U.S. government to one degree or another. As a superpower, the United States has military bases in Europe, East Asia, the Pacific Basin, and Central and South America. In 1950, the United States gave economic and military aid to approximately forty countries; by the mid-1980s, more than $6 billion in foreign aid was being pumped into the economies of more than one hundred nations.[3] The virtual explosion in international commerce, moreover, has expanded government oversight of everything from foreign currency transactions to customs inspections of imported products. When we add a wealth of technological changes, from global satellite communications to the revolution in travel brought about by the jet age, it is easy to see government's expanding responsibilities.

The growth of the bureaucracy has also stimulated considerable apprehension and criticism. Few issues in American politics have been so hotly debated in recent years as how to put a brake on the reach and costs of government. Ronald Reagan's pledge to trim the costs and role of the federal bureaucracy was a cornerstone of both of his successful campaigns for the presidency. Indeed, to many Americans, the bureaucracy has become the major symbol of governmental waste and inefficiency, a symbol few of the Constitution's framers could have fully imagined.

Staffing the Bureaucracy

As the bureaucracy has grown, so has the concern over how it should be staffed. Where should all of the bureaucrats come from, and how should they be selected and supervised?

Before the Civil War, presidents commonly appointed to the bureaucracy people who had demonstrated partisan loyalty. Providing a job on the federal payroll was a handy way for a newly elected chief executive to reward someone for his support during the campaign. This practice, known widely as the **spoils system** (from the saying "To the victor belong the spoils"), was used to fill not only cabinet and other high governmental posts but also such lesser positions as postal clerk and justice of the peace. And with each turnover in administrations, a large number of civil servants were sacked and replaced by supporters of the other party. To put it mildly, job security was hardly a major benefit of a federal appointment.

Following the Civil War, the patronage system came under increased attack. Many people saw the bureaucracy as riddled by political corruption and staffed by incompetents. Then, in 1881, a Chicago lawyer named Charles Guiteau assassinated President James Garfield. Guiteau was apparently disappointed that he did not get the patronage job he expected, so he shot Garfield in the back. (Guiteau was later hanged.) The push for reform soon reached fever pitch, and in 1883 Congress passed the Pendleton Act, setting up a bipartisan Civil Service Commission to recruit and regulate federal employees.

Today about 90 percent of all federal jobs are filled under the rules and regulations of the **civil service** system. Most federal employees are hired through competitive examinations, are promoted on the basis of evaluations by their superiors, and are largely protected from dismissal for partisan reasons. Only about 6,500 top policy-making positions, such as the heads of the cabinet departments and independent agencies, are still filled directly by the president.

This is not to say that political considerations and personal favoritism have been entirely removed from the civil service system. Despite examinations and other controls, a person with pull can still manage to land a federal job. Many bureaus and agencies occasionally use special referral procedures to bypass normal channels and make room for people with political connections or special skills.

Nor has the present system guaranteed equal opportunities in job advancement. Although minority groups and women are well represented in most agencies, they tend to be concentrated at the lower grades. Women, for example, hold about 48 percent of all white-collar positions in the federal bureaucracy, but only about 7 percent of the highest-salaried positions.[4]

In fact, critics have been demanding changes in civil service procedures since the system was created. Instead of attacking the way federal employees are hired, however, they have been critical of the way incompetent and inefficient employees are retained and even promoted. In 1978, President Carter finally persuaded Congress to pass a Civil Service Reform Act. The act provided for the reorganization of the Civil Service Commission by splitting it into two new entities: (1) a Merit System Protection Board to handle employees' complaints and protect their rights, and (2) an Office of Personnel Management to conduct civil service examinations, regulate employees' salaries and benefits, and stimulate productivity. The act was designed to eliminate the schizophrenic quality of a commission that was responsible for overseeing employees' rights and encouraging their productivity at the same time.

★ Most of the people who work for the government obtain their jobs by taking a civil service examination. This person is processing income tax forms for the IRS.

Carter agreed with critics who contended that it was easier to promote or transfer an incompetent employee than it was to fire one. He cited Alan Campbell, Chairman of the Civil Service Commission, who reported that only 226 of 2.8 million federal workers were discharged for incompetence in 1977. That was no way, Carter said, to run a farm, a factory, or a government. He also observed that "there is not enough merit in the merit system; there is inadequate motivation because we have too few rewards for excellence and too few penalties for unsatisfactory work."[5] As a result, the Civil Service Reform Act also set up a merit-pay system for middle-level management, modified provisions for firing incompetent workers, and even established a special board to protect whistle-blowers, employees who emerge from the bureaucratic shadows to expose governmental waste and corruption.

★ The Bureaucratic Network

Since the Constitution does not spell out how the federal bureaucracy should be organized, it has been left to the president and Congress to decide which bureaucrats will perform which duties and in which building. They determine when new agencies will be established, what their responsibilities will be, and how much officials will be paid. As a result, we have inherited an administrative enterprise formed in sporadic and piecemeal fashion. Like a small village that has taken centuries to grow into a metropolis, with its streets and boulevards laid out in a haphazard pattern formed by years of circumstance and changing needs, the federal bureaucracy has gradually evolved into its present form (see figure 14-1). For a federal bureaucracy we have inherited not the planned symmetry of a central Paris, but the unplanned sprawl of a Los Angeles.

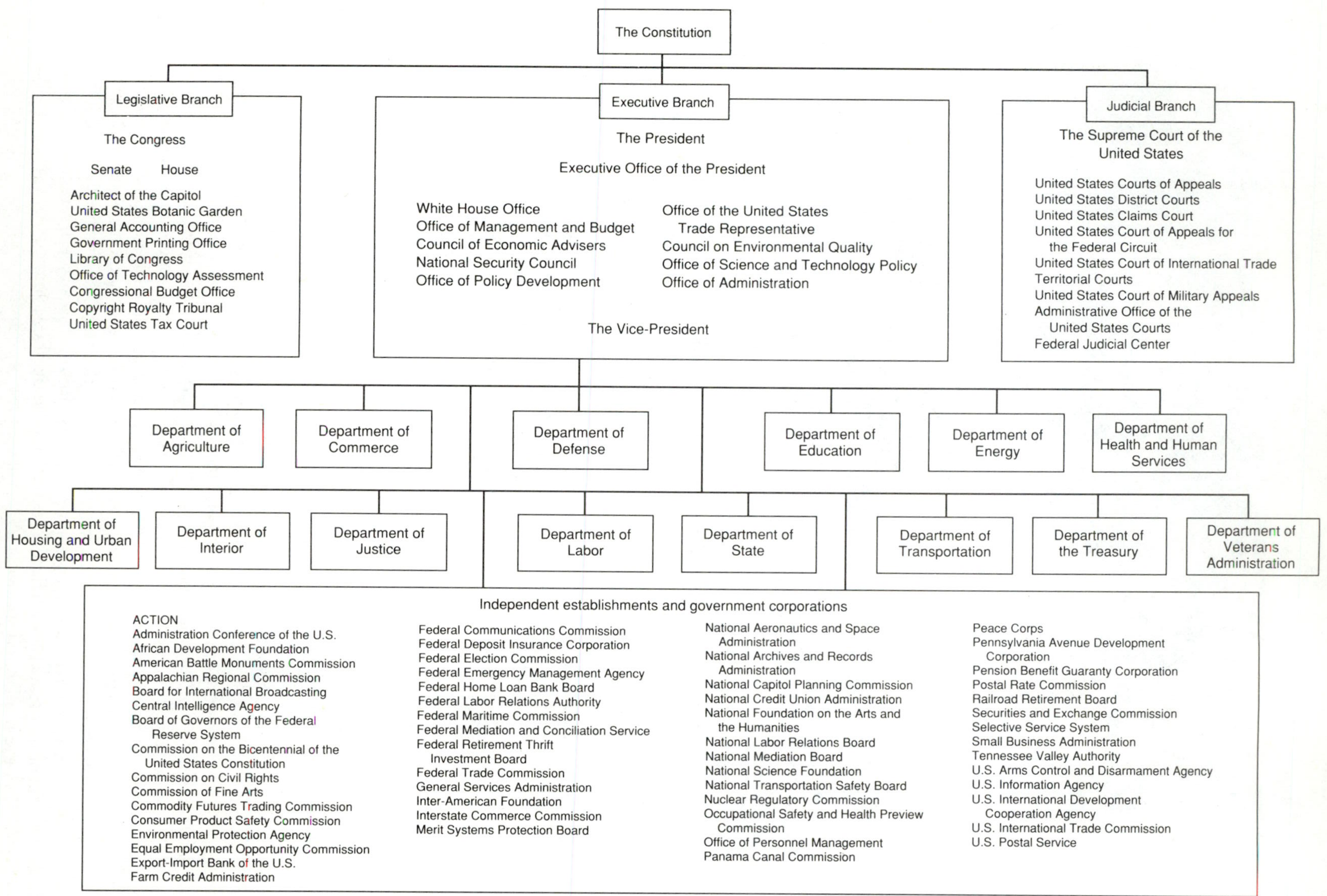

★ **Figure 14-1**
Organizational chart of the government of the United States

★ Table 14-2
The cabinet departments and their duties, 1988

Department	*Founded*	*Major duties*
State	1789	Advises president on foreign policy; negotiates treaties; oversees foreign aid programs
Treasury	1789	Enforces federal revenue laws; coins money; collects taxes
Interior	1849	Oversees national parks, natural resources, and Indian reservations
Agriculture	1862	Supports farm productivity research; administers crop surplus subsidies
Justice	1870	Enforces federal laws; represents federal government in legal matters
Commerce	1903	Promotes U.S. foreign trade; administers Census Bureau and Patent Office
Labor	1913	Enforces minimum wage laws and labor safety regulations; oversees pension programs; arbitrates labor disputes
Defense	1947	Maintains and directs U.S. military forces; awards defense contracts; conducts foreign military operations
Health and Human Services	1953	Administers food and drug laws, public health research, and social security programs
Housing and Urban Development	1965	Coordinates urban renewal and public housing assistance
Transportation	1966	Oversees federal highway and mass transit programs; enforces auto and air safety standards
Energy	1977	Coordinates U.S. energy research and development programs, including nuclear power
Education	1979	Administers federal education programs
Veterans Affairs	1988	Administers programs for veterans

For the sake of description, we can lump most of the agencies of the federal bureaucracy into four basic groups: the cabinet-level departments, the independent agencies, the government corporations, and the regulatory commissions. Let us first look at the cabinet departments.

The Cabinet Departments

The largest and most important agencies of the federal bureaucracy are the fourteen cabinet-level **executive departments** (or "line agencies," as they are sometimes called). They deal with the most pressing national concerns—defense, foreign policy, the economy—and provide many of the social services and carry out most of the laws passed by Congress (see table 14-2). They vary in size from the Education Department, with roughly 4,500 employees, to the mammoth Defense Department, with more than a million employees. While some of the departments—such as State and Treasury—have been around since the nation's founding, others—such as Health and Human Services, Housing and Urban Development (HUD), and

Veterans Affairs—are relative newcomers whose staffs and responsibilities have mushroomed in response to the nation's growth.

Each department is headed by a secretary (an attorney general in the case of the Justice Department) appointed by the president with the consent of the Senate. The secretaries enjoy considerable public prestige as members of the president's cabinet, and are assisted by at least one undersecretary and several assistant secretaries, also appointed by the president. Each department is splintered into many smaller bureaus and divisions that handle special functions or serve particular geographical areas (for an example, see figure 14-2).

The structures of the departments, however, vary considerably. While some are neatly centralized with authority flowing in clear vertical lines, others are little more than collections of relatively independent bureaus with their own concerns and clientele. The Federal Bureau of Investigation (FBI) in the Justice Department, for example, and the Army Corps of Engineers in the Defense Department have considerable autonomy in carrying out their functions.

Furthermore, although the official duties of the departments are to provide essential governmental services and apply the laws, some of the departments also have a third mission: to represent the interests of client groups. The Department of Agriculture, for instance, was set up in 1862 primarily to assist and regulate the farm industry. Similarly, the Department of Labor came into being in 1913 largely in response to demands for cabinet representation of labor interests. In late 1988 the Veterans Administration was elevated to a cabinet-level department to give veterans a stronger voice in the government. Presidents usually face considerable political pressure to appoint department secretaries who are sympathetic to their department's client groups.

The Independent Agencies

In addition to the cabinet departments, dozens of **independent agencies** also answer to the president. They are "independent" only in that they exist outside the cabinet departments; they are not free of presidential oversight. The directors of these agencies are appointed by the president with the consent of the Senate and may be removed from their posts by the president.

These independent agencies vary considerably in size, organization, and power. Some are headed by a single administrator; others are headed by a board or commission. They are alike only in that they tend to be more specialized than the major departments and are not represented in the president's cabinet. Among the best known of the independent agencies are the Central Intelligence Agency (CIA), the National Aeronautics and Space Administration (NASA), and the General Services Administration (GSA).

The Government Corporations

Among the agencies known as **government corporations** are the U.S. Postal Service, the Federal Deposit Insurance Corporation (FDIC), the Tennessee Valley Authority (TVA), and the National Railroad Passenger Corporation (Amtrak). They are organized and run somewhat like private corporations, with governing boards appointed by the president with the consent of the Senate. Because they either are

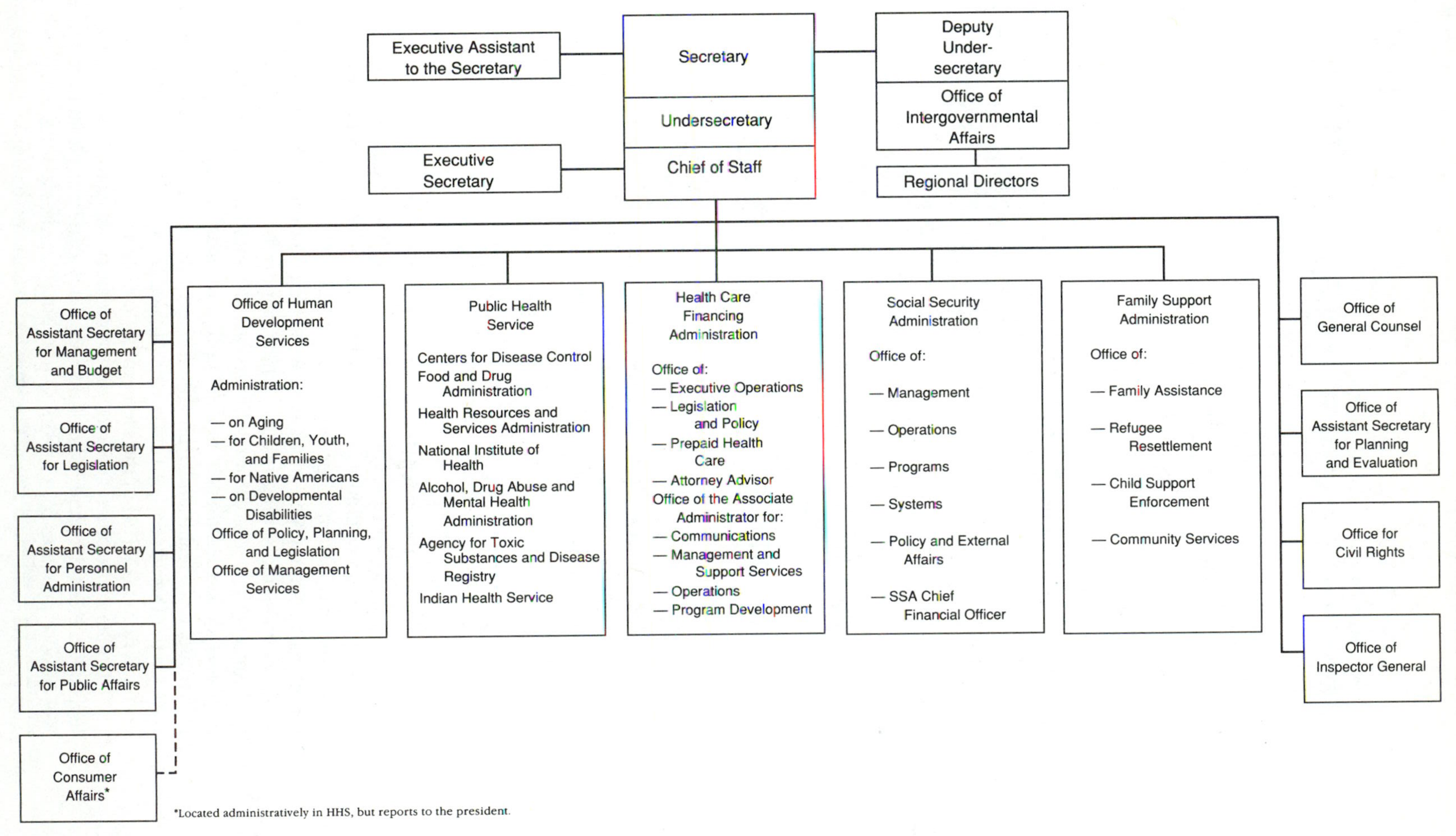

★ **Figure 14-2**
Department of Health and Human Services

★ Table 14-3
Background on some regulatory commissions

Commission	*Founded*	*Major duties*	*Number of commissioners*
Interstate Commerce Commission	1887	Regulates rates and routes of interstate railroads, trucking and bus companies, and pipelines	7
Federal Reserve Board	1913	Regulates banking industry and sets monetary and credit policy	7
Federal Trade Commission	1914	Enforces antitrust laws, prohibits unfair competition, and enforces truth-in-labeling laws	6
Federal Communications Commission	1934	Licenses television and radio stations and regulates interstate telephone services	5
Securities and Exchange Commission	1934	Regulates stock exchanges and investment companies	5
Consumer Product Safety Commission	1972	Sets product safety standards and initiates recall notices for defective products	5

self-financing or receive long-term appropriations from Congress, they do not have to present operating budgets to Congress each fiscal year. This arrangement is supposed to provide these agencies with the freedom and flexibility to operate efficiently.

The Regulatory Commissions

Finally, there are the independent **regulatory commissions,** whose activities reach into virtually every corner of our society. These bodies are charged with regulating certain operations in the private sector of the economy and with protecting the public from corporate abuses. They perform such duties as setting rates for interstate commerce, issuing licenses for television and radio stations, enforcing antitrust laws, and setting product safety standards. (Table 14-3 shows a selected list.) Among these regulatory commissions are some agencies that operate within a cabinet department, such as the Food and Drug Administration (FDA) in the Department of Health and Human Services, the Federal Aviation Administration (FAA) in the Department of Transportation, and the Occupational Safety and Health Administration (OSHA) in the Department of Labor.

Unlike most other agencies, the regulatory commissions wield a blend of legislative, executive, and judicial powers. They issue rules that have the effect of law, impose penalties for violations, and settle disputes among conflicting parties. The Federal Communications Commission (FCC), for example, has the power to decide who shall receive a license to operate a television or radio station, and can revoke a license if a station fails to satisfy certain operating conditions. Barring federal court action, the FCC's judgment is final.

Because the regulatory commissions have such a range of powers, they are supposed to remain relatively independent of both the president and Congress. They are headed by boards of several members instead of by single individuals, for example, and must be bipartisan. And even though commissioners are appointed by the president, they do not report directly to him and cannot easily be removed. Most serve long, overlapping terms so that no one president can make all of the appointments.

However, the "independence" of the regulatory commissions is only partial. The president designates the head of each commission—thus exercising some measure of control over policy direction—while Congress controls the flow of money to keep the commission operating. In addition, the regulatory commissions are often criticized for yielding to pressures from the industries they are supposed to regulate. Because a commission's rulings can directly affect the profits of an industry, as when it bans a company's product or denies an operating license, regulatory commissions face intense efforts to persuade them to support rather than challenge the industry. These efforts are often successful, especially since commission members are frequently snatched from the same industries they oversee. As critics have noted, some of the commissions seem more concerned with promoting the interests of industry groups than with protecting the public from corporate abuses. More on this point later.

Overlapping Responsibility

One might easily assume that each department or agency enjoys a defined area of competence and responsibility: the Department of Commerce takes care of business (so to speak), Defense is alert to foreign threats, and the Department of Agriculture is busy ensuring that our tables are filled with nature's bounty. In reality, there is substantial overlap of responsibility among agencies. Take, for example, America's relations with other nations. One would assume that the Department of State (working with the president, Congress, and Department of Defense) would take care of foreign policy. And while it is true that the Departments of State and Defense are vitally concerned with foreign relations, the list of government agencies and departments concerned with the international sphere is extensive. According to the Department of State, a partial list of agencies and departments that are routinely involved in making and implementing foreign policy includes the following:

Central Intelligence Agency
Department of Defense
Federal Bureau of Investigation
National Security Agency
Department of State
Department of Agriculture
Department of Commerce
U.S. Customs Service
Drug Enforcement Agency
Export-Import Bank
Immigration and Naturalization Service
Department of Labor
Overseas Private Investment Corporation
Department of the Treasury

★ Having to pass through an airport check is one way citizens experience directly the policy-making powers of bureaucratic agencies.

The smooth development and implementation of policy by such a diverse group of agencies is a continuing challenge to American government. Inefficiency and lack of coordination abound. Along with the predictable problems that arise when such a diverse group of large organizations is involved is the less expected phenomenon of interagency rivalry and competition. As we shall see, jealousy and political in-fighting are common traits of bureaucracies—traits that can lead, in some dramatic instances, to near-disasters for the nation.

★ How the Bureaucracy Affects Our Lives

To most people the agencies and departments just described are little more than vaguely familiar names. The officials who run them are largely unknown, tucked away in massive buildings along the Mall in Washington, D.C., and in other cities across the country. Yet in several respects the decisions of these anonymous men and women affect us more directly than those of any other governmental officials—more than those of the members of Congress, state legislators, city council members, and presidents we elect to office. Each day they issue regulations governing virtually all aspects of our lives, from the softness of our mattresses to the shape of our toilet seats. They tell us whether we can use sugar substitutes in our coffee, whether our hair sprays and shave creams can come in aerosol cans, and whether our children's pajamas are to be treated with flame-retardant chemicals.

Theoretically, bureaucrats are supposed to do what elected officals tell them to do, which is to implement or administer the laws. In practice, however, they have great discretionary authority. Although such agencies as the Food and Drug Administration (FDA) and the Internal Revenue Service (IRS) administer policies made by Congress and the White House, policies rarely are so specific that these agencies cannot use discretion in carrying them out. For instance, when Congress

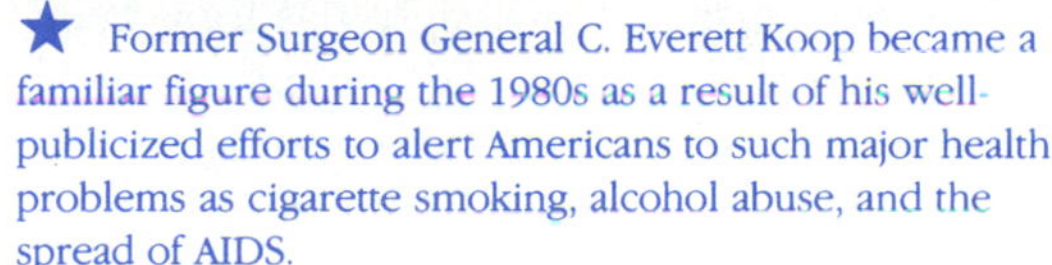
★ Former Surgeon General C. Everett Koop became a familiar figure during the 1980s as a result of his well-publicized efforts to alert Americans to such major health problems as cigarette smoking, alcohol abuse, and the spread of AIDS.

★ Because of Koop's efforts to stop the spread of AIDS, private companies not involved with the federal bureaucracy have also committed their time and resources to the same cause.

stipulated that new drugs on the market had to be safe and effective, the Food and Drug Administration was handed the power to establish the actual standards of safety and effectiveness. It was given the authority to make policy decisions concerning the kinds of products that reach consumers—in effect, to determine both the health and well-being of millions of Americans and the economic fate of entire industries. Consider, too, the threat to public health represented by the Acquired Immune Deficiency Syndrome (AIDS) epidemic. When the federal government resolved in the mid-1980s to stop the spread of AIDS, the Public Health Service, then under the direction of Surgeon General C. Everett Koop, set out to find specific ways to alert the public to the dangers of this disease and publicize some of the practical ways to avoid acquiring it.

Agencies of the federal bureaucracy, in fact, play an important role in every stage of the policy-making process. Agency heads (and the people under them) often provide expert information to legislators, helping even to draw up and initiate new policy. And the ways in which these agencies choose to implement acts of Congress or executive orders of the president can have a great effect on their outcomes.

In some cases, Congress has found it necessary to amend policies to prevent them from being carried out. Consider the artificial sweetener saccharin. According to a law passed by Congress, the Food and Drug Administration had no choice but to ban the sweetener once tests on laboratory animals linked its use to cancer. Such an outcry arose against the ban, however, that Congress had to revise the policy that guided the FDA. In other cases, Congress has been so distrustful of federal agencies that it has drastically limited their actions. It was distrust of the CIA that led Congress to pass the Boland Amendment, specifically ordering the agency not to provide military assistance to the Contras in Nicaragua.

Still, neither the president nor Congress can be everywhere at once, and there are several reasons why policy-making power has been handed to nonelected bureaucrats. One is that such power is an unavoidable consequence of a growing technological society. Many social and economic problems have become so highly complex that people with technical expertise are required to handle them. Elected officials, including members of Congress, usually do not have such expertise and therefore must delegate considerable policy-making authority to bureaucrats.

Another reason is that the challenges of our economic system—unemployment, price fixing, contamination of the environment, unsafe working conditions, consumer fraud, imbalances in foreign trade and competition—have placed increased responsibilities on bureaucratic officials charged with solving social and economic problems. The FDA, for example, has been handed its enormous policy-making authority in recognition of the fact that consumers require some protection against the occasional abuses of the food and drug industries. Without the scientific expertise and governmental authority commanded by the FDA and other federal agencies, it is extremely doubtful whether safety standards for many of the products we use would have been achieved.

Although the need for administrative expertise and oversight has long been accepted as a necessary part of government, the rash of new regulations in recent years—for consumer product quality, industrial safety, and environmental protection—has sparked new debates about the highly visible regulatory aspect of the bureaucracy. Have bureaucratic officials, as some critics contend, been handed too much power to regulate American society? Have they been properly serving the interests of American citizens, or have they instead been serving the interests of the industries they are supposed to regulate?

Because the outcome of this debate could have a profound impact on our lives, we should examine some of the criticisms and justifications of the bureaucracy's regulatory activities. By exploring the debate over this major function of the bureaucracy we should gain some insight into the principles and problems of the bureaucracy as a whole.

The Uses of Regulation

Some years ago it was revealed that the Firestone Tire and Rubber Company was continuing to market defective steel-belted radial tires suspected of causing the deaths of forty-one people in auto accidents. Despite alarming data on the tires compiled by the National Highway Traffic and Safety Administration (NHTSA), and despite protests from consumer action groups such as the Center for Auto Safety, Firestone persisted in dumping its inventories of the tires in Florida and Alabama. Finally, in October 1978, Firestone yielded to government pressure and agreed to recall more than ten million tires, one of the largest recalls in the nation's history.

Although not all corporations show disregard for human safety and health, the sad fact is that citizens cannot rely exclusively on the good intentions of profit-oriented enterprises. Some additional mechanisms are needed to protect us against fraud and against products that could endanger our health. Experience has shown that governmental programs in such areas as drug regulation, food inspection, and industrial and product safety have served legitimate public needs.

Consider one dramatic example. In the early 1960s, Dr. Frances Kelsey of the FDA received national publicity for keeping out of the nation's drugstores a drug

★ Before many products can be marketed and sold in the United States, they must be tested and approved by the Food and Drug Administration, a process that may take years to complete. Critics accuse the FDA of moving too slowly when potentially life-saving medications are discovered. Supporters respond that caution is necessary to avoid approving drugs with unforeseen side effects.

called Thalidomide, intended to control nausea during pregnancy. She resisted a drug company's efforts to introduce the product into the American market, even though it already had been widely prescribed in Europe. As it turned out, the drug was found to have caused thousands of European children to be born deformed.

This does not mean that all regulatory officials should be viewed as fearless knights protecting us against hordes of vicious corporate scoundrels. As we shall see, many federal regulators have been criticized for permitting themselves to be "captured" by the industries they are supposed to oversee. Nevertheless, federal regulators such as Dr. Kelsey can check abuses of private industry that we, as consumers, may be unable to detect or prevent. As we said earlier, without the scientific expertise and governmental authority commanded by federal regulators, it is extremely doubtful whether many of the safety standards we take for granted today would have been implemented.

The Negative Side of Regulation

A number of criticisms, however, have been lodged against federal regulators. One target of criticism has been the sheer cost of all the regulations the agencies issue. Officials in President Ford's administration once estimated that the average American family ends up paying several thousand dollars a year above its income taxes to help foot the bill.[6] Equipment mandated by the federal government, for example, adds hundreds of dollars to the average price of a new car and thousands to the price of a new house. And this cost does not include the enormous amount of paperwork generated. One governmental commission established to study the problem claimed that the federal bureaucracy issues enough regulations and documents each year to fill a number of major league baseball stadiums.[7]

To make matters worse, federal regulators occasionally have been shown to be inconsistent and inept. In the early 1970s, for example, the Consumer Product Safety Commission (CPSC) demanded that children's sleepwear be treated with flame-retardant chemicals such as Tris. The requirement immediately resulted in a 20 percent price hike in children's pajamas, imposed by manufacturers to cover the added expense of treatment. Then, several years later, the same commission, concerned about reports that Tris was a suspected cancer-causing agent, banned the use of the chemical in children's sleepwear. It was unable to explain to parents why they had been required earlier to pay higher prices to expose their children to a potential carcinogen.

An even more serious criticism of the regulatory bureaucracy is that it fails to do enough for the consumer. Despite the occasional heroism of a Dr. Kelsey, federal agencies have not responded quickly and effectively enough to many of the harmful products that show up in the marketplace. The CPSC, for example, issued mandatory safety standards for only three kinds of products from 1973 to 1978: swimming pool slides, architectural glass, and matchbook covers.[8] In view of the fact that an estimated 20 million Americans are injured or killed annually by defective products, the commission's limited actions during those five years hardly demonstrated a high commitment to consumer safety.

Many observers also fault bureaucratic agencies for failure to respond strongly and quickly enough to such problems as waste management, especially in the nuclear power industry. Toxic wastes continue to contaminate the environment. Leakage from nuclear power plants is a constant threat. Perhaps no event in recent times has more effectively dramatized the absence of adequate regulatory controls than the Three Mile Island nuclear reactor accident near Middletown, Pennsylvania, in April 1979. Over a period of days, radioactive steam periodically escaped from the nuclear plant into the surrounding atmosphere, prompting thousands of local residents to flee the area. As nuclear power foes had argued for years, the industry's fail-safe systems proved to be as fallible as the humans who designed and operated them. The reactor accident cast a shadow not only over the future of the nuclear power industry but also over the performance of the Nuclear Regulatory Commission (NRC), which is charged with licensing and inspecting all commercial power reactors. Critics argued that the NRC was aware of design flaws at Three Mile Island and had been lax about safety standards at nuclear plants around the country. They charged that NRC inspectors tended to rely too heavily on test results provided by the builders of the nuclear plants and not enough on independent on-site investigations. The General Accounting Office (GAO), a watchdog agency responsible to Congress, joined the chorus of criticism, chastising the NRC for not requiring detailed emergency and evacuation plans. The Chernobyl nuclear reactor disaster in the Soviet Union in 1986, when radioactive material escaped into the atmosphere to contaminate neighboring European countries, further increased demand for more careful regulatory oversight of the nuclear industry in the United States.

One common explanation for bureaucratic inaction is that regulatory agencies are often too close to the industries they regulate. The NRC, FDA, and other regulatory commissions have been staffed at the highest levels with former industry members who compromise the independence of the commissions' decision making. (A study by Common Cause, for example, revealed that 65 percent of NRC staffers had been employed by companies licensed by or holding contracts with

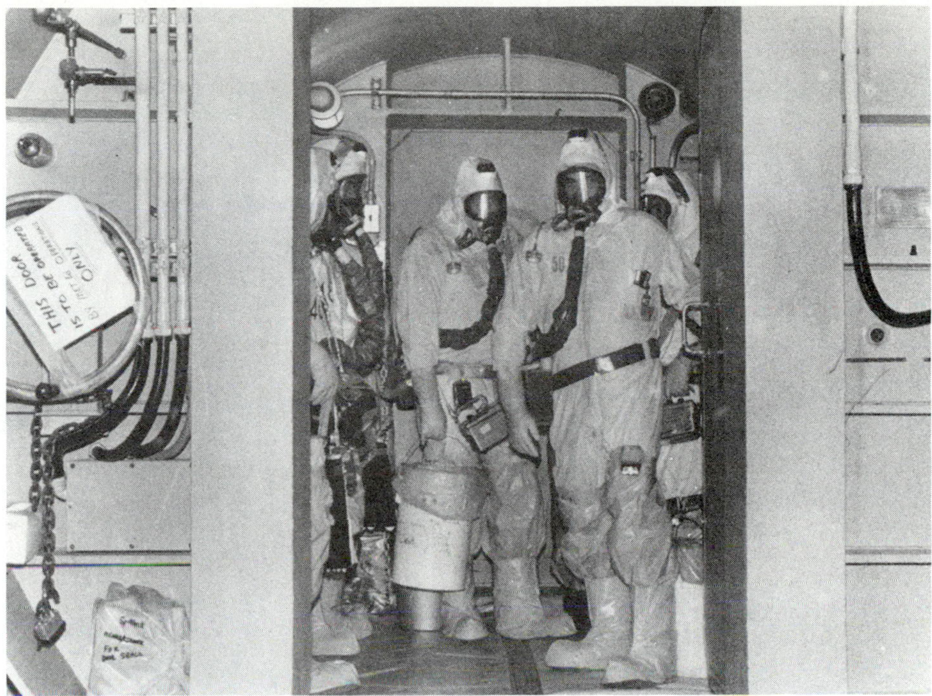

★ Technicians in protective gear enter the Three Mile Island nuclear facility following the worst nuclear accident in U.S. history, an accident some critics blamed on inadequate oversight by the Nuclear Regulatory Commission.

the commission.) Here we see one of the paradoxes of a modern bureaucracy. In many cases, only the people who have been directly involved in a particular industry have the level of technical expertise necessary to oversee that industry. Yet, while we desire expertise in the bureaucracy, we also want impartial public servants.

These regulatory officials often enjoy the support of key members of congressional committees who are sympathetic to the industries they regulate. Together they form two legs of an "iron triangle": bureaucrats, members of Congress, and industry lobbyists.[9] Although a major function of regulatory agencies is to provide private industry with central services, such as maintaining a healthy climate of competition and arbitrating disputes, the interests of ordinary citizens have often been slighted or overlooked. Instead of championing the rights of consumers, regulatory agencies have often served as defenders of the industries they are supposed to oversee, protecting the interests of their client groups. This allegation, of course, is not reserved for purely regulatory agencies. The Defense Department, among others, has also been accused of having too close and friendly a relationship with the enormous corporations that supply the military.

Some regulators insist, however, that they are not given enough support by the White House and Congress to meet their responsibilities. This concern became especially evident during the Reagan administration, when many agencies saw their staffs and budgets slashed. Early in his first term, Reagan established a Task Force on Regulatory Relief, headed by Vice-President George Bush, to find ways to cut

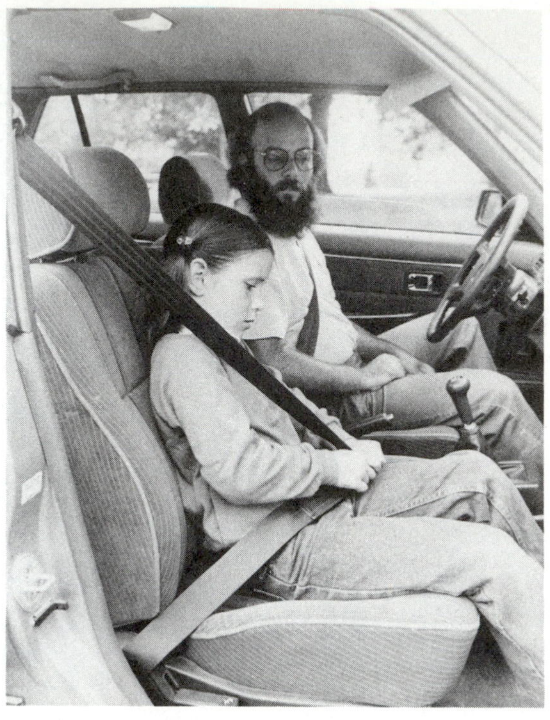

★ Requiring automobile companies to install seatbelts in their cars is an example of federal regulatory efforts to improve auto safety. While many Americans applaud these actions, others express concern about preserving freedom of choice.

back on the flow and cost of regulations. One target was the CPSC, which eventually saw its staff cut from 975 employees in 1981 to 519 in 1988. Its annual budget during the same period fell from $42 million to $34 million—roughly equivalent to the cost of operating the Defense Department for one hour. The result of such cuts is that bureaucrats can become caught in the middle between political ideology and public demands for product safety. While the public clamors for more consumer protection, bureaucrats claim they are unable to obtain sufficient funds and staffs to carry the added load. The FDA, for example, may take several years to complete the testing of a new drug. Since hundreds of new drugs are submitted for approval each year and thousands of other drugs are already on the market, the pressure to satisfy all parties is simply too great to bear under present conditions.

Moreover, regulators argue, they are constantly dealing with highly charged issues of individual rights. The growing demand for consumer protection has brought with it the contradictory criticism that regulatory agencies are intruding too much into people's lives. For each person who demands greater passenger protection in the event of an auto accident, there is another who resents a seat belt that must be buckled before the car will start. For example, the FDA's disapproval of the cancer drug Laetrile prompted enormous controversy during the late 1970s. While the FDA claimed that the drug (derived from apricot pits) had little medical value and refused to certify it, Laetrile supporters insisted that cancer patients should have the freedom to use it if their doctor approved. (Before he died of cancer, the film star Steve McQueen, among others, sought medical treatment with the drug in Mexico, where it is legally prescribed.) The controversy was sufficiently intense to inspire nearly a dozen states to try to bypass the FDA by legalizing the drug within their boundaries.

Finally, many issues and concerns expressed by Americans cannot be readily dealt with by federal agencies alone because the problems are global in scope. For

The Bald Eagle: A Government Success Story

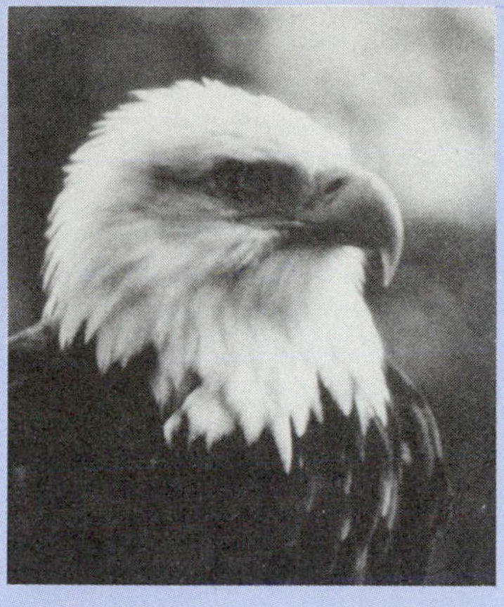

★ The bald eagle.

Despite frequent criticisms of government agencies and their programs, there are occasional success stories. America's national symbol, the bald eagle, once on the brink of extinction, has rebounded dramatically, thanks in large measure to the federal endangered-species program. Working with state agencies and private organizations, federal officials have stepped up efforts to enforce stiff sentences for poachers, to mount publicity campaigns, and to ban such pesticides as DDT, which damage the birds' eggs. By 1989, more than two thousand breeding pairs of bald eagles—up from about eight hundred in 1960—soared in the skies over the continental United States. Though more than three hundred domestic animal species remain on the endangered list, other species besides the bald eagle—among them the gray wolf, the peregrine falcon, and the grizzly bear—have similarly seen their chances for survival greatly improve as a result of the efforts of government agencies. ★

example, concerns that the rising incidence of skin cancer among Americans may be due in part to the depletion of the earth's ozone layer, which helps filter out harmful solar rays, cannot be addressed solely on the domestic front. Many other nations besides the United States have become dependent on the use of chlorofluorocarbons, which are believed to be contributing to the ozone depletion. International cooperation to ban the use of chlorofluorocarbons is required.

The same frustration can be found in other areas as well—in efforts to prevent the extinction of animal species outside U.S. borders, to halt the deforestation of tropical rain forests, to preserve the great whales, and to guard against contamination of the world's shorelines by oil spilled from supertankers. In an increasingly interdependent world, many hard questions must be addressed. Are we Americans willing to pay the added costs required to confront these and other threats on a global scale? Are we prepared and willing to hand government agencies even greater power and discretion to do so? Should we, in fact, as a nation attempt to tell, or even force, other nations to clean up their act, in the same way a federal agency may confront and punish a negligent corporation for marketing a defective product or polluting a domestic river? If we are indeed a global community, how far do we go to regulate matters of interest to us all?

In the final analysis, people's attitudes toward governmental regulation and the bureaucracy in general tend to reflect their political views or personal experiences. Those who deplore in principle any large-scale regulation of free enterprise, for example, will continue to object to the government's butting into business activities, no matter how many instances of corporate insensitivity are cited. Similarly, those who have been hassled or mistreated by the Postal Service, the IRS, or any other bureaucratic agency will not be enthusiastic about expanding governmental influence over their lives. Some people even see the activities of governmental regulators as an insufficient response to the basic defects of a capitalist economy. Merely banning an occasional product or slapping a few industrialists' wrists will not dramatically alter the deficiencies of the present economic system.

★ Bureaucracy in a Changing World: Hidden Consequences

In many respects, bureaucracy and regulation are necessary evils, providing less than perfect mechanisms to implement public policy. Along with the problems of size, inefficiency, and a sometimes too cozy relationship between the regulators and the regulated, there are many less obvious ways a large bureaucracy can affect American politics. A dramatic example of how bureaucracy can influence the smooth operation of government can be found in the foreign policy arena.

In October 1962 the Soviet Union began to install offensive missiles in Cuba, putting the threat of atomic attack less than one hundred miles from Florida. The resulting Cuban missile crisis was one of the most dangerous periods in American history (see chap. 19). With the aid of hindsight, scholars have learned a great deal about the way American leaders responded to the crisis, including the part played by the bureaucracy.

In our study of government we generally assume that policy making is a rational process. By "rational" we mean that decision making takes place through a logical sequence. It begins with identification of the problem and continues with consideration of alternative courses of action, a choice of the most appropriate action, and finally the implementation of policy. The officials involved in the decision are also considered rational in that they come to agree on what is best for the nation and are not distracted by personal or partisan concerns. In this model of decision making, the national interest is foremost in each official's mind.

This image of government decision making was seriously challenged in Graham T. Allison's ground-breaking study of the Cuban missile crisis, *Essence of Decision.*[10] In looking at government procedures before and during the crisis, Allison found that bureaucracy can affect the development of policy in many ways. One such influence involves bureaucracy's reliance on **standard operating procedures (SOPs)**. SOPs are often the heart and soul of large governmental organizations; things must be done "by the book." SOPs abound because predictable, regulated action is presumed to be the key to a smoothly running bureaucracy. SOPs had a curious effect on the evolution of the Cuban missile crisis.

Once Soviet leaders had decided to risk putting missiles in Cuba, the job of installation was turned over to the military and intelligence bureaucracies. Assuming that secrecy was a major priority (to prevent a U.S. attack before the missiles became operational), the Soviets made obvious blunders in carrying out their assignment. Working by the book, the technicians designed and built missile sites similar to those already in existence in the Soviet Union. The use of proven methods may have been efficient, but it also made discovery of the Cuban sites easier for American intelligence officials already familiar with Soviet medium-range missile installations. Once American U-2 spy planes photographed the sites, it was fairly easy to determine that the Soviets were not building swimming pools or tennis courts in Cuba.

SOPs also influenced America's response to the installation of the missiles. According to Allison, information about the missiles was not made available to President Kennedy until about three weeks after intelligence officials suspected their presence in Cuba. The reasons for this delay were clearly bureaucratic:

> The job of intelligence requires an incredibly complex organization, coordinating large numbers of actors, processing endless piles of information. That this organization must function according to established routines and standard procedures is a simple fact. . . . Information does not pass from the tentacle to the top of the organization instantaneously. Facts can be "in the system" without being available to the head of the organization.[11]

Thus the intelligence bureaucracy, with its cautious reliance on well-worn procedures, allowed the president little time to respond before the missiles would become operational.

America's response to the Soviet threat was shaped not only by the structure of the bureaucracy but also by competition among the various departments and agencies involved in the crisis. Once evidence of the missiles' presence began to mount, a disagreement flared between the CIA and the Air Force over who should fly the U-2 spy mission over Cuba. This disagreement was based, in Allison's view, not solely on a rational assessment of the relative merits of CIA and Air Force pilots, but also on the desire of each organization to promote its own interest and image before the public. Competition between government organizations is a subtle factor that continues to influence American politics.

We are all aware of friendly interservice rivalry, played out in the Army–Navy football game and by many other means. But friendly competition can give way to empire building and a tendency to confuse the welfare of the organization with the welfare of the nation. In the Cuban missile crisis, Allison found the various branches of the military competed for the honor of destroying the missile sites, and their recommendations sometimes seemed to be influenced more by organizational self-interest than by the quest for the most rational solution. "The 'leaders' who sit on top of organizations are not a monolithic group," he wrote. "Rather, each individual in this group is, in his own right, a player in a central game. The name of the game is politics: bargaining along regularized circuits among players positioned hierarchically within the government."[12]

Allison's revelation of bureaucratic in-fighting may not be surprising, except that it occured during a crisis of global importance. Americans are well aware of organizational rivalry at the workplace, at school, and in social clubs as well as in Washington. As we have noted, politics often involves competition for scarce resources. Obtaining a large budget and taking on prestigious tasks can become goals that rival the organization's basic responsibilities. Bureaucracies can take on a life of their own with their own expectations, norms of behavior, and political battles. The task of balancing bureaucratic politics with the responsibility of carrying out public policy (while cutting through the red tape of standard operating procedures) is a continuing challenge for both government agencies and the American people.

★ Who Controls the Bureaucracy?

As we have seen, there is the view that the bureaucracy is an omnipotent force in its own right, a powerful and independent "fourth branch" of government elected by and seemingly accountable to no one. With its army of obedient officials, it reaches into every corner of our society, creating and enforcing rules that sometimes bear little relation to reason or justice. How valid is this view? Does it represent an accurate portrait of the federal bureaucracy?

It can be argued that such a view exaggerates the power and independence of the bureaucracy by ignoring the important interplay of political forces in our society. In light of the checks and balances in the American political system, bureaucratic agencies can hardly remain immune to the influences of other governmental and political interests. As participants in the policy-making process, bureaucratic agencies must share power with other governmental institutions and be subject to legal and political restraints.

Congress, for example, not only has the constitutional authority to set up the agencies in the first place; it also holds the power of the purse. Congress regulates the flow of money to pay for bureaucrats' salaries and paper clips, and thus can doom agencies and programs by cutting off their funds. Moreover, through appropriations hearings and special investigations, members of Congress can review the activities of bureaucratic agencies and amend the laws under which they operate.

These congressional restraints are supplemented by others imposed by the White House. Though the president can hardly keep a close watch on thousands of administrators, he does screen all agency requests for funds through the Office of Management and Budget (OMB). He can appoint and remove many key officials, and, together with Congress, can reorganize or eliminate federal agencies.

Even the courts have an impact, albeit a more limited one, on bureaucratic behavior. The courts can overturn a regulatory action if it is not in accord with the law the agency is supposed to enforce. Just as the courts can exercise the power of judicial review over the actions of the president and Congress, they can impose their will on administrators. Indeed, many citizens who believe they have been wronged by an administrative act have successfully challenged agency rules and procedures in the courts.

There are other checks as well, including the influence of powerful interest groups, the press and public opinion, and even—as some observers have noted—the professional norms and conduct of the bureaucrats themselves.[13] In fact, it can be argued that if the bureaucracy has not been adequately restrained, it is because the president and Congress have been lax in exercising control. Congress frequently has been accused of incompetence in carrying out its legislative oversight responsibilities. Bureaucratic irregularities and mismanagement often slip by unnoticed or are tacitly accepted by members of Congress, who are too involved in legislative and other pursuits to deal with them. As one scholar has noted, even in cases "where the public interest and a committee-defined constitutional mandate

© Signe Wilkinson

govern committee roles, there is still little, if any, systematic concern for comprehensive oversight."[14]

A balance, of course, must be struck between responsiveness and responsibility. A bureaucracy that surrenders all of its autonomy to elected officials can pose almost as much danger as one that shows its independence. As the Watergate and Iran-Contra investigations revealed, there is always a danger that a president may abuse his influence over such agencies as the Internal Revenue Service, National Security Council, Central Intelligence Agency, Department of State, and Federal Bureau of Investigation by setting them against his political opponents or circumventing the will of Congress. Without proper limits on the compliance of the bureaucracy with the directives of elected officials, citizens could face the double threat of an imperial presidency aligned with an omnipotent bureaucracy.

The bureaucracy, for all its growth and influence, cannot prevail on its own. It can grow and multiply only with the consent of the White House and Congress. If the president and Congress should decide to trim the bureaucracy, to scrap certain agencies or reform their procedures, the constitutional authority exists for them to do so. As the elected representatives of the people, they must carry the major responsibility for the character and performance of the federal bureaucracy.

★ Taking On the Bureaucracy: Citizen Access to Federal Agencies

During the past two decades, citizens and public interest groups have intensified their efforts to influence bureaucratic decision making. Citizens have descended on governmental agencies in growing numbers to demand fuller participation in their proceedings.[15]

Because bureaucrats are not elected at the polls, broadened citizen participation has long been advocated as a way to improve bureaucratic responsiveness and accountability. Direct citizen involvement—through advisory boards, public

The Freedom of Information Act and the Privacy Act

38 *The CIA and the Cult of Intelligence*

events of another country is frequently the stimulus that either sparks the CIA into action or permits its operators to launch a dubious operation. Only then does the apparatus get into motion; only then do the analysts become meaningless. But "only then" means "almost always."

Tactics

In his talk at the Council on Foreign Relations, Bissell listed eight types of covert action, eight different ways that the CIA intervenes in the domestic affairs of other nations:

> (1) political advice and counsel; (2) subsidies to an individual; (3) financial support and "technical assistance" to political parties; (4) support of private organizations, including labor unions, business firms, cooperatives, etc.; (5) covert propaganda; (6) "private" training of individuals and exchange of persons; (7) economic operations; and (8) paramilitary [or] political action operations designed to overthrow or to support a regime (like the Bay of Pigs and the program in Laos). These operations can be classified in various ways: by the degree and type of secrecy required by their legality, and, perhaps, by their benign or hostile character.

Bissell's fifth and eighth categories—covert propaganda and paramilitary operations—are so large, so important, that they will be discussed at length in later chapters; they are, as well, somewhat self-defining. But the other six categories need some explanation at this point.

The first three categories—political advice and counsel, subsidies to an individual, and financial support and technical assistance to political parties—are usually so closely related that they are nearly impossible to separate.

8 LINES DELETED

The reporters who covered that affair on April 10, 1971, apparently failed to notice anything unusual about the guests. Seated in the State Dining Room at long white tables forming a large E was the usual assortment of foreign dignitaries, high U.S. government officials, and corporate executives

The Clandestine Theory 39

who had become fixtures at such occasions during the Nixon years. The guest list supplied by the White House Press office gave the titles and positions for almost all the diners.

19 ½ LINES DELETED

years later, he was elected mayor of West Berlin. Throughout this period,

8 ½ LINES DELETED

He was a hard-working politician in Allied-occupied Berlin, and his goal of making the Social Democratic party a viable alternative to communism

15 LINES DELETED

And that evening after dinner, singer Pearl Bailey entertained the White House crowd in the East Room. The *Washington Post* reported the next day that she had "rocked" the White House. *During the same Cold War years . . . the CIA . . . was also secretly funding and providing technical assistance . . . to the Christian Democratic party . . . in Italy. Most of these payments were terminated in the 1950s, . . .*

In certain countries where the CIA has been particularly active, the agency's chief of station (COS) maintains closer ties with the head of state than does the U.S. ambassador. Usually, the ambassador is kept informed of the business transacted between the COS (who is officially subordinate to the ambassador) and the head of state (to whom the ambassador is officially accredited as the personal representative of the President of the United States). But Bissell mentioned cases in which the CIA's relationship with the local head of state was so special that the American ambassador was not informed of any of the details, because either the Secretary of State or the head of the host government preferred that the ambassador be kept ignorant of the relationships.

A notable example of such a "special relationship" is Iran, where a CIA organized coup d'etat restored the Shah to power in 1953. . . .

Still another example of a country where the CIA enjoys a special relationship is Nationalist China. In Taiwan, however,

★ These two pages from *The CIA and the Cult of Intelligence* show that the publisher deliberately left large blank spaces to indicate the locations and amount of material deleted by the CIA.

SOURCE: *The CIA and the Cult of Intelligence* by Victor Marchetti and John D. Marks. Copyright © 1974, 1980 by Victor Marchetti and John D. Marks. Reprinted by permission of Alfred A. Knopf, Inc.

Government agencies, such as the FBI, the IRS, the CIA, and the Census Bureau, traditionally have been able to decide what information they will release to the public. In 1966, however, Congress passed the Freedom of Information Act, which requires federal agencies to make documents and records available to citizens who request them, unless the material falls into one of nine exempted categories. Exempted from disclosure, for example, are personnel and medical files, sensitive national security information, and criminal investigation records.

In 1974, Congress amended the act (over President Ford's veto) to make it even stronger. Agencies are now required to reply to requests within ten working days and to charge reasonable fees for the information they provide. These amendments were designed to discourage agencies from dragging their feet in response to requests and from charging expensive "search fees" to discourage requests for documents. Citizens are permitted to appeal to the courts if an agency refuses to comply; and it is up to the agency to prove that information should be withheld for national security or other reasons.

Congress also passed the Privacy Act of 1974 to protect citizens from invasions of privacy by federal agencies. It permits individuals to inspect personal records about them compiled by government agencies and to challenge or correct any inaccurate information. It also prohibits an agency from making an individual's file available to other agencies without that individual's consent.

Although these two acts have given reporters, public interest groups, and ordinary citizens greater access to government agencies, they have not been entirely successful in encouraging disclosure of information to the public. Agencies have been successful in limiting the types of information officials and former officials can release about their experiences while they served in the government.

Former officials of the CIA, for example, must submit any manuscripts about their work in the murky world of intelligence and covert operations for censorship before publication. In 1972, when a former CIA employee, Victor Marchetti, teamed with the writer John D. Marks to produce an account of his work as a CIA operative, the government went to court to prevent its publication. The government based its case on the fact that all CIA employees sign a contract when they accept employment, agreeing to submit for review anything they may write. Marchetti responded that censorship would violate his First Amendment right of free speech. The court, agreeing that the issue was the contract and not the First Amendment, allowed the CIA to censor Marchetti's manuscript. The book, *The CIA and the Cult of Intelligence,* was finally published in 1974. ★

hearings, and local councils—is thought to contribute to better decision making by exposing administrators to a broader range of views. Although there is always a danger that such labels as "public interest," "consumer," and "environmental" may be abused by individuals and groups in pursuit of their own selfish aims, positive benefits are seen in admitting people who speak for a variety of public concerns into agency proceedings.

During most of this century, participation in bureaucratic decision making was limited primarily to well-heeled corporate interests. Legal and financial obstacles tended to prevent other groups from gaining access to federal agencies so that they could voice their concerns. But in the mid-1960s, a series of court rulings defined new rights of citizen participation. Federal agencies were ordered to admit citizen groups into more of their proceedings. These court rulings were bolstered by legislation authorizing financial support for citizen groups that wanted to participate in certain regulatory areas, such as those partly covered by the Federal Trade Commission, the Environmental Protection Agency, and the Consumer Product Safety Commission. The community action programs started in the 1960s also provided federal grants to encourage the "maximum feasible participation" of the poor in local antipoverty programs, while a few agencies set up special in-house advocacy units to represent consumer and other interests.

More recently, efforts have been made to improve citizen access to all federal agencies and to provide additional financial support for people who want a voice in bureaucratic decision making. Despite past court rulings and legislation, many citizens still cannot afford the attorneys' fees and other expenses that are sometimes necessary to penetrate the bureaucracy and compete effectively against well-financed corporate interests. In 1978, President Carter pushed for legislation to help citizens cover the costs of participating in federal agency proceedings. The money would go to citizens and groups, such as the elderly, consumers, and small business interests, who represent important segments of the community but who do not have sufficient funds to promote their cause on an ongoing basis. Not surprisingly, Carter's proposal was endorsed by such groups as Common Cause, the Consumers' Union, and the National Council of Senior Citizens. Opposing it were the National Association of Manufacturers, the Grocery Manufacturers of America, and several utility and nuclear power firms. The proposal gained little support in either the House or the Senate and died a quiet death in committee.

Many people doubt their ability to influence the federal bureaucracy, with or without financial assistance. Apart from the high costs, one needs time and expertise to become effectively involved. The rule-making process of a federal agency is often lengthy and complicated, requiring great patience and the ability to master the procedural maze. In view of the usual pressures of working at a full-time job and supporting a family, the average citizen, if he or she is to become involved at all, may find it difficult to do more than testify at a local hearing or dash off an occasional letter to an administrator.

Even people who have participated in the process have sometimes come away disillusioned. Citizens who have testified at agency hearings or have even gained representation on advisory and policy-making boards have complained of not being taken seriously. Their feeling has been that administrators do not value citizen input as much as the information obtained from special interests and community leaders. In fact, some observers believe that agencies often use citizen participation to gain public support for their policies and to co-opt or pacify potential forces of opposition.

Indeed, citizen participation in bureaucratic decision making still has a long way to progress. Citizen groups that wish to sway the minds and hearts of bureaucrats will have to continue to press for greater access and for more support from government. And there is every indication they will do so. As long as bureaucratic agencies affect the quality of so many American lives, there will be demands for more citizen participation in agency deliberations.

★ Reform of the Bureaucracy

The growing concern over the inefficiencies, unresponsiveness, and excesses of bureaucracy has inspired numerous proposals for reform. Some of these proposals have been offered by people who see the "capture" of federal agencies by private industry as the primary obstacle to effective regulation. They have suggested that Congress adopt more rigorous conflict-of-interest laws and that more consumer-oriented officials be recruited outside of private industry.

Other suggestions have been offered by people who want more controls on government spending. One proposal has been to expand the use of **zero-base budgeting,** which requires agencies to defend every dollar they plan to spend each fiscal year, not just request increases over last year's appropriations. Another has been to adopt the kinds of **sunset laws** used in several states, which require agencies to justify their existence every few years or face abolition.

There have even been moves toward whittling down the number of regulations and rewriting them in plainer English. In the late 1970s, for example, the Federal Trade Commission, traditionally one of the worst enemies of the English language, hired Rudolph Flesch, the author of *Why Johnny Can't Read,* as a consultant to work on its regulations. His job was to eliminate the linguistic gobbledygook that infests so many documents and letters to citizens. In an agency where such phrases as "ongoing collaborative discussion revision process" are thrown around, his assigned task was monumental.

The most dramatic calls for reform have come from critics who wish to see the structure of the federal bureaucracy overhauled. Among these critics was Jimmy Carter, who pledged to do something about "the horrible Washington bureaucracy" if he was elected. After taking office, he persuaded Congress to extend the Reorganization Act of 1949, which had expired in 1973. The act, originally proposed by President Truman, authorized the president to submit plans for reshaping the federal bureaucracy, subject to congressional veto. Presidents from Truman to Nixon had used the act to create new federal agencies, such as the Office of Management and Budget (OMB) and the Environmental Protection Agency (EPA), and to try to extend presidential control over the bureaucracy by reshuffling the lines of authority. Though most of their plans were approved by Congress, they did not greatly simplify the operations of government. Carter hoped that by reinstating presidential authority to reorganize the executive branch, he would succeed where others had failed. He intended to streamline the bureaucracy by making deep cuts in the number of agencies and to improve governmental efficiency.

Certainly few dispassionate observers of the bureaucracy dispute the need for reorganization. Demands for revamping the bureaucracy have ranged from decentralization of decision making to consolidation of administrative functions into fewer agencies. Perhaps the greatest impetus for reform has been the overlap-

Gobbledygook

Bureaucracies are known for issuing memos and regulations that are impossible to understand. In fact, every issue of *The Washington Monthly* includes a "memo of the month," sent in by an amused bureaucrat who wants to share some governmental wisdom. Here is one such memo:

FM BROADCAST APPLICATIONS
ACCEPTED FOR FILING AND
NOTIFICATION OF
CUT-OFF DATE
Report no. B-36
Released: March 21, 1983
CUT-OFF DATE: April 29, 1983

NOTICE is hereby given that the applications listed in the attached appendix are accepted for filing. Because the applications listed in the attached appendix are in conflict with applications which were accepted for filing and listed previously as subject to a cut-off date for conflicting applications, no application which would be in conflict with the applications listed in the attached appendix will be accepted for filing. ★

SOURCE: *Washington Monthly,* June 1983.

ping and duplicating efforts of various agencies and departments. "Examples of mission redundancy," notes one observer, "abound within national administration. . . . The Federal Trade Commission and the Justice Department have jurisdiction in the anti-trust field. The Justice Department shares civil rights enforcement authority with the Civil Rights Commission. Jurisdiction over the airwaves is divided between the Federal Aviation Agency and the Civil Aeronautics Board."[16] Sometimes the competition and overlap reach absurd levels. In one case, the Occupational Safety and Health Administration (OSHA) ordered all vehicles used on work sites to be equipped with back-up beepers. The order was then challenged by the Environmental Protection Agency (EPA) because the beepers made too much noise.[17]

Yet resistance to change has also been marked. Many groups in and out of government have established firm ties to existing agencies and regard proposals for reorganization as a potential threat to their influence. In the early 1970s, for instance, President Nixon proposed to combine seven cabinet departments (Agriculture; Commerce; Health, Education, and Welfare; Housing and Urban Development; Interior; Labor; and Transportation) into four new superdepartments organized in such broad categories as Community Development, Economic Affairs, Human Resources, and Natural Resources. His plan ran into such strong opposition from interest groups and Congress that it was dropped.

President Carter tried to soften the opposition to his own reorganization plans by courting key legislators and interest groups in advance of his proposed reforms. In his eagerness to trim bureaucratic waste, he eliminated close to five hundred advisory committees, including the Board of Tea Exports, the Condor Advisory Committee, and even the National Peanut Advisory Committee. He also reduced the number of units within the executive office and, as we saw earlier, reorganized the Civil Service Commission. In 1978 he also signed a bill gradually phasing out the Civil Aeronautics Board (CAB), which regulated the routes and fares of interstate airlines. The bill was passed to reduce governmental restraints on free-market competition among passenger airlines, allowing them to drop (or raise) fares and scrap unprofitable routes.

In 1979, Carter considered a major reorganization of governmental agencies concerned with economic assistance, education, and natural resources. He persuaded Congress to create a separate Department of Education, removing it from

the Department of Health, Education and Welfare (renamed the Department of Health and Human Services). Carter's most publicized achievement, however, was the creation of a new Department of Energy in 1977. The new department absorbed dozens of energy-related functions spread throughout the federal government. It consolidated the Energy Research and Development Administration (ERDA), the Federal Power Commission (FPC), and the Federal Energy Administration (FEA). It also absorbed the energy-related functions of several cabinet departments, including those of Defense, Interior, and Commerce.

Yet, as a sign of the continuing controversy surrounding reorganization, the new Energy Department quickly drew fire. Before the department could even obtain office space for its new employees, doubts were expressed whether lumping separate energy functions into a single package was a good idea after all. A spokesman for the environmental group Friends of the Earth commented, "We don't believe the creation of this superagency will provide anything except a monolithic structure that is much bigger, more rigid, and more inaccessible to the public than the existing energy agencies."[18] During his first term in office, President Reagan vowed to get rid of the Department of Energy, as well as the Department of Education. But his threat did not materialize. In fact, he elevated the Veterans Administration to cabinet status, creating a new department in his second term.

As a presidential candidate, Reagan had also pledged to do something about the bloated federal bureaucracy. Unlike Carter, however, he made few changes in the structure of the bureaucracy itself. And despite his commitment to reduce the regulation of the economy, he did little to eliminate or reorganize the regulatory agencies. As we will see in chapter 18, Reagan's efforts were directed mainly at trimming the budgets and personnel of the agencies, and at appointing officials who could be counted on to cut back on the number of regulations issued and to limit their enforcement. As a result, with smaller staffs and less incentive to regulate industry, federal agencies under the Reagan administration made fewer inspections and issued fewer citations for violations in the areas of environmental protection, worker safety, and consumer affairs than they had issued under Reagan's predecessors.

The problems of reorganization are complex and perhaps are unlikely to be resolved. Observers who desire multiple routes of access to bureaucratic decision making will continue to suspect plans to combine separate agencies into one monolithic agency. Likewise, those who attack the overlapping and competitive efforts of separate agencies will continue to criticize any presidential failure to pursue a course of consolidation. Although the needs of both groups may not be mutually exclusive, differing perceptions of what reorganization means in terms of efficiency and responsiveness will probably continue to stall sweeping reform of the bureaucracy.

★ Summary

The bureaucracy has become a major force in American politics. In the federal government, "bureaucracy" refers principally to the executive agencies and departments under the president's command which carry out the laws passed by Congress. Interestingly, the Constitution says very little about the bureaucracy. The framers did not anticipate the enormous growth in the sizes and numbers of the agencies that would be created to deal with modern problems and the demands placed on government by its citizens.

As the bureaucracy has grown over the decades, so has the concern about its staffing. Before the Civil War, presidents usually appointed people to the bureaucracy on the basis of political loyalty. Today, although the most important positions are still filled by the president on the basis of party loyalty or other political criteria, most federal employees are hired on a nonpartisan basis through the civil service system.

Since the Constitution does not clearly spell out how the federal bureaucracy should be organized, it has been left to the president and Congress to establish the various types of agencies. In general, the federal bureaucracy consists of four basic groups: the cabinet-level departments, the independent agencies, the government corporations, and the regulatory commissions. Each group has certain features that distinguish it from the others.

At various times the bureaucracy has been criticized for its large size, enormous expenditures, overlapping responsibilities, inconsistencies, and intrusions into people's lives. The regulatory commissions have been especially controversial. Some observers insist that the commissions play an essential role in protecting citizens from corporate and other abuses, while others insist that their powers are too sweeping and need to be curtailed. In the final analysis, bureaucratic agencies must share power with other governmental institutions and are subject to legal and political restraints. In the years to come, we can expect continued demands for reform of the federal bureaucracy, ranging from more controls on spending to a sweeping reorganization or elimination of many existing agencies.

★ Key Terms

bureaucracy
civil service
executive department
government corporation
independent agency
regulatory commission
spoils system
Standard Operating Procedures (SOPs)
sunset laws
zero-base budgeting

★ Notes

1. C. Northcote Parkinson, *Parkinson's Law* (Boston: Houghton Mifflin, 1957), p. 2.
2. *International Encyclopedia of the Social Sciences,* 2d ed. (New York: Free Press, 1977), 2:206.
3. U.S. Department of State, *Atlas of United States Foreign Relations,* 2d ed. (Washington, D.C.: U.S. Government Printing Office, December 1985), pp. 79–81.
4. U.S. Bureau of the Census, *Statistical Abstract of the United States, 1989* (Washington, D.C.: U.S. Government Printing Office, 1989), p. 318.
5. See *Newsweek,* March 13, 1978, p. 26; *U.S. News & World Report,* March 13, 1978, pp. 21–24.
6. *U.S. News & World Report,* June 30, 1975, p. 24.
7. *Time,* January 2, 1978, p. 48.
8. *Congressional Quarterly Weekly Report,* February 18, 1978, p. 391.
9. See, for example, Douglass Cater, *Power in Washington* (New York: Pegasus, 1969).
10. Graham T. Allison, *The Essence of Decision: Explaining the Cuban Missile Crisis* (Boston: Little, Brown, 1971).
11. Ibid., pp. 118–120.
12. Ibid., p. 144.
13. See, for example, W. Lloyd Warner et al., *The American Federal Executive* (New Haven, Conn.: Yale University Press, 1963).
14. William L. Morrow, *Public Administration* (New York: Random House, 1975), p. 114.
15. See, for example, "Symposium on Neighborhoods and Citizen Involvement," *Public Administration Review* 32 (May/June 1972).
16. Morrow, *Public Administration,* p. 84.
17. *Newsweek,* December 15, 1975, p. 35.
18. Quoted in *Newsweek,* July 11, 1977, p. 59.

★ For Further Reading

Bryner, Gary S. *Bureaucratic Discretion.* New York: Pergamon, 1987.

Derthick, Martha, and Paul J. Quirk. *The Politics of Deregulation.* Washington, D.C.: Brookings Institution, 1985.

Fritschler, A. Lee. *Smoking and Politics: Policy-Making and the Federal Bureaucracy.* Englewood Cliffs, N.J.: Prentice-Hall, 1983.

Goodsell, Charles T. *The Case for Bureaucracy,* 2d ed. Chatham, N.J.: Chatham House, 1985.

Michael, James R., ed. *Working on the System: A Comprehensive Manual for Citizen Access to Federal Agencies.* New York: Basic Books, 1974.

Pressman, Jeffrey, and Aaron Wildavsky. *Implementation,* 3d ed. Berkeley: University of California Press, 1984.

Rourke, Francis E. *Bureaucracy, Politics, and Public Policy,* 3d ed. Boston: Little, Brown, 1984.

Seidman, Harold, and Robert S. Gilmour. *Politics, Position, and Power,* 4th ed. New York: Oxford University Press, 1986.

Wilson, James Q. *The Politics of Regulation.* New York: Basic Books, 1980.

Scarcely any political question arises in the United States that is not resolved, sooner or later, into a judicial question.

—*Alexis de Tocqueville*

CHAPTER FIFTEEN

JUDICIARY

★★★★★★★★★★★

Politicians in Black Robes: The Judicial Branch

Many Americans who are disgusted by politicians and bureaucrats retain a certain reverence for the Supreme Court. In contrast to members of Congress, presidents, and lobbyists, who appear to be locked forever in partisan battle, the robed justices who sit on the high bench—though certainly not immune to controversy—are seen to tower above the usual pettiness and strife of political ambition. If public opinion polls are to be believed, the justices of the Supreme Court have enjoyed greater prestige and public confidence than any other officials in government.[1]

Yet, while the popular image of Supreme Court justices may suggest an aloofness from partisan politics, the justices are as much practitioners of political art as any other elected or appointed officials. Indeed, they must be viewed in the same light as presidents and members of Congress: as individuals who have achieved positions of power and whose exercise of that power is guided by their personal views and perceptions. As we will see, President Reagan's controversial and unsuccessful nominations of Robert Bork and Douglas Ginsburg in 1987 demonstrated that the Supreme Court can be a battleground for competing ideological forces. And once appointed to the Supreme Court, justices do not relinquish their claims to personal opinion or forego prejudice and political ambition.

Some observers have cynically suggested that the justices enjoy great prestige because of the public's overall ignorance of their activities. If people knew more about the way justices are appointed and understood the motivations for their rulings, public respect for them would be no greater than for other governmental officials.

Whatever the merits of this observation, social scientists have discovered that an overwhelming majority of Americans scarcely know what the Court is doing. Few can name more than a handful of the Court's nine justices, describe its procedures, or recount the nature and history of its role in the political system. And, apart from a few highly controversial cases—such as those concerning abortion and prayer in the public schools—most Court decisions stir little public interest. The courts, moreover, rarely if ever deal with the dramatic international events that dominate TV's nightly news. One study revealed that more than 55 percent of Americans could not describe any recent Supreme Court rulings.[2]

The Court's press coverage, of course, has not been as extensive as that of the president and Congress, and many of the Court's decisions have abounded in legal technicalities that defy most people's understanding. Moreover, most Americans have neither the opportunity nor the desire to become intimately acquainted

★ The Justices of the Supreme Court, 1990. With this picture as a prompt, how many justices can you name?

with the Court's activities. They do not write letters to the justices, are unable to penetrate the secrecy in which most of the Court's work is accomplished, and have few of the required resources to bring an injustice to the Court's attention. Some scholars aptly conclude that among the various governmental institutions in this country, the Supreme Court remains one of the least open to citizen scrutiny and influence—a conclusion that, if shared by most Americans, may indeed inhibit understanding and awareness.

★ The Power to Nullify Laws

Ignorance of the Supreme Court's activities should not be permitted to obscure the enormous power the nine justices command in the political system. Nor should it obscure the occasional storms of controversy that accompany their decisions. During the past few decades alone, the justices have handed down opinions that affect the very fabric of American society.

From the standpoint of political action, for example, the role of the justices has been profound. Their decisions have ranged over a wide area of political expression, touching on voting rights, freedom of speech, freedom of the press, and freedom of association. Their rulings on the issue of what constitutes permissible acts of public protest have carried broad implications for seekers of constitutional protection for political expression. In response to widespread civil rights and anti–Vietnam war protests during the 1960s, the justices confronted federal, state, and local laws restraining public speech and assembly. For example, the Court

★ Young people burned their draft cards in protest against the Vietnam war. This and other symbolic acts of defiance resulted in a number of rulings by the Supreme Court on the proper limits of free expression.

upheld the right of almost two hundred students to demonstrate on the South Carolina state capitol grounds, ruling that the students were exercising "basic constitutional rights in their most pristine and classic form."[3] Similarly, the Court upheld a sit-in by five black adults to protest the segregationist policies of a regional library.[4] In other cases, however, the Court came down hard against political protest. It sustained the convictions of two hundred college students who had demonstrated against a segregated county jail on the grounds that the jail was not on public property.[5] And it upheld the convictions of four persons who had burned their draft cards in violation of federal law.[6]

Court rulings of the 1980s also affected the rights of high school students. The Court declared that many protections guaranteed by the Bill of Rights stop at the schoolhouse gates. The Court upheld the right of school officials to conduct searches of students' lockers and to censor student publications. The right to privacy and free expression, the justices stated, must be balanced against the responsibilities of school officials.

The basis for these and other rulings is the justices' sweeping power to exercise **judicial review.** By law and tradition, the nine Court justices can overturn decisions of Congress, the president, the state legislatures, and lower courts which in their opinion conflict with the Constitution. The president and members of Congress also continually interpret the Constitution through their actions, but the Supreme Court justices have the final word on the document's meaning. As former chief justice Charles Evans Hughes stated bluntly in 1907, "We are under a Constitution, but the Constitution is what the judges say it is."[7]

Take one dramatic example. In July 1974, the Supreme Court justices held an extraordinary midsummer hearing on whether President Nixon had to surrender sixty-four White House tape recordings sought by Special Prosecutor Leon Jaworski. The case of *The United States of America* v. *Richard M. Nixon* marked the first

★ One of the Supreme Court's most dramatic uses of judicial review came in 1974, when it ordered President Nixon to release the secret tape recordings of conversations in the White House that implicated him in the cover-up of the Watergate scandal.

appearance of the Watergate scandal in the highest court. In their historic decision, the justices ruled against President Nixon, upholding a previous order by District Court Judge John Sirica requiring the president to hand over the tapes as evidence in the trial of six former Nixon aides charged with conspiracy, burglary, and illegal wiretapping in connection with the Watergate break-in.

Simply stated, the justices rejected Nixon's sweeping assertion that only a president can decide what White House materials can be used as evidence in criminal proceedings. The doctrine of separation of powers and the need for confidential communication within the executive branch, the justices ruled, does not give the president absolute privilege to withhold material from the courts. In a criminal case such as the cover-up trial, where the claim of confidentiality is not based on grounds of military or diplomatic secrecy, the president's assertion of **executive privilege** must yield to the need for evidence. The president, the Court found, was using executive privilege to avoid a criminal prosecution, not to protect the national security. "The generalized interest in confidentiality . . . ," the Court stated, "cannot prevail over the fundamental demands of due process of law in the fair administration of criminal justice."[8]

Clearly, the case represented one of the most significant disputes over governmental powers in American history and strongly bolstered the Court's position in relation to that of the president in the area of law. Nixon's compliance with the ruling reaffirmed the Court's preeminence among the three branches of government in interpreting the Constitution. Revelation of the contents of Nixon's tapes ultimately contributed to his resignation in the face of impending impeachment by the House of Representatives. More than a decade later, President Reagan, facing a congressional investigation of the Iran-Contra arms scandal in 1987, made little reference to executive privilege and was generally more cooperative with investigators.

Interpreting the Constitution is not all that the Court does, of course. Much of its time is also spent interpreting the meanings of acts of Congress and rules of federal regulatory agencies. Because federal laws and regulations are often ambiguously worded, the Court frequently is asked to resolve conflicts of statutory interpretation. And in interpreting the law, the Court is also *making* law. Thus, in matters ranging from federal trade practices and corporate mergers to taxation and welfare, the Court's rulings are often as important in policy making as its rulings on constitutional issues.

How Judicial Review Began

In view of the fact that judicial review is the Court's most awesome power, it is interesting to realize that the Constitution does not specifically authorize the Court to exercise it. Although Article III stipulates that the justices may consider "all cases, in law and equity, arising under the Constitution," this provision does not clearly empower them to strike down acts they consider to be unconstitutional.

Many historians have pointed out, however, that the use of judicial review had been anticipated before the Constitution was drafted and that many state courts already had invalidated acts that conflicted with state constitutions. Furthermore, many members of the Constitutional Convention in 1787 had championed judicial review as one of the vital functions of the Court.[9] An early study by the historian Charles Beard revealed that at least seventeen of the twenty-five most influential delegates to the convention were "on the record in favor of the proposition that the Judiciary would in the natural course of things pass upon the constitutionality of acts of Congress." And of the less prominent delegates, Beard found, six "understood and approved" the doctrine.[10]

Moreover, in *Federalist* no. 78, Alexander Hamilton pleaded for the right of the judicial branch to decide whether legislative acts were constitutional. "The complete independence of the courts of justice is peculiarly essential in a limited constitution," he argued, and such a limited constitution "can be preserved in practice no other way than through the courts of justice, whose duty it must be to declare all acts contrary to the manifest tenor of the Constitution void. Without this, all the reservations of particular rights or privileges would amount to nothing." In fact, in the Judiciary Act of 1789 (which established the federal court system), Congress handed Supreme Court justices limited power over state court decisions. By doing so, many historians contend, Congress implied that the justices could overturn laws that contradicted the federal Constitution.

But because the Constitution was silent on the Court's right to review congressional or presidential acts (for reasons still being debated), the justices gradually acquired this power through their own interpretations of the document. The celebrated case of *Marbury* v. *Madison* (1803) was especially important in this regard, since it set the precedent for judicial review of acts of Congress. The case developed in 1801 when John Adams, just before stepping down from the presidency, hurriedly appointed a number of Federalist party judges, among them William Marbury, whom he named justice of the peace in the District of Columbia. When Thomas Jefferson, Adams's Republican successor, learned that Marbury's commission had not been delivered within the required time span, he decided to appoint someone else. Marbury, evidently disappointed and angered by Jefferson's refusal to honor his appointment, appealed directly to the Supreme Court. He insisted that the justices should force Jefferson's secretary of state, James Madison, to deliver the commission. He based his appeal on the fact that Congress, in the Judiciary Act of

1789, had stated that requests for a **writ of mandamus** (an order demanding that a public official do his duty) could be taken directly to the Supreme Court; that is, such requests were part of the Court's **original jurisdiction.**

Clearly the justices were placed in an uncomfortable position. On the one hand, if they ordered Madison to deliver the commission, Madison would probably just ignore the order and thereby humiliate the Court. On the other hand, if they refused to support Marbury, they would be admitting their own weakness.

Chief Justice John Marshall's majority opinion was a masterpiece of strategy. He wrote that Marbury should be given his commission, but that the justices did not have the power to help him get it, because the section of the Judiciary Act authorizing them to honor direct requests for writs of mandamus was unconstitutional. Congress had no authority, Marshall said, to enlarge the Court's original jurisdiction by handing the justices the added authority to issue such writs. The Court's original jurisdiction is limited by the Constitution to disputes involving diplomats or one of the states and cannot be enhanced by Congress. And because Marbury was neither a diplomat nor a state, the justices had no right to issue a write of mandamus on his behalf. Thus, even though Marbury did not benefit by this decision, the justices and the Court clearly did. By ruling that a section of the Judiciary Act was unconstitutional, they avoided a fight with the Jefferson administration and simultaneously established the Court's authority to interpret the constitutionality of congressional acts.

In the years since the *Marbury* decision, Supreme Court justices have not overturned many other acts of Congress: only about one hundred such acts have been declared totally or partly unconstitutional. Most of the Court's judicial review power has been directed instead against the states. More than one thousand state and local acts have been thrown out by the Court. In the opinion of some observers, in fact, the power to review state acts has been more important than the power to review legislation of Congress. Without the power to interpret state acts, there would be little to prevent the states from going their independent legal ways, to the detriment of the federal Constitution. As former justice Oliver Wendell Holmes concluded, "I do not think the United States would come to an end if we lost our power to declare an act of Congress void. I do think the Union would be imperiled if we could not make that declaration as to the laws of the several states."[11]

Justifications for Judicial Review

What possible justification can we find for allowing Supreme Court justices to exercise judicial review? Why should nine robed judges who never face the voters command the awesome power to overturn the decisions of elected officials? Such power would appear to conflict with the democratic ideal that no group, particularly an elite appointed for life, should determine policy for a majority of citizens.

One justification, as we saw in chapter 2, is that our political system is based on more than majority rule, that ultimately it rests on a foundation of constitutional law. As Alexander Hamilton wrote in *Federalist* no. 78 and as Chief Justice John Marshall ruled in *Marbury* v. *Madison,* the Constitution must be regarded as the supreme law of the land, superior to any act of Congress, the president, a lower court, or a state legislature. And because the responsibility of the courts is to interpret the law, Supreme Court justices must be the ultimate interpreters of the Constitution. They must determine whether any legislation passed by Congress or another legislative body is in accord with it. If the justices should find a conflict between such legislation and the Constitution, it is their duty to declare that legislation invalid.

Related to this legalistic justification is the more obvious fact that many of the framers were not willing to put full trust in the majority or in their elected representatives. They feared that the majority might trample on the rights of those individuals or groups who happened to offend the prevailing prejudices of the times. And because every citizen is likely to be a member of some minority at one time or another, no individual might be spared persecution by the many. "It is of great importance in a republic," James Madison warned in *Federalist* no. 51, "not only to guard the society against the oppression of its rulers, but to guard one part of the society against the injustice of the other.... If a majority be united by a common interest, the rights of the minority will be insecure."

Thus, in the opinion of many of the framers, it would be unrealistic to entrust members of Congress or of state legislatures with the sole responsibility to define the boundaries of their authority or the rights of minorities. These bodies are elected by temporary majorities, whose prejudices might at any moment be unleashed against unpopular groups. In contrast, Supreme Court justices, who are not elected by the voters and who serve for life, are in a more independent position to protect individual rights guaranteed by the Constitution.

Supreme Court justices have not always provided such protection however. As we will see, constraints have been imposed on the Court to prevent the justices from challenging the majority will for long periods of time. In fact, Supreme Court justices have even aided the repression of individual rights at various times in history. In *Dred Scott* v. *Sanford* (1857), they ruled that descendants of slaves were not United States citizens and that Congress could not halt the expansion of slavery into the territories. In *Plessy* v. *Ferguson* (1896), a majority of the justices supported the concept of "separate but equal" facilities for blacks and whites. And in *Korematsu* v. *United States* (1944), a similar majority upheld President Roosevelt's order placing thousands of loyal Japanese Americans in makeshift detention camps during World War II. While these rulings may be regarded as exceptional in the Court's history, they offer little reassurance to those who expect judicial knights in shining armor always to wield their swords of judicial review to defend the rights of individuals in distress.

★ History of the Supreme Court

The exercise of judicial review by Supreme Court justices has had an interesting and somewhat mixed history. The rulings of the Court during the past two hundred years reveal that the orientations of the justices have tended to shift quite remarkably, reflecting changes in both social concerns and legal perspectives. It is possible, in fact, to distinguish several periods in the Court's history during which certain issues dominated the justices' attention.

1789–1865

During the initial period of the Court's history, from 1789 until the Civil War, the justices were involved primarily in power disputes between the federal government

★ During the late nineteenth and early twentieth centuries, child labor flourished in America's factories. The Supreme Court generally refused to support laws designed to curb its abuse.

and the states. Under Chief Justice John Marshall (1801–1835), they labored not only to establish the Court as the supreme interpreter of the Constitution but to strengthen the authority of the federal government. They ruled in *McCulloch* v. *Maryland* (1819), for instance, that the states could not interfere with the authority of Congress to create a national bank by the use of their taxing power. They also declared in *Gibbons* v. *Ogden* (1824) that Congress, not the states, had the ultimate authority to regulate interstate commerce. Because the federal government, Marshall stated, is "emphatically, and truly, a government of all the people," its decisions in certain matters must prevail.

Even after Marshall's death in 1835, the justices continued to be preoccupied with the nation–state issue. Under Chief Justice Roger B. Taney (1836–1864), however, they retreated from the strong support previously given to the claims of the federal government and gave greater (although not exclusive) support to the claims of the states. They asserted that the two levels of government were basically coequal and that powers delegated to the federal government were clearly limited by the powers reserved to the states by the Tenth Amendment. The reputation of the Taney Court was badly tarnished, however, by the notorious *Dred Scott* decision in 1857, stating that Congress had no right to exclude slavery from the new territories. This decision greatly undermined the Court's prestige in the North for more than a generation and provided yet another spark to ignite the Civil War.

1865–1941

From the Civil War until the New Deal in the 1930s, the Court turned its attention from the nation–state issue toward the perceived need to guard capitalist industrial development against governmental regulation. Although previous justices under Marshall and Taney had been concerned with business and property rights as well, most of the justices during this second period reflected the general spirit of the times and sided with business interests in their efforts to ward off governmental regulation of free enterprise. Under a succession of chief justices, the Court held that a provision of the Fourteenth Amendment (ratified in 1868) prohibiting the taking of a person's property without "due process" also protected business enterprises from governmental interference. It ruled that corporations were "persons," and that employers and employees had a right to bargain in any way they wished. In due course, it struck down the federal income tax in 1895, overturned legislation curbing child labor in 1918, and repealed minimum wage laws for women in 1923.[12] These and similar rulings were condemned by the Progressives, who viewed the justices as merely defenders of industrial robber barons.

Interestingly, the Great Depression of the 1930s brought the Court's probusiness orientation into direct conflict with Franklin Roosevelt's New Deal. Maintaining a laissez-faire philosophy, the Court declared more than eleven major New Deal initiatives unconstitutional. President Roosevelt sharply attacked the justices' destruction of his policies and vowed revenge. In a message to Congress in 1937, he asked for legislation to increase the Court's size from nine to fifteen justices and thereby ensure a majority sympathetic to the New Deal. Although this "Court-packing" plan failed to win congressional support, the president's determination eventually sparked some changes. Several of the justices switched their positions ("the switch in time that saved nine"), and vacancies on the bench finally allowed Roosevelt to appoint new justices who favored his policies. As a result, the Court upheld both the Social Security Act and the National Labor Relations Act as valid federal legislation.

1941–1969

Following the United States' entry into World War II, the major concern (and controversy) facing the Court involved the issues of equal rights and due process. At various times during this twenty-eight-year period, a majority of justices were found on both sides of these issues. During the reigns of Chief Justice Harlan F. Stone (1941–1946) and Chief Justice Fred M. Vinson (1946–1953), the Court generally refused to challenge the federal government's restrictions on individual rights. The justices upheld the executive order incarcerating thousands of Japanese Americans in detention camps during World War II. They also, in *Dennis* v. *United States* (1951), upheld the Smith Act, which denied freedom of speech to certain political groups.

During Earl Warren's reign as chief justice (1953–1969), the Court actively employed judicial review to extend the protections of the Bill of Rights. The Warren Court ruled in numerous cases that the provisions of the Bill of Rights applied not only to the federal government but to the states as well, through the due process and equal protection clauses of the Fourteenth Amendment. Thus the states had to recognize and uphold the rights guaranteed by the first ten amendments, and state laws that violated those rights were unconstitutional. (The Supreme Court, in *Gitlow* v. *New York* [1925], had already ruled that freedom of speech and of the press—protected by the First Amendment from abridgement by Congress—was also protected by the due process clause of the Fourteenth Amendment from abridgement by the states.) Thus, among its other rulings, the Warren Court struck down state laws supporting segregation in the public schools, required the states to furnish an attorney for any defendant who could not afford one, and prohibited state prosecution of criminal suspects who had not been notified of their rights or provided with counsel during interrogations.[13] These and other rulings won favorable notice from Americans who felt that individual rights had too long been ignored or resisted by other governmental agencies. But they also won a surprising amount

★ The Supreme Court under Chief Justice Earl Warren drew criticism during the 1950s and 1960s from the John Birch Society and other right-wing critics for its landmark rulings in civil rights and criminal justice cases.

of criticism from those who thought the justices' decisions had gone too far in the direction of social reform.

1969–1980

Many observers expected that Richard Nixon's appointments of four so-called judicial conservatives, beginning in 1969, would initiate a new period for the Supreme Court. Under Chief Justice Warren Burger, the Court was expected to retreat from the strong activist philosophy touted by its immediate predecessor. Burger frequently asserted, for instance, that Americans had come to rely too heavily on the Court to solve pressing social problems. Instead of seeking the Court's intervention, he declared, they should lobby Congress and state legislatures to enact laws requiring policy changes. And in keeping with this view, the Burger Court began to impose procedural roadblocks (such as restrictions on the use of class-action suits) limiting access to the Court by civil rights and other plaintiffs.[14]

In stating this position, Burger echoed the views of those who had criticized the Warren Court for making policy decisions they felt belonged to the elected branches of the government. They had argued that Supreme Court justices should keep their hands off social problems and not substitute their own social values for statutes passed by elected officials. Taking a similar view, President Nixon had promised to appoint only **strict constructionists**—justices who would interpret the Constitution in accordance with the precise meaning of its words. "It is my belief," he declared, "that it is the duty of a judge to interpret the Constitution and not to place himself above the Constitution or outside the Constitution. He should not twist or bend the Constitution in order to perpetuate his personal political and

★ Former Chief Justice Warren Burger (1969–1986) was one of four conservative justices nominated to the Supreme Court by President Nixon.

social values."[15] Thus he expected that his appointees—Burger, Harry A. Blackmun, Lewis F. Powell, Jr., and William H. Rehnquist—would force the Court to conform with his standards of judicial conservatism and not make sweeping changes in existing law.

As many scholars have pointed out, such labels as "strict constructionist" and "judicial conservative" are oversimplifications. Certainly many of the Burger Court's decisions—notably its 1973 ruling striking down state laws against abortion[16]—reflected as broad an interpretation of the Constitution as any decision handed down by the Warren Court. Few justices are likely to pass up the chance to apply their own values to legal interpretations or to ignore completely their unique opportunity to influence American life. In fact, the vagueness of key phrases in the Constitution—such as "due process of law" and "probable cause" for arrest, search, or seizure—compels the justices to apply their own criteria, to choose among alternative and competing values.

In several respects, the Burger Court's patchwork of rulings defied most efforts to determine its judicial character and direction. While it upheld many rulings of the Warren Court, it weakened others. It was especially unpredictable in the area of individual rights. While it continued to rule against sex and race discrimination and extended the rights of prisoners, it also weakened the rights of criminal suspects, sustained the death penalty, made it easier for local officials to define and crack down on "obscenity," and upheld the Bank Secrecy Act, allowing governmental officials broad access to citizens' banking records.[17] It was also criticized for being inconsistent in its judgments. For example, the Court's 1973 rulings upholding the right to abortion were partly undermined four years later by rulings upholding the denial of public funds for abortions for women who could not afford to pay for them.[18] The Court, as we shall see, also made several rulings in the areas of national security and foreign relations that limited citizens' access to information.

The most interesting thing about both the Warren and Burger Courts, however, was their enormous impact on governmental policy. Despite the avowed intentions of Burger and Nixon to restrain the Court's activist role, the Burger Court followed in the Warren Court's footsteps in telling elected officials what they must do. As one scholar noted, the tendency of courts in the past was

> to *restrict* the executive and legislature in what they could do. The distinct characteristic of more recent activist courts has been to *extend* the role of what the government could do, even when the government did not want to do it. The *Swann* and *Keyes* decisions meant that government *must* move children around to distant schools against the will of their parents. The *Griggs* decision meant that government *must* monitor the race and ethnicity of job applicants and test-takers.[19]

In these and other decisions, the Burger Court continued rather than discarded the activist policy-making role assumed by the Warren Court.

1980–1988

In 1986 Warren Burger retired as chief justice, leaving a vacancy for President Reagan to fill with someone who shared his brand of conservative philosophy. Reagan selected Associate Justice William Rehnquist, one of the most conservative members of the Court in recent times. (He had been appointed to the Court by President Nixon in 1971.) And to fill Rehnquist's empty chair, he nominated Antonin Scalia, another conservative judge on the federal appeals court. During his first term, Reagan had chosen the first woman to sit on the Court, Sandra Day O'Connor, a conservative classmate of Rehnquist's at Stanford Law School.

Like Nixon before him, Reagan vowed to shift the ideological balance of the Court, to mold it in his own conservative image. He wanted a Court that would

★ Judge Robert H. Bork, Ronald Reagan's controversial nominee to the Supreme Court in 1987, was turned down by a majority of the Senate, who disapproved of, among other things, his conservative judicial views.

take a more constrained approach to the interpretation of law, yet one that reflected a more conservative position on such social issues as abortion, prayer in the public schools, and affirmative action.

Reagan's ideological bent reached a climax of sorts in 1987, when he tried but failed to win Senate approval of his third nominee, Judge Robert H. Bork, a controversial former Yale law professor whom Reagan had appointed to the federal appeals court. The nomination of Bork had sparked a fierce battle among politicians and special-interest groups, many of whom feared, on the basis of Bork's writings and earlier public statements, that he would support a wholesale attack on the Warren and Burger Courts' rulings on privacy, abortion, and civil rights. Reagan accused the anti-Bork forces of launching a political assault on the judicial nominating process—a charge, incidentally, that was also leveled against Reagan for his appointment of such a conservative ideologue.

In the end, the Senate's rejection of Bork proved to be one of Reagan's biggest defeats. He responded by nominating a second controversial and unsuccessful candidate for the Court, Douglas Ginsburg. At forty-one years of age, Ginsburg was one of the youngest nominees in history and, like Bork, had strong conservative credentials. However, following revelations that he had smoked marijuana both as a student and as a law professor at Harvard, Ginsburg withdrew his name from nomination. Whereas Reagan's first failed nominee had been rejected by the Senate because of his views, Ginsburg foundered over lifestyle. Reagan eventually settled for Appeals Court Judge Anthony Kennedy, a moderate conservative, who was confirmed by the Senate in 1988. (The composition of the Supreme Court at the end of Reagan's second term is shown in table 15-1.)

Despite these setbacks, Reagan was able to exert considerable influence on the Court's future. Because Reagan had the opportunity to name three of its nine members, together with hundreds of judges of lower courts, he put a conservative

★ Table 15-1
The Supreme Court, 1989

	Appointed by	*Year of appointment*	*Year of birth*	*Party*	*Home state*
Chief justice					
William Rehnquist[a]	Reagan	1986	1924	R	Arizona
Associate justices					
William J. Brennan, Jr.	Eisenhower	1956	1906	D	New Jersey
Byron R. White	Kennedy	1962	1917	D	Colorado
Thurgood Marshall	Johnson	1967	1908	D	New York
Harry A. Blackmun	Nixon	1970	1908	R	Minnesota
John Paul Stevens	Ford	1975	1920	R	Illinois
Sandra Day O'Connor	Reagan	1981	1930	R	Arizona
Antonin Scalia	Reagan	1986	1936	R	Illinois
Anthony Kennedy	Reagan	1988	1936	R	California

[a]Appointed associate justice by Nixon in 1971.

stamp on the Court and judicial system for many years to come. How much the Reagan legacy would depart from or conform to the activist tendencies of the Warren and Burger Courts is something that observers and historians of the 1990s will have to determine.

A final point to remember is that the Court's policy-making role has been criticized by different sides at different times in history. While many self-proclaimed conservatives, for example, lambasted the frequent use of judicial review by the Warren Court in the 1950s and 1960s, they applauded its use in the 1930s when an earlier Court overturned many of Franklin Roosevelt's New Deal policies. Similarly, while many self-professed liberals were gratified to see the Warren Court flex its judicial review muscles, they have been strongly critical of such displays by the currently more conservative Court. In view of such changes of opinion, it is apparent that the major issue has been not the Supreme Court's activism or restraint but rather the substantive nature of its decisions. To put it more bluntly, support or rejection of the Court's activist role has often depended on whose ox is being gored by its rulings.

★ The Courts and a Changing World: The Political Thicket

During most of this country's history the Supreme Court has preferred not to become involved in controversial issues involving American foreign policy. When issues of war and peace have produced lawsuits, the courts have tended to consider such disputes political questions to be settled on the floor of Congress or in the polling booth. When the Supreme Court did hear a case, it usually came down firmly on the side of the president and executive branch as the primary source of foreign policy.

Presidential Ascendance

The most far-reaching recognition of presidential dominance in foreign affairs by the Supreme Court was handed down in *United States* v. *Curtiss-Wright Export Corporation* in 1936. The case arose out of a congressional resolution granting President Roosevelt great latitude in prohibiting the sale of arms to Bolivia and Paraguay, two South American nations locked in the bloody Chaco War. The Chaco War, which ultimately cost 100,000 soldiers their lives, threatened stability on the South American continent. The American-based Curtiss-Wright Corporation was indicted in 1934 for attempting to sell fifteen machine guns to Bolivia.

Curtiss-Wright argued its innocence on a variety of grounds, including the charge that Congress had unconstitutionally delegated broad legislative authority to the president. According to Curtiss-Wright, Congress's resolution was far too vague, allowing the president to "legislate" the specifics of the arms embargo. The case eventually found its way to the Supreme Court on appeal. The Court, in deciding against Curtiss-Wright, set the precedent for a broad interpretation of presidential powers in foreign affairs.

The Court made a distinction between internal and external presidential powers. Internally, the president and the federal government are limited to powers specifically delegated by the Constitution (and, as we saw in chap. 2, implied powers that are "necessary and proper"). In the external or foreign realm, federal power is not so limited. Sounding like modern-day international relations scholars, the justices reasoned that as a member of the family of nations, the federal government by its very nature possesses certain implied powers:

> The powers to declare and wage war, to conclude peace, to make treaties, to maintain diplomatic relations with other sovereignties, if they had never been mentioned in the Constitution, would have been vested in the federal government as necessary concomitants of nationality.

Moreover, they said, the bulk of this power resides with the president:

> In this vast external realm, with its important, complicated, delicate and manifold problems, the President alone has the power to speak or listen as a representative of the nation. He makes treaties with the advice and consent of the Senate; but he alone negotiates. Into the field of negotiation the Senate cannot intrude and Congress itself is powerless to invade it.

Thus the degree of presidential influence on foreign policy which we take for granted today can be traced in part to the Supreme Court's decision in *Curtiss-Wright* in 1936.

During the Carter presidency, several interesting disputes between Congress and the executive found their way into the courts. One dispute involved the Panama Canal Treaty. In 1978, sixty members of the House of Representatives, unable to prevent Senate ratification of the treaty, filed suit in federal court charging that return of the canal to Panama constituted a disposal of federal property. Transfer of federal property, the suit claimed, was limited to Congress under Article IV of the Constitution. The lower court, echoing the Curtiss-Wright case, stated that in the international sphere the president's power to negotiate agreements included the right to transfer property to another nation by treaty.

A second case involved Carter's decision in 1978 to terminate the Mutual Defense Treaty with Taiwan. A group of senators challenged this action in court, arguing that since the Senate must ratify treaties, it should also be consulted when

★ During World War II, thousands of Americans of Japanese descent on the West Coast were forcibly relocated to makeshift detention camps, an action upheld by the Supreme Court in *Korematsu* v. *United States* (1944). More than forty years later, Congress approved reparations to those victimized by this action.

treaties are terminated. The Supreme Court refused to hear the case; four of the justices openly argued that the dispute was a political rather than a legal question.

One of the most important challenges to presidential authority has yet to find its way into the court system. The 1973 War Powers Resolution, passed over President Nixon's veto, places direct limits on the ability of the commander in chief to engage U.S. troops abroad. (The War Powers Resolution is discussed more fully in chap. 19.) Although no president has formally acknowledged the resolution's authority or constitutionality, none has directly violated its principles to the point of forcing a showdown with Congress. When and if a president directly ignores the resolution's requirements, which include informing Congress when troops are sent abroad in a hostile situation and withdrawing them upon request, a constitutional battle of major proportions will ensue. The courts, no doubt, will be in the thick of the fight.

National Security and the Courts

Curtiss-Wright and other cases have established presidential ascendance in foreign affairs. But what happens when the distinction between a purely external matter, such as the return of the Panama Canal, and an internal, domestic issue becomes blurred? As we have stressed, few issues today are purely international or purely domestic. To put this question another way, how far will the courts allow the government to go when its concern for national security infringes on the individual's basic constitutional rights? Historically, the courts have given the president great latitude during times of war. In dramatic situations, such as the internment of Japanese Americans during World War II, presidential authority seemed nearly absolute. Still, the courts have drawn a constitutional line that the president, even during a national emergency, cannot cross. A good example of judicial nullification of a presidential action is seen in the case of *Youngstown Sheet and Tube Company* v. *Sawyer.*

During the Korean conflict in 1952, President Truman ordered the seizure of the Youngstown steel mills in order to avoid a strike. When his action was challenged in court, Truman's counsel argued that seizure of a militarily important industry was within the president's power as commander in chief. The Court, however, responded that the president's action was an unconstitutional exercise of legislative power. Legislative authority, under the constitutional doctrine of separation of powers, resides in Congress, not in the executive. Had Congress passed legislation authorizing seizure of the steel mills under its power of eminent domain, then the president would be properly fulfilling his obligation to enforce the law. By acting without congressional approval, Truman had exceeded his authority. The lesson from the Youngstown case was clear: the commander in chief commands great power, but that power does not include making law in areas specifically reserved for Congress.

In more recent times, executive branch action in the name of national security has ignited several controversies that have found their way into the courts. One such case involved the public's right to know versus the government's need for secrecy in foreign affairs.[20] Daniel Ellsberg, a former employee of the Defense Department, obtained papers revealing the government's secret history of the Vietnam war, which he leaked to the *New York Times.* These so-called Pentagon Papers revealed that the government had been less than truthful to the American people about Vietnam. Claiming an inherent right to exercise prior restraint over publication of material that might threaten national security, the Nixon administration in 1971 sought to prevent the *Times* from printing the documents. The Supreme Court, traditionally reluctant to limit First Amendment rights, declared that the executive branch has no inherent power of censorship in the area of foreign affairs. Censorship in the name of national security during peacetime may be possible, according to the Court, but only if it is mandated by Congress and will prevent the release of information that would "inevitably, directly and immediately" cause harm equivalent to that of disclosure in wartime. Material contained in the Pentagon Papers, much of which had already been made public, did not pose such a dire threat.

Interdependence and the Courts

Many of the stickiest issues involving war, peace, and diplomacy are purposely avoided by the courts as being "political." It is only when an issue threatens the separation of powers or the basic protections afforded by the Bill of Rights that the courts have found it necessary to enter the political thicket. But along with these dramatic, precedent-setting decisions, the courts increasingly find themselves involved in international issues in other ways.

One area of growing concern for the federal court system surrounds the treaties that America makes with other nations. When the United States signs a treaty (and it is ratified by the Senate), the treaty becomes part of American law. Treaties cover a rich diversity of subjects, ranging from the extradition of suspected

★ The Supreme Court building.

lawbreakers to the protection of migrating birds. When disputes arise over the interpretation or enforcement of a treaty, citizens may go to court for a resolution.

A relatively new area of involvement in international issues concerns efforts to apply the human rights provisions of the United Nations Charter in American courts. Congress itself has passed legislation, such as the Alien Torts Statute, giving foreigners an opportunity to sue their government in U.S. courts for damages arising from human rights violations. These complex and controversial cases can push the courts further into the political thicket.

★ Constraints on Judicial Action

Although ruling elite theorists and others may consider the Supreme Court to be one of the nation's most elite institutions, the justices are under considerable constraint. The president, Congress, even ordinary citizens can employ weapons against the justices to circumvent their rulings. Let us first consider Congress.

Congress

If members of Congress become sufficiently upset by the decisions of the justices, they have several alternative weapons to employ. They may impeach a justice in an attempt to intimidate or remove him from the Court. When Gerald Ford was House

The World Court

The International Court of Justice (ICJ) is the closest the world comes to a global courtroom where nations locked in conflict can "have their day in court." The ICJ, popularly known as the World Court, was created in 1946 as one of the six principal organs of the United Nations. Its purpose is to hear disputes between nations, not individuals or organizations.

The ICJ, with its stately headquarters in the picturesque Dutch city of The Hague, is made up of fifteen justices elected to nine-year terms by the United Nations General Assembly and Security Council. In addition to hearing disputes between nations, the ICJ is also empowered to deliver advisory opinions at the request of U.N. officials.

Jurisdiction

Formally, all members of the United Nations are subject to the jurisdiction of the ICJ. With some important exceptions, however, participation in a case brought before the Court is entirely at the discretion of the two nations involved. In other words, both nations *must* agree to have the ICJ hear their case. Some nations, in the hope of strengthening the ICJ, have agreed to grant compulsory jurisdiction to the Court in the following areas:

- the interpretation of a treaty
- any question of international law
- the existence of any fact that, if established, would constitute a breach of an international obligation
- the nature or extent of the reparation to be made for the breach of an international obligation

The agreement to accept compulsory jurisdiction, however, is usually made with many qualifications and reservations limiting a nation's actual obligation to take part in a case. Moreover, fewer than fifty of the 159 members of the United Nations have agreed to compulsory jurisdiction.

Cases

Given the limited jurisdiction of the ICJ, it is not surprising that it has heard only a few cases over the years. Since 1946, the Court has heard fewer than sixty cases between nations and has delivered fewer than twenty advisory opinions. Most of the cases have been of a technical nature—determining a boundary dispute or ensuring free travel on the high seas or in the air.

The United States and the ICJ

Historically, the United States has been a firm backer of the ICJ. It agreed in 1946 (with omnibus reservations) to accept compulsory jurisdiction. During the height of the Cold War, it brought numerous unsuccessful cases against the Soviet Union and its allies, stemming from border incidents. In perhaps the most dramatic use of the Court, the United States successfully brought action against Iran after its diplomats were seized in Tehran in 1979.

During the Reagan presidency, however, the United States rejected the ICJ as an acceptable forum for international conflict resolution. In 1986, following the World Court's decision to hear a case brought by the government of Nicaragua (requesting redress for damage resulting from American paramilitary action and support for the Contra rebels), the United States withdrew its agreement to participate in the ICJ. The Bush administration, on the other hand, indicated that, with the cooperation of the Soviet Union, the United States may be willing to again lend its support to the ICJ.

(continued)

minority leader in 1970, he introduced a resolution to impeach Justice William O. Douglas on charges of taking outside income. Ford apparently also disliked the "radical" political views expressed in Douglas's book *Points of Rebellion,* excerpts of which surfaced in an issue of *Evergreen* magazine that featured photographs of nudes. Ford's threat to impeach the reputable justice was based on the elusive constitutional provision that judges "shall hold their offices during good behavior,"

Effectiveness of the ICJ

Like most international organizations, the success of the ICJ in global problem solving is in direct proportion to the political importance of the dispute. By and large, nations are not yet willing to turn issues of national interest over to a distant international body. The ICJ thus hears few important cases. Even when the World Court renders a decision, it (and the United Nations) has little meaningful enforcement power. But the Court *does* focus the world's attention on important issues. The United States' refusal to take part in the case brought by Nicaragua did not improve America's image around the world. If nations are truly concerned about their image abroad, then the ICJ can play a role in promoting solutions to international conflict. ★

★ The judges of the World Court: *(from left)* Raghunandan S. Pathak (India), Gilbert Guillaume (France), Jens Evensen (Norway), Mohammed Bedjaoui (Algeria), Stephen M. Schwebel (United States), Shigeru Oda (Japan), Manfred Lachs (Poland), President José María Ruda (Argentina), Taslim Olawale Elias (Nigeria), Roberto Ago (Italy), Robert Jennings (United Kingdom), Ni Zhrengya (China), Nikolai Konstantinovich Tarassov (Soviet Union), Mohamed Shahabuddeen (Guyana). Not present: Vice-president Kèba Mbaye (Senegal).

SOURCE: John Tessitore and Susan Woolfson, eds. *Issues Before the 43rd General Assembly of the United Nations* (Lexington, MA.: Lexington Books, 1989) and Robert E. Riggs and Jack C. Plano, *The United Nations: International Organization and World Politics* (Pacific Grove, Calif.: Brooks/Cole, 1988).

as well as Ford's own remarkable view that "an impeachable offense is whatever a majority of the House of Representatives considers it to be at a given moment in history." Ford's efforts fizzled, however, when the House Judiciary Committee concluded that sufficient grounds for impeachment did not exist.

Actually, impeachment has not been a potent weapon against Supreme Court justices. Although four lower-court judges have been removed by Congress, not a single member of the Supreme Court has been deposed. The only Supreme Court justice who has been impeached—that is, formally accused of an offense by the House—was Samuel Chase, who was accused in 1805 of making seditious public statements against the Jefferson administration; but the Senate did not find Chase guilty.

Members of Congress also have the constitutional power to take away the justices' appellate jurisdiction in certain kinds of cases. Article III states that, except for original jurisdiction in a few areas, the Court's right to hear appeals on federal questions is subject to "such exceptions, and under such regulations as the Congress shall make." Although Congress has not exercised this power in more than one hundred years, it remains a potentially significant threat to the Court's independence.

If members of Congress are reluctant to impeach Court justices or strip them of their appellate jurisdiction, they can always try to pass constitutional amendments reversing their decisions. As we have seen, the Constitution empowers Congress to amend the Constitution if it can muster the support of three-fourths of the state legislatures. In 1909, for example, Congress proposed the Sixteenth Amendment (ratified by the states in 1913), establishing the federal income tax. This amendment overturned an earlier Court ruling that such a tax would be unconstitutional.[21] Although this and other procedures have not been resorted to often, the possibility of congressional retaliation always exists.

The President

Supreme Court justices must be concerned about the challenges of the president as well as those of Congress. Though the president's weapons may not be so dramatic as those of Congress, his influence tends to be more immediate and direct. For one thing, he can alter the philosophy of the Court by appointing new justices. Some presidents have had little opportunity to place new justices on the bench (John F. Kennedy, for example, appointed only one), but others have appointed sufficient numbers to affect the Court's judicial orientation. Ronald Reagan, by filling three vacancies on the Court, and naming the chief justice, had the opportunity to influence considerably the Court's philosophical character during his two terms in office.

Equally significant is the president's command of the bureaucracy that enforces the law. Because Supreme Court justices can boast no police or army of their own—that is, no independent enforcement machinery—they must rely on the president and the Justice Department to carry out their decisions. If they were to make a decision offensive to the president (as well as to Congress and most other Americans), they might find themselves helpless. When President Lincoln suspended the writ of habeas corpus during the Civil War, the Court could not even muster the courage to complain about his actions until after he had died. And after the Court ruled in 1954 that segregation in the public schools was unconstitutional, many schools throughout the country remained—and still remain—segregated. Neither President Eisenhower nor state officials made much effort to enforce the Court's ruling. Echoing Andrew Jackson more than a century earlier, the governor of Texas stated flatly in 1956, "The Supreme Court passed the law, so let the Supreme Court enforce it."

★ Despite such Supreme Court rulings as *Brown* v. *Board of Education* (1954), segregation of buses, restaurants, hotels, and schools persisted as local officials either ignored or defied the Court.

The Lower Courts

The Supreme Court must also depend on lower courts to carry out its rulings. Although we may believe that lower courts jump to attention whenever the Supreme Court sneezes, the fact is that they sometimes delay or alter the Court's broad interpretations of federal law to fit local and specific situations. The lower courts often have a great deal of discretion in interpreting the Court's rulings, especially when the Court provides less than a clear mandate in its opinions. They may even openly defy its rulings in response to local pressures or out of a basic difference in philosophy. Efforts to undermine the Court by distorting the meaning of its interpretations have been seen in such highly emotional and controversial areas as school segregation, school prayers, and reapportionment of legislative districts.[22]

The People

Indeed, the justices' reliance on public support can significantly constrain their power. In the opinion of many scholars, Supreme Court justices must remain sensitive to the changing climate of opinion or run the risk of sacrificing the Court's legitimacy. Because the justices ultimately depend on the president and the cooperation of the public to enforce their rulings, they cannot afford to make too many decisions that run counter to the political temper of the times. In the words of the late Justice Felix Frankfurter, "The Court's authority—possessed neither of the purse nor the sword—ultimately rests on sustained public confidence in its moral sanction." Even the justices' support of individual rights can never extend too far beyond the tolerance of majority opinion. If it did, the public could ignore their decisions and encourage Congress to supersede the justices' authority through a constitutional amendment.

Attempts have been made to measure the impact of Supreme Court decisions and to determine the extent of public compliance with its rulings. One conclusion is that although most court decisions are obeyed—especially those requiring the compliance of only a few officials, such as a ruling on the death penalty—other decisions directed toward major social reform have been more difficult to enforce.[23] On matters of racial discrimination, for example, justices have found their decisions on school desegregation, busing of schoolchildren, and open housing ignored for long periods of time by large segments of the population. Such decisions have aggravated deeply ingrained prejudices and depend for their effectiveness on the cooperation of millions of people.

The Justices

Finally, Supreme Court justices observe their own restrictions on judicial review. Because their jurisdiction is primarily appellate, they cannot take the initiative. They must wait for a case to be appealed to the Court before they can pass judgment. And even when such an appeal surfaces, at least four of the justices must agree on the importance of the case before it can be considered.

Furthermore, justices tend to fashion their own doctrine of judicial restraint. Although they are not likely to pass up every temptation to wield the powers of their office, they know that political realities require them to resist such temptations. They must at least retreat from cases that might jeopardize the Court's independence. With some notable exceptions, as we have seen, most justices have been reluctant to interfere with presidential decisions in foreign and military affairs, even when those decisions have raised serious constitutional questions. In 1970, the Massachusetts state legislature filed suit to challenge the constitutionality of the United States' involvement in Vietnam. The suit requested the justices to declare American participation "unconstitutional in that it was not initially authorized or subsequently ratified by Congressional declaration." But a majority of the justices refused to review the suit, just as they refused to entertain suits challenging the legality of the draft in an undeclared war and the right of President Nixon to send troops into Cambodia without formal congressional authorization. Given the Court's long-standing reluctance to enter the political thicket of foreign affairs, as well as the fear that the president would ignore the Court's ruling anyway, little serious thought was given to challenging executive authority in military matters. The challenge to Nixon's use of troops came not from the Court but from Congress, in the form of the War Powers Resolution.

This reluctance has frustrated many citizens who have looked to the Court for help in defeating foreign policy and other decisions with which they disagree. Their attempts to gain access to the Court have been shadowed by the political considerations that may cause the justices to decline to hear a case, regardless of its constitutional implications. Because the justices may refuse to consider the constitutionality of a governmental policy and may be unable to enforce a ruling if they make one, citizens have faced innumerable obstacles in their efforts to confront certain laws and practices through the Court.

★ Clarence Gideon demonstrated that sometimes an individual can change the judicial system. In response to his appeal from a Florida prison cell, the Supreme Court handed down the landmark case *Gideon* v. *Wainwright* (1963), which requires the states to make sure that anyone charged with a serious crime who cannot afford an attorney is provided with one.

★ Approaching the Bench: Access to the Court

Since judicial review can be exercised only after a case is brought before the Court, we should consider some of the ways in which a case may reach the Court. Occasionally we hear people proclaim defiantly that they will fight an issue "all the way to the Supreme Court." What these people may not realize is that, even if they could afford to spend thousands of dollars to appeal a case to the highest court, they could have no assurance that the case would be heard. Apart from political considerations, a case will not be heard unless it raises constitutional questions that have greater significance than the outcome of a single dispute. The kinds of cases that reach the Court typically involve issues that affect a large segment of society.

In fact, the justices severely limit the number of cases they review to a small fraction of the petitions that pour in each year. Unlike members of Congress, Supreme Court justices have no committee system to divide the work load; they must all help decide each case. In a typical year they may receive petitions to hear more than 4,500 cases. If they had to rule on all of the petitions they receive, they would have to decide more than fifteen cases a day! They usually rule on fewer than two hundred cases, or roughly 5 percent of the appeals they receive.

This does not mean that citizens face impossible odds in winning a Supreme Court hearing. In exceptional cases, even individuals with little money and no legal support have successfully brought civil rights and criminal justice cases before the Court. In the early 1960s, a prisoner in Florida named Clarence Gideon submitted a handwritten petition asking the Court to review his conviction. According to federal statutes, persons too poor to pay the usual costs of a court appeal may proceed in forma pauperis (in the manner of a pauper). Thus, although Gideon had little money and had drafted his petition in pencil on lined paper, the justices accepted his case. And in the landmark decision *Gideon* v. *Wainwright* (1963), they ruled that because Gideon had not had the benefit of an attorney at his original trial, his conviction was invalid.[24]

Indeed, many citizens and interest groups have achieved as much success by taking their cases to the courts as by trying to win public support or to pressure legislative and executive officials into taking action. The National Association for the Advancement of Colored People (NAACP), for example, has for years relied on litigation as a tactic to fight school segregation and job discrimination. By persuading the Supreme Court in 1954 to outlaw segregation in the public schools (*Brown* v. *Board of Education*), the NAACP won a legal victory as important as any gained through legislation in Congress. (Of course, as we saw earlier, the Court's inability to enforce its own rulings may retard the full fruition of victory.)

Even a lawsuit filed by an individual can achieve wide-ranging political reform. In 1959, a registered voter in Tennessee named Charles Baker brought a suit against the state's election officials. Baker charged that they had violated his constitutional rights by their failure to reapportion the legislative districts to reflect changes in population since 1901. Their inaction, he insisted, diluted his vote by permitting rural districts—some with fewer than four thousand people—to have the same representation as large urban ones, such as his own, with more than seventy thousand people. In Tennessee's senate, 37 percent of the voters controlled more than 60 percent of the seats. Baker's victory in the Supreme Court three years later (*Baker* v. *Carr*, 1962) opened the way for citizens throughout the country to file similar suits demanding reapportionment of their state legislative and congressional districts.

Because of the large financial commitment required to bring a lawsuit, some citizens and groups prefer to become involved in court actions by submitting amicus curiae (friend of the court) briefs. As we noted in chapter 10, interested persons who are not direct litigants in a case may petition the court for permission to file a written argument outlining their own legal views on an issue. In an amicus brief they can try to help one side in a dispute by presenting new information and arguments not provided by the person who originally filed the suit. This tactic has been commonly used by the NAACP and the American Civil Liberties Union in civil rights and civil liberties cases.

Another tactic is to join a **class-action suit**—a suit brought by one or more persons with a legal complaint who share the costs and other burdens of suing in court. The suit is initiated on behalf of the plaintiff and "all others similarly situated." A suit might be brought, for example, on behalf of all women in a large corporation who faced sex discrimination in hiring and promotion. The Supreme Court, however, has placed several restrictions on class-action suits. The Court has ruled that in order to sue for damages in a federal court, each individual in the suit must claim a certain level of financial interest. In addition, persons who initiate a federal class-action suit must notify all other class members at their own expense. The more widespread the injustice, in other words, the greater the difficulty of bringing a class-action suit.

Jurisdiction of the Court

Essentially, two principal ways exist to gain access to the Supreme Court (see figure 15-1). The first is to rely on the Court's original jurisdiction which, as described in the Constitution, permits a case to be brought directly before the Court. Because the Supreme Court is the final arbiter or umpire of the federal system, settlement of major disputes between different levels and branches of government fall within

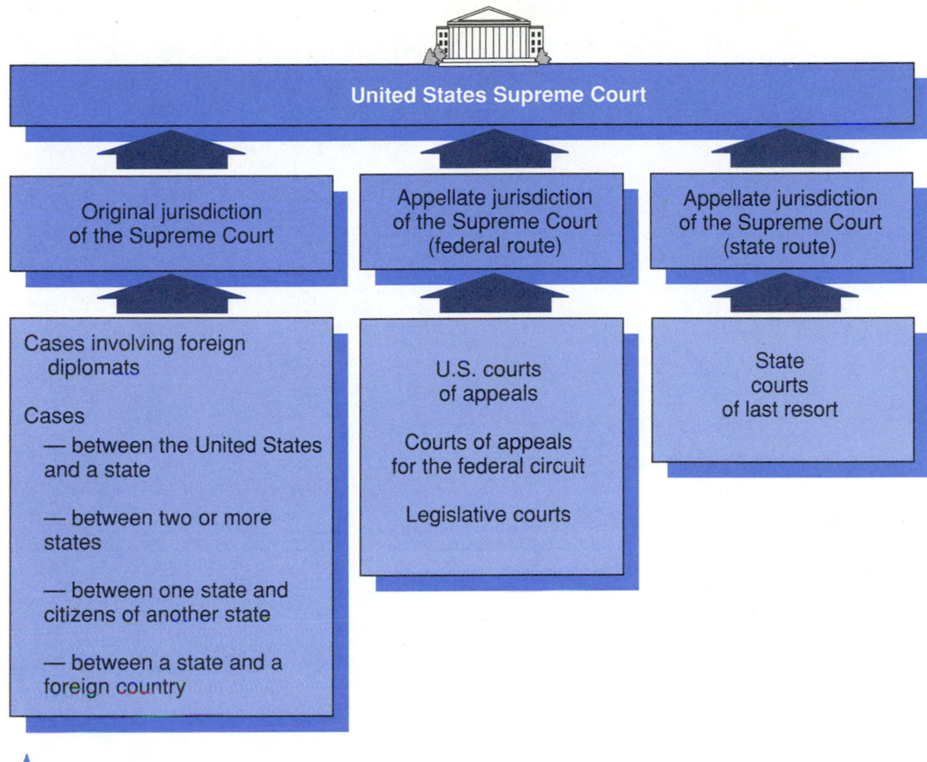

★ **Figure 15-1**
The organization and jurisdiction of the courts

its original jurisdiction. Normally, however, the Court hears such disputes only when they involve "ambassadors, other public ministers and consuls, or . . . a state." In fact, such original cases have been quite rare; only about 150 such cases have been settled by the Court. An example is the 1963 dispute between Arizona and California over rights to the water of the Colorado River.

A more common path to the Court is through its **appellate jurisdiction,** as established by Congress. The Supreme Court will entertain a request for a hearing from any citizen whose case raises a substantial federal question (such as a potential violation of the Bill of Rights). The losing party in a case heard by a state or lower federal court may make a formal request for review, claiming that the judge wrongly interpreted the Constitution. Although the Supreme Court has a basic obligation to hear certain kinds of cases on **appeal**—as when a federal court strikes down a state law—most cases that reach the Court do so through a petition for a discretionary **writ of certiorari** (Latin for "to be informed"). Essentially, such a petition is a request by the losing party that the Supreme Court order a lower court to send up the records of the case for review. Normally, the justices will agree to issue a writ (to hear the case) only when at least four of them believe that the issue at stake involves a serious constitutional question or falls within the Court's jurisdiction. In fact, the decision to hear or reject a case may even be based on the unique policy interests of the justices who happen to be sitting on the Court at the time. And as we have seen, those policy interests may vary considerably from one

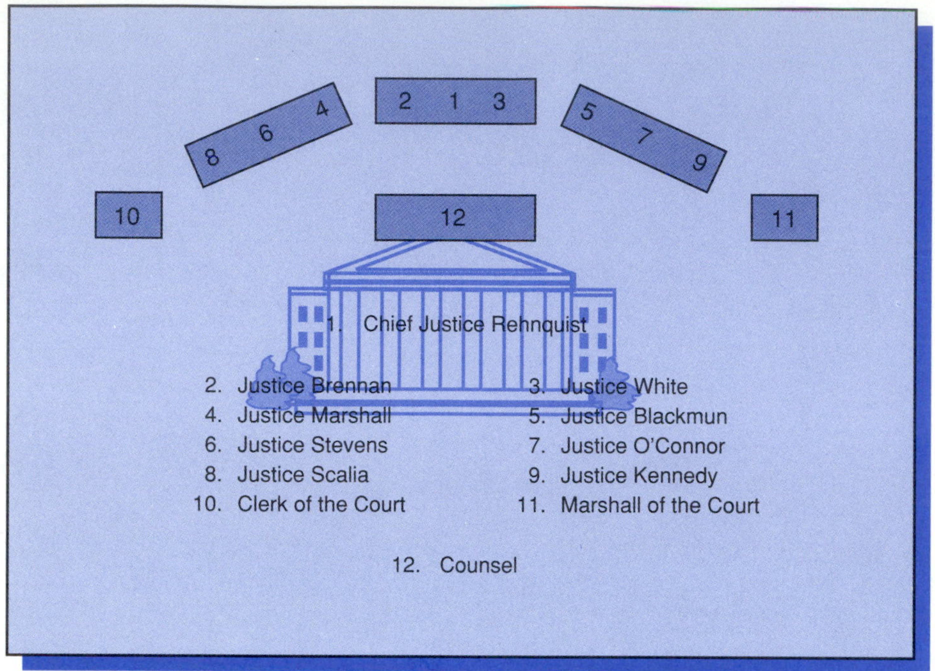

★ **Figure 15-2**
The arrangement of the Supreme Court justices and the clerk of the Court, marshall of the Court, and counsel

historical period to another.[25] Though the Court may be flooded by thousands of petitions for a writ of certiorari each year, the justices grant only a few hundred; the decision as to which cases to accept is entirely up to them.

Deciding the Cases

How, then, do the nine justices process the cases they agree to hear? Usually they hear cases in open court two weeks each month during the October–June term, scheduling the other two weeks for research and opinion writing. On the Mondays through Thursdays when open court sessions are held, the justices march into the marble-columned courtroom at precisely 10:00 A.M. dressed in flowing black robes (see figure 15-2). (No wigs are worn, however; the justices do not mimic this aspect of the British judicial system.)

After the justices have read their decisions on previously heard cases, the chief justice calls for the first case of the day, to be presented by opposing attorneys seated at the counsel tables in front of the bench. Although the justices have already reviewed the written briefs of all sides of the case, they allow the lawyers to present brief oral arguments. They usually allow only thirty minutes for each side, though in some important cases they allot more time. To the chagrin of the lawyers, the justices may interrupt their speeches to ask questions or challenge their arguments. At times the justices may even talk among themselves, scribble notes, or, as in the

exceptional case of Oliver Wendell Holmes, who frequently had already made up his mind, take a nap.

As imposing as these public sessions may be, the real work of the justices takes place behind the scenes. Each justice spends most of his or her time researching and studying cases alone or with law clerks. Then, for a day or two each week, the justices assemble in an ornate conference room to decide which new petitions for review to accept and to vote on the cases already presented in chamber. These conferences may last all day and are totally confidential—not even law clerks or secretaries are allowed to attend. The junior justice (the last member appointed to the Court) usually acts as the "guardian of the door," dashing from the conference table to accept or deliver messages.

It is difficult to learn what goes on in these meetings, but we do know that the chief justice presides and usually begins by summarizing the cases and arguing how they should be decided. The chief justice then yields to the others, who take turns voicing their opinions. After a case has been decided, a majority opinion must be drafted explaining the Court's decision. If the chief justice sides with the majority, he writes the opinion or assigns the task to another justice who supported the same view; otherwise, the senior associate justice in the majority makes the assignment.

The drafting of an opinion is an intricate process that usually takes weeks or even months to complete. An initial draft typically circulates among the justices for many rewritings until it is approved by everyone in the majority. Those justices who disagree with the majority may write a dissenting opinion. Sometimes justices who write a dissenting opinion manage to persuade their colleagues to change their minds before the final decision is read in open court.

★ William H. Rehnquist, one of the most conservative of the Supreme Court's nine justices, became chief justice in 1986. He was first appointed to the Court by President Nixon in 1971.

Ironically, some observers see this practice of dissenting as weakening the Court's prestige by revealing its internal divisions. The fact that many important Court decisions have been split 5 to 4 or 6 to 3 convinces some critics that the Court often cannot provide a definitive solution to a legal controversy. Yet many powerful legal expressions have been voiced in dissenting opinions, such as in those by Oliver Wendell Holmes, Louis Brandeis, and Hugo Black. In fact, many dissenting opinions eventually become the Court's majority opinion, a reflection of changes in the times and new perspectives on legal issues. (Indeed, since 1789 the Supreme Court has reversed itself at least 150 times.)

The Chief Justice

Judicial influence is not shared equally by all nine justices. Just as some members of Congress exert disproportionate influence on policy making, some justices, by virtue of their superior legal skills, exert considerably greater influence than others on judicial decisions.

The role of the chief justice is important in this regard, for if he is an especially forceful individual, he can stamp his own character on the Court. The chief justice gains special authority by presiding over open court sessions and by directing the secret conferences. Although, like other justices, he has but one vote, he sets time limits on debate, establishes the ground rules for discussion, and assigns the writing of Court opinions. In addition, he is the Court's symbolic head and holds in some respects the highest governmental office next to that of the president. By virtue of his position, he may guide the Court toward making a profound and lasting imprint on national policy.

★ Recruitment to the High Court

As we would expect, a major influence on judicial decision making is the background of each person appointed to the Court. Yet, though the Constitution outlines legal requirements for other political officeholders, such as the president and members of Congress, it is silent about the qualifications of a Supreme Court justice. As far as the Constitution is concerned, a justice could be foreign born (and not even a United States citizen), too young to vote, and totally without legal training.

In fact, the Constitution does not even specify how many justices there should be. This responsibility was handed to Congress. In the beginning, the Court was composed of only six members; but this number was changed half a dozen times until Congress finally settled on nine justices in 1869.

Although the Constitution does not specify any formal legal qualifications for a Supreme Court justice, some informal qualifications have tended to prevail. The backgrounds of justices, like those of presidents and members of Congress, have not been representative of the general population. Most have been Protestant, financially independent, and about fifty-five years of age at the time of their appointment. Only about 10 percent have been Catholic or Jewish; only one has been black; and so far, only one has been a woman.

Interestingly enough, although every Supreme Court justice has had some legal background, some have had little prior experience as a judge. Almost half of the justices in the Court's history, including some of the Court's most eminent members—John Marshall, Louis Brandeis, Felix Frankfurter, Earl Warren—have had no judicial training at all. Instead, some have come from positions in government, as former members of Congress, cabinet officials, governors, or even (as in the case of William Howard Taft) president of the United States.

The Role of the President

Although a seat on the high bench is a top prize for anyone who seeks political influence, it cannot be campaigned for like a seat in Congress or won through a public popularity contest. Like other federal judgeships, a Supreme Court seat must be filled by presidential appointment, subject to Senate approval.

Though each president has pledged to appoint federal judges strictly on the basis of merit, the selection process has tended to be a political one. Federal district judges have tended to be appointed on the recommendations of state party officials or senators of the states concerned; vacancies on the Supreme Court and courts of appeals have been filled after the president has received recommendations from a variety of sources, including members of Congress, judges, interest groups, and bar associations. Presidents have sometimes made an effort to maintain some religious, ethnic, and geographic balance on the Court to help legitimize its decisions and gain the political support of influential groups. As we have seen, however, such considerations have not applied to most minority groups or to women, who generally have been greatly underrepresented in the appointment process.

Historically, presidents have tended to select justices who reflect their own political and judicial philosophies, using the appointment process to augment their political influence. Because Supreme Court rulings can greatly affect national policy, the appointment of justices has been a prime way for presidents to implant their own ideas on American law. As Richard Nixon once stated, "There is probably no more important legacy that a President of the United States can leave in these times than his appointments to the Supreme Court. . . . You will recall, I am sure, that during my campaign for the Presidency I pledged to nominate to the Supreme Court individuals who shared my judicial philosophy."[26] Given this perspective, it should not be surprising that about 90 percent of all Supreme Court justices and lower federal court judges appointed since 1789 have belonged to the same party as the appointing president. Of the judges appointed to the federal courts by President Reagan during his two terms in office, 98 percent were Republicans. Reagan and his advisors carefully screened candidates to ensure that any person nominated would take a conservative position on abortion and other social issues.

Naturally, the ability of presidents to shape the Court to their own philosophies has been limited by the necessity of winning Senate approval. President Nixon saw two of his nominees, Clement Haynesworth and G. Harrold Carswell, rejected by the Senate in 1969 and 1970. And as we noted earlier, in 1987 the Senate refused to confirm Ronald Reagan's nominee Robert Bork, a former Yale law professor whom Reagan had earlier appointed to a federal appeals court. The record for rejections, however, is held by John Tyler (1841–1844), who saw four of his nominees turned down. Although the Senate does not customarily resist presidents' wishes in such fashion, at least one of every five nominations has been either withdrawn, rejected, or not acted on at all.[27]

Presidents sometimes make mistakes and discover that their appointees take positions contrary to their expectations. Supreme Court justices tend to become quite independent once they reach the bench, especially since they are appointed for life. President Eisenhower, for example, was less than happy to find Earl Warren—a California Republican governor whom he appointed chief justice in 1953—leading one of the most activist Courts in American history. The appointment of Warren, Eisenhower reportedly lamented, was "the biggest damn fool mistake I ever made." As we will see, some critics suggest that Supreme Court justices, rather than being appointed by the president, should be elected by the voters.

★ Other Courts, Other Judges

Although Supreme Court justices stand at the pinnacle of the federal judicial system, the rulings of lower federal and state court judges also can have tremendous political and legal significance. Without the diligence of District Court Judge John Sirica (*Time* magazine's "Man of the Year" in 1973), the Watergate scandal might have attracted considerably less attention than it did. It was Judge Sirica, a Republican who headed the federal district court in the nation's capital, who presided at the trial of the seven Watergate burglars and who broke open the case by agreeing to review their penalties if they talked—as James McCord eventually did. Not only did the disclosures in Judge Sirica's courtroom help elevate the original burglary into a national scandal, but it was there that the White House, the Senate Watergate Committee, and the special prosecutor battled over possession of the elusive White House tapes. It was Judge Sirica, not the justices of the Supreme Court, who first pitted the judicial branch against the president of the United States by ordering Richard Nixon to turn over the tapes for court inspection.

Given the latent political importance and the legal power of judges in the American judicial system, we should consider the structures and duties of their

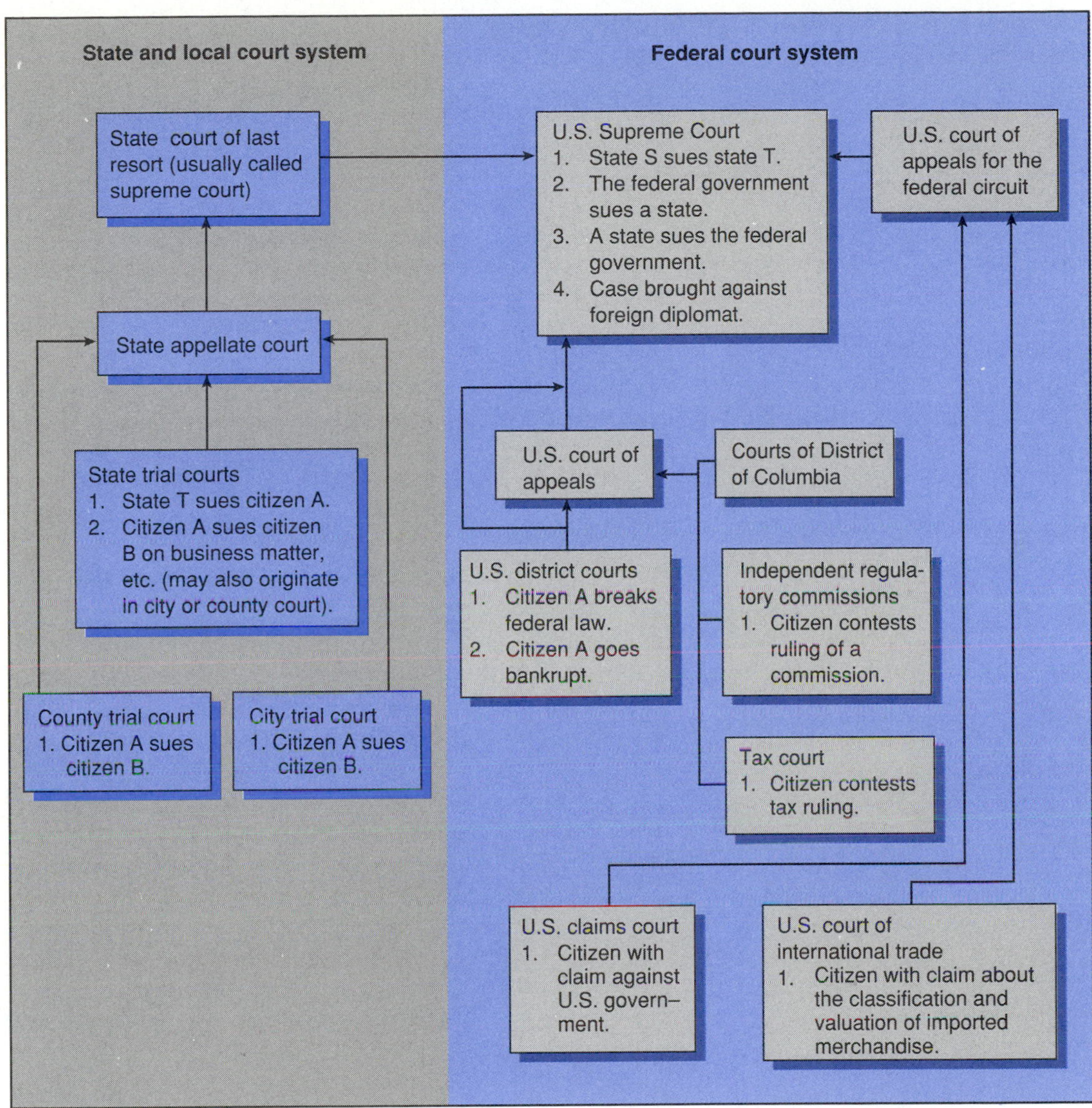

★ **Figure 15-3**
How cases go through the state and local court systems and the federal court systems to get to the Supreme Court

courts (see figure 15-3). Article III of the Constitution specifies that "the judicial power of the United States shall be vested in one supreme Court, and in such inferior Courts as the Congress may from time to time ordain and establish." Thus the Constitution specifically provides for the Supreme Court, but it gives Congress the sole authority to determine the number and jurisdiction of other federal courts. Beginning with the Judiciary Act of 1789, which established the first federal district and circuit courts, Congress has been creating an increasing number of federal courts to accommodate the country's growing population and judicial work load.

★ Table 15-2
U.S. courts of appeal

Circuits	*States served*
First circuit	Maine, Massachusetts, New Hampshire, Rhode Island, Puerto Rico
Second circuit	Connecticut, New York, Vermont
Third circuit	Delaware, New Jersey, Pennsylvania, Virgin Islands
Fourth circuit	Maryland, North Carolina, South Carolina, Virginia, West Virginia
Fifth circuit	Louisiana, Mississippi, Texas
Sixth circuit	Kentucky, Michigan, Ohio, Tennessee
Seventh circuit	Illinois, Indiana, Wisconsin
Eighth circuit	Arkansas, Iowa, Minnesota, Missouri, Nebraska, North Dakota, South Dakota
Ninth circuit	Arizona, California, Idaho, Montana, Nevada, Oregon, Washington, Hawaii, Alaska, Guam
Tenth circuit	Colorado, Kansas, New Mexico, Utah, Oklahoma, Wyoming
Eleventh circuit	Alabama, Florida, Georgia
Twelfth circuit	Court of Appeals for District of Columbia

Federal District Courts

The most numerous of the federal courts are those at the base of the federal judicial system, the district courts. At present there are ninety-four federal district courts in the United States, with at least one in each state and territory. Containing anywhere from two to twenty-seven judges each, these district trial courts settle civil disputes between citizens of different states, resolve federal questions arising under the Constitution (such as the constitutional controversy surrounding the White House tapes), and try persons accused of violations of federal law (such as counterfeiting, illegal immigration, and mail fraud). These district courts have original jurisdiction only; that is, they do not hear cases on appeal.

Courts of Appeals

Because the rulings of district court judges are occasionally controversial or imprecise, the federal judicial system also provides twelve courts of appeals to review their decisions (see table 15-2). Each court of appeals serves one of the twelve judicial circuits into which the country has been divided and contains anywhere from six to twenty-eight judgeships. These courts have the responsibility not only to hear appeals from the lower district courts but occasionally to review decisions of the federal regulatory agencies. Because they hear cases only on appeal, they do not use juries; instead, these judges normally sit as a panel to hear each case.

The federal courts of appeals also received publicity during the Watergate scandal, when the court of appeals in Washington, D.C. upheld Judge Sirica's order directing President Nixon to hand over the White House tapes. Although Nixon later appealed a similar case to the Supreme Court, he obeyed the appeals court's ruling in the first confrontation, setting a precedent that future presidents may find difficult to ignore.

Special Federal Courts

In addition to the district and appeals courts, a number of other federal courts have been created by Congress to deal with special kinds of cases. These courts include the United States Court of Claims, Customs Court, Court of Customs and Patent Appeals, Tax Court, Court of Military Appeals, and the territorial courts. The judges of these courts, like the judges of the district and appeals courts, are appointed by the president with the consent of the Senate. The decisions of these courts also may be appealed to the Supreme Court.

State Courts

Finally, we should remember that there are two different sets of courts in the United States: federal and state. Each of the fifty states has its own court system to handle cases not within the judicial power granted to the federal courts by the Constitution and Congress. Theoretically, neither set of courts is inferior to the other, but the state courts must obey the rulings of the United States Supreme Court in cases involving constitutional issues.

State courts not only possess the power to interpret acts of state legislatures and other state officials, but they, not federal courts, try most of the nation's civil and criminal cases. The bulk of criminal and civil laws—such as those concerning divorce, burglary, and homicide—are enacted by the states and not by the federal government. Thus, although most Americans probably will never be a party to a federal court case, there are few who will not at some time at least challenge a traffic ticket in a municipal court, which is part of the state judicial system.

Though the names and nature of state courts vary throughout the country, their hierarchies tend to be similar: at the bottom of the structure, municipal and justice courts; above them, superior (or county) courts; then district courts of appeals; and at the top a state supreme court. And, in contrast to all federal judges, who are appointed by the president with the approval of the Senate, in most states the judges are elected at the polls.[28]

★ The Court and Its Critics

In its long history the Supreme Court has faced many reform proposals. Some of these proposals have been made by people who support an activist role for the Court but who feel it urgently needs reorganizing and streamlining. Still other proposals have been made by people who are critical of the justices' exercise of power and who wish to see such power curtailed. The two types of reform proposals overlap in some ways.

Reducing the Work Load

The practice of hearing cases for only two weeks each month might seem to give Supreme Court justices a great deal of time to research and study cases. Yet there have been complaints that their work load has become increasingly hard to bear. As the number of appeals and petitions for certiorari filed each year has climbed from about a thousand cases in the early 1950s to close to five thousand cases today, concern has been expressed that the justices have become entangled in too much legal paperwork. With so many cases to consider each year, the justices have not had enough time to oversee the judicial process properly. And with so many cases competing for the justices' attention, citizens with legitimate grievances find the opportunities for judicial redress restricted.

One proposal to meet this problem was made in the early 1970s by a study group headed by Paul Freund, a Harvard law professor. This study group, appointed by former chief justice Warren Burger, recommended the creation of a national court of appeals composed of judges chosen on a rotating basis from the federal courts of appeals. This new court would screen all cases now referred to the Supreme Court and would decide which cases were important enough for the highest court to consider. Supreme Court justices would retain the right to hear any case they wanted, but would be relieved of handling the large volume of mostly trivial and insubstantial petitions.

A number of people denounced the study group's proposal on the grounds that the Supreme Court justices would only lose much of the independent authority to decide which new petitions to consider. Former chief justice Earl Warren, for instance, believed that the creation of a new national court of appeals would do "irreparable harm to the prestige, the power and the function of the Supreme Court." It would simply add to the bureaucracy of justice and impose goals and values that conflicted with those expressed by the high Court. Moreover, it would serve as another means of restricting access to the Supreme Court by ordinary citizens, adding another procedural roadblock to those already imposed by the Burger Court. Despite serious consideration by the Senate in the mid-1980s, the proposal to establish an intermediary court of appeals has not been put into effect.

Curbing the Court's Powers

Far more dramatic suggestions for reforming the Court have been offered as a result of repeated criticisms of its decisions. As we have seen, Supreme Court justices have had their share of criticism and accusations of wielding too much power. The justices were attacked in the 1930s for obstructing the policies of the New Deal and in the 1960s, 1970s, and 1980s for their rulings on police procedures, prayer in public schools, flag burning, and abortion. Such criticisms have given rise to proposals of measures to curb the justices' powers, such as a requirement that more than a simple 5-to-4 majority be obtained to render any law or action unconstitutional.

Perhaps the most dramatic suggestion has been to elect justices for limited and fixed terms. Critics argue that because the Court plays a major role in policy making, justices should be elected at the polls rather than appointed by the president for life terms. There is adequate precedent for such a change, since most states currently elect their highest court judges for terms ranging from six to twelve years. Though these state court judges also exercise judicial review, the voters still have an opportunity to express their disapproval without the need to resort to impeachment.

This proposal has not been vigorously championed, however, partly because the constraints on the justices already mentioned have been considered adequate. The public, through the president and Congress as well as through their own actions, ultimately can circumvent unpopular Court decisions. In addition, there has been a reluctance to extend majority control over the Court for reasons discussed earlier. If the justices of the nation's highest court were required to run periodically for reelection, they might be subjected to greater pressures by special interests and would lose much of their independent authority to protect individual and minority rights from majority prejudices. "The very purpose of having a written Constitution," former chief justice Burger stated, "is to provide safeguards for certain rights that cannot yield to public opinion. . . . The Justices' duty is to stand firm in defense of basic constitutional values, as they see them, even against momentary tides of public opinion."[29] In any event, as two scholars have concluded in their review of California's judicial system, "There are problems with both methods: executive appointment may result in numerous political hacks on the bench, while election assumes that the people are knowledgeable in the area of judicial qualifications and care enough to become informed."[30]

★ Summary

In contrast to the presidency and Congress, the Supreme Court tends to receive little public scrutiny. Most Americans are unfamiliar with the Court's proceedings, history, and rulings. Yet such widespread ignorance should not obscure either the Court's enormous power or the controversies that sometimes accompany its rulings. The court's power of judicial review, though not specifically granted by the Constitution, has been used to overturn decisions of Congress, the president, state legislatures, and the lower courts.

Though the power of judicial review had been anticipated and used by lower courts before the Constitution was drafted, it was the Supreme Court's ruling in *Marbury* v. *Madison* (1803) that firmly established its use by the highest Court. It has been justified as an important tool in the Court's efforts to interpret the Constitution's meaning and check for the possible excesses of popularly elected legislators and executives.

Throughout its history, the rulings of the Court have tended to reflect shifting orientations. It is possible to discern several periods when certain issues dominated the Court's attention: federal-state relations; government regulation of private enterprise; and equal rights and due process. Moreover, depending on the composition and philosophy of its members, the Court has leaned toward either judicial restraint or judicial activism. Today the dispute continues over which approach is best for the nation. Though the justices sometimes avoid foreign policy disputes, they have ruled in a variety of cases involving international relations. As globalization expands America's economic and political role in the world, the Court may find itself venturing further and further into the thicket of foreign policy. Thus the Court does not exist in a vacuum. It must be sensitive to the political climate of the times and to the substantial impact of both Congress and the president. This impact can be perceived with special clarity in the making of foreign policy, which the Court (with some exceptions) has tended to regard as the prerogative of the president and Congress.

There are several avenues by which citizens can have a case heard by the Supreme Court; the most common means is a petition for a writ of certiorari. It is up to the justices to decide whether to hear a case under such circumstances. Of the thousands of petitions submitted each year, only a few hundred are likely to receive a hearing.

The drafting of an opinion by the Court is a complex process in which all nine justices participate. They research the cases alone and discuss them in conference before a vote is taken. Those justices who disagree with the majority's position may submit a dissenting opinion, which perhaps years later may eventually turn into the Court's majority view.

Although the Constitution does not specify the qualifications for a justice, or even how many justices there should be, certain informal qualifications tend to prevail. The selection of a new justice, who serves for life, is up to the president, with the advice and consent of the Senate. While some presidents have been unable to fill any vacancies on the Court, other presidents have been able to select a sufficient number to influence the Court's philosophical character and direction for years to come.

Finally, in addition to the Supreme Court, our judicial system comprises lower federal and state courts. Like the Supreme Court, these courts wield significant influence on the lives of American citizens.

★ Key Terms

appeal
appellate jurisdiction
class-action suit
executive privilege
judicial review
original jurisdiction
strict constructionists
writ of certiorari
writ of mandamus

★ Notes

1. See, for example, James Allen Davis and Tom W. Smith, *General Social Surveys, 1972–1988* (Chicago: National Opinion Research Center, 1988), subfiles 1986, 1987 (machine-readable data file); also *Gallup Report,* December 1988.
2. Walter F. Murphy and Joseph Tanenhaus, "Public Opinion and the United States Supreme Court," in *Frontiers of Judicial Research,* ed. Joel B. Grossman and Joseph Tanenhaus (New York: Wiley, 1969).
3. Edwards v. South Carolina (1962).
4. Brown v. Louisiana (1966).
5. Adderly v. Florida (1967).
6. United States v. O'Brien (1968).
7. Merlo Pusey, *Charles Evans Hughes* (New York: Macmillan, 1952), p. 204.
8. Quoted in James A. Nathan and James K. Oliver, *Foreign Policy Making and the American Political System,* 2d ed. (Boston: Little, Brown, 1987), p. 241.
9. See Edward S. Corwin, ed., *The Constitution of the United States of America: Analysis and Interpretation* (Washington, D.C.: U.S. Government Printing Office, 1953).
10. Charles Beard, "The Supreme Court—Usurper or Grantee?" *Political Science Quarterly,* March 1912, pp. 1–35.

11. Oliver Wendell Holmes, "Law and the Court," in *The Occasional Speeches of Oliver Wendell Holmes,* comp. Mark De Wolfe Howe (Cambridge, Mass.: Belknap Press of Harvard University Press, 1962), p. 172.
12. Pollock v. Farmer's Loan and Trust Company (1895); Hammer v. Dagenhart (1918); Adkins v. Children's Hospital (1923).
13. Brown v. Board of Education (1954); Gideon v. Wainwright (1963); Miranda v. Arizona (1966).
14. See Stephen L. Wasby, *Continuity and Change: From the Warren Court to the Burger Court* (Pacific Palisades, Calif.: Goodyear, 1976), chap. 2.
15. Richard M. Nixon, speech of October 21, 1971.
16. Roe v. Wade (1973).
17. Harris v. New York (1971); Gregg v. Georgia (1976); Miller v. California (1973); California Bankers Association v. Schultz (1974).
18. Beal v. Doe (1977); Maher v. Roe (1977).
19. Nathan Glazer, "Towards an Imperial Judiciary?" *Public Interest,* Fall 1975, p. 109. Glazer refers to Swann v. Charlotte–Mecklenburg County Board of Education (1971); Keyes v. School District No. 1, Denver, Colorado (1973); Griggs v. Duke Power Company (1971).
20. New York Times Company v. United States (1971).
21. Pollock v. Farmer's Loan and Trust Company (1895).
22. See, for example, Theodore L. Becker and Malcolm M. Feeley, eds., *The Impact of Supreme Court Decisions,* 2d ed. (New York: Oxford University Press, 1973); Neil Romans, "The Role of State Supreme Courts in Judicial Policy Making," *Western Political Quarterly,* March 1974, pp. 38–59.
23. Becker and Feeley, *Impact of Supreme Court Decisions.*
24. For more on this case, see Anthony Lewis, *Gideon's Trumpet* (New York: Random House, 1964).
25. See Lawrence Baum, "Policy Goals in Judicial Gatekeeping: A Proximity Model of Discretionary Jurisdiction," *American Journal of Political Science,* February 1977, pp. 13–36.
26. Richard M. Nixon, speech of October 21, 1971.
27. *Congressional Quarterly's Guide to Congress,* 2d ed. (Washington, D.C., 1976), p. 647.
28. For more information, see Henry J. Abraham, *The Judicial Process,* 3d ed. (New York: Oxford University Press, 1975).
29. "The Chief Justice Talks about the Court," *Reader's Digest,* February 1973.
30. Ruth A. Ross and Barbara S. Stone, *California's Political Process* (New York: Random House, 1973), p. 140.

★ For Further Reading

Abraham, Henry J. *The Judicial Process.* 5th ed. New York: Oxford University Press, 1986.

——. *Justices and Presidents: A Political History of Appointments to the Supreme Court.* 2d ed. New York: Oxford University Press, 1985.

Baum, Lawrence. *American Courts: Process and Policy.* Boston: Houghton Mifflin, 1986.

——. *The Supreme Court.* 2d ed. Washington, D.C.: Congressional Quarterly Press, 1985.

Horowitz, Henry J. *The Judicial Process.* 5th ed. New York: Oxford University Press, 1986.

Johnson, Charles A., and Bradley C. Cannon, *Judicial Politics: Implementation and Impact.* Washington, D.C.: Congressional Quarterly Press, 1984.

Rohde, David W., and Harold J. Spaeth. *Supreme Court Decision Making.* San Francisco, W. H. Freeman, 1976.

Woodward, Bob, and Scott Armstrong. *The Brethren: Inside the Supreme Court.* New York: Simon & Schuster, 1979.

PART FOUR

Government to the Rescue? American Politics in Action at Home and Abroad

CHAPTER SIXTEEN

The history of governmental intervention has been the history of the growing ineffectiveness of the private conscience as a means of social control. The only alternative is the growth of the public conscience, whose natural expression is the democratic government.

—*Arthur M. Schlesinger, Jr.*

In this present crisis, government is not the solution to our problem; government is the problem.

—*Ronald Reagan*

PUBLIC POLICY

★★★★★★★★★★★★★

Public Policy Making: How Governments Solve Problems

Imagine that you were given the task of eliminating poverty in the United States. What would you do? Create jobs for every able-bodied adult? What if some of those jobs did not pay enough to bring workers above the poverty line? How would you define the poverty line? If the private sector did not create enough jobs, should the government do so? Who should care for the preschool children of those workers? Who should be taxed to pay for government-sponsored jobs, child care, and benefits to parents of young children? Alternatively, would you give poor people a certain amount of money each year to spend as they saw fit? Would such a plan discourage people from seeking work?

Imagine further that you had the task of eliminating world poverty. How would you feed, clothe, house, and heal the world's poor? How much should Americans be taxed to pay for your antipoverty programs around the world?

Poverty is only one of many difficult problems that nations must face. We routinely ask our governments to solve complex problems in such areas as health care, transportation, taxation, the environment, civil rights, and foreign policy. Governments try to solve problems by a variety of measures. Sometimes they work. At other times they seem to make matters worse. How can we tell when a proposed measure will work? Can we borrow measures from other countries?

Governmental attempts to solve social problems are called public policies. In this chapter, we will look at the way public policies emerge. First we will examine the conflict at the root of public policy making: governments versus markets. Then we will consider how public policy making sometimes pits experts against politicians. Finally, we will see how policies have to make their way through five stages in the public policy-making process. This chapter focuses mainly on *how* policies are made; chapter 17 examines the substance of specific controversial policies.

★ Public Policy: Governments vs. Markets

To solve social problems, government officials must make **public policy:** they must forge new laws that, in effect, will determine how the burdens and benefits of social programs will be distributed. They must decide who will pay for those programs and who will reap the major benefits from them.

Indeed, public policies reveal a nation's priorities; for example, should we spend more money to defend our shores or to educate our children? There are

★ Even though we live in one of the world's wealthiest nations, we are often made painfully aware that American affluence does not extend to all our citizens and that poverty grips many people around the world. While some Americans look to private relief and charitable organizations to remedy U.S. and world poverty, many expect governments to provide workable solutions to the problem of poverty both at home and abroad.

always alternatives to existing policies and so government officials must consider the costs and consequences of various alternatives.

Although governments borrow public policy solutions from each other, comparative studies show that nations differ considerably when it comes to the question of whether the government (the public sector) or markets (the private sector) should solve social problems. Much of the current debate between liberals and conservatives in American politics centers on the proper roles of governments and markets as problem solvers.

This question of the proper relation between governments and markets as problem solvers gave birth to public policy as a distinct field of study. The grandfather of public policy was Adam Smith, a Scottish economist whose *Wealth of Nations* was published in 1776—the year we declared our independence. Smith criticized his government's inefficient commercial policies. He wanted to take economic policy making out of the hands of government and put it under the control of market forces. Smith supported a **free-market economy,** with little government regulation; an economy in which buyers and sellers would arrive at a fair price for goods and services. Such an arrangement, he believed, would make the economy as a whole better off, or more efficient.[1] Smith believed that governments should not waste taxpayers' hard-earned money; rather, they should seek the most cost-efficient solutions to social problems.

But public policy involves more than efficiency. Many citizens also want policies that are equitable. Equity, or fairness, is an equally important consideration in public policy. For many people, an efficient solution that makes the rich richer and the poor poorer is hard to justify in a democracy. As we saw in chapter 3, the fact that the federal income tax has always been progressive (with wealthier people paying at higher rates than the poor) reflects a liberal concern for equity.

Concerns about efficiency and equity are often drawn along partisan lines. While neither side has a monopoly on either concern, conservative Republicans

Adam Smith and Franklin D. Roosevelt: Markets vs. Governments

Should we turn to markets or governments to solve social problems and promote the general welfare? In one corner stands Adam Smith, champion of markets, and in the other, Franklin Roosevelt, defender of governments.

The first policy analyst, Adam Smith (1723–1790), argued in his *Wealth of Nations* that a nation's welfare is best served when the government leaves markets alone to produce wealth and to satisfy consumers (the doctrine of **laissez-faire**). If individual producers and consumers are free to pursue their own gain, everyone will be better off. An invisible hand promotes the public interest as each individual pursues his or her own interest. According to Smith:

> Every individual necessarily labors to render the annual revenue of the society as great as he can. He generally indeed neither intends to promote the public interest, nor knows how much he is promoting it. . . . He intends only his own gain, and he is in this, as in many other cases, led by an invisible hand to promote an end which was no part of his intention. . . . By pursuing his own interest he frequently promotes that of society more effectually than when he really intends to promote it. I have never known much good done by those who affected to trade for the public good. [*Wealth of Nations,* bk. 4, chap. 2]

Smith recognized certain types of market failures and instances of positive government action. But he put the burden of proof on those who recommended government intervention in a free market.

One of the most famous responses to this challenge came from Franklin D. Roosevelt (1882–1945), thirty-second president of the United States (1933–1945). In the face of a collapsed economy, with slackened production and high unemployment, Roosevelt used government spending to recharge the economy. In his view, the private pursuit of individual gain had failed to steer the invisible hand in the right direction, and the general good demanded action by the public sector.

But Roosevelt did not come to the presidency convinced of the **Keynesian economics** he eventually came to practice. Keynesian economic theory calls for the government to fuel demand in a depressed economy, an interven-

(continued)

tend to be in the efficiency camp, while liberal Democrats tend to stress the importance of equity. In considering foreign aid to developing nations, for instance, conservatives generally seek to limit direct American aid in favor of a more "efficient" encouragement of economic growth. Liberals, in contrast, often look at the unequal distribution of wealth in these nations and believe that American monetary aid may directly benefit the poor. Conservatives say that efficiency results in an economic pie expanded by the private sector, which makes everyone better off; liberals respond that equity makes sure that the rich do not end up with more than their fair share of the pie.

Similarly, liberals and conservatives tend to differ over the effectiveness of governments versus markets as problem solvers. In the tradition of Adam Smith, conservatives tend to trust the market and distrust government to arrive at good solutions. They see Big Brother's intrusion into their lives as a threat to the sanctity of individualism, which we described in chapter 6 as a core American value. In the tradition of President Franklin Roosevelt, however, liberals are more optimistic about public-sector solutions. They like to tinker with a variety of programs in areas where, in their view, market forces have not produced satisfactory results.

To see the difference between conservatives and liberals, let us consider educational policy. Some conservatives advocate the use of vouchers, or redeem-

★ During his presidency, Franklin D. Roosevelt used government measures to influence market activity.

★ In his *Wealth of Nations,* Adam Smith made the case for government's leaving markets alone to produce wealth.

tion opposed by the classical economic theory of Adam Smith. After the British economist John Maynard Keynes first visited the new president, he remarked with disappointment, "I'm afraid your president knows little about economics." At first Roosevelt ignored the advice of Keynesians in his administration and tried to reduce expenditures to cure a new recession. But in 1937 the situation worsened, and that was the last time a president was to try to cut expenditures during an economic downturn.

Roosevelt approached economic policy with the same receptivity to new ideas that marked his other New Deal innovations. He was not afraid of failure and presented his policy initiatives as experiments: if a program did not work, he would introduce something else until he hit upon something that did work.

The legacies of Roosevelt and Smith to the field of public policy go beyond their respective economic theories. From Roosevelt comes a pragmatic, can-do, trial-and-error attitude toward government problem solving. And from Smith comes a reminder that government policies should make the most cost-efficient use of taxpayers' hard-earned money. ★

SOURCES: Richard Pious, *The American Presidency* (New York: Basic Books, 1979); Arthur Schlesinger, Jr., *The Coming of the New Deal* (Boston: Houghton Mifflin, 1958).

able coupons issued by the government. Parents could use these vouchers to send their children to quality public or private schools, thus pressuring low-quality schools to improve in order to avoid being driven out of business by lack of demand in the marketplace. Liberals, in contrast, often point to the virtues of our public educational system as a major source of upward mobility for immigrants and underprivileged Americans. In their view, citizens' tax dollars and energies should go toward making all schools equally good, rather than supporting only an elite few. They note that our system of public education has historically been a force in opening opportunities to underprivileged Americans—in contrast to the education systems of many other Western industrial nations, where only a privileged few receive a quality education.

Liberals also tend to support the expansion of our **social welfare state** (a nation whose government provides extensive health, educational, and welfare services). We have more extensive educational policies than other Western industrial nations, but our health and welfare policies lag behind theirs. The social welfare state first sprang up in the 1880s in Germany, under the rule of a conservative, Otto von Bismarck. The irony that a conservative adopted liberal social welfare policies is explained by the fact that Bismarck wanted to undermine the popularity of his rivals, the German Socialists, by introducing social insurance programs. These are

government-sponsored programs to which people make regular contributions in order to obtain protection against future disabilities. Today most Western European nations have more comprehensive government-sponsored programs than the United States in such areas as child care, family allowance, maternity leave, health care, housing allowances, and income supplements for the poor.[2] The term "social welfare," as we saw in chapter 6, tends to have fewer negative associations for Europeans than for Americans. Europeans tend to believe that social welfare programs benefit everyone. In the United States, "welfare" tends to be more class-specific and stigmatizing. Ask an average class of students how many are receiving "welfare," and few are likely to raise their hands. Ask how many receive some form of student aid, and probably many will.

Americans have made a trade-off—a choice between conflicting alternatives. We pay less in taxes than our Western European counterparts but receive fewer social welfare services (see figure 16-1). We choose to leave money in private hands and purchase such social services as health care and child care in the marketplace. How do we know if this, or any other public policy trade-off, is worth the price it entails? How do we as citizens make intelligent judgments about the relative advantages and disadvantages of alternative public policy options? These are the questions policy analysts attempt to answer.

★ The Science of Public Policy: Policy Analysis

In using **public policy analysis,** we try to determine which among alternative policies is best for achieving a given set of goals. Take, for example, the goal of improving students' reading and writing abilities. How is this goal best achieved? By buying more books for classroom and library use? By raising teachers' salaries to attract better teachers? By changing curricula to include more reading and writing assignments?

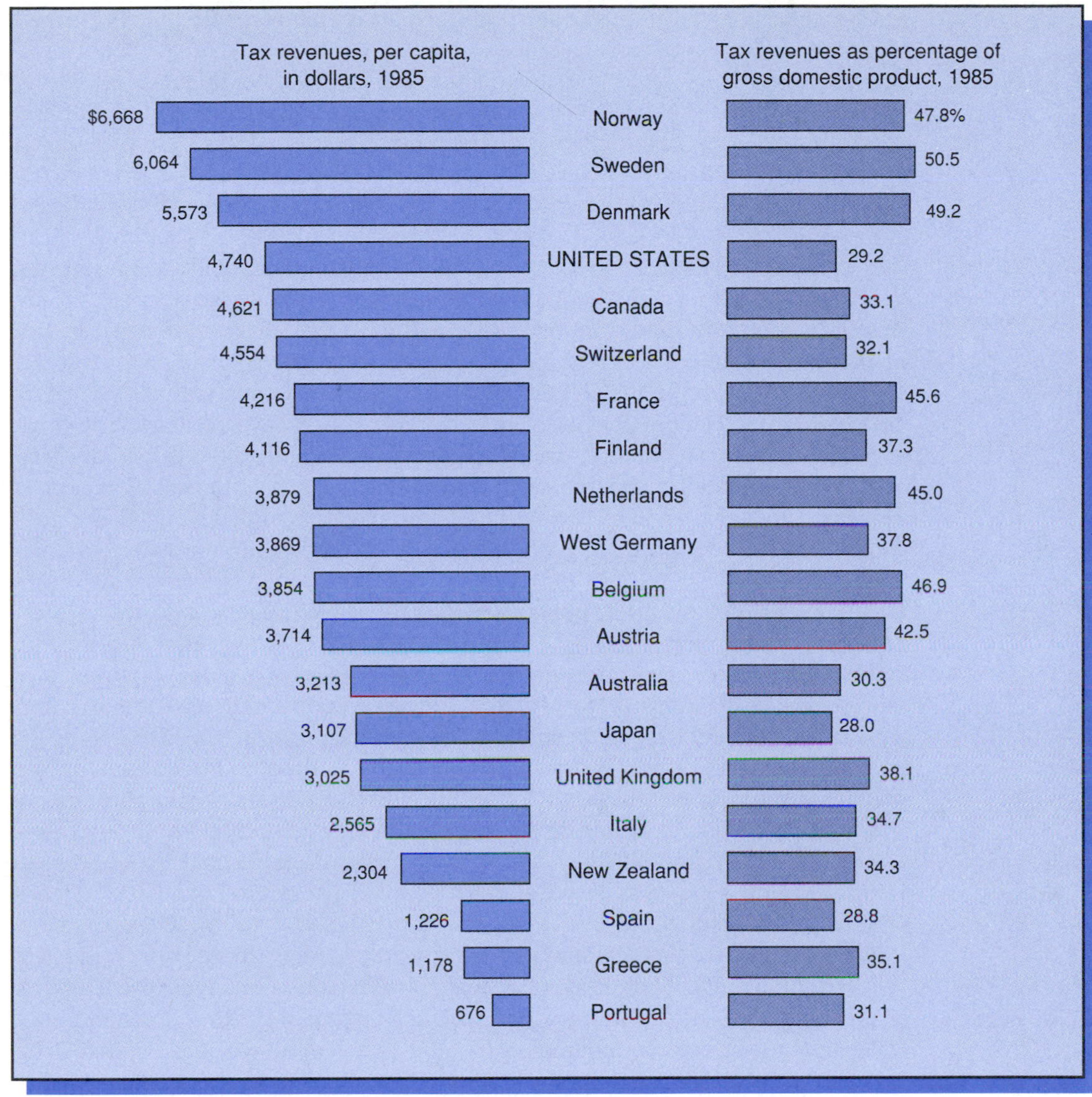

★ **Figure 16-1**
Tax revenues and tax revenues as a percentage of gross domestic product for selected countries, 1985
SOURCE: U.S. Bureau of the Census, *Statistical Abstract of the United States, 1988* (Washington, D.C.: U.S. Government Printing Office, 1987), p. 810.

The Difficulties of Policy Analysis

Policy analysis is extremely difficult. Just when we think we have found the perfect solution to a problem, we find that things are not so simple as we thought. One difficulty is unanticipated consequences, or unforeseen results of a policy. During the 1950s, for example, the federal government launched a program to expand interstate highways. This program succeeded in its goal of enabling troops and private citizens to cross the country more quickly than ever before. But it had significant unanticipated consequences. Highways contributed to the decay of inner cities. Many workers could now move to the suburbs and commute to the city to work. Most of these suburbanites were white and relatively affluent. The poor and minorities were left in the inner city, which now had a small tax base with which to fund public services. Highways also wreaked havoc on the railroad system. Cars, buses, and trucks started to replace trains as the quickest and most efficient means to move people and goods.

A second challenge for policy analysts is the complexity of social problems. Most social problems defy easy answers. By using policy analysis, we attempt to be systematic, objective, and comprehensive, and to rely on proper information. But what if information is severely limited? United States foreign policy toward the Soviet Union, for example, has been hampered by the fact that until very recently the USSR has been a closed society, reluctant to publish vital social and economic data. And in our own country, even when data are available, experts may disagree in their interpretations. Experts routinely disagree on such matters as whether the death penalty deters criminals, whether group day care impedes infant development, whether certain chemicals cause cancer, and whether nuclear weapons make the world less safe.

Another difficulty with policy analysis is that it is slow and costly. Political decision makers often must make policy choices before information is complete. Cancer, for instance, may take decades to develop following initial exposure to a cancer-causing agent. How much evidence does the Food and Drug Administration (FDA) need before it bans a potentially cancer-causing product? The FDA tests drugs for a longer period of time than its counterparts in many other nations before permitting them to be marketed. Yet politicians feel pressure from constituents who have seemingly incurable diseases, such as Acquired Immune Deficiency Syndrome (AIDS), to allow them to use experimental drugs without FDA approval. Vietnam veterans exposed to the herbicide called Agent Orange claim they are suffering from health problems related to this exposure. Yet the Department of Veterans Affairs counters that studies demonstrating such a link are not conclusive.

An additional limitation of policy analysis is that it cannot tell us which aspects of a problem deserve most attention. Let us say that we are concerned about violence in the streets. What dimension of this problem do we address first? Drug use? Poor schools? Violent domestic relations? Unemployment? The easy availability of guns? Our violent and materialistic culture? Personality disorders? The most important causes of a problem may be things the government can do least about. Certainly it is easier to upgrade schools and cushion the effects of unemployment than it is to change a culture that glorifies cheap thrills, violence, and materialism.

Finally, policy analysts are often baffled by conflicts in values. We can say that public policies ought to serve "the public interest," but who gets to define what the public interest is? Should we use the utilitarian yardstick: the greatest good for the greatest number of people? Should we use economists' measure of utility or "satisfaction maximization": satisfying the wants of all? Or are some wants more deserving than others? These are not just abstract questions. They come into play routinely for policy analysts.

Consider the controversial health policy introduced by Oregon in 1987. State legislators shifted $11 million from organ transplants to prenatal care. For this amount of money, the state could provide for either thirty organ transplants or prenatal care for fifteen hundred poor women. Prenatal care was deemed to be

Do Americans Want More for Less?

Even though 62% of the American public say that income taxes are too high, they want the government to spend more money for some programs. In figure 16-2, people were asked to indicate whether they would like to see more or less government spending in each area. They were reminded that if they indicated "much more," it might require a tax increase to pay for it. You will notice that in the areas of education, health, law enforcement, environment, and retirement benefits, the public wanted more money spent. ★

Education	21.4 much more	43.0 more	31.0 same	3.9 less	
Health	13.0 much more	45.0 more	34.2 same	6.1 less	
The police and law enforcement	9.8 much more	42.2 more	42.3 same	4.8 less	
Environment	10.3 much more	33.3 more	43.4 same	11.0 less	
Retirement benefits	12.6 much more	31.0 more	42.5 same	11.2 same	
Unemployment benefits	7.9 much more	18.4 more	49.2 more	17.0 less	7.5 much less
The military and defense	7.7 much more	12.1 more	37.1 same	28.7 less	14.4 much less
Culture and the arts	4.4 much more	10.9 more	41.9 same	26.4 less	16.4 much less

much more · more · same · less · much less

★ **Figure 16-2**

Attitudes on need for government involvement in eight policy areas, 1985

SOURCE: James Allan Davis and Tom W. Smith, *General Social Survey, 1972–1988* (Chicago: National Opinion Research Center, 1988), subfile 1985 (machine-readable data file).

more economical in the long run, since it reduced the incidence of low-birth-weight babies. Such babies tend to have health problems that drain state resources over the years. State-funded transplants are restricted to those that have high success rates, such as transplants of kidneys and corneas. Less successful transplants—of bone marrow for leukemia victims, say—are not covered by state funds. This policy decision may sound rational and cost-effective. But implicit in it is a value decision about whose lives are worth saving. Shortly after this policy went into effect, a seven-year-old boy died of leukemia after the state refused to pay for his bone marrow transplant. His relatives had raised $70,000 of the $100,000 needed for the operation before he died.

This case illustrates a key point: that public policy involves both political analysis and value judgments. Analysts can be objective up to a point, but ultimately their values enter into their analyses. The analysts who persuaded Oregon legislators to adopt this health-care policy made implicit value judgments about whose lives were worth saving and at what costs. And Oregon legislators themselves made similar value judgments. There were certain political assumptions as well: that bone-marrow transplants are a private, not a public, responsibility, and that the health budget could not be expanded because of taxpayer pressure to keep down the cost of government.

Every day we ask our lawmakers to make hard policy choices. In a world of unlimited resources, there would be enough money to satisfy everyone. But legislators enjoy no such luxury. During the 1960s, the economy was booming and the Kennedy and Johnson administrations waged an increasingly costly war on two fronts: in Vietnam and against domestic poverty and discrimination. These administrations enlisted experts in the hope that rational analysis and a can-do mentality would enable the federal government to solve pressing foreign and domestic problems.[3] Then during the 1970s and early 1980s the economy worsened, and the Nixon and Reagan administrations saw government programs as the problem, not the solution. They viewed the market as the solution to social problems.

Whether an administration sees government as the problem or the solution depends on its politics and philosophical perspective. In either case, politicians have come to rely increasingly on policy analysts. Politicians employ their analyses as a form of power: to persuade opponents that a certain course of action is best. Despite the limitations of policy analysis, politicians and the public want rational consideration of policy alternatives and the best use of taxpayers' money.

Cost-Benefit Analysis

The most common form of scrutiny to which analysts subject public policies is **cost-benefit analysis:** they assign a monetary value to the positive and negative features of a project. A project should produce benefits to society greater than its costs; when a choice must be made among projects, the one that yields the greatest net benefits should be selected. Cost-benefit analysis takes into account **opportunity costs,** or the benefits that must be forgone when one project is rejected in favor of another. The cost of doing *A* is that you cannot do *B.* If you have a limited supply of labor and concrete, for example, you can build a dam, but if you do, you cannot build a highway.

Suppose we apply cost-benefit analysis to the example of government construction of a new dam.[4] Time is one factor to take into account. Both the costs and the benefits of such a project are spread out over a number of years. Costs are usually greatest at the outset and stabilize over time. Benefits are often slow to appear and eventually diminish over time.

Other factors come into play in determining whether this project is worth doing. In assigning monetary values to aspects of the dam project, one must make both technical and value choices. How would you attach dollar amounts to the following hypothetical costs and benefits of the dam project?

Costs	*Benefits*
Construction	Hydroelectric power
Flooded lands	Flood control
Relocation of families	Irrigation
Loss of recreation (canoeing)	New recreation (water skiing)

The market provides guidance for calculating some of these dollar amounts, as in the case of the property value of flooded lands. But it is of limited help in others, such as the relative value of canoeing versus water skiing. Furthermore, we expect the public sector, unlike the private sector, to take into account social costs and benefits, such as the costs to a family of relocating from an ancestral family farm, or the benefits of preserving natural beauty.

★★★★★★★★★★★★
Defense

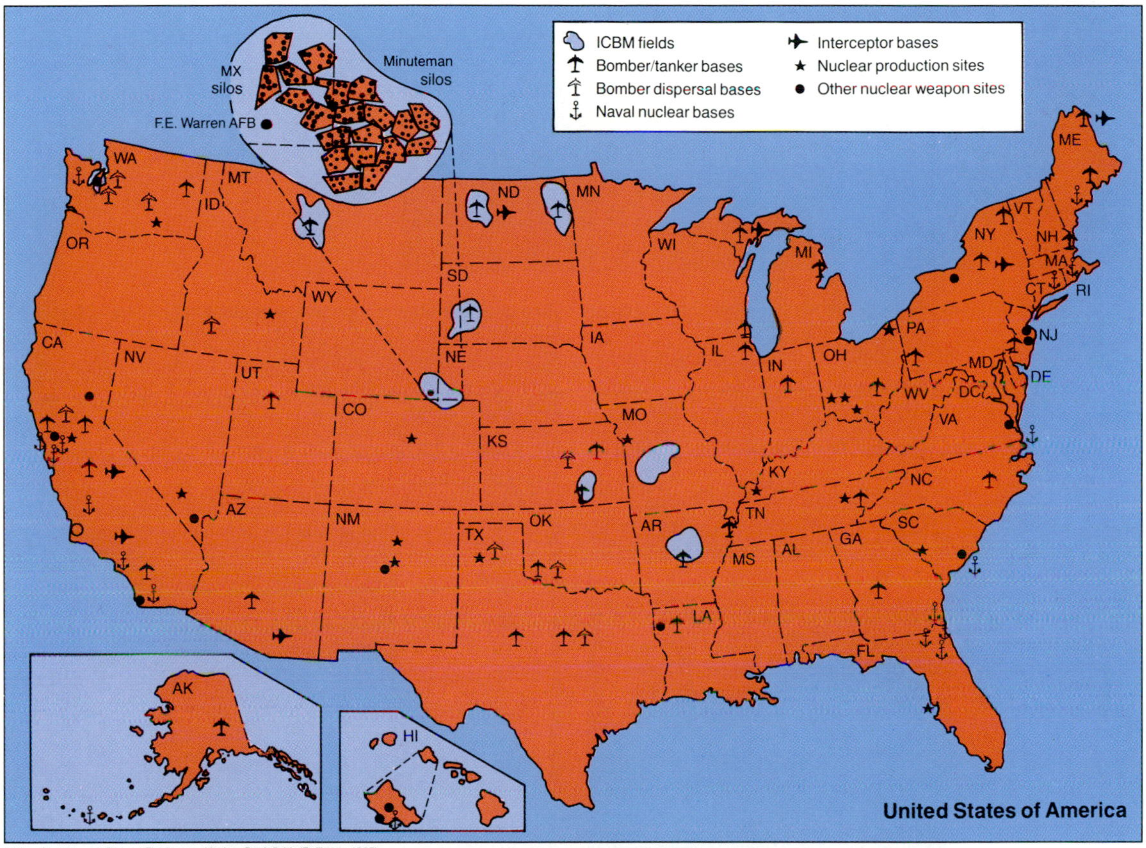

ICBM fields
Bomber/tanker bases
Bomber dispersal bases
Naval nuclear bases
Interceptor bases
Nuclear production sites
Other nuclear weapon sites
MX silos
Minuteman silos
F.E. Warren AFB
United States of America

William M. Arkin and Richard Fieldhouse, *Nuclear Battlefields* (Ballinger, 1985)

Much of the American population remains unaware of the extent of our nuclear preparedness. Yet only nine states in the country do not contain a bomb base, missile silo, submarine base, or command center. Some of these locations are underground sites, often invisible to the above-ground observer. The NORAD (North American Aerospace Defense Command) command center, for instance, is located deep underground in the Cheyenne mountains of Colorado.

CLEARANCE 10FT 5IN
CHEYENNE MTN COMPLEX

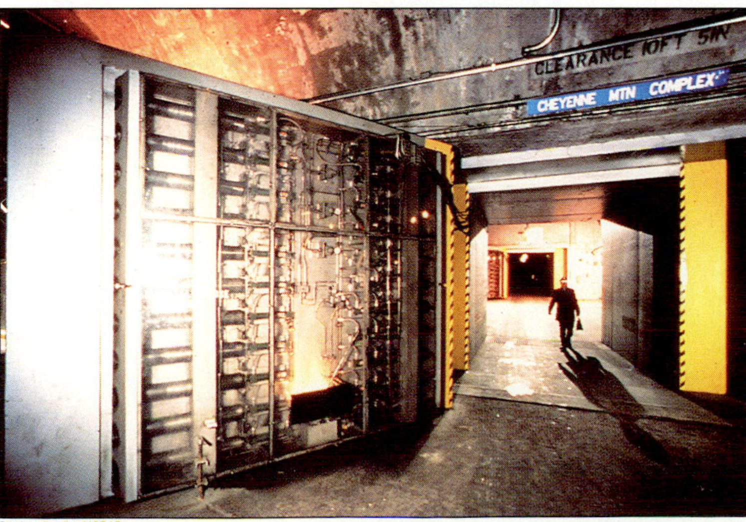

Stephen Forsling/NORAD

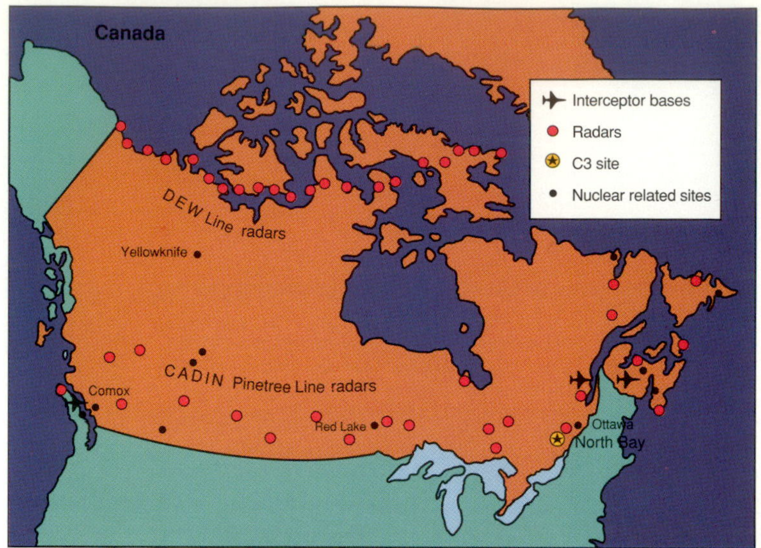

William M. Arkin and Richard Fieldhouse, *Nuclear Battlefields* (Ballinger, 1985)

Great Britain, one of our chief allies, has a nuclear strike capacity of its own (depicted on the map), consisting primarily of bombers and submarine-launched missiles whose targets lie within the Soviet Union and Eastern Europe. In addition, the United States stores nuclear weapons in Britain (as it does in many other countries) in nondescript sites similar to the one shown above. (The United States actually stores more nuclear weapons in Great Britain than exist in the entire British arsenal.)

Rene Burri/Magnum Photos, Inc.

William M. Arkin & Richard Fieldhouse, *Nuclear Battlefields* (Ballinger, 1985)

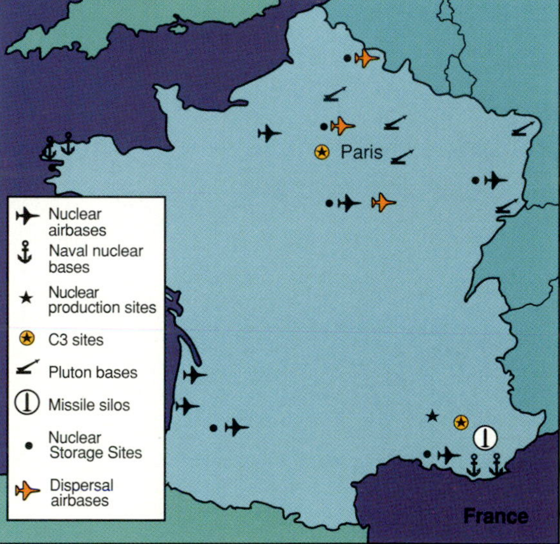

William M. Arkin and Richard Fieldhouse, *Nuclear Battlefields* (Ballinger, 1985)

France also maintains nuclear forces on its soil. By the middle of the 1990s, with remodeling and innovations in its system, it is expected that France will be able to strike over 500 enemy targets.

Our two most formidable nuclear adversaries remain the USSR and China. Most Soviet nuclear forces and installations are located in the western part of the country and along the path of the Trans-Siberian Railroad. Bases in the Arctic provide launching sites for bombers going over the North Pole to North American targets.

It is not possible to be sure of the location of all of China's nuclear forces, especially missile sites. China moves its forces often and keeps them as hidden as possible. The map depicts, to the best of our knowledge, China's nuclear framework.

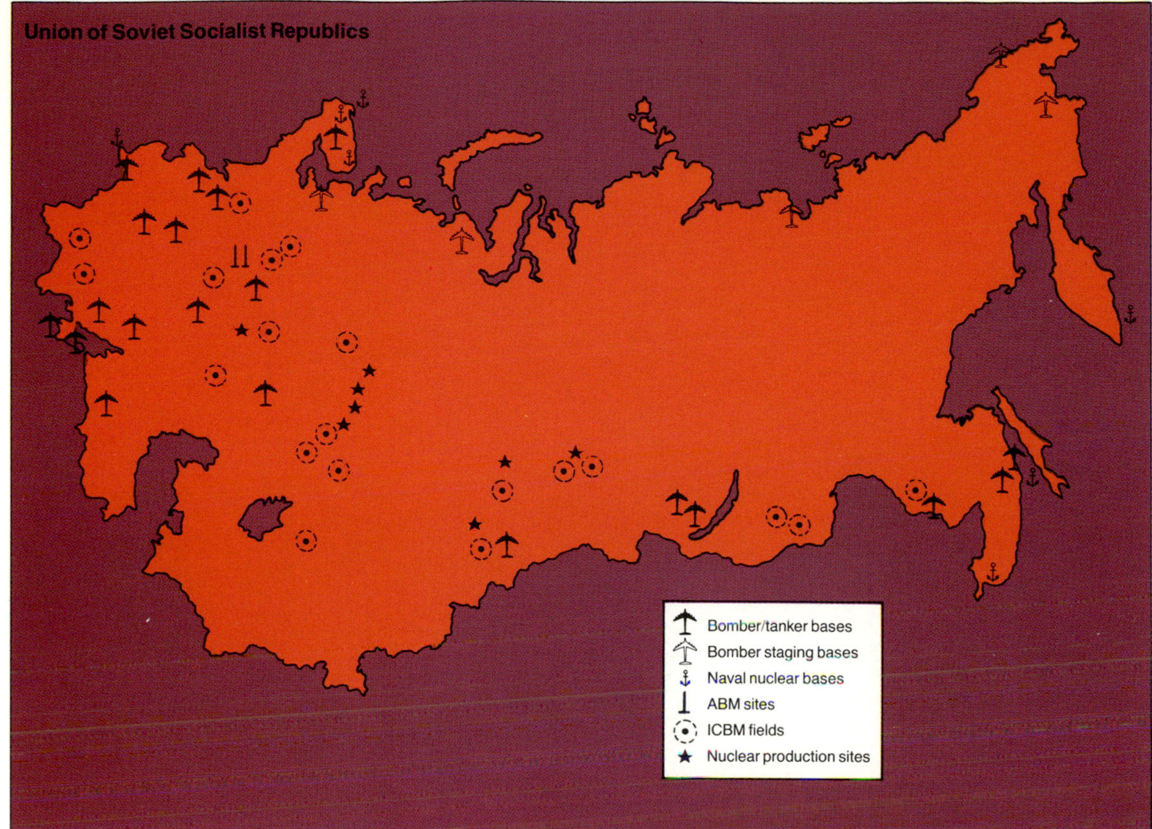

William M. Arkin and Richard Fieldhouse, *Nuclear Battlefields* (Ballinger, 1985)

Dept. of the Air Force/Kirtland Air Force Base

Tyndall Air Force Base

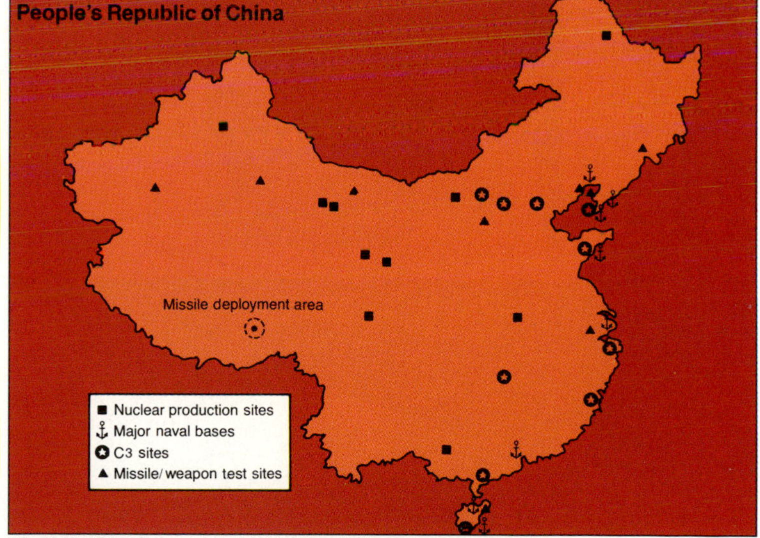

William M. Arkin & Richard Fieldhouse, *Nuclear Battlefields* (Ballinger, 1985)

Our concern for defense against possible nuclear attack goes further than simply establishing weapons' arsenals and launch sites. Planes like this new Air Force B-1B bomber are tested on "the trestle" at Kirtland Air Force Base in New Mexico. Electric shocks are pumped through aircraft to see if the planes could survive the electromagnetic impulses created by nuclear explosions.

The United States also has an early warning system to defend against surprise attack. Supplementary ground-based radar, satellites, and even blimps provide surveillance information. "Fat Albert" is the name given to each of the two blimps pictured here. They are equipped with an extensive radar system capable of detecting signals that higher flying aircraft cannot.

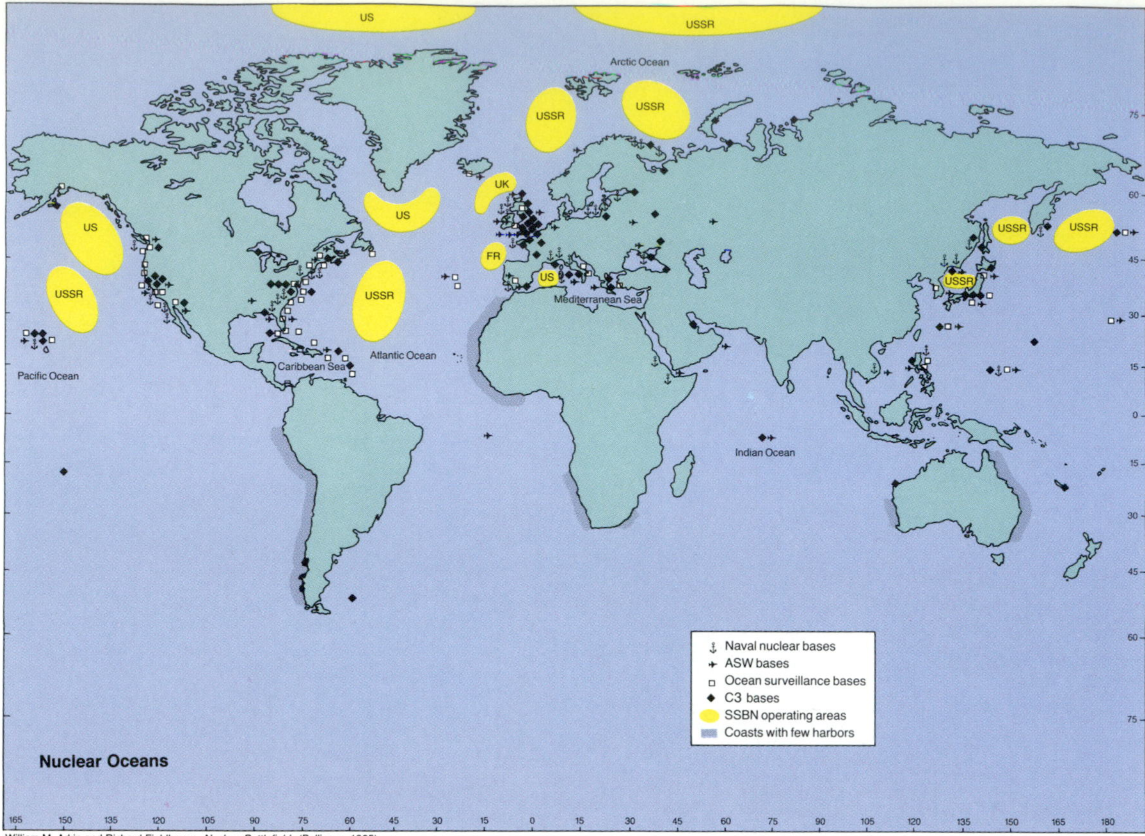

William M. Arkin and Richard Fieldhouse, *Nuclear Battlefields* (Ballinger, 1985)

Nuclear preparedness is not confined to land bases. The United States maintains bases with nuclear-capable ships and planes all over the world, as you can see on this map. Countering antisubmarine warfare strategies is a significant aspect of nuclear war planning. Before a submarine is sent out, it undergoes a process called magnetic silencing (shown on the left), which minimizes the chances of its being detected by the enemy.

U.S. Navy/Submarine Base, Puget Sound

Space is also being charted for its defense and strike capabilities. Here you see an artist's rendering of part of the Strategic Defense Initiative (SDI), popularly known as "Star Wars." This space-based sensor surveillance system will attempt to detect, track, and discriminate among objects—such as missile warheads, decoys, and debris—in low earth orbit.

NASA

The question remains: Does the increasing involvement of the global community in nuclear warfare and its accoutrements make it more or less likely that such a nuclear war will occur? As with all such questions there is a risk-benefit issue: How much is at risk and what benefits derive from this global network? Do they balance each other?

NOTES FOR A NEW ADMINISTRATION

You can pretend teens don't have sex. But the evidence is hard to ignore.

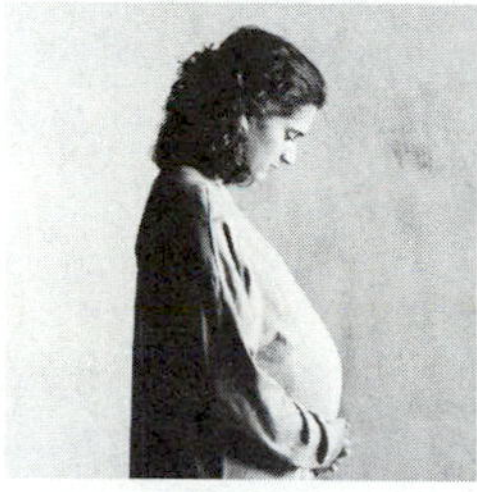

READY FOR THE FACTS of life? Three-quarters of American teens have had sex by the time they're 19.

But only a third of teens use birth control every time. And that's why more than half of the girls get pregnant unintentionally.

In fact, we have the highest teen pregnancy rate in the entire industrialized world. Not because our teens are more active — frequency is about the same. Our teens are simply more ignorant, confused and stymied about sex.

Given a chance to behave responsibly, they do. Studies of sex education and family planning services prove it.

Most kids, however, aren't given the chance. Adults spend more time trying to suppress teen sexuality than prevent teen pregnancy. Facts are few and far between, but commercial tease is as close as the TV.

The only sexual mystery left is contraception. It's never mentioned.

What can we do, as a nation?

Be honest. Neither sexual hype nor hypocrisy gives our children any guidance.

While our children acquire values from their parents at home, they need to get the facts at school. Comprehensive sex education is needed at all grade levels.

Meanwhile, there's no reason to keep contraceptive advertising off the air. And plenty of reasons to urge the mass media (especially television) to treat sexuality in an accurate, non-exploitive way.

Few teens visit a family planning clinic before they become sexually active. Most come a year later — when they think they might be pregnant. It's time to eliminate every barrier to confidential birth control services, low-cost or free, for any sexually active teen.

Everyone agrees that teen pregnancy is a serious national problem. Direct health and welfare costs have reached $18 billion. But experience right here in the U.S. shows that every $1 invested in preventing teen pregnancy can save taxpayers $3.

It's a matter of facing the facts of life. And about time our leaders set the example.

A KINDER, GENTLER NATION BEGINS WITH FAMILY PLANNING.

★ In this 1989 advertisement, Planned Parenthood used a cost-benefit argument to send its message to the Bush administration. Noting that teen pregnancy costs taxpayers $18 billion, it calculated that every $1 invested in preventing teen pregnancy would save taxpayers $3 over the long run.

Although cost-benefit analysis can help us make policy decisions, it has some serious shortcomings. First of all, it is most useful when it is applied to capital-intensive projects, such as our dam, where market guidelines help determine the monetary value of costs and benefits. Critics of cost-benefit analysis say that it is less useful when the quality of life is at issue or in such cases as the Oregon transplant controversy. Where social welfare policies are concerned, it is difficult to attach a monetary value to such matters as lives saved, literacy, nutrition, and disease prevention. Is the monetary value of a human life the amount that that person would have earned had he or she lived? Or is it the going rate awarded to plaintiffs in malpractice cases?

Second, cost-benefit analysis cannot tell us what we owe our posterity. Projects designed for future generations take away resources from present consumption. We are glad that our ancestors built the roads, bridges, and dams we now enjoy. What are we obliged to sacrifice for future generations?

Third, cost-benefit analysis ignores the equity or fairness of a project. Suppose you had to choose between projects *A* and *B*. Project *A* would increase the wealth of a millionaire by $2 million and would be financed by a regressive tax (one that placed a greater burden on the poor than on the rich) of $100,000. Project *B* would produce $900,000 in benefits for unemployed workers and would be financed by a progressive tax (one that placed a greater burden on the rich than on the poor) of $200,000.[5]

Advocates of cost-benefit analysis would probably contend that society as a whole would be better off with project *A* because it would produce the greatest increase in benefits. Winners could compensate losers. Benefits would trickle down to others indirectly, as in the creation of new jobs. Critics respond that in reality winners rarely compensate losers, in part because it is hard to identify losers in public policy trade-offs. There is a third position here: conduct the analysis in such a way that any positive change in the salaries of low-income people has bonus points attached to it.[6]

Finally, critics of cost-benefit analysis question its two underlying assumptions: that money is an appropriate measure of value and that society's dominant value is economic wealth, so that more is always better. These assumptions may be adequate in economics and if efficiency is one's sole concern. But democracies are also concerned with politics and with equity. As one observer has noted, "Only when the results of [cost-benefit] analysis are integrated with other forms of analysis, such as ethical analysis, and are combined with sound political judgment can the 'correct decisions' ever be made."[7]

In their attempts to combine cost-benefit and other forms of analysis, policy analysts often rely on studies produced by **think tanks**—private research institutions that receive government and foundation grants to conduct social science studies of public policies. Among the most important think tanks are the American Enterprise Institute (Washington, D.C.), the Brookings Institution (Washington, D.C.), the Heritage Foundation (Washington, D.C.), the Hoover Institution (Stanford, Calif.), the Institute for Policy Studies (Washington, D.C.), the Rand Corporation (Santa Monica, Calif.), and the Urban Institute (Washington, D.C.). Some have reputations for advancing partisan agendas, such as the Heritage Foundation on the right and the Institute for Policy Studies on the left. The Brookings Institution is often referred to as the "Democratic party in exile" during Republican administrations, and the American Enterprise Institute houses many Republican analysts during Democratic administrations.

Think tanks are not the only sources of government studies, of course. Policy analysts are also found on university campuses and in government agencies: at the state level in offices of legislative analysis and at the federal level in the General Accounting Office, Congressional Budget Office, and Office of Management and Budget, to name but a few. In most areas of public policy, governments are awash in a sea of statistical studies of alternative policy choices.

Given this vast array of experts and studies, why should sound policies have such a difficult time making their way through the American political process? The answer lies in the politics of public policy.

★ The Politics of Public Policy: Science Doesn't Win Elections

The cold, calculating character of cost-benefit analysis and other scientific tools stand in stark contrast to the rough-and-tumble world of American politics as we usually think of it. In politics, the "best" solution to a public policy problem sometimes has to wait until our political institutions are ready to accept it. For example, it took over two decades for Medicare to win approval in Congress. Politicians often bargain away parts of rationally crafted bills in order to get them passed. They are hesitant to make bold breaks with past programs, preferring to build on what has been tried before. Getting reelected, not making technically perfect policy, is the primary concern of most politicians. And while they rely on studies to make good policy, they know that some studies are used for partisan purposes.

Scholars point to at least five factors that make it difficult to obtain rational, scientific policies from our irrational political process: fragmented power, iron triangles, weak political parties, interest-group power, and the imprecision of voting as a policy guide. Let us consider each in turn.

Fragmented Power

As we saw earlier, the framers fragmented power both horizontally (separation of powers) and vertically (federalism). Because of the separation of powers, there are numerous points at which a bill embodying the "best" public policy solution can be killed before it sees the light of day as a viable program. It has to leap the hurdles of subcommittees, committees, floor votes, a potential filibuster, appropriations committees, a conference committee, and a possible presidential veto. Under federalism, states and localities often have great discretion in administering federal programs, and sometimes their politics are at odds with federal policies.

As a result of this fragmentation of power, it is much easier to obstruct or prevent a policy than it is to initiate and carry one out. Furthermore, it is difficult to obtain the intended result of a policy and to assign responsibility when things go wrong. And it is possible for policies to cancel each other out. When the Kennedy administration cut the federal income tax, for example, states and localities hiked their tax rates. The net result was that Americans ended up paying at the same rate overall as they had paid before the federal tax cut. And in a related area, as we saw in chapter 3, the progressive nature of the federal income tax is counteracted by the regressive tendencies of many state and local sales and property taxes. Most Americans end up paying about the same proportion of their income in their total tax package, about 20 percent.

Fragmented power also sometimes leads to contradictory policies. With one hand, Congress subsidizes the tobacco industry, and with the other, the surgeon general warns us that cigarettes are hazardous to our health. While the Commerce and State departments dole out millions in aid to build the economies of our Caribbean neighbors, the Agriculture Department cuts in half the amount of sugar these nations can sell to the United States. And fragmented power lends itself to local inconsistencies in the administration of public policies as well. During the Vietnam war, for example, there were wide disparities in the deferment criteria and practices of the nation's four thousand local draft boards, so that similarly situated men were treated very differently across the country.[8]

Iron Triangles

Another reason why the "best" policies may be hard to develop is the existence of iron triangles, also called subgovernments or subsystems. As we mentioned in chapter 10, the three sides of the triangle are a bureaucratic agency, a congressional

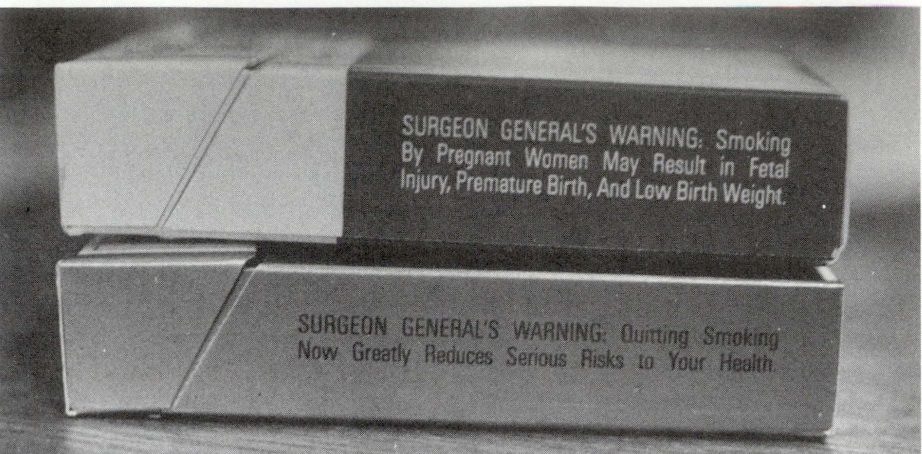

★ The fragmentation of power in the American political system sometimes results in contradictory public policies coming from different branches or levels of government. While Congress appropriates millions of dollars to subsidize the tobacco industry, for instance, the president's surgeon general warns us about the health risks of smoking cigarettes.

committee or subcommittee, and an interest group. All three share a common policy concern and develop a cozy relationship. Such a triangle may be formed by lobbyists for defense contractors, members of the military appropriations subcommittees, and Pentagon officials. Lobbyists provide campaign funds and information. Members of Congress deliver strategic votes. And Pentagon bureaucrats want to see their programs survive and their budgets grow with expanded programs to administer.

While iron triangles may produce policies that ensure the survival of all three sides, such policies are not necessarily coherent. They tend to reflect a policy feudalism: each subsystem carves out its own policy turf, with no overarching consistency among policies. The exchange of favors common in Congress makes it easy to do whatever furthers one's career and to avoid making the hard choices that policy analysts frequently advocate. At times iron triangles can lead to corruption, as in the scandal involving a defense contractor in 1988. Some observers even say the national defense can be compromised when inferior and dangerous weapons are selected under the influence of iron triangles.

Weak Political Parties

Our political parties also contribute to inconsistencies in the policy-making process. As we saw in chapter 8, American political parties seem weak in comparison with parties in other industrial societies. Unlike parties in Britain, for example, American parties are not disciplined. Party leaders in Congress cannot force members to vote the party line on a consistent set of policies. Consequently, a Democratic-controlled Congress, for example, does not ensure a coherent range of Democratic domestic or foreign policies. In 1981, a Democratic House of Representatives passed President Reagan's tax cuts and budget-reduction measures. These tax cuts benefited the rich disproportionately and the budget reductions sliced into many social welfare programs that had enjoyed the Democrats' support in the past.

★ Given the influential role played by interest groups in formulating public policy, pressing social problems without group representation often get neglected by policy makers. The plight of the homeless, who do not have well-heeled lobbyists to represent them in Washington, is a case in point. (This homeless child and his family now have their own home.)

Thus Democratic and Republican legislators are forced to forge coalitions across party lines to ensure the passage of legislation. This necessity results in what some observers call "policy making at the lowest common denominator." By the time a consensus is reached, a policy may have lost its effectiveness to deal with the problem it was designed to solve. In a parliamentary system with centralized, disciplined parties, in contrast, all members can stand or fall together in a vote of no confidence. If enough members of the majority party defect to vote no confidence, the government might have to call for a new election. Legislators have more incentive to support coherent party platforms agreed upon before elections.

Interest-Group Power

The power of interest groups is another obstacle to sound policy production. As we saw in earlier chapters, members of Congress depend on contributions from political action committees (PACs) for their reelection. Three-fourths of PAC money goes to incumbents, and about 90 percent of incumbents in Congress get reelected. Interest groups want insurance policies to protect their favored programs and to be able to cash in on favors when these measures come up for a vote.

Interest groups wield the power of information as well as that of money. Because of this power, they are often directly involved in policy making. The direct involvement of interest groups in political decision making is called corporatism.[9] **Corporatism** is a system in which individuals and groups are represented not as residents of a geographical area but as members of interests in society (such as management, labor, doctors, farmers, educators, the elderly, the poor).

Gary Markstein/Copley News Service

While many countries have moved more in this direction than the United States has done, we do include interest groups in key policy-making posts. For example, neighborhood associations were required to participate in some of the antipoverty programs of President Johnson's Great Society. Both labor and management organizations participated on President Nixon's Wage and Price Stabilization Board, which implemented wage and price controls in the 1970s. Farmers' organizations monitor and implement some crop-allotment programs of the U.S. Department of Agriculture. And county medical organizations serve in local professional standards review organizations, which monitor costs and quality control of Medicare and Medicaid programs.[10] Interest groups that participate in the making of public policy wield a double-edged sword. On the one hand, these groups provide expert knowledge, thus enhancing the quality of the policy-making process. On the other hand, they promote their own interests, which may bias the policy in a way unfair to those whose voices are not heard in the clamor of interest-group politics.

Imprecision of Voting as a Policy Guide

Finally, it is hard to develop effective policies under the guidance of voters' preferences. While politicians frequently claim to enjoy a mandate on certain policies, such claims are usually tenuous at best. Politicians can never be sure if voters liked them or simply disliked their opponents more. A case in point was the 1980 election, in which much of Reagan's "mandate" probably represented an anti-Carter vote. And what kind of mandate can any politician claim when most elections have such a low voter turnout rate? A plurality of votes in an election with a 40 percent turnout (typical for local elections) could mean that one's so-called mandate came from only 25 percent of the eligible electorate.

Furthermore, it is hard to measure the intensity of voters' preferences for public policies. Perhaps a policy has 51 percent lukewarm support and 49 percent strongly felt opposition. Members of Congress may consider more than two thousand bills in a legislative session. They have neither the time nor the money to conduct polls to gauge the level of their constituents' interest in and support for

★ **Table 16-1**
Characteristics of analysis and politics in the policy-making process

	Analysis	*Politics*
Process	Scientific procedure based on information; rational comparison of alternatives	Democratic procedure: elections, bargaining, trading of favors, exercise of power
Analysis	Objectivity, impartial pursuit of truth	Partisan pursuit of interests
Knowledge	Systematic presentation of problem, weighing of alternatives	Trial and error; piecemeal, incremental learning from past
Experts	Reliance on intellectual elite of experts for whom truth prevails over partisanship	Mistrust of any one policy maker; encouragement of competition among experts because partisanship is inevitable

SOURCE: Charles E. Lindblom, *The Policy-Making Process,* 2d ed. (Englewood Cliffs, N.J.: Prentice-Hall, 1980), chaps. 1–5.

each measure they consider. Even if they did, many policies are so technical and involve such sophisticated terminology that rational deliberation of them would be dominated by highly educated professionals. Senators and representatives have staffs to help them wade through complicated policies. The average citizen has few such aids. These political factors muddy the pristine waters of "scientific" public policies. Table 16-1 summarizes the tension between pure analysis and political realities.

The political considerations we have raised call forth an important question about public policy in a democracy. How do we resolve the tension between the experts' concern about rationality and efficiency and the citizens' lack of technical expertise? Recent polls indicate, for example, that only about 5 percent of adult Americans are "scientifically literate," possessing an understanding of basic scientific facts. One-quarter of the respondents in a 1988 survey did not know that the earth revolved around the sun. In an election year in which voters were being asked to think about the global effects of acid rain, the greenhouse effect, and the Star Wars missile defense system, only about a third of respondents knew what lasers (a critical component of Star Wars) were.[11]

Do we resign ourselves to relying on experts as a new priest class with their technical jargon? For example, as we shall see in chapter 17, current debate on health-care policy employs the following terms: PSROs (professional standards review organizations), DRGs (diagnostic related groups), HMOs (health maintenance organizations), HSAs (health systems agencies), certificates of need, and national health insurance. Or do we educate ourselves about existing public policies and their alternatives as part of our citizenship training?[12] Is a bias inherent in this suggestion—will only the better educated become truly informed citizens? Does this alternative place an obligation on you, as a citizen relatively privileged by your education, to become more policy literate?

In an attempt to increase policy literacy, we now turn to the five stages of making public policy: agenda setting, lawmaking, budgeting, implementation, and evaluation (see figure 16-3).

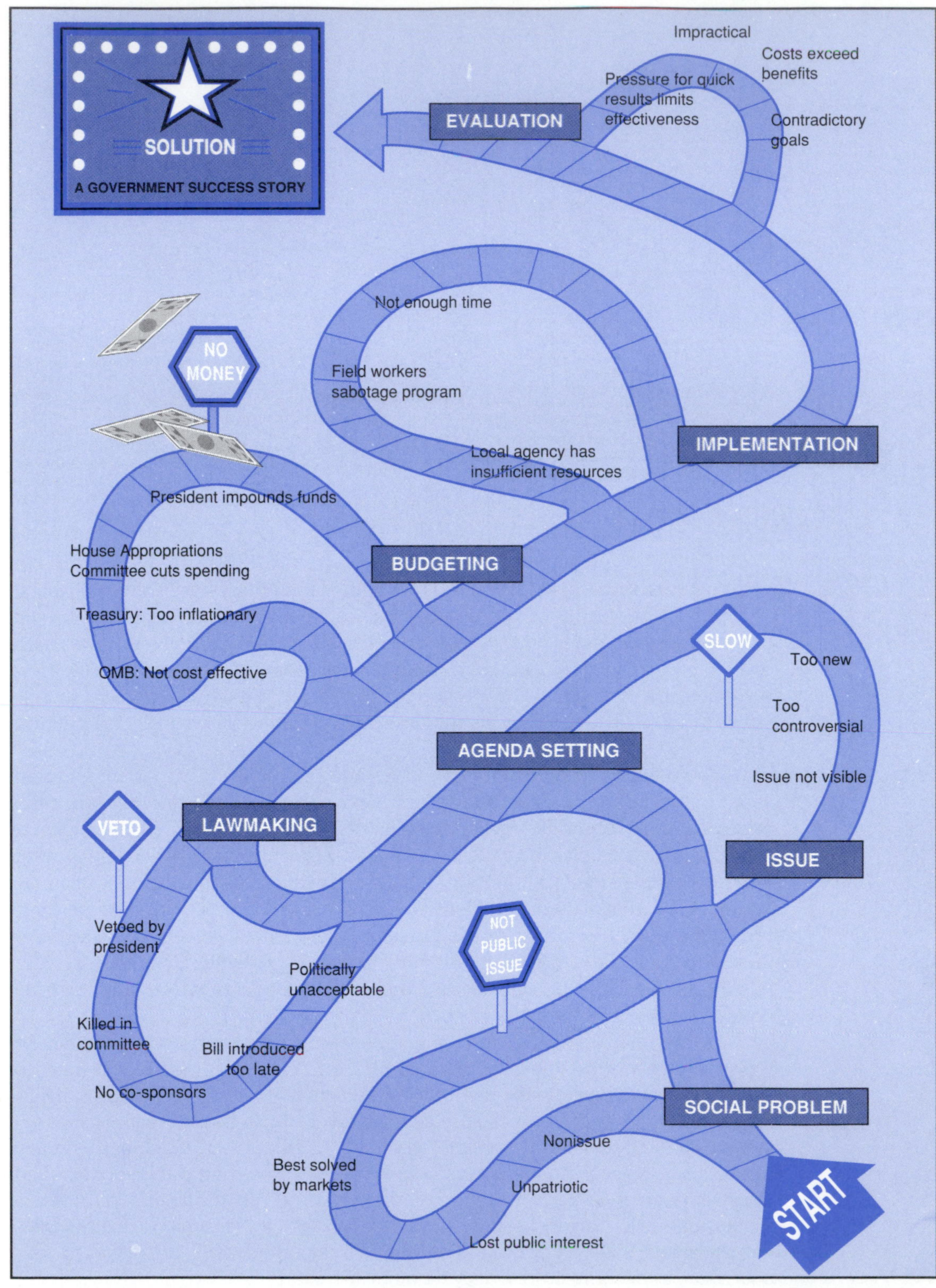

Figure 16-3
Public policy as problem solving. Pitfalls abound at every turn.

★ Countries have different ideas about what constitutes a problem worthy of government attention. Practices such as the mandatory veiling of women in public, which would lead to public protest in some places, is part of an accepted tradition and is not considered a matter of government concern in other areas.

★ The Stages of Making Public Policy

Now that we know that public policy results from a compromise between scientific, rational analysis and real-world politics, we can take a closer look at the way policies get made. Of course, what ultimately matters is results—*what* our government does to solve social problems. But it is also true that these results are largely shaped by *how* our government undertakes its tasks. Therefore, let us briefly consider how policies are affected by the five stages of the public policy-making process. These stages present obstacles that any sound policy idea has to surmount to see the light of day as a viable public policy.

Agenda Setting

Agenda setting occurs when a social problem becomes transformed into a public issue. A public issue is a matter that receives government attention and requires deliberation of alternative solutions. Of course, something first has to be thought of as an issue before it can get onto a government agenda. Issues vary from country to country. We are sometimes surprised to learn about practices in other countries that we consider abhorrent but other governments do not: torture of political prisoners, legal racial segregation, diversion of humanitarian aid for partisan purposes, and laws prohibiting women from appearing unveiled in public.

Every government has certain items it does not want to see on its agenda. These **nonissues** are matters that challenge the basic structure or powerful elites of a nation. All governments indoctrinate their citizens, teaching them that certain issues are not worth considering. It is easy to recognize indoctrination in other countries, but it is harder to see it in our own. Among our nonissues are a

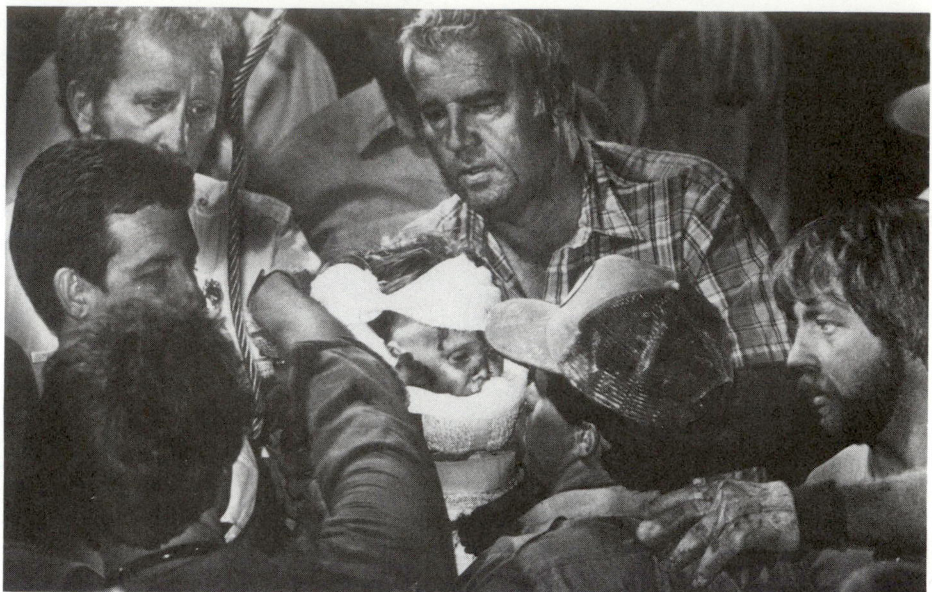

★ Thanks to television, rescue efforts make their way onto public agendas. Viewers around the nation watched the human drama of Jessica McClure's rescue. An engineer from California who watched the TV drama flew to Texas with the device that finally bore through the rock to free the toddler. Other volunteers joined official government workers in their round-the-clock, costly rescue efforts.

parliamentary system to replace our presidential form of government, public as opposed to private ownership of major industries, radical redistribution of wealth, and unilateral military disarmament. Until relatively recently, racial segregation was a nonissue in many parts of this country. President Jimmy Carter said of his childhood in southern Georgia: "As a child, I rode the bus to school each day with the other white students, while the black students walked, and never gave a thought to the lack of equality inherent in the separateness."[13]

In the process of reaching our government's agenda, issues are subject to attention cycles by the public and media. One observer, focusing on the ecology issue, noted that the alarmed discovery of a problem and proposed governmental solutions tend eventually to give way to sober realization of the costs of solving the problem. The subsequent loss of media and public interest is followed by a bureaucratic government response. Once an issue becomes routine, the media and the public are hungry for new problems. Thus the cycle of enthusiasm and inattention begins again.[14]

Certain kinds of issues are most likely to secure a place on the government's agenda. The first are those that pose a widespread threat to public health and safety—AIDS, say, and fear of nuclear war. Other issues that make their way onto agendas are geographically concentrated and highly visible. When unemployment is spread across the United States, it is not so noticeable as it was in Michigan in the summer of 1980, when about one-quarter of that state's work force was laid off by a slowdown in automobile production. Or take the case of a strapped earthquake or hurricane victim or of Jessica McClure, the toddler who was trapped for days in an abandoned well in Texas in 1987. Such incidents quickly mobilize costly, round-the-clock government rescue responses.

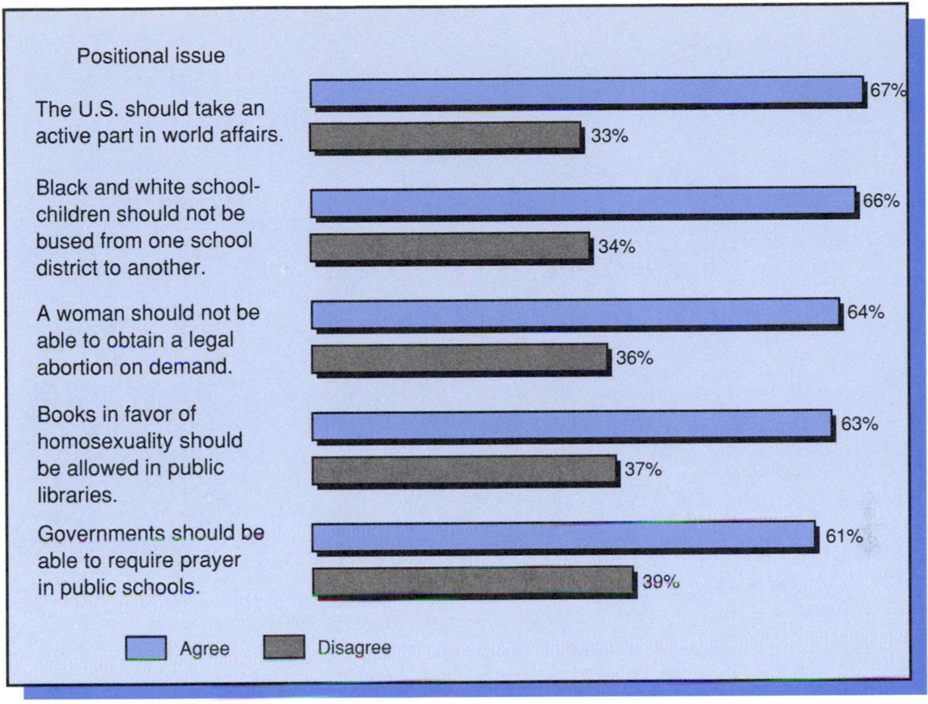

★ **Figure 16-4**

Responses to questions asked about some positional issues, 1988 (in percentage)

SOURCE: James Allan Davis and Tom W. Smith, *General Social Survey, 1972–1988* (Chicago: National Opinion Research Center, 1988), subfile 1988 (machine-readable data file).

Citizens and groups interested in getting their issues onto the public agenda have discovered several helpful strategies. One is to make a new issue appear to be an old issue. Proponents of Medicare, for example, portrayed the program as looking less like socialized medicine and more like something familiar by making it part of social security, which had already been widely accepted as a legitimate program. In addition, activists have found that an issue benefits from the power of national symbols. For example, our attempt to bolster elementary and secondary education in the wake of the Soviet launching of *Sputnik* was the National Defense Education Act, which associated education with the powerful symbol of defense. It also helps to portray one's issue as a valence issue. A **valence issue** is one that ignites a strong, fairly uniform emotional response and does not have an adversarial quality. Incest and drug pushing are such issues. Most issues, however, are **positional issues,** sparking alternative and often highly conflictual responses. Abortion and prayer in school are positional issues (see figure 16-4).[15]

Finally, an issue is likely to get on the government agenda if it involves a public good. A **public good**—a concept borrowed from economics—is a benefit or service that can be enjoyed by many people, whether or not they pay for it. The private sector is unwilling to produce such goods because they cannot be effectively priced. "Free riders" could enjoy the benefits of the good without paying for it. One public good is national defense. In the event of attack, our government could not selectively defend only those individuals who chose to pay for defense, so it forces everyone to pay for defense through taxation.

★ People use various tactics to mobilize support to get an issue on the public agenda. In recent years, some citizens have drawn public and governmental attention to the AIDS epidemic through a unique demonstration called The Names Project. Friends and families made a quilt in memory of those who died from the disease. The enormous quilt was assembled in front of Capitol Hill in October 1987 and again in October 1989.

No matter how favorable the conditions, issues cannot get on the government agenda unless people mobilize to put them there. Who sets the agenda? People who support the pluralist theory answer that different groups have power in different policy arenas. Teachers' associations, for example, influence the educational policy agenda, and medical associations set our health policy agenda. New groups can be mobilized to draw attention to new issues. In recent decades, blacks, Hispanics, and women have added civil rights to the agenda.

Supporters of the ruling elite theory respond that the public agenda is controlled by the privileged few who have the money, time, and skills to mobilize support for their causes. The energy agenda, for example, is set by the oil industry. Major oil companies control the production and distribution of oil, natural gas, coal, uranium, and synthetic fuels. They secure policies favorable to their interests and keep nationalization of their firms off the national agenda, though the oil industries of many other industrialized countries are nationalized. Oil companies have been able to keep nationalization of their industry a virtual nonissue in the United States.

A third response comes from those who adopt the "state-centric" approach: the view that the government sets much of its own agenda. Bureaucratic agencies suggest programs to keep their budgets and personnel thriving. Legislators generate issues to further their careers. One study claimed that Congress was the source of continued expansion of public programs.[16] Another study placed the source of new policy ideas in the bureaucracy as much as in Congress.[17]

Agenda Setting from Within. Insight into the way the government sets its own agenda can be gained from Barbara Nelson's case study of how child abuse got on

★ **Table 16-2**
Innovations in three policy areas, including duration of adoption process and number of states adopting innovations

Innovation	*Time period*	*No. of states adopting*
Education		
State boards of education	1784–1949	40
Chief state school officer	1835–1912	37
Compulsory school attendance	1852–1918	48
Degree requirement for teaching in elementary school	1930–1969	46
Degree requirement for teaching in high school	1896–1966	44
Welfare		
Merit system for state welfare department	1883–1942	48
Old age assistance	1923–1938	48
Aid to the blind	1898–1945	48
Aid to families with dependent children	1911–1937	48
Civil rights		
Antidiscrimination in public accommodations	1947–1966	31
Fair housing (public or private)	1937–1965	19
Fair employment	1945–1966	28

SOURCE: Virginia Gray, "Innovation in the States: A Diffusion Study," *American Political Science Review* 67 (December 1973): p. 1175.

the agenda in the United States.[18] While the government drew on outside research, one bureaucratic agency, the U.S. Children's Bureau, was responsible for keeping the issue alive and handing it over to the states and Congress.

The Children's Bureau learned about the problem of child abuse from two reports. The first was released in 1955 by the American Humane Association (AHA), a charitable organization engaged in research on maltreatment of children and animals. The AHA report looked at the extent of physical child abuse and the adequacy of governmental response. The second report was a 1962 article in the *Journal of the American Medical Association (JAMA)* on the battered-child syndrome. The AHA study defined the problem and the *JAMA* article suggested a governmental solution. The Children's Bureau sponsored further research, which provided the information on which subsequent public activism was based. In 1963 the Children's Bureau proposed to the states a model statute to encourage the reporting of child abuse.

The Children's Bureau's model statute shifted agenda setting to state governments. Between 1963 and 1967, every state and the District of Columbia passed a law on the reporting of child abuse. This new idea spread rapidly—five times more quickly than average policy innovations between 1933 and 1966 and much more rapidly than innovations in education, welfare, and civil rights (see table 16-2).[19] Nelson attributed the speed of this diffusion to several factors, primarily the emotional quality of the issue. State legislators saw the laws as a way of doing good at little cost. However, they were soon faced with an unanticipated consequence.

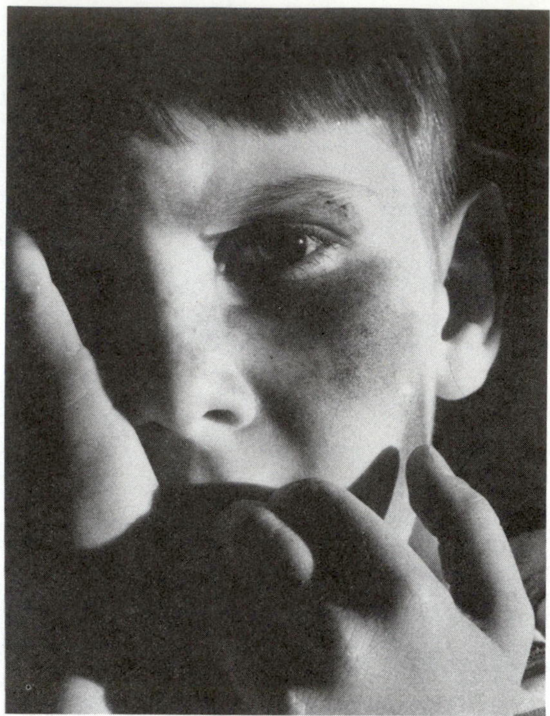

★ Sometimes an issue secures a place on the public agenda because of the persistent efforts of a government agency. Child abuse made its way onto state and federal agendas thanks largely to measures taken by the U.S. Children's Bureau during the 1960s.

Reporting laws unwittingly created a huge demand for legal and social welfare services. Legislators had no idea how prevalent the problem was. In 1970, for example, Florida authorities received seventeen reports of suspected child abuse. In 1971, the state began to take reports over a well-publicized hot line and the number of cases that year exploded to 19,120.[20]

In contrast to the speed at which child abuse made its way onto state agendas, about ten years passed before the issue reached the agenda of Congress. The issue first surfaced in 1964, a year after the Children's Bureau model statute went to the states. The District of Columbia Committee, acting in its capacity as "city council" for the District, introduced legislation mandating reporting of child abuse in the District. This measure failed for two reasons: the low status of this committee in Congress and the lack of an effective solution to the problem raised in the bill. Then in 1969, Representative Mario Biaggi (D-New York) introduced a bill requiring uniform reporting laws and social services nationwide. His concern for the issue stemmed from his twenty-three-year exposure to the problem as a New York police officer. Though his bill never got out of committee, his interest set the stage for congressional recognition of child abuse. It was the leadership of Senator Walter Mondale (D-Minnesota) that secured the issue's eventual recognition and its place on the agenda. As chair of the Senate Subcommittee on Children and Youth, Mondale had an institutional power base from which to mobilize Congress. He became interested in the issue in 1973; in 1974 Congress passed the $86 million Child Abuse Prevention and Treatment Act.

Agenda setting, however, is just the first step in the policy-making process. With any luck, an issue proceeds to the second stage: lawmaking.

Lawmaking

Policies are mandated by laws. Though our focus here is on laws passed by Congress and signed by the president, it should not be forgotten that federal policies are also created by regulatory agencies and courts. The Occupational Safety and Health Administration, for example, issued 4,600 regulations in its first two years in existence.[21] And school desegregation was mandated not by Congress but by the Supreme Court in its 1954 decision *Brown* v. *Board of Education.* It should also be remembered that the 80,000 state and local governments in America are responsible for many of the policies that affect our everyday lives.

Congress and the president are the primary producers of major federal policies. We have already discussed their powers and operations in earlier chapters, but it is worth taking a brief look here at their policy-making roles. Members of Congress and the executive branch have institutional tricks up their sleeves with which to alter the substance of a policy as it wends its way through the lawmaking process. Nowhere are these tricks seen to better advantage than in Eric Redman's book *The Dance of Legislation.*[22]

Redman describes how in 1970, fresh from college, he worked in Washington, D.C., as a junior staffer for Senator Warren Magnuson (D-Washington), who was trying to pass a health bill. The National Health Service Corps (NHSC) was Magnuson's solution to the "doctor distribution" problem. Doctors are concentrated in affluent areas and are in short supply in many rural and inner-city communities. The federal government would pay the tuition for medical students who agreed to serve for two years in areas where doctors were scarce. The federal government would pay their salaries and exempt them from military service (U.S. troops were in Vietnam at this time). The ultimate goal was to encourage NHSC doctors to establish their practices in needy communities.

Redman soon faced many challenges in his efforts to get Magnuson's bill passed intact. The first challenge was to present the issue in a politically acceptable way. For example, the NHSC raised the specter of "socialized medicine." At one point, a key legislator withdrew support when headlines in his local newspaper read, "Bill Seeks Care of Poor by Government Doctors." One tactic Redman used to counteract this association was to have members of the medical profession, who presumably would have the most to lose by socialized medicine, testify in favor of the bill during Senate hearings.

Another stigma he had to avoid was that of the NHSC as just another do-good antipoverty program that sounded nice but was unlikely to pass, given the prevailing political climate. The Nixon administration and the public mood had become increasingly critical of what were seen as the excesses of President Lyndon Johnson's Great Society social programs. Trying to tailor Magnuson's measure to the political climate in Congress, Redman portrayed the bill as a low-cost, experimental program.

A second challenge was presented by congressional deadlines. Congressional sessions last two years. Bills introduced late in the session have difficulty passing,

★ Aides are indispensable to members of Congress and their policies. Eric Redman *(right)*, an aide to Senator Warren Magnuson (D-Washington) *(left)*, was instrumental in both preserving the essence of a policy written by Magnuson and getting it passed by Congress in 1970.

so legislators use various shortcuts. Magnuson had only six months and tried three legislative strategies to sneak the NHSC through Congress without any new legislation. The first was an "earmarking strategy." He tried to add a few million dollars to an existing appropriations bill, earmarking the money (specifying its use in the bill or accompanying report) for an NHSC-type experiment. While this earmarking strategy was politically feasible, Magnuson eventually decided against it on advice from the Senate legislative counsel's office. Then Magnuson attempted an amendment-in-committee strategy. He tried to graft the NHSC onto a related bill being voted upon in another committee. But Nixon's invasion of Cambodia disrupted Senate business: staff members were redirected to respond to constituent mail. By the time Redman returned to the bill in question, it had already been voted out of committee. Finally, Magnuson tried to obtain an amendment on the floor, a politically risky maneuver because it infringes on committee prerogatives. Committee chairs do not appreciate it when their bills are tampered with on the floor. Floor amendments are typically used only for technical changes, not to introduce new policy ideas. This strategy failed when Redman was unable to draft the floor amendment in time. These time-saving measures ended up using four of the six months left in the congressional session. Failing in his attempts to sneak a simplified version of his policy through Congress, Redman had no choice at this point but to have Magnuson introduce a new bill for the NHSC.

The next hurdle to confront was the politics of introducing a bill. Successful introduction of a bill involves co-sponsorship. Legislators accumulate and discharge political debts by co-sponsoring one another's bills. A co-sponsor is legally superfluous but politically advantageous to a bill's passage. Co-sponsorship is one of the lubricants of the legislative process, as bipartisan support makes a bill more attractive to undecided legislators. Next, one has to prevent the introduction of a duplicate bill, which dilutes support for a program. Redman had to persuade the staffer of a junior senator not to introduce another NHSC-type bill. Then one has to appease the opposition. In this case it was the military, who feared that the NHSC would steal "their" drafted doctors. Redman was able to secure a promise from Magnuson's junior colleague from Washington, Senator Henry "Scoop" Jackson, chair of the Senate Armed Forces Committee, that he would not stall the bill in the Senate on behalf of the military. Finally, one has to win over the support of committee chairs who have jurisdiction over the bill in the House and Senate. Unsympathetic chairs have several parliamentary means at their disposal to delay or even kill a bill in committee. Failure to obtain chair support may be the kiss of death for a bill.

Once a bill has been successfully introduced, the next challenge is to survive committee hearings and meetings. Universities and think tanks provide policy analysts to testify at committee hearings about the costs and benefits of a bill; interest groups send witnesses to influence legislators; and executive agencies furnish bureaucrats to advance the president's agenda. In committee meetings, bills are typically amended as compromises are forged between liberals and conservatives. The "best" policy solutions often have to give way to the politically feasible ones. In the NHSC case, the conservative senator Peter Dominick (R-Colorado) deleted a provision for a national advisory council and in the process inadvertently deleted a local-control provision that he favored. The Senate committee added Republican co-sponsors and the House committee included provisions on malpractice insurance.

The next hurdle Redman faced was floor management of the bill. In the NHSC case, this step took on surreal dimensions. A bill's sponsor or its committee chair typically manages a bill when it comes up for a vote on the floor. Because both Magnuson and the committee chair were out of town when the NHSC bill came up for a vote, Redman quickly secured a roll-call vote to stall for time to find someone to manage the bill. Looking around, he saw that the only supporters on the floor were so liberal that they would alienate conservatives. He persuaded Peter Dominick to manage the bill, and to read a speech he had drafted for the committee chair. A Republican senator amended the bill to add the local-control provision that Dominick had inadvertently deleted in committee. As conservatives strolled onto the floor and saw who was managing the bill, they assumed it was acceptable and added no further amendments. The content of the policy was preserved, thanks to Redman's luck in getting Dominick to manage the bill.

A final challenge was the inevitable tension between Congress and the executive branch. In the post–World War II period, Republican administrations have typically faced Democratic Congresses, with resultant public policy battles drawn along predictable partisan lines. The NHSC got caught in the cross-fire. The Department of Health, Education, and Welfare (HEW) and the surgeon general were under orders from the Nixon White House to oppose the bill. HEW never testified at Senate hearings. Nor did it follow through with promised help in providing research requested by Redman or in drafting the legislation. The HEW lobbyist on Capitol Hill said he was still "studying the issues." The surgeon general, who personally favored the bill, was forced to testify against it in House hearings under threat of being fired if he refused.

After the NHSC bill made its way against all odds through the closing days of Congress, President Nixon's advisers urged him to pocket-veto the bill. However, Nixon had just become embroiled with Congress in a constitutional crisis over his

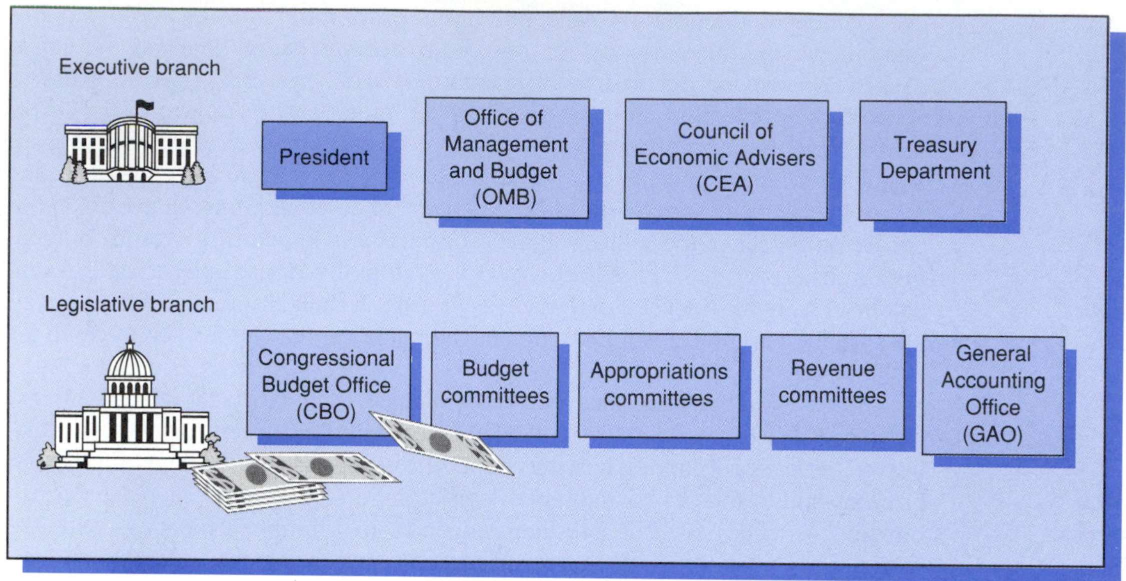

★ **Figure 16-5**
Budget players

use of the pocket veto. (He claimed he could pocket-veto bills within ten working days of congressional *recess* for Christmas; Congress claimed the Constitution said the relevant time period was ten working days before the *adjournment* of the session, which had been prolonged by a Senate filibuster.) The disputed pocket veto was of another health bill, encouraging family practice, and Nixon probably did not want to press his luck with the NHSC bill as well. He signed it during the last hours of the congressional session. Again Redman was in luck. In the absence of this crisis, President Nixon probably would have prevented Magnuson's policy from seeing the light of day.

A bill that survives the legislative process becomes a law that authorizes a program. The next step is to appropriate the money to be spent on that program. Appropriating and actually spending money on a program are part of the budgeting process, to which we now turn.

Budgeting

No money can be spent on a program until members of Congress and the president pass an appropriations bill, which instructs the Treasury to release funds to the agency in charge of carrying out the program. Every year Congress produces appropriations bills, corresponding to the different cabinet departments in the executive branch. The appropriations process is part of a larger budgetary process (see figure 16-5).

The federal budget is the president's financial plan for government during a fiscal year (FY). The government's fiscal year is its budgeting year, beginning October 1 of the prior calendar year. FY 1995, for example, begins October 1, 1994.

★ Table 16-3
Budget-making functions of House and Senate committees

Function	*House*	*Senate*
To set overall budget picture	House Budget Committee	Senate Budget Committee
To authorize programs and spending levels	House Standing Committees	Senate Standing Committees
To pass appropriations bills allocating funds to be spent	House Appropriations Committee	Senate Appropriations Committee
To pass revenue bills	House Ways and Means Committee	Senate Finance Committee

Each fall, the Office of Management and Budget (OMB) drafts the president's budget. OMB gets estimates from the cabinet-level departments and other executive agencies, which tell OMB how much money they want in the next fiscal year's budget.

One of the most important features of budgeting is **incrementalism,** or expansion of a budget by a certain percentage of the previous year's expenditures. Each agency asks OMB for the amount it was budgeted last year plus an additional increment. In the budgetary process, all agencies ask for more than they expect to receive and assume that their requests will get cut somewhere along the way.[23] Incrementalism often wins out over the advice of the president's "troika." The troika consists of the president's three budget-making agencies.

Each plays a distinctive role and tries to influence the president's thinking. OMB represents the expenditure community, the agencies that request money from it. The Council of Economic Advisers (CEA) provides technical forecasting to the president and tries to get him to see the long-term budget picture. And the Treasury Department represents the financial community of bankers and investors. It promotes a balanced budget, issues government bonds to cover the national debt, and has links with the International Monetary Fund, an international lending agency.[24]

Each winter the president presents his budget to Congress. The president and Congress have until the following October 1 to agree on a budget. If no agreement is reached in time (as happened during the Reagan presidency), Congress passes a **continuing resolution.** This is a measure passed by one or both houses of Congress instructing federal agencies to spend at last year's level until a new budget can be agreed upon.

Members of Congress divide their work on the budget among four powerful kinds of committees in each chamber. This division of labor is shown in table 16-3.

Budget committees work closely with the Congressional Budget Office (CBO), Congress's budgetary agency. Together they look at long-term budget considerations and try to keep other committees in line with a coherent congressional budget. Appropriations and other standing committees determine where to spend money, while the Ways and Means and Finance committees figure out how to raise money. The House Appropriations Committee has a reputation for cutting the spending levels of programs, and the Senate Appropriations Committee is known for frequently restoring such cuts. Both appropriations committees are supposed to have completed the markup of all the appropriations bills (that is, have made all the necessary changes in them) before submitting them for final passage, so that they will have an idea of the overall level of spending.

Congress can seriously weaken a program by failing to appropriate enough funds for it. By the same token, as we saw with Redman's NHSC, members of Congress can also use the appropriations process to try to sneak their pet projects past their unsuspecting colleagues.

When appropriations bills are finally presented to the president, he must sign or veto them as a total, multibillion-dollar package. Unlike most governors, he does not have the constitutional power of an item veto. This is the power to veto one line item, or category of expenditure, in an appropriations bill. George Bush and many other conservatives favor a constitutional amendment giving the president the item veto so that it would be easier to trim the federal budget. Without an item veto, presidents cannot target specific programs by cutting off appropriations.

An alternative way for a president to reduce spending is **impoundment:** the president simply refuses to spend money appropriated for a specific program; he instructs the Treasury not to release funds to the agency in charge of administering that program. Throughout most of American history, presidents have used this power sparingly and usually when Congress agreed. Thomas Jefferson, for example, impounded money that had been appropriated to build Mississippi River gunboats, and President Truman waited until it was determined where World War II veterans had settled before releasing funds to build hospitals for them.

No other president, however, resorted to impoundment so often as Richard Nixon. He impounded money on an unprecedented scale (about $30 billion between 1971 and 1973 alone), and he killed programs that were not in keeping with his conservative philosophy but were supported by a liberal Democratic Congress. When a president refuses to spend money on policies he disagrees with ideologically, the tactic is called **policy impoundment.**

In 1974 Congress passed the Budget and Impoundment Control Act, which limited the president's power to impound funds that Congress had appropriated. Now the president has to inform the comptroller general (head of the General Accounting Office [GAO], Congress's auditing agency) of his intentions. The comptroller general classifies the impoundment as either a rescission (termination of funds, as in Jefferson's gunboat case) or a deferral (delay in the spending of funds, as in Truman's hospital case). If it is a rescission, the funds are automatically released within forty-five days unless both the House and the Senate agree not to spend them. If it is a deferral, the money must be released if either the House or the Senate so determines.

Congress also uses the GAO to postaudit federal expenditures. The GAO sends an annual report to Congress outlining deviations from congressional intent in the way federal agencies spent money appropriated for them. The GAO is Congress's watchdog, on the lookout for cost overruns. A policy beset by massive cost overruns is often in jeopardy the next time it faces legislative scrutiny. The GAO also detects bureaucratic sabotage of congressional intent in the implementation of policies, the next stage in the policy-making process. In recent years, President Reagan sought to terminate the spending of over $25 billion of funds appropriated by Congress (see table 16-4).

★ **Table 16-4**
Presidents' budget rescission requests, 1977–1986 (in thousands of dollars)

Item	*1977*	*1978*	*1979*	*1980*	*1981*	*1982*	*1983*	*1984*	*1985*	*1986*
Funds appropriated to the president	41,500	40,200	000	000	000	10,629	15,133	000	105,399	39,760
Agriculture	000	000	000	000	000	2,000	77,301	000	310,218	1,062,681
Commerce	2,025	000	000	000	34,493	19,000	000	000	325,371	196,632
Defense-military	878,950	000	000	000	000	000	000	000	000	000
Defense-civil	6,600	000	000	000	000	000	000	000	16,200	000
Education	000	000	000	000	321,729	1,157,205	1,230,381	000	173,939	1,080,200
Energy	000	000	50,000	000	101,926	20,000	69,000	000	21,112	000
Health and human services	000	000	227,258	104	344,218	000	000	000	26,838	787,417
Housing	000	000	608,167	000	10,000	9,421,639	000	331,431	260,057	4,625,677
Interior	47,500	000	3,127	000	000	000	63,500	30,000	72,389	116,104
Justice	000	000	000	18	000	000	000	000	13,659	122,109
Labor	000	000	000	000	000	4,095	000	1,700	276,566	416,037
State	12,000	5,000	000	000	10,185	000	000	000	2,432	000
Transportation	6,803	000	000	000	000	9,623	28,200	000	49,327	356,051
Treasury	000	000	000	000	000	000	000	000	9,530	788,395
Independent agencies	60,000	10,055	26,140	000	433,240	10,877	000	25,418	55,338	717,995
Total	1,055,378	55,255	914,692	122	1,255,791	10,655,068	1,483,615	388,549	1,718,375	10,309,058

NOTE: Rescissions are decisions by presidents not to spend funds already appropriated by Congress. Under the Budget and Impoundment Control Act of 1974, presidents must notify Congress by rescission requests. Congress can deny the request by a resolution passed by either house.

SOURCE: Gary King and Lyn Ragsdale, ***The Elusive Executive**: Discovering Statistical Patterns in the Presidency* (Washington, D.C.: Congressional Quarterly Press, 1988), pp. 180–181. [Based on U.S. Executive Office of the President, ***Budget of the United States***, 1978–1987.]

Implementation

The fact that a program obtains funding does not necessarily mean that those funds will be spent in accordance with legislators' intentions. **Implementation** means putting legislation into effect. About three million federal bureaucrats carry out the laws of the land as employees of cabinet departments, independent agencies, regulatory commissions, and government corporations (discussed in chap. 14). An additional fourteen million administrators work for state and local governments.[25] Thus implementation is the most substantial stage of the policy-making process as measured by the people engaged in it and the funds spent on it.[26]

Implementation involves a great amount of bureaucratic discretion. As we saw in chapter 14, administrators often must use their own judgment in implementing policy. Think of the discretion of police officers assigned to enforce speed limits, for instance. Which streets should they patrol? At what speed should they pull drivers over? Should certain kinds of cars be targeted more than others?

Administrative discretion stems from several sources. One is the inadequacy of resources to carry out the law fully. Obviously, there are not enough police to catch every speeding motorist. And consider the Drug Enforcement Administration's struggle with limited resources to stem the flow of illegal drugs into this country. Another reason for discretion is the vagueness of legislative guidelines. Legislators cannot possibly foresee all the wrinkles that may emerge in a program once it is in place out in the field. Abstract goals are much harder to implement than concrete ones. Rules against sex or race discrimination by an employer, for example, are harder to enforce than rules against price discrimination by a railroad.[27]

Implementation involves various forms of bureaucratic politics. A common form of bureaucratic politics is seen when an agency is captured by its constituency (the group it serves). Here we see a reflection of the iron triangle: an agency's cozy relationship with the interest groups it frequently deals with. As we saw in chapter 14, many economic regulatory agencies are prone to this sort of relationship. The Interstate Commerce Commission (ICC), for instance, has often forged policy guidelines favorable to the railroads.[28] However, such relations are less common in the newer, noneconomic regulatory agencies, such as the Consumer Product Safety Commission.

A more benign form of an agency's cozy relationship with its constituency is known as "going native." When appointed administrators are more sympathetic to their agency's needs than they are to the president's priorities, they are said to have gone native. Such administrators usually do not last long in their posts, or else they experience intense pressure from the administration, as the surgeon general did in the NHSC case. Although he supported the bill, he was forced to testify against it under threat of being fired.

Bureaucratic politics also emerges in the tension between central and field staffs. This conflict is often partisan. When Ronald Reagan replaced Jimmy Carter, for example, a conservative Republican administration inherited liberal Democratic civil servants in the field to administer its programs. In any case, field staffs are often more sympathetic to their clients than are their more distant managers. Welfare caseworkers for instance, may be more inclined than their supervisors to bend the rules out of sympathy for a client. Finally, fieldworkers may find that in order to uphold the spirit of a law, they have to violate the letter of the law in some cases.

Partisan officials as high in the chain of command as the president are often frustrated by the behavior of their bureaucratic underlings. In 1952 President Truman predicted that if General Eisenhower won the upcoming election, he would be in for quite a surprise. "He'll sit here," Truman said, tapping his desk for emphasis, "and he'll say, 'Do this! Do that!' And nothing will happen. Poor Ike—it won't be a bit like the Army. He'll find it very frustrating." Sure enough, well into his second term, an aide said of Eisenhower, "The President still feels that when he's decided something, that ought to be the end of it . . . and when it bounces back undone or done wrong, he tends to react with shocked surprise."[29]

Government officials are not the only ones to be frustrated by bureaucracies. Average citizens, as well, are sometimes put off by standard operating procedures (SOPs). These are an organization's routine procedures for processing information and formulating responses. Such procedures are extremely useful in routine situations. By providing uniform responses to problems, they minimize favoritism. And they allow a more rapid response than would be possible if a new decision had to be made in each case. This is one reason why SOPs are so prevalent in military and police organizations, where a quick response can make the difference between life and death. As we all know, however, SOPs can serve as blinders in novel situations that require a more flexible response. In fact, SOPs can have enormous consequences for effective policy making.

A standard operating procedure that prevented effective implementation can be seen in a case study of an attempt by the Economic Development Administration (EDA) to create new jobs for the unemployed of Oakland, California.[30] The EDA was set up in 1965 to administer Great Society programs designed to provide jobs for minorities in areas with high unemployment rates. Before the Oakland project, most of its programs were administered in Appalachia. It had developed SOPs appropriate for an economically depressed *region*, and then applied them to Oakland, which was an economically depressed *neighborhood* in an economically prosperous region, the San Francisco Bay area.

For poor regions, capital-intensive projects such as roads, airports, and ports are appropriate. Such projects draw upon local labor, create new jobs, and help develop the region. In accordance with these regional SOPs, the EDA decided to fund the construction of an airport hangar, marine terminal, and highway overpass in Oakland. This regional approach, however, proved inappropriate for Oakland. The region did not need these new structures, and there was no guarantee that the jobs provided by these projects would go to the people who needed them.

The implementation process can be distorted not only by inappropriate SOPs but also by the filtering of information. Information about policies tends to be specialized at the bottom ranks of administrators and generalized at the top echelons. The people at the bottom typically transmit only what those at the top want to hear, or what makes them look good. Top-level administrators use a variety of means to counteract information distortion. One method is to rely on several channels of information simultaneously. President Franklin Roosevelt was a master at this. He strove to maintain personal ties with low-level bureaucrats as well as with his cabinet advisers. Sometimes he gave the same policy problem to several of his advisers, who competed with one another in arguing their cases before the president.

Another way presidents can combat information distortion is by creating a **task force,** a group of experts from various organizations called together temporarily to study or solve a problem. After the problem is addressed, the group disbands. One of the most famous task forces was the group convened by President

John Kennedy during the Cuban missile crisis of 1962, when American spy planes discovered Soviet offensive missile sites in Cuba. This task force presented Kennedy with a range of options, from military intervention to diplomatic negotiations. In the Oakland case, the head of the Economic Development Administration created a special task force to expedite the Oakland project. It was able to cut through bureaucratic channels and demonstrate innovation. EDA personnel, however, resented the task force's special treatment and arrangements, and the antibureaucratic personnel of the task force did not remain with the project long enough to see their program carried out. Implementation needs both imagination and perseverance.[31]

Despite the best efforts of government decision makers, effective implementation is often a casualty of time constraints. In the Oakland case, the EDA had four months to process $300 million worth of projects before the fiscal year ended. If it did not spend the money, members of Congress might conclude that it was not doing its job when they engaged in the next round of budget deliberations. The last thing an agency wants is a cut in its budget. As the EDA had no time to do the *best* thing, it opted to do *something* quickly. EDA administrators decided to concentrate on one city, Oakland, to achieve early, dramatic results from their experiment. They picked Oakland because they had had some prior dealings with it, so contacts would be easy. Another reason was Oakland's riot potential. Other urban areas with a high unemployment rate had been hit by riots, and the federal government wanted to prevent such an outburst in Oakland. Good policies are often casualties of the rush to meet budget deadlines.

There are other timing problems as well. For one thing, bureaucratic response often lags behind need. Military bureaucracies are often chided for fighting the last war, inappropriately using methods that worked in one setting (World War II, say), in another (Korea). Another instance of delayed response is seen in the failure to build enough schools to accommodate the large number of children born in the years after World War II.

Another problem occurs when an agency's cyclical responses are not timed properly. Take the federal government's macroeconomic (unemployment and inflation) policies. These are called "countercyclical" measures because they are used to counteract economic cycles of unemployment and inflation. During an inflationary cycle, when more money is circulating in the economy than goods are available to purchase, the Federal Reserve Board raises the interest rates on money it loans to member banks, which in turn increase the interest they charge to consumers like us. We are less likely to borrow money at high interest rates, so consumer demand slackens. If such measures are not properly timed—in this case, if inflation has already given way to recession—then the Federal Reserve Board's action only makes matters worse.

Finally, bureaucratic agencies often work at cross-purposes. Four agencies were working at cross-purposes in the Oakland project. The Economic Development Administration wanted to stimulate economic growth and create jobs. The Small Business Administration was the cautious banker, hesitant to lend federal money to marginal businesses that could not secure it in the private sector. The General Accounting Office questioned EDA's grant/loan ratio for port-development projects. And the Department of Health, Education, and Welfare wanted to see funds for job training going through a skills center with which it had ties.

In short, implementation of a policy in accordance with policy makers' intentions can never be assured. And it rarely occurs as quickly as policy makers hope.

★ A task force is called together by an executive to try to counteract the information distortion that sometimes characterizes agency advice. During the 1962 Cuban missile crisis, President John Kennedy *(far right, with head bent)* convened a task force to pit agency perspectives against one another. He did not want to repeat the error of the previous year, when he relied too heavily on one agency—the CIA—for advice about the ill-fated invasion of Cuba at the Bay of Pigs.

For example, Redman's bill for a National Health Service Corps took six months to emerge from Congress and had no real impact until a year and a half later. The Nixon administration employed several delaying tactics. The Office of Management and Budget, for instance, insisted that the NHSC had to pay its own way within a few years with fees collected from patients, though the law contained no such requirement. And the Department of Health, Education, and Welfare spent $1 million of the first NHSC appropriation on studies by private consulting firms, despite restrictions limiting such expenditures to 1 percent of total program funds (it was a $16 million project at the time). One million dollars would have funded about sixty doctors in the field. Although the bill passed in December 1970, it was not until the American Medical Association endorsed the program in 1973 that the Nixon administration fully implemented it.

Evaluation

The final stage in the public policy-making process is **program evaluation**—the process of determining the effectiveness and efficiency of a public program. Evaluators specify the goals of a program, measure its effects, and apply a set of values to judge the program's success. Evaluation research has become increasingly popular in recent years. Some laws require periodic evaluation of the programs they create. The American public and its legislators want effective programs that show results. However, this is easier said than done. It is very difficult to isolate the goals, measure the effects, and specify the values used in the evaluation of a program.[32]

The goals of a program are often difficult to specify. Sometimes they are even contradictory. The goal of one foreign aid program was "to assist those nations in greatest need as well as those that would most likely use the money to produce significant developmental effects."[33] But the neediest nations have the fewest resources to produce sustained economic development.

How Do We Know What Our Foreign Aid Accomplishes?

How do we evaluate the success or failure of U.S. foreign aid programs? We want to see economic results, yet many of the world's poorest nations are plagued by problems of such magnitude that it is next to impossible to determine what effect our aid has had on a nation's well-being. Some poor nations are engaged in civil wars that divert scarce resources into arms purchases, disrupt agricultural production, and block the delivery of food and medicine into disputed territory. Still other countries suffer from overpopulation or are beset by natural disasters such as drought, floods, and locusts.

Poor nations need investment capital for "infrastructure" projects such as roads, bridges, dams, telephones, sewers, electricity, and running water. But it is hard for people with annual incomes under $500 (the price of a good VCR in the United States) to save money and put it in the bank to be lent out for needed public works projects. Nor can governments extract much in the way of taxes from people with so little income.

When Americans send their tax dollars abroad as foreign aid, how much of an improvement in the lives of the world's have-nots can they expect and how quickly? Should the money go for direct relief or for the production of facilities that increase economic self-sufficiency over the long run? How can we find out what these nations really need as opposed to what works for us? For example, large tractors that are effective on the wide, open plains of Kansas are inappropriate on the hilly terrains of many countries.

If it is difficult to evaluate "what works" in our domestic policies, it is even more of a challenge to assess what works when it comes to U.S. aid to nations with economies, histories, and cultures vastly different from ours. ★

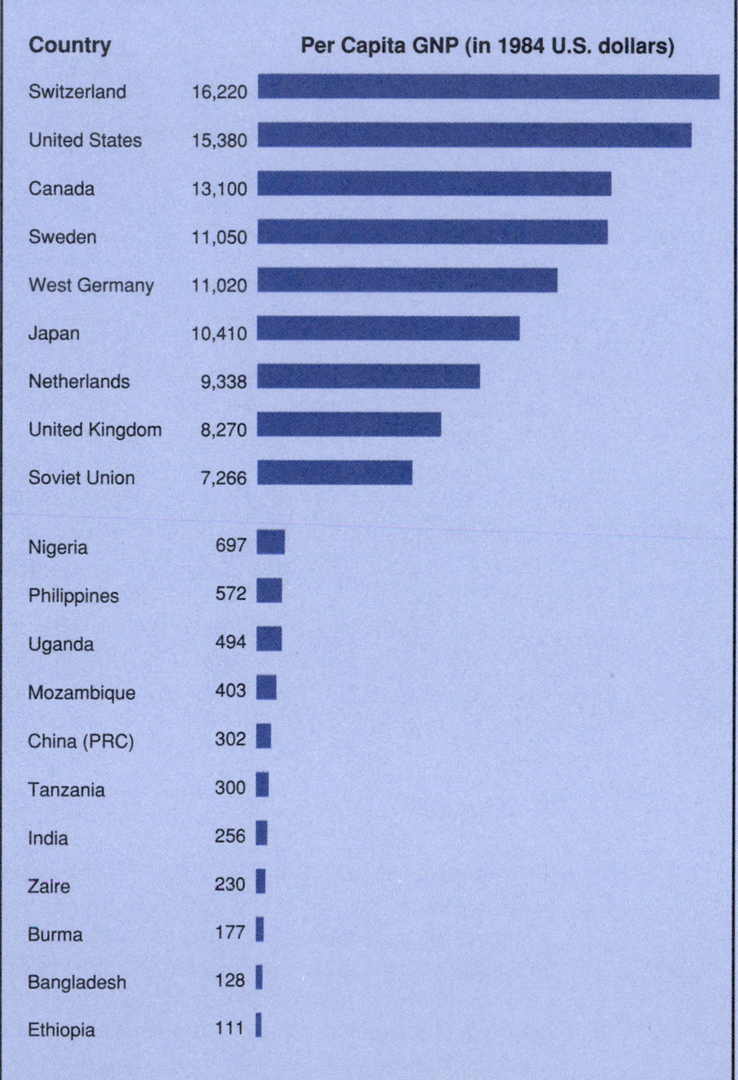

 **Figure 16-6**

The world's haves and have-nots

SOURCE: U.S. Bureau of the Census, *Statistical Abstract of the United States, 1988* (Washington, D.C.: U.S. Government Printing Office, 1987), p. 805.

Moreover, a program's goals may be modified once they are in operation. After the United States landed astronauts on the moon, administrators of the space program pushed for new goals of planetary exploration. Now they set their sights on Mars, Jupiter, and Saturn.

And a program's goals may not be practical. The goal of the 1946 Employment Act was "full employment." "Full" employment was defined as 4 percent unemployment when the act was passed; the definition has since been revised upward, to 5 percent.

Even harder than specifying a program's goals is measuring its effects. Sometimes it is hard to say what a program produces. How does one know which of many weapons systems, if any, ultimately deters an enemy? One way to find out would be to dismantle weapons systems selectively. But, as we shall see in chapter 17, unilateral disarmament is not politically feasible. Even if it were, we might discover that our adversaries were deterred from attacking us by something other than our formidable weapons systems, such as internal political problems.

Political pressure to achieve quick results compounds the difficulty of measuring the effects of a program. We saw in the Oakland case that agencies and legislators felt pressured to produce quick and tangible evidence of the success of their program: an increase in the employment rate and large building projects. But this rush to beat the budget clock may be shortsighted.

How long does one give a program before deeming it a failure or a success? Some scholars claim that many Great Society antipoverty programs created during the Johnson administration were not given enough time or money to work properly. Education and job-training programs may not yield results for years. In fact, the Vietnam war diverted federal money from many social programs. Results may be slow to come for economic as well as for social programs. Researchers point out that it took thirty years for New Deal land relief programs to demonstrate significant results in the rural South.[34]

The effects of many government programs are difficult to measure also because the factors involved in them cannot be held constant. Should reductions in disease rates among the poor be attributed to the passage of Medicaid, better nutrition, or expanded housing programs? If we use experimentation to evaluate a policy, there is the danger that participants' behavior may change because they know they are part of an experiment. Those who favor the program may go out of their way to make it work, while those who oppose it may try to make it appear ineffective.[35]

Sometimes programs may be effective, but not in reaching the groups they were intended to serve. Medicare, for example, has not improved the health of the neediest elderly as much as it has improved the health of the elderly as a whole, because all Medicare recipients must pay part of their hospitalization costs. Many programs are voluntary and depend on people's willingness and ability to avail themselves of the benefits to which they are entitled. In many cases poverty, language difficulties, lack of education, and the difficulty of obtaining information pose barriers for target groups. Many people who are eligible to receive public assistance and food stamps do not apply for them. Government studies found, for example, that in 1984 only about half of those people who were eligible received food stamps: less than 15 million of the 30 million who were entitled to them. Experts said applicants were sometimes discouraged from participating in the program by cumbersome state and local procedures.[36] Language barriers and mistrust of the Immigration and Naturalization Service caused many eligible undocumented workers to miss the May 1988 deadline to apply for amnesty.

★ Although the New Deal's land relief programs were created to help the rural poor, it took many years for them to yield results in the South. This sharecropper in Louisiana lived with no electricity or indoor plumbing and farmed the land using methods from the 1800s.

Because of the difficulties of measuring the effects of a policy, procedure is often measured instead of substance.[37] What matters is not so much *what* is produced but *how* agencies go about producing it. If an agency meets its management, budgeting, and accounting requirements in a timely and efficient way, then it may be thought to have administered an effective program. Activity becomes a substitute for results. There is pressure to spend rather than to spend wisely.

Policy evaluation ultimately reflects the values of the analysts. Researchers can emphasize different factors in their evaluations of the same program. A case in point is an evaluation of a Comprehensive Employment and Training Act (CETA) program performed by both the John F. Kennedy School of Government at Harvard and the Graduate School of Public Policy at the University of California at Berkeley. These two schools stressed different values in their evaluations of the CETA program. The Harvard researchers concentrated on economic costs and benefits and reached one set of conclusions. The Berkeley investigators put more value on the political and participatory aspects of the program and reached another set of conclusions.[38]

If evaluation is so fraught with problems, why bother doing it? Policy analysts answer that it is an important way to learn how to make better public policies. Evaluation often uncovers unforeseen problems and leads to better-informed and more realistic expectations.[39] Evaluation is the final hurdle of the policy-making process. Governments at all levels are subjecting more and more of their policies to formal evaluation. A policy that survives this hurdle joins the ranks of government success stories.

★ Summary

Public policy is what a government does to solve social problems. It distributes burdens and benefits among citizens in its efforts to solve these problems and it reveals a nation's priorities. Policy analysts consider the costs and benefits of alternative policies. Governments borrow alternatives from each other. Analysts and governments look for more efficient and equitable solutions to social problems. While conservatives usually look to the market economy for such solutions, liberals tend to trust the government to find them.

Policy analysts in the government, universities, and think tanks often employ cost-benefit analysis to assess the value of public projects. Citizens and politicians bring ethical and political judgments to bear on public policies. Public policies in a democracy reflect partisan politics, bargaining, trial and error, interest-group pressure, and voter preferences.

The process of making public policies consists of five stages: agenda setting, lawmaking, budgeting, implementation, and evaluation. Policies are typically transformed by the distinctive politics that characterize each stage.

★ Key Terms

agenda setting
continuing resolution
corporatism
cost-benefit analysis
free-market economy
implementation
impoundment
incrementalism
Keynesian economics
laissez-faire
nonissues
opportunity costs
policy impoundment
positional issue
program evaluation
public good
public policy
public policy analysis
social welfare state
task force
think tanks
valence issue

★ Notes

1. See Charles E. Lindblom, *The Policy-Making Process,* 2d ed. (Englewood Cliffs, N.J.: Prentice-Hall, 1980), p. 1.
2. See Kenneth M. Dolbeare, *American Public Policy: A Citizen's Guide* (New York: McGraw-Hill, 1982).
3. For foreign policy, see David Halberstam, *The Best and the Brightest* (New York: Penguin, 1984). For domestic policy, see Henry J. Aaron, *Politics and the Professors* (Washington, D.C.: Brookings Institution, 1978).
4. This example is drawn from B. Guy Peters, *American Public Policy: Promise and Performance,* 2d ed. (Chatham, N.J.: Chatham House, 1986), pp. 299–305.
5. Ibid., p. 308.
6. Ibid.
7. Ibid., p. 309.
8. See Dolbeare, *American Public Policy,* p. 51.
9. See Frederick B. Pike and Thomas Stritch, eds., *The New Corporatism* (Notre Dame, Ind.: University of Notre Dame Press, 1974).
10. Peters, *American Public Policy,* p. 28.
11. *San Francisco Chronicle,* October 24, 1988, pp. 1, 18.
12. This position is advocated by Dolbeare, *American Public Policy.*

13. Jimmy Carter, *Keeping Faith: Memoirs of a President* (New York: Bantam, 1982), p. 141.
14. Anthony Downs, "Up and Down with Ecology—'The Issue Attention Cycle,'" *Public Interest* 32 (Summer 1972): 38–50.
15. Angus Campbell et al., *Elections and the Political Order* (New York: Wiley, 1966), pp. 170–174.
16. Advisory Commission on Intergovernmental Relations, *The Federal Role in the Federal System: The Dynamics of Growth* (Washington, D.C., 1980).
17. B. Guy Peters, "The Problem of Bureaucratic Government," *Journal of Politics,* February 1981, pp. 56–82.
18. Barbara Nelson, *Making an Issue of Child Abuse: Political Agenda Setting for Social Problems* (Chicago: University of Chicago Press, 1984).
19. See Jack L. Walker, "The Diffusion of Innovation among the American States," *American Political Science Review* 63 (September 1969): 895.
20. Nelson, *Making an Issue of Child Abuse,* p. 80.
21. Albert Nichols and Richard Zeckhouser, "OSHA after a Decade: A Time for Reason," in *Case Studies in Regulation,* ed. Leonard W. Weiss and Michael W. Klass (Boston: Little, Brown, 1981), pp. 202–234.
22. Eric Redman, *The Dance of Legislation* (New York: Simon & Schuster, 1973).
23. See Aaron Wildavsky, *The Politics of the Budgetary Process,* 4th ed. (Boston: Little, Brown, 1984).
24. Peters, *American Public Policy,* pp. 106–107.
25. Harold W. Stanley and Richard G. Niemi, *Vital Statistics on American Politics* (Washington, D.C.: Congressional Quarterly Press, 1988), pp. 264–265.
26. Lindblom, *Policy-Making Process,* p. 64.
27. Theodore Lowi, *The End of Liberalism,* 2d ed. (New York: Norton, 1979), pp. 42–63.
28. Ibid.
29. Richard E. Neustadt, *Presidential Power* (New York: Wiley, 1976), p. 77.
30. Jeffrey Pressman and Aaron Wildavsky, *Implementation,* 3d ed. (Berkeley: University of California Press, 1984).
31. Ibid., p. 132.
32. This discussion draws on several examples cited in Peters, *American Public Policy,* chap. 7.
33. Ibid., p. 134.
34. Lester M. Salamon, "The Time Dimension in Policy Evaluation: The Case of New Deal Land Relief Programs," *Public Policy* 27 (Spring 1979): 129–183.
35. Donald T. Campbell and Julian C. Stanley, *Experimental and Quasi-Experimental Designs for Research* (Chicago: Rand McNally, 1963).
36. *New York Times,* November 15, 1988, p. A12.
37. Peters, *American Public Policy,* p. 141.
38. Michael Nelson, "What's Wrong with Policy Analysis?" *Washington Monthly,* September 1979, pp. 53–60.
39. See, for example, Garry Brewer and Peter de Leon, *The Foundations of Policy Analysis* (Pacific Grove, Calif.: Brooks/Cole, 1983), pp. 363–366.

★ For Further Reading

Allison, Graham T. *The Essence of Decision: Explaining the Cuban Missile Crisis.* Boston: Little, Brown, 1971.

Gelb, Joyce, and Marian Lief Palley. *Women and Public Policies.* Rev. ed. Princeton, N.J.: Princeton University Press, 1987.

Henig, Jeffrey R. *Public Policy and Federalism: Issues in State and Local Politics.* New York: St. Martin's Press, 1985.

Liechter, Howard M., and Harrell R. Rodgers, Jr. *American Public Policy in a Comparative Context.* New York: McGraw-Hill, 1984.

Mazmanian, Daniel A., and Paul A. Sabatier. *Implementation and Public Policy.* Glenview, Ill.: Scott, Foresman, 1983.

Nelson, Richard R. *The Moon and the Ghetto: An Essay on Public Policy Analysis.* New York: Norton, 1977.

Schwarz, John E. *America's Hidden Success: A Reassessment of Public Policy from Kennedy to Reagan.* Rev. ed. New York: Norton, 1988.
Shuman, Howard E. *Politics and the Budget: The Struggle between the President and Congress.* 2d ed. Englewood Cliffs, N.J.: Prentice-Hall, 1988.
Wildavsky, Aaron. *Speaking Truth to Power.* New York: Wiley, 1979.

CHAPTER SEVENTEEN

With the exception of preventing war, this is the greatest challenge our country will face during our lifetimes. The energy crisis has not yet overwhelmed us, but it will do so if we do not act quickly. . . . This difficult effort will be the 'moral equivalent of war.' . . .

—Jimmy Carter

At the present rate, women workers won't have wage parity with men until the year 2020 or so.

—Representatives Barbara Kennelly (D-CT) and Claudine Schneider (R-RI)

POLICY CASES

★★★★★★★★★★★★★

Approaching the Year 2000: A Sampler of Public Policies

In chapter 16 we looked at the public policy-making process: *how* our government makes policies. In this and subsequent chapters, we turn to substantive public policy areas: *what* our government does to solve problems. In their attempt to solve social problems, government officials are always on the lookout for alternative solutions. Here, we will consider some of the available alternatives they face in five areas of public policy: health care, income maintenance (social security and welfare), women's concerns, energy, and arms control.

Daily newspaper headlines alert readers to "crises" in these areas as we approach the year 2000. We are running out of oil (the energy crisis), latchkey children are turning to drugs (the child-care crisis), welfare handouts spawn teen pregnancies (the welfare crisis), families are driven to financial ruin by astronomical medical bills (the health-care crisis), there won't be any money left in the pot for this generation of workers (the social-security crisis), and the economies of the United States and the Soviet Union are being drained by a costly arms race (the arms-control crisis). As the federal government strives to deal with these seemingly insurmountable problems, the American public has become increasingly involved in the debate as to the best means to solve them.

★ Health-Care Policy

Americans like to think of themselves as having the most advanced health-care system in the world. Many infectious diseases, such as smallpox and polio, have been virtually eliminated, thanks to inoculation practices. Women rarely die during childbirth and high-tech machines keep three-pound premature infants alive. Precision instruments detect signs of cancer, stroke, and other problems in time for life-saving treatments.

Yet the wonders of modern medicine are not available to all Americans. Even when they are within reach, their costs can spell financial ruin for families and local governments.

Two of the most important problems in health-care policy are the spiraling costs of medical care and the limited coverage of health-care insurance. How did these problems come about and what solutions are viable?

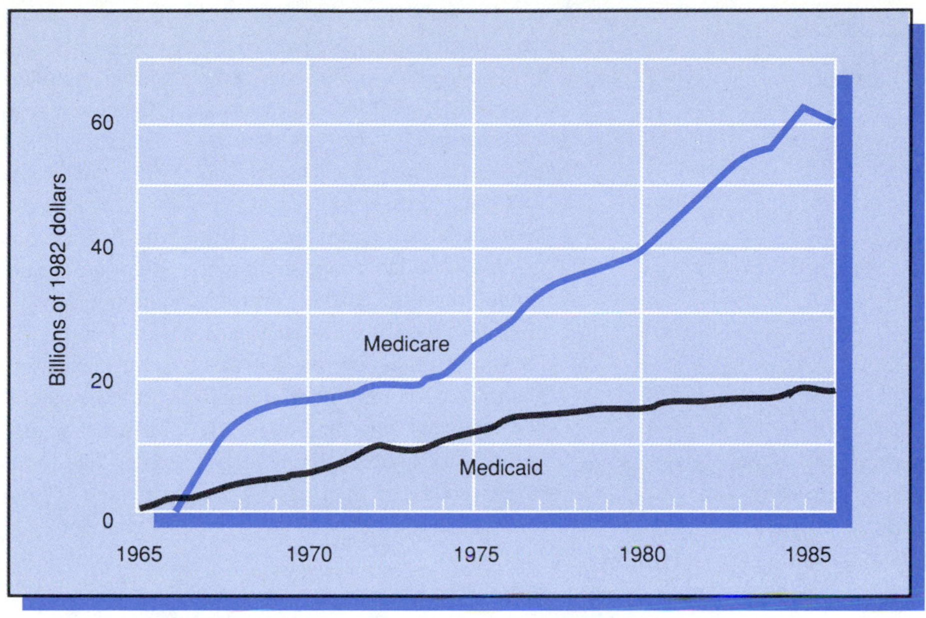

★ **Figure 17-1**
Health entitlement outlays, fiscal years 1965–1986
SOURCE: R. Kent Weaver, "Controlling Entitlements," in John E. Chubb and Paul E. Peterson (eds.), *The New Direction in American Politics* (Washington, D.C.: Brookings, 1985), p. 317. [Based on Office of Management and Budget, *Fiscal Year 1986, Historical Tables.*]

The High Cost of Medical Care

Getting sick is becoming increasingly expensive. Since 1970, medical costs have risen faster than the consumer price index (CPI), a federal government measure of changes in the price of consumer goods.

One cause of rising medical costs is the increase in medical services provided to two groups whose medical bills are partially covered by the government: the elderly and the poor. People are living longer than they used to. The life expectancy of Americans born in 1920 was fifty-four years; for those born in 1985, it was seventy-four years.[1] Older people have become increasingly likely to receive medical services ever since Medicare went into effect in 1965. **Medicare** is a program of government assistance that pays a portion of the medical expenses of the elderly. (It does not pay the full costs until a patient has paid $1,370 out of pocket each year. If a physician charges more than Medicare will pay, the additional amount the patient must pay does not count toward the $1,370.) Poor people have also been more likely to receive medical care since the adoption of Medicaid in 1965. **Medicaid** covers part of the medical expenses of the poor (see figure 17-1).

Health-care costs have also been driven up by hospitals. Their costs have risen the fastest of the three components of medical-care costs—hospitals, physicians, and commodities.[2] In competition for physicians and patients, hospitals have invested in expensive X-ray and CAT-scan machines, the costs of which are covered by increases in room prices and other charges.[3] In addition, hospital labor costs have gone up as many health-care workers have unionized and bargained for higher

Medicare and Medicaid: The Major Federal Health Policies

Medicare

Medicare came into existence in 1965 as part of the social security program. It is a federally financed and administered health insurance program that insures about 28 million elderly and 3 million disabled citizens against the costs of hospital, physicians', and related medical care. In FY 1986, Medicare paid out $75 billion in benefits, about three-quarters of total federal spending on health care. It has two components. Part A consists of hospital insurance (HI), financed through social security payroll taxes levied on both employers and employees. In 1986 the part of the social security tax that went to Medicare was 1.45 percent of the first $42,000 earned. HI covers hospitalization up to a point. Part B consists of supplemental medical insurance (SMI), financed through a combination of general revenues (that is, revenues other than social security taxes) and premiums paid by participants. Medicare costs have risen 17 percent annually since 1974 and HI spending is expected to grow almost 60 percent faster than payroll tax revenues in the 1990s.

Medicaid

Medicaid also was established in 1965. It is a state-administered entitlement program (that is, people are automatically entitled to benefits if they meet certain income requirements). Medicaid is jointly financed by federal and state governments, insuring poor people against the costs of medical and long-term care. It covers about 40 percent of the poverty population. In 1986 it served 22 million people, of whom 70 percent were recipients of aid to families with dependent children (AFDC) and the remainder were aged and disabled. In FY 1985, the federal share was $22 billion; the states paid a roughly equal amount for a total of about $41 billion for the entire Medicaid program. States set eligibility and benefit levels. Since 1982, increases in Medicaid spending have slowed to about half the annual growth rate between 1979 and 1981, which was 18 percent. ★

SOURCES: U.S. Bureau of the Census, *Statistical Abstract of the United States, 1988* (Washington, D.C.: U.S. Government Printing Office, 1987), p. 70; and John L. Palmer and Isabel V. Sawhill, eds., *The Reagan Record: An Assessment of America's Changing Domestic Priorities* (Cambridge, Mass.: Ballinger, 1984).

wages. And the cost of maintaining empty beds and expensive emergency room services is passed along to patients.

Physicians have contributed to mounting medical costs by practicing defensive medicine. They often order costly tests and procedures to protect themselves in the event of a malpractice lawsuit. These tests raise the nation's health-care tally as funds go to the clinics and hospitals that conduct the procedures. And physicians jack up their fees to cover skyrocketing malpractice insurance premiums. In 1988, average annual rates for physicians' malpractice insurance was $50,000 in California, $80,000 in New York, and $136,000 in Florida.[4]

Finally, increased health-care costs can be traced to our system of **third-party payments.** These are payments made to health-care providers by insurance programs, both private (such as Blue Cross and Blue Shield) and public (Medicare and Medicaid). Over 90 percent of all hospital costs and 70 percent of all medical expenses are paid by insurers.[5] Thus neither doctors nor patients have an incentive to save because "someone else" is paying the bill. This attitude contributes to increases in unnecessary services and ultimately to higher insurance premiums.

Various programs have been put into effect in recent years in efforts to bring down medical costs. Hospitals' practice of overpurchasing expensive equipment to attract doctors, who in turn pass on costs to third-party insurers, has been addressed by health systems agencies (HSAs) and state certificate-of-need laws. The 1974

Health Planning Act created HSAs, which are local planning bodies that monitor the development of medical care facilities. State certificate-of-need laws establish guidelines for demonstrating a need before the local HSA can allow the construction of a new health-care facility. These laws cover new hospital facilities and all capital equipment valued at $150,000 or more.

Health systems agencies represent an opportunity for average citizens to change our medical treatment system. Their staffs consist largely of consumers and government officials, with only a minority of health-care providers. More than two hundred local HSAs have the legal power to approve or disapprove applications for federal grant funds, new construction of facilities, and the reimbursement of providers under Medicare and Medicaid. These are significant powers to direct the future of medical care in this country. Citizens have a chance to steer HSAs toward preventive medicine, which benefits consumers, rather than acute-care medicine, which benefits members of the medical profession who command high fees for their services.

Congress has attempted to trim Medicare and Medicaid costs by setting up agencies to review provider practices and by setting flat fees for services. Professional standards review organizations (PSROs) were established by Congress in 1972 to police the quality and pricing of services provided to Medicare and Medicaid patients. PSROs are staffed primarily by physicians affiliated with county medical organizations. They have achieved mixed results. Some have been able to secure substantial savings, while others have had no effect in disciplining physicians or hospitals.[6]

PSROs are a good example of corporatism (discussed in chap. 16): a mixed bag of information and bias. The government wants and needs knowledgeable people on these boards. Yet PSROs have been criticized for being ineffectual because doctors are reluctant to police other physicians. The original goal of PSROs was to limit unnecessary costly practices. But opposition by the American Medical Association (AMA) has refocused attention from scrutiny of individual physicians toward a general concern for quality and effective use of health resources.[7]

Diagnostic related groups (DRGs) represent another cost-reduction measure. Under this 1983 program, the federal government reimburses a hospital for care of a Medicare or Medicaid patient on the basis of the specific diagnostic group to which the patient's disease or condition is assigned. Each of the more than four hundred DRGs is assigned a fixed dollar amount. A hospital that treats a patient for less than that amount can retain the difference; one that goes over the amount must absorb the loss. Some observers fear that this program may create tension between hospital administrators (who want to keep costs low), and physicians (who want to provide treatment they consider appropriate, regardless of cost), or that it may lead hospitals to send patients home before they are able to care for themselves. DRGs illustrate one of the dilemmas of cost-benefit analysis: short-term versus long-term costs. Reductions in short-term costs may end up being quite costly in the long run if patients are released so early that they require rehospitalization when complications arise.

Finally, the federal government has encouraged the creation of **health maintenance organizations (HMOs).** These are programs of prepaid medical care, such as Kaiser-Permanente, which has enrolled more than three million members and three thousand physicians. Members pay an annual fee for virtually all of their medical care. HMOs were set up to alleviate two costly features of American medical care: fee-for-service medicine and acute rather than preventive care. Physicians who practice fee-for-service medicine are paid for each service they perform, so they have an incentive to perform many services. Physicians who practice acute-care medicine are oriented toward treatment of disease rather than the prevention of disease. HMOs get around these two problems by having doctors share in the profits of the organization. Thus physicians have an incentive not to prescribe unnecessary treatments and to keep members healthy by practicing preventive medicine. Preventive measures focus on checkups, diet, and exercise to prevent diseases or to catch them at an early stage so that they never require costly acute care.

The main critics of HMOs are some members of the medical profession, especially the AMA. Many doctors complain that HMOs represent unfair competition with their private practices because they are subsidized by the federal government. Beginning in 1973, Congress provided grants to develop HMOs, and federal agencies have subsequently curbed attempts by physicians and insurers to reduce the competitive threat of HMOs. The chief defenders of HMOs are organized labor and some business groups, who see HMOs as an important way to reduce workers' medical costs. The federal government joined the HMO cost-cutting bandwagon in 1984, when the Reagan administration allowed Medicare and Medicaid patients the option of joining HMOs for medical care. HMOs provide lower costs to consumers than do private insurance systems that pay fees for services. It is not yet clear how much of the reduction in cost is due to preventive efforts. But one source of reduced costs has been identified: HMOs have much lower rates of hospitalization and surgery than do fee-for-service practices.[8]

Limited Health-Care Insurance

Adding to the political controversy over high health-care costs is the fact that many Americans lack health-care insurance. In 1985, 13 percent of Americans (31 million people) were not covered by private or government health insurance.[9] Many jobs, especially those that are part-time, seasonal, or low-skilled, provide no health-care benefits.

As we mentioned earlier, only 40 percent of the poor are covered by Medicaid. Economics is the biggest barrier blocking access to medical care. One-third of all low-income children did not see a doctor for any purpose during the mid-1970s.[10] It is not that we do not have enough doctors. In 1980, the United States had one doctor for every 580 persons, a ratio exceeded only by Israel and the Soviet Union.[11] But this ratio has not translated into delivery of quality health care to the poor. Not only do doctors shun poor areas, but they are increasingly specialists, not generalists (primary-care physicians). The United States has a much lower ratio of general practitioners to specialists than any other industrialized nation: about 20 percent as compared with more than 50 percent in Sweden, West Germany, and Great Britain.[12]

The elderly, who have access to Medicare when they reach age sixty-five, still pay about 35 percent of their own medical bills. Medicare picks up about 40 percent and other government programs and private health insurance cover about 25 percent of the tab.[13] Medicare has three loopholes: deductibles (amounts patients must pay each year before coverage becomes effective), copayment requirements (percentages of costs that must be paid by the patient), and coverage limitations (limits beyond which the coverage ceases, usually ninety days). Catastrophic illnesses can

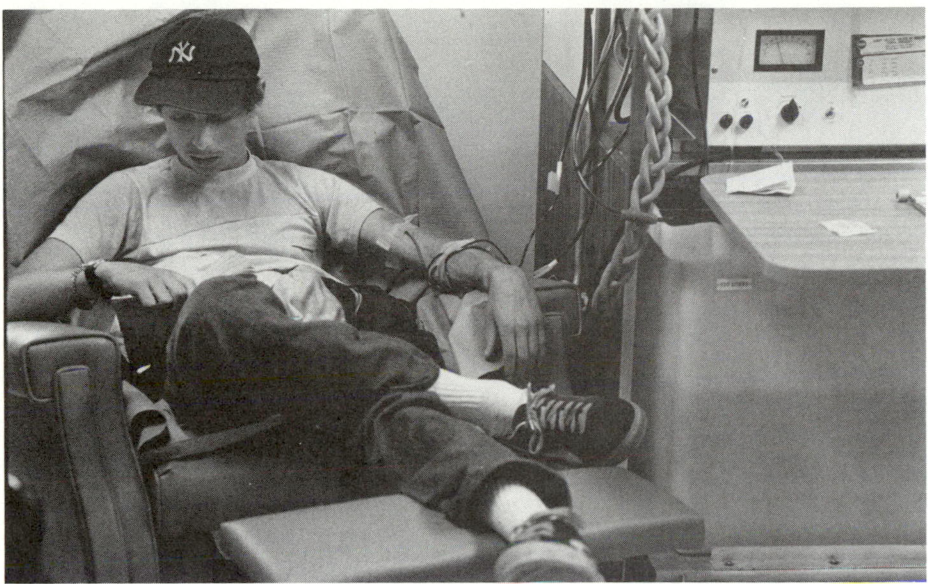

★ Americans want quality health care available to everyone, such as this boy, who is on a hemodialysis machine. Yet they cannot agree on how the costs for various medical services should be divided among patients, taxpayers, employers, and employees.

spell economic disaster for all but the very wealthy. Recall the case cited in chapter 16, of the parents of the boy with leukemia who tried in vain to raise $100,000 for his bone-marrow transplant.

Efforts toward National Health Insurance

Citizens disturbed by the limitations of health-care insurance have called for some form of national health insurance. The United States is the only Western industrialized nation without such insurance, even though 14 percent of Americans depend upon government for health care and 43 percent of health-care expenditures in the United States are made by government agencies.[14] Most industrialized nations not only spend less per capita than the United States on health care but also outrank the United States in many key health and mortality indicators.[15] Infant mortality rates, for example, are lower in eighteen other industrialized nations than in the United States. Each year about forty thousand American infants die before their first birthday.[16] And this figure conceals a vast racial disparity. The mortality rate for black infants is twice that for white infants.[17]

Attempts to implement national health insurance in the United States began under the Truman administration in 1945. Introduced as part of social security, it was thwarted by the American Medical Association and conservative business organizations, who denounced it as "socialized medicine."

Opponents were worried that the adoption of Medicare in 1965 represented a partial victory for supporters of a national health insurance program. As we mentioned earlier, Medicare covers hospitalization up to a point, doctor's fees, and outpatient services. It does not cover many other essentials, such as prescriptions,

Our Health Care System in Comparative Perspective

Advanced industrial nations vary widely in their health-care systems. At one end of the spectrum are nations with the philosophy that health care is primarily a private responsibility and government should play a limited role in providing this service. At the other end of the spectrum are countries whose philosophical position is that health care is an absolute right of citizenship and the government should control its provision. Other key differences are whether physicians should operate private businesses or work as state employees; whether health-care facilities should be privately or publicly owned; and whether costs should be shouldered directly by the patient or indirectly by all citizens through taxes.

The following table depicts five models of health-care systems around the world. ★

★ Models of health-care systems

Characteristics of the system	*Market, free enterprise*	*Mixed*	*Insurance, social security*	*National health system*	*Socialized*
Philosophical assumptions	Health care is a personal responsibility	Health care is a shared public and private responsibility but primarily private	Health care is a shared responsibility but primarily a concern of the government	Health care is an absolute right of citizenship	Health care is an absolute right of citizenship
Role of government	Minimal	Decentralized, indirect	Centralized, direct	Centralized, direct	Total
Position of physician	Private enterprise	Private enterprise	Private enterprise	Private enterprise	State employees
Ownership of health-care facilities	Private	Private and public	Private and public	Mostly public	Entirely public
Financing	Direct patient to doctor	Some direct and indirect*	Mostly direct	Mostly direct	Entirely indirect
Examples	U.S., Western Europe, tsarist Russia in 19th century	U.S. and South Africa	Sweden, France, Japan, Canada, Italy, Switzerland	Great Britain	Soviet Union, Eastern Europe

*Includes public and private insurance.

SOURCE: Howard M. Leichter and Harrell R. Rodgers, Jr., *American Public Policy in a Comparative Context* (New York: McGraw-Hill, 1984), p. 69. [Adapted with permission from *Social Science and Medicine,* 14A, Mark Field, "The Health System and the Polity: A Contemporary American Dialectic," 1980, Pergamon Press plc.]

eye and dental treatment, inoculations, and extended care. Pressure has mounted for increased coverage and insurance for the entire population. In 1973, a majority of Americans polled favored some form of public health insurance.

Three types of national health insurance were proposed in the late 1970s.[18] At the liberal end of the spectrum, Massachusetts Senator Edward Kennedy's plan was the most comprehensive and had the support of organized labor. It relied on private carriers and did not establish a separate, publicly funded insurance plan. It would require all citizens to have medical insurance, with no deductibles of co-insurance provisions. That is, citizens would have no out-of-pocket medical expenses. It would be financed by premiums paid by employers and employees, the latter being liable for up to 35 percent of premium costs, and there would be provisions for cost containment. Congress would plan the annual health budget to increase at the same rate as the gross national product.

A second approach was the Carter administration's proposal, which was directed primarily at catastrophic coverage. It sought coverage for catastrophic expenses for all Americans, who would pay for some portion of the coverage. Individuals would be liable for $2,500 in medical expenses annually, plus a portion of the medical insurance premiums. This deductible was intended to reduce overuse of the system. Existing insurance companies would write the insurance, with employers absorbing most of the costs. There would be a 9 percent annual cap on hospital costs.

The third plan was a catastrophic coverage plan proposed by a group of Republican senators. Their proposal would cover expenses beyond $5,000 and sixty days in the hospital. It would be carried by existing insurance companies and would be jointly financed by employees and employers, with federal subsidies for smaller employers. Medical coinsurance and deductibles would be reduced. There would be few cost-control provisions in this plan.

During the 1980s, debate centered on plans to cover catastrophic expenses. Congress bogged down in the question of how much of the cost should be borne by employers, employees, and taxpayers. The Reagan administration was not eager to drive up the cost of doing America's business or to impose new taxes. And unions were not eager to see workers foot the bill out of their paychecks.

In 1988 President Reagan signed the Medicare Catastrophic Coverage Act, which placed the entire burden of financing the program on the elderly. All taxpayers aged sixty-five and over paid a premium based on the amount of income taxes they owed, whether or not they were covered by Medicare. (Many people continue to work past age sixty-five and so do not receive social security or Medicare benefits.) Critics deluged Congress with mail, forcing lawmakers to go back to the drawing board in 1989 to devise a different way to finance catastrophic insurance coverage.

Thus our steps toward a national health program comparable to those of our European neighbors continue to be sidetracked by the difficult question of who should pay the costs imposed by our system of private health care.

★ Income-Maintenance Policy

The United States has several programs to help people in times of need. The largest income-maintenance programs, in terms of costs and number of beneficiaries, are

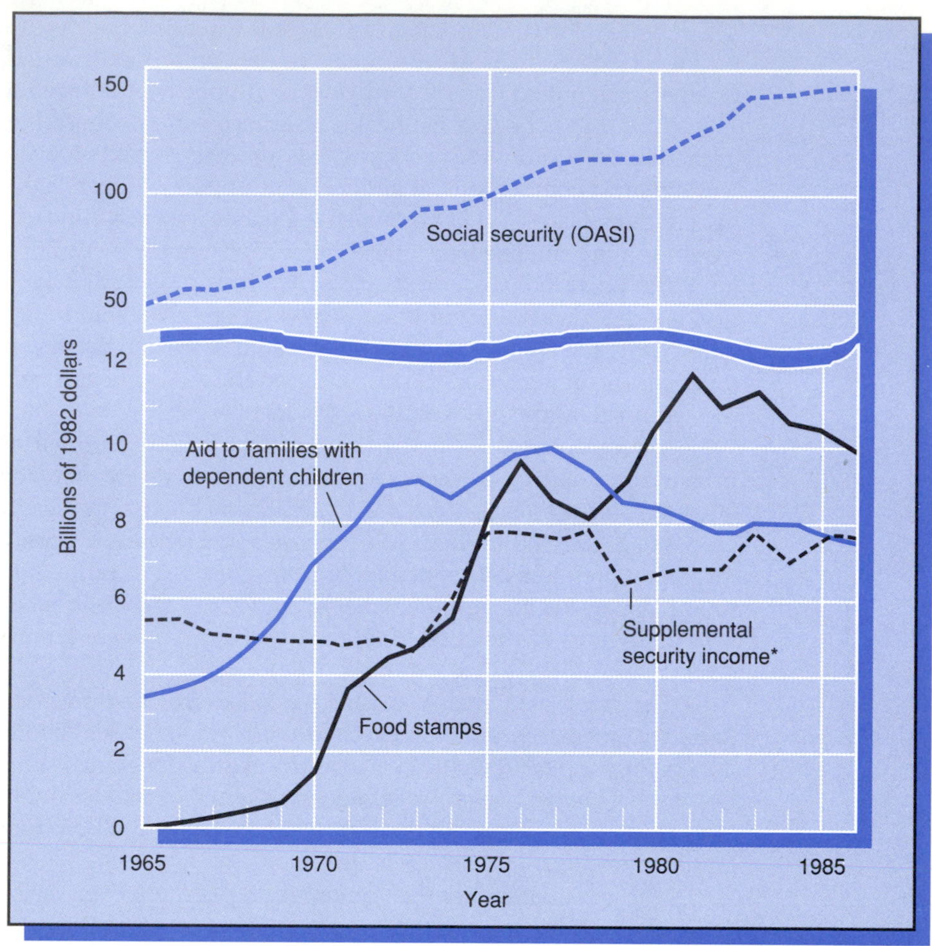

★ **Figure 17-2**

Public assistance program outlays, fiscal years 1965–1986

* Includes federal expenditures for predecessor programs to SSI: aid to the permanently and totally disabled, aid to the blind, and old-age assistance.

NOTE: Data for 1985 and 1986 are projected and social security data exclude social security disability payments.
SOURCE: R. Kent Weaver, "Controlling Entitlements," in John E. Chubb and Paul E. Peterson (eds.), *The New Direction in American Politics* (Washington, D.C.: Brookings, 1985), p. 314–315. [Based on Office of Management and Budget, *Fiscal Year 1986, Historical Tables;* Department of Health and Human Services; and Committee Print, House Committee on Ways and Means, 1985.]

social security, unemployment compensation, food stamps, supplemental security income (SSI), and aid to families with dependent children (AFDC, or "welfare") (see figure 17-2). The most problematic of these programs, and the ones most in need of reform, are social security and AFDC.

Social Security

Social security is the nation's most important safety-net program, helping millions of people to stay above the poverty line. A 1988 Census Bureau report concluded that social security payments reduced the inequality of Americans' income more than the progressive tax system and more than other social welfare programs. In

1986, social security benefits lifted fifteen million people out of poverty and reduced the poverty rate from 21 percent to 14 percent. The program was responsible for an even more dramatic reduction in the poverty rate of the elderly, from 47 percent to 14 percent.[19]

Any attempt to tinker with a program of such vital importance to almost half of the nation's elderly is met with a quick response not only from current recipients—the elderly—but also from future recipients—the current work force. Active workers are especially concerned that social security should remain solvent well into the twenty-first century, when it will be their turn to collect benefits.

Enough Money to Go Around? One of the biggest problems with social security is how to finance it. Given the rising number of elderly Americans, active workers are increasingly burdened to finance the needs of retired workers and their survivors. Today one retiree is financed by approximately three workers; by 2025, the number of workers per retiree will fall to two.

In the 1960s, fears began to be expressed that social security's trust fund was going bankrupt. Government officials concluded that increased longevity and a declining birth rate threatened to deplete the trust fund. By the early 1980s, the federal government announced that social security reserves faced imminent liquidation unless quick action was taken.

Rescuing Social Security from Insolvency. In 1983 Congress took action to avert the imminent insolvency of the social security trust fund. To solve short-run funding problems, Congress added $128 billion in revenues by increasing the payroll tax, taxing half of the social security benefits of recipients whose incomes exceeded a certain level, extending coverage to all new federal workers and nonprofit employees (thereby generating more payroll taxes), transferring general revenues to social security to compensate for military-service credits that increased benefits, and delaying for six months the 1983 cost-of-living increases.[20]

Several other reforms have been discussed as well: raise the retirement age (it is currently sixty-five and will be sixty-seven early in the next century), reduce survivors' benefits, trim cost-of-living increases, eliminate the income threshold beyond which no payroll tax is withheld, boost the employers' contributions along the lines of those of most Western European nations, remove Medicare from the payroll tax and finance it through general revenues, and impose a tax on benefits received by the wealthy.

Perhaps the most far-reaching proposal for financing social security through general revenues is a value-added tax (VAT). This is a tax that is levied on the value added by each pair of hands through which the components of a product pass and is reflected in the price of the product. When a pair of shoes is produced, for example, a tax is levied on the hides purchased by the tanner to make leather, on the leather bought by the manufacturer to be made into shoes, on the shoes purchased by a retailer to be sold in a store, and again on the shoes when a customer buys them. The VAT is in effect a national sales tax collected at every stage of production and marketing. Liberals favor it as a means of financing needed social programs and conservatives criticize it as a hidden way to expand the social welfare state. The conservative view prevailed until the latter 1980s, when many economists proposed adoption of a VAT to supplement the payroll tax for social security. Although most states and localities have sales taxes, there is no national sales tax comparable to the VATs collected by most European countries, which generate about 15 percent

★ Most welfare recipients also qualify for food stamps, or coupons redeemed for food at retail stores. Many AFDC recipients cannot afford to get off welfare because they cannot find jobs that pay enough to match the combined dollar value of the AFDC, food stamps, and Medicaid.

of those nations' revenues. The United States raises about 6 percent of its total revenues (federal, state, and local) through sales taxes.[21]

As the government's largest income-maintenance program—over $200 billion strong—social security is a prime target of federal budget cutters. But attempts to reduce social security benefits have been effectively countered by the voting bloc of elderly Americans, "gray power." As we saw in chapter 9, older Americans are much more likely to vote than are this country's younger citizens. For some older Americans, social security is a matter of survival. They have to make their monthly check cover their expenses. Whether poor or rich, the elderly feel entitled to benefits from a program to which they have contributed for decades. To alienate the voting bloc of older voters would be political suicide in many congressional districts.

AFDC (Welfare)

While social security is the most important income-maintenance program for the elderly poor, **AFDC (welfare)** is the safety net that keeps parents and their dependent children afloat. Welfare is a godsend to mothers who worry about how they are going to provide for their young children. Two-thirds of welfare recipients are children and about 90 percent of adult recipients are women. To qualify for AFDC, a parent must have dependent children, virtually no income ($3,200 in 1986), and no one living in the household who is capable of supporting the children.

Welfare may be a godsend to its recipients, but in the public imagination it conjures up images of abuse and fraud. It is probably the most maligned government program. As Americans head toward the year 2000, liberals and conservatives alike agree that something has to be done about the "welfare mess."

The Welfare Mess. AFDC has come under attack on several fronts. It is said to have spawned a bloated bureaucracy of caseworkers, who process reams of paper-

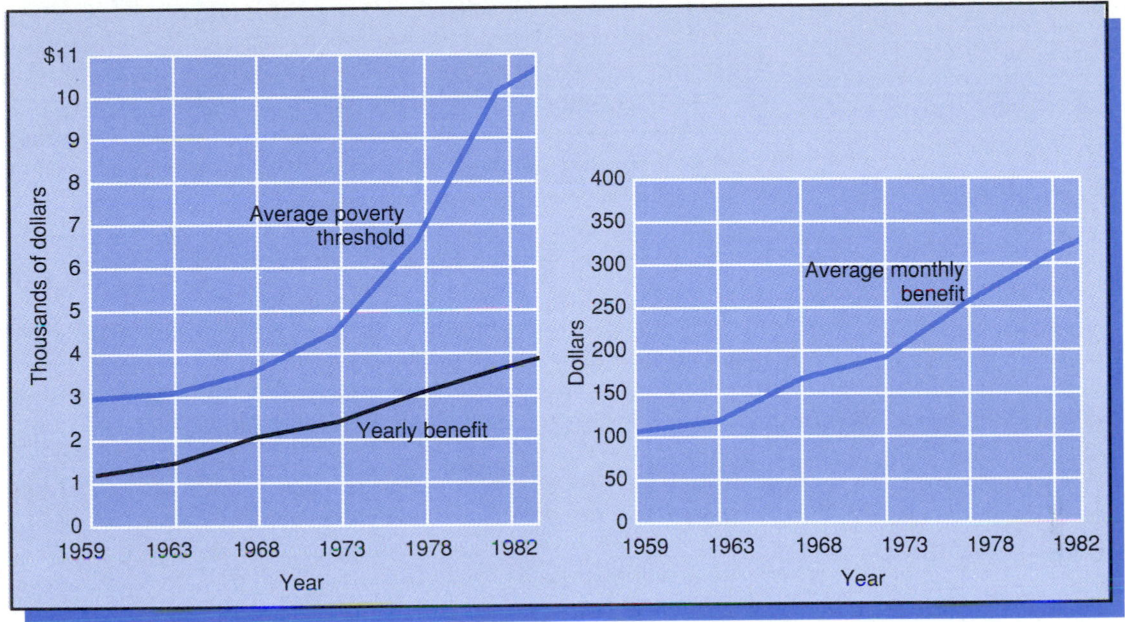

★ **Figure 17-3**

Aid to families with dependent children versus the poverty line, 1959–1984

NOTE: Average AFDC benefits are for three- to four-member families. Poverty threshold is for a family of four persons.

SOURCE: Adapted from Harold W. Stanley and Richard G. Niemi, *Vital Statistics on American Politics* (Washington, D.C.: Congressional Quarterly Press, 1988), p. 325. [Based on U.S. Bureau of the Census, *Statistical Abstract of the U.S.* data.]

work and investigate such minute details as the price of the last pair of shoes a mother bought for her child. Some recipients have been humiliated by caseworkers' prying into such private matters as the sources of their income, the kinds of household goods they buy, and the presence of a boyfriend around the house. Many women who are eligible for AFDC benefits do not apply for them because of the stigma attached to the program. Contrary to the popular myth, few women make a career of welfare. About 60 percent of welfare families are off the rolls in three years or less; only about 7 percent of them remain on welfare more than ten years.[22]

Some studies claim that children raised in AFDC households later come to rely on the program as teenagers. (Other studies, however, find no such dependency effect.) Thus AFDC is criticized for fostering the recent dramatic increase in teenage out-of-wedlock pregnancies. It has become the new "husband" for young girls who want the status of heading their own households at the taxpayers' expense.

Finally, many people take issue with AFDC's work penalty. Individuals who are on welfare are severely penalized if they work. They can work no more than a certain number of hours per month, no matter how low the pay. After a certain amount is earned each year, the recipient has to return $2 in benefits for every $3 earned, which amounts to an income tax at a higher rate than any other in our tax system. Recipients have little incentive to work for another reason as well: if they take a job, they may lose food stamps and Medicaid. Conservative critics say AFDC benefits are too high, promoting dependency on the program. Liberals view benefits as too low, preventing a decent standard of living. Benefits averaged $303 a month in 1986. See figure 17-3 for benefits in earlier years.

Income-Maintenance Programs

Social Security

Old Age, Survivors, and Disability Insurance (OASDI), popularly known as social security, was established in 1935 as part of President Franklin Roosevelt's New Deal. It is a federal program that protects most workers and their families against loss of income due to retirement, disability, or death of a breadwinner. It is financed by a payroll tax on employees and employers. In 1989 both employees and employers paid 7.5 percent on incomes up to $42,000. Social security does not distribute income across classes, but rather across time and generations. Social security funds are earmarked for social security payments only; they are not part of the general fund (general revenues of the federal government, which can be spent on any program). About 90 percent of the American work force are covered; government employees joined the system in 1984. Benefits are based on a worker's earnings history, from a low of 24 percent of a high-wage earner's last year of earnings to a high of 63 percent for low-wage workers. Thus there is a slight redistributional effect. In 1984 the average monthly benefit for retired and disabled workers was $450. That year there were about 36 million beneficiaries: 25 million retired, 7 million survivors, and 4 million disabled. In FY 1986, $205 billion went to social security, the single largest federal income program.

Unemployment Compensation

Unemployment insurance (UI) was passed as part of the 1935 Social Security Act. This joint federal-state program pays benefits to most unemployed workers who meet a test of recent work experience. Benefits are paid from state accounts in a federal trust fund financed by a payroll tax on each state's employers. States have sole authority to set taxes above a federally required minimum. States also set eligibility criteria and benefit levels. Most states pay compensation for up to twenty-six weeks of unemployment; benefits range from 50 to 60 percent of previous wages up to a maximum. In addition, a jointly financed federal-state extended benefit program is triggered in states with high unemployment levels to provide compensation for up to thirteen additional weeks. The Trade Adjustment Assistance program may provide compensation after UI benefits are exhausted for workers unemployed because of foreign competition. In FY 1984 the federal government spent $26 billion to

(continued)

Reforming Welfare. Several reforms of welfare have been proposed. One is the family allowance, which is a policy maintained by virtually every other industrial society. All families that include dependent children receive a monthly check from the government. Much of this money is returned in taxes by affluent families, while for the poor it constitutes a major source of income. The stigma of welfare is reduced because all households with children receive it. And administrative costs are substantially less than they are for AFDC, whose caseworkers scrutinize family finances in accordance with rigid eligibility standards.

A negative income tax would have the same advantages of eliminating stigma and reducing administrative overhead. Each family would file a tax statement. Those whose earnings fell below an established minimum level would receive a rebate. The working poor would be better off than they are under AFDC, as their benefits would be reduced by only one-third or one-half for money earned (depending on their tax bracket), instead of AFDC's two-thirds penalty. President Nixon's 1969 proposal for a family assistance plan would have operated much like a negative income tax. It was defeated by a coalition of liberals, who criticized its meager benefits, and conservatives, who were ideologically opposed to the idea of a guaranteed minimum income. Many social workers, who saw their jobs threatened by provide unemployment insurance for 4.7 million people.

Food Stamps

Food stamps became a federal program in 1970. This federally financed and state-administered program provides aid on the basis of need, without regard to other family or individual characteristics. Food coupons are dispensed by state agencies and redeemed for food at retail stores. In 1984, the maximum monthly allotment was $76 for a single person and $253 for a family of four. Benefits are automatically adjusted for annual increases in food costs. In FY 1984, outlays of $11 billion went to 21 million recipients.

Supplemental Security Income

Supplemental security income (SSI) went into effect in 1974. This federally funded and administered program provides cash assistance to low-income aged, blind, and disabled persons. Benefits are automatically adjusted for inflation each year. Maximum monthly benefits in 1984 were $312 for a single person and $472 per couple. About half of the states supplement federal payments at their own expense by an average of about 12 percent. In FY 1984, SSI outlays were $8 billion for 3.4 million recipients.

Aid to Families with Dependent Children

Aid to families with dependent children (AFDC) had its origins in the 1930s, when a federal program to provide aid to dependent children (ADC) distributed benefits to widows and "deserving deserted" mothers. It became AFDC in 1961, when families with unemployed fathers became eligible. AFDC is a state-administered cash assistance program financed jointly by federal and state governments for families with dependent children and a parent who is absent, incapacitated, or, in some states, unemployed, whose income falls below a stipulated amount. States determine benefit levels and eligibility criteria under broad federal guidelines. In 1984, the maximum monthly benefit, which is received by nearly 90 percent of all recipients, ranged from a low of about $120 to a high of $600 for a family of four. Federal outlays in 1984 were $8 billion. The case load was 3.8 million families, or 10.9 million persons. ★

SOURCES: Kenneth Dolbeare, *American Public Policy: A Citizen's Guide* (New York: McGraw-Hill, 1982); John L. Palmer and Isabel V. Sawhill, eds., *The Reagan Record: An Assessment of America's Changing Domestic Priorities* (Cambridge, Mass.: Ballinger, 1984); B. Guy Peters, *American Public Policy: Promise and Performance*, 2d ed. (Chatham, N.J.: Chatham House, 1986); and U.S. Bureau of the Census, *Statistical Abstract of the United States, 1988* (Washington, D.C.: U.S. Government Printing Office, 1987).

a program that placed the burden of establishing eligibility on recipients, also opposed the plan.[23]

One program that has been tried in several states is **workfare,** which requires recipients to work for their benefits. Michael Dukakis touted the success of workfare in Massachusetts during his 1988 presidential campaign. Typically, workfare clients work enough hours to earn their benefits as if they had been paid at the minimum wage. They also receive an allowance to cover the costs of going to work. Many of them work in public service jobs. While workfare has the advantage of redeeming the work ethic, it has the disadvantages of placing recipients in low-skill jobs and increasing costs by the expenses of finding jobs, providing work allowances, and subsidizing child care.

Of course, yet another solution would be a full employment economy, which would eliminate many of the problems of AFDC by guaranteeing jobs rather than benefits. Though full employment has been the stated goal of the federal government ever since the 1946 Full Employment Act was adopted, the unemployment rate since that time has fluctuated between 3.5 and 9.5 percent.[24] In the 1970s, the federal government's Comprehensive Employment and Training Act (CETA) enabled people to acquire job skills by working with local public and private contractors

★ Table 17-1
Percentage of population living below official poverty level, 1965–1986

	1965	1969	1970	1975	1980	1983	1986
Total	17.3	14.7	12.6	12.3	13.0	15.2	13.6
Blacks	NA	41.8	33.5	31.3	32.5	32.7	31.3
Children under 6	NA	18.1	16.6	18.2	20.3	25.0	22.1
Female-headed households	NA	39.8	38.1	37.5	36.7	40.2	34.2
Over age 65	NA	28.5	24.5	15.3	15.7	14.1	12.4

NOTE: NA = not available.

SOURCE: *National Journal*, September 8, 1984, p. 1650; U.S.Bureau of the Census, *Statistical Abstract of the United States, 1988* (Washington, D.C.: U.S. Government Printing Office, 1987), pp. 434–437.

and to work for a period of time in subsidized jobs until they were able to earn a living wage in the labor market. The program was eventually curtailed amid charges of corruption and complaints that people were being trained to fill nonexistent jobs and that too many trainees were being placed in the public rather than the private sector.

The most far-reaching set of alternatives to welfare was President Johnson's War on Poverty legislation in the 1960s. This package of programs attempted to address the long-term causes of poverty and to involve the poor themselves in the design and implementation of programs. In order to get around the bureaucratic commitment of the Department of Health, Education, and Welfare to entrenched social insurance programs, Johnson set up the Office of Economic Opportunity (OEO) in the White House Office to administer the War on Poverty. Head Start was a preschool program that prepared poor children to compete with other children when they entered kindergarten. The Neighborhood Youth Corps and Job Corps prepared young people for jobs and placed them in temporary public service jobs. The work-study program subsidized the college expenses of students from low-income families.

By the early 1980s, many of these programs had been dismantled, reduced, or modified for several reasons. The war in Vietnam diverted attention and money from domestic programs, particularly the new antipoverty measures, which lacked the political power base and institutionalized bureaucracy of the iron triangle (discussed in chap. 16). Goals were often so unrealistic that it was easy to deem the programs a failure. Some were funded only as pilot programs and not given enough time to be tested. And the Republican administrations of Nixon, Ford, and Reagan reversed the impetus for new antipoverty measures.

Supporters of the War on Poverty say that it led to a dip in the poverty rate. As table 17-1 indicates, the poverty rate did decline in the late 1960s and the 1970s. The table also shows that the poor in this country are decreasingly the elderly and increasingly children. To the extent that government programs have helped alleviate the problem of poverty, they have been more successful in maintaining the incomes of the elderly (social security) than in providing incomes for fatherless

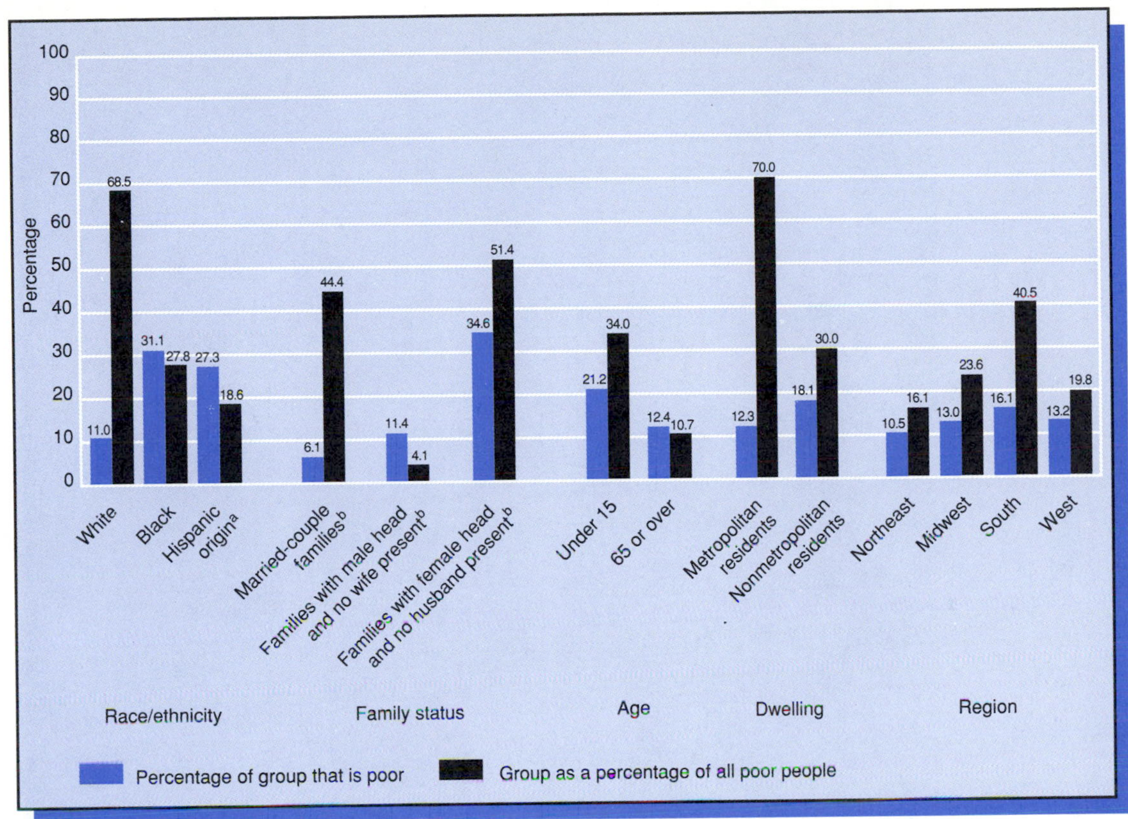

★ **Figure 17-4**

Persons and families below the poverty line, 1986

[a] Persons of Hispanic origin may be of any race.

[b] Percentages based on numbers of families.

SOURCE: Harold W. Stanley and Richard G. Niemi, *Vital Statistics on American Politics* (Washington, D.C.: Congressional Quarterly Press, 1988), p. 318. [Based on U.S. Bureau of the Census, Current Populations Report, "Money Income and Poverty Status of Families and Persons in the U.S., 1986."]

families through AFDC (see figure 17-4). If current trends continue, by the year 2000 almost the entire poverty population will consist of women and their children. This trend, already visible, has been termed the **feminization of poverty.**

★ Women and Public Policy

In recent years women have joined the labor force in steadily increasing numbers. In the 1950s, one-third of all women were employed; by the 1980s, over one-half were. Today a majority of married women, even those with children under six years of age, are working outside the home.[25] Women's participation in the labor force has been accompanied by a host of problems. The two we will look at here are inequities in employment and the inadequacy of provisions for child care.

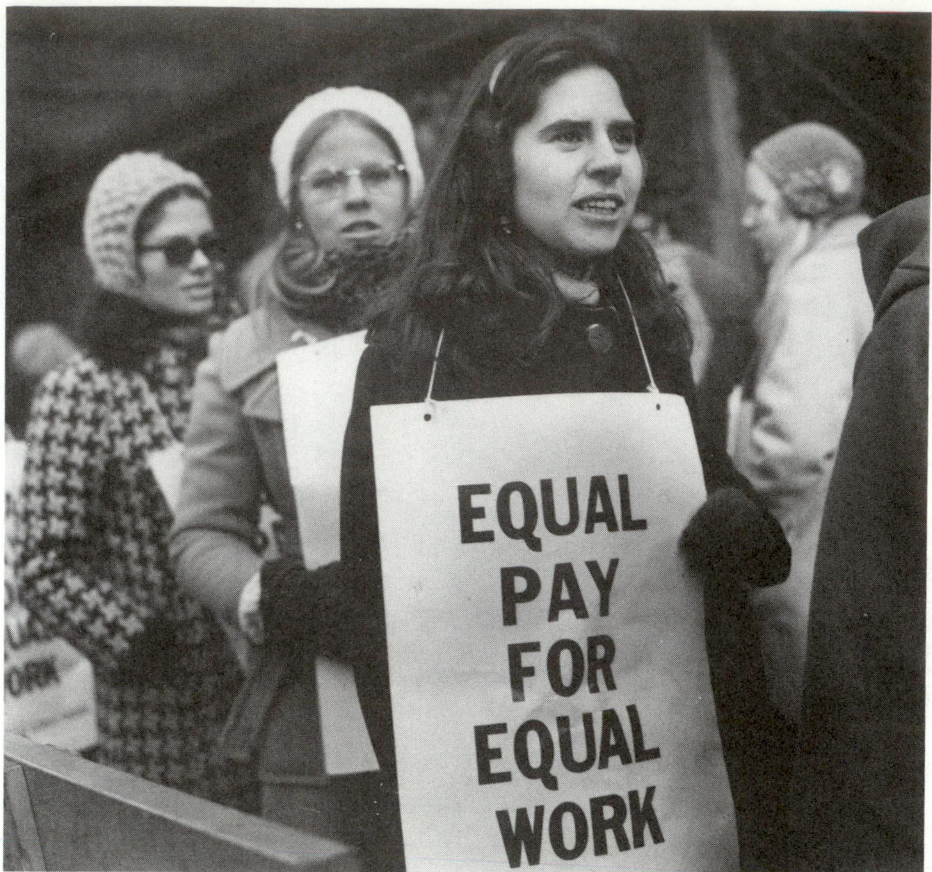

★ In spite of three decades of women's activism and a federal law mandating equal pay for equal work, women earn only about 70 percent of what men do.

Employment Inequities

Women's entrance into the labor force has been a boon to many women and their families. Many women enjoy the freedom that comes from earning their own money and the satisfaction of challenging work outside the home. But for most women and their families, paid work is an economic necessity. Most women in the work force are either single, divorced, or married to men who earn less than $15,000 a year. With the skyrocketing cost of homeownership (the 1989 median home price nationwide was $118,400)—particularly in a state such as California, where only one in five families could afford to buy a home in 1989—a woman's paycheck has increasingly become the ticket to middle-class family status.[26]

Problems in the Job Market. As we approach the year 2000, the trend of women's participation in the labor force will continue to rise. But certain inequalities in the job market still plague women, despite government measures to correct them.

Socialization pressures and overt sexism have led many women to choose jobs that have traditionally been thought of as "women's work." Eighty percent of

★ Table 17-2
Women as a percentage of all workers in selected occupations, 1975 and 1986

Occupation	Women as percentage of total employed	
	1975	1986
Architect	4.3%	9.7%
Auto mechanic	0.5	1.0
Bartender	35.2	48.8
Bus driver	37.7	50.4
Carpenter	0.6	1.4
Child care worker	98.4	97.4
Computer programmer	25.6	34.0
Computer systems analyst	14.8	34.4
Data entry keyer	92.8	91.1
Data-processing equipment repairer	1.8	11.1
Dental assistant	100.0	99.0
Dentist	1.8	4.4
Economist	13.1	39.3
Editor, reporter	44.6	50.5
Garage, gas station attendant	4.7	5.8
Lawyer, judge	7.1	18.1
Librarian	81.1	85.9
Mail carrier	8.7	20.6
Physician	13.0	17.6
Registered nurse	97.0	94.3
Social worker	60.8	65.0
Teacher		
elementary school	85.4	85.2
college/university	31.1	36.0
Telephone operator	93.3	87.9
Waiter/waitress	91.1	85.1
Welder	4.4	5.1

SOURCE: Sara E. Rix (ed.), *The American Woman, 1988–89: A Status Report* (New York: Norton, 1988), p. 382. [Based on Bureau of Labor Statistics, *Employment and Earnings,* Jan. 1976, Table 2, and Jan. 1987, Table 22.]

employed women are clustered in what has become known as the "pink-collar ghetto" of female-dominated jobs such as dental assistant and telephone operator. Many of these jobs provide low-paying, dead-end work and few benefits. Women have only recently made headway into nontraditional, male-dominated occupations in the professions and skilled trades (see table 17-2). Most working women complain of some form of sexual harassment on the job (unwanted sexual advances by one's superiors at work).[27] There is also a sizable earnings gap in the workplace (see figure 17-5). Women's wages remained at about 60 percent of men's wages throughout the 1960s and 1970s; by the late 1980s women were making 70 percent as much as men. Wage discrepancies are greatest in clerical and sales jobs and least in the professions.[28] The average annual salary of female college graduates is less than that of men who have gone no further than high school (see table 17-3).

★ **Table 17-3**
Average earnings of year-round, full-time workers age 25 and over by sex and educational attainment, 1985 (in dollars)

Educational attainment	*Women*	*Men*
Fewer than 8 years	$ 9,681	$15,039
1–3 years of high school	12,317	19,241
High school graduates	14,903	22,852
1–3 years of college	17,229	26,705
College graduates	21,362	35,400
1 or more years postgraduate	26,348	44,478
All education levels	17,033	27,430

SOURCE: Sara E. Rix (ed.), *The American Woman, 1988–89: A Status Report* (New York: Norton, 1988), p. 389. [Based on Bureau of the Census, Current Population Reports, 1985, Series P-60, No. 156, Table 36.]

Addressing Inequities in Employment. Several measures have been proposed and enacted to counter these inequities. One federal policy adopted to help women gain entrance into nontraditional jobs is **affirmative action,** which requires employers who hold federal contracts to hire women and minorities to rectify the effects of past discrimination. Affirmative action is implemented by the Office of Federal Contract Compliance, which has the power to cancel government contracts and deny future ones. About one-third of the labor force works for employers who receive money from the federal government.

The policy of affirmative action originated in two executive orders issued by President Lyndon Johnson in the 1960s. In 1965, federal contractors were prohibited from discriminating in hiring on the basis of "race, color, religion, or national origin," and were required to undertake affirmative action programs. In 1967, under pressure from the National Organization for Women, "sex" was added to the earlier order.[29] In 1978, specific goals and timetables were established under the executive order to increase the participation of women in skilled trades. By 1981, women were to comprise at least 6.9 percent of the workers in each trade area on federally assisted projects. In 1988, women made up only 2 percent of the nontraditional construction work force and only 4 percent of blue-collar apprenticeships. At that rate, the 1981 goal of 6.9 percent would not be reached until the year 2020.[30]

The federal government has also made it possible to seek redress for sexual harassment through the courts. Sexual harassment is an illegal form of sex discrimination in employment, barred by Title VII of the 1964 Civil Rights Act. However, few women have the time and resources for a protracted court battle. Most victims endure the harassment, quit, or are fired.[31]

In 1963, Congress passed the **Equal Pay Act,** one of the first federal laws requiring that men and women workers be paid the same wages for "equal work on jobs the performance of which requires equal skill, effort and responsibility and which are performed under similar working conditions."[32] Despite this legis-

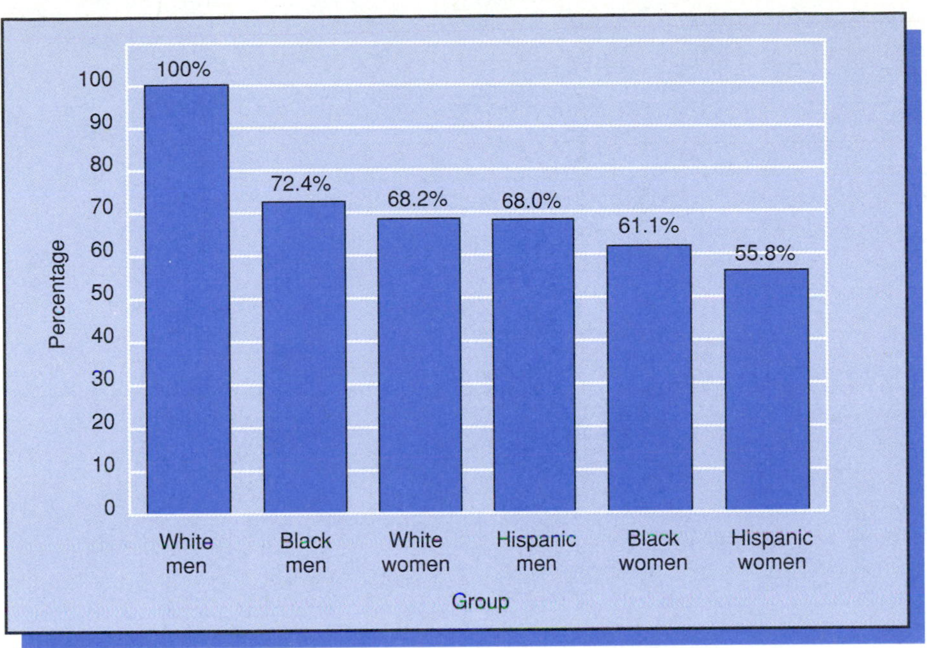

Figure 17-5
Earnings as percentage of white men's earnings, 1987
SOURCE: Sara E. Rix (ed.), *The American Woman, 1988-89: A Status Report* (New York: Norton, 1988), p. 386. [Based on Bureau of Labor Statistics, *News*, USDL 88-43, 1988, Table 5.]

lation, the earnings gap between men and women has not changed: data from the U.S. Bureau of the Census and the U.S. Bureau of Labor Statistics indicate that women still earn about 70 percent of what men do.

A final effort to address inequities in the workplace is the policy of **comparable worth,** also known as pay equity. Comparable worth is not the same thing as equal pay for equal work; it is equal pay for work of comparable value to the employer. The intent of the policy is to remedy the fact that "women's work" has been systematically undervalued in the marketplace. Equal pay for equal work does little to close the earnings gap when most women do not hold the same kinds of jobs that men do: 80 percent of women work in female-dominated occupations. Two-thirds of all employed women and men would have to change jobs in order for sex-linked occupational segregation to disappear.[33]

Undervaluation of female-dominated jobs was documented in a 1981 report by the National Academy of Sciences, which found that after education, experience, and weekly hours of work were taken into account, a 15 percent gap between male and female wages remained unexplained. The report attributed the gap to undervaluation of women's work. "Not only do women do different work than men," the report concluded, "but the work women do is paid less, and the more an occupation is dominated by women, the less it pays."[34]

In order to upgrade the value of women's work, comparable worth policy begins with a job evaluation study conducted by an employer, with the help of outside consultants. Jobs are ranked according to the demands they make on the worker with respect to skill, knowledge, responsibility, and working conditions. Points are assigned for each of these factors; jobs with equal points should be paid

★ Table 17-4
Illustrations of the wage gap

Location	Job title	Number of points	Monthly salary	Difference
Minnesota	Registered nurse (F)	275	$1,723	$537
	Vocational education teacher (M)	275	2,260	
San Jose, California	Senior legal secretary (F)	226	665	375
	Senior carpenter (M)	226	1,040	
	Senior librarian (F)	493	898	221
	Senior chemist (M)	493	1,119	
Washington State	Administrative services manager A (F)	506	1,211	500
	Systems analyst III (M)	426	1,711	
	Dental assistant I (F)	120	608	208
	Stockroom attendant II (M)	120	816	
	Food service worker (F)	93	637	332
	Truck driver (M)	94	969	

SOURCE: Ronnie Steinberg and Lois Haignere, "Separate but Equivalent: Equal Pay for Work of Comparable Worth," in Women's Research and Education Institute (WREI), *Gender at Work* (Washington, D.C.: WREI, 1984), p. 18.

the same amount (see table 17-4). Job evaluation studies have found substantial undervaluation of women's work.[35]

Many states and hundreds of local governments have conducted studies to evaluate the jobs of their employees. And adjustments have been made in many jurisdictions. Minnesota has been the comparable worth trendsetter. In 1982 it passed a plan for state employees, which was to be implemented over four years at a cost of about $40 million. And in 1984 it became the first state to require all local jurisdictions to prepare plans to implement comparable worth policies for public employees.[36] One of the first cities to embrace the concept of comparable worth was San Jose, California, which adjusted salaries by $1.75 million between 1981 and 1986.[37]

As we noted in chapter 3, the federal government has lagged behind other jurisdictions on this policy. Pay equity for federal employees was debated in Congress throughout the 1980s as part of the 1981 Economic Equity Act. Federal court rulings in the 1980s gave mixed messages, pivoting on the thorny issue of intent to discriminate. In 1981 the U.S. Supreme Court's decision in *Gunther* v. *County of Washington, Oregon* opened the door for comparable worth litigation. The Court ruled that Title VII of the 1964 Civil Rights Act could be applied to jobs that were not identical. In this case, even though male and female prison guards had different job responsibilities, the fact that the county paid the women less than the amount indicated by a job evaluation study was cited as evidence of intent to discriminate. Then in 1983 a federal district court found the state of Washington guilty of sex discrimination for failing after twelve years to implement pay adjustments based on a state job evaluation survey. The court ordered Washington to pay over $500

© Huck/Rothco

million in back pay and raises. But this decision was overturned by an appellate court in 1985, on the grounds that there was no evidence of intentional discrimination on the part of the state. As it turned out, Washington state agreed to pay $482 million to settle the issue.

In addition to attempting to remedy employment inequities for women, governments have turned their attention to the inadequacy of provisions for day care for the children of working mothers.

Inadequate Provision for Child Care

The most dramatic change in women's labor-force participation since the end of World War II has been the entry of mothers with young children into the job market. Before World War II, most mothers of preschool children stayed home to rear them. As these mothers sought employment outside the home, the problem of who would care for their children became a growing public concern (see figure 17-6).

Because of traditional beliefs about woman's role as nurturer, child care remains predominantly a "woman's issue." Of course, men and women alike share a concern about the younger generation. Nevertheless, it has been women who have pressured government for child-care measures to ease working women's double duty as workers and primary caretakers of their children.

Lack of Affordable Child Care. Most children have mothers in the work force. By the year 2000, two-thirds of preschool children and three-quarters of older children will need child care.[38] Among two-thirds of married couples with children under eighteen, both partners are in the work force. As we mentioned earlier, most women work out of economic necessity. Two-thirds of women working outside the home are either the sole providers for their children or have husbands who earn less than $15,000 a year. In the 1980s, the number of single mothers who provided their children's sole support jumped 40 percent.[39] Only about a third of the nearly

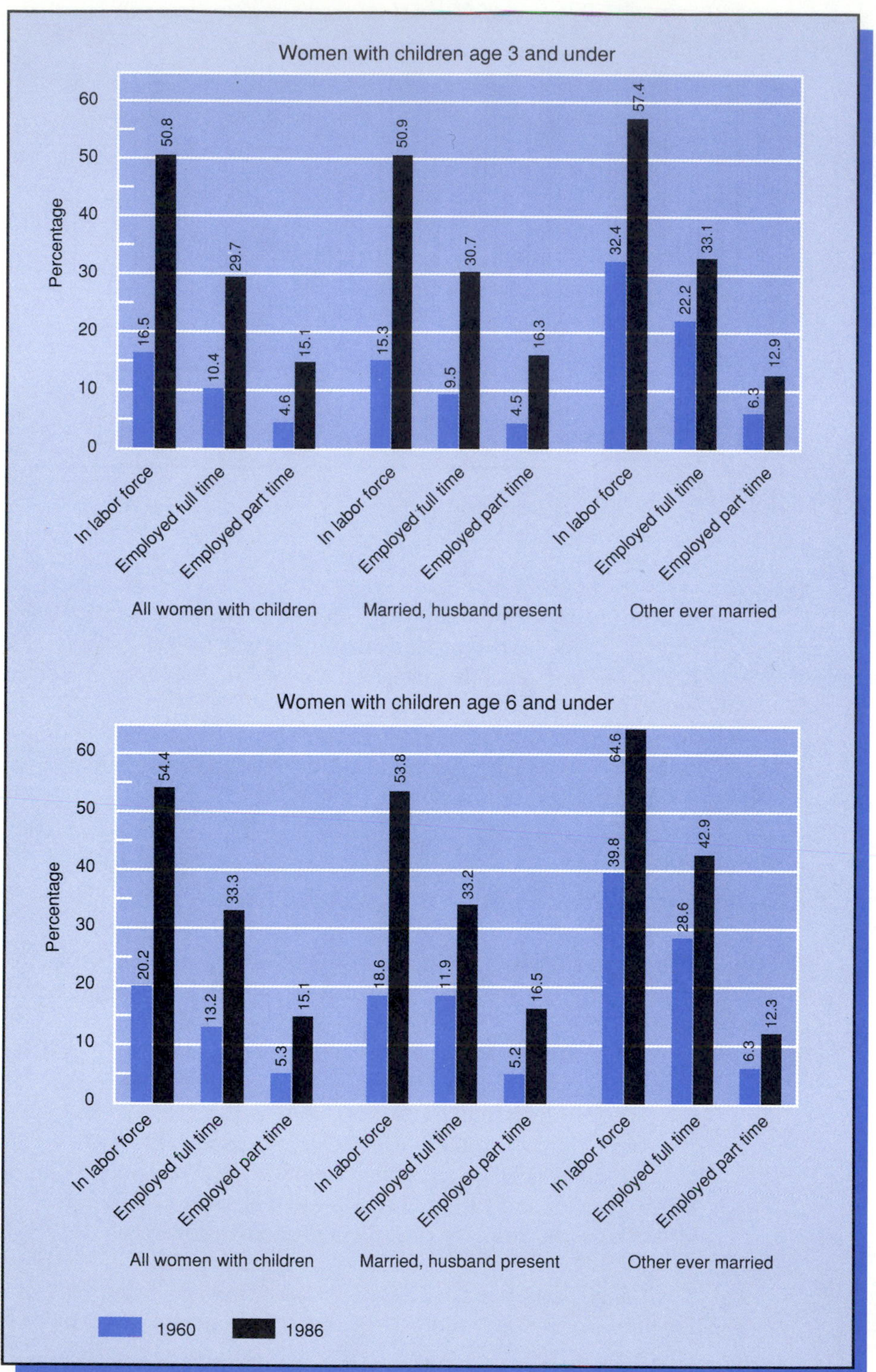

★ **Figure 17-6**

Labor force and employment experience of women with young children, 1960 and 1986

SOURCE: Sara E. Rix (ed.), *The American Woman, 1988-89: A Status Report* (New York: Norton, 1988), p. 375. [Based on Bureau of Labor Statistics (BLS), 1961, and unpublished BLS data.]

★ Table 17-5
Child support awards and payments, 1978 and 1985 (numbers in thousands)

	1978		1985	
Award and recipient status[a]	*Number*	*Percent*	*Number*	*Percent*
Awarded	4,196	59.2%	5,396	61.3%
Should have received payments	3,424	48.3	4,381	49.7
Received full amount	1,675	23.6	2,112	24.0
Received partial amount	779	11.0	1,131	12.8
Did not receive payments	969	13.7	1,138	12.9
Not supposed to receive payments	772	10.9	1,015	11.5
Not awarded[b]	2,898	40.9	3,411	38.7
Total	7,094		8,808	

[a]Payments from absent fathers to women with children under age 21.

[b]Reasons for nonaward include: final agreement pending; property settlement in lieu of award; joint custody granted; did not want child support.

SOURCE: Sara E. Rix (ed.), *The American Woman, 1988–89: A Status Report* (New York: Norton, 1988), p. 360. [Based on Bureau of the Census Current Population Reports, Series P-23, No. 112, 1981, Table A; and Series P-23, No. 152, 1987, Table A.]

eight million women who rear children alone receive child-support payments (see table 17-5). One of every two children living in poverty is from a single-parent home, and that parent is almost always the mother. Over half of mothers with infants, toddlers, and preschoolers are employed.[40] The lack of affordable child care has become an increasingly pressing problem as we approach the year 2000.

Child-Care Proposals. Numerically, the biggest part of the problem is the estimated five million so-called latchkey children, school-age children who go home to empty houses after school. They represent more than half of the children in need of day care. One proposal for meeting their needs is a change in our school system: open schools earlier in the morning and keep them open later in the afternoon and during the summer. Part of the school building would be for teaching, while another part would be for child care and supervision, performed by certified day-care workers, not teachers.[41]

Child-care needs for infants and toddlers have elicited a wide range of proposals. One is for infancy care leave for one or both parents, a policy of every industrialized nation except the United States and South Africa. One policy expert proposed six months' leave, with three months of it at 75 percent of the parent's regular salary, financed by joint employer-employee contributions.[42] In the late 1980s, Congress considered an infant-care plan of ten weeks of unpaid leave, the Family and Medical Leave Bill.

Once a parent returns to work, infant and toddler care becomes so expensive that, in the view of most experts, a government subsidy or a negative income tax is a necessity. At present three types of care are available for these children: home care (a friend, relative, or other caregiver comes to the child's home), family care

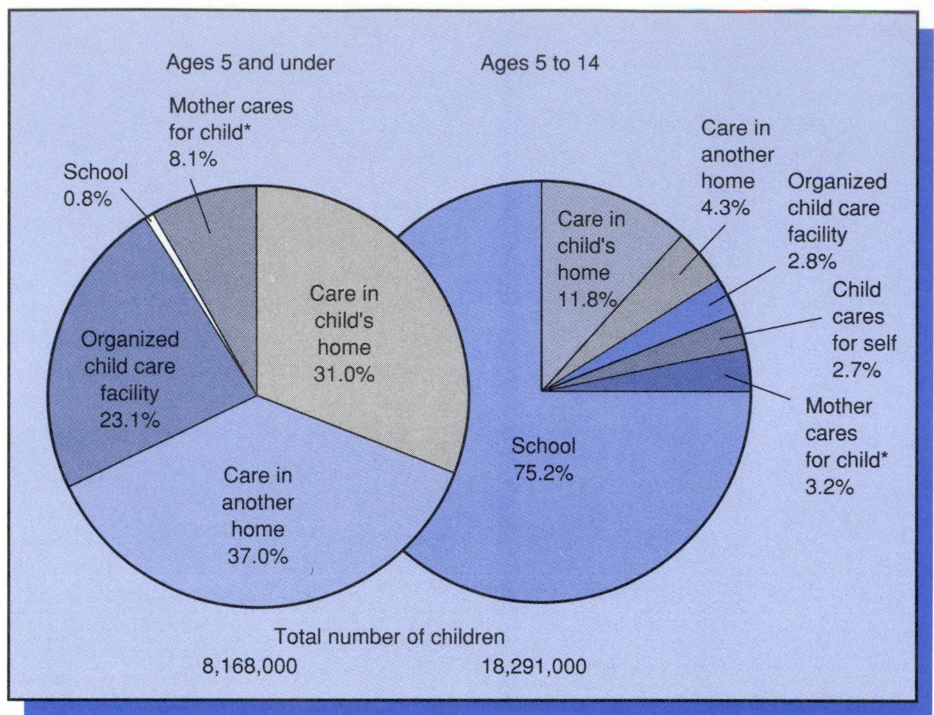

★ **Figure 17-7**
Primary child-care arrangements for children with employed mothers, 1984-1985
* Includes mothers working at home or away from home.
SOURCE: Sara E. Rix (ed.), *The American Woman, 1988-89: A Status Report* (New York: Norton, 1988), p. 377. [Based on Bureau of the Census, Current Population Reports, Series P-70, No. 9, 1987, Table B.]

(a caregiver takes a small group of children into her or his home), and center-based care (parents leave children at an organized center). (See figure 17-7.) These arrangements cost on average about $3,000 per year per child. Americans spend a total of between $75 billion and $100 billion a year on private care. These arrangements vary in quality, and child development specialists have drawn up standards they have been unable to get through Congress for twenty years. Currently, states set standards for safety, staff-child ratios, and health issues.[43]

The United States came close to having a national child-care policy in 1971, when Congress passed the Comprehensive Child Development Act. But it was vetoed by President Nixon, who objected to the "family weakening implications" of "communal approaches to child rearing over against the family-centered approach." This legislation outlined an extensive network of federally funded day-care centers with comprehensive medical, educational, nutritional, and social services for preschool and school-age children.[44]

Child care returned to the federal agenda in 1988, when proposals by both liberals and conservatives were debated in Congress. That election year was dubbed "the year of the child" as both parties raced to get the votes of two-income families. The liberal proposal was the Act for Better Child Care Services (ABC). It would help states improve child-care services for all while making them more affordable for low- and moderate-income families. It would authorize funding to the states rather than directly to local programs. Federal funds would be allocated on the

★ Americans spend about $100 billion a year on private child-care programs. Congress is currently debating who should foot the bill for caring for our nation's preschoolers and whether the federal or state governments should set child-care program standards.

basis of a state's median income, the number of children under five, and the number of children receiving reduced-price and free school lunches.

Most of the ABC funds would be targeted for subsidizing, on a state-designed sliding scale, working families who earned up to 115 percent of a state's median income. States could either contract for services or provide vouchers. Some funds would extend existing part-day programs, such as Head Start. Remaining funds would develop state and local resource and referral systems, provide grants and low-interest loans to establish and expand programs, recruit and train child-care providers, fund family care providers to enable them to meet government standards, and ensure adequate salaries for child-care workers. The ABC would also create a national advisory committee to enforce minimum federal standards, including staff-child ratios, group size, parent involvement, caregiver qualifications, and health and safety provisions for all child-care facilities.[45]

Republican proposals were on a smaller scale than the ABC and relied more heavily on the private sector, primarily through the provision of tax credits to parents. Funds would be provided for vouchers, scholarships for low-income children, state projects with sliding-scale fees, start-up costs for employer-sponsored child care, and provision of training for caregivers and for after-school centers. Employers who established on-site programs would receive tax credits. Family care providers could file their tax returns as individuals rather than as small businesses. There would be state liability insurance pools and a statute of limitations on civil cases involving providers.[46]

The federal government currently subsidizes child care in two ways that help the poor and the well-to-do but leave the middle class without much relief. It was

★ Table 17-6
World energy consumption, by region and energy source, 1970–1985 (in tons of coal equivalent)

Region and energy source	Per capita (kilograms)			Percent distribution		
	1970	1980	1985	1970	1980	1985
Region						
North America*	7,825	7,480	6,768	38.9%	32.7%	29.7%
United States	10,811	10,386	9,563	34.4	27.7	24.9
South America	749	1,046	967	2.2	2.9	2.8
Europe	3,745	4,433	4,364	26.7	25.1	23.5
Asia	386	607	687	14.0	18.5	21.3
Japan	3,246	3,726	3,715	5.2	5.1	4.9
Soviet Union	4,132	5,549	6,131	15.5	17.2	18.7
Oceania	3,675	4,572	4,816	1.1	1.2	1.3
Energy source						
Solid fuels	586	591	629	33.5	30.8	33.3
Liquid fuels	770	848	746	44.0	44.2	39.5
Natural gas	351	412	425	20.1	21.5	22.5
Electricity	42	68	88	2.4	3.5	4.7
World total	1,748	1,919	1,888	100.0	100.0	100.0

*Includes Central America.

SOURCE: U.S. Bureau of the Census, *Statistical Abstract of the United States, 1988* (Washington, D.C.: U.S. Government Printing Office, 1987), p. 543.

the needs of this middle class that politicians, both Republican and Democratic, tried to address in the proposals we have described. The Dependent Care Tax Credit allows families to deduct between 20 and 30 percent of annual child-care expenses. This tax credit benefits only those families whose incomes are high enough to give them significant tax liabilities. Title XX of the Social Security Act addresses the needs of poor families by providing 75 percent matching funds to the states for various social services, including child care. In the 1980s, about one-quarter of Title XX funds were spent on child care, serving about three-quarters of a million of the more than six million children under age six who lived below the poverty line.[47]

★ Energy Policy

As we approach the year 2000, probably no other word has so frequently been followed by "crisis" as "energy". The "energy crisis" following the 1973 oil embargo by the Organization of Petroleum Exporting Countries (OPEC) helped to reveal the United States' dependence on the global economy and the need to examine prospects for greater self-sufficiency in energy (see table 17-6 and table 17-7). Presidents have proclaimed that access to Middle East oil fields is vital to our

★ **Table 17-7**
World primary energy production, by region and energy source, 1975–1985 (in quadrillion BTU*)

Region and energy source	1975	1980	1985
Region			
North America	71.1	80.6	84.1
United States	59.8	64.7	64.6
Central and South America	10.6	12.1	13.1
Western Europe	21.4	28.7	34.8
Eastern Europe and Soviet Union	55.9	67.7	78.9
Middle East	43.5	41.8	24.9
Africa	13.3	17.2	17.5
Far East and Oceania	29.3	37.3	48.5
Energy source			
Crude oil	111.6	125.5	113.3
Natural gas	43.9	52.9	60.3
Natural gas liquids	4.4	5.5	6.7
Coal	66.3	75.8	85.8
Hydroelectric power	15.0	18.2	20.8
Nuclear	3.9	7.5	14.9
World total	245.6	285.6	301.8

*BTU: British thermal units

SOURCE: U.S. Bureau of the Census, *Statistical Abstract of the United States, 1988* (Washington, D.C.: U.S. Government Printing Office, 1987), p. 543.

national security. President Carter bolstered a rapid deployment force and President Reagan ordered the navy to escort oil tankers to keep shipping lanes open in the Middle East.

Energy policies can reach crisis proportions not only with respect to international vulnerability but also with regard to environmental consequences. We can no longer afford to pollute and heat up the atmosphere at the current rate without causing irreversible damage to the world's ecosystem.

Government policy makers face two different but related energy problems: How do we increase our energy supply? And how do we decrease our demand for energy? Solutions must take into account both the global economy and the global ecology.

Increasing Energy Supplies

One way out of the energy bind is to develop programs that increase the nation's supply of energy. Government officials recognize the economic and ecological costs of developing new energy sources. But they see these costs as the price we have to pay for greater self-sufficiency in energy.

Our Costly Energy Dependence. Most of the energy consumed by Americans comes from three sources: oil (about 45 percent), natural gas (about 25 percent), and coal (about 20 percent). About 30 percent of our oil is imported, which means

★ **Table 17-8**
Crude oil imports into United States by country of origin: 1970–1986

Country of origin	Percent distribution 1970	1980	1986
Canada	50.7%	3.8%	13.6%
Mexico	–	9.6	14.9
Norway	–	2.7	1.2
Trinidad-Tobago	–	2.2	2.2
United Kingdom	–	3.3	7.6
OPEC	46.0	73.4	50.6
Algeria	.4	8.7	1.8
Ecuador	–	.3	1.5
Gabon	–	.5	.6
Indonesia	5.4	6.0	7.1
Iran	2.5	.2	.5
Iraq	–	.5	1.9
Kuwait	2.5	.5	.7
Libya	3.5	10.4	–
Nigeria	3.5	16.0	10.5
Qatar	–	.4	.3
Saudi Arabia	3.1	23.8	14.8
United Arab Emirates	4.8	3.3	.9
Venezuela	20.3	3.0	10.0
Other	3.3	4.9	9.8
Total	100.0	100.0	100.0

NOTE: "–" represents less than .05 percent.

SOURCE: U.S. Bureau of Census, *Statistical Abstract of the United States, 1988* (Washington D.C.: U.S. Government Printing Office, 1987), p. 544.

that about 13 percent of the total U.S. energy supply consists of imported oil.[48] (See table 17-8.) Our dependence on imported oil has been increasing as it becomes more difficult and more costly to extract domestic supplies. Dependence on oil imports can fuel inflation if oil producers raise prices, and it can add to our trade and balance-of-payments deficits.

Currently almost all of our natural gas comes from domestic sources. However, we have only between thirty-five and sixty years' worth of proven reserves available at current and predicted rates of consumption.[49] Therefore, natural gas is not a viable long-term solution to our energy needs. Furthermore, since it is valued for its commercial uses (in the production of plastics and synthetic fibers), it may be inefficient to use it to heat buildings and cook meals.[50]

Coal is our most abundant energy resource. We have about a two-hundred-year supply; we export coal to Japan and Europe. Reliance on coal as an energy source, however, entails serious environmental consequences. When coal is burned, it forms sulfur dioxide, which, when combined with water, makes acid rain. Acid rain threatens forests and wildlife in the northeastern United States and Canada and creates political tension between the two neighbors. In addition, as the deeply

★ Tugboats move a giant oil-drilling rig to a new location off the Rhode Island coast. Offshore drilling for oil increases our supply of energy, but it has been met with resistance from environmentalists and coastal residents for fear of major oil spills.

embedded coal in the eastern part of the country becomes more dangerous and costly to mine, producers have been increasingly turning to the strip mining of coal nearer the surface in the western United States. This procedure has been severely criticized by environmentalists. While some of this land is restored and reclaimed, much of it is rendered unusable for centuries. Finally, while coal can be used to generate electricity and heat, it cannot be used for transportation (which accounts for 26 percent of U.S. energy use), and it is more difficult to transport than oil or natural gas (which move readily through pipelines).

Ways to Increase Our Energy Supplies. Oil, natural gas, and coal are fossil fuels in limited supply. The scarcity of these resources involves more than serious economic issues. It also involves national security. The United States needs energy to defend the homeland and project its power abroad. Today's carrier battle groups—the vast armadas of ships, planes, and submarines that are the backbone of America's naval strategy—burn thousands of gallons of fuel every hour. Time and again, in the Middle East, the Caribbean, and elsewhere, the United States has wielded its military might and suffered serious casualties in order to ensure access to energy supplies. Given the international importance of energy, it is not surprising that there has been an ongoing search for solutions to this major problem.

One set of solutions to the energy-supply problem centers on the development of new domestic supplies of fossil fuels. A second type of solution focuses on devising alternative, renewable energy sources: nuclear, solar, wind, and biomass. We will begin with the measures to increase domestic supplies of fossil fuels.

Several steps have been taken and proposed to make us less dependent on imported fuels. In the 1970s, federal lands in Alaska were opened for oil and gas exploration and a major oil pipeline was built to connect the northern deposits to a port in the southern part of the state. The federal government has made similar attempts to drill for offshore oil, but these efforts have frequently been resisted by state governments and environmental groups, particularly after the devastating Exxon oil tanker spill in Alaska in 1989. Both Michael Dukakis and Jesse Jackson made clear their opposition to offshore drilling in the Democratic California primary in 1988. The Reagan administration leased some federal lands for coal mining, but the favorable price offered to private coal companies when the coal market was glutted was criticized as poor resource management.[51] Many of the presidential candidates in 1988 supported oil import quotas to make imported oil more expensive and to give domestic producers an incentive to drill for new supplies.

Several measures have been taken to encourage a switch from oil and natural gas to coal. A 1978 law prohibited new utility plants from burning oil or gas and required existing plants to convert to coal by 1990. In 1980, Congress appropriated $3.6 billion to assist in the conversion of thirty-eight plants. This was a reduction from President Carter's request for $10 billion to convert 107 plants and a blow to the goal of doubling the amount of coal used by 1990.[52] Since most American coal deposits are located west of the Mississippi, and much of that coal is needed to heat the East, two proposals are aimed at reducing transportation costs. One is to provide federal subsidies to railroads to upgrade their equipment and roadbeds. The other is to build pipelines in which pulverized coal mixed with water can be transported hundreds of miles to midwestern users or to transfer points for shipment to the East. Thus far, efforts to build such pipelines have been blocked by railroad interests (who want the business of transporting coal) and by ranchers and environmentalists (who are concerned about land damage and water supplies).

A final attempt to make us less dependent on fossil fuels focuses on the development of synthetic fuels, or "synfuels": oil produced from shale rock, and oil and gas made from coal. Oil can be recovered from shale rock when it is heated. The potential is enormous, as shale rock reserves exceed all known petroleum reserves in the world.

Most domestic shale is located on western federal lands, where oil companies have invested heavily in leases since the early 1970s. The production of shale oil requires costly facilities and large amounts of water for cooling purposes. It is politically controversial because it requires the strip mining of enormous tracts of land. But if the price of imported oil goes high enough, some companies believe they can produce and sell shale oil profitably.[53]

Oil and gas can be produced from coal that is heated under pressure. This process, too, requires costly facilities and large amounts of water for cooling. Plants would be located near western coal reserves, mostly on federal lands. The oil and gas produced could be transported through existing pipelines.

The Energy Security Act of 1980 established the federal Synthetic Fuels Corporation to promote the development of synfuels through loans and guarantees to private investors. Oil companies are the main investors. About 10 percent of oil companies' research and development expenditures in the 1970s went into efforts to make oil and gas from coal.[54]

A second set of measures has been directed at increasing alternative, renewable sources of energy. The most controversial of these measures, on both economic and environmental grounds, has been the construction of nuclear power plants. Their nuclear reactors split atoms of uranium 235 (fission) to heat water to run steam turbines and generate electricity. Throughout the 1960s and 1970s, these plants seemed to be the answer to America's growing need for electricity.

In 1974, a government report estimated that nuclear power could provide 40 percent of electricity-generating capacity by the year 2000, instead of the 6 percent it then provided. Between 1970 and 1974, 145 orders for new reactors were placed by utility companies. By 1980, however, both demand for new plants and estimates of their electricity-generating capacity had declined substantially. Plants faced drops in demand during the recession of 1974–1975, increases in construction costs,

JUST SAY NO.

America is hooked on foreign oil. Today, we import almost 40 percent of the oil we use—even more than in 1973, when the Arab embargo plunged us into gas lines, rationing, and recession.

The more we can use nuclear energy, instead of imported oil, to generate electricity, the less we have to depend on foreign nations.

The 110 nuclear plants in the U.S. have cut our foreign oil dependence by over three billion barrels since 1973. And they have cut foreign oil payments by over one hundred billion dollars.

But 110 nuclear plants will not be enough to meet our growing electricity demand. More plants are needed.

To help kick the foreign oil habit, we need to rely more on our own energy sources, like nuclear energy.

For a free booklet on nuclear energy, write to the U.S. Council for Energy Awareness, P.O. Box 66103, Dept. SN01, Washington, D.C. 20035.

U.S. COUNCIL FOR ENERGY AWARENESS

Nuclear energy means more energy independence.

©1989 USCEA

★ An advertisement promoting the use of nuclear energy.

deficiencies in fuel reprocessing and waste disposal that heightened concern for safety, and public opposition, particularly after the near-disaster at Three Mile Island in Pennsylvania in 1979.[55] As of 1984, there were eighty nuclear power plants in the United States, producing 3 percent of the total energy supply. During the 1980s, the disposal of nuclear wastes became an increasingly serious problem. The 1986 disaster at Chernobyl in the Soviet Union increased public skepticism about the safety of nuclear power plants. Opposition from antinuclear groups has forced numerous operational delays and even the closing of nuclear power plants from New Hampshire to California.

The federal government has left the development of nuclear fission technology to the private sector and has focused its research on breeder reactors, which produce more fuel than they use. Breeder reactors solve the problems of the limited supply and high cost of uranium, but they introduce another problem: the fuel used and produced is plutonium—the primary ingredient in nuclear weapons—which is even more radioactive than uranium. The half-life of plutonium (the time required for half of its nuclear activity to be exhausted) is 24,000 years.

★ The cooling towers of the Three Mile Island nuclear power plant loom over homes in Harrisburg, Pennsylvania. Ever since the near-disaster at this facility in 1979, Americans have become less than enthusiastic about the construction of such plants in their own communities.

★ Solar panels such as the ones on this house collect the sun's heat and transfer it through a building. Proponents of solar energy praise the minimal adverse environmental effects of this form of energy production as compared to energy generated by nuclear fission, coal, and natural gas.

Other renewable sources are less risky. The sun, the ultimate renewable energy source, produces energy that can be captured for use. "Active" panels bolted on a roof can collect the sun's heat and transfer it through water or air piped through a building. Solar heat can also be transferred into electricity by means of photovoltaic cells. Solar energy is obviously most cost-effective in warmer parts of the country. It is estimated that it could provide between one-quarter and one-third of our total energy needs.[56] Widespread adoption of solar technology will depend on the availability of government tax incentives and loan guarantees. The Energy Tax Act of 1978, for example, gave tax credits for solar modifications to homes and businesses. Like solar power, wind power is used on a small scale to generate electricity. But the unreliability of the source and lack of effective ways to store electricity limit the attractiveness of windmills.

Another alternative energy source is "biomass," plant material converted to methane gas and used like natural gas. Biomass can also be used to produce gasohol, a combination of gasoline and methyl (wood) alcohol. Biomass energy is renewable. It will not disrupt the environment if agricultural by-products or rapidly growing plants are used. Unlike the products of solar or wind power, gasohol can be burned in automobiles.

Finally, two far-reaching proposals have been discussed for increasing America's energy supplies. One is to break up oil monopolies and create a public energy corporation. Of the seven leading companies that dominate world oil production (the "Seven Sisters"), five are based in the United States (Exxon, Mobil, Texaco, Gulf, and Standard of California). These oil companies have both vertical and horizontal control over domestic energy supplies. Vertically, they control the production, transportation, refinement, and marketing of oil and natural gas. Horizontally, they have controlling interest not only in oil and natural gas (the source of 70 percent of the total energy used in the United States) but increasingly in coal, uranium, shale, and synfuels as well.

© Signe Wilkinson

Some observers say that only a vertical and horizontal breakup of the oil companies' holdings and expanded competition will make possible an effective energy program. They point out that the antitrust route has not been seriously pursued since 1911, when John D. Rockefeller's Standard Oil Trust was broken up into what are now Exxon, Mobil, SoCal, and Amoco.[57] The creation of a public energy corporation has been advocated to stimulate competition in the development of alternative energy supplies, to create new jobs in solar power, and to break the oil companies' monopoly of information about the actual costs and performance of their industry.[58]

Decreasing Energy Demand

Trimming demand is the other key energy proposal. Conservationists and others argue that the economic and ecological costs of increasing energy supplies are prohibitive. Over the long run, the United States has to recognize what other advanced industrial countries have known since the end of World War II, when many of them lay in ruins: that the world cannot afford to have its industrial giants squandering limited resources. As we approach the year 2000, American politicians are warning their constituencies that we have run out of places to dump our wastes and can no longer afford our profligate ways.

The Problem of Wasteful Energy Consumption. The ecology movement has taken Americans to task for their wasteful habits—driving gas-guzzling cars and using electricity as though there were no tomorrow. The United States has only 5 percent of the world's population but consumes 23 percent of the world's energy. We use 98 percent more energy per capita than does Sweden and 10 percent more per capita than does Canada (which is closer to the size of the U.S. than Sweden

★ As landfills across the country are reaching their capacity, local governments are encouraging citizens to recycle paper, glass, and metal goods. Some locations have even mandated curbside pickup of products to be recycled. At the same time, members of environmental groups such as Greenpeace use novel methods to try to get Americans to change their wasteful ways.

is), yet both countries have standards of living similar to ours.[59] By some estimates, the United States could consume 30 to 40 percent less energy with no decline in our standard of living if we made a serious commitment to use energy efficiently.[60]

Some analysts have traced Americans' profligate ways to the frontier mentality. As we saw in chapter 6, this nation has been richly endowed with land and other resources. This condition fostered an attitude of limitless room in which to maneuver—environmentally, economically, and socially. But with the advent of the international ecology movement in the 1970s, Americans realized that it would only be a matter of time before they would face the high gasoline prices Europeans pay at their pumps and they would start to think "recycle" instead of "throw away."

Curbing Our Wasteful Habits. One way to encourage Americans to consume less oil and natural gas is to raise their prices. The Natural Gas Policy Act of 1978 lifted price controls on natural gas in several stages through 1985. In 1979 President Carter phased out price controls on domestic oil, letting prices rise to then-current world levels. These measures resulted in windfall profits for oil companies, estimated to top $227 billion by 1990. So in 1980 Congress passed a windfall profits tax, taxing new profits realized through decontrol of domestic oil prices. Oil companies retained about 22 percent of the net profits from decontrol. Of the sum raised in taxes, 25 percent went to help the poor pay their bills to oil companies, 15 percent was set aside for energy development and mass transit, and 60 percent was designated for future tax reduction.

Throughout the 1970s, the federal government took other measures to encourage conservation. It set standards for automobile fuel efficiency, taxed new gas-guzzling cars (those rated at less than 15 miles per gallon), set guidelines for energy efficiency in new buildings and appliances, and provided tax credits for energy-saving modifications to homes and businesses. In 1973 Congress used the leverage of federal highway funds to persuade states to lower their speed limits to 55 miles per hour. Advocates of the measure said it would save between 130,000

★ **Table 17-9**
Number of U.S. and Soviet intercontinental weapons

	United States	*Soviet Union*
Intercontinental ballistic missiles	996	1,389
Warheads	2,312	6,400
Submarine-launched ballistic missiles	640	969
Warheads	5,632	2,941
Bombers*	363	160
Warheads	3,890	840
Total		
Launchers	1,999	2,518
Warheads	11,834	10,181

* Does not include Soviet TU-22 "Backfire" bomber.

NOTE: Figures are approximate and the deployment of weapons systems is subject to frequent change.

SOURCE: U.S. Bureau of the Census, *Statistical Abstract of the United States, 1989* (Washington, D.C.: U.S. Government Printing Office, 1989), p. 334.

and 165,000 barrels of gasoline each day. State and local governments have attempted to reduce gasoline consumption by encouraging carpooling (as through the introduction of highway lanes restricted to cars carrying three or more people).

By the 1980s, conservation measures resulted in decreased demand for oil in the United States and there was a glut of oil on the world market. And the 55-mile-per-hour speed limit was repealed on some interstates. However, political battles continued to be waged between oil drillers and environmentalists, and between pro- and anti-nuclear-power activists.

★ Public Policy in a Changing World: The Arms-Control Debate

How to control the nuclear arms race while keeping America secure from attack is one of the most perplexing problems facing the nation. With each of the superpowers possessing tens of thousands of nuclear weapons (and lesser powers having hundreds each), arms control is a highly emotional and controversial subject (see table 17-9). Emotion and controversy, of course, surround many public policy issues. Yet the arms-control debate has aspects that set it apart from the other public policy cases we have so far discussed.

In the first place, nuclear weapons policy and arms control, like many other aspects of national security, are often shrouded in secrecy. The public debate over arms control is conducted with imperfect or incomplete information. The government, for a variety of reasons, may mislead the public as to the numbers, locations, and performance of its own weapons systems and those of the Soviet Union.

Second, the arms race involves highly technical issues. It takes detailed study to understand the distinctions among land-based missiles, cruise missiles, and submarine-launched missiles (not to mention MIRVs and Star Wars).

Successful arms control also requires cooperation among governments, especially between the United States and the Soviet Union. The compromise and concession that produce American arms-control policy are only the first steps in a tedious process that requires agreement by our allies, by Soviet leaders, and by our own military-industrial complex. This process can take years, and by the time they all are ready to agree on an arms-control pact, the political climate in the United States or in the Soviet Union may no longer favor the agreement. In order to understand how policy is made, let's begin with a brief look at the history of arms control.

The Problem: Controlling Nuclear Weapons in a Hostile World

Throughout recorded history, humankind has sought to regulate the conduct of war and the bloodshed caused by increasingly deadly weapons. In recent times, the Covenant of the League of Nations, the 1928 Kellogg-Briand Pact, and the United Nations Charter were all aimed at limiting arms races and other forms of competition between major powers. With the advent and use of atomic weapons by the United States during World War II and the development of Soviet bombs in 1949, the world faced yet another escalation in the age-old saga of arms races.

As the cold war began, tentative efforts were made to control the arms race. The unsuccessful Baruch Plan, put forward by the United States in 1947, sought to "internationalize" the bomb under United Nations control. The Soviet Union, outvoted in the UN and lacking a bomb of its own at the time, was not interested in the U.S. proposal. Each side made more unsuccessful arms-control proposals during the 1950s. In the 1960s, agreements were hammered out to establish the "hot line" linking Washington and Moscow and a partial ban on testing nuclear weapons (see chap. 19). These tentative steps at superpower cooperation aside, the placing of real limits on the deployment of nuclear weapons would have to wait until the 1970s.

In the twenty years that followed the dawning of the superpower nuclear arms race, both sides were virtually unrestrained in the pursuit of new, more powerful weapons. Beginning with bombs dropped from long-range bombers, each side proceeded to develop increasingly sophisticated weapons. Eventually both the United States and the Soviet Union possessed a triad of weapons systems: intercontinental ballistic missiles (ICBMs), submarine-launched ballistic missiles (SLBMs), and long-range bombers. As neither superpower had the ability to prevent a sudden attack, weapons were designed to withstand or evade attack and deliver a devastating counterblow on the enemy's population centers. National defense came to rely on a policy of mutually assured destruction (MAD) (see chap. 19). While neither side was pleased about its vulnerability, the "logic" of MAD offered some security but also mandated the building of increasingly deadly weapons to maintain the delicate balance of terror.

Arms control seemed to offer a way out. But meaningful arms-limitation discussions between the two superpowers were not possible until three preconditions had been satisfied. First, there had to be rough equivalence (or parity) in the nuclear arsenals of both sides. Although the type and quality of weapons systems varied between the United States and the Soviet Union, by the end of the 1960s each side had built thousands of missiles, as well as sophisticated bombers and nuclear-missile-carrying submarines, and a rough balance of power prevailed. Since neither power would negotiate an arms-control agreement from an inferior position, the achievement of rough equivalence in weapons encouraged both sides to control the expensive and dangerous arms race.

The second precondition for arms control was the development of independent means to verify compliance with any agreement reached. Since neither side placed much trust in the other, the two sides would not proceed with meaningful talks until they had the technical means to confirm that limits on weapons were being adhered to. By the end of the 1960s, spy satellites and other electronic means of eavesdropping made it possible for the superpowers to check up on each other, thus creating a climate favorable to arms control.

Finally, each side needed the political will to engage in arms control. Until the 1970s, U.S. leaders and the American public were generally content with the "security" that nuclear weapons provided. Although a ban-the-bomb movement existed in the 1950s and 1960s, most Americans felt that the national defense needed more nuclear weapons, not fewer. Indeed, as a presidential candidate in 1960 John Kennedy attracted many supporters when he charged that the Eisenhower administration had permitted a "missile gap" to develop, leaving the nation vulnerable to the Soviets. After Richard Nixon was elected in 1968, however, he soon realized that new weapons, especially the costly and potentially destabilizing antimissile systems, would cause an uncontrollable escalation in the arms race. This concern, along with the tremendous economic and human cost of the Vietnam war, led Nixon to conclude that some form of agreement with the Soviets was necessary. The Soviets, for slightly different reasons, also welcomed the opportunity to curtail the expensive arms race that was bleeding their underdeveloped economy.

Possible Solutions to the Arms-Race Problem

As the 1970s began, the three preconditions for meaningful arms control had, in varying degrees, been met. The United States and the Soviet Union signed major agreements on anti-ballistic missile systems (the ABM Treaty) and temporary limits on deployment of weapons (the **Strategic Arms Limitation Treaty,** or **SALT I**) in 1972, and an interim agreement in 1974 to continue restraints on the most deadly weapons until a more specific treaty known as SALT II could be hammered out. The road to these agreements was hardly smooth, however, and the debate over arms-control policy in the United States was often intense.

President Nixon's signing of the SALT I and ABM treaties in 1972 initiated the debate over arms control in the United States. Soon after the ink dried on the treaties, conservative critics were charging that Nixon had given the Soviets too much in exchange for too little. Defenders of arms control also organized to defend SALT I and to push for more stringent treaties. The debate resulted in more interest groups, industry lobbyists, and other concerned segments of American society demanding a voice in arms-control policy. Today there are many well-organized supporters and critics of arms-control policy in the United States.

Indeed, the arms-control controversy, like many other public policy issues, has engaged the far left and right, as well as the more moderate political center. Conservatives on the far right generally reject arms control as a "surrender" to the Soviet Union. In their view, arms control is a devious plot by the Soviets to fool a gullible and peace-loving America into a position of military inferiority. "Our country is in a period of danger," warned the Committee on the Present Danger, "and the danger is increasing. . . . The principal threat to our nation, to world peace, and

★ Many citizens who support arms-control agreements with the Soviet Union do so to prevent the damage nuclear weapons would wreak on the global ecosystem.

★ Groups such as Peace Through Strength mistrust the Soviet Union and call for military superiority to the Soviets instead of arms-control agreements with them.

to the cause of human freedom is the Soviet drive for dominance based upon an unparalleled military buildup."[61] Conservative groups thus tend to promote a policy of "peace through strength." The American Conservative Union sent out more than 950,000 letters condemning the proposed SALT II treaty in the late 1970s.[62] At the extreme, anti-arms-control groups feel that the Soviets cannot be trusted at all, and that the United States should build and deploy every new weapon it can invent.

On the far left, some individuals and groups have called for unilateral disarmament: if the United States would begin to destroy its nuclear arsenal, they say, the Soviets would follow suit. Some even see the arms race as entirely the fault of an aggressive United States. The Soviet Union, they point out, did not start the arms race. The United States built the first atomic bombs; the Soviet Union only sought to achieve a balance of power. If the United States abandoned its deadly arsenal, according to some people on the left, the Soviets would surely withdraw from the dangerous and expensive arms race. Other supporters of arms control, especially some religious groups, say that unilateral disarmament is the morally correct way to pursue peace.

Still other groups, though not calling for unilateral disarmament, lobby for steps to reduce each side's nuclear arsenal. Some call for a nuclear freeze on the development of new weapons. While some people worry about an accidental war, others feel that the superpowers already possess far more destructive power than they need to keep the peace.

The priority given to a military buildup during the Reagan administration encouraged greater activism on the part of many arms-control supporters. Some traditional American institutions, such as the Roman Catholic church, took a bold public stand in support of arms control. At the end of the 1980s more than thirty groups were working at the national level to encourage continued progress on arms control. Among them are the following:

American Friends Service Committee
Arms Control Association
Clergy and Laity Concerned
Council for a Livable World
Federation of American Scientists
Ground Zero
Physicians for Social Responsibility
SANE/Freeze
Women's International League for Peace and Freedom

Among groups that oppose arms control are:

American Conservative Union
American Security Council
Committee for the Survival of a Free Congress
Committee on the Present Danger
Conservative Caucus
Emergency Coalition against Unilateral Disarmament
Heritage Foundation
Peace through Strength

The political center, comprised of moderates in both major parties, has rejected proposals from both the left and the right. Unilateral disarmament or a freeze on deployment of new weapons, the moderates argue, would violate the principle of arms negotiations which says that there must be rough equality in the military balance of power. According to the Department of Defense, a freeze on nuclear forces would build in Soviet advantages, especially in ICBMs, and "experience demonstrates that the Soviets will not negotiate seriously . . . unless they see proof that the U.S. is 1) determined to rectify existing imbalances, and 2) insistent on achieving equitable and verifiable mutual reductions."[63] Moderates also reject the "peace through strength" argument on similar grounds. They maintain that a massive buildup of U.S. weapons, including deployment of a Star Wars space-based missile defense, would destroy the military balance necessary for arms control.

With neither a freeze nor a massive buildup of nuclear weapons likely to produce secure, verifiable arms control, most American leaders support cautious negotiations based on the **Strategic Arms Reduction Talks (START,)** which began during the Reagan administration. Although it took nearly all of Reagan's eight years in office, he was able to reach agreement in principle with Soviet leader Mikhail Gorbachev to work to reduce strategic nuclear forces by 50 percent. Along the way, important confidence-building measures were approved by both superpowers, including on-site inspection to verify compliance, the Soviets' willingness to make deep asymmetrical reductions in land-based ICBMs, and the signing of the landmark **Intermediate-Range Nuclear Force (INF) Treaty** in 1987. In this treaty, the U.S. and the Soviet Union agreed to destroy all of their intermediate-range missiles stationed in Europe (see table 17-10).

A number of important problems remain, nonetheless, which could block progress on arms control. Verification is a continuing issue as weapons become smaller and relatively easy to conceal. Cruise missiles, for example, can be hidden in small sheds and moved about with relative ease. Another potential roadblock to

★ Table 17-10
Arms control and disarmament agreements

Issue	*Participants*
Nuclear weapons	
To prevent the spread of nuclear weapons	
Antarctic Treaty, 1959	32 countries[a]
Outer Space Treaty, 1967	125 countries[a]
Latin American Nuclear-Free Zone Treaty, 1967	31 countries[a]
Nonproliferation Treaty, 1968	136 countries[a]
Seabed Treaty, 1971	108 countries[a]
To reduce the risk of nuclear war	
Hot Line and Modernization Agreements, 1963	United States and Soviet Union
Accident Measures Agreements, 1971	United States and Soviet Union
Prevention of Nuclear War Agreement, 1973	United States and Soviet Union
To limit nuclear testing	
Limited Test Ban Treaty, 1963	127 countries[a]
Threshold Test Ban Treaty, 1974[b]	United States and Soviet Union
Peaceful Nuclear Explosions Treaty, 1976[b]	United States and Soviet Union
To limit nuclear weapons	
ABM Treaty (SALT I) and Protocol, 1972	United States and Soviet Union
SALT I Interim Agreement, 1972[c]	United States and Soviet Union
SALT II, 1979[d]	United States and Soviet Union
Intermediate Range Missiles Treaty, 1987	United States and Soviet Union
Other weapons	
To prohibit use of gas	
Geneva Protocol, 1925	130 countries
To prohibit biological weapons	
Biological Weapons Convention, 1972	131 countries
To prohibit techniques changing the environment	
Environmental Modification Convention, 1977	73 countries
To control use of inhumane weapons	
Inhumane Weapons Convention, 1981	22 countries[e]
To reduce risk of war	
Notification of Military Activities, 1986	35 countries

[a]Number of parties and signatories as of December 1986.

[b]Not yet ratified.

[c]Expired by its terms on October 3, 1977.

[d]Never ratified. If the treaty had entered into force, it would have expired by its terms on December 31, 1985.

[e]Convention entered into force December 1983. The United States is not a signatory.

SOURCE: Harold W. Stanley and Richard G. Niemi, *Vital Statistics on American Politics* (Washington, D.C.: Congressional Quarterly Press, 1988), p. 295. [Based on data from U.S. Arms Control and Disarmament Agency, *World Military Expenditures and Arms Transfers*, 1983.]

arms control is the issue of the Star Wars antimissile defense system. If the United States deployed such a system, the Soviets would interpret the action as a dangerous and destabilizing escalation of the arms race.

There are also many potential political roadblocks to arms control. Despite Gorbachev's apparent efforts to ease tensions with the West, both sides remain distrustful of each other, and the confidence that has slowly emerged in recent years could be shattered by a conflict in the Middle East or other global hot spot. The defense establishments of the superpowers—weapons manufacturers, bureaucrats, the military services—may oppose arms control for other reasons. By and large, weapons manufacturers oppose arms control as a threat to future lucrative contracts. The military, though bound to obey their commander in chief, certainly try to influence Congress through their testimony and the public through speeches and writings.

The influence of the defense establishment on arms policy can be seen in the aftermath of President Carter's decision in 1977 not to build the B-1 bomber. Carter opposed the B-1 primarily on economic and technical grounds, but he also felt it would impede progress on arms control with the Soviets. Working to change Carter's mind was the Air Force, the prime contractor on the $24.8 billion B-1 project (Rockwell International), the 1.5-million-member United International Union of Automobile, Aerospace, and Agricultural Implement Workers of America, and the AFL-CIO.[64] Although the members of the military establishment did not win Carter over, they encouraged Ronald Reagan to make the bomber a campaign issue in 1980. Once in office in 1981, President Reagan reinstated the B-1 program.

The Future of Arms Control

Both superpowers now recognize that the danger and expense of a never-ending arms race probably exceed the security afforded by the weapons. Barring unforeseen international setbacks, the internal political climate in the United States and the Soviet Union will determine the pace of arms-control negotiations. What conclusions can we draw about the way arms-control policy is made in the United States? As we will see in chapter 19, the president and the executive branch take the initiative in this crucial area of national security. Republican presidents have had more success than Democratic presidents. After a seven-year, $1-trillion-plus arms buildup, hard-line anti-Soviet Ronald Reagan had little trouble winning congressional and public support for the 1987 INF Treaty. Indeed, arms control had become so well accepted on the American political scene that it was not even an issue in the 1988 presidential election. Jimmy Carter in 1979, on the other hand, had little luck in his efforts to persuade the Senate or the American people to support his SALT II treaty.

International events are often of crucial importance to happenings on the domestic front. In 1979, President Carter faced an uncooperative Soviet Union that was engaged in a massive buildup of weapons and the invasion of Afghanistan. President Reagan, on the other hand, outlived three Soviet leaders, and found the fourth, Mikhail Gorbachev, an energetic leader on important arms-control issues. America's allies in Europe, moreover, were also eager to move the arms-control process along after years of facing antimissile demonstrations in the streets of their cities.

Finally, although Congress and interest groups act primarily in response to presidential initiatives, their responses can be crucial. Conservatives' dissatisfaction with the terms of the SALT I Treaty helped create a public debate. After President Reagan succeeded in building vast new weapons systems, peace groups picked up where their conservative opponents left off, ensuring that the arms-control debate will continue well into the twenty-first century.

★ Summary

The federal government has debated alternatives and enacted programs to meet important challenges as we approach the year 2000. This chapter looked at programs and alternatives in five public policy areas. In the area of health-care policy, proposed solutions to the high costs of medical care and limited coverage of health-care insurance range from government curbs on costs to a national health insurance policy. In the area of income-maintenance policy, proposals for reform of social security and welfare include a value-added tax and a family allowance, two measures borrowed from European nations. Two of the most important policy concerns of women are workplace inequalities and inadequate provisions for child care. Possible solutions include comparable worth and government-subsidized child care. We looked at ways to increase energy supplies and decrease demand for energy. Proposals range from increased production of coal and synthetic fuels to conservation measures to curb our wasteful ways. Finally, we considered the arms-control debate: progress and roadblocks in arms-control agreements between the United States and the Soviet Union. This sampler of challenging policies illustrates how the federal government is continually searching for better alternatives, often borrowing ideas from state and local governments and from other countries.

★ Key Terms

AFDC (welfare)
affirmative action
comparable worth
Equal Pay Act
feminization of poverty
health maintenance organizations (HMOs)
Intermediate-range Nuclear Force Treaty (INF)
Medicaid
Medicare
social security
Strategic Arms Limitation Treaty (SALT I)
Strategic Arms Reduction Talks (START)
third-party payments
workfare

★ Notes

1. U.S. Bureau of the Census, *Statistical Abstract of the United States, 1988* (Washington, D.C.: U.S. Government Printing Office, 1987), p. 70.
2. B. Guy Peters, *American Public Policy: Promise and Performance,* 2d ed. (Chatham, N.J.: Chatham House, 1986), p. 188.
3. Henry Aaron, *Painful Prescription* (Washington, D.C.: Brookings Institution, 1984).
4. Helen Nakdimen, "Cesarean Myths," *Ms. Magazine,* May 1988, p. 22.

5. Health Insurance Association of America, *Source Book on Health Insurance Data*, 1983–84 (Washington, D.C., 1984), table 5.5.
6. Congressional Budget Office, *The Impact of PSROs on Health Care Costs* (Washington, D.C.: U.S. Government Printing Office, 1981).
7. Darryl D. Enos and Paul Sultan, *The Sociology of Health Care* (New York: Praeger, 1977), pp. 133–134.
8. Jordan Braverman, *Crisis in Health Care* (Washington, D.C.: Acropolis, 1978), p. 160.
9. *Statistical Abstract of the United States, 1988,* p. 92.
10. *Changes in the Environment Affecting the Health Care System,* Health Planning Information Series no. 1, Trends Affecting the U.S. Health Care System (Washington, D.C.: U.S. Department of Health, Education, and Welfare, 1976), table 5.4.
11. *New York Times,* September 14, 1980, p. 22E.
12. Ruth Hauft, "Health Manpower," in *Health Care Delivery in the United States,* ed. Steven Jonas (New York: Springer, 1977), pp. 67–95.
13. Kenneth M. Dolbeare, *American Public Policy: A Citizen's Guide* (New York: McGraw-Hill, 1982), p. 165.
14. Peters, *American Public Policy,* pp. 203, 183.
15. Dolbeare, *American Public Policy,* p. 179.
16. *New York Times,* August 5, 1988, p. A10.
17. Peters, *American Public Policy,* pp. 184–185.
18. Ibid., pp. 203–205.
19. *New York Times,* December 28, 1988, pp. A1, A12.
20. John L. Palmer and Isabel V. Sawhill, eds., *The Reagan Record: An Assessment of America's Changing Domestic Priorities* (Cambridge, Mass.: Ballinger, 1984), p. 377.
21. Peters, *American Public Policy,* p. 174.
22. Emily Stoper, "State and Local Policies on Motherhood," in *Political Women: Current Roles in State and Local Government,* ed. Janet A. Flammang (Beverly Hills, Calif.: Sage, 1984), pp. 260–276.
23. M. Kenneth Bowler, *The Nixon Guaranteed Income Proposal: Substance and Process in Policy Change* (Cambridge, Mass.: Ballinger, 1974).
24. U.S. Bureau of the Census, *Statistical Abstract of the United States, 1982–83* (Washington, D.C.: U.S. Government Printing Office, 1982), p. 375.
25. *Statistical Abstract, 1988,* pp. 373–374.
26. *San Francisco Chronicle,* January 10, 1989, pp. A1, A14.
27. Susan Ehrlich Martin, "Sexual Harassment: The Link Joining Gender Stratification, Sexuality, and Women's Economic Status," in *Women: A Feminist Perspective,* 4th ed., ed. Jo Freeman (Mountain View, Calif.: Mayfield, 1989), pp. 57–75.
28. U.S. Department of Labor, Women's Bureau, *The Earnings Gap between Men and Women* (Washington, D.C.: U.S. Government Printing Office, 1979).
29. Jo Freeman, *The Politics of Women's Liberation* (New York: David McKay, 1975).
30. U.S. Congress, House, Congressional Caucus for Women's Issues, *Update* (Washington, D.C.: U.S. Government Printing Office, 1988), pp. 8–9.
31. Catharine A. MacKinnon, *Sexual Harassment of Working Women* (New Haven, Conn.: Yale University Press, 1979).
32. E. Robert Livernash, ed., *Comparable Worth: Issues and Alternatives* (Washington, D.C.: Equal Employment Advisory Council, 1980), pp. 217–218.
33. Heidi I. Hartmann and Barbara Reskin, "Job Segregation: Trends and Prospects," in *Occupational Segregation and Its Impact on Working Women: A Conference Report,* ed. Cynthia Chertos et al. (Albany, N.Y.: Center for Women in Government, 1983), pp. 52–78.
34. Donald Trieman and Heidi Hartmann, eds., *Women, Work, and Wages: Equal Pay for Jobs of Equal Value* (Washington, D.C.: National Academy Press, 1981), p. 28.
35. Ronnie Steinberg, "'A Want of Harmony': Perspectives on Wage Discrimination and Comparable Worth," in *Comparable Worth and Wage Discrimination,* ed. Helen Remick (Philadelphia: Temple University Press, 1984), pp. 3–27.
36. Sara M. Evans and Barbara J. Nelson, "Comparable Worth for Public Employees: Implementing a New Wage Policy in Minnesota," in *Comparable Worth, Pay Equity, and Public Policy,* ed. Rita Mae Kelly and Jane Bayes (Westport, Conn.: Greenwood, 1988), pp. 191–212.
37. Janet A. Flammang, "The Implementation of Comparable Worth in San Jose," in Kelly and Bayes, *Comparable Worth,* pp. 159–190.
38. Mary McNamara, "A Major Push for Child Care," *Ms. Magazine,* February 1988, pp. 17–19.

39. Congressional Caucus for Women's Issues, *Update,* pp. 5–6.
40. Robert J. Trotter, "What Are We Going to Do about Day Care?" *San Francisco Examiner's This World,* January 10, 1988, pp. 12–14.
41. Ibid.
42. Proposed by Yale University psychologist Edward Zigler, quoted in ibid.
43. Ibid.
44. Jill Norgren, "In Search of a National Child-Care Policy: Background and Prospects," in *Women, Power, and Policy,* ed. Ellen Boneparth (New York: Pergamon, 1982), pp. 124–143.
45. McNamara, "Major Push for Child Care."
46. Ibid.
47. Ibid. and Carole Joffe, "Why the United States Has No Child-Care Policy," in *Families, Politics, and Public Policy,* ed. Irene Diamond (New York: Longman, 1983), pp. 168–182.
48. *Statistical Abstract of the United States, 1988,* p. 661.
49. U.S. Congress, Office of Technology Assessment, *Analysis of Prepared National Energy Plan,* (Washington, D.C.: U.S. Government Printing Office, 1979).
50. Peters, *American Public Policy,* p. 254.
51. Ibid, p. 259.
52. Dolbeare, *American Public Policy,* p. 137.
53. *New York Times,* August 4, 1980.
54. Robert Stobaugh and Daniel Yergin, eds., *Energy Future: Report of the Energy Project at Harvard Business School* (New York: Random House, 1979), p. 105.
55. Dolbeare, *American Public Policy,* p. 140.
56. Barry Commoner, *The Poverty of Power* (New York: Knopf, 1976).
57. See, for example, John Blair, *The Control of Oil* (New York: Pantheon, 1976).
58. William W. Winpisinger, president of the International Association of Machinists and Aerospace Workers, speech in Boston, March 1978, cited in Richard Grossman and Gail Daneken, *Energy Jobs and the Economy* (Boston: Alyson, 1979), p. 84.
59. United Nations Statistical Office, *Yearbook of World Energy Statistics, 1981* (New York, 1983), table 1.
60. Stobaugh and Yergin, *Energy Future,* p. 136.
61. Committee on the Present Danger, "Common Sense and the Common Danger," in *The Nuclear Predicament,* ed. Donna Gregory (New York: St. Martin's Press, 1986), p. 205.
62. Ronald J. Hrebenar and Ruth K. Scott, *Interest Group Politics in America* (Englewood Cliffs, N.J.: Prentice-Hall, 1982), p. 238.
63. Defense Department testimony before Congress, August 1985, in Gregory, *Nuclear Predicament,* p. 235.
64. Norman J. Ornstein and Shirley Elder, *Interest Groups, Lobbying, and Policymaking* (Washington, D.C.: Congressional Quarterly Press, 1978), p. 194.

★ For Further Reading

Cherlin, Andrew J., ed. *The Changing American Family and Public Policy.* Lanham, Md.: Urban Institute Press, 1988.

Derthick, Martha. *Policymaking for Social Security.* Washington, D.C.: Brookings Institution, 1979.

Garfinkel, Irwin, and Sara S. McLanahan. *Single Mothers and Their Children: A New American Dilemma.* Lanham, Md.: Urban Institute Press, 1986.

Kamerman, Sheila, and Alfred Kahn. *Child Care, Family Benefits, and Working Parents.* New York: Columbia University Press, 1981.

Marmor, Theodore, ed. *Political Analysis and American Medical Care.* New York: Cambridge University Press, 1983.

Rosenbaum, Walter A. *Energy, Politics, and Public Policy.* 2d ed. Washington, D.C.: Congressional Quarterly Press, 1987.

Sweet, William. *The Nuclear Age: Atomic Energy, Proliferation, and the Arms Race.* 2d ed. Washington, D.C.: Congressional Quarterly Press, 1988.

Women's Research and Education Institute of the Congressional Caucus for Women's Issues. *Gender at Work: Perspectives on Occupational Segregation and Comparable Worth.* Washington, D.C., 1984.

We meant to change a nation and instead we changed a world.

—Ronald Reagan, 1989

When the United States sneezes, the rest of the world catches a cold.

—Popular Third World saying

CHAPTER EIGHTEEN

POLITICAL ECONOMY

★★★★★★★★★★★

Economic Policy: Political Solutions to Economic Problems

The "Reagan revolution" of the 1980s set in motion national changes with international repercussions. The essence of President Reagan's revolution was a scaling back of the role of government in the economy. Much to his surprise, he found that his desire to reduce taxes, cut social spending, curb regulation of industry, and promote free trade was shared by many other nations. In the battle of governments against markets described in chapter 16, markets seemed to carry the day throughout the 1980s. Even countries with highly regulated economies, such as China and the Soviet Union, backed off from central control and permitted more private enterprise. And many of our capitalist trading partners, such as Canada and Great Britain, jumped on the conservative bandwagon of limited government and free trade.

Students of **political economy** analyze the relationship between governments and their economies. In a world of growing political and economic interdependence, whenever the U.S. government alters its stance toward domestic and international economic matters, the rest of the world stands up and takes notice.

The U.S. economy is the shared responsibility of individuals and government. Individuals buy and sell goods and services. And government steps in to harness the market activities of individuals in the name of the public good. In this chapter we look at government attempts to manage the economy. We begin with an overview of the major features of the U.S. economy with which government must contend. We then turn to the government's efforts to manage the economy through a combination of monetary, fiscal, regulatory, and subsidy policies. Finally, we consider how government policies affect America's role in a global economy, policies that attempt to meet the challenges of growing international economic competition.

It is no easy task to harness the activities of an economy with a $5 trillion gross national product. Even if the government could control major aspects of the economy, it is not of one mind about what best serves the public's welfare. Some of the questions government officials and others must address follow:

- What is the best mix of free enterprise and central planning?
- Should the government favor the needs of small businesses or those of multinational corporations?
- Should wealth and income be more equitably distributed?
- Which should be tackled first, inflation or unemployment?
- What do we do about our national debt and what some people regard as an unfair tax system?

- To what extent should government regulate business practices?
- Should government subsidize businesses or let them fall prey to market forces?
- How do we increase our competitive edge in the world economy and reduce our growing dependence on imports?
- What are the risks associated with being the banker for the world's developing nations?

★ Features of the U.S. Economy

Before we can assess the ways in which the U.S. government attempts to control domestic and international economic behavior, it is important to discuss four key features of the U.S. economy with which government must contend: markets, types of businesses, economic sectors, and wealth and income distribution.

Our Economic System: Market or Mixed?

Economic systems are concerned with the production and consumption of goods and services. The American economy is part of a larger, international economic system. This international system is comprised of economies of three general types: market, command, and mixed.

★ Leaders of the industrially advanced capitalist nations often meet to discuss economic matters. Here President Ronald Reagan (*far left*) joined other world leaders at an economic summit in Williamsburg, Virginia, in 1983.

★ The Soviet Union and China have government-directed command economies. In recent years, however, the Soviet and Chinese governments have increasingly allowed individuals to sell their goods in private markets. Here a Soviet couple sell garlic and Chinese women sell fish in open markets.

A **market economy** is based on free markets and private property. In a free market, demand and supply determine price. Such an economy is based on the idea of consumer sovereignty. Consumers have power by virtue of their spending in the marketplace, which determines what and how much is produced. In other words, if consumer demand for product *A* decreases, producers will shift their resources to make product *B*. Producers of product *A* will lay off workers, while makers of product *B* will hire more workers. Resources are reallocated and consumer demand is satisfied without the need for government direction or control of the production process.

A free market is also based on the principle of private property, which holds that individuals have the right to buy, sell, own, and accumulate property. Property takes the form of real assets (land, buildings, cars, and so forth), financial assets (stocks, bonds, insurance, and so on), and liquid assets (cash, checking and savings accounts, and the like). The right to private property protects individuals from government seizure of property. In market economies, the means of production (land, factories, farms, and businesses) are owned by individuals, not by the government. Individuals may be sole proprietors of a firm, partners in a business enterprise, or stockholders in a corporation.

In a **command economy,** in contrast, the government owns the means of production. Production decisions are determined not by consumer demand but by the "command" of a central economic planning authority. Command economies are government-directed rather than price-directed. Governments, not individuals, own and operate the farms, factories, and firms that produce goods and services.

The Soviet Union is commonly cited as a command economy, while the United States is typically seen as a market economy. However, while it may be convenient to place the two superpowers at opposite ends of a market–command continuum, the American government has actually been increasing its role in the economy

Misconceptions about Some Economic Issues Are Widespread

By George Gallup, Jr.

PRINCETON, N.J. — A new survey reveals a wide disparity in Americans' knowledge of economic affairs.

Most have at least a superficial understanding of widely covered topics such as the federal budget deficit, the savings-and-loan crisis, the trade deficit and foreign investment in the United States. Many, however, are uninformed or misinformed about matters important to [our] economic policies.

Misconceptions about the current status of the social security budget also are widespread. Nearly half (45 percent) are aware that the amount collected is greater than the amount distributed as benefits. But about as many think receipts are less than disbursements (28 percent) or that income and outlay are in balance (16 percent).

Survey participants were scored on the number of questions they answered correctly. People who gave 9–14 correct responses rated "high," those having 6–8 right responses were rated "medium," and those with five or fewer correct answers were rated "low."

The accompanying chart gives the key findings, which are based on in-person interviews with 2,048 adults, conducted nationwide from Jan. 27 to Feb. 5, 1989. The margin of error is within 3 percentage points in either direction. ★

Knowledge of economic affairs (percentage giving correct response)

The U.S. has a trade deficit with Japan	83%
Defense is one of the two largest components of the federal budget	81
Foreign investment in the U.S. has increased over the last 10 years	78
The federal budget deficit is larger than it was 10 years ago	74
Savings and loan institutions are having financial difficulties	73
Gasoline taxes are lower in the U.S. than in Western Europe	53
The U.S. has a trade deficit with South Korea	53
The amount of money collected for social security is greater than the amount paid out to people receiving social security	45
The U.S. has a trade deficit with the countries of Western Europe	38
Americans pay a smaller percentage of their income in taxes than Western Europeans do	37
The annual federal budget deficit is between $100 and $200 billion	18
The U.S. has a trade deficit with Canada	16
Foreign investors own less than 5 percent of privately owned U.S. real estate	4

Social characteristics and level of knowledge of economic affairs

	High	*Medium*	*Low*
Nationwide	24%	47%	29%
Men	35	44	21
Women	15	50	35
Whites	27	48	25
Nonwhites	8	41	51
18–29 years	13	49	38
30–49 years	26	47	27
50 and older	30	47	23
College grads	47	43	10
Some college	24	56	20
High school grads	20	48	32
Not high school grads	14	42	44
$50,000 and over	36	46	18
$30,000-$49,999	29	46	25
$15,000-$29,999	20	50	30
Under $15,000	17	45	38
Republicans	30	46	24
Democrats	21	47	32
Independents	24	48	28
East	23	43	34
Midwest	29	50	21
South	21	46	33
West	25	51	24

SOURCE: *San Jose Mercury News,* Sunday, April 30, 1989, p. 22A.

while the Soviet government has been experimenting with market incentives. At the center of this continuum is a **mixed economy,** which combines elements of a market economy with some government involvement in production and distribution of goods and services.

Most Western industrialized nations have mixed economies. One measure of a government's involvement in its economy is ownership of key industries. The British government, for example, owns the coal and steel industries, but has left its financial enterprises to the free market. France has nationalized its banks, while Mexico, Italy, and Venezuela, among others, have government-run oil industries. Even the United States has never had a pure market economy. Market economies are geared toward profit, and some socially desirable goods are not profitable. Our government has taken a leading role in providing for education, roads, dams, bridges, canals, and airports, activities that aid private business in many ways. Our government also intervenes when firms fail to cover all the costs of production, such as cleaning up air and water pollution, or toxic waste dump sites. Government also insures bank deposits and helps to bail out financial institutions if they fail.

Another measure of a government's involvement in the economy is the amount of gross national product (GNP) the government generates. The U.S. government accounts for about 22 percent of the American GNP. The governments of most European countries account for roughly 35 percent of their nations' GNPs; the figure for Sweden's government is more than 40 percent.[1]

While the American economy has never been a pure market type, it has been dominated by powerful businesses that both respond to consumer demand and help to create that demand through advertising. Let us take a closer look at the types of firms that dominate the American economy.

Types of Businesses: Competitive, Oligopolistic, Multinational

The kinds of businesses that produce goods and services in the American economy range from the family-run neighborhood shoe-repair or jewelry store to the giant multinational corporation that operates in many nations, employs thousands of workers around the world, and reaps billions in profits. It is necessary to understand the various types of businesses before we can address the question of what control, if any, the United States government can exercise over their economic activities.

By the mid-1980s, sixteen million businesses were operating in the United States. Almost three-quarters of them were proprietorships, or unincorporated businesses owned by one person. About 10 percent were partnerships, or unincorporated businesses owned by two or more persons, each of whom has a financial interest in the business. The remaining firms were corporations. A **corporation** is a business that is legally incorporated under state laws and that pools the resources of many owners, with ownership rights freely transferable between persons. No one owner is liable in a financial sense for any losses other than his or her own investment. With this limited investment risk, corporations can attract investors more easily than other forms of business. Corporations are "persons" in the eyes of the law, enjoying many of the rights of citizens. While corporations constitute only one-fifth of American businesses, they generate 90 percent of sales and reap over three-quarters of all business profits, as table 18-1 indicates.

★ **Table 18-1**
Number of businesses and sales and profits, by type of business, 1984

	Businesses		*Sales*		*Profits*	
Type of business	*Number*	*Percent*	*Billions of dollars*	*Percent*	*Billions of dollars*	*Percent*
Proprietorship	11,262,000	70%	516	6%	71	24%
Partnership	1,644,000	10	375	4	−3	−1
Corporation	3,171,000	20	7,861	90	233	77
All businesses	16,077,000	100%	$8,752	100%	$301	100%

SOURCE: U.S. Bureau of the Census, *Statistical Abstract of the United States, 1988* (Washington, D.C.: U.S. Government Printing Office, 1987), p. 495.

★ **Table 18-2**
Sales, profits, and assets of top 500 and second 500 manufacturing and retailing corporations, 1981 (billions of dollars)

	Top 500	*Second 500*
Sales	$1,773	$121
Profits	84	6
Assets	1,282	91

SOURCE: U.S. Bureau of the Census, *Statistical Abstract of the United States, 1982–83* (Washington, D.C.: U.S. Government Printing Office, 1982), p. 543.

Not only is economic power concentrated in corporate hands, but the five hundred largest corporations account for the bulk of corporate economic activity. Where we compare sales, profits, and assets, we find that the top five hundred firms account for thirteen times the economic activity of the second five hundred corporations (see table 18-2).

Thus free-market competition is tempered by the existence of **oligopolies,** a few large firms that control more than half of the production of a certain good or service. Oligopolies control more than half of the assets in such areas as mining, manufacturing, transport, utilities, banking, and finance.[2] Not only do a few giant firms dominate markets, but these companies also are tied together with other large businesses, thus reducing competition and a "pure" market economy. One of the many ways in which large firms are tied together is through **interlocking directorates.** When an individual sits on the board of directors of two or more companies, these enterprises are informally "locked" together. Only fifteen of the largest two hundred nonfinancial companies and one of the largest fifty financial firms have no interlocks.[3]

Moreover, these larger firms are not so susceptible to the ups and downs of the marketplace as are the smaller, more vulnerable firms, the partnerships and proprietorships. For some people, these large companies, linked together by interlocking directorates, signal a healthy market where talented entrepreneurs produce popular products and earn a large share of the profits of a product sector. Other people, however, see the dominance of a few giant companies as detrimental to a free, competitive marketplace.

This economic concentration has important political significance as well. Many of these firms are **multinational corporations,** whose production activities take place in several countries. They are headquartered in major industrial nations and have subsidiaries in countries with cheap labor and/or raw materials. Multinationals account for a dominant share of the nation's production of manufactured goods, computers, industrial instruments, and pharmaceuticals. They control many raw materials in developing countries, including oil, copper, zinc, and bauxite. In the financial sector, they set up their own banks abroad to facilitate their business dealings, expanding the amount of U.S. dollars used in the world economy in support of international trade and finance. This form of stateless money is controlled solely by private banking and business interests with little regulation by the U.S. government. By the early 1980s, American dollars abroad had grown to over $1 trillion, about three times the amount of the domestic money supply.[4]

Politically, many large corporations, especially the multinationals, operate beyond the control of the U.S. government. They are financed by unregulated dollars held abroad; they sometimes close profit-making plants in the United States in order to make even greater profits with cheaper labor abroad; and they often go abroad to avoid environmental controls at home. They sometimes even pursue their own foreign policy goals. In 1954, for instance, the United Fruit Company instigated the U.S.-orchestrated overthrow of the government of Guatemala, and in 1970 International Telephone and Telegraph worked with the CIA to overthrow the government of Chile. In both cases, these corporations opposed the host government's attempts to regulate their business activities. Thus large corporations wield considerable economic power and can be formidable adversaries of government attempts to control their economic activities.

Economic Sectors: Agricultural, Manufacturing, Service

A third important set of distinctions to keep in mind consists of those among the three sectors of contemporary economies: the agricultural, manufacturing, and service sectors. The United States began as an agricultural economy. Most people lived in rural areas and either engaged in subsistence farming or planted cash crops such as cotton and tobacco. Following the Civil War, industrialization increased rapidly, and by 1920 more people were living in urban than in rural areas. People flocked to the cities to work in factories, and huge numbers of immigrants swelled the urban labor force. As a result, manufacturing constituted an ever-growing share of the nation's GNP.

Since the end of World War II, the United States has witnessed yet another change in the relative importance of the three sectors (see figure 18-1). A declining manufacturing sector has given way to a robust service sector. By 1948, service-

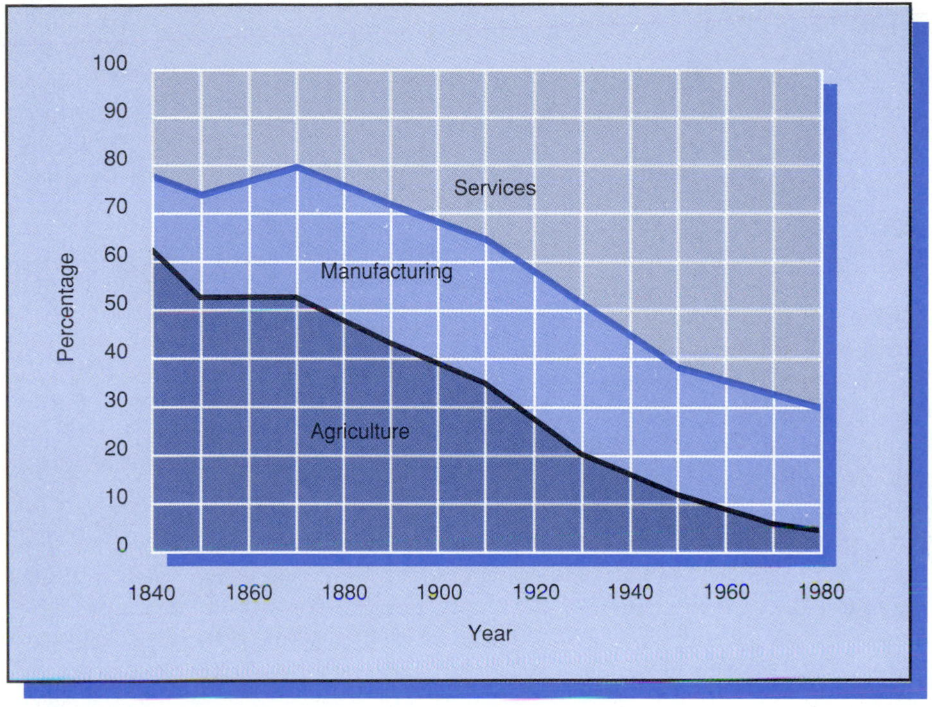

★ **Figure 18-1**
Percentage of labor force in three economic sectors, 1840–1980
SOURCE: *Economic Report of the President* (Washington, D.C.: U.S. Government Printing Office, 1988), p. 190.

producing industries, such as transportation, communications, public utilities, wholesale and retail trade, finance, insurance, and real estate, accounted for nearly 58 percent of all nonfarm payroll employees, and contributed more than 59 percent of the total GNP. Over the years, the service sector's share of employment has increased faster than its share of GNP. Currently, three-quarters of all workers have jobs in this sector, which now accounts for two-thirds of GNP. Manufacturing's share of employment and GNP, by contrast, is about 20 percent. And only about 3 percent of the labor force work in the agricultural sector, which produces about 15 percent of GNP.[5]

Since the bulk of the nation's work force and GNP are found in the service sector, the United States has been called a "postindustrial society," a reflection of the diminishing importance of the manufacturing and agricultural sectors.

Government attempts to control the economy must respond to the economic and political consequences of the changes in these sectors. For instance, government has to decide how much it should subsidize its farmers with price supports and protect its factories with import quotas. Farms and factories may employ a shrinking proportion of the work force, but they are still critical factors in the economic health of the nation. Moreover, government is concerned with the way workers adjust to these structural changes. The expanded service sector has particularly affected women: 80 percent of the new jobs created during the early 1980s were filled by women.[6] It has also benefited people with technical skills (such as

A Growing International Service Economy

One of the most significant developments of recent years has been the huge growth of international service conglomerates. They account for about 40 percent of all existing foreign direct investment and about 50 percent of all new investment, according to the United Nations. The size and character of the sector is also being transformed by the increasing importance of advertising, research, product development, legal issues, and public relations. Many companies find it cheaper to buy specialized services rather than build in-house expertise, while deregulation of the world's financial centers has allowed banks and other financial agents to become financial supermarkets, offering pensions, investment and property services.

New computer-related technologies have created demand for services such as software and data bases, and permitted more services to be delivered long-distance, including banking, accountancy and library services. In addition, higher personal incomes have increased foreign travel, with a corresponding growth in the number of hotels and tourist services.

SOURCE: *South*, No. 97, November 1988, p. 18. [Based on IMF Balance of Payment Statistics.]

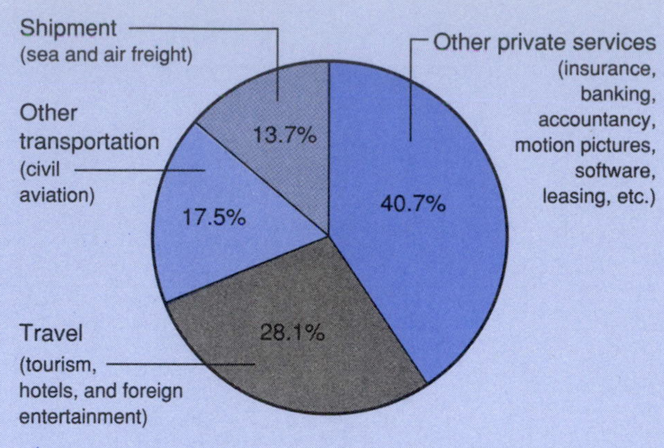

Figure 18-2
How trade in services divides up: World services in 1986 (measured on the credits side of the accounts).

computer programmers) and those willing to work for low wages (such as workers in fast-food restaurants). Hardest hit are industrial workers, who are accustomed to earning high wages in skilled and semiskilled occupations.

Wealth and Income Distribution

Finally, government attempts to control the economy must grapple with the consequences of vast disparities in wealth and income. Wealth consists of income and assets, such as stocks, bonds, loans, real estate, artwork, and precious metals. Income consists of wages, salaries, tips, and interest. Wealth provides greater economic security than income, which for most people is only as secure as their current job. Wealthholders can live wholly or in part on income generated by their assets.

The federal government does not routinely collect data on wealth distribution. As a presidential candidate John Kennedy "discovered" poverty while he campaigned in Appalachia; and when he became president in 1961, he instructed the Federal Reserve Board to conduct a study of the way wealth was distributed in the U.S. population. The results of the board's 1962 study were startling: the richest 20 percent of the population held 76 percent of U.S. wealth, while the poorest 20

★ **Table 18-3**
Percentage shares of family income, 1940–1985, by income rank

Income rank	*1940*	*1950*	*1960*	*1970*	*1980*	*1985*
Lowest 20%	4.1%	4.5%	4.8%	5.4%	5.1%	4.6%
Second 20%	9.5	11.9	12.2	12.2	11.6	10.9
Middle 20%	15.3	17.4	17.8	17.6	17.5	16.9
Fourth 20%	22.3	23.6	24.0	23.8	24.3	24.2
Highest 20%	48.8	42.7	41.3	40.9	41.6	43.5
Top 5%	24.0%	17.3%	15.9%	15.6%	16.2%	16.7%

SOURCE: U.S. Bureau of the Census, *Statistical Abstract of the United States,* relevant years (Washington, D.C.: U.S. Government Printing Office, relevant years).

percent held only 0.2 percent.[7] The top 6 percent of Americans owned 57 percent of the nation's wealth.[8]

Two decades later another government study found that wealth was still concentrated in the hands of a tiny fraction of America. A 1985 study by the Joint Economic Committee of Congress reported that one-half of 1 percent of the population held 35.1 percent of U.S. wealth, an increase of 10 percent over the previous decade. Furthermore, between 1965 and 1985, the percentage of total wealth held by the bottom 90 percent of Americans fell from 34.9 percent to 28.2 percent.[9]

The distribution of income is less skewed toward the rich than is wealth. The Internal Revenue Service and the Census Bureau routinely collect statistics on personal income. Since 1940, income distribution has changed very little. The top 20 percent of the population account for about 42 percent of family income and the bottom 20 percent for about 5 percent. The main change since 1940 has been a decline in the percentage held by the top 5 percent of U.S. families: from 24 percent to 16.7 percent (see table 18-3).

The federal government takes patterns of wealth and income distribution into account when it attempts to control the economy by means of tax policy and benefit programs. So-called redistributive programs, for example, seek to transfer money from the rich to the poor. Many liberals note that there has been no change in the status of the bottom ranks in spite of federal income-maintenance programs, which have taken increasingly larger chunks out of the federal budget since 1940. Conservatives respond that liberals ignore the value of noncash public benefits, such as food stamps, Medicare, Medicaid, and housing subsidies. When the value of these benefits is taken into account, they say, the poverty rate is lower than official statistics indicate (see table 18-4).

Having outlined the essential features of the American economy—a market/mixed economy dominated by large and increasingly multinational firms in a post-industrial society with skewed patterns of wealth and income distribution—let us now turn to the tools the federal government has at its disposal to impose political solutions on economic problems, both domestic and global.

Table 18-4
Percentage of U.S. population living in poverty, 1979–1983, by alternative definitions of poverty

	1979	1980	1981	1982	1983
Current approach	11.7%	13.0%	14.0%	15.0%	15.2%
Market-value approach[a]	6.8	7.9	9.0	10.0	10.2
Recipient-value approach[b]	9.0	10.4	11.7	12.7	13.0
Poverty budget share approach[c]	9.1	10.4	11.5	12.5	12.9

[a]Income calculated to include estimated value of in-kind benefits in the marketplace.

[b]Income calculated to include estimated cash value that recipients would exchange for benefits.

[c]Based on Census Bureau estimate of value of benefits in relation to consumption patterns of poor families.

SOURCE: *National Journal,* August 18, 1984, p. 1564.

Government Intervention in the U.S. Economy

The four most important tools the federal government uses to affect the nation's economy are monetary, fiscal, regulatory, and subsidy policies.

Monetary Policy

Monetary policy consists of government measures to control the amount of money circulating in the economy. The aim of monetary policy is to ensure public access to sound banks and to maintain a stable money supply.

A sound banking system was of paramount importance to the founders of this country, particularly to such Federalists as Alexander Hamilton and George Washington. As the first secretary of the treasury, Hamilton championed a stable national economy to protect investments, loans, and the value of currency. He supported a national bank so that the federal government could assume the debts the states had incurred to finance the Revolutionary War. During the war, paper currency fell in value at an alarming rate. In 1787, Washington complained that he had to sell at a rate of 20 for 1 the certificates that Congress paid him to fight the war.[10] Federalists supported a tight-money policy, which benefited creditors. Anti-Federalists, in contrast, advocated cheap money and state banks, which benefited debtors.

In 1832, President Andrew Jackson donned the Anti-Federalist mantle and vetoed the renewal of the charter of the Bank of the United States, which he saw as a tool to make the rich richer. His 1832 reelection campaign slogan was "No bank and Jackson—or bank and no Jackson." Throughout the nineteenth century, debtors and farmers made continual demands for easy credit. Such populists as William Jennings Bryan advocated silver-backed currency to provide cheaper dollars for ordinary citizens. At the 1896 Democratic Convention, presidential nominee Bryan gave his famous "Cross of Gold" speech, attacking the tight-money policy of backing currency with gold: "You shall not press down upon the brow of labor this cross of thorns, you shall not crucify mankind upon a cross of gold." With the 1896 victory of the Republican William McKinley over Bryan, however, the gold standard was officially adopted.

The Federal Reserve System. Until 1913, monetary policy was coordinated by the Treasury Department, which ever since Hamilton has had a reputation for close ties to the nation's financial community of bankers and investors. The Federal Reserve Act of 1913 established the national monetary and banking system known as the **Federal Reserve System.** It established twelve Federal Reserve banks as the central banks of their districts, governed by the Federal Reserve Board. The system was created to boost investors' confidence in banks by requiring banks to keep money on reserve to cover their outstanding loans. Its other purpose was to regulate the amount of money in circulation—to pursue a tight-money policy to protect the value of investments.

The Federal Reserve Board is composed of seven members appointed by the president with Senate approval. The board and its banks are set up to be independent of the executive authority of the president. Members of the Federal Reserve are supposed to exercise their judgment as bankers rather than submit to the control of public officials, who may want to manipulate the money supply for personal or political gain. Often the board goes against the wishes of a president. During Lyndon Johnson's administration, for example, the board chairman refused Johnson's request to increase the money supply more rapidly to ease the financial pressure created by his expanding domestic programs and the war in Vietnam.[11]

The Federal Reserve uses three tools to conduct monetary policy: open-market operations, the discount rate, and reserve requirements. The Federal Reserve's open-market operations, its most commonly used tool, consist of the buying and selling of securities issued by the Federal Reserve Board. To reduce the money supply, it sells securities to take cash out of circulation. To enlarge the money supply, it purchases securities to increase cash in circulation.

A more drastic measure is changing the discount rate. The discount rate is the rate of interest at which member banks can borrow money from the Federal Reserve bank. To take money out of circulation, the Federal Reserve Board raises the discount rate, so that money becomes more expensive to borrow and customers will be less likely to take out loans from their banks. To add money to the economy, the Federal Reserve Board lowers the discount rate, encouraging customers to borrow money.

Finally, the Federal Reserve Board can change the reserve requirement. The reserve requirement is the amount of money member banks of the Federal Reserve System are required to keep on deposit at the Federal Reserve banks to cover outstanding loans. The reserve requirement is a percentage of a bank's total loans, usually around 20 percent. When the Federal Reserve Board increases the reserve requirement, banks must keep on deposit money they would otherwise lend, so the amount of money in circulation is reduced. Lowering the reserve requirement has the opposite effect: banks have more money to lend, and the amount of money in circulation is increased.

The Federal Reserve has historically pursued a conservative economic policy of tight money. The board is typically composed of bankers and business people

★ The seven members of the Board of Governors of the Federal Reserve System determine general monetary, credit, and operating policies for the system as a whole.

responsive to the financial community. Liberals frequently criticize the Federal Reserve's tight-money policy for producing hardship and slowing economic growth. Conservatives applaud the system's role in stabilizing the U.S. economy. Conservatives tend to be monetarists, people who identify a stable rate of growth in the money supply as the key to economic stability. The conservative economist Milton Friedman is a well-known advocate of this view. Like many other conservatives, Friedman is critical of liberals' attempts to use fiscal policies (the government's taxing and spending powers) to achieve economic stability and prosperity.

Fiscal Policy

Fiscal policy is a more recent development than monetary policy. **Fiscal policy** is the government's use of its taxing and spending powers to achieve economic stability and prosperity. The federal government turned to fiscal policies to solve economic problems in earnest in the 1930s, during the liberal Democratic administration of President Franklin Roosevelt. On October 24, 1929, the bottom fell out of the stock market, precipitating an economic crisis. Banks failed, investments became worthless, borrowers defaulted, businesses closed or cut back, unemployment soared, and incomes plummeted. The United States' economy slid into the worst depression of its history. A **depression** is a phase in the business cycle characterized by low output and high unemployment. The depression of the 1930s was so severe that it is known as the Great Depression.

Roosevelt became president in 1933, at the height of the Great Depression. Total economic output had fallen to about half of its 1929 level, unemployment hovered at 25 percent, and people stood in bread lines to get food distributed by charitable organizations. All quarters turned to the federal government for help: business, labor, state and local governments, and religious and charitable groups.

During the first hundred days of the Roosevelt administration, Congress passed fifteen major pieces of fiscal legislation to remedy falling production, the crisis in the banking industry, and the poverty of the elderly and farmers. These were the first of Roosevelt's New Deal programs, measures that ushered in our social welfare state of government programs.

In 1936, after most of the major New Deal measures (see Appendix D) had been passed by Congress, the theoretical justification for government intervention to restore the nation's economy was provided by the British economist John Maynard Keynes. Keynes argued that governments should reduce unemployment by increasing aggregate demand. Aggregate demand is the combined demand for goods and services of consumers, businesses, and government. The government can boost aggregate demand by cutting taxes (so consumers have more money to spend) and increasing government spending for goods and services. When less revenue comes in than the government spends, the federal budget shows a deficit. A **budget deficit** is an excess of government expenditures over government receipts in a given budget year. The economic growth stimulated by government spending, Keynes reasoned, would generate the revenues needed to offset the deficit. In Keynes's view, a government should also stimulate the economy through income redistribution. Consumption was the key to his economic argument. By distributing money more evenly among citizens, Keynes believed, government could stimulate consumer spending.

Keynesian economics became the dominant economic philosophy in the postwar period. The Employment Act of 1946 committed the national government to maintaining "maximum employment, production and purchasing power." It also created the President's Council of Economic Advisers, mandated an annual economic report by the president, and established the Joint Economic Committee of Congress to consider the president's recommendations. These groups are supposed to head off such economic problems as recessions and depressions. A **recession** is a phase in the business cycle characterized by a decline in output and employment. The government uses Keynesian measures to promote economic recovery and prevent recessions from becoming depressions.

Inflation, Stagflation, and Supply-Side Economics. By the time of President Lyndon Johnson's administration, confidence that the economy could be fine-tuned with Keynesian fiscal measures was so high that the federal government turned its attention to spending on domestic social programs and the war in Vietnam. However, this spending resulted in substantial budget deficits that contributed to the inflationary spiral of the 1970s. **Inflation** is a rise in the prices of goods and services, which causes a decline in purchasing power: "too much money chasing too few goods." Inflation is measured by the consumer price index, the price of an assortment of goods and services typical of consumer purchases. Each month the U.S Bureau of Labor Statistics publishes this index. Between 1970 and 1980, inflation totaled more than 100 percent: in 1980 a family needed $10,000 to purchase something that cost $5,000 in 1970. The Keynesian solution for inflation was the opposite of that for recession/depression: increase taxes and reduce government spending. Politicians avoided these politically unpopular measures, however, practicing "one-eyed Keynesianism," reading Keynes's passages about recessions but skipping over those about inflation.[12]

The 1970s saw not only a high rate of inflation but also high levels of unemployment (between 5 and 8 percent), in spite of the budget deficits of Presidents

Richard Nixon, Gerald Ford, and Jimmy Carter. The combination of low economic growth, high unemployment, and inflation came to be called **stagflation,** a word coined from "stagnation" and "inflation." Stagflation challenged conventional wisdom about monetary and fiscal policies. High unemployment and inflation were not supposed to happen at the same time. Monetary and fiscal policies were designed to deal with each set of conditions separately, not with the two together. As if inflation and unemployment weren't bad enough, the 1970s also saw the Organization of Petroleum Exporting Countries (OPEC) drive up oil prices from $2.70 a barrel in 1969 to $34 in 1980.

With mounting stagflation, Keynesian fiscal policy fell into disrepute. Some observers claim that the failure of Keynesian economics to deal with stagflation was due to both domestic and global factors beyond the scope of the theory that did not exist at the time Keynes wrote; namely, growing price rigidity in the market, caused by the enormous size of corporations, contracts that tied wages to the cost-of-living index, and increased oil prices on the international markets. Others felt it was time to turn from the demand-management policies of Keynes to the supply-side economics of Ronald Reagan.

When President Reagan took office in 1981, unemployment had reached 7.5 percent and inflation 10.5 percent. His solution to stagflation was **supply-side economics,** which focused its efforts on encouraging producers to supply goods and services rather than on enabling consumers to buy them. Reagan cut taxes and provided other investment incentives to increase the supply of goods and services the economy produced. Tax cuts for business, he reasoned, would stimulate investment, and tax cuts for consumers would promote savings and investment. Ultimately, economic recovery, job opportunities, and higher wages would benefit everyone, even the poorest. According to this trickle-down theory, the benefits of economic growth eventually would work their way down to the poor.

The centerpiece of supply-side economics was the Economic Recovery Tax Act of 1981, which sliced the average income tax by 23 percent over four years. Tax cuts benefited people in higher income brackets, presumably those most likely to invest. The immediate impact of the tax cut was a massive increase in the federal deficit. While the Reagan administration managed a significant reduction in the rate of inflation, it also oversaw the creation of more new debt than the combined deficits of all previous administrations.

Deficits and Debt. A government's budget shows a deficit when its outlays exceed its receipts in a fiscal year. When receipts are greater than outlays, there is a budget surplus for that fiscal year. Since the end of World War II, only two budgets have run a surplus: those of FY 1960 and FY 1969. The sum total of deficits over time is the **national debt.** Each year the federal budget includes payments for the interest on this accumulated debt. During the 1980s, about 15 cents of every dollar the federal government spent went to pay off our national debt (see figure 18-3). This debt grew from $367 billion in 1969 to an estimated $2.4 trillion in 1987, as shown in table 18-5 (on p. 682).

In response to the alarming growth in deficits and debt during the Reagan administration, several policy solutions were proposed. One was the Gramm-Rudman-Hollings Act, which was passed by Congress in 1985. This legislation mandated budget deficit reductions of $36 billion annually for five years, beginning in FY 1987, to achieve a balanced budget by FY 1991. It originally provided for the General Accounting Office to make mandatory cuts if Congress and the president

★★★★★★★★★★★★★

Economy

Sarah Putnam/Sudan Pictures

Mark Peterson/JB Pictures

Peter Charlesworth/JB Pictures

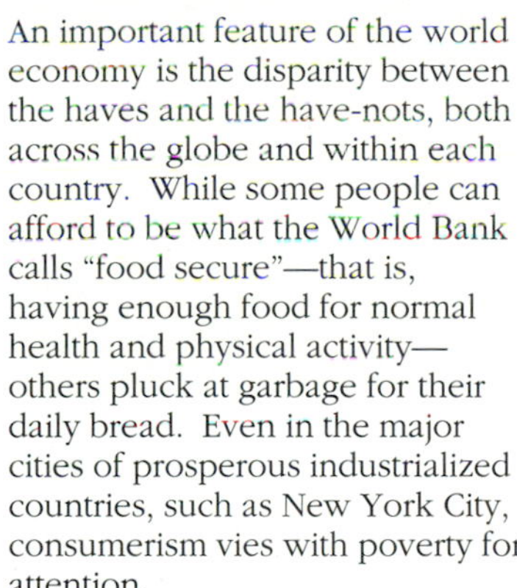

An important feature of the world economy is the disparity between the haves and the have-nots, both across the globe and within each country. While some people can afford to be what the World Bank calls "food secure"—that is, having enough food for normal health and physical activity—others pluck at garbage for their daily bread. Even in the major cities of prosperous industrialized countries, such as New York City, consumerism vies with poverty for attention.

Drought, political conflict, and the search for employment drive populations to the edges of cities, where they set up huts such as the one shown here *(top left)* outside Khartoum, Sudan. In an economy in which there is not enough work for adults, a "working child" from the Philippines sifts through the garbage for valuables to sell. In Mozambique, two mothers wrapped in food sacks stand with their babies and wait for assistance in a local clinic. Meanwhile, in London, a woman, perhaps another mother, selects food from a well-stocked market for her family.

Aarhus/JB Pictures

Peter J. Kaplan

What are the effects of these disparities? What kinds of political pressures do they produce as the have-nots are increasingly bombarded with images of affluence? Is America morally obligated to help the world's poor? How will wealth disparities affect political stability?

Herman Koko/Black Star

Economic problems often lead to armed conflict and a sellers' market in weapons. Americans debate the issue of gun control, and government leaders discuss nuclear arms control among the superpowers; yet, conventional arms trafficking is big business, and most countries, including ours, profit from it. In fact, during the Gulf War between Iran and Iraq (1980-1988), at least twenty-seven countries where known to be selling $10 billion worth of weapons a year to Iran and Iraq, with some countries selling to both parties.

Robert Nickelsberg/Gamma–Liaison

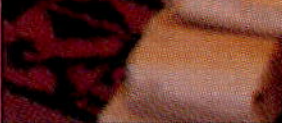

Tom O'Brien/Picture Group

And where do warring countries go to find these weapons? Purchasers could have gone to the Paris Air Show in 1988 and ordered their bombs and fighter planes of choice. Soldiers in Afghanistan could have taken a short trip across the border to Peshawar, Pakistan, to a munitions "supermarket" for a supply of weapons and ammunitions.

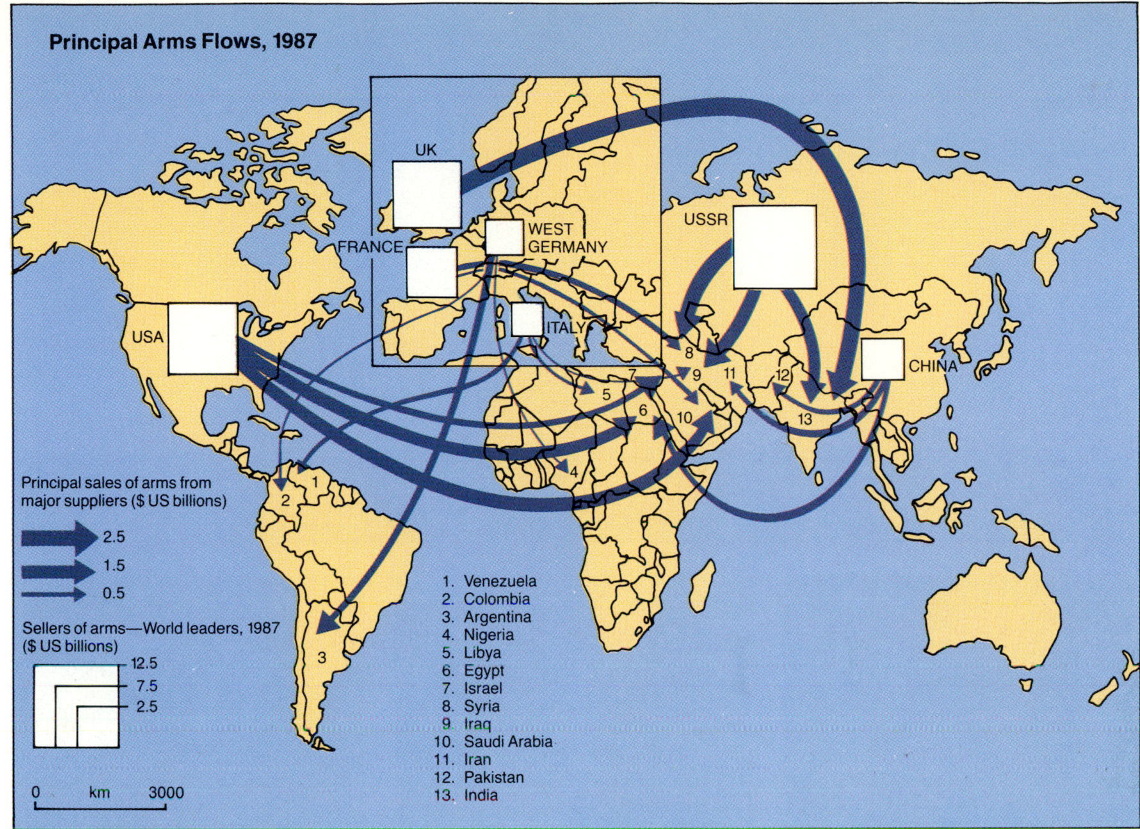

Gary Haley/*Geographical Magazine*, January 1989

Although much of the arms market is a matter of private enterprise, many governments are arms merchants, as you can see from the table. Do governments sell weapons to achieve balance of power or to balance the budget? And when private enterprise and government interests become intertwined, as they did in the Iran-Contra scandal, what purposes are really served?

The World's Leading Arms Sellers in 1987

Soviet Union	$12.5 billion	24.9%
United States	9.2 billion	18.3
Great Britain	8.6 billion	17.1
France	4.5 billion	8.9
China	3.2 billion	6.3
West Germany	2.7 billion	5.4
Italy	2.0 billion	3.9
Japan	1.8 billion	3.5
Sweden	1.3 billion	2.5
Poland	1.2 billion	2.3
Israel	0.9 billion	1.7
Czechoslovakia	0.8 billion	1.5
Canada	0.7 billion	1.3
Brazil	0.5 billion	0.9
India	0.3 billion	0.5

SOURCE *Geographical Magazine*, January 1989, p.15.

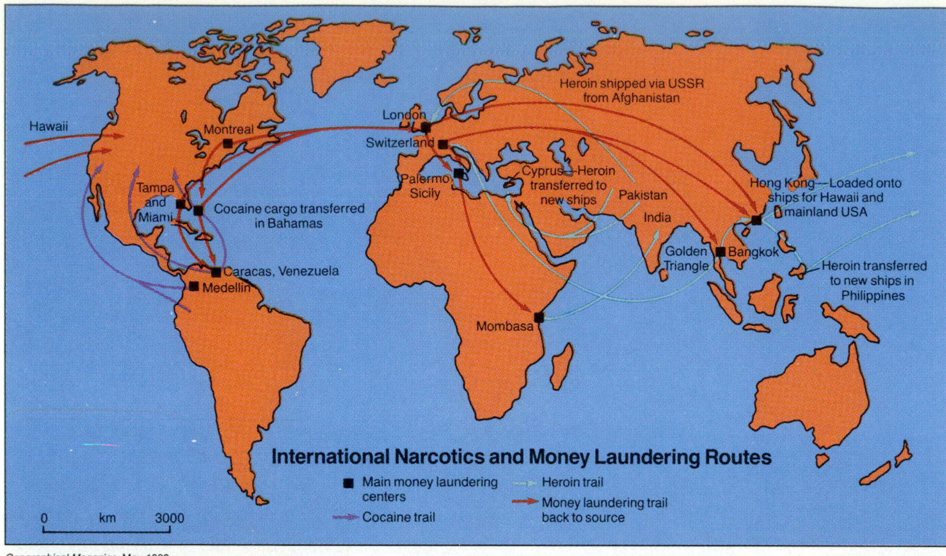

Geographical Magazine, May 1989

Drug trafficking also creates an international market. Indeed, drug money has become the foundation of a growing number of economies. For example, almost half of Peru's export revenue is derived from the export of coca leaves or their derivatives.

Greg Smith/Picture Group

Psiameek Keystone/Picture Group

Timothy Ross/Picture Group

The economic incentive to grow coca is great. A Peruvian farmer gets $4,500 per hectare for coca leaves but only $600 per hectare for planting coffee or cocoa beans. It is no surprise, then, that the Peruvian farmers produce almost $900 million worth of coca leaves a year. Drug traffickers turn the leaves into cocaine paste, netting $2,400 million per year. By the time the cocaine reaches New York, a major target city, it has increased in value to $76,000 billion.

While governments try to destroy crops through aerial spraying and bombing in South America or by burning opium crops in the Golden Triangle in Southeast Asia, the sellers fight back. Columbia's Medellin drug cartel, for example, assassinated scores of judges and bombed the newspaper *El Spectador (above right),* which had launched a vigorous antidrug campaign. Meanwhile, many people live off the drug trade indirectly.

Frederic Alban/Gamma–Liaison

For example, Peruvian guerrillas (the Senderos Luminosos) forbid the farmers under their control to produce extra food for the cities (which are considered politically corrupt) but permit them to grow coca leaves for sale. The

Omar Bradley/Picture Group

resulting income can then be used to buy weapons for their cause.

If selling drugs is seen as the vehicle for some people's economic and political survival or prosperity, can we eradicate drug trafficking without providing an economic substitute—especially when the United States provides the most lucrative market for the traffickers? When people and countries reap great profit through illegal means, what alternatives can be suggested? And how can any one country, acting alone, curb the flow of an international commodity?

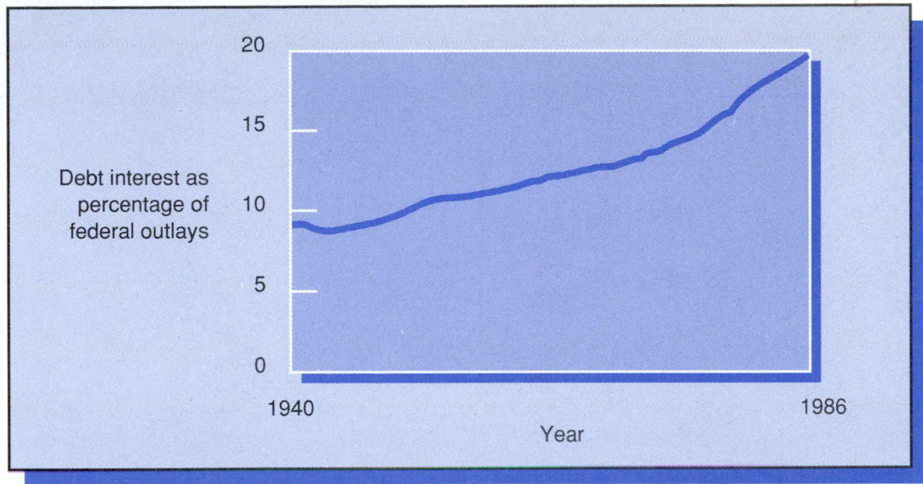

★ **Figure 18-3**
Interest the federal government paid on public debt, 1940–1986
SOURCE: U.S. Bureau of the Census, *Statistical Abstract of the United States, 1988* (Washington, D.C.: U.S. Government Printing Office, 1987), p. 297.

failed to reach stipulated goals in their annual budget. But this provision was declared unconstitutional by the U.S. Supreme Court. Subsequent budgets fell short of Gramm-Rudman goals. The financial community's fears that Washington was unable to handle the deficit problem sparked a dramatic decline in the stock market in October 1987. In response to the worst crash since 1929, Congress and President Reagan reached an agreement on spending cuts to bring down the deficit in future budgets.

There are two ways to achieve immediate and dramatic reductions in the budget deficit, and thereby in the national debt: cut spending and increase taxes. Although neither option is politically popular, cutting spending is particularly difficult because many programs are uncontrollable. Funds for them cannot be increased or decreased by presidential decision without a change in existing federal laws. Beneficiaries of the so-called entitlement programs—social security, Medicare, Medicaid, unemployment insurance, and the like—are entitled to payments by law; and the government cannot fail to make payments it has previously contracted to pay, such as those for interest on the national debt, farm price supports, and multiyear defense contracts. In 1986, 75 percent of the budget consisted of these relatively uncontrollable outlays, leaving only 25 percent subject to congressional and presidential manipulation for deficit reduction.[13]

With few options on the cutting side, analysts in the late 1980s considered raising taxes. Liberal Democrats discussed a repeal of the 1981 tax cuts, which reduced revenues during the Reagan years by about $200 billion. They accused the Reagan administration of deliberately incurring deficits to create a fiscal crisis in order to keep Congress from spending money on social programs. With his tax cuts and dramatic increases in military spending, there was little left for new or expanded social programs. In 1988, Reagan's OMB director predicted how each party would solve the deficit problem: "Republicans will have a 20 percent revenue increase and 80 percent reduction in services. The Democrats will be 50–50."[14]

★ Table 18-5
Federal budgets, deficits, and debt, 1969–1987 (actual, in billions of dollars)

Fiscal year	*Receipts*	*Outlays*	*Surplus or deficit (−)*	*Budget era of president*[a]	*Debt*[b]
1969	$186.9	$ 183.6	$ 3.2	Johnson	$ 367.1
1970	192.8	195.6	− 2.8	Nixon	382.6
1971	187.1	210.2	−23.0	Nixon	409.5
1972	207.3	230.7	−23.4	Nixon	437.3
1973	230.8	245.7	−14.9	Nixon	468.4
1974	263.2	269.4	− 6.1	Nixon	486.2
1975	279.1	332.3	−53.2	Nixon	544.1
1976	298.1	371.8	−73.7	Ford	631.9
1977	355.6	409.2	−53.6	Ford	709.1
1978	399.6	458.7	−59.2	Carter	780.4
1979	463.3	503.5	−40.2	Carter	833.8
1980	517.1	590.9	−73.8	Carter	914.3
1981	599.3	678.2	−78.9	Carter	1,003.9
1982	617.8	745.7	−127.9	Reagan	1,147.0
1983	600.6	808.3	−207.8	Reagan	1,381.9
1984	666.5	851.8	−185.3	Reagan	1,576.7
1985	734.1	946.3	−212.3	Reagan	1,827.2
1986	769.1	989.8	−220.7	Reagan	2,132.9
1987[c]	842.4	1,015.6	−173.2	Reagan	2,372.4

[a]The budget era of a president begins with the first full fiscal year of that administration, reflecting the first budget for which a president is responsible, and continues through the last fiscal year for which a president is responsible.

[b]Outstanding gross debt.

[c]Estimated.

SOURCE: U.S. Bureau of the Census, *Statistical Abstract of the United States, 1988* (Washington, D.C.: U.S. Government Printing Office, 1987), p. 291.

During the 1988 presidential campaign, George Bush said he opposed tax increases. He and other conservative Republicans advocated three alternatives: a balanced-budget amendment, the line-item veto, and across-the-board spending cuts. A balanced-budget amendment is a proposed amendment to the Constitution requiring the federal government to adopt a balanced budget except in time of war. During peacetime, Congress would need a three-fifths vote to authorize deficit spending, instead of the simple majority it now needs. Proponents say that such an amendment would make it harder to go into debt and that similar provisions in many state constitutions have kept state governments out of debt. In response, opponents note that the federal government needs to maintain its flexibility in case of crises other than war (such as the Great Depression) and that such an amendment would strain state and local budgets, which derive 20 percent of their revenues from federal funds. By July 1984, the legislatures of thirty-two states (just two fewer

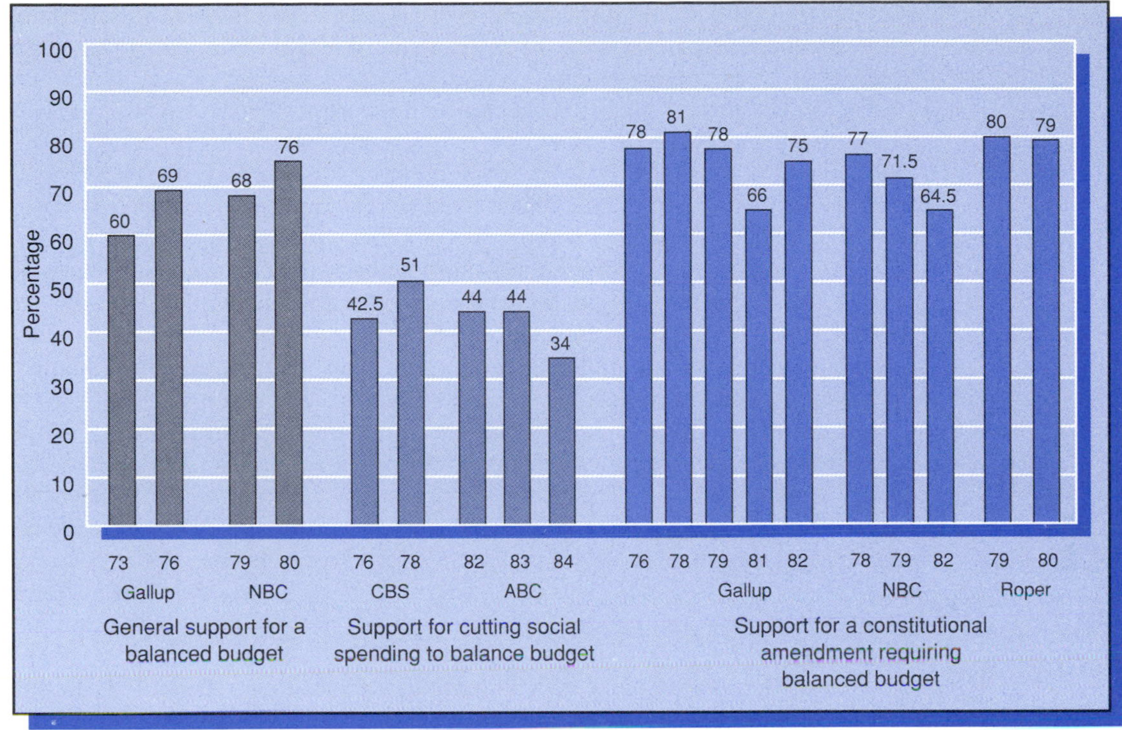

★ **Figure 18-4**
Support for a balanced budget, as indicated by polls, 1973–1984
SOURCE: Paul E. Peterson, "The New Politics of Deficits," in John E. Chubb and Paul E. Peterson (eds.), *The New Direction in American Politics* (Washington, D.C.: Brookings, 1985), p. 387.

than the two-thirds required by the Constitution) had submitted petitions to Congress requesting that a constitutional convention be held to propose a balanced-budget amendment. In fact, a 1983 Gallup poll showed 71 percent of respondents in favor and only 21 percent opposed to such an amendment.[15] (See figure 18-4.)

A line-item veto would also have to be introduced as a constitutional amendment. It would give the president the power to delete specific items from appropriations bills, a power that most governors have. Without this power, the president must veto an entire, multi-billion-dollar appropriations bill even if he finds only parts of it objectionable. Both Reagan and Bush supported the line-item veto, but it has not enjoyed the same groundswell of popular support that the balanced-budget amendment has. Some observers insist it would undermine the framers' intent to give the people control of the purse strings through their elected representatives in Congress.

Finally, some conservatives support across-the-board spending cuts as a solution to the deficit crisis. Across-the-board cuts would require every government agency to reduce its spending by the same percentage, say 3 to 4 percent. This measure would have the advantage of forcing all agencies to tighten their belts equally and could be easily enforced. But it has the disadvantage of failing to distinguish between good and bad programs and between fat and lean programs.

Taxes. While the problem of a ballooning national debt is a relative newcomer on the fiscal scene, the problem of an equitable tax system is one of the oldest problems faced by makers of fiscal policy. Everyone seems to want someone else to carry the tax burden. Surveys have indicted that about 90 percent of Americans believe the federal income tax is unfair.[16] Certainly, tax policy is technical and legalistic, and is controlled by a few key legislators (in particular the members of the House Ways and Means and Senate Finance committees), making it easy prey for special interests.

The federal government generates most of its revenue from individual income taxes (about 40 percent), social security taxes (about 35 percent), and corporate income taxes (about 12 percent). Since 1960, the proportion from income taxes has remained fairly stable, while dependence on social security taxes has doubled and reliance on corporate income taxes has been cut nearly in half.

In chapter 17 we saw how social security funds are earmarked for social security entitlement programs. A change in this tax would affect the scale of social security expenditures, but not other programs. It is politically risky to advocate reductions in social security benefits, as President Reagan found when he made his initial budget-trimming proposal in 1981. Older Americans are very much concerned about this issue and they vote in large numbers. As Reagan's OMB director noted, "The Democrats took the Republicans to the cleaners on Social Security in the '82 elections."[17]

Liberal Democrats want corporations to shoulder a greater tax burden, noting how their contribution to the federal Treasury has declined from 20 percent under President Kennedy to 12 percent under Presidents Reagan and Bush. Conservatives respond that corporations simply pass the cost of increased taxes along to consumers in the form of higher prices.

Excise taxes are taxes on items the government wants you to consume less of, such as alcoholic beverages and cigarettes (hence the nickname "sin tax"). The proportion of revenues generated by excise taxes has dropped from 12 percent in 1960 to 4 percent in 1987. They play a relatively minor role in the total revenue picture.

Although efforts have been made to revise corporate, excise, and social security taxes, most energy has been spent in the area of personal income taxes. In 1913, the Sixteenth Amendment to the Constitution gave Congress the power to collect personal income taxes. (A constitutional amendment was necessary, as we have noted, because the U.S. Supreme Court had declared income taxes unconstitutional in 1895.) The individual income tax has always been structured as a progressive tax, with the tax rate increasing as income climbs. The top rate has fluctuated dramatically over the years (see figure 18-5).

Before the 1980s, the last major changes in the tax law had been made during World War II, when, in order to finance the war, Congress introduced withholding of taxes from wages and changed rates so that most Americans became subject to a federal income tax for the first time.

Almost every administration since that of President John Kennedy has tried to reform the tax system, but special interests have effectively lobbied Congress to protect and expand their tax breaks. Tax breaks are called **tax preferences** (or "tax expenditures," because taxes that are not collected are lost to the Treasury). Between 1967 and 1987, tax preferences increased nearly tenfold, to $320 billion.[18] Table 18-6 shows some of the largest loopholes.

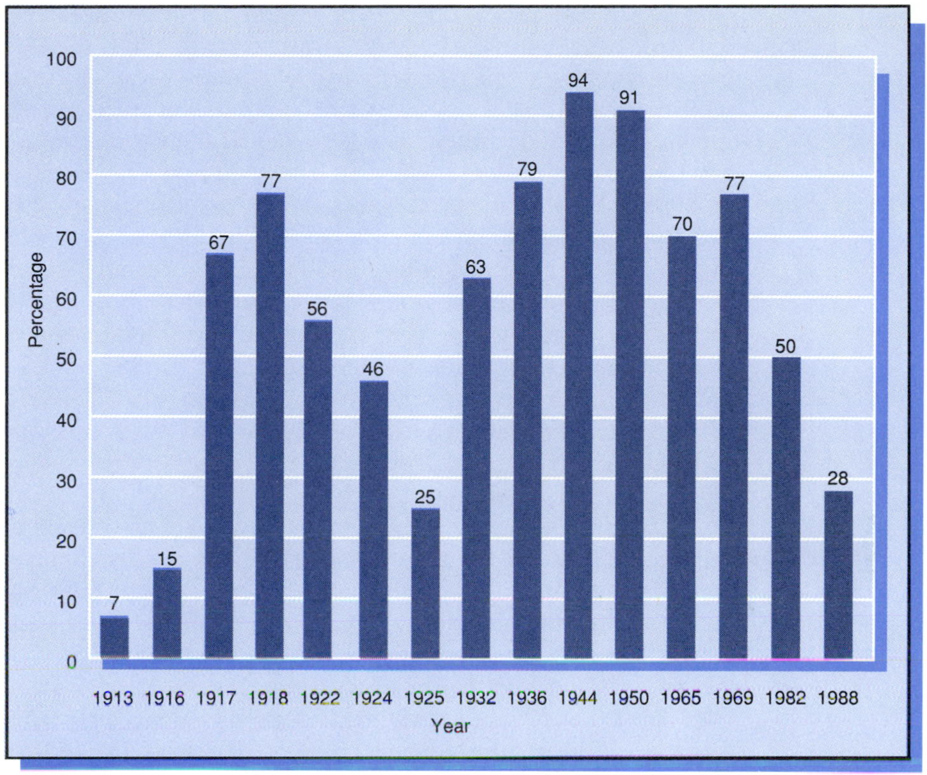

★ Figure 18-5

Top individual income tax rates, 1913–1988

SOURCE: Gary L. Klott, *The New York Times Complete Guide to the New Tax Law* (New York: Times Books, 1986), p. 10.

★ Table 18-6

Largest tax preferences, 1987 (billions of dollars)

Exclusion of employers' pension contributions	$45.7
Accelerated depreciation of machinery and equipment	32.8
Deductibility of mortgage interest	24.9
Capital gains	23.4
Deductibility of state and local taxes	18.8
Investment credits	14.1
Exclusion of Individual Retirement Accounts	13.8
Exclusion of Social Security benefits	12.9
Deductibility of interest on consumer credit	12.0
Exclusion of interest on state and local debt	10.2
Deductibility of charitable contributions	9.5

SOURCE: U.S. Bureau of the Census, *Statistical Abstract of the United States, 1988* (Washington, D.C.: U.S. Government Printing Office, 1987), p. 296.

As tax preferences proliferated, debate intensified about fairness and unproductive tax incentives. Why should businesses be able to write off the costs of factory equipment when most individuals cannot write off the costs of their automobiles? Why should homeowners be able to deduct their mortgage interest while renters cannot deduct their rent? Why should the tax system nourish tax shelters and other wasteful investments that have led to billions of dollars of misallocated resources? Movie stars, professional athletes, doctors, and other wealthy professionals often invest in shopping centers or office buildings to whittle their tax bills down to little or nothing. Why should some corporations be able to pay no corporate income taxes even though they reap millions of dollars in profits? In 1978, for instance, fourteen large corporations paid no federal income tax; among them were U.S. Steel, Occidental Petroleum, American Airlines, and Southern California Edison.

By the 1980s, concerns about fairness and misdirected tax incentives had reached such a crescendo that the president and Congress were able to revamp the tax code in a radical way with the 1986 Tax Reform Act. According to Dan Rostenkowski (D-Illinois), chair of the House Ways and Means Committee, a concern for fairness was the reason Capitol Hill was finally able to beat back special interests and pass comprehensive tax reform. "It wasn't low tax rates or larger paychecks that brought working men and women behind tax reform," he noted. "It was fairness—knowing they weren't subsidizing a loophole for the guy down the street, or the corporation across town."[19]

The Tax Reform Act of 1986 made the most sweeping changes in the seventy-three-year history of the federal income tax. It sharply lowered tax rates and closed many tax loopholes. It lowered the top individual income tax rate from 50 percent to 28 percent and condensed the old fifteen-bracket system into just two rate brackets of 15 and 28 percent. Corporate tax rates were reduced from 46 to 34 percent. To pay for reduced rates, the law set up a timetable to phase out tax loopholes by 1991. It eliminated deductions for state and local sales taxes, the charitable deduction for nonitemizers, the deduction for interest on personal and consumer loans, and the deduction for contributions to an individual retirement account (for certain taxpayers covered by a company pension plan). Business people could deduct only 80 percent of the cost of wining and dining clients. Students had to pay taxes on part of their scholarship income. Unemployment compensation became fully taxable. Capital gains (money earned from the sale of property) became taxed at the same rates as other income.

The tax cuts for individuals were designed to shift more of the burden onto corporations. Between 1987 and 1991, businesses were slated to pay about $120 billion more, and individual income taxes were to be reduced by a similar amount. Some industries fared better than others. The 1986 law curtailed a long list of investment incentives and special tax breaks for particular industries, such as heavy manufacturers, real estate developers, large financial institutions, and multinational corporations. While they suffered from the loss of tax breaks, other firms that never had such breaks for investment incentives—including retailers, media companies, high-tech firms, and service-oriented businesses—benefited from the lowered rates.[20]

The 1986 reform fell short of being perfectly fair, however. Among the complaints were that it unfairly changed the rules in the middle of the game for many taxpayers; that homeowners retained interest deductions but renters got no corresponding break; that oil and gas industries retained most of their special tax breaks while other industries lost theirs; and that several hundred companies, private organizations, and civic projects were able to get their members of Congress

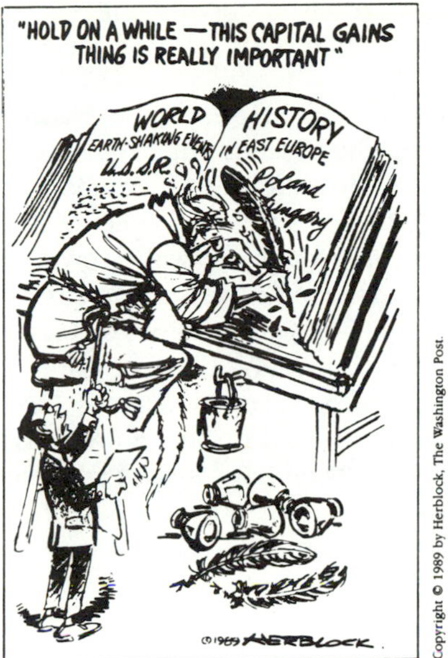

to obtain specially tailored transition rules to preserve some tax benefits for projects already in the works.[21]

Regulatory Policy

The federal government can use means other than monetary and fiscal policies to control the American economy. One of the most controversial tools at the government's disposal is regulatory policy, by which the federal government tries to reconcile private economic power with broader public purposes. Some regulations affect overall economic growth by making it more or less profitable to engage in certain economic activities. Other regulatory activities, such as antitrust legislation, affect the overall economic structure of the United States. Naturally, the level of government regulatory activity arouses considerable controversy between advocates of a market economy and those who favor a mixed economic system.

Wage and Price Controls. A drastic form of economic regulation is **wage and price controls.** During times of war Congress has authorized the president to set wages and prices for a specified period of time. President Nixon implemented such controls in 1971, when the United States' involvement in Vietnam was having an inflationary impact on the economy. Nixon imposed a ninety-day freeze on wages, prices, rents, and interest rates to stem runaway inflation. Controls were implemented by a Cost of Living Council with a separate Pay Board and Price Commission staffed by representatives of labor, business, and public-interest groups. Most economists agree that such controls work in the short run but are of questionable use in the long run. Inflation is built on psychology as well as economics. During the 1970s, wage and price controls were popular with the public because they gave people the feeling that the government was trying to do something equitable to curb inflation.[22] The program worked politically through the 1972 elections, but not economically. As if to make up for lost time, prices shot up after the program stopped. The wealthy relied on income from stock dividends and capital gains, and executives received stock options, which were not subject to controls. The burden of controlling inflation fell on citizens less favored.[23]

Antitrust Legislation. Another form of economic regulation is **antitrust legislation,** which calls for the regulation or breaking up of firms that dominate their markets in order to restore economic competition. The Interstate Commerce Act of 1887, for instance, was directed at the railroads. Instead of nationalizing the railroads, in accordance with growing popular sentiment at the time, Congress established the Interstate Commerce Commission (ICC) to regulate them. The 1887 law was the first significant piece of regulatory legislation passed by Congress, and the ICC was our nation's first regulatory agency, with independent power to control the business practices of railroads. Two pieces of legislation passed to break up monopolies were the Sherman Anti-Trust Act of 1890 and the Clayton Anti-Trust Act of 1914. These laws sought to reduce the existing market power of firms, to monitor mergers and prevent those that would decrease competition, and to eliminate price fixing. Antitrust laws are enforced by the Antitrust Division of the U.S. Department of Justice. Lawsuits can be brought by the attorney general against violators.

Antitrust legislation has proved to be a limited government tool, however. It is often poorly written, awkward to enforce, and time-consuming to implement. Decades of court battles are frequently necessary to prove collusion and anticompetitive practices. For many large firms, the benefits of a delayed ruling outweigh the costs of a trial. The government has won some major cases, however, most notably the breakup of the Standard Oil trust in 1911 and of American Telephone and Telegraph in 1983. But the requirements for evidence and the difficulty of proving a case make antitrust laws a slow remedy at best. Between 1950 and 1967, one of the most active merger periods in our history, 199 cases were filed by the Antitrust Division and in only 48 cases were companies forced to divest themselves of anything.[24]

Deregulation. Regulatory activity in the United States grew in two spurts: economic regulatory activity increased in response to the Great Depression of the 1930s, and social regulatory activity developed in response to the social movements of the 1960s. Economic regulatory agencies exert economic controls on firms' market behavior, while social regulatory agencies regulate firms' nonmarket behavior in such matters as hiring, safety, health, fraud, and discrimination. In both cases, government regulations affect the cost of doing the nation's business.

Among economic regulatory agencies are the Interstate Commerce Commission (ICC), the Federal Trade Commission (FTC), the Federal Communications Commission (FCC), and the Securities and Exchange Commission (SEC). Some social regulatory agencies are the Equal Employment Opportunity Commission (EEOC), the Food and Drug Administration (FDA), the Environmental Protection Agency (EPA), and the Occupational Safety and Health Administration (OSHA).

In the 1970s, the private sector went on the offensive to push for deregulation of their economic activities. Many executives resented being told by government agencies whom to hire and fire and how to produce. They objected to the costs of filling out forms to prove compliance, of cleaning up the environment, and of improving safety measures at the workplace. In 1972, some of the largest corporations formed the Business Roundtable, an umbrella organization to lobby Congress and federal agencies for rules more compatible with the needs of business.[25]

★ Regulation in action: Chemists at the Environmental Protection Agency conduct water purity tests to see whether water departments and companies are providing their customers with safe drinking water.

Many business people blamed regulation for contributing to the inflation of the 1970s. A former chair of the Council on Wage and Price Stability said that regulation was the source of a ¾ to 1½ percent increase in the cost of living each year.[26] Executives claimed that the time and energy spent complying with federal directives could be more profitably spent on research and development. Regulations contributed to a slackened growth rate for the U.S. economy and loss of our nation's competitive advantage worldwide. Small businesses said they could not afford to comply with the same rules devised for big corporations and could not handle the same amount of paperwork. Large firms contended that they were being penalized for their success.

Proponents of deregulation emphasized the economic costs of regulations. One study estimated that regulation cost the private sector $120 billion in 1980.[27] A study by the Business Roundtable found that the cost to forty-eight corporations of regulations by the EPA, EEOC, OSHA, FTC, and the Departments of Energy and Labor was $2.6 billion.[28] Another study concluded that FDA rules cost Americans three to four times as much as the economic benefits they produced, and that auto safety devices had no effect on the post-1965 accident death rate.[29] Proponents of deregulation say the direct and indirect costs of regulation average $100 billion a year and that the private sector is motivated by profits to seek safer working conditions and products. Unsafe working conditions raise insurance costs and wages for dangerous work. And unsafe products invite lawsuits and raise insurance costs.

Defenders of government regulations counter that critics emphasize the costs and downplay the benefits of regulations. They argue that the figures on the cost of regulation are not offset by the savings in medical bills, damaged crops, property erosion, and expenses that would otherwise be borne by victims of pollution. They contend that most accounts of the inflationary impact of government regulation do not calculate such savings, adding that many benefits do not have a direct monetary value. Clean air, for instance, is not traded on the market. Regulation defenders list the positive accomplishments of social regulatory agencies: a decline in racial and sexual discrimination, increased consumer information (such as the listing of ingredients on food packages) that permits informed product choice, a decline in accidental workplace deaths by half since OSHA and its sister agency regulating coal mines came into existence, improved air quality (between 1972 and 1976, for instance, carbon monoxide levels in eight cities declined 46 percent), improved water quality, a decline in accidental childhood poisonings, and a decline in highway deaths (a 15 percent drop between 1965 and 1972, even before the post-OPEC speed reductions).[30]

Defenders of regulation argue that regulation has become a scapegoat for industry woes. Susan and Martin Tolchin cite the case of Anaconda Copper, which closed its plant in Anaconda, Montana, in 1980. The corporation said it had to close because of the prohibitive costs ($300–400 million) of compliance with regulations. Skeptics said the real reasons were a costly labor dispute, poor management that sacrificed technological innovation for short-term profits, and the nationalization of its mines in Chile. Government regulators said the compliance costs were not as high as the company said (more like $134 million) and that they were willing to negotiate a flexible timetable.[31]

It is much more difficult to compare the costs and benefits of social regulations than to compare those of economic regulations. Although the costs are easily identified and fall heavily on business, the benefits are hard to measure and are reaped by the population as a whole. Proponents of social regulations cite studies showing that the lives saved, injuries prevented, and productivity increased by regulation save billions of dollars each year for society.[32] They note that the private sector is quick to want "government off its back" when it comes to regulations, but eager to have government on its side when it comes to subsidies that benefit them or bail them out of trouble.

Subsidy Policy

The fourth tool the government has at its disposal to control the economy is subsidy policy. **Subsidies** are governmental measures that work through the market system to achieve goals without increasing regulation. They encourage production or maintain income.

Tariffs. One of the oldest forms of subsidy in the American political economy is the **tariff,** a tax on imported goods. Tariffs make imported goods more expensive so that consumers will purchase domestically produced goods instead. It also "protects" new domestic industries that cannot compete internationally without government help. The use of tariffs, sometimes called protectionism, is the opposite of a free-trade policy, which permits imports and exports to flow freely between countries.

The tariff was one of the key economic issues during the last half of the nineteenth century. The Morrill Tariff Act of 1860 was the first systematic effort to protect American industry from foreign competition. The result was an increase in the price of manufactured goods. The South, a net importer of such goods, had opposed protective tariffs for decades. The difference between the tariff price and the market price represents a sort of private tax taken from the consumer to subsidize business prosperity. It also brought revenue to the federal government and helped avoid an income tax on the emerging corporate elite. A high-tariff policy prevailed until World War I. Shortly after the war ended, the income tax began to replace the tariff as the major source of federal revenue. Most major American

★ During an embargo on the export of grain to the Soviet Union, the United States had an excess of grain to store. One place that was available to store the overflow was a street in a midwestern town.

industries, such as steel, developed with the help of tariffs. As we shall see, tariffs, protectionism, and free trade continued to be major political issues throughout the 1980s.

Price Supports. In addition to subsidizing industry, the federal government has supported the agricultural sector of the economy. Agricultural subsidies began in 1933, when the federal government passed measures to forestall bankruptcies among farmers. **Price supports** are government guarantees of the prices of certain agricultural commodities. In return for the guarantee of favorable prices, farmers accept certain regulations on the amount of land they can work in a given year. The purpose of keeping land out of production is to keep crop output down and prices up. Historically, price-support programs have benefited larger, more profitable farmers more than smaller, poorer ones.[33]

In 1982 the cost of direct payments to farmers, subsidies, loans, and storage charges totaled over $12 billion. Despite these government outlays, the farm sector became increasingly depressed because of high interest rates, expensive energy, and falling commodity prices and land values. The government began a new program: payments in kind (PIK). Farmers were paid partly in cash but mostly in kind to idle their land. Prices were not affected and many family farms were lost to foreclosure. PIK cost $19 billion in 1983 and mostly benefited large corporate farms. In 1985 Congress passed new legislation that reduced price supports in the hope of lowering prices and thereby stimulating the export trade and reducing agricultural surpluses.[34] And in 1988 Congress passed a $3 billion relief package to aid drought-striken farmers.

The effectiveness of price supports is severely curtailed by U.S. foreign policy and by European countries' subsidization of their agricultural exports. In the early 1980s, for example, huge amounts of American grain were stockpiled as a consequence of an embargo on the export of grain to the Soviet Union. President Jimmy

Carter's embargo in response to the Soviet invasion of Afghanistan in 1979 increased the domestic glut but imposed little hardship on the Soviet Union, which purchased grain from Canada, Australia, and Argentina. Whereas the Soviet Union imported 74 percent of its grain from the United States in 1979, by 1987 it imported only 17 percent. As a result of the embargo, American taxpayers were paying to store millions of metric tons of corn and wheat, farmers faced low commodity prices, and the United States gained a reputation as an unreliable trade partner. Not only does the European Community have a reputation for more reliable service, but it also subsidizes its agricultural exports much more heavily than the United States does. It spent about $7 billion on export subsidies in fiscal 1983, in comparison with the United States' $1.25 billion.[35]

Loan Guarantees. The federal government has subsidized not only sectors of the economy but also major cities and private corporations through loan guarantees. A **loan guarantee** is a government promise to a bank to back a loan the bank makes to a creditor. If the creditor, in this case a city or a corporation, defaults on the loan, the federal government picks up the tab.

Perhaps the most notable case of the rescue of a city by the federal government occurred in 1975, when New York City was in danger of default. An enormous deficit and large annual payments on short-term and long-term debt created a crisis situation. Lenders feared for the value of their New York City bonds and the city's credit rating dropped. The city turned to the state and federal governments for aid. Congress appropriated more than $2 billion in loans and loan guarantees to prevent the financial collapse of the city. Supporters of the bailout pointed to New York City's unique role as an immigration hub for the nation, to the fact that the city sent to the federal government more money in taxes than it received from federal programs, and to the importance of protecting bondholders' investments for the future of all American cities. Opponents contended that city employees were overpaid and that the private sector was better able to revitalize cities. They supported such measures as urban enterprise zones—urban areas in which businesses are encouraged to locate in order to take advantage of low-interest loans and tax incentives. Such zones are created to attract job-creating businesses to inner cities. Jobs and businesses would increase the tax base of distressed cities, thereby alleviating their budget problems.[36]

The federal government has also bailed out private corporations. In 1980, for example, the government provided Chrysler Corporation with $1.5 billion in loan guarantees. Chrysler has since repaid its loans and experienced more favorable progress than had been anticipated.

But the loan, unprecedented in scale, sparked considerable controversy. Proponents argued that the economy could not afford the collapse of its tenth-largest corporation. An estimated 131,000 Chrysler employees and 250,000 suppliers and dealers would have been affected. And the Treasury would have lost close to $3 billion in revenues. Organized labor strongly supported Chrysler's request, pointing out that 27 percent of the company's employees were minorities. Some conservative economists, however, argued that Chrysler should have gone bankrupt so that workers and facilities could be transferred to more efficient areas of the economy. One senator advanced the free-market position during Senate hearings on the Chrysler bailout: "What we are doing is rewarding bad management, ignoring the decisions of the marketplace, and distorting the forces of competition."[37] Moreover, some people saw the bailout as a surrender to the corporate-banking

★ One of the most pervasive symbols of the growth of U.S. trade abroad is the American fast-food restaurant, which can be found in virtually every major world city. Here in Hamburg, West Germany, the hamburger returns to its city of origin.

sector. The government put the people's money at risk to ensure continued private profit. And it demonstrated its bias toward helping large corporations and ignoring small businesses (the millions of small businesses received altogether only $10.4 billion in loan guarantees, as against the $1.5 billion received by one giant, Chrysler).[38]

In an even more dramatic bailout, in 1988 the Federal Home Loan Bank Board orchestrated a $38 billion assistance package for insolvent savings and loan associations. The government closed more than two hundred failing savings and loan institutions and arranged for them to be taken over by new investors, promising loan guarantees and direct subsidies.

★ The U.S. Economy in a Changing World

Since the end of World War II, the U.S. government has played a dominant role not only in the national economy but also in the world economy. Before the war, trade represented less than 5 percent of the U.S. gross national product. Between 1970 and 1980 the trade portion of GNP doubled, from 11 percent to 22 percent. With only 5 percent of the world's population, America produced nearly 20 percent of global exports. The United States also came to dominate international banking and finance. Today, other countries owe U.S. banks billions of dollars, and the dollar serves as the key currency for virtually all major international transactions. Financial crises in America reverberate around the globe.

Economic domination helped America become a military and political superpower. The United States derived significant political benefits from its domination

The Stock Market Crash of 1987

On October 19, 1987, a warning flashed across computer screens in high-tech control rooms around the globe: RED ALERT! Was this the first word of a dreaded nuclear sneak attack? Had an atomic power plant suffered a massive meltdown, spreading radiation to the four winds? No. This was a threat of a different nature. These computer screens were not part of a great power's supersecret situation room. This network linked the world's leading financial markets and the news hit like a 100-megaton bomb—STOCK MARKET CRASH ON WALL STREET!

The 1987 Wall Street crash, which saw the Dow Jones average plunge 508 points in one day, had many causes. Although the drop cost an estimated $1 trillion in paper wealth and cut investors' confidence, it did not damage the American economy so severely as the great crash of 1929. In the long run, the "how" of the crash was as important as the "why." The "how" involved the internationalization of the American economy and the technological changes that linked the world's major financial capitals.

Information, along with the ability to transfer funds and complete transactions, is what greases the wheels of today's stock exchanges. In the past, transfer of information and execution of business decisions moved with glacier-like speed. Now, with satellite networks and high-speed computers, London, Tokyo, Hong Kong, New York, and Paris pulse to the beat of fax machines and display terminals. Commodities, stocks, precious metals, oil, and even the fast-food empires that fuel students everywhere are bought and sold in a global shopping mall that is open twenty-four hours a day.

If good news travels fast in the global shopping mall, bad news travels at close to the speed of light. A crop failure in America's farm belt can send commodity prices soaring. Political unrest in the Middle East can raise doubts about oil supplies. A drop in stock prices on Wall Street is mirrored in other markets. In the immediate aftermath of "Black Monday" on Wall Street, most foreign stock markets shut down for several days to avoid chaos. When they reopened on October 26, aftershocks were still reverberating around the globe: Tokyo down 5 percent, Hong Kong down 33 percent, London down 6 percent, Frankfurt down 6 percent, and New York down 8 percent.

Since October 1987, stock market and government officials have taken steps to temper some of the practices that led to the crash. But reformers were cautious, for fear of killing the golden goose. By and large, global trading has provided new sources of investment for the United States and many other countries. The key challenge for America is to determine how to reap the benefits of global financial markets without sacrificing local autonomy and control. ★

SOURCE: Lewis M. Simons, "As Goes Tokyo, So Goes the World," *San Jose Mercury News*, November 1, 1987, pp. 1E, 10E.

of global trade and banking after World War II. The strong dollar made it possible to station troops in some forty nations overseas, a vital part of the cold war strategy of "containing" the Soviet Union. Friendly relations abroad were also reinforced through U.S. investment and foreign aid. Today millions of Americans are linked to the global economy as producers, consumers, and investors.

Trade Policy

The United States has been more nearly self-sufficient than many other industrialized nations. Japan and most of Western Europe, for example, are completely dependent on imported oil. Still, Americans have come to recognize that in order to enjoy a strong economy and an effective foreign policy, the United States must maintain a healthy trading relationship with the rest of the world (see figure 18-6).

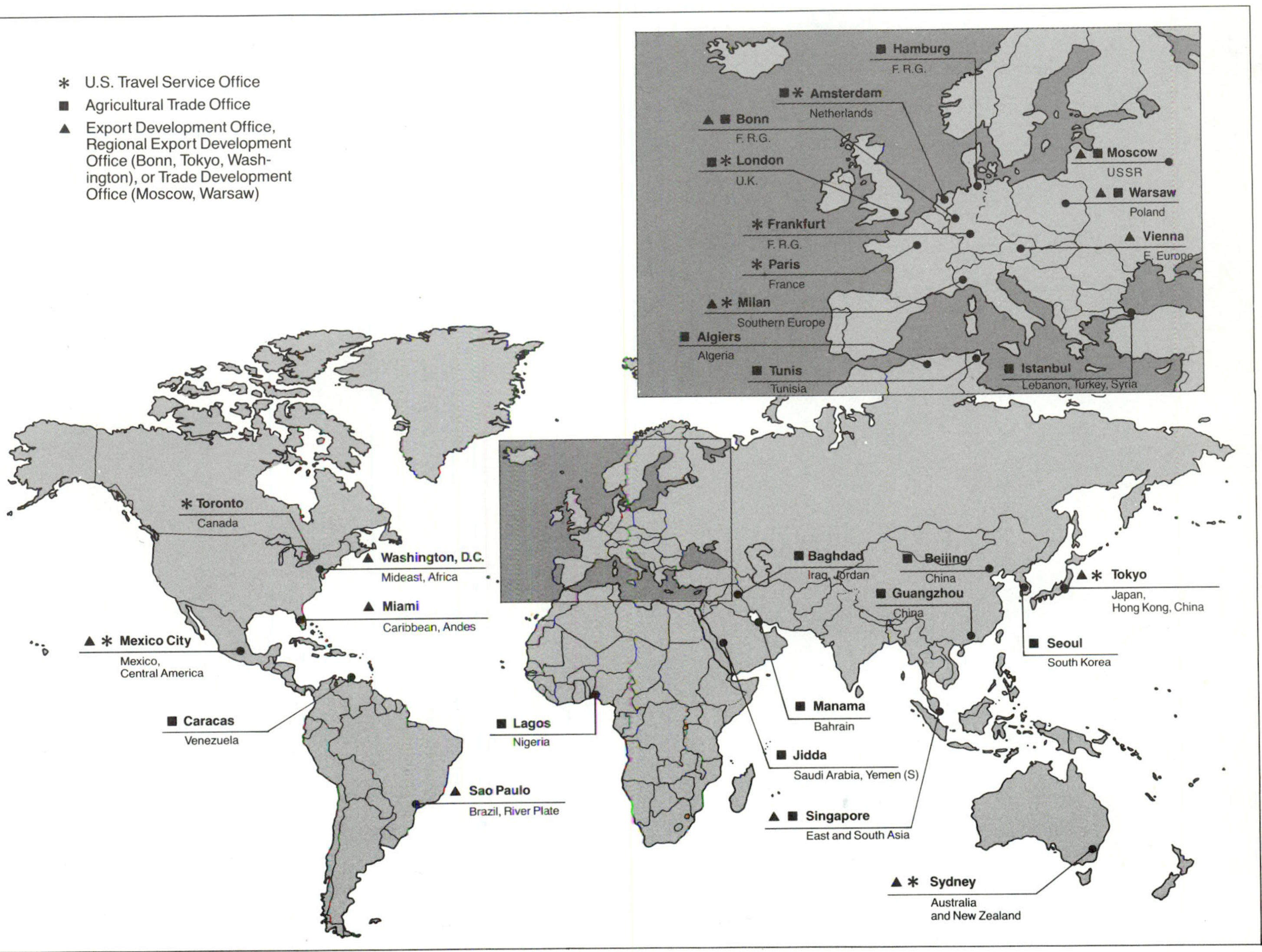

★ **Figure 18-6** Trade promotion offices abroad. SOURCE: U.S. Government Printing Office.

★ First a novelty, now a necessity: Since the end of World War II, Americans' growing demand for imported automobiles has contributed to an increase in our trade deficit. The United States is no longer the world's leading producer of cars.

The most universally recognized measure of a nation's trade position is the **balance of trade.** The balance of trade indicates payment for imported and exported goods. A nation that spends more on imports than it earns on exports faces a negative balance of trade. The balance of trade, however, is only one component of a nation's overall international economic transactions, reflected in its balance of payments. The **balance of payments** is a complex computation that counts all financial flows in and out of a country. Along with the obvious category of trade, many other transactions go into the balance of payments: foreign investment, profits sent back to the United States from American companies operating abroad, foreign aid sent to other countries, military spending abroad, money spent by American tourists abroad and by foreign tourists here, and even money sent to relatives in "the old country."

Of all the components of the balance of payments, the balance of trade is the most visible and the most politically controversial. After decades of enjoying trade surpluses, in the 1970s the United States experienced sporadic trade deficits, which reached around $124 billion in 1985.

The causes of this decline were complex. One factor was an artificially strong dollar. A country's trade position is affected by the exchange rate of its currency. The exchange rate reflects the value of a country's currency in a foreign currency. Throughout most of the 1980s, the dollar was worth a lot in foreign currencies, in part because our high interest rates attracted foreign money into the United States. Foreign investors, seeking high interest earnings in U.S. banks and government bonds, readily exchanged their local currencies for dollars, and the resulting demand kept the international value of the dollar strong. A highly valued dollar was great

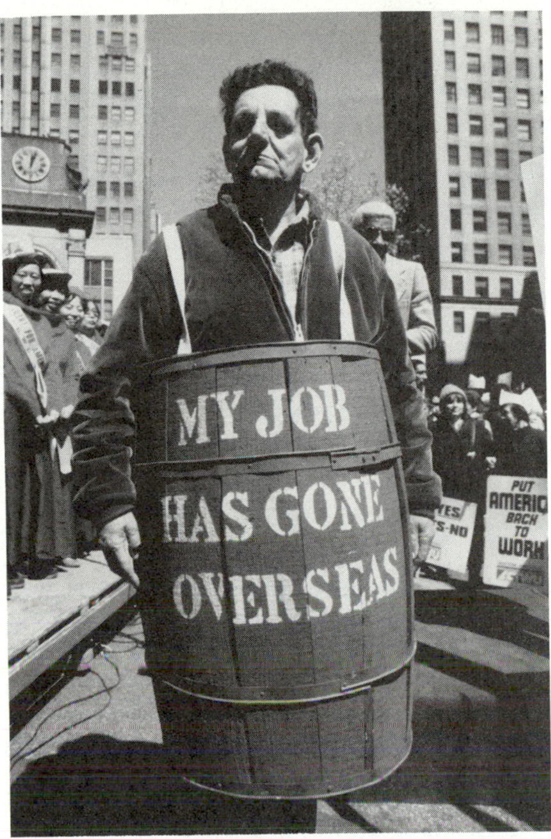

★ Many unemployed Americans have blamed their plight either on what they see as unfair foreign competition or on U.S. industries that have relocated in nations with cheaper labor costs.

for American tourists, who could buy a lot abroad, and for retailers, who imported boatloads of electronic gadgets from Japan and elsewhere. For American businesses that depended on exports, however, the overvalued dollar made American products very expensive overseas.

Another factor that hurt U.S. exports was a recession that hit many less developed nations. Negative economic growth in combination with the high prices of U.S. goods meant that many foreign consumers simply had to go without. A sluggish economic growth rate in Western Europe also hurt U.S. exports. American consumers, with more money in their pockets, spent freely on imported goods while their European counterparts were more frugal.

In the late 1980s, the federal government responded to political pressure on several fronts to do something about the trade deficit. It let the value of the dollar fall to boost exports. But nagging budget deficits continued to attract foreign investors, whose purchase of U.S. bonds financed much of our national debt. Moreover, the government extended credit through the Export-Import Bank, a government bank established in 1934 to help finance U.S. exports through loans, guarantees, and insurance so that exporters and private banks can finance ventures with reduced

© Signe Wilkinson

risk. In 1987 Congress appropriated $100 million for use as grants in combination with loans. Overall, the bank does about $40 billion worth of business.[39]

Despite the complexity of the technical factors that have cut U.S. exports, many workers, especially those in steel, autos, and other heavy industries, found a simple scapegoat—unfair foreign competition. Claiming that other nations such as Japan restricted imports while offering subsidies to their own exporting industries, segments of U.S. labor and business called for protection. As we have seen, the cry for protectionism was hardly new. The difference lay in the number and diversity of industries affected. Labor and management, though unlikely allies, sometimes banded together to demand that tariffs and other means be adopted to discourage imports.

Complicating the problem of imports was the relocation of some industries to less developed nations with lower labor and other overhead costs. The issue of so-called runaway shops affected electronics, agriculture, textiles, and other industries. Some communities even banded together to try to retain established firms or attract new ones.

Regardless of the proposed solution, foreign competition became an increasingly controversial issue in the 1980s. President Reagan staunchly opposed protectionism and advocated open markets and free trade. His administration argued that America had not, in fact, lost jobs to foreign competition. A high-ranking State Department official put the administration's case this way:

> It is said that we have "exported jobs." But where are they? In other countries, unemployment has not fallen as it has here. Those jobs that some would have you believe were exported have simply been shifted around in this country, and more than 7 million new jobs have been added.[40]

These statistics meant little, of course, to the worker unable to keep pace with a shifting job market. Thus President Reagan, bowing to political pressure, often

Forms of U.S. Aid to Other Countries

Development assistance is project support used for education, management training, and some small business development. It also funds development of the private sector and agriculture, and finances health and nutrition programs: all of these to increase the incomes of poor rural families to meet their basic needs.

Food for Peace, commonly called PL 480, provides food from U.S. Department of Agriculture stockpiles to those nations that are too poor to feed all of their people adequately. The food provided alleviates hunger and malnutrition and improves health. One of our most successful programs, it also generates local currency, in some countries, that is recycled to fund agricultural development, infrastructure improvements, rural education, and health programs.

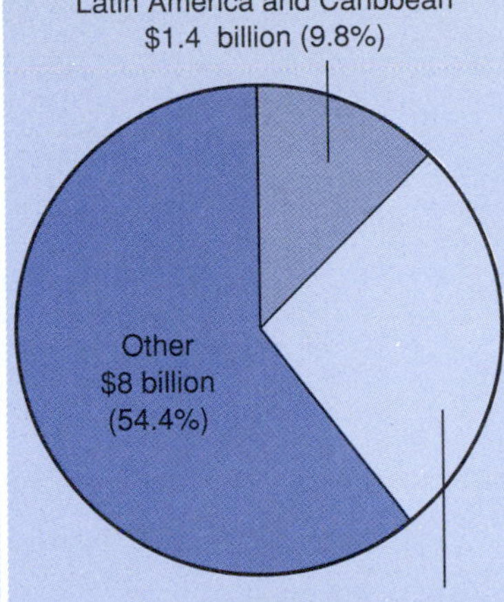

Figure 18-7
U.S. bilateral assistance, 1990 request

The economic support fund (ESF) advances U.S. economic interests by offering grant or loan economic assistance. These funds are used primarily to provide quick-disbursing balance-of-payments support to allow time for local economic and financial adjustments to take effect.

Through the provision of international narcotics control assistance, the U.S. Government works with drug-producing and -trafficking countries to encourage cooperation in eradicating crops at their source, interdicting narcotics as they are trafficked, and in reducing the demand for drugs in foreign countries.

The foreign military sales financing program (FMSF) provides grant funds for procurement of defense articles and services to help strengthen defense capabilities. Without grant aid, many countries in this hemisphere would have to divert scarce domestic resources from economic development efforts in order to purchase military training and equipment. FMSF essentially replaces the military assistance program (MAP) funding in FY 1990.

The international military education and training (IMET) program is a grant-aid, low-cost instrument that gives the U.S. Government an extremely valuable channel of communication and influence with foreign military organizations and promotes a concept of professionalism that includes respect for democracy, human rights, and social justice. Education and training for the professionalization of military officers have long been considered to be the most cost-effective form of security assistance.

SOURCE: U.S. Department of State.

spoke of "fair" as well as "free" trade. Behind the scenes he frequently urged Japan and other major trading partners to accept more U.S. exports. And in 1988 he reluctantly signed a so-called plant-closing bill, which requires companies to give sixty days' notice to their workers before the operation is shut down or transferred to another country.

The U.S. Economy and the Third World

The nations of the Third World (the less developed countries of Latin America, Africa, and Asia) have traditionally been recipients of American exports, investment,

Table 18-7
Largest recipients of U.S. economic and military aid, 1986 (millions of dollars)

	Economic aid	*Military aid*	*Total*
Israel	$1,898	$1,723	$3,621
Egypt	1,069	1,246	2,315
Turkey	120	619	739
Pakistan	263	312	575
Philippines	351	105	456
El Salvador	268	122	390

SOURCE: U.S. Bureau of the Census, *Statistical Abstract of the United States, 1988* (Washington, D.C.: U.S. Government Printing Office, 1987), pp. 766–767.

and foreign aid. Many American firms have a direct financial interest in Third World nations. In recent years, about 40 percent of U.S. merchandise exports have gone to the Third World. The rate of return per dollar invested in the Third World tends to be double that of investments in Europe. About 40 percent of U.S. foreign investment earnings come from the Third World. Thus it is not surprising that American businesses often act individually and through interest groups to influence U.S. trade policy.[41] The Third World, moreover, has often been the stage where cold war political conflicts have been played out. Thus the economic situation in the Third World, especially the poverty, hunger, and other symptoms of underdevelopment, have been of continuing interest to the United States because of their potential impact on foreign policy.

Imports also link the Third World to the United States. The nations of the Third World supply a vast array of raw materials that fuel U.S. industries. Of special importance are the so-called strategic materials vital to America's industrial and military capability. Along with about 30 percent of its oil, the United States receives more than 90 percent of its chromium, platinum, and cobalt from abroad. Some of these strategic materials come from somewhat unreliable sources, such as South Africa and the Soviet Union. Lacking reliable internal sources, the United States remains dependent on other nations.

The United States is also a supplier of aid to the Third World. With a foreign aid budget of around $15 billion a year, the United States contributes more military and economic help to other nations than any other country in the world. Although some aid is given for humanitarian and other reasons, it is rooted primarily in American political and economic self-interest. When America grants economic and military aid, it expects to reap certain benefits. Table 18-7 shows the major recipients of U.S. aid. Obviously, aid does not necessarily flow to the most needy nations of Asia, Africa, and Latin America. El Salvador is not objectively poorer than Haiti or the Dominican Republic. What sets the troubled nation of El Salvador apart is its political importance to the United States.

Foreign aid serves U.S. economic interests as well. Of the billions of dollars that flow abroad each year, a large percentage is returned through recipients' pur-

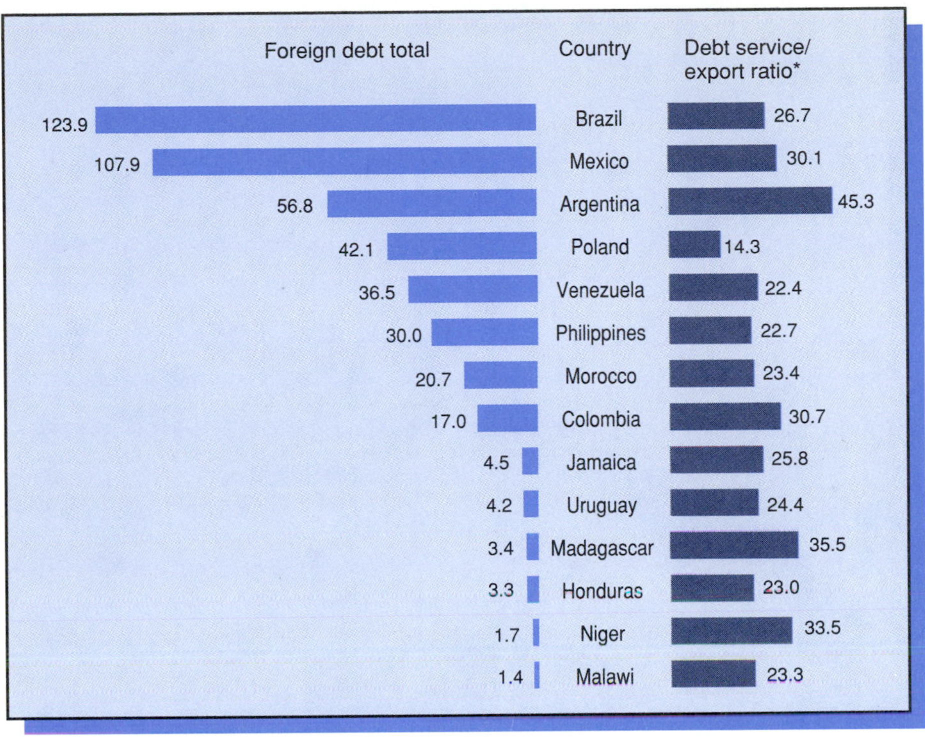

★ **Figure 18-8**
Third World debt of selected countries, 1987 (in billions of dollars)

chases of U.S. goods and services. In addition, dollars are recycled to U.S. banks. Consider the current debt crisis that affects Argentina, Mexico, and many other Third World nations. With Third World debt approaching $1 trillion, many debtor nations must spend at least one-fourth of their yearly export earnings just to pay the interest on their debts (see figure 18-8). Much of this debt, moreover, is owed to private U.S. commercial banks. About fifteen hundred banks across the United States have extended loans to developing nations. Some banks have had to close down when Third World nations have been unable to make timely payments. Even the massive Bank of America suffered setbacks in the late 1980s as a result of such loans. Should there be a large-scale default on these loans, the American banking system and economy would suffer. Thus foreign aid, much of it in the form of loans to enable debtor nations to make payments on earlier loans, is also closely linked to the U.S. economy.

The World's Banker

The United States' role in the global economy is not limited to trade, direct investment, or foreign aid. For more than forty years the United States has also been one of the world's major bankers. In 1984, about $850 billion was owed to private U.S. banks by Third World and Eastern European countries.[42] America's role as world banker began soon after the end of World War II, when a financially strong America

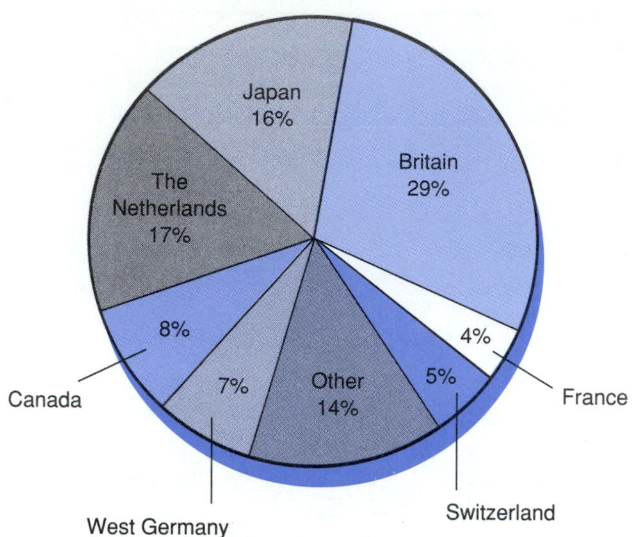

★ **Figure 18-9**
The foreign owners. Total foreign direct investment in the United States at the end of 1988 was $304.2 billion.
SOURCE: *The New York Times*, May 28, 1989, p. 3–1.

provided private investment and foreign aid to a war-ravaged Europe. Through such massive aid programs as the Marshall Plan, the United States pumped billions of dollars into Europe, and the dollar became the currency that virtually all nations used to conduct their international transactions. The United States also played a vital roie in the International Monetary Fund and the World Bank, which gave loans and grants to Europe and, more recently, to struggling Third World countries.

U.S. investment and aid helped rebuild Europe and Japan, and in the process forged a strong economic relationship to underpin political-military alliances. By the 1970s, the formerly war-torn nations had recovered to the point of competing with the United States in both trade and financial services. Today the United States no longer dominates international banking and other financial services. London, Tokyo, and Hong Kong are now also important financial centers. The growth of a global financial network has been facilitated by the development of vast computer systems and satellite communications links. These new markets offer both opportunities and dangers to the U.S. economy. With the service sector playing a larger role in the American economy, the global financial arena can create new jobs and profits for many firms. But in order to take advantage of these opportunities, the United States must be able to compete with the financial wizards of Europe and Asia.

Participation in the global financial market also diminishes the ability of the government to control the economy. Earlier in this chapter we discussed the various steps that the federal government can take to control the economy (monetary supply, discount rate, and so on). With billions of U.S. dollars held abroad by foreign banks and corporations, implementation of economic policy is much less certain than it once was and often depends on the cooperation of other governments (see figure 18-9). The dollars held abroad, often called **Eurodollars,** have a profound influence on U.S. monetary policy and the economy as a whole. By the early 1980s, the amount of Eurodollars had grown to over $1 trillion, about three times as large as the U.S. domestic money supply.[43] Eurodollars form a significant part of the world's monetary reserves. They can create international credit in a matter of seconds in an arcane system described by the Joint Economic Committee of Congress as a "financial black box into which goes American money and from which comes credit for foreigners."[44] *Business Week* magazine described Eurodollars as having created a "world of stateless money," which "has in turn bred a stateless banking system in which national boundaries mean very little. . . . Now international commerce is totally dependent on this new supranational banking system."[45] The importance of Eurodollars reveals dramatically how the U.S. economy is tied to the international economy.

Preparing the U.S. Economy for Global Challenges

Keeping the economy healthy at home and abroad is a key task confronting America's political leaders. While many economic questions are highly technical, they are also profoundly political. What presidential candidate, for instance, can risk alienating big labor or big business? Given the volatility of economic issues, politicians are often tempted to pursue economic policies that will win votes. In 1988, a presidential election year, Congress passed, and President Reagan reluctantly signed, a trade bill that included the following provisions:

- Tax relief for U.S. industries hurt by foreign competition.
- Investigation of and retaliation against foreign countries that unfairly compete with U.S. firms.
- $2.5 billion in subsidies for farmers hurt by foreign trade barriers.
- A $1 billion program to help workers displaced by foreign competition.

The Trade Bill of 1988, while offering short-term assistance to some businesses and workers, did not address the fundamental problems America faces in the highly competitive global economic environment of the 1990s. Many observers conclude that government, business, and the public must take a hard look at the way we plan and finance America's economy, both at home and abroad. Proposals for long-term reforms of the economy include the development of a national industrial policy, encouragement of savings and capital development, and control of military spending. The growing importance of the international economy has reinvigorated the debate about the relative merits of free markets and government regulations.

A National Industrial Policy. As we saw at the beginning of this chapter, the United States' economy has undergone a dramatic sectoral shift in recent years. High-paying industrial jobs have declined in favor of lower-paying service-sector jobs. Our industrial edge in the international marketplace has been slipping as well. In many high-tech industries, such as pharmaceuticals, electrical equipment, plastics, industrial chemicals, and scientific instruments, foreign companies have outpaced us in technology and manufacturing.

In the 1984 presidential elections, the Democratic party proposed to replace the current hodgepodge of bailouts, subsidies, and tax incentives with a **national industrial policy,** a coordinated strategy for industrial competition developed by

★ Some analysts call for a national industrial policy that revitalizes American smokestack industries, such as the steel mill in Birmingham, Alabama, where this man used to work.

government in cooperation with business and labor. The Democratic party debated two basic versions of a national industrial policy: (1) reviving the smokestack industries and (2) channeling energies into emerging high-tech industries, letting most of the smokestack industries die.[46]

The smokestack approach aimed at bringing back some of the 1.5 million jobs that had been lost during the 1970s and protecting workers from unfair foreign trade practices. Proponents of this approach argued that the only way to ensure well-paying jobs was to protect the industrial sector, whose jobs paid more on average than those in the rapidly growing service areas. As we shall see, many people also considered steel and other basic industries vital to national defense. Since foreign governments subsidized their basic industries, this approach advocated, among other proposals, instituting quotas or negotiating voluntary restraints on their exports; requiring local co-production ventures and some U.S.-made parts in foreign products; and enforcing antidumping laws, which would impose fines on companies that sold products in the American market at prices below their production cost. This practice had forced many American firms out of business, whereupon the foreign firms, having captured the market, raised their prices.

In the high-tech approach, industrial policy would be directed by an economic coordinating council of business, labor, and government representatives. High-tech industries would receive tax incentives and low-interest loans. Tax credits would be given to corporations that trained displaced workers for new high-tech jobs. And the government would fund more scientific and technical education in the nation's universities. Proponents of this approach note that other countries, especially West Germany and Japan, have been able to capture larger market shares in high-tech products in part because of coordinated planning by their governments. Our high-tech planning has been directed by the Pentagon, for military applications, a practice that limits our ability to capitalize on our technological advances for commercial purposes.

The Role of Government Planning. Many liberals include elements of planning and public ownership in their industrial policy proposals. They point to the successes of government planning in Japan, France, and Sweden, where managers and economists use planning information to guide some of their investment decisions. They note that in Western Europe, public ownership of business has been used to improve aspects of the economy, provide public services, and increase public control over investments. During the Great Depression and World War II, European governments nationalized key industries and remained involved in them after the crises subsided. France and Italy have the most nationalized economies. American liberals admit that in a mixed economy such as ours, where government plays a significant role but investment decisions remain in the private sector, the government can nudge but it cannot command. Still, planning can be useful for clarifying the long-term picture; for coordinating federal regulation, taxes, credits, and subsidies; and for redirecting investment flows to certain industries.[47]

Most American liberals do not call for full-scale nationalization of American industries. But they point to the crucial economic services provided by U.S. public corporations such as Amtrak, which took over deteriorating passenger rail service from the private sector. And they want more public control over major investment decisions, particularly in the area of energy policy. They say oil companies have gone after short-term profits rather than developing a viable long-term energy plan. To this end, the government could develop a public energy corporation to compete with the private oil industry.[48]

While Republicans have steered away from the centralized planning aspects of the Democrats' industrial policy proposals, they have supported other measures, such as the 1988 Trade Bill. They agreed with a 1985 report by the President's Commission on Industrial Competitiveness, which advocated new trade reciprocity laws that would penalize unfair competition, a relaxation of antitrust restraints in high-tech areas so that American firms could collaborate on research and development, and new tax incentives, tax credits, and federal funds for research and development.

Savings and Capital Development. Conservatives and liberals agree that Americans spend too much and save too little. Low rates of savings reduce the amount of capital available to finance industrial expansion. The United States has one of the lowest savings rates among Western industrial nations. Conservatives attribute our low rate of savings to high taxes on the wealthy and their investments. Liberals trace the problem to the low rate of interest paid by savings institutions and earlier tax laws that allowed citizens to deduct interest on credit accounts, thus encouraging them to go into debt. Conservatives were pleased with the 1982 tax cuts for upper-income groups. Liberals welcomed the phasing out of the consumer interest deduction in the 1986 tax reforms, but wanted other measures to encourage middle- and low-income groups to save. At least some of the interest earned on savings accounts, they say, should be exempt from taxes.[49]

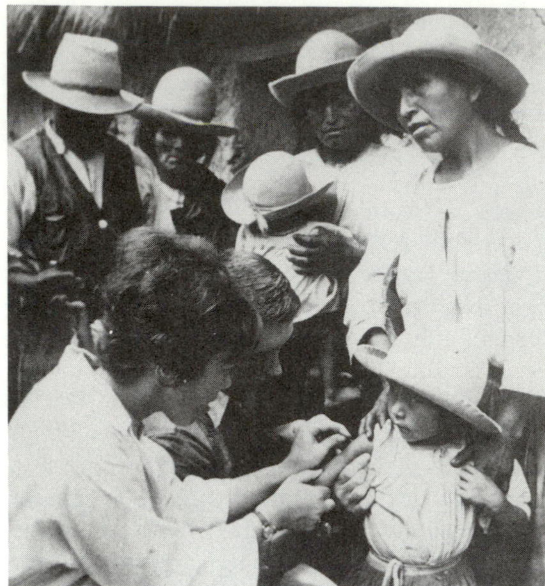

★ Critics of the military industrial complex fault it not only for channeling the American economy along military instead of commercial lines, but also for exporting armaments, which fuel military conflicts. Such critics applaud the efforts of American Peace Corps Volunteers, pictured here administering vaccinations and digging irrigation ditches.

Both liberal and conservative economists have suggested that the federal government resurrect a version of the New Deal Reconstruction Finance Corporation (RFC). During the Great Depression, the RFC provided capital and management assistance to failing industries. A new RFC would provide industries with additional capital, tax breaks, and management and technological aid. Liberals envision an RFC that would finance experiments in worker ownership and worker democracy, promote balanced regional growth, rejuvenate cities in the Midwest and the East, and encourage industrial competition.[50]

Some observers cite corporations' practice of concentrating on short-term profits as one reason the United States is losing its competitive edge. Instead of adapting to international competition, U.S. corporations are generating quick profits through mergers and tax loopholes. "Paper entrepreneuralism" has replaced a more productive capitalism.[51] Government should discourage this behavior and encourage a more productive use of industrial assets.

Control of the Military Industrial Complex. Finally, liberals contend that our industrial priorities have been distorted by the political clout of the military-industrial complex. The armed forces and the industries that supply them are criticized for channeling too much of the nation's industrial research, development, and production along military rather than commercial lines. The defense industry employs about 7 percent of the work force, accounts for 20 percent of employment in manufacturing industries, and provides nearly 40 percent of manufacturing in Connecticut, California, and Washington.[52]

With so much money at stake, the defense iron triangle is a strong one. Defense contractors are notorious for cost overruns and overcharges. The GAO found charges of $436 for a $7 hammer and $3,100 for three plastic stool caps

★ Table 18-8
Arms trade, selected countries, 1985 (in millions of dollars)

Country	*Total*	*Arms imports as percent of total imports*
Exporters		
Canada	$ 178	.1%
China: Mainland	327	.3
Czechoslovakia	772	2.2
France	3,087	.1
Poland	655	3.2
Soviet Union	8,325	.9
United Kingdom	538	.4
United States	8,793	.2
West Germany	538	.4
*Arms trade, world total**	*$26,990*	*1.4%*

Country	*Total*	*Arms imports as percent of total imports*
Importers		
*Developed**	*$6,674*	.5%
Canada	47	.1
East Germany	374	1.8
Japan	702	.6
Soviet Union	725	.9
United Kingdom	440	.4
United States	538	.2
West Germany	655	.4
*Developing**	*$20,310*	*4.4%*
Angola	412	25.9
Egypt	1,029	11.0
El Salvador	84	9.4
Ethiopia	365	39.3
India	1,777	13.0
Iraq	1,964	19.9
Libya	1,216	24.0
Nicaragua	112	14.1
North Korea	281	17.4
Saudi Arabia	2,339	(NA)
South Korea	355	1.2
Spain	122	.4

*Includes countries not shown separately.

NOTE: NA means "not available."

SOURCE: U.S. Bureau of the Census, *Statistical Abstract of the United States, 1988* (Washington D.C.: U.S. Government Printing Office, 1987), p. 318.

worth 34 cents each. To some critics, the defense industry is not receiving proper government scrutiny, and military products represent a misdirection of resources away from products that would make the United States more competitive in the world commercial market. Instead, we have become a major arms supplier, especially to Third World nations. In 1985 the United States sold almost $9 billion worth of armaments abroad, accounting for about one-third of the total world arms trade (see table 18-8).

We spend a greater proportion of our GNP on defense than our industrial trading partners do. In 1985, military spending accounted for 6.6 percent of the United States' GNP (that is, $6.60 of every $100 in the economy was spent by the military). Most of our major trade competitors spend between 2 and 4 percent of their GNP on defense. Critics of defense spending note that there is an inverse relationship between military expenditures and economic growth: rising military spending is correlated with declining investment in civilian enterprises.[53] The capital needs of defense contractors often clash with the need to invest in business to rebuild our industrial base. The Pentagon's demand for goods raises industrial prices, increasing the need to import products from abroad, to the detriment of our trading position.[54] The more our industrial base concentrates on military hardware, the more of our technological edge in the world marketplace is lost.[55]

★ Summary

The United States is becoming more and more a mixed economy as the federal government expands its role in the production and consumption of goods and services. Our economy is dominated by large firms that increasingly are multinational in scale. In recent years a robust service sector has overshadowed the manufacturing and agricultural sectors. Both wealth and income are concentrated in the hands of the richest 20 percent of the population.

The federal government attempts to control the economy in several ways. Its monetary policies control the money supply. Its fiscal policies (taxing and spending) target the problems of unemployment, inflation, stagflation, deficits, the national debt, and tax reform. The government's regulatory tools include wage and price controls, antitrust laws, and the rules issued by numerous economic and social regulatory agencies. The government subsidizes economic activities through tariffs, price supports, and loan guarantees.

The U.S. government also intervenes in the economy to enhance the nation's role in the global economy. It seeks a favorable balance of trade, amid controversy about free trade versus protectionism. It also wants a positive balance of payments and a strong dollar. Our economy is closely tied to the economies of Third World nations through trade, foreign aid, and repayment of debts to our commercial banks. The United States plays the role of one of the world's major bankers through the Export-Import Bank, International Monetary Fund, and World Bank. But there are some domestic economic activities over which the government has little influence, most notably those of U.S.-based multinational corporations and their Eurodollar transactions. Finally, contemporary debate about means to improve America's competitive edge in an interdependent global economy centers on a national industrial policy, the role of government planning, domestic savings patterns, and control of the military-industrial complex.

★ Key Terms

antitrust legislation
balance of payments
balance of trade
budget deficit
command economy
corporation
depression
Eurodollars
Federal Reserve System
fiscal policy
inflation
interlocking directorates
loan guarantee
market economy
mixed economy
monetary policy
multinational corporations
national debt
national industrial policy
oligopolies
political economy
price supports
recession
stagflation
subsidies
supply-side economics
tariff
tax preferences
wage and price controls

★ Notes

1. Kenneth M. Dolbeare, *American Public Policy: A Citizen's Guide* (New York: McGraw-Hill, 1982), p. 5.
2. Denise E. Markovich and Ronald E. Pynn, *American Political Economy* (Pacific Grove, Calif.: Brooks/Cole, 1988), pp. 91–92.
3. Edward S. Herman, *Corporate Control, Corporate Power* (New York: Cambridge University Press, 1981), p. 201.
4. Howard M. Wachtel, *The Money Mandarins: The Making of a New Supranational Economic Order* (New York: Pantheon, 1986), p. 16.
5. *Economic Report of the President* (Washington, D.C.: U.S. Government Printing Office, 1988), pp. 64–65.
6. Andrew Hacker, "Women at Work," *New York Review of Books,* August 14, 1986, pp. 26–32.
7. Executive Office of the President, Office of Management and Budget, *Social Indicators, 1973* (Washington, D.C.: U.S. Government Printing Office, 1973), p. 164.
8. Dorothy S. Projector and Gertrude S. Weiss, *Survey of Financial Characteristics of Consumers* (Washington, D.C.: Board of Governors of the Federal Reserve System, August 1966), p. 136.
9. Markovich and Pynn, *American Political Economy,* pp. 119–120.
10. Charles Beard, *An Economic Interpretation of the Constitution of the United States* (New York: Free Press, 1935), p. 146.
11. B. Guy Peters, *American Public Policy: Promise and Performance* (Chatham, N.J.: Chatham House, 1986), p. 166.
12. Richard Rose and B. Guy Peters, *Can Government Go Bankrupt?* (New York: Basic Books, 1979), pp. 135–141.
13. U.S. Bureau of the Census, *Statistical Abstract of the United States, 1988* (Washington, D.C.: U.S. Government Printing Office, 1987), p. 295.
14. James C. Miller 3d, quoted in Martin Tolchin, "Paradox of Reagan Budgets Hints Contradiction in Legacy," *New York Times,* February 16, 1988, pp. 1, 12.
15. Austin Ranney, "What Constitutional Changes Do Americans Want?" in *This Constitution: A Bicentennial Chronicle,* published by Project '87 of the American Historical Association and the American Political Science Association, Winter 1984, pp. 13–18.
16. Karyl A. Kinsey, *Survey Data on Tax Compliance: A Compendium and Review* (Chicago: American Bar Foundation, 1984), p. 4.
17. James C. Miller 3d, quoted in Tolchin, "Paradox of Reagan Budgets," p. 12.
18. U.S. Bureau of the Census, *Statistical Abstract of the United States, 1988* (Washington, D.C.: U.S. Government Printing Office, 1987), p. 296.
19. Gary L. Klott, *The New York Times Complete Guide to the New Tax Law* (New York: Times Books, 1986), p. 11.
20. Ibid., pp. 1, 5.
21. Ibid., pp. 7, 11.
22. Lawrence C. Pierce, "Wage and Price Controls: Economic Necessity or Political Expedience," in *What Government Does,* ed. Matthew Holden, Jr., and Dennis L. Dresang (Beverly Hills, Calif.: Sage, 1977), pp. 77–78.

23. Marvin Kosters, *Controls and Inflation* (Washington, D.C.: American Enterprise Institute, 1975), pp. 47–53.
24. Richard J. Barnet and Ronald E. Muller, *Global Reach: The Power of the Multinational Corporations* (New York: Simon & Schuster, 1974), p. 231.
25. David Vogel, "The 'New' Social Regulation in Historical and Comparative Perspective," in *Regulation in Perspective,* ed. Thomas K. McCraw (Cambridge, Mass.: Harvard University Press, 1981), p. 176.
26. Barry Bosworth, quoted in Jules Backman, "The Problem of Regulation," in *Regulation and Deregulation,* ed. Backman (Indianapolis: Bobbs-Merrill, 1981), p. 23.
27. Ibid., p. 20.
28. Congressional Quarterly, *Regulation: Process and Politics* (Washington, D.C., 1982), pp. 29–30.
29. Barry Crickmer, "Regulation: How Much Is Enough?" *Nation's Business,* Vol. 68, March 1980, pp. 26–33.
30. Steven Kelman, "Regulation That Works," *New Republic,* Vol. 179, November 25, 1978, pp. 16–20.
31. Susan J. Tolchin and Martin Tolchin, *Dismantling America: The Rush to Deregulate* (New York: Oxford University Press, 1983), chap. 1.
32. Study prepared for the U.S. Senate by the Center for Policy Alternatives at the Massachusetts Institute of Technology, cited in Congressional Quarterly, *Regulation,* p. 30.
33. Charles L. Schultze, *The Distribution of Farm Subsidies* (Washington, D.C.: Brookings Institution, 1971).
34. *Congressional Quarterly Almanac, 1978* (Washington, D.C., 1979), p. 188; Markovich and Pynn, *American Political Economy,* pp. 170–171.
35. Markovich and Pynn, *American Political Economy,* p. 171.
36. Ibid., pp. 171, 174.
37. U.S. Senate, Committee on Banking, Housing, and Urban Affairs, *Hearings: Chrysler Corporation Loan Guarantee Act of 1979,* 96th Cong., 1st sess. (1979), p. 169.
38. Dolbeare, *American Public Policy,* pp. 99–100.
39. *U.S. Government Manual, 1987–88* (Washington, D.C.: U.S. Government Printing Office, 1987), p. 534.
40. U.S. Department of State, Under Secretary Allen Wallis, "Open Markets: Key to a Stronger, Richer, and Freer America," *Current Policy,* no. 754 (October 1985).
41. Joan E. Spero, *The Politics of International Economic Relations,* 4th ed. (New York: St. Martin's Press, 1985), p. 175.
42. World Bank, *World Development Report, 1985* (New York: Oxford University Press, 1985), p. 23.
43. Wachtel, *Money Mandarins,* pp. 15–16.
44. U.S. Congress, Joint Economic Committee, *Some Questions and Brief Answers about the Eurodollar Market* (Washington, D.C.: U.S. Government Printing Office, 1977), p. 1.
45. "Stateless Money: A New Force on World Economies," *Business Week,* August 21, 1978, pp. 76–77.
46. Simon Lazarus and Robert Litan, "The Democrats' Coming Civil War over Industrial Policy," *Atlantic,* Vol. 225, September 1984, pp. 92–98.
47. Howard M. Leichter and Harrell R. Rodgers, Jr., *American Public Policy in a Comparative Context* (New York: McGraw-Hill, 1984), pp. 171–173.
48. Ibid., pp. 173–174.
49. Ibid., chap. 5.
50. Alfred J. Watkins, "Felix Rohatyn's Biggest Deal," *Working Papers,* September–October 1981, pp. 44–52.
51. Richard R. Reich, "The Next American Frontier," *Atlantic,* March 1983, pp. 43–58.
52. Markovich and Pynn, *American Political Economy,* p. 94.
53. Bruce Russett, *What Price Vigilance?* (New Haven, Conn.: Yale University Press, 1970).
54. *The Defense Buildup and the Economy,* Joint Economic Committee staff study (Washington, D.C.: U.S. Government Printing Office, February 1982).
55. Simon Ramo, *America's Technology Slip* (New York: Wiley, 1980).

★ For Further Reading

Ferguson, Thomas, and Joel Rogers, eds. *The Political Economy: Readings in the Politics and Economics of American Public Policy*. Armonk, N.Y.: M. E. Sharpe, 1984.

Greider, William. *The Secrets of the Temple: How the Federal Reserve Runs the Country.* New York: Touchstone/Simon & Schuster, 1989.

Levy, Frank. *Dollars and Dreams: The Changing American Income Distribution.* New York: Russell Sage Foundation, 1987.

Markovich, Denise E., and Ronald E. Pynn. *American Political Economy: Using Economics with Politics.* Pacific Grove, Calif.: Brooks/Cole, 1988.

Pechman, Joseph A. *Federal Tax Policy.* 5th ed. Washington, D.C.: Brookings Institution, 1987.

Reich, Robert B. *The Next American Frontier.* New York: Times Books, 1983.

Savas, E. S. *Privatization: The Key to Better Government.* Chatham, N.J.: Chatham House, 1987.

CHAPTER NINETEEN

We, as Americans, share a strong consensus on our basic American interests and objectives. As a people and a nation, we are seeking to:

- Uphold the principles of freedom, the rule of law, and observance of fundamental human rights;
- Promote our domestic prosperity;
- Protect the security of our nation and its institutions, as well as those of our allies and friends;
- Contribute to a safer world by reaching equitable and verifiable arms reductions agreements with the Soviet Union;
- Assist the economic development of poorer nations; and
- Act in a manner consistent with our humanitarian instincts.

—U.S. Department of State, 1988

FOREIGN POLICY

The lofty goals listed on the first page of this chapter reinforce the point we have stressed throughout this book: that American politics is firmly tied to a network of increasingly complex international forces. While the United States has always been involved with other nations, since World War II the scope and intensity of our involvement in the international arena has grown dramatically. Technical, political, economic, and cultural changes have globalized politics and brought the world to small-town America. Whether Americans fully appreciate it or not, the international system is an integral part of American politics and life.

The purpose of this chapter is twofold: first, it brings together the diverse examples we have discussed—Vietnam, the arms race, conflict in Central America, defense spending, foreign trade—through a historical review of major themes and events in American foreign policy. This review, by no means all-inclusive, should answer some questions that may have come up along the way about America's role in the world.

Second, we will consider how American political institutions—the Constitution, the presidency, Congress, public opinion, and interest groups—help shape foreign policy. This look at foreign policy making can serve as a review of material presented in earlier chapters. As we examine American foreign policy, you can conduct your own review by asking a few simple questions: How have the president, Congress, the courts, the bureaucracy, interest groups, and the citizenry affected American foreign policy over the past two centuries? In what ways have our basic political institutions developed as the United States has become more involved with the world? And what changes in foreign policy making have been brought about by such developments as atomic weapons, improvements in global communications, and the growing dependence on other countries for oil, raw materials, and markets? You may find that, like politicians and political scientists, you have more questions than answers.

★ Survival in a Competitive World: The Basic Themes of American Foreign Policy

> We have to be so strong that no other nation on earth will dare to violate the peace.
>
> —*Ronald Reagan, 1980*

A properly conceived and executed foreign policy is essential to the survival of every nation. Indeed, the ability to defend one's national borders and maintain territorial integrity is part of the fundamental definition of what constitutes a nation-state. In this regard the United States does not differ from any other country in the world. Maintaining national security has always been the primary goal of American foreign policy.

A crucial aspect of national security is the maintenance of the balance of power. In the words of one scholar:

> The aspiration for power on the part of several nations, each trying to maintain or overthrow the status quo, leads of necessity to a configuration that is called the balance of power and to policies that aim at preserving it.[1]

The idea that one nation must balance the power of other nations is based on the assumption that each state will do almost anything to maintain or improve its economic and political situation. Thus, if a country believes it has sufficient strength to grab territory from other states, it will do so unless another country or countries act to deter the aggression. This desire to deter aggressive states has been a primary cause of arms races, alliances, political and economic competition, and wars throughout history. The post–World War II bipolar world, divided into two major military/political alliances (North Atlantic Treaty Organization, or NATO, versus Warsaw Pact), is a classic example of the balance of power at work.

In today's complex world, of course, foreign policy involves a great deal more than simply keeping the nation free from attack. Along with the basic goal of national security, American foreign policy is also aimed at defending the national interest. Broadly defined, the national interest involves all of the goals and aspirations of the American political system as interpreted and pursued by the national government. The national interest has a strong economic component—foreign trade, investment, access to raw materials—and an equally strong political component—maintenance of beneficial relations with allies and promotion of American values around the globe. What constitutes the national interest at any given time can be a highly controversial political issue.

At times the national security and the national interest have been seen as best served by a withdrawal from international politics. In his farewell address in 1796, George Washington insisted that the United States should "steer clear of permanent alliances" with European countries. "Europe," he proclaimed, "has a set of primary interests which to us have none or a very remote relation. Hence she must be engaged in frequent controversies, the causes of which are essentially foreign to our concerns." Aided by geographic separation, an element of isolationism thus began to flow through American foreign policy. Physical separation helped the United States to maintain its independence from the political intrigues of Europe.

Yet, even in its earliest manifestations, isolationism was selectively pursued, and directed mostly to European entanglements. In a sustained effort to extend its borders, the United States purchased the Louisiana Territory from France, fought battles with Native Americans to acquire western land, annexed Texas, and seized California and parts of the Southwest in the war with Mexico (1846–1848). It also purchased Alaska from Russia, annexed the Hawaiian Islands, and acquired the Philippines, Guam, and Puerto Rico in the Spanish-American War (1898). The United States then reduced newly independent Cuba to a virtual colony and in 1903 connived with local dissidents to obtain the right to construct and fortify the Panama Canal, making the new state of Panama (formerly a part of Colombia) a virtual American outpost.

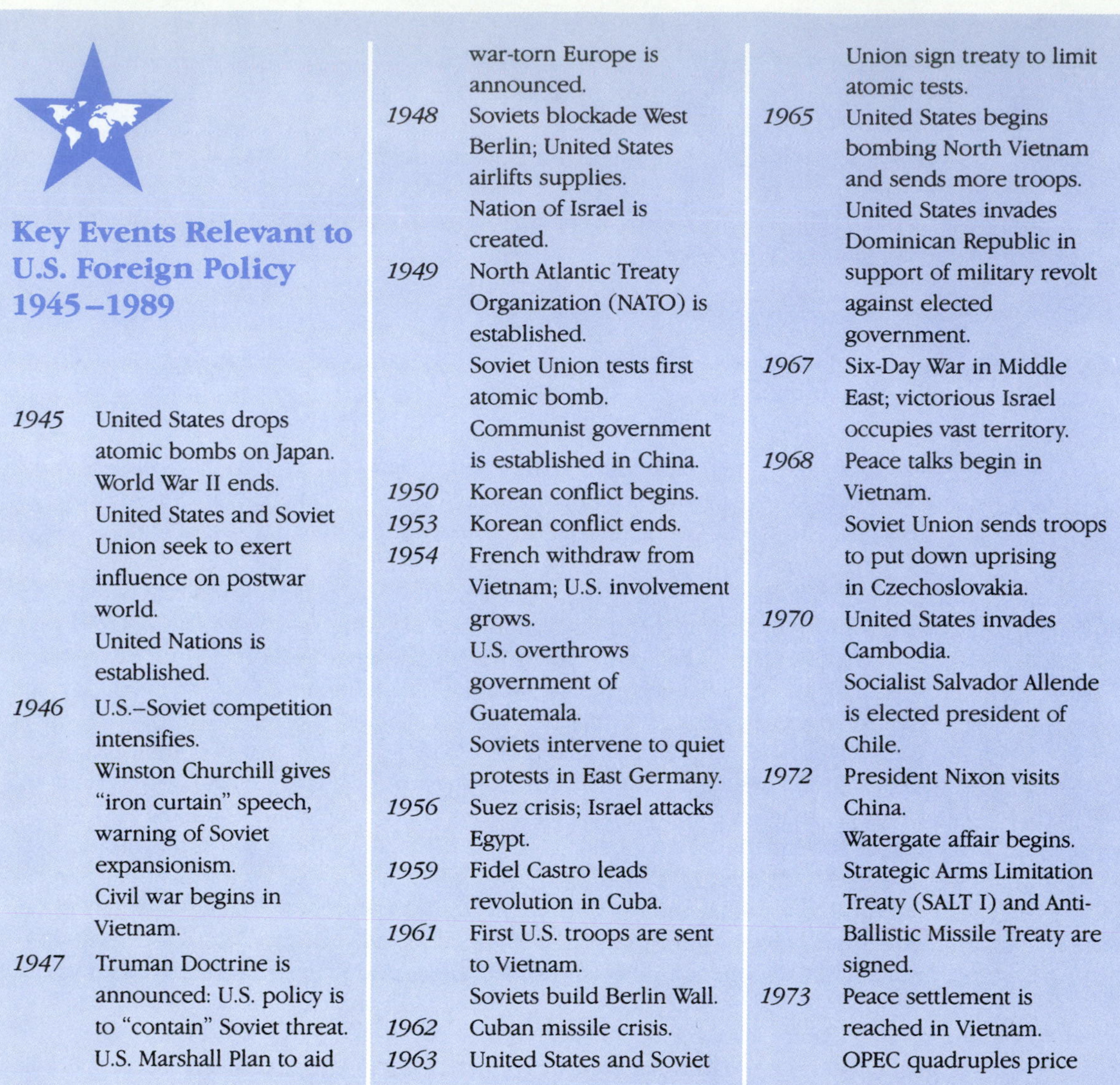

Key Events Relevant to U.S. Foreign Policy 1945–1989

1945	United States drops atomic bombs on Japan.
	World War II ends.
	United States and Soviet Union seek to exert influence on postwar world.
	United Nations is established.
1946	U.S.–Soviet competition intensifies.
	Winston Churchill gives "iron curtain" speech, warning of Soviet expansionism.
	Civil war begins in Vietnam.
1947	Truman Doctrine is announced: U.S. policy is to "contain" Soviet threat.
	U.S. Marshall Plan to aid war-torn Europe is announced.
1948	Soviets blockade West Berlin; United States airlifts supplies.
	Nation of Israel is created.
1949	North Atlantic Treaty Organization (NATO) is established.
	Soviet Union tests first atomic bomb.
	Communist government is established in China.
1950	Korean conflict begins.
1953	Korean conflict ends.
1954	French withdraw from Vietnam; U.S. involvement grows.
	U.S. overthrows government of Guatemala.
	Soviets intervene to quiet protests in East Germany.
1956	Suez crisis; Israel attacks Egypt.
1959	Fidel Castro leads revolution in Cuba.
1961	First U.S. troops are sent to Vietnam.
	Soviets build Berlin Wall.
1962	Cuban missile crisis.
1963	United States and Soviet Union sign treaty to limit atomic tests.
1965	United States begins bombing North Vietnam and sends more troops.
	United States invades Dominican Republic in support of military revolt against elected government.
1967	Six-Day War in Middle East; victorious Israel occupies vast territory.
1968	Peace talks begin in Vietnam.
	Soviet Union sends troops to put down uprising in Czechoslovakia.
1970	United States invades Cambodia.
	Socialist Salvador Allende is elected president of Chile.
1972	President Nixon visits China.
	Watergate affair begins.
	Strategic Arms Limitation Treaty (SALT I) and Anti-Ballistic Missile Treaty are signed.
1973	Peace settlement is reached in Vietnam.
	OPEC quadruples price

Admittedly, the notion that America can isolate itself behind safe borders is still popular in some quarters today. As we discussed in chapter 7, isolationism has found periodic support among a significant minority of Americans. But we also saw that fewer and fewer citizens see isolationism as a viable alternative in today's highly interdependent world. President Washington's advice to avoid entangling alliances in Europe has been replaced by a vast web of collective security pacts, including NATO, whereby the United States has promised to defend Western Europe at all costs, including nuclear war.

Since World War II, several themes have pushed aside American isolationist tendencies including:

- Containment of Soviet expansion
- Improving relations with the Soviet Union
- Promoting capitalism and free trade
- American exceptionalism

of oil; Arab nations embargo oil shipments to United States.

1977 Panama Canal Treaty is signed.

1979 Camp David Middle East peace plan is approved.

1979 Iranian Revolution.
Nicaraguan Revolution.
SALT II Treaty is signed.
Soviet Union invades Afghanistan.

1980 President Carter removes SALT II Treaty from Senate consideration.
Iraq attacks Iran.

1981 United States begins multibillion-dollar military spending program.

1982 United States initiates Caribbean Basin aid package.
United States begins efforts to overthrow government of Nicaragua.
Argentina and Britain go to war over Falkland/ Malvinas Islands.

1983 President Reagan launches "Star Wars" program.
Soviets shoot down Korean passenger plane that strays into its territory.
241 U.S. military personnel die in Lebanon.
United States invades Caribbean island of Grenada.
NATO begins deployment of medium-range missiles.

1984 U.S. troops leave Lebanon.
United States mines harbors in Nicaragua.

1985 U.S.–Soviet summit in Geneva; arms talks begin.
United States is target of increased terrorist activities in Middle East.

1986 United States initiates direct funding of Contra rebels in Nicaragua.
President Jean-Claude (Baby Doc) Duvalier of Haiti flees country.
President Ferdinand Marcos of Philippines flees country.
United States bombs Libya.
President Reagan admits selling weapons to Iran.

1987 Iran-Contra scandal unfolds.
President of Costa Rica announces new Central American peace plan.

1988 United States reaches agreement with Soviets on medium-range missiles in Europe.
Iran and Iraq agree to cease-fire.
United States shoots down Iranian commercial jet over Persian Gulf.
Mikhail Gorbachev offers large troop reductions in Eastern Europe.

1989 Elections in Panama are nullified by the military.
Open elections are held in Poland and the Soviet Union.
United States and Soviet Union continue to explore reductions in conventional and nuclear forces.
Student movement for political reforms is crushed by the military in China.
Berlin Wall falls. ★

These themes provide threads that tie together the specifics of recent American international policies. Let us, then, discuss modern American foreign policy in relation to these four general concepts.

★ Containment of Soviet Expansion

For a brief while, some Americans hoped to avoid the crisis that seemed destined to consume Europe as the 1930s came to a close. But the spread of nazism and competition with the Japanese in the Pacific, which culminated in the attack on Pearl Harbor on December 7, 1941, brought America into the war. Seeking to maintain the balance of power around the globe, the United States was once again involved in a major foreign entanglement—an entanglement that fundamentally changed its role in the world.

By the end of the war in 1945, the United States had become a superpower among nations. Having ushered in the nuclear age with a devastating attack on Japan, the United States was virtually unrivaled in military might. At the same time, whereas both the winners and the losers in Europe found their nations in ruins, the United States' vast economic strength was untouched. Though the task of rebuilding Europe was formidable, it also held great promise for the nation's business community. America seemed to face a bright, peaceful, and prosperous future. It soon found itself, however, in a new kind of struggle, a **cold war,** with vague rules and certain dangers.

Origins of Containment: The Cold War

> At the present moment in world history nearly every nation must choose between alternative ways of life. The choice is often not a free one. One way of life is based upon the will of the majority, and is distinguished by free institutions. . . . The second way of life is based upon the will of a minority. . . . It relies upon terror and oppression . . . and the suppression of personal freedoms.
>
> —*Harry S Truman*

President Truman's speech, delivered to a joint session of Congress in March 1947, captured the essence of America's image of the Soviet Union as the cold war unfolded. With the gift of hindsight, it is clear that the two budding superpowers had long been on a collision course. Marxism, as adapted to the Russian situation by Lenin and Stalin, was seen as alien to American political culture. In the civil war that followed the Bolshevik takeover in 1917, the United States briefly intervened with 14,000 troops in Siberia, suffering 100 casualties.[2] The U.S. intervention, though of little military significance, was an early hint of the conflict to come. Angered by the Soviets' refusal to honor the tsar's debts and appalled by the harsh excesses of Stalin's rule, the United States did not extend diplomatic recognition to the Soviet Union until 1933.

After World War II, Winston Churchill, in his now-famous speech in 1946, proclaimed that the Soviet Union's territorial advances in Eastern Europe had caused an "iron curtain" to descend across the continent. Many Americans, convinced that the Soviet Union was bent on world domination, felt it was the duty of the United States to defend the world against this expansionist threat. The U.S. response was suggested in part by a high-ranking diplomat named George F. Kennan. Writing in *Foreign Affairs,* Kennan argued that "the main element of any United States policy toward the Soviet Union must be that of a long-term vigilant containment of Russian expansive tendencies."[3] Thus **containment** of the anticipated Soviet threat became the foremost theme of American foreign policy in the postwar era.

Containment in Europe

Containment was first given substance in what has come to be called the **Truman Doctrine.** Although a civil war in Greece in 1947 was President Truman's specific inspiration, his concern was global. Fearing that local communists would gain control in Greece and Turkey, Truman called for direct U.S. assistance to the two nations. "I believe that it must be the policy of the United States," he declared, "to

★ Allied leaders *(left to right)* Winston Churchill, Harry S Truman, and Joseph Stalin attended the Potsdam Conference, July–August 1945, to discuss the shape of the postwar world. Cooperation soon gave way to the cold war, and America's global interests and responsibilities multiplied dramatically.

support free peoples who are resisting attempted subjugation by armed minorities or by outside pressures." Congress agreed and voted over $400 million in aid.

But the Truman Doctrine implied more than just military containment. As the cold war progressed, the United States added economic and political components to build an alliance against the Soviets. America's European allies, suffering serious economic problems and facing large internal communist parties seeking to exploit those problems, needed immediate assistance if they were to help contain the Soviets. The response was the **Marshall Plan** (named after Secretary of State George C. Marshall). By providing over $17 billion in economic aid between 1948 and 1952, the plan helped the sixteen participating European states to begin to exceed prewar levels of production. While Marshall Plan aid was justified on political and humanitarian grounds, it also made good sense to American businesses, which had been locked out of European markets before World War II. Another link in the chain of containment was forged.

As U.S.-Soviet relations continued to deteriorate, especially over the issue of Western access to Berlin, which the Soviet Union had tried to close off in 1948, Truman concluded that economic aid and uncoordinated military programs for Europe were not enough. Containment also required collective defense arrangements unprecedented in peacetime. Thus, in 1949, the United States helped found NATO. The NATO allies, comprising the United States, Canada, and ten Western European nations (followed later by West Germany, Greece, Turkey, and Spain), pledged to "unite their efforts for collective defense." They agreed that "an armed attack against one or more of them in Europe or North America shall be considered an attack against them all."

As figure 19-1 shows, this collective defense approach was extended to other regions of the world when the United States also formally aligned itself with countries of Latin America (the Organization of American States, or OAS, 1948); with Australia and New Zealand (ANZUS, 1951), and with the countries of Southeast Asia (the Southeast Asia Treaty Organization, or SEATO, 1954). In addition, the United States concluded mutual defense pacts with South Korea, the Philippines, Taiwan, and Japan. The Soviet Union, meanwhile, formed the Warsaw Pact (1955) with the countries of Eastern Europe.

Korea: Containment's First Test

Containment faced a major test in 1950, when communist North Korea invaded South Korea. The United States, together with fifteen other nations fighting under the United Nations flag, intervened on the side of South Korea, while the Soviet Union was aligned with the North. To a large extent American strategists, concerned about Japan and the Philippines, considered Korea peripheral to the balance of power in the region. To them Korea was a local matter and thus "the wrong war in the wrong place at the wrong time."

President Truman, however, viewed the Korean conflict as a direct test of containment. If the United States failed to honor its commitment to South Korea, Truman reasoned, then the entire policy of collective security would be in doubt. It mattered not that Korea itself was of little strategic importance.[4] Using arguments that were to be echoed by President Nixon about Vietnam and President Reagan about Central America, Truman outlined the basic logic of the cold war: regardless of the country or the issue, a gain for the Soviet Union was, by definition, a loss for the United States.

Domestically, the war sparked a bitter debate. After three years of fighting, at a cost of more than 54,000 American, 14,000 allied, and untold numbers of Korean and Chinese lives, a stalemate truce was signed, with the borders between North and South Korea virtually unchanged. Some critics argued that the United States should have gone all out, invading North Korea and using atomic weapons against China if necessary. Others felt that the war lacked global importance. Looming large in the debate was the fear that a local conflict could escalate into a direct military confrontation between the United States and the Soviet Union. In Korea, America was thus introduced to the baffling dilemma of limited war.

Nor was Korea the end of American military engagements. In 1954 the United States helped to oust a democratically elected reformist regime in Guatemala, and in 1958 it sent 6,000 troops to quash a leftist revolt in Lebanon.

The 1960s: Active Containment around the Globe

In the 1960 presidential campaign, John Kennedy made military preparedness a major issue. He set in motion an ambitious program to expand land-based intercontinental missiles and submarine-launched missiles to complement America's long-range bomber fleet. With the advice of Secretary of Defense Robert McNamara, Kennedy sought to develop options to the Eisenhower administration's rigid and deadly strategy of massive retaliation by implementing a policy of "flexible response" in Europe. By expanding conventional forces, flexible response was intended to

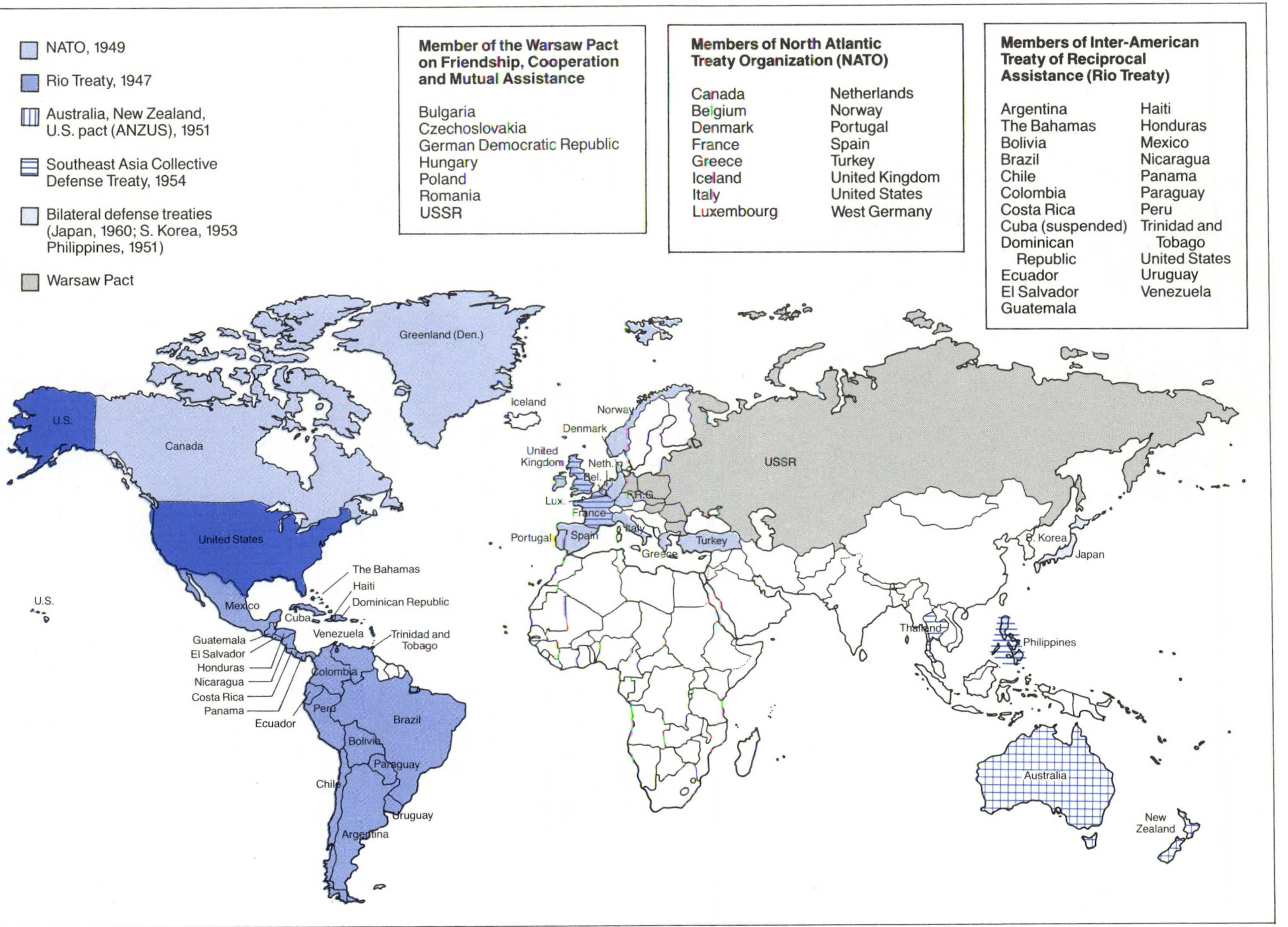

★ **Figure 19-1** U.S. collective defense treaties and the countries of the Warsaw Pact, 1955
SOURCE: U.S. Department of State, *Atlas of United States Foreign Relations,* 2d ed. (Washington, D.C.: U.S. Government Printing Office, 1985), p. 83.

★ Fidel Castro, leader of the Cuban Revolution. Cuba's ties with the Soviet Union and support for anti-government movements in Latin America have presented a continuing challenge for U.S. foreign policy-makers.

offer a range of options short of total nuclear war with the Soviets. With the advent of flexible response, NATO adopted a policy of limited nuclear war as one step in a chain of measures designed to deter a Soviet attack.

Kennedy's policy for the Third World was equally dynamic. In keeping with both the Monroe Doctrine and Truman's containment policy, the United States attempted unsuccessfully to overthrow the government of Fidel Castro by directing an invasion by Cuban refugees in 1961. Kennedy also helped create the Special Forces units of the military, trained to conduct counterinsurgency operations in the Third World. In the nonmilitary realm, the Kennedy administration sought to reduce the poverty that led to Third World unrest through such economic assistance programs as the Latin American–based Alliance for Progress. Third World economic programs, of course, were also designed to expand opportunities for U.S. investment and trade.

It was also in the Third World that cold war competition put the United States at the brink of a nuclear showdown with the USSR. In the summer of 1962, the Soviets decided to bridge the widening arms gap with a quick, low-cost solution—placing missiles in Cuba, only a short distance from U.S. shores. After an agonizing week of deliberations, Kennedy ordered a naval blockade of Cuba and warned that a Cuban-based missile attack on the United States would result in an immediate counterattack on the Soviet homeland. Faced with the prospect of a nuclear war in which it was seriously outgunned, the Soviet Union agreed to remove the missiles in exchange for a promise from Kennedy that no further military action would be taken against Cuba.

The Cuban crisis had a variety of effects on global relations. On the one hand, it forced the Soviets to abandon the low-cost weapons policy of Nikita Khrushchev and engage in a massive buildup. The Kremlin vowed never again to be subjected to nuclear blackmail by the United States. On the other hand, walking the tightrope of nuclear war so frightened both nations that they began to consider methods to reduce tension. Thus the "hot line" direct link between Washington and Moscow was established to improve communication during times of crisis. Another consequence, according to some observers, was that the United States' success in the

Cuban crisis boosted confidence in its military and foreign policy capabilities—a confidence that helped carry America into the mire of Vietnam.

As we will see in a later section, Vietnam was one of the most costly and controversial wars in American history. It raised serious doubts about the wisdom of America's military activities abroad. Above all, opposition to the war began a prolonged public dialogue about the wisdom of containment and confrontation with the Soviet Union.

★ Improving Relations with the Soviet Union

The 1970s introduced a new word to the American vocabulary and a new theme to the nation's foreign policy. **Détente,** roughly translated, means a process of gestures, negotiations, and agreements designed to lessen tension between the superpowers. Détente, although always controversial, was the predominant theme of American foreign policy in the 1970s. It returned, draped in various disguises and using several aliases, during the second Reagan administration.

When Richard Nixon took office in 1969, he, like many other Americans, began to feel that the containment crusade had to be modified. The nation, in this view, could no longer expect to impose its ideology on the world or maintain its we-will-go-anywhere policies of the previous decades:

> This is the message of the doctrine I announced at Guam—the "Nixon Doctrine." Its central thesis is that the United States will participate in the defense and development of allies and friends, but that America cannot—and will not—conceive *all* the plans, design *all* the programs, execute *all* the decisions and undertake *all* the defense of the free nations of the world. We will help where it makes a real difference and is considered in our interest.[5]

The Nixon Doctrine, which stated that the United States could not shoulder the entire military or economic burden of the Western alliance alone, represented a major reassessment of America's twenty-year policy of containment. Drawing upon the balance-of-power views of his top adviser, Henry Kissinger, President Nixon offered a classic "realist" perspective: while lofty goals are admirable, American economic and military interests come first.

The cornerstone of the Nixon-Kissinger foreign policy was the conviction that the use of an occasional carrot instead of the traditional stick in dealings with the Soviets and Chinese Communists could reap real benefits. By the 1970s, it was clear that neither regime was likely to collapse, as many U.S. policymakers had secretly hoped. Rather than continue to isolate them, Nixon reasoned, why not give China and the Soviet Union cause to cooperate through trade, arms control, and similar incentives? This strategy was the foundation for America's pursuit of détente with its traditional adversaries.

A key component of this strategy was the creation of so-called linkages—connections between various unrelated goals. In effect, the United States was saying to the Soviets, "If you want trade with us, stop supporting revolution in the Third World," or "If you want arms control, cooperate on human rights." Through such a policy of détente (or reduced tension) it was hoped that the crisis atmosphere of the cold war could be calmed. Central to this balancing act with the Soviets was another key part of détente—improved relations with the People's Republic of

★ Table 19-1
Action/reaction in the superpower arms race

Initiator/Year	*Action*	*Reactor/Year*
U.S., 1945	Atomic bomb	USSR, 1949
U.S., 1948	Intercontinental bomber	USSR, 1955
U.S., 1952	Thermonuclear bomb	USSR, 1953
USSR, 1957	Intercontinental ballistic missile	U.S., 1958
USSR, 1957	Earth-launched satellite	U.S., 1958
U.S., 1959	Photo-reconnaissance satellite	USSR, 1962
U.S., 1960	Submarine-launched ballistic missile	USSR, 1968
U.S., 1966	Multiple warhead	USSR, 1968
USSR, 1968	Anti-ballistic missile system	U.S., 1972
U.S., 1970	Multiple independently targeted warhead	USSR, 1975
USSR, 1977	Medium-range ballistic missile	U.S., 1983
U.S., 1982	Long-range cruise missile	USSR, 1984
U.S., 1985	New strategic bomber	USSR, 1987
U.S., 1986	Anti-satellite missile	USSR, *
U.S., 1988	Stealth bomber	USSR, *
U.S., *	Star Wars space weapons	USSR, *

*Under development.

SOURCE: Adapted from Ruth Leger Sivard, *World Military and Social Expenditures, 1985* (Washington, D.C.: World Priorities, 1985), p. 16.

China. As we will see, Nixon flew to China in 1972, ending several decades of official "nonrecognition" of the most populous nation on earth.

Détente and the Arms Race

Although Nixon sometimes denied it, a basic goal of the effort to improve relations with China was to gain bargaining power with the Soviets. The creation of a so-called triangular relationship among the three nations would allow the United States to expand détente and ensure stability through selective use of economic and political incentives. It seemed that the United States had little choice but to seek accommodation with its Communist adversaries. Having once enjoyed an overwhelming lead in the nuclear arms race, the United States now faced a Soviet arsenal that, though lacking in diversity and technical sophistication, boasted hundreds of intercontinental ballistic missiles (ICBMs) with very powerful warheads. U.S. strategic forces had expanded from 1,278 bombers and missiles in 1963 to 2,110 in 1970. During the same period Soviet forces increased from 387 to 1,957. As table 19-1 shows, the action/reaction cycle of the arms race seemed to have no end.

Arms races, of course, have existed throughout history. They are the product of the quest for a balance of power that has always characterized international relations. What sets the nuclear arms race apart is the destructive power of the weapons. Describing the dilemma presented by nuclear weapons, the strategist Bernard Brodie observed in 1946 that "thus far the chief purpose of our military

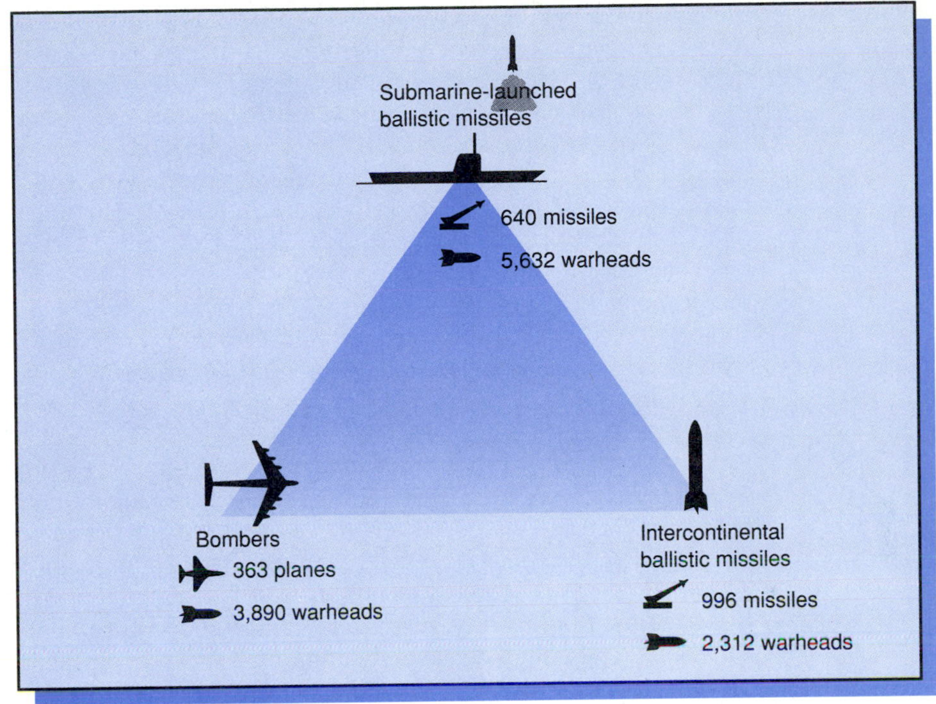

★ **Figure 19-2**
U.S. strategic triad
SOURCE: U.S. Bureau of the Census, *Statistical Abstract of the United States, 1989* (Washington, D.C.: U.S. Government Printing Office, 1989), p. 334.

establishment has been to win wars. From now on its chief purpose must be to avert them. It can have almost no other useful purpose."[6]

Given this reality, as the superpowers continued to build complex new weapons they gradually arrived at a nuclear stalemate, a "balance of terror." This global game of chicken was given a high-sounding name—**mutually assured destruction,** or **MAD** for short.

The logic of MAD was impeccable. Each side possessed a sufficient number of nuclear weapons to absorb an attack and launch a devastating counterattack against the enemy's cities. The threat of instant retaliation presented an unacceptable risk, thus deterring a nuclear first strike. To ensure survivability of weapons, both sides placed their missiles in underground silos or on submarines hidden in the sea's depths. Through MAD each superpower, in effect, held the other's population hostage. Figure 19-2 shows America's strategic triad.

Neither superpower was happy with the deadly logic of MAD. It ran counter to every military principle on which the modern nation-state was founded. "What in the name of God is strategic superiority?" asked Henry Kissinger in 1974. "What is the significance of it, politically, militarily, operationally, at these numbers? What do you do with it?"

There was also the problem of cost. The need to maintain a credible deterrent meant building new and more expensive weapons to counter real or imagined advances by the other side. By 1972 the United States was allocating 35 percent of the government's budget to the military ($748 billion in 1979 dollars). The Soviets in 1972 devoted 67 percent of their budget to the military ($824 billion).[7] Add to these issues the danger of accidental war, and it becomes easy to see why Nixon and his counterparts in Moscow were willing to consider some form of arms control.

As we saw in chapter 17, the idea of arms control was certainly not new. Since the cold war began, both the Americans and the Soviets had made numerous proposals to curb the spiraling arms race. For the most part, these proposals were offered either for propaganda purposes or as vain efforts to formalize one or the other's temporary advantage. One roadblock to arms control was overcome when rough strategic equivalence was reached in the late 1960s. The prospects for arms control were also improved when technical means of verification became possible. With satellite surveillance, the long-standing Soviet refusal to permit on-site inspection became less of a barrier to arms control.

In 1969, the Strategic Arms Limitations Talks (SALT) were begun in Helsinki, Finland. As signed by President Nixon and Soviet leader Leonid Brezhnev in Moscow in 1972, the SALT I treaty limited the deployment of anti-ballistic missile systems (ABMs) and placed a five-year ceiling on the number of strategic launching vehicles each side could possess. The ABM portion of the treaty was highly significant. By limiting the deployment of ABMs to a token 100 for each nation, SALT I was intended to prevent a costly and potentially destabilizing new aspect of the arms race. In forgoing a defensive buildup, both superpowers enshrined the notion of MAD—as long as each side's cities were vulnerable, stability would be maintained.

SALT I's limits on strategic launching vehicles (primarily ICBMs) were more symbolic in nature. The Soviets, because of their technical inferiority, were allowed more launching systems. The United States, able to pack a greater punch per launcher thanks to its multiple independent reentry vehicle (MIRV) technology, still maintained an overall warhead advantage of approximately 5,700 to 2,500. (Bombers and medium-range systems in Europe were not counted.) By permitting continued research and by focusing primarily on launchers rather than on warheads, each side was actually able to improve its arsenal under SALT I—a fact that did not escape the notice of the treaty's critics.

The Limits of Détente and Arms Control

A variety of factors combined to slow Nixon's policy of détente, including the Watergate scandal, which forced him from office. Many Americans, moreover, were skeptical of détente; whereas many liberals felt that arms control and other tension-relieving measures did not go far enough, conservatives were distrustful of the Soviets and feared that SALT I had given them a built-in advantage. President Ford attempted to continue the SALT process, signing in 1974 the interim Vladivostok agreement, which limited each side to 2,400 missiles and bombers, 1,320 of which could be armed with MIRV warheads. Despite the success at Vladivostok, it took five more years for the superpowers to complete the SALT II treaty. By then, relations had turned so sour that President Carter did not bother to submit the treaty to the Senate for ratification.

President Ford's problems with détente and arms control return us to some important subjects we have discussed earlier. Throughout Ford's term in office (1974–1976), many Americans continued to support arms control. Who was it, then, that created political problems for the president? Think back to our discussions of political behavior, political parties, elections, and interest groups (chaps. 7–10). Conservative interest groups, for instance, were certainly not comfortable with détente. Comprised mostly of citizens who took a hard-line internationalist view, these groups made matters difficult for Ford.

But can a minority of interest groups successfully pressure a president who serves all the people? In order to seek reelection in 1976, Ford first had to win the nomination of the Republican party. The well-organized conservative wing of the party, representing important sources of campaign finance, were openly being wooed by Ronald Reagan. In these circumstances, the conservative Republicans became crucial to Ford's campaign hopes. "So virulent was the right wing criticism," according to one analyst, "that in his 1976 campaign for the presidential nomination Ford explicitly renounced further official use of the word détente; and in the 1976 Republican National Convention the Reagan forces were able to insert anti-détente and anti-Kissinger planks in the platform."[8]

Détente by Any Other Name: The Carter Years

Disillusioned over Vietnam and Watergate, and hurting in the pocket from global recession, Americans looked for a fresh start in world affairs. In our examination of public opinion in regard to international affairs in chapter 7 we learned that in the 1970s Americans seemed more inclined toward isolationism. Reflecting this caution, Carter sought selective engagement, turning America's attention back to its neighbors in Latin America and emphasizing economic prosperity at home. Though Carter understood that many Americans were leery of activist/interventionist policies abroad, he still believed that America's well-being was linked to that of the global community.

The interdependence of the world's nations, according to Carter, actually reduced the need to rely on overt military action. By creating (or breaking) economic, political, and cultural forms of interdependence, the United States could influence other nations without resorting to direct confrontation or military intervention. He hoped to avoid the naked realism of the Nixon years and rekindle the belief that America stood for human rights. Carter improved America's image in Latin America by successfully negotiating the Panama Canal Treaty and rejecting use of the "big stick" when civil war in Nicaragua led to the ouster of the dictator Anastasio Somoza in 1979. Hoping to reduce the risk of nuclear war, Carter continued the SALT discussions with the Soviets.

But many Americans found Carter's low-key approach confusing. The United States seemed unable to deal with an increasingly hostile world. Alarmed by the Soviets' continued arms buildup, their invasion of Afghanistan, and the taking of hostages in Iran, a generation raised during the height of U.S. power in the 1950s wondered how America's position in the world could have declined so far. The public's flirtation with isolationism, ultimately a reaction to a unique set of circumstances, was brief. By the end of the 1970s, Carter abandoned many of his early policies and returned to a more traditional internationalist cold war stance. In the so-called Carter Doctrine, he warned Americans that they must be prepared to fight to protect access to Persian Gulf oil and other vital interests. But the damage had already been done. A well-organized campaign to restore what were called basic American values was being launched by a charismatic actor-turned-politician from California.

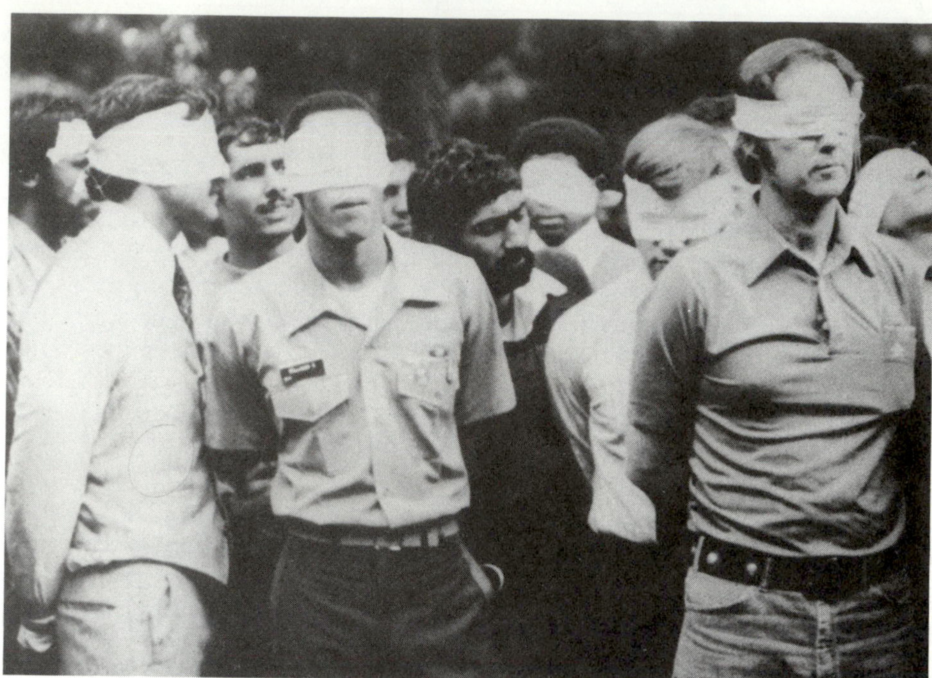

★ The Iran hostage crisis shook the nation and tarnished Jimmy Carter's foreign policy. In 1980, Ronald Reagan's promise to restore America's power abroad put him in the White House and détente on the back burner.

Ronald Reagan's campaign for the White House emphasized military toughness and the maintenance of the balance of power. Although he would eventually pursue his own brand of détente, Reagan was a classic cold warrior. At the heart of his message rested another basic theme underlying U.S. foreign policy: America was a unique nation with a special mission to promote freedom, prosperity, and democracy around the globe.

★ Promoting Capitalism and Free Trade

> A strong and prosperous American economy that relies on private enterprise and initiative is the most important pillar of a successful U.S. foreign economic policy. . . . We support and promote market-oriented economic policies that maximize economic opportunity and individual welfare throughout the globe as well as keep the U.S. economy strong.
>
> —*U.S. Department of State, 1988*

Throughout this book we have seen that growing economic interdependence with the rest of the world has altered American life in many ways. In our discussion of public opinion in chapter 7 we saw that people's basic philosophies of international relations can change when their economic well-being is involved. We have also explored how trade, foreign competition, and American access to oil and other raw materials abroad create political challenges for Congress, the president, interest groups, and the general public. At times, America's ideological commitment to free

★ President General Augusto Pinochet, the dictator who seized power in Chile in 1973. Pinochet's belief in capitalism and free trade helped him win U.S. economic and political backing. In the 1980s, however, U.S. support was tied to respect for human rights and a restoration of democracy. Here Pinochet is voting in a 1988 election to determine if his rule should continue.

enterprise and an open global trading system has also seemed messianic. As we learned in chapter 18, trade, foreign investment, and the role of U.S. corporations abroad are highly controversial issues in American politics.

Having concluded that the protectionist practices of many nations in earlier decades (including America's highly restrictive Smoot-Hawley tariff of 1930) had helped produce the global depression of the 1930s, the United States emerged from World War II with a strong commitment to increased global trade and investment. Along with many other industrialized nations, the United States helped form the General Agreement of Trade and Tariffs in 1947 (GATT), an organization dedicated to removing barriers to trade. The United States also was a founding member of the International Monetary Fund (IMF) and the International Bank for Reconstruction and Development (the World Bank). Through the Marshall Plan, it sent billions of dollars in aid to Western Europe.

As the United States came to dominate global trade and banking after World War II, the nation enjoyed significant political and economic benefits. A strong dollar made it possible to station troops around the globe, a vital part of containment. By 1950 the United States was producing 40 percent of the world's goods and services.[9] Between 1970 and 1980 the trade portion of the gross national product doubled, from 11 percent to 22 percent; an estimated five million Americans worked in export-related fields; and additional millions became linked to the global economy as consumers.

America's belief in capitalism went beyond promotion of free trade. The United States often made acceptance of free enterprise and rejection of socialism and communism a prerequisite for its political and economic assistance. In international organizations, including the United Nations and IMF, American representatives have been consistently outspoken in favor of policies that support market economies and diminish the state's role in local economies.

Like so many other aspects of our political life, America's commitment to free trade has, in practice, been compromised on many occasions. In the 1960s, the United States applied a total trade and financial embargo on the communist government of Cuba. President Carter in 1979 embargoed millions of tons of grain destined for the Soviet Union in retaliation for the invasion of Afghanistan. And in 1985 President Reagan, attempting to bring the Sandinista government down, ordered a suspension of trade with Nicaragua.

Suspension of trade for political reasons is but one of many ways in which America strays from strict adherence to free-trade principles. The most important deviation results from foreign competition and America's declining share of the world's trade. American farm exports, for example, dropped from a peak of $44 billion in 1981 to $28 billion in 1987. Arguing that producers in Europe, Asia, and Latin America subsidized their farmers unfairly, Congress passed the Farm Act of 1985, increasing various forms of assistance to American agriculture.[10]

The effort to support U.S. agriculture is one example of America's concern with foreign competition. As we saw in chapter 18, the growing debate over protectionism involves Congress, interest groups, foreign governments, and the general public. Whereas only 15 percent of U.S. business executives polled in 1980 favored import restrictions, by 1985 44 percent said that some limits should be instituted.[11] As America searches for a solution to its trade deficit, which reached $171 billion in 1987, we must remember that protectionist sentiments do not reflect a diminished belief in capitalism or free trade. Indeed, the Reagan and Bush administrations consistently argued that more, not less, free trade was the key to American and global prosperity. As for the Third World, nations that hope to remain on good economic and political terms with the United States must seek more free enterprise and foreign investment. Nations that pursue development through highly nationalistic and/or socialist methods run the risk of violating one of the most basic values of postwar American foreign policy.

★ American Exceptionalism

> There can be no question of our ceasing to be a world power. . . . The stage is set, the destiny disclosed. It has come to us by no plan of our conceiving, but by the hand of God who led us into this way. . . . America shall in truth show the way.
>
> —*Woodrow Wilson, 1918*

Throughout the nation's history, many citizens and leaders have believed that the very nature of their democracy made America an exceptional country. **American exceptionalism** is the belief that U.S. foreign policy is motivated by lofty moral values and goals rather than narrow self-interest. America, in other words, is an exception to the "realist" view, which sees all nations, regardless of political system, seeking to expand their wealth and power. "While other nations have interests," someone once quipped, "America has only ideals." Thus when the United States did get involved, it was in a "holy cause."

Very early in America's history, its political culture began to reflect this belief that the United States was fundamentally different from other nations. America's early military and economic expansionism in the Pacific and Latin America, for

example, was viewed as the nation's **manifest destiny,** a righteous cause linked to the will of God. It is "our manifest destiny," boasted John L. O'Sullivan, editor of the *New York Morning News* in 1845, "to overspread and to possess the whole of the continent which providence has given us for the development of the great experiment in liberty and federative self-government entrusted to us." The moralistic tone of manifest destiny was later given an international flavor by President William McKinley, who claimed that America's real goal in colonizing the Philippines was "to educate the Filipinos, and uplift and civilize and Christianize them." While many Americans found this righteous crusade hard to swallow, others saw it as a natural corollary to America's expanding power and wealth.

American exceptionalism has produced what one observer has called a certain dualism in U.S. foreign policy.[12] "Dualism" here refers to conflicting images of the nation's role in the world. American leaders speak with pride about the nation's revolutionary war for independence and democracy. But at the same time, America supports law and order, and its leaders tell oppressed peoples to use "ballots, not bullets," in their quest for freedom. This confusing dualism can lead to conflicting policies. During the 1980s, for instance, the Reagan administration funded antigovernment rebels in Nicaragua and Angola while sending military advisers to help the government of El Salvador suppress a popular insurrection.

A second conflicting message in U.S. foreign policy involves the use of force. On the one hand, America has built a massive arsenal of weapons, which it uses when necessary, often against nearly defenseless nations such as the Caribbean microstate of Grenada. The need for the use of force by other nations, however, is rarely accepted. As one observer noted, "When other nations act as we do, often in quite similar circumstance, we frown, grumble, or condemn. The use of force, the threat of force, the preparations to use force by our opponents are evil."[13] Thus America often applies a dual standard to foreign policy. Seeing itself as the world's most enlightened and benevolent nation, the United States claims to use force only when it is essential to a just cause. Other nations, especially America's foes, are depicted as using force solely in pursuit of narrow, selfish interests.

Idealism and Exceptionalism in the Postwar Era

Perhaps no event symbolizes American exceptionalism better than the Vietnam war. John Kennedy characterized Vietnam as "the cornerstone of the Free World in Southeast Asia." It represented "a proving ground of democracy in Asia . . . a test of American responsibility and determination." As his words imply, the Vietnam war was, in many respects, a logical and tragic result of American exceptionalism. The guerrilla insurgency in South Vietnam was widely viewed not merely as a nationalist, anticolonialist movement but as an instance of the threat of world communism. Many top U.S. officials subscribed to the **domino theory,** which held that a failure to thwart communist advances anywhere in the world would only inspire similar problems elsewhere. If South Vietnam "fell'" to communism, they argued, then other nations in Southeast Asia would collapse like a row of dominoes. While the domino theory drew upon the balance-of-power logic of containment, it was also rooted in the ideological belief that America had a moral obligation to fight communism around the globe. America, as an exceptional nation, could do no wrong even when it supported a dictatorship in South Vietnam or bombed civilian targets.

American interest in Vietnam began at the close of World War II with assistance to the French, who were struggling against determined anticolonialist forces in Indochina. After the decisive defeat of the French at Dienbienphu in 1954, the United States decided to support the regime of Ngo Dinh Diem in the south. Fearing the popularity of local Communists, Diem, with U.S. backing, refused to hold elections. In response to this refusal, and to the fact that Diem's regime was seen as corrupt and autocratic by many Vietnamese, guerrilla warfare erupted. By 1957, communist guerrillas (the Viet Cong) had expanded their attacks throughout the south, with support provided by North Vietnam, China, and the Soviet Union.

Fearing that an insurrection would topple Diem's government, Presidents Eisenhower and Kennedy gradually stepped up military and economic aid. By November 1963, the month both Kennedy and Diem were assassinated, more than 16,000 U.S. military "advisers" were fighting in Vietnam. Thus began what today is sometimes called the "Vietnam syndrome"—America's gradual involvement in an undeclared war in which the issues are unclear, the military options are limited by the threat of superpower involvement, and the nation is confused as to the proper course of action.

By 1968 the Johnson administration had committed more than 540,000 troops and thrown the massive weight of America's conventional air and naval forces into the battle. The American people, however, remained divided over Vietnam. Dissent over Vietnam led President Johnson not to seek a second term. The Nixon administration, with its "Vietnamization" policy, aimed at replacing U.S. troops with the army of South Vietnam, fared little better. After four years of war and negotiation, which saw massive U.S. bombing of North Vietnam, the invasion of Cambodia (1970), and hundreds of U.S. prisoners of war held as virtual hostages, a cease-fire agreement was reached in 1973. President Nixon's insistence on "peace with honor" had achieved neither. Two years later, the South Vietnamese government collapsed under a North Vietnamese–Viet Cong offensive.

The war had been extremely costly for America and the people of Southeast Asia. By the time the war ended in 1975, the United States had lost more than 56,000 lives, suffered more than 300,000 wounded, and spent more than $140 billion. The total number of Vietnamese deaths is reported to have exceeded one million.

Another casualty for many Americans was the credibility of their government.

★ April 1975: Planes evacuating U.S. personnel from Nha Trang are besieged by refugees fleeing the opposing forces advancing on the cities in South Vietnam.

The war divided the American people more than had any other conflict since the Civil War. U.S. support for a series of corrupt and repressive regimes, the questionable right of the United States to become involved in what seemed to be a local political struggle, the reports of napalm bombing and the massacre of civilians at My Lai and elsewhere, and the widespread belief that government officials were lying to the nation about the conduct of the war, fueled a mounting wave of angry protest. This anger, combined with the Watergate scandal and other revelations of political improprieties, further corroded Americans' faith in their government.

The tension between the idealism of American exceptionalism and the reality that the United States was pursuing its own narrow interest in Central America, South Africa, and the Middle East continued throughout the 1980s. Before we examine how the Reagan and Bush administrations dealt with these and other issues, it will be helpful to consider how foreign policy is actually made.

★ Making Foreign Policy: The Major Players

Throughout our study of American politics we have stressed that public policy flows from both the formal institutions of government (the executive, Congress, and the courts) and the individuals and groups that make up our diverse society. Thus we must examine political culture as well as the Constitution; we must study public opinion and participation as well as the president and the courts.

Foreign policy decisions result from the same interaction of people and institutions, including people and institutions outside our borders. With global interdependence politicizing many dimensions of American life, foreign policy decisions are sometimes reached in a highly emotional atmosphere, with intense media attention and wide-ranging public debate. Since these decisions involve our nation's basic values (and sometimes survival itself), it is no surprise that they are bathed in controversy.

Many of the tools needed to analyze foreign policy making have already been supplied in our discussion of the presidency, Congress, interest groups, and public policy. Still, decisions involving international politics present many unique challenges. Why, for instance, should a congressional representative from a rural agricultural district know or care about apartheid in South Africa? Yet we know that in overseeing the executive branch, our representatives in Congress routinely deal with issues far removed from their local districts. We may also ask why the president, the only person in America with both total access to classified information and the power of the commander in chief, should have his hands tied by Congress. Addressing these and similar questions can illuminate the complex issue of foreign policy making while simultaneously acting as a review for material presented in early chapters.

The President

On December 8, 1941, President Franklin Roosevelt addressed a joint session of Congress:

> Yesterday, December 7, 1941—a date which will live in infamy—the United States of America was suddenly and deliberately attacked by naval and air forces of the empire of Japan. . . . As Commander in Chief of the Army and Navy I have directed that all measures be taken for our defense, that always will our whole nation remember the character of the onslaught against us. . . . I ask that the Congress declare that since the unprovoked and dastardly attack by Japan on Sunday, December 7, 1941, a state of war has existed between the United States and the Japanese Empire.[14]

During an international crisis, Americans look almost instinctively to the president for inspiration and leadership. The office is certainly larger than any individual who occupies it. Who could not be moved by the dramatic swearing in of Lyndon Johnson on *Air Force One* a few brief hours after President Kennedy was felled by an assassin's bullets? The chain of command must not be broken.

As chapter 13 points out, the president is central to the foreign policy process. As commander in chief of the armed forces and as the nation's principal spokesperson on the world stage, the president sets the general tone of American foreign policy. The Constitution grants the president the power "to make Treaties, provided two-thirds of the Senators present concur," to "appoint Ambassadors, other public Ministers and Consuls," to "receive Ambassadors and other public Ministers," and to serve as "Commander in Chief of the Army and Navy of the United States." From these provisions other presidential powers flow: he may choose to recognize or sever relations with governments of other nations; he may conclude executive agreements with foreign nations without formal Senate approval; and he may send armed forces abroad at any time.

In chapter 7 we learned that the public mood usually ebbs and flows in response to dynamic presidential actions. When Lyndon Johnson decided to begin bombing North Vietnam, a once-skeptical public temporarily rallied round. Indeed, many Americans today have come to accept the idea that the president should dominate military and foreign policy. With the vast technological changes of the nuclear age, it seems that only the president can respond to emergencies with appropriate speed and decisiveness. It is estimated that the president may have only thirty minutes' warning of a nuclear attack, hardly time enough for a detailed policy review by Congress. Only the president is supplied with daily intelligence reports compiled by the Central Intelligence Agency and the State and Defense Departments, and thus has the information and expertise needed to act decisively. It is partly for these reasons, in fact, that Congress has been reluctant to curb the president in military and foreign policy matters—although that reluctance has been waning.

The president, of course, must act within bounds set by events outside his control. Not only is he tied to many of the policies of his predecessors—foreign aid programs, mutual defense pacts, treaties, and so on—but his plans are constantly subject to changes occurring in other nations. A new foreign leader may come to power, a poor nation may default on debts owed to U.S. banks, or a war between two strategically important nations may erupt. In 1982, for instance, America found itself in a highly embarrassing situation when two long-time friends, Argentina and Great Britain, went to war over the Falkland/Malvinas Islands in the South Atlantic, forcing President Reagan to take sides. In choosing to support loyal ally Britain over Argentina, which had seized disputed territory by force, the president knew that relations with Latin America would suffer. A president faces such no-win choices daily.

Within the legal boundaries of the Constitution and the constraints imposed by a hostile and often uncooperative world, the president has considerable room for initiative and creativity in foreign policy. This is where the personality and leadership style of the president can truly change history. One such presidential initiative was Richard Nixon's decision to reestablish diplomatic contact with the People's Republic of China.

Presidential Creativity: Nixon's Opening to China

When President Nixon stepped off *Air Force One* in February 1972 and into the waiting arms of the once-dreaded Chinese Communists, many people felt that this was his finest hour. The opening of China marked not only a major turning point in U.S. foreign relations but the culmination of one of the most remarkable personal political comebacks in American history. Nixon's China trip also ensured that this comeback would not be cut short by electoral defeat in November.

To be sure, the opening to China was inextricably tied to the major foreign policy issues of the day: the Vietnam war and relations with the Soviets. At the same time it was an intensely personal goal for Nixon, a goal linked directly to domestic political problems and the president's preoccupation with his image in history. Ironically, Nixon had been closely associated early in his political career with the so-called China lobby, a group dedicated to maintaining U.S. support for Chiang Kai-Shek's government in Taiwan. In the 1950s Nixon and the China lobby relentlessly opposed recognition of the communist government on the Chinese mainland. As early as 1960, however, Nixon recognized that the world's largest nation could not be ignored forever. "In the long view," Nixon wrote in 1967, "we simply cannot afford to leave China forever outside the family of nations.[15]

★ President Nixon and Chairman Mao confer during their historic meeting in 1972. Not only was Nixon's journey to China a diplomatic coup; it also bolstered the president's sagging popularity at home.

Once in the White House, Nixon began tiptoeing around the idea of an approach to China as early as November 1969. Such a dramatic change in U.S. policy held many political risks, both foreign and domestic. But risk was nothing new to the man who had risen from the ashes of political humiliation in the 1960s to the nation's highest office:

> My own attitude toward crisis is best expressed in the way the word "crisis" is written in the Chinese language. Two characters are combined to form the one: One brush stroke stands for "danger" and the other character stands for "opportunity."[16]

Once the decision to approach the Chinese Communists was made, President Nixon and his national security adviser, Henry Kissinger, began a series of maneuvers befitting a spy novel. Between 1969 and 1971, an intricate web of back-channel communications and diplomatic signaling was spun that ranged from secret contacts through France, Romania, Pakistan, and Norway to exchange visits by American and Chinese table tennis players (the much-celebrated "Ping-Pong diplomacy").

By 1971, the opening to China was no longer simply desirable but a political imperative for the survival of the Nixon presidency. Deep in the Vietnam quagmire and facing bloody demonstrations at home, Nixon hoped the Chinese would help him attain "peace with honor." An opening to China could also provide leverage over the Soviets in arms talks, and the potential trade opportunities for U.S. business would build popularity at home. The Chinese leaders, displaying a keen appreciation of the president's political need for a diplomatic success, drove a hard bargain. At one point in early 1971, the Chinese hinted that they might invite the front-running Democrats—Edward Kennedy, Edmund Muskie, and George McGovern—for a visit. This storm was weathered, no such invitations were forthcoming, and after a series of concessions on both sides (China pressuring North Vietnam to accept a peace plan, the United States loosening its commitment to Taiwan), Nixon's trip was on.

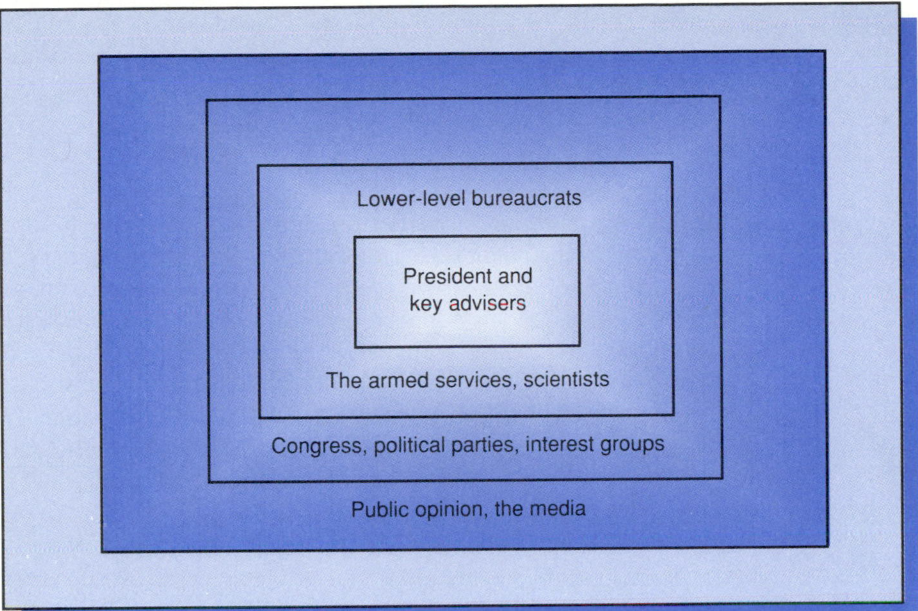

★ **Figure 19-3**
Levels of foreign policy decision making in the United States
SOURCE: Adapted from Charles W. Kegley, Jr., and Eugene W. Wittkopf, *American Foreign Policy: Pattern and Process,* 3d ed. (New York: St. Martin's Press, 1987), p. 335. Originally formulated by Roger Hilsman in *To Move a Nation* (New York: Doubleday, 1967), pp. 541–544.

Nixon's China trip was indeed a political bonanza, complete with intense media coverage: Nixon exchanging toasts with Chinese Communists, Nixon at the Great Wall, Nixon meeting Chairman Mao Zedong. This political angle offered an important lesson. A major foreign policy event is never entirely international in scope. The complex calculations that propelled Nixon toward China sprang not only from the crisis-laden atmosphere of the Pentagon and State Department but also from the gut-level instincts of the politician. In summarizing the impact of the China opening on American voters, the journalist Seymour Hersh has written that "although the President would continue to use dirty tricks and illegalities in the campaign, none of the Democratic candidates, after the summit, would pose a serious threat to his lead in the polls."[17]

The President's Inner Circle

A multitude of government and nongovernment organizations and personal advisers help the president to make foreign policy (see figure 19-3). Depending on the president's style of leadership, the number of experts and aides who form the inner circle of the White House foreign policy team may vary greatly. Along with personal political advisers, those closest to the president in foreign affairs often include the secretary of state, the secretary of defense, the White House chief of staff, the ambassador to the United Nations, and a person whose position grew greatly in power during the Nixon administration, the national security adviser.

The National Security Council

This inner circle comes together under the auspices of the National Security Council (NSC). Formally consisting of the president, vice-president, secretary of state, and secretary of defense, the NSC draws upon a wide-ranging group of executive branch officials and is supported by a staff of military, political, and economic specialists. The NSC was formed by Congress in 1947 to "advise the President with respect to the integration of domestic, foreign, and military policies relating to the National security." In other words, the NSC aids the president by condensing the wealth of information that pours in from around the globe and then setting out policy options.

Officially, the NSC's task is to advise the president, not to make or implement policy. In reality, the NSC's tasks and importance have varied from administration to administration (see figure 19-4). The Tower Commission, which investigated the Iran-Contra affair, reported in February 1987:

> The National Security Council has from its inception been a highly personal instrument. Every President has turned for advice to those individuals and institutions whose judgment he has valued and trusted. For some Presidents, such as President Eisenhower, the National Security Council served as a primary forum for obtaining advice on national security matters. Other Presidents, such as President Kennedy, relied on more informal groupings of advisors, often including some but not all of the Council members.[18]

As we shall see, one of the more dramatic (and controversial) uses of the NSC occurred during the Reagan administration, when staff members turned from their purely advisory role to actually making and carrying out crucial policy initiatives without informing the president.

The National Security Adviser

The **national security adviser** (officially known as the special assistant for national security affairs), though not a statutory member of the NSC, is closely associated with foreign policy decision making. Reliance on the national security adviser has varied greatly from president to president. President Nixon's national security adviser, Henry Kissinger, became the focal point of policy making; his influence often overshadowed that of the departments of State and Defense. Recognizing that knowledge is power, Kissinger came to sit at the crucial intersection where information from the far-flung branches of government converge. According to a member of the NSC staff, Kissinger was "like a freight yard with 500 tracks coming in and one going out."[19]

Jimmy Carter's national security adviser was a vital member of the foreign policy team but never achieved the preeminence of Henry Kissinger. When President Reagan took office in 1981, he hoped to reorganize foreign policy making with a less visible and more managerial style for the national security adviser. Ironically, Reagan's fourth national security adviser, Vice-Admiral John M. Poindexter, pursued policies far beyond his authority, policies that led to the

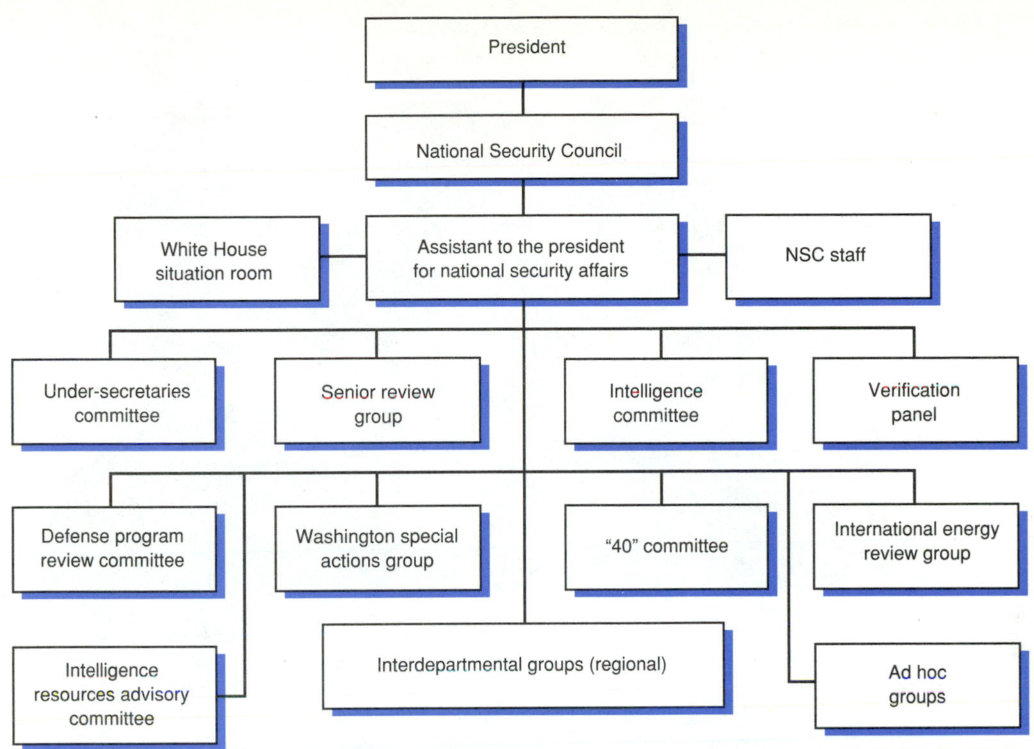

The Nixon National Security Council, 1969–1974

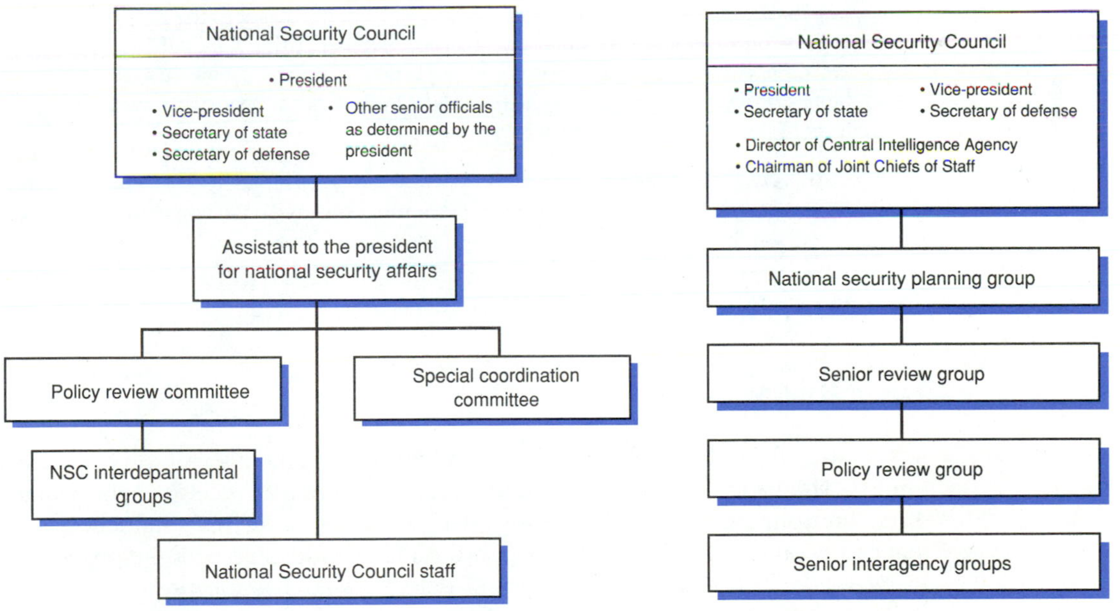

The Carter National Security Council, 1977–1981

The Reagan National Security Council, 1987

★ **Figure 19-4**

The NSC is organized differently with each new president. Three past presidents chose their own way to organize the NSC: Nixon *(top)*, Carter *(left)*, and Reagan *(right)*.

SOURCES: Nixon, Congressional Research Service, Library of Congress; Carter, prepared by the Carter White House, 1977; Reagan, based on documents prepared by the Reagan White House, 1987.

★ The military is big business, and its economic clout (combined with its technical and strategic expertise) gives the Pentagon brass a major voice in U.S. foreign policy.

Iran-Contra scandal. The Tower Commission pointed out the danger of personal advocacy on the part of the national security adviser:

> As the "honest broker" of the NSC process, the National Security Advisor must ensure that the different and often conflicting views of the NSC principals are presented fairly to the President. But as an independent advisor to the President, he must provide his own judgment. To the extent that the National Security Advisor becomes a strong advocate for a particular point of view, his role as "honest broker" may be compromised and the President's access to the unedited views of the NSC principals may be impaired.[20]

Ultimately the president alone determines who will sit in the inner circle. Presidents surround themselves with advisers whom they trust, regardless of their formal position in government. President Kennedy often consulted his brother Robert, the attorney general; both Carter and Reagan were reported to rely on their wives when difficult decisions were to be made.

The Military

A step away from the president's inner circle lies the remainder of the executive branch. The various branches of the military, for example, receive their civilian direction from the secretary of defense. The secretary of defense's influence, like that of any other cabinet member, depends on his relationship with the president. In most administrations, the secretary of defense serves as the president's chief military adviser and plays a central role in shaping defense policy. He is responsible for supervising the military budget, advising the president and Congress on new weapons systems, and funneling presidential directives to the military, among other things.

Much of the secretary's influence derives from his position as head of the largest department in the federal bureaucracy. He is boss of about one million civilians and more than two million military personnel. In fact, not only is the Defense Department the government's largest employer, it is also the largest single

customer of American business, awarding defense contracts totaling more than $158 billion a year. As the 1980s came to an end, the department was responsible for a military budget of about $300 billion a year.

Budget oversight has become a highly volatile issue as allegations of illegal practices by major defense contractors anger a tax-conscious public. Add to this distress the outcry that accompanies other excesses, such as the Pentagon's $7,600 coffeemaker for the C-5 cargo plane, and we can see why the secretary must pay close attention to spending priorities.

The military itself, a major component of government, also influences policy formation. At times, advocacy by a popular military official can cause open conflict with political leaders. General Douglas MacArthur's public disagreement with President Truman over Korea led to his dismissal by the commander in chief. At other times military influence is more subtle but no less important. In chapter 14, we discussed the crucial role that government agencies and interservice rivalry can play at tense times, as during the Cuban missile crisis. Competition among branches of the military service (and government agencies, for that matter) continues to cloud decisions on weapons purchases and strategy. Some observers feel that the desire to include the army, air force, and navy in the invasion of Grenada in 1983, for instance, led to a costly and dangerous lack of coordination.

Many segments of American society, of course, are concerned with the military and its spending. In our examination of interest groups in chapter 10, we saw that a long list of individuals and organizations influence government policy. In chapter 3, moreover, we learned that local politicians may seek construction of a military facility in their town, in order to benefit from jobs and new business. The late senator Henry Jackson was lightheartedly called "the senator from Boeing" because of his concern for the giant aerospace company in his home state of Washington. That decisions are sometimes made for economic rather than security reasons is a notable aspect of American military spending.

The Intelligence Community

> Covert activities place a great strain on the process of decision making in a free society.
>
> —*Tower Commission Report, 1987*

The intelligence community is also a major player in U.S. foreign policy. The major members of the "community" include:

Air Force Intelligence	Federal Bureau of Investigation
Army Intelligence	Marine Corps Intelligence
Central Intelligence Agency	National Security Agency
Defense Intelligence Agency	Naval Intelligence
Drug Enforcement Agency	State Department
Department of Energy	Treasury Department

Primary among these many agencies charged with keeping track of world events is the Central Intelligence Agency (CIA). Created by Congress in 1947, the CIA serves directly under the National Security Council, supplying it with information gathered from both covert and open sources. Its director, appointed by the president and confirmed by the Senate, is responsible for coordinating the activities and flow of information from other government agencies.

The CIA's intelligence-gathering activities have, for the most part, been accepted by the American public as a basic aspect of national security. A nation with wide-ranging global concerns must have up-to-date information about its international rivals. Controversy develops, however, when the CIA goes beyond information gathering and attempts to influence events in other nations through covert operations.

A covert operation may be as mundane as an effort to discredit a foreign public official by implicating him in drug use, illicit sex, or bribery; or it may involve the funding and operation of full-scale military activities. A CIA recruitment pamphlet says:

> Besides its primary job of collecting intelligence, the Clandestine Service ... seeks to change adversaries into friends or neutrals through covert operations by political, psychological, or paramilitary means. It works with friendly intelligence services toward mutual goals. It also defends itself and the government against hostile penetration and attack.

The CIA has toppled the governments of Iran (1953), Guatemala (1954), and South Vietnam (1963); directed the ill-fated Bay of Pigs invasion of Cuba (1961); aided the overthrow of the constitutionally elected government of Salvador Allende in Chile (1973); and worked with the Contra opposition in Nicaragua (1981). It has also plotted the assassination of several foreign leaders, including Rafael Trujillo of the Dominican Republic, Fidel Castro of Cuba, the Congo's Patrice Lumumba, and Muammar Qaddafi of Libya.[21] Such actions have sparked resentment among citizens of other nations and have helped inflame anti-American sentiment abroad.

Because many of the CIA's operations have been conducted in secrecy, however, the full extent of its activities has been difficult to determine. Following revelations about the CIA's covert operations (and its alleged involvement in internal spying on American citizens), Congress in the mid-1970s began to take a closer

★ CIA headquarters. From its facilities in Virginia, the CIA operates a vast intelligence and covert operations network.

look at the agency's budget and activities. In 1976 the Senate established a Select Committee on Intelligence to oversee the CIA and other intelligence agencies. The House of Representatives followed suit in 1977. The primary motivation for congressional oversight was excessive covert operations, not the agency's intelligence-gathering activities. Thus congressional interest did not portend a dismantling of the CIA. In fact, according to Senator Daniel Patrick Moynihan of New York, a long-time member of the Senate's Select Committee on Intelligence, "like other legislative committees, ours came to be an advocate for the agency it was overseeing."[22] The overall intelligence budget tripled between 1976 and 1986.

Congressional oversight, nonetheless, was too constricting for President Reagan's CIA director, William Casey. According to testimony given during the Iran-Contra congressional hearings in 1987, Casey attempted to establish a permanent nongovernmental group to engage in covert operations free of congressional scrutiny. Thus, despite the recognized need for intelligence gathering, covert operations can become highly controversial when there is no firm agreement among the branches of government or the public about America's proper role in its dealings with other nations. The most dramatic controversy over covert operations in recent times was the Iran-Contra scandal, which erupted in November 1986.

The Iran-Contra Scandal and the Inner Circle

The Iran-Contra scandal reveals the difficulties that arise when Congress, the president, and the people cannot agree on U.S. foreign policy. The scandal evolved from a dispute between the Reagan administration and Congress over military versus political strategies in Central America. Out of what seemed to be a typical

★ American adviser trains Contra troops in Central America. Disagreement between the White House and Congress over help to the Contras to overthrow the government of Nicaragua set one branch of government against another.

disagreement between Congress and the president came one of the major political dramas of our day.

The controversy began in 1981 when President Reagan ordered U.S. economic support and military training for the forces, known as Contras, opposing the government of Nicaragua (see figure 19-5). Congress showed its disapproval by passing the Boland Amendment, barring the CIA or Department of Defense from attempting to overthrow the government of Nicaragua. The Boland Amendment, however, did not outlaw the use of U.S. funds to put pressure on the Nicaraguan government to stop aiding revolutionary movements in El Salvador and elsewhere in the region. The White House, exploiting this loophole, continued to aid the Contras.

The controversy intensified in the summer of 1983 when it was learned that the CIA had directed the mining of Nicaraguan harbors and had worked closely with the Contras at many levels. The distinction between pressuring Nicaragua and trying to overthrow the government was becoming increasingly murky. In December 1983 Congress further limited CIA and Defense Department work with the Contras and in October 1984 all U.S. funding to the Contras was cut. By this time, President Reagan, who referred to the Contras as "freedom fighters," had adopted their cause as his own, and he was determined to continue to provide them with support. Thus the stage was set for a classic confrontation between the executive and legislative branches of government.

The Reagan administration's solution was both creative and of questionable legality. The National Security Council, the president's advisory inner circle, was to become an active player in delivering weapons to the Contras. If Congress prohibited the CIA or Department of Defense from providing military assistance, then

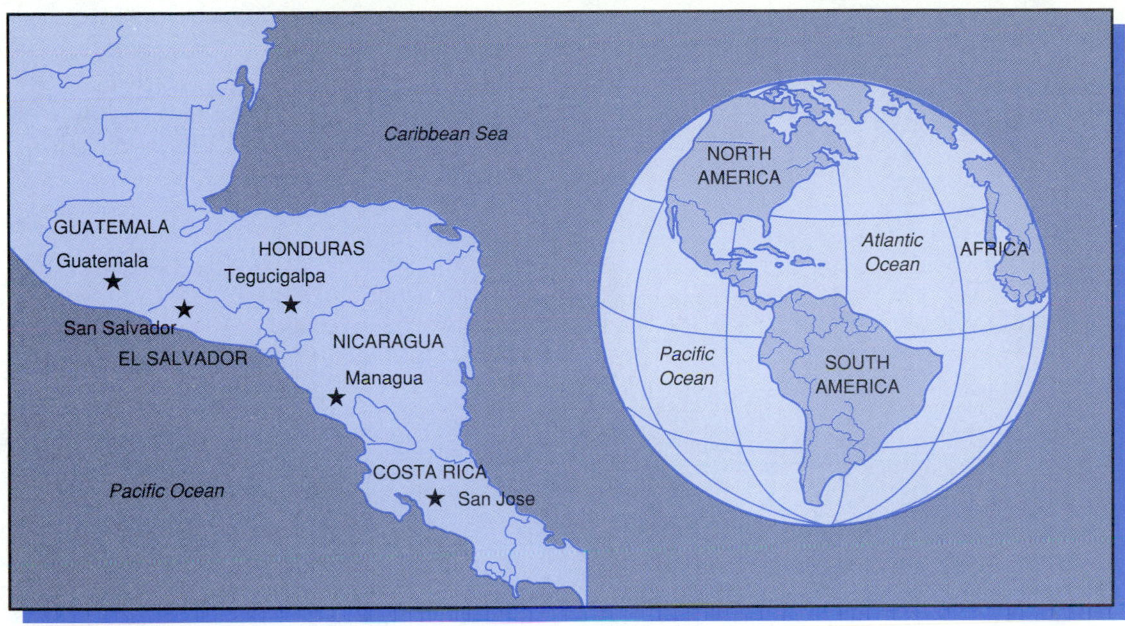

Figure 19-5
Central America, a region where U.S. security and human rights goals often clash.
SOURCE: U.S. Department of State, "U.S. Support for Democracy and Peace in Central America," (Washington, D.C.: Bureau of Public Affairs, March 1989).

the military experts on the NSC staff, according to the Tower Commission, would fill the void:

> After October 2, 1984, the NSC staff—particularly Oliver North—moved to fill the void left by the Congressional restrictions. Between 1984 and 1986, Lt. Col. North, with the acquiescence of the National Security Advisor [John Poindexter], performed activities the CIA was unable to undertake itself, including the facilitation of outside fund-raising efforts and oversight of a private network to supply lethal equipment to the Contras.[23]

The NSC's operational activities in Central America, problematic in their own right, soon became entangled with other administration covert operations. Ronald Reagan, like presidents before him, was engaged in a long and often futile search for solutions to the perennial problems in the Middle East. He was especially concerned about Iran and its apparent support for terrorism and the taking of American hostages in Lebanon. After many unsuccessful initiatives toward Iran, the NSC determined that a diplomatic opening was possible through the sale of weapons needed in Iran's bloody war with Iraq.

President Reagan was first informed of the efforts to improve relations with Iran from his national security adviser, Robert McFarlane, in 1985. The president gave formal written approval of arms sales in January 1986, but shipments through Israel had actually begun in August 1985. The profits from the sales, according to NSC staff member Colonel Oliver North, were eventually used to avoid congressional restrictions and assist the Contras in Nicaragua. The organization for supplying arms to Iran and transferring profits to the Contras was provided by former

Iran-Contra Chronology of Events

December 1981
President Reagan authorizes covert assistance to Contras.

Summer 1983
CIA offers direct assistance with Contra attacks in Nicaragua.

March 1984
William Buckley, CIA station chief in Lebanon, is kidnapped

August 1984
National Security Adviser Robert McFarlane asks government agencies to reassess policy toward Iran.

October 1984
Congress bans all aid to Contras.

July 1985
President Reagan directs McFarlane to contact Iran.

August 1985
Arms are shipped to Iran by way of Israel under direction of National Security Adviser McFarlane. Role of president is uncertain.

December 1985
Colonel Oliver North of NSC staff tells Israelis that profits from arms sales to Iran will be used to fund Nicaraguan Contras.

January 1986
President Reagan authorizes arms shipments to Iran.

April 1986
Memo from North outlining diversion of profits from arms sales to Contras is given to Admiral John Poindexter for relay to President Reagan. Poindexter claims memo was never delivered.

June 1986
Congress authorizes $100 million in aid to Contras.

November 1986
Attorney General Edwin Meese announces Iran-Contra arms arrangements. National Security Adviser Poindexter resigns and Colonel North is dismissed from NSC staff. President Reagan indicates that this is the first he knew of Iran-Contra arms connection.

February 1987
Tower Commission finds that top presidential advisers were responsible for Iran-Contra program and faults the president for being out of touch with staff operations.

May 1987
Congress begins hearings of Iran-Contra affair.

July 1987
Colonel North testifies that CIA director William Casey was aware of Iran-Contra arms deals. Admiral Poindexter testifies that he did not tell the president to afford him "plausible deniability."

November 1987
Congressional Iran-Contra committee issues final report.

July 1988
Oliver North is indicted.

May 1989
North is found guilty on three counts, not guilty on nine counts on which evidence or testimony indicated he had been following the orders of higher authorities. ★

SOURCE: *New York Times,* November 19, 1987, p. 8.

U.S. military personnel and private citizens under the direction of the NSC and CIA. These activities were apparently conducted without the knowledge of Congress, the State Department, the Department of Defense, or the president.

The Iran-Contra policy became public in November 1986. The public's initial shock at learning that President Reagan would approve the sale of weapons to a nation that he continually accused of terrorism turned to amazement as the extent of the intrigue came to light. The Iran-Contra scandal, part spy thriller, part soap opera, captivated the nation as the story unfolded during special congressional hearings held in the spring and summer of 1987.

Congress and the public focused on why the president sold arms to Iran, and asked if he knew that the profits were being used for the Contras. Reagan said that the provision of aid to Iran represented an effort to improve relations with a strategically important nation, and though no ransom was intended, the arms may have indirectly helped release American hostages in Lebanon. Ultimately, the president admitted that the policy was "flawed and mistakes were made."[24] But the president steadfastly denied any knowledge that the NSC or any other administration officials were supplying funds or weapons to the Contras. The final report of Congress offered no conclusive proof that the president had approved the diversion of funds to the Contras.

Behind the drama of the Iran-Contra scandal were serious issues. Obviously, the NSC's effort to establish a private network to conceal administration activities from Congress (perhaps with the aid of the CIA) threatened the constitutional mandate for co-equal branches of the government. The decision by the president's closest advisers deliberately to shield him from their efforts to aid the Contras was equally troubling. Many citizens wondered if Reagan should have been more dynamic in running his administration. And what of George Bush? Did he, as vice-president, know of the illegal aid to the Contras and the equally illegal sale of weapons to Iran? These and a wealth of other questions stemming from the Iran-Contra scandal continue to offer ample food for thought for any student of American politics.

The State Department and Its Bureaucracy

Although the State Department has one of the smallest budgets and staffs of any cabinet department, it is the oldest in the executive branch (1789) and one of the most influential. In addition to advising the president on foreign policy, it represents the United States in such international organizations as the United Nations and in every foreign nation with which we have formal relations. It also helps negotiate treaties, operates cultural exchange programs, assists business transactions, and issues passports and visas. About half of its employees—including U.S. ambassadors, Foreign Service officers, and country desk officers—are stationed in embassies and consulates overseas.

The head of the department, the secretary of state, is the highest-ranking cabinet member (he is fourth in line to succeed the president) and often serves as the chief adviser and spokesperson for the president on foreign affairs. The actual amount of influence wielded by the secretary of state, however, depends on his relationship with the president. In past administrations his influence has sometimes been eclipsed by the president's national security adviser, the secretary of defense, and other governmental officials.

Congress

As we have seen, American politics is based on the sharing of powers and responsibilities by the three branches of government. It should come as no surprise that Congress has a major influence on American foreign policy. Although the president has tended to dominate foreign policy making, Congress also has wide-ranging responsibilities. The Constitution grants Congress the power to declare war, regulate commerce with foreign nations, provide for the common defense, and "raise and support Armies." In addition, it grants the Senate the power to approve treaties and diplomatic appointments. As should be obvious in the light of the Iran-Contra scandal, a president ignores Congress at his own risk.

Indeed, Congress's constitutional powers can be formidable. The power of the purse was the weapon Congress used to limit the Reagan administration's support for the Nicaraguan Contras. The power to declare war and fund the military usually requires the president to consider the wishes of Congress. The mandate to regulate commerce means America's multi-billion-dollar foreign trade is subject to congressional control, as is the granting of foreign economic and military aid. The Senate's power to approve treaties can severely limit a president's foreign policy agenda, as Woodrow Wilson learned when his much-prized Treaty of Versailles was rejected by the Senate. The Senate can also send the president a strong message by rejecting a diplomatic appointment.

These constitutional powers notwithstanding, Congress was more or less content to let the president dominate foreign policy up until the 1970s. In the early 1970s, however, Congress began to reassert its powers and to challenge executive authority in various areas of foreign policy making. Many congressional representatives felt they had been misled by Johnson and Nixon about Vietnam, and acted to place limits on the president's warmaking prerogatives. Their dissatisfaction culminated in the passage of the War Powers Resolution, limiting the use of U.S. forces abroad without congressional approval.

Thinking back to chapters 12 and 13 on Congress and the presidency, we know the War Powers Resolution was a controversial effort to redefine the relationship between the executive and legislative branches of government. Although no president had acknowledged the constitutional validity of the resolution, none yet has directly challenged it. Thus when U.S. troops have been sent abroad, as to Lebanon in 1982–1984, to Grenada in 1983, and to the Persian Gulf in 1987, President Reagan, while not acknowledging the resolution's validity, claimed to have remained within its provisions. Though some members of Congress disagreed, no formal action was taken. By and large, both Congress and the executive concur that invoking the War Powers Resolution would produce a highly partisan struggle at a time when tension both at home and abroad ran high, as at the time of the bombing of Libya in 1986.

When we consider Congress's influence on foreign policy, we cannot forget its ability to investigate (and publicize its findings in the media). Time and again, congressional hearings have brought to light administration policies that, as in the case of the Iran-Contra hearings, have sparked nationwide debate on American foreign policy and the separation of powers. While the president may enjoy great power in foreign policy, it is not absolute.

The Public and Foreign Policy

Last but certainly not least in the foreign policy process is the American public. As we noted earlier, the problems of distance and misinformation present barriers to the public's full participation in foreign policy decisions. At the same time, such issues as arms reductions, human rights, global pollution, instability in the Third World, and foreign economic competition have tremendous emotional impact. Often it is an individual's membership in a church, labor union, or other group that heightens his or her awareness of international events.

Along with the general public, special interests, such as transnational corporations, often demand specific policies toward other nations. In the early 1970s, for example, the ITT Corporation—anxious to prevent nationalization of its investments in Chile—moved to persuade President Nixon to help overthrow the socialist government of Salvador Allende.

Lobbying efforts aside, the public's role in foreign policy is primarily reactive. The technological imperatives of the nuclear age have reinforced the president's domination of the foreign policy process. Still, neither the public nor Congress can be ignored for long. Congress can cut funds and turn up the heat by publicizing unpopular policies. The public can influence policy at the polls or, in such extreme cases as Vietnam, in the streets.

The Human Element

In looking at institutions and formal decision making, we should never lose sight of the human drama of diplomacy: the drama of Roosevelt meeting with Stalin and Churchill at Yalta or Jimmy Carter agonizing over the fate of American hostages in Iran. Sometimes the drama will be played out in public, as with President Reagan's open effort to sell "covert" operations in Central America. At other times it will be cloaked in secrecy worthy of a spy novel, as with Kissinger's use of back-channel communications to strike a deal with China and George Bush's efforts to remove Panamanian strong-man General Manuel Noriega from power. Foreign policy may be rooted in rational calculation of national interest, but the political and economic goals are interpreted and pursued by mortal men and women. Given the high stakes, foreign policy may be complex, confusing, and highly emotional, but it is never boring.

★ From Reagan to Bush: Looking toward the 1990s

> Quite obviously, the widespread desire for a safer and more humane world is—by itself—not enough to create such a world. In pursuing our worthy goals, we must go beyond honorable intentions and good will to practical means.
>
> —*Ronald Reagan, 1986*

In many ways the Reagan presidency embodied many of the foreign policy themes we have discussed here. Though Reagan and his supporters recognized America's vast international interests and responsibilities, they seemed to long for a simpler time when Americans could at least toy with the idea of isolationism. Reagan was also a fierce cold warrior with a strong foundation in traditional balance-of-power politics. Reagan's world view had much in common with the views of his predecessors in the 1940s and 1950s, and he was quite at home with the policy of "containing" the Soviet Union. And he firmly believed that America was an exceptional nation, genuinely interested in promoting the general welfare of all peace-loving nations. Somewhat surprisingly, in his second term President Reagan reached broad agreements with the Soviet Union, opening up the possibility of a new era of détente with the nation he had once labeled an "evil empire."

★ Table 19-2
U.S. and Soviet military spending, 1975–1990 (billions of dollars)

	United States	Soviet Union
1975	$ 90.9	$128.0
1980	144.0	201.0
1981	169.9	221.0
1982	196.4	237.0
1983	217.2	250.0
1984	237.1	264.0
1985	265.8	275.0
1986	281.4	290.0
1987	279.5	295.0
1988	283.1	293.0[a]
1989	283.8	280.0[a]
1990	300.0[b]	275.0[a]

[a]Estimate

[b]Preliminary request

SOURCE: United States Arms Control and Disarmament Agency, *World Military Expenditures and Arms Transfers, 1987* (Washington, D.C.: U.S. Government Printing Office, 1987), pp. 77, 81 and United States Budget, 1988, 1989.

The Arms Race Revisited

> We must not forget that the Soviet Union has acquired awesome military capabilities. That was a fact of life for my predecessors. And that's always been a fact of life for our allies. And that is a fact of life for me.
>
> —*George Bush, 1989*

Ronald Reagan had based his presidential campaign in part on the notion that the Soviets' deployment of new strategic weapons created a "window of vulnerability," leaving the United States seriously behind in the arms race. Blaming the Carter administration for failing to keep pace, Reagan charged that the Soviets had gained a dangerous lead, especially in accurate, land-based missiles with large nuclear warheads. Although these charges were based on a highly controversial reading of the military balance, Congress agreed and America embarked on a $1.7 trillion, five-year military spending program (see table 19-2[25]).

The U.S. expansion program included restoration of the B-1 bomber project (suspended by President Carter), the MX missile, and the Trident submarine and missile. Along with these intercontinental systems came the highly controversial medium-range Pershing II and cruise missiles being deployed by NATO in Europe to counter the Soviets' potent SS-20 missile. Conventional ground, air, and sea forces were also expanded and modernized.

Many Americans (and Europeans) grew increasingly uneasy at the pace of the arms race. The cost and number of weapons being developed aroused concern, and the accuracy and power of the new systems were especially worrisome. Even more troubling to some people was the United States' position that under certain circumstances it might be necessary to launch a preemptive first strike against the

★ For some Americans, peace requires strength—strength in the form of a Trident submarine and other sophisticated weapons. Other Americans believe that controlling and eliminating nuclear weapons is the only way to a safe, secure nation.

Soviets. This policy, first announced by President Carter, was echoed by Reagan aides who spoke of "war-fighting capabilities" and "limited nuclear war." The Soviets, adding to the controversy, countered that they had no use for limited war, that any attack would inevitably lead to global nuclear war.

The public's response was predictable. While some Americans supported the arms buildup to achieve "peace through strength," others sought a nuclear freeze and mobilized under the banner "Arms control now!" As we saw in chapter 3, some local communities even declared themselves to be nuclear-free zones. A 1986 Gallup poll found that 62 percent of Americans believed arms control to be "very important" and another 25 percent said it was "important." Only 8 percent thought that arms control was "unimportant or very unimportant."

Arms Control Revisited

The Reagan administration was initially quite wary of arms control. Having denounced the proposed SALT II treaty as "fatally flawed" and citing alleged Soviet violations of previous arms-control agreements, the president was not disposed to negotiate with the Soviets. Preferring to develop a space-based shield against Soviet attack, the Strategic Defense Initiative (or "Star Wars," as most people called it), Reagan gave arms control low priority during his first term. By building weapons with first-strike capabilities and researching antimissile defenses, the Reagan administration appeared to reject the basic principles of MAD.

During the second Reagan administration, however, movement toward arms control gained momentum. Reagan's meetings with Soviet leader Mikhail Gorbachev in 1986, 1987, and 1988 improved the climate for arms control. In December

U.S.–Soviet Arms Agreements, 1963–1988

1963 *"Hot line" agreement* established communications link between Moscow and Washington for use in times of crisis.

1963 *Partial Test Ban Treaty* prohibited atmospheric testing of nuclear devices.

1967 *Outer Space Treaty* banned placement of nuclear weapons in orbit or on celestial bodies; also prohibited establishment of military bases on celestial bodies.

1968 *Nonproliferation Treaty* prohibited transfer of nuclear weapons to other countries.

1971 *Nuclear Accidents Agreement* provided for immediate notification in case of accidental detonation of a nuclear weapon.

1972 *Anti-Ballistic Missile Treaty* limited deployment of anti-ballistic missile systems.

1972 *Strategic Arms Limitation Treaty* (SALT I) set five-year numerical limit on deployment of nuclear missiles.

1973 *Prevention of Nuclear War Agreement* obligated each side to refrain from threat or use of nuclear force; required consultation if war seemed imminent.

1974 *Threshold Test-Ban Treaty* limited size of underground nuclear tests.

1976 *Peaceful Nuclear Explosions Treaty* limited size of nonweapon underground nuclear tests.

1979 *Strategic Arms Limitation Treaty* (SALT II) expanded and clarified limits set by SALT I. The treaty was never ratified by the U.S. Senate, but both sides generally followed its provisions until the United States exceeded the ceiling on missiles in 1986.

1988 *Intermediate-Range Nuclear Force Treaty* (INF), signed in 1987 and ratified by the Senate in 1988, banned production of medium-range missiles and required the phased withdrawal and destruction of existing weapons in Europe. ★

1987 the two superpowers signed a ground-breaking treaty agreeing to dismantle all of their medium-range missiles. The Intermediate-Range Nuclear Force (INF) Treaty was ratified by the Senate in 1988. History has taught us that both superpowers are most comfortable when the balance of power is roughly equal. Dramatic new announcements regarding the Soviets' willingness to reduce their military forces continued throughout 1988 and were greeted with optimism as President Reagan brought his second term to a close.

The Bush administration continued to explore the avenues of cooperation opened by Reagan and Gorbachev. Discussions were held with the Soviets on a variety of military issues, including conventional and short-range nuclear forces in Europe, further limitations on underground nuclear testing, a ban on chemical weapons, and steep cuts in strategic weapons. Strategic weapons—deadly long-range missiles and bombers—are the cornerstone of the arms race. Both the Soviet Union and the United States possess massive strategic arsenals. The aim of the Strategic Arms Limitations Talks (START), conducted periodically in Geneva, Switzerland, initially aimed to set an overall ceiling of 6,000 warheads for each side, with specific limits placed on types of delivery systems.

President Bush, like Ronald Reagan before him, pledged to negotiate from a position of strength. Development of the MX and Midgetman missiles, along with research on the Strategic Defense Initiative, would continue.

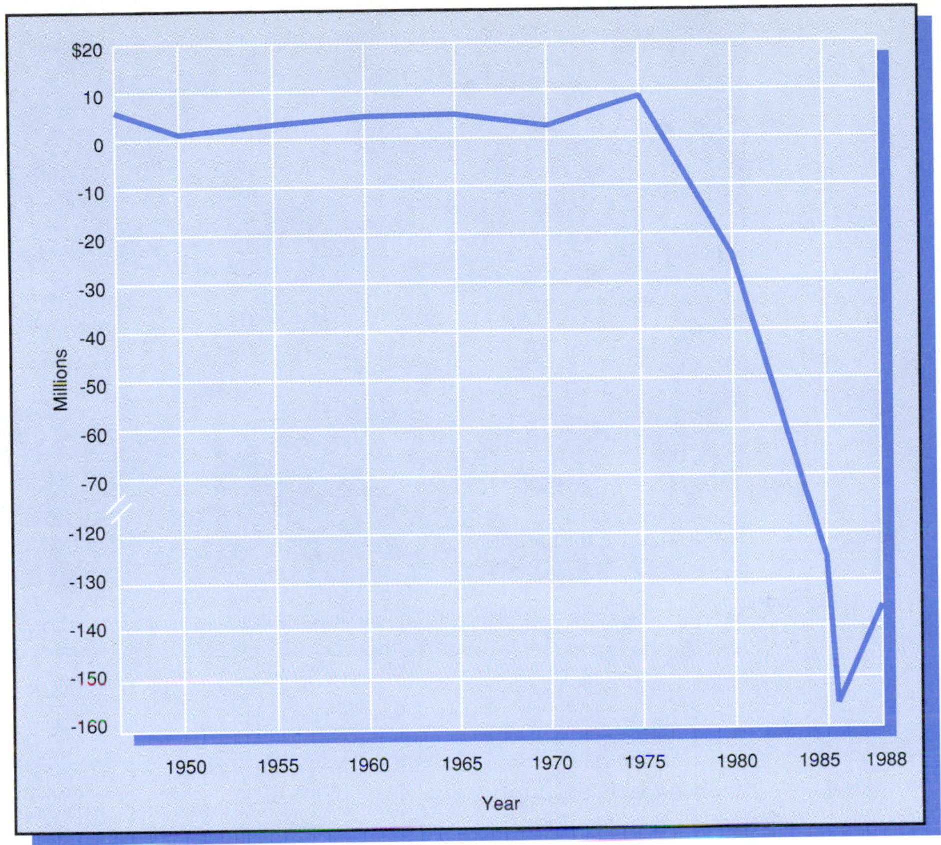

★ **Figure 19-6**
U.S. balance of trade, 1946–1988 (in millions of dollars)
SOURCE: Harold W. Stanley and Richard G. Niemi, *Vital Statistics on American Politics* (Washington, D.C.: Congressional Quarterly Press, 1988), p. 309.

In any event, following years of spending on expensive weapons, each side seemed to have many economic and political incentives to negotiate. One thing is certain: given the incalculable cost of nuclear war, the arms race will be a major issue of the 1990s and beyond.

Trade and Economic Prosperity

As Reagan entered office, America's domination of world trade seemed to have come to an end. After decades of enjoying trade surpluses, the United States actually began to import more than it exported. America's balance of trade went from a surplus of $9 billion in 1980 to a deficit of around $156 billion in 1986. Deficits continued to grow in 1987 and 1988 (see figure 19-6). Although the causes of this decline were complex, many workers, especially those in such traditional heavy industries as steel and autos, complained of unfair foreign competition.

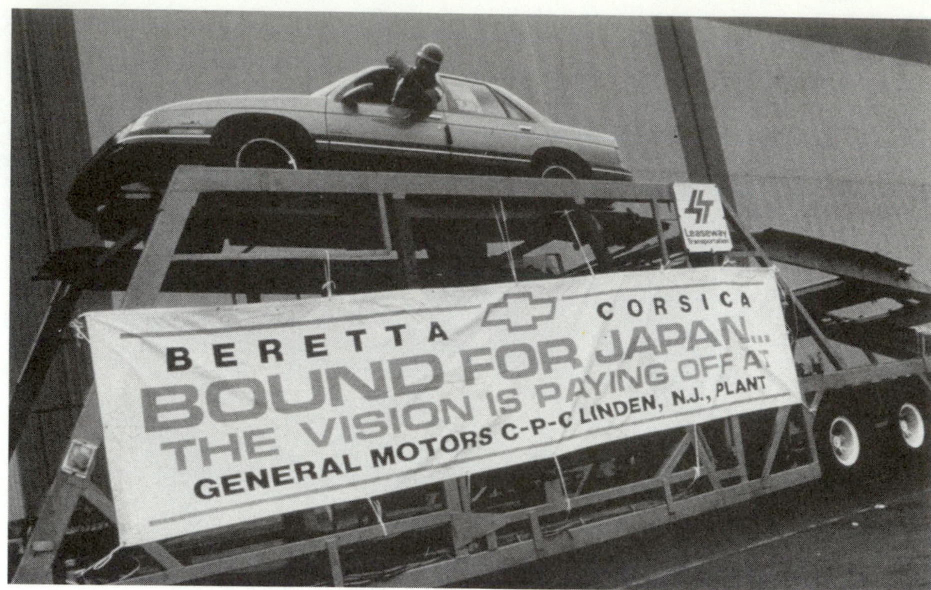

★ In an effort to restore the balance of trade both economically and symbolically, the United States has begun to export cars to Japan. The exporting of cars may also create more jobs in the United States.

As we have seen in chapter 18, Reagan firmly opposed overt protectionism. A strong believer in the open market and free trade, he argued that America had not, in fact, lost jobs to foreign competition. To workers unable to keep pace with a shifting job market, however, these arguments meant little. Thus President Reagan, bowing to political pressure, often spoke of "fair" as well as "free" trade. Behind the scenes he frequently lobbied Japan and other major trading partners to accept more U.S. exports.

The Bush administration promises to be equally concerned about America's trade imbalance. Under White House direction, the Commerce Department pressures many U.S. trading partners and threatens to apply sanctions should practices it considers discriminatory continue.

Conflict in the Third World

Because of the dangers inherent in a confrontation between the superpowers, U.S. foreign policy makers were most active in the Third World in the 1980s. Though its language was tough, the Reagan administration was fairly cautious in its first term, choosing to react to world events rather than to lead. Some critics pointed to a lack of clear objectives in President Reagan's policies, citing the disastrous decision to send U.S. Marines to Lebanon (1982–1984), which resulted in the death of 241 servicemen and a serious blow to the nation's prestige.

The Middle East is indicative of the complicated problems that global interdependence presents for the people who make U.S. foreign policy. From our vantage point today, the Middle East conjures up an array of images: terrorist attacks, vast oil reserves, and seemingly fanatical movements sworn to destroy the West. As with many other international problems, the issues in the Middle East have deep

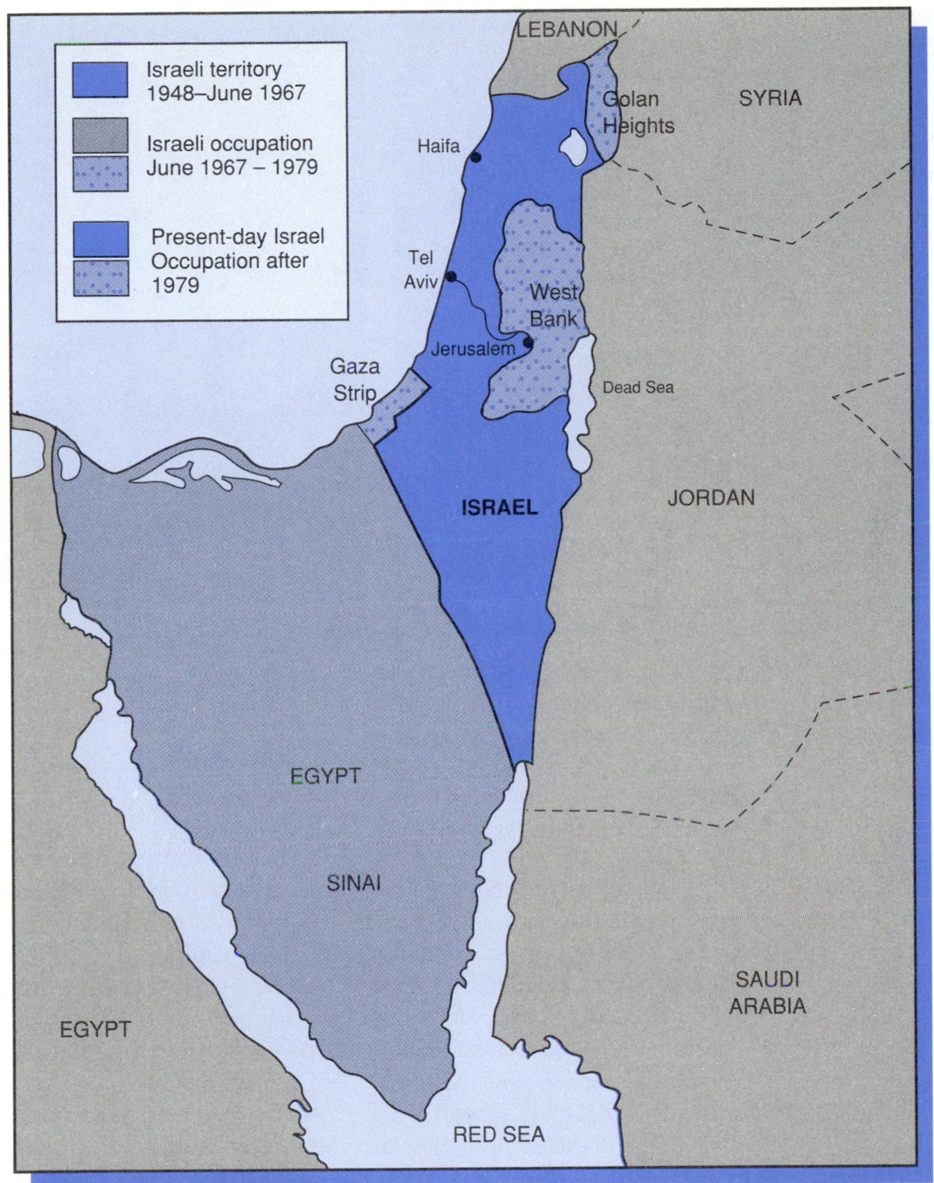

★ **Figure 19-7**
This map shows Israel and its boundaries for three time periods. The first period is from 1948 to June 1967; the second period is from June 1967 to 1979, after the Camp David Accords; the third time period is present day. Note that the Gaza Strip and the West Bank are areas that are still disputed.

historical roots and are highly complex. The principal issues in the area for the United States are Israel's security, access to oil, maintenance of friendly, stable governments, the limiting of Soviet influence, and the fate of the Palestinian people. On many occasions solutions to these problems have seemed mutually exclusive.

When the United Nations in 1948 partitioned Palestine into Arab and Israeli states, close to one million Arabs fled Israel for refuge in neighboring Arab countries (see figure 19-7). Most of the Arab countries, however, refused to accept the

★ Palestinian youth fight for autonomy in Israel. Americans demonstrate against apartheid and call for stiffer U.S. sanctions against the government of South Africa.

Palestinians as permanent residents, preferring to confine them in refugee camps. As a result, an entire generation of Palestinians grew up hoping to return to a "homeland" they had never seen. Some insisted on the destruction of the Israeli state, and supported international terrorism as a means to achieve that end.

Between 1948 and 1973 Israel and its Arab foes fought several major wars. For a variety of reasons, including the strong influence of America's own Jewish population, the United States supported Israel. During his first term, Reagan sought to build a coalition between moderate Arab states (such as Saudi Arabia) and Israel. Unable to produce such an unlikely marriage, the United States gave its tacit approval to Israel's invasion and occupation of Lebanon in 1982. U.S. policy changed dramatically in Reagan's second term, especially in regard to the Middle East. Tension in the region eased following a cease-fire in the bloody Iran-Iraq war, and the United States was able to reduce its controversial naval commitments in the area. In December 1988, for the first time in history, U.S. diplomats held formal talks with the Palestine Liberation Organization (PLO), raising the possibility of a negotiated solution to one of modern history's most complex and tragic issues.

Terrorism was another problem faced by the Reagan administration. The subject of terrorism sparked continuing controversy among politicians and the public. One problem in regard to terrorism, according to critics of the Reagan administration, was the matter of definition. Some felt that U.S. training and funding of antigovernment forces in Nicaragua, for example, was a form of terrorism. Revelations that the Reagan administration had sold arms to Iran, a nation often blamed for terrorism against Americans, further confused the public. Although many Americans supported the U.S. bombing raid against Libya in 1986, others felt it was an act of frustration that would only accelerate the cycle of violence.

Meanwhile, in Central America, Africa, and other Third World hot spots, Reagan promised to shun the noninterventionist "idealism" of the Carter years, and to pursue what he called the "new realism." In a reprise of the era of containment, the United States would meet the Soviet challenge wherever it arose. Carrying containment a step further with the so-called Reagan Doctrine, the president promised actively to support the development of democratic regimes. When the Reagan administration helped to bring about the fall of such dictators as Ferdinand Marcos of the Philippines, the Reagan Doctrine seemed more than just campaign rhetoric. Yet the sending of massive aid and American military advisers to El Salvador, the invasion of little Grenada in 1983, and the creation and funding of the Contra opposition in Nicaragua hardly represented new policies in an area long dominated by the United States.

The United States' actions in the Third World, as in its war on terrorism, were limited by the natural concerns imposed by the nuclear age, global interdependence, and a weary American public still fearful of the "Vietnam syndrome." When a 1985 *New York Times* poll asked: "Should the United States try to change a dictatorship to a democracy where it can, or should the United States stay out of other countries' affairs?" 62 percent said stay out and 28 percent said try to change.

The Reagan administration was certainly not without concrete accomplishments in the Third World. When George Bush moved into the Oval Office in January 1989, accords were being finalized to end the Soviet intervention in Afghanistan and the long-running conflict between Angola and South Africa over the territory of Namibia.

The situation in Central America, on the other hand, was anything but calm. The Contras were rapidly losing ground in Nicaragua. Bush was able to persuade Congress to provide funds to maintain the Contras in their bases in Honduras, but they were no longer capable of sustained military activity in Nicaragua. In El Salvador, the civil war continued to rage, and in Panama, with its vital canal and strategic location, the military was a roadblock to the establishment of a freely elected civilian government.

A New Era in American Foreign Policy?

> The characteristics of the cold war should be abandoned. The arms race, mistrust, . . . ideological struggle, all those should be things of the past.
>
> —*Mikhail Gorbachev, 1989*

> We stand at the threshold of a brand new era of U.S.–Soviet relations.
>
> —*George Bush, 1989*

As America faces the 1990s, it is reasonable to ask if we are entering a new era in international relations. Has the bipolar world of cold war with the Soviets really become a thing of the past? Economic and political reforms, which swept the Soviet Union and Eastern Europe in recent years, set in motion by Mikhail Gorbachev, seem to challenge many of the basic assumptions of the cold war. Many Americans did agree with President Bush that "a new breeze is blowing across the steppes and the cities of the Soviet Union." A December 1989, *New York Times*/CBS poll showed that 37% of Americans believed that the cold war was indeed over. Moreover, 67% said that the Soviet Union would not be in control of most Eastern European nations by Christmas, 1990.

But old ways die hard. "Although this is a time of great hope," cautioned President Bush after a summit with Gorbachev in December 1989, "we must not blur the distinction between promising expectations and present realities." While the superpowers talk peace, they and the rest of the world continue to spend more

★ The removal of the Berlin Wall, even a piece at a time, is a dramatic symbol of the changes in East–West relations that took place in late 1989.

and more on weapons. Many U.S. citizens remain distrustful of the Soviet Union. The brutal repression of the student-led movement for political reform that rocked China in 1989 fueled people's skepticism of liberalization in the communist world. Outside the communist world, moreover, social unrest in South Africa, Central and South America, the Middle East, and other troubled regions still casts a shadow over superpower cooperation.

Despite the potential roadblocks to improved U.S.–Soviet relations in the 1990s, many people believe that the cold war may be winding down. Our interdependent global community, besieged by devastating poverty, ecological disaster, the international drug trade, and many other problems, could certainly use a rest from the military and political conflicts that consume vast amounts of human and natural resources.

A significant improvement in relations with the Soviet Union would force a rethinking of American foreign goals. Citizens may ask, should the United States, which once intervened in the Caribbean basin to prevent the spread of communism, now consider invading countries that produce dangerous drugs? What about countries that destroy the environment? Should the United States, which used economic sanctions to punish Cuba and Nicaragua during the cold war, now apply the same pressure to Brazil to prevent deforestation of the Amazon basin? These and other unforeseen global issues will surely confound citizens and politicians alike. How America reacts to the challenges of a post–cold war world, of course, is what politics is all about.

★ The United Nations General Assembly. The United States and the Soviet Union have expressed an interest in expanding the role of the United Nations in global conflict resolution.

★ Summary

As the 1980s drew to a close, U.S. foreign policy seemed a far cry from President Washington's advice to stay clear of foreign entanglements. Today virtually every aspect of American life, from sports, fashion, culture, and economics to our very survival, is closely linked to the outside world. Beneath the fast-paced life of modern America, however, we can discern the major trends in U.S. foreign policy: containment of Soviet expansion, détente with the Soviet Union, promotion of capitalism and free trade, and American exceptionalism.

Foreign policy is made and implemented by the president and the inner circle of White House advisers. The Pentagon, Department of State, CIA, and other agencies play important roles in the policy-making process. Congress, with its constitutional oversight responsibilities, warmaking powers, and control of the national budget, can influence foreign policy in many ways. Although the American people are not always well informed about international issues and usually can only react to rather than initiate changes in foreign policy, they can have a say in such matters through their votes and other political activities.

The 1990s are certain to present a variety of challenges. Technological innovation in weaponry will continue to outstrip humankind's ability to manage political conflict peacefully. Flash points in the Third World—South Africa, the Middle East, Central America, and the Caribbean—will test America's political leaders. Behind blaring media reports of the latest crisis, the unseen human tragedies of hunger, disease, and denial of human rights await solution. The key dilemma for the United

States in the 1990s is easy to identify but hard to resolve: how to employ its vast power not only in its own self-interest but as a positive influence in a world besieged by poverty, inequality, and war.

★ Key Terms

American exceptionalism
cold war
containment
détente
domino theory
manifest destiny
Marshall Plan
mutually assured destruction (MAD)
national security adviser
Truman Doctrine

★ Notes

1. Hans J. Morgenthau, *Politics among Nations,* 5th ed. (New York: Knopf, 1973), p. 167.
2. Walter S. Jones, *The Logic of International Relations,* 5th ed. (Boston: Little, Brown, 1985), p. 17.
3. *X* [George F. Kennan], "The Sources of Soviet Conduct," *Foreign Affairs,* July 1947, pp. 566–582.
4. John Spanier, *American Foreign Policy since World War II,* 10th ed. (New York: Holt, Rinehart & Winston, 1985), p. 61.
5. Richard M. Nixon, "United States Foreign Policy for the 1970s: A New Strategy for Peace" (1970), in *A Reader in American Foreign Policy,* ed. James M. McCormick (Itasca, Ill.: Peacock, 1986), pp. 115–116.
6. Bernard Brodie, "The Development of Nuclear Strategy," in *Arms Control and Security: Current Issues,* ed. Wolfram F. Hanrieder (Boulder, Colo.: Westview, 1979), pp. 19–38.
7. U.S. Arms Control and Disarmament Agency, *World Military Expenditures and Arms Transfers, 1971–1980* (Washington, D.C.: U.S. Government Printing Office, March 1983). As comparisons between the two economies are difficult, figures should be taken as estimates only.
8. Seyom Brown, *The Crises of Power: Foreign Policy in the Kissinger Years* (New York: Columbia University Press, 1979), p. 15.
9. John Spanier and Eric M. Uslaner, *American Foreign Policy Making and the Democratic Dilemmas,* 5th ed. (Pacific Grove, Calif.: Brooks/Cole, 1989), p. 329.
10. U.S. Department of State, *Fundamentals of U.S. Foreign Policy* (Washington, D.C.: U.S. Government Printing Office, March 1988), p. 36.
11. Spanier and Uslaner, *American Foreign Policy Making,* p. 333.
12. Stanley Hoffmann, *Gulliver's Troubles, or The Setting of American Foreign Policy* (New York: McGraw-Hill, 1968), pp. 179–180.
13. Ibid.
14. Franklin D. Roosevelt, "For a Declaration of War against Japan," in *The World's Great Speeches,* eds. Lewis Copeland and Lawrence Lamm (New York: Dove, 1958), pp. 531–532.
15. Quoted in Seymour M. Hersh, *The Price of Power: Kissinger in the Nixon White House* (New York: Summit, 1983), p. 350.
16. Quoted in Brown, *Crises of Power,* p. 1.
17. Hersh, *Price of Power,* p. 502.
18. *Tower Commission Report* (New York: Times Books, 1987), p. 7.
19. Quoted in Charles W. Kegley, Jr., and Eugene R. Wittkopf, *American Foreign Policy,* 2d ed. (New York: St. Martin's Press, 1982), p. 337.
20. *Tower Commission Report,* pp. 10–11.
21. See, for example, U.S. Senate, Select Committee to Study Governmental Operations with Respect to Intelligence Activities, "Alleged Assassination Plots Involving Foreign Leaders" (Washington, D.C.: U.S. Government Printing Office, 1975).
22. *New York Times,* July 7, 1986, pp. 1, 8.
23. *Tower Commission Report,* p. 452.
24. Ronald Reagan, radio address to the nation, December 6, 1987.
25. Spending figures are offered for general comparisons only. There are significant methodological difficulties in equating the U.S. and Soviet economic systems.

★ For Further Reading

Brewer, Thomas L. *American Foreign Policy: A Contemporary Introduction.* 2d ed. Englewood Cliffs, N.J.: Prentice-Hall, 1986.

Brown, Seyom. *The Faces of Power: Constancy and Change in United States Foreign Policy from Truman to Reagan.* New York: Columbia University Press, 1983.

Hanrieder, Wolfram F., ed. *Technology, Strategy, and Arms Control.* Boulder, Colo.: Westview, 1986.

Kegley, Charles W., Jr., and Eugene R. Wittkopf. *American Foreign Policy: Pattern and Process.* 3d ed. New York: St. Martin's Press, 1987.

Levine, Herbert M., and David Carlton, eds. *The Nuclear Arms Race Debated.* New York: McGraw–Hill, 1986.

Nathan, James A., and James K. Oliver. *Foreign Policy Making and the American Political System.* 2d ed., Boston: Little, Brown, 1987.

Spanier, John, and Eric M. Uslaner. *American Foreign Policy Making and the Democratic Dilemmas.* 5th ed. Pacific Grove, Calif.: Brooks/Cole, 1989.

Ungar, Sanford J., ed. *Estrangement: America and the World.* New York: Oxford University Press, 1985.

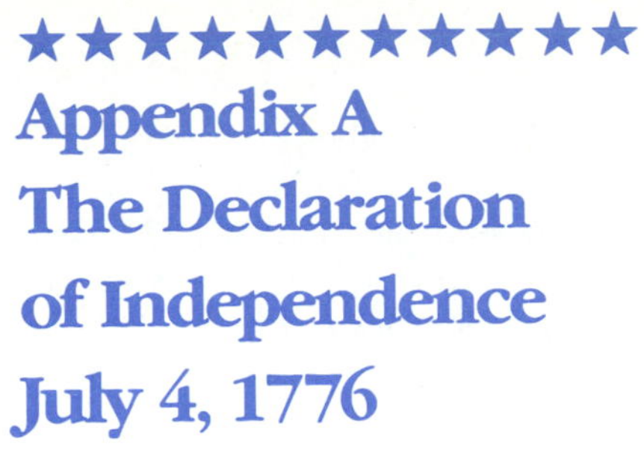

Appendix A The Declaration of Independence July 4, 1776

The unanimous declaration of the thirteen United States of America

When, in the course of human events, it becomes necessary for one people to dissolve the political bands which have connected them with another, and to assume, among the powers of the earth, the separate and equal station to which the laws of nature and of nature's God entitle them, a decent respect to the opinions of mankind requires that they should declare the causes which impel them to the separation.

We hold these truths to be self-evident: That all men are created equal; that they are endowed by their Creator with certain unalienable rights; that among these are life, liberty, and the pursuit of happiness; that, to secure these rights, governments are instituted among men, deriving their just powers from the consent of the governed; that whenever any form of government becomes destructive of these ends, it is the right of the people to alter or to abolish it, and to institute new government, laying its foundation on such principles, and organizing its power in such form, as to them shall seem most likely to effect their safety and happiness. Prudence, indeed, will dictate that governments long established should not be changed for light and transient causes; and accordingly all experience hath shown that mankind are more disposed to suffer, while evils are sufferable, than to right themselves by abolishing the forms to which they are accustomed. But when a long train of abuses and usurpations, pursuing invariably the same object, evinces a design to reduce them under absolute despotism, it is their right, it is their duty, to throw off such government, and to provide new guards for their future security. Such has been the patient sufferance of these colonies; and such is now the necessity which constrains them to alter their former systems of government. The history of the present King of Great Britain is a history of repeated injuries and usurpations, all having in direct object the establishment of an absolute tyranny over these states. To prove this, let facts be submitted to a candid world.

He has refused his assent to laws, the most wholesome and necessary for the public good.

He has forbidden his governors to pass laws of immediate and pressing importance, unless suspended in their operation till his assent should be obtained; and, when so suspended, he has utterly neglected to attend to them.

He has refused to pass other laws for the accommodation of large districts of people, unless those people would relinquish the right of representation in the legislature, a right inestimable to them, and formidable to tyrants only.

He has called together legislative bodies at places unusual, uncomfortable, and distant from the depository of their public records, for the sole purpose of fatiguing them into compliance with his measures.

He has dissolved representative houses repeatedly, for opposing, with manly firmness, his invasions on the rights of the people.

He has refused for a long time, after such dissolutions, to cause others to be elected; whereby the legislative powers, incapable of annihilation, have returned to the people at large for their exercise; the state remaining, in the mean time, exposed to all the dangers of invasions from without and convulsions within.

He has endeavored to prevent the population of these states; for that purpose obstructing the laws for naturalization of foreigners; refusing to pass others to encourage their migration hither, and raising the conditions of new appropriations of lands.

He has obstructed the administration of justice, by refusing his assent to laws for establishing judiciary powers.

He has made judges dependent on his will alone, for the tenure of their offices, and the amount and payment of their salaries.

He has erected a multitude of new offices, and sent hither swarms of officers to harass our people and eat out their substance.

He has kept among us, in times of peace, standing armies, without the consent of our legislatures.

He has affected to render the military independent of, and superior to, the civil power.

He has combined with others to subject us to a jurisdiction foreign to our constitution, and unacknowledged by our laws, giving his assent to their acts of pretended legislation:

For quartering large bodies of armed troops among us;

For protecting them, by a mock trial, from punishment for any murders which they should commit on the inhabitants of these states;

For cutting off our trade with all parts of the world;

For imposing taxes on us without our consent;

For depriving us, in many cases, of the benefits of trial by jury;

For transporting us beyond seas, to be tried for pretended offenses;

For abolishing the free system of English laws in a neighboring province, establishing therein an arbitrary government, and enlarging its boundaries, so as to render it at once an example and fit instrument for introducing the same absolute rule into these colonies;

For taking away our charters, abolishing our most valuable laws, and altering fundamentally the forms of our governments;

For suspending our own legislatures, and declaring themselves invested with power to legislate for us in all cases whatsoever.

He has abdicated government here, by declaring us out of his protection and waging war against us.

He has plundered our seas, ravaged our coasts, burned our towns, and destroyed the lives of our people.

He is at this time transporting large armies of foreign mercenaries to complete the works of death, desolation, and tyranny already begun with circumstances of cruelty and perfidy scarcely paralleled in the most barbarous ages, and totally unworthy the head of a civilized nation.

He has constrained our fellow-citizens, taken captive on the high seas, to bear arms against their country, to become the executioners of their friends and brethren, or to fall themselves by their hands.

He has excited domestic insurrection among us, and has endeavored to bring on the inhabitants of our frontiers the merciless Indian savages, whose known rule of warfare is an undistinguished destruction of all ages, sexes, and conditions.

In every stage of these oppressions we have petitioned for redress in the most humble terms; our repeated petitions have been answered only by repeated injury. A prince, whose character is thus marked by every act which may define a tyrant, is unfit to be the ruler of a free people.

Nor have we been wanting in our attentions to our British brethren. We have warned them, from time to time, of attempts by their legislature to extend an unwarrantable jurisdiction over us. We have reminded them of the circumstances of our emigration and settlement here. We have appealed to their native justice and magnanimity; and we have conjured them, by the ties of our common kindred, to disavow these usurpations, which would inevitably interrupt our connections and correspondence. They, too, have been deaf to the voice of justice and of consanguinity. We must, therefore, acquiesce in the necessity which denounces our separation, and hold them, as we hold the rest of mankind, enemies in war, in peace friends.

We, therefore, the representatives of the United States of America, in General Congress assembled, appealing to the Supreme Judge of the world for the rectitude of our intentions, do, in the name and by the authority of the good people of these colonies, solemnly publish and declare, that these United Colonies are, and of right ought to be, FREE AND INDEPENDENT STATES; that they are absolved from all allegiance to the British crown, and that all political connection between them and the state of Great Britain is, and ought to be, totally dissolved; and that, as free and independent states, they have full power to levy war, conclude peace, contract alliances, establish commerce, and do all other acts and things which independent states may of right do. And for the support of this declaration, with a firm reliance on the protection of Divine Providence, we mutually pledge to each other our lives, our fortunes, and our sacred honor.

Signed by fifty-six representatives from the thirteen original colonies

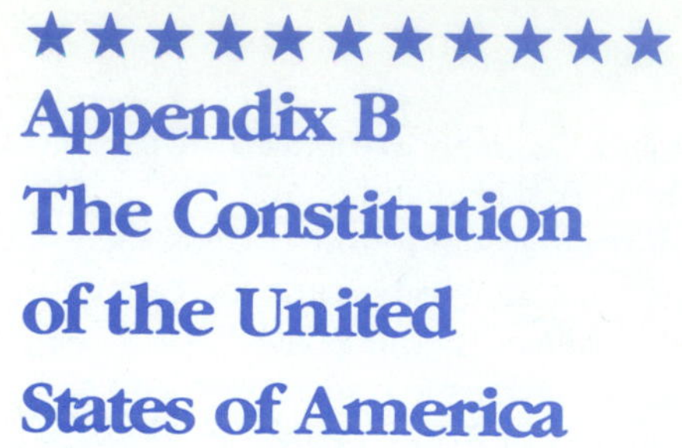

Appendix B The Constitution of the United States of America

We the people of the United States, in order to form a more perfect union, establish justice, insure domestic tranquility, provide for the common defense, promote the general welfare, and secure the blessings of liberty to ourselves and our posterity, do ordain and establish this Constitution for the United States of America.

★ Article I

Section 1. All legislative powers herein granted shall be vested in a Congress of the United States, which shall consist of a Senate and House of Representatives.

Section 2. The House of Representatives shall be composed of members chosen every second year by the people of the several states, and the electors in each state shall have the qualifications requisite for electors of the most numerous branch of the state legislature.

No person shall be a representative who shall not have attained to the age of twenty-five years, and been seven years a citizen of the United States, and who shall not, when elected, be an inhabitant of that state in which he shall be chosen.

Representatives and direct taxes shall be apportioned among the several states which may be included within this union, according to their respective numbers, *which shall be determined by adding to the whole number of free persons, including those bound to service for a term of years,* and excluding Indians not taxed, *three-fifths of all other persons.*[1] The actual enumeration shall be made within three years after the first meeting of the Congress of the United States, and within every subsequent term of ten years, in such manner as they shall by law direct. The number of representatives shall not exceed one for every thirty thousand, but each state shall have at least one representative, and until such enumeration shall be made, the state of New Hampshire shall be entitled to choose three, Massachusetts eight, Rhode Island and Providence Plantations one, Connecticut five, New York six, New Jersey four, Pennsylvania eight, Delaware one, Maryland six, Virginia ten, North Carolina five, South Carolina five, and Georgia three.

When vacancies happen in the representation from any state, the executive authority thereof shall issue writs of election to fill such vacancies.

[1]Superseded by the Fourteenth Amendment. Throughout, italics indicate passages altered by subsequent amendments.

The House of Representatives shall choose their Speaker and other officers; and shall have the sole power of impeachment.

Section 3. The Senate of the United States shall be composed of two senators from each state, chosen by the *legislature thereof,*[2] for six years; and each senator shall have one vote.

Immediately after they shall be assembled in consequence of the first election, they shall be divided as equally as may be into three classes. The seats of the senators of the first class shall be vacated at the expiration of the second year, of the second class at the expiration of the fourth year, and of the third class at the expiration of the sixth year, so that one-third may be chosen every second year; *and if vacancies happen by resignation, or otherwise, during the recess of the legislature of any state, the executive thereof may make temporary appointments until the next meeting of the legislature, which shall then fill such vacancies.*[3]

No person shall be a senator who shall not have attained to the age of thirty years, and been nine years a citizen of the United States, and who shall not, when elected, be an inhabitant of the state for which he shall be chosen.

The vice-president of the United States shall be president of the Senate, but shall have no vote, unless they be equally divided.

The Senate shall choose their other officers, and also a president pro tempore, in the absence of the vice-president, or when he shall exercise the office of president of the United States.

The Senate shall have the sole power to try all impeachments. When sitting for that purpose, they shall be on oath or affirmation. When the president of the United States is tried, the chief justice shall preside: And no person shall be convicted without the concurrence of two-thirds of the members present.

Judgment in cases of impeachment shall not extend further than to removal from office, and disqualification to hold and enjoy any office of honor, trust or profit under the United States: but the party convicted shall nevertheless be liable and subject to indictment, trial, judgment and punishment, according to law.

Section 4. The times, places and manner of holding elections for senators and representatives, shall be prescribed in each state by the legislature thereof; but the Congress may at any time by law make or alter such regulations, except as to the places of choosing senators.

The Congress shall assemble at least once in every year, and such meeting shall be on the first Monday in December, unless they shall by law appoint a different day.[4]

Section 5. Each house shall be the judge of the elections, returns and qualifications of its own members, and a majority of each shall constitute a quorum to do business; but a smaller number may adjourn from day to day, and may be authorized to compel the attendance of absent members, in such manner, and under such penalties as each house may provide.

Each house may determine the rules of its proceedings, punish its members for disorderly behavior, and, with the concurrence of two-thirds, expel a member.

[2]See Seventeenth Amendment.

[3]See Seventeenth Amendment.

[4]See Twentieth Amendment.

Each house shall keep a journal of its proceedings, and from time to time publish the same, excepting such parts as may in their judgment require secrecy; and the yeas and nays of the members of either house on any question shall, at the desire of one-fifth of those present, be entered on the journal.

Neither house, during the session of Congress, shall, without the consent of the other, adjourn for more than three days, nor to any other place than that in which the two houses shall be sitting.

Section 6. The senators and representatives shall receive a compensation for their services, to be ascertained by law, and paid out of the treasury of the United States. They shall in all cases, except treason, felony and breach of the peace, be privileged from arrest during their attendance at the session of their respective houses, and in going to and returning from the same; and for any speech or debate in either house, they shall not be questioned in any other place.

No senator or representative shall, during the time for which he was elected, be appointed to any civil office under the authority of the United States, which shall have been created, or the emoluments whereof shall have been increased during such time; and no person holding any office under the United States, shall be a member of either house during his continuance in office.

Section 7. All bills for raising revenue shall originate in the House of Representatives; but the Senate may propose or concur with amendments as on other bills.

Every bill which shall have passed the House of Representatives and the Senate, shall, before it become a law, be presented to the president of the United States; if he approve he shall sign it, but if not he shall return it, with his objections to that house in which it shall have originated, who shall enter the objections at large on their journal, and proceed to reconsider it. If after such reconsideration two-thirds of that house shall agree to pass the bill, it shall be sent, together with the objections, to the other house, by which it shall likewise be reconsidered, and if approved by two-thirds of that house, it shall become a law. But in all such cases the votes of both houses shall be determined by yeas and nays, and the names of the persons voting for and against the bill shall be entered on the journal of each house respectively. If any bill shall not be returned by the president within ten days (Sundays excepted) after it shall have been presented to him, the same shall be a law, in like manner as if he had signed it, unless the Congress by their adjournment prevent its return, in which case it shall not be a law.

Every order, resolution, or vote to which the concurrence of the Senate and House of Representatives may be necessary (except on a question of adjournment) shall be presented to the president of the United States; and before the same shall take effect, shall be approved by him, or being disapproved by him, shall be repassed by two-thirds of the Senate and House of Representatives, according to the rules and limitations prescribed in the case of a bill.

Section 8. The Congress shall have power to lay and collect taxes, duties, imposts and excises, to pay the debts and provide for the common defense and general welfare of the United States; but all duties, imposts and excises shall be uniform throughout the United States;

To borrow money on the credit of the United States;

To regulate commerce with foreign nations, and among the several states, and with the Indian tribes;

To establish an uniform rule of naturalization, and uniform laws on the subject of bankruptcies throughout the United States;

To coin money, regulate the value thereof, and of foreign coin, and fix the standard of weights and measures;

To provide for the punishment of counterfeiting the securities and current coin of the United States;

To establish post offices and post roads;

To promote the progress of science and useful arts, by securing for limited times to authors and inventors the exclusive right to their respective writings and discoveries;

To constitute tribunals inferior to the Supreme Court;

To define and punish piracies and felonies committed on the high seas, and offenses against the law of nations;

To declare war, grant letters of marque and reprisal, and make rules concerning captures on land and water;

To raise and support armies, but no appropriation of money to that use shall be for a longer term than two years;

To provide and maintain a navy;

To make rules for the government and regulation of the land and naval forces;

To provide for calling forth the militia to execute the laws of the union, suppress insurrections and repel invasions;

To provide for organizing, arming, and disciplining, the militia, and for governing such part of them as may be employed in the service of the United States, reserving to the states respectively, the appointment of the officers, and the authority of training the militia according to the discipline prescribed by Congress;

To exercise exclusive legislation in all cases whatsoever, over such district (not exceeding ten miles square) as may, by cession of particular states, and the acceptance of Congress, become the seat of the government of the United States, and to exercise like authority over all places purchased by the consent of the legislature of the state in which the same shall be, for the erection of forts, magazines, arsenals, dockyards, and other needful buildings;—and

To make all laws which shall be necessary and proper for carrying into execution the foregoing powers, and all other powers vested by this Constitution in the government of the United States, or in any department or officer thereof.

Section 9. The migration or importation of such persons as any of the states now existing shall think proper to admit, shall not be prohibited by the Congress prior to the year one thousand eight hundred and eight, but a tax or duty may be imposed on such importation, not exceeding ten dollars for each person.

The privilege of the writ of habeas corpus shall not be suspended, unless when in cases of rebellion or invasion the public safety may require it.

No bill of attainder or ex post facto law shall be passed.

No capitation, or other direct, tax shall be laid, unless in proportion to the census or enumeration herein before directed to be taken.

No tax or duty shall be laid on articles exported from any state.

No preference shall be given by any regulation of commerce or revenue to the ports of one state over those of another: nor shall vessels bound to or from, one state, be obliged to enter, clear, or pay duties in another.

No money shall be drawn from the treasury, but in consequence of appropriations made by law; and a regular statement and account of the receipts and expenditures of all public money shall be published from time to time.

No title of nobility shall be granted by the United States: and no person holding any office of profit or trust under them, shall, without the consent of the Congress, accept of any present, emolument, office, or title, of any kind whatever, from any king, prince, or foreign state.

Section 10. No state shall enter into any treaty, alliance, or confederation; grant letters of marque and reprisal; coin money; emit bills of credit; make anything but gold and silver coin a tender in payment of debts; pass any bill of attainder, ex post facto law, or law impairing the obligation of contracts, or grant any title of nobility.

No state shall, without the consent of the Congress, lay any imposts or duties on imports or exports, except what may be absolutely necessary for executing its inspection laws: and the net produce of all duties and imposts, laid by any state on imports or exports, shall be for the use of the Treasury of the United States; and all such laws shall be subject to the revision and control of the Congress.

No state shall, without the consent of Congress, lay any duty of tonnage, keep troops, or ships of war in time of peace, enter into any agreement or compact with another state, or with a foreign power, or engage in war, unless actually invaded, or in such imminent danger as will not admit of delay.

★ Article II

Section 1. The executive power shall be vested in a president of the United States of America. He shall hold office during the term of four years, and, together with the vice-president, chosen for the same term, be elected, as follows:

Each state shall appoint, in such manner as the legislature thereof may direct, a number of electors, equal to the whole number of senators and representatives to which the state may be entitled in the Congress: but no senator or representative, or person holding an office of trust or profit under the United States, shall be appointed an elector.

The electors shall meet in their respective states, and vote by ballot for two persons, of whom one at least shall not be an inhabitant of the same state with themselves. And they shall make a list of all the persons voted for, and of the number of votes for each; which list they shall sign and certify, and transmit sealed to the seat of the government of the United States, directed to the president of the Senate. The president of the Senate shall, in the presence of the Senate and House of Representatives, open all the certificates, and the votes shall then be counted. The person having the greatest number of votes shall be the president, if such number be a majority of the whole number of electors appointed; and if there be more than one who have such majority, and have an equal number of votes, then the House of Representatives shall immediately choose by ballot one of them for president, and if no person have a majority, then from the five highest on the list the said House shall in like manner choose the president. But in choosing the president, the votes shall be taken by states, the representation from each state having one vote: a quorum for this purpose shall consist of a member or members from two-thirds of the states, and a majority of all the states shall be necessary to a choice. In every case, after the choice of the president, the person having the greatest number of votes of the electors shall be the vice-president. But if there should remain two or more who have equal votes, the Senate shall choose from them by ballot the vice-president.[5]

The Congress may determine the time of choosing the electors, and the day on which they shall give their votes; which day shall be the same throughout the United States.

No person except a natural born citizen, or a citizen of the United States, at the time of the adoption of this Constitution, shall be eligible to the office of president; neither shall any person be eligible to that office who shall not have attained to the age of thirty-five years, and been fourteen years a resident within the United States.

In case of the removal of the president from office, or of his death, resignation, or inability to discharge the powers and duties of the said office, the same shall devolve on the vice-president, and the Congress may by law provide for the case of removal, death, resignation or inability, both of the president and vice-president, declaring what officer shall then act as president, and such officer shall act accordingly, until the disability be removed, or a president shall be elected.[6]

The president shall, at stated times, receive for his services, a compensation, which shall neither be increased nor diminished during the period for which he shall have been elected, and he shall not receive within that period any other emolument from the United States, or any of them.

Before he enter on the execution of his office, he shall take the following oath or affirmation:—"I do solemnly swear (or affirm) that I will faithfully execute the office of president of the United States, and will to the best of my ability, preserve, protect and defend the Constitution of the United States."

Section 2. The president shall be commander in chief of the army and navy of the United States, and of the militia of the several states, when called into the actual service of the United States; he may require the opinion, in writing, of the principal officer in each of the executive departments, upon any subject relating to the duties of their respective offices, and he shall have power to grant reprieves and pardons for offenses against the United States, except in cases of impeachment.

He shall have power, by and with the advice and consent of the Senate, to make treaties, provided two-thirds of the senators present concur; and he shall nominate, and by and with the advice and consent of the Senate, shall appoint ambassadors, other public ministers and consuls, judges of the Supreme Court, and all other officers of the United States, whose appointments are not herein otherwise provided for, and which shall be established by law: but the Congress may by law vest the appointment of such inferior officers, as they think proper, in the president alone, in the courts of law, or in the heads of departments.

The president shall have power to fill up all vacancies that may happen during the recess of the Senate, by granting commissions which shall expire at the end of their next session.

Section 3. He shall from time to time give to the Congress information of the state of the union, and recommend to their consideration such measures as he shall judge necessary and expedient; he may, on extraordinary occasions, convene

[5]Superseded by the Twelfth Amendment.

[6]See Twenty-fifth Amendment.

both houses, or either of them, and in case of disagreement between them, with respect to the time of adjournment, he may adjourn them to such time as he shall think proper; he shall receive ambassadors and other public ministers; he shall take care that the laws be faithfully executed, and shall commission all the officers of the United States.

Section 4. The president, vice-president, and all civil officers of the United States, shall be removed from office on impeachment for, and conviction of, treason, bribery, or other high crimes and misdemeanors.

★ Article III

Section 1. The judicial power of the United States, shall be vested in one Supreme Court and in such inferior courts as the Congress may from time to time ordain and establish. The judges, both of the Supreme and inferior courts, shall hold their offices during good behavior, and shall, at stated times, receive for their services, a compensation, which shall not be diminished during their continuance in office.

Section 2. The judicial power shall extend to all cases, in law and equity, arising under this Constitution, the laws of the United States, and treaties made, or which shall be made, under their authority;—to all cases affecting ambassadors, other public ministers and consuls;—to all cases of admiralty and maritime jurisdiction;—to controversies to which the United States shall be a party;—to controversies between two or more states;—*between a state and citizens of another state;*[7]—between citizens of different states;—between citizens of the same state claiming lands under grants of different states, *and between a state or the citizens thereof, and foreign states, citizens, or subjects.*[8]

In all cases affecting ambassadors, other public ministers and consuls, and those in which a state shall be party, the Supreme Court shall have original jurisdiction. In all the other cases before mentioned, the Supreme Court shall have appellate jurisdiction, both as to law and fact, with such exceptions, and under such regulations as the Congress shall make.

The trial of all crimes, except in cases of impeachment, shall be by jury; and such trial shall be held in the state where the said crimes shall have been committed; but when not committed within any state, the trial shall be at such place or places as the Congress may by law have directed.

Section 3. Treason against the United States, shall consist only in levying war against them, or in adhering to their enemies, giving them aid and comfort. No person shall be convicted of treason unless on the testimony of two witnesses to the same overt act, or on confession in open court.

The Congress shall have power to declare the punishment of treason, but no attainder of treason shall work corruption of blood, or forfeiture except during the life of the person attained.

[7]See Eleventh Amendment.

[8]See Eleventh Amendment.

★ Article IV

Section 1. Full faith and credit shall be given in each state to the public acts, records, and judicial proceedings of every other state. And the Congress may by general laws prescribe the manner in which such acts, records, and proceedings shall be proved, and the effect thereof.

Section 2. The citizens of each state shall be entitled to all privileges and immunities of citizens in the several states.

A person charged in any state with treason, felony, or other crime, who shall flee from justice, and be found in another state, shall on demand of the executive authority of the state from which he fled, be delivered up, to be removed to the state having jurisdiction of the crime.

No person held to service or labor in one state, under the laws thereof, escaping into another, shall, in consequence of any law or regulation therein, be discharged from such service or labor, but shall be delivered up on claim of the party to whom such service or labor may be due.[9]

Section 3. New states may be admitted by the Congress into this union; but no new state shall be formed or erected within the jurisdiction of any other state; nor any state be formed by the junction of two or more states, or parts of states, without the consent of the legislatures of the states concerned as well as of the Congress.

The Congress shall have power to dispose of and make all needful rules and regulations respecting the territory or other property belonging to the United States; and nothing in this Constitution shall be so construed as to prejudice any claims of the United States, or of any particular state.

Section 4. The United States shall guarantee to every state in this union a republican form of government, and shall protect each of them against invasion; and on application of the legislature, or of the executive (when the legislature cannot be convened), against domestic violence.

★ Article V

The Congress, whenever two-thirds of both houses shall deem it necessary, shall propose amendments to this Constitution, or, on the application of the legislatures of two-thirds of the several states, shall call a convention for proposing amendments, which, in either case, shall be valid to all intents and purposes, as part of this Constitution, when ratified by the legislatures of three-fourths of the several states, or by conventions in three-fourths thereof, as the one or the other mode of ratification may be proposed by the Congress; provided that no amendment which may be made prior to the year one thousand eight hundred and eight shall in any manner affect the first and fourth clauses in the ninth section of the first article; and that no state, without its consent, shall be deprived of its equal suffrage in the Senate.

[9]See Thirteenth Amendment.

★ ARTICLE VI

All debts contracted and engagements entered into, before the adoption of this Constitution, shall be as valid against the United States under this Constitution, as under the Confederation.

This Constitution, and the laws of the United States which shall be made in pursuance thereof; and all treaties made, or which shall be made, under the authority of the United States, shall be the supreme law of the land; and the judges in every state shall be bound thereby, anything in the constitution or laws of any state to the contrary notwithstanding.

The senators and representatives before mentioned, and the members of the several state legislatures, and all executive and judicial officers, both of the United States and of the several states, shall be bound by oath or affirmation, to support this Constitution; but no religious test shall ever be required as a qualification to any office or public trust under the United States.

★ ARTICLE VII

The ratification of the conventions of nine states, shall be sufficient for the establishment of this Constitution between the states so ratifying the same.

Done in convention by the unanimous consent of the states present the seventeenth day of September in the year of our Lord one thousand seven hundred and eighty-seven and of the Independence of the United States of America the twelfth. In witness whereof we have hereunto subscribed our names.

Articles in addition to, and amendment of, the Constitution of the United States of America, proposed by Congress, and ratified by the several states, pursuant to the fifth Article of the original Constitution:

AMENDMENT I

(Ratification of the first ten amendments was completed December 15, 1791.)

Congress shall make no law respecting an establishment of religion, or prohibiting the free exercise thereof; or abridging the freedom of speech, or of the press; or the right of the people peaceably to assemble, and to petition the government for a redress of grievances.

AMENDMENT II

A well-regulated militia, being necessary to the security of a free state, the right of the people to keep and bear arms, shall not be infringed.

AMENDMENT III

No soldier shall, in time of peace be quartered in any house, without the consent of the owner, nor in time of war, but in a manner to be prescribed by law.

AMENDMENT IV

The right of the people to be secure in their persons, houses, papers, and effects, against unreasonable searches and seizures, shall not be violated, and no warrants shall issue, but upon probable cause, supported by oath or affirmation, and particularly describing the place to be searched, and the persons or things to be seized.

AMENDMENT V

No person shall be held to answer for a capital, or otherwise infamous crime, unless on a presentment or indictment of a grand jury, except in cases arising in the land or naval forces, or in the militia, when in actual service in time of war or public danger; nor shall any person be subject for the same offense to be twice put in jeopardy of life or limb; nor shall be compelled in any criminal case to be a witness against himself, nor be deprived of life, liberty, or property, without due process of law; nor shall private property be taken for public use, without just compensation.

AMENDMENT VI

In all criminal prosecutions, the accused shall enjoy the right to a speedy and public trial, by an impartial jury of the state and district wherein the crime shall have been committed, which district shall have been previously ascertained by law, and to be informed of the nature and cause of the accusation; to be confronted with the witness against him; to have compulsory process for obtaining witnesses in his favor, and to have the assistance of counsel for his defense.

AMENDMENT VII

In suits at common law, where the value in controversy shall exceed twenty dollars, the right of trial by jury shall be preserved, and no fact tried by a jury, shall be otherwise reexamined in any court of the United States, than according to the rules of the common law.

AMENDMENT VIII

Excessive bail shall not be required, nor excessive fines imposed, nor cruel and unusual punishments inflicted.

AMENDMENT IX

The enumeration in the Constitution, of certain rights, shall not be construed to deny or disparage others retained by the people.

AMENDMENT X

The powers not delegated to the United States by the Constitution, nor prohibited by it to the states, are reserved to the states respectively, or to the people.

AMENDMENT XI (1798)

The judicial power of the United States shall not be construed to extend to any suit in law or equity, commenced or prosecuted against one of the United States by citizens of another state, or by citizens or subjects of any foreign states.

AMENDMENT XII (1804)

The electors shall meet in their respective states and vote by ballot for president and vice-president, one of whom, at least, shall not be an inhabitant of the same state with themselves; they shall name in their ballots the person voted for as president, and in distinct ballots the person voted for as vice-president, and they shall make distinct lists of all persons voted for as president, and of all persons voted for as vice-president, and of the number of votes for each, which lists they shall sign and certify, and transmit sealed to the seat of the government of the United States, directed to the president of the Senate;—the president of the Senate shall, in the presence of Senate and House of Representatives, open all the certificates and the votes shall then be counted;—the person having the greatest number of votes for president, shall be the president, if such number be a majority of the whole number of electors appointed; and if no person have such majority, then from the persons having the highest numbers not exceeding three on the list of those voted for as president, the House of Representatives shall choose immediately, by ballot, the president. But in choosing the president, the votes shall be taken by states, the representation from each state having one vote; a quorum for this purpose shall consist of a member or members from two-thirds of the states, and a majority of all the states shall be necessary to a choice. And if the House of Representatives shall not choose a president whenever the right of choice shall devolve upon them, *before the fourth day of March next following,*[10] then the vice-president shall act as president, as in the case of the death or other constitutional disability of the president. The person having the greatest number of votes as vice-president shall be the vice-president, if such number be a majority of the whole number of electors appointed, and if no person have a majority, then from the two highest numbers on the list, the Senate shall choose the vice-president; a quorum for the purpose shall consist of two-thirds of the whole number of senators, and a majority of the whole number shall be necessary to a choice. But no person constitutionally ineligible to the office of president shall be eligible to that of vice-president of the United States.

[10]Altered by the Twentieth Amendment.

AMENDMENT XIII (1865)

Section 1. Neither slavery nor involuntary servitude, except as a punishment for crime whereof the party shall have been duly convicted, shall exist within the United States, or any place subject to their jurisdiction.

Section 2. Congress shall have the power to enforce this article by appropriate legislation.

AMENDMENT XIV (1868)

Section 1. All persons born or naturalized in the United States, and subject to the jurisdiction thereof, are citizens of the United States and the state wherein they reside. No state shall make or enforce any law which shall abridge the privileges or immunities of citizens of the United States; nor shall any state deprive any person of life, liberty, or property, without due process of law; nor deny to any person within its jurisdiction the equal protection of the laws.

Section 2. Representatives shall be apportioned among the several states according to their respective numbers, counting the whole number of persons in each state, excluding Indians not taxed. But when the right to vote at any election for the choice of electors for president and vice-president of the United States, representatives in Congress, the executive and judicial officers of a state, or the members of the legislature thereof, is denied to any of the male inhabitants of such state, being twenty-one years of age, and citizens of the United States, or in any way abridged, except for participation in rebellion, or other crime, the basis of representation therein shall be reduced in the proportion which the number of such male citizens shall bear to the whole number of male citizens twenty-one years of age in such state.

Section 3. No person shall be a senator or representative in Congress, or elector of president and vice-president, or hold any office, civil or military, under the United States, or under any state, who, having previously taken an oath, as a member of Congress, or as an officer of the United States, or as a member of any state legislature, or as an executive or judicial officer of any state, to support the Constitution of the United States, shall have engaged in insurrection or rebellion against the same, or given aid or comfort to the enemies thereof. But Congress may by a vote of two-thirds of each house, remove such disability.

Section 4. The validity of the public debt of the United States, authorized by law, including debts incurred for payment of pensions and bounties for services in suppressing insurrection or rebellion, shall be questioned. But neither the United States nor any state shall assume or pay any debt or obligation incurred in aid of insurrection or rebellion against the United States, or any claim for the loss or emancipation of any slave; but all such debts, obligations, and claims shall be held illegal and void.

Section 5. The Congress shall have power to enforce, by appropriate legislation, the provisions of this article.

AMENDMENT XV (1870)

Section 1. The right of citizens of the United States to vote shall not be denied or abridged by the United States or by any state on account of race, color, or previous condition of servitude.

Section 2. The Congress shall have power to enforce this article by appropriate legislation.

AMENDMENT XVI (1913)

The Congress shall have power to lay and collect taxes on incomes, from whatever source derived, without apportionment among the several states, and without regard to any census or enumeration.

AMENDMENT XVII (1913)

The Senate of the United States shall be composed of two senators from each state, elected by the people thereof, for six years; and each senator shall have one vote. The electors in each state shall have the qualifications requisite for electors of the most numerous branch of the state legislatures.

When vacancies happen in the representation of any state in the Senate, the executive authority of such state shall issue writs of election to fill such vacancies: *provided,* that the legislature of any State may empower the executive thereof to make temporary appointments until the people fill the vacancies by election as the legislature may direct.

This amendment shall not be so construed as to affect the election or term of any senator chosen before it becomes valid as part of the Constitution.

AMENDMENT XVIII (1919)

Section 1. After one year from the ratification of this article the manufacture, sale, or transportation of intoxicating liquors within, the importation thereof into, or the exportation thereof from the United States and all territory subject to the jurisdiction thereof for beverage purposes is hereby prohibited.

Section 2. The Congress and the several states shall have concurrent power to enforce this article by appropriate legislation.

Section 3. This article shall be inoperative unless it shall have been ratified as an amendment to the Constitution by the legislatures of the several states, as provided in the Constitution, within seven years from the date of the submission hereof to the states by the Congress.[11]

AMENDMENT XIX (1920)

The right of citizens of the United States to vote shall not be denied or abridged by the United States or by any state on account of sex.

Congress shall have power to enforce this article by appropriate legislation.

AMENDMENT XX (1933)

Section 1. The terms of the president and vice-president shall end at noon on the 20th day of January, and the terms of senators and representatives at noon on the 3rd day of January, of the years in which such terms would have ended if this article had not been ratified; and the terms of their successors shall then begin.

Section 2. The Congress shall assemble at least once in every year, and such meeting shall begin at noon on the 3rd day of January, unless they shall by law appoint a different day.

Section 3. If, at the time fixed for the beginning of the term of the president, the president elect shall have died, the vice-president elect shall become president. If a president shall not have been chosen before the time fixed for the beginning of his term, or if the president elect shall have failed to qualify, then the vice-president elect shall act as president until a president shall have qualified; and the Congress may by law provide for the case wherein neither a president elect nor a vice-president elect shall have qualified, declaring who shall then act as president, or the manner in which one who is to act shall be selected, and such person shall act accordingly until a president or vice-president shall have qualified.

Section 4. The Congress may by law provide for the case of the death of any of the persons from whom the House of Representatives may choose a president whenever the right of choice shall have devolved upon them, and for the case of the death of any of the persons from whom the Senate may choose a vice-president whenever the right of choice shall have devolved upon them.

Section 5. Sections 1 and 2 shall take effect on the 15th day of October following ratification of this article.

Section 6. This article shall be inoperative unless it shall have been ratified as an amendment to the Constitution by the legislatures of three-fourths of the several states within seven years from the date of its submission.

[11]Repealed by the Twenty-first Amendment.

AMENDMENT XXI (1933)

Section 1. The eighteenth article of amendment to the Constitution of the United States is hereby repealed.

Section 2. The transportation or importation into any state, territory, or possession of the United States for delivery or use therein of intoxicating liquors, in violation of the laws thereof, is hereby prohibited.

Section 3. This article shall be inoperative unless it shall have been ratified as an amendment to the Constitution by conventions in the several states, as provided in the Constitution, within seven years from the date of the submission hereof to the states by the Congress.

AMENDMENT XXII (1951)

Section 1. No person shall be elected to the office of the president more than twice, and no person who has held the office of president, or acted as president for more than two years of a term to which some other person was elected president shall be elected to the office of president more than once. But this article shall not apply to any person holding the office of president when this article was proposed by the Congress, and shall not prevent any person who may be holding the office of president, or acting as president, during the term within which this article becomes operative from holding the office of president or acting as president during the remainder of such term.

Section 2. This article shall be inoperative unless it shall have been ratified as an amendment to the Constitution by the legislatures of three-fourths of the several states within seven years from the date of its submission to the states by the Congress.

AMENDMENT XXIII (1961)

Section 1. The district constituting the seat of government of the United States shall appoint in such manner as the Congress may direct:

A number of electors of president and vice-president equal to the whole number of senators and representatives in Congress to which the district would be entitled if it were a state, but in no event more than the least populous state; they shall be in addition to those appointed by the states, but they shall be considered, for the purposes of the election of president and vice-president, to be electors appointed by a state; and they shall meet in the district and perform such duties as provided by the twelfth article of amendment.

Section 2. The Congress shall have power to enforce this article by appropriate legislation.

AMENDMENT XXIV (1964)

Section 1. The right of citizens of the United States to vote in any primary or other election for president or vice-president, for electors for president or vice-president, or for senator or representative in Congress, shall not be denied or abridged by the United States or any state by reason of failure to pay any poll tax or other tax.

Section 2. The Congress shall have the power to enforce this article by appropriate legislation.

AMENDMENT XXV (1967)

Section 1. In case of the removal of the president from office or of his death or resignation, the vice-president shall become president.

Section 2. Whenever there is a vacancy in the office of the vice-president, the president shall nominate a vice-president who shall take office upon confirmation by a majority vote of both houses of Congress.

Section 3. Whenever the president transmits to the president pro tempore of the Senate and the Speaker of the House of Representatives his written declaration that he is unable to discharge the powers and duties of his office, and until he transmits to them a written declaration to the contrary, such powers and duties shall be discharged by the vice-president as acting president.

Section 4. Whenever the vice-president and a majority of either the principal officers of the executive departments or of such other body as Congress may by law provide, transmit to the president pro tempore of the Senate and the Speaker of the House of Representatives their written declaration that the president is unable to discharge the powers and duties of his office, the vice-president shall immediately assume the powers and duties of the office as acting president.

Thereafter, when the president transmits to the president pro tempore of the Senate and the Speaker of the House of Representatives his written declaration that no inability exists, he shall resume the powers and duties of his office unless the vice-president and a majority of either the principal officers of the executive departments or of such other body as Congress may by law provide, transmit within four days to the president pro tempore of the Senate and the Speaker of the House of Representatives their written declaration that the president is unable to discharge the powers and duties of his office. Thereupon Congress shall decide the issue, assembling within forty-eight hours for that purpose if not in session. If the Congress, within twenty-one days after receipt of the latter written declaration, or, if Congress is not in session, within twenty-one days after Congress is required to assemble, determines by two-thirds vote of both houses that the president is unable to discharge the powers and duties of his office, the vice-president shall continue to discharge the same as acting president; otherwise, the president shall resume the powers and duties of his office.

AMENDMENT XXVI (1971)

Section 1. The right of citizens of the United States, who are 18 years of age or older, to vote shall not be denied or abridged by the United States or any state on account of age.

Section 2. The Congress shall have the power to enforce this article by appropriate legislation.

Appendix C

Winners and losers in presidential elections, 1789–1988

Year	Winner	Winner's party	Loser	Loser's party
1789	George Washington[a]			
1792	George Washington[a]			
1796	John Adams	Federalist	Thomas Jefferson	Democratic Republican
1800	Thomas Jefferson	Democratic Republican	John Adams	Federalist
1804	Thomas Jefferson	Democratic Republican	Charles E. Pinckney	Federalist
1808	James Madison	Democratic Republican	Charles E. Pinckney	Federalist
1812	James Madison	Democratic Republican	De Witt Clinton	Federalist
1816	James Monroe	Democratic Republican	Rufus King	Federalist
1820	James Monroe	Democratic Republican	John Quincy Adams	National Republican
1824	John Quincy Adams	National Republican	Andrew Jackson	Democratic Republican
1828	Andrew Jackson	Democratic	John Quincy Adams	National Republican
1832	Andrew Jackson	Democratic	Henry Clay	National Republican
1836	Martin Van Buren	Democratic	William Henry Harrison	Whig
1840	William Henry Harrison[b]	Whig	Martin Van Buren	Democratic
1844	James K. Polk	Democratic	Henry Clay	Whig
1848	Zachary Taylor[c]	Whig	Lewis Cass	Democratic
1852	Franklin Pierce	Democratic	Winfield Scott	Whig
1856	James Buchanan	Democratic	John C. Fremont	Republican
1860	Abraham Lincoln	Republican	Stephen A. Douglas	Democratic
1864	Abraham Lincoln[d]	Republican	George B. McClellan	Democratic
1868	Ulysses S. Grant	Republican	Horatio Seymour	Democratic
1872	Ulysses S. Grant	Republican	Horace Greeley	Democratic
1876	Rutherford B. Hayes	Republican	Samuel J. Tilden	Democratic
1880	James A. Garfield[e]	Republican	Winfield S. Hancock	Democratic
1884	Grover Cleveland	Democratic	James G. Blaine	Republican
1888	Benjamin Harrison	Republican	Grover Cleveland	Democratic
1892	Grover Cleveland	Democratic	Benjamin Harrison	Republican
1896	William McKinley	Republican	William Jennings Bryan	Democratic

(continued)

★

Winners and losers in presidential elections, 1789–1988 *(continued)*

Year	*Winner*	*Winner's party*	*Loser*	*Loser's party*
1900	William McKinley[f]	Republican	William Jennings Bryan	Democratic
1904	Theodore Roosevelt	Republican	Alton B. Parker	Democratic
1908	William Howard Taft	Republican	William Jennings Bryan	Democratic
1912	Woodrow Wilson	Democratic	Charles Evans Hughes	Republican
1916	Woodrow Wilson	Democratic	Charles Evans Hughes	Republican
1920	Warren G. Harding[g]	Republican	James M. Cox	Democratic
1924	Calvin Coolidge	Republican	John W. Davis	Democratic
1928	Herbert Hoover	Republican	Alfred E. Smith	Democratic
1932	Franklin D. Roosevelt	Democratic	Herbert Hoover	Republican
1936	Franklin D. Roosevelt	Democratic	Alfred M. Landon	Republican
1940	Franklin D. Roosevelt	Democratic	Wendell L. Willkie	Republican
1944	Franklin D. Roosevelt[h]	Democratic	Thomas E. Dewey	Republican
1948	Harry S Truman	Democratic	Thomas E. Dewey	Republican
1952	Dwight D. Eisenhower	Republican	Adlai E. Stevenson	Democratic
1956	Dwight D. Eisenhower	Republican	Adlai E. Stevenson	Democratic
1960	John F. Kennedy[i]	Democratic	Richard M. Nixon	Republican
1964	Lyndon B. Johnson	Democratic	Barry M. Goldwater	Republican
1968	Richard M. Nixon	Republican	Hubert H. Humphrey	Democratic
1972	Richard M. Nixon[j]	Republican	George McGovern	Democratic
1976	Jimmy Carter	Democratic	Gerald Ford	Republican
1980	Ronald Reagan	Republican	Jimmy Carter	Democratic
1984	Ronald Reagan	Republican	Walter Mondale	Democratic
1988	George Bush	Republican	Michael Dukakis	Democratic

[a]Unopposed.

[b]Died 1841; succeeded by John Tyler.

[c]Died 1850; succeeded by Millard Fillmore.

[d]Died 1865; succeeded by Andrew Johnson.

[e]Died 1881; succeeded by Chester A. Arthur.

[f]Died 1901; succeeded by Theodore Roosevelt.

[g]Died 1923; succeeded by Calvin Coolidge.

[h]Died 1945; succeeded by Harry S Truman.

[i]Died 1963; succeeded by Lyndon B. Johnson.

[j]Resigned 1974; succeeded by Gerald Ford.

★★★★★★★★★★★★

Appendix D Major New Deal Legislation and Agencies

Agricultural Adjustment Act (AAA, 1933) Authorized payments to farmers to reduce production and control acreage

Civilian Conservation Corps (CCC, 1933) Provided for government employment of men aged 18–25 in natural resources projects

Civil Works Administration (1933) Provided for government employment on construction projects (dams, bridges, buildings)

Emergency Banking Relief Act (1933) Provided for government purchase of stock in banks; authorized Federal Reserve to extend credit on unconventional assets

Emergency Farm Mortgage Act (1933) Provided immediate relief against farm foreclosures

Federal Deposit Insurance Corporation (FDIC, 1933) Provided for federal insurance of bank deposits to instill confidence and forestall mass withdrawals

Federal Emergency Relief Administration (FERA, 1933) Provided relief to needy states and localities

National Industrial Recovery Act (NIRA, 1933) Established codes of competition giving industries license to limit production, fix prices, and specify wages and hours of labor (declared unconstitutional by U.S. Supreme Court)

National Labor Relations Act (Wagner Act, 1935) Recognized labor's right to organize and bargain collectively; established National Labor Relations Board (NLRB) to mediate disputes between labor and management

Public Works Administration (PWA, 1935) Authorized jobs on public construction projects for unemployed, paying union wages

Securities and Exchange Commission (SEC, 1934) Established to regulate the stock market to prevent manipulation of securities

Social Security Act (1935) Provided for retirement benefits based on contributions by workers and employers

Tennessee Valley Authority (TVA, 1933) Established to undertake flood control and economic development of Tennessee Valley

Works Progress Administration (WPA, 1935) Provided for employment on local public projects

Glossary

accommodationist One willing to compromise in a dispute with another nation.

achievement The ideal that accomplishments are brought about by persistence, resolve, and hard work.

acid rain The combination of sulfur dioxide (from burning coal) and water that causes environmental damage to lakes and forests.

adversary relationship A relationship characterized by conflict between the press and government.

advise and consent The constitutional functions of the Senate to advise the president and to grant or withhold approval of treaties and of certain presidential appointments.

AFDC (welfare) Aid to Families with Dependent Children, a government program to provide income to families of children who have no wage-earning parent in the household.

affirmative action A policy of actively recruiting the hiring of members of minority groups and women as a means of remedying past discrimination.

agenda setting The process through which issues come to be considered worthy of a political response.

aggregate demand The combined demand for goods and services of consumers, businesses, and government.

American exceptionalism The presumed superiority of American ideals and policies over those of other countries.

amicus curiae "Friend of the court"; a brief or argument filed by an individual or group that is not a direct party to a suit but seeks to influence the court's decision.

Anti-Federalists A group consisting of small farmers and others who opposed a strong central government and argued against ratification of the Constitution.

antitrust legislation Laws that prohibit the formation of monopolies.

appeal (*a*) A legal proceeding in which a case is brought from a lower court to a higher court for review. (*b*) A case brought to the U.S. Supreme Court as a matter of right.

appellate jurisdiction The authority of a court to try a case on appeal (to review a decision of a lower court).

appropriations bill A bill granting money to carry out a governmental program authorized by Congress.

Articles of Confederation The first constitution of the original thirteen states, adopted in 1781 and replaced by the present Constitution in 1789.

attention cycles The process by which issues are adopted and then abandoned by the public, government, and media.

authority Where a demand is regarded as legitimate and right by virtue of position.

balanced budget amendment A proposed change in the Constitution that would prohibit the government from spending more than it collects in taxes and fees, except in time of war.

balance of payments The monetary value of exports minus the monetary value of imports.

balance of trade The ratio of the monetary value of a country's imports to that of its exports.

bicameral legislature A legislature composed of two houses or chambers.

bill of attainder A legislative act that singles out an individual for punishment without benefit of trial; forbidden by the Constitution.

Bill of Rights The first ten amendments to the U.S. Constitution, added shortly after ratification.

biomass A renewable source of energy derived from plant material.

blip culture A pattern of knowledge and behavior associated with the computer age, in which more attention is paid to unconnected events than to long-term considerations.

block grant A federal grant of money for purposes of the recipient's choosing within a general policy area.

budget deficit An excess of government expenditures over government receipts in a given budget year.

bureaucracy (*a*) The organization of bureaus, agencies, and departments within the executive branch that administers the laws and services of government. (*b*) Any administrative system based on specialization of duties, a hierarchy of command, and formal rules and regulations.

cabinet An advisory body within the executive branch composed of the heads of the major executive departments, the vice-president, and possibly other high-ranking officials, who convene with the president to discuss problems and policies.

capital gains Income derived from investments rather than earnings.

casework Work performed by a member of Congress on behalf of individual constituents, as opposed to groups of constituents.

categorical grant A federal grant of money to be used for a specific purpose.

caucus (*a*) A meeting of party members in a legislative chamber to select leaders or adopt policy positions. (*b*) A closed meeting of state or local party leaders to nominate candidates for office.

Central Intelligence Agency An agency created to oversee the U.S. government's worldwide network of intelligence collection and analysis.

certiorari, writ of A writ issued by a higher court ordering a lower court to send up the records of a case for review.

checks and balances The overlapping powers of the executive, legislative, and judicial branches of government that permit each branch to restrain the actions of the others. *See also* **separation of powers.**

chief executive The position of the president in the capacity to administer (or direct the administration of) the laws of the land.

citizens' lobby *See* **public interest group.**

city upon a hill Coined by John Winthrop to illustrate the exemplary nature of the first Puritan community in New England.

civil liberties Freedoms granted to individuals.

civil service (*a*) A system by which government jobs are filled through competitive examinations, without regard to political affiliation. (*b*) The body of civilian employees who hold such jobs.

class-action suit A lawsuit brought by one or more persons on behalf of a larger number of people with a similar legal complaint.

closed primary A primary election in which only registered members of a party may vote.

cloture rule A procedure for shutting off debate on a bill in the Senate, requiring a three-fifths vote of the entire membership to succeed.

coalitions A temporary alliance of groups or individuals united to achieve a common goal.

cold war The conflict over ideological differences between the United States and the Soviet Union in the years following World War II, carried out by means short of military action.

colonial mentality An attitude characteristic of a dominant country toward a colony, based on the belief that the colony exists primarily for the benefit of the dominant country.

command economy An economic system in which the state owns the means of production, all land, and all resources.

commander in chief The president as head of the armed forces.

communications revolution The developments in the manner and speed with which news is disseminated around the world, which have political, social, and economic effects on all countries.

community The first stage of the socialization process, in which the child learns to discriminate "us" from "them."

comparable worth A policy of equal pay for work of comparable value to the employer.

Compromise of 1808 A provision of the Constitution that protected the importation of slaves until 1808.

concurrent powers Powers granted by the Constitution to both the national government and the states, such as the power to levy taxes.

confederation An alliance of independent states, with a central government that has only limited authority.

conference A meeting of party members in a legislative chamber to select leaders or adopt policy positions.

conference committee A

committee composed of members of both the House and the Senate, who meet to reconcile differences between House and Senate versions of a bill.

congressional caucus Informal associations of like-minded members who meet to discuss policy concerns.

Connecticut Compromise A compromise adopted at the Constitutional Convention in 1787 that called for a two-house legislature with equal representation of the states in the Senate and representation by population in the House.

conservative (*a*) A person who wishes to maintain the existing order, values tradition, and prefers change to be gradual. (*b*) A person who opposes the expansion of governmental activities.

constituents The residents of a legislator's district, to whom the legislator is responsible.

constitution The principal legal statement of a political system, prescribing the powers and procedures of its governmental institutions.

constitutionalism (constitutional government) A system of government that imposes legal limits on the powers of those who govern.

consumer price index The price of an aggregation of goods and services typical of consumer purchases, expressed as a number indicating the increase or decrease in relation to the price of a similar aggregation in an earlier period.

containment A policy adopted by the United States after World War II that sought to prevent the expansion of Soviet power and the spread of communism.

continuing resolution A measure passed by Congress instructing federal agencies to spend at last year's budget level until a new budget can be agreed upon.

Contras A military group opposed to the leftist Sandinista government of Nicaragua.

convention system A political system whereby party delegates meet to nominate candidates for office and/or adopt a policy platform.

cooperative federalism A view of national, state, and local governments as partners in performing government functions.

corporation A business that is legally incorporated under the laws of a state and that pools the resources of many owners, with ownership rights freely transferable between persons.

corporatism A system in which individuals and groups are represented not as residents of a geographical area but as members of interests in society (e.g., labor, doctors, the elderly).

cost-benefit analysis An economic analysis that assigns a monetary value to the positive and negative features of a project.

Council on Foreign Relations A highly influential, private research and planning organization that serves as an informal forum for the elite to discuss American foreign policy.

creative federalism The involvement of all three levels of government in coming up with solutions to social problems.

cross-pressure Sociological traits that pull people in opposite directions.

de facto segregation Segregation of the races caused by residential patterns rather than by law (*de jure*).

deficit An excess of government expenditures over government receipts.

delegated powers (enumerated powers) Powers specifically granted by the Constitution to the national government, such as Congress's power to tax and to declare war.

delivery systems Various means used to transport nuclear weapons to their targets.

democracy (*a*) A political system in which citizens enjoy a relatively high degree of access to and influence over their government. (*b*) A system in which ultimate political authority rests with the people.

depression A phase in the business cycle characterized by low output and high unemployment.

deregulation The removal of government regulations on a certain sector of the economy.

détente A relaxation of tensions and improvement of relations between two nations.

direct action A form of political action aimed at achieving an end directly, usually through disruptive or obstructionist means (e.g., boycotts or sit-ins).

direct primary A preliminary election in which voters select the candidates who will run on the party's ticket in the general election.

discount rate The rate of interest at which member banks can borrow money from the Federal Reserve Bank.

domino theory A theory that holds that if one nation "falls" to communism, neighboring countries will topple like a row of dominoes.

double jeopardy Subjection to trial for an offense for which one has already been tried; a practice forbidden by the Constitution.

dual (layer-cake) federalism The idea that there is a fixed distribution of power between the two levels of government, with the states operating on an equal basis with the federal government.

due process The requirement that laws be reasonable and that they be administered in a fair manner, such that an individual has an opportunity to be heard and to confront opposing witnesses before he or she can be deprived of life, liberty, or property.

efficiency In terms of public policy, it generally means the most expeditious or cost effective ways to pursue a policy.

electoral college The body of electors chosen by the states who, following the presidential election in November, formally elect the president and vice-president.

elite (*a*) The few individuals who have the most of the things valued by the society, such as money and influence. (*b*) Those people who dominate major institutions and who have a major impact on political, economic, and social decision making.

enumerated powers *See* **delegated powers.**

environmental perspective Akin to the "nature" position of the formation of human personality, this explanation focuses on non-human factors involved in the development of national character.

equality The idea that persons are naturally imbued with the same intrinsic value.

Equal Pay Act A federal law passed in 1963 requiring that men and women be paid the same for "equal work on jobs the performance of which requires equal skill, effort and responsibility and which are performed under similar working conditions."

equal time requirement A rule of the Federal Communications Commission that requires broadcasters to give equal air time to candidates for public office other than the presidency.

equity In terms of public policy, it generally means fairness.

Eurodollars U.S. dollars held abroad.

evaluation The assessment of a program to determine its effectiveness and efficiency after it has been implemented.

exclusionary rule A rule established by the Supreme Court that requires evidence obtained illegally to be excluded from trial proceedings.

executive agreement An agreement between the president and a foreign nation that has the effect of a treaty but does not require formal approval by the Senate.

executive department A major agency of the national government headed by a presidential appointee with cabinet rank (e.g., the State Department, the Justice Department).

Executive Office of the President The group of top staff agencies (e.g., the Office of Management and Budget, the Council of Economic Advisers, the White House Office) that report directly to the president and provide him with information and advice.

executive order A presidential directive given to a federal agency.

executive privilege A presumed right of a president to withhold sensitive information requested by Congress or the courts.

Exportation Compromise A compromise reached during the Constitutional Convention whereby the South agreed to abide by uniform import tariffs in exchange for the banning of export tariffs.

ex post facto law A law that subjects a person to punishment for an act that was not illegal at the time it was committed. Such a law is forbidden by the Constitution.

fairness doctrine A requirement of the Federal Communications Commission that broadcasting stations provide opportunities for the airing of conflicting views on important issues.

family allowance A monthly benefit distributed to all families by the government.

Federal Communications Commission (FCC) A body appointed by the president and approved by the Senate to regulate radio and television broadcasting in the United States.

Federal Election Campaign Act An act passed in 1974 to limit the amount individuals or groups can contribute to presidential or congressional campaigns.

Federal Election Commission A group set up to administer and oversee the laws created by the Federal Election Campaign Act.

federalism A governmental system in which power is divided between a central (national) government and regional (state) governments.

Federalist Papers A series of essays written by James Madison, Alexander Hamilton, and John Jay in 1787–1788 explaining and defending the newly proposed U.S. Constitution.

Federalists Persons who favored a strong central government and supported the adoption of the Constitution.

Federal Reserve System The monetary and banking system of the federal government.

feminization of poverty The increasing tendency of the poverty population to consist of women and their children.

filibuster An obstructionist tactic used in the U.S. Senate whereby a minority of senators try to block action on a bill by endless speeches and debate, refusing to yield the floor so that a vote may be taken.

fiscal federalism The sharing of economic policies among national, state, and local governments.

fiscal policy The use of government taxing and spending powers to achieve economic stability and prosperity.

floor leader Assistant to the Speaker of the House, and often a stepping-stone to the job of Speaker.

fossil fuels The fuels such as oil, coal, and natural gas that are contained in the earth.

freedom The idea that people are free to do as they choose without fear of being coerced or constrained.

free-market economy An economy in which demand and supply determine prices.

free-trade policies Policies that favor the reduction of international tariffs.

friend of the court See amicus curiae.

full employment The stated goal of the U.S. government to provide all Americans with jobs.

gatekeepers The few people—editors, assignment editors, TV network anchors, radio disc jockeys—who select stories for coverage by the newspapers and the networks.

global village The world as a place whose prospects and problems are shared by all of its inhabitants.

government The combination of institutions, rules, and policy makers principally involved in settling disputes and distributing benefits. *See also* **politics.**

government corporation A governmental agency organized like a private corporation to perform a public commercial function (e.g., the U.S. Postal Service, the Federal Deposit Insurance Corporation).

grace According to Puritan belief, unmerited assistance granted by God to some persons whom He has chosen for salvation.

Gramm-Rudman Hollings Act Legislation enacted in 1985 to mandate reductions in the federal budget deficit beginning in 1987.

grandfather clause A provision of a law that excuses some persons from its coverage on the basis of some prior qualification.

grant-in-aid Financial aid from the federal government to state or local governments.

guerrilla war A war involving irregular troops and unconventional combat tactics.

habeas corpus, writ of A court order requiring an enforcement official to show cause for holding a person in custody.

hard-liner One unwilling to compromise in regard to foreign policy objectives.

head of state A government official (in the United States, it is the president) who is the symbolic representative of the people and performs ceremonial functions.

health maintenance organizations (HMOs) Programs of prepaid medical care.

human rights Basic rights of human beings, regardless of nationality.

image politics Focusing on style as much as, if not more than, substance in presidential speeches and appearances.

impeachment Formal charges of misconduct voted by the House of Representatives against a president, federal judge, or other high federal official that could lead to his or her removal from office upon conviction by the Senate.

imperial presidency The concentration of foreign and domestic policy making in the office of the president.

implementation The putting into practice of a policy proposal.

implied powers Powers that are not specifically granted by the Constitution to Congress but that are "necessary and proper" to carry out those powers that are listed. *See also* **necessary and proper clause.**

impoundment Refusal by a president to spend money appropriated by Congress. *See also* **policy impoundment.**

income Consists of wages, salaries, tips, and interest.

incrementalism The practice of changing bits of policies without a major revamping.

independent agency A governmental agency responsible to the president that is not a cabinet-level executive department (e.g., the General Services Administration, the Central Intelligence Agency).

independent voter A voter who is not registered as a member of any political party and claims to identify with none.

infancy care leave The policy of giving one or both parents leave from work when a child is born.

inflation A rise in the price of goods and services that causes a decline in purchasing power.

influence A form of political power relying on persuasion, reason, or tangible rewards.

initiative A device in some states that permits citizens to petition for laws that are then accepted or rejected by the voters at the polls.

institutional power Where society's key institutions "socialize" Americans to characteristic ways of thinking.

interdependence The mutual dependence of the world's nations, such that national policies have international implications.

interest group A group with shared goals banded together to influence governmental policy.

intergovernmental lobbies Associations of government officials organized to help their various jurisdictions compete for federal grant monies.

interlocking directorates Disparate boards of directors whose members include one or more of the same individuals simultaneously.

Intermediate-range Nuclear Force (INF) Treaty An agreement signed by the United States and the Soviet Union in 1988 where both agreed to dismantle all their medium-range missiles.

internationalist One who believes that America's proper role in the world is to be a political, economic, and moral leader.

investigative reporting Modern-day muckraking, where reporters attempt to unearth facts that might be embarrassing to people in high places.

iron triangle Members of a congressional subcommittee, lobbyists, and bureaucrats who jointly pursue shared policy goals.

isolationist One who desires to retreat from international affairs.

item veto The power possessed by some governors to strike out only sections of a bill while leaving the remainder intact.

joint committee A committee composed of members from both the House and the Senate who meet to iron out differences between House and Senate versions of the same bill.

judicial review The power of a court to determine whether federal laws are in violation of the Constitution.

Keynesian economics The economic theory advanced by John Maynard Keynes, who held that economic decline can be counteracted by an increase in government spending.

laissez-faire An economic doctrine opposed to governmental interference in economic affairs.

legislative oversight Congressional review of the performance of the executive branch, to determine whether the federal bureaucracy is properly administering the laws.

libel A false or malicious written statement that damages a person's reputation.

liberal (*a*) One who favors political reform and social change, and who supports expanded governmental programs to eliminate poverty and other social ills. (*b*) Originally, one who opposed governmental restraints on individual liberty.

liberalism The political theory that is based on the idea that all persons are equal and capable of self-government.

literacy tests Tests administered to citizens to determine their competence to vote; in practice, a device to exclude black voters from the polls.

litigation The process of bringing a case before the courts.

loan guarantee A government promise to a bank to back a loan.

lobbyist A representative of an interest group who seeks to influence legislation through direct contact with policy makers.

majority leader (*a*) The head of the majority party in the Senate. (*b*) The second ranking member of the majority party in the House.

mandamus, writ of A court order demanding that a public official perform some duty required by law.

manifest destiny The doctrine, subscribed to by many Americans in the nineteenth century, that it was the destiny of the United States to expand its territories across the North American continent and beyond.

marble-cake federalism When federal, state, and local activities are interdependent, and distinctions among the three levels are blurred.

market economy An economy based on free markets and private property.

Marshall Plan A post–World War II foreign aid program, initiated by Secretary of State George C. Marshall, to help restore the war-ravaged economies of Western Europe.

mass media Means of communication, such as television, radio, books, newspapers, and magazines, designed to reach large numbers of people.

mass society According to C.

Wright Mills, the majority of citizens who have little or no influence over policy making.

materialism A preoccupation with the amassing of wealth.

Medicaid A government program that pays a portion of the medical expenses of the poor.

Medicare A government program that pays a portion of the medical expenses of the elderly.

military-industrial complex A presumed alliance between the military and large corporations (especially defense contractors), who have a mutual interest in keeping military spending at a high level.

mixed economy An economy that combines a market economy and government involvement in production and distribution of goods and services.

monetarists Persons who identify a stable rate of growth in the money supply as the key to economic stability.

monetary policy Government measures to control the amount of money circulating in the economy.

Monroe Doctrine A unilateral declaration of American foreign policy, first promulgated by President James Monroe in 1823, opposing any European intervention in the Western Hemisphere and pledging that the United States would not interfere in the internal affairs of Europe.

muckraking The practice of investigating and reporting corruption among public officials.

multinational corporations (MNCs) Corporations whose production activities take place in several countries.

mutually assured destruction (MAD) The ability of the United States and of the Soviet Union to withstand a nuclear attack and retaliate with devastating effect; presumably a deterrent to nuclear attack by either nation.

national character A personality type presumed to be characteristic of a nation's citizens.

national debt The sum total of federal budget deficits over time.

national health insurance Government health insurance that would cover all Americans.

national industrial policy A coordinated strategy for industrial competition developed by government in cooperation with business and labor.

national interest The goals and aspirations of the American political system as interpreted by the national government.

nationalism Overriding attachment to one's country.

national security The ability of a nation to defend its national borders and maintain territorial integrity.

national security adviser A cabinet-level person on the president's staff, responsible for advising the president on foreign affairs.

necessary and proper clause The language of Article I, Section 8, of the Constitution that grants Congress the power to pass laws "necessary and proper" for carrying out the specific powers granted by the Constitution; provides the basis for Congress's implied powers.

negative income tax A rebate on taxes for families earning below a certain income level.

new conservatism The term that applies to conservatism in the 1980s.

New Deal coalition The various groups that supported President Franklin Roosevelt's policies of increased government intervention in the economy and social welfare.

new federalism The state-centered philosophy of conservative Republican administrations that gives states and localities discretion in using federal grant money.

New Jersey Plan A proposal introduced at the Constitutional Convention in 1787, and backed by most of the smaller states, that called for a one-house legislature with equal representation of the states.

Nineteenth Amendment An amendment passed in 1920 that gave women the right to vote.

Nixon Doctrine The policy proclaimed by President Nixon that although the United States would help protect the security of allied nations, those nations would have to bear the major burden of their own defense.

nondecisions Matters that never make it on the formal political agenda.

nonissues Matters that challenge the basic structure or powerful elites of a nation, and therefore are not permitted a place on the public agenda.

nuclear freeze The position that both the United States and the Soviet Union should "freeze" their production of nuclear weapons and pursue meaningful arms control.

nullification The action of a state to prevent the enforcement of a federal law within its boundaries.

nullification doctrine When a state declares that a position of the national government is not applicable in that state.

oligopolies Large firms that strongly affect but do not control the market for the goods and services they provide.

open-market operations The procedures by which the Federal Reserve Bank sells government securities to control the money supply and thereby regulate the availability of credit.

open primary A primary election in which any registered voter may participate, regardless of party affiliation.

opinion leader A person who commands respect and influences the political opinions of others.

opportunity costs Benefits that must be forgone when one project is rejected in favor of another.

original jurisdiction The authority of a court to try a case for the first time (as opposed to appellate jurisdiction).

pack journalism Reportage by journalists who depend on reports prepared by one of their number and press releases handed out by the staff of the person they are covering.

party caucus or conference A meeting of party members in a legislative chamber to select leaders or adopt policy positions. (Democrats call them caucuses and Republicans call them conferences.)

party convention A gathering of party officials and delegates at which final candidate selections and changes to the party platform are made.

party whip See **whip.**

paternalism A relationship that presumes that a dominant or paternal figure knows better than subordinates what is best for them.

peace through strength The view that America should pursue a position of nuclear superiority and shun arms control with the Soviet Union.

photo opportunities Staged media events that are designed to portray a favorable image of the president.

pluralist theory A theory of government that holds that power is widely dispersed among many separate and competing groups held in check by various social and political forces.

plurality Electoral mechanism whereby the candidate with the most votes is the winner in an election.

plural-member district system A legislative district represented by more than one legislator.

pocket veto The president's power to kill a bill received within ten days before Congress adjourns by allowing it to remain on his desk unsigned.

policy impoundment Refusal by a president to spend money appropriated by Congress for policies with which he disagrees ideologically.

Political action committee (PAC) An organization that has legal authority to collect contributions and donate them to political candidates.

political economy The economy of a nation in relation to its government.

political party An organization that seeks to gain control of government by running candidates for public office.

political science The study of politics and government, often broken into sub-fields like political theory, comparative politics, international relations, and American government.

political socialization The lifelong learning process by which individuals acquire political attitudes and values.

political survey Opinion polls designed to measure people's political attitudes and voting preferences.

politicization When citizens come to see society's problems as falling within the realm of politics and government.

politics The process of settling disputes and distributing benefits, of deciding "who gets what, when, and how."

poll tax A fee imposed as a requirement for voting.

pork-barrel legislation Legislation providing federal funds for local government projects that are not always critically needed but that may help politicians look good in the eyes of their constituents (*slang*).

positional issue An issue that arouses alternative and often highly conflictual responses (e.g., defense, welfare).

positive apathetics Those who do not vote because they are satisfied with the status quo.

post-industrial society Reflects the increasing importance of the service sector and the diminishing importance of the manufacturing and agricultural sectors.

power The ability to affect the behavior of others and to influence political outcomes.

power elite According to C. Wright Mills, the triumvirate of top business, military, and government leaders that controls the key resources for decision making in America.

president pro tempore A member of the majority party chosen to preside over the Senate in the absence of the vice-president.

presidential succession The order that officers should succeed the president if the president is removed from office or dies.

press conferences Meetings called by the president where the press is free to ask questions.

pressure group *See* **interest group.**

price supports Government guarantees of the prices of certain agricultural commodities.

prior restraint Action taken to prevent certain material from being published.

private sector The markets and private business as opposed to government.

procedural rights Rights guaranteeing citizens protection against arbitrary actions by governmental officials. No individual may be deprived of life, liberty, or property except through well-defined procedures prescribed by law. *See also* **due process.**

program evaluation The process of determining the effectiveness and efficiency of a public program.

proportional representation An electoral system in which parties are assigned seats in the legislature in proportion to their percentages of the popular vote.

proprietorship An unincorporated business owned by one person.

protectionist legislation A law providing for a tariff on imported goods, designed to protect domestic producers from foreign competition.

pseudo-events Events that occur as a result of careful planning by the president's staff, for the purpose of controlling the news reported by the media.

public energy corporation A governmental alternative to relying on the major oil companies for developing alternative energy sources.

public good A good or service that can be enjoyed by many people, whether or not they pay for it (e.g., clean air).

public interest group A group that claims to represent the interests of society as a whole rather than those of its own members alone.

public policy The body of laws that determine how the benefits and burdens of social programs are distributed.

public policy analysis The process of attempting to determine which among alternative policies is best for achieving a given set of goals.

public sector The government as opposed to private business or markets.

puritanism A reform movement within the Church of England during the sixteenth and seventeenth centuries that believed in the doctrine of predestination.

quiet diplomacy The policy followed by the Reagan administration of using subtle economic and political pressures on a government to improve its record on human rights.

random sample A group of individuals selected at random in a poll to represent a larger population, in such a way that all persons have an equal chance of being polled.

realigning elections Elections in which normal partisan ideologies and attachments are significantly disrupted.

reapportionment Redrawing of the boundaries of legislative districts to reflect changes in population distribution. To ensure that legislative districts contain equal populations, redistricting is usually carried out approximately every ten years, following the census.

recall A procedure by which voters can remove an official from office before the end of his or her term.

recession A phase in the business cycle in which output and employment begin to decline.

redistributive programs Social programs designed to transfer money from the rich to the poor.

referendum A procedure for referring legislative measures directly to the voters for approval or rejection.

regulatory commission A governmental agency with legislative, executive, and judicial powers charged with regulating a given sector of the economy (e.g., the Federal Communications Commission, the Federal Trade Commission).

reinforcement theory of the campaign The theory that campaigns reinforce people's previously held opinions rather than change them.

republic A representative democracy, in which power ultimately rests with the people and is exercised by elected officials responsible to the citizens who elected them. Republican government usually is distinguished from a direct democracy, in which political decisions are made by the people directly, and from a monarchy, in which power is exercised by a nonelected hereditary ruler.

rescission An impoundment in which the president decides to terminate funds.

reserved powers Powers reserved by the Constitution to the states.

revenue sharing The return of federal money to state and local governments with few or no strings attached.

rider A provision, unlikely to pass on its own, which is added to an important bill in the hope that the president will accept it rather than veto the entire bill.

rules committee The committee that determines the sequence and ways in which bills will be taken up on the House floor.

ruling elite theory A theory of government that holds that political and economic resources are concentrated in the hands of a relatively small and cohesive group that dominates the major policy-making institutions.

secret government Executive intelligence agencies that have resorted to controversial means of pursuing their goals of preventing the spread of communism.

select committee A congressional committee established for a limited time period and for a specific purpose, such as to conduct a special investigation.

selective attention A tendency to pay attention only to information that coincides with beliefs already held.

selective benefits Benefits that are available only to members of a certain group; a device sometimes used by interest groups to attract and keep members.

selective incorporation The process of applying, through the interpretations of the Supreme Court, the protections of the Bill of Rights to the states.

selective perception A tendency to pay attention only to those views and opinions with which one already agrees.

self-interest A central tenet of liberalism, self-interest means that the only thing people can be trusted to do is pursue their own interests.

senatorial courtesy A custom by which the president, before appointing a federal judge, consults the senator or senators of his own party who represent the state in which the appointee is to serve.

seniority system The practice of assigning a House or Senate committee chair to the member of the majority party who has had the longest continuous service on the committee.

sensationalism Reporting on (and frequently exaggerating) dramatic stories involving sex and violence to increase sales.

separation of powers The division of governmental power among the executive, legislative, and judicial branches of the national government. *See also* **checks and balances.**

service sector The sector of the economy that provides services rather than goods.

sexism Discrimination on the basis of sex.

single-issue group A political organization formed to promote an issue rather than a general political philosophy.

single-member district system An electoral system in which only one legislative member may be elected from a district, regardless of the number of candidates running.

social explanation Akin to the "nurture" position in the formation of human personality, this explanation focuses on the human factors involved in the development of national character.

social security A public insurance program, funded by taxes on wages paid by workers and employers, that provides income to retired people and surviving dependents of deceased workers.

social welfare state A nation whose government provides extensive health, educational, and welfare services.

socioeconomic status One's relative position in society, determined by income, education, and occupation.

solar energy A renewable source of energy derived from the sun.

Speaker of the House The presiding officer of the House of Representatives.

split-ticket voting Voting for candidates of more than one party for different offices.

spoils system The practice of awarding government jobs to friends and political supporters.

spot commercial A short television commercial in political campaigns to project either a favorable or an unfavorable image of a candidate.

Sputnik The first Earth-orbiting satellite that was launched by the Soviet Union on October 4, 1957.

stagflation The coincidence of inflation and recession.

standard operating procedures Bureaucratic methods established to facilitate fair and consistent behavior in given situations.

standing committee A permanent committee in the Senate or House of Representatives that considers bills within a given subject area.

"Star Wars" *See* **Strategic Defense Initiative.**

State of the Union message A yearly speech given by the president to report to the Congress on the general condition of the nation, as required by the Constitution.

Strategic Arms Limitation Treaty (SALT I) An agreement signed by the United States and the Soviet Union in 1972, setting temporary limits on deployment of weapons.

Strategic Arms Reduction Talks (START) A series of talks between U.S. and Soviet leaders on reductions in strategic nuclear weapons.

Strategic Defense Initiative A space-based antimissile defense program ("Star Wars") begun by the Reagan administration.

strategic deterrence The notion that the best security

against aggression is the maintenance of nuclear superiority, based on the assumption that peace can be preserved so long as each side has sufficient nuclear retaliatory capability to deter the other side from attacking.

strategic leaks Pieces of information conveyed surreptitiously to the press by a member of the government to test public reaction to a proposed policy or to embarrass an opponent.

strict constructionists Judges and others who hold the view that the Constitution should be interpreted narrowly, in accordance with the precise meaning of its words.

subsidies Governmental measures that work through the market system to achieve goals without increasing regulation.

substantive rights Rights essential to individual liberty and of value in themselves, such as freedom of speech, assembly, and religion.

sunset laws Statutes requiring automatic abolition of governmental agencies or programs after a specified period of time unless the legislature acts to reestablish them.

superdelegates Persons who are guaranteed places as delegates at a party convention.

supply-side economics An economic theory that focuses on stimulating producers to supply goods and services rather than on enabling consumers to demand them.

supremacy clause A provision of the Constitution declaring national laws to have precedence over state and local statutes.

synfuels Oil produced from shale rock, and oil and gas made from coal.

tariff A tax on imported goods.

task force A group of experts from various government agencies called together temporarily to study or solve a problem.

tax preferences Economic activities that the government encourages by levying no taxes on the gains they produce; also called "loopholes."

televised debate A debate between two candidates for high office, who appear together on television in an effort to present a favorable image to the public.

think tank A private research institution that receives government and foundation grants to conduct social science studies of public policies.

third party A political party in the United States other than the Democratic or Republican party.

third-party payments Payments made to health-care providers by insurance programs.

Third World The group of generally poor nations of Africa, Asia, Latin America, and the Middle East that are not aligned with either the communist or the noncommunist bloc.

ticket-splitting Voting for candidates of different parties in the same election.

trade deficit The excess in value of goods imported over goods exported.

trade-off A decision to be made between conflicting alternatives or choices.

trade surplus The excess in value of goods exported over goods imported.

treaty A formal agreement negotiated between two or more nations. In the United States, a treaty requires approval by a two-thirds vote of the Senate.

trickle-down theory The theory that holds that the benefits of economic growth work their way down to the poor.

Trilateral Commission Formed by David Rockefeller in the 1970s to coordinate the political and economic polices of Western capitalist nations.

Truman Doctrine A 1947 policy calling for U.S. economic and military aid to the governments of Greece and Turkey to prevent them from falling into communist hands.

unanticipated consequences The unforeseen or unplanned results of a policy.

unicameral legislature A legislature with a single house or chamber.

unilateral disarmament The position that the United States should start destroying its nuclear arsenal in the hopes that the Soviet Union would follow suit.

unitary system A political system in which power is concentrated in a central government.

Universal Declaration of Human Rights Adopted by the United Nations General Assembly in 1948, it enumerates in great detail the basic political and economic rights that all humans should enjoy.

urban enterprise zone An urban area where businesses are encouraged to locate by offers of low-interest loans and tax incentives.

valence issue An issue that arouses a strong, fairly uniform emotional response that does not have an adversarial quality (e.g., incest, drug pushing).

value-added tax A tax levied on the value added to a good at each stage of production.

veto The president's refusal to sign a bill passed by Congress, which thus fails to become law.

A two-thirds vote of both houses of Congress is required to override a veto. *See also* **item veto; pocket veto.**

veto groups Subgroups that balance each other by competing for opposing interests and policy goals.

vice-president The one who serves as constitutional successor to the president and President of the Senate.

Virginia Plan A proposal introduced at the Constitutional Convention in 1787, and generally favored by the larger states, that called for a strong two-house legislature with state representation based on population.

vouchers Coupons issued by the government that are redeemable at parents' choice of schools.

wage and price controls Legislation authorizing the president to set wages and prices for a specified period of time.

war on poverty The "Great Society" programs during the 1960s that were designed to address the long-term causes of poverty.

War Powers Resolution of 1973 An act that limits the president's unilateral use of troops abroad by specifying that the president must inform Congress in advance and obtain congressional approval for their continued use within a specific time frame.

Watergate An apartment and office complex in Washington, D.C., where in 1972 persons hired by Richard Nixon's Committee to Reelect the President broke into Democratic party headquarters; by extension, the wider pattern of illegalities and abuses committed by the Nixon administration and brought to light by the apprehension of the burglars.

wealth The combination of income plus assets such as stocks, bonds, and real estate.

welfare *See* **AFDC.**

whip An assistant to a congressional party leader, responsible for getting the party's members to vote when and as the party leadership wishes.

White House Office (WHO) A staff of persons within the Executive Office of the President who provide personal services to the president and serve as policy advisers.

white primary A primary election in which only white persons may vote; outlawed in 1944.

wire services Services to provide stories for newspapers unable to maintain their own reporters in distant cities and nations.

workfare A governmental income-maintenance program that requires employment as a condition of assistance.

writ of certiorari *See* **certiorari, writ of.**

writ of mandamus *See* **mandamus, writ of.**

yellow journalism Reporting of sensational or scandalous events or of ordinary news in a sensationally distorted manner.

zero-base budgeting A type of budgeting that requires governmental agencies to justify the money they plan to spend each year, not merely to request an increase in funds over the amount received in the preceding year.

★★★★★★★★★★★

Index

Photo Credits

These pages constitute an extension of the copyright page.

Chapter 1
3: Courtesy of NASA; **5:** Jacques Langevin/SYGMA; **6:** (left) © Fred Ward/Black Star, (right) © Rio Branco/Magnum Photos, Inc.; **8:** AP/Wide World Photos; **12:** © Dagmar Fabricius/Uniphoto Picture Agency; **14:** Atlan/SYGMA; **17:** © Graig Davis/SYGMA; **18:** (left) © Patsy Davidson/The Image Works, (right) Norbert Schiller, AFP; **19:** © Alexandra Tsiaras/Photo Researchers, Inc.; **21:** John Chiasson/Gamma-Liaison; **22:** © Bob Daemmrich/Uniphoto Picture Agency; **23:** (left) John Running/Stock, Boston, (right) © Costa Manos/Magnum Photos, Inc.

Chapter 2
27: © Michael Evans/SYGMA; **30, 31:** Culver Pictures, Inc.; **33, 35:** The Bettmann Archive; **37:** Culver Pictures, Inc.; **43:** © Arthur Grace/SYGMA; **44:** The Bettmann Archive; **54:** © Alex Webb/Magnum Photos, Inc.

Chapter 3
57: © 1989 Arthur Montes De Oca/Light Images, Inc.; **61:** Culver Pictures, Inc.; **63:** (left) Photo Researchers, Inc., (right) © Uniphoto Picture Agency; **65:** Culver Pictures, Inc.; **68:** (left) Culver Pictures, Inc., (right) UPI/Bettmann Newsphotos; **74:** Mark Richards/PhotoEdit; **78:** © 1980 Herb Levart, Photo Researchers, Inc.; **80:** Shel Hershorn/Black Star; **84:** © Dennis Budd Gray/Stock, Boston; **85:** © Eugene Richards/Magnum Photos, Inc.; **91:** AP/Wide World Photos; **92:** Nan Wintersteller, El Paso Herald Post.

Chapter 4
101: © 1989, ABC News; **105:** Jerome Friar; **107:** © Susie Fitzhugh/Stock, Boston; **108:** Magnum Photos, Inc.; **109:** Culver Pictures, Inc,; **110:** UPI/Bettmann Newsphotos; **111:** Connolly/Gamma-Liaison; **115:** Jerome Friar; **117:** UPI/Bettmann Newsphotos; **119:** UPI/Bettmann Newsphotos; **122:** (left) UPI/Bettmann Newsphotos, (right) © Bruce Roberts, Photo Researchers, Inc.; **125:** © David Powers/Stock, Boston; **126:** © Jean-Claude Lejeune/Stock, Boston; **132:** Magnum Photos, Inc.

Chapter 5
139: Ray Ellis © 1983/Photo Researchers, Inc.; **142:** Stock, Boston; **146:** (left) UPI/Bettmann Newsphotos, (right) © Bettina Cirone/Photo Researchers, Inc.; **151:** 1980 Blair Seitz/Photo Researchers; **159:** (left) © Magnum Photos, Inc., (right) Susan Biddle, The White House; **160:** Jerome Friar; **163:** U.S. Army Photograph; **166:** © John Feingersh/Uniphoto.

Chapter 6
171: © David R. White/Stockfile; **173:** Magnum Photos, Inc.; **175:** Culver Pictures, Inc.; **177, 178:** The Bettmann Archive; **179:** Culver Pictures, Inc.; **182:** © Mary Evans Picture Library/Photo Researchers, Inc.; **183, 186:** The Bettmann Archive; **187:** Michael Lloyd/The Oregonian; **189:** AP/Wide World; **193:** The Bettmann Archive; **194:** Mark Richards/PhotoEdit; **195:** Ralph Morse, LIFE Magazine © 1958 Time, Inc.; **198:** © James B. Adair/SYGMA; **199:** Douglas Kirkland/SYGMA; **202:** Kira Godbe.

Chapter 7

209: © 1980 Janet Fries/Black Star; **211:** UPI/Bettmann Newsphotos; **213:** UPI/Bettmann Newsphotos; **216:** Mark Antman/The Image Works; **220:** © 1989 George C. Dritsas/Light Images, Inc.; **225:** © Van Bucher/Photo Researchers, Inc.; **233:** © Shooting Star.

Chapter 8

243: United Press International, Inc.; **255:** Library of Congress; **260:** Carter Library; **262:** © David Powers/Stock, Boston; **268:** (left) UPI/Bettmann Newsphotos, (right) AP/Wide World Photos; **272:** United Press International Photo; **274:** The Bettmann Archive.

Chapter 9

281: UPI/Bettmann Newsphotos; **283:** Reuters/Bettmann Newsphotos; **285:** © Bob Adelman/Magnum Photos, Inc.; **287:** (left) and (middle) Culver Pictures, Inc., (right) The Bettmann Archive; **288:** Photo Researchers, Inc.; **304:** Young & Rubicam, Inc.; **309:** UPI/Bettmann Newsphotos; **317:** UPI/Bettmann Newsphotos; **319:** © David Burnett.

Chapter 10

325: Alain Keler/SYGMA; **329, 331:** Jerome Friar; **337:** D. Dietz/Stock, Boston; **342:** Courtesy of Common Cause; **343:** (left) Courtesy of Handgun Control, (right) Courtesy of the National Rifle Association of America; **344:** © Bruce Davidson/Magnum Photos, Inc.; **350:** © 1988 George Lange; **352:** © Les Schofer/SYGMA; **355:** © Thomas England/Photo Researchers, Inc.

Chapter 11

363: Jerome Friar; **367:** UPI/Bettmann Newsphotos; **368:** Eric Neurath/Stock, Boston; **370:** © Berle Cherney/Uniphoto Picture Agency; **372:** Magnum Photos, Inc.; **377:** Reuters/Bettmann Newsphotos; **379:** © Stephen Ferry/J. B. Pictures; **380:** Paul Schutzer, LIFE Magazine © 1960 Time, Inc.; **385:** UPI/Bettmann Newsphotos; **386:** (left) © Donald Patterson/Stock, Boston, (right) © Christopher Brown/Stock, Boston; **390:** Uniphoto Picture Agency.

Chapter 12

409: © John Aikens/Uniphoto Picture Agency; **416:** © Paul Fusco/Magnum Photos, Inc.; **418:** UPI/Bettmann Newsphotos; **419:** © J. P. Leffont/SYGMA; **420:** (left) B/C Library, (right) AP/Wide World Photos; **424:** © J. P. Leffont/SYGMA; **427:** AP/Wide World Photos; **430:** UPI/Bettmann Newsphotos; **435:** (left) and (right) UPI/Bettmann Newsphotos; **422, 446:** UPI/Bettmann Newsphotos; **499:** © 1989 George C. Dritsas/Light Images, Inc. Courtesy of the League of Women Voters.

Chapter 13

455: David Burnett/Contact; **457:** Reuters/Bettmann Newsphotos; **461:** © Mary Evans Picture Library/Photo Researchers, Inc.; **463:** © Cornall Capa/Magnum Photos, Inc.; **467:** UPI/Bettmann Newsphotos; **469:** Photo Researchers, Inc.; **471:** T. Matsumoto/SYGMA; **474, 477:** UPI/Bettmann Newsphotos; **491:** Maison/Blanche/SYGMA.

Chapter 14

499: © 1988 Bill Weems/Woodfin Camp & Associates; **503:** © Arthur Grace/Stock, Boston; **505:** UPI/Bettmann Newsphotos; **512:** Alan Carey/The Image Works, © All Rights Reserved; **513:** (left) UPI/Bettmann Newsphotos, (right) Kenneth Cole Productions, Inc.; **515:** © Dean Abramson/Stock, Boston; **517:** UPI/Bettmann Newsphotos; **518:** © Gale Zucker/Stock, Boston; **519:** Dept. of Fish and Game, Redding, CA.

Chapter 15

533: AP/Wide World Photos; **535:** The Supreme Court Historical Society; **536:** © Burt Glinn/Magnum Photos, Inc.; **537:** UPI/Bettmann Newsphotos; **541:** Photo Researchers, Inc.; **543:** © Danny Lyon/Magnum Photos, Inc.; **544:** Wide World Photos; **546:** UPI/Bettmann Newsphotos; **549, 551, 555** and **562:** UPI/Bettmann Newsphotos; **553:** J. Van Der Plas (The Hague); **557:** Flip Schulke/Black Star.

Chapter 16

575: © Michael J. Howell/Light Images, Inc.; **577:** (left) Mike Douglas/The Image Works, (right) © Paul Fusco/Magnum Photos, Inc.; **579:** (left) Culver Pictures, Inc., (right) The Bettman Archive; **585:** Reprinted by permission. Planned Parenthood® Federation of America; **588:** Mark Antman/The Image Works; **589:** David Wells/The Image Works; **593:** Owen Franken/Stock, Boston; **594:** UPI/Bettmann Newsphotos; **596:** Jerome Friar; **598:** Frank Siteman/Stock, Boston; **600:** Heller, Ehrman, White, and McAliffe; **609:** UPI/Bettmann Newsphotos; **612:** Culver Pictures, Inc.

Chapter 17

617: © Baron Wolman/Stockfile; **623:** Alan Carey/The Image Works; **628:** Michael Weisbrot/Stock, Boston, Inc.; **634:** Photo Researchers, Inc.; **643:** Elizabeth Crews/Stock, Boston, Inc.; **647:** Arthur Grace/Stock, Boston; **649:** U. S. Council for Energy Awareness; **650:** (left) © David Wells/The Image Works, (right) Camerique Stock Photography; **652:** (left) © Dennis Capolongo/Black Star, (right) © Robert Kalman/The Image Works; **656:** (left) and (right) Jerome Friar.

Chapter 18

665: © Lynn Melaren, Rapho/Photo Researchers, Inc.; **667:** © Lionel Delevingne/Stock, Boston; **668:** (left) © Jim Harrison/Stock, Boston, (right) Stock, Boston; **678:** © Dennis Brack/Black Star; **689:** Alan Carey/The Image Works; **691:** © 1985 Ken Jarecke/Contact Press Images; **693:** © Margo Granitsas /Photo Researchers, Inc.; **696:** © John Maher /Stock, Boston; **697:** © Charles Steiner, Picture Group; **704:** Oliphant; **706:** (left) © Donald Wright Patterson, Jr./Stock, Boston, (right) David C. Boyer © National Geographic Society.

Chapter 19

713: Reuters/Bettmann Newsphotos; **719:** Photo Researchers, Inc.; **722:** AP/Wide World Photos; **728:** UPI/Bettmann Newsphotos; **729:** AP ColorPhoto; **733:** UPI/Bettmann Newsphotos; **736:** © Magnum Photos, Inc.; **740:** © Peter Menzel/Stock, Boston; **743:** UPI/Bettmann Newsphotos; **746:** Jason Bleibtreu/SYGMA; **751:** (left): © 1981, Scott MacClay/Black Star, (right) © 1989 George C. Dritsas/ Right Images, Inc.; **754:** Rick Maiman/SYGMA; **756:** (left) © James Nachtwey/Magnum Photos, Inc., (right) © Paul Fusco/Magnum Photos, Inc.; **758:** © J. Langevin/SYGMA; **759:** United Nations Photo/ Milton Grant.